THE ROUGH GUIDE TO

Peru

This ninth edition updated by

Kiki Deere, Anna Kaminski, Phillip Tang
and Greg de Villiers

In memory of Dilwyn Jenkins

Public Library San Mateo, CA

roughguides.com

Contents

Introduction to
Peru

Trekking through the awe-inspiring Andes to the world-famous Inca citadel of Machu Picchu is the main draw for most travellers to Peru but, truth be told, this takes in only a fraction of the treasures that lie within one of South America's most diverse countries. Peru is home to a staggering array of landscapes – puzzling geoglyphs in the arid plains of Nazca, two of the world's deepest canyons outside the colonial town of Arequipa, the lush Amazon jungle in the east and excellent surf in the northwest – offering boundless potential for adventure. Peru's Andean culture is one of the most exciting in the Americas, with tucked-away highland towns that explode into colour on market day, and vibrant local fiestas that have been celebrated with unbridled enthusiasm for centuries.

Peru's immense wealth of sights and experiences has its roots in one of the world's richest heritages, topped by the **Inca Empire** and its fabulous **archeological gems**, not to mention the monumental adobe temples and pre-Inca ruins along the desert coast. While Machu Picchu is undoubtedly one of the world's most important archeological sites, Peru is home to a host of other archeological riches – and important new discoveries are constantly being unearthed.

Boasting access to the highest tropical mountain range in the world as well as one of the best-preserved areas of virgin Amazon rainforest, Peru's **wildlife** is as diverse as you'd expect, and sights such as jaguars slinking through the jungle, caimans sunning themselves on riverbanks and dazzling macaws gathering at Amazon clay licks are all within the visitor's grasp. For those looking for adrenalin-fuelled fun, a host of **outdoor activities** are on offer, from trekking ancient trails and whitewater rafting to paragliding and hurtling through the desert on dune-buggy rides.

Equally, a trip to Peru could focus on more restful pursuits. Widely touted as one of the world's **culinary hotspots**, the country – and Lima in particular – offers an array of exotic tastes to appeal to curious palates, as well as a laidback, vibrant dining scene, ranging from backstreet cevicherías to gourmet restaurants. And in the big cities, you can expect buzzing **nightlife** too.

Despite it all, simple, unaffected pleasures remain in place. The country's prevailing attitude is that there is always enough time for a chat, a ceviche or another drink. Peru is accepting of its visitors – it's a place where the resourceful and open-minded traveller can break through barriers of class, race and language far more easily than most of its inhabitants can. Even the Amazon jungle region – covering nearly two-thirds of the country's landmass, but home to a mere fraction of its population – is accessible for the most part, with countless tour operators on hand to organize trips to even the furthest-flung corners. Now all you have to do is figure out where to start.

Where to go

You're most likely to arrive in the buzzing and at least fitfully elegant capital, **Lima**; a modern city, it manages effortlessly to blend traditional Peruvian heritage with twenty-first-century glitz. **Cusco** is perhaps the most obvious place to head from here. A beautiful and bustling colonial city, it was once the ancient heart of the Inca Empire, and is surrounded by some of the most spectacular mountain landscapes and palatial ruins in Peru, and by magnificent hiking country. The world-famous **Inca Trail**, which culminates at the lofty, fog-shrouded Inca citadel of **Machu Picchu**, is just one of several equally scenic and challenging treks in this region of Peru alone.

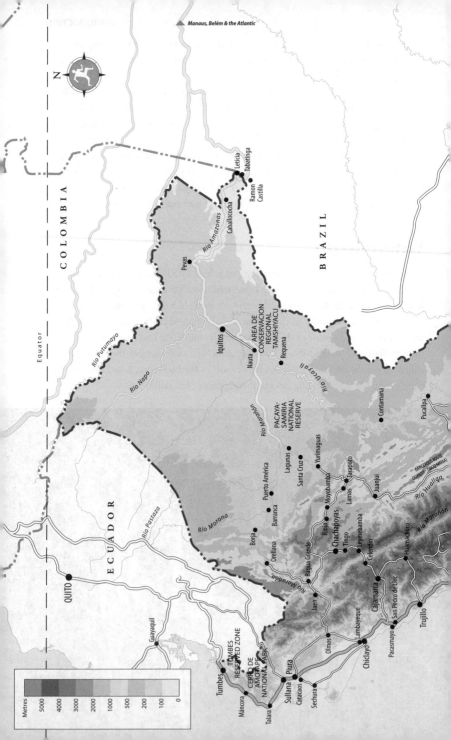

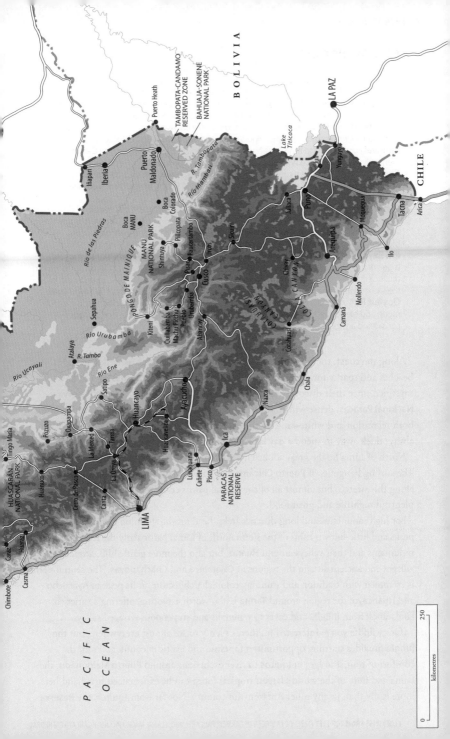

BEST OF THE FIESTAS

Peruvians love any excuse for a celebration. In Andean towns and villages, especially, communities host a huge number of **festivals**. Most of these have some link to the religious calendar, and the major Christian holidays of Christmas and Easter – infused with indigenous elements – still provide the basis for the biggest festivities. **Cusco** in particular is a great place for holidays that involve some sort of Inca ritual, **Puno** is renowned as the capital of Andean music and folkloric tradition, and in the hills around **Huaraz**, it's common to stumble across a village fiesta, with its explosion of human energy and noise, bright colours and a mixture of pagan and Catholic symbolism.

Carnival For a grand old time just about anywhere, you can't go wrong during **Carnival** (generally late February), a wholesale licence to throw water at everyone and generally go crazy.

Corpus Christi About two months after Easter Sunday, Peruvians celebrate Corpus Christi, honouring the saints. Processions are the most vibrant in Cusco, where church officials carry ornate sacred icons through the streets.

Fiesta de la Virgen del Carmen At this festival, which takes place in the pueblo of Paucartambo near Cusco (see box, p.270), usually on the second or third weekend in July, the villagers enact symbolic dramas, dressing up as Spanish colonists and wearing hideous blue-eyed masks with long hairy beards.

Inti Raymi At the end of June, Inti Raymi (see p.218) – Quechua for "resurrection of the sun" – is one of the largest festivals in South America, drawing visitors from all over the world. Based on the Inca ritual of the same name (held on the winter – June – solstice to honour and welcome the sun god and request his return), the festival is celebrated in the fortress of Sacsayhuaman.

Qoyllur Rit'i Just before Corpus Christi, the festival of Qoyllur Rit'i (see p.218) is held on a full moon and blends Catholic and indigenous traditions. Pilgrims trek to the foot of a glacier – considered an *apu*, or mountain god – to recharge their spirits.

Along the **coast**, there are more fascinating archeological sites as well as glorious beaches and sparky towns. South of Lima are the bizarre **Nazca Lines**, which have mystified since their discovery some seventy years ago, as well as the vast **Reserva Nacional Paracas**, dense with wildlife, and the oasis resort of **Huacachina**, which offers both relaxation and white-knuckle thrills. If that all sounds too active, you could always duck away to spend a day lazily sipping wine at the many **Ica Valley bodegas**.

North of Lima lie the great adobe city of **Chan Chan** and the **Valley of the Pyramids**. The surfing hangouts of **Puerto Chicama** and trendy **Máncora** beach are big draws along this stretch, but almost all of the coastal towns come replete with superb beaches, plentiful nightlife and great food.

For high mountains and long-distance treks, head for the stunning glacial lakes, snowy peaks and little-known ruins of the **sierra** north of Lima, particularly the ice-capped mountains and their valleys around **Huaraz**, but also the more gentle hills, attractive villages and ancient sites in the regions of **Cajamarca** and **Chachapoyas**. The central sierra is crammed with tradition and stunning colonial architecture, at its peak in **Ayacucho** and **Huancayo**; the region around **Tarma** is also worth exploring, offering a variety of landscapes, from jungles and caves to waterfalls and stupendous terraced valleys.

If it's wildlife you're interested in, there's plenty to see almost everywhere, but **the jungle** provides startling opportunities for close and exotic encounters. From the comfort of tourist lodges in **Iquitos** to river excursions around **Puerto Maldonado**, the fauna and flora of the world's largest tropical forest can be experienced first-hand here more easily than in any other Amazon-rim country. Not far from Iquitos, the **Reserva**

FACT FILE

• Potatoes are native to what is today southern Peru – they were domesticated here around 7000 to 10,000 years ago. Today there are over 3000 varieties of potato grown in the country.

• Peru is home to the largest segment of the Amazon rainforest after Brazil, with over 60 percent of Peruvian territory covered in dense forest.

• Guinea pigs (*cuy*) are widely consumed in Peru; it is said approximately 65 million guinea pigs are eaten every year.

• The Cotahuasi Canyon is the world's deepest, with a depth of over 3500m – twice that of the Grand Canyon.

• The popular children's character Paddington Bear is from Darkest Peru and is based on the native spectacled bear.

• The Cerro Blanco sand dune is the highest in the world at 2070m above sea level and 1176m from base to summit.

Nacional Pacaya-Samiria is a remote and stunningly beautiful, though little-visited region; while close to Cusco, just below the cloud forest, the Manu Biosphere Reserve is another wildlife hotspot. Further towards the Bolivian and Brazilian jungle frontier, the **Reserva Nacional Tambopata–Candamo** holds some of the most exciting and varied wildlife in the world.

When to go

Picking the best time to visit Peru's various regions is complicated by the country's physical characteristics; temperatures can vary hugely across the country (see box, p.45). Summer along the **desert coast** more or less fits the expected image of the southern hemisphere – extremely hot and sunny between December and March (especially in the north), cooler and with a frequent hazy mist between April and November – although only in the polluted environs of **Lima** does the coastal winter ever get cold enough to necessitate a sweater. Swimming is possible all year round, though the water itself (thanks to the Humboldt Current) is cool-to-cold at the best of times; to swim or surf for any length of time you'd need to follow local custom and wear a wetsuit. Apart from the occasional shower over Lima it hardly ever rains in the desert. The freak exception, every ten years or so, is when the shift in ocean currents of **El Niño** causes torrential downpours, devastating crops, roads and communities all down the coast. One of the heaviest was in 1983, though there have been several El Niños since including the devastating 1997–98 event that created a vast lake in the Sechura Desert along the northern Pacific Ocean coast.

In **the Andes**, the seasons are more clearly marked, with heavy rains from December to March and a warm, relatively dry period from June to September. Inevitably, though, there are always some sunny weeks in the rainy season and wet ones in the dry. A similar pattern dominates **the jungle**, though rainfall here is heavier and more frequent, and it's hot and humid all year round.

Taking all of this into account, the **best time to visit** the coast is around January while it's hot, and the mountains and jungle are at their best after the rains, from May until September. Since this is unlikely to be possible on a single trip there's little point in worrying about it – the country's attractions are broad enough to override the need for guarantees of good weather.

Author picks

Our intrepid authors have travelled to every corner of Peru, trekking through Andean plateaus, whitewater rafting through some of the world's deepest canyons and rowing down narrow creeks in the Amazon jungle. Here are some of their highlights:

Beach life Around 2000km long, Peru's desert coastline is one very big beach. Of the resorts, Máncora (p.414) is the most popular, while those who want peace and quiet will head right out to Punta Sal (p.416) or Las Pocitas (p.416).

Canyons and condors Colca (p.178) is great for the stunning new resorts for wealthier travellers, but Cotahuasi (p.185) is exactly what the more adventurous types coming to Peru are looking for: quiet and relatively unvisited with spectacular scenery and pre-Inca towns tucked up next to the river and high up on the cliff.

Lima's peñas and salsódromos Mostly located in Barranco, Lima's *peñas* are the surest bet for listening to authentic Andean folk, although some also specialize in Peruvian criolla (p.91).

Inca citadels A masterpiece of urbanism, architecture and engineering that blends in with the natural environment, Machu Picchu (p.255) is the country's greatest archeological attraction, but Peru abounds in strikingly perpendicular sites such as Choquequirao (p.265) and Pisac (p.238).

Peruvian cuisine Try traditional favourites like seafood ceviche at *Caplina* in Lima (p.88) or *Limo* in Cusco (p.227), as well as *novoandino* fusion cuisine at *Astrid y Gastón* in Lima (p.88) and *Tres Keros* in Urubamba (p.244), which uses fresh organic ingredients from the Sacred Valley.

Trekking Peru offers endless hiking opportunities, with most travellers heading to the glacial landscapes around Cusco or the Cordillera Blanca mountains around Huaraz (see p.321).

The jungle In the south, the Río Tambopata (p.440) and Manu (p.442) are best for spotting wildlife, while the central (p.448) and northern selva (p.461) also offer excellent tours into the unspoilt Amazon and its communities.

> Our author recommendations don't end here. We've flagged up our favourite places – a perfectly sited hotel, an atmospheric café, a special restaurant – throughout the Guide, highlighted with the ★ symbol.

28
things not to miss

It's not possible to see everything that Peru has to offer in one trip – and we don't suggest you try. What follows, in no particular order, is a selective taste of the country's highlights: colourful towns, awe-inspiring ruins, spectacular hikes and exotic wildlife. Each highlight has a page reference to take you straight into the Guide, where you can find out more. Coloured numbers refer to chapters in the Guide section.

1 MACHU PICCHU
Page 255
With mysterious temples and palaces nestling among hundreds of terraces, this fabulous Inca citadel is awe-inspiring.

2 PERUVIAN WILDLIFE
Page 508
Whether spotting a three-toed sloth in the Amazon treetops or crossing paths with a *vicuña* while hiking in the Andes, Peru's sheer variety of flora and fauna never fails to amaze.

3 MARCAHUASI
Page 283
At an altitude of 4000m, the little village of Marcahuasi makes an excellent overnight trip from Lima. The mysterious rock shapes in the nearby plateau must be seen to be believed.

4 TEXTILES
Page 229
Peru has been producing fine cotton textiles for over three thousand years.

15

11 TRUJILLO
Page 352
Though it doesn't attract the hype of Lima or Cusco, Peru's third city charms with its colonial architecture and cosmopolitan atmosphere.

12 BALLESTAS ISLANDS
Page 116
Often called the Peruvian Galapagos, these islands located off the coast of Pisco are teeming with bird and marine life.

13 CEVICHE
Page 33
Seafood ceviche is a popular alternative version of Peru's national dish, which is typically made from fresh fish soaked in lime juice and chillies.

14 SHIPIBO TRIBAL ARTS AND CRAFTS
Page 460
Dressed in traditional skirts and colourful seed jewellery, the women of this tribe travel all over Peru to sell their craft goods.

15 RAINFOREST CANOPY WALKWAY
Page 475
Peru's jungle can be viewed at its best from the Amazon's longest tree-top canopy walkway, reaching 35m above ground at the Amazon Explorama Field Station.

16 RESERVA NACIONAL PARACAS
Page 116
Just a few hours out of Lima, Paracas is a coastal wildlife haven, boasting some fantastic beaches alongside archeological sites.

16

20

21

17 CORDILLERA BLANCA
The Cordillera Blanca mountain range offers some of the best hiking and climbing in South America.

18 AREQUIPA
This white stone city, beautiful and intriguing, is watched over by the awesome, ice-capped volcano of El Misti.

19 AYACUCHO
Bustling streets, impressive churches, passionate religious processions and unique artesanía make this Andean city a standout.

20 SACSAYHUAMAN
The zigzag megalithic defensive walls of this Inca temple-fortress are home to the annual Inti Raymi Festival of the Sun.

21 CHAVÍN DE HUANTAR
Dating back over 2500 years, this large temple has many striking stone carvings and gargoyles, both externally and within its subterranean chambers.

22 PUERTO BELÉN
This frenetic floating jungle port has been nicknamed the "Venice of the Peruvian Jungle".

22

26

27

28

Itineraries

First-time visitors will inevitably try to fit in most of the major sites of the south; for those with ample time on their hands, the northern circuit offers an offbeat array of destinations to suit all tastes. You could also take an adventurous trip into the Amazon rainforest, staying at one of its many eco-lodges.

THE GRAND TOUR

Taking in the main attractions of the south of Peru, this tour can be covered in a couple of weeks, but could very easily absorb an extra week or two.

❶ Paracas and the Ballestas Islands A few hours south of Lima, this beachside area offers boat trips to islands of penguins and sea lions, great beaches, desert scenery, a scattering of pre-Inca sites and fine seafood. **See p.115**

❷ Huacachina At this desert oasis, its lagoon ringed by palm trees, you can relax and enjoy the scenery, or hit the dunes on a sandboard or dune buggy. **See p.128**

❸ Nazca Located in an attractive desert valley, Nazca sits next to a huge plain on which an ancient civilization etched enormous animal figures, as well as geometric shapes and perfectly straight lines. **See p.132**

❹ Arequipa and canyon country Arequipa is a stunning city with a colonial heart, built of white volcanic stone. The rugged regions around the city offer access to two of the world's deepest canyons – Colca and Cotahuasi. **See p.154**

❺ Puno and Lake Titicaca One of the most desolate yet scenic corners of Peru, Puno sits at the edge of the enormous Lake Titicaca. Take in its lively and vibrant music and festivals scene, and visit the lake's peaceful islands. **See p.188**

❻ Cusco Capital of the Inca Empire, Cusco today embodies outdoor activities, great dining, lively nightlife and craft shopping as much as it does ancient history. **See p.206**

❼ Machu Picchu Easily accessible from Cusco, this magnificent Inca citadel makes a fitting culmination to any trip. **See p.255**

THE NORTHERN CIRCUIT

The main focus of the little-visited north is beaches and surfing, coastal archeology and a chain of ancient mountain citadels and tombs, with the option of a jungle trip tagged on for those with more than two weeks to spare.

❶ Caraz to Trujillo bus ride If you'd like a hairy adventure, take the bus from Caraz to Trujillo – it pushes on nervously along the edge of small canyons for over an hour. **See p.332**

❷ The Mochica Trail The ancient Mochica civilization developed an important centre around the Huacas del Sol y de la Luna (see p.362) and is also in evidence at the richly endowed tombs of El Señor de Sipán and the Valley of the Pyramids. **See p.403**

❸ Ventanillas de Otuzco A huge pre-Inca necropolis of *ventanillas* (windows) where Cajamarca chieftains were once buried in niches cut into volcanic rock. **See p.379**

❹ Máncora and the beaches Máncora is the trendy focus of several stunning sandy beaches – all good for surfing, fishing and diving, as well as Cabo Blanco further south. **See p.414**

❺ Chachapoyas and Kuélap Inland and high up in the northern Andes, the Chachapoyas region abounds in waterfalls, cliff-bound mausoleums and little-explored trails and is home to Kuélap, a mountain citadel with 20m-high walls. **See p.382**

❻ Tarapoto and the jungle Head from Chachapoyas down to the jungle frontier city of Tarapoto – you can travel by river as far as the Reserva Nacional Pacaya-Samiria or Iquitos, for a taste of Peru's rainforest. **See p.390**

AMAZON HIGHLIGHTS

To get the most out of a jungle visit, allow at least four days (three nights), otherwise you're likely to spend most of the time in a bus, plane and/or boat.

❶ Tambopata A wide selection of lodges lies along the Río Tambopata and nearby Río Madre de Dios, offering access to luxuriant jungle and unrivalled wildlife-spotting in the Reserva Nacional Tambopata–Candamo. **See p.440**

❷ Manu The Manu Biosphere Reserve ranges from lowland tropical rainforest to cloud forest, teeming with monkeys, jaguars, giant otters, deer and wild boar. **See p.442**

❸ Pampa Hermosa Located in stunning cloud forest, this national reserve boasts a well-populated lek, where Peru's national bird, the cock-of-the-rock, can be seen dancing every morning. **See p.450**

❹ Iquitos and around Peru's liveliest jungle town, accessible only by air or riverboat, friendly Iquitos is home to clubs, bars and restaurants, while nearby eco-lodges offer the chance to see pink river dolphins, wild tapirs and jaguars. **See p.461**

❺ Riverboat trips Float down the Amazon River from Iquitos on an ecotourism riverboat featuring cabins, hammock areas, decks and restaurant-bars, with some offering five-star luxury. **See p.431**

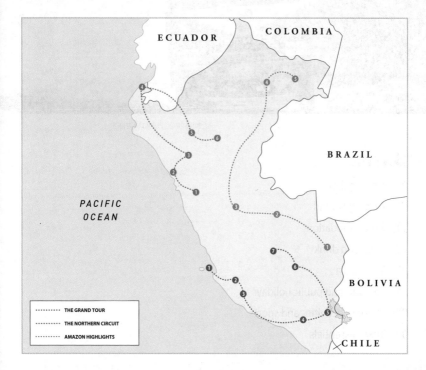

BUS TRAVEL, PERUVIAN ANDES

Basics

Getting there

Unless you're travelling overland through South America, you'll need to fly to reach Peru. Although prices vary depending on the time of year, how far in advance you buy and the type of ticket, the main airlines seem to hold fares fairly steady and tickets can easily be bought online. Apart from Christmas and to a lesser extent Easter, high season is roughly from late May to early October.

You can sometimes cut costs by going through a specialist **flight or travel agent**, who, in addition to dealing with discounted flights, will occasionally also offer special student and youth fares and a range of other travel-related services such as insurance, car rental, tours and the like.

Most people arrive at Jorge Chavez airport in Lima (see p.79). There's an airport hotel (☎017 112 00, ⑩ramada.com), but it's a fair distance to downtown areas of Lima – Miraflores, San Isidro, Barranco – or even the old Lima Centro. A taxi to downtown Lima takes 35 to 55 minutes (S/45–50). Inside the airport is the official Taxi Green service (⑩taxigreen.com.pe). It is strongly advised to use this service and not take one of the local taxis outside the airport, which have a reputation for robbing passengers. Alternatively, make sure you organize pickup with your hotel.

Flights from the UK

As there are no **direct flights** from the UK to Peru, getting there always involves switching planes somewhere in Europe or America. From Heathrow you can expect the journey to take anywhere between 16 and 22 hours, depending on the routing and stopovers. The permutations are endless, but the most common routes are **via Amsterdam** on KLM (⑩klm.com), **via Madrid** on Iberia (⑩iberia.com), **via Frankfurt** on Lufthansa (⑩lufthansa.com) or **via Miami, Atlanta, New York** or **Houston** on one of the US airlines.

Fares (usually £650–1200) vary almost as much as route options, and the closer to departure you buy, the higher the price is likely to be, so it is worth **booking in advance**. KLM and Iberia tend to offer the most competitive rates.

There's also a wide range of **limitations** on the tickets (fixed-date returns within three months etc), and options such as "open-jaw" flights are available (flying into Lima and home from Río, for example). Having established the going rate, you can always

check these prices against those on offer at **discount flight outlets** and other travel agents listed in the press.

It's best to avoid buying international air tickets in Peru, where prices are inflated by a **high tax** (and are not cheap to begin with). If you're uncertain of your return date, it will probably still work out cheaper to pay the extra for an **open-ended return** than to buy a single back from Peru.

Flights from the US and Canada

Nearly all flights to Peru from the US go **via Miami, Houston or Atlanta**. Delta (⑩delta.com), and American Airlines (⑩aa.com) are the traditional carriers serving Peru from the US. Most airlines can book connecting flights to Miami, Houston or Atlanta from a range of cities throughout the US. A number of airlines fly from Miami to Lima, including American, Copa (⑩copaair.com), Avianca (⑩avianca.com) and LAN (⑩lan.com); the fare is usually US$1000–1500 return. Fares **from New York** (via Miami) cost no more than fares from Miami.

Flights **from Toronto** straight to Lima start at about Can$900 with LAN (⑩lan.com); it costs around the same price when flying from Montréal via Toronto.

There are a huge variety of **tours and packages** on offer from the US and Canada to Peru, starting from around US$1500 for a two- to three-day package and ranging up to US$4000–5000. You'll also find a number of packages that include Peru on their itineraries as part of a longer **South American tour**.

Flights from Australia, New Zealand and South Africa

Scheduled flights to Peru from Australia and New Zealand are rather limited and tend to involve changing planes, usually in the US. In Australia, New Zealand and South Africa, **high season** is December to February; low season is the rest of the year.

LAN (⑩lan.com) flies from Sydney to Lima via Auckland, Miami, Buenos Aires or Santiago de Chile, while Delta (⑩delta.com) flies from Sydney to Lima via the US; Air Canada flies via Canada; their cheapest tickets start at about Aus$2500. American Airlines (⑩aa.com) fly regularly **from Melbourne** via Sydney and the US (stopovers available) with fares starting at about Aus$2200.

Air New Zealand (⑩airnewzealand.com) flies to LA **from Auckland and Wellington** but has no specific connections to Peru. Qantas (⑩qantas.com.au) has flights from Auckland to LA via Sydney or

A BETTER KIND OF TRAVEL

At Rough Guides we are passionately committed to travel. We believe it helps us understand the world we live in and the people we share it with – and of course tourism is vital to many developing economies. But the scale of modern tourism has also damaged some places irreparably, and climate change is accelerated by most forms of transport, especially flying. All Rough Guides' flights are carbon-offset, and every year we donate money to a variety of environmental charities.

Melbourne and also flies to Dallas and New York from Sydney, from where there are connecting flights to Lima; prices start from about NZ$1300. **Round-the-world (RTW)** tickets including Peru are usually a good investment.

All flights from South Africa to Lima involve making connecting flights. British Airways (**W** british airways.com) flies **from Johannesburg** to Heathrow and Toronto, which gives the option of flying Heathrow-to-Madrid (to connect with Iberia flights for Lima) or connecting with Air Canada flights to Lima. Lufthansa also flies from Johannesburg to Frankfurt where there's a change for Lima flights via Caracas (ZAR18,500). South African Airways (**W** flysaa.com) flies to Lima from Cape Town via Johannesburg, with a changeover in São Paulo (ZAR11,000–16,000).

Buses from neighbouring countries

Peru neighbours five other South American countries: Brazil, Ecuador, Colombia, Bolivia and Chile. **From Brazil**, you can drive directly into Peru via Puerto Maldonado on the Transoceanic Highway; Puerto Maldonado is just two to three hours from Peru's side of the frontier.

Arriving in southern Peru **from Bolivia** requires catching a bus, either directly or in stages, from La Paz across the altiplano to Copacabana or Desaguaderos, both near Lake Titicaca, and on to Puno, or even straight to Cusco. **From Chile** it's a similarly easy bus ride, across the southern border from Arica to Tacna, which has good connections with Lima and Arequipa.

From Ecuador, there are two routes, the most popular being a scenic coastal trip, starting by road from Huaquillas, crossing the border at Aguas Verdes and then taking a short bus or taxi ride on to Tumbes, from where there are daily buses and flights to Chiclayo, Trujillo and Lima. An alternative – and also rather scenic – crossing comes into Peru from Macará in Ecuador over the frontier to La Tina, from where there are daily buses to Peru's coast.

Boats from neighbouring countries

It's possible to take a boat ride up the Amazon from the **three-way frontier** between Brazil, Colombia and Peru (see p.476) to Iquitos. This is a twelve-hour to three-day ride depending on the type of boat. **From Leticia**, just over on the Colombian side of the three-way frontier (see p.476), there are speedboats up the Río Amazonas more or less daily to Iquitos. Taking the slow boat is usually a memorable experience – you'll need a hammock (unless you book one of the few cabins) and plenty of reading material.

AGENTS AND OPERATORS

Adventure tours or customized packages are often good value, but always check in advance exactly what's included in the price. Other specialist companies organize **treks** and **overland travel**, often based around some special interest, such as the rainforest, birdwatching, native culture or Inca sites.

Abercrombie & Kent UK ☎ 01242 851 877, **W** abercrombiekent .co.uk. With long-established contacts with the best authentic and luxury hotels and specialists in everything from art to archeology, A&K also offers a 'guardian angel' service out of Cusco, which means someone is on hand 24/7 for any requests, big or small.

Adventure US ☎ 1 855 698 5186, **W** adventure.com. Hiking and "soft adventure" specialists with some tours in Peru, including food and photography tours.

Adventure Associates Australia ☎ 02 8916 3000, **W** adventureassociates.com. Tours and cruises to Central and South America, including Peru and the Amazon.

Adventure Travel New Zealand ☎ 0800 269 000 or ☎ 04 494 7180, **W** adventuretravel.co.nz. Off-the-beaten path treks to Machu Picchu, tours around Lake Titicaca, food tours of Lima, as well as family trips and adventures by bike and kayak.

Adventure World Australia ☎ 1 300 295 049, **W** adventureworld.com.au. Agents for a vast array of international adventure travel companies that operate trips to every continent, with several options for Peru.

Backroads US ☎ 1 800 462 2848 or ☎ 510 527 1555, **W** backroads.com. Cycling, hiking and multi-sport tour offerings including Peru.

Classic Journeys US ☎ 1 800 200 3887, **W** classicjourneys.com. Offers cultural walking adventures and family trips to Machu Picchu.

Dragoman UK ☎ 01728 888 081, Ⓦ dragoman.com. Extended overland journeys in expedition vehicles through the Americas, covering Machu Picchu, Titicaca, Arequipa, Colca, Nazca and other sites in Peru.

Exodus UK ☎ 0845 805 5482, Ⓦ exodus.co.uk. Adventure-tour operators taking small groups on tours to South America, usually incorporating Peru's main destinations. They also provide specialist programmes including adventure, activity and walking trips.

Explore Worldwide UK ☎ 01252 883 879, Ⓦ explore.co.uk. Big range of small-group tours, treks and expeditions on all continents, including the Cusco and Lake Titicaca areas of Peru.

Mountain Travel Sobek US ☎ 1 888 831 7526, Ⓦ mtsobek.com. Hiking, river-rafting and trekking in Peru.

Nature Expeditions International ☎ 1 800 869 0639 or ☎ 954 693 8852, Ⓦ naturexp.com. Offers luxury wildlife, adventure and cultural tours in 25 countries around the world.

North South Travel UK ☎ 01245 608 291, Ⓦ northsouthtravel .co.uk. Friendly, competitive travel agency, offering discounted fares worldwide. Profits are used to support projects in the developing world, especially the promotion of sustainable tourism.

On the Go Tours UK ☎ 020 7371 1113, Ⓦ onthegotours.com. Seven- to fifteen-day tours in Peru; highlights include treks to Machu Picchu and the Amazon.

Overseas Adventure Travel US ☎ 1 800 995 1925, Ⓦ oattravel .com. Offers a wide variety of adventure trips around the planet, including some South American combinations, like Machu Picchu and the Galapagos.

Peru For Less US ☎ 1 877 269 0309 or ☎ 1 817 230 4971, UK ☎ 0203 002 0571; Ⓦ peruforless.com. Specializes in travellers who seek worry-free, fully customizable tours and services combined with personalized attention from their Peru tour experts - budget, luxury or boutique.

Real World UK ☎ 0113 2625329, Ⓦ realworldholidays.co.uk. South America specialists providing personalized tours of Peru for individuals, couples and small groups. As well as visits to the usual suspects, they have good and up-to-date local knowledge to help you get off the beaten track.

Select Latin America UK ☎ 0207 4071478, Ⓦ selectlatinamerica .co.uk. Specializes in bespoke journeys to all parts of Peru, not just Machu Picchu, with meticulous planning. Good rates for small boutique accommodation and local guides that are experts in culture, wildlife, archeology or birdwatching.

STA Travel UK ☎ 0333 321 0099, US ☎ 1 800 781 4040, Australia ☎ 134 782, New Zealand ☎ 0800 474 400, South Africa ☎ 0861 781 781; Ⓦ statravel.co.uk. Worldwide specialists in independent travel; also student IDs, travel insurance, car rental, rail passes and more. Good discounts for students and under-26s.

The Surf Travel Co Australia ☎ 02 9222 8870, New Zealand ☎ 09 473 8388; Ⓦ surftravel.com.au. Packages and advice for catching the waves (or snow) in the Pacific region, including main sites on the Peruvian coastline such as Chicama, Pacasmayo and Punta Huanchaco.

Trailfinders UK ☎ 0207 368 1200, Republic of Ireland ☎ 01 677 7888; Ⓦ trailfinders.com. One of the best-informed and most efficient agents for independent travellers.

Travel CUTS Canada ☎ 1 800 667 2887, Ⓦ travelcuts.com. Canadian youth and student travel firm.

USIT Republic of Ireland ☎ 01 602 1906, Australia ☎ 1 800 092 499; Ⓦ usit.ie. Ireland's main student and youth travel specialists.

World Expeditions Australia ☎ 02 8270 8400, New Zealand ☎ 09 368 4161, UK Freephone ☎ 0800 0744135 or ☎ 020 8545 9030, US toll free ☎ 1 800 567 2216 or ☎ 1 613 241 2700; Ⓦ worldexpeditions.com. Adventure company offering several programmes focused on the Peruvian jungle.

Getting around

With distances in Peru being so vast, many Peruvians and other travellers are increasingly flying to their destinations, as all Peruvian cities are within a two-hour flight of Lima. Most Peruvians, however, still get around the country by bus, a cheap way to travel with routes to almost everywhere. In a few cases, it's possible to arrive by train – an interesting and sought-after experience itself – though these trips are considerably slower than the equivalent bus journeys.

By plane

There's a good **domestic air service** in Peru these days. Some places in the jungle can only sensibly be reached by plane, and Peru is so vast that the odd flight can save a lot of time. There are three main established airline companies: LAN (Ⓦ lan .com), a Chilean-owned company, who fly to all of the main cities and many smaller destinations; StarPerú (Ⓦ starperu.com), a Peruvian airline that began operating in 2005; and Avianca (Ⓦ avianca .com). More recently, Peruvian Airlines (Ⓦ peruvian .pe) has set up to compete with these three, along with Bolivian-run Amazonas (Ⓦ amazonas.com) and Andes Air (Ⓦ andesair.com).

Most tickets for all these domestic airlines can be booked and bought online as well as from travel agents or airline offices in all major towns. The most popular domestic routes cost upwards of S/215 (US$80) and are generally cheaper if booked well in advance. In high season some Lima–Cusco flights are fully booked months in advance. Less busy routes tend to be less expensive per air mile and can be booked the day before. On all flights it's probably wise to **confirm your booking** two days before departure.

Flights are often cancelled or delayed, and sometimes they even leave earlier than scheduled – especially in the jungle where the weather can be a problem. If a passenger hasn't shown up **an hour**

ADDRESSES

Addresses are frequently written with just the street name and number: for example, Pizarro 135. Officially, though, they're usually prefixed by Calle, Jirón or Avenida (abbreviated to C, Jr and Av in listings throughout this guidebook). The **first digit** of any street number (or sometimes the first two digits) represents the block number within the street as a whole. Note that in Cusco some streets have two street names in order to honour Inca/Quechua heritage – the official Spanish name and an Inca/Quechua equivalent. This is not, however, a challenge for foreigners as the default names are still the official ones.

before the flight, the company may give the seat to someone on the waiting list, so it's best to be on time whether you're booked or are merely hopeful. The luggage allowance on internal flights can range from 10–16kg, so make sure you pack lightly.

Note that there is a "gringo tax" on internal flights. The cheapest fares offered by Avianca ("Promo" and "Econo") and LAN for Lima to Cusco, for example, are for Peruvians only, but it isn't always obvious. You may be charged up to US$170 at the airport if you can't show papers to prove that you are a Peruvian resident. Make sure you read the small print carefully before purchasing your ticket.

By bus

Peru's **buses** are run by a variety of private companies, all of which offer remarkably low fares, making it possible to travel from one end of the country to the other (over 2000km) for under US$35. Long-distance bus journeys cost from around US$2 per hour on the fast coastal highway, and are even cheaper on the slower mountain and jungle routes. The condition of the buses ranges from the efficient and relatively luxurious Cruz del Sur fleet that runs along the coast, to the older, more battered buses used on local runs throughout the country. Some of the better bus companies, including Cruz del Sur (Ⓦcruzdelsur.com.pe) and Ormeño (Ⓦgrupo-ormeno.com.pe), offer excellent onboard facilities including sandwich bars and video entertainment. The major companies generally offer two or three levels of service, and many companies run the longer journeys by night with a **bus-cama**

(comfortable deeply reclining seat) option. Cruz del Sur operates an excellent website with timetables and ticket purchase option (credit cards accepted). Oltursa (Ⓦoltursa.pe) and Movil Tours (Ⓦmoviltours.com.pe) are also reputable companies, and have services to most major destinations throughout the country.

As the only means of transport available to most of the population, buses run with surprising regularity, and the coastal Panamerican Highway and many of the main routes into the mountains have now been paved (one of ex-President Fujimori's better legacies), so on such routes services are generally **punctual**. On some of the rougher mountainous routes, punctures, arguments over rights of way and, during the rainy season, landslides may delay the arrival time by several hours.

Peru is investing in a series of **terminal terrestres**, or *terrapuertos*, centralizing the departure and arrival of the manifold operators. Lima does not have this facility and, in any case, it's always a good idea to double-check where the bus is leaving from as some companies such as Cruz del Sur operate from their individual terminals around town. If you can't get to a bus depot or *terminal terrestre*, you can try to catch a bus from the exit roads or **police checkpoints** on the outskirts of most Peruvian cities, though there's no guarantee of getting a ride or a seat.

For intercity rides, it's best to **buy tickets in advance** direct from the bus company offices; for local trips, you can buy tickets on the bus itself. On long-distance journeys, try to avoid getting seats right over the jarring wheels, especially if the bus is tackling mountain or jungle roads.

By taxi

Taxis can be found anywhere at any time in almost every town. Any car can become a taxi simply by sticking a taxi sign up in the front window; a lot of people, especially in Lima, take advantage of this to supplement their income, although beware – robberies are not unheard of on illegal taxis, and it's certainly not advised to use them especially if you're a single female traveller. It's always best to call a reliable taxi company (your hotel or restaurant can do so for you). Whenever you get into a taxi, always fix the price in advance (in nuevo soles rather than in US dollars) since few of them have **meters**. Taxi drivers in Peru do not expect tips.

Relatively short journeys in **Lima** generally cost around S/5–10 (US$2–4), but it's cheaper elsewhere in the country. Radio taxis, minicabs and airport taxis tend to cost more. Even relatively long taxi rides in Lima are likely to cost less than S/20 (US$7), except to and from the airport, which ranges from S/30 to S/60 (US$11–22); prices depend on how far across the city you're going and how bad the traffic is.

By mototaxi

In many rural towns, you'll find small cars – mainly motorcycle rickshaws, known variously as **mototaxis**, all competing for customers. They are cheap, starting at S/1 for short rides, if slightly dangerous and not that comfortable, especially if there's more than two of you or if you've got a lot of luggage. In a rural town, you might find normal car taxis (eg Toyotas) and mototaxis competing for business; a ride across town might cost S/5–8 in a normal taxi or S/2–3 in a mototaxi.

By colectivo

Colectivos (shared taxis) are a very useful way of getting around that's peculiar to Peru. They connect all the coastal towns, and many of the larger centres in the mountains. Like the buses, many are ageing imports from the US – huge old Dodge Coronets – though, increasingly, fast new Japanese and Korean minibuses run between the cities.

Colectivos tend to be faster than the bus, though they are often as much as twice the price. Most **colectivo cars** manage to squeeze in about seven people including the driver (three in the front and four in the back), and can be found in the centre of a town or at major stopping places along the main roads. If more than one is ready to leave it's worth bargaining a little, as the price is often negotiable. **Colectivo minibuses**, also known as combis, can squeeze in twice as many people, or often more.

In the cities, colectivos have an appalling reputation for **safety**. There are crashes reported in the Lima press every week, mostly caused by the highly competitive nature of the business. There are so many combis covering the same major arterial routes in Lima that they literally race each other to be the first to the next street corner. They frequently crash, turn over and knock down pedestrians. Equally dangerous is the fact that the driver is in such a hurry that he does not always wait for you to get in. If you're not careful he'll pull away while you've still got a foot on the pavement, putting you in serious danger of breaking a leg.

By train

Peru's spectacular **train journeys** are in themselves a major attraction, and you should aim to take at least one long-distance train ride during your trip, especially as the trains connect some of Peru's major tourist sights. At the time of writing, the **Central Railway**, which climbs and switchbacks its way up from Lima into the Andes as far as Huancayo on the world's highest standard-gauge tracks, only runs about twice a month between April and September (see box, p.283).

There are two rail companies operating out of Cusco. PeruRail (W perurail.com) offers passenger services inland from Puno on Lake Titicaca north to Cusco, from where another line heads out down the magnificent Urubamba Valley as far as Machu Picchu Pueblo. On the Cusco-to-Machu Picchu line there is also Inca Rail (W incarail.com).

The trains move slowly, allowing ample time to observe what's going on outside. For all train journeys, it's advisable to buy **tickets** a week or two before travelling and even further in advance during high season.

By car

Driving around Peru is generally not a problem outside of Lima, and allows you to see some out-of-the-way places that you might otherwise miss. However, road traffic in Lima is abominable, both in terms of its recklessness and the sheer volume. Traffic jams are ubiquitous between 8 and 10am and again between 4 and 7pm every weekday, while air pollution from old and poorly maintained vehicles is a real health risk, particularly in Lima and Arequipa.

If you bring a car into Peru that is not registered there, you will need to show (and keep with you at all times) a **libreta de pago por la aduana** (proof of customs payment) normally provided by the relevant automobile association of the country you are coming from. **Spare parts**, particularly tyres, should be carried, along with a tent, emergency water and food. The chance of **theft** is quite high – the vehicle, your baggage and accessories are all vulnerable when parked.

International driving licences are valid for six months in Peru, after which a permit is required from the Touring y Automóvil Club del Perú, Av Trinidad Moran 698, Lince, Lima (Mon–Fri 9am–4.45pm; T 01 611 9999, W touringperu.com.pe).

Renting a car costs much the same as in Europe and North America. The major rental firms all have offices in Lima, but outside the capital you'll generally find only local companies are represented. You may find it more convenient to rent a car in advance online – expect to pay from around US$40 a day, or US$200 a week for the smallest car. In jungle cities it's usually possible to rent **motorbikes** or **mopeds** by the hour or by the day: this is a good way of getting to know a town or being able to shoot off into the jungle for a day.

By boat

There are no coastal **boat services** in Peru, but in many areas – on Lake Titicaca and especially in the jungle regions – water is the obvious means of getting around. From Puno, on Lake Titicaca, there are currently no regular services to Bolivia by ship or hydrofoil – though check with the tour agencies in Puno (see p.191) – but there are plenty of smaller boats that will take visitors out to the various islands in the lake. These aren't expensive and a price can usually be negotiated down at the port.

In the jungle areas **motorized canoes** come in two basic forms: those with a large outboard motor and those with a Briggs and Stratton **peque-peque** engine; the outboard is faster and more manoeuvrable, but they cost a lot more to run. Your best option is to **hire a canoe** along with its guide/ driver for a few days. This means searching around in the port and negotiating, but you can often get a *peque-peque* canoe from around S/150–240 (US$50–80) per day, which will invariably work out cheaper than taking an organized tour, as well as giving you a choice of guide and companions. Obviously, the more people you can get together, the cheaper it will be per person.

On foot

Even if you've no intention of doing any serious hiking, there's a good deal of walking involved in checking out many of the most enjoyable Peruvian attractions. Climbing from Cusco up to the fortress of Sacsayhuaman, for example, or wandering around at Machu Picchu, involves more than an average Sunday afternoon stroll. Bearing in mind the rugged terrain throughout Peru, the absolute minimum **footwear** is a strong pair of running shoes. Much better is a pair of hiking boots with good ankle support.

Hiking – whether in the desert, mountains or jungle – can be an enormously rewarding experience, but you should go properly equipped and bear in mind a few of the **potential hazards**.

Never stray too far without food and water, something warm and something waterproof to wear. The weather is renowned for its dramatic changeability, especially in the mountains, where there is always the additional danger of altitude sickness (see box, p.210). In the jungle the biggest danger is getting lost (see p.431).

In the mountains it's often a good idea to hire a **pack animal** to carry your gear. Llamas can only carry about 25–30kg and move slowly; a *burro* (donkey) carries around 80kg and a mule – the most common and the best pack animal – will shift 150kg with relative ease. Mules can be hired at about S/90 a day, and they normally come with an *arriero*, a muleteer who'll double as a guide. It is also possible to hire mules or horses for **riding** but this costs a little more. With a guide and beast of burden it's quite simple to reach even the most remote valleys, ruins and mountain passes, travelling in much the same way as Pizarro and his men did over four hundred years ago.

Hitching

Hitching in Peru usually means catching a ride with a truck driver, who will almost always expect payment. Always agree on a price before getting in as there are stories of drivers stopping in the middle of nowhere and demanding unreasonably high amounts (from foreigners and Peruvians alike) before going any further. Hitching isn't considered dangerous in Peru, but having said that, few people, even Peruvians, actually hitch. Trucks can be flagged down anywhere but there is greater choice around markets, and at police controls or petrol stations on the outskirts of towns. Trucks tend to be the only form of public transport in some less accessible regions, travelling the roads that buses won't touch and serving remote communities, so you may end up having to sit on top of a pile of potatoes or bananas.

Hitchhiking in **private cars** is not recommended, and, in any case, it's very rare that one will stop to pick you up.

Organized tours

There are hundreds of **travel agents** and **tour operators** in Peru, and reps hunt out customers at bus terminals, train stations and in city centres. While they can be expensive, **organized excursions** can be a quick and relatively effortless way to see some of the popular attractions and the more remote sites, while a prearranged trek of something like the Inca Trail can take much of the worry out of camping preparations and ensure that you get decent campsites, a sound meal and help with carrying your equipment in what can be difficult walking conditions.

Many **adventure tour companies** offer excellent and increasingly exciting packages and itineraries – ranging from mountain biking, whitewater rafting, jungle photo-safaris, mountain trekking and climbing, to more comfortable and gentler city and countryside tours. Tours cost US$45–300 a day and, in Cusco and Huaraz in particular, there's an enormous selection of operators to choose from (note that most tour operators in Peru charge in US dollars). **Cusco** is a pretty good base for hiking, whitewater rafting, canoeing, horseriding or going on an expedition into the Amazonian jungle with an adventure tour company; **Arequipa** and the **Colca Canyon** offer superb hiking; **Huaraz** is also a good base for trekking and mountaineering; **Iquitos**, on the Amazon River, is one of the best places for adventure trips into the jungle and has a reasonable range of tour operators. Several of these companies have branches in Lima, if you want to book a tour in advance. Reliable tour operators are listed in the relevant sections throughout the Guide.

Accommodation

Peru has the typical range of Latin American accommodation, from top-class international hotels at prices to compare with any Western capital down to basic rooms or shared dorms in hostels. The biggest development over the last ten years has been the rise of the mid-range option, reflecting the growth of both domestic and international tourism. Camping is frequently possible, sometimes free and perfectly acceptable in most rural parts of Peru, though there are very few formal campsites.

Accommodation denominations of *hotel*, *hostal*, *residencial*, *pensión* or *hospedaje* are almost meaningless in terms of what you'll find inside. Virtually all upmarket accommodation will call itself a **hotel** or, in the countryside regions, a **posada**. In the jungle, **tambo lodges** can be anything from somewhere quite luxurious to an open-sided, palm-thatched hut with space for slinging a hammock. Technically speaking, somewhere that calls itself a

pensión or **residencial** ought to specialize in longer-term accommodation, and while they may well offer discounts for stays of a week or more, they are just as geared up for short stays. There's no standard or widely used **rating system**, so, apart from the information given in this book, the only way to tell whether a place is suitable or not is to walk in and take a look around – the proprietors won't mind this, and you'll soon get used to spotting places with promise.

Many of the major hotels will request a **credit card number** to reserve rooms in advance; be careful, since if you fail to turn up they may consider this a "no-show" and charge you for the room anyhow. Always check beforehand whether the quoted price includes **IGV tax** (as a tourist, if you register your passport and tourist card with the hotel, they don't charge you this tax, which is currently eighteen percent). It's not advisable to pay **travel agents** in one city for accommodation required in the next town; by all means ask agents to make reservations but do not ask them to send payments as it is always simpler and safer to do that yourself.

The **prices** quoted for accommodation throughout the Guide are for the **cheapest double room in high season**, except where noted.

Hotels

Peru's cheaper **hotels** are generally old – sometimes beautifully so, converted from colonial mansions with rooms grouped around a courtyard. They tend to be within a few blocks of a town's central plaza, general market or bus or train station. For a night in a no-frills place, expect to pay S/60.

You can find a good, clean single or double room in a **mid-range hotel** (generally three-star), with a private bathroom, towels and hot water, for S/75–180 (US$25–60). Quality hotels, not necessarily five-star, but with good service, truly comfortable rooms and maybe a pool or some other additional facility, can be found in all the larger Peruvian resorts as well as some surprisingly offbeat ones. Out of season some are relatively inexpensive, at S/150–250 (US$50–80).

There are quite a few **five-star hotels** in Peru (usually costing upwards of S/675 or US$225 for a double room), nearly all in Lima, Arequipa, Cusco, Trujillo and Iquitos. Even **four-star hotels** (S/330–675 or US$110–225) offer excellent service, some fine restaurants and very comfortable rooms with well-stocked minibars.

A little haggling is often worth a try, and if you find one room too pricey, another, perhaps very similar, can often be found for less: the phrase "Tiene un cuarto más barato?" ("Do you have a cheaper room?") is useful. Savings can invariably be made, too, by **sharing rooms** – many have two, three, even four or five beds. A double-bedded room ("con cama matrimonial") is usually cheaper than a twin ("doble" or "con dos camas").

Hostels

Not to be confused with "hostales" which are simple guesthouses, most of Peru's **hostels** are unaffiliated to Hostelling International, though there are dozens (see ⓦhihostels.com), spread throughout Peru, including in Arequipa, Cusco, Iquitos, Lima, Máncora, Puno, Tumbes and Trujillo. Most of the hostels that are linked to Hostelling International don't bother to check that you are a member, but if you want to be on the safe side, you can join up at the Asociación Peruana de Albergues Turísticos Juveniles, Av Casimiro Ulloa 328, Miraflores, Lima (☎01 446 5488, ⓦlimahostell.com.pe).

While not the standardized institution found in Europe, Peru's hostels are relatively cheap and reliable; expect to pay S/21–30 (US$7–10) for a bed (the most expensive ones are in Lima and Cusco). All hostels are theoretically open 24 hours a day and most have cheap cafeterias attached. They are always great places to meet up with other travellers and tend to have a party scene of their own.

YOUTH HOSTEL ASSOCIATIONS

US AND CANADA

Hostelling International–American Youth Hostels US ☎1 240 650 2100, ⓦhiusa.org.
Hostelling International Canada Canada ☎1 613 237 7844, ⓦhihostels.ca.

UK AND IRELAND

Youth Hostel Association (YHA) UK ☎0800 019 1700, ⓦyha .org.uk.
Scottish Youth Hostel Association UK ☎0845 293 7373 or ☎01786 891 400, ⓦsyha.org.uk.
Irish Youth Hostel Association Ireland ☎01 830 4555, ⓦanoige.ie.
Hostelling International Northern Ireland Northern Ireland ☎028 9032 4733, ⓦhini.org.uk.

AUSTRALIA, NEW ZEALAND AND SOUTH AFRICA

Australian Youth Hostels Association Australia ☎02 9261 1111, ⓦyha.com.au.

ACCOMMODATION ALTERNATIVES

These useful websites provide some interesting alternatives to standard hotel and hostel accommodation:
CouchSurfing ⓦcouchsurfing.org.
Vacation Rentals by Owner ⓦvrbo.com.
Airbnb ⓦairbnb.com.

Youth Hostelling Association New Zealand New Zealand ☎0800 278 299 or ☎03 379 9970, ⓦyha.co.nz.
Hostelling International South Africa South Africa ☎021 424 2511, ⓦhisouthafrica.com.

Camping

Camping is possible almost everywhere in Peru, and it's rarely difficult to find space for a tent; since there are only one or two organized campsites in the whole country (costing between S/10–15 per person), it's also largely free. Moreover, camping is the most satisfactory way of seeing Peru, as some of the country's most fantastic destinations are well off the beaten track: with a tent – or a hammock – it's possible to go all over without worrying if you'll make it to a hostel.

It's usually okay to set up camp in the fields or forest beyond the outskirts of settlements, but ask **permission** and advice from the nearest farm or house first. Apart from a few restricted areas, Peru's enormous sandy coastline is open territory, the real problem not being so much where to camp as how to get there; some of the most stunning areas are very remote. The same can be said of both the mountains and the jungle – camp anywhere, but ask first, if you can find anyone to ask.

Reports of **robberies**, particularly along such popular routes as the Inca Trail, are not uncommon, so travelling with someone else or in groups is always a good idea. There are a few basic precautions that you can take: let someone know where you intend to go; be respectful, and try to communicate with any locals you may meet or who you are camping near (but be careful who you make friends with en route).

Camping equipment is easy to find in Peru, but good-quality gear is hard to obtain. Several places sell, rent or buy secondhand gear, mainly in Cusco, Arequipa and Huaraz, and there are some reasonably good, if quite expensive, shops in Lima. It's also worth checking the noticeboards in the popular travellers' hotels and bars for equipment that is no longer needed or for people seeking trekking companions. Camping Gaz butane canisters are available from most of the above shops and from some *ferreterías* (hardware stores) in the major resorts. A couple of essential things you'll need when camping in Peru are a mosquito net and repellent, and some sort of water treatment system.

Food and drink

Peruvian cuisine is rated among the best in the world and is currently experiencing a period of flourishing self-confidence and great popularity overseas. The country's chefs are adept at creating innovative new fusions with its fantastic wealth of food products, most of which are indigenous.

As with almost every activity, the style and pattern of eating and drinking varies considerably between the three main regions of Peru. The food in each area, though it varies depending on the availability of different regional ingredients, is essentially a *mestizo* creation, combining indigenous cooking with four hundred years of European – mostly Spanish – influence.

Guinea pig (*cuy*) is the traditional dish most associated with Peru, and you can find it in many parts of the country, especially in the mountain regions, where it is likely to be roasted in an oven and served with chips. It's likely however, that you may encounter more burgers and pizza than guinea pig, given that fast food has spread quickly in Peru over the past two decades.

Snacks and light meals

All over Peru, but particularly in the large towns and cities, you'll find a wide variety of traditional **fast foods** and snacks such as *salchipapas* (chips with sliced sausage covered in various sauces), *anticuchos* (a shish kebab made from marinated lamb or beef heart) and *empanadas* (meat- or cheese-filled pies). These are all sold on street corners until late at night. Even in Peru's villages you'll find cafés and restaurants that double as bars, staying open all day and serving anything from coffee and bread to steak and chips, or even lobster. The most popular sweets in Peru are made from either *manjar blanco* (sweetened condensed milk) or fresh fruits.

In general, the **market** is always a good place to stock up – you can buy food ready to eat on the spot or to take away and prepare – and the range and prices are better than in any shop. Most food prices are fixed, but the vendor may throw in an orange, a bit of garlic or some coriander leaves for good measure. Smoked meat, which can be sliced up and used like salami, is normally a good buy.

Restaurants

All larger towns in Peru have a fair choice of **restaurants**, most of which offer a varied menu. Among them there are usually a few **Chinese** (*chifa*) places, and nowadays a fair number of **vegetarian** restaurants too. Most establishments in larger towns stay open daily from around 11am until 11pm, though in smaller settlements they may close one day a week, usually Sunday. Often they will offer a **set menu**, from morning through to lunchtime, and another in the evening. Ranging in price from S/8 to S/25, these most commonly consist of three or four courses: soup or other starter, a main dish (usually hot and with rice or salad), a small sweet or fruit-based third plate, plus tea or coffee to follow. Every town, too, seems now to have at least one restaurant that specializes in *pollos a la brasa* – spit-roasted chickens.

Seafood

Along the coast, not surprisingly, **seafood** is the speciality; the Humboldt Current keeps the Pacific Ocean off Peru extremely rich in plankton and other microscopic life forms, which attract a wide variety of fish. **Ceviche** is the classic Peruvian seafood dish and has been eaten by locals for over two thousand years. It consists of fish, shrimp, scallops or squid, or a mixture of all four, marinated in lime juice and chilli peppers, then served "raw" with corn, sweet potato and onions. *Ceviche de lenguado* (sole) and *ceviche de corvina* (sea bass) are among the most common, but there are plenty of other fish and a wide range of seafood is utilized on most menus. You can find ceviche, along with fried fish and fish soups, in most restaurants along the coast from S/15–25.

Escabeche is another tasty fish-based appetizer, this time incorporating peppers and finely chopped onions. The coast is also an excellent place for eating **scallops** – known here as *conchitas* – which grow particularly well close to the Peruvian shoreline; *conchas negras* (black scallops) are a delicacy in the northern tip of Peru. Excellent **salads** are also widely available, such as *huevos a la rusa* (egg salad), *palta rellena* (stuffed avocado), or a straight tomato salad, while *papas a la Huancaina* (a cold appetizer of potatoes covered in a spicy, light cheese sauce) is great too.

TIPPING

In budget or average restaurants **tipping** is normal, though not obligatory and you should rarely expect to give more than about ten percent. In fancier places you may well find a **service charge** of at least ten percent as well as a **tax** of eighteen percent (IGV) added to the bill. In restaurants and *peñas* where there's live music or performances a **cover charge** is generally also applied and can be as high as US$5 a head. Even without a performance, additional cover charges of around US$1 are sometimes levied in the flashier restaurants in major town centres.

Mountain food

Mountain food is fairly basic – a staple of potatoes and rice with the meat stretched as far as it will go. *Lomo saltado*, or diced prime beef sautéed with onions and peppers, is served anywhere at any time, accompanied by rice and a few French fries. A delicious snack from street vendors and cafés is *papa rellena*, a potato stuffed with vegetables and fried. **Trout** is also widely available, as are cheese, ham and egg sandwiches. *Chicha*, a **corn beer** drunk throughout the sierra region and on the coast in rural areas, is very cheap with a pleasantly tangy taste. Another Peruvian speciality is **pachamanca**, a roast prepared mainly in the mountains but also on the coast by digging a large hole, filling it with meats and vegetables, thereafter placing stones and lighting a fire over them, then using the hot stones to cook a wide variety of tasty meats and vegetables.

Jungle food

Jungle food is quite different from food in the rest of the country. **Bananas** and **plantains** figure highly, along with *yuca* (a manioc rather like a yam), rice and plenty of fish. There is **meat** as well – mostly chicken supplemented occasionally by **game** (deer, wild pig or even monkey). Every settlement big enough to get on the map has its own bar or café, but in remote areas it's a matter of eating what's available and drinking coffee or bottled drinks if you don't relish the home-made *masato* (cassava beer).

Drinking

Beer, wines and spirits are served in almost every bar, café or restaurant at any time, but there is a **deposit** on taking beer bottles away from a shop (canned beer is one of the worst inventions to hit Peru in recent years – some of the finest beaches are littered with empty cans).

Nonalcoholic drinks

Soft drinks range from mineral water, through the ubiquitous Coca-Cola and Fanta, to home-produced favourites like the gold-coloured Inka Cola, with rather a home-made taste, and the very sweet Cola Inglesa. **Fruit juices** (*jugos*), most commonly papaya or orange, are delicious and prepared fresh in most places (the best selection and cheapest prices are generally available in a town's main market), and you can get **coffee** and a wide variety of herb and leaf **teas** almost anywhere. Surprisingly, for a good coffee-growing country, the coffee in cafés outside Lima, Cusco and Arequipa leaves much to be desired, commonly prepared from either *café pasado* (previously percolated coffee mixed with hot water to serve) or simple powdered Nescafé. Increasingly it's possible to find great coffee in larger towns where certain cafés prepare good fresh espresso, cappuccino or filtered coffee. *Starbucks* (complete with wi-fi) can be found in several of Peru's cities and is everywhere you turn in Lima.

Beer and wine

Most **Peruvian beer** – except for *cerveza malta* (black malt beer) – is bottled lager almost exclusively brewed to five percent alcohol content, and extremely good. Traditional Peruvian beers include Cristal, Pilsen and Cusqueña (the last, originating from Cusco, is generally preferred, and has even reached some UK supermarkets in recent years). In Trujillo on the north coast, they drink Trujillana beer, again quite similar; and in Arequipa they tend to drink Arequipeña beer. There are several new lager beers now on the market, including the Brazilian brand Brahma. Peru has been producing **wine** (*vino*) for over four hundred years. Among the better ones are Vista Alegre (the Tipo Familiar label is generally OK) – not entirely reliable but only around S/8 a bottle – and, much better, Tabernero or Tacama Gran Vino Reserva (white or red) from about S/25–45 a bottle. A good Argentinian or Chilean wine will cost from US$10 upwards.

Spirits

As for **spirits**, Peru's main claim to fame is **pisco**. This is a white-grape brandy with a unique, powerful and very palatable flavour – the closest equivalent elsewhere is probably tequila. Almost anything else is available as an import – Scotch **whisky** is cheaper here than in the UK, but beware of the really cheap whisky imitations or blends bottled outside Scotland which can remove the roof of your mouth with ease. The jungle regions produce a sugar-cane rum, **cashassa** (basically the Peruvian equivalent of Brazilian *cachaça*), also called *aguardiente*, which has a distinctive taste and is occasionally mixed with different herbs, some medicinal. While it goes down easily, it's incredibly strong stuff and is sure to leave you with a hangover the next morning if you drink too much.

The media

English language, or non-Spanish, magazines and newspapers are hard to find in Peru; some are available in Miraflores, Lima, and they can occasionally be found in airports or bookshops in Cusco. BBC World Service and VOA can be picked up if you have the right receiver.

There are many poor-quality newspapers and magazines available on the streets of Lima and throughout the rest of Peru. Many of the **newspapers** stick mainly to sex and sport, while **magazines** tend to focus on terrorism, violence and the frequent deaths caused by major traffic accidents. Meanwhile, many get their news and information from **television** and **radio**, where you also have to wade through the panoply of entertainment-oriented options.

Newspapers and magazines

The two most established (and establishment) **daily newspapers** are *El Comercio* (Ⓦ elcomercio .pe) and *Expreso* (Ⓦ www.expreso.com.pe), the latter having traditionally devoted vast amounts of space to anti-Communist propaganda. *El Comercio* is much more balanced but still tends to toe the political party of the day's line. *El Comercio*'s daily *Seccion C* also has the most comprehensive cultural listings of any paper – good for just about everything going on in Lima. In addition, there's the sensationalist tabloid *La República* (Ⓦ larepublica .pe), which takes a middle-of-the-road to liberal approach to politics; and *Diario Ojo* (Ⓦ ojo.pe), which provides interesting tabloid reading.

International newspapers are fairly hard to come by; your best bet for English papers is to go to the British Embassy in Lima (see p.96), which has a selection of one- to two-week-old papers, such as *The Times* and *The Independent*, for reference only. US papers are easier to find; the bookstalls around Plaza San Martín in Lima Centro and those along Avenida Larco and Diagonal in Miraflores sell *The Miami Herald*, the *International Herald Tribune*, and *Newsweek* and *Time* magazines, but even these are likely to be four or five days old.

One of the better weekly **magazines** is the fairly liberal *Caretas* (Ⓦ caretas.com.pe), generally offering mildly critical support to whichever government happens to be in power.

Television and radio

Peruvians watch a lot of **television** – mostly football and soap operas, though TV is also a main source of news. Many programmes come from Mexico, Brazil and the US, with occasional eccentric selections from elsewhere and a growing presence of manga-style cartoons. There are nine main terrestrial channels; the govern-ment-run channel 7 has the most cultural and educational content. **Cable and satellite TV** is increasingly forming an important part of Peru's media, partly due to the fact that it can be received in even the remotest of settlements.

Alternatively, you can tune in to **Peruvian radio stations**, nearly all of which play music and are crammed with adverts. International pop, salsa and other Latin pop can be picked up most times of the day and night all along the FM wave band, while traditional Peruvian and Andean folk music can usually be found all over the AM dial. Radio Moda (97.3FM) mainly plays latino and reggaeton; Radio Planeta (107.7FM) plays rock and pop in English while Studio 92 (92.5FM) plays popular hits from rap to latino; RPP Noticias (89.7FM) and Radio Capital (96.7FM) are best for the news, while Radio Felicidad and Radio Mágica (88.3FM) play old school tracks. A useful website is Ⓦ radios.com.pe.

Festivals and public holidays

Public holidays, Carnival and local fiestas are all big events in Peru, celebrated with an openness and gusto that gives them enormous appeal for visitors; note that everything shuts down, including banks, post offices, information offices, tourist sites and

museums. The main national holidays take place over Easter, Christmas and during the month of October, in that order of importance. It is worth planning a little in advance to make sure that you don't get caught out.

In addition to the major regional and national celebrations, nearly every community has its own saint or patron figure to honour at town or **village fiestas**. These celebrations often mean a great deal to local people, and can be much more fun to visit than the larger countrywide events. Processions, music, dancing in costumes and eating and drinking form the core activities of these parties. In some cases the villagers will enact **symbolic dramas** with Indians dressed up as Spanish colonists, wearing hideous blue-eyed masks with long hairy beards. In the hills around towns like Huaraz and Cusco, especially, it's quite common to stumble into a village fiesta, with its explosion of human energy and noise, bright colours and a mixture of pagan and Catholic symbolism.

Such celebrations are very much **local affairs**, and while the occasional traveller will almost certainly be welcomed with great warmth, none of these remote communities would want to be invaded by tourists waving cameras and expecting to be feasted for free. The dates given below are therefore only for established events that are already on the tourist map, and for those that take place all over the country.

FESTIVALS AND PUBLIC HOLIDAYS

JANUARY

1 New Year's Day. Public holiday.

FEBRUARY

2 Candlemas. Folklore music and dancing throughout Peru, but especially lively in Puno at the Fiesta de la Virgen de la Candelaria and in the mountain regions.

Date varies Carnival. Wildly celebrated immediately prior to Lent, throughout the whole country.

MARCH/APRIL

Date varies Semana Santa (Holy Week). Superb processions all over Peru (the best are in Cusco and Ayacucho); the biggest is on Good Friday and in the evening on Easter Saturday, which is a public holiday.

MAY

1 Labour Day. Public holiday.

2–3 Fiesta de la Cruz (Festival of the Cross). Celebrated all over Peru in commemoration of ancient Peruvian agro-astronomical rituals and the Catholic annual calendar.

JUNE

Beginning of the month Corpus Christi. This takes places exactly nine weeks after Maundy Thursday, and usually falls in the first half of June. It's much celebrated, with fascinating processions and feasting all over Peru, but is particularly lively in Cusco.

24 Inti Raymi. Cusco's main Inca festival (see p.218).

29 St Peter's Day. A public holiday all over Peru, but mainly celebrated with fiestas in all the fishing villages along the coast.

JULY

15–18 Virgen del Carmen. Dance and music festivals at Pisac (see p.237) and Paucartambo (see box, p.270).

28–29 National Independence Day. Public holiday with military and school processions.

AUGUST

13–19 Arequipa Week. Processions, firework displays, plenty of folklore dancing and craft markets take place throughout Peru's second city.

30 Santa Rosa de Lima. Public holiday.

SEPTEMBER

End of the month Festival of Spring. Trujillo festival involving dancing – especially the local *marinera* dance and popular Peruvian waltzes (see p.356).

OCTOBER

8 Public holiday to commemorate the Battle of Angamos.

18–28 El Señor de Los Milagros (Lord of Miracles). Festival featuring large and solemn processions (the main ones take place on October 18, 19 and 28); many women wear purple for the whole month, particularly in Lima, where bullfights and other celebrations continue throughout the month.

NOVEMBER

1 Fiesta de Todos los Santos (All Saints Day). Public holiday.

2 Día de los Muertos (All Souls Day). A festive remembrance of dead friends and relatives that is taken very seriously by most Peruvians; it is a popular time for baptisms and roast pork meals.

1–7 Puno Festival. One of the mainstays of Andean culture, celebrating the founding of Puno by the Spanish conquistadores and also the founding of the Inca Empire by the legendary Manco Capac and his sister Mama Ocllo, who are said to have emerged from Lake Titicaca. October 5 is marked by vigorous, colourful community dancing.

1–30 International Bullfighting Competitions. Bullfights take place throughout the month, and are particularly spectacular at the Plaza de Acho in Lima.

12–28 Pacific Fair. One of the largest international trade fairs in South America – a huge, biennial event, which takes place on a permanent site on Av La Marina between Callao and Lima Centro.

DECEMBER

8 Feast of the Immaculate Conception. Public holiday.

25 Christmas Day. Public holiday.

Outdoor activities and sports

Few of the world's countries can offer anything remotely as varied, rugged and stunningly beautiful as Peru when it comes to ecotourism, trekking, mountain biking and river rafting. Apart from possessing extensive areas of wilderness, Peru has the highest tropical mountain range in the world, plus the Amazon rainforest and a long Pacific coastline, all offering different opportunities for outdoor activities and adventure. Football is Peru's sport of passion, closely followed by women's volleyball, at which they are remarkably good, often contending at the very top international levels. Bullfighting has a strong heritage both in Lima and small Andean villages.

Trekking and climbing

The most popular areas for **trekking and climbing** are: north and south of Cusco; the Colca Canyon; and the Cordillera Blanca. But there are many other equally biodiverse and culturally rich trekking routes in other *departamentos*: Cajamarca and Chachapoyas both possess challenging but rewarding mountain trekking, and the desert coast, too, has exceptional and unique eco-niches that are most easily explored from Lima, Trujillo, Chiclayo, Nazca, Pisco, Ica and Arequipa, where there is some tourism infrastructure to support visits.

The main tours, treks and climbs have been listed throughout the Guide in their appropriate

> **TOP 5 TREKS**
> **Ausangate** See p.268
> **The Chiquián Loop** See p.340
> **Choquequirao** See p.265
> **The Inca Trail** See p.250
> **The Llanganuco-to-Quebrada Santa Cruz Loop** See p.330

geographical context. Chapter Six, which includes Huaraz and the Cordillera Blanca, contains further information on climbing, mountaineering and trekking in the Andes, or **Andinismo**, as it's long been known (see box, p.324). The Cusco and Arequipa chapters also contain extensive listings of tour and trek operators as well as camping and climbing equipment rental.

TREKKING AND CLIMBING INFORMATION

Regional trekking resources can also be found in the relevant chapters of the Guide.

Asociación de Guías de Montaña del Peru (AGMP) Parque Ginebra 28-G Ancash, Huaraz (☎ 043 421811, ⊛ agmp.pe). Base for the Huaraz and Cordillera Blanca mountain guides association (see p.327).

CAMYCAM ⊛ camycam.org. A well-run, reliable mountain climbing organization set up in 1994.

Club de Andinismo de la Universidad de Lima Av Javier Prado Este, Lima 33 ☎ 01 437 6767 ext 30775. Peru's leading mountaineering club.

Canoeing and whitewater rafting

Peru is hard to beat for **canoeing** and **whitewater rafting**. The rivers around Cusco and the Colca Canyon, as well as Huaraz and, nearer to Lima, at Lunahuana, can be exciting and demanding,

A WALK ON THE WILD SIDE: ECOTOURISM IN PERU

Ecotourism is most developed in the Amazon rainforest region of Peru, particularly around Manu, which is considered one of the most biodiverse regions on Earth; Iquitos in the northern jungle and the Tambopata region around Puerto Maldonado are similar ecotourism hotspots. These areas, and others in Peru's extensive rainforest, all offer a wide choice of operators leading tours up rivers to **jungle lodges**, which themselves function as bases from which to explore the forest on foot and in smaller, quieter canoes. Naturally, the focus is on wildlife and flora; but there are often **cultural elements** to tours, including short visits to riverside communities and indigenous villages, and sometimes even mystical or healing work with jungle shamans. Prices vary and so does the level of service and accommodation, as well as the degree of sustainability of the operation.

Ecotourism is very much alive in the Peruvian **Andes** too, with several tour operators offering expeditions on foot or on horseback into some of the more exotic high-Andes and cloud-forest regions.

NATIONAL PARKS AND RESERVES

Almost ten percent of Peru is incorporated into some form of **protected area**, including thirteen national parks, fifteen national reserves, nine national sanctuaries, four historical sanctuaries, twelve reserved zones, six buffer forests, two hunting reserves and an assortment of communal reserves and national forests.

The largest of these protected areas is the **Reserva Nacional Pacaya-Samiria**, an incredible tropical forest region in northern Peru. This is closely followed in size by the **Manu Biosphere Reserve**, another vast and stunning jungle area, and the **Reserva Nacional Tambopata–Candamo and Parque Nacional Bahuaja-Sonene**, again an Amazon area, with possibly the richest flora and fauna of any region on the planet. Smaller but just as fascinating to visit are the **Parque Nacional Huascarán** in the high Andes near Huaraz, a popular trekking and climbing region, and the less-visited **Reserva Nacional Pampas Galeras**, close to Nazca, which was established mainly to protect the dwindling but precious herds of *vicuña*, the smallest and most beautiful member of the South American camelid family.

Bear in mind that the parks and reserves are enormous zones, within which there is hardly any attempt to control or organize nature. The term "park" probably conveys the wrong impression about these huge, virtually untouched areas, which were designated by the **National System for Conservation Units (SNCU)**, with the aim of combining conservation, research and, in some cases (such as the Inca Trail) recreational tourism.

In December 1992, the **Peruvian National Trust Fund for Parks and Protected Areas (PROFONANPE)** was established as a trust fund managed by the private sector to provide funding for Peru's main protected areas. It has assistance from the Peruvian government, national and international non-governmental organizations, the World Bank Global Environment Facility and the United Nations Environment Program.

VISITING THE PARKS

There's usually a small **charge** (usually around S/30 a day) to visit the national parks or nature reserves; this is normally levied at a reception hut on entry to the particular protected area. Sometimes, as at the Parque Nacional Huascarán, the cost is a simple daily rate (1 day S/10; 2 days S/65 includes camping fee); at others, like the Reserva Nacional Paracas on the coast south of Pisco, you pay a fixed sum to enter (S/10), regardless of how many days you might stay. For really remote protected areas, like Pacaya-Samiria, or if for some reason you enter an area via an unusual route, it is best to check on permissions – for Pacaya-Samiria you can pay the fee within the reserve itself. Most frequently visited National Parks will have an official hut for registration and paying of entry fees (which range from S/5 up to S/30 a day). For details, check with the protected areas national agency **SERNANP** at Calle Diecisiete 355, Urb El Palomar, San Isidro, Lima (☏01 717 7500, ⍟ sernanp.gob.pe), the South American Explorers' Club in Lima (see p.81) or at the local tourist office.

though there are always sections ideal for beginners. **Cusco** is one of the top rafting and canoeing centres in South America (see box, p.223), with easy access to a whole range of river grades, from 2 to 5 on the Río Urubamba (shifting up grades in the rainy season) to the most dangerous whitewater on the Río Apurímac (level 6). On the Río Vilcanota, some 90km south of Cusco, at Chukikahuana, there's a five-kilometre section of river that, between December and April, offers constant level-5 rapids. One of the most amazing trips from Cusco goes right down into the **Amazon Basin**. It should be noted that these rivers can be very wild and the best canoeing spots are often very remote, so you should only attempt river running with reputable companies and knowledgeable local guides.

The main companies operating in this field are listed in the relevant chapters. Trips range from half-day excursions to several days of river adventure, sometimes encompassing both mountain and jungle terrain. **Transport, food and accommodation** are generally included in the price where relevant; but the costs also depend on levels of service and whether overnight accommodation is required.

Cycling

In Peru, **cycling** is a major national sport, as well as one of the most ubiquitous forms of transport available to all classes in towns and rural areas virtually everywhere. Consequently, there are bike shops and bicycle-repair workshops in all major cities and larger towns. Perhaps more importantly, a number of tour companies offer **guided cycling tours** which can be an excellent way to see the best of Peru. Huaraz and Cusco are both popular destinations for bikers. For further information check the relevant chapter sections or contact the Federación Peruana de Ciclismo, Av San Luis 1308, Villa Deportiva La Videna, San Luis, Lima Centro (☎ 01 346 3493, ✆ fedepeci.org).

Surfing

People have been **surfing** the waves off the coast of Peru for thousands of years and the traditional *caballitos de totora* (cigar-shaped ocean-going reed rafts) from the Huanchaco (p.363) and Chiclayo (p.394) beach areas of Peru are still used by fishermen who ride the surf daily. Every year around twelve thousand surfers come to Peru whose best beaches – Chicama, Cabo Blanco, Punta Rocas – rival those of Hawaii and Brazil. Good websites to find out more about the scene include: ✆ perusurfguides.com, ✆ peruecosurf.com and ✆ vivamancora.com/english/surf.htm.

Diving and fishing

For information on **diving** and **fishing** contact the Federación Deportiva Peruana de Actividades Subacuáticas (✆ fedepasa.org). Aquasport, Av Conquistadores 805, San Isidro, Lima (☎ 01 221 1548, ✆ aquasport.com), stocks a good range of watersports gear.

Football

Peru's major sport is **football** and you'll find men and boys playing it in the streets of every city, town and settlement in the country down to the remotest of jungle outposts. The big teams are **Cristal**, **Alianza** and **El U** in Lima and **Ciencianco** from Cusco. The "Classic" game is between Alianza, the poor man's team from the La Victoria suburb of Lima, and El U ("U" from "Universitario"), generally supported by the middle class. To get a flavour for just how popular football is in Peru try a visit to the *Estadio Restaurant* in Lima (p.88), which has great murals, classic team shirts and life-size models of the world's top players.

Volleyball

Volleyball (*vóley*) is a very popular sport in Peru, particularly for women. The national team

---

> ## BARGAINING
>
> You are generally expected to **bargain** in markets and with taxi drivers (before getting in). Nevertheless, it's worth bearing in mind that travellers from Europe, North America and Australasia are generally much wealthier than Peruvians, so for every penny or cent you knock them down they stand to lose plenty of nuevo soles. It's also sometimes possible to haggle over the price of hotel rooms, especially if you're travelling in a group. Food, except at markets, and shop prices, however, tend to be fixed.

frequently reaches World Cup and Olympic finals, and they are followed avidly on TV. Even in remote villages, most schools have girls' volleyball teams. For more information, check out ✆ vivevoley.com.

Bullfighting

Although **bullfighting** is under threat from the pro-animal lobby, and has diminished significantly in popularity in the twenty-first century, in many coastal and mountain haciendas (estates), bullfights are still often held at fiesta times. In a less organized way they happen at many of the village fiestas, too – often with the bull being left to run through the village until it's eventually caught and mutilated by one of the men. This is not just a sad sight, it can also be dangerous for unsuspecting tourists who happen to wander into a seemingly evacuated village. The Lima bullfights in October (see box, p.68), in contrast, are a very serious business; even Hemingway was impressed.

Travel essentials

Costs

Peru is certainly a much **cheaper** place to visit than Europe or the US, but how much so will depend on where you are and when. As a general rule low-budget travellers should – with care – be able to get by on around S/45–90/US$15–30/£10–20/€13–26 per day, including transport, board and lodging. If you intend staying in mid-range hotels, eating in reasonable restaurants and taking the odd taxi, S/150–270/US$50–90/£33–60/€42–77 a day should be adequate, while S/300–600/US$100–200/£65–130/€85–170 a day will allow you to stay in comfort and sample some of Peru's best cuisine.

In most places in Peru, a good **meal** can still be found for under S/30 (US$10), **transport** is very reasonable, a comfortable **double room** costs S/60–180 (US$20–60) a night, and **camping** is usually free, or under S/15 (US$5) per person. Expect to pay a little more than usual in the larger towns and cities, especially Cusco and Lima, and also in the jungle, as many supplies have to be imported by truck. In the villages and rural towns, on the other hand, some basic commodities are far cheaper and it's always possible to buy food at a reasonable price from local villages or markets.

In the more popular parts of Peru, costs vary considerably with the **seasons**. Cusco, for instance, has its best weather from June to August, and many of its hotel prices go up by around 25–30 percent. The same thing happens at **fiesta** times – although on such occasions you're unlikely to resent it too much. As always, if you're travelling alone you'll end up spending considerably more than you would in a group of two or more people.

Tipping is expected in restaurants (ten per cent) and upmarket hotels, but not in taxis.

Student and youth discounts

It's also worth taking along an international **youth/student ID card**, if you have one, for the occasional reduction (up to fifty percent at some museums and sites). Cards generally cost US$20–25, but, once obtained, they soon pay for themselves in savings. Full-time students are eligible for the International Student ID Card (ISIC) or ITIC, Youth, VIP, YHA or Nomads card, most of which entitle the bearer to special air, rail and bus fares and discounts at museums, theatres and other attractions. For US citizens there's also a **health benefit**, providing emergency medical and hospital coverage, plus a 24-hour hotline to call in the event of a medical, legal or financial emergency.

You only have to be 26 or younger to qualify for the International Youth Travel Card, which carries the same benefits. Teachers qualify for the International Teacher Card, offering similar discounts. All these cards are available in the UK, US, Canada and South Africa from STA (Ⓦstatravel.com) and from Hostelling International (Ⓦhihostels.com) in Australia and New Zealand. Several other travel organizations and accommodation groups also sell their own cards, good for various discounts.

Crime and personal safety

The biggest problem for travellers in Peru is arguably **theft**, for which the country once had a bad reputation. While pickpockets are remarkably ingenious in Peru, as far as violent attacks go, you're probably safer here than in the backstreets of New York, Sydney, Durban or London; nevertheless, muggings do happen in certain parts of Lima (eg in the main shopping areas, La Victoria district, Barranco late at night and even in the parks of Miraflores), Cusco, Arequipa and, to a lesser extent, Trujillo.

Theft

While the overall situation has improved, **robbery** and **pickpocketing** are still real dangers; although you don't need to be in a permanent state of paranoia and watchfulness in busy public situations, common sense and general alertness are still recommended. Generally speaking, **thieves** (*ladrones*) work in teams of often **smartly dressed** young men and women, in crowded markets, bus depots and train stations, targeting anyone who looks like they've got money. One of them will distract your attention (an old woman falling over in front of you or someone splattering an ice cream down your jacket) while another picks your pocket, cuts open your bag with a razor or simply runs off with it. Peruvians and tourists alike have even had earrings ripped out on the street.

Bank **ATMs** are a target for **muggers** in cities, particularly after dark, so visit them with a friend or two during daylight hours or make sure there's a policeman within visual contact. **Armed mugging** is rare but does happen in Lima, and it's best not to resist. The horrific practice of "strangle mugging" has been a bit of a problem in Cusco and Arequipa, usually involving night attacks when the perpetrator tries to strangle the victim into unconsciousness. Again, be careful not to walk down badly lit streets alone in the early hours.

Theft from cars and even more so, theft of car parts, is rife, particularly in Lima. Also, in some of the more popular **hotels** in the large cities, especially Lima, bandits masquerading as policemen break into rooms and steal the guests' most valuable possessions while holding the hotel staff at gunpoint. Objects left on restaurant floors in busy parts of town, or in unlocked hotel rooms, are obviously liable to take a walk.

Precautions

You'd need to spend the whole time visibly guarding your luggage to be sure of keeping hold of it; even then, though, a determined team of thieves will stand a chance. However, a few simple **precautions** can make life a lot easier. The most important is to keep your ticket, passport (and tourist card), money and travellers' cheques on your person at all times (under your pillow while sleeping and on your person when washing in communal hotel bathrooms). **Money belts** are a good idea for travellers' cheques and tickets, or a holder for your passport and money can be hung either under a shirt or from a belt under trousers or skirts. Some people go as far as lining their bags with chicken wire (called *maya* in Peru) to make them knife-proof, and wrapping wire around camera straps for the same reason (putting their necks in danger to save their cameras).

Cities are most dangerous in the early hours of the morning and at **bus or train stations** where there's lots of anonymous activity. In rural areas robberies tend to be linked to the most popular towns (again, be most careful at the bus depot) and treks (the Inca Trail for instance). Beyond that, **rural areas** are generally safe. If you're camping near a remote community, though, it's a good idea to ask permission and make friendly contact with some of the locals; letting them know what you are up to will usually dissolve any local paranoia about tomb-robbers or kidnappers.

The only certain precaution you can take is to **insure** your gear and cash before you go (see p.46). Take refundable travellers' cheques, register your passport at your embassy in Lima on arrival (this doesn't take long and can save days should you lose it) and keep your eyes open at all times. If you do have something stolen, report it to the tourist police in larger towns, or the local police in more remote places, and ask them for a certified **denuncia** – this can take a couple of days. Many insurance companies will require a copy of the police *denuncia* in order to reimburse you. Bear in mind that the police in popular tourist spots, such as Cusco, have become much stricter about investigating reported thefts, after a spate of false claims by dishonest tourists. This means that genuine victims may be grilled more severely than expected, and the police may even come and search your hotel room for the "stolen" items.

Terrorism

You can get up-to-date information on the **terrorism** situation in each region from the South American Explorers' Club (see p.49), Peruvian embassies abroad (see p.43) or your embassy in Lima (see p.96). Essentially, though, **terrorism** is not the problem it was during the 1980s and 1990s when the two main **terrorist groups** active in Peru were the Sendero Luminoso (the Shining Path) and Tupac Amaru (MRTA).

The police

Most of your contact with the **police** will, with any luck, be at frontiers and controls. Depending on your personal appearance and the prevailing political climate, the police at these posts (Guardia Nacional and Aduanas) may want to **search your luggage**. This happens rarely, but when it does, it can be very thorough. Occasionally, you may have to get off buses and **register documents** at the police controls which regulate the traffic of goods and people from one *departamento* of Peru to another. The controls are usually situated on the outskirts of large towns on the main roads, but you sometimes come across a control in the middle of nowhere. Always stop, and be scrupulously polite – even if it seems that they're trying to make things difficult for you.

In general the police rarely bother travellers but there are certain sore points. The possession of (let alone trafficking of) either soft or hard **drugs** (basically marijuana or cocaine) is considered an extremely serious offence in Peru – usually leading to at least a ten-year jail sentence. There are many foreigners languishing in Peruvian jails after being charged with possession, some of whom have been waiting two years for a trial – there is no bail for serious charges.

Drugs aside, the police tend to follow the media in suspecting all foreigners of being **political subversives** and even gun-runners or terrorists; it's more than a little unwise to carry any Maoist or **radical literature**. If you find yourself in a tight spot, don't make a statement before seeing someone from your embassy, and don't say anything without the services of a reliable translator. It's not unusual to be given the opportunity to pay a **bribe** to the police (or any other official for that matter), even if you've done nothing wrong. You'll have to weigh up this situation as it arises – but remember, in South America bribery is seen as an age-old custom, very much part of the culture rather than a nasty form of corruption, and it can work to the advantage of both parties, however irritating it might seem. It's also worth noting that all police are **armed** with either a revolver or a submachine gun and will shoot at anyone who runs.

Tourist Police

It's often quite hard to spot the difference between **Tourist Police** and the normal police. Both are wings of the Guardia Civil, though the tourist police sometimes wear white hats rather than the standard green. Increasingly, the Tourist Police have taken on the function of informing and assisting tourists (eg in preparing a robbery report or *denuncia*) in city centres.

If you feel you've been ripped off or are unhappy about your treatment by a tour agent, hotel, restaurant, transport company, customs, immigration or even the police, you can call the 24-hour **Tourist Protection Service** hotline for the Tourist Police in Lima (Lima North ☏01 423 3500; Lima South ☏980 121 463). There are also Tourist Police offices throughout the country, including all major tourist destinations, such as Cusco, Arequipa and Puno.

Customs and etiquette

The most obvious cultural idiosyncrasy of Peruvians is that they **kiss** on one cheek at virtually every meeting between friends or acquaintances. In rural areas (as opposed to trendy beaches) the local tradition in most places is for people, particularly women, to **dress modestly** and cover themselves (eg longish skirts and T-shirts or blouses, or maybe traditional robes). In some hot places men may do manual labour in shorts, but they, too, are generally covered from shoulder to foot. Travellers sometimes suffer **insults** from Peruvians who begrudge the apparent relative wealth and freedom of tourists. Remember, however, that the terms "gringo" or "mister" are not generally meant in an offensive way in Peru.

Punctuality has improved in Peru in the last twenty years or so, but for social happenings can still be very lax. While buses, trains or planes won't wait a minute beyond their scheduled departure time, people almost expect friends to be an hour or more late for an appointment (don't arrange to meet a Peruvian on the street – make it a bar or café). Peruvians stipulate that an engagement is *a la hora inglesa* ("by English time") if they genuinely want people to arrive on time, or, more realistically, within half an hour of the time they fix.

Try to be aware of the strength of **religious belief** in Peru, particularly in the Andes, where churches have a rather heavy, sad atmosphere. You can enter and quietly look around all churches, but in the Andes especially you should refrain from taking photographs.

Electricity

220 volt/60 cycles AC is the standard **electrical current** all over Peru, except in Arequipa where it is 220 volt/50 cycles. In some of Lima's better hotels you may also find 110 volt sockets to use with standard electric shavers. Don't count on any Peruvian power supply being one hundred percent reliable and, particularly in cheap hostels and hotels, be very wary of the wiring (especially in electric shower fittings).

Entry requirements

Currently, EU, US, Canadian, Australian, New Zealand and South African citizens can all stay in Peru as tourists for up to one hundred and eighty three days without a visa. However, the situation does change periodically, so always check with your local Peruvian embassy some weeks before departure. All nationalities need a **tourist/embarkation card** (*tarjeta de embarque*) to enter Peru, issued at the frontiers or on the plane before landing in Lima. Tourist cards are usually valid for between sixty and ninety days. Unless you specifically ask for ninety days when being issued a Tourist Card on arrival, you may only receive sixty. For your own safety and freedom of movement a copy of the tourist card should be kept on you, with your passport, at all times – particularly when travelling away from the main towns.

Should you want to **extend your visa** (between thirty and sixty additional days), there are two basic options: either cross one of the borders and get a new tourist card when you come back in; or go through the bureaucratic rigmarole at a Migraciones office, which involves form filling, taking a photocopy of your passport and visa (or tourist card) and a visit to the Banco de la Nación to pay the required fee (US\$20) to the State, where you get issued an official receipt (*recibo de pago*). This process is easiest in Lima, where it can be all be done in the same building, but even there it can take a couple of hours or more. A further US\$11.70 is needed for legalizing the Migraciones form (usually issued at reception), and you may also be asked to provide evidence of a valid exit ticket from Peru. Migraciones is also the place to sort out new visas if you've **lost your passport** (having visited your embassy first) and to get passports re-stamped.

Student visas (which last twelve months) are best organized as far in advance as possible through your country's embassy in Lima, your nearest Peruvian embassy or the relevant educational institution. **Business visas** only become necessary if you are to be paid by a Peruvian organization, in which case ask your Peruvian employers to get this for you.

PERUVIAN EMBASSIES AND CONSULATES

An up-to-date list of Peruvian diplomatic missions can be accessed in Spanish on ⓦrree.gob.pe.

AUSTRALIA

Peruvian Embassy 40 Brisbane Ave, 2nd floor, Office 1B, Barton 2606 ACT, Canberra ☎ 02 6273 7351, ⓦembaperu.org.au
Peruvian Consulate 157 Main St, Croydon, Melbourne ☎ 03 9725 4655, ⓦconsulperuau.org.
Peruvian Consulate Suite 1001, 84 Pitt St, Sydney ☎ 02 9235 0300, ⓦconsulperuau.org.

CANADA

Peruvian Embassy 1901–130 Albert St, Ottawa ☎ 613 233 2721.

NEW ZEALAND

Peruvian Embassy Level Eight, Cigna House, 40 Mercer St, Wellington ☎ 04 499 8087.

SOUTH AFRICA

Peruvian Consulate 200 Saint Patricks St, Muckleneuk Hill, Pretoria ☎ 012 440 1030.

UNITED KINGDOM

Peruvian Embassy 52 Sloane St, London SW1X 9SP ☎ 020 7235 1917.

US

Peruvian Embassy 1700 Massachusetts Ave NW, Washington, DC ☎ 202 833 9860.

Gay and lesbian travellers

Homosexuality is pretty much kept underground in what is still a very macho society, though in recent years Lima has seen a liberating advance and transvestites can walk the streets in relative freedom from abuse. However, there is little or no organized gay scene. **The Peruvian Homosexual and Lesbian Movement** can be contacted at C Mariscal Miller 828, Jesús María, Lima (☎01 433 5314, ⓦmhol.org.pe). There are few specialist gay organizations, hotel facilities, restaurants or even clubs (where they exist they are listed in the relevant sections of the Guide). Further information can be accessed at the following websites: ⓦpurpleroofs.com, ⓦglobalgayz.com, ⓦperuesgay.com and ⓦgayperu.com.

Health

No inoculations are currently required for Peru, but a **yellow fever vaccination** is sometimes needed to enter the jungle, as well as being generally recommended. It's always a good idea to check with the embassy or a reliable travel agent before you go. Your doctor will probably advise you to have some **inoculations** anyway: typhoid, cholera, rabies and, again, yellow fever shots are all sensible precautions, and it's well worth ensuring that your polio and tetanus-diphtheria boosters are still effective. Immunization against hepatitis A is also usually recommended.

In case you don't get your shots before you leave for Peru, there is a useful 24-hour vaccination service at the Sanidad de la Fuerza Aérea on the first floor of Jorge Chávez airport in Lima (☎01 575 1745); remember to bring your passport as you will need to show it before getting the vaccination (S/85).

Yellow fever

Yellow fever breaks out now and again in some of the jungle areas of Peru; it is frequently obligatory to show an inoculation certificate when entering the Amazon region – if you can't show proof of immunization you'll be jabbed on the spot. This viral disease is transmitted by mosquitoes and can be fatal. Symptoms are headache, fever, abdominal pain and vomiting, and though victims may appear to recover, without medical help, they may suffer from bleeding, shock, and kidney and liver failure. The only treatment is to keep the patient's fever as low as possible and prevent dehydration.

Malaria

Malaria is quite common in Peru these days, particularly in the Amazon regions to the east of the country, and it's very easy to catch without prophylactics. If you intend to go into the jungle regions, malaria tablets should be taken – starting a few weeks before you arrive and continuing for some time after. Make sure you get a supply of these, or whatever is recommended by your doctor in advance of the trip. There are several commonly recommended malarial **prophylactics** recommended for the Peruvian jungle regions; some are more expensive than others and some are not recommended for prolonged periods. You should investigate your options with your GP, ideally more than a month prior to your departure for Peru. To avoid getting bitten in the rainforest wear long sleeves, long trousers, socks and a mosquito-proof net hat and sleep under good mosquito netting or in well-proofed quarters. For more information check out ⓦcdc.gov/travel/regionalmalaria.

Dengue fever

Like malaria, **dengue fever** is another illness spread by mosquito bites; the symptoms are similar, plus aching bones. Dengue-carrying mosquitoes are particularly prevalent during the rainy season, with urban jungle areas often the worst affected; they fly during the day, so wear insect repellent in the daytime if mosquitoes are around. The only treatment is complete rest, with drugs to assuage the fever – unfortunately, a second infection can be fatal.

Diarrhoea

Diarrhoea is something everybody gets at some stage, and there's little to be done except to drink a lot of water and bide your time. You should also replace salts either by taking oral rehydration salts or by mixing a teaspoon of salt and eight teaspoons of sugar in a litre of purified water. You can minimize the risk by being sensible about what you eat, and by not drinking **tap water** anywhere (see below). Peruvians are great believers in herbal teas, which often help alleviate cramps.

Dysentery and giardia

If your diarrhoea contains blood or mucus, the cause may be dysentery (one of either two strains; see below) or giardia. Combined with a fever, these symptoms could well be caused by **bacillic dysentery** and may clear up without treatment. If you're sure you need it, a course of antibiotics such as tetracyclin or ampicillin (travel with a supply if you are going off the beaten track for a while) should sort you out, but they also destroy "gut flora" which help protect you, so should only be used if properly diagnosed or in a desperate situation. Similar symptoms without fever indicate **amoebic dysentery**, which is much more serious, and can damage your gut if untreated. The usual cure is a course of metronidazole (Flagyl), an antibiotic which may itself make you feel ill, and should not be taken with alcohol.

Similar symptoms, plus rotten-egg-smelling belches and gas, indicate **giardia**, for which the treatment is again metronidazole. If you suspect you have any of these illnesses, seek medical help, and only start on the metronidazole (250mg three times daily for a week for adults) if there is definitely blood in your diarrhoea and it is impossible to see a doctor.

Water and food

Water in Peru is better than it used to be, but it can still trouble non-Peruvian (and even Peruvian) stomachs, so it's a good idea to only drink **bottled water** (*água mineral*), available in various sizes, including litre and two-litre bottles from most corner shops or food stores. Stick with known brands, even if they are more expensive, and always check that the seal on the bottle is intact, since the sale of bottles refilled with local water is not uncommon. Carbonated water is generally safer as it is more likely to be the genuine stuff. You should also clean your teeth using bottled water and avoid raw foods washed in local water.

Apart from bottled water, there are various methods of **treating water** while you are travelling, whether your source is tap water or natural groundwater such as a river or stream. **Boiling** is the time-honoured method, which is an effective way to sterilize water, although it will not remove any unpleasant tastes. A minimum boiling time of five minutes (longer at higher altitudes) is sufficient to kill microorganisms. In remote jungle areas, **sterilizing tablets** are a better idea, although they leave a rather bad taste in the mouth. Pregnant women or people with thyroid problems should consult their doctor before using iodine sterilizing tablets or iodine-based purifiers. There are also several portable **water filters** on the market. In emergencies and remote areas in particular, always check with locals to see whether the tap water is OK (*es potable?*) before drinking it.

Peruvian **food** cooked on the street has been frequently condemned as a health hazard, particularly during rare but recurrent **cholera outbreaks**. Be careful about anything bought from street stalls, particularly seafood, which may not be that fresh. **Salads** should be avoided, especially in small settlements where they may have been washed in river water or fertilized by local sewage waters.

The sun

The sun can be deceptively hot, particularly on the coast or when travelling in boats on jungle rivers when the hazy weather or cool breezes can put visitors off their guard; remember, **sunstroke** can make you very sick as well as burnt. Wide-brimmed hats, sunscreen lotions (factor 60 advisable since the sun high up in the Andes is deceptively strong) and staying in the shade whenever possible are all good precautions. Note that suntan lotion and sunblock are more expensive in Peru than they are at home, so take a good supply with you. If you do run out, you can buy Western brands at most *farmacias*, though you won't find a very wide choice available, especially in the higher factors. Also make sure that you increase your water intake, in order to prevent **dehydration**.

Altitude sickness

Altitude sickness – known as *soroche* (see box, p.210) in Peru – is a common problem for visitors, especially if you are travelling quickly between the coast or jungle regions and the high Andes. The best way to prevent it is to eat light meals, drink lots of coca tea and water and spend as long as possible acclimatizing to high altitudes (over 2500m) before carrying out any strenuous activity. Anyone who suffers from headaches or nausea should rest; more seriously, a sudden bad cough could be a sign of **pulmonary edema** and demands an immediate descent and medical attention – altitude sickness can kill. People often suffer from altitude sickness on trains crossing high passes; if this happens, don't panic, just rest and stay on the train until it descends. Most trains are equipped with oxygen bags or cylinders that are brought around by the conductor for anyone in need. **Diamox** is used by many from the US to counter the effects of *soroche*. It's best to bring this with you from home since it's rarely available in Peruvian pharmacies.

Insects

Insects are more of an irritation than a serious problem, but on the coast, in the jungle and to a lesser extent in the mountains, the **common fly** is a definite pest. Although flies can carry typhoid, there is little one can do; you might spend mealtimes swatting flies away from your plate but even in expensive restaurants it's difficult to monitor hygiene in the kitchens.

A more obvious problem is the **mosquito**, which in some parts of the lowland jungle carries malaria. Repellents are of limited value – it's better to cover your arms, legs and feet with a good layer of clothing. Mosquitoes tend to emerge after dark, but the daytime holds even worse biting insects in the jungle regions, among them the **manta blanca** (or white blanket), so called because they swarm as a blanket of tiny flying insects. Their bites don't hurt at the time but itch like crazy for a few days afterwards. **Antihistamine creams** or tablets can reduce the sting or itchiness of most insect bites, but try not to scratch them – if it gets unbearable go to the nearest *farmacia* for advice. To keep hotel rooms relatively insect-free, buy some of the spirals of incense-like **pyrethrin**, available cheaply everywhere.

HIV and AIDS

While Peru does not have as bad a reputation for **HIV** and **AIDS** (also known as **SIDA** in Latin America) as neighbouring Brazil, they are a growing problem in South America and you should still take care. Although all hospitals and clinics in Peru are supposed to use only sterilized equipment, many travellers prefer to take their own sealed hypodermic syringes in case of emergencies.

Contraception

Condoms *(profilacticos)* are available from street vendors and some *farmacias*. However, they tend to be expensive and often poor quality, so bring an adequate supply with you. **The Pill** is also available from *farmacias*, officially on prescription only, but frequently sold over the counter. You're unlikely to be able to match your brand, however, so it's far better to bring your own supply. It's worth remembering that if you suffer from moderately severe **diarrhoea** on your trip the Pill (or any other drug) may not be in your system long enough to take effect.

Pharmacies

For **minor ailments** you can buy most drugs at a pharmacy (*farmacia* or *botica*) without a prescription. Antibiotics and malaria pills can be bought over the counter (it is important to know the correct dosage), as can antihistamines (for bite allergies) or medication for an upset stomach (try Lomotil or Streptotriad). You can also buy Western-brand **tampons** at a *farmacia*, though they are expensive, so it's better to bring a good supply. For any serious illnesses, you should go to a doctor or hospital; these are listed throughout the Guide, or ask your hotel or the local tourist office for the best clinic around.

AVERAGE TEMPERATURES AND RAINFALL

	Oct–April	May–Sept	Temp. range (approx) °C/°F	Annual rainfall mm/in
COAST	Sunny season	Some coastal cloud	13–30/55–86	0.55/0.02
ANDES	Rainy season	Dry season	0–18/32–64	400–1000/16–39
JUNGLE	Rainy season	Dry season	20–35/68–95	2000–3900/79–154

Alternative medicines

Alternative medicines have a popular history going back at least two thousand years in Peru and the traditional practitioners – *herbaleros, hueseros* and *curanderos* – are still commonplace. **Herbaleros** sell curative plants, herbs and charms in the streets and markets of most towns. They lay out a selection of ground roots, liquid tree barks, flowers, leaves and creams – all with specific medicinal functions and sold at much lower prices than in the *farmacias*. If told the symptoms, a *herbalero* can select remedies for most minor (and apparently some major) ailments. **Hueseros** are consultants who treat diseases and injuries by bone manipulation, while **curanderos** claim diagnostic, divinatory and healing powers, and have existed in Peru since pre-Inca days.

MEDICAL RESOURCES

UK AND IRELAND

Hospital for Tropical Diseases Travel Clinic ☎ 0203 456 7891, Ⓦ thehtd.org.

MASTA (Medical Advisory Service for Travellers Abroad) Ⓦ masta.org for the nearest clinic.

Tropical Medical Bureau Ireland ☎ 1850 487 674, Ⓦ tmb.ie.

US AND CANADA

Canadian Society for International Health ☎ 613 241 5785, Ⓦ csih.org. Extensive list of travel health centres.

CDC ☎ 1 800 232 4636, Ⓦ cdc.gov/travel. Official US government travel health site.

International Society for Travel Medicine ☎ 1 404 373 8282, Ⓦ istm.org. Has a full list of travel health clinics.

AUSTRALIA, NEW ZEALAND AND SOUTH AFRICA

The Travel Doctor – TMVC ☎ 1300 658 844, Ⓦ tmvc.com.au. Lists travel clinics in Australia, New Zealand and Thailand.

Insurance

Insurance (see box below) is definitely a good idea for a destination like Peru. Most worldwide policies offer a range of options to cover different levels of adventurous activities. Some of the extreme sports, including kayaking and bungee jumping, may not be covered by standard policies.

Internet

Peru has good **internet** connections, with cybercafés, internet cabins and wi-fi in the most unlikely of small towns. There is wi-fi virtually everywhere in Lima and Cusco, including at hotels, hostels, restaurants and cafes, closely followed by Arequipa, Huaraz, Puno, Iquitos and Trujillo. Wi-fi is generally free, while the rate is typically S/3 an hour at Internet cafés, though thirty- and fifteen-minute options are often available.

Language lessons

You can learn **Peruvian Spanish** all over Peru, but the best range of schools is in Lima, Cusco, Arequipa and Huancayo. Check the relevant Directory sections in the Guide.

Laundry

Mid- to high-end hotels frequently offer a **laundry** service and some basic hotels have communal washrooms where you can do your own washing. It's no great expense to get your clothes washed by a *lavandería* (laundry) on the street, normally upwards of S/3 per kg.

Living and working in Peru

There is a certain amount of **bureaucracy** involved if you want to work (or live) officially in Peru. Your only real chance of **earning money** here is by teaching English in Lima, or, with luck, teaching English or working in an expat bar in Arequipa or Cusco. In the more remote parts of the country it may sometimes be possible to find board and lodging in return for a little building work or general labour.

ROUGH GUIDES TRAVEL INSURANCE

Rough Guides has teamed up with Ⓦ WorldNomads.com to offer great travel insurance deals. Policies are available to residents of over 150 countries, with cover for a wide range of adventure sports, 24-hour emergency assistance, high levels of medical and evacuation cover and a stream of travel safety information. Roughguides.com users can take advantage of their policies online 24/7, from anywhere in the world – even if you're already travelling. And since plans often change when you're on the road, you can extend your policy and even claim online. Roughguides.com users who buy travel insurance with Ⓦ WorldNomads.com can also leave a positive footprint and donate to a community development project. For more information, go to Ⓦ roughguides.com/travel-insurance.

For biology, geography or environmental science graduates there's the chance of free board and lodging, and maybe a small salary, if you're willing to work very hard for at least three months as a **tour guide** in a jungle lodge, under the Resident Naturalist schemes. One or two lodges along the **Río Tambopata** offer such schemes and other research opportunities. For more details, it's best to contact lodges such as the *Tambopata Research Centre* (see p.441) directly. Arrangements need to be made at least six months in advance. There are plenty of charities you can help out at, including the Arequipa-based not-for-profit **Traveller Not Tourist** organization (Ⓦtravellernottourist.org) that helps volunteers work directly to support children in poverty.

Teaching English

There are two options if you'd like to teach English in Peru: find work before you go, or just wing it and see what you come up with while you're out there, particularly if you already have a degree, teaching experience or a relevant ELT or TEFL qualification. The British Council website (Ⓦbritishcouncil.org) has a list of English-teaching vacancies and Overseas Jobs Express (Ⓦoverseasjobs.com) also lists jobs.

STUDY AND WORK PROGRAMMES

AFS Intercultural Programs US ☎ 1 800 237 4636, Canada ☎ 1 800 361 7248, Australia ☎ 1300 131 736, NZ ☎ 0800 600 300, SA ☎ 0861 237 468; Ⓦ afs.org. Intercultural exchange organization with programmes in over 50 countries.
American Institute for Foreign Study US ☎ 1 866 906 2437, UK ☎ 020 7581 7300, Australia ☎ 02 8235 7000; Ⓦ aifs.com. Language study and cultural immersion, as well as au pair and Camp America programmes.
BUNAC US ☎ 1 800 462 8622, UK ☎ 0333 999 7516; Ⓦ bunac.org. Organizes working holidays in a range of destinations for students.
BTCV (British Trust for Conservation Volunteers) UK ☎ 01302 388 883, Ⓦ btcv.org.uk. One of the largest environmental charities in Britain, with a programme of national and international working holidays (as a paying volunteer).
Council on International Educational Exchange (CIEE) US ☎ 1 207 553 4000, Ⓦ ciee.org. Leading NGO offering study programmes and volunteer projects around the world.
Earthwatch Institute UK ☎ 01865 318 838, US ☎ 978 461 0081, Australia ☎ 03 9016 7590; Ⓦ earthwatch.org. Scientific expedition project that spans over fifty countries, with environmental and archeological ventures worldwide.

Mail

The Peruvian **postal service** – branded as Serpost – is reasonably efficient, if slightly irregular and a little expensive. Letters from Europe and the US generally take around one or two weeks to arrive – occasionally less – while outbound letters to Europe or the US seem to take between ten days and three weeks. Stamps for postcards and airmail letters to the UK, the US and to Australia, New Zealand and South Africa cost around S/3–7.

Be aware that **parcels** take about one month to arrive and are particularly vulnerable to being opened en route – in either direction – and expensive souvenirs can't be sure of leaving the building where you mail them. Never send money through the Peruvian post!

Maps

Maps of Peru fall into three basic categories. A standard **road map** should be available from good map-sellers just about anywhere in the world or in Peru itself from street vendors or *librerías*; the Touring y Automóvil Club de Perú, Av Trinidad Morán 698, Lince Lima (☎01 611 9999, Ⓦtouring peru.com.pe), is worth visiting for its good route maps. **Departmental maps**, covering each *departamento* (Peruvian state) in greater detail, albeit often very out of date, are also fairly widely available. **Topographic maps** (usually 1:100,000) cover the entire coastal area and most of the mountainous regions of Peru. In Lima, they can be bought from the Instituto Geográfico Nacional (Ⓦwww.ign.gob.pe), and they're also available at the South American Explorers' Club (see p.49), along with a wide variety of hiking maps and guidebooks for all the most popular hiking zones, and quite a few others.

Money

The **currency** in Peru is the **nuevo sol**, still simply called a "sol" on the streets, and whose symbol is S/. The sol remains relatively steady against the US dollar, and at time of writing,the exchange rate for the nuevo sol was roughly US$1 = S/3, £1 = S/4.5, Aus$1 = S/2.5, NZ$1 = S/2.3, ZAR1 = 26¢.

Dollars are also accepted in many places, including smart hotels, tour companies, railway companies and classy restaurants. The main supermarkets in Lima also take dollars, as do some taxi drivers (especially those picking up from airports).

ATMs are common in all of Peru's cities and main towns, with the BCP (Banco de Crédito del Peru) probably being the most common, but all the main banks' ATMs seem to work well with standard credit and debit cards. Travellers' cheques and cash dollars or euros can be cashed at **casas de cambio**. Cash can be changed on the street, sometimes at a slightly better rate than the banks or casas de cambio, but with a greater risk of being short-changed.

Opening hours

Most **shops** and **services** in Peru open Monday to Saturday 9am to 5pm, or 6pm. Many are open on Sunday as well, if for more limited hours. Of Peru's **museums**, some belong to the state, others to institutions and a few to individuals. Most charge a small admission fee and are open Monday to Saturday 9am to noon and 3 to 6pm.

Peru's more important **ancient sites** and ruins usually have opening hours that coincide with daylight – from around 7am until 5pm or 6pm daily. Smaller sites are rarely fenced off, and are nearly always accessible 24 hours a day. For larger sites, you normally pay a small admission fee to the local guardian – who may then walk around with you, pointing out features of interest. Only Machu Picchu charges more than a few dollars' entrance fee – this is one site where you may find it worth presenting an ISIC or FIYTO student card (which generally gets you in for half-price).

Churches open in the mornings for Mass (usually around 6am), after which the smaller ones close. Those which are most interesting to tourists, however, tend to stay open all day, while others open again in the afternoon from 3 to 6pm. Very occasionally there's an admission charge to churches, and more regularly to monasteries (*monasterios*).

Phones

It's easy to make **international calls** from just about any town in the country, either with a pre-paid phonecard or via a telephone cabin, which can be found in all town centres. **Mobiles** are expensive to use, but almost everyone seems to have one these days. Using your own mobile almost always works out to be the most expensive form of telephone communication, but it may be worth checking with your provider before departure. It is certainly cheaper to buy a local mobile phone and sim card (available in shops everywhere from around S/105–135 or US$35–45) and use this for in-Peru calls. Probably the most popular mobile company is Claro.

Phonecards (eg Telefónica Tarjeta 147) are the cheapest way to communciate by phone either domestically or internationally; indeed, international calls from a fixed phone often work out cheaper than ones to Peruvian mobiles or between Peruvian cities. Each card has directions for use (in Spanish) on the reverse and most are based on a scratch-card numeral basis. You can buy phonecards from corner shops, *farmacias* or on the street from cigarette stalls in the centres of most towns and cities. With free wi-fi available in most places, Skype is probably the most convenient form of long-distance calling.

Photography

The light in Peru is very bright, with a strong contrast between shade and sun. This can produce

---

USEFUL NUMBERS AND DIALLING CODES

USEFUL TELEPHONE NUMBERS
Directory enquiries ☎103
Operator ☎100
Emergency services ☎105
International operator ☎108

CALLING HOME FROM ABROAD
To make an international call, dial the international access code (in Peru it's +51 then the destination's country code, before the rest of the number. Note that the initial zero is omitted from the area code when dialling the UK, Ireland, Australia and New Zealand from abroad.
Australia + 61
New Zealand + 64
UK + 44
US and Canada + 1
Republic of Ireland + 353
South Africa + 27

a nice effect and generally speaking it's easy to take good **photographs**. One of the more complex problems is how to take photos of people without upsetting them. You should always talk to a prospective subject first, and ask if she/he minds if you take a quick photo ("*una fotita, por favor?*" – "a little photo please"); most people react favourably to this approach even if all the communication is in sign language, although don't be surprised if you're asked for a sol or two.

Digital photography is by far the most common format for Peruvians and travellers alike. Digital cameras, memory cards, batteries and accessories are now widely available pretty much everywhere in Peru. Most internet cafés can also help download memory cards. Camera film is expensive to buy, and not readily available outside of the main cities; colour Kodak and Fuji films are easier to find, but black-and-white film is rare.

Senior travellers

Senior travellers in reasonable health should have no problems in Peru. Anyone taking medication should obviously bring enough supplies for the duration of the trip, though most drugs are available over the counter in Lima and other cities. The altitude is likely to be the most serious concern, so careful reading of our section on altitude sickness (see p.45) becomes even more crucial; so does taking great care with what food you eat (see p.44).

As far as accommodation for senior travellers goes, most middle- to top-range hotels are clean and comfortable; it's mostly a matter of clearly asking for what you need when booking or on arrival at the hotel. This is particularly true if you have special requirements such as a ground-floor room.

Shopping

Peru is one of those places where you want to buy something from virtually every street corner. Apart from all the fine alpaca sweaters and blankets, there are baskets, musical instruments, paintings and a whole raft of quite well-known **artesanía** (craft goods).

Of course, most Peruvians live in cities with massive supermarkets and a pharmacy on each street corner. **Shopping centres** are springing up all over Lima, each more or less a replica of the other. Traditional craft goods from most regions of Peru can be found in **markets** and independent shops in Lima. Woollen and alpaca products,

though, are usually cheaper and often better quality in the mountains – particularly in Cusco, Juliaca and Puno; carved gourds are imported from around Huancayo; the best places to buy ceramic replicas are Trujillo, Huaraz, Ica and Nazca; and the best jungle crafts are from Pucallpa and Iquitos.

If you get offered an "ancient" pot or necklace, remember that **Peruvian law** stipulates that no items of archeological or historical value or interest may be removed from the country. Many of the **jungle crafts** which incorporate feathers, skins or shells of rare Amazonian animals are also banned for export – it's best not to buy these if you are in any doubt about their scarcity. If you do try to export anything of archeological or biological value, and get caught, you'll have the goods confiscated at the very least, and may find yourself in a Peruvian court.

Time

Peru keeps the same hours as **Eastern Standard Time**, which is five hours behind GMT.

Tourist information

These days, **iPerú** (☎01 574 8000, ⓦperu.info) is the key government source of tourist information. They have offices in most major cities, often operating in parallel with a local municipal service. They will provide information by email and their website is useful.

The **South American Explorers' Club** is also a great source of relevant and up-to-date travel information both before you leave home and when you arrive in Lima. It is a nonprofit organization that was founded in 1977 to support scientific and adventure expeditions and to provide services to travellers. In return for membership (from US$60 a year) you receive the monthly E-newsletter, and you can use the club's facilities, which in Lima include an excellent library, a map collection, trip reports, listings, a postal address and storage space. The club also provides discounts on maps and guidebooks, information on visas, doctors and dentists, and access to a network of experts with specialist information. Some trip reports are now also available online. They have clubhouses in Lima (see p.81), and Cusco (see p.221), as well as Quito – check the website for further details.

GOVERNMENT WEBSITES

Asociación Peruano de Tursimo Receptivo e Interno ⓦapoturperu.org.
Australian Department of Foreign Affairs ⓦdfat.gov.au.

British Foreign & Commonwealth Office Ⓦ fco.gov.uk.
Canadian Department of Foreign Affairs Ⓦ international
.gc.ca.
Instituto Geográfico Nacional Ⓦ ign.gob.pe.
Irish Department of Foreign Affairs Ⓦ foreignaffairs.gov.ie.
Ministerio de Cultura Ⓦ cultura.gob.pe.
New Zealand Ministry of Foreign Affairs Ⓦ mfat.govt.nz.
US State Department Ⓦ state.gov.
South African Department of Foreign Affairs Ⓦ dfa.gov.za.

Travelling with children

South Americans hold the family unit in high regard and **children** are central to this. Prices can often be cheaper for children; tours to attractions can occasionally be negotiated on a **family-rate** basis and entry to sites is often half-price or less (and always free for infants). Children under 10 generally get half-fare on local (but not inter-regional) buses, while trains and boats generally charge full fare if a seat is required. Infants who don't need a seat often travel free on all transport except planes, when you pay around ten percent of the usual fare.

Travelling around the country is perhaps the most difficult activity with children. **Bus and train journeys** are generally long (twelve hours or more). Crossing international borders is a potential hassle; although Peru officially accepts children under 16 on their parents' **passports**, it is a good idea for them to have their own to minimize problems. For more information you can try *The Rough Guide to Travel with Babies and Young Children*.

Health

Most types of nappies, creams, wet-wipes and children's medication can be bought easily in main **chemists** and larger supermarkets in Lima, Arequipa and Cusco, but outside these places it's wise to arrive prepared. Consult your doctor before leaving home regarding health matters. **Sunscreen** is important, as are sun hats (cheap and readily available), and you might consider a parasol for very small children. Conversely, it can get cold at night in the Andes, so take plenty of **warm clothing**. In the mountains, the **altitude** doesn't seem to cause children as many problems as it does their elders, but they shouldn't walk too strenuously above 2000m without full acclimatization.

The major risk around the regions is a bad stomach and **diarrhoea** (see p.44) from water or food; you should be ready to act sooner than usual when treating children under 10 with rehydration salts. In **Lima**, where the water is just about good enough to clean your teeth, but not to drink, the

issues for local children are mainly bronchial or asthmatic, with humid weather and high pollution levels causing many long-lasting chest ailments. This shouldn't be a problem for any visiting children unless they already have difficulties.

Food and drink

The **food and drink** in Peru is varied enough to appeal to most kids. Pizzas are available almost everywhere, as are good fish, red meats, fried chicken, chips, corn on the cob and nutritious soups, and vitamin supplements are always a good idea. There's also a wide range of **soft drinks**, from the ubiquitous Coca-Cola and Sprite to Inka Cola (now owned by Coca-Cola). Recognizable commercial **baby food** (and nappy brands) is available in all large supermarkets. **Restaurants** in Peru cater well for children and some offer smaller, cheaper portions; if they don't publicize it, it's worth asking.

Hotels

Like restaurants, **hotels** are used to handling kids; they will sometimes offer discounts, especially if children share rooms or beds. Lower- to mid-range accommodation is the most flexible in this regard, but even expensive places can be helpful. Many hotels and hostels have collective rooms large enough for families to share at reasonable rates.

Travellers with disabilities

Peru is not well set up in terms of access infrastructure for welcoming **travellers with disabilities** (even the best buses have mostly ordinary steps), but nevertheless, in a moment of difficulty many Peruvians will support and help. **Airlines** have facilities and will assist in most of Peru's airports.

While there are still few hotels or resorts that are well designed enough to ensure access for all, Peru, and Lima in particular, has made progress in recent years. The hotel chain Sonesta Posadas del Inca (Ⓦ sonesta.com) caters well for disabilities and has places in Lima, Cusco, Arequipa, Puno and the Sacred Valley; other pioneers in Peru include the travel agency Apumayo Expediciones (Ⓦ apumayo .com), Rainforest Expeditions (Ⓦ perunature.com) and InkaNatura Travel (Ⓦ inkanatura.com). Accessible Journeys (Ⓦ disabilitytravel.com), meanwhile, offers tours specifically designed for travellers with physical disabilities, including a thirteen-day trip to Lima, Cusco, the Sacred Valley, Machu Picchu and Nazca. Additional information on access for travellers in Peru with disabilities can be obtained from the South American Explorers' Club (see p.49).

Women travellers

Machismo is well ingrained in the Peruvian male mentality, particularly in the towns, and female foreigners are almost universally seen as liberated and therefore sexually available. On the whole, the situations female travellers will encounter are more annoying than dangerous, with frequent comments such as *qué guapa* ("how pretty"), intrusive and prolonged stares, plus whistling and hissing in the **cities**. Worse still are the occasional rude comments and groping, particularly in crowded situations such as on buses or trains. Blonde and fair-skinned women are likely to suffer much more of this behaviour than darker, Latin-looking women.

Mostly these are situations you'd deal with routinely at home but they can seem threatening without a clear understanding of Peruvian Spanish and slang. To avoid getting caught up in something you can't control, any provocation is best ignored.

In a public situation, however, any real harassment is often best dealt with by loudly drawing attention to the miscreant.

In the predominantly Indian, **remote areas** there is less of an overt problem, though surprisingly this is where physical assaults are more likely to take place. They are not common, however – you're probably safer hiking in the Andes than walking at night in most British or North American inner cities.

Personal safety

Two obvious, but enduring, pieces of advice are to **travel with friends** (being on your own makes you most vulnerable), and if you're **camping**, it's a good idea to get to know the locals, which can give a kind of acceptance and insurance, and may even lead to the offer of a room – Peruvians, particularly those in rural areas, can be incredibly kind and hospitable. It's also sensible to check with the South American Explorers' Club (see p.49), particularly in Cusco, for information.

Lima and around

PLAZA DE ARMAS, LIMA

1

Lima and around

Crowded into the mouth of the arid Rimac river valley, with low sandy mountains closing in around its outer fringes, Lima is a boisterous, macho sprawl of a city, full of beaten-up cars chasing Mercedes and 4WDs: this is a place where money rules, with an irresistible, underlying energy. A large part of the city's appeal is its fascinating mix of lifestyles and cultures: from the snappy, sassy, cocaine-influenced criolla style to the easy-going, happy-go-lucky attitude of Lima's poorer citizens. Somehow, though, it still manages to appear relaxed and laidback in the barrios and off the beaten track, and the noisy, frenetic craziness of it all is mellowed somewhat by the presence of the sea and beaches. Even if you choose not to spend much time here, you can get a good sense of it all in just a few days: Limeño hospitality and kindness are almost boundless once you've established an initial rapport.

Considered the most beautiful city in Spanish America during the sixteenth and seventeenth centuries and long established as Peru's seat of government, Lima retains a certain elegance, particularly in colonial Lima Centro. The city still brims with culture and history, though it may not be obvious at first. Top of its attractions are some excellent **museums** – the best of which should definitely be visited before setting off for Machu Picchu or any of Peru's other great Inca ruins – as well as fine Spanish **churches** in the centre, and some distinguished **mansions** in the wealthy suburbs of Barranco and Miraflores. Add to this some outstanding **restaurants** and hedonistic **nightlife**, and you'll find there's plenty to explore in Peru's distinctive capital.

As a transport and communications hub, Lima also makes a good base for exploring the surrounding region, and the immediate area offers plenty of reasons to delay your progress on towards Arequipa or Cusco. Within an hour's bus ride south is the coastline – often deserted – lined by a series of attractive **beaches**. Above them, the imposing fortress-temple complex of **Pachacamac** sits on a sandstone cliff, near the edge of the ocean. In the neighbouring **Rimac Valley** you can visit the pre-Inca sites of **Puruchuco** and **Cajamarquilla**, and, in the foothills above Lima, intriguingly eroded rock outcrops and megalithic monuments surround the natural amphitheatre of **Marcahuasi** (see p.283). To the north, meanwhile, the oldest stone pyramids in the world sit abandoned in the desert of **Caral**.

A MASK OF THE SICÁN DEITY, MUSEO LARCO

Highlights

❶ Huaca Pucllana A vast pre-Inca adobe pyramid mound in the middle of suburban Miraflores, this is a good place to get your bearings and a taste of ancient Lima. **See p.69**

❷ Parque Kennedy The central park in downtown Lima's Miraflores district draws locals and tourists alike to its small craft market every evening, and there are some fun cafés and restaurants located along its edges too. **See p.69**

❸ Fishermen's Wharf At the southern end of Lima's cliff-hemmed beaches, a small wooden jetty is home to the fishermen of Chorrillos, whose morning catch is landed just in time for the ceviche kiosks next door to prepare inexpensive, but fantastically fresh, fish lunches. **See p.75**

❹ Museo Larco One of the city's most unusual museums, and the largest private collection of Peruvian archeology, containing more than 400,000 excellently preserved ancient ceramics, including an extensive erotic section. **See p.76**

❺ El Cordano One of Lima's last surviving traditional bar/restaurants, bustling with locals. **See p.86**

❻ Lima restaurants Enjoy a lazy lunch in one of Lima's excellent restaurants – you can't go wrong with the ceviche served up by seafood specialists, *Caplina*. **See p.88**

HIGHLIGHTS ARE MARKED ON THE MAP ON PP.58–59

1 Lima

Laid out across a wide, flat, alluvial plain, Lima's buildings fan out like a concrete phoenix in long, straight avenues and roads from its centre. The old colonial heart, **Lima Centro**, is of both architectural and cultural interest as well as being the seat of government and religion. South of here, along and just inland from the ocean clifftop, the modern centre of **Miraflores**, where most tourists stay, buzzes with shoppers by day and partiers by night. East along the coast a few kilometres, what was once a separate seaside suburb and artists' quarter, **Barranco**, still boasts both tradition and a vibrant atmosphere. Between Miraflores and Lima Centro, jammed between the Paseo de la República and the Avenida Arequipa main roads that connect them, rise the skyscraping banks of **San Isidro**, Lima's heaving commercial centre.

To the west, the city reaches a fine finger of low-lying land pointing into the Pacific; this is **Callao**, the rather down-at-heel port area, close to the airport. The **shantytowns** that line the highways, meanwhile, continue to swell with new arrivals from the high Andes, responsible in large part for the dramatic surge in Lima's population in recent years.

Lima's **climate** seems to set the city's mood: in the height of summer (Dec–March) it fizzes with energy and excitement, though during the winter months (June–Sept) a low mist descends over the arid valley in which the city sits, forming a solid grey blanket – what Limeños call **garua** – from the beaches almost up to Chosica in the foothills of the Andes; it's a phenomenon made worse by traffic-related air pollution, which dampens the city's spirit, if only slightly.

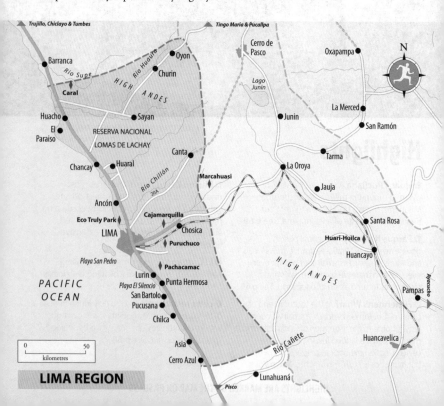

LIMA REGION

Brief history

1

When the Spanish first arrived here in 1533, the valley was dominated by three important **Inca**-controlled urban complexes: **Carabayllo**, to the north near Chillón; **Maranga**, now partly destroyed, by the Avenida La Marina, between the modern city and the Port of Callao; and **Surco**, now a suburb within the confines of greater Lima but where, until the mid-seventeenth century, the adobe houses of ancient chiefs lay empty yet painted in a variety of colourful images. Now these structures have faded back into the sandy desert terrain, and only the larger pyramids remain.

The sixteenth century

Francisco Pizarro founded **Spanish Lima**, nicknamed the "City of the Kings", in 1535. The name is thought to derive from a mispronunciation of Río Rimac, while others suggest that the name "Lima" is an ancient word that described the lands of Taulichusco, the chief who ruled this area when the Spanish arrived. Evidently recommended by mountain Indians as a site for a potential capital, it proved a good choice – apart perhaps from the winter coastal fog – offering a natural harbour nearby, a large well-watered river valley and relatively easy access up into the Andes.

Since the very beginning, Lima was different from the more popular image of Peru in which Andean peasants are pictured toiling on Inca-built mountain terraces. By the 1550s, the town had developed around a large **plaza** with wide streets leading through a fine collection of elegant mansions and well-stocked shops run by wealthy merchants, rapidly developing into the capital of a Spanish viceroyalty which encompassed not only Peru but also Ecuador, Bolivia and Chile. The **University of San Marcos**, founded in 1551, is the oldest on the continent, and Lima housed the Western Hemisphere's headquarters of the Spanish Inquisition from 1570 until 1820. It remained the most important, the richest, and – hardly believable today – the most alluring city in South America, until the early nineteenth century.

The seventeenth century

Perhaps the most prosperous era for Lima was the **seventeenth century**. By 1610 its **population** had reached a manageable 26,000, made up of forty percent black people (mostly slaves); thirty-eight percent Spanish people; no more than eight percent pure indigenous peoples; another eight percent (of unspecified ethnic origin) living under religious orders; and less than six percent *mestizo*, today probably the largest proportion of inhabitants. The centre of Lima was crowded with shops and stalls selling silks and fancy furniture from as far afield as China. Rimac, a suburb just over the river from the Plaza Mayor, and the port area of Callao, both grew up as satellite settlements – initially catering to the very rich, though they are now fairly run down.

The eighteenth century

The **eighteenth century**, a period of relative stagnation for Lima, was dramatically punctuated by the tremendous **earthquake of 1746**, which left only twenty houses standing in the whole city and killed some five thousand residents – nearly ten percent of the population. From 1761 to 1776 Lima and Peru were governed by **Viceroy Amat**, who, although more renowned for his relationship with the famous Peruvian actress **La Perricholi**, is also remembered for spearheading Lima's rebirth. Under his rule, the city lost its cloistered atmosphere, and opened out with broad avenues, striking gardens, Rococo mansions and palatial salons. Influenced by the Bourbons, Amat's designs for the city's architecture arrived hand in hand with other transatlantic reverberations of the Enlightenment, such as the new anti-imperialist vision of an independent Peru.

The nineteenth century

In the **nineteenth century** Lima **expanded** still further to the east and south. The suburbs of Barrios Altos and La Victoria were poor from the start; above the beaches at

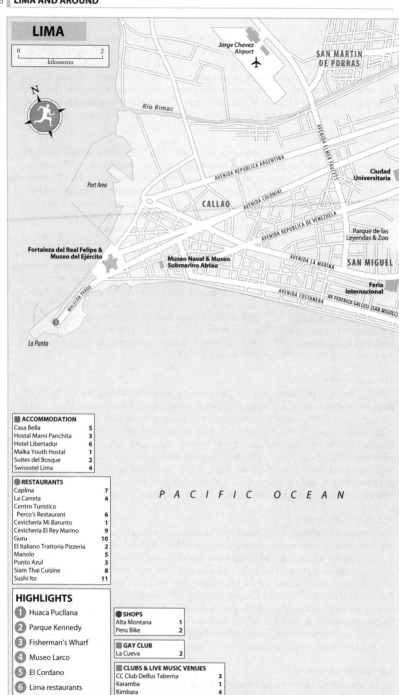

LIMA

0 ——— 2
kilometres

N

Jorge Chavez Airport

SAN MARTIN DE PORRAS

Río Rimac

AVENIDA ELMER FAUCETT

AVENIDA REPUBLICA ARGENTINA

Ciudad Universitaria

Port Area

CALLAO

AVENIDA COLONIAL

AVENIDA REPUBLICA DE VENEZUELA

Parque de las Leyendas & Zoo

Fortaleza del Real Felipe & Museo del Ejército

Museo Naval & Museo Submarino Abtao

AVENIDA LA MARINA

SAN MIGUEL

Feria Internacional

MALECÓN PARDO

AVENIDA COSTANERA

AV. FEDERICO GALLESI (SAN MIGUEL)

La Punta

PACIFIC OCEAN

ACCOMMODATION
Casa Bella	5
Hostal Mami Panchita	3
Hotel Libertador	6
Malka Youth Hostal	1
Suites del Bosque	2
Swissotel Lima	4

RESTAURANTS
Caplina	7
La Carreta	4
Centro Turístico Perco's Restaurant	6
Cevichería Mi Barunto	1
Cevichería El Rey Marino	9
Guru	10
El Italiano Trattoria Pizzeria	2
Manolo	5
Punto Azul	3
Siam Thai Cuisine	8
Sushi Ito	11

HIGHLIGHTS
1 Huaca Pucllana
2 Parque Kennedy
3 Fisherman's Wharf
4 Museo Larco
5 El Cordano
6 Lima restaurants

SHOPS
Alta Montana	1
Peru Bike	2

GAY CLUB
La Cueva	2

CLUBS & LIVE MUSIC VENUES
CC Club Delfus Taberna	3
Karamba	1
Kimbara	4

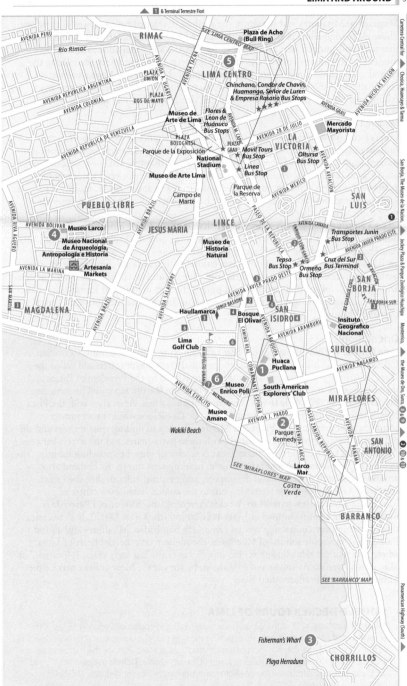

& Terminal Terrestre Fiori

RIMAC

Río Rimac

AVENIDA PERU

AVENIDA REPUBLICA ARGENTINA

AVENIDA COLONIAL

AVENIDA REPUBLICA DE VENEZUELA

AVENIDA RIVA AGÜERO

AVENIDA TACNA

AVENIDA G. UGARTE

PLAZA UNION

PLAZA DOS DE MAYO

Plaza de Acho (Bull Ring)

SEE LIMA CENTRO MAP

5

LIMA CENTRO

Chinchano, Condor de Chavin, Huamanga, Señor de Luren & Empresa Rosario Bus Stops

Museo de Arte de Lima

PLAZA BOLOGNESI

Flores & León de Huánuco Bus Stops

Parque de la Exposición

National Stadium

Museo de Arte Lima

Campo de Marte

AVENIDA BRAZIL

PUEBLO LIBRE

Museo Larco

4

AVENIDA BOLÍVAR

Museo Nacional de Arqueología, Antropología e Historia

Artesanía Markets

AVENIDA LA MARINA

MAGDALENA

SAN MARTIN

JESÚS MARIA

Museo de Historia Natural

AVENIDA SALAVERRY

AVENIDA BRAZIL

AVENIDA 28 DE JULIO

PLAZA GRAU

Movil Tours Bus Stop

LA VICTORIA

Mercado Mayorista

AVENIDA GRAU

AVENIDA NICOLÁS AYLLON

Oltursa Bus Stop

AVENIDA AVIACIÓN

Linea Bus Stop

Parque de la Reserva

AVENIDA MEXICO

SAN LUIS

LINCE

PASEO DE LA REPÚBLICA

AVENIDA CANADA

AVENIDA JAVIER PRADO ESTE

Transportes Junin Bus Stop

ENRIQUE CANAVAL

Tepsa Bus Stop

Cruz del Sur Bus Terminal

Ormeño Bus Stop

AVENIDA JAVIER PRADO OESTE

3

2

JORGE BASADRE

Haullamarca

5

Bosque El Olivar

2

1

SAN ISIDRO **4**

CAMINO REAL

SAN BORJA

AV. DEL AIRE

SAN BORJA SUR

Instituto Geográfico Nacional

SURQUILLO

Lima Golf Club

6

COMANDANTE ESPINAR

AVENIDA ARAMBURU

AVENIDA ARE QUIPA

AVENIDA ANGAMOS

AVENIDA EJÉRCITO

MENDIBURU

6

Museo Enrico Poli

AVENIDA 2 DE MAYO

Huaca Pucllana

1

South American Explorers' Club

MIRAFLORES

Museo Amano

Wakiki Beach

AVENIDA J. PARDO

Parque Kennedy

AVENIDA LARCO

PASEO ZANJON REPÚBLICA

SAN ANTONIO

AVENIDA PANAMA

Larco Mar

SEE 'MIRAFLORES' MAP

Costa Verde

BARRANCO

SEE 'BARRANCO' MAP

Fisherman's Wharf **3**

Playa Herradura

CHORRILLOS

Carretera Central for ▶ Chosica, Huancayo & Jarma

San Boja, The Museo de la Nación ▶

Jockey Plaza & Parque Zoológico-Huachipa ▶

Montericco, the Museo de Oro, Surco ● ⑧ ⑨ ▶

② ⑩ ⑪ ▶

Panamerican Highway (South) ▶

1

Magdalena, Miraflores and Barranco, the wealthy developed new enclaves of their own. These were originally separated from the centre by several kilometres of farmland, at that time still studded with fabulous pre-Inca *huacas* and other adobe ruins. Lima's first modern facelift and expansion was effected between 1919 and 1930, revitalizing the central areas. Under orders from **President Leguia**, the Plaza San Martín's attractive colonnades and the *Gran Hotel Bolívar* were erected, the Palacio de Gobierno was rebuilt and the city was supplied with its first drinking-water and sewerage systems.

Modern Lima

Lima's rapid **growth** has taken it from 300,000 inhabitants in 1930 to over nine million today, mostly accounted for by the massive immigration of peasants from the provinces into the *pueblos jovenes* ("young towns", or **shantytowns**) now pressing in on the city. The ever-increasing traffic is a day-to-day problem, yet **environmental awareness** is rising almost as fast as Lima's shantytowns and neon-lit, middle-class suburban neighbourhoods, and air quality has improved over the last ten years for the people who live here.

Lima continues to grow, perhaps faster than ever, and the country's **economy** is booming even in the face of serious slowdowns in some of Peru's traditional markets, namely Europe and the US. The city is as varied as any in the developing world: while many of the thriving middle class enjoy living standards comparable to, or better than, those of the West, and the elite ride around in chauffeur-driven Cadillacs and fly to Miami for their monthly shopping, the vast majority of Lima's inhabitants endure a constant struggle to put either food on the table or the flimsiest of roofs over their heads.

Orientation

Lima Centro, the old city, sits at the base of a low-lying Andean foothill, Cerro San Cristóbal, and focuses on two plazas: the colonial **Plaza Mayor** (often still called the Plaza de Armas) – itself separated from the Río Rimac by the Presidential Palace and the railway station – and the more modern **Plaza San Martín**, separated by some five blocks along the **Jirón de la Unión**, a major shopping street. At its river end, the Plaza Mayor is fronted by the Catedral and Palacio de Gobierno, while there's greater commercial activity around Plaza San Martín. The key to finding your way around the old part of town is to acquaint yourself with these two squares and the streets between.

From Lima Centro, the city's main avenues reach out into the sprawling suburbs. The two principal routes are **Avenida Venezuela**, heading west out to the harbour area around the suburb of Callao and the airport, and perpendicular to this, the broad, tree-lined **Avenida Arequipa** stretching out to the coastal downtown centre of Miraflores. More or less parallel to Avenida Arequipa, the 50-year-old **Paseo de la República**, more fondly known in Lima as **El Zanjón** (the Great Ditch), is a concrete, three-lane highway connecting central Lima with San Isidro, Miraflores and almost to Barranco. The seaside suburb of **Miraflores**, the modern commercial heart of Lima, where much of the city's businesses have moved over the last forty years, is located 7 or 8km down Avenida Arequipa and El Zanjón, by the ocean. Most visitors make either Lima Centro or Miraflores their base.

DOUBLE-DECKER TOURS OF LIMA

Mirabus (☎01 476 4213, ⓦ mirabusperu.com) operates a fleet of double-decker buses, with an **open roof** on the upper deck, for exploring the sites in and around Lima. They offer day- or night-tours of Lima, colonial tours of the city, and trips out to places like the Pachacamac archeological site (see p.97) some 30km south of the city centre. **Tickets** (ranging from S/8 to S/65) can be bought from the tourist information kiosk in the Parque Kennedy, Miraflores' central park (see p.69).

Lima Centro

With all its splendid architectural attractions, **Lima Centro** might well be expected to have a more tourist-focused vibe than it does. In reality, though, the neighbourhood is very much a centre of Limeños' daily life. The main axis is formed by the parallel streets – Jirón de la Unión and Jirón V Carabaya – connecting the grand squares of the **Plaza San Martín** and **Plaza Mayor**. Here the roads are narrow and busy, bringing together many of the city's office workers with slightly downmarket shops and their workers. There are many fine buildings from the colonial and Republican eras, overhung with ornate balconies, yet apart from a few – notably the **Presidential Palace** and **Torre Tagle** – these are in a poor state of repair. To the north you'll find the slightly run-down, but fascinating **Rimac suburb**, home to the city's bullring. South of the two main plazas, some lavish parks and galleries are within walking distance.

Plaza Mayor

The heart of the old town is **Plaza Mayor** – also known as the Plaza de Armas, or Plaza Armada as the early conquistadores called it. There are no remains of any Indian heritage in or around the square; standing on the original site of the palace of Tauri Chusko (Lima's indigenous chieftain at the time the Spanish arrived) is the relatively modern Palacio de Gobierno, while the cathedral occupies the site of an Inca temple once dedicated to the puma deity, and the Palacio Municipal lies on what was originally an Inca envoy's mansion.

Palacio de Gobierno

Plaza Mayor • Changing of the guard Mon–Sat warm-up at 11.45am, start at noon; tours daily 9.30am–noon; pre-register at Departamento de Actividades, office 201, Jr de la Unión, block 2, Plaza Peru (also known as Plaza Pizarro) • Tours free • ☎ 01 426 7020 or ☎ 01 311 3908 ext 378, ⓦ presidencia.gob.pe

The **Palacio de Gobierno** – also known as the Presidential Palace – was the site of the house of **Francisco Pizarro** (see p.486) long before the present building was conceived. It was here that he spent the last few years of his life, until his assassination in 1541. As he died, his jugular severed by the assassin's rapier, Pizarro fell to the floor, drew a cross, then kissed it; even today some believe this ground to be sacred.

The **changing of the guard** takes place outside the palace – it's not a particularly spectacular sight, though the soldiers look splendid in their scarlet-and-blue uniforms. There are free guided **tours** in English and Spanish, which include watching the changing of the guard; to go on a tour you have to register with the Departamento de Actividades at least 24 hours in advance. The tour also takes in the imitation Baroque **interior** of the palace and its rather dull collection of colonial and reproduction furniture.

La Catedral and Museum of Religious Art and Treasures

Plaza Mayor • **Catedral** Mon–Fri 10am–4pm, Sat 10am–1pm • Free • ☎ 01 427 9647 • **Museum** Daily 10am–4pm • S/5

Southeast across the square, less than 50m away from the Palacio de Gobierno, the squat and austere **Catedral**, designed by Francisco Becerra, was modelled on a church in Seville, and has three aisles in a Renaissance style. When Becerra died in 1605, the cathedral was far from completion, with the towers alone taking another forty years to finish. In 1746, further frustration arrived in the guise of a devastating **earthquake**, which destroyed much of the building. Successive restorations over the centuries have resulted in an eclectic style; the current version, which is essentially a reconstruction of Becerra's design, was rebuilt throughout the eighteenth and nineteenth centuries, then remodelled once again after another quake in 1940.

The building is primarily of interest for its **Museum of Religious Art and Treasures**, which contains seventeenth- and eighteenth-century paintings and some superb **choir stalls** – exquisitely carved in the early seventeenth century by Catalan artist Pedro Noguero. Its other highlight is a collection of human remains thought to be **Pizarro's**

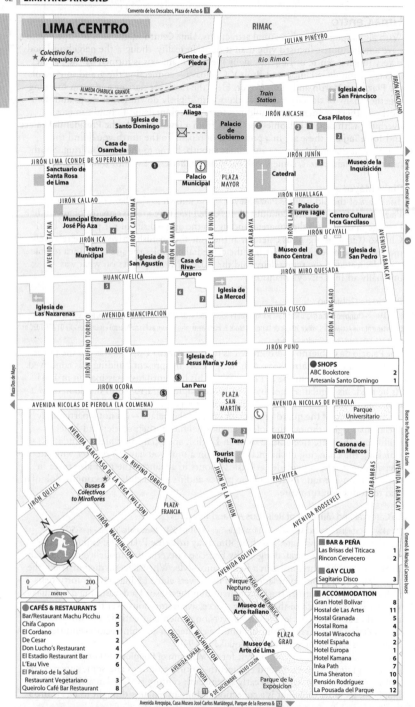

LIMA CENTRO

RIMAC

Convento de los Descalzos, Plaza de Acho & 🚌 ▲

JULIAN PINÉYRO

★ Colectivo for
Av Arequipa to Miraflores

Puente de Piedra

Río Rimac

ALMEDA CHABUCA GRANDE

Train Station

Iglesia de San Francisco

JIRÓN AYACUCHO

Casa Aliaga

JIRÓN ANCASH

Casa Pilatos

Iglesia de Santo Domingo

Palacio de Gobierno

Casa de Osambela

JIRÓN LIMA (CONDE DE SUPERUNDA)

Sanctuario de Santa Rosa de Lima

Palacio Municipal

PLAZA MAYOR

Catedral

JIRÓN JUNÍN

Museo de la Inquisición

JIRÓN CALLAO

JIRÓN HUALLAGA

Palacio Torre Tagle

Centro Cultural Inca Garcilaso

AVENIDA TACNA

Muncipal Etnográfico José Pío Aza

JIRÓN CAYLLOMA

JIRÓN CAMANÁ

JIRÓN DE LA UNION

JIRÓN CARABAYA

JIRÓN LAMPA

JIRÓN UCAYALI

AVENIDA ABANCAY

JIRÓN ICA

Teatro Municipal

Iglesia de San Agustín

Casa de Riva-Aguero

Museo del Banco Central

Iglesia de San Pedro

HUANCAVELICA

JIRÓN MIRO QUESADA

Iglesia de La Merced

Iglesia de Las Nazarenas

AVENIDA EMANCIPACION

AVENIDA CUSCO

JIRÓN RUFINO TORRICO

MOQUEGUA

JIRÓN PUNO

JIRÓN AZÁNGARO

Iglesia de Jesus María y José

Plaza Dos de Mayo

JIRÓN OCOÑA

Lan Peru

PLAZA SAN MARTÍN

SHOPS
ABC Bookstore	2
Artesanía Santo Domingo	1

AVENIDA NICOLAS DE PIEROLA (LA COLMENA)

AVENIDA NICOLAS DE PIEROLA

Parque Universitario

Buses to Pachacamac & Lurín

AVENIDA GARCILASO DE LA VEGA (WILSON)

JR. RUFINO TORRICO

Tans

MONZON

Casona de San Marcos

AVENIDA ABANCAY

Tourist Police

PACHITEA

COTABAMBAS

JIRÓN QUILCA

Buses & Colectivos to Miraflores

PLAZA FRANCIA

JIRÓN DE LA UNION

AVENIDA ROOSEVELT

Ormeró & Mariscal Cáceres buses

JIRÓN WASHINGTON

N

0   200
metres

AVENIDA BOLIVIA

Parque Neptuno

PASEO DE LA REPUBLICA

BAR & PEÑA
Las Brisas del Titicaca	1
Rincon Cervecero	2

GAY CLUB
Sagitario Disco	3

CAFÉS & RESTAURANTS
Bar/Restaurant Machu Picchu	2
Chifa Capon	5
El Cordano	1
De Cesar	2
Don Lucho's Restaurant	4
El Estadio Restaurant Bar	7
L'Eau Vive	6
El Paraiso de la Salud Restaurant Vegetariano	3
Queirolo Café Bar Restaurant	8

Museo de Arte Italiano

Museo de Arte de Lima

PLAZA GRAU

CHOTA

JIRÓN WASHINGTON

AVENIDA ESPAÑA

9 DE DICIEMBRE PASEO COLÓN

Parque de la Exposición

ACCOMMODATION
Gran Hotel Bolívar	8
Hostal de Las Artes	11
Hostal Granada	5
Hostal Roma	4
Hostal Wiracocha	3
Hotel España	2
Hotel Europa	1
Hotel Kamana	6
Inka Path	7
Lima Sheraton	10
Pensión Rodríguez	9
La Pousada del Parque	12

Avenida Arequipa, Casa Museo José Carlos Mariátegui, Parque de la Reserva & 🚌 ▼

Barrio Chino & Central Market

Ormeró & Mariscal Cáceres buses

1

body (quite fitting since he placed the first stone shortly before his death), which lie in the first chapel on the right. Although gloomy, the interior retains some of its appealing Churrigueresque (or highly elaborate Baroque) decor.

Palacio Municipal

Plaza Mayor • Mon–Fri 9am–1pm • Free

The square-set edifice directly across the plaza from the cathedral is the **Palacio Municipal**, usually lined with heavily armed guards and the occasional armoured car, though actual civil unrest is fairly uncommon. Built on the site of the original sixteenth-century city hall and inaugurated in 1944, it's a typical example of a half-hearted twentieth-century attempt at Neocolonial architecture, designed by Alvarez Emilio Harth Terré and Ricardo de Jara Malachowski, and fronted by grand wooden balconies.

The elegant **interior** is home to the **Pinacoteca Ignacio Merino Museum**, which exhibits a selection of Peruvian paintings, notably those of Ignacio Merino from the nineteenth century. For those with an interest in Peruvian constitutional history, the library displays the city's **Act of Foundation and Declaration of Independence**.

Iglesia de San Francisco

Jr Ancash • Daily 9.30am–5pm; tours at least hourly • S/7, including tour

Jirón Ancash leads east from the Palacio de Gobierno towards one of Lima's most attractive churches, **San Francisco**, a majestic building that has withstood the passage of time and the devastation of successive earth tremors. A large seventeenth-century construction with an engaging stone facade and towers, San Francisco's vaults and columns are elaborately decorated with Mudéjar (Moorish-style) plaster relief.

The **Convento de San Francisco**, part of the same architectural complex and a museum in its own right, contains a superb library and a room of **paintings** by (or finished by) Zurbarán, Rubens, Jordaens and Van Dyck. You can take a 45-minute guided tour of the monastery and its **subterranean crypt**, both of which are worth a visit. The museum is inside the monastery's vast crypts, which were only discovered in 1951 and contain the skulls and bones of some seventy thousand people.

Casa Pilatos

Jr Ancash 390 • Mon–Fri 11am–1.30pm • Free, but advance booking necessary • ☎ 01 427 5814

Opposite the Iglesia de San Francisco is the **Casa Pilatos**, today home to the constitutional courts; although you can't enter the building, you can get as far as the central courtyard. Quite a simple building, and no competition for Torre Tagle (see p.64), it is nevertheless a fine, early sixteenth-century mansion with an attractive courtyard and a stone staircase leading up from the middle of the patio. The wooden carving of the patio's balustrades adds to the general picture of opulent colonialism.

Museo de la Inquisición

Jr Junín 548 • Daily 9am–5pm, by guided tour only • Free • ☎ 01 311 7777

Behind a facade of Greek-style classical columns, the **Museo de la Inquisición** was the **headquarters of the Inquisition** for the whole of Spanish-dominated America from 1570 until 1820, and contains the original tribunal room with its beautifully carved mahogany ceiling. Beneath the building, you can look round the **dungeons** and torture chambers, which contain a few gory, life-sized human models, each being put through unbearably painful-looking antique contraptions, mainly involving stretching or mutilating.

Mercado Central and Barrio Chino

The few blocks east of Avenida Abancay are taken over by the **Mercado Central** (Central Market) and **Barrio Chino** (Chinatown). Perhaps one of the most fascinating sectors of

1

Lima Centro, the Barrio Chino (which can be entered by an ornate Chinese **gateway**, at the crossing of Jirón Ucayali with Capon) houses Lima's best and cheapest *chifa* (Chinese **restaurants**). Many Chinese came to Peru in the late nineteenth century to work as labourers on railway construction; many others came here in the 1930s and 1940s to escape cultural persecution in their homeland. The shops and street stalls in this sector are full of all sorts of inexpensive goods, from shoes to glass beads, though there is little of genuine quality.

Iglesia de San Pedro
Jirones Ucayali and Azángaro • Mon–Sat 7am–12.30pm & 5–8pm • Free

At the corner of Jirón Ucayali, the **Iglesia de San Pedro** was built and occupied by the Jesuits until their expulsion in 1767. This richly decorated colonial church is home to several religious art treasures, including paintings from the Colonial and Republican periods, and a superb main altar which was built in the late nineteenth century after the Jesuits returned; definitely worth a look around.

Palacio Torre Tagle
Jr Ucayali 323 • Mon–Fri 9am–5pm; book two days in advance • Free • ☎ 01 3112400

The spectacular **Palacio Torre Tagle** is the pride and joy of the old city. A beautifully maintained mansion, it was built in the 1730s and is embellished with a decorative facade and two elegant, dark-wood balconies, typical of Lima architecture in that one is larger than the other. The **porch and patio** are distinctly Andalucian, with their strong Spanish colonial style, although some of the intricate **woodcarvings** on pillars and across ceilings display a native influence; the *azulejos*, or **tiles**, also show a combination of Moorish and Limeño tastes. In the left-hand corner of the patio you can see a set of **scales** like those used to weigh merchandise during colonial times, and the house also contains a magnificent sixteenth-century **carriage** (complete with mobile toilet). Originally, mansions such as Torre Tagle served as refuges for outlaws, the authorities being unable to enter without written and stamped permission – now anyone can go in (afternoons are the quietest times to visit).

Museo del Banco Central de Reserva del Peru
Jirones Lampa and Ucayali • Tues–Fri 10am–4.30pm, Sat & Sun 10am–1pm • Free • ☎ 01 613 2000 ext 2655

The **Museo del Banco Central de Reserva del Peru** holds many antique and modern **Peruvian paintings**, as well as a good collection of **pre-Inca artefacts**, including some ancient objects crafted in gold; most of the exhibits on display come from grave robberies and have been returned to Peru only recently. The museum also has a numismatic display and sometimes shows related short films for kids.

Centro Cultural Inca Garcilaso
Jr Ucayali 391 • Tues–Sun 11am–7pm • Free • ☎ 01 311 2756

By Torre Tagle, you'll find the **Centro Cultural Inca Garcilaso**, built in 1685 as the Casa Aspillaga but restored during the late nineteenth century and again in 2003. It contains an art gallery (mainly temporary photographic or sculpture exhibtions) but is most interesting for its Neoclassical Republican-style architecture.

Casa Aliaga
Jr de la Unión 224 • Tours S/5 • Book tours through Lima Tours at ☎ 01 619 5000 or ☎ 01 619 6911

Heading north from the Plaza Mayor you pass the **Casa Aliaga**, an unusual mansion, reputed to be the oldest in South America, and occupied by the same family since 1535, making it the oldest colonial house still standing in the Americas. It's also one of the most elaborate mansions in the country, with sumptuous reception rooms full of Louis XIV mirrors, furniture and doors. It was built on top of an Inca palace and is largely made of wood divided stylishly into various salons.

Iglesia de Santo Domingo

Mon–Sat 9am–noon & 3–6pm, Sun & holidays 9am–1pm • Church free, tombs S/7 • ☎ 01 427 6793

Just off the main square, a block behind the Palacio Municipal, is the church and monastery of **Santo Domingo**. Completed in 1549, Santo Domingo was presented by the pope, a century or so later, with an alabaster statue of Santa Rosa de Lima. The **tombs** of Santa Rosa, San Martín de Porres and San Juan Masias (a Spaniard who was canonized in Peru) are the building's great attractions, and much revered. Otherwise the church is not of huge interest or architectural merit, although it is one of the oldest religious structures in Lima, built on a site granted to the Dominicans by Pizarro in 1535.

Casa de Osambela

Jr Conde de Superunda 298 • Mon–Fri 9am–4pm • Free; guided tours, donation appreciated

The early nineteenth-century **Casa de Osambela** has five balconies on its facade and a lookout point from which boats arriving at the port of Callao could be spotted by the first owner, Martín de Osambela. This mansion is home to the Centro Cultural Inca Garcilaso de la Vega, which offers **guided tours** of the building.

Sanctuario de Santa Rosa de Lima

First block of Av Tacna • Mon–Sat 9am–1pm & 3–6pm • Free

Two traditional sanctuaries (see box below) can be found on the western edge of old Lima, along Avenida Tacna. Completed in 1728, the **Sanctuario de Santa Rosa de Lima** is a fairly plain church named in honour of the first saint canonized in the Americas. The construction of Avenida Tacna destroyed a section of the already small church, but in the patio next door you can visit the saint's **hermitage**, a small adobe cell; there's also a 20m-deep well where devotees drop written requests.

Museo Etnográfico José Pío Aza

Jr Callao 562 at Av Tacna • Mon–Sat 10am–5pm • S/3 • ☎ 01 431 0771

A short stroll down Avenida Tacna from the Sanctuario de Santa Rosa takes you to the fascinating **Museo Etnográfico José Pío Aza**, containing crafts, tools, jewellery and weapons from jungle tribes, as well as some photographs of early missionaries.

Iglesia de San Agustín

Jirones Ica and Camaná • Daily 8.30am–noon & 3.30–7pm • Free

The southern stretch between the Plaza Mayor and Plaza San Martín is the largest area of Old Lima, home to several important churches, including **San Agustín**, founded in 1592. Although severely damaged by earthquakes (only the small side-chapel can be visited nowadays), the church retains a glorious **facade**, one of the most complicated examples of Churrigueresque–Mestizo architecture in Peru; it originally had a Renaissance doorway, traces of which can be seen from Jirón Camaná.

EARTHQUAKES AND MIRACLES

Despite its small size and undistinguished appearance, the **Iglesia de las Nazarenas** (daily 7am–noon & 4–8pm; free; ☎01 423 5718), on the corner of Avenida Tacna and Huancavelica, has an unusual history. After the severe **1655 earthquake**, a mural of the Crucifixion, painted by an Angolan slave on the wall of his hut and originally titled *Cristo de Pachacamilla*, was the only object left standing in the district. Its survival was deemed a miracle – the cause and focus of popular processions ever since – and it was on this site that the church was founded in the eighteenth century. The widespread and popular **processions for the Lord of Miracles**, to save Lima from another earthquake, take place every spring (Oct 18, 19, 28 & Nov 1), and focus on a silver litter, which carries the original mural. **Purple** is the colour of the procession and many women in Lima wear it for the entire month.

1

Casa de Riva-Aguero

Jr Camaná 459 • Daily 10am–1pm & 2–7pm • S/3 • ☎ 01 427 9275

Across the road from San Agustín, the **Casa de Riva-Aguero** is a typical colonial house, built in the mid-eighteenth century by a wealthy businessman and later sold to the Aguero family. Its patio has been laid out as a **Museo de Arte y Tradiciones Populares**, displaying crafts and contemporary paintings from all over Peru.

Iglesia de la Merced

Jr de la Unión 621 and Av Miro Quesada • Mon–Sat 8am–12.45pm & 4–8pm, Sun 7am–1pm & 4–8pm; cloisters daily 8am–noon & 5–6pm • Free • Cloisters ☎ 01 423 5718, guided visits ☎ 01 427 8199

Perhaps the most noted of all religious buildings in Lima is the **Iglesia de la Merced**, two blocks south of the Plaza Mayor. Built on the site where the first Latin Mass in Lima was celebrated, the original sixteenth-century church was demolished in 1628 to make way for the present building whose ornate granite facade, dating back to 1687, has been adapted and rebuilt several times – as have the broad columns of the nave – to protect the church against tremors.

By far the most lasting impression is made by the **Cross of the Venerable Padre Urraca** (La Cruz de Padre Urraca El Venerable), whose silver staff is witness to the fervent prayers of a constantly shifting congregation, smothered by hundreds of kisses every hour. If you've just arrived in Lima, a few minutes by this cross may give you an insight into the depth of Peruvian belief in miraculous power. Be careful if you get surrounded by the ubiquitous sellers of candles and religious icons around the entrance – **pickpockets** are at work here. The attached **cloisters** are less spectacular, though they do offer a historical curiosity: it was here that the Patriots of Independence declared the Virgin of La Merced their military marshal.

Iglesia de Jesus María y José

Jirones Camaná and Moquegua • Daily 7am–1pm & 3–7pm • Free

Close to the Plaza San Martín stands the **Iglesia de Jesus María y José**, home of Capuchin nuns from Madrid in the early eighteenth century; its particularly outstanding interior contains sparkling Baroque gilt altars and pulpits.

Plaza San Martín

A large, grand square with fountains at its centre, the **Plaza San Martín** is almost always busy by day, with traffic tooting its way around the perimeter. Nevertheless, it's a place where you can sit down for a few minutes – at least until hassled by street sellers or shoeshine boys.

Ideologically, the Plaza San Martín represents the sophisticated, egalitarian and European spirit of intellectual liberators like San Martín himself, while remaining well and truly within the commercial world. The plaza has attracted most of Lima's major **political rallies** over the past hundred years, and rioting students, teachers or workers and attendant police with water cannons and tear gas are always a (rare) possibility here.

Plaza Dos de Mayo

The city's main rallying point for political protests is **Plaza Dos de Mayo**, linked to the Plaza San Martín by the wide Avenida Nicolás de Piérola (also known as La Colmena). Built to commemorate the repulse of the Spanish fleet in 1866 – Spain's last attempt to regain a foothold in South America – the plaza is markedly busier and less visitor-friendly than Plaza San Martín. It sits on the site of an old gate dividing Lima from the road to Callao.

Casona de San Marcos

Av Nicolás de Piérola 1222 • Mon–Sat 9am–5.30pm • S/5 • ☎ 01 619 7000, ⊕ ccsm-unmsm.edu.pe

East of Plaza San Martín, Avenida Nicolás de Piérola runs towards the **Parque Universitario**, site of South America's first university. Right on the park itself, the

1

Casona de San Marcos is home to the Centro Cultural de San Marcos and the Ballet de San Marcos. Once lodgings for the Jesuit novitiate San Antonio Abad (patron saint of everything from animals to skin complaints), it's a pleasant seventeenth-century complex with some fine architectural features including colonial cloisters, a Baroque chapel, a small **art and archeology museum**, exhibitions and a great café. The **amphitheatre** in the park is sometimes used for free public performances by musicians and artists.

Museo de Arte Italiano
Paseo de la República 250, Parque Neptuno • Tues–Sun 10am–5pm • S/6 • ☎ 01 423 9932

South of Plaza San Martín, Jirón Belén leads down to the Paseo de la República and the shady **Parque Neptuno**, home to the pleasant **Museo de Arte Italiano**. Located inside a relatively small and highly ornate Neoclassical building that's unusual for Lima, built by the Italian architect Gaetano Moretti, the museum exhibits oils, bronzes and ceramics by Italian artists, and offers a welcome respite from the hectic city outside.

Parque de la Cultura Peruana
Tues–Sun 10am–8pm

The Museo de Arte is at the city end of the extensive, leafy **Parque de la Cultura Peruana**, originally created for the International Exhibition of Agricultural Machines in 1872. Conspicuously green for Lima, the park is where lovers meet at weekends and students hang out amid greenery, pagodas, an amphitheatre, a small lake and organized music and dance performances at fiesta times. The park stretches a couple of hundred metres down to Avenida 28 de Julio, from where it's just a few blocks to the Estadio Nacional and **Parque de la Reserva** (see below).

Museo de Arte de Lima
Paseo Colón 125 • Tues–Fri & Sun 10am–8pm, Sat 10am–5pm • S/12 • ☎ 01 204 0000, ⓦ mali.pe

A couple of minutes' walk south of the Museo de Arte Italiano is the commanding **Museo de Arte**, housed in the former International Exhibition Palace, built in 1868. The museum holds interesting permanent collections of colonial art, as well as many fine crafts from pre-Columbian times, and also hosts frequent international exhibitions of modern photography and video as well as contemporary Peruvian art. Film shows and lectures are offered on some weekday evenings (check the website, *El Comercio* newspaper listings or posters in the lobby).

Casa Museo José Carlos Mariátegui
Jr Washington 1946 • Mon–Fri 9am–1pm & 2–5pm, Sat 9am–1pm • Free

Not far from the Parque de la Cultura Peruana is the **Casa Museo José Carlos Mariátegui**, an early twentieth-century one-storey house – home for the last few years of his life to the famous Peruvian political figure, ideologist and writer Mariátegui – which has been restored by the Instituto Nacional de Cultura. The period furnishings reveal less about this man than his writings, but the house is kept alive in honour of one of Peru's greatest twentieth-century political writers.

Parque de la Reserva
Between the Paseo de la República and Av Arequipa, beside the Estadio Nacional • Wed–Sun & hols 3–10.30pm; fountains go off at 7.15pm, 8.15pm & 9.30pm • S/5 • ⓦ parquedelareserva.com.pe

The **Parque de la Reserva**, next to the Estadio Nacional, was superbly and imaginatively refurbished in 2007 to create the **circuito mágico del agua** (see box, p.68), a splendid array of fountains, each with a different theme, set to go off at specific times.

Puente de Piedra
It's a short walk north up Jirón de la Unión from the Plaza Mayor to the **Puente de Piedra**, the stone bridge that arches over the Río Rimac – usually no more than a

1

FUN WITH FOUNTAINS

A popular haunt, the **circuito mágico del agua** (or "magical water circuit"; Wed–Sun 3–10.30pm; S/5), in the Parque de la Reserva near blocks 5–8 of Avenida Arequipa, boasts fifteen colourful and well-lit **fountains**, some of which spurt some 80m into the air. Watch out for the Fuente de Fantasía, which moves to music, and the Cupula Visitable, which you can get drenched climbing inside, as well as the beautiful water pyramid and the Tunel de Sorpresas (Tunnel of Surprises), which you can walk through; it all makes for one of Lima's most memorable evening attractions, especially for kids who run through the fountains.

miserable trickle – behind the Palacio de Gobierno. Initially a wooden construction, the current brick structure was built in the seventeenth century, using egg whites with sand and lime to improve the consistency of its mortar.

Rimac

The function of the Puente de Piedra was to provide a permanent link between the centre of town and the Barrio of San Lázaro, known these days as **Rimac**, or, more popularly, as **Bajo El Puente** ("below the bridge"). This district was first populated in the sixteenth century by African slaves, newly imported and awaiting purchase by big plantation owners; a few years later Rimac was beleaguered by outbreaks of leprosy. Although these days its status is much improved, Rimac is still one of the most run-down areas of Lima. It can be quite an aggressive place after dark, when drug addicts and thieves abound, and it's **dangerous** to walk this area alone at any time of day. Take a taxi direct to where you want to go.

Museo Taurino de Acho

Jr Hualgayoc 332 • Mon–Sat 9am–6pm • S/5 • ☎ 01 481 3433

Rimac is home to the **Plaza de Acho**, Lima's most important **bullring** (see box below), which also houses the **Museo Taurino de Acho**, or Bullfight Museum, containing some original **Goya engravings**, several related paintings and a few relics of bullfighting contests.

The Alameda de los Descalzos and Paseo de Aguas

A few blocks to the right of the bridge, you can stroll up the **Alameda de los Descalzos** (though best not to do so alone, even in daylight), a fine tree-lined walk designed for courtship, and an afternoon meeting place for the early seventeenth- to nineteenth-century elite (the railings were added in 1853). Along the way stands the **Paseo de Aguas**, built by Viceroy Amat in the eighteenth century. It leads past the foot of a distinctive hill, the **Cerro San Cristóbal**, and, although in desperate need of renovation, it still possesses twelve appealing marble **statues** brought from Italy in 1856, each one representing a different sign of the zodiac.

At the far end of the Alameda is a fine Franciscan monastery, **Convento de los Descalzos** (Mon & Wed–Sun 10am–1pm & 3–6pm; S/3, usually including a 40min tour; ☎01 481 0441 or ☎01 481 3433), dating from 1592 and housing a collection of colonial and

BULLFIGHTING IN LIMA

Bullfighting has been a popular pastime among a relatively small wealthy elite from the Spanish Conquest to the present day, despite some 185 years of independence from Spain. Pizarro himself brought out the first *lidia* bull for fighting in Lima, and the controlling families of Peru – the same families who breed fighting bulls on their haciendas – maintain the tradition. They invite some of the world's best bullfighters from Spain, Mexico and Venezuela, offering them significant sums for an afternoon's "sport" at the prestigious **Plaza de Acho** in Rimac. **Tickets** can be bought in advance from major shops such as the Wong and Metro chain of superstores throughout the city. Fights happen mostly on Sunday afternoons in October and November.

1

Republican paintings from Peru and Ecuador; its chapel – **La Capilla El Carmen** – possesses a beautiful Baroque gold-leaf altar. The monastery was built in what was then a secluded spot beyond the town, originally a retreat from the busy heart of the city at the base of Cerro San Cristóbal. Now, of course, the city runs all around it and way beyond.

Lima's suburbs

The old centre of Lima is surrounded by a number of sprawling **suburbs**, or *distritos*, which spread across the desert between the foothills of the Andes and the coast. A short drive south of Lima Centro lies the lively suburb of **Miraflores**, a slick, fast-moving mini-metropolis, which has become Lima's business and shopping zone, with a coast walk watched over by expensive apartments. South of Miraflores begins the oceanside suburb of **Barranco**, one of the oldest and most attractive parts of Lima, above the steep sandy cliffs of the **Costa Verde**, hosting a small nightlife enclave. Sandwiched between Lima Centro and Miraflores is the plush suburb of **San Isidro**, boasting both the city's main commercial and banking sector and a golf course surrounded by sky-scraping apartment buildings. West of here, **Pueblo Libre** is older, an established home to several good museums. To the east lies **San Borja**, a more recently constructed district with another fine museum, the Museo de la Nación. The city's port area, **Callao**, is an atmospheric, if rather old and insalubrious zone tapering into the western peninsula of **La Punta**, with its air of slightly decayed grandeur. The suburb of **La Victoria**, on the other side of central Lima from Callao, contains some once-fine plazas and buildings, but is better known these days for its bus depots and pickpockets. Lima city's sprawl means that there are massive urbanizations to the north, the south, and into the western foothills of the Andes, where the upmarket suburb of **Monterrico** is found.

Most of Lima's popular city **beaches**, like the surfers' hangout of **Playa Wakiki**, are directly below the sea-facing cliffs of Miraflores, visible from the Larco Mar commercial complex and accessible on foot from Parque Kennedy.

Miraflores

As far as Lima's inhabitants are concerned, **Miraflores** is the major focus of the city's action and nightlife, its streets lined with cafés and the capital's flashiest shops. **Larco Mar**, a modern entertainment district built into the cliffside at the bottom of Miraflores' main street, adds to its swanky appeal. Although still connected to Lima Centro by the long-established Avenida Arequipa, which is served by frequent colectivos, another generally faster road – Paseo de la República (also known as the Vía Expressa and El Zanjón) – provides the suburb with an alternative route for cars and buses.

Huaca Pucllana

General Borgoño 800 • Mon & Wed–Sun 9am–4.30pm • S/12 • ☎ 01 617 7138, ⓦ huacapucllanamiraflores.pe/english • A 5min walk from Av Arequipa, on the right as you come from Lima Centro at block 44

A good place to make for first is the **Huaca Pucllana**, a temple, pre-Columbian tomb and administrative centre in the middle of suburban Miraflores. This vast pre-Inca adobe mound continues to dwarf most of the houses around and has a small site museum, craft shop and very good restaurant (see p.89). From the top of the *huaca* you can see over the office buildings and across the flat roofs of the multicoloured houses in the heart of Miraflores.

Parque Kennedy

Av Arequipa • Market daily 6–9pm

Miraflores' central area focuses on the attractive, almost triangular **Parque Kennedy** (or Miraflores Central Park or Cat Park: so named because of the many docile cats that roam here) at the end of Avenida Arequipa. Neatly grassed and with some attractive flowerbeds, the park divides into four areas of activity: at the top end is the pedestrian

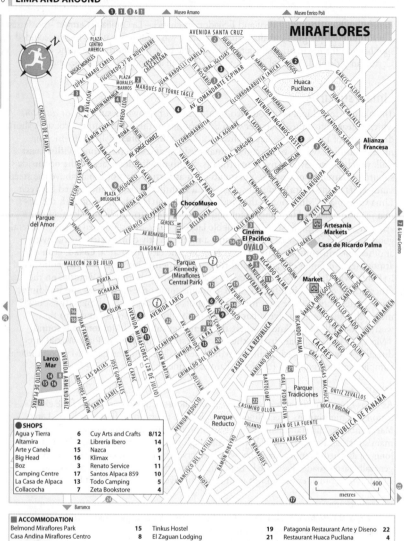

MIRAFLORES

SHOPS
Agua y Tierra	6
Altamira	2
Arte y Canela	15
Big Head	16
Boz	3
Camping Centre	17
La Casa de Alpaca	13
Collacocha	7
Cuy Arts and Crafts	8/12
Librería Ibero	14
Nazca	9
Klimax	1
Renato Service	11
Santos Alpaca 859	10
Todo Camping	5
Zeta Bookstore	4

■ ACCOMMODATION
Belmond Miraflores Park	15
Casa Andina Miraflores Centro	8
Casa de Baraybar	1
Casa del Mochilero	2
Colonial Inn	5
Embajadores Hotel	16
Explorer's House	4
Faraoña Grande Hotel	11
Friends House	13
HI Hostel Lima	22
Hospedaje Flying Dog	12
Hostal Antigua Miraflores	6
Hostal Buena Vista	20
Hostal Martinika	7
Hostal Pariwana	9
Hostal El Patio	14
Marieta Bed & Breakfast Inn	3
Miraflores Colón Inn	8
Pensión José Luís	23
Radisson	10
Sonesta Posada del Inca – Miraflores	17
Tinkus Hostel	19
El Zaguan Lodging	21

● CAFÉS & RESTAURANTS
Arabica Espreso Bar	10
Astrid y Gastón	19
Bio Leben	21
El Bodegon	7
Las Brujas de Cachiche	9
Café Café	13
Café Haiti	14
Café Verde	2
Club Suizo	23
D'nnos Pizza	7
La Emolientería	9
La Hamaca	14
El Kapallaq	3
La Lucha Sanguchería	18
Madre Natura	1
Mama Lola	24
La Mar	8
Patagonia Restaurant Arte y Diseno	22
Restaurant Huaca Pucllana	4
Restaurant Tai-i Vegetariano	11
La Rosa Nautica	20
Scena Restaurant Bar	12
El Señor de Sulco	6
La Tiendacita Blanca	17

■ BARS, CLUBS, PEÑAS & LIVE MUSIC VENUES
Aura	8
The Brenchley Arms	3
Gotica	8
Habana Café Bar	5
Jazz Zone	7
The Old Pub	4
Peña Sachún	1
Satchmo	7

■ GAY CLUBS
Downtown Vale Todo	6
Legendaris	2

THE ORACULAR ORIGINS OF THE HUACA PUCLLANA

One of a large number of *huacas* and palaces that formerly stretched across this part of the valley, little is known about the **Huaca Pucllana**, though it seems likely that it was originally named after a pre-Inca chief of the area. It has a hollow core running through its cross section and is believed to have been constructed in the shape of an enormous **frog**, symbol of the rain god, who spoke to priests through a tube connected to the cavern at its heart. This site may well have been the mysteriously unknown **oracle** after which the Rimac (meaning "he who speaks") Valley was named; a curious document from 1560 affirms that the "devil" spoke at this mound.

junction where the shoeshiners hang out; further down there's a small amphitheatre, which often has mime acts or music; next you come to a raised and walled, circular concrete area, which has a good **craft and antiques market** set up on stalls every evening; and just down from here is a small section of gardens and a children's play area. Throughout, you'll see people taking selfies with the ubiquitous cats. Painters sell their artwork in and around the edges of the park, particularly on Sundays – some quite good, though it's aimed at the tourist market. The streets around the park are lined with smart cafés and bars, and crowded with shoppers, flower-sellers and car-washers.

Larco Mar

The flash development at the bottom of Avenida Larco, **Larco Mar**, has done an excellent job of integrating the park end of Miraflores with what was previously a rather desolate clifftop area. Essentially a shopping zone with patios and walkways open to the sky, sea and cliffs, Larco Mar is also home to several bars, ice-cream parlours, reasonably good restaurants, a host of cinema screens and a couple of trendy clubs.

Parque del Amor

From the end of Avenida Arequipa, Avenida Larco and Diagonal fan out along the park en route to the ocean about a kilometre away. Near where the continuation of Diagonal reaches the clifftop, the small but vibrant **Parque del Amor** sits on the clifftop above the Costa Verde and celebrates the fact that for decades this area has been a favourite haunt of young lovers, particularly poorer Limeños who have no privacy in their often overcrowded homes. Mosaics with romantic quotes, and a huge sculpture of a loving Andean couple clasping each other rapturously is usually surrounded by pairs of real-life lovers walking hand-in-hand or cuddling on the clifftop, especially on Sunday afternoons. In recent years there have been reports of muggings around here, but it's become relatively safe again.

Casa de Ricardo Palma

General Suarez 189 • Mon–Fri 10am–1pm & 3–5pm • S/6 • ☏ 01 617 7115 or ☏ 01 445 5836

Miraflores' only important mansion open to the public is the **Casa de Ricardo Palma**, where Palma, Peru's greatest historian, lived for most of his life. Located between Avenida Arequipa and the Paseo de la República, just behind the artesanía markets on Petit Thouars (see p.95), the nineteenth-century house has some architectural merit, but is mostly visited for an insight into Palma's lifestyle, through the household furnishings, and mind, through some first editions of his written works and some diary extracts. The set of spacious rooms includes a music room, bedrooms, patio and bathroom, all of which can be explored.

Museo Enrico Poli

Lord Cochrane 466 • S/60 per person; minimum five people • Tues–Fri 4–6pm, by appointment only; call ☏ 01 422 2437

Within a few blocks of the Ovalo Gutierrez in Miraflores, the **Museo Enrico Poli** contains some of the finest pre-Inca archeological treasures in Lima, including ceramics, gold and silver. The highlight of this private collection is the treasure found at **Sipán** in northern Peru, in particular four golden trumpets, each over a metre long and over a thousand years old.

1

LIMA FROM THE AIR

To see Lima from a completely different perspective, jump off the coastal cliffs in Miraflores on a tandem **paragliding flight**. Flights take around ten to fifteen minutes, and you're in the safe hands of expert guides and teachers Mike Fernandez, from Aeroextreme (Tripoli 350, Dpto 302, Miraflores; ☎ 01 242 5125 or ☎ 999 480 954, @ 2mike@aeroextreme.com), and Marco Mercado of Tandem Flights (Tripoli 340, Dpto 402, Miraflores; ☎ 01 241 7370 or ☎ 994 092 537, ✆ Tandemperu .com) throughout. No previous experience is necessary, and prices start at around S/200.

Museo Amano

C Retiro 160, by block 11 of Av Angamos Oeste • Mon–Fri, opening and tours by appointment but usually 3 or 4pm • Entry by donation • ☎ 01 441 2909

The private **Museo Amano**, off block 11 of Angamos Oeste, merits a visit for its fabulous exhibition of beautifully displayed **textiles**, mainly Chancay weavings (among the best of pre-Columbian textiles), as well as some beautiful **ceramics**.

ChocoMuseo

C Berlín 375 • Daily 11am–7.30pm • Free • ☎ 01 445 9708

A museum, café and gift store, Lima's **ChocoMuseo** explores the history and process of chocolate making in Peru; the knowledgeable guides can answer all your questions, leading you around a model cacao tree, sacks of real cacao beans to run your fingers through and taste tests of every stage from cacao to chocolate. Detailed plaques in English and Spanish explain the process from bean to cup. The tour finishes with a blatant sales pitch, but the products – chocolate tea, liqueurs, fresh hot chocolate and raw chocolate (using unroasted cacao) – are all delicious. There are also free chocolate-making workshops.

Parque Reducto

Av Benavides, by Paseo de la República

The greatest attraction of the **Parque Reducto** is arguably the Saturday-morning organic food and sustainable products **market** (8am–noon), which takes place along its southern edge. There's also a good kids' play area, and a **museum** (Mon–Sat 7am–5pm; free) dedicated to the Municipality of Miraflores and the Peruvian army, in particular to the latter's battle against invading forces from Chile – the 1881 Battle of Miraflores. Exhibits include war memorabilia, photographs, small cannons and guns.

Barranco

Some 3km south of Larco Mar and quieter than Miraflores, **Barranco** overlooks the ocean and is scattered with old mansions, including fine colonial and Republican edifices, many beginning to crumble through lack of care. This was the capital's seaside resort during the nineteenth century and is now a kind of Limeño Left Bank, with young artists, writers, musicians and intellectuals taking over some of the older properties. Only covering three square kilometres, Barranco is quite densely populated, with some 40,000 inhabitants living in its delicately coloured houses. The area's primary attractions are its **bars, clubs and cafés**, and there's little else in the way of specific sights, though you may want to take a look at the clifftop remains of a **funicular rail-line**, which used to carry aristocratic families from the summer resort down to the beach.

Plaza Municipal de Barranco and south

The small but busy and well-kept **Plaza Municipal de Barranco** is the hub of the area's **nightlife**: the bars, clubs and cafés clustered around the square buzz with frenetic energy after dark, while retaining much of the area's charm and character. A couple of museums near here are worth a browse: the **Museo de Electricidad**, Pedro de

FROM TOP PARQUE DEL AMOR (P.71); EL CORDANO (P.86) >

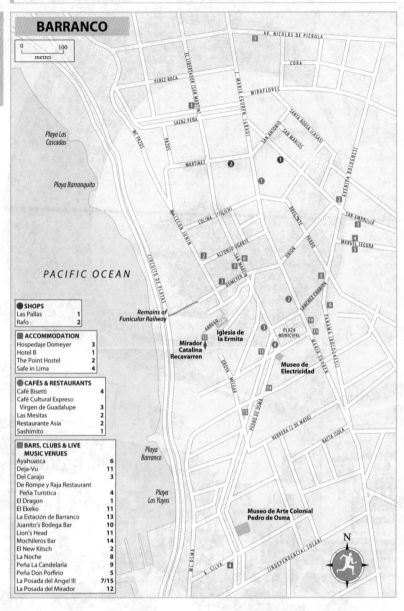

BARRANCO

0   100
metres

Playa Las
Cascadas

Playa Barranquito

PACIFIC OCEAN

Remains of
Funicular Railway

Mirador
Catalina
Recavarren

Iglesia de
la Ermita

Museo de
Electricidad

Playa
Barranco

Playa
Los Yuyos

Museo de Arte Colonial
Pedro de Osma

N

● **SHOPS**

Las Pallas	1
Rafo	2

■ **ACCOMMODATION**

Hospedaje Domeyer	3
Hotel B	1
The Point Hostel	2
Safe in Lima	4

● **CAFÉS & RESTAURANTS**

Café Bisetti	4
Café Cultural Expreso Virgen de Guadalupe	3
Las Mesitas	2
Restaurante Asia	2
Sashimito	1

■ **BARS, CLUBS & LIVE MUSIC VENUES**

Ayahuasca	6
Deja-Vu	11
Del Carajo	3
De Rompe y Raja Restaurant Peña Turística	4
El Dragon	1
El Ekeko	11
La Estación de Barranco	13
Juanito's Bodega Bar	10
Lion's Head	11
Mochileros Bar	14
El New Kitsch	2
La Noche	8
Peña La Candelaria	9
Peña Don Porfirio	5
La Posada del Angel III	7/15
La Posada del Mirador	12

Osma 105 (daily 9am–5pm; free; phone in advance for tours on ☎01 477 6577), displays a wide range of early electrical appliances and generating techniques; and just down the road, at Pedro de Osma 421, the **Museo de Arte Colonial Pedro de Osma** (daily 10am–1.30pm & 2.30–6pm; S/10; ☎01 467 0063, ⊛museopedrodeosma.org) holds a number of treasures and antiques such as oil paintings, colonial sculptures and silverware.

1

Iglesia de la Ermita and around

One block inland of the funicular, the impressive **Iglesia de la Ermita** (Church of the Hermit) sits on the cliff, with gardens to its front. Local legend says that the church was built here after a miraculous vision of a glowing Christ figure on this very spot. Beside the church is the **Puente de los Suspiros**, a pretty wooden bridge crossing a gully – the Bajada de Baños – which leads steeply down to the ocean, passing exotic dwellings lining the crumbling gully sides. A path leads beside the church along the top edge of the gully to the **Mirador Catalina Recavarren**, boasting lovely sea views. There's a uniquely situated pub, *La Posada del Mirador*, at the end of the path, as well as some other pleasant cafés and bars, buzzing on weekend evenings.

Costa Verde

Down beside the pounding rollers lies the **Costa Verde** beach area, so named because of vegetation clinging to the steep sandy cliffs. A bumpy road follows the shore from an exclusive yacht club and the Chorrillos Fishermen's Wharf northwest past both Barranco and Miraflores, almost to the suburb of Magdalena. The sea is cold here, but the surfers still brave it. The **Fishermen's Wharf** (around S/1) is always an interesting place for a stroll, surrounded by pelicans and, early in the day, fishermen unloading their catch, which is delivered immediately to the neighbouring market. The outdoor restaurants here compete vigorously for customers; all of them are pretty good and, not surprisingly, have a reputation for serving the freshest **ceviche** in Lima.

San Isidro

Unless you're shopping, banking or looking for a sauna or disco, there are few reasons to stop off in **San Isidro**. The exception is to take a stroll through the **Bosque El Olivar**, 150m west from block 34 of Avenida Arequipa: one of Lima's relatively few large, open, green spaces. A charming grove first planted in 1560, it's now rather depleted in olive trees but you can still see the old press and millstone, and the grove has developed its own **ecosystem**, which is home to over thirty different **bird species** including doves, flycatchers and hummingbirds. There's also a stage where concerts and cultural events are often held.

LIMA'S ART AND PHOTOGRAPHY GALLERIES

Lima's progressive culture of **art and photography** is deeply rooted in the Latin American tradition, combining indigenous ethnic realism with a political edge. The city boasts a few permanent galleries – all free – with temporary exhibitions on display in many of the main museums.

Artco C Rouad y Paz Soldan 325, San Isidro ☎ 01 221 3579. One of the most happening painters' galleries in Lima, usually well worth checking out. Mon–Fri 11am–8pm, Sat 10.30am–1.30pm & 3.30–7.30pm.

Centro Cultural de la Municipalidad de Miraflores Avenidas Larco and Diez Canseco, Miraflores ☎ 01 617 7266. Hosts a series of innovative photography exhibitions. Daily 10am–10pm.

Centro Cultural Ricardo Palma Av Larco 770, Miraflores ☎ 01 617 7263. Hosts fixed and changing exhibitions of paintings, photographs and sculpture. Daily 10am–9pm.

Centro Cultural de la Universidad Católica Av Camino Real 1075, San Isidro ☎ 01 616 1616. Art gallery hosting visiting exhibitions by foreign artists. Daily 10am–10pm.

Corriente Alterna Las Dalias 381, Miraflores ☎ 01 242 8482. Often presents shows by non-Peruvian painters. Mon–Fri 10am–8pm.

Galeria L'Imaginaire Av Arequipa 4595, Miraflores ☎ 01 610 8000. Usually exhibits Latin American painters and sculptors. Mon–Sat 5–9pm.

Sala Cultural del Banco Wiese Av Larco 1101, Miraflores ☎ 01 446 5240. A contemporary, international art gallery in the Banco Weise in the heart of downtown Miraflores. Mon–Sat 10am–2pm & 5–9pm.

Trapecio Av Larco 743, Miraflores ☎ 01 444 0842. Specializes in oils and sculpture. Mon–Sat 5–9pm.

1

Huallamarca

Nicolás de Rivera 201, just off Av El Rosario • Tues–Sun 9am–5pm • S/5

A few blocks northwest of the Bosque El Olivar and a few north of Lima Golf Club, the impressive reconstructed adobe *huaca*, **Huallamarca**, is now surrounded by wealthy suburbs. Like Pucllana (see p.69), this dates from pre-Inca days and has a small **museum** displaying the archeological remains of ancient Lima culture, such as funerary masks and artwork found in the *huaca* – including textiles oddly reminiscent of Scottish tartans.

Jesús María

The workaday suburb of **Jesús María**, west of San Isidro and Lince, south of Lima Centro, has only one real attraction: the little-visited, but quite fascinating **Museo de Historia Natural Jesús María**, Av Arenales 1256 (Mon–Fri 9am–3pm, Sat 9am–4.30pm, Sun 9am–12.30pm; S/10, tours S/30 per group; ☎01 471 0117). The museum presents a comprehensive if dusty overview of Peruvian wildlife and botany. One highlight is the sun fish: one of only three known examples of this colourful fish that can be found in the American coastal waters. There are also great **gardens** with botany displays, as well as a **geology** section.

Pueblo Libre

The quiet backstreets of **Pueblo Libre**, a relatively insalubrious suburb lying between San Isidro and Callao, on the western edge of Lima, is now home to two of Lima's major **museums**. These are quite tucked away, so it may be worth taking a taxi.

Museo Nacional de Arqueología, Antropología e Historia del Peru

Plaza Bolívar, San Martín and Antonio Pola • Tues–Sat 9am–4pm, Sun 9am–3pm • S/12, tours S/10 • Phone in advance for tours on ☎ 01 463 5070 • Take a taxi, or one of the microbuses that run along avenidas Brasil or Sucre

First among Pueblo Libre's attractions is the **Museo Nacional de Arqueología, Antropología e Historia del Peru**, which possesses a varied collection of pre-Inca artefacts and a number of historical exhibits relating mainly to the Republican period (1821 until the late nineteenth century). The liberators San Martín and Bolívar both lived here for a while. Although there's plenty to see, even more of the museum's immense collection is in storage, though some has permanently shifted to the Museo de la Nación (see p.78).

Renovated displays give a detailed and accurate perspective on Peru's prehistory, a vision that comes as a surprise if you'd previously thought of Peru simply in terms of Incas and conquistadores. The galleries are set around two colonial-style courtyards, with exhibits including stone **tools** some 8000 years old, Chavín-era **carved stones** engraved with felines and serpents, and the Manos Cruzados or Crossed Hands stone from Kotosh, evidence of a mysterious cult from some five thousand years ago. From the Paracas culture there are sumptuous **weavings** and many excellent examples of deformed heads and trepanned **skulls**: one shows post-operative growth, and a male mummy, "frozen" at the age of 30 to 35, has fingernails still visible and a creepy, sideways glance fixed on his misshapen head. From Nazca there are incredible **ceramics** representing marine life, agriculture, flora, sexuality, wildlife, trophy-heads and scenes from mythology and everyday life. The **Mochica** and **Chimu cultures** (see pp.482–483) are represented, too, and there are also exhibits devoted to the **Incas**. The national history section shows off some dazzling antique clothing, extravagant furnishings and other period pieces, complemented by early Republican paintings.

Museo Larco

Av Bolívar 1515 • Daily 9am–10pm • S/30 • ☎ 01 461 312, ⓦ museolarco.org • Take a taxi or bus #23 (passes Av Abancay in Lima Centro) • From the Museo Nacional de Historia, follow the blue path painted on the pavement north up Av Sucre, then west for ten blocks

Within a fifteen-minute walk from the district's two other museums is one of Lima's most unusual attractions, the **Museo Larco**, which contains hundreds of thousands of

1

excellently preserved **ceramics**, many of them Chiclin or Mochica pottery from around Trujillo. The mansion itself is noteworthy as a stylish *casa Trujillana*, in the style of the northern city where this collection was originally kept. The museum houses the largest collection of Peruvian antiquities in the world and is divided into three sections: the **main museum**, which contains an incredible range of household and funerary ceramics; the **warehouse museum**, with shelf after shelf stacked with ceramics; and the **erotic art museum**, holding a wide selection of sexually themed pre-Inca artefacts – mainly from the explicit Mochica culture – which tends to attract the most interest.

Parque de las Leyendas and the zoo

Av Las Leyendas 580, San Miguel • Daily 9am–6pm • S/10 • ☎ 01 717 7456 • Take yellow bus #48 from the Plaza Mayor or a taxi

Located in a deserted spot on the sacred site of the ancient Maranga culture, but close to block 24 of Avenida La Marina, the **Parque de las Leyendas** is laid out according to the three regions of Peru – *costa, sierra* and *selva*. The park and **zoo** have been much improved in recent years, though there's little attempt to create the appropriate habitats and the animals are caged. Nevertheless, it does offer a glimpse of many of Peru's animal and bird species: condors, jaguars, sea lions, snakes, pumas, king vultures, bears and other exotica. It's also a fine spot for a picnic and there's an interesting **botanical garden**. Just outside there are often some interesting **artesanía** stalls selling cases of dead insects, including colourful Amazonian butterflies and tarantulas.

Callao and La Punta

Isolated on a narrow, boot-shaped peninsula, **Callao** and **La Punta** (The Point) form a natural annexe to Lima, looking out towards the ocean. Originally founded in 1537 and quite separate from the rest of the city, Callao was destined to become Peru's principal treasure-fleet port before eventually being engulfed by Lima's other suburbs during the course of the twentieth century. These days it's a crumbling but attractive and atmospheric area full of restaurants and once-splendid houses. The land is very low-lying and, at La Punta itself, the surf feels as though it could at any moment rise up and swallow the small rowing-boat-dotted beach and nearby houses.

Still the country's main commercial harbour, and one of the most modern ports in South America, Callao lies about 14km west of Lima Centro. The suburb also has its slum zones, nameless areas located in the backstreets infamous for prostitution and gangland assassins, considered virtually **no-go areas** for visitors – but if you keep to the main streets, you will find some of the best **ceviche restaurants** anywhere on the continent.

Fortaleza del Real Felipe

Av Saenz Peña, 1st block, Plaza Independencia • Daily 9.30am–3.30pm; museum Mon–Fri 9.30am–4pm • S/8 • ☎ 01 465 8394

Away from Callao's rougher quarters and dominating the entire peninsula is the great **Fortaleza del Real Felipe**, built after the devastating earthquake of 1764, which washed ships ashore and killed nearly the entire population of Callao. This is a superb example of the military architecture of its age, designed in the shape of a pentagon. Although built too late to protect the Spanish treasure-fleets from European pirates like Francis Drake, it was to play a critical role in the **battles for independence**. Its firepower repulsed both Admiral Brown (1816) and Lord Cochrane (1818), though many Royalists (Peruvians loyal to the Spanish Crown) starved to death here when the

---

GETTING TO CALLAO AND LA PUNTA

To reach Callao, take **bus #25** from Plaza San Martín, which runs all the way here – and beyond to La Punta – or take a bus marked "La Punta" from Avenida Arequipa west along either Avenida Angamos or Avenida Javier Prado.

1

stronghold was besieged by the Patriots (those patriotic to Peru but keen to devolve power from the Spanish colonial authorities) in 1821, just prior to the Royalist surrender. The fort's grandeur is marred only by a number of storehouses, built during the late nineteenth century when it was used as a customs house. Inside, the **Museo del Ejercito** (Military Museum) houses a good collection of eighteenth- and nineteenth-century arms, and has various rooms dedicated to Peruvian war heroes.

Museo Naval

Av Jorge Chavez 123, off Plaza Grau • Mon–Fri 9.30am–2.30pm • S/5 • ☎ 01 429 4793 ext 6794, ⓦ museonaval.com.pe

If your interest in military matters has been piqued by the Fortaleza, head for the **Museo Naval**, displaying the usual military paraphernalia, uniforms, paintings, photographs and replica ships. Outside is the **Canon del Pueblo**, a large gun installed in a day and a night on May 2, 1866, during a battle against a Spanish fleet; it is also claimed to have deterred the Chilean fleet from entering Lima during the War of the Pacific in 1880.

Museo Submarino Abtao

Av Jorge Chavez, 1st block, waterside • Tues–Sun 9.30am–4.30pm • S/10 • ☎ 01 795 6900, ⓦ submarinoabtao.com

From the same building as the Naval Museum, there's also access to the nearby **Museo Submarino Abtao**, or Submarine Museum, actually a real sub that literally opened its hatches in 2004 to allow public access for thirty-minute guided tours, including a simulated attack by enemy submarine. A Sierra-type vessel, this torpedo-firing battle sub was built in Connecticut, US, between 1952 and 1954, when it first arrived in Peru. You can touch the periscope, visit the dorms and enter the engine and control rooms, which were responsible for over five thousand submersions during 48 years of service.

La Punta

Out at the end of the peninsula, what was once the fashionable beach resort of **La Punta** is now overshadowed by the Naval College and Yacht Club. Many of its old mansions, slowly crumbling, are very elegant, though others are extravagant monstrosities. Right at the peninsula's tip, an open and pleasant **promenade** offers glorious views and sunsets over the Pacific and the nearby offshore islands such as **Fronton** (with its small, isolated prison), **San Lorenzo** (with evidence of human occupation, fishing and the use of both cotton and maize going back to 2500 BC) and **Isla Palomino** (with a colony of sea lions). Meanwhile, at the back of the strand, there are some excellent **restaurants** serving traditional food (many are difficult to find, so ask locally).

Museo de la Nación

Av Javier Prado Este 2465, San Borja • Tues–Sun 9am–5pm • Free • ☎ 01 476 9878 • Take a colectivo along Av Javier Prado east from Av Arequipa; after 10min, you'll see the vast, concrete building on the left

The **Museo de la Nación**, situated in the suburb of **San Borja** just east of San Isidro, is Lima's largest modern museum, with exhibitions covering most of the important aspects of Peruvian archeology, art and culture, including regional peasant costumes from around the country, and life-sized and miniature models depicting life in pre-Conquest times. Frequent high-profile temporary exhibits, displayed in vast salons, are usually worth the trek out of town.

Museo de Oro

Av Alonso de Molina 1100, Monterrico • Daily 11.30am–7pm • S/35 • ☎ 01 345 1292 • Taxi from Miraflores or Lima Centro S/12–15 one way

Housed in a small, fortress-like building set back in the shade of tall trees and owned by the high-society Mujica family, the **Museo de Oro** is located along Avenida Javier Prado Este, in the suburb of **Monterrico**. As it's difficult to find and quite far from Miraflores and Lima Centro, it's best to take a taxi.

The upper floor holds some excellent **tapestry** displays, while the ground level boasts a vast display of **arms and uniforms**, which bring to life some of Peru's bloodier historical episodes. The real gem, however, is the basement, crammed with original and replica pieces from **pre-Columbian** times. The pre-Inca weapons and wooden staffs and the astounding Nazca yellow-feathered poncho designed for a noble's child or child high-priest are especially fine. Look out for the **skull** with a full set of pink quartz teeth.

Parque Zoológico Huachipa

Av Las Torres, Vitarte • Daily 9.30am–5.30pm •S/13, children 2–12 S/6 • ☎ 01 356 3666, ⬚ zoohuachipa.com.pe • Take a taxi (S/20–25) or any bus going west from Lima Centro marked "Vitarte"

Much newer and more appealing than the Parque de las Leyendas zoo, if a long way out to the east of Lima in the Vitarte district, the **Parque Zoológico Huachipa** offers a diverse, man-made habitat with lakes and rides, and plenty of animals and birds. There's an African savanna section, another dedicated to carnivores (including tigers), a kangaroo enclosure and an aquatic area.

ARRIVAL AND DEPARTURE   LIMA

Most visitors arrive in Lima by **plane**, landing at the Jorge Chavez airport, or by **bus**, concluding their long journeys either in the older, central areas of the city, or in one of the modern terminals en route to the busy commercial suburb of San Isidro, or close to the Avenida Javier Prado Este. **Driving** into the city is only for the truly adventurous: the roads are highly congested and the driving of a generally poor standard.

BY AIR

Jorge Chavez airport is 7km northwest of the centre (☎ 01 511 6055, ⬚ lap.com.pe). Many hotels, even mid-range ones, will arrange for free or relatively inexpensive airport pick-up; otherwise, the best way into town is to take a taxi. **Facilities** You'll find an ATM at the top of the stairs by the internet cabins at the north end of the building. There are 24hr exchange counters with reasonably competitive rates in both the arrivals baggage reclaim area and near the departure gates, but you'll get slightly better rates in the centre of Lima or Miraflores.

Official taxis The quickest way into the city is by taxi, which will take around 45min to Lima Centro or downtown Miraflores. The simplest way is to book or find on arrival an official taxi from the Taxi Green kiosk (☎ 01 484 2734), or official drivers with laminated badges inside the terminal. To most parts of Lima the cost is S/55. Returning to the airport is cheaper and should be S/40 from Miraflores.

Non-official taxis It is possible, though not easy without good Spanish, to negotiate with non-official taxi drivers outside the terminal building and agree a price as low as S/35; however the streets here are quite rough and have a reputation for theft. If you don't use the official service, it's very important to fix the price in Peruvian soles with the driver before getting in. It can be in US$, if required, but the important thing is to be clear both about the amount and the currency. Take extra care when looking for a taxi outside the perimeter at the roundabout or on the road into Lima, as there are often thefts in these areas.

Domestic airline contacts Aeroica (☎ 01 444 3026, ⬚ aeroica.net); Aeroparacas, Santa Fe 270, Higuereta, Surco (☎ 01 449 4768, ⬚ aeroparacas.com); Lan, at Jr de la Unión 958, Lima Centro (☎ 01 213 8200), also at C Las Begonias 780, San Isidro, Tienda 102, Centro Comercial,

Jockey Plaza, Surco, and Av José Pardo 513, Miraflores (☎ 01 213 8200, ⬚ lan.com); Star Peru, Av Comandante Espinar 331, Miraflores (☎ 01 705 9000, ⬚ starperu.com); TACA Peru (☎ 01 213 6060, ⬚ Taca.com); TANS, Av Arequipa 5200, Miraflores (☎ 01 241 8510).

International airline contacts Aerolineas Argentinas, Carnaval y Moreyra 370 (☎ 0800 52200, ⬚ aerolineas .com); Air Canada (☎ 0800 52073, ⬚ aircanada.com); Air France, Av Alvarez Calderon 185, 6th floor, San Isidro (☎ 01 213 0200, ⬚ airfrance.com); American Airlines, Jr Juan de Arona 830, 14th floor, San Isidro (☎ 01 211 7000 or ☎ 0800 40350, ⬚ americanairlines.com); Avianca, Av Paz Soldan 225, Oficina C-5, Los Olivos, San Isidro (☎ 01 444 0747, ☎ 01 444 0748 or ☎ 0800 51936, ⬚ avianca.com); Continental Airlines, Victor Andrés Belaunde 147, Oficina 101, Edificio Real, San Isidro (☎ 01 221 4340 or ☎ 0800 70030, ⬚ continentalairlines.com); Delta Airlines (☎ 01 211 9211, ⬚ delta.com); Iberia, Av Camino Real 390, Oficina 902, San Isidro (☎ 01 4417801, ⬚ iberia.com); KLM, Av Alvarez Calderon 185, 6th floor, San Isidro (☎ 01 213 0200, ⬚ klm.com); Japan Airlines (☎ 01 221 7501, ⬚ jal.com); Lan Chile, Av José Pardo 269, Miraflores (☎ 01 213 8200 or ☎ 0801 11234, ⬚ lan.com).

Destinations Arequipa (1 daily; 1hr 20min); Chiclayo (1 daily; 1hr 40min); Cusco (several daily; 1hr); Iquitos (2 daily; 2hr); Jauja for Huancayo (1 weekly; 30min); Juliaca for Puno (1 daily; 2hr); Piura (1 daily; 2hr); Pucallpa (1 daily; 1hr); Rioja/Moyabamba (1 weekly; 2hr); Tacna (1 weekly; 2hr 30min); Tarapoto (1 weekly; 1hr 30min); Trujillo (1 daily; 1hr); Tumbes (1 daily; 2hr 30min).

BY BUS

Lima doesn't have one bus terminal, but multiple individual private bus companies with their own offices and depots in

1

different locations (see below). Whichever terminal you arrive at, your best bet, particularly if you have luggage, is to hail a taxi and fix a price – about S/8–20 to pretty much anywhere in Lima.

Long-distance and inter-regional buses The bus terminals of the main operators – Cruz del Sur, Ormeño and Tepsa – are on Av Javier Prado Este. Plenty of buses and colectivos pass by here (those marked Todo Javier Prado), and can be picked up on Av Javier Prado or where Av Arequipa crosses this road. Many operators have alternative depots in the suburbs, to avoid the worst of Lima Centro's traffic.

Local and intercity buses Some of the smaller buses serving the area north of Lima depart from the Terminal Terrestre Fiori, block 15 of Av Alfredo Mendiola in San Martín de Porres; other companies arrive at small depots in the district of La Victoria, including those that connect with the Central Sierra and jungle regions; some arrive on the Paseo de la República, opposite the Estadio Nacional. Other common arrival points nearby include Jr García Naranjo, C Carlos Zavala (in the Cercado district) and Av Luna Pizarro. Destinations Arequipa (12 daily; 14–16hr); Chincha (8 daily; 2–3hr); Cusco (10 daily, some change in Arequipa; 30–40hr); Huacho (12 daily; 2–3hr); Huancayo (12 daily; 6–8hr); Huaraz (10 daily; 9–10hr); Ica (every 15min; 3–4hr); La Merced (8 daily; 7–8hr); Nazca (10 daily; 6hr); Satipo (2 daily; 12–14hr); Pisco (6 daily; 3hr–3 30min); Tacna (6 daily; 18–20hr); Tarma (8 daily; 6–7hr); Trujillo (10 daily; 8–9hr).

BUS OPERATORS
The best and most reliable bus companies – Cruz del Sur, Ormeño, Tepsa and Oltursa – can deliver you to most of the popular destinations up and down the coast, and to Arequipa or Cusco. Cruz del Sur is the best choice – if not the cheapest – for the big destinations. Below is a list of bus companies and the destinations they serve. Note that the addresses given below are of the companies' offices, and buses often depart from elsewhere: always check which terminal your bus is departing from when you buy your ticket.

Chanchamayo Manco Capac 1052, La Victoria ☎ 01 470 1189. Tarma, La Oroya, San Ramon and La Merced.

Chinchano Av Carlos Zavala 171, La Victoria ☎ 01 427 5679. The coast as far as Cañete, Chincha and Pisco.

Cial Av Abancay 947 and Av República de Panamá 2469–2485, Santa Catalina, La Victoria ☎ 01 207 6900, ⓦ expresocial.com. North coast including Máncora, Cajamarca and Huaraz.

El Condor Av Carlos Zavala 101, Lima Centro ☎ 01 427 0286. Trujillo and Huancayo.

Condor de Chavín Montevideo 1039, La Victoria ☎ 01 428 8122. Callejón de Huaylas, Huaraz and Chavín.

Cruz del Sur Av Javier Prado Este 1109 and Nicolás Arriola, on the border of San Isidro and La Victoria ☎ 01 3115050, ⓦ cruzdelsur.com.pe. Chiclayo, Trujillo,

Máncora, Piura, Tumbes, Ica, Nazca, Tacna, Arequipa, Puno, Cusco, Huaraz, Huancayo and Ayacucho.

Empresa Huaral 131 Av Abancay, Lima Centro ☎ 01 428 2254. Huaral, Ancon and Chancay.

Empresa Rosario Jr Ayacucho, La Victoria 942 ☎ 01 534 2685. Huánuco and La Unión.

Flores Buses Calles Paseo de la República and 28 de Julio, La Victoria ☎ 01 424 3278. Arequipa and south coast.

Huamanga Jr Montevideo 619 and Luna Pizarro 455, La Victoria ☎ 01 330 2206. Ayacucho, Chiclayo, Moyobamba, Yurimaguas and Tarapoto; you'll probably need to change bus at Pedro Ruiz for Chachapoyas.

León de Huánuco Av 28 de Julio 1520, La Victoria ☎ 01 424 3893. Cerro de Pasco, Huánuco, Tarma and La Merced.

Libertadores Av Grau 491, Lima Centro ☎ 01 426 8067. Ayacucho, Satipo and Huanta.

Línea Paseo de la República 979, La Victoria ☎ 01 424 0836. Buses to all north coast as far as Piura, plus Huaraz and Cajamarca.

Lobato Buses 28 de Julio 2101–2107, La Victoria ☎ 01 4749411. Tarma, La Merced and Satipo.

Mariscal Caceres Av 28 de Julio 2195, La Victoria ☎ 01 474 7850. The coast and some other sectors, including Huancayo.

Movil Tours Paseo de la República, opposite the Estadio Nacional, La Victoria ☎ 01 716 8000; other depot at Av Carlos Izaguirre 535, Los Olivos. Huaraz, Tarapoto and Chachapoyas.

Oltursa Av Aramburu 1160, La Victoria ☎ 01 708 5000. Máncora and Tumbes, down south all the way to Arequipa, as well as to Cusco, Huancayo and Huaraz.

Ormeño Av Javier Prado Este 1059, on the border of San Isidro and La Victoria ☎ 01 4721710; some buses also pass through the depot at Carlos Zavala 177, Lima Centro ☎ 01 427 5679, ⓦ grupo-ormeno.com.pe. Good for big national and international services along the north coast, south coast to Tacna and Arequipa and Puno, and also Cusco and into Ecuador, Bolivia, Brazil, Argentina and Chile.

Palomino Av 28 de Julio 1750, La Victoria ☎ 01 428 6356. Cusco via Nazca and Abancay.

Señor de Luren Manco Capac 611, La Victoria ☎ 01 479 8415. Nazca.

Soyuz/Peru Bus Av Carlos Zavala y Loyaza 221 and Av Mexico 333, La Victoria ☎ 01 4276310 or ☎ 01 2661515. Nazca, Ica and the coastal towns en route.

Tepsa Av Javier Prado Este 1091, on the border of San Isidro and La Victoria ☎ 01 617 9000. Good buses serving the whole coast, north and south (Tacna to Tumbes) as well as Cajamarca, Huancayo, Abancay, Cusco and Arequipa.

Transportes Junin Av Nicolás Arriola 240, C Av Javier Prado, La Victoria ☎ 01 326 6136. Tarma, San Ramon, La Merced and the Selva Central.

Transportes Rodríguez Av Paseo de la República 749, La Victoria ☎ 01 428 0506. Huaraz, Caraz and Chimbote.

INFORMATION

TOURIST INFORMATION

Some of the commercial tour companies (see below) are also geared up for offering good tourist information, notably Fertur Peru and Lima Vision. The South American Explorers' Club at C Piura 135, Miraflores (☎01 444 2150, ⓦsaexplorers.org) has good information, including maps, listings and travel reports, available to its members.

Airport Información y Asistencia al Turista, run by i-Peru, has a kiosk at the airport (☎01 574 8000).

Lima Centro The main public municipal office of Información Turística is hidden away in a small office behind the Palacio Municipal on the Plaza Mayor at C Los Escribanos 145 (daily 9am–5pm; ☎01 315 1505 or ☎01 315 1300 ext 1542).

Miraflores There's a small tourist information kiosk in the central Parque Kennedy (daily 9am–2pm & 2.30–7pm). Maps, leaflets and information can also be obtained from the Central de Información y Promoción Turística, Av Larco 770 (Mon–Fri 9am–1pm & 2–5pm; ☎01 446 3959 ext 114, ⓦmiraflores.gob.pe and ⓦregionlima.gob.pe). There are other kiosks on the corner of Av Petit Thouars and Enrique Palacios, close to the craft stores – the Petit Thoars Mercado Indio – and also in Larco Mar (☎01 445 9400, ⓔiperuLarco Mar@promperu.gob.pe).

San Isidro The office of Información y Asistencia al Turista is run by i-Peru from Jorge Basadre 610 in San Isidro (Mon–Fri 8.30am–6pm; ☎01 421 1627, ⓦperuinfo.org).

LISTINGS

Published monthly in Peru, the *Peru Guide* gives up-to-date information on Lima, from tours and treks to hotels, shopping, events and practical advice; it's readily available in hotels, tour and travel agents, and information offices.

MAPS

Buy city maps from kiosks in Lima Centro or the better bookshops in Miraflores; the best is the *Lima Guía "Inca" de Lima Metropolitan* (US$15).

TRAVEL AGENTS AND TOURS

For standard tours, tickets, flights and hotel bookings, the best agencies are below. A number of companies also organize specialist outdoor activities in and around Lima (see box, p.82).

Class Adventure Travel San Martín 800, Miraflores ☎01 444 1652, ⓦcat-travel.com. Organizes excellent tours and packages including Lima culinary tours, Nazca and desert experiences.

Fertur Peru Jr Junín 211, Lima Centro ☎01 427 2626, ⓦfertur-travel.com; or in Miraflores at Schell 485 ☎01 242 1900. Top service in tailor-made visits around Peru, as well as overland, air or other travel needs and accommodation.

Highland Tours Av Pardo 231, Oficina 401, Miraflores ☎01 242 6292, ⓦhighlandperu.com. Offers tours and will arrange travel around Peru plus accommodation when required.

Lima Tours Jr de la Unión (ex-Belén) 1040, near Plaza San Martín ☎01 619 6900, ⓦlimatours.com.pe. One of the more upmarket companies, with an excellent reputation.

Lima Vision Jr Chiclayo 444, Miraflores ☎01 447 7710, ⓦlimavision.com. A variety of city tours, plus a range of archeological ones: Pachacamac, Nazca and Cusco.

Marilí Tours Av Primavera 120, Oficina 306, Chacarilla ☎01 241 0142, ⓦmarilitours.com.pe. Tours to most of Peru, including Cusco, Madre de Dios, Puno and the northern desert region.

Overland Expeditions Jr Emilio Fernández 640, Santa Beatrice ☎01 424 7762. Specialize in the Lachay Reserve.

Paracas Tours Av Rivera Navarette 723, San Isidro ☎01 222 2621, ⓦparacastours.com.pe. A small office with a very professional air-ticketing service.

GETTING AROUND

BY COLECTIVO

Colectivos vary in appearance, but are usually either microbuses (small buses) or combis (minibuses); both tend to be crowded and have flat rates (from around S/1). Quickest of all Lima transport, combi-colectivos race from one street corner to another along all the major arterial city roads; microbuses generally follow the same routes, albeit usually in a more sedate fashion.

Avenida Arequipa colectivos The Av Arequipa colectivos start their route at Puente Rosa in Rimac, running along Tacna and Garcilaso de La Vega (formerly Av Wilson) in the centre, before picking up on the Av Arequipa which will take you all the way down to Miraflores, passing the Ovalo (a large roundabout), going down Diagonal to C José González before starting the route back to the centre, up Larco, then via Av Arequipa.

Barranco colectivos To reach Barranco from Miraflores, pick up one of the many colectivos or buses (marked Barranco or Chorrillos) travelling along Diagonal (which is one-way, from the central park towards Larco Mar and the ocean).

BY BUS

The modern Lima Metropolitana bus system (☎01 203 9000, ⓦmetropolitano.com.pe) connects Chorrillos and Barranco in the south with Independencia to the north of the city. Much of the route follows a dedicated track in the

1

ADVENTURE TRIPS AND TOURS AROUND LIMA

Many of Lima's travel agents (see p.81) can organize trips to the most popular destinations; the operators below specialize in adventure tours. There are a huge range of trips on offer, from paragliding above the city (see box, p.72) to trekking and mountain biking.

TREKKING

For advice on **trekking and mountain climbing** and trail maps, visit the Trekking and Backpacking Club, Jr Huascar 1152, Jesús María (☎01 423 2515), the Asociación de Andinismo de la Universidad de Lima, based at the university on Avenida Javier Prado Este (☎01 437 6767; meets Wed evenings), or the South American Explorers' Club (see p.81).

Most trekking companies run trips to the Cordillera Blanca and Colca, as well as around the Cusco area and along the Inca Trail.

Incatrek Av Pardo 620, Oficina 11, Miraflores ☎01 242 7843, ⓦincatrekperu.com. This outfit sometimes runs tours to Lima's Museo de Oro, the ancient site of Caral, Ica and Paracas, Tarma, Oxapampa, Pozuzo and Satipo.

Peru Expeditions C Colina 151, Miraflores ☎01 447 2057, ⓦperu-expeditions.com. A professional, helpful company specializing in adventure travel,

particularly on the coast (Paracas and Ballestas, Nazca), Arequipa and Colca areas. It offers trekking, mountain biking and 4WD tours.

Rainforest Expeditions Av Larco 1116, Dep-S, Miraflores ☎01 719 6472, ⓦperunature.com. Arguably Peru's best eco-tourism operator, with three lodges in the Peruvian Amazon; check website for toll-free telephone details.

WHITEWATER RAFTING

For **whitewater rafting** around Cusco and Huaraz, contact Explorandes or Mayuc (see below) or check for other operators in Cusco, Lunahuana or Huaraz (see relevant chapter listings).

Explorandes San Fernando 320, Miraflores ☎01 445 0532, ⓦexplorandes.com. Offering itineraries to most areas of Peru, this company tailors trips to individual interests as well as pre-packaged expeditions.

Mayuc Portal Confituras, Cusco ☎084 242 824, ⓦmayuc.com. One of Peru's best and longest-established operators; while specializing in rafting, it also operates tours to Nazca, Colca and Titicaca.

DIVING AND BOAT TRIPS

Motor Yachts Contact through Ecocruceros, Av Arequipa 4960, of 202, Miraflores ☎01 226 8530, ⓦislaspalomino.com. Offer trips from Lima to the nearby islands, Islas Palomino, to see marine mammals,

including a sea lion colony; a pleasant trip in clear weather.

Nature Expeditions ☎946 096 753, ⓦnature -expeditions-peru.com. Diving and scuba are popular sports in Peru – this is the best operator for trips.

---

centre of the Paseo de la República, and the bus track can be accessed via the road bridges across the multi-lane freeway. There are "regular" and "expreso" buses (every 10min; daily 6am–9.50pm), the former stopping at all stations, the latter at certain set ones. Tickets (*tarjeta inteligente*) can be bought at the station entry points, mainly from machines. You can catch other (non-Lima Metropolitana) buses to most parts of the city from Av Abancay in the centre; to catch a bus to a destination covered in this chapter look for the suburb name (written on the front of all buses).

BY TAXI

Taxis are a fast and cheap way to get around Lima, and can be hailed pretty well anywhere on any street at any time.

Official taxis Official taxis are based at taxi ranks and licensed by the city authorities (most but not all their cars have taxi signs on the roof; some of the larger taxi

companies are radio-controlled). Short rides cost S/5–10 for ten blocks or so, say from Parque Kennedy in Miraflores to Barranco, while longer rides will set you back S/10–25, for example from Miraflores to Lima Centro or the Museo de Oro in Monterrico. Taxis can be rented for the day from about S/150. You should always fix the price to your destination in soles before getting in, and pay in soles only at the end of your journey. Reliable 24hr taxi companies include: Taxi Seguro ☎01 536 6956; Taxi Amigo ☎01 349 0177; and Taxi Movil ☎01 422 6890.

Unofficial taxis Unofficial taxis abound in the streets of Lima; they're basically ordinary cars with temporary plastic "taxi" stickers on their front windows, and are cheaper than official taxis.

BY CAR

Driving in Lima is incredibly anarchic. It's not too fast, but it is assertive, with drivers, especially *taxistas*, often finding gaps in traffic that don't appear to exist; this means you have to be brave as a visitor to take the wheel. Given the city's size and spread, however, this is still an option, particularly if you want to visit sites just north or south of the city (such as Caral, Pachacamac or the beaches).

Car rental Budget, Av Larco 998, Miraflores (☎01 444 4546, ⓦ budgetperu.com); Hertz, Cantuarias 160, Miraflores (☎01 447 2129, ⓦ hertzperu.com.pe).

Van and driver hire Backpacker Van Express, Av Comandante Espinar 611, Miraflores (☎01 447 7748);

Transporte Manchego Turismo (☎01 420 1289 ⓦ manchegoturismo.com.pe); LAC Dolar, Av La Paz, Miraflores (☎01 717 3588).

BY BIKE

Bike Tours of Lima C Bolívar 150, Miraflores ☎01 445 3172, ⓦ biketoursoflima.com. Bilingual themed bike tours, as well as bike rentals, from S/20 for 2hr to S/50 for a full day.

Rentabike C Alcanfores 132, Miraflores ☎01 692 1082. Bike tours and rentals.

ACCOMMODATION

There are three main areas in which to stay. Most travellers on a budget end up in **Lima Centro**, in one of the traditional gringo dives around the Plaza Mayor or the San Francisco church. These are mainly old buildings and tend to be full of backpackers, but they aren't necessarily the best choices in the old centre, even in their price range, as most of them are poorly maintained. If you can spend a little bit more and opt for mid-range, you'll find some interesting old buildings bursting with atmosphere and style. If you're into nightlife and want to stay somewhere with a downtown feel, with access to the sea, opt for a hotel further out of the city in **Miraflores**, which is still close to the seafront as well as home to most of Lima's nightlife, culture and shops. However, most hostels here start at around S/50 per person, and quite a few hotels go above S/350. Higher-end hotels aimed at foreigners give their prices in US$ and are listed here in that format. The trendy ocean-clifftop suburb of **Barranco** is increasingly the place of choice for the younger traveller. Apart from the artists'-quarter vibe and the clubs and restaurants, though, the area has little to offer in the way of sights. Other suburban options include **San Isidro**, mainly residential but close to some of the main bus terminals; and **San Miguel**, a mostly rather down-at-heel suburb, close to the clifftop and extending from Miraflores towards La Perla and Callao.

LIMA CENTRO

★**Gran Hotel Bolívar** Jr de la Unión 958 ☎01 619 7171, US toll-free ☎888 790 5264, ⓦ granhotelbolivar .com.pe; map p.62. This old, elegant and luxurious hotel is well located and full of old-fashioned charm, dominating the northwest corner of the Plaza San Martín. Even if you don't stay here, you should check out the cocktail lounge (famous for its Pisco Sour Cathedral) and restaurant, which host live piano music most nights (8–11pm). Great-value online deals. S/245

Hostal de Las Artes Chota 1460 ☎01 433 0031; map p.62. At the southern end of Lima Centro, this clean, gay-friendly place is popular with travellers, located as it is in a large, attractive house. Some rooms have a private bathroom, and there's also a dorm with shared bathroom; avoid the downstairs rooms, which can be a little gloomy. English is spoken and there's a book exchange, as well as a nice patio. Dorms S/30, doubles S/70

Hostal Granada Huancavelica 323 ☎01 428 7338;

map p.62. This place could be more welcoming, but it's in a great location and the service is efficient. It has large, tidy rooms, private bathrooms, wi-fi and double glazing on streetside windows. S/65

Hostal Roma Jr Ica 326 ☎01 4277576 or ☎01 427 7572, ⓦ hostalroma.8m.com; map p.62. A pleasant, safe place that's always popular, so book online in advance. It's conveniently located a few blocks from the Plaza Mayor, offers a choice of private or communal bathrooms (but only one shower for women) and a reliable luggage storage service. There's a TV room and a café in the entrance area. S/60, communal bathroom S/40

Hostal Wiracocha Jr Junín 284 ☎01 427 1178; map p.62. Run by the same owners since 1975, it's located on the second level of this building, a block from Plaza Mayor. Rooms are quite spacious, if simply furnished, and fairly clean. S/50

Hotel España Jr Azángaro 105 ☎01 428 5546, ⓦ hotelespanaperu.com; map p.62. A converted nineteenth-century Republican-style house very popular

---

CATCH A COLECTIVO

Almost every corner of Lima is linked by the ubiquitous, regular and privately owned **colectivos**. Generally speaking, colectivos chalk up their **destination or route** on the windscreen and shout it out as they pull to a stop. So, for instance, you'll see "Todo–Arequipa" or "Tacna–Arequipa" chalked up on their windscreens, which indicates that the colectivo runs the whole length of Avenida Arequipa, connecting Lima Centro with downtown Miraflores. The driver will call out the destination sing-song style, competing with market-stall holders and the like for the attention of prospective passengers.

1

with backpackers, this secure hostel has rooms available with or without private bathroom. There's also a dorm with shared bathroom. Amenities include a nice courtyard and rooftop patio, internet connection, book exchange and safe. Dorms S/25, doubles S/65

★**Hotel Europa** Jr Ancash 376 ☎01 427 3351; map p.62. One of the best-value budget pads, conveniently located opposite the San Francisco church, with a lovely courtyard. It's a good place to meet fellow travellers and as such is very popular and fills up quickly. Dorms S/17.50, doubles S/38

★**Hotel Kamana** Jr Cámana 547 ☎01 426 7204, ⓦhotelkamana.com; map p.62. An adequate, small hotel in the heart of Lima Centro, with friendly staff; TVs and showers in all of the nicely furnished rooms. Facilities include a 24hr café, room service, security-guarded entrance, wi-fi and money exchange. S/190

Inka Path Jr de La Unión 654 ☎01 426 1919, ⓦhotelinkapath.com; map p.62. About as central as you could wish for, *Inka Path* has very comfortable, if overly minimal, rooms. Beds are queen size and bathrooms private, with 24hr hot water. Price includes breakfast and internet. S/155

Lima Sheraton Paseo de la República 170 ☎01 315 5000, ⓦsheraton.com.pe; map p.62. A top-class, modern international hotel – concrete, tall and blandly elegant, though past its heyday. It also boasts a casino, a spa and a good restaurant. S/350

Pensión Rodríguez Av Nicolás de Piérola 730, Dept 201 ☎01 423 6465, ⓔjotajot@terra.com.pe; map p.62. Excellent value but often crowded, with shared rooms and bathrooms, and prone to noise from the road outside. The pension staff will organize airport pick-up if required. Look for the buzzer on the inner-left at the street entrance. Dorms S/30, doubles S/70

★**La Pousada del Parque** Parque Hernan Velarde 60, Santa Beatriz ☎01 433 2412, ⓦincacountry.com; map p.62. A wonderful boutique hotel in a large, quiet and stylish house close to Lima Centro and the Parque de La Exposición, but just south of the centre's busy sectors. The rooms are excellently kept and well furnished, and there are good breakfasts. Internet access available. S/150

MIRAFLORES

Belmond Miraflores Park Av Malecón de la Reserva 1035 ☎01 610 4000 or US toll-free ☎800 237 1236, ⓦbelmond.com; map p.70. Conspicuously modern hotel for the area, with a day spa, great restaurant, pub-style bar and lovely views over Miraflores, the city and the Pacific. In short, total luxury. S/350

★**Casa Andina Miraflores Centro** Av Petit Thouars 5444 ☎01 213 9700, ⓦcasa-andina.com; map p.70. Occupying five floors, this popular, well-appointed place is close to most of Miraflores' shops and nightlife, though

rooms are neither spacious nor grand. It's hard to beat for value at the top end; all rooms have private bathrooms and TV, and the price includes an exceptional buffet breakfast. S/462

Casa de Baraybar C Toribio Pacheco 216 ☎01 441 2160, ⓦcasadebaraybar.com; map p.70. Located between blocks 5 and 6 of Av El Ejercito, this hotel has ten spacious rooms, all with comfortable beds, private bathroom, 24hr hot water and cable TV. Continental breakfast is included, and there's a 10–20 percent daily discount if you stay for a few nights. S/180

Casa del Mochilero Jr Cesareo Chacaltaña 130A, 2nd floor ☎01 444 9089, ⓔpilaryv@hotmail.com; map p.70. Within walking distance of central Miraflores, this place has bunk-bed rooms. Though none too big, rooms do come with hot water and cable TV, and there are kitchen facilities too. The very friendly and helpful staff will arrange airport pick-up. Dorms S/17, doubles S/50

Colonial Inn Av Comandante Espinar 310 ☎01 203 2840 or ☎01 241 7471; map p.70. Great service and exceptionally clean, if slightly away from the fray of Miraflores. Light sleepers should ask for a room away from the (very busy) road. The English spoken by the staff is hit and miss. S/95

Embajadores Hotel Juan Fanning 320 ☎01 242 9127, ⓦembajadoreshotel.com; map p.70. Part of the Best Western chain, this is located in a quiet area of Miraflores, just a few blocks from Larco Mar and the seafront. Small but pleasant, the hotel has comfortable rooms and access to a mini-gym, small rooftop pool and restaurant. S/125

Explorer's House Av Alfredo Leon 158 ☎01 241 5002, ⓔevaaragon_9@hotmail.com; map p.70. A short walk from the action of Parque Kennedy and close to the sea, this ramshackle hostel has a homely feel, thanks to the cheerful owner who speaks good English. Basic breakfast, guest kitchen, internet, wi-fi and hot water are all included. Some doubles have private bathroom and cost a little more. Book ahead as it is small and popular. Dorms S/21, doubles S/60

Faraoña Grande Hotel C Manuel Bonilla 185 ☎01 446 9414, ⓦfaraonagrandhotel.com; map p.70. A plush, secure, quite modern hotel in a central part of this busy suburb; there's a rooftop pool and a pretty good restaurant with Peruvian, international and vegetarian dishes. Live piano music performed daily in the bar 7–10pm. S/397

Friends House Jr Manco Capac 368 ☎01 446 6248, ⓔfriendshouse_peru@yahoo.com.mx; map p.70. Located on the second level of this building, this is a small but well-maintained and popular hostel in a superb Miraflores location; comfortable and clean rooms, hot water, cable TV and open kitchen. You can't tell that it's a hostel from outside; look for the green-coloured house. Dorms S/25, doubles S/54

HI Hostel Lima Casimiro Ulloa 328 ☎01 446 5488, ⓦlimahostell.com.pe; map p.70. A great deal, this hostel is a base for International Youth Hostels in Peru. It's located just over the Paseo de la República highway from Miraflores in the relatively peaceful suburb of San Antonio, in a big, fairly modern and stylish house with a pool. There's also a restaurant and bar with views to the garden, and they'll pick up from the airport. Dorms S/46, doubles S/157

★**Hospedaje Flying Dog** Av Diez Canseco 117 ☎01 445 0940, ⍟flyingdogperu.com; map p.70. A clean and homely, B&B-style backpackers' hostel right in the middle of Miraflores. Most rooms are shared but the maximum size is four beds; you also have the option of a double with private bathroom. There's an open kitchen facility and cable TV lounge, as well as internet access. Price includes breakfast. It has an annexe over the road at Lima 457 (☎01 444 5753). Dorms S/33, doubles S/99

Hostal Antigua Miraflores Av Grau 350 ☎01 241 6116, ⍟peru-hotels-inns.com; map p.70. Within walking distance of downtown Miraflores, the *Antigua* is an expanding mock mansion with professional and helpful service, and spacious, well-appointed and very quiet rooms. There's also a small restaurant with reasonable food. Good breakfast included. S/106

Hostal Buena Vista Av Grimaldo del Solar 202 ☎01 447 3178, ⍟hostalbuenavista.com; map p.70. Located in a distinctive house in downtown Miraflores, the *Buena Vista* offers large rooms with private bathroom, and there's also outside space in the form of gardens and rooftop patios. Staff are friendly and helpful, and a buffet breakfast is included in the price. S/60

Hostal Martinika Av Arequipa 3701 ☎01 422 3094, ⍟martinika@terra.com.pe; map p.70. Very reasonably priced and centrally located within the greater city area – it's close to the boundary of Miraflores and San Isidro – if a little noisy in the mornings. It's also comfortable and friendly, offering fairly large rooms with private bathroom. Airport pick-up available. S/150

★**Hostal Pariwana** Av Larco 189 ☎01 242 4350, ⍟pariwana-hostel.com; map p.70. With a wide, grand stairway entrance including spectacular stained-glass window, this converted mansion is a veritable backpackers' haven and a great meeting place for young travellers. It's also in a lovely location, overlooking the main park in Miraflores. There are dorms (including a women-only option) as well as private rooms, mainly with shared bathroom, as well as games, free internet, kitchen access, rooftop terrace, tours and a good bar and café, which serves very tasty late breakfasts. Dorms S/32, doubles S/125

★**Hostal El Patio** Av Diez Canseco 341 ☎01 444 2107, ⍟hostalelpatio.net; map p.70. A very agreeable, family-friendly and secure little place right in the heart of Miraflores, with comfy beds and private – albeit small – bathrooms. More expensive mini-suites and full suites are also available, and it's often fully booked, so reserve in advance. S/156

Marieta Bed & Breakfast Inn Malecón Cisneros 840 ☎01 446 9028, ✉gato@amauta.rcp.net.pe; map p.70. A small but spotless B&B in a lovely house in one of Lima's more exclusive locations overlooking the ocean, with private bathrooms and a terrace. The family that runs the B&B also operates a number of tours in and around Lima and will pick guests up from the airport for a reasonable fee. Advance bookings only. S/115

Miraflores Colón Inn Colón 600 ☎01 610 0900, ⍟mirafflorescolonhotel.com; map p.70. Located near the corner of Juan Fanning. Rooms are spacious, clean and equipped with bathtubs, while rooms equipped with jacuzzi and hydro-massage baths are also available. Breakfast included. S/145

Pensión José Luís Francisco de Paula de Ugarriza 727 ☎01 444 1015; map p.70. Comfortable, modern house, in a good location, within walking distance of central Miraflores and the ocean, and popular with English-speaking travellers. Most rooms have city views, and all come with private bathroom, basic breakfast and wi-fi. S/150

Radisson Av 28 de Julio 151 ☎01 625 1241, ⍟radisson .com/miraflores.pe; map p.70. Entering the *Radisson* resembles boarding a spaceship: lobby and bars alike have a sci-fi ambience. The rooms are as modern and luxurious as you'd expect from this famous chain. Cheaper rates than here can be found online. S/744

Sonesta Posada del Inca – Miraflores C Alcanfores 329 ☎01 241 7688, ✉reservas@sonestaperu.com; map p.70. This very plush, excellently run and modern downtown hotel offers cable TV, a/c and a decent 24hr restaurant. Airport pick-up is available. S/120

Tinkus Hostel Av La Paz 608 ☎01 242 0131, ⍟hoteltinkus.com; map p.70. Well located just a few blocks from Av Larco in central Miraflores, *Tinkus* is a good-value option. The lobby is larger and more salubrious-looking than the rooms, though the larger ones aren't too bad. Service is friendly, although the breakfast of instant coffee, bread and jam is rather insubstantial. S/140

El Zaguan Lodging Av Diez Canseco 736 ☎01 446 9356, ⍟elzaguanlodging.com; map p.70. Located in a relatively tranquil street near the Parque Tradiciones, yet within a stone's throw of the heart of the district, this B&B offers eminently accommodating rooms set around leafy courtyards, with private bathrooms and generous breakfasts. S/120

BARRANCO

Hospedaje Domeyer Jr Domeyer 296 ☎01 247 1413, ⍟domeyerhostel.net; map p.74. Close to the Plaza Municipal and nightlife of Barranco, this is a beautiful old mansion from the outside with a bohemian, colourful interior. Shared and private rooms available, and most are small but comfortable, with hot water and cable TV; price includes breakfast. Dorms S/50, doubles S/150

1

Hotel B Av San Martín 301 ☎01 206 0800, ⓦhotelb
.pe; map p.74. A boutique hotel with a strong personality,
Hotel B showcases both traditional and modern art by mostly
Peruvian artists, curated by one of the owners (who has a
gallery next door). Every room and suite in this converted
Belle Époque mansion is different, but all are spacious, white
and light with high ceilings, some with freestanding bathtubs.
The breakfast buffet and afternoon teas in the "library" are
exceptional in variety and quality; and many Limeños drop by
just for a drink in the chic-casual restaurant-bar. **S̲/360**

The Point Hostel Malecón Junín 300 ☎01 2477997,
ⓦthepointhostels.com; map p.74. A B&B hostel with
twelve rooms created by two *mochilleros* (backpackers) in a
colonial house with relaxing gardens; the shared kitchen
and billiard room are further bonuses. There's often music
playing, sometimes live jams among travellers, sometimes
rock and reggae CDs, but rarely so loud it interferes with
others' sleep. The managers are helpful and offer sensible
travel information. Dorms **S̲/27**, doubles **S̲/70**

Safe in Lima Alfredo Silva 150 ☎01 252 7330,
ⓦsafeinlima.com; map p.74. This Belgian-run
guesthouse offers a quiet bolt-hole in Barranco, just off
block 5 of Pedro de Osma, not far from the action. Pleasant
rooms and good service; there's airport pick-up (S/51) and
tours within the city and the country as a whole on offer. A
simple but ample breakfast is included in the price. **S̲/55**

SAN ISIDRO

Casa Bella Las Flores 459 ☎01 421 7354,
ⓦcasabellaperu.net; map pp.58–59. A modern hotel
located one block from the Country Club and Golf Club in
San Isidro (behind *Los Delfines Hotel*), offering exceptionally
pristine rooms with state-of-the-art finishing in a
redesigned mansion from the early 1930s. Staff can help

with tours and tickets. **S̲/190**

Hotel Libertador Los Eucaliptos 550 ☎01 518 6300,
ⓦlibertador.com.pe; map pp.58–59. A top-class hotel
with a convenient location in this well-to-do Lima suburb.
The service and room standards are excellent. The website
offers much better prices than you'll get in person. **S̲/82**

Malka Youth Hostal Los Lirios 165 ☎01 442 0162,
ⓦyouthhostelperu.com; map pp.58–59. Well located,
Malka is cheerful and intimate as well as being good value for
this part of the city. There are several airy rooms, one with
views over the garden, and a few with private bathrooms
that cost a bit more. Dorms **S̲/35**, doubles **S̲/112**

Suites del Bosque Av Paz Soldan 165 ☎01 616 2121,
ⓦsuitesdelbosque.com; map pp.58–59. Though
essentially a business hotel with conference centre, the
suites themselves are smartly furnished, complete with
dining/living room, cable TV, internet access, heating and
a/c. There's also a restaurant and bar, a jacuzzi and great
buffet breakfasts. **S̲/780**

Swissotel Lima Vía Central 150, Centro Empresarial
Real ☎01 421 4400, ⓦswissotel.com; map pp.58–59.
Conveniently located near banks, bus depots and some
department stores and supermarkets, this is luxurious
accommodation with all the modern conveniences you'd
expect, aimed largely at the business traveller. **S̲/650**

SAN MIGUEL

Hostal Mami Panchita Av Federico Gallesi 198
☎01 263 7203, ⓦmamipanchita.com; map pp.58–59.
Located in the suburb of San Miguel, this is a very
approachable hostel in lovely gardens with a well-
appointed, shared dining room, TV lounge and bar. Both
English and Dutch are spoken, and they also offer airport
pick-up (just 20min away). Price includes breakfast. **S̲/135**

EATING

Lima boasts some of the best **restaurants** in the country, serving cuisines from all over the world. What makes traditional
Peruvian dishes (see box opposite) so special is a combination of diverse cultural ingredients (Andean, Spanish, Italian,
African and Chinese in particular) alongside varied indigenous edible plants. Regardless of class or status, virtually all
Limeños eat out regularly – and a meal out usually ends up as an evening's entertainment in itself. Many of the more
upmarket places fill up very quickly, so it's advisable to **reserve in advance**. In recent years a large number of **cafés** have
sprung up around Miraflores and Barranco, many offering free wi-fi and providing snacks as well as coffee. Lima Centro is
less well served by cafés, though there are a few appealing options.

CAFÉS

LIMA CENTRO

Bar/Restaurant Machu Picchu Jr Ancash 318; map
p.62. A busy place opposite San Francisco church, serving
inexpensive snacks such as omelettes and sandwiches or
even *cuy picante* (spicy guinea pig); it offers cheap, set-
menu lunches and it's a good spot for meeting up with
other travellers. Daily 9am–6pm.

★**El Cordano** Jr Ancash 202 ☎01 427 0181; map p.62.
Across the street from the Palacio de Gobierno, this is one of

the city's last surviving traditional bar/restaurants with
mirrored walls, racks of bottles and old-style waiters, who
are curt but efficient, even charming in an old-fashioned
way. Worth visiting if only to soak up the atmosphere,
sample the excellent ham sandwiches and see first-hand
the exquisite late nineteenth- and early twentieth-century
decor. Mon–Sat 8am–9pm.

El Paraiso de la Salud Restaurant Vegetariano Jr
Cámana 344 ☎01 428 4591; map p.62. Offering a
delivery service, this vegetarian option does good

1

LIMA SPECIALITIES

Widely acclaimed as one of the world's great culinary destinations, Lima is a paradise for food enthusiasts. As well as a wide array of delicious meat-, rice- and vegetable-based **criolla dishes**, you'll come across the highly creative **novo andino cuisine**, often pairing alpaca steaks with berries or cheese sauces from lush Andean farms, and best appreciated in Lima's finest restaurants. Below are a few specialities that your taste buds will thank you for trying.

Ceviche Seafood is particularly good in Lima, with ceviche – raw fish or seafood marinated in lime juice and served in dozens of possible formulas with onions, chillis, sweetcorn and sweet potatoes – a must-try.

Chorros a la Chalaca These spicy mussels are best sampled near the port area of Callao.

Cabrito a la Norteña This traditional goat feast has made its way to Lima from the northern coast of Peru; as well as tender goat meat, the dish incorporates a sauce made with *chicha de jorra* (rustic maize beer), yellow chillis, *zapallo* squash, onions and garlic, plus *yuca* and lots of fresh coriander, served with rice.

Arroz con Pato a la Chiclayana From northern Peru, this is a dish of duck and rice prepared as in the city of Chiclayo, with oranges, spices, beer, brandy, peas and peppers. It's such a popular dish you'll probably come across it in all regions of the country.

Asado A good cut of beef roasted in a red sauce, usually served with *pure de papas* (smooth, garlic-flavoured mashed potatoes).

Chicken broaster The staple at the thousands of broaster restaurants found in every corner of Peru: essentially, spit- or oven-roasted chicken with chips, and often a very meagre salad on the side.

Cuy This is the Inca word for guinea pig, one of the most common foods for Andean country folk, but also something of a delicacy which can be found everywhere from backstreet cafés to the best restaurants in Lima, Cusco and Arequipa. There are various ways to prepare *cuy* for the plate, but *cuy chactado* (deep-fried) is one of the most common.

Pisco Sour Pisco is Peru's clear, grape-based brandy, which forms the heart of the national drink – pisco sour. The pisco, crushed ice, fresh lime juice, plus a sweetener and egg white, are whisked together with a bitter added at the end. It's refreshing and sometimes surprisingly potent.

---

breakfasts, as well as yogurt, juice, salads, wholemeal breads and smoothies. It's a large space but gets busy at lunch, when it serves delicious plates such as steamed broccoli and lentil tortillas. There are three other vegetarian restaurants on the same street. Daily 8am–10pm.

Queirolo Café Bar Restaurant Jirones Cámana 900 and Quilca; map p.62. This is a classic meeting place for poets, writers and painters, and is worth a visit just for the splendour of its old Lima Cason-style architecture and bohemian atmosphere. It serves comida criolla, sandwiches, beer and pisco; great for inexpensive but good-quality set lunches. Mon–Sat 9am–2am.

MIRAFLORES

Arabica Espreso Bar General Recavarren 269 ☎ 01 715 2152; map p.70. A narrow space with small patio and coffee-roasting equipment out back, this place serves arguably the best coffee in Lima. There are great cakes, too, as well as free wi-fi. Mon–Fri 8am–9pm, Sat 10am–10pm, Sun 11am–9pm.

Café Café Pasaje Martir Olaya 250 ☎ 01 4451165; map p.70. Located just off Diagonal in downtown Miraflores, this is a hip, gay-friendly coffee shop that plays good rock music and serves a variety of sandwiches, salads, paellas,

pastas and Peruvian dishes, as well as a selection of cocktails. Daily 10am–midnight.

Café Haiti Diagonal 160 ☎ 01 4463816; map p.70. The most popular meeting place for upper-middle-class Limeños, based near the Cinema El Pacífico in the heart of Miraflores. It offers excellent snacks, such as stuffed avocado or *ají de gallina*, and a decent range of soft and alcoholic drinks, although it's not cheap. Daily 8am–2am.

Café Verde Av Santa Cruz 1305 ☎ 01 6527682; map p.70. One of the best places for coffee in Lima is this small café, which roasts on site. Mon–Sat 8am–7pm.

La Emolientería José Galvez and Diagonal ☎ 4445579; map p.70. Very hip ambience, with plenty of glass, a science-lab inspired bar, wooden interior balcony and two floors of colour and artwork. The staff and drinkers are young and cool; there's ceviche and bar food but their speciality is *emolientes*, Peruvian "medicinal" cocktails. Mon–Thurs & Sun 7.30am–1am, Fri & Sat 11am–3am.

La Tiendacita Blanca Av Larco 111 ☎ 01 445 1412; map p.70. Located right on the busiest junction in Miraflores, this is a popular meeting place, with a superb range of Peruvian and Swiss foods, plus cakes and pastries, though they are pricey. Live piano music Mon–Fri 7–8pm. Daily 7am–7pm.

1

BEST OF LIMA'S RESTAURANTS

Fine dining *Astrid y Gastón* is one of the world's best p.88
Ceviche Classics at *Caplina* or upmarket at *La Mar* p.88 & p.89
Dinner with a view *La Rosa Nautica* has ocean views, and *Restaurant Huaca Pucllana* faces a *huaca* p.89
Local ambience *El Cordano* overflows with old-world charm p.86
Something different *L'Eau Vive* has French and Peruvian dishes cooked by nuns p.88

BARRANCO

Café Bisetti Av Pedro de Osma 116 ☎ 01 713 9565; map p.74. On the Plaza Municipal, this place serves really excellent coffees and very good snacks. The dark chocolate slice is incredible. It's a large space with plenty of tables and a pleasant garden, and it also roasts coffee on the premises. Occasional live music on Saturdays. Daily 8am–10pm.

Las Mesitas Av Grau 341 ☎ 01 477 4199; map p.74. A tasteful café serving delicious snacks, meals and scrumptious sweets including excellent *humitas*, tamales, juices and sandwiches. Daily noon–2am.

RESTAURANTS

LIMA CENTRO

Chifa Capon Jr Ucayali 774 ☎ 01 427 2969; map p.62. An excellent and traditional Limeño-Chinese fusion restaurant, the best in this block of Chinatown. It offers a range of authentic, moderately priced *chifa* dishes. Daily noon–2/3am.

De Cesar Jr Ancash 300 ☎ 01 428 8740; map p.62. Great little café/restaurant and bar right in the heart of old Lima, with a buzzing atmosphere. The spacious interior is sometimes a bit dark but the food is fine and cheap, the service very friendly and the range of breakfasts and juices endless. Daily 7.30am–10pm.

Don Lucho's Restaurant Jr Carabaya 346; map p.62. Just off the Plaza Mayor, this is a busy lunchtime spot with a fan-cooled interior, popular with local office workers and offering fast service and decent set-menu meals, with a ceviche option, for less than S/10. Daily 7.30am–6pm.

El Estadio Restaurant Bar Av Nicolás de Piérola 926, Plaza San Martín ☎ 01 4288866, ⓦ estadio.com.pe; map p.62. A restaurant with a strong football theme with walls covered in sports paraphernalia: fascinating even for those only remotely interested in the sport. You can even take your picture next to a life-size bust of Pele. Both the food and bar are excellent and sometimes there are club nights in the basement. There's a Peruvian food festival every Friday and Saturday. Mon–Wed 12.15–11pm, Thurs 12.15pm–midnight, Fri & Sat 12.15pm–3am, Sun 12.15–6pm.

L'Eau Vive Jr Ucayali 370 ☎ 01 427 5612; map p.62. Opposite the Palacio Torre Tagle, this interesting restaurant serves superb French and Peruvian dishes cooked by nuns. It offers a reasonable set menu at lunch and dinner, and closes after a chorus of *Ave Maria* most evenings. Mon–Sat 12.30–3pm & 7.30–9.30pm.

MIRAFLORES

★**Astrid y Gastón** Cantuarias 175 ☎ 01 2425387, ⓦ astridygaston.com; map p.70. A trendy, colonial-style signature restaurant run by the world-renowned Peruvian chef Gastón Acurio. Possibly the best in Lima, and voted one of the world's top fifty restaurants, it is stylish and expensive (expect to spend from around S/70), with a menu blending Peruvian criolla and Mediterranean-style cooking. Acurio has opened restaurants in six other Latin American countries, plus Spain, flying the flag for Peruvian cuisine. Daily 12.30–11.30pm.

Bio Leben C Alcanfores 416; map p.70. A great vegetarian restaurant, and a cheerful place to shelter from the bustle of the Miraflores streets. Daily 8am–10pm.

El Bodegon Tarapaca 197–199 ☎ 01 445 6222; map p.70. This place serves up Mediterranean, vegetarian and *novo andino* cuisine in pleasant surroundings, with creative alpaca dishes, among others, with French or European influence, and a good selection of wines and piscos. Mon–Sat 11am–11pm.

Las Brujas de Cachiche Av Bolognesi 460 ☎ 01 477 1883; map p.70. Very trendy and expensive, this top-class restaurant and bar serves mainstream Peruvian dishes as well as a range of pre-Columbian and *novo andino* meals, such as seafood ceviche and maize-based dishes made using only ingredients available more than a thousand years ago. Daily noon–11pm.

★**Caplina** Mendiburu 793 ☎ 01 475 3404; map pp.58–59. A good cevichería on the outskirts of Miraflores, serving tasty, classic ceviche as well as a range of other seafood dishes, around an attractive, almost Japanese, pebble pond. They also prepare seafood *a la Chalaca* (traditional Callao-style, often spicy hot and one of the best) and *a la Chiclayana*, as well as meat and Italian pasta dishes. Daily 9am–5pm.

Club Suizo Genaro Iglesias 550, La Aurora, Miraflores ☎ 01 445 9230; map p.70. Located level with block 17 of Avenida Benavides, this fine place offers exquisite Swiss cuisine, including extravagant fondues combining four cheeses, in a very pleasant environment. Tues–Sat 11am–11pm, Sun 11am–4pm.

D'nnos Pizza Comandante Espinar 408 ☎ 01 219 0909; map p.70. This flashy, brightly lit restaurant offers some of the best pizza in Lima, as well as relatively fast service and delivery. Daily noon–midnight.

La Hamaca Av Arequipa 4698 ☎01 242 7978; map p.70. This Lima stalwart serves quality criollo meals. Its *ají de gallina* (a chillied chicken dish with ancient roots) is spectacular, and the colonial museum-mansion it's based in is almost as good. Daily 6–10.30pm.

El Kapallaq Av El Reducto 1505 ☎01 444 4149; map p.70. Recently opened in a new, 1950s-style renovated house on the border between Miraflores and Barranco, this excellent restaurant focuses on a fusion of north-coast and Lima seafood cuisine. Service and food are both excellent. Advance booking necessary. Mon–Sat 11am–5pm.

La Lucha Sanguchería Diagonal and Pasaje Martir Olaya ☎01 241 5953; map p.70. The best place to discover what makes a Peruvian *sanguch* (S/10) so much more than a couple of neat triangles. The crispy, panini-like buns come with a variety of meaty fillings and creamy sauces – the smoked, pulled chicken is delicious with a spicy *ají* sauce and rustic wedges. Expect to queue for a seat. Mon–Thurs & Sun 8am–1am, Fri & Sat 8am–3am.

Madre Natura Jr Chiclayo 815; map p.70. Located by block 4 of Av Comandante Espinar, this cafetería serves tasty but healthy snacks and meals in a courtyard. It's in the Madre Natura complex behind an organic and health products store, an eco gifts centre and a wholemeal bakery. Mon–Sat 8am–9pm, Sun 9am–2pm.

Mama Lola Av Diez Canseco 119 ☎01 241 6335; map p.70. Right in the heart of Miraflores, near the bottom end of the park, this welcoming trattoria and pizzeria buzzes at night with locals and tour groups. *Mama Lola* serves great Italian dishes such as onion soup and spinach ravioli with ricotta, as well as Peruvian dishes like *tacu tacu*, black beans and seafood. Daily 11.30am–11pm.

La Mar Av La Mar 770 ☎01 421 3365, ✆lamarcebicheria .com; map p.70. Easily Lima's trendiest and liveliest cevichería, *La Mar* is stylish, swanky and very, very busy. Noisy but with great salsa music and strong pisco sours, the restaurant serves a wide range of ceviche in all sorts of regional styles, such as *tiraditos* (thin slivers of fish in sweet sauces) in innovative combinations such as the *tiradito poderoso* with sea urchin and black scallops in a lemon and olive oil vinaigrette. Get there before 12.30pm to avoid the queues. Tues–Sun noon–7pm.

Patagonia Restaurant Arte y Diseno C Bolívar 164 ☎01 446 8705; map p.70. With walls full of photos and paintings, plus a space for theatre and music performances, this place offers a slightly different dining experience. Specialities include Italian–Argentine cuisine, and the *pasta fresca* is excellent. Good wines available. Mon–Sat 6pm–2am.

Restaurant Huaca Pucllana General Borgoño, block 8 ☎01 445 4042; map p.70. Tasty, international cuisine with a French flavour and quality Peruvian dishes, including *novo andino* and excellent traditional *cuy*, *cabrito* (goat) and various fish offerings. The service is outstanding, and the restaurant has an elegant terrace that looks out onto the ancient monument of the Huaca Pucllana (see p.69). Mon–Sat 12.30pm–midnight, Sun 12.30–4pm.

Restaurant Tai-i Vegetariano Av Petit Thouars 5232 ☎01 242 6654; map p.70. Handily located opposite the artesanía markets, this veggie standby offers simple, inexpensive and satisfying food in the shape of set-lunch menu meals, plus a range of great Asian dishes. Daily 8am–8pm.

La Rosa Nautica Espigon 4, Costa Verde ☎01 447 5450; map p.70. With excellent ocean views thanks to its pier location, this is one of Lima's more expensive seafood restaurants. The menu offers a wide range of Latin American and European dishes. Jazz performances every Thursday evening. Daily 12.30pm–12.30am.

Scena Restaurant Bar C San Francisco de Paula Camino 280 ☎01 241 8181; map p.70. Ultra modern in design, this restaurant's dishes are a fusion of flavours based on the chef's own interpretation of *cocina Peruana*, with good meat and fish. Mon–Fri 12.30–4pm, Sat 7.30pm–12.30am.

El Señorio de Sulco Malecón Cisneros 1470 ☎01 441 0183; map p.70. Specializing in Peruvian cuisine, including *novo andino*, this restaurant uses the finest ingredients to prepare mainly traditional dishes, many cooked in earthen pots. This type of meal can be found on street stalls all over Peru, but here the chef is top quality – and this is reflected in the prices. Mon–Sat noon–midnight.

BARRANCO

★**Café Cultural Expreso Virgen de Guadalupe** Av Prol San Martín 15A ☎01 252 8907; map p.74. A unique, atmospheric restaurant and bar situated right beside the Puente de los Suspiros, serving typical international and Peruvian fare inside an ornate nineteenth-century railway carriage. Live music at weekends. Daily 5pm–midnight.

Restaurante Asia Av Grau 323 ☎01 249 4582; map p.74. A large restaurant with a traditional wood-and-paper-screen interior that is so tasteful that you'd be surprised to know that the prices are budget. The usual Chinese set menus are fresh and nicely presented. Daily 11.30am–11.30pm.

Sashimito Av Grau 614 ☎01 248 8212; map p.74. A small sushi bar that serves fresh maki rolls with good seafood and vegetarian options to eat in or to go. Mon–Sat 1–11pm, Sun 1–9pm.

SAN ISIDRO

La Carreta Av Rivera Navarrete 740 ☎01 442 2690; map pp.58–59. One of Lima's best *churrascarías* (Brazilian-style steakhouses), close to San Isidro's Centro Comercial. Designed to resemble an old hacienda, this place serves

1

SELF-CATERING

Lima offers plenty of options for DIY lunches. **Surquillo market** (daily 6.30am–5.30pm), a couple of blocks from Miraflores over the Av Angamos road bridge, on the eastern side of the Paseo de la República freeway, is a colourful place fully stocked with a wonderful variety of breads, fruits, cheeses and meats. Pickpockets are at work here, though, so keep your wallet and passport close.

Of Lima's **supermarkets**, Metro has the best range at reasonable prices. You'll find this chain across the city, notably at the San Isidro Comercial Centre, the Ovalo Gutierrez in Miraflores and next to Ripley's on Calle Schell in the centre of Miraflores. All branches accept and change US dollars. **Bakeries and delicatessens** can be found in most urban districts – try Avenida Larco in Miraflores, within a few blocks of Larco Mar. *Madre Natura*, Jr Chiclayo 815, off Avenida Comandante Espinar, in Miraflores, stocks a wide range of **health foods** and ecological products, as well as having its own café (p.89) and wholemeal bakery.

dishes that are mainly Peruvian or international, and there's a spectacular bar with quality wines. Daily noon–midnight.

Centro Turístico Perco's Restaurant C Elias Aguirre 166 ☎01 445 6697; map pp.58–59. Don't be put off by the name: this is Lima's one and only restaurant specializing in the cuisine of the jungle region. They offer venison, wild pig, *paiche* fish and many other tasty and reasonably priced dishes. Daily 8am–11pm.

Punto Azul Avenidas Javier Prado and Petit Thouars ☎01 221 3747; map pp.58–59. One of a chain of excellent and unpretentious cevicherías, this one is unusual in that you eat outside at tables overlooking one of Lima's busiest junctions. Mon–Sat 11.30am–6pm.

LA VICTORIA

Cevichería Mi Barunto Jr Sebastián Barranca 935 ☎01 427 2066; map pp.58–59. Close to the Alianza football stadium, this popular cevichería is full of club regalia and has a great atmosphere. It's a large space but often full. Daily 11am–6pm.

El Italiano Trattoria Pizzeria C Enrique León García 376 ☎01 472 1281; map pp.58–59. A locals' place, not at all touristy. Unlike most pizzerias or Italian restaurants in Peru, all food is freshly prepared on the premises. Tues–Sun 1–4pm & 6–11pm.

SURQUILLO

Cevichería El Rey Marino Clara Barton Lte. 10, La

Calera, Surquillo ☎01 448 8667; map pp.58–59. Located close to block 43 of Av Aviación, this is a brilliant and unpretentious cevichería with very friendly service and good Peruvian music. Best at lunch. Daily 11am–6pm.

SURCO AND MONTERRICO

Guru Av Benavides 3796, Monterrico ☎01 273 5658; map pp.58–59. If you like spice, this is the place. A small but excellent curry and kebab house, located in the district of Surco, but easily accessible by taxi from Miraflores. The owner is an English-speaking African-Asian. Daily noon–10pm.

Siam Thai Cuisine Av Caminos del Inca 467, Surco ☎01 372 0680; map pp.58–59. Superb Thai food in a delightful, tranquil environment with small indoor gardens and very reasonable service and prices. Best to take a taxi (S/12 from Miraflores). Daily 11.30am–10.30pm.

Sushi Ito Av El Polo 740, Monterrico ☎01 435 5817; map pp.58–59. Located in the Centro Comercial El Polo, this is an excellent, posh sushi restaurant serving *sashimi* and *maki-temaki*, among other dishes. Mon–Sat noon–4pm & 7pm–midnight.

CALLAO

Manolo Malecón Pardo, block 1, La Punta ☎01 453 1380; map pp.58–59. A fine seafood restaurant and bar on the seafront (best sampled when sunny rather than windy) that's an oasis in this run-down area. The food is very fresh; try the *chicharones de pulpo* (battered and fried octopus nuggets) or the *ceviche de pescado*. Daily 11am–4pm.

DRINKING AND NIGHTLIFE

Lima's nightlife is more urban, modern and less traditional than in cities such as Cusco and Arequipa; **Barranco** is the trendiest and liveliest place to hang out. The city has an exciting **club** scene, with the majority of its popular **bars** and discos located out in the suburbs of San Isidro and Miraflores. In the summer months (Jan–March) the party sometimes carries on down the coast to the resort of **Asia**, 110km south (see p.100), where there are some surprisingly sophisticated nightclubs.

As far as the **live music scene** goes, the great variety of traditional and hybrid sounds is one of the best reasons for visiting the capital, with folk group *peñas*, Latin jazz, rock, reggae and reggaeton all popular. All forms of **Peruvian music** can be found here, some – like **salsa** and **Afro-Peruvian** (see p.503) – better than anywhere else in the country. Even Andean folk music can be close to its best here (though Puno, Cusco and Arequipa are all more probable contenders).

Entrance charges and policies Most clubs charge an entrance fee of around S/20–50, which often includes a drink and/or a meal. Many clubs have a members-only policy, though if you can provide proof of tourist status, such as a passport, you usually have no problem getting in.

Listings The daily *El Comercio* provides the best information about music events, and its Friday edition carries a comprehensive nightlife supplement – easy to understand even if your Spanish is limited. Things are at their liveliest on Friday and Saturday nights.

BARS

Ayahuasca Av Prol San Martín 130, Barranco ☏ 01 445 9680; map p.74. A fantastic venue, this place is based in a lovingly restored mansion with several interesting bar areas; it's not cheap but the drinks are inventive and there are great snacks too. Very busy after 10pm at weekends. Mon–Sat 8pm–2am.

The Brenchley Arms Atahualpa 174, Miraflores ☏ 01 445 9680; map p.70. An attempt to replicate an English pub, *The Brenchley Arms* has a pleasant atmosphere and three bars stocked with good beer. Rock music is occasionally performed live. Thurs–Sun 6.30pm–late.

El Dragon Av Nicolás de Piérola 168, Barranco ☏ 01 715 5043; ⓦ eldragon.com.pe; map p.74. A dark, often packed-out and fun cultural bar, *El Dragon* almost always has live music, frequently good Latin rock and jazz. Tues–Sat 8pm–2am.

Habana Café Bar Av Manuel Bonilla 107, Miraflores ☏ 01 446 3511; map p.70. Live music Fri and Sat (10pm–1am), particularly Cuban, but also great jazz and nostalgic rock. Serves an excellent range of rum and cocktails. Tues–Sun 7pm–late.

Juanito's Bodega Bar Av Grau 274, Barranco; map p.74. Probably the most traditional of the neighbourhood's bars; facing onto the Parque Municipal, it's small and basic and offers an excellent taste of Peru as it used to be. The music policy is strictly criolla and traditional Peruvian folk, and the front bar is open until very late. Closed during World Cup finals, when the owners travel to watch the games. Mon–Sat 4pm–2am.

Lion's Head Av Grau 268, Barranco; map p.74. Located on the second floor of the building is this British-style pub with dartboard, pool table, newspapers, sports TV and, of course, English beers. Daily 5pm–late.

Mochileros Bar Av Pedro de Osma 135, Barranco ☏ 01 247 1225; map p.74. Located in a fine old Barranco mansion, now converted into an *albergue* and live music bar. It has outside tables and good cocktails (the house speciality is El Beso del Diablo, consisting of pisco, tequila and grenadila). Tues–Sat 8am–11pm.

The Old Pub C San Ramón 295, Miraflores ☏ 01 242 8155; map p.70. The most authentic of the English-style pubs in Lima – it's run by an Englishman – and easy to find, just a block or two from the park in Miraflores, at the far end of Little Italy (San Ramón). There's good music and a dartboard, and sandwiches, salads, chips and roast-beef meals are available. Daily noon–1am.

La Posada del Mirador On the clifftop point behind the Puente de Suspiros and church, Barranco; map p.74. A popular evening bar with great views and a lively atmosphere. Daily 10am–10pm.

Rincon Cervecero Jr de la Unión 1045A, Lima Centro ☏ 01 428 8866; map p.62. An original Lima bar but in Germanic style, with satisfyingly large pitchers of draught beer and shots, and a buzzing atmosphere. The kitchen serves original recipes, and there's a beer festival in Oct. Mon–Thurs 10am–midnight, Fri & Sat 10am–3am.

CLUBS

Aura Larco Mar, Miraflores ☏ 01 242 5516, ⓦ aura .com.pe; map p.70. Well respected for its weekend shows and electronica prowess; now and then international DJs make an appearance. Special events are generally Thurs–Sat. Tues–Sat 10pm–3am.

Deja-Vu Av Grau 294, Barranco ☏ 01 247 6989; map p.74. A heaving dance club from Mon through to Sat night. Music mainly ranges from trance to techno, but also live music, mainly rock, sessions at weekends. Best Thurs–Sat. Mon–Sat 10pm–3am.

Gotica Larco Mar, Miraflores ☏ 01 628 3033, ⓦ gotica .com.pe; map p.70. A fairly exclusive but popular disco with excellent music and an even better sound system:

LIMA'S DANCE SCENE

Lima's **peñas** – some of which only open at weekends and nearly all located in Barranco – are the surest bet for listening to authentic **Andean folk**, although some of them also specialize in **Peruvian criolla**, which brings together a unique and very vigorous blend of Afro-Peruvian, Spanish and, to a lesser extent, Andean music. These days it's not uncommon for some of Lima's best *peñas* to feature a fusion of criolla and Latin jazz. Generally speaking, *peñas* don't get going until after 10pm and usually the bands play through to 3 or 4am, if not until first light.

Lima is also an excellent place to experience the Latin American **salsa** scene, and there are *salsódromos* scattered around many of the suburbs. They play a mix of tropical music, salsa, merengue and technocumbia. Most are open Friday and Saturday 10pm–3am.

expect anything from hip-hop and punk to Latin rock, salsa and reggaeton, as well as occasional live bands at weekends. Tues–Sun 9pm–2am.

Karamba Jr Manuel Asencio Segura, Blvd Los Olivos, Los Olivos, north Lima ☏ 01 208 0920, ⊕ boulevard losolivos.com; map pp.58–59. This is a hectic *salsódromo* based north of Lima Centro in the district of Los Olivos. Split into two levels with its walls painted in coconuts, the club has a hot, tropical feel and plays heavy electronica as well as salsa. Nearby, also on the Boulevard, is another popular club, *Kokos*. Thurs–Sun 9pm–3am.

El New Kitsch Av Bolognesi 743, Barranco ☏ 01 445 3856; map p.74. A funky and gay-friendly disco-bar with weird decor, known for playing lots of 1970s and 1980s tunes; it gets hotter later on. Thurs–Sun 10pm–2am.

PEÑAS AND SALSÓDROMOS

★**Las Brisas del Titicaca** Jr Wakulski 168, Lima Centro ☏ 01 332 1901, ⊕ brisasdeltiticaca.com; map p.62. One of the busiest and most popular venues for tourists in the know and locals alike; excellent bands and yet this is one of the cheapest of the city's *peñas*. Thurs–Sat 8.30pm–5am (shows 10.30pm–2.30am).

★**Del Carajo** Jr San Ambrosia 328, Barranco ☏ 01 241 8904, ⊕ delcarajo.com.pe; map p.74. A lively and popular *peña* playing a range of criolla, Andean and coastal traditional and modern music. Some of Latin America's top criolla muscians play here. Thurs–Sat 10pm–3am.

La Estación de Barranco Av Pedro de Osma 112, Barranco ☏ 01 247 0344; map p.74. Just across the road from the suburb's main plaza, this established *peña* regularly varies its flavour between folklore, criolla and even Latin jazz or rock at times, with a lively atmosphere most Fridays and Saturdays. Tues–Sat 9pm–3am.

Kimbara Paseo de la República 1401, La Victoria ☏ 01 265 5831; map pp.58–59. This is a sprawling, unpretentious choice, with vibrant salsa music, sometimes performed live at weekends. Top Peruvian criolla musicians sometimes play here. Thurs–Sat 9pm–2am.

Peña La Candelaria Av Bolognesi 292, Barranco ☏ 01 247 1314, ⊕ lacandelariaperu.com; map p.74. An enormous venue presenting live music and dance from the three regions (coast, Andes and Amazon). Thurs, Fri & Sat 9pm–3am.

Peña Don Porfirio C Manuel Segura 115, Barranco ☏ 01 477 3119; map p.74. Possibly the only traditional-style *peña* left in Lima. Offers dance lessons during the week. Fri from 10pm.

Peña Sachún Av del Ejercito 657, Miraflores ☏ 01 441 0123; map p.70. Very lively and popular tourist restaurant with a good reputation for live folkloric music and criolla dancing. Tues–Sat 8.30pm–3am.

De Rompe y Raja Restaurant Peña Turística C Manuel Segura 127, Barranco ☏ 01 247 3271, ⊕ derompeyraja .pe; map p.74. Located between blocks 5 and 6 of Av Bolognesi, this *peña* presents live Peruvian music from 10pm. Ideal for groups, with big tables and entertainment. Thurs–Sat 9pm–midnight.

JAZZ, ROCK AND LATIN JAZZ

CC Club Delfus Taberna Av San Martín 587, San Borja ☏ 01 943 1211; map pp.58–59. Live rock music every Friday and Saturday night, with open jam sessions on Tues and Thurs. Wed–Sat 9pm–2am.

El Ekeko Av Grau 266, by the Plaza Municipal, Barranco ☏ 01 247 3148; map p.74. Often has Latin jazz at weekends, though also hosts Peruvian Andean and coastal music, mainly criolla. It's best to call first to make sure there's live music on when you go. Wed–Sun 9pm–late.

Jazz Zone Av La Paz 656, Miraflores ☏ 01 241 8139; map p.70. Located in the Pasaje El Suche, *Jazz Zone* offers cutting-edge live Latin or Brazilian rock, salsa and jazz, as well as fine examples of avant-garde Andean folk and occasionally Peruvian ballad singers. Daily 8pm–2am.

La Noche Av Bolognesi 307, El Boulevard Pazos, Barranco ☏ 01 247 2186, ⊕ lanoche.com.pe; map p.74. Don't let the slightly risqué website put you off: this is a top club located at the top end of the Boulevard, and is arguably the best venue in Barranco for meeting people; it gets really packed at weekends. Musically, it specializes in Latin rock and electronica, with free jazz sessions on Mon evenings. Live music (Fri & Sat 10pm–2am) comes with a small entry fee. Daily 9pm–2am.

★**La Posada del Angel III** Av Prol San Martín 157, Barranco ☏ 01 247 5544; map p.74. This is the largest of three *Posada del Angel* venues, all within a stone's throw of each other in Barranco. Well known for its Trova and Latino live music sessions, it has a great bar and also serves snacks and meals. All three locations are richly – and kitschly – decorated; the other two are at Pedro de Osma 164 & 218. Tues–Sat 6.30pm–midnight.

Satchmo Av La Paz 538, Miraflores ☏ 01 442 8425; map p.70. A large, traditional indoor live venue, best at weekends when performances range from Latino and Peruvian criolla music to jazz and blues. It's reasonably priced and food is also available. Fri–Sun 8pm–late.

GAY AND LESBIAN LIMA

Since the **gay and lesbian scene** is relatively small, there are few gay meeting places, though the main park and **Larco Mar** centre in Miraflores (see p.96) can be cruisey in the evenings. Although there are gay saunas in Miraflores, the busiest in Lima, Baños Turcos 240, is in an isolated part of Lima Centro that is dangerous to reach without a taxi. Lima society has

1

begun to grow more tolerant, but this does depend on which area you're in. The male culture, however, is still primarily macho, so, as a visitor, keeping a relatively low profile makes for an easier time. Most clubs here have a cover charge that includes a complimentary drink after a certain time, with free entry earlier in the evening.

GAY BARS AND CLUBS

La Cueva Av Aviación 2514, San Borja ☎ 993 484 532; map pp.58–59. A simple gay and lesbian club with drag shows and special bear nights. Great shows on Friday and Saturday, usually peaking around 3am. Thurs–Sun 10.30pm–late.

Downtown Vale Todo Pasaje Los Pinos 160, Miraflores ☎ 01 444 6433; map p.70. Arguably the best gay club in Lima; now and then there are caged go-go dancing boys, occasional striptease acts and a cruise bar. A mixed young crowd that is gayest on Saturdays. Mon–Thurs & Sun 8pm–1am, Fri & Sat 8pm–3am.

Legendaris C Berlín 363, Miraflores ☎ 01 446 3435; map p.70. Fashionable *Legendaris* is a large, comfortable club with personalized service, good drinks and shows, particularly on Sat night. Wed–Sun 10pm–late.

Sagitario Disco Av Wilson 869, Lima Centro ☎ 01 424 4383; map p.62. The longest-established gay club, in the heart of Lima, has cruising balconies filled with young people – a large number of them gay – and dancing through the night, often until 11am the next day. Daily 8pm–late.

ARTS AND ENTERTAINMENT

Going to the **cinema** and **theatre** is an important part of life in Lima. Peruvians are a well-cultured people with a passion and intuitive understanding of everything from Latin music and fine arts to ancient textiles and traditional Andean dance forms. **Peruvian culture** is very much alive and most locals know dozens of songs and several folk dances, as well as being able to dance salsa with the best of them. Lima's **cultural centres**, some associated with one of the local universities, are often the best places to catch innovative films, music shows and drama. The best source of **information** about film, theatre, sporting events and exhibitions is the daily *El Comercio*, especially its Friday supplement.

CINEMAS

There are clusters of cinemas around the Plaza San Martín, Jr de la Unión and Av Nicolás de Pierola in Lima Centro, on the fringes of the park in Miraflores, at Larco Mar and in some of the suburban shopping malls.

Cinemark Peru Jockey Plaza 12, Av Javier Prado, Surco ☎ 01 437 0222.

Cinemark Plaza Lima Sur 7 Av Prol Paseo de la República, Chorrillos ☎ 01 437 0222.

Cineplanet Alcazar 1–8 Santa Cruz 814, Miraflores ☎ 01 452 7000.

Cineplanet Centro Jr de la Unión, Lima Centro ☎ 01 452 7000.

Cineplanet Primavera Av Angamas Este 2684, San Borja ☎ 01 452 7000.

Cinerama El Pacífico Av Pardo 121, Miraflores ☎ 01 243 0541.

UVK Multicines Larco Mar 1–12 Parque Salazar, Larco Mar, Miraflores ☎ 01 446 7336.

CULTURAL CENTRES

Centro Cultural de la PUCP (Universidad La Católica) Av Camino Real 1075, San Isidro ☎ 01 616 1616. One of the most active cultural centres in Lima, with innovative theatre, cinema and video, as well as art exhibitions, a library and cafetería.

Centro Cultural de la UNMSM (Universidad de San Marcos) Av Nicolás de Piérola 1222, Parque Universitario, Lima Centro ☎ 01 428 0052. Often presents folk music and dance performances. The centre is run by the Universitario de San Marcos (see p.57), on the Parque Universitario, and performances are publicized on the noticeboard at the entrance.

Centro Cultural Ricardo Palma Av Larco 770, Miraflores ☎ 01 446 6164. Often hosts excellent concerts of Andean music, but doesn't have the same participatory feel as the *peñas* (see p.92). It does, however, boast a library, two exhibition rooms and occasional cinema festivals, plus jazz, dance and theatre performances.

THEATRE, BALLET AND CLASSICAL MUSIC

Lima possesses a prolific and extremely talented **theatre** circuit, with many of its best venues based in Miraflores. In addition to the major theatres, short performances sometimes take place in the bars of the capital's top theatres. The country's major prestige companies, however, are the **National Ballet Company** and the **National Symphony**, both based seasonally at the Teatro Municipal (see below).

Satchmo Av La Paz 526, Miraflores ☎ 01 444 4957.

Teatro Britianico Jr Bellavista 527, Miraflores ☎ 01 447 1135.

Teatro Larco Larco 1036, Miraflores ☎ 01 330 0979.

Teatro Municipal Block 3 of Jr Ica, Lima Centro ☎ 01 428 2302.

SHOPPING

When it comes to **shopping** in Peru's towns and cities, Lima is the most likely to have what you're looking for. It's certainly your best bet for **shoes and clothing**, particularly if you want a large selection to choose from. The same is true of

electronic goods, **stationery** and **music**, though bear in mind that most Limeños who can afford it do their main shopping in Miami. Lima also has a good selection of reasonably priced **arts and crafts** markets and shops.

Shopping hours The usual shopping hours are Mon–Sat 10am–7pm, though in Miraflores, the main commercial area, many shops and artesanía markets stay open until 8pm and sometimes later. Some shops, but by no means all, shut for a two-hour lunch break, usually 1–3pm, and most shops shut on Sundays, though the artesanía markets on avenidas La Marina and Petit Thouars tend to stay open all week until 7pm.

ANTIQUES
Collacocha C Colón 534, Miraflores ☎01 447 4422; map p.70. Parallel to block 11 of Av Larco, this place has good-quality antiques, as well as arts and crafts.
Rafo Martinez de Pinillos 1055, Barranco ☎01 247 0679; map p.74. Quality antiques and a good lunchtime restaurant too.

ARTS AND CRAFTS
Agua y Tierra Av Diez Canseco 298, Miraflores ☎01 444 6980; map p.70. A wide range of ethnic and traditional healing or *curanderos'* artefacts.
Artesanía Santo Domingo Jr Lima Conde de Superunda 221–223, Lima Centro; map p.62. This little square pavement area, just a stone's throw from the Correo Central in Lima Centro, is good for beads, threads and other artesanía items.
La Casa de Alpaca Av La Paz 665, Miraflores; map p.70. High-quality but expensive alpaca clothing and unique fabrics, masks and figurines you won't find in the markets. A similar artesanía store is across the road.
Cuy Arts and Crafts Av Larco 1175 & 874, Miraflores; map p.70. Dodge the T-shirts and usual souvenirs and you'll find some good handmade crafts of all kinds.
Las Pallas Cajamarca 212, Barranco ☎01 477 4629; map p.74. A fascinating, veritable museum of artesanía,

run by a British woman who has spent most of her life collecting fine works and who may be able to show you the rest of her collection (ring for an appointment).
Santos Alpaca 859 Av Larco 859, Miraflores; map p.70. Excellent-quality pima cotton and alpaca products at quite reasonable prices.

BOOKS
ABC Bookstore Av Colmena 689, Lima Centro; map p.62. Well supplied with all kinds of works in English. The same street (aka Nicolás de Pierola) has a few other shops stocking English-language books.
Librería Ibero Larco 199, Av Oscar Benavides 500 & Comandante Espinar, by the Ovalo Gutierrez, Miraflores; map p.70. The best bookshops are in Miraflores. This bookshop has three branches, which generally have a wide range of books and magazines in English.
Zeta Bookstore Comandante Espinar 219, Miraflores; map p.70. Has a small selection of new English paperbacks.

CAMPING, SURF AND SPORTS EQUIPMENT
Altamira Arica 800, Miraflores; map p.70. A block from the Plaza Agustín Gutierrez roundabout, this shop sells a good range of quality camping equipment.
Alta Montana Av Julio Bailetti 610, San Borja ☎01 346 3010; map pp.58–59. Probably the best place for climbing gear.
Big Head Larco Mar, Miraflores; map p.70. Good surf store. There's a second branch in the Jockey Plaza Shopping Centre (see p.96).
Boz Av Angamos Oeste 1130, between Miraflores and San Isidro ☎01 440 1033; map p.70. Specializes in surfing equipment.

CRAFT-SHOPPING IN LIMA

Lima is a treasure-trove of **Peruvian artesanía**, with woollen goods, crafts and gemstones among the best souvenirs. Artesanía shops tend to cluster in particular areas, and there are some dedicated craft markets too. **Avenida La Paz** in Miraflores boasts several shops selling precious metals, gemstones and antiques, with many places devoted to silverwork and other jewellery. Some of the cheapest traditional crafts in Peru can be found in an artesanía market area en route to Callao (or the Parque de Las Leyendas), located by the roadside blocks 6–8 of **Avenida La Marina**, in Pueblo Libre. The **Mercado Indio**, on Avenida Petit Thouars between blocks 48 and 54 (between avenidas Ricardo Palma and Angamos) is much more central, reasonably priced and home to the best craft and souvenir stalls and shops, all well within walking distance of Miraflores centre. **Artesanía Gran Chimu**, Av Petit Thouars 5495, has a wide range of jewellery and carved wooden items, as does **Mercado Artesanal**, Av Petit Thouars 5321. At La Rotunda, the small circular area towards the bottom (ocean) end of Parque Kennedy in Miraflores, a small selection of reasonable-quality crafts and antiques is displayed every evening (6–9pm).

1

Camping Centre Av Benavides 1620, Miraflores ☎01 242 1779; map p.70. Has a good range of tents and other equipment in a small space.

Klimax C José González 488, Miraflores ☎01 442 1685; map p.70. Good for surf gear.

Peru Bike Parque Nueva Castilla, C A, d-7, Surco ☎01 449 8435; map pp.58–59. Good range of bikes and related accessories.

Todo Camping Av Angamos Oeste 350, Miraflores; map p.70. Has a range of tents and other equipment.

JEWELLERY

Arte y Canela Larco Mar, Miraflores; map p.70. Stocks fine silver jewellery.

Nasca Av La Paz 522, Miraflores; map p.70. Has a nice range of less expensive jewellery, particularly silverware.

PHOTOGRAPHIC EQUIPMENT

Renato Service 28 Julio 442, Miraflores; map p.70. For excellent camera and video equipment. The store is not very obvious from the street.

SHOPPING MALLS

Jockey Plaza Av Javier Prado Este 4200, Surco. The largest of the shopping malls, with over two hundred shops including two massive department stores (Saga and Ripley), a bowling alley, twelve cinema screens and dozens of restaurant-cafés. Take any colectivo or bus marked "Todo Javier Prado" heading east from the junction of avenidas Javier and Arequipa.

Centro Comercial Larco Mar At the clifftop end of Av Larco, Miraflores. This compact centre has more than seventy shops complemented by thirty restaurant-cafés, cinema screens, a few nightclubs and bars, and a bowling alley.

DIRECTORY

Embassies and consulates Australia, Av Victor Belaunde 147, Office 1301, Torre Real 3, San Isidro (☎01 222 8281); Bolivia, C Los Castaños 235, San Isidro (☎01 440 2095); Brazil, Av José Pardo 850, Miraflores (☎01 421 5660); Canada, C Bolognesi 228, Miraflores (☎01 319 3200); Chile, Av Javier Prado Oeste 790, San Isidro (☎01 710 2211); Ecuador, Las Palmeras 356, San Isidro (☎01 421 7050); Ireland, Paseo de la República 5353B, San Antonio, Miraflores (☎01 242 9516); New Zealand, Los Nogales 510, Piso 3, San Isidro (☎01 422 7491); South Africa, Av Victor Andres Belaunde 147 (office 801), Edificio Real Tres, San Isidro (☎01 440 9996); UK, Torre Parque Mar, Av Larco 1301, 22nd floor, Miraflores (☎01 617 3000); US, La Encalada, block 17, Monterrico (☎01 434 3000).

Health For an ambulance call ☎01 440 0200 or ☎01 372 6080, but if you can, take a taxi – it'll be much quicker. The following hospitals are well equipped, with emergency departments which you can use as an outpatient, or which you can phone for a house call: Clínica Anglo Americana, Av Salazar, San Isidro (☎01 221 3656); Clínica Internacional, Washington 1475, Lima Centro (☎01 428 8060); Clínica Ricardo Palma, Av Javier Prado Este 1066, San Isidro (☎01 224 8027); and Clínica San Borja, Av Guardia Civil 337, San Borja (☎01 475 3141). For anti-rabies vaccinations and emergency treatment contact Antirabico (☎01 425 6313). If you just need to see a doctor, try one of the following: Dr Jorge Bazan works as a "backpackers medic" and will make house calls to hostels (☎997 352 668, ✉backpackersdr @yahoo.com); Dr Aste, C Antero Aspillaga 415, Oficina 101, San Isidro (☎01 441 7502), speaks English; Dr Alicia Garcia, Instituto de Ginecología, Av Monterrico 1045, Surco (☎01 434 2650); or Dr Raul Morales, Clínica Padre Luis Tezza, Av del Polo 570, Monterrico (☎01 434 6990), speaks good English. The best pharmacy is Boticas Fasa, Av Benavides 847, Miraflores (☎01 619 0000), with 24hr delivery; they

accept major credit cards. There's a comprehensive Mifarma pharmacy in Lima Centro at Av Abancay 601. Inka Farma (☎01 619 8000) is a delivery service.

Internet You can find internet cafés virtually anywhere in Lima, particularly in Miraflores, where Dragonfans, Tarata 230, and Larconet, Av Larco 675, are the best. Wi-fi is available in many cafés.

Language schools Hispana Spanish School, C San Martín 377, Miraflores (☎01 446 3045, ⊛hispanaidiomas.com); Ecela, Gen Recavarres 542, Miraflores (☎01 4442279); Lima School of Languages, Av Grimaldo del Solar 469, Miraflores (☎01 242 7763, ⊛elsol.idiomasperu.com), where you can start any Monday for small-group or private tuition, full- or part-time; El Tulipán, José Galvez 426, Miraflores (☎01 447 7403, ⊛eltulipanperu.com), which offers a good Spanish survival course.

Laundry Many hotels will do this cheaply, but there are numerous *lavanderías* in most areas; the Lavandería Saori, Av Grimaldo del Solar 175, Miraflores (Mon–Sat 8am–7pm; ☎01 444 3830), is fast; LavaQueen, Av Larco 1158, Miraflores, does washing by the kilo at reasonable prices.

Money and exchange Banco de la Nación, Av Nicolás de Piérola 1065 and Av Abancay 491; Banco de Credito, Jr Lampa 499, Av Larco 1099, Miraflores (well run and with small queues) and Juan de Arona, San Isidro; Banco Continental, Av Larco, Miraflores. Casas de cambio sometimes offer better rates and are often the only places where travellers' cheques will be accepted. Try casa de cambio, Ocoña 211A; LAC Dollar, Av Camaná 779, 2nd floor; and another office in Miraflores at La Paz 211.

Police Peru's Tourist Police are based at Jr Colón 246, Miraflores (☎01 225 8698 or ☎01 423 3500), and in the Museo de la Nación at Av Javier Prado Este 2465 (☎01 225 8698).

Post office The main post office is at Pasaje Piura, Jr Lima, block 1 near the Plaza Mayor (Mon–Sat 8am–8pm, Sun

8am–2pm), with other branches in Miraflores, at Av Petit Thouars 5201 (Mon–Fri 8am–8pm). The best bet for sending large parcels is to use KLM (Av Elmer Faucett 2823, Oficina 404, Lima Cargo City, Callao; ☎01 575 5270), who charge about US$12/kilo to Europe. Concas Travel, C Alcanfores 345, Oficina 101, Miraflores (☎01 241 7516), can arrange larger shipments.

The coast around Lima

Stretching out along the coast in both directions, the **Panamerican Highway** runs the entire 2600km length of Peru, with Lima more or less at its centre. Towns along the sometimes arid coastline immediately north and south of the capital are of minor interest to most travellers, though there are some glorious **beaches**, mostly to the south, with next to no restrictions on beach camping. The best of the beaches begin about 30km out, at the impressively hulking pre-Inca ruins of **Pachacamac**, a sacred citadel that still dominates this stretch of coastline.

Pachacamac

Daily 9am–5pm • S/10, guides S/20 for a small group • ☎01 430 0168

Originally one of the most important centres of pilgrimage on the Peruvian coast, **PACHACAMAC** functioned from around the time of Christ as a very sacred location that, even in pre-Inca days, housed a miraculous wooden idol (see box below). It's by far the most interesting of the Rimac Valley's ancient sites, and well worth making time for even if you're planning to head out to Cusco and Machu Picchu; allow a good two hours to wander around the full extent of the ruins. The site can easily be combined with a day at one or other of the beaches, and it's little problem to get out there from the capital.

The museum

The entry fee for the citadel includes admission to the site **museum**, which merits a quick browse on the way in, if only to get a look at the wooden idol of Pachacamac (see box below) and a 3D site model; there are nice gardens attached, and a café serving snacks.

IDOLS AND ORACLES

"Pachacamac" means (more or less) "Earth's Creator", and the site was certainly occupied by 500 AD and probably for a long time before that. When other *huacas* were being constructed in the lower Rimac Valley, Pachacamac was already a temple-citadel and centre for mass pilgrimages. The god-image of Pachacamac was believed to express his or her anger through **tremors and earthquakes**, and was an **oracle** used for important matters affecting the State: the health of the ruler, the outcome of a war and so on. Later this became one of the most famous **shrines** in the Inca Empire, with Pachacamac himself worshipped along with the sun. The Incas built their Sun Temple on the crest of the hill above Pachacamac's own sacred precinct.

In 1533, **Francisco Pizarro** sent his brother Hernando to seize Pachacamac's treasure, but was disappointed by the spoils, which consisted of little more than a **wooden idol** representing, through intricate carvings, a two-faced humanoid. This wooden representation of Pachacamac may well have been the oracle itself: it was kept hidden inside a labyrinth and behind guarded doors – only the high priests could communicate with it face to face. When Hernando Pizarro and his troops arrived they had to pass through many doors to arrive at the main idol site, which was raised up on a "snail-shaped" (or spiralling) platform, with the wooden carving stuck into the earth inside a dark room, separated from the world by a jewelled curtain. Pizarro ended up burning the complex to the ground, dissatisfied with the relatively small amounts of gold on offer.

As well as earthquakes, Pachacamac's powers extended to the absence or presence of **disease and pestilence**. His wife, or female counterpart, was believed to dominate **plant and fish life**.

1

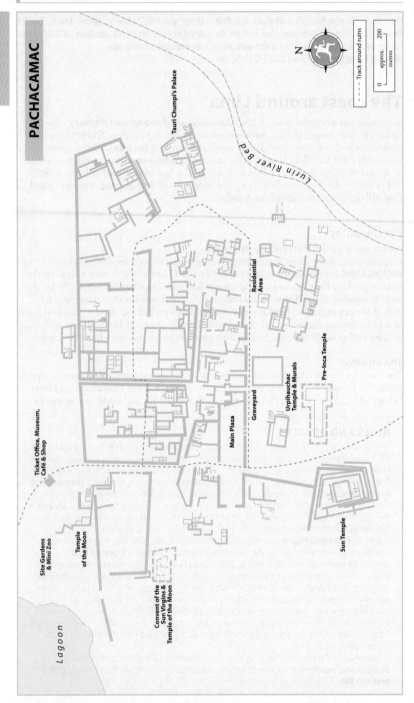

PACHACAMAC

Tauri Chumpi's Palace

Lurin River Bed

N

0   approx.   200
          metres

--- Track around ruins

Ticket Office, Museum,
Café & Shop

Site Gardens
& Mini Zoo

Temple
of the Moon

Lagoon

Convent of the
Sun Virgins &
Temple of the Moon

Residential
Area

Main Plaza

Graveyard

Urpihuachac
Temple & Murals

Pre-Inca Temple

Sun Temple

The ruins

Entering the ruins, after passing the restored sectors, which include the **Templo de la Luna** (Temple of the Moon) and the **Convento de las Virgenes del Sol** (Convent of the Sun Virgins, or *Mamaconas*), you can see the later Inca construction of the **Sun Temple** directly ahead. Constructed on the top level of a series of pyramidical platforms, it was built tightly onto the hill with plastered adobe bricks, its walls originally painted in gloriously bright colours. From the very top of the Sun Temple there's a magnificent **view** west beyond the Panamerican Highway to the beach (Playa San Pedro) and across the sea to a sizeable yet uninhabited island, which resembles a huge whale approaching the shore. Below the Sun Temple is the **main plaza**, once covered with a thatched roof supported on stilts, and thought to have been the area where pilgrims assembled in adoration. The rest of the ruins, visible though barely distinguishable, were once dwellings, storehouses and palaces.

ARRIVAL AND DEPARTURE | PACHACAMAC

By bus Buses leave every 2hr for Pachacamac from Av Abancay in Lima Centro and around the Parque Universitario on Jr Montevideo at the corner with Jr Ayacucho (1hr). Buses can also be picked up from one of the bus-stop lay-bys on the Panamericana Sur (south direction); the spot where Av Angamos Este crosses the Panamericana is a good bet.

By taxi A taxi to Pachacamac and back from Miraflores can be found from around S/100.

By tour Many of the tour agencies in Lima offer half-day tours to the site (see p.81).

Lomas de Lucumo

Taxi from Lima (S/120–180) or Pachacamac (S/15)

Going away from the Pachacamac site via the pueblo of the same name you pick up a hard road heading for the Quebrada Verde area. Within a few kilometres you come across the **Lomas de Lucumo**, a beautiful natural ecosystem at the edge of the desert replete with shrubs and the odd flower thriving on little more than seasonal coastal fog.

Southern beach towns

South from Pachacamac lie some of Lima's most attractive **beaches**. Closest to the ruins, just a couple of kilometres away, is **Playa San Pedro**, a vast and usually deserted strip of sand. Constantly pounded by rollers, however, it can be quite dangerous for swimming. Though much more sheltered, the bay of **El Silencio**, 6km to the south, occasionally suffers from low-level pollution that can appear here from the local beachside developments. You may be better off heading to one of the excellent **seafood restaurants** on the cliff above, or to the smaller, more secluded bays a short drive further down the coast.

Santa María and San Bartolo

At **Punta Hermosa**, about ten minutes on the bus beyond El Silencio, you come to an attractive clifftop settlement and, down below, what's becoming Lima's leading surf resort, **Santa María**, a great family haunt, with plenty of hotels and a reasonable beach. Just south of here the surf and beach resort of **San Bartolo** offers hostels, restaurants and reasonably good waves.

Pucusana, Chilca and around

South of San Bartolo lies the fishing village of **Pucusana**, clustered on the side of a small hilly peninsula, which is now perhaps the most fashionable of the beaches – a holiday resort where Limeños actually stay rather than just driving out for a swim.

Continuing south, the road cruises along the coast, passing the long beach and salt pools of **Chilca** after 5km, and the curious lion-shaped rock of **León Dormido** (Sleeping Lion) after another 15km or so.

1

Asia and further south

Spread out along the roadside from Km 95 to Km 103, **Asia** has turned from a small agricultural town, producing cotton, bananas and corn, to a modern, trendy resort with hotels and fashionable **clubs** alongside its long **beach**. Archeological finds in local graveyards have revealed that this site was occupied from around 2500 BC by a pre-ceramic agricultural community associated also with the earliest examples of a trophy-head cult (many of the mummies were decapitated). About 20km on from Asia is the growing surfers' resort of **Cerro Azul**.

ARRIVAL AND GETTING AROUND

By bus Buses to San Bartolo (45min) and Pucusana (35min) can be picked up in Lima from one of the bus-stop lay-bys on the Panamericana Sur (south direction); wait at the spot where Av Angamos Este crosses the Panamericana. Some buses start from the corner of jirones Montevideo

SOUTHERN BEACH TOWNS

and Ayacucho every 2hr, passing Pachacamac, San Pedro, El Silencio, Punta Hermosa and Santa María on the 65km journey. For Asia and Cerro Azul take the Peru Bus (Av Mexico 280, La Victoria; ☎01 205 2370, ⓦperubus .com.pe).

ACCOMMODATION AND EATING

Doña Paulina About 20km south of Chilca on the highway, where it bypasses the town of Malfa. At this cafetería, you can sample the best *chicharones* (chunks of deep-fried pork) in the region. Daily 9am–7pm.
Penascal Surf Hotel Av Las Palmeras 258, San Bartolo

☎01 430 7436, ⓦsurfpenascal.com. These apartments with oceanfront views are part of a surfing school (also offering Spanish lessons). Rates include breakfast, parking and laundry. **S/205**

East of Lima

Several destinations in the **foothills of the Andes** are within relatively easy reach in the east, inland from Lima. The most spectacular is the mystical plateau of **Marcahuasi** (see p.283) in the northeast, a weekend trip from the city; much closer to Lima are the impressive sites of **Puruchuco** and **Cajamarquilla**, which are typical of ruins all over Peru and make a good introduction to the country's archeology. The attractive mountain towns of **Tarma**, **Huancayo** and **Huancavelica**, all interesting destinations, are within a day's easy travelling of the capital, fanning out from northeast to southeast (see Chapter Five).

Puruchuco and around

Between Km 4 and Km 5 of the Carretera Central • Daily 9am–5pm • S/5 • ☎01 494 2641 • Take any bus marked Vitarte or Chaclacayo and get off in Villa Vitarte, where the entrance is signposted from the Carretera Central (quite close to the football stadium)

An 800-year-old, pre-Inca settlement, **PURUCHUCO** is a labyrinthine villa. Nearby is the small but interesting **Museo de Sito Puruchuco**, containing a complete collection of artefacts and attire found at the site (all of which bears a remarkable similarity to what Amazon Indian communities still use today). The name itself means "feathered hat or helmet", and recent building work in the locality discovered that the Puruchuco site was also a massive **graveyard**, revealing greater quantities of buried pre-Incas than most other sites in Peru. The villa's original adobe structure was apparently rebuilt and adapted by the Incas shortly before the Spanish arrival: it's a fascinating ruin, superbly restored in a way which vividly captures what life was like before the Conquest.

Very close by, in the Parque Fernando Carozi (ask the site guard for directions), two other ruins – **Huaquerones** and **Catalina Huaca** – are being restored, and at **Chivateros** there's a quarry dating back some twelve thousand years.

Cajamarquilla

Huachipa, Carretera Central • Daily 9am–5pm • S/5 • Take any bus marked Chaclacayo and get off at Santa Clara junction; cross over the river from here and turn right along the signposted road, from where it's 3km to the site

First occupied in the Huari era (600–1000 AD), **CAJAMARQUILLA** flourished under the **Cuismancu culture**, a city-building state contemporary with the better-known Chimu in northern Peru. It was an enclosed city containing thousands of small, complex dwellings clustered around a higher section, probably nobles' quarters, and numerous small plazas. The site was apparently abandoned before the Incas arrived in 1470, possibly after being devastated by an earthquake. Pottery found here in the 1960s by a group of Italian archeologists suggests habitation over 1300 years ago.

Today the site is a vast and almost overwhelming labyrinth of cracked and weathered adobe-built corridors, rooms and small plazas, and feels almost as if it was only recently deserted after a massive earthquake.

ARRIVAL AND DEPARTURE   PURUCHUCO AND CAJAMARQUILLA

Both Puruchuco and Cajamarquilla lie near the beginning of the Central Highway, the road that climbs up behind Lima towards Chosica, La Oroya and the Andes. The two sites are only 6km apart.

By tour The sites are most easily visited on a half-day guided tour from Lima (see p.81).

By colectivo You could take a colectivo from

C Montevideo, La Victoria (daily from 7am; S/8; 35min), and return by waving down passing buses on the main Carretera Central; the Chosica-to-Lima bus will be the most likely to have spare seats. For Cajamarquilla, the colectivo will drop you off at the refinery turn-off before Km10 of the Carretera Central; then it's about 4km, or an hour's walk to the ruins, which are well hidden next to an old hacienda.

Parque Zoológico Huachipa

Av Las Torres, Vitarte; close to the Cajamarquilla turn-off • Daily 9am–5.30pm • S/13, children S/6 • ☎ 01 356 3141, ⓦ zoohuachipa.com .pe • Take any bus marked Chaclacayo and get off at Santa Clara junction; it's on the right and well signposted before you reach the river and bridge, just a short walk along Av Las Torres

The **Parque Zoológico Huachipa**, a theme park and zoo, is fun for kids. There's a walk-on pirate boat, a waterworld area, an imaginative play area and a zone full of exotic animals, including zebras, tigers and giraffes, not to mention an array of brightly coloured reptiles.

San Juan de Pariachi

Km 12.5 of the Carretera Central

A few kilometres east of the Parque Zoológico Huachipa is an archeological site on the right bank of the Río Rimac: the Inca administrative centre now known as **San Juan de Pariachi**, dating from at least a thousand years ago.

Chosica and around

Into the foothills through sprawling developments, the road comes to the town of **Chosica**, a narrow settlement squeezed between the steepening dry and rocky foothills and the turbulent river below. Just 35km from Lima, Chosica has long been a traditional weekend escape from the city, particularly during winter, when it provides some respite from Lima's mist and smog. There's not much to visit here, just some country clubs, mostly private, in the valley below. Above Chosica the road starts to climb fast, winding its way past some impressive-looking hydro power stations into the Andes towards Ticlio and way beyond to the beautiful **Mantaro Valley**.

ARRIVAL AND DEPARTURE

By bus Catching a bus from Chosica to Huancayo, Tarma or Huánuco can be tricky: although they pass through here, they may well be full already. Colectivos or shared taxis may be an easier solution. Buses from Lima to Chosica will usually drop passengers off and pick them up around the Parque Central.

CHOSICA AND AROUND

By colectivo There are plenty of minibus colectivos connecting Lima with Chosica for around S/10 (45min–1hr 10min); in San Isidro, they leave from behind the Cine Orantia; in Lima Centro they depart from the corner of Jr Ayacucho with Av Nicolás de Piérola.

ACCOMMODATION AND EATING

Hospedaje Chosica Av 28 de Julio 134 ☎ 01 361 0841. Pleasant and good value, this is a family-run place. It has four rooms with baths and six without. $\overline{S/85}$
Restaurant Liluzca Jr Chiclayo 250. It's difficult to do

better than this place, in a small side-street off the main road by the plaza; it has outside seating and serves decent food, though it usually closes before 7pm.

North of Lima

To the north of Lima, the desert stretches up between the Pacific Ocean and the foothills of the Andes. A couple of short trips north of Lima are becoming increasingly popular as long-weekend breaks. One of these is a horseshoe loop connecting the **Chillón and Chancay valleys** via the beautiful town and region of Canta in the foothills of the Andes. Another route, further out from Lima, heads up the Huara Valley from Huacho; although the road can be traced all the way to Huánuco, most people only get as far up into the Andes as **Churin**, where their efforts are pleasantly rewarded with a visit to the hot springs. Futher north again, yet still feasible as a day-trip from Lima, the recently discovered pyramids of **Caral** are considered to be the most ancient ruins in the Americas.

The Chillón and Chancay valleys

Leaving Lima and heading north, the Panamerican Highway – or Panamericana Norte – passes through the **Chillón Valley**, dotted with ancient **ruins**, of which the most important are on the south side of the Río Chillón within 3 or 4km of the Ventanilla road. The most impressive is the 2000- to 3000-year-old **Temple El Paraiso**, which was built by a sedentary farming community of probably no more than 1500 inhabitants and consists of three main pyramids built of rustic stones.

From here, the Panamerican Highway passes the yacht and tennis clubs that make up the fashionable beach resort of **Ancón**, about 30km from Lima, then crosses a high, often foggy, plateau from the Chillón to the **Chancay Valley**. Still covered by sparse vegetation, this was a relatively fertile *lomas* area (where plants grow from moisture in the air rather than rainwater or irrigation) in pre-Inca days, and evidence of winter camps from five thousand years ago has been found. The highway bypasses the market town of Huaral and runs through **Chancay**, some 65km north of Lima.

Eco Truly Park

Km 63 on the Panamericana Norte • Lima contact: Av Javier Prado Este 185, San Isidro • ☎ 01 4210016, ⓦ ecotrulypark.org • Coastal buses headed for Chancay, Barranca or Chimbote can drop off here

The unique domes of **Eco Truly Park** appear along the beach at Km 63 on the Panamerican Highway, by Chacra y Mar beach. Set at the foot of desert cliffs and close to the pounding ocean, this ashram offers guided tours of their adobe huts and organic gardens, plus yoga and meditation, hikes and workshops on ecology. Always book visits in advance.

Reserva Nacional Lomas de Lachay

Signposted off the Panamericana Norte between Chancay and Huacho, before the police controls at Doña María • Daily 7am–7pm

North of Chancay, the road passes through stark desert for 20km until at Km 105 you reach the **Reserva Nacional Lomas de Lachay**, a protected area of unique *lomas* habitat some 5000 hectares in extent and around 600m above sea level. Run by the Ministry of Agriculture, the centre maintains the footpaths that thread through the reserve's beautiful scenery. Formed by granite and diorite rocky intrusions some seventy million years ago, the **lomas** – at its best between June and December when it is in full bloom – is home to more than forty types of **bird**, including hummingbird, parrot, partridge, peregrine and even condor; you may also spot various species of reptile and native deer.

ARRIVAL AND DEPARTURE	RESERVA LOMAS DE LACHAY
By tour The easiest way to get to the reserve is with an organized tour from Lima (see p.81). **By car or taxi** In a car or taxi from Chancay (S/20 each way; 45min), continue up the Panamericana Norte for	about 6km beyond the turning for Sayan and Churin. The turn-off to the reserve is signposted at the top of a hill, but from the road it's still an hour's walk along a sandy track to the interpretive centre at the entrance to the reserve.

El Paraíso and Huacho

A little north of the Reserva Nacional Lomas de Lachay, at Km 133 of the Panamericana Norte, a track turns off onto a small peninsula and leads to the secluded bay of **El Paraíso** – a magical beach perfect for camping, swimming and scuba diving. Crossing bleaker sands, the Panamericana Norte next passes through **Huacho**, an unusual place with some interesting colonial architecture and a ruined church in the upper part of town, but mostly made up of recent concrete constructions. As it's so close to Lima, it was one of the first towns to be hit by expanding and migratory populations, as well as wealthy Lima families taking on a second home or farmstead.

The Huara Valley

Just beyond Huacho a side road turns east into the **Huara Valley** and the foothills of the Andes to reach **Sayan**, a small farming town where little has changed for decades – the church here has a very attractive colonial interior.

Churin

Further up the valley from Sayan lies **CHURIN**, a small thermal spa town popular with Limeños during holidays, located in the district of Pachangara 210km from Lima. Most of the farmland on the valley floor and the Sayan-to-Churin road was washed away in the 1998 El Niño, and a new, rough road has been carved out between the boulders littering the valley floor. There are two spas in town, both fairly cool, with private and communal baths; the **El Fierro spa** (all baths cost S/2–3) is the hottest and reputed to be the most curative. It's a ten-minute ride by colectivo from town (S/1.50).

Churin is also a good base from which to explore a number of traditional communities as well as archeological **ruins**, such as Ninash, Kutun, Antasway and Kuray. For climbers, there are also some challenging **peaks** in the Cordillera Raura (up to 5700m). The main **festival** here is San Juan, between June 23 and 25, which includes a ritual procession to the river for a cleansing bath, to ensure health in the coming year.

Huancahuasi

Baths S/5

An excellent day-trip from Churin can be made to more thermal baths at **Huancahuasi**. There are two sets of hot baths here, and traditional snacks such as *pachamanca* (meat and vegetables on pre-heated rocks covered with earth and left for a few hours) are

1

prepared outside them. En route to Huancahuasi you'll spot a remarkable, early colonial, carved facade on the tiny church at **Picoy**.

ARRIVAL AND DEPARTURE — THE HUARA VALLEY

By bus There are several buses to Sayan and Churin from Lima daily (6–7hr), the best run by Transportes Estrella Polar, Av Luna Pizarro 330–338, La Victoria (⚓ 01 332 8182; expect to pay around S/12).

By colectivo Colectivos run between Sayan and Huacho every 30min. Colectivos to Huancahuasi leave from Churin church at around 8am (S/12 return; 30min), returning mid-afternoon.

ACCOMMODATION AND EATING

There are many places to stay in Churin, but they all get packed out in the main holiday periods, when prices double. All of the **hotels** are within a couple of blocks of each other in the town centre. Churin has some good restaurants and cafés too, mostly around the main plaza. Local specialities include honey, *alfajores*, *manjar blanca* and cheeses.

Hotel Las Termas Av Larco Herrera 411, Churin ⚓ 01 237 3094. This well-located place has pleasant rooms, good service and a pool, as well as a private terrace and gardens. S/70

Caral

Supe Valley, accessed via Carretera Caral-Las Minas Ambar from Supe Town • Daily 7am–5.30pm • S/10 • ⚓ 01 431 2235, Ⓦ caralperu.gob.pe

North up the coast from Huacho, only the town and port of Supe breaks the monotonous beauty of desert and ocean, until you reach Barranca and the labyrinthine ruins of the Fortress of Paramonga (see p.341). Inland from Supe, however, along the desert coast in a landscape that looks more lunar than agricultural, archeologists have uncovered one of the most important finds of the past century. Thought to be the oldest city in the Americas at around five thousand years old, the **ancient pyramids of Caral** are now a UNESCO World Heritage Site.

Brief history

From humble beginnings (see box below), Caral developed into one of the earliest metropolises, representing human achievements that took place four thousand years earlier than the Incas: the stone ceremonial structures here were flourishing a hundred years before the Great Pyramid at Giza was even built.

Archeologists have studied its temples, houses and plazas, and the artefacts unearthed here, to form a picture of the ancient Caral culture, which focused heavily on agriculture and construction. There's evidence of ceremonial functions, too, and music was also important: a collection of coronets and flutes have been found on site.

THE ORIGINS OF CARAL

Before the advent of urban living and stone ceremonial pyramids here, the region was only populated by a few **coastal villages**, each with around a hundred inhabitants. Around 2700 BC it appears that a number of larger villages emerged, principally, it seems, based around the successful domestication and early cultivation of the cotton-bush plant. The early use of **cotton** was nothing short of a bio-technological revolution, not only providing cloth for garments but more importantly permitting the fabrication of nets for fishing in the rich coastal waters, as well as net or woven bags for carrying produce and fish back home to their settlements. The introduction of cotton fishing nets transformed the lives of coastal communities, giving them sufficient protein, more spare time to evolve social and religious practices, and surplus food to trade with neighbouring communities, laying the groundwork for what was to become a thriving urban centre.

1

The site

The heart of the site covers about 150 acres. There are two large, sunken circular plazas, the base of the tallest mound measurimg 154m by 138m, making it the largest pyramid yet found in Peru. Excavations have revealed that this **Piramide Mayor** (main pyramid) was terraced, with a staircase leading up to an atrium-like platform, culminating in a flattened top housing enclosed rooms and a ceremonial fire pit. Some of the best artefacts discovered here include 32 **flutes** made from pelican and animal bones and engraved with the figures of birds and even monkeys, demonstrating a connection with the Amazon region.

The six mounds, or pyramids, are arranged together around a large plaza. Archeologists believe that the pyramids were constructed in a maximum of two phases, which suggests a need for particularly complex social structures for planning, decision-making and the mobilization of a large sector of the population to provide sufficient labour as and when it was required. Around the pyramids is evidence of many residential structures.

ARRIVAL AND DEPARTURE   **CARAL**

By bus and colectivo Transportes Paramonga (Av Luna Pizarro 251, La Victoria; ☎ 01 423 6338, ⓦ turismo paramonga.com.pe) runs buses every day to Supe, usually leaving around 6.20am. From here, if unguided, you'd need to take a colectivo (S/6; 45min); they leave regularly from near the market in Supe centre.

By car Easier to reach with your own car, Caral is connected to the Panamericana by a badly rutted dirt-track road that starts at Km 184 of the highway and continues for 23km to the site.
By tour Fertur Peru (see p.81) offers a day-trip from around US$80 per person, including guide, bus and taxi to the site.

Nazca and the south coast

PARACAS NATIONAL RESERVE

Nazca and the south coast

South of Lima, a beautiful dry desert stretches the entire 1330km to Chile. In places just a narrow strip of desert squashed between Andes and Pacific, it is followed diligently by the Panamericana Sur Highway. The region harbours one of South America's greatest archeological mysteries – the famous Nazca Lines – as well as offering access to coastal wildlife and stunning landscapes. Once home to at least three major pre-Inca cultures – the Paracas (500 BC–400 AD), the influential Nazca (500–800 AD) and the Ica culture – this region of Peru was eventually taken over by the Incas. Today, Nazca and Paracas are very much part of the tourist trail and are often visited en route between Lima and Cusco.

Once beyond Lima's beaches, the first significant town is **Cañete**, which is of little interest itself, but is a gateway to the attractive **Lunahuana** valley, well known as a river-rafting centre as well as for its vineyards. Just south of here, near the town of **Pisco** and the coastal resort of **Paracas** (previously known as El Chaco), **Paracas National Reserve** and the offshore **Islas Ballestas** offer an exciting mix of wildlife – including sea lions, dolphins and sharks – boat trips and ancient archeology.

Just inland from Pisco, the adobe Inca remains of **Tambo Colorado** are an interesting diversion, perhaps rounded off by a great seafood dinner at the fisherman's wharf in **San Andrés**. Hidden in sand dunes just outside the city of **Ica**, the resort of **Huacachina** combines peaceful desert oasis with sandboarding and dune buggies. A couple of hours' drive south, the geometric shapes and giant figures of the **Nazca Lines** are etched over almost 500 square kilometres of bleak pampa. Nazca also offers access to the outstanding, rare *vicuña* reserve of **Pampa Galeras** (in the Andes above Nazca).

Further south, just before the town of Chala, **Puerto Inca** is a stunning but still relatively undeveloped beach resort, at one time a coastal port for the nobles of Inca Cusco. Also nearby is a small, unique national park, **Las Lomas de Atiquipa**, where rugged hills are tucked up against the sea. Once past the town of Camaná, south of Chala, the **Panamericana Sur Highway** runs inland to within almost 40km of Arequipa (see Chapter Three), where there's a fast road connection into the city. From here the highway cuts south across undulating desert to the calm colonial town of **Moquegua**, a springboard for the region's archeological heritage, before heading south another 150km to **Tacna**, the last pit stop before the **frontier with Chile**.

GETTING AROUND   THE SOUTH COAST

Transport is not usually a problem along the south coast, with local buses connecting all the towns with each other and with Lima, and express buses ploughing along the coastal road between Lima and Arequipa day and night.

By bus The best bus companies serving the south coast are Cruz del Sur (☎01 324 6332, ⊚cruzdelsur.com.pe) and

Excluciva (☎01 418 1111, ⊚excluciva.com.pe) which offers seating reminiscent of airline business class, with service to

Highlights

❶ Lunahuana This beautiful coastal valley is almost always sunny, and a focus for whitewater rafting and mountain biking as well as good local wines and piscos. **See p.111**

❷ Islas Ballestas Within a morning's boat ride from the town of Pisco, these guano islands with their much-photographed rock arches are home to an impressive range of bird and mammalian marine life. **See p.116**

❸ Paracas National Reserve A beautiful peninsula with stunning desert landscapes touching the Pacific Ocean; both beaches and sea are a haven for wildlife, and there is a museum dedicated to the ancient Paracas culture. **See p.116**

❹ Huacachina A magical oasis surrounded by giant sand dunes, Huacachina is a must visit for those looking for desert adventure or a place to wind down after pisco tasting in neighbouring Ica. **See p.128**

❺ Nazca Lines The world-famous Nazca Lines, including stylized geometric and animal figures, were etched, seemingly impossibly, into a massive desert pampa. **See p.130**

❻ Puerto Inca This small but secluded resort lies in an area of coast teeming with rare Inca remains as well as offering great access to beaches, coves, fishing and excellent diving. **See p.142**

HIGHLIGHTS ARE MARKED ON THE MAP ON P.110

THE SOUTH COAST

- Porocacha
- Cañete
- Lunahuana
- Incahuasi
- Islas Ballestas
- Bahía de Paracas
- Río Topara
- Chincha
- Huaca Centinela
- Pisco
- Tambo Colorado
- Paracas
- Castrovirreyna
- PARACAS NATIONAL RESERVE
- Laguna Grande
- Pozo Santo
- Guadalupe
- Ica
- Cachiche
- Huacachina
- Ocucaje
- Ayacucho
- Palpa
- Nazca Lines
- Cahuachi
- Nazca
- Chauchilla Cemetery
- Pampa Galeras Vicuña Reserve
- Sacaco
- Puquio
- Las Lomas
- LAS LOMAS DE ATIQUIPA
- Chumpi
- Puerto Inca
- Chala
- Lago Parinacochas
- PANAMERICAN HIGHWAY
- Cotahuasi
- Atico
- Chuquibamba
- Ocoña
- Aplao
- Toro Muerto
- Corire
- Colca Canyon
- Camaná
- Chivay
- Mollendo
- Arequipa
- Mejía Bird Sanctuary
- Chapi
- PACIFIC OCEAN
- Torata
- Ilo
- Moquegua
- Tarata
- Tacna
- CHILE
- Arica
- Huancavelica
- Cusco

HIGHLIGHTS

1. Lunahuana
2. Islas Ballestas
3. Paracas National Reserve
4. Huacachina
5. Nazca Lines
6. Puerto Inca

0 — 100 kilometres

---

match. A more frequent service from Lima to all towns as far south as Ica, is the Soyuz/Peru Bus, Av México 333, La Victoria (☎01 427 6310, ⊚www.soyuz.com.pe); these buses leave every 10min during the day (every 30min at night) and can also be picked up from obvious bus stops along the Panamericana Sur Highway in Lima (where the highway is crossed by either Av Javier Prado Este or Av Benavides Este).

By colectivo from Ica White Mercedes minivans run routes between most of the towns and cities in the south. They are safe and comfortable, usually with a/c; the only downside is that they don't have set departure times, only leaving when full. You can generally find them outside of the standard bus terminals, but just ask around for the 'sprinters' and somebody will be able to point you in the right direction.

Cañete

Two hours' or so drive from Lima brings you to the busy market town of **CAÑETE**. This is not an obviously attractive town in itself, despite some colonial flavour, but the surrounding marigold and cotton fields and easy access to the nearby district and small town of Lunahuana (see opposite) grant it a certain appeal. Cañete and its surrounding area is the nearest place from Lima where you can get a feel for the rural desert coast and there is almost constant sunshine year round. New roads extend nearly all the way from Lima, but this particular valley has not yet been overdeveloped or populated with factories or *pueblos jovenes* (shanties).

ARRIVAL AND DEPARTURE   CAÑETE

BY BUS

Most buses on the south-coast road pass through Cañete and stop briefly where Av Dos de Mayo meets the old Panamericana, but you should check this with the bus company before buying your ticket if you need to get off, since there's a new stretch of Panamericana which now bypasses Cañete, taking a route between the town and the ocean.

Bus companies Peru Soyuz Bus (Jr Unanue 20; ☎01 5811391, ⊚soyuz.com.pe) and Ormeño (Av Carlos Zavala 177; ☎01 4275679) connect with Paracas, Ica and Nazca as well as north with Lima. Non-direct Cruz del Sur buses usually stop on Dos de Mayo. For Lunahuana take a bus for Yauyos (usually leaves daily around 3pm), which departs from Dos de Mayo. ETAS buses run once or twice a week from Cañete to Huancayo via Lunahuana.

Destinations Huancayo (1 or 2 per week; 10–15hr); Ica (every 20min; 2hr 30min); Lima (hourly; 2–3hr);

Lunahuana (several daily; 1hr); Nazca (every 20min; 4hr 15min); Paracas (every 20min; 2hr); Yauyos (1 or 2 per week; 5–8hr).

BY COLECTIVO

Colectivos all arrive on the old Panamericana in town, opposite the intersection with Dos de Mayo or on Dos de Mayo itself. As with most colectivos, these are informal operators with no specific depot. Colectivos generally leave during the day for Lunahuana from Dos de Mayo or from Jr Ayacucho and Av Ramos in Imperial, a district to the north of Cañete proper.

Lunahuana

2

Just 35km east of Cañete, the pleasant river-based resort of **LUNAHUANA** is home to several hotels and a wide variety of tour agencies offering trekking, mountain biking, valley tours, whitewater rafting or canoeing. The place varies in feel considerably depending on whether it is the busy time (mainly Dec–March, when the rapids can reach up to class IV, plus one week either side of the national holiday on July 28) – when there are festivals for the grape harvest combined with rafting competitions. Outside these, it's empty and laidback. Although numbers of foreign visitors are growing, it mainly sees a young and sporty crowd from Lima.

Lunahuana and the surrounding area consist of beautifully sculpted, dusty mountainsides surrounding a narrow, irrigated and fertile green valley floor. As well as abundant vineyards, which can be visited on tours (see below), the valley is also dedicated to cultivating maize, cotton, rice, avocados, chillies, limes, papayas and bananas. And as well as adventure sports, Lunahuana is a great base for exploring the local Inca archeological complex of **Incahuasi**.

On the plaza there's a fine colonial church with a cool interior and a sky-blue wooden vaulted ceiling. Within easy striking distance there's a horse dressage (*caballos de paso*) centre, a traditional hanging bridge, plus rustic **pisco haciendas**, such as the *Bodega Fidelina Candela*, (Anexo Jita, at Km 37, ☎012 841 030) dotted along the Cañete-Yauyos route on either side of Lunahuana.

Incahuasi

Incahuasi was established by the Inca Emperor Pachacuti (1438–71), who created his empire by expanding the territorial base out of the Cusco Valley. This was one of his coastal palaces, a hunting lodge and an optimum spot for his administrators and soldiers to control the flow of goods and people in and out of the Andes. What remains are scattered low stone and mud walls in a dominant position overlooking the northern section of Lunahuana town and the cemetery.

ARRIVAL AND DEPARTURE
LUNAHUANA

By bus Buses stop on Jr Grau, within walking distance of the Plaza de Armas.
By colectivo Colectivos drop you on Jr Grau or the Plaza de Armas. The far end of Jr Grau is close to the river and *Camping Lunahuana*.
By taxi Taxis to Lunahuana from Cañete (S/30) are usually available in the town centre, around the bus stops on the main through-road.

TOURS

Candela Tours Peru ☎996 299 266, ⓦcandelatours peru.com. Covers most adventure sports available in the area, from trekking to rafting. It offers a full day tour from Lima including a tour of the town and surrounds, taking in the nearby hanging bridge, a drive through the valley and a stop at an artisan market. The tour continues on to a winery, rafting or ziplining and a visit to a nearby beach at Cerro Azul. From S/135 per person.

Cicloturismo Peru ☎01 497 1660, ⓦcicloturismoperu .com. An online source of information about cycling tours, bike rentals and events, it also offers one- or two-night bike trips to Lunahuana.
Lunahuana Rafting Jr Grau 180 ☎999 579 709, ⓦlunahuanarafting.com. Tours for trekking and adventure action; rafting usually costs S/40 for about an hour on the river – including guide, transport and training

– depending on the season (price will be reduced in the low season, May–Oct).

Río Cañete Expediciones Jr Grau 284 ☎ 012 841 271, ⓦ riocanete.com. Offer guided runs from 21km to 5km, and also a two-day package that includes rafting, hiking and climbing.

ACCOMMODATION

Las Antorchas Carretera Central Km 31.5 ☎ 940 398 997. Comfortable, clean rooms, mostly reliable wi-fi and pleasant lounging areas make this a good mid-range option. The on-site restaurant out in the garden serves up wood-fired oven pizzas and great *camarón* (river shrimp) dishes; the owner is friendly and knowledgeable about all the sports and activities in the area. **S/105**

Camping Lunahuana Entry at the opposite end of Jr Grau to the Plaza de Armas. A well-set-up campground, with electricity, on the banks of the Cañete River, busy on weekends or holidays. Prices are likely to rise in high season. **S/15**

Camping El Tambo Annexo Condoray Km 41.2 ☎ 997 377 423, ⓦ lunahuanaeltambo.com. Carmen Hererra runs a clean and pleasant campsite with toilets, a nice garden and swimming pool, shared with the hotel of the same name, at Km 41.2, some 10km up the valley from town. **S/15**

★**La Confianza** Carretera Cañete ☎ 968 213 093, ⓦ laconfianza.com.pe. Out in the countryside, a 15min drive from town, this is the best place to really get out and relax in the area. Bungalows and wooden A-frames are set in a lush green space up against the river, and the surrounding landscape is stunning. The restaurant, set in an old bodega is excellent, offering a well-prepared and -presented range of local dishes – don't miss the trout ceviche. **S/210**

Hostal Casurinas Jr Grau 295 ☎ 01 284 1045. Cheap option with clean, hot showers and basic rooms, located near the action within the main Lunahuana settlement and near the Plaza de Armas. Rooms are more expensive during busy weekends and national fiestas. **S/40**

Refugio de Santiago C Real 33, Paullo Km 31 ☎ 01 436 2717, ⓦ refugiodesantiago.com. A beautifully furnished hostel inside a colonial-style house, with an internal courtyard bar and a few acres of gardens with outside tables, this has one of the finest restaurants (dishes based around indigenous and ancient fruits, herbs and vegetables) south of Lima. They also offer camping in the garden, and run walking and minibus tours to sites around the valley. Price is per person and includes all meals. Camping **S/10**, doubles **S/190**

EATING

Piscopollo Plaza de Armas. Everybody loves *Piscopollo*. The owner is a local legend, extremely knowledgeable about the area and makes a killer pollo with his not-so-secret recipe (S/20–45). Daily 1–10pm.

El Refugio de Santiago C Real 33, Paullo Km 31. This place provides undoubtedly the best cuisine in the valley, served out in the gardens in fine weather. The owner-chef takes great pride in cooking fresh home-grown herbs and vegetables; unfortunately, it is not always open to day-visitors. Call in advance and check opening times outside high season (S/25–60). Daily noon–6pm.

Valle Hermoso Piscuy Anexo San Jeronimo Km 33. A simple, homely place with friendly owners, and a menu including *cuy* marinated in pisco – one of the best dishes in the valley (S/50). The *chicharron de conejo* (fried rabbit) is also a winner. Daily, lunch only.

DIRECTORY

Banks and exchange Banco de la Nación, Jr Grau 398, is the only option, although the exchange rate can be poor so it's best to bring enough soles with you when visiting the area.

Internet Most hotels have wi-fi but there are little internet cabins close to the main Plaza, at Jr Grau 311.

Chincha

Languishing at the top of a cliff, **CHINCHA** is a relatively rich oasis that appears after a stretch of almost Saharan landscape – and a mightily impressive sand dune. A rather crowded and noisy little coastal centre renowned for its cheap wines and variety of **piscos**, Chincha is a strong cultural hub for **Afro-Peruvian culture**. The town was developed during the early colonial period when Africans (mainly from Guinea) were brought over as slaves to work on the cotton plantations. Chincha is dominated by two roads running north to south; most hotels and restaurants are on the main Panamericana itself. For the passing tourist, Chincha isn't particularly attractive, and musically it's a bit dry outside the festivals. Nearby El Carmen has more charm, and you'll be more likely to find some Afro-Peruvian music and dance, with the rhythm of the *cajon*, a traditional, boxlike wooden percussion instrument, setting the pace.

The Huacas of Chincha

A taxi from Chincha will take you to the sites for S/40–50, depending on how long you want the driver to wait

The area has a number of ruins, with the **Huacas of Chincha** lying scattered about the oasis. Dominated in pre-Inca days by the Cuismancu (or Chincha) state, activity focused around what were probably ceremonial pyramids. One of these, the majestic **Huaca Centinela** – also known as the little city of Chinchacamac – sits in the valley between the Chincha plateau and the ocean, around thirty minutes' walk from the town, some 8km off the Panamericana. Not far away, 40km up the Castrovirreyna road (which leaves the Highway at Km 230) is another impressive Cuismancu ruin, Tambo Colorado (see p.122).

2

Hacienda San José

Pueblo San José • Daily 9am–6pm • Free; catacomb tours 45min, US$3 • ☎ 056 221 458 • Continue along the Panamericana Sur until Km 203, turn left and continue 10km until just before El Carmen, when you will see a sign for the hacienda; turn right and continue 2km until you see the hotel

Don't miss the **Hacienda San José** – now converted into a hotel (see below) – set 9km southeast of Chincha in an extensive plantation. Its morbid history includes the tale of an owner murdered on the house's main steps by his slaves, and it still sports impressive Churrigueresque-domed towers built in the 1680s. Non-guests can use the pool and watch local folklore shows, and there are **tours** around the labyrinthine **catacombs** containing prison cells still clearly showing the poor conditions in which slaves were once shackled; a horrific but important reminder.

ARRIVAL AND DEPARTURE   CHINCHA

By bus Most bus connections to and from Chincha are at the Terminal Terrestre on Av Benavides, close to the big bend in the Panamericana Sur as it enters the urban areas of town from the north. Peru Soyuz Bus (Av Benavides 704; ☎056 269 239, ⓦsoyuzonline.com.pe) connects every 20min south with Paracas, Ica and Nazca as well as north with Lima.

By colectivo Colectivos and taxis drop off and pick up on main Panamericana Sur, as well as around the big bend in the highway as it enters town from the north and crosses over Jr Santo Domingo.

ACCOMMODATION

Casa Albergue Huaranjapo Panamerica Sur Km 203 ☎ 998 785 286, ⓦhuaranjapo.com. A welcoming house set in the middle of a large green space with fruit trees. Plenty of options to keep you busy, from a volleyball pitch to an inviting hammock area. **S/170**

Hacienda San José Panamericana Sur Km 203 ☎056 313 332, ⓦcasahaciendasanjose.com. A stunningly restored building with a dark history, this old-style hacienda and ex-slave plantation offers the chance to experience the luxury of another era, but also reminds what this luxury was built upon. Stunning rooms and the grounds are a pleasure to explore, but there's not much to do nearby; come for pure relaxation. **S/180**

Punto Sur Lodge C Los Eucaliptos s/n ☎ 056 267 528, ⓦpuntosurlodge.com. Simple and friendly with a particularly nice pool and garden area. **S/100**

CHINCHA'S FESTIVALS

The main local festival – **National Pisco Day** – takes place on the third Saturday in September, when things really get lively along this section of the coast. The area is also well known for its traditionally rhythmic music and annual dance festival, **Verano Negro**, at the end of February. In November, the **Festival de Danzas Negras** is excellent, a vibrant dance event based on Afro-Peruvian traditions; in both cases the celebrations are liveliest in El Carmen, 10km southeast of Chincha.

EATING AND DRINKING

Bodega Naldo Navarro Pasaje Santa Rosa, Sunampe ☎ 056 271 356, ⓦ vinosnaldonavarro.com. A 100-year-old bodega that's one of the best places for pisco and local wine (*vino dulce*) (S/10–25). Based 1km north of Chincha, it offers free guided tours and samples; call to check opening times and when there are special music events.

El Batan Panamericana Sur 791 Km 197.5. A petrol station diner right on the Panamericana with gourmet aspirations – and it delivers. International and local creole favourites are all superbly prepared (S/15–45). Great *empañadas*. Daily 8am–6pm.

El Refugio de Mamainé Cacerio Guayabo, El Carmen. Just before El Carmen lies one of the region's best-loved restaurants, run by the gregarious queen of creole flavours, Esther Cartagena. Nothing fancy, just great food, abundant and affordable. The best place to try all the local favourites such as *carapulcra* (a spicy pork and dried potato stew) and *pollo con sopa seca* (basil pasta with chicken), *tacu tacu* (a fried rice and bean cake) and *cau cau* (tripe stew), all between S/15 and S/30. There's a good chance you'll be treated to some live music. Daily, lunch only.

Pisco and around

Less than three hours by bus from Lima, the old port town of **PISCO** is the gateway to neighbouring town, **Paracas**, 12km away and previously known as **El Chaco**. Pisco is a cheaper and less touristy base for visiting the **Paracas National Reserve**, **Ballestas Islands** and the well-preserved Inca coastal outpost of **Tambo Colorado**. The two towns are also decent stop-offs before heading up into the Andes: you can take roads from here to Huancavelica and Huancayo, as well as to Ayacucho and Cusco.

Pisco today, however, is a shadow of its former self. An 8.0 magnitude earthquake hit in the evening of August 15, 2007, devastating the town and the surrounding area. Some 70 percent of the town's buildings were destroyed, hundreds of people were killed and over 15,000 left homeless. Much of the emergency relief money never made it to the people who most needed it, and government promises of rapid redevelopment have, by and large, failed to materialize.

Plaza de Armas

Pisco's focus of activity is the **Plaza de Armas** and adjoining **Jirón Comercio**; every evening the plaza is crowded with people walking and talking, buying *tejas* (small sweets made from pecan nuts) from street sellers or chatting in one of several laidback cafés and bars around the square. Clustered about the plaza, with its statue of liberator San Martín poised in the shade of ancient ficus trees, are a few fine colonial showpieces, including the mansion where San Martín stayed on his arrival in Peru, half a block west of the plaza. Unusual in its Moorish style, the **Consejo Provincial** (or Municipal Palace), just to the left if you're facing the earthquake-destroyed church on the Plaza de Armas, is painted in striking blue and white in memory of San Martín's own colours.

Avenida San Martín

If you have an hour or so to spare, it's worth exploring **Avenida San Martín** from the plaza west (fifteen to twenty minutes' walking to the sea), but beware – there have been tourist muggings here in recent years, so go in a group. Here you can see the decaying remains of the old pier, second in size only to the Muelle de Pacasmayo in the north of Peru, and notice just how much further out the sea edge is today than it clearly was a hundred or so years ago.

San Andrés

Reached via taxi from Pisco (S/10). Moving on, there are usually at least two buses hourly on to the El Chaco wharf in El Balneario, where boats leave for the Ballestas Islands (see p.116)

South along the shore from Pisco town towards Paracas, the road keeps close to the shoreline and there's a fisherman's jetty at **SAN ANDRÉS**, where fresh fish is received and

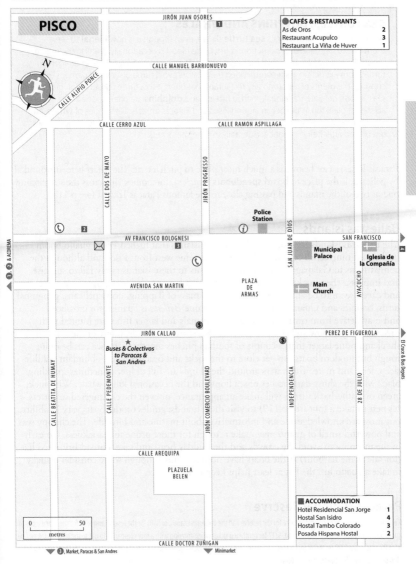

PISCO

N

CAFÉS & RESTAURANTS

As de Oros	2
Restaurant Acupulco	3
Restaurant La Viña de Huver	1

JIRÓN JUAN OSORES

CALLE ALIPIO PONCE

CALLE MANUEL BARRIONUEVO

CALLE CERRO AZUL

CALLE RAMON ASPILLAGA

CALLE DOS DE MAYO

JIRÓN PROGRESSO

Police Station

SAN JUAN DE DIOS

SAN FRANCISCO

AV FRANCISCO BOLOGNESI

Municipal Palace

Iglesia de la Compañía

AVENIDA SAN MARTIN

PLAZA DE ARMAS

Main Church

AYACUCHO

& ACOREMA

JIRÓN CALLAO

PEREZ DE FIGUEROLA

★ Buses & Colectivos to Paracas & San Andres

CALLE BEATITA DE HUMAY

CALLE PEDEMONTE

JIRÓN COMERCIO BOULEVARD

INDEPENDENCIA

28 DE JULIO

El Cruce & Bus Depots

CALLE AREQUIPA

PLAZUELA BELEN

ACCOMMODATION

Hotel Residencial San Jorge	1
Hostal San Isidro	4
Hostal Tambo Colorado	3
Posada Hispana Hostal	2

0   50
metres

CALLE DOCTOR ZUÑIGAN

Market, Paracas & San Andres   Minimarket

taken straight to the nearby restaurants or to Pisco market. This is a great place to enjoy a lunchtime ceviche.

Paracas

Paracas, lying on the road from San Andrés past the Pisco air force base, is a decidedly more scenic place to base yourself than Pisco. Also known as El Balneario or El Chaco, it was once a spot for wealthy Limeños, whose expensive resort hotels and large bungalows line the beach close to the entrance to the reserve, but plenty of reasonably priced hostels and restaurants have appeared of late. It's also possible to **camp** on the sand, though the nearby

2

> ## SEA TURTLES, DOLPHINS AND WHALES
>
> San Andrés is still known for its **sea turtle** dishes, even though it is now **illegal** to serve them due to the danger of extinction. Warm turtle blood is occasionally drunk in the region, reputedly as a cure for bronchial problems. These days, in order to save these endangered turtles from extinction, it's recommended that visitors avoid turtle dishes and perhaps even consider the merits of reporting any restaurant that offers it to a turtle conservation group. The seas around here are traditionally rich in fish life, and **dolphins** are often spotted. The abundant plankton in the ocean around Pisco and Paracas attracts five species of **whale**, and in 1988 a new, small species – the *Mesoplodon peruvianus*, which can be up to 4m long – was discovered after being caught accidentally in fishermen's nets.

Paracas Reserve (see below) is a much nicer place to pitch a tent. The wharf here, surrounded by pelicans, is the place to board **speedboats** (*lanchas*), for a quick zip across the sea, circling one or two of the islands and passing close to the famous Paracas Trident (see p.118).

Ballestas Islands

The **Ballestas Islands** (one of a whole string of islands that fuelled Peru's guano boom in the mid-nineteenth century), lie off the coast due west from Pisco and although the comparisons to Galapagos seem optimistic, visits to these islands rarely fail to surprise and impress. These rocky outposts, parts of which have eroded into impressive arches and caves, seem to be alive and moving with a mass of flapping, noisy pelicans, penguins, terns, boobies and Guanay cormorants. The name *Ballesta* is Spanish for crossbow, and may derive from times when marine mammals and larger fish were hunted with mechanical crossbow-style harpoons. There are scores of islands, many of them relatively small and none larger than a couple of football pitches together. The sea can be quite rough but modern boats can get close to the rocks and beaches where abundant wildlife sleep, feed and mate. The waters around the islands are full of life, sometimes sparkling black with the shiny dark bodies of sea lions and the occasional killer whale. With luck, green or leatherback turtles will make an appearance, or even the endangered sea otters. It's best to take a **tour** (see p.119) to visit these islands; guides on the boats vary in ability, but most are knowledgeable and informative about marine and bird life. The choppy seas and powerful smell of guano may make it tough for those prone to seasickness. Go early in the morning to avoid the crowds and the midday heat, and take a broad-brimmed hat (for sale at the harbour) as the boats have no shade and although some consider it lucky to take a guano hit, the hat at least helps keep it off the face.

Paracas National Reserve

Reserve 6am–6pm • S/22 combined price for the reserve and the Ballestas Islands, or S/10 for the reserve and S/15 for the islands; pay at guard booth, located on the entrance road. S/17 for combined ticket when entering with a tour company • To get to the reserve, take a taxi from Paracas (from S/20 per hr) or join a tour organized with one of the local agents (see p.119) or hotels • **Paracas Visitor Centre** Lies 2km beyond guard booth • Daily 7am–6pm • Free

With even more wildlife than the Ballestas Islands (see above), the **Paracas National Reserve**, a few kilometres south of Paracas, was established in 1975, mainly to protect the marine wildlife. Its bleak 1170 square kilometres of pampa are frequently lashed by strong winds and sandstorms (*paracas* means "raining sand" in Quechua). Home to some of the world's richest seas (a couple of hundred hectares of ocean is included within the reserve's borders), an abundance of marine plankton gives nourishment to a vast array of fish and various marine species including octopus, squid, whale, shark, dolphin, bass, plaice and marlin. This unique desert is also a staging point for a host of migratory birds and acts as a sanctuary for many endangered species. Schools of dolphins play in the waves offshore; condors scour the peninsula for food; small desert foxes come down to

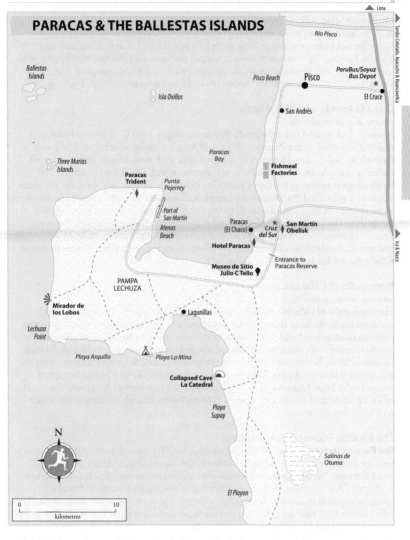

PARACAS & THE BALLESTAS ISLANDS

Río Pisco

Lima

Ballestas
Islands

Isla Ovillos

Pisco Beach

Pisco

**PeruBus/Soyuz
Bus Depot**

El Cruce

San Andrés

Three Marias
Islands

Paracas
Bay

**Fishmeal
Factories**

**Paracas
Trident**

Punta
Pejerrey

Port of
San Martín

Atenas
Beach

Paracas
(El Chaco)

Cruz
del Sur

**San Martín
Obelisk**

Hotel Paracas

**Museo de Sitio
Julio C Tello**

Entrance to
Paracas Reserve

PAMPA
LECHUZA

**Mirador de
los Lobos**

Lagunillas

Lechuza
Point

Playa Arquillo

Playa La Mina

**Collapsed Cave
La Catedral**

Playa
Supay

Salinas de
Otuma

El Playón

N

0 — 10
kilometres

Tambo Colorado, Ayacucho & Huancavelica

Ica & Nazca

the beaches looking for birds and dead sea lions; and lizards scrabble across the hot sands. People have also been active here – predecessors of the pre-Inca Paracas culture arrived here some 9000 years ago, reaching their peak between 2000 and 500 BC.

On the way from Pisco to the reserve, the road passes some unpleasant-smelling fishmeal-processing factories, which are causing environmental concern due to spillages of fish oil that pollute the bay, endangering bird and sea-mammal life. Just before the entrance to the reserve, you'll pass a bleak concrete obelisk vaguely shaped like a nineteenth-century sailing boat, built in 1970 to commemorate the landing of San Martín here on September 8, 1820, on his mission to liberate Peru from the Spanish stranglehold.

Cycling is encouraged in the reserve, though there are no rental facilities and, if you do enter on a bike, keep on the main tracks because the tyre marks will damage the surface of the desert.

Museo de Sitio Julio C Tello

Located 2km beyond the reserve entrance and park office at Km 27 of the Carretera Pisco • Mon–Sun 9am–5pm • S/6

Right between the two major Paracas archeological sites – Cerro Colorado and Cabeza Largas – this **museum** depicts human life here over the last 9000 years, with interpretative exhibits relating to the national park and a wide range of Paracas artefacts – mummies, ceramics, funerary cloths and a reconstructed dwelling.

Cerro Colorado and Wari Kayan

East of the Museo de Sitio Julio C Tello

It was at and around **Cerro Colorado** that archeologist Julio C. Tello made the first major discoveries of the Paracas culture and found remains which could be dated as far back as 3000 years. He unearthed burial sites with two distinct styles: a deeper, earlier technique denominated Paracas Cavernas which saw mummies buried in bottle-shaped tombs at depths of up to 7m below the surface, while on the northern slope, at a site called **Wari Kayan,** he found shallower gravesites like small rooms where some mummies were found seated, facing the sea, among ceramics, weapons and foodstuffs. The burial cloths of this Paracas Necropolis stage are the best-known Paracas embroideries, whose intricate and colourful designs are considered among the best pre-Columbian textile work; many of which can be seen at the **Museo Regional Adolfo Bermúdez Jenkins** in Ica (see p.125).

Necropolis of Cabeza Largas

Just outside the Museo de Sitio at Km 27

The **Necropolis of Cabeza Largas** is another Paracas Necropolis site, where several excellent examples were found of the deformed, elongated craniums which have also come to be associated with the Paracas of this era. Most mummies were wrapped in *vicuña* skins or rush matting, and buried along with personal objects like shell beads, bone necklaces, lances, net bags and cactus-spine needles. A little further on, near the beach where dozens of pink flamingoes gather between July and November (they return to the high Andean lakes for breeding from December to May), are the remains of a Chavín-related settlement, known as **Disco Verde**, though all there is left to see now are a few adobe walls.

The Paracas Trident (El Candelabro)

The **Paracas Trident**, a massive 128-metre-high by 74-metre-wide candelabra carved into the tall sea cliffs and facing out towards the Pacific Ocean, is one of Paracas's main features. No one knows its function or its creator, though Erich von Däniken, author of *Chariots of the Gods*, speculated that it was a sign for extraterrestrial spacecraft, pointing the way (inaccurately as it happens) towards the mysterious Nazca Lines (see p.131) that are inland to the southeast; others suggest it was constructed as a navigational aid for eighteenth-century pirates. It seems more likely, however, that it was a kind of pre-Inca ritual object, representing a cactus or tree of life, and that high priests during the Paracas or Nazca eras worshipped the setting sun from this spot. A poorly signposted trail leads 15km across the desert from the Museo de Sitio (see above); the first 2km follow the main park road, and then just before the modern port complex of San Martín, a sandy side-road leads away from the sea and around the hills on the outer edge of the peninsula towards the Trident. The best way to appreciate the Trident is on the outward journey to the Ballestas Islands, just as you pass the peninsula.

Lagunillas and around

The tiny and likeable port of **Lagunillas**, some 6km from the entrance to the park, is a fishing hamlet with a few huts serving *conchitas* (scallops) and other great seafood. Try *La Tia Chela* and *El Che*, two favourites in the area. Lagunillas is the only place within the Paracas reserve where you can buy a meal and drinks – but there's no accommodation. From here, it's possible to appreciate the unique and very beautiful peninsula, so flat that if the sea rose just another metre the whole place would be submerged. Pelicans and sea lions hang around the bobbing boats waiting for the fisherman to drop a fish, and little trucks regularly arrive to carry the catch back into Pisco.

Beaches near Lagunillas

Lagunillas is home to a few lovely **beaches**, including **La Mina** – just a 20min walk away and a good place for **camping** – and **Yimaque**, an empty beach where you can stay for days, often without seeing anyone. A track goes off 5km north from Lagunillas to a longer sandy beach, **Arquillo**; on the cliffs a few hundred metres beyond there's a **viewing platform** (Mirador de los Lobos) looking out over a large colony of sea lions. To the north is Atenas, a stony beach known for one particular resident, El Griego. From Thursdays to Sundays he serves the best grilled scallops in the area, at a very decent price, while nearby *Intimar* is a peaceful place to stop over for the night on the beach. Another path leads north from here, straight across the peninsula to the Trident and on to Punta Pejerrey. There have been **reports of stingrays** on some of the beaches, so take care, particularly if you're without transport or company; check first with the fishermen at Lagunillas which beaches are the safest.

ARRIVAL AND DEPARTURE   PISCO AND AROUND

By bus All buses pass through El Cruce (also known as San Clemente or Repartición), where the Panamericana meets the turn-off to Pisco. Several kilometres further along the Panamericana another road turns off right to the Paracas settlement, in the bay around El Chaco wharf, a few kilometres before the entrance to the National Reserve. Peru Soyuz Buses (☎ 056 269 239) has a depot at El Cruce. Cruz del Sur (☎ 056 536 636) goes direct to Paracas, where

it has a depot at the entrance to the town on Av Principal. The Oltursa bus from Lima (☎ 994 616 492) also stops in Paracas, on Av Chaco, next to the hotel *Refugio del Pirata*. From El Cruce, there are regular colectivos from here to Pisco (S/2; 10min) and Paracas (S/5; 25min); to continue south, get a ticket at the Soyuz depot.

Destinations Ica (several daily; 1hr); Lima (several daily; 3–4hr); Nazca (several daily; 3–4hr).

GETTING AROUND

Most travellers use one of the local tour companies (see below) located in town or affiliated to hostels to get the most out of their time in and around Pisco and Paracas.

By taxi Pisco is small enough to explore on foot. Should you need one, a taxi anywhere in the central area should cost around S/4. A taxi from Pisco to Paracas is around S/20,

while colectivos leave from near the market or on Callao and Pedemonte and cost S/3 (15min).

INFORMATION AND TOURS

Tourist information At the regional tourism directorate (Mon–Fri 8am–7pm; ⓦ pisco.info) in the Subprefectura's office next to the police station on the Plaza de Armas; they also have a list of official guides in the area and sometimes maps or photocopied information on the town, islands and local beaches. A somewhat better information service is offered by the staff at the *Posada Hispana Hostal* (see p.120), who provide informed details about most of the local sites of interest and worthwhile places to eat.

Tours The companies below operate package excursions to the Ballestas Islands (see p.116) and Paracas National Reserve (see p.116) with good guides and a reliable service.

A speedboat takes you out to the Ballestas Islands; after this most people continue on the tour from the Playa El Chaco wharf (Paracas Bay) to the main sights in the Paracas National Reserve. It's a standard package costing S/35 (2–3hr) for the islands morning trip and a further S/35 for the afternoon tour of the reserve. Most of these companies also organize tours to Tambo Colorado (see p.122) and offer a discount for ten or more people. Choose from: Paracas Overland, C San Francisco 111 (☎ 056 533 855, ⓦ paracasoverland.com.pe); Paracas Explorer, Av Paracas Mz D Lote 5 (*Hostal Los Frayles*), El Chaco (☎ 056 545 141); Zarcillo Connections, C Independencia A20, Pisco (☎ 056 536 636, ⓦ zarcilloconnections.com). From Lima, go with

2

Haku Tours (☎983 473 724, ⓦhakutours.com), a well-run and friendly non-profit operation with a strong social responsibility programme. A flyover of the Nazca Lines from the Pisco airport is possible, but is considerably longer (around 1hr 40min) and much more expensive – around S/840. Also try Tikariy, Amador Merino Reyna 551 Lima (☎01 712 7000).

ACCOMMODATION

Most of the accommodation options below are located 12km south along the seafront and by Paracas Bay, pleasantly away from noisy Pisco town centre; Paracas is quickly being developed as a resort.

PISCO

Hotel Residencial San Jorge Barrionuevo 133 ☎056 532 885. A modern hotel, three short blocks north of the town centre, and with two entrances: one on the Barrio Nuevo road, one block nearer the plaza than the Jr Juan Oscores entrance. Rooms are clean and well-furnished, with private bath, and there's a bit of a garden with ample parking. S̲/̲1̲3̲0̲

Hostal San Isidro San Clemente 103 ☎056 536 471, ⓦsanisidrohostal.com. In a relatively peaceful and safe area of Pisco, this place is friendly and clean and there is a pool to cool off in. Wi-fi works most of the time. Tours can be arranged via staff. S̲/̲7̲0̲

Hostal Tambo Colorado Av Bolognesi 159 ☎056 531 379, ⓦhostaltambocolorado.com. Just around the corner from the Plaza de Armas, this is about as good as it gets in Pisco for quality and price. Great staff with plenty of local knowledge who can also organize tours. Rooms aren't exactly stylish but are impeccably clean and comfortable with great showers and surprisingly good wi-fi. Breakfasts are good, but cost S/8–10 extra. S̲/̲7̲0̲

Posada Hispana Hostal Av Bolognesi 222 ☎056 536 363, ⓦposadahispana.com. One of the best choices in Pisco – very safe and well decorated, with friendly and helpful staff who are always happy to provide good tourist information. All rooms are clean and equipped with a TV, telephone, private bath and reliable hot water. Laundry facilities are available, and breakfast is served on the rooftop patio. S̲/̲6̲0̲

PARACAS

La Hacienda Bahia Paracas Urb Sto Domingo Lote 25 ☎056 581 370, ⓦhoteleslahacienda.com. Among the best of the resort style hotels along the beach, La Hacienda has all the luxuries and comforts necessary for complete relaxation. Rooms have a tiny private terrace and overlook the huge pool and the sea. Breakfasts are delicious and the sea views from the restaurant a winner. S̲/̲6̲6̲0̲

Hostal El Mirador El Chaco ☎056 545 086, ⓦelmiradorhotel.com. A popular place close to the ocean best loved for its large pool; they also have a games room and serve a decent breakfast. The staff are friendly and can help organize tours. Rooms are showing some age, with

dated furniture, but are spacious. Best to make reservations in advance. S̲/̲2̲1̲0̲

Hotel Paracas Av Paracas 173, Ribera del Mar, El Balneario ☎056 581 333, ⓦstarwoodhotels.com. A luxurious option that hits all the notes of a high-end resort, with infinity pools, an excellent bar and restaurant (open to non-residents) all stylishly designed and right on the ocean. S̲/̲9̲6̲0̲

Icthus Paracas Asociacion San Martín Mz J1 Lt 29 ☎989 178 278. All you need from a backpackers' – cheap, clean dorms and rooms, wi-fi and a well-equipped shared kitchen. The owners are nearly always present and can help arrange every step of your stay. Dorms S̲/̲1̲8̲, doubles S̲/̲5̲0̲

Kokopelli Hostel Paracas Av Paracas 128 ☎056 311 824, ⓦhostelkokopelli.com. Clean, cool common spaces with colourfully painted walls, a lively bar day and night and the beachfront location make this the most popular backpackers' in town. The beds are comfortable in the dorms, and the private rooms are light, spacious and welcoming. Dorms S̲/̲3̲6̲, doubles S̲/̲8̲0̲

Refugio del Pirata Av Paracas D-6 ☎056 545 054, ⓦrefugiodelpirata.com. Some of the tidy rooms have sea views; there is a parking area, also wi-fi and cable TV. S̲/̲1̲8̲0̲

Residencial Los Frayles José de San Martín, Mz J1 Lote 4 ☎056 531 487, ⓦhotelresidenciallosfrayles.com. Genuinely welcoming and well located in the centre of town, this is one of the best options for those not splashing out on one of the expensive resorts. The rooms are standard, the wi-fi decent and the pool area with bar and sun loungers good for relaxing after a day of tours. S̲/̲1̲7̲0̲

PARACAS NATIONAL RESERVE

Camping The reserve's natural attractions include plenty of superb, deserted beaches where you can camp wherever you like for days without seeing anything except the lizards and birdlife, and maybe a couple of fishing boats. F̲r̲e̲e̲

LAGUNILLAS

Intimar Atenas beach ☎991 350 656, ⓦinti-mar.com. A four-room hostel offering absolute peace and quiet, stunning views, great food (and pisco) and plenty of wildlife – including a scallop farm. S̲/̲2̲4̲0̲

2

EATING AND DRINKING

Most Pisco restaurants specialize in a wide range of locally caught fish and seafood. Nightlife is restricted to the lively pubs and bars, on or within a block or two of the main plaza, as well as on the beach and in hotels out in the Paracas area.

PISCO

As de Oros San Martín 472 ☎056 532 010. A local classic, the *As* has been around for over 35 years; now grown up and moved to a bigger, fancier location with outdoor seating next to a swimming pool. Still, nothing has taken away from the flavour; the food – regional creole favourites – is still among the town's best. Try the *parihuela* (S/30), a powerful seafood soup. Tues–Sat 11.30am–11pm, Sun until 10pm.

Puro Pisco Av Genaro Medrano N0 460, San Andrés ☎056 542 384. Fresh seafood, well prepared and all round views of the sea and the harbour. Prices range form S/25 to S/35, and portions big. Go for sunset. Daily 9am–5pm.

Restaurant Acapulco Av Genaro Medrano 620, San Andrés ☎956 757 575. Located just fifty yards or so from the main fishermen's wharf at San Andrés, this is one of the more traditional and popular seafood restaurants in the region, serving massive fish dishes at reasonable prices (S/20–35). Mon–Sat 11.30am–8.30pm, Sun 11.30–5.30pm.

Restaurant La Viña de Huver Prolongación Cerro Azul, next to the Parque Zonal ☎056 536 456. Just a little way from the centre of town, this is one of the busiest

lunch spots in Pisco, serving excellent, huge and relatively inexpensive ceviche (S/30) and other seafood dishes in a bustling and appealing environment. Wed–Mon 11am–5.30pm.

PARACAS

Il Covo Av San Martín s/n ☎056 530 324, ⓦilcovo.pe. The smartest place in town outside the excellent resort hotel restaurants, *Il Covo* simply serves up great Italian food in a classy dining room. Can't go wrong with anything on the menu, and the pizza (S/30–40) is always a good option. Pricey, with most dishes over S/40, but worth it for a change. Tues–Sun 12–3.30, Tues–Sat 7.30–11pm.

Restaurant La Brisa Marina El Malecón. Open for lunch only, this restaurant offers very tasty seafood out at Paracas; on the promenade close to El Chaco wharf and San Andrés, it has excellent fresh fish and clams. Daily 11am–3pm.

Restaurant Paracas Opposite the pier at El Chaco ☎056 535 138. Up on the fourth floor, the view overlooking the pier and harbour are worth the visit alone. The seafood dishes (S/40) are excellent and the service good, although it can get very busy and service inevitably suffers. Daily 8am–11pm.

DIRECTORY

Banks and exchange Banco de Credito, Perez de Figuerola 162, and Banco Continental, next door on the corner of the Plaza and Independencia. Most hotels and the tour companies (see p.119) will change dollars for cash. The best rates are from the *cambistas* on the corner of the

pedestrian boulevard between Comercio and Progreso and Plaza de Armas.

Health The hospital is at C San Juan de Dios 350.

Police Plaza de Armas, C San Francisco ☎056 227 673.

Post office Av Bolognesi 173 (Mon–Sat 8am–7pm).

Tambo Colorado

☎056 233 881 • Mon–Fri 8am–7pm, Sat & Sun 8am–6pm • Entry S/5

Some 48km northeast of Pisco, and 327km south of Lima, the ruins at **TAMBO COLORADO** were originally a fortified administrative centre, probably built by the Chincha before being adapted and used as an Inca coastal outpost. Its position at the base of steep foothills in the Pisco river valley was perfect for controlling the flow of people and produce along the ancient road down from the Andes. You can still see dwellings, offices, storehouses and row upon row of barracks and outer walls, some of them even retaining traces of coloured paints. The rains have taken their toll, but even so this is considered one of the best-preserved **adobe ruins** in Peru – roofless, but otherwise virtually intact.

ARRIVAL AND DEPARTURE   TAMBO COLORADO

By bus It's best to visit Tambo Colorado with one of the local tour agents (see p.119) but you can also travel there independently from Pisco: take the Ormeño bus from J San Francisco or the Oropesa bus from C Comercio (both leave most mornings, but check first with the bus company as

departure times and frequencies vary from day to day; approximately S/12 each way). The bus takes the surfaced Ayacucho road, which runs straight through the site, and the ruins are around 20 minutes beyond the village of Humay.

South from Pisco

South from Pisco, the Panamericana Sur Highway sweeps some 70km inland to reach the fertile wine-producing Ica Valley, a virtual oasis in this stretch of bleak desert. **Pozo Santo**, the only real landmark en route, is distinguished by a small, towered and whitewashed chapel, built on the site of an underground well. Legend has it that when Padre Guatemala, the friar Ramón Rojas, died on this spot, water miraculously began to flow from the sands. Now there's a restaurant here where colectivo drivers sometimes stop for a snack, but little else.

Beyond Pozo Santo, the Panamericana crosses the Pampa de Villacuri and, further down the highway, the pretty roadside village of **Guadalupe** (at Km 293) signals the beginning of the Ica oasis.

2

Ica

An old but busy city with around 170,000 inhabitants, **ICA** sits in a fecund valley, close to enormous sand dunes some 400m above sea level and around 50km from the ocean. It's one of the first places south of Lima where you can virtually guarantee **sunny weather** most of the year.

The surrounding region is famous throughout Peru for its wine and pisco production. The city's foundation (1563) went hand in hand with the introduction of grapevines to South America, and for most Peruvian visitors it is the **bodegas**, or wineries, that are the town's biggest draw. However, the **Museo Regional**'s superb collections of pre-Columbian ceramics and Paracas, Ica and Nazca cultural artefacts would alone make the city worth an excursion, despite some damage by the 2007 quake.

Ica's streets and plazas are crowded from early morning to evening with hundreds of little *tico* taxis, all beeping their horns to catch potential passengers' attention and making crossing the streets a dangerous affair. Aside from the traffic and the occasional pickpocket – particularly round the market area – Ica is a pleasant place with a friendly population. After a day or less, though, most visitors are ready to head for the desert oasis of **Huacachina**, a few kilometres to the southwest. On the edge of town is the rather ramshackle suburb of **Cachiche**, known throughout Peru as a traditional sanctuary for white witches (see box, p.128).

Brief history

Founded in 1563, and originally called Villa de Valverde de Ica, the settlement was moved (due to regional earthquake activity) after only five years, and renamed **San Jerónimo de Ica**. It was subsequently moved several times until finding itself in its present position in a relatively sheltered river valley protected slightly from the coastal weather (especially the mists) by large sand dunes, but still quite a way from the foothills of the Andes to the east.

The Plaza de Armas

Ica's colonial heart – the **Plaza de Armas**, site of the 1820 declaration of independence from Spain – remains its modern centre, smart and friendly, with the inclusion of an obelisk and fountains. The **cathedral** on the plaza was first constructed in the eighteenth century then remodelled in 1814 with a Neoclassical exterior and a Baroque altar and pulpit. Running east from the plaza, the modern commercial spine is the busy Avenida Grau with the market area parallel, a couple of blocks to the north. Walking alone east of this area is not recommended, as **muggings** are not unheard of.

ACCOMMODATION
Diamond Monkey Lodge	3
Hostal Sol de Ica	7
Hotel Arameli	1
Hotel Villa Jazmin	4
Hotel Viñas Queirolo	8
Ica Wasi Hospedaje	5
Ica's Desert House	6
Sol y Luna	2

CAFÉS & RESTAURANTS
Calor Iqueno	3
Don Juan Tejas y Chocotejas	4
El Otro Peñoncito	6
La Olla de Juanita	1
Restaurant Galindo	2
Restaurant La Estación	7
Restaurant Pastelería Anita	5
Restaurant Rumi Wasi	8

Ica's churches

Open to the public during regular church hours

Apart from the cathedral, Ica's important churches are within a few blocks of the plaza. The church of **La Merced**, southwest of the plaza, contains Padre Guatemala's tomb – said to give immense good fortune if touched on New Year's Day. Around the corner on Avenida Municipalidad is the more recent, grander **San Francisco** church, whose stained-glass windows dazzle against the strong sunlight. Quite a stroll south of the plaza, down Jirón Lima, then left along Prolongación Ayabaca, stands a third major church, **El Santuario de Luren**. Built on the site of a hermitage founded in 1556, the present construction, Neoclassical in style and with three brick-built *portales*, houses the Imagen del Señor de Luren, an image of the patron saint of the town, a national shrine and a centre for procession and pilgrimage at Easter as well as on the third Sunday in October.

Ica's mansions

There are a few **mansions** of note near the plaza, including the **Casona del Marqués de Torre Hermosa**, block 1 of Calle Libertad. Now belonging to the Banco Continental, it

FIESTAS IN ICA

There are several important **fiestas** in Ica throughout the year. The best is in **March** after the grape harvest, when there are open-air concerts, fairs, handicraft markets, cockfighting and *caballo de paso* meetings (horse dressage – where Peruvian Paso horses are trained by riders to dance and prance for events or competitions). Over the **Semana de Ica** (June 12–19), based around the colonial founding of Ica, there are more festivities, including religious processions and fireworks, and again in the last week of September for the **Semana Turística**. On July 25, there's the nationwide **Día Nacional de Pisco**, a big celebration for the national brandy (rather than the town of the same name), mostly held in the bodegas south of Lima, particularly around Ica. As in Lima, **October** is the main month for religious celebrations, with the focus being the ceremony and procession at the church of El Santuario de Luren (main processions on the third Sunday and following Monday of October).

2

is one of the few examples of colonial architecture to survive in this earthquake-stricken city. In the first block of Calle Dos de Mayo, you can find the **Casona de José de la Torre Ugarte**, once home to the composer of the Peruvian national anthem. The **Casona Alvorado**, now belonging to the Banco Latino, at Cajamarca 178, is the region's only example of a copy of the Greco-Roman architectural style, while the **Casona Colonial El Porton**, C Loreto 233, conserves some fine colonial architecture.

Museo de Piedras Grabadas de Ica

Bolívar 170 • Guided tours by arrangement S/30; the museum doors are usually closed, so knock on the door or call in advance •
📞 056 227 676

On the Plaza de Armas, the **Museo de Piedras Grabadas de Icas** contains a controversial collection of engraved stones, assembled by the late Dr Javier Cabrera who claimed that the stones are several thousand years old. Few people believe this – some of the stones depict patently modern surgical techniques and, perhaps more critically, you can watch artesans turning out remarkably similar designs over on the pampa at Nazca. Nevertheless, the stones are fine works of art and one enthusiastic local guidebook claims that "dinosaur hunts are portrayed, suggesting that Ica may have supported the first culture on earth."

Museo Regional Adolfo Bermúdez Jenkins

Block 8 of Av Ayabaca • 📞 034 234 383 • Mon–Fri 8am–7pm, Sat & fiestas 9am–6pm • S/12, extra if you want to take photos • Head west from Plaza de Armas along Av Municipalidad, then turn left onto C Elias; continue south for half a kilometre, then turn right onto C Ayabaca and the museum is just over the road. Or take bus #17 from Plaza de Armas

The **Museo Regional Adolfo Bermúdez Jenkins** is one of the best archeological museums in Peru. While there are exhibits from various ancient cultures, including Paracas, Nazca, Ica, Huari and Inca, the most striking of the museum's collections is its display of **Paracas textiles**, the majority of them discovered at Cerro Colorado on the Paracas peninsula by Julio Tello in 1927. Enigmatic in their apparent coding of colours and patterns, these funeral cloths consist of blank rectangles alternating with elaborately woven ones – repetitious and identical except in their multidirectional shifts of colour and position. One of the best and most priceless pieces was stolen in October 2004, so security is tight.

The first room to the right off the main foyer contains a fairly gruesome display of **mummies**, **trepanned skulls**, **grave artefacts** and **trophy heads**. It seems very likely that the taking of trophy heads in this region was related to specific religious beliefs – as it was until quite recently among the head-hunting Jivaro of the Amazon Basin. The earliest of these skulls, presumably hunted and collected by the victor in battle, come from the Asia Valley (north of Ica) and date from around 2000 BC.

ICA'S BODEGAS

The best way to pass Ica's hot desert afternoons is to wander around the cool chambers and vaults, and sample the wines at one of the town's **bodegas** or wineries. Many of the region's best wine and piscos can be sampled from stores in and around the Plaza de Armas in Ica, but if you have the time, it's well worth visiting the producer haciendas located outside the town.

Bodega Ocucaje Mon–Fri 9am–noon & 2–5pm, Sat 9am–noon; ☎056 408 011. Any bus or colectivo heading south will get you to within a few kilometres of the bodega. A taxi from Ica costs around S/30 one way. About 35km south of Ica, the oasis of Bodega Ocucaje is one of Peru's finest vineyards. You can stay here at the *Hotel Ocucaje* and explore the surrounding desert, particularly the Cerro Blanco site where whalebone remains have been found.

Bodega Tacama Tue–Sun 9.30am–4.30pm; ☎056 581 030 ext.1039, ⓦtacama.com. Follow the road beyond Vista Alegre for another 6km. Some microbuses pass this way; a taxi costs S/15 each way. Bodega Tacama is a large and successful wine producer located about 3km from the centre of Ica. The vineyards here are still irrigated by the Achirana Canal, which was built by the Inca Pachacutec (or his brother Capac Yupanqui) as a gift to Princess Tate, daughter of a local chieftain. Apparently it took 40,000 men just ten days to complete this astonishing canal, which brings cold, pure water down 4000m from the Andes to transform what was once an arid desert into a startlingly fertile oasis. Clearly a romantic at heart, Pachacutec named it Achirana – "that which flows cleanly towards that which is beautiful". Guided tours and tastings are available.

Destileria La Caravedo By appointment; ☎056 313 963, ⓔyanina@lacaravedo.com. Guadalupe,

go by taxi, about S/25 each way. One of the area's oldest bodegas, restored as part of the massively funded Pisco Porton project. TV celebrity and pisco expert Johnny Schuler renovated the old bodega and hacienda, as well as building one of the most modern refineries in Peru to produce his Pisco Porton. Tours are by appointment only and include a visit to the new and old bodega, a tasting of their piscos and a horseback ride around the grounds. Free for a basic tour, around S/60 for a more complete tasting and snacks.

Tres Generaciones Daily 9am–6pm; ☎056 403 565. Fundo Tres Esquinas, on the outskirts of town; the taxi shouldn't cost more than S/12. The current owner of this traditional distillery that was founded in 1856 is Doña Juanita Martinez, generally acknowledged as Ica's queen of pisco. You can take a tour of the bodega, learning the entire production process and followed by a tasting of their excellent piscos. Their restaurant, *La Olla de Juanita*, is also a treat.

Vista Alegre Daily 9am–4.30pm; ☎056 222 919. Orange microbus #8 from Av Grau or the market. This well-known bodega is based in an old hacienda still chugging happily along in a forgotten world of its own. There's usually a guide who'll show you around free of charge, then arrange for a wine- and pisco-tasting session at the shop.

The main room

The museum's main room is almost entirely devoted to pre-Columbian **ceramics and textiles**, possibly the finest collection outside Lima. There are some spectacular Paracas urns – one is particularly outstanding, with an owl and serpent design painted on one side, and a human face with arms, legs and a navel on the other. There is some exquisite Nazca pottery, too, undoubtedly the most colourful and abstractly imaginative designs found on any ancient Peruvian ceramics. The last wall consists mainly of artefacts from the Ica-Chincha culture – note the beautiful **feather cape**, with multicoloured plumes in almost perfect condition. Also in the main room are several **quipus**, ancient calculators using bundles of knotted strings as mnemonic aids, also used for the recitation of ancient legends, genealogies and ballads. Thanks to the dry desert climate, they have survived better here on the coast than in the mountains, and the Ica collection remains one of the best in the country. Behind the museum there's an excellent large-scale model of the Nazca Lines.

ARRIVAL AND DEPARTURE   ICA AND AROUND

By bus The main bus services from Lima and Pisco have their own stations in Ica. Ormeño (Jr Lambayeque 180

☎056 215 600), Cruz del Sur (☎056 223333), Soyuz PeruBus (☎056 224 138), Flores (152 ☎056 212 266) and

Transportes Civa (☏ 056 523 019) arrive near Matias Manzanilla and Lambayeque. Orange buses to Huacachina (see p.128) leave from outside the Santuario de Luren (every 20min or so).

Destinations Arequipa (several buses daily; 12hr); Lima (several buses daily; 4–5hr); Nazca (several buses daily; 2–3hr).

By colectivo Colectivos from Nazca drop you off within two or three blocks of the Plaza de Armas, the same small depots from where they depart back to Nazca.

By taxi Taxis to Huacachina cost S/10; mototaxis cost S/6.

GETTING AROUND

By taxi and mototaxi Most people take taxis, generally small, flimsy and dangerous *tico* cars (try to use one of the rarer, but larger and more solid vehicles), with journeys within town rarely costing more than S/5. Cheaper still (S/2–3 for anywhere in town and under S/10 to Huacachina) are the mototaxis (motorcycle rickshaw taxis)

which can be hailed anywhere in town.

By microbus For longer journeys to the outlying parts of town, take one of the microbuses, which leave from Jr Lima or Prolongación Lambayeque and have their destinations up on their windscreens.

INFORMATION AND TOURS

Tourist information Available from some of the bodegas (see box opposite) and tour offices on the Jr Lima side of the Plaza de Armas.

Tour operators There are several tour operators in town offering excursions such as Ica City Tour (including Huacachina, wine bodegas, the Museo Regional and the barrio of Cachiche), buggy rides in the desert and also trips to the Palpa Valley, various Nazca archeological attractions, the Ballestas Islands and Paracas; most have shopfronts on

the Plaza de Armas and all can arrange for flights over the Nazca Lines: Huacachina Tours, Av Angostura 355, L-47, close to *Hotel las Dunas* entrance ☏ 056 256 582, ⓦ huacachinatours.com; Las Brujas de Cachiche, Los Diamantes K-16 ☏ 056 254 893, 956710069, ⓦ lasbrujasdecachichetours.com; Desert Travel and Service, Lima 171 (in Tejas Don Juan shop) ☏ 056 227 215; and Dolphin Travel, Av Municipalidad 132, Oficina 04 ☏ 056 218 920, ⓦ av-dolphintravelperu.com.

ACCOMMODATION

There are plenty of options in Ica, but very little of particular quality or note. For style or range of choice, most people go to Huacachina (see p.128) or one of the other out-of-town places.

Diamond Monkey Lodge Urb Santa Margarita A-15 ☏ 955 951 555. Hot water, simple, clean rooms and an accommodating and friendly host. Close to the plaza, there are plenty of restaurants nearby. Owner Danillo also runs great tours of local bodegas. **S/80**

Hostal Sol de Ica Jr Lima 265 ☏ 056 236 168, ⓦ hotelsoldeica.com. Well located although quite noisy due to heavy traffic. Modern and clean, with a nice swimming pool, though the building has suffered some earthquake damage and no longer looks its best. **S/140**

Hotel Arameli Jr Tacna 239 ☏ 056 239 107. A basic modern-style hotel; all rooms are plain but have a private bath and hot water, and it's clean, central and very friendly. **S/60**

Hotel Villa Jazmin Los Girasoles Mz C-1, Lote 7 ☏ 056 258 179, ⓦ villajazmin.net. In a quiet neighbourhood on the outskirts of Ica, this is one of the most pleasant and peaceful places to stay in town. A big pool area with sun loungers and all the little luxuries of a higher-end hotel. Rooms are tastefully designed and spacious. **S/230**

Hotel Viñas Queirolo Carretera a Los Molinos s/n ☏ 056 254 119, ⓦ hotelvinasqueirolo.com. First-class

luxury in the vineyards of the bodega Queirolo, an unbeatable rural setting and beautiful, well-furnished rooms, some with vineyard views. The pool area is the perfect place to try their wines and the restaurant serves superb food at decent prices. **S/420**

Ica Wasi Hospedaje Fermin Tauguis 194 and Luis Medina ☏ 966 787 343, ⓔ icawasi@hotmail.com. A small, simple hostel, with great service and attention to detail. Rooms are clean and bright, the wi-fi works, and the location is close to the plaza, but removed enough to afford a little peace and quiet. Free bus station pickups and excellent information on tours. Dorms **S/30**, doubles **S/60**

Ica's Desert House Urb Las Casuarinas Primera Etapa M-25 ☏ 956 029 153, ⓦ gohananperu.com. A friendly family home turned hostel, this is the perfect balm for the chaotic streets of Ica. Rooms and beds are impeccable, and the common spaces comfortable. Slightly out of the way, but taxis are cheap. Dorms **S/28**

Sol y Luna Salaverry 292 ☏ 056 227 241. A modern, very clean hotel. Service and facilities such as a laundry, cafetería and room service are superior to others of a similar price. **S/60**

2

EATING AND DRINKING

Most of the restaurants in Ica are within a block or two of the Plaza de Armas. Their quality in terms of food and general ambience varies enormously, but there is ample choice from breakfast to the dinner. Ica is famous for its sweets, too, and this is reflected in several shops near the plaza.

Calor Iqueno Av Grau 103. Small and fairly quiet, this snack bar/coffee shop has great hot drinks, yogurt and local *empañadas* (pasties filled with meat, onions and olives). Daily 8am–8pm.

Don Juan Tejas y Chocotejas Jr Lima 171, Plaza de Armas. Some of the best local *dulces* in town, including traditional *tejas* (sweets made from *manjar blanco* and pecan nuts). Daily 7.30am–9pm.

La Olla de Juanita Fundo Tres Esquinas 121, Subtanjalla ☏ 056 403 317. One of Ica's pleasant rural restaurants, set in the bodega Tres Generaciones, this is a perfect lunch stop after visiting a few distilleries. Excellent local dishes, a good *chilcano* (a refreshing pisco cocktail with ginger ale) and pleasant outdoor seating right next to the vineyard. Daily 11am–5pm.

El Otro Peñoncito Jr Bolívar 255 ☏ 056 233 921. Less than a block from the plaza, this stylish restaurant has walls tastefully adorned with artwork from Andean cosmology by an Iqueño artist; their speciality is *pollo iqueño* – chicken stuffed with spinach and pecan nuts topped with a pisco sauce. Daily 7pm–midnight.

Restaurant Galindo Jr Callao 145, just off the Plaza de Armas ☏ 056 223 650. A popular locals' dive serving big portions and sometimes the Ica speciality *carapulcra* (pork, chicken and potato casserole). A busy atmosphere with a loud TV. Daily 7am–9pm.

★ **Restaurant La Estación** Panamericana Sur Km 307, ☏ 056 237 164. Its location at the rear of a Primax petrol station may not inspire much faith, but don't hesitate: inside they cook up some of the best local and creole Peruvian dishes around. The dishes are abundant and delicious; don't miss the *tacu tacu con mariscos* (a fried cake of rice and beans with a seafood sauce) and the *picamuseo de piedrante de pallares* (broad beans). Daily 7am–9pm.

Restaurant Pastelería Anita C La Libertad 137, Plaza de Armas. This is Ica's slightly upmarket downtown eating and meeting place serving fine traditional cuisine, including excellent *lomo saltado* (see p.34) and lots of sweets and pastries for eating in or out. Has a relatively inexpensive set-lunch menu. Daily 10am–10pm.

Restaurant Rumi Wasi Urb Rinconada de Huacachina B–3 ☏ 056 235 518. Best-loved for the *chancho al palo*, a Peruvian version of spit-roasted pig. Although relatively new, Rumi Wasi has achieved nationwide fame after several appearances at Mistura, Peru's biggest culinary festival. Tues–Sun noon–6pm.

DIRECTORY

Banks and exchange Banco de Credito, Av Grau 105 (Mon–Fri 9am–6pm), has an ATM; Caja Municipal, Av Municipalidad 148 (Mon–Fri 9am–6.45pm); and the Banco de la Nación, Av San Martín and C Huánuco (Mon–Fri 9am–6pm). For dollars cash try any of the *cambistas* on the corners of the Plaza de Armas.

Police The Tourist Police are on block 1 of Prolongación Lambayeque (☏ 056 232 449 or ☏ 056 235 421).

Post office San Martín 156, not far from the Plaza de Armas (Mon–Sat 8am–8.30pm).

Huacachina

According to myth, the lagoon at **HUACACHINA**, about 5km southwest of Ica, was created when a princess stripped off her clothes to bathe. When she looked into a

THE WITCHES OF CACHICHE

In the down-at-heel suburb of Cachiche, history and mythology have merged into a legend of a local group of **witches**. The story dates back to the seventeenth century, when Spanish witches were persecuted for their pagan beliefs during the Inquisition. Seeking religious refuge, the witches emigrated to Lima, where they were also persecuted for their beliefs before finally settling in the countryside, in particular the Ica Valley, in a village called Cachiche. For hundreds of years, the Cachiche witches operated in secret until the 1980s, when there was a renewed interest in alternative health practices and even the Peruvian presidents of the 1980s and 1990s openly consulted them about health matters. The popularity of Cachiche healing methods grew even more when a powerful congressman was dramatically cured of a terminal illness on TV by a Cachiche witch. Similar to witchcraft and shamanism along the Peruvian coast, Cachiche practices involve the use of San Pedro, a psychedelic cactus containing mescaline.

mirror and saw that a male hunter was watching her she dropped the mirror, which then became the lagoon. More prosaically, during the late 1940s, the **lagoon** became one of Peru's most elegant and exclusive resorts, surrounded by palm trees, sand dunes and waters famed for their curative powers. Since then the lagoon's subterranean source has grown erratic and it is supplemented by water pumped up from artesian wells, making it less of a red-coloured, viscous syrup and more like a green, salty lagoon. The **curative powers** of the lagoon attract people from all over: mud from the lake is reputed to cure arthritis and rheumatism if you plaster yourself all over with it; and the sand around the lagoon is also supposed to benefit people with respiratory problems, so it's not uncommon to see locals buried up to the neck in the dunes. In recent days though, the water is looking considerably murkier and as a result of increased visitors, increasingly polluted with trash. Swimming in it now could do more harm than good.

The settlement is still small, but the growing backpacker atmosphere and associated clubs is changing the focus from relaxation to adventure sports and parties. Street noise can be a problem almost everywhere in the oasis. If, however, you go in the low season, the serene and romantic air of Huacachina's glory days can still be felt. Climb the dunes at the end of the lake and take in the views from the top early in the morning, before it gets too hot and prior to the noisy dune-buggy runs.

ARRIVAL AND INFORMATION   HUACACHINA

By mototaxi or taxi All taxis drop off and pick up passengers at the top end of the lagoon, within 100m of the lake edge. On arrival, you'll find a small wooden kiosk, frequently staffed by the local tourist police; they have information sheets and rather poor maps, and will also direct you to accommodation or other services. Take a stroll around and make your choice based on what you see, not what taxi drivers recommend – they work on a commission basis.

ACTIVITIES

Local tour operators are everywhere and can also help organize the following activities:

Sand-boarding On the higher slopes, sand-boarding is all the rage and you can rent boards for around S/10 per hour from the cafés and hotels along the shoreline.
Dune buggies Adrenalin rides are offered at some of the cafés, hotels and independent kiosks and shops.
Boating You can rent boats for rowing or peddling on the lagoon.

ACCOMMODATION

As well as the accommodation listings below, it's possible to **camp** anywhere in the sand dunes around the lagoon for free; it's rarely cold enough to need more than a blanket.

Banana's Adventure Av Perotti s/n ☎ 056 237 129, ⓦ bananasadventure.com. The most popular hostel in town for good reason – friendly, helpful staff, clean rooms and great gardens, bar and chillout area. It's expensive, but includes your choice of tour and breakfast. The restaurant is average, but affordable. S/160
★ La Casa de Bamboo Av Perotti next to Hostería Suiza ☎ 056 776 649. Small family place for those looking to escape the party, but not pay a fortune. Rooms are small and simple, but light and cool, and some even have a small balcony. The owners are great and the garden restaurant/café is a treat. Excellent wi-fi connection. S/80
Hostería Suiza Av Perotti 264 ☎ 056 238 762, ⓦ hosteriasuiza.com.pe. Comfort well in line with the higher price paid, it is cosy and quiet, located at the far end

of the lake, with a touch of old-world elegance. One of the best swimming pool areas around. S/320
Hotel El Huacachinero Av Perotti s/n ☎ 056 217 435, ⓦ elhuacachinero.com. A nice choice with the better (and quieter) rooms giving onto the spacious green garden and pool. There are good views of the dunes, and a calm, pleasant atmosphere. Rooms are on the basic side, but the ceiling fan can be a life-saver. S/190
Hotel Mossone Nicolás Ariola, block 4, Santa Catalina ☎ 056 213 630. This large place is luxurious and elegant, once the haunt of politicians and diplomats who listened to concerts while sitting on the colonial-style veranda overlooking the lagoon. The interior and some of the rooms, however, are quite run down and in need of renovation. S/210

2

EATING

La Casa de Bamboo Av Perotti next to Hostería Suiza ☎056 776 649. True to its simple, healthy and friendly style, there is no pretension, just great food. This tiny restaurant offers delicious vegetarian dishes, has a great espresso and a Thai curry that everybody loves – all at very comfortable prices S/10–22. The go-to spot to feed the sweet tooth. Daily 8am–10pm.

Desert Nights Balneario de Huacachina ☎056 228 458. A simple place that serves a bit of everything at a good price (S/18–32). Can't really go wrong. Daily 8am–10pm.

Hotel Mossone Nicolás Ariola, block 4, Santa Catalina ☎056 213 630. This plush hotel of faded glory has a stylish restaurant serving a wide range of Peruvian and international cuisine, but it's very pricey with the lunch set menu at S/40. Daily 7am–11pm.

Restaurant Trattoria Novaro A stone's throw from the lake, and close to the *Mossone* (see above), it's very popular in the evenings with its wide range of Italian and Peruvian dishes. Daily 11.30am–9/10pm.

The Nazca Lines

One of the great mysteries of South America, the **NAZCA LINES** are a series of animal figures and geometric shapes, some up to 200m in length, drawn across some five hundred square kilometres of the bleak, stony **Pampa de San José** or, as more simply referred to, the Nazca Plain. If you plan to visit the lines by air or on foot, you'll have to spend at least one night in Nazca, more to do it justice. If you're staying over, base yourself in either the small town of **Palpa** or larger **Nazca town**. When it comes to visiting the Lines, by far the best way is by **air** (see box, p.134). If you're keen to keep your feet on the ground, though, make for the **mirador** (viewpoint), 2km north of Palpa.

The Lines are a combination of straight lines continuing for many kilometres in some cases across the sandy, stone-strewn plateau; others look like trapezoidal plazas, perfectly created by clearing the stones from the surface for the required pattern. Around seventy other "lines" are actually stylized line drawings of birds and animals (some over fifty metres wide), believed to symbolize both astrological phases and possible ancient Nazca clan divisions, with each figure representing, perhaps, the totem of a particular sub-group of this pre-Inca society and that clan's animal ally in the spirit world. Theories discussing their purpose and origin are as varied as the patterns themselves (see box opposite).

ARRIVAL AND DEPARTURE   NAZCA LINES

Approaching from Ica in the north, you first have to cross a wide desert plain and pass through a couple of valleys, including Palpa, before arriving at the Pampa de San José and the Nazca Lines proper. The Lines themselves begin on the tableland above the small town of Palpa, about 90km south of Ica on the Panamericana.

By bus It's best to visit the Lines with a tour (see p.136), but if you want to travel independently, take a local bus from Nazca (S/2) or one of the intercity buses for Ica and Lima, which leave every couple of hours from the corner of the Panamericana and Jirón Lima on the outskirts of Nazca and let you off at the main *mirador* on the road between Palpa and Nazca. It's usually easy enough to get a lift with a

bus back to town. Buses leave every hour for the Nazca airstrip, from the corner of Grau with Jirón Bolognesi and are normally marked "B-Vista Alegre".

By colectivo/taxi A taxi to the Lines from Nazca town costs S/30, and it will wait and bring you back again. Colectivos link the airstrip with Jirón Bolognesi and Av Grau in town. It's also fairly easy to get a colectivo back from the Nazca Lines.

Palpa

Palpa is a one-street town, but there are a few archeological sites in the area and incipient signs of tourism infrastructure are beginning to emerge.

Just 2km to the north of Palpa there's a *mirador*, or viewing tower, from which geometric lines forming a pattern known locally as a Solar Clock, or **Reloj Solar**, can be seen on the lower valley slopes. It's said that during the equinox, seers can tell from the Reloj Solar what kind of harvest there will be. Some 8km by navigable dirt track from

THEORIES ABOUT THE NAZCA LINES

The Lines remain one of the world's biggest archeological mysteries and attract thousands of visitors every year to Peru's south coast. Theories abound as to their purpose and creation.

MARIA REICHE

The greatest expert on these mammoth desert designs was **Maria Reiche**, who escaped from Nazi Germany to Peru in the 1930s and worked at Nazca almost continuously from 1946 until her death in 1998. Standing on the shoulders of US scientist Paul Kosok, a colleague of hers, she believed that the Lines were an astronomical calendar designed to help organize planting and harvesting around seasonal changes rather than the fickle shifts of weather. When certain stars lined up with specific lines, shapes or animals, it would signal a time for planting, the coming of the rains, the beginning or end of summer, the growing season or the time for harvesting. It also gave the elite high priests, who possessed this knowledge, a large element of control over the actions of the populace. In a desert area like Nazca, where the coastal fog never obscures the night sky, there was a strong emphasis on relating earthly matters to the movements of the heavens and how they in turn relate to nature's cycles. Reiche's theories are thought to have established some alignments, many of which were confirmed by the computer analysis (particularly those for the solar solstices) of astronomer Gerald Hawkins (world famous for "decoding" Stonehenge in England), who himself spent much of the 1960s working on the Nazca Lines. Much, however, was left unexplained, and this has allowed more recent theorists to fill out the picture.

THEORIES OF RITUALS

Toribio Mejía Xesspe, a Peruvian archeologist, actually "discovered" the site in 1927 and believed that the lines were made for walking or dancing along, probably for ritual purposes.

In 2000, Dr Anthony Aveni, a leading archeoastronomer, agreed that at least some of the Nazca Lines were **pathways** meant to be walked in rituals, perhaps consciousness-changing like labyrinths, but also relating to the acquisition of water. A statistically significant number of the Lines point towards a section of the horizon where the sun used to rise at the beginning of the rainy season, suggesting that perhaps they were created to help worship or invoke their gods, particularly those related to rain. According to Aveni, air and ground surveys revealed that "most of the straight lines on the pampa are tied to water sources".

IT'S IN THE WATER

In 2003, David Johnson (University of Massachusetts) proposed that the ancient Nazcans mapped the desert to mark the surface where aquifers appeared. His work suggested that large underground rivers run under the pampa and many of the figures are connected to this, creating a giant map of what's happening under the earth. Zigzag lines indicate a lack of underground water, while trapezoids point towards the source of it. Archeological research also suggests that Nazca experienced a serious drought around 550 AD, at the same time as the main ceremonial centre – Cahuachi – was abandoned on the plain, and more or less contemporaneous with the construction of the trapezoid spaces where evidence of ritual offerings has been found.

MORE IDEAS...

Further theories on the purpose of the Lines include the concept of shamanic flight or out-of-body experience, with the symbolic "flight path" already mapped out across the region. Such an experience is induced by some of the "teacher plants", such as the mescaline cactus San Pedro, which are still used by traditional healers in Peru. Visually, there are clear links and similarities between the animal figures found on the plain and those elaborately painted onto Nazca's fine ceramics. Animal totems or spirit helpers are commonly used, even today, by traditional Peruvian healers to communicate with the "other world".

Most of the above theories are fairly compatible; taken together, they form a matrix of interrelated explanations – agro-astonomical, environmental, spiritual and ritual. However, just how the ancient Nazca people ever constructed the Lines is possibly the biggest mystery of all – not least since they can't even be seen from the ground. In the early 1970s the populist writer Erich von Däniken claimed that the Lines were built as runways for alien space ships. Less controversially, perhaps, in the 1980s a local Nazca school tried building its own line and from its efforts calculated that a thousand patient and inspired workers could have made them all in less than a month.

2

Palpa it's possible to see the **petroglyfos de Casa Blanca**, where stone human figures and cubic shapes have been etched on one sunken but upright stone. Roughly 4km further on is a series of petroglyphs on the scattered volcanic boulders, known as the **petroglyfos de Chicchictara**. The images depict two-headed snakes, a sunburst, a moon and various animals.

If you happen to be in town around August 15, your visit will coincide with the annual Fiesta de la Naranja (Orange Festival), which sees a few days of processions, dancing, singing and drinking.

Mirador Metálico and Museum Maria Reiche

Mirador S/2 • **Museum** Mon–Sat 9am–5pm • S/15 • A tour with an operator (see p.136) to the *mirador* on the Palpa road and the Casa Museo Maria Reiche takes 2hr 30min and costs from S/36

At Km 420 of the Panamericana, a tall metal **mirador** (viewing tower) has been built above the plain. Unless you've got the time to climb up onto one of the hills behind, or take a flight over the Lines (see box, p.134), this is the best view of the Lines you'll get.

The rather underdeveloped **Casa Museo y Mausoleo Maria Reiche**, about 1km beyond the *mirador*, consists of three main rooms containing displays of photos, drawings and ceramics relating to the Nazca Lines and the studies of **Maria Reiche**, a premier Nazca Lines researcher (see box, p.131). Housed in her old adobe home, the museum includes one room dedicated solely to Reiche's personal possessions, showing the spartan reality of her daily life here, right down to her flip-flops.

Nazca and around

The colonial town of **NAZCA** spreads along the margin of a small coastal valley some 20km south of the viewing tower (see above). The river is invariably dry, but the valley remains green and fertile through the continued use of an ancient Nazca subterranean aqueduct, and though it was badly affected by an earthquake in 1996, necessitating the rebuilding of half the town, it's still an interesting and enjoyable place to stay.

There are plenty of fascinating local sites, like the pre-Inca and Inca remains of **Paredones** and the aqueducts or canals of **Cantalloc**. Others, like the ancient Nazca ceremonial and urban centre of **Cahuachi** and the early Nazca graveyard at **Chauchilla** lie a little further away in the desert. They can only be reached by car or with a tour bus, and are poorly signposted so you will need a guide.

Museo Antonini

Av de la Cultura 600 • Daily 9am–7pm • S/15 • ☎ 056 523 444

Walking east across Nazca's main plaza and heading along Avenida de la Cultura you soon come to the town's best museum – the fascinating **Museo Antonini**, an Italian pre-Columbian archeological research and study centre. Opened in 1999, the museum presents excellent interpretative exhibits covering the evolution of Nazca culture, a good audiovisual show and scale-model reconstructions of local remains such as the Templo del Escalonado at Cahuachi. The museum complex extends to almost ten thousand square metres and includes an archeological park that contains the Bisambra aqueduct (fed by the reservoir higher up the valley) and some burial reconstructions.

The market and Barrio San Carlos

South along Calle Arica from the Plaza de Armas, the town's **main market**, offering the usual food and electronic goods, is based in a ramshackle collection of huts and stalls on the left just before the river bridge on Calle Arica.

Slightly further afield, the **Taller Artesanía**, Pasaje Torrico 240, over the river in the **Barrio San Carlos**, south of the plaza over the bridge, is worth a visit for its wonderful ceramics produced by the maestro Andrés Calle Flores for over twenty years. As long

Aqueducts of Cantayoc ▲ 10 ▲

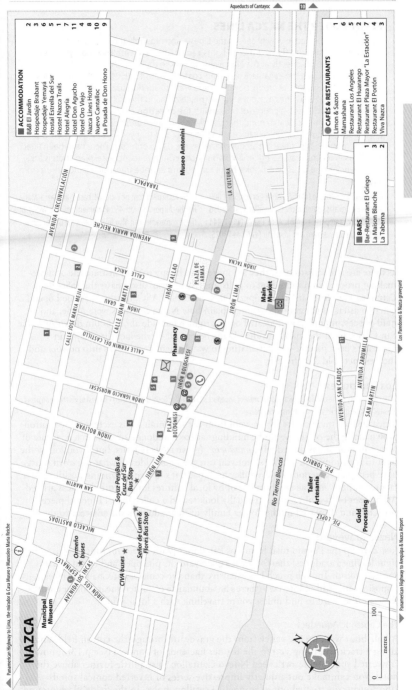

Panamerican Highway to Lima, the mirador & Casa Museo y Mausoleo Maria Reiche ▲

NAZCA

ACCOMMODATION
B&B El Jardin	2
Hospedaje Brabant	6
Hospedaje Yemayá	3
Hostal Estrella del Sur	5
Hostal Nazca Trails	7
Hotel Alegria	1
Hotel Don Agucho	11
Hotel Oro Viejo	4
Nazca Lines Hotel	8
Nuevo Cantálloc	10
La Posada de Don Hono	9

CAFÉS & RESTAURANTS
Limon & Sazon	1
Mamashana	6
Restaurant Los Angeles	5
Restaurant El Huarango	7
Restaurant Plaza Mayor "La Estación"	4
Restaurant El Portón	3
Viva Nazca	2

BARS
Bar-Restaurant El Griego	1
La Maison Blanche	3
La Taberna	2

Museo Antonini

Main Market

Taller Artesania

Gold Processing

Los Paredones & Nazca graveyard ▶

Panamerican Highway to Arequipa & Nazca Airport ▶

0 — 100 metres

N

Municipal Museum

Soyuz PeruBus & Cruz del Sur Bus Stop
Ormeño buses
CIVA buses
Señor de Luren & Flores Bus Stop

2

2

FLYING OVER THE NAZCA LINES

A pricey but spectacular way of seeing the Lines – and arguably the only way to fully appreciate them – is to **fly** over them. Flights can be arranged with **tour companies** in Nazca (see p.136) or directly at the Nazca airstrip (where they depart), about 3km south of Nazca (at Km 447 on the Panamericana), and **cost** from US$45–250 a person depending on the season, the size of the group, how long you want to spend buzzing around (eg if you want to include Palpa lines as well) and how much demand there is on the day. Flights can last from ten minutes to a couple of hours, with the **duration** of the average package being 30–45 minutes. Bear in mind that the planes are small and bounce around in the changeable air currents, which can cause airsickness, and that you'll get a better **view** on an early morning trip, since the air gets hazier as the day progresses. There have been fatal accidents in recent years, so prices and regulations continue to increase. Many hotels and tour agencies (see p.136) will book a flight for you and arrange transport to the airport from your hotel.

Airlines Alas Peruana (📞 056 522 444 or in US +1 800 548 5486, 🌐 alasperuanas.com), AeroParacas (📞 956 698 332, 🌐 aeroparacas.com), Aero Diana (📞 01 444 3075, 🌐 aerodiana.com) and Travel Air (📞 01 444 3075, 🌐 travelairperu.com.pe) are all based at Nazca Maria Reiche Airport on Km 452 Panamericana Sur. Many of these companies can also fly in from Ica, Pisco or Lima.

as there are a few customers, they are more than happy to demonstrate the ceramic-making process from moulding to polishing. San Carlos also boasts the **Taller de Cerámica Juan José**, at Pasaje López 400, Ceramicas LASC, nearby at Pasaje López 125, where masters of the craft show and explain how Nazca ceramics were made, and a **gold-processing** operation, located on the right-hand side about 500m down Avenida San Carlos from the market bridge. Don't be put off by the fact that they're in someone's back garden – it's fascinating to watch them grind rocks into powder and then extract gold dust from it.

Los Paredones

S/25: covers entry to the nearby Inca graveyard, Cantalloc Aqueduct and Cantalloc Geoglyphs (El Telar) • It's best to visit them on a tour as the sites lack good information and transport is sparse

Once an Inca trade centre where wool from the mountains was exchanged for cotton grown along the coast, the adobe buildings at **Los Paredones** are now in a bad state of repair and the site is dotted with *huaqueros'* (grave robbers') pits, but if you follow the path to the prominent central sector you can get a good idea of what the town must have been like. Overlooking the valley and roads, it's in a commanding position – a fact recognized and taken advantage of by local cultures long before the Incas arrived. At the foot of the ruins, you can usually look round a collection of funereal pieces collected and displayed by the Pomez family in their adobe home adjacent to the site.

Nazca graveyard

Just 2km up the Puquio road from Los Paradones (with Nazca in front of you, turn right leaving Paradones) there's a **Nazca graveyard**, its pits open and burial remains spread around. Though much less extensive than the cemetery at Chauchilla (see opposite), it is still of interest – there's an abundance of subterranean galleries, but they're rather hard to find unless you're travelling with a local guide.

The Cantalloc Aqueduct

A half-hour walk up the valley from the graveyard through the cotton fields and along a track will bring you to the former hacienda of **Cantayo** (see p.138), now a converted spa hotel resort called Nuevo Cantalloc. Just a little further above the hotel, you can make out a quietly impressive series of inverted conical spirals laboriously constructed out of stone, like swallow-holes, in the fields. Each around

4m across they function as air vents for a vast underground **canal system** that siphons desperately needed water from rivers higher in the valley. The spirals allow walking access to the bottom, which allowed the drawing of water and maintenance. Designed and constructed by the Nazca, it is still in use today and plays an essential role in the continuing agriculture in the Nazca Valley. It's worth going down into the openings and poking your head or feet into the canals – they usually give off a pleasant warm breeze and sometimes you can see small fish swimming in the flowing water.

Cantalloc Geoglyphs (El Telar)

From the Aqueducts, across the fields and on the other side of the Panamericana (best accessed with a car or tour), is a viewpoint over the **Cantalloc Geoglyphs (El Telar)** – a giant geoglyph that consists of trapezoids and spirals theorized to represent Nazca textile and weaving.

Chauchilla Cemetery

Tours need to be arranged in advance • 2hr 30min • S/35–45 per person • Drive 27km southeast of Nazca along the Panamericana Sur to Km 464.2, then take a dirt road beside the Poroma riverbed

Some 27km southeast of Nazca, **Chauchilla Cemetery** certainly rewards the effort it takes to visit. Once you reach the atmospheric site you realize how considerable a civilization the riverbanks must have maintained in the time of the Nazca culture. The desert landscape rolls gently down towards a small river and copses of *huarango* trees on the northern side. To the south are several rain-destroyed adobe pyramids, difficult to discern against the sand. Scattered about the dusty ground are thousands of graves, most of which have been opened by grave robbers, leaving the skulls and skeletons exposed to the elements, along with broken pieces of pottery, bits of shroud and lengths of braided hair, as yet unbleached by the desert sun. Further up the track, near Trancas, there's a small ceremonial **temple** – Huaca del Loro – and beyond this at Los Incas you can find the Quemazon **petroglyphs**. These last two are not usually included in the standard tour, but if you hire your own guide, you can negotiate with him to take you there – expect to pay S/15 extra.

Cahuachi

Tours need to be arranged in advance • 4hr • Approx S/150–225 for 4 or 5 people

The ancient centre of Nazca culture, **Cahuachi** lies to the west of the Lines, about 30km from the city and some 20km from the Pacific. Cahuachi is typical of a Nazca ceremonial centre in its use of natural features to form an integral part of the structure. Their everyday homes showed no such architectural aspirations – indeed there are no major towns associated with the Nazca, who tended to live in small clusters of adobe huts, villages at best.

The landscape between Nazca Town and the distant coastline is a massive, very barren desertscape – almost always hot, dry and sunny. It's hard to imagine how ancient peoples managed to sustain such an advanced civilization here; but, as in northern Peru, it had much to do with a close religious and technical relationship with natural water sources, all the more important because of their scarcity. The site consists of a religious citadel split in half by the river, with its main temple (one of a set of six) constructed around a small natural hillock. Adobe platforms step the sides of this twenty-metre mound and though badly weathered, you can still make out the general form. Separate courtyards attached to each of the six pyramids can be distinguished, but their exact purpose is unknown.

Templo Escalonado

The only section of Cahuachi to have been properly excavated so far is the **Templo Escalonado**, a multilevel temple on which you can see wide adobe walls and, on the temple site, some round, sunken chambers. A hundred metres away, from the top of what is known as the main pyramid structure, you can look down over what was once the main ceremonial plaza, though it's difficult to make out now because of the sands.

El Estaquería

Quite close to the main complex is a construction known as **El Estaquería**, the Place of the Stakes, retaining a dozen rows of *huarango* log pillars. *Huarango* trees (known in the north of Peru as *algarrobo*) are the most common form of desert vegetation. Their wood, baked by the sun, is very hard, though their numbers are much reduced nowadays by locals who use them for fuel. The Estaquería is estimated to be 2000 years old, but its original function is unclear, though other such constructions are usually found above tombs. The bodies here were buried with ceramics, food, textiles, jewellery and *chaquira* beads. Italian archeologist Giuseppe Orefici has worked on Cahuachi for nearly twenty years and has uncovered over three hundred graves, one of which contained a tattooed and dreadlocked warrior. Also around 2000 years old, he's a mere whippersnapper compared with other evidence Orefici has unearthed relating to 4000-year-old pre-ceramic cultures.

ARRIVAL AND GETTING AROUND

NAZCA AND AROUND

By bus Most people arrive in Nazca by bus from Lima, Arequipa or Cusco. Nearly all bus companies have depots or offices around the *óvalo* (roundabout) at the northern entry to town. Cruz del Sur buses (☎ 056 720 440) and the regular Soyuz PeruBus for Ica, Pisco or Lima (☎ 056 521 464, ⓦ soyuzonline.com.pe) drop off close to the *ovalo* on C Lima and San Martín at the entrance to town. Ormeño buses (☎ 056 522 058, ⓦ grupo-ormeno.com.pe) arrive close by at Av de los Incas 112; Civa, block 1 of Av Guardia Civil (☎ 056 523 019), though note that there's a restaurant out front; Señor de Luren, at the roundabout near *Restaurant La Kañada*; Flores (Av Los Incas 120 ☎ 01 332 1212, ⓦ floreshnos.net), from near the *óvalo*, have Mercedes buses to and from Arequipa and Cusco.

By colectivo White colectivo minivans (see p.29), leaving from near the *óvalo* a few doors down from the Civa bus office, connect Nazca to Ica to the north and Chala to the south. They only leave when full; the best time is the morning and early afternoon.

Destinations Abancay (2 or 3 daily; 10–11hr); Arequipa (several daily; 9–11hr); Chala (several daily; 3hr); Cusco (2–3 daily; 14–16hr); Lima (several daily; 5–6hr); Pampa Galera (2–3 daily; 5hr); Puquio (2–3 daily; 5–6hr).

By taxi *Tico* taxis or mototaxis can be hailed anywhere and compete to take you into – or around – town cheaply; you shouldn't pay more than S/5 for the car or S/2 for the mototaxi for any destination in town.

INFORMATION AND ACTIVITIES

Tourist information and tours There is an excellent tourist information office at the airport (☎ 979 980 622) and the following Nazca-based operators can provide general information, as well as tours and activities: Alegria Tours, Jr Lima 166 (☎ 056 522 497, ⓦ alegriatoursperu.com), who also run the *Hotel Alegria* (see p.138); Great Nazca Tours, Pasaje Bisambra 255 (☎ 056 523 100, ⓦ greatnazcatours .com); Jat Peru Adventures Travel Agency, C Los Jardines Mz C Lote 2 (☎ 056 521 430, ⓦ jatperu.com); Mystery Peru,

C Simon Bolivar 221 (☎ 056 522 379, ⓦ mysteryperu.com).
Activities Cerro Blanco, one of the biggest dunes in the world, provides expansive views and a perfect spot for sand-boarding trips. It is a 1–2hr drive up towards Puquio from Nazca, best visited on a tour.
Festivals September is one of the best times to visit for fiestas, when the locals venerate the Virgen de Guadalupe (Sept 8) with great enthusiasm. In May, the religious and secular festivities of the Fiesta de las Cruces go on for days.

ACCOMMODATION

NAZCA

B&B El Jardin C José María Mejia E01 ☎ 056 522 956. A home turned B&B with colourful local decoration and a stone-paved garden area to relax in and have breakfast. Rooms have balconies overlooking the garden, plus there is a pool and good wi-fi. It's a bit of a stroll to the centre, but

it's worth it for this friendly, attractive spot. S̲/̲1̲0̲0̲
Hospedaje Brabant C Juan Matta 878 ☎ 056 524 127. An excellent budget choice a block from the plaza. Plenty of young travellers, decent wi-fi and a terrace with hammocks to sip a beer and watch the sunset over the city. You get what you pay for: it's very basic but clean. No breakfast, but

2

there is a fridge you can use. There is only one shared bathroom/shower. Dorms $\overline{S/16}$, doubles $\overline{S/45}$

Hospedaje Yemayá Jr Callao 578 ☎056 523 146, ⓦhospedajeyemaya.com. Another well-located budget option near the plaza, Yemayá is a little dark in the corridors, but the rooms are impeccable and cool, and have fans for hot nights. There is a terrace on the roof and good wi-fi throughout. No breakfast. $\overline{S/50}$

Hostal Estrella del Sur Jr Callao 568 ☎056 522 764, ⓔestrelladelsurhotel@yahoo.com.mx. Good value, TV in most rooms, private baths, very clean and with friendly service. Pick your room carefully, since only some of the compact rooms have windows. Staff can help organize tours. Breakfasts included. $\overline{S/70}$

Hostel Nasca Trails C Fermin Del Castillo 637 ☎056 522 858. Excellent budget choice, the rooms are clean, beds comfortable and the showers decent. Wi-fi is quick and there is a gravel covered internal patio with some slumping sofas and hammocks. Extremely friendly owner runs quality tours. $\overline{S/70}$

Hotel Alegria Jr Lima 166 ☎056 522 702, ⓦhostalalegria.com. This popular hotel has rooms with private baths set around an attractive garden with a fine pool; it also runs a café that serves tasty, affordable meals and their travel agency can arrange tours and bus connections to Lima or Arequipa. Spacious parking area at back. $\overline{S/135}$

Hotel Don Agucho Av San Carlos 100 ☎056 522 048. One of the nicest options in and around Nazca, this hacienda-style place has comfortable rooms, with bath and TV, entered via cactus-filled passages. There's also a pool and a bar-restaurant; breakfast included in the price. $\overline{S/120}$

Hotel Oro Viejo Jr Callao 483 ☎056 523 332, ⓦhoteloroviejo.net. An excellent mid-range option with big rooms around a well-maintained courtyard and a very welcome pool considering the heat in Nazca. Good, if limited breakfast. Conveniently located close to bus stations. $\overline{S/200}$

★**Nazca Lines Hotel** Jr Bolognesi 147 ☎056 522 293, ⓔreservas@dmhoteles.pe. Luxurious hotel, with its own well-kept pool (which non-residents can use for approximately US$5 a day) and an excellent restaurant. $\overline{S/427}$

Nuevo Cantalloc 3km from Nazca on Route 26 to Cusco, close to the Cantalloc Aqueducts ☎056 522 264, ⓦhotelnuevocantalloc.com. Located 15min from the town centre in an old hacienda, this is a stylish luxury spa and hotel resort spread over six hectares of pools, helipad, fine gardens, gym, sauna, martial arts *dojo* and a yoga programme; lovely if you can afford it. Service is top-notch. $\overline{US$160}$

La Posada de Don Hono Av María Reiche 112 ☎056 523 991, ⓔlaposadadedonhono1@hotmail.com. Simple but well-located hotel just off the main plaza. A great deal if you can get one of the bungalows at the back which are pleasant and have a little terrace with touches of green. Parking available. $\overline{S/100}$

AROUND NAZCA

★**Hostal Wasipunko** Km 462, Panamericana Sur, Pajonal ☎056 631 183, ⓦwasipunko.com. A delightful rustic hostel set in an impressive patch of green in an otherwise desert landscape, with its own small ecological and archeological museum. There's no electricity, but it's very clean, and rooms (some with private bath) are set around a courtyard, and the restaurant specializes in tasty pre-Inca dishes utilizing guinea pigs and local vegetables. There are plenty of activities to keep you busy in the area. It's signposted on the right of the highway some 15km south of Nazca; a taxi from town will cost around S/15, or take one of the local buses or colectivos heading south from Nazca's main *óvalo*. Camping $\overline{S/25}$, doubles $\overline{S/233}$

Hotel Majoro (ex de la Borda) Km 447, Panamericana Sur ☎056 522 481. A recent refurbishment to go with the change of name has created an idyllic place to relax outside Nazca, but close to the airstrip. The rooms lack some style, but the grounds are stunning, and there is even a friendly pet *vicuña* to keep you company as you lounge by the pool. The hotel also runs tours, including some to wildlife havens on the nearby coast. $\overline{S/330}$

Pampa Galeras Vicuña Reserve Provincia de Lucanas, Departamento de Ayacucho (90km from Nazca on the Nazca–Puquio route) ☎(central office) 056 522 770, ⓔaflores@sernanp.gov.pe. A beautiful reserve in a unique landscape with large populations of *vicuña* and *guanaco*, some Andean fox and over 20 species of birds. There is a basic concrete shack with no beds, or a space for camping. Email or call in advance, and they will ensure there is a park warden to meet you as you enter. Come prepared for cold nights. Camping $\overline{Free}$

EATING

Eating in Nazca offers more variety than you might imagine given the town's small size. Most places are in or around Jr Bolognesi and Jr Lima. There's also a small market on Jr Lima, opposite the Banco de la Nación as well as the Panificadora La Esperanza bakery at Jr Bolognesi 389.

Limon & Sazon Av Los Incas 202 ☎056 522 540. A slightly more refined than average cevichería. There is a great selection of classic Peruvian seafood dishes (S/19–25) if you just can't wait until you get back to the coast. Daily 9am–6pm.

Mamashana Jr Bolognesi 270 ☎056 521 286. The best of the row of restaurants on Bolognesi, the menu here is varied and the dishes all very well prepared. The pizzas are decent, but they're best at creole dishes – try the classic *lomo saltado* (stir-fried beef strips, tomatoes, rice and potato chips, S/28) or the delicious pasta with *huancaína* sauce and beef cutlet (S/32). Spread over two levels, the open upper deck is particularly nice and surprisingly without much noise from the street below. Daily 11am–late.

Restaurant Los Angeles Bolognesi 266. A very nice family-run restaurant with a wide range of freshly cooked foods, from burgers and omelettes to pizza, French fries and more traditional Peruvian food like *lomo saltado* (S/18–25). Mon–Sat 9.30am–9pm.

★**Restaurant El Huarango** C Arica 602 ☎056 522 141. Offering a covered rooftop patio and a great ambience, this place serves delicious food, mostly traditional coastal Peruvian dishes such as *ají de gallena* (chilli chicken) but also including some more international cuisine. Daily 11am–11pm.

Restaurant Plaza Mayor "La Estación" C Arica and Jr Bolognesi, on main plaza ☎056 237 164. A large, popular central restaurant on three levels, the *Plaza Mayor* serves plenty of meat dishes, mainly *parrillas*, amid interesting decor, with Andean godlike figurines on the walls and the feel of a large, chunky, wooden structure. Daily lunch–11pm.

NAZCA CERAMICS

In 1901, when Max Uhle "discovered" the Nazca culture, it suddenly became possible to associate a certain batch of beautiful **ceramics** that had previously been unclassifiable in terms of their cultural background: the importance of Nazca pottery in the overall picture of Peru's pre-history asserted itself overnight. Many of the best pieces were found in Cahuachi (see p.135).

Unlike contemporaneous Mochica ware, Nazca ceramics rarely attempt any realistic imagery. The majority – painted in three or four earthy colours and given a resinous surface glaze – are relatively stylized or even completely abstract. Nevertheless, two main categories of subject matter recur: naturalistic designs of bird, animal and plant life, and motifs of mythological monsters and bizarre deities. In later works it was common to mould effigies to the pots. During Nazca's decline under the Huari-Tiahuanaco cultural influence (see p.483), the workmanship and designs were less inspired. The style and content of the early pottery, however, show remarkable similarities to the symbols depicted in the **Nazca Lines**, and although not enough is known about the Nazca culture to be certain, it seems reasonable to assume that the early Nazca people were also responsible for the drawings on the Pampa de San José. With most of the evidence coming from their graveyards, though, and that so dependent upon conjecture, there is actually little to characterize the Nazca and not much is known of them beyond the fact that they collected heads as trophies, that they built a ceremonial complex in the desert at Cahuachi, and that they scraped a living from the Nazca, Ica and Pisco valleys from around 200–600 AD.

2

Restaurant El Portón Jr Ignacio Morseski 120 ☎ 056 523 490. A lively hangout at night, especially at weekends with frequent live folk music, a dancefloor and bar. Pastas, meat and seafood dishes are complemented by the colonial mansion-style decor. Best espresso in town. Daily 8am–10pm.

Viva Nasca C Bolognesi 464 ☎ 994562477. Rather small and over-lit, this is a typical Peruvian sandwich restaurant, but with friendly staff and delicious sandwiches and burgers. The fresh juices are just the thing to ease the throat after a long day exploring in the heat and the sand. Mon–Sat 9am–11pm.

DRINKING

What little nightlife exists is mainly based around restaurants and bars, particularly on Jr Lima, Plaza de Armas and Jr Bolognesi. Alcohol can also be bought at the Licoria liquor store at C Arica 401.

Bar-Restaurant El Griego Jr Bolognesi 287 ☎ 056 521 480. A friendly local eating-house with fine food and decent drinks at reasonable prices. Good breakfasts and can be fun in the evening when it functions less as a restaurant and more as a bar. Daily 10.30am–midnight.

La Maison Blanche Jr Bolognesi 388 ☎ 056 522 361. Great for crepes and coffee during the day, and the little terrace out front is the perfect for a cold beer in the

evening. The sandwiches are a bit of a let-down and service can be a little sluggish, but the staff is friendly. Good wi-fi. Daily 8am–10pm.

La Taberna Jr Lima 321. Serves a good selection of local and international dishes, plus a variety of drinks; its walls are covered with graffiti scrawled over the years by passing groups of travellers. Live folk music plays until around midnight most evenings. Daily 11am–12pm.

DIRECTORY

Banks and exchange Banco de Credito, Jr Lima and C Grau Mon-Fri 9am-6pm; Banco de la Nación, Jr Lima 465. The best rates for dollars cash are with the *cambistas* in the small park outside the *Hotel Nasca Lines,* where Jr Bolognesi and Jr Lima merge, or outside the Banco de Credito.

Health Pharmacies include Botica Central, Jr Bolognesi 355 and Jr Fermin del Castillo; Botica Alejandra, C Arica 407.

Internet Available all over Nazca, but in particular next door to the *Restaurant El Portón*. Also at Fox Internet, Jr Bolognesi block 1; Mundo Virtual, Jr Bolognesi 395 and Jr Bolognesi 225.

Police Av Los Incas s/n ☎ 056 522 084.

Post office Jr Fermin del Castillo 379; Mon–Sat 8am–8pm.

Pampa Galeras Vicuña Reserve

Get off one of the main daily Nazca–Cusco buses, or go with the Tour Huari that runs to Puquio at around 4pm; ask the driver to tell you where to get off

Some 90km inland from Nazca, and well signposted at Km 89 of the Nazca–Cusco road, the **Pampa Galeras Vicuña Reserve** is one of the best places in Peru to see the **vicuña**, a llama-like animal with very fine wool. The *vicuña* have lived for centuries in the area of reserve, which contains more than five thousand of the creatures.

The *vicuña* themselves are not easy to spot. When you do notice a herd, you'll see it move as if it were a single organism. They flock together and move swiftly in a tight wave, bounding gracefully across the hills. The males are strictly territorial, protecting their patches of scrubby grass by day, then returning to the rockier heights as darkness falls. Try to visit for the Chaccu, a rowdy traditional roundup and shearing of the *vicuña* that needs hundreds of helping hands. The main festival is on June 24, but it also takes place at various times between May and November

Puquio, Chumpi and Lago Parinacochas

Chumpi and Lago Parinacochas can only be accessed by private car, tour groups (see p.136) or irregular local buses and colectivos from or via Puquio

Located east of the Pampa Galeras Vicuña Reserve along the Cusco road, **PUQUIO** is a quiet, relatively uninteresting stop-off, but if you have to break your journey, there's a choice of several unexceptional hostels, most within a block or two of the plaza. As soon as you cross over the metal bridge at the entrance to the village, you get a real sense that the desert coast is left behind and the Andean ecology and landscapes abruptly take over. In fact, Puquio was an isolated community until 1926, when the townspeople built their own road link between the coast and the sierra.

The road divides at Puquio, with the main route continuing over the Andes to Cusco via Abancay. A side road goes south for about 140km along the mountains to Lago Parinacochas; although frequently destroyed by mudslides in the rainy season, the road always seems full of passing trucks, which will usually take passengers there for a small price. Continuing to **Chumpi**, an ideal place to camp, there is some exceptionally stunning sierra scenery. Within a few hours' walk of the town is the beautiful lake, **Lago Parinacochas**, named after the many flamingoes that live there and probably one of the best unofficial nature reserves in Peru. If you're not up to the walk, you could take a day-trip from Nazca for about US$40; try Alegria Tours (see p.136). From Chumpi you can either backtrack to Puquio, or continue down the road past the lake, before curving another 130km back down to the coast at Chala.

The Panamericana Sur Highway

From Nazca, the **Panamericana Sur Highway** continues for about 1000km to the border with Chile. Apart from Chala and Camaná, the road only passes the occasional fishing village or squatter settlement until it reaches the Arequipa turn-off; from there, it's straight south across the northern altiplano desert to Tacna. The desert landscape immediately south of Nazca is stunningly bleak and there's relatively little of specific interest in the 170km of desert between Nazca and Chala. If you can, stop at the unexpected patch of green that is Yauca, a little valley dedicated entirely to the production of olive oil. Some of the olive trees are ancient, supposedly all grown from a single plant stolen from the gardens of San Isidro in Lima in the 1500s.

Las Lomas

Las Lomas is a remote fishing village with a **beach** that's especially good for spotting pelicans, about 90km to the south of Nazca and off the Panamericana. It can only be reached in a private car or with a tour group from Nazca.

Sacaco

Km 539, Panamericana Sur, on the left (heading south). From here it's a 30min walk along a sand track into the desert, away from the road. Ask at the house in daylight hours for the guardian to open the museum, which is a few hundred metres further • Daily 9am–3pm • Voluntary payment (S/5–10 per person recommended)

The remarkable paleontological site of **Sacaco** gives access to fossilized whale remains sitting in the desert near a small museum about 96km south of Nazca, just after the Las Lomas turn-off. One fossilized whale skeleton is housed within the museum building itself with some interpretative material about the geology and paleontology of the region on the walls. It can be reached on some tours and also by hopping off one of the Nazca-to-Chala (or Lima-to-Arequipa) buses, Be aware that getting back to Nazca or heading further south could be tricky as buses passing on the Panamericana are often full or refuse to stop.

Las Lomas de Atiquipa

Panamericana Sur Km 597; turn right and 2km further you'll find the village of Atiquipa. To go further you need a 4WD • You can camp for free or stay in a small hotel built by the community (S/30)

Near the village of **Atiquipa** is a small reserve housing one of the most impressive remaining examples of a unique micro-climate that once stretched all along the Peruvian coast, and is now reduced to a few enclaves north and south of Lima. The *lomas* are small hills right on the coast which trap the fog coming in off the sea and so support a low, bushy forest and a surprising amount of wildlife. A heroic job of reforestation and promotion of this area has been done by locals Roberto and Julietta de la Torre, whom you should call before visiting for directions and information (☎993 623 013 or ☎999 376 396). Some basic accommodation is available, or visitors can stay at the rustic, but well-appointed beachside homes just before the reserve at Jihuay (⊕jihuay.com). There are two independent and fully furnished homes with views over the bay for rent (US$200 a night, six people and US$100 a night, three people); at extra cost someone can come in and prepare meals.

Puerto Inca

Open access • Free • To get to the ruins, take a taxi from Chala (about S/20 each way; specify a time for pickup and pay then), or catch an Arequipa-bound bus along the Panamericana Sur and ask to be dropped off at Km 610. It's an easy 2–3km walk downhill from here along a windy dirt road following a narrow gully to the beach

The ruins of **Puerto Inca**, the Incas' main port for Cusco, stand 10km before Chala. There's an excellent **beach**, and fine diving and fishing here. The ruins are expansive and interesting, although with only a little information, and are just a short stroll up past, the *Puerto Inka* hotel (see below) and beach. Within a half-day's walk there are caves, grottos, hidden coves, rock formations and plenty of opportunity for getting lost in the desert coastline, birdwatching or even spotting Humboldt penguins if you're patient and lucky enough.

Chala

A small, quietish town, **Chala** was the main port for Cusco until the construction of the Cusco–Arequipa rail line. Now, it's a more or less agreeable little fishing town serving the mines in the area and set on a low cliff overlooking a long empty beach. If you avoid the chaos in the centre, and don't mind rather basic accommodation, Chala can be a very pleasant stop on your trip south. Pass your time overindulging in fresh seafood, the best of which is found near the pier and small main beach at the southern edge of town.

Camaná

About 200km south from Chala, **CAMANÁ** is a popular Arequipeño beach resort from December to March, when the weather is hot, dry and relatively windless, although outside high season it has little to offer. The most popular **beach** is at **La Punta**, around 5km along the Arequipa road. The town is unexceptional and is a little removed from the beach, while the jumbled seaside developments are aimed at a young, local crowd there to party long hours and with very little care as to the quality of the accommodation. This is not a beach for quiet relaxation during high season.

Continuing towards Arequipa (see p.154), the sealed road keeps close to the coast wherever possible, passing through a few small fishing villages and over monotonous, arid plains before eventually turning inland for the final uphill stretch into the land of volcanoes and Peru's second largest city. At Km 916 of the Panamericana, a road leads off into the Majes Valley towards the Toro Muerto petroglyphs, the Valley of the Volcanoes and the spectacular but little-visited **Cotahuasi Canyon** (see p.185). At Rapartición, the road splits: east to Arequipa and south towards Mollendo, Moquegua, Tacna and Chile.

ACCOMMODATION	THE PANAMERICANA SUR HIGHWAY

PUERTO INCA

Puerto Inka Km 610, Panamericana Sur ☎054 692 596, ⊕puertoinka.com.pe; or contact in Arequipa at C Arica 406a, Yanahuara ☎054 252 588. The hotel is spread out across several bungalows overlooking the sea; it offers a reasonable restaurant, big parking area, campsite and quick access to the beach. Check the website for deals. No wi-fi. Camping <u>S/10</u>, bungalows <u>S/190</u>

CHALA

Hotel Grau C Comercio 701 (in front of the hospital) ☎ 054 551 009. Run down, but the front rooms with a shared terrace, offer great views over Chala's long curved beach. A bargain if you're not fussy about patchy wi-fi, saggy beds and cold water. **S/25**

Hotel de Turistas de Chala C Comercio 601 ☎ 054 551 111, ⓦ hoteldeturistaschala.com. Old-fashioned but comfortable hotel. Recent refurbishments include a more modern wing and a swimming pool with ocean views. **S/133**

CAMANÁ

Sun Valley Km 850, Panamericana Sur ☎ 054 796 180, ⓔ sunvalleycamana@hotmail.com. Easily the best option in town, *Sun Valley* is tucked up against a sand dune on the far end of the beach. It is on the highway, not next to the sea, but has a private plot with umbrellas on the beach for guests. The bungalows around the pool area are the best, and owner Alvaro Rosas is a passionate food man, so you can be assured of eating well. Camping **S/10**, doubles **S/100**

Mollendo and Mejía

Near to the **Reserva Nacional de Mejía**, a marvellous lagoon-based bird sanctuary, **MEJÍA** is a pleasant seaside village with beautiful 1940s'-style wooden houses kept in impeccable shape as summer houses for wealthy Arequipeños. There's a decent stretch of **beach** and a laidback atmosphere, but accommodation is sparse, limited to a few rundown and unappealing hostels on the noisy main road far from the sea. Camping, although not strictly allowed, can be an option; have a chat with the lifeguards on the beach and they'll point you the right way. Some 15 minutes further along is the town of **MOLLENDO,** which has grown massively due to the industrial port nearby, but still has some charm if you visit outside the peak tourist season of December to March. The best places to stay are near the plaza, a block or so from the promenade that overlooks the beach. The buildings are throwbacks from its previous life as a seaside resort similar to Mejía, but they are now run down and the whole area is a little shabby. Still, plenty of eating options, a great market for getting a juice and sandwich in the morning and a long beach; although the sand is a bit grey, and tends to be riddled with beach umbrellas, it will serve for a beach break.

The National Sanctuary and Lakes of Mejía

Daily 7am–5pm • S/5 • Take an Empresa Aragon bus from Arequipa (see p.165); you'll see the lagoons just before you get to Tambo Valley; alternatively, get a colectivo (every 10min) from the top end of C Castilla in Mollendo

The **National Sanctuary and Lakes of Mejía**, 7km south of Mollendo, is an unusual ecological niche consisting of almost 700 hectares of lakes separated from the Pacific Ocean by just a sand bar, and providing an important habitat for many thousands of migratory birds. Of the 157 species, such as blue-footed boobies, pelicans, penguins and Inca terns, sighted at Mejía, around 72 are permanent residents; the best time for sightings is early in the morning.

ARRIVAL AND DEPARTURE   **MOLLENDO AND MEJÍA**

By colectivo The buses that run the route to and from Arequipa are slow and old; the best way to get in or out are the Mercedes minivans which leave across from the market behind the main terminal in Arequipa, and in Mollendo, from the Terminal Terrestre outside of town. They are quick, comfortable and safe. There are various options; one is Empresa de Transportes Cristo del Pacífico (several daily; 2–3hr; S/25). From Moquegua, get any bus heading to Arequipa and ask to get off at Fiscal (2hr); from there,

colectivos leave regularly for Cocachacra where another car or a combi will take you on to Mejía or Mollendo. Combis run constantly between Mollendo and Mejía. To head on south, you can go back to Fiscal and hope for a space on a passing bus, or go to Ilo by van from the terminal, where you can easily connect with Moquegua and Tacna by bus or minivan.

Destinations Arequipa (several daily; 2–3hr); Ilo (several daily; 2hr)

2

ACCOMMODATION AND EATING

Hostal Cabaña C Comercio 240 ☏ 054 534 671. Inexpensive rooms in a down-at-heel but lovely wooden building with verandas and patio; rooms with shared and private bath are available, with hot water (although water pressure is an issue), average service and wi-fi. The rooms overlooking the plaza, though noisy, have a glimpse of the sea. **S/60**

Hostal La Casona C Arequipa 188 ☏ 054 533 160. Like so many hotels here, the interior lacks a little attention, but the rooms and bathrooms are spacious, and the beds decent. Just around the corner from the plaza. **S/70**

Hostal Plaza C Arequipa 209 ☏ 054 532 460. The most expensive option near the plaza, but it feels calmer and better cared for. The rooms are also cleaner and more welcoming than most options in town and the service is friendly. **S/100**

Marco Antonio C Comercio 258 ☏ 054 534 258. A modern, stylish design announces Marco Antonio as the coolest place in town, but it's not just a pretty face. The menu is seafood-focused and the dishes come out fresh and tasty. Good for a midday ceviche or something more elaborate like a *corvina* in a seafood sauce. Daily 9am–10pm.

Pizzería 1900 C Arica 183 ☏ 054 533 769. Low lit with smooth music and a tartan and leather interior design that is oddly closer to Scotland than Napoli, but charming nevertheless. The owner is friendly and the pizzas have a decently thin, crispy base. Daily 6pm–midnight.

Pizza Plaza C Arequipa 213 ☏ 054 532 383. Despite the name, don't go for the pizzas, rather focus on the meat they're grilling on the barbecue out on the street. Daily noon–11pm.

DIRECTORY

Banks and exchange If you need to change money, you'll get the best rates for dollars from the *cambistas* on Plaza Bolognesi; ATMs available at the Banco de la Nación, Arequpa 243 and the Banco de Credito, Comercio 323.

Moquegua

Situated on the northern edge of the Atacama Desert, most of which lies over the border in Chile, the **MOQUEGUA** region is traditionally and culturally linked to the Andean region around Lake Titicaca, and many ethnic Colla and Lupaca from the mountains live here. The local economy today is based on copper mining, fruit plantations and wine and Moquegua has a reputation for producing excellent **pisco**. Historically, this area is an annexe of the altiplano, which was used as a major thoroughfare first by the Tiahuanacu and later the Huari peoples. In the future it may well be the main route for the gas pipeline out of Peru's eastern rainforest regions to the coast. Right now, though, located in a relatively narrow valley, the rather flavourless town of Moquegua has an attractive plaza with some old colonial houses to peer into nearby. As with all growing Peruvian towns, however, move away from the centre and things get considerably more rowdy.

Few non-Peruvians come to Moquegua to visit the local attractions, as most are in a hurry to get into or out of Chile. That said, the area has plenty of little-visited but interesting sites, from wine and pisco bodegas and volcanoes to petroglyphs and

---

MOQUEGUA'S BODEGAS

Initially established during the colonial era, Moquegua's bodegas have various lines in piscos (including *italia* and *mosto verde*), cognacs, aniseed liqueurs and wines.

Bodega Biondi Km 1143, Panamerica Sur ☏ 053 461 889; Mon–Fri 8am–3pm. Consistently ranked among the best producers in Peru, particularly well known for its aromatic varieties, Moscatel and Albilla. Visits must be arranged in advance.

Bodega Norvil C Ayacucho 1370 ☏ 053 461 229; Mon–Sat 8am–noon & 2–5pm. Welcoming bodega run by Alberto Villegas Vargas, grandson of the original founder Norberto Villegas Talavera, one of the town's benefactors.

Bodega Paredes Fundo la Chimba, on the road to Rayo ☏ 053 461 972; Mon–Fri 9am–1pm and 3–5pm, Sat–Sun 9am–5pm. Produces fine piscos from *quebranta* and *italia* grapes. Time your visit to take in a show by the family's Peruvian Paso horses in a traditional dance called La Marinera, and stay for lunch in the on-site restaurant.

archeological remains. All of these require personal car transport, or, better, going with a local tour company (see p.146).

Catedral de Santo Domingo

C Tacna and C Ayacucho • Mon–Sat 7am–noon & 4–7pm • Free

Standing close to the plaza – which has an ornate metal fountain designed in 1877 by Gustave Eiffel – the **Catedral de Santo Domingo** was restored after an earthquake in 1868 and now contains a large single nave, two finely worked *retablos* and the first clock to arrive in Moquegua from London (in 1798). The cathedral also houses the relics of Santa Fortunata whose remains were excavated from their original resting place in Spain and brought to Peru in the nineteenth century.

Museo Contisuyo

Jr Tacna 294 • Wed–Mon 8am–1pm & 2.30–5.30pm, Tue 8am–12pm & 4pm–8pm • ☎ 053 461 844, ⦿ museocontisuyo.com

On the western side of town, just half a block from the main plaza, there's the **Museo Contisuyo**, an archeological museum that exhibits relics from the region including stone arrow points, ceramics, textiles, gold and silver objects and specimens from the Tiahuanuco and Huari cultures as well as the local ancient coastal Chiribaya and Tumilaca cultures.

Torata

Bus from Carretera Binacional (S/3; 30min)

About 24km away from Moquegua on the main road to Puno, **TORATA** is a picturesque district and settlement of country homes made with traditional *mojinete* (slanted and gable ended) roofs. There's also an imposing church and old stone mill, both from the colonial period, as well as some restaurants. The **petroglyphs of Torata**, which depict llamas, geometric shapes and what look like maps and water symbols, are within relatively easy reach of Moquegua by following the small *quebrada*, a dry canyon which runs east 200m from the bridge at Km 120.45 of the Carretera Binacional.

Cerro Baúl

One of the bigger sites around is the archeological remnant of a Huari (600–1100 AD) citadel that is easily visited by taxi from Moquegua. Sitting atop a truncated hill – **Cerro Baúl**, after which the ruins are named – some 17km northeast of the town, this commanding site once offered its ancient inhabitants a wide view around the Moquegua Valley, allowing them to control the flow of goods and people at this strategic point.

The volcanoes and Omate

Within striking distance of Moquegua are the majestic Ubinas (5673m, with a 350m crater) and Huaynaputina (4800m) **volcanoes**. Visiting these is an adventurous operation that demands 4WD support from one of the local travel agencies (see p.146). Also in the sierra is the remote town of **Omate**, 130km (3hr) from Moquegua on the back mountain road to Arequipa. Surrounded by unique and impressive terrain formed by rock, volcanic ash and sands, it's also famous for its crayfish. Check out the natural **thermal baths** of Ulucan (3100m; daily 8am–5.30pm; S/2), just 10km from Omate.

Toquepala

Into the hills southeast of Moquegua, the town of **Toquepala** and nearby mysterious **caves** (2500m) can be visited in a day. The caves – occupied by a group of hunter-gatherers from the Archaic era around nine thousand years ago – are fascinating but rarely visited. These caves contain roughly drawn pictures of cameloid animals, hunting scenes and Andean religious symbols. Again, the best way to find this site is by taking a short tour with a local travel agency (see below).

The Chen Chen geoglyphs

The little-seen **geoglyphs of Chen Chen** can be accessed by car from Moquegua, by taking the track towards Toquepala which leaves the Panamericana Sur between Km 98 and 97; the track passes along the base of some hills where the geoglyphs, mainly large Nazca-like representations of llamas, are scattered around, some hidden from over the road.

ARRIVAL AND GETTING AROUND   MOQUEGUA

Moquegua is a busy nodal point for two important roads into the Andes: the Carretera Transoceanica connecting Ilo on the coast to Puno and Juliaca, and the Carretera Binacional to Desaguadero, which shears off from it some distance after Torata.

BY BUS

Most people arrive in town by bus, at the new bus terminal which covers blocks 2 and 3 of Avenida Ejercito or Avenida La Paz, several long blocks from the centre and worth the S/3–5 taxi ride, or S/1.5 in a combi from over the road. **Bus companies** Cruz del Sur, (☎053 462 005) serves Lima, Tacna, Arequipa and Desaguadero; as does Tepsa (☎053 461 171); and Flores (☎053 462 181). Civa serves most destinations in Peru, while Oltursa covers major coastal destinations south of Lima except Arequipa. There are various small companies that have routes up to Desguadero, Juliaca and Puno, but they are not reliable or particularly comfortable. A better bet is to take a bus from Arequipa. Destinations There are several buses daily to: Arequipa (3hr); Desaguadero (5hr); Lima (18hr); Puno (6hr); Tacna (2hr).

BY COLECTIVO

Colectivos run much the same routes as buses (see opposite), though without set itineraries. They all leave from Av Ejercito by the corner with C Cáceres. Mili Tours run several cars daily to Desaguadero (5–6hr), as well as two or three cars a day to Arequipa (3–4hr). Comite 1, Comite 11 and El Buen Samaritano all serve Tacna, each taking four or five passengers daily. El Buen Samaritano, Av del Ejercito, also serves Desaguadero and offers *expresso* services to take passengers anywhere they like.

BY CAR

For car rental, try Explorer Rent a car, C Ayacucho 712 (☎053 463 180 ⓦ explorerrentacar.com), from around S/300 a day.

INFORMATION AND TOURS

Tourist information Main tourist office, C Ayacucho and C Ancash, the Regional Tourism Directorate at C Ayacucho 344 (☎053 464 053), and Ledelca Tours, C Ayacucho 625 (☎053 462 953, ✉ledelca@viabcp.com), provide information; also, some historical information is available from the Museo Contisuyo just north of the Plaza de Armas. **Tour operators** Ledelca Tours, C Ayacucho 625

(☎053 462 953), sells airline tickets and is the local representative for DHL. They offer city tours (3hr) and countryside tours (3hr), which generally include a visit to a bodega, or a longer tour to the Chen Chen geoglyphs, the archeological site of Cerro Baúl (4hr) and, if requested, Ubinas and other local volcanoes (4–6hr) in 4WDs.

ACCOMMODATION

Hostal Atlantis C Lima 417 ☎053 462 920. Basic yet fairly comfortable and good-value hostel with private bathrooms, wi-fi and a small terrace on the third floor. **S/50**
Hotel El Mirador Alto de Villa ☎053 424 193, ⓦ dematourshoteles.com. One of the smartest options in town with swimming pool and all mod-cons, if somewhat dated. **S/200**
Hotel Moquegua C Junin 431 ☎053 506 861. Spacious,

light and comfortable rooms with bar fridges and there is decent wi-fi. Corridors are too dimly lit, but everything is clean. **S/120**
Residencial Moquegua C Cusco 454 ☎053 462 316, ⓦ residencialmoquegua.com. The rooms are impeccable, everything looks quite new and some have large windows that open up to a tiny balcony to let in light and fresh air. Breakfast and wi-fi included. Great service. **S/80**

EATING AND DRINKING

Bandido Pub C Moquegua 333. One of the few bars in town and a place where they play good music and serve pizzas cooked in wood-fired earth ovens, as well as reasonably priced drinks. Mon–Sat 6pm–midnight.

Mr Papaya's Caja China C Ancash 428 ☎ 953 776 478. Mr Papayas started life on the far side of town near the market but has recently moved to this prime spot due to popular demand. Weekdays they serve a great lunch menu and their famous pork in the *caja china*, a Peruvian barbecue box where the coals are placed on the steel lid (S/20). Weekends they serve up delicious local dishes. Daily, 11am–3.30pm.

El Piurano C Moquegua 934 ☎ 987 988 549. A few blocks up from the plaza, *El Piurano* serves tasty, no-frills Peruvian food. The selection goes a little bit broader than the rest of the lunch menus in town (S/10), and the quick service and friendly atmosphere make it a top choice. Try the owner/cook's star dish, avocado with local river shrimp. Daily, lunch time.

Restaurante Moral y C Lima and C Libertad ☎ 053 463 084. This is a traditional and stylish restaurant in the town centre with a reputation for great breakfasts and good service. Arrive early for the set-lunch menu (S/12), it sells out quickly. Daily 7am–7pm.

Restaurante Recreo Turístico Las Glorietas C Antigua de Samegua ☎ 053 461 181. Located on the outskirts of town, this is the restaurant best loved by locals. Large and lively, it serves good local food in a traditional atmosphere. Tue–Sun 11am–6pm.

DIRECTORY

Banks and exchange Cash can be changed at the Banco de la Nación, Jr Lima 616; the Banco de Credito has an ATM on the corner at Moquegua 861; or there are the *cambistas* outside Plaza Bolívar.

Internet Sybernet, Jr Moquegua 434, half a block from the plaza (daily 8am–11pm), and Café Internet, Jr Moquegua 418, which serves drinks (daily 8am–10pm).

Post office C Ayacucho 560, Plaza de Armas (Mon–Sat 8am–8pm).

Ilo

About 95km southeast of Moquegua, **ILO** is a busy port on the Peruvian Atacama Desert coastline, with a population of over 65,000 inhabitants and an economy based around fishing and mining. The most strategically, and economically, important port in Peru, Ilo doesn't see many foreign visitors, but it is growing as a local tourist destination and has some interesting features such as its attractive promenade and the nearby beaches.

Templo de San Geronimo

Plaza de Armas • Daily 6am–6pm

The Plaza de Armas is the civic heart of the city, dominated by the **Templo de San Geronimo**. The temple was built originally in 1871 and contains an antique font created with a seashell and brought here from Paris. It has a single rectangular nave and central tower, and one of the three church bells was crafted in 1647.

Malecón costero

Museo Naval Daily 9am–6pm • US$1.50

The *Malecón Costero* (seaside promenade) and the seafront developments lie two blocks away from the Templo. La Glorieta, an iron bandstand structure built onto a huge boulder overlooking the sea is the main draw here. In the Capitano del Puerto's offices, there's a small **Museo Naval** with documents and artefacts relating to the maritime past, including manuscripts pertaining to Admiral Miguel Grau. Next to the nineteenth-century iron pier, you can find a busy wharf used by artisan fishermen who use small boats and simple nets, and a seafood market.

Ilo's beaches

Ilo is known for its fifteen or so **beaches** spreading out both north and south of the town. The nearest and most popular is the **Playa Pozo de Lisas**, close to the airport; it's extensive and usually empty except weekends in December and January. At the other end of town, to the north, the **Playa Boca del Río** has fine sand and good views back to the city. About 20km further north, the **Playa Pocoma** is ideal for camping; the nicer **Playa Waikiki** is another 4km further north.

2

Museo de Sitio El Algarrobal

Municipalidad El Algarrobal • Daily 7am–5pm • ☎ 053 837 103 • S/5 • Take a taxi from Ilo, S/30 for the round trip

The most interesting local attraction is the **Museo de Sitio El Algarrobal**, about 15km east of town. The museum presents exhibits from the pre-Hispanic cultures of the Ilo region, including textiles from the local Chiribaya culture and mummies, and offers views over the valley of Algarrobal and the old hacienda Chiribaya (1000–1350 AD).

ARRIVAL AND DEPARTURE   ILO

BY BUS

Arriving at Ilo, most buses come in on or close to Jr Matara. Buses to Bolivia leave from the corner of Matara and Junín.

BY COLECTIVO

Cars and minivans run between Ilo and Mollendo.
Bus companies Cruz del Sur (☎053 482 071) serves

Moquegua, Lima and Arequipa, and set off from the corner of Matara and Jr Moquegua. Oltursa (☎053 570 390) has a direct bus from Lima (15hr). Cial (☎053 630 511), Civa (☎053 483 555) and Flores (☎053 482 512) leave regularly from Moquegua terminal (2hr). Buses for Tacna and Arica in Chile leave daily with Flores from the corner of Jr Ilo with Matara.

ACCOMMODATION AND EATING

Calienta Negros Costanera Sur Km 02 ☎053 482 839, ⓦcalientanegros.pe. Just out of town, and on the beach of the same name, this is one of the better and most popular restaurants for most types of creole Peruvian dishes (S/25–40) and a few standard international regulars; can also cater for vegetarians. Tues–Sun 11am–5pm.

Le Gran Hotel Ilo Av Cáceres 3007 ☎053 782 411, ⓦlegrandhotelilo.com. Surely inspired by the French prefix it picked up with the remodelling in 2014, this the most comfortable hotel in town: it has over 60 well-kept rooms, a private beach, pool, car park and restaurant. S/210

Hotel Vip Jr Dos de Mayo 608 ☎053 481 492, ⓦviphotelilo.com. This is a very modern five-storey hotel whose bar and restaurant area on the top floor has good views over the nearby port; rooms are carpeted and well equipped with TV, fridge-bar and good bathrooms. S/180

Sargoloco Cevichería C Moquegua 506 ☎953 682 100. They make a killer ceviche (S/16) and serve up a good range of other seafood dishes (average S/22). Popular, and so at times service gets slow. Well located near the plaza. Daily 11am–5pm.

DIRECTORY

Money and exchange Banco de Credito, Jr Zepita 402, has an ATM; and there's the casa de cambio Dolares Vilca, 28 de Julio 331 ☎053 782 728.
Post office Av Mariano Urqueta, block 3 (Mon–Sat

8am–7.30pm).
Tour agencies Tropical Travel, Jr Moquegua 608 (☎053 483 865), offers local travel and tour packages as well as car hire services.

Tacna

Over three hours south of Moquegua and five times larger, **TACNA**, at 552m above sea level, is the last stop in Peru. The only reason to stay here is if you're coming from or going over the border into **Chile** (see box, p.150) and the border-crossing timing demands you stop, or if you feel like a break in your overland journey. Tacna is designated a **Zona Franca** (a tax- or duty-free zone) where visitors can spend up to US$1000 in any one trip (with a limit of US$3000 in a year) on a range of tax-free electronic, sports and other luxury items. Tacna is also a centre for **cyclists**, particularly in August when there's usually a bicycle festival attracting competitors and enthusiasts from Bolivia and Chile as well as Peru.

Brief history

Founded as San Pedro de Tacna in 1535, just three years after the Spanish first arrived in Peru, Tacna was established by Viceroy Toledo as a *reducción de indígenas*, a forced concentration of normally scattered coastal communities, making them easier to tax and use as labour. Almost three hundred years later, in 1811, Francisco Antonio de Zela began the first struggle for independence from Spanish colonialism here. The people of Tacna suffered Chilean occupation from May 1880 until the Treaty of Ancón was signed in August 1929, after a local referendum. Nowadays, unfortunately, it's better known as an expensive city, infamous for both its contraband and its pickpockets. The reputation is worse than the reality: the usual precautions (see p.40) are adequate and it's not a violent place.

Plaza de Armas

The main focus of activity in this sprawling city is around the **Plaza de Armas** and along the Alameda Bolognesi. At the centre of the plaza, the ornamental *pileta*, designed by Gustave Eiffel, has a Neoclassical base depicting the four seasons, while on top of the main fountain are four children holding hands. The nearby Arco Parabólico was erected in honour of the Peruvian dead from the War of the Pacific. Fronting the plaza is the **Catedral**, designed by Eiffel in 1870 (though not completed until 1955) and built from *cantera* stones quarried from the hills of Intiorko and Arunta. The **Alameda Bolognesi**, located in the civic centre near the *Hotel de Turistas*, is an attractive, palm-lined avenue constructed in 1840; it's dotted with busts of local dignitaries and also one in fine marble of Christopher Columbus.

Some 8km north of Tacna (10–15min by taxi; S/8 one way), on Cerro Intiorko, the eight steel sculptures of **Campo de Alianza** stand in memory of the war heroes; there's also the small Museo de Sitio (daily 8am–5pm; free) which houses some old uniforms, arms and missiles left over from the historic battles.

Tacna's museums

There are a few museums in town. The **Museo Histórico Regional de Tacna** (Jr Apurímac 202; Mon–Sat 9am–6pm; free) combines ceramics and textiles from ancient cultures with exhibitions related to the nineteenth-century wars with Chile. The **Casa de Zela** (C Zela 542; Mon–Fri 8am–noon & 3–7pm) houses a small archeological museum exhibiting ceramics largely discovered in the region; the building itself has been a recognized historic monument since 1961. There is also the **Museo Ferroviario** on the corner of Calle Albarracin and Avenida Dos de Mayo (daily 8am–5.30pm; US$1), which is a must for rail enthusiasts; five minutes' walk from the plaza, it contains locomotives, machinery and documents mainly relating to the now defunct Tacna–Arica line, but also a collection of train-related stamps from around the world. On Avenida Grau, there's also **Parque de la Locomotora**, built in 1977, dedicated exclusively to housing the antique Locomotive No. 3, which carried troops to the historic battle of Morro de Arica in 1879.

ARRIVAL AND GETTING AROUND   TACNA

BY BUS

You'll most likely alight at one of the Terminal Terrestres. It's easy enough to walk to the centre of town from the Manuel Odria Terminal, but better to take a taxi from the Bolognesi Terminal, where they are easy enough to find. Most long-distance and international buses leave from the Manuel Odria Terminal on C Hipólito Unanue (☎ 052 427 007), or from outside the train station on Av 2 de Mayo; shorter-distance local buses for the interior of the region leave from the Bolognesi Terminal on Av Circunvalación (☎ 052 411 786).

2

Destinations Arequipa (several daily; 6hr); Arica (several daily; 1–2hr); Cusco (several daily; 14–16hr); Desaguadero (daily; 6hr); La Paz (daily; 10–12hr); Lima (several daily; 20hr); Moquegua (several daily; 2–3hr); Puno (daily; 10hr).

BY PLANE
The airport, Aeropuerto Carlos Ciriani Santa Rosa, is out on the Panamericana Sur at Km 5 (☎ 052 314 672). The main

airline offices are Lan Perú, Apurimac 101 (☎ 01 213 8200), and Peruvian Airlines (☎ 052 480 011).
Destinations Lima (daily; 2hr).

BY TAXI
Taxis can be stopped anywhere in the centre with ease at any time of day and the fare for destinations within the city should not be any more than S/5–7.

INFORMATION
Tourist information Available from the tourist office at C Deustua 364, a few blocks from Plaza de Armas (Mon–Fri 9.30am–1pm & 4–7pm; ☎ 052 242 777), or IPeru (Av San

Martín 491; ☎ 052 425 514). Failing that, try the Dirección Regional de Industria y Turismo, Jr Blondell 506 (☎ 052 246 944), or check out ☎ turismotacna.com.

ACCOMMODATION
Gran Hotel Tacna Bolognesi 300 ☎ 052 424 193, ☎ granhoteltacna.com. This traditional hotel is located a few blocks from the Plaza de Armas. The interior belongs to another era, but then so do the courteous staff. There is a

spacious garden and good-sized pool. S/250
Hostal Hogar 28 de Julio 146 ☎ 052 426 811, ☎ hostalhogartacna.com. Good value in a secure hostel which has nice rooms with private baths, cable TV and wi-fi; it

---

CROSSING THE CHILEAN BORDER

The border with Chile (daily 9am–10pm) is about 40km south of Tacna. Arica, the first town in Chile, lies 25km beyond the border. There are a couple of hotels and plenty of restaurants. Bus and air services from here to the rest of Chile are excellent.

PERU–CHILE

By bus and colectivo Regular buses and colectivos to Arica leave from the modern bus terminal, on Hipolito Unanue, in Tacna. Tepsa (Leguis 981) and Ormeño (Araguex 698) buses leave the bus terminal every couple of hours or so for the one- to two-hour journey to Arica (S/12). Colectivos (normally around S/20) are quicker and slightly more expensive than the bus, but well worth it given the hassle saved, as they'll wait at the border controls while you get your Peruvian exit stamp and Chilean tourist card.
Customs You clear Peruvian customs control on your way out of Tacna, along the Panamericana.

CHILE–PERU

Coming into Peru from Arica is as simple as leaving. Colectivos run throughout the day. Though unlikely these days, night travellers might be required to have a *salvoconducto militar* (safe-conduct card), particularly in times of tension between the two countries; if so, your driver will likely organize it. If you intend to travel at night, check first with the tourist office in Arica, C Prat 305, on the second floor.

ACCOMMODATION IN ARICA

End of the Trail Esteban Alvarado 117 ☎ +56 991 518 479, ☎ endofthetrail-arica.cl. Five minutes from the bus station, the rooms are more than adequate with clean, comfortable beds, a great breakfast and outstanding service. US$15
Hostal Sunny Days Tomas Aravena 161 and Pedro de Valdivia ☎ +56 582 241 038, ☎ sunny-days -arica.cl. A short stroll from the beach and the bus station, this nice and clean hostel has a great atmosphere thanks to the ever-present kiwi owner who has a ready smile and plenty of advice to give. There are both private and shared rooms, and the

breakfast is a feast. Dorms US$15, doubles US$40
Hotel Avenida Diego Portales 2422, Arica ☎ +56 582 583 656, ☎ hotelavenida.cl. A modern three-storey hotel with lovely gardens, a large pool and ample-sized bedrooms, some with kitchenette; wi-fi and cable TV available throughout. US$70
Hotel Casa Beltran Rafael Sotomayor 266 ☎ +56 582 253 839, ☎ hotelcasabeltran.com. A well-done boutique hotel experience for those wanting a bit of luxury during their stay in Arica. Quality in the details and stylish all round. Don't miss the restaurant downstairs. US$120

is centrally located half a block from the Plaza de Armas. S/90
Hotel Las Lido Av San Martín 876 ☎052 577 001.
Comfortable rooms in a well-looked-after basic hotel; just off the Plaza de Armas. S/50

EATING

El Caquique C José Rosa Ara 1903 ☎052 414 582. The local *picantería* – a traditional eating place specializing in spicy and usually abundant local dishes (S/25–40) – and probably the best place to try guinea pig. Daily 11am–5pm.

Comedor Mercado Central, Zona Monumental. The central market is the best place for a tasty and very cheap meal for under S/10; also excellent juice stands where you can select your own mix for S/4–6. Busiest between 7 and 11am. Daily 7am–6pm.

Mar Adentro Av Pinto 28 ☎052 426 027. A dressed up cevichería with modern stone walls and soft natural light filtering through the roof; the prices are higher than average, but it is well worth it if you're looking for a last treat before leaving Peru. Go for the *ronda fría* (S/70 for three people; a selection of four different seafood dishes, including a ceviche and a *causa*) to try a bit of everything, or their fish of the day with a seafood sauce is delicious (S/30). Daily 11am–4pm.

La Olla de Barro Billinghurst 951 ☎052 503 501. Prides itself on Peruvian dishes typical of the region, such as the Combinado Triple (S/26), a delicious *choclo con queso* (sweetcorn and cheese) or the spicy *picante de Tacnena* (duck in a chili and oregano sauce – S/17). Daily 11am–9pm.

DIRECTORY

Banks and exchange Cash and travellers' cheques can be changed at the Banco de la Nación, San Martín 321 ☎052 426 130, on the Plaza de Armas; Banco Continental, San Martín 665 and the Banco de Credito, San Martín 574. *Cambistas* hang around on avenidas Bolognesi and Mendoza. It's a good idea to get rid of your extra nuevo soles before going into Chile (exchange them for US dollars or, if not, Chilean pesos), and the *cambistas* in Tacna usually offer better rates than those in Santiago or Arica anyway.

Post office Av Bolognesi 361 ☎052 724 221 (Mon–Sat 8am–8pm).

2

Arequipa and Lake Titicaca

STONE ARCH, LAKE TITICACA

Arequipa and Lake Titicaca

While the southern coast of Peru boasts all manner of intriguing cultural sites, the adjacent interior of the south is much better known for its extremely beautiful geographical features. The Andes take hold here, punctuated by spectacular lakes, towering volcanoes and deep, stark canyons – a landscape well suited to adventurous outdoor pursuits like trekking, canoeing, climbing or mountain biking. The region has two distinct areas: one focused around Arequipa, not far removed from the coast though high above sea level; the other, the Titicaca Basin, high in the east at the northern end of the immense Altiplano, which stretches deep into Bolivia. Both are detached from the rest of the country, something reflected as much in political leanings as their landscapes, themselves unique in Peru.

3

Arequipa, second city of Peru and a day's journey from Lima, sits poised against an extraordinary backdrop of volcanic peaks. Located 2335m above sea level, the city enjoys a distinctly poetic appearance. If you're coming from the north, it's one of the last places to really merit a stop before continuing on south to the **Chilean border** (see p.150). White local stone from the surrounding mountains has been heavily incorporated into the city's buildings and was a major factor in Arequipa being designated a UNESCO World Heritage site. Trekkers from across the world are attracted by the startlingly varied countryside within the city's reach: from the gorges of both the **Colca Canyon** – massive but dwarfed by the glaciers and volcanoes on either side of the valley – and the more distant **Cotahuasi Canyon**, to the unsettling isolation of the **Valley of the Volcanoes**.

Further inland from Arequipa, you'll probably want to spend time at the world's highest lake, **Lake Titicaca**. The surrounding area is renowned for its folk dances and Andean music and this is an obvious place to break a journey from Arequipa to Cusco or into **Bolivia**. Visit and stay on one of the huge lake's islands to experience life in a very traditional Andean household or get to know its main town and port – **Puno**, a high, quite austere city with a cold climate and incredibly rarefied air. **Juliaca**, to the north of Puno, makes an alternative, if dull and unattractive, base for exploring the lake, or the countryside of this poor, largely peasant area.

Arequipa

A wealthy city with a population of almost 800,000, **AREQUIPA** maintains a rather aloof attitude towards the rest of Peru. Most Arequipans feel themselves distinct, if not culturally superior, and resent the idea of the nation revolving around Lima. This confident image arose in the nineteenth century when the city found itself wealthy on the back of the wool trade with England.

Arequipeña delicacies p.169
Traditional folk music in Arequipa p.171
Colca Canyon tourist tickets p.179
Trekking in and around the Colca
   Canyon p.180
Hats in the Colca Canyon p.181

Titicaca's aquatic inhabitants p.188
Puno festivals p.190
The Uros p.196
Weaving and knitting on Taquile p.198
The Gateway of Amaru Muru p.200

HOT SPRINGS OF LA CALERA

Highlights

❶ **Monasterio de Santa Catalina** Exploring the labyrinthine, sunlit streets of this Arequipa convent is a calming, even spiritual, experience in its own right. **See p.160**

❷ **La Calera** Wallow, swim and relax in the fantastic hot springs of La Calera, a short distance from Chivay at the head of Colca Canyon. **See p.177**

❸ **Mirador Cruz del Condor** A breathtaking viewpoint on the rim of Colca Canyon, offering daily sightings of wild condors swooping above and below. **See p.181**

❹ **Sangalle** Trek down into the heart of the arid Colca Canyon to Sangalle, an oasis of greenery with palm and fruit trees – and a couple of

inviting swimming pools too. **See p.181**

❺ **Cotahuasi Canyon** Not only one of the deepest canyons in the world, this is also one of the most remote valleys that can be reached relatively easily by bus in the Peruvian Andes. **See p.185**

❻ **Sillustani** The ring of tower-like *chullpa* tombs at this ancient temple/cemetery overlooks Titicaca from a little peninsula in Lake Umayo. **See p.194**

❼ **Taquile and Amantani islands** These Lake Titicaca islands offer a genuinely fascinating glimpse of what life must have been like five hundred years ago. **See p.196 & p.198**

HIGHLIGHTS ARE MARKED ON THE MAP ON P.156

Situated at the foot of an ice-capped volcano – **El Misti** (5821m) – and close to four other prominent volcanoes, Arequipa has long been famous for having one of the most beautiful settings and pleasant climates of all Peru's cities. Despite a disastrous earthquake in 1687, it's still endowed with some of the country's finest colonial **churches** and **mansions**, many of which were constructed from white volcanic *sillar*, cut from the surrounding mountains and often flecked with black ash.

Characterized by arched interior ceilings, Arequipa's architectural beauty comes mainly from the colonial period. In general, the style is stark and almost clinical, except where Baroque and *mestizo* influences combine, as seen on many of the fine sixteenth- to eighteenth-century facades. A huge number of religious buildings are spread about the old colonial centre. The architectural design of the **Monasterio de Santa Catalina**, a convent complex enclosing a complete world within its thick walls, constitutes perhaps the city's main appeal to travellers. Further out, but still within walking distance, you can visit the attractive suburbs of **San Lázaro**, **Yanahuara** and **Cayma**, this last being particularly renowned for its dramatic views of the valley.

Brief history

Arrowheads and rock art are proof of human occupation around Arequipa for over ten thousand years. This began with early groups of hunter-gatherers arriving here on a seasonal basis for several millennia from 8000 BC to around 1000 BC when horticulture and ceramic technology began to appear in small settlements along streams and rivers. Initially influenced by the Paracas culture and later by the

AREQUIPA AND LAKE TITICACA

HIGHLIGHTS
1. Monasterio Santa Catalina
2. La Calera
3. Mirador Cruz del Condor
4. Sangalle
5. Cotahuasi Canyon
6. Sillustani
7. Taquile and Amantani islands

Tiahuanaco-Huari, two major local groups emerged sharing the area: the **Churajone** living in the far northwest section of the Arequipa region, and the **Chuquibamba** who thrived higher up in the Andean plateaus above Arequipa until the arrival of the Incas.

The name Arequipa is derived from the **Quechua** phrase "*ari quepay*", meaning "let's stop here", which, according to local legend, is exactly what the fourth Inca emperor, **Mayta Capac**, said to his generals on the way through the area following one of his conquest trips.

Colonial development

The Incas were not alone in finding Arequipa to their liking. When **Pizarro** officially "founded" the city in 1540, he was moved enough to call it Villa Hermosa, or Beautiful Town, and *Don Quixote* author Miguel de Cervantes extolled the city's virtues, saying that it enjoyed an eternal springtime. The lovely white stone lent itself to extravagant buildings and attracted master architects to the city.

The wool trade

During the eighteenth and nineteenth centuries, this mountainous region became an important source of sheep and alpaca **wool exports**, largely to the UK. Connected to the rest of Peru only by mule track until 1870, Arequipa was slow to become the provincial capital it is today. Money made mainly from exports kept the economy growing enough to establish an electric urban tramway in 1913 and then a road up to Puno in 1928.

Political upheaval

Having acquired a reputation as *the* centre of **right-wing political power**, while populist movements have tended to emerge around Trujillo in the north, Arequipa has traditionally represented the solid interests of the oligarchy. Important politicos, such as Francisco Javier de Luna Pizarro, who was president of Congress on many occasions in the nineteenth century, came from Arequipa. Sanchez Cerro and Odria both began their **coups** here, in 1930 and 1948 respectively, and Belaunde, one of the most important presidents in pre- and post-military coup years, sprang into politics from one of the wealthy Arequipa families. By 1972 the city's population had reached 350,000. Twenty years later it passed half a million, with many people arriving from the Andean hinterland to escape the violence of Peru's civil war.

The **social extremes** are quite clear today; despite the tastefully ostentatious architecture and generally well-heeled appearance of most townsfolk, there is much poverty in the region and there's been a huge increase in the number of street beggars in Arequipa. Social polarization came to a head in 2002, when the city's streets were ripped up in political protest against President Toledo's plans to sell off the local electric utility.

Plaza de Armas

The **Plaza de Armas**, one of South America's grandest, is very much the focus of the city's social activity in the early evenings, dotted with palms, flowers and gardens. At its heart sits a bronze fountain, topped by an angel fondly known as *turututu* because of the trumpet it carries. The east and west sides of the plaza are dominated by fine granite portals and colonial-style wooden balconies, while the southern edge is taken up by a municipal building.

La Catedral

Plaza de Armas • **Cathedral** Mon–Sat 7–10am & 5–7pm, Sun 9am–1pm • Free • **Museum** Mon–Sat 9am–5pm • S/10 • ☎ 054 213 149, ⓦ museocatedralarequipa.org.pe

The arcades and elegant white facade of Arequipa's seventeenth-century **Catedral** demand attention, even drawing your eyes away from El Misti towering behind. Displaying some French influence in its Neo-Renaissance style, it looks particularly beautiful when lit up in the evenings. Consecrated in 1556, the cathedral building was subsequently gutted by

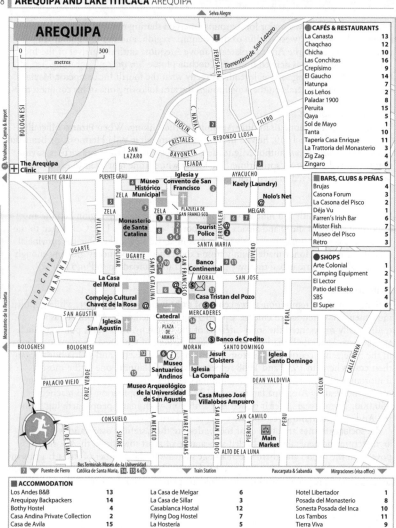

Selva Alegre

AREQUIPA

0 _____ 300
metres

fire in 1844 and restored in 1868 by Lucas Poblete, before coming to grief again in 2001 when its impressive Neoclassical towers were seriously damaged in an earthquake. The cathedral's pulpit was brought over from Lille in France in 1879, while the large organ with a height of 15m, shipped over to Peru in 1854, is one of the largest in South America. Entry to the adjacent Museo de la Catedral, which houses impressive religious artefacts, grants access to the bell tower from where there are wonderful views of the city and beyond.

Iglesia La Compañía

Calles General Moran and Alvarez Thomas • Mon–Sat 9am–12.30pm & 3–6pm, Sun 9.30am–12.30pm & 3–6pm • Free

On the southeast corner of the Plaza de Armas, opposite the Catedral, and more exciting architecturally, sits the elaborate **Iglesia La Compañía**. The original church, built in 1573, was destroyed eleven years later by an earthquake. The present structure was completed in 1660, when the magnificently sculpted **doorway**, with a locally inspired zigzagging *mestizo*-Baroque stone relief, was crafted using only shadow to outline the figures of the frieze. Inside, by the main altar, hangs a *Virgin and Child* by Bernardo Bitto, which arrived from Italy in 1575.

Jesuit Cloisters

Cloisters open 24hr; Chapel of San Ignacio de Loyola Mon–Sat 9am–1pm & 3–6pm, Sun 9am–1pm • S/4 • ☎ 054 212 141

Next door to the Iglesia La Compañía are the **Jesuit Cloisters**, superbly carved back in the early eighteenth century. In the first cloister, squared pillars support white stone arches and are covered with intricate reliefs showing angels, local fruits and vegetables, seashells and stylized puma heads. The second cloister is, in contrast, rather austere, although it is home to the stunning seventeenth-century **Chapel of San Ignacio de Loyola,** whose cupola depicts images of warriors, angels and Evangelists, along with parrots, fruits and flowers with Spanish and Arab influences. Both cloisters are today home to crafts and clothes shops.

3

Iglesia Santo Domingo

Calles Santo Domingo and Rivero • Daily 7.30am–9.30pm & 3.30–6pm • Free

East of the Iglesia La Compañía and the plaza you'll find the exquisitely restored **Iglesia Santo Domingo**, originally built in 1553 by Gaspar Baez, the first master architect to arrive in Arequipa. Most of what you see today was built between 1650 and 1698, but suffered major damage during the earthquakes of 1958 and 1960. The large main door represents an interesting example of Arequipa's *mestizo* craftsmanship – an Indian face amid a bunch of grapes, leaves and cacti – and the side door is said to be the oldest in the city.

Casa de Tristan del Pozo

C San Francisco 108 • Mon–Fri 9am–1pm & 4–6pm, Sat 9am–1pm • Free • ☎ 054 215 060 ext 252

Opposite the northeast corner of the Catedral stands a particularly impressive colonial mansion, **Casa de Tristan del Pozo**, also known as La Casa Rickets. Built in 1738 as a seminary, it later became the splendid residence of the Rickets family, who made their fortune from the wool trade in the late nineteenth century. The building boasts an extremely attractive traditional facade and courtyard. The stonework above the main door depicts Christ's genealogy, with highly stylized plants supporting five discs, or Jesuit medallions, with JHS (the abbreviation for the name Jesus) at the centre, Mary and Joseph to the side of this, and Joachim and Anna on the extremes. Now owned and lavishly restored by the Banco Continental, the mansion houses three art galleries.

Complejo Cultural Chavez de la Rosa

C Santa Catalina 101 • Mon–Fri 8am–8.30pm • Free • ☎ 054 204 482

North of the Plaza de Armas, the Casa Arróspide (also known as the Casa Iriberry) is home to the **Complejo Cultural Chavez de la Rosa**. This attractive 1743 colonial building belongs to the law faculty of the University of San Agustín and hosts changing selections of modern works by artists (mostly Peruvian). It possesses three main galleries with works that change every fortnight.

La Casa del Moral

C Moral 318 • Mon–Sat 9am–5pm • S/5 • ☎ 054 285 371

Around the corner from the Casa Arróspide sits the seventeenth-century **Casa del Moral** (literally "Mulberry House"), lovingly restored and refurbished with period pieces. Its most engaging feature is a superb stone gateway, carved with motifs that are similar to those on Nazca ceramics – puma heads with snakes growing from their mouths – surrounding a Spanish coat of arms. The mansion's name comes from an ancient *mora* tree, still thriving in the central patio.

Iglesia San Agustín

Calles Bolívar and San Agustín • Daily 8am–12.30pm & 5–8pm • Free

One block from La Casa del Moral, the elegant 1575 **Iglesia San Agustín** has one of the city's finest Baroque facades, added later in the late eighteenth century. Its old convent cloisters are now attached to the university, while inside only the unique octagonal sacristy survived the 1868 earthquake.

Monasterio de Santa Catalina

C Santa Catalina 301 • Daily: May–Dec 8am–5pm; Jan–April 9am–5pm; Tues & Thurs open till 8pm • S/40; guides are optional at around S/20 (1hr) • ⊕ santacatalina.org.pe

Two blocks north of the Plaza de Armas the vast walls of the **Monasterio de Santa Catalina** shelter a convent that housed almost two hundred secluded nuns and three hundred servants from the late sixteenth century until 1970, when it opened some of its outer doors to the public. The most important and prestigious religious building in Peru, its enormous complex of rooms, cloisters and tiny plazas takes an hour or two to explore. Some thirty nuns still live here today, though they worship in the main chapel only outside opening hours.

Originally the concept of Gaspar Baez in 1570, though only granted official licence five years later, the convent was funded by the Viceroy Toledo and the wealthy María de Guzmán, who later entered the convent with one of her sisters and donated all her riches to the community. The most striking feature is its predominantly Mudéjar style, adapted by the Spanish from the Moors, but which rarely found its way into their colonial buildings. The quality of the design is emphasized and harmonized by a superb interplay between the white stone and brilliant colours in the ceilings, the strong sunlight and deep-blue sky above the maze of narrow interior streets.

Los locutorios

Once you enter, you file left along the first corridor to a high vaulted room with a ceiling of opaque *huamanga* stone imported from the Ayacucho Valley. Beside here are **los locutorios** – little cells where on holy days the nuns could talk, unseen, to visitors.

The Novices Cloister and Orange Tree Cloister

The **Novices Cloister**, beyond the *locutorios*, is built in solid *sillar*-block columns, with antique wall paintings depicting the various qualities to which the devotees were expected to aspire and the Litanies of the Rosary. Off to the right, the **Orange Tree Cloister** (Claustro Naranjal), painted a beautiful blue with birds and flowers over the vaulted arches, is surrounded by a series of paintings showing the soul evolving from a state of sin to the achievement of God's grace. In one of the side rooms, dead nuns were mourned, before being interred within the monastic confines.

La lavandería

Calle Cordoba runs from the Orange Tree Cloister past a new convent, where the nuns now live. The road continues as Calle Toledo, a long, very narrow street that's the oldest part of the monastery and connects the main dwelling areas with **la lavandería**, or communal washing sector, brought to life with permanently flowering geraniums. There are several rooms off here worth exploring, including small chapels, prayer rooms and a kitchen. The *lavandería* itself, perhaps more than any other area, offers a captivating insight

3

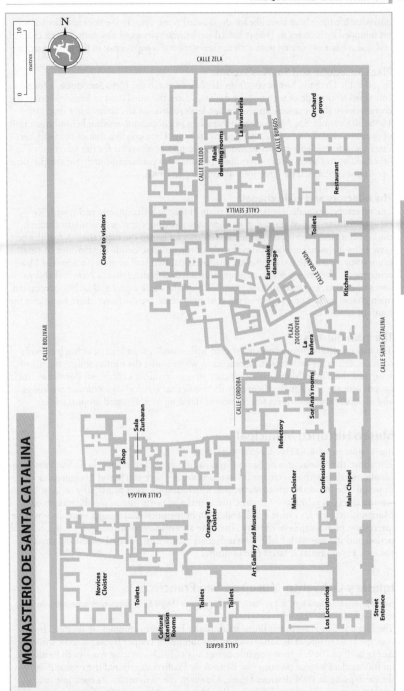

MONASTERIO DE SANTA CATALINA

N

0 — 10 metres

CALLE BOLIVAR

CALLE ZELA

Closed to visitors

La lavanderia

Main dwelling rooms

CALLE TOLEDO

CALLE BURGOS

Orchard grove

CALLE SEVILLA

Restaurant

Toilets

Earthquake damage

CALLE GRANADA

Kitchens

PLAZA ZOCODOVER

La bañera

CALLE SANTA CATALINA

Sor Ana's rooms

CALLE CORDOBA

Refectory

Sala Zurbaran

Shop

CALLE MALAGA

Orange Tree Cloister

Art Gallery and Museum

Main Cloister

Confessionals

Main Chapel

Novices Cloister

Toilets

Cultural Extension Rooms

Toilets

Toilets

CALLE UGARTE

Los Locutorios

Street Entrance

into what life must have been like for the closeted nuns; open to the skies and city sounds yet bounded by high walls. Twenty halved earthenware jars stand alongside a water channel, and it also has a swimming pool with sunken steps and a papaya tree in the lovely garden.

Plaza Socodobe and Sor Ana's rooms

Broad Calle Granada brings you from the *lavandería* to the **Plaza Socodobe**, a fountain courtyard to the side of which is the *bañera*, where the nuns used to bathe. Around the corner, down the next little street, are **Sor Ana's rooms**. By the time of her death in 1686, 90-year-old Sor Ana was something of a phenomenon, leaving behind her a trail of prophecies and cures. Her own destiny in Santa Catalina, like that of many of her sisters, was to castigate herself in order to offer up her torments for the salvation of other souls – mostly wealthy Arequipan patrons who paid handsomely for the privilege. Sor Ana was beatified by Pope John Paul II in the 1990s.

The refectory and main chapel

The **refectory**, immediately before the main cloisters, is deceptively plain, with its exceptional star-shaped stained-glass windows shedding dapples of sunlight through the empty space. Nearby, confessional windows look into the **main chapel**, but the best view of its majestic cupola is from the top of the staircase beside the cloisters. A small room underneath these stairs has an intricately painted wall niche with a Sacred Heart centrepiece. The ceiling is also curious, illustrated with three dice, a crown of thorns and some other, less recognizable items. Within the quite grand and lavishly decorated **main chapel** itself, but not part of the tour these days, are the lower choir room and the tomb of Sor Ana.

The main cloisters

The **main cloisters** themselves are covered with murals on an intense ochre base with cornices and other architectural elements in white stone; the murals follow the life of Jesus and the Virgin Mary. Although they were originally a communal dormitory, their superb acoustics now make them popular venues for classical concerts and weddings and the space can absorb up to 750 people standing or 350 seated around tables.

Museo Histórico Municipal

Plaza de San Francisco 407 • Daily 8.30am–5pm • S/10 • ☎ 054 221 017

Just above the Monasterio de Santa Catalina, the small, leafy Plazuela de San Francisco, usually buzzing with students and townspeople, is where you'll find Arequipa's city museum, the **Museo Histórico Municipal**, which devotes itself principally to local heroes – army chiefs, revolutionary leaders, presidents and poets (including the renowned Mariano Melgar). It's rather a dull collection of memorabilia, though some rooms have interesting photographs of the city. There are also displays of artefacts from the colonial period and the war with Chile. The university's museums, located on the outskirts of the city, are of greater interest (see opposite).

Iglesia y Convento-Museo de San Francisco

Plaza de San Francisco • Church Mon–Sat 7.15–9am & 4–8pm, Sun 7.15am–12.45pm & 6.15–8pm; convent/museum Mon–Sat 9am–noon & 3–6pm • Church free, museum S/5 • ☎ 054 223 048

The Plaza de San Francisco is home to a striking Franciscan complex, dominated by a convent and the **Iglesia de San Francisco**. Yet another of Gaspar Baez's projects, this one dating back to 1569, it shows an interesting mix of brick and *sillar* work both inside and on the facade. Original paintings by Baltazar de Prado once covered the central nave, but the earthquake of 1604 destroyed these. However, the nave retains its most impressive feature – a pure-silver altar. Adjoining the church are rather austere convent cloisters and the very simple **Capilla de la Tercera Orden**, its entrance decorated with modest *mestizo* carvings of St Francis and St Clare, founders of the first and second orders.

Monasterio de Santa Teresa

C Melgar 303 • Tues–Sun 9am–5pm, Fri until 8pm • S/20 • ☎ 054 281 188, ⓦ museocarmelitas.com

Close to the centre of town, the **Monasterio de Santa Teresa** has thirteen exhibition spaces set around beautiful cloisters dating from 1750 to 1753. The monastery's most valuable piece is the **custodia**, decorated with more than 2000 pearls and 250 precious and semi-precious stones including diamonds, rubies and amethysts, which continues to be used every year during Semana Santa (Holy Week) processions. Among the other objects on display are antique Chinese porcelain ceramics dating back to the era of Emperor Wanli (1573–1619) – to this day it is not known how or why they came to the monastery from the Far East. Nuns continue to call the building home – if you're visiting around noon you will hear them ring the monastery bells as they enter the premises to pray.

Monasterio de La Recoleta

C La Recoleta 117 • Mon–Sat 9am–noon & 3–5pm • S/10 • ☎ 054 270 966

The **Monasterio de La Recoleta** is located on the western side of the Río Chili, which runs its generally torrential course through Arequipa from Selva Alegre, dividing the old heart of the city from what has become a more modern downtown sector, including Yanahuara (see p.164) and Cayma (see p.164). This large Franciscan monastery stands conspicuously alone on Callejón de La Recoleta, just ten to fifteen minutes' walk east of the Plaza de Armas.

The stunning major and minor cloisters were built in 1651; in 1869 it was converted to an Apostolic Mission school administered by the Barefoot Franciscans. It is the archeology and natural history **museums** that really draw people here though. Open to the public since 1978, they house: two rooms of pre-Columbian artefacts including textiles and ceramics; an Amazon room showing artefacts from jungle Indian tribes and examples of forest flora and fauna; a religious and modern art gallery displaying both Cusqueña and Arequipeña classical works; plus a renowned historic library with some 25,000 sixteenth- and seventeenth-century volumes.

Museo Santuarios Andinos

C La Merced 110 • Mon–Sat 9am–6pm, Sun 9am–3pm • S/20 • ☎ 054 215 013

The **Museo Santuarios Andinos**, part of the Universidad Católica de Santa María, is arguably the most important museum in Arequipa today, with displays of some nineteen Inca mummies and a range of archeological remains; guides are obligatory but their fee, which is additional, is negotiable. The main exhibit is **Juanita**, the ancient 13-year-old "princess" uncovered in her icy ritual grave on September 8, 1995, by an expedition that included the archeologists Johan Reinhard and José Chavez, along with the well-known *Andinista* Miguel Zarate. Her gravesite, located at the incredible altitude of 6380m on Ampato Volcano, is estimated to be about 500 years old. It is thought that Juanita was sacrificed to the Apu Ampato and killed, after a time of fasting and herbal sedation, with a blow to the head by a five-pointed granite mace. The museum also contains fine examples of associated grave goods like textiles, precious metals and Inca ceramics.

Museo de Arqueología de la Universidad Católica de Santa Maria

C Cruz Verde 303 • Mon–Fri 8am–5pm • Free, includes a guided tour; donations expected • ☎ 054 221 083, ⓦ ucsm.ed.pe

Distinct from Santuarios Andinos, but also a university affiliate, is the **Museo de Arqueología de la Universidad Católica de Santa María**. This museum has seven rooms concentrating on items from pre-Conquest cultures such as the Huari, Tiahuanuco,

Chancay and Inca, and boasts around a thousand different pieces such as stone weapons, ceramics, textiles, grave goods, as well as other worked and ancient stone, wood and metal objects.

Museo Arqueológico de la Universidad de San Agustín

C Alvarez Thomas 200 • Mon–Fri 9am–4pm • S/2 • ☎ 054 288 881, ⓦ unsa.edu.pe

The largest of Arequipa's archeological museums, the **Museo Arqueológico de la Universidad de San Agustín**, has good collections of everything from mummies and replicas of Chavín stones to Nazca, Huari and Inca ceramics, as well as colonial paintings and furniture. There are more than 14,000 pieces held here at the university campus.

Casa Museo José Villalobos Ampuero

C Alvarez Thomas 206 • Mon–Sat 9.30am–5pm • S/20 includes 45min guided tour • ☎ 054 220 855, ⓦ casamuseovillalobos.com

The beautiful **Museo José Villalobos Ampuero** offers a glimpse into the wealthy home of José Villalobos, the former mayor of Arequipa. Built in the early twentieth century, the building's Art Nouveau facade with curving wavy columns was constructed using materials exclusively from Europe, including Italian granite and marble. The sumptuous interiors contain antique wooden furniture, porcelain ornaments, a Titian painting and a one-tonne chandelier embellished with statuettes of the Greek goddess Minerva. Note the seventeenth-century cross in the bedroom, which was decorated with diamond nails. To this day the house continues to be used on special occasions by family members.

San Lázaro

The oldest quarter of Arequipa – and the first place the Spanish settled in this valley – is the barrio of **San Lázaro**, an uncharacteristic zone of tiny, curving streets stretching around the hillside at the top end of Calle Jerusalén, all an easy stroll north from the plaza. If you feel like a walk, and some good views of El Misti, you can walk down to the river from here and cross over Puente Grau towards Yanahuara suburb (10min away) where there's a superb vantage point.

Yanahuara

Until the railway boom of the late nineteenth century, which brought peasant migrants to Arequipa from as far away as Cusco, **Yanahuara** was a distinct village. It is now built up, though it still commands stunning views across the valley, above all from its **churches**. There are also one or two fine **restaurants** in this sector. The municipal plaza possesses a beautiful **viewing point** (*mirador*), which has been made famous by postcards.

To get here, catch a bus or colectivo from the junction of Puente Grau and Calle Santa Catalina, or walk from San Lázaro (see above).

Iglesia Yanahuara

Yanahuara Plaza • Mon–Fri 9am–noon & 4–8pm, Sat 9.30am–2.30pm • Free • ☎ 054 253 664

The small **Iglesia Yanahuara** on the tranquil main plaza dates to the middle of the eighteenth century, and its Baroque facade is particularly fine, with a stone relief of the tree of life incorporating angels, flowers, saints, lions and hidden Indian faces.

Cayma

From Puente Grau, a longish stroll takes you across to the west bank of the Chili, along Avenida Ejercito and out to the suburb of **Cayma** (3–4km); there are also buses available (see below). Another kilometre or so further out than Yanahuara, the area was once a small suburb with views over the city, but now reflects the commercial, even flashy side of Arequipa, with large shops and even one or two nightclubs. The suburb also offers good views of the Chachani Volcano.

Iglesia de San Miguel

Main plaza • Mon–Sat 8am–noon • Free • ☎ 054 251 459

The **Iglesia de San Miguel**, built in the early eighteenth century, houses an image of the Virgen de la Candelaria, donated to the city by King Carlos V. It's possible to climb up to the roof of the church which offers great views across Yanahuara and towards the volcanoes to the north.

Puente de Fierro

South of the city centre, Arequipa's very impressive black-iron viaduct, or **Puente de Fierro**, provides a great vantage point for views over the city to El Misti. Although spanning half a kilometre, it was well designed by Gustave Eiffel and built to such high standards by the railway baron Henry May that it has successfully vaulted the city's bubbling **Río Chili** and withstood the test of Arequipa's severe earthquakes and tremors for over a hundred years.

3

ARRIVAL AND DEPARTURE   AREQUIPA

Arequipa is a popular stopping-off point between Lima and the Titicaca, Cusco and Tacna regions, and is a hub for most journeys in the southern half of Peru. From Arequipa you can continue to Cusco, or Titicaca by bus or plane. There's no passenger train between Arequipa and Puno or Cusco, but it is easy enough to travel by bus. **Bolivia** is also within a day's bus journey, while Tacna and the **Chilean frontier** (see p.150) are even more accessible from Arequipa by road.

BY PLANE

Flights by LAN (ⓦ lan.com), Peruvian (ⓦ peruvian.pe) and Avianca (ⓦ avianca.com) land at Arequipa's Aeropuerto Alfredo Rodríguez Ballón, 8km northwest of town (☎ 054 443 464). A taxi to the centre costs S/25 (30min).

Destinations Cusco (3 daily; 1hr); Juliaca, for Puno (2 daily; 40min); Lima (several daily; 1hr); Tacna (1 daily; 30min).

BY BUS

Most long-distance buses arrive at the Terminal Terrestre bus station (☎ 054 427 798) about 4km south from the centre of town, or at the Terrapuerto next door; there are regular buses from outside the station on Av La Marina west of the city centre (30–40min); a taxi to the Plaza de Armas is about S/15.

Destinations Cabanaconde (4 daily; 6–8hr); Chivay (8 daily; 4hr); Cusco (several daily; 9–12hr); Desaguadero (2 daily; 7–9hr); Ica (5 daily; 4hr 30min–5hr); Lima (several daily; 14–18hr); Moquegua (4 daily; 3–4hr); Nazca (10 daily; 5–6hr); Puerto Maldonado (2 daily; 16hr); Puno (6 daily; 6hr); Tacna (hourly; 5hr).

BUS OPERATORS

Del Carpio Terminal Terrapuerto (☎ 054 427 049 or ☎ 054 430 941). Services to the Majes Valley, Aplao and Pampacolca.

Civa Terminal Terrapuerto (☎ 054 432 208). Services to Cusco, Puno, Lima and Tacna.

Cruz del Sur Terminal Terrapuerto (☎ 054 720 444, ⓦ cruzdelsur.com.pe). Services to Lima, Nazca, Paracas, Ica, Cusco, Tacna and Puno.

Flores Terminal Terrestre (☎ 054 431 646). Services to Tacna, Moquegua and Ilo.

Jacantay Terminal Terrestre. Services to Juliaca, Puno, Desaguadero and La Paz.

Julsa Terminal Terrestre (☎ 054 430 843). Services to Puerto Maldonado.

Mendivil Terminal Terrestre (☎ 974 210 329). Services to Puerto Maldonado.

Moquegua Turismo Terminal Terrapuerto (☎ 054 431 545). Services to Tacna and Moquegua.

Oltursa Terminal Terrapuerto (☎ 054 423 152). Services to Lima, Nazca, Paracas and Ica.

Ormeño Terminal Terrapuerto (☎ 054 427 788). Services to Puno.

Reyna Terminal Terrestre (☎ 054 425 812). The best services to Chivay and Cabanaconde.

Tepsa Terminals Terrestre and Terrapuerto (☎ 054 424 135). International services, as well as to Lima.

Turismo Alex Av Olímpico 203 (☎ 054 202 863). Services to Andaray and Chuquibamba.

GETTING AROUND

On foot The centre of Arequipa is compact and it's easy enough to walk around.

By taxi If you want a taxi make sure you order a cab over the phone; taxis on the city streets are not necessarily safe – many are illegal and robberies have taken place in the past. Recommended firms include Aló 45 (☎054 454 545), Aló Cayma (☎054 458 282) and Taxi Plus (☎054 438 070).

By car Given the number of nearby attractions accessible by road, renting a car (with or without *chófer*) can work out well. A number of companies rent out 4WD vehicles, among them Hertz GyG at Palacio Viejo 214 (☎054 282 519, ⓦgygrentacar.com), DGA Rent a Car at Palacio Viejo 302A (☎054 281 741, ⓦrentacar.com) and Atix Rent a Car at C Ugarte 216 (☎054 224 327, ⓦatixrentacar.com).

INFORMATION

Tourist information The main iPeru office is on the Plaza de Armas (Mon–Sat 9am–8pm, Sun 9am–1pm; ☎054 223 265, ⓔiperuarequipa@promperu.gov.pe), with a branch at the airport that meets incoming flights.

TOURS AND ACTIVITIES

Taking a **guided tour** is the easiest way to negotiate the otherwise quite difficult region around Arequipa. It's tricky to get around here in a number of ways – the sheer terrain is inhospitable, massive and wild, and the altitude changes between Arequipa city and, say, Chivay, can affect you for a couple of days (mountain sickness with headaches), which makes driving your own rented car dicey until you're properly adjusted.

CITY TOURS

All operators tend to offer similar packages, with city tours lasting around three hours and usually including the Monasterio de Santa Catalina, La Compañía, La Catedral, Iglesia San Agustín and the Yanahuara *mirador*.

Bustour Portal San Agustín 111 ☎054 203 434, ⓦbustour.com.pe. Offers a half-day bus tour of the city and its outskirts – it starts near the Monastery of Santa Catalina and includes stops such as Puente Grau, Yanahuara and Carmen Alto. The tour (S/45) takes a circular route, with two daily departures at 9am and 2pm.

COUNTRYSIDE TOURS

Countryside tours (*tur de campiña*) usually consist of a roughly three-hour trip to the rural churches of Cayma and Sachaca, the old mill at Sabandia, Tingo lagoon and local *miradores* (private tours from S/240 for two people). Bus Tour (ⓦbustour.com.pe) has daily buses leaving at 9am and 2pm (S/45) although note this is in a large tour bus. Most companies also offer private one- to three-day trips out to the Colca Canyon (S/200–1500 per person; sometimes with very early morning starts) or to the petroglyphs at Toro Muerto (from S/350 per person, depending on group size). Trips to the Valley of the Volcanoes and the Cotahuasi Canyon are only offered by a select few companies (private tours from S/800 upwards). Specialist adventure activities, such as rafting in the Colca Canyon, mountaineering or serious trekking can cost anything from S/400–2000 for a three- to six-day outing. Of course, all prices vary according to the season, the quality you demand (in terms of food, transport to start point and whether you have *arrieros* with mules to carry your gear) and the size of the group. Mountain-bike rental ranges from S/40 to S/100 per day.

Carlos Zarate Adventures C Santa Catalina 204 ☎054 202 461, ⓦzarateadventures.com. A good expedition outfitter and a leading trekking and climbing company with decades of experience. It uses only professional and qualified guides such as Carlos Zarate, the internationally renowned founder. Treks include rock climbing and canoeing in the usual places such as Colca, El Misti and Cotahuasi, but there are also more adventurous routes including a trip from Colca to the Valley of the Volcanoes, and another to Nevado Mismi (see p.178).

Colca Trek C Jerusalén 401B ☎054 206 217, ⓦcolcatrek .com.pe. A well-established company operating its own lodge in the Colca Canyon, which serves as the start for several walks in the area, as well as more demanding climbs such as the one to Ampato, where the famous Juanita mummy was found. The company organizes climbing, rafting, biking and trekking, and also has equipment for rent.

Expediciones y Aventuras C Santa Catalina 219 ☎054 221 653, ⓦexpedicionesyaventuras.com. This company specializes in adventure activities including rafting down the ríos Chili and ríos Majes; canoeing in the Colca and Cotahuasi Canyons; body boarding along the Pacific Coast; rock climbing for beginners and advanced levels; and 4WD trips. It also arranges downhill and cross-country mountain biking trips, including to Chachani Volcano (6057m), where experienced bikers can descend all the way to Arequipa from an altitude of 4000m.

Naturaleza Activa C Santa Catalina 211 ☎968 969 544 or ☎988 227 723, ⓔnaturactiva@yahoo.com. This company deals in single-track, off-road and downhill biking along the coast and volcanoes, as well as in the Colca and Cotahuasi canyons. It also organizes treks in the canyons, as well as in the Valley of the Volcanoes, and arranges mountain climbing trips. You can rent camping equipment here, too.

Pablo Tour C Jerusalén 400A ☎054 203 737, ⓦpablotour.com. This reliable well-established company pioneered tourism in the Colca Canyon in the 1990s, and has since been operating tours to Cabanaconde and the surrounding areas. It has excellent links to hostels and local guides in the canyon, and also arranges trips to myriad other places including the Cotahuasi Canyon, the Valley of the Volcanoes and to the source of the Amazon River. Its registered mountain guides have the latest equipment including satellite phones and oxygen.

ACCOMMODATION

Arequipa has a good selection of accommodation in all price ranges, with most of the better options mainly within a few blocks of the **Plaza de Armas** or along **Calle Jerusalén**.

HOTELS

Casa Andina Private Collection C Ugarte 403 ☎054 226 907, ⓦcasa-andina.com. Previously housing the city's old Mint, this upmarket hotel just a stone's throw from the Monasterio de Santa Catalina features a range of rooms, from superiors with run-of-the-mill decor to lavishly furnished senior suites (S/1080) set around a beautiful colonial courtyard. **S/800**

Casa de Avila Av San Martín 116, Vallecito ☎054 213 177, ⓦcasadeavila.com. Accommodation is set around a large peaceful garden area shaded by a beautiful tree where friendly pet turtle Paca roams freely. Rooms feature faux-wooden floors and while they're perfectly comfortable with en-suite bathrooms, the decor and furnishings are somewhat uninspiring. The hotel's real draw is the friendly atmosphere and fun and educational cooking classes (S/65) that are held most days of the week. **S/180**

★**La Casa de Melgar** C Melgar 108 ☎054 222 459, ⓦlacasademelgar.com. A beautiful eighteenth-century colonial building with arched ceilings and thick stone walls, this was once the house of the Bishop of Arequipa who is remembered as having erected a cross on the summit of El Misti. The spacious rooms are set around a series of pretty courtyards with potted plants and feature beautiful parquet floors and antique furnishings. Breakfast is served in a bright blue courtyard, home to lofty cacti. **S/168**

La Casa de Sillar C Rivero 504 ☎054 284 249, ⓦlacasadesillar.com. A pleasant option especially for those on a bit of a budget wanting to stay somewhere quiet. Located in a beautiful colonial building with a pretty patio, the doubles with private bath are more welcoming than those with shared bath, with decorative wall paintings, lamps made using natural materials and clay floors. The quadruple mezzanine room (S/140) with a vaulted ceiling is a great choice for groups, there's a small rooftop terrace with hammock and a kitchen for guests' use, too. **S/70**

★**Casablanca Hostal** Puente Bolognesi 104 ☎054 221 327, ⓦcasablancahostal.com. This very agreeable place constructed with volcanic blocks of stone right by the main plaza features eight spacious rooms with private bathrooms and lovely parquet floors. Some rooms have private balconies overlooking the street, and there's an open-plan kitchen that guests are welcome to use. **S/120**

★**La Hostería** C Bolívar 405 ☎054 289 269, ⓦlahosteriaqp.com.pe. This little gem of a place has a pretty courtyard with fountain, colourful flowers and two caged parakeets, and is attractively furnished with beautifully carved wooden benches, a piano and old curios. Superior rooms (S/285) are more stylish and spacious and worth the extra cost. There's a little indoor pool and a sauna, too. **S/240**

Hotel Libertador Plaza Bolívar s/n ☎054 215 110, ⓦlibertador.com.pe. A pleasing, upmarket choice with efficient service and well-appointed rooms with modern amenities in a quiet neighbourhood a short walk north of town. Breakfast can either be enjoyed in the dining area or in the spacious garden with swimming pool. **S/720**

Posada del Monasterio C Santa Catalina 300 ☎054 206 565, ⓦhotelessanagustin.com.pe. Housed in a welcoming eighteenth-century *casona* (mansion), which once formed part of the Monasterio de Santa Catalina, this pleasant hotel with thick stone walls, vaulted ceilings and antiques offers comfortable rooms – carpeted or with faux-wooden floors – with orange bedspreads and private bathroom right in the heart of town. **S/375**

Sonesta Posada del Inca Portal de Flores 116 ☎054 215 530, ⓦsonesta.com. Located on the main square, this friendly hotel offers carpeted rooms with dark furnishings. There's a rooftop pool with lounge chairs and lovely views over the square and beyond, as well as a restaurant area with terrace overlooking the cathedral. **S/645**

Los Tambos Puente Bolognesi 129 ☎054 600 900, ⓦlostambos.com.pe. A central choice with neat and tidy rooms brightened up with a single yellow-painted wall and autumnal abstract paintings. All rooms have flat-screen TV and double glazing, a welcome addition in the centre of town where cars seemingly honk at all times of the day. The modern bathrooms are decked out in shades of grey. **S/259**

Tierra Viva C Jerusalén 202 ☎054 234 161. This is an excellent mid-range choice offering nicely appointed rooms with carpeted floors and comfortable beds with orthopaedic mattresses draped with alpaca blankets. Rooms are bright and equipped with modern amenities, including flat-screen TV and wi-fi, and the breakfast area is fronted by oversized pots of plants that add a unique touch. **S/390**

HOSTELS

Los Andes B&B La Merced 123 ☎054 330 015, ⓦlosandesarequipa.com. A stone's throw from the Plaza de Armas, this is a very decent budget choice with a large, open-plan kitchen perfect for self-caterers, as well as a breezy terrace area complete with TV lounge. Accommodation is in dorms and spacious privates with parquet flooring or carpets. Dorms S̲/̲2̲5̲, doubles S̲/̲8̲5̲

Arequipay Backpackers Pasaje O'Higgins 224 ☎054 234 560, ⓦarequipaybackpackers.com. A fun, brightly painted hostel with two movie rooms with flat-screen TV and PlayStation, a pool room and a pleasant patio with hammocks and barbecue set. Dorms are comfortable if a bit cramped, with sturdy beds, lockers and shared bathrooms. The simply decorated doubles and twins feature polished parquet floors and communal bathrooms. Dorms S̲/̲2̲0̲, doubles S̲/̲7̲0̲

Bothy Hostel Puente Grau 306 ☎054 282 438, ⓔbothyhostel@gmail.com. This colourful, laidback hostel in a seventeenth-century building just a few steps from Arequipa's nightlife centre features quirky murals and bean bags where travellers sit back and socialize at all times of the day. Dorms, mixed and female-only, have lockers and colourful linen. Dorms S̲/̲2̲7̲, doubles with private bathroom S̲/̲7̲0̲

★**Flying Dog Hostel** C Melgar 116 ☎054 231 163, ⓦflyingdogperu.com. This lovely hostel offers clean and welcoming rooms giving onto a couple of colourful courtyards dotted with cacti. There's a cavernous bar that's a good spot to meet fellow travellers, and there's a kitchen for self-caterers, too. Breakfast is served in a pretty patio area, and a cute little dog and cat guard the premises. Dorms S̲/̲3̲0̲, double with shared bathroom S̲/̲7̲5̲, double with private bathroom S̲/̲9̲0̲

3

EATING

As it's not too far from the Pacific, the town's better restaurants are also renowned for their excellent fresh seafood. **Picanterías** – traditional Peruvian eating houses serving spicy seafood – are particularly well established here.

CAFÉS

La Canasta C Jerusalén 115 ☎054 211 820, ⓦlacanastaaqp.com. This popular bakery tucked away off C Jerusalén offers *empañadas* (S/3.80), sandwiches (S/8), savoury pastries (S/5) and *quinoa* and cheese croissants (S/1.50) that can be enjoyed at little tables in the peaceful courtyard. Mon–Sat 8.30am–8pm.

★**Chaqchao** C Santa Catalina 204 ☎054 234 572, ⓦchaqchao.com. A chocolate lover's paradise specializing in chocolate and only chocolate – there's even (complimentary) chocolate tea, made from cocoa husks, and chocolate lip balm and soap available for purchase.

Here you can feast on home-made brownies (S/6), double chocolate cake (S/8) and exquisite hot chocolate (S/8) as you watch life go by from the little balcony overlooking C Santa Catalina. There are daily chocolate-making classes (S/60), too. Daily 11am–9pm.

Crepísimo C Santa Catalina 208 ☎054 206 620, ⓦcrepisimo.com. This popular two-storey restaurant located in the Alianza Francesa building offers a whopping one hundred types of sweet and savoury crepes; it's a great spot for a morning snack or a light lunch, and you can happily linger here for longer than planned. The café's *crepísimo* with ham, cheese and egg (S/16) remains its

---

AREQUIPEÑA DELICACIES

Arequipa's restaurants are famous across Peru for a range of delicious dishes that make use of local food resources such as *rocoto* (an indigenous type of pepper), guinea pig, peanuts, maize, potatoes, chillis and river shrimps. The city is particularly well known for the following dishes:

Adobo Typically eaten for breakfast in Arequipa. This is a pork dish where the meat and bones are soaked and cooked in maize-beer sediment or vinegar, onions, garlic, boiled small *rocotos* and chillis.

Chupe de camarones River shrimp casserole incorporating squashes, cheeses, chillis and potatoes.

Cuy chactado The name comes from the flat, round stone – or *chaqueria* – which is placed on top of a gutted and hung guinea pig to splay it out flat in a large frying pan, while cooking it in ample olive oil; it is usually served with toasted maize and a sauce made from chillis and the herb *huacatay* (black Andean mint).

Ocopa A cold appetizer that originated in this city but can be found on menus across Peru. it is made with potatoes, eggs, olives and a fairly spicy yellow chilli sauce, usually with ground peanuts added.

Rocoto relleno A spicy Andean pepper usually stuffed with minced pork meat and blended with garlic, tomato paste, eggs and mozzarella.

bestseller, and the great lunch deal (S/26) includes salad, crepe, dessert and drink. There's Old Speckled Hen beer (S/12) on tap, too, as well as book exchange, wi-fi and board games. Mon–Sat 8am–midnight, Sun 8am–10pm.

Tanta C Santa Catalina 210 ☏ 054 287 360, ⊕ tantaperu. com. This upmarket café displays a mouthwatering selection of delectable cakes and other sweet delights including macaroons (S/3) and truffles (S/3.50). The open-air courtyard with seating is a pleasant spot to enjoy a mid-afternoon snack or a more substantial meal (mains S/30), too. Mon–Sat 8.30am–10pm, Sun 8.30am–8pm.

RESTAURANTS

Chicha C Santa Catalina 210 ☏ 054 287 360, ⊕ chicha .com.pe. Renowned chef Gastón Acurio is behind this top-quality restaurant with a sister establishment in Cusco (see p.227). The setting, a fine colonial mansion, is a pleasant spot to enjoy a pre- or post-prandial drink. The menu includes Arequipa's famous *rocoto relleno* (S/28), deer *adobo* (S/39) and *quinoa* burgers (S/29). Mon–Sat noon–11pm, Sun noon–8pm.

★ **Las Conchitas** Av San Martín 200 ☏ 054 223 672. This small and friendly local hangout has been serving excellent fresh fish and seafood dishes at very reasonable prices since 2004. The crab *empañadas* (S/5) are delicious, as are the ceviche (S/21) and steamed fish with yucca or rice (S/35). Tues–Sun 10am–4pm.

El Gaucho Portal de Flores 112 ☏ 054 220 301. Right in the heart of town, this cosy basement restaurant with wooden interiors, lanterns and draped cow hide specializes in grilled meats. The set-lunch menu comprises salads, steak, potatoes, dessert and a glass of sangria. Mon–Sat noon–11.30pm.

Hatunpa C Ugarte 208 ☏ 054 212 918. This cheap and cheerful restaurant attracts a young foreign crowd with its potato-based dishes (S/12.50). Everything on the menu features potatoes with a topping of choice, including meat or veggies. The food is cooked in front of your eyes in the little open-plan kitchen. Mon–Sat 12.30–9.30pm.

Los Leños C Jerusalén 407 ☏ 054 281 818. This little place with stone walls and wooden tables rustles up decent wood-fire oven pizzas (S/18) served on rustic wooden boards. The Provençal pizza topped with aubergines, peppers, onion and black olives is particularly good (S/23). The menu also includes a handful of pasta dishes (S/18). Daily 5–11pm.

Paladar 1900 C San Francisco 227 ☏ 054 226 295. This upmarket yet quirky place with oversized armchairs and hanging white umbrellas offers delicious Peruvian food with a hint of Mediterranean and Japanese. The menu includes creative dishes such as the French-sounding *comantutapel* (breast of duck with green risotto and passionfruit sauce; S/37) and *tukurukuy* (grilled alpaca and *quinoa* risotto with vegetables and tomato sauce; S/33). Daily noon–midnight.

Peruita Palacio Viejo 321 ☏ 054 212 621. This Italian-owned and -run pizzeria with chequered red-and-white tablecloths serves tasty wood-fire-oven pizzas (S/26). The menu also features pasta, ravioli and lasagne (S/20), and there's an excellent-value set lunch for just S/15. Mon–Sat 1–3pm & 5.30–10.30pm.

Qaya C Ugarte 207 ☏ 054 235 687, ⊕ qaya.pe. This Peruvian restaurant serves tasty dishes including *rocoto relleno* (S/36) in a crimson-coloured dining area giving onto an interior courtyard. The food is particularly tasty, and there are great-value three-course lunch meals for S/28 (Tues–Fri only). Tues–Sat noon–4pm & 7–11pm, Sun noon–4pm.

Sol de Mayo C Jerusalén 207, Yanahuara ☏ 054 254148, ⊕ restaurantsoldemayo.com. Located in a different C Jerusalén (in the suburb of Yanahuara) to the one that bisects Arequipa's centre, this place has tables set within and around attractive gardens, live music and superbly prepared, traditional Peruvian dishes, all enjoyed in a convivial atmosphere. It's quite expensive, with main dishes starting at around S/30, but worth the S/5 taxi ride out here; alternatively it's a 15min walk over Puente Grau, then a few blocks up Av Ejercito. Call to reserve a table, since it's very popular. Daily 11am–6pm.

Tapería Casa Enrique C Jerusalén 212 ☏ 054 213 060, ⊕ restauranteytapasenrique.com. This laidback place offers Spanish favourites including tortilla, *chorizo* and manchego cheese, and you can enjoy Spanish and South American wines with a cheese or meat platter (S/60). The excellent-value set lunch (S/12; Mon–Sat) includes a starter, main (normally *paella*) and dessert. Daily noon–10pm.

★ **La Trattoria del Monasterio** C Santa Catalina 309 ☏ 054 204 062, ⊕ latrattoriadelmonasterio.com. Located within the grounds of the Monasterio de Santa Catalina, this is one of the city's best restaurants. The interior is warm and welcoming with three partitioned dining areas, while the cuisine offers superb fusion dishes that combine the best of Italian and Peruvian flavours. The ravioli and fettuccine are all home-made, and the creamy *Arequipa* risotto with lima beans, peas and shrimps is delicious. Mon–Sat noon–3pm & 7–11pm, Sun noon–3pm.

★ **Zig Zag** C Zela 210 ☏ 054 206 020, ⊕ zigzagrestaurant.com. A wonderful restaurant, with a cosy vaulted interior, specializing in sizzling, volcanic-stone-cooked meats and fish. The "alpine" menu includes Swiss favourites such as cheese fondue (S/74 for two people) and there's a great-value three-course lunch menu at S/49. The wine list features a great selection of South American labels, as well as a few European, and the adjacent bar and lounge area with fireplace is the perfect spot for a pre- or post-prandial drink. Daily noon–midnight.

Zingaro C San Francisco 309 ☏ 054 217662, ⊕ zingaro -restaurante.com. In the heart of town, this restaurant with bare-brick walls serves tasty Peruvian dishes in a rather smart setting. The menu includes boneless trout stuffed with mint and bacon (S/38) and alpaca *lomo* *saltado* (S/33), while the extensive wine list lists more than three hundred bottles; there's a convivial little bar area, too. Daily noon–11pm.

DRINKING AND NIGHTLIFE

Most of Arequipa's nightlife takes place on Calle San Francisco, lined with bars, pubs and clubs that get particularly busy on weekend evenings. There are establishments to suit all tastes, from laidback boozers to smarter bars serving pricey creative cocktails.

BARS

Brujas C San Francisco 300. On Arequipa's busy nightlife strip, this relaxed bar with a cosy wooden interior and low lighting is a great spot for those wanting to enjoy a beer (S/10, or three for S/25) and a chat without their voices being drowned out by pumping music. Daily 6pm–3am.

★ **La Casona del Pisco** C San Francisco 319 ☎ 054 231 809, ⓦ casonadelpisco.com. This classy gastro-bar has four ancient earthenware jugs used to store pisco in the first of a series of vaulted rooms where tastings take place. There's a patio with outdoor heaters, an open-fronted glass kitchen in the back garden and a terrace with spectacular views of the church of San Francisco. At the time of research there were plans to possibly open during the day, too. Mon–Wed & Sun 6pm–midnight, Thurs–Sat 6pm–2am.

Farren's Irish Bar Pasaje Catedral 107. This Irish pub-type bar tucked away behind the cathedral offers a wide range of drinks and imported beers, including Old Speckled Hen (S/20) and Abbot Ale (S/20), board games and a few tables spilling onto the pedestrianized street. Major sporting events are screened here, too. Mon–Sat 10am–midnight.

Museo del Pisco Calles Santa Catalina and Moral ☎ 054 281 583. The people behind the happening bar in Cusco (see p.229) have now opened up this establishment in Arequipa. With dozens of labels to choose from, it's the perfect spot for a pisco sour, particularly if you're after a quiet place where you can socialize over a drink or two. Mon–Thurs & Sun noon–midnight, Fri & Sat noon–1am.

CLUBS AND LIVE MUSIC

Casona Forum C San Francisco 317 ☎ 054 204 294, ⓦ casonaforum.com. This three-storey complex houses some of Arequipa's best nightspots, such as *Zero Pub & Pool*, with pool tables. The basement *Forum* disco is the place to see and be seen among young *Arequipeños*, with a lively tropical decor including palm trees, pools and a large artificial waterfall. Mon–Sat 7pm–late.

Déja Vu C San Francisco 319B ☎ 054 221 904, ⓦ dejavuaqp.com. This popular place gets particularly busy in the evenings as its appealing terrace, with sofas and views over town, is a particularly pleasant spot for a sundowner. It morphs into a club at night, mainly playing an eclectic mix of salsa and dance music on the ground floor and electronica on the first floor. There's a S/10 entry charge on weekends after 11.30pm. Mon–Wed & Sun 11am–3am, Thurs, Fri & Sat 11am–5am.

Mister Fish Av Variante Ucumayo s/n. This large club on the outskirts of Arequipa is one of the city's most popular nightlife spots, with dance and electronic music from late afternoon on Thursdays and creole music on Fridays, while on Saturday revellers go wild to club beats. Entry S/60. Thurs 3pm–5am, Fri & Sat 9pm–5am.

Retro C San Francisco 317 ☎ 054 204 294, ⓦ casonaforum.com. Located in the Casona Forum, this is Arequipa's only bar hosting bands early on in the week. Rock groups hit the stage Tuesday through Saturday at 10pm, occasionally backed up by some salsa, reggaeton and 1970s, 1980s and 1990s combos. Mon–Sat 7pm–2am.

ENTERTAINMENT

Alianza Francesa C Santa Catalina 208 ☎ 054 215 579 ⓦ wafarequipa.org.pe. The French Alliance houses a gallery displaying local artists' work.

Centro Cultural Peruano Norteamericano Melgar 109 ☎ 054 391 020 ⓦ cultural.edu.pe. Hosts workshops, photography exhibitions and theatre shows.

TRADITIONAL FOLK MUSIC IN AREQUIPA

Arequipa has a very strong tradition of **folk singing** and **poetry**, and folk musicians will wander from *peña* to *peña*. They often perform the region's most authentic music, *yaraví*, which involves lamenting vocalists accompanied by a guitar. In recent years the youth of Arequipa have developed a preference for Latin- and Cuban-style **ballads** (troubador singing) accompanied by electric guitars, drums and sometimes keyboards, so the choice at weekends can be quite extensive.

Instituto Cultural Peruano-Aleman C Ugarte 207 ☎054 218 567, ⓦicpa.org.pe. The Peruvian-German culture institute shows good films in Spanish and German and sometimes has children's theatre. It also has a cultural events noticeboard.

SHOPPING

CENTRAL MARKET
Mercado de San Camilo A couple of blocks down from Iglesia Santo Domingo. Arequipa's central market is one of the biggest and liveliest in Peru, though it's also a prime spot for pickpockets. It sells all sorts of food, leatherwork, musical instruments, inexpensive artesanía and even llama and alpaca meat, while offering an excellent range of hats, herbs and even cheap shoe repairs. You can also get a selection of fruit juices, including some combined with eggs and dark, sweet, stout beer. On Sundays and public holidays not all market stalls operate. Daily 6am–5pm.

ARTESANÍA
Patio del Ekeko C Mercaderes 141 ☎054 215 861, ⓦelekeko.pe. A plush shopping mall with silverware, artesanía, clothing and quality food – a good place to buy gifts. Mon–Sat 10am–9pm, Sun 11am–8pm.

ANTIQUES
Arte Colonial C Santa Catalina 312 ☎054 335 611. Of the numerous antique shops on C Santa Catalina, this is probably one of the best. Its two rooms are jam-packed with displays, including colonial furniture, paintings, jewellery, carvings and more. Mon–Sat 9.30am–8pm, Sun 11am–4pm.

BOOKSTORES
El Lector C San Francisco 213 ☎054 288677, ⓦlibreriaellector.com. Stocks a wide range of English-language books, including many on the history and wildlife of Peru. Mon–Sat 9am–8pm.
SBS C San Francisco 125 ☎054 205 317, ⓦsbs.com.pe. Has a range of English-language books, plus novels in other European languages. Mon–Sat 9.30am–7.45pm.

CAMPING EQUIPMENT
Camping Equipment C Jerusalén 300 ☎054 213 384. A number of tour agencies rent out camping equipment. Otherwise, there are several camping stores clustered close together on C Jerusalén, among them this decently stocked shop selling a range of camping accessories including tents, walking boots and torches. Mon–Sat 9am–1pm & 2–8pm.

SUPERMARKET
El Super Portal de la Municipilidad 130 ☎054 202 573. Located right on the main square, this is the city's most central supermarket, offering a range of goods from fruits and vegetables to toiletries. Mon–Sat 8.30am–10pm, Sun 9.30am–8pm.

DIRECTORY

Consulates Brazil, C Luna Pizarro 401, Vallecito ☎054 206 562; Chile, C Mercaderes 212 ☎054 223 947; Holland, León XIII D-13, Cayma ☎054 257 436; UK, La Recoleta 146 Dpto.203-A, Residencial La Recoleta ☎054 255 006.
Health For hospital treatment, try the Arequipa Clinic, at puentes Bolognesi and Grau (24hr; ☎054 599 000, ⓦclinicarequipa.com.pe).
Immigration Migraciones, Urb. Quinta Tristan, 2nd park, Distrito José Bustamante y Rivero ☎054 421 759 (Mon–Fri 8am–4.15pm, Sat 9am–noon).
Internet There are a handful of internet cafés north of town on calles Melgar, Rivero and Jerusalén; try Nolo's.net at C Rivero 400 (daily 7.30am–9pm; S/1 per hr).
Language schools Ceica Peru, C Los Arces 257A (☎054 250 722, ⓦceica-peru.com) and Rocio Language Classes,

Ayacucho 208, Oficina 22 (☎054 224 568, ⓦspanish-peru .com) both offer Spanish courses to suit all levels.
Laundry There are plenty of laundry places on C Jerusalén to the north of the plaza. Try Kaely at no. 412 (☎054 691 777; Mon–Sat 8am–8pm, Sun 8am–5pm; S/3/kg).
Money and exchange For foreign cards the best is Banco de Credito at C San Juan de Dios 125 (ATM); Banco Continental is at Block 1 of C San Francisco.
Police Tourist Police, C Jerusalén 315 (24hr; ☎054 201 258).
Post office Moral 118 (Mon–Sat 8am–8pm, Sun 8am–1.30pm).
Volunteering Traveller Not Tourist, C Los Arces 257A (☎054 250 722 or ☎959 910 196, ⓦtravellernottourist .org). Offers volunteering opportunities with various community projects.

Around Arequipa

The spectacular countryside around Arequipa rewards a few days' exploration, with some exciting and adventurous possibilities for trips from the city. Most people visit these sites on an **organized trip** with one of the tour companies in Arequipa (see p.166).

If you are prepared to put up with the extra hassle, you can visit many of the sites by much cheaper **public transport**.

The attractive village of **Sabandia** and the historic **Mansión del Fundador** are both within 20km of the city centre; further afield the Inca ruins of **Paucarpata** at the foot of El Misti volcano offer excellent scenery, great views and a fine place for a picnic. Climbing **El Misti** is a very demanding but rewarding trek, but should not be attempted without a professional guide. The attractive village of **Chapi** makes a good day-trip, while the **Cuevas de Sumbay**, just a few hours' drive from Arequipa on the road towards Caylloma, contain hundreds of unique prehistoric paintings.

Yet the greatest attraction here is easily the **Colca Canyon**, some 200km to the north of Arequipa, usually accessed via the quaint town of **Chivay**; second only to Machu Picchu in its ability to attract tourists, it is developing fast as a trekking and canoeing destination (best in the dry season, May–Sept). On route to Colca, the road passes through the **Reserva Nacional de Aguada Blanca**, a good place for wildlife. One of the canyon's pulls is the **Mirador Cruz del Condor**, where several condors, symbols of the Andes, can be seen flying most days. Called the "Valley of Marvels" by the Peruvian novelist Mario Vargas Llosa, it is in places nearly twice the depth of Arizona's Grand Canyon and one of the country's most extraordinary natural sights.

Around 120km west of Arequipa, you can also see the amazing **Toro Muerto petroglyphs** and perhaps go on to hike amid the craters and cones of the **Valley of the Volcanoes**, roughly 25km to the northeast. A little further north is the **Cotahuasi Canyon**, which some people believe could usurp Colca's claim to being the deepest canyon in the world.

Paucarpata

Colectivos leave every 30min from Av Salverry and C San Juan de Dios in Arequipa (30min)

Set against the backdrop of El Misti, **PAUCARPATA** is a fine place to while away an afternoon with some wine and a picnic lunch. About 7km out of central Arequipa, this large village is surrounded by farmland based on perfectly regular pre-Inca terraces, or *paucarpata* – the Quechua word from which it takes its name. On the southwestern edge of the suburb there's a small colonial church that contains a few Cusqueña School paintings.

Sabandia

Mill Daily 9am–5pm • S/5 • A return taxi trip from Arequipa costs S/40; Correcaminos and Characato colectivos from Av La Paz (every 10min; 50min)

Another 2–3km beyond Paucarpata lies **SABANDIA**, where you'll find a reconstructed colonial **mill** fronted by lawns with alpacas and llamas, and an attractive riverbank nearby. Built in 1661 to supply the city, along with three others in the region, the mill operated continuously for some three hundred years and was capable of milling 800kg of grain in one eight-hour shift with a single operator; it was only abandoned when industrial milling took root. The surrounding scenery, characterized by Inca terracing and broad vistas of surrounding mountains, is also home to a restored seventeenth-century **windmill**, which makes for an interesting visit.

Mansión del Fundador

Daily 9am–5pm • S/15 • ☎ 054 213 423 • Return taxi from Arequipa S/50 (20min); colectivo from Av Independencia (55min) with an M (for Mansion) on signboard

Ten kilometres beyond Sabandia, through the fertile Socabaya Valley, the **Mansión del Fundador** houses a colonial museum with period furnishings and attractive gardens. Once owned by Garcia Manuel de Carbajal, the original founder of Arequipa, it became the property of the Jesuits, who built a small chapel within the mansion. The mansion

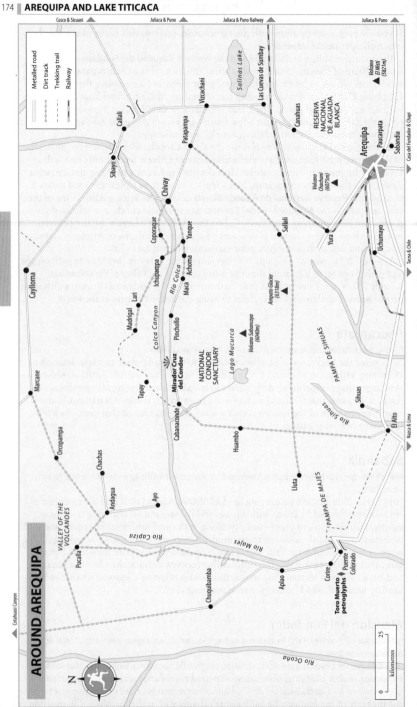

AROUND AREQUIPA

Metalled road
Dirt track
Trekking trail
Railway

Cusco & Sicuani
Juliaca & Puno
Juliaca & Puno Railway
Juliaca & Puno

Salinas Lake

Las Cuevas de Sumbay

Vizcachani

Callali

Patapampa

Canahuas

Sibayo

Chivay

RESERVA
NACIONAL
DE AGUADA
BLANCA

Volcano
El Misti
(5827m)

Arequipa

Paucarpata

Sabandia

Casa del Fundador & Chapi

Coporaque

Yanque

Volcano
Chachani
(6075m)

Cayllomа

Ichupampa

Achoma

Maca

Rio Colca

Sallali

Yura

Uchumayo

Tacna & Chile

Lari

Madrigal

Colca Canyon

Pinchollo

Ampato Glacier
(6318m)

PAMPA DE SIHUAS

Marcane

Mirador Cruz
del Condor

Tapay

NATIONAL
CONDOR
SANCTUARY

Lago Mucurca

Volcano Sabancaya
(6040m)

Sihuas

Rio Sihuas

Orcopampa

Cabanaconde

Huambo

El Alto

Nazca & Lima

Chachas

Andagua

Ayo

Lluta

PAMPA DE MAJES

VALLEY OF THE
VOLCANOES

Rio Capiza

Pucalla

Rio Majes

Chuquibamba

Aplao

Cotire

Puente
Colorado

Toro Muerto
petroglyphs

Rio Ocoña

Cotahuasi Canyon

N

0   25
kilometres

was restored in 1821 by Archbishop José Sebastián de Goyeneche y Barreda, one of Arequipa's greatest nineteenth-century benefactors, who converted the building into a country estate and rural palace for ecclesiastical and civic dignitaries. After the Jesuits were expelled from Peru, the building was bought at auction then resold to the Goyeneche family, who kept it until 1947 when the estate was sold off. It was lovingly restored once again in the late 1980s by some local architecture enthusiasts.

Chapi

Buses and colectivos leave from Av Andrés Avelino Cáceres (every 30min; 1hr 30min; S/20)

CHAPI, 45km southeast of Arequipa, is easily manageable as a day's excursion. Though less dramatic than the Colca Canyon, the landscape here is still magnificent, surrounded as it is by mining territory but few peaks much over 5000m. Chapi itself is famous for its white church, the **Santuario de la Virgen de Chapi**, set high above the village at the foot of a valley, which itself is the source of a natural spring. Thousands of pilgrims come here annually on May 1 to revere the image of the Virgin – a marvellous burst of processions and fiesta fever. There's no hotel, so if you intend to stay overnight you'll need a **tent**, but there are several basic places to eat.

El Misti

Colectivos (marked "Chiguata"; every 20min; 1hr) leave from Av Sepulveda in Arequipa and will drop you at the trailhead

If you feel compelled to climb **EL MISTI** (5821m), 20km northeast of Arequipa, bear in mind that it's considerably further away and higher than it looks from Arequipa. That said, it's a perfectly feasible hike if you allow two days for the ascent and another to get back down. Buses will drop you at the trailhead, from where there's a seven- to eight-hour hike to **base camp**. To spend the night here you'll need at the very least food, drink, warm clothing, boots and a good sleeping bag. Your main enemies will be the altitude and the cold night air, and during the day you'll need to wear some kind of hat or sunblock as the sunlight is particularly strong. Note that the climate is changeable and that water is scarce. From the base camp it's another breathless seven hours to the summit, with its excellent panoramic **views** across the whole range of accompanying volcanoes. Any of the tour companies listed (see p.166) can drop walkers off at a higher starting point than Chiguata, cutting a few hours off the first day. Although some tourists decide to tackle this trek on their own, you are strongly advised to seek the assistance of a guide. In recent years tourists have got lost in the area, and robberies are not uncommon.

Reserva Nacional de Aguada Blanca

Covering some 300,000 hectares of plateau behind El Misti is the **Reserva Nacional de Aguada Blanca**, the largest protected area in this region, located at 4000m above sea level. A cold and dry *puna* (a high Andean ecological zone located above the treeline), it's a great place to spot groups of wild *vicuñas*, while its reservoirs – El Farile and Aguada Blanca – are known for their excellent trout fishing. This reserve is crossed by vehicles during the first hour on the Chivay and Colca road from Arequipa as it climbs high above Arequipa's valley floor.

Las Cuevas de Sumbay

S/5 • Daily 9am–4pm • It is only possible to stop here with a private tour group or in your own vehicle

There are signposts showing the entrance to **Las Cuevas de Sumbay** from the main road that continues towards Chivay and also Cusco. To stay at Sumbay you'll have to **camp**, but if you have a vehicle it's easy enough to stop for an hour or so en route, following the signpost (at Km 103 from Arequipa) down a bad track to the village of Sumbay (4532m), about 1.5km away. At this point you'll need to find the guardian of the cave (often just a small shepherd child) who can open the gate for your car to continue another kilometre to a parking area.

From the gate it's a ten-minute walk to the caves, down into a small canyon just before the bridge. The guardian will have to unlock another gate to give you access to the site. Although small, the main Sumbay cave contains a series of 8000-year-old rock paintings representing shamans, llamas, deer, pumas and *vicuñas*. The surrounding countryside is amazing in itself: herds of alpacas roam gracefully around the plain looking for *ichu* grass to munch, and vast sculpted rock strata of varying colours mix smoothly together with crudely hewn gullies.

Chivay and around

Surrounded by some of the most impressive and intensive ancient terracing in South America, **CHIVAY**, 163km north of Arequipa and just four hours by bus from there, lies at the heart of fantastic hiking/mountain biking country. Although notable as a market town, it is not actually a good place from which to observe the canyon. Chivay is nevertheless bustling with gringos using the town as a base for exploring the Colca Canyon region.

The **market** itself is located along Avenida Salaverry, where you'll also find a slew of artesanía shops. The town has a growing range of accommodation options, restaurants and bus services for these visitors, making it a reasonable place to stay while you acclimatize to the high altitude. Serious trekkers will soon want to move on to one of the other canyon towns, probably **Cabanaconde** (see p.181).

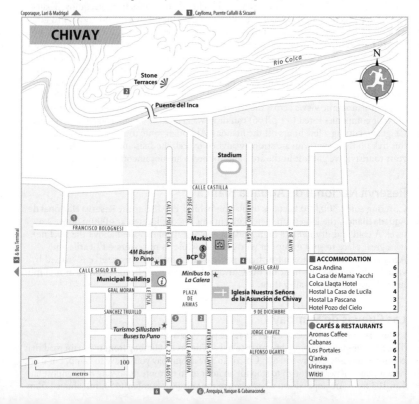

La Calera

Hot springs Daily 4am–7pm • S/15 • Colectivos leave approx every 20min from between the main plaza and the local market

Just 5km east of Chivay, slightly further up the Colca Canyon, the road passes mainly through cultivated fields until it reaches the tiny settlement of **LA CALERA**, which boasts one of Chivay's main attractions – a wonderful series of **hot-spring pools**, fed by the bubbling, boiling brooks that emerge from the mountain sides all around at an average natural temperature of 85°C. Said to be good for curing arthritis and rheumatism these clean and well-kept thermal baths are not to be missed. There's also a **small museum** on site with models and artefacts demonstrating local customs, such as making an offering to the *pacha mama*, Mother Earth. There is a zipline (ⓦcolcaziplining.com) just by the hot springs.

ARRIVAL AND DEPARTURE

By bus Buses from Arequipa stop off at the terminal in Chivay, a 10min stroll from the main plaza; some continue on to Cabanaconde. There are three main companies – Reyna (☎054 430 612), Andalucía (☎054 424 932) and Turismo Milagros (☎054 298 090), all of which travel about five times daily from Arequipa (3hr). From Chivay it's about 2hr 30min to Cabanaconde. Turismo Sillustani (Av 22

CHIVAY AND AROUND

Agosto, Chivay and Jr Lima 440, Puno, ☎951 024 758 ⓦturismosillustani.com; US$35 one way) and the more reliable 4M (C La Merced 125, Galerías Unicentro no. 111, Arequipa, ☎054 452 296, ⓦ4m-express.com; US$50 one way) operate daily services from Puno to Chivay leaving around 6am (5hr 30min), returning at 1.15pm. The buses stop off at a few scenic spots en route.

INFORMATION

Tourist information Autocolca on the Plaza de Armas (Mon–Fri 8am–1pm & 2.30–5.30pm, Sat 9am–1pm; ☎054 531 143) can supply information on the local area.

Services There's a BCP ATM on the main plaza and a cashpoint just opposite the market, although it's probably wise to bring some spare cash from Arequipa.

ACCOMMODATION

Chivay is not the most appealing of towns, although it does have a few decent places to stay. If you're planning on exploring more of the Colca Canyon, you're much better off staying in the little town of Cabanaconde, where you can descend deep down into the canyon.

Casa Andina Huayna Cápac s/n ☎054 531 020, ⓦcasa-andina.com. For top-quality accommodation in Chivay this tranquil oasis in the heart of town is arguably the place to choose. Stone walkways lead to a series of tastefully decorated rooms in thatched bungalows, and there's a planetarium and shaman hut where coca readings take place, too. S/400

La Casa de Mama Yacchi Coporaque, 7km west of Chivay ☎054 531 004, ⓦlacasademamayacchi.com. Just arriving at this place is pleasing enough: a lovely, picture-perfect building with thatched roof, pretty flowers and pre-Inca ruins in the front garden. Some of the rooms have wonderful views (make sure to book one well in advance), and all feature rustic wicker lamps and en-suite bathrooms with hot water. There are no TVs and no wi-fi – perfect for those who want to get away from it all. S/200

Colca Llaqta Hotel C José Gálvez s/n ☎054 531 280, ⓦcolcallaqtahotel.com. This pleasant hotel just a short walk from the main square offers nicely decorated, spacious rooms with rustic open-fronted wardrobes and flat-screen TVs. The overall atmosphere is peaceful and welcoming. S/220

Hostal La Casa de Lucila C Grau 131 ☎054 284 211. This small but homely place offers comfortable rooms set on two floors that give onto a leafy garden area with stone walkway and potted plants. It's by far the best budget place in town. S/150

Hostal La Pascana Av Siglo XX 106 ☎054 531 001, ⓦhostal-lapascana.com. Located just by the main square, this yellow budget hotel is where 4M buses drop off passengers from Puno. The simple rooms give onto balconies with wooden banisters and brightly painted murals; all have en-suite facilities and 24hr hot water. S/120

Hotel Pozo del Cielo Huascar s/n ☎054 346 545, ⓦpozodelcielo.com.pe. Set on a sloping road overlooking town, the cosy rooms with low ceilings are decorated with wooden statuettes and local fabrics; each has an armchair or sofa, most have lovely views over Chivay and beyond, and all have TV, heating and en-suite bathrooms. Take a look at a couple of rooms before settling in, as some are more inviting than others. S/255

EATING

Aromas Caffee Plaza de Armas 301 ☏054 796 512, ⓦaromascaffee.com. This small coffee joint is a great spot to grab a refreshing frappuccino (S/7) on a hot day or a warming hot chocolate (S/5) on a nippy evening. Seating is at little wooden tables, each with a glass compartment full of coffee beans. Daily 8am–10pm.

Cabanas Plaza de Armas 607 ☏054 531 114. Right on the main plaza, this popular restaurant featuring stone walls and columns offers a range of good-value set menus for S/16, including vegetarian and light, as well as more substantial set menus for S/27. It also serves American (S/10) and continental breakfasts (S/7) and freshly squeezed juices (S/5), too. Daily 7am–10pm.

Los Portales C Arequipa 603 ☏054 531 101, ⓦlosportalesdechivay.com. This popular restaurant buzzes with tour groups at lunchtime for its decent eat-all-you-can buffet (S/28). There's plenty to choose from, including quinoa- and meat-based dishes and some veggie options and soups. The free wi-fi comes in handy, too. Daily 11am–2.30pm.

Q'anka C Salaverry 105, 3rd floor ☏958 296 914. This is a pleasant restaurant with walls decorated with masks and tables adorned with mud vases. The specialities here are hot stone steaks, with a particularly tasty lomito de alpaca (S/30), and pizzas (S/15), also served sizzling on hot stones. Daily 11am–10pm.

Urinsaya C Francisco Bolognesi 1026 ☏054 531 235. Tucked away off a dusty side road, this pleasant restaurant featuring a large condor mural and thatched roof offers a very good buffet lunch for S/30. There are occasional live folkloric bands that liven up the scene. Daily 11am–3pm.

Wititi Av Siglo XX 328 ☏054 531 036. A pleasant restaurant offering the usual lunch buffet deal for S/28. You can also choose à la carte, with mains costing about S/20. Daily 11am–2pm.

Colca Canyon

Claimed by some to be the deepest canyon in the world at more than 1km from cliff-edge to river bottom, the **COLCA CANYON** may be an impressive sight but is actually estimated to be 170m shallower than its more remote rival, the Cotahuasi Canyon (see p.185). Both of these canyons are among several in the world that claim to be the biggest or deepest on the planet, depending on exactly how you measure them. In places the canyon's sides are so steep that it is impossible to see the valley bottom, while the higher edges of Colca are punctuated with some of the finest examples of pre-Inca terracing in Peru, attributed in the main to the Huari cultural era. Craggy mountains, huge herds of llamas and traditionally dressed Andean peasants complete the picture.

The canyon was formed by a massive geological fault between the two enormous volcanoes of Coropuna (6425m) and Ampato (6318m): the Río Colca forms part of a gigantic watershed that empties into the Pacific near Camana. Despite being one of Peru's most popular tourist attractions, the area's sharp terraces are still home to more-or-less traditional Indian villages. To the north of Colca, meanwhile, sits the majestic **Nevado Mismi**, a 5597m-high snow-capped peak that belongs to the Chila mountain range, and which, according to *National Geographic*, is the official source of the Amazon River; long the subject of argument and speculation, the precise location of the source was finally pinpointed in 2000 by a five-nation National Geographic Society expedition using cutting-edge GPS navigational equipment. The team, headed by 46-year-old maths teacher Andrew Pietowski, identified the spot on Nevado Mismi. Most tourists just see the Colca Canyon as somewhere for a day or overnight trip, but there are a number of beautifully sited rustic lodges and upmarket hotels sprinkled around the Colca Canyon which make it perfect for a longer stay.

Brief history

Francisco Pizarro's brother, Gonzalo, was given this region in the 1530s as his own private *encomienda* (colonial Spanish landholding) to exploit for economic tribute. In the seventeenth century, however, Viceroy Toledo split the area into *corregimientos* that concentrated the previously quite dispersed local populations into villages. This had the effect of a decline in the use of the valley's agricultural terracing, as the locals switched to farming the land nearer their new homes.

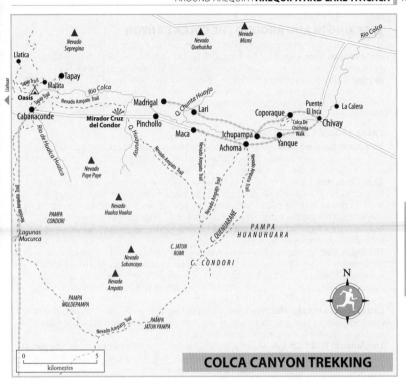

COLCA CANYON TREKKING

The *corregimientos* created the fourteen main settlements that still exist in the valley today, including Chivay, Yanque, Maca, Cabanaconde, Corporaque, Lari and Madrigal. Most of the towns still boast unusually grand, Baroque-fronted **churches**, underlining the importance of this region's silver mines during the seventeenth and eighteenth centuries. During the Republican era, Colca's importance dwindled substantially and interest in the zone was only rekindled in 1931 when aerial photography revealed the astonishing natural and man-made landscape of this valley to the outside world – particularly the exceptionally elaborate terracing on the northern sides of bordering mountains.

Yanque

From Chivay, the first village the road winds through is **YANQUE**. The mountains to the southwest are dominated by the glaciers of Ampato and Hualca, and sometimes the volcano Sabancaya can be seen smoking away in the distance. Yanque boasts a fine white church, a small archeology museum, thermal baths down by the river,

---

COLCA CANYON TOURIST TICKETS

Arriving at Chivay by road, a tourism checkpoint issues standard, mandatory **Colca Boleto Turísticos** (general tourist tickets), which cost S/70 and offer "free" entry to the Mirador Cruz del Condor, other main *miradors* and all the major churches in the valley. These tickets are required just for entry to the Colca National Park area, essentially most of the valley, regardless of whether or not you visit the Mirador Cruz del Condor. The ticket is sold in three places: checkpoints on the road at **Chivay** (see p.176), at **Pinchollo** (see p.181) and also in the tourist office at **Cabanaconde** (see p.181).

TREKKING IN AND AROUND THE COLCA CANYON

There are dozens of trekking routes in the Colca Canyon, but if you're planning on descending to the **canyon floor**, even if just for the day, it's best to be fit and prepared for the altitude – it's tough going and becomes quite dangerous in sections. Make sure to check whether **oxygen** is provided by your tour operator – even a bus trip to Chivay can bring on mountain sickness (see p.210) if you've only recently arrived from sea level. If you start trekking from Cabanaconde you can organize guides, *arrieros* (muleteers), mules and horses at the *Valle del Fuego* guesthouse (see p.182).

TREKS FROM CABANACONDE

Mirador Achachiwa Walk A fifteen-minute stroll from the plaza in Cabanaconde takes you past the bullring to the Mirador Achachina, a good spot for spotting condors and viewing the western end of the valley from above.

Basic Colca Trek The start of the classic route from Cabanaconde to the bottom of the Colca Canyon is just ten minutes' walk along a fairly clear track beyond *Casa de Santiago*, itself a five-minute walk from the plaza. The descent from here follows an incredibly steep path, quite dangerous in parts, down to the *Oasis* (see p.182), a rustic lodge and campsite right in the bottom of the canyon; it takes one and a half to two hours to descend and four or five to get back up. Many people stay the night.

The Tapay Trail This well-used trekking route connects Cabanaconde with the small settlement of Tapay via the *Oasis* (see p.182). It is a two- to four-day return hike through fine scenery, immense canyons, tiny hamlets such as Cosñirhua (2350m) and Malata as well as various Inca and pre-Inca ruins. Save for the aforementioned campsite – which you'll pass on the first morning – there are no facilities at all in the area.

Cabanaconde to Lake Mucurca There is a popular eight-hour hike from Cabanaconde that culminates at Lake Mucurca (4000m). At its end point the astonishingly beautiful Ampato volcano is reflected in the lake's crystalline waters.

The Ampato Trail From Lake Mucurca the adventurous, fully acclimatized and well-prepared can trek all the way around snowcapped Ampato (4–6 days). The Ampato Trail has one very high pass – around 4850m at the crossing of two trails on Cerro Quenahuane, above the Quebrada Condori – and most of the walking is at over 4200m. Local guides are a good idea and you will need food and camping equipment. Be prepared for snow and ice; the weather can change very fast. On the last downhill leg of the trek you can choose to follow trails back to Achoma, Maca or Cabanaconde.

THE COLCAS DE CHICHINIA TREK

A relatively easy two-hour walk from the village of **Corporaque** (15min by car or bus from Chivay, on the opposite side of the Colca Canyon to Maca and the Mirador Cruz del Condor), takes in the **Colcas de Chichinia**, a semi-intact set of pre-Inca Huari tombs; today they lie exposed at the foot of the cliffs on Cerro Yurac Ccacca (also known as Cerro San Antonio). A path leads out a couple of blocks just below the plaza in Corporaque, crossing the stream as you leave the settlement behind and climbing steadily towards a prominent, pink rocky outcrop. Because it's little visited, the entry path to the site isn't marked and more or less leaves you to find your own route; given this, it's important to take care not to damage the stone walls and agricultural plots you have to find your way through.

The tombs are just below the 4000m contour line where several overhangs have been partially filled in with stone as permanent thrones for pre-Inca **mummies**, placed here ceremoniously to spend eternity watching over the valley and gazing east towards several sacred mountain peaks. These days, after the ravages of time and grave-robbers, all that is left of the mummies are skulls and skeletons, some with hair and a few with remnants of the rope and cloth they were originally wrapped in.

To the southwest, a partly tumbled down, but still impressive **Huari village** can be clearly seen stretching from the tombs down to a major *tambo*-style (Quechua for house or resting place) building on the bottom corner, which commands views around the valley. To get back to Corporaque, you can either drop down to the road and trace this back up to the settlement, or go along the small aqueduct that follows the contour of the hill from the *tambo* back to where you started.

horseriding facilities, mountain-bike rental and, after Maca, some of the area's best-preserved pre-Inca ruins. The town lies directly on a fault line and is subject to frequent tremors: the visible effects can be seen in various land movements, abandoned houses and deep fissures around the area.

Maca

The road from Yanque continues on through a very dark tunnel until just beyond **MACA**, a small community which sits on the lower skirts of the volcano Sabancaya and the Nevado Hualca Hualca, some 23km west of Chivay. Immediately after this tunnel, a number of hanging pre-Inca tombs – *las chullpas colgantes* – can be seen high up in seemingly impossible cliff-edge locations, facing perhaps the best example of agricultural terracing in Peru across the valley.

Mirador Cruz del Condor

Colca Canyon tourist tickets S/70 (see box, p.179); all tours come here and public buses will stop briefly

The **Mirador Cruz del Condor** is the most popular point for viewing the canyon – it's around 1200m deep here – and you can almost guarantee seeing several condors circling up from the depths against the breathtaking scenery. The condors are best spotted from 7 to 9am; the earlier you get there the more likely you are to have fewer other spectators around. These days it's a popular spot, and most mornings there will actually be more tourists here than in the Plaza de Armas in Arequipa. For safety's sake, stand well back from the edge.

The gateway to the Mirador, the settlement of **Pinchollo** has a small museum and a tourist information office with photos and a model representing the canyon.

Cabanaconde and around

The small but growing town of **CABANACONDE** (3300m), 10km on from Pinchollo, is a good base from which to descend into the canyon. An impressive high wall and painted gateway mark the town's eighteenth-century cemetery. The town is also home to several semi-destroyed stone buildings and doorways from the late colonial (or Viceregal) era. If you can make it for the **Fiesta de la Virgen del Carmen** (usually between 14–18 July), you'll see the bullring in action and the town in the throes of a major religious festival and party.

The main reason to visit Cabanaconde, though, is to trek down to the verdant **Valle de Sangalle**, an oasis of palm and fruit trees lying at the heart of the Colca Canyon.

Valle de Sangalle

It's a three-hour walk down a stony path from Cabanaconde to Sangalle, and as you slowly wind your way down the canyon the view becomes increasingly impressive, with the emerald-green Colca River gushing through the valley. Even more rewarding is the swimming pool of *Oasis Paraíso Camping Lodge* – visible from the path and a refreshing welcome after the tiring trek down the canyon.

ARRIVAL AND DEPARTURE   COLCA CANYON

By bus Most people arrive and leave the Colca Canyon by bus from Arequipa via Chivay, getting off at their particular village: Yanque, Maca or Cabanaconde. There are daily bus services from Puno to Chivay, too (see p.177).

HATS IN THE COLCA CANYON

The indigenous communities of the Colca Canyon form two distinct ethnic groups: the Aymara-speaking **Collaguas** and the Quechua-speaking **Cabanas**. Traditionally, both groups used different techniques for deforming the heads of their children. The Collaguas elongated them and the Cabanas flattened them – each trying to emulate the shape of their respective principal *apu* (mountain god). Today it is the shape of their **hats** (taller for the Collaguas and round, flat ones for the Cabanas), rather than heads, which mainly distinguishes the two groups.

3

GETTING AROUND AND TOURS

By bus The plaza in Cabanaconde is the drop-off and pick-up point for buses, where agencies sell tickets of the main bus companies connecting this settlement with Arequipa and Chivay. Andalucía buses depart Arequipa's Terminal Terrestre at 7am and 11.30am, while Turismo Milagros departs at 2pm and Reyna at 1am. Departures from Cabanaconde to Arequipa are at 7am (Reyna), 9am (Andalucía), 11am (Turismo Milagros), 2pm (Andalucía) and 10pm (Milagros). All services stop off briefly to pick up passengers in Chivay. There are daily tourist buses too, which stop off at the Cruz del Condor, Maca, Chivay's thermal baths and other points of interest along the way, leaving around 9.30am. Yamil at the *Hostal Valle del Fuego* (see below) can organize tickets.

Tours Guides for the region can be organized through Yamil at the *Hostal Valle del Fuego* (see below); they generally cost S/80–100 per day, plus more for mules and an *arriero*.

ACCOMMODATION AND EATING

YANQUE

Alpaca Chef Colca Manzanayoc s/n ☎ 054 035 783. This thatched-roofed restaurant has a pleasant interior with clay floors, colourful Peruvian-style tablecloths and a mud oven. Reservations must be made one day in advance, and meals will set you back about S/30. Open for reservations.

★ **Colca Lodge** Fundo Puye s/n ☎ 054 282 177, ⓦ colca-lodge.com. This wonderful lodge offers smart rooms with rustic furniture in a beautiful riverside setting. The junior suites, with stylish bathrooms, are worth the splurge. The hotel owns an alpaca ranch just across the river where guests are invited to learn about the friendly creatures, and fishing rods are available from reception for those who fancy a bit of angling. The open-air steaming-hot thermal pools are a real treat, especially after a long day's trekking. S/440

Hotel Las Casitas del Colca ☎ 959 671 435, ⓦ lascasitasdelcolca.com. A lovely hotel located outside Yanque with twenty *casitas*, or chalets, that are stylishly furnished with leather sofas, stone floors and fireplace. Each has its own hot tub, and there's a spa and open-air pool, too, as well as plenty of complimentary activities including alpaca feeding, cooking classes, pisco sour lessons, fishing and baking lessons for children. S/1720

Tradición Colca C Argentina 108 ☎ 054 424 926, ⓦ tradicioncolca.com. This French-run place offers clean and well-kept rooms with private bathroom just a short walk from Yanque's main square. The great facilities include three jacuzzis, a sauna, astronomy dome and wi-fi in communal areas. Staff can organize treks in the local area, as well as horseriding trips. S/180

CABANACONDE AND AROUND

La Casa de Santiago C Grau, Cabanaconde ☎ 054 203 737 or ☎ 959 611 241, ⓦ lacasadesantiago.com. A peaceful guesthouse with rooms built around a pleasant garden area with seating, where it's easy to while away an afternoon reading or soaking in the surrounding mountain views. Rooms all have en-suite bathrooms and hot water, there's all-day tea, and breakfast is served in the communal area with sofas and TV. S/100

Hostal Valle del Fuego Calles Grau and Bolívar, Cabanaconde ☎ 054 668 910, ⓦ valledelfuego.com. This backpackers' pad is run by friendly Yamil, who welcomes guests with a potent pisco sour. There are two welcoming dorm rooms with bare-brick walls and en-suite bathrooms, as well as simple doubles, most with lovely mountain views. There's a little patio with colourfully painted stone walls, laundry facilities and a camping area out of town just a 10min walk from the Cruz del Condor. You can hire horses (S/90 for 3–4hr), mules (S/70 for 5–6hr, plus an *arriero* for S/60) and rent mountain bikes (S/60 per day). An atmospheric sister restaurant, dotted with couches and old curios, serves great pizzas. Camping S̲/̲1̲0̲, dorms S̲/̲2̲0̲, doubles S̲/̲7̲0̲

Hotel Kuntur Wassi On the hill above the Plaza de Armas, Cabanaconde ☎ 054 233 120, ⓦ arequipacolca .com. A comfortable hotel sitting 80m above Cabanaconde's plaza, whose name translates as "The House of the Condor". The lobby area has a water feature and a splash of greenery, while the attractive rooms with clay tiles feature open-fronted wardrobes built using natural materials. Bathrooms have hot-water showers heated with solar panels, and there's a lovely restaurant and bar area with views over town and beyond. S/175

★ **Oasis Paraíso Camping Lodge** Valle de Sangalle, bottom of Colca Canyon, 3–4hr walk from Cabanaconde ☎ 054 630 611. You'll want to stay longer than planned at this rustic place with simple rooms overlooking a lush garden area with swimming pool. Meals are served in the open-fronted restaurant, made from the produce that grows abundantly in Sangalle oasis, including tomatoes, spinach, carrots and onions. It's happy hour 4–6pm, and there are cooking classes (S/30 per person) that begin with you picking your ingredients from the vegetable garden. Camping S̲/̲1̲0̲ per person, dorms S̲/̲1̲5̲, doubles S̲/̲6̲0̲, en-suite doubles S̲/̲8̲0̲

Pachamama C San Pedro 209, Cabanaconde ☎ 054 767 277, ⓦ pachamamahome.com. A popular backpacker pad offering simple rooms, with or without bathroom, tucked away behind a cosy restaurant area with candlelit tables where pizzas are cooked in a wood-fire

OPPOSITE ALPACAS GRAZE NEAR THE COLCA CANYON (P.178) >

oven. Guests tend to congregate here and socialize until the early hours over a drink or two. Dorms S/25, doubles S/50, en-suite doubles S/60
La Posada del Conde C San Pedro s/n, Cabanaconde ☎ 054 631 749, ⓦ posadadelconde.com. In the centre of

town, just a short walk from the main square, this place offers darkish olive-green rooms with private bathroom. The restaurant serves good local dishes, with mains at about S/20. S/60

Corire

Located 160km northwest of Arequipa, **CORIRE** is a small town of around two thousand people. Of very little interest to tourists in its own right, it is a primarily agricultural settlement based on rice and wheat production, although there are a handful of good riverfront restaurants serving tasty crayfish dishes between April and December. Corire's claim to fame is really its proximity to the **Toro Muerto petroglyphs**.

Toro Muerto petroglyphs

Daily 6am–6pm • S/5, students S/2 • Travelling from Arequipa, hop off on the main road and walk from there (30min) or catch a taxi from Corire (10–15min; approx S/30–50 including waiting time)

Reached by bus or car from Arequipa, the **Toro Muerto petroglyphs** consist of carved boulders strewn over a kilometre or two of hot desert. More than a thousand rocks of all sizes and shapes have been crudely, yet strikingly, engraved with a wide variety of distinct representations. No archeological remains have been directly associated with these images but it is thought that they date from between 1000 and 1500 years ago; they are largely attributed to the **Wari culture**, though with probable additions during subsequent Chuquibamba and Inca periods of domination in the region. The engravings include images of humans, snakes, llamas, deer, parrots, sun discs and simple geometric motifs. Some of the figures appear to be dancing, others with large round helmets look like spacemen – obvious material for the author Erich Von Däniken's extraterrestrial musings (he based his book *Chariots of the Gods* on several archeological sites in Peru). Some of the more abstract geometric designs are very similar to those of the Huari culture, which may well have sent an expeditionary force in this direction, across the Andes from the Ayacucho basin, around 800 AD.

The route to the **petroglyphs** is signalled by a small site museum, but it is a good thirty-minute walk from the road, and at least 500m above it. What you're looking for is a vast row of **white rocks**, believed to have been scattered across the sandy desert slopes by a prehistoric volcanic eruption – the natural setting is almost as magnificent as the hundreds of petroglyphs.

ARRIVAL AND DEPARTURE   CORIRE

By bus There are hourly buses to Corire from Arequipa's Terrapuerto terminal (3hr). Buses to Arequipa run from the Plaza de Armas in Corire and, unless full, can be flagged down on the main road at the Toro Muerto turn-off.

ACCOMMODATION AND EATING

Hostal Willy's Plaza Principal, avenidas Progreso and Moran ☎ 054 472 046. The simple rooms all have hot water, although don't be surprised to see paint peeling off the walls here and there. It's a decent enough choice nonetheless – certainly for a remote town like Corire, anyway. S/50
Hotel El Molino Av Progreso 121 ☎ 054 472 056, ⓔ hotelmolinocorire@hotmail.com. The tiled rooms here are kept clean and bright with regular touch-ups of white paint. All are en suite, and some have TVs. Rates include breakfast, and there's wi-fi throughout and parking facilities. Staff can help organize trips in the local area. S/80
Laguna Azul Riverfront ☎ 959 918 545. About 1km east of town, this laidback, wood-and-thatch riverfront restaurant serves tasty crayfish dishes between April and December; when the river water level rises in January, the restaurant moves a few metres inland and, until April, specializes in seafood. A meal will set you back about S/30. Daily 7am–8pm.

Aplao

Continuing on from Corire towards the Cotahuasi Canyon for about 20km you come across the little town of **APLAO**. Although it's of little interest to tourists, the surrounding area offers excellent whitewater rafting on the Río Majes (level 3–4). The climate here is dry year-round and the arid, desert-like scenery contrasts dramatically with the lush river valley.

ACCOMMODATION   APLAO

Majes River Lodge Valle de Majes, Aplao ☎ 054 660 219, ⓦ majesriver.com. Ten kilometres north of Aplao, this welcoming place specializing in rafting and kayaking on the Majes River is run by a warm and welcoming couple. The simple rooms overlook a swimming pool area, while at the back of the premises is a wine cellar (guests here at the right time can even take part in the grape harvest) that brims with character, packed with curios including an old camera, typewriter and vinyl disc player; within the grounds is also a bullring dating from the 1970s, which still hosts occasional bullfights. **S/80**

Valley of the Volcanoes   3

Following some 65km of the Río Andagua's course, the **VALLEY OF THE VOLCANOES** (Valle de los Volcanes) skirts along the presently dormant Mount Coropuna, the highest volcano in Peru (6425m) and the highest peak in southern Peru. At first sight just a pleasant Andean valley, this is in fact one of the strangest geological formations you're ever likely to see. A stunning lunar landscape, the valley is studded with extinct craters varying in size and height from 200 to 300m. About 200,000 years ago, these small volcanoes erupted when the lava fields were degassed (a natural release of volcanic gas through soil, volcanic lakes and volcanoes) – at the time of one of Coropuna's major eruptions.

The best overall view of the valley can be had from Anaro Mountain (4800m), looking southeast towards the Chipchane and Puca Maura cones. The highest of the volcanoes, known as Los Gemelos (The Twins), are about 10km from Andagua. To the south, the Andomarca volcano has a pre-Inca ruined settlement around its base.

ARRIVAL AND INFORMATION   VALLEY OF THE VOLCANOES

By bus Buses to Andagua from Arequipa's Terminal Terrestre leave daily between 3 and 4pm with Reyna (10hr); Transporte Trebol has services Wednesday and Thursday afternoons, usually leaving around 5–6pm.

On foot You can trek to the Valley of the Volcanoes from Cabanaconde (5–6 days); this expedition will require mules, a guide and cook and costs about S/2000–3000. Treks can be organized through one of the tour agencies in Arequipa.

Maps The main section of the valley is about 65km long; to explore it in any detail you'll need to get maps (two adjacent ones are required) from the South American Explorers' Club in Lima or Cusco (see p.81 & p.221), the Instituto Geográfico (ⓦ www.ign.gob.pe) or the Ministerio de Cultura in Arequipa (Alameda San Lázaro 120, Cercado; ☎ 054 213 171). Pablo Tour in Arequipa (see p.168) also has detailed maps of the area for sale.

ACCOMMODATION AND EATING

If you plan to camp here you'll need good supplies, especially water and a sunhat; the sun beating down on the black ash can get unbelievably **hot** at noon. Because this is a rarely visited region, where most of the people are pretty well self-sufficient, there are only the most basic of **shops** – usually set up in homes. Local people are also generally very hospitable, often inviting strangers they find **camping** in the fields to sleep in their houses (try Dora, who rents out a couple of rooms, on ☎ 973 610 375).

Hostel El Trebol Quince de Agosto 106, Andagua ☎ 959 214 355. Probably the best option in the area, with twelve simple rooms with private bathroom and hot water. Breakfast is not included in the rates. **S/45**

Cotahuasi Canyon

First navigated by a Polish expedition in 1981 and declared a Zona de Reserva Turística Nacional in 1988, the magnificent **COTAHUASI CANYON** (Cañon de Cotahuasi), 378km from Arequipa, has since opened up to visits that don't involve major rafting trips.

However, getting to this wild and remote place is even more adventurous and less frequently attempted than the trip to the Valley of the Volcanoes. One of the world's deepest canyons, along with nearby Colca and the Grand Canyon in the US, it is around 3400m deep and over 100km long.

Arriving from the south along the difficult road from Arequipa (some 375km long) the route passes along the bottom part of the canyon, where the main settlement, **Cotahuasi** (2684m), can be found. This remote and attractive settlemenet boasts quaint narrow streets and a small seventeenth-century church. It has a variable climate but isn't particularly cold and is rapidly developing a name as an adventure travel destination, offering by far the best local facilities.

Continuing north to the village of **Alca** (near the hot springs of Luicho), the road forks. To the right, it heads into the deeper part of the canyon where you'll find the village of **Pucya**; further up the valley, heading pretty well northwest you end up at the astonishingly beautiful plateau of Lauripampa, from where you can walk down into the canyon or admire the massive *Puya raimondii* hereabouts. The left fork continues to the pueblo of **Pampamarca**, where the locals weave lovely woollen blankets. Above the pueblo there is a fabulous trail that leads to the Uscuni waterfalls on one side of the valley and the natural rock formations of the Bosque de Piedras on the other. A little further on you'll find the thermal springs of Josla, an ancient spa that's a joy for tired legs after a long hike.

About 40km from Cotahuasi, the Wari ruins of **Marpa** can be seen straddling both sides of the river, but another hour away is the larger and better-preserved Wari city of **Maucallacta**.

ARRIVAL AND DEPARTURE   COTAHUASI CANYON

By bus or guided tour Reyna and other operators have daily bus services to Cotahuasi from Arequipa (11–12hr), though the easiest (and quickest) way to get here is on a guided tour from Arequipa (see p.166).

ACCOMMODATION AND EATING

Hatunhuasi Hotel C Centenario 307–309, Cotahuasi ☎ 054 581 054, ⓦ hatunhuasi.com. This small, family-run hotel features eleven simple rooms giving onto a garden area with a handful of potted plants. The owner can cook meals upon request. S/55

Hotel Valle Hermoso C Tacna 106, Cotahuasi ☎ 054 581 057, ⓦ hotelvallehermoso.com. A very pleasant guest-house with rooms set around a lovely garden area with avocado, orange and fig trees and a couple of grazing llamas.

The rooms have welcoming little touches, such as lamps with old irons as stands, and breakfast includes home-made jams and bread, as well as freshly squeezed juice. S/140

★ **Linda Cotahuasina** C Arequipa 117, Cotahuasi ☎ 054 660 113. Unlike most restaurants in Cotahuasi where food is pre-cooked and served as part of a menu, friendly owner Carmen prepares everything to order, with a handful of tasty meat dishes and vegetarian meals as required. Daily 6am–11pm.

Lake Titicaca

An undeniably calming and majestic sight, **LAKE TITICACA** is the world's largest high-altitude body of water. At 284m deep and more than 8300 square kilometres in area, it is fifteen times the size of Lake Geneva in Switzerland and higher and slightly bigger than Lake Tahoe in the US. An immense region both in terms of its history and the breadth of its magical landscape, the **Titicaca Basin** makes most people feel like they are on top of the world. Usually placid and mirror-like, the deep blue water reflects the vast sky back on itself. All along the horizon – which appears to bend away from you – the green Andean mountains can be seen raising their ancient backs towards the sun; over on the Bolivian side it's sometimes possible to make out the icecaps of the Cordillera Real mountain chain. The **high altitude** (3827m above sea level) means that recent arrivals from the coast should take it easy for a day or two, though those coming from Cusco will already have acclimatized.

A **National Reserve** since 1978, the lake has over sixty varieties of bird, fourteen species of native fish and eighteen types of amphibian. It's often seen as three separate regions: Lago Mayor, the main, deep part of the lake; Wiñaymarka, the area incorporating various archipelagos that include both Peruvian and Bolivian Titicaca; and the Golfo de Puno, essentially the bay encompassed by the peninsulas of Capachica and Chucuito. The villages that line its shores depend mainly on grazing livestock for their livelihood, since the altitude limits the growth potential of most crops. These days, **Puno** is the largest settlement and port in the whole of Lake Titicaca. Densely populated well before the arrival of the Incas, the lakeside Titicaca region is also home to the curious and ancient tower-tombs known locally as **chullpas**: rings of tall, cylindrical stone burial chambers, often standing in battlement-like formations. These were built by the Colla people, an Aymara-speaking tribe who preceded the Incas and once dominated the lake.

There are over seventy islands in the lake, the largest being the **Isla del Sol** (Island of the Sun), an ancient Inca temple site on the Bolivian side of the border; Titicaca is an Aymara word meaning "Puma's Rock", which refers to an unusual boulder on the island. The island is best visited from Copacabana in Bolivia (see p.201), or trips can be arranged through one of the tour companies in Puno (see p.190).

On the Peruvian side of the lake you can visit the unusual **Uros islands**. These floating platform islands are built out of reeds – weird to walk over and even stranger to live on, they are now a major tourist attraction. More spectacular by far are two of the populated, fixed islands, **Amantani** and **Taquile**, where the traditional lifestyles of these powerful communities give visitors a genuine taste of pre-Conquest Andean Peru.

Brief history

The scattered population of the region is descended from two very ancient Andean ethnic groups – the **Aymara** and the **Quechua**. The Aymara's Tiahuanaco culture

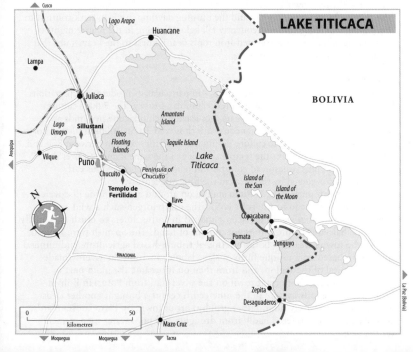

LAKE TITICACA

BOLIVIA

Cusco

Lago Arapa
Huancane
Lampa
Juliaca
Lago Umayo
Sillustani
Amantani Island
Uros Floating Islands
Taquile Island
Vilque
Puno
Chucuito
Peninsula of Chucuito
Lake Titicaca
Island of the Sun
Island of the Moon
Templo de Fertilidad
Ilave
Amarumur
Juli
Pomata
Copacabana
Yunguyo
BINACIONAL
Zepita
Desaguaderos
Mazo Cruz

Arequipa

La Paz (Bolivia)

0   50
kilometres

Moquegua   Moquegua   Tacna

TITICACA'S AQUATIC INHABITANTS

Not surprisingly, **fish** are still an important food source for Titicaca's inhabitants, including the islanders, and for the ibises and flamingoes that can be seen along the pre-Inca terraced shoreline. The most common fish – the **carachi** – is a small piranha-like specimen. **Trout** also arrived in the lake, after swimming up the rivers, during the first or second decade of the twentieth century. **Pejerey** (kingfish) established themselves only some thirty years ago but have been so successful that there are relatively few trout left – *pejerey* fishing is an option for visitors.

pre-dates the Quechua's Inca civilization by over three hundred years and this region is thought to be the original home for the domestication of a number of very important plants, not least the potato, tomato and the common pepper.

Puno

A crossroads for most travellers en route to Bolivia or Chile, **PUNO** lacks the colonial style of Cusco or the bright glamour of Arequipa's *sillar* stone architecture, but it's a friendly place and one of the few Peruvian towns where the motorized traffic seems to respect pedestrians. Busy as it is, there is less of a sense of manic rush here than in most coastal or mountain cities. On the edge of the town spreads vast **Lake Titicaca** – some 8400 square kilometres of shimmering blue water enclosed by white peaks. Puno's port is a vital staging-point for exploring the northern end of Lake Titicaca, with its floating islands just a few hours away by boat.

There are three main points of reference in Puno: the spacious **Plaza de Armas**, the **train station** several blocks north, and the vast, strung-out area of old, semi-abandoned docks at the ever-shifting **Titicaca lakeside port**. It all looks impressive from a distance, but, in fact, the real town-based attractions are few and quickly visited.

The climate here is generally dry and the burning daytime sun is in stark contrast to the icy evenings (temperatures frequently fall below freezing in the winter nights of July and August). Sloping corrugated-iron roofs bear witness to the heavy rains that fall between November and February.

Brief history

Puno is immensely rich in living traditions – in particular its modern interpretations of folk dances – as well as fascinating pre-Columbian history. The **Pukara culture** emerged here some three thousand years ago, leaving behind stone pyramids and carved standing stones contemporaneous with those of Chavín 1600km further north. The better-known **Tiahuanaco culture** dominated the Titicaca basin between 800 and 1200 AD, leaving in its wake the temple complex of the same name just over the border in Bolivia, plus widespread cultural and religious influence. This early settlement was conquered by the Incas in the fifteenth century.

The first Spanish settlement at **Puno** sprang up around a silver mine discovered by the infamous Salcedo brothers in 1657. The camp forged such a wild and violent reputation that the Lima viceroy moved in with soldiers to crush and finally execute the Salcedos before things got too out of hand. The Spanish were soon to discover the town's wealth – both in terms of tribute-based agriculture and mineral exploitation based on a unique form of slave labour. In 1668 the viceroy made Puno the capital of the region, and from then on it became the main port of Lake Titicaca and an important town on the silver trail from **Potosí** in Bolivia. The arrival of the railway, late in the nineteenth century, brought another boost, but today it's a relatively poor, rather grubby sort of town, by Peruvian standards, and a place that has suffered badly from droughts and poor water management over the years.

PUNO

0 ————————— 100
metres

N

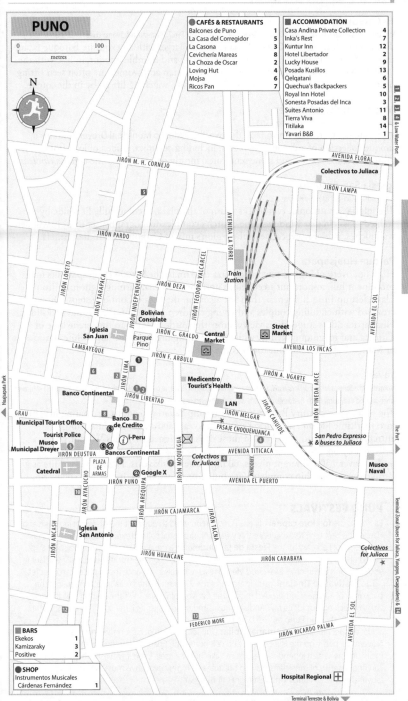

CAFÉS & RESTAURANTS

Balcones de Puno	1
La Casa del Corregidor	5
La Casona	3
Cevichería Mareas	8
La Choza de Oscar	2
Loving Hut	4
Mojsa	6
Ricos Pan	7

ACCOMMODATION

Casa Andina Private Collection	4
Inka's Rest	7
Kuntur Inn	12
Hotel Libertador	2
Lucky House	9
Posada Kusillos	13
Qelqatani	6
Quechua's Backpackers	5
Royal Inn Hotel	10
Sonesta Posadas del Inca	3
Suites Antonio	11
Tierra Viva	8
Titilaka	14
Yavari B&B	1

3

JIRÓN M. H. CORNEJO

AVENIDA FLORAL

Colectivos to Juliaca

JIRÓN LAMPA

JIRÓN PARDO

AVENIDA LA TORRE

JIRÓN LORETO

JIRÓN TARAPACA

JIRÓN INDEPENDENCIA

JIRÓN DEZA

JIRÓN TEODORO VALCÁRCEL

*Train
Station*

AVENIDA EL SOL

**Bolivian
Consulate**

JIRÓN C. GRALDO

**Iglesia
San Juan**

Parque
Pino

**Central
Market**

*Street
Market*

LAMBAYEQUE

JIRÓN F. ARBULU

AVENIDA LOS INCAS

Huajsapata Park

JIRÓN LIMA

**Medicentro
Tourist's Health**

JIRÓN A. UGARTE

Banco Continental

JIRÓN LIBERTAD

LAN

JIRÓN MELGAR

JIRÓN CAHUIDE

JIRÓN PINEDA ARCE

GRAU

**Banco
de Credito**

Municipal Tourist Office

PASAJE CHOQUEHUANCA

*San Pedro Expresso
& buses to Juliaca*

Tourist Police

i-Peru

**Museo
Municipal Dreyer**

JIRÓN DEUSTUA

Bancos Continental

AVENIDA TITICACA

*Colectivos
for Juliaca*

WENDORFF

Catedral

PLAZA
DE
ARMAS

Google X

JIRÓN MOQUEGUA

**Museo
Naval**

The Port

JIRÓN AYACUCHO

JIRÓN PUNO

AVENIDA EL PUERTO

JIRÓN AREQUIPA

JIRÓN ANCASH

**Iglesia
San Antonio**

JIRÓN CAJAMARCA

JIRÓN TACNA

JIRÓN HUANCANE

JIRÓN CARABAYA

*Colectivos
for Juliaca*

AVENIDA EL SOL

Terminal Zonal (buses for Juliaca, Yunguyo, Desaguadero) &

FEDERICO MORE

JIRÓN RICARDO PALMA

BARS

Ekekos	1
Kamizaraky	3
Positive	2

SHOP

Instrumentos Musicales
Cárdenas Fernández	1

Hospital Regional

La Catedral

Plaza de Armas • Mon–Fri 8am–noon & 3–6pm, Sat 8am–noon & 3–7pm, Sun 7.30am–noon & 3–5pm • Free

The seventeenth-century **Catedral** is surprisingly large, with an exquisite Baroque facade from 1657 and, unusually for Peru, a very simple and humble interior, in line with the local Aymaras' austere attitude to religion. Local men and women are often seen sitting on the church steps, sometimes in traditional dress, watching life go by in the square.

Museo Municipal Dreyer

Conde de Lemos 289 • Mon–Sat 9am–7pm • S/15

Opposite the Catedral's north face, the two-floor **Museo Municipal Dreyer** contains a unique collection of archeological pieces, including ceramics, golden objects from Sillustani, some textiles and stone sculptures, mostly removed from the region's *chullpas*.

Iglesia San Antonio

Jr Ayacucho • Mon–Sat 8am–6pm • Free

The **Iglesia San Antonio**, two blocks south of the plaza, is colourfully lit inside by ten stained-glass circular windows. The church's complex iconography, set into six wooden wall niches, is highly evocative of the region's mix of Catholic and Indian beliefs.

Parque Huajsapata

High up, overlooking the town and Plaza de Armas, the **Parque Huajsapata** sits on a prominent hill, a short but steep climb up Jirón Deustua, turning right into Jirón Llave, left up Jirón Bolognesi, then left again up the Pasaje Contique steps. Often crowded with cuddling couples and young children playing on the natural rockslides, Huajsapata offers stupendous views across the bustle of Puno to the serene blue of Titicaca and its unique skyline, while the pointing finger on the large white statue of Manco Capac reaches out towards the lake.

Yavari

Moored by the *Sonesta Posada del Inca Hotel*, Sesquicentenario 610, Sector Huaje, or cruising Lake Titicaca as a B&B (see p.193) • Museum when moored daily 8am–6pm • By donation • ☎ 051 369 329, ⓦ yavari.org

The nineteenth-century British-built steamship **Yavari** provides a fascinating insight into maritime life on Lake Titicaca over 150 years ago and the military and entrepreneurial mindset of Peru in those days. Designed by James Watt, it was delivered by boat from England to Arica on the coast, and then carried 560km by mule in over 1300 different pieces, taking a total of six years. Having started life as a Peruvian navy gunship complete with bullet-proof windows, it ended up delivering

---

PUNO FESTIVALS

Famed as the **folklore capital** of Peru, Puno is renowned throughout the Andes for its music and dance. The best time to experience this wealth of traditional cultural expression is during the first two weeks of February for the **Fiesta de la Candelaria**, a great folklore dance festival, boasting incredible dancers wearing devil masks; the festival climaxes on the second Sunday of February. If you're in Puno at this time, it's a good idea to reserve hotels in advance (hotel prices can double).

The **Festival de Tinajani**, usually around June 27, is set in the bleak altiplano against the backdrop of a huge wind-eroded rock in the Canyon of Tinajani. Off the beaten trail, it's well worth checking out for its raw Andean music and dance, plus its large sound systems; ask at the tourist offices in Puno or Cusco for details.

Just as spectacular, the **Semana Jubilar** (Jubilee Festival) occurs in the first week of November, partly on the Isla Esteves, and celebrates the Spanish founding of the city and the Incas' origins, which legend says are from Lake Titicaca itself. Even if you miss the festivals, you can find a group of musicians playing brilliant and highly evocative music somewhere in the labyrinthine town centre on most nights of the year.

mail around Lake Titicaca, and at times had to use llama dung as fuel. In 2015 the *Yavari* was certified for passenger use and today travels the lake as a unique B&B. When moored it functions as a museum.

ARRIVAL AND DEPARTURE   PUNO

BY PLANE
The closest airport to Puno is Aeropuerto Manco Capac (☎ 051 328 226) near Juliaca, about 49km north of the city. Flights arrive and depart most days for Lima, Arequipa and Cusco with LAN (ⓦ lan.com) and Avianca (ⓦ avianca.com). Rossy Tours (☎ 051 366 709) offers colectivo taxis from the airport, dropping passengers off at their hotels in Puno for S/15 per person, although travellers organizing this pick-up service have reported buses arriving late or not at all.

BY TRAIN
If you're coming in from Cusco by train, you'll arrive at the station at Av la Torre 224 (☎ 051 369 179). Taxis leave from immediately outside the station and will cost about S/5 to anywhere in the centre of town. Trains to and from Cusco leave at 8am (April–Oct Mon, Wed, Fri & Sat; Nov–March Mon, Wed & Sat), arriving at their destination at 6pm. Tickets are available from agents or direct from PeruRail (☎ 084 581 414, ⓦ perurail.com).

BY BUS
Buses from Arequipa, Cusco, Tacna, Moquegua, Copacabana and La Paz use the Terminal Terrestre at Jr Primero de Mayo (☎ 051 364 733). Buses from local provincial destinations such as Juliaca or along the edge of Lake Titicaca come in at the Terminal Zonal, Av Costanera 451, Barrio Progreso. Ignore anyone who offers you help, unless you have already booked with them (there are thieves operating as touts for hotels or tours).
Destinations Arequipa (several daily; 6hr); Chivay (2 daily; 5hr 30min); Copacabana (9 daily; 2–3hr); Cusco (several daily; 6hr); Desaguadero (4 daily; 2–3hr); La Paz (10 daily; 5–6hr); Lima (3 daily via Arequipa; 20hr); Moquegua (7 daily; 8hr); Tacna (7 daily; 9hr 30min).

BUS OPERATORS
4M Express Jr Arequipa 736 ☎ 051 452 296, ⓦ 4m-peru .com. Has one daily service to Chivay (for the Colca Canyon),

inclusive of hotel pickup.
Cruz del Sur Terminal Terrestre and Jr Lima 394 ☎ 051 205 824, ⓦ cruzdelsur.com.pe. Services to Arequipa, Cusco and Lima.
Expreso Sagitario Terminal Terrestre ☎ 051 321 519. Serves Moquegua and Tacna.
Expreso Turismo San Martín Terminal Terrestre ☎ 951 677 730. Serves Moquegua and Tacna, via Laraqueri or Desaguardero.
Ormeño Terminal Terrestre ☎ 051 352 780, ⓦ grupo -ormeno.com.pe. Services to Arequipa, Lima and La Paz via Desaguadero.
El Pino (TEPSA) Terminal Terrestre ☎ 051 205 103, ⓦ tepsa.com. Services to Arequipa and Lima.
Tour Perú Terminal Terrestre and Jr Tacna 285, room no. 105 ☎ 051 206 088, ⓦ tourperu.com.pe. Serves Cusco, Copacabana and La Paz.
Transportes Internacional Titicaca Bolivia Terminal Terrestre and Jr Tacna 285, room no. 104 ☎ 051 363 830. Serves Copacabana and La Paz.
Transzela Terminal Terrestre ☎ 051 353 822, ⓦ transzela .com.pe. Serves Cusco.
Turismo Sillustani Jr Lima 440 ☎ 051 353 214, ⓦ turismosillustani.com. One daily service to Chivay (for the Colca Canyon).

BY COLECTIVO
Colectivos from Desaguadero and Yunguyo serve the Terminal Zonal. Combis from Juliaca terminate here but also stop off at a number of places in town, including the corner of Jr Lampa close to Pasaje Maldonado.

BY BOAT
The main port, used by boats from Bolivia as well as the Uros islands, Taquile and Amantani, is a 10–15min ride from the Plaza de Armas It's generally best to take a taxi or mototaxi to and from the port (S/5–7).

INFORMATION

Tourist information iPeru is on the Plaza de Armas, at jirones Lima and Deustua (Mon–Sat 9am–6pm, Sun 9am–1pm; ☎ 051 365 088, ✉ iperupuno@promperu.gob. pe). On Sundays only it operates a kiosk at the Terminal Terrestre (2–4pm), while the airport branch opens for incoming flights (☎ 051 639 549).

TOURS

The streets of Puno are full of touts selling guided tours and trips, but don't be swayed – always go to a respected, established **tour company**, such as one of those listed below. There are four main local tours on offer in Puno, all of which will reward you with views of abundant bird and animal life, immense landscapes and genuine living traditions. The trip to **Sillustani** normally involves a 3–4hr tour by minibus and costs S/40. Most other tours involve a combination of visits to the nearby **Uros Floating Islands** (half-day tour; S/35), **Taquile and the Uros islands** (full day from S/60, or S/110 overnighting in Amantani) and **Amantani** (2 days, 1 night S/110).

All Ways Travel Jr Deustua 576 ☎051 353 979, ⌨titicacaperu.com. This reliable tour company located in the historic Casa del Corregidor runs the usual tours to Uros and Sillustani, and offers trips to the wildlife haven of Anapia, close to the Bolivian border, where it works with locals on a sustainable tourism project. The company is involved in social tourism in the Capachica Peninsula and the three islands of Anapia where it helps with educational projects in the community.

Cusi Expeditions Teodoro Valcarcel 155 ☎051 369 072. A reliable company offering all the usual tours at reasonable prices: Sillustani, Uros, Taquile and Amantani.

Edgar Adventures Jr Lima 328 ☎051 353 444, ⌨edgaradventures.com. Edgar leads a number of off-the-beaten-track tours such as Titicaca Express, which visits remote parts of Taquile island, thereby avoiding large crowds of tourists. He also offers kayaking trips, as well as the usual tours to Uros, Taquile and beyond.

Leon Tours Jr Libertad 176 ☎051 352 771, ⌨peru -titicaca.com. A recommended travel agent specializing in catamaran trips to Bolivia (full day by bus to Copacabana, catamaran to Isla del Sol, then bus to La Paz). It also runs tours to Sillustani, Uros, Amantani, Taquile and Tinajani, *turismo rustico* with a local shaman, either on Amantani or near Juli, and adventure tourism, mainly in the Cordillera Carabaya (around 5000m) and down to the rainforest along the Inambari with boats and 4WD vehicles.

ACCOMMODATION

There is no shortage of **accommodation** in Puno for any budget, but most of it is bland compared with Arequipa or Cusco. The streets in the city centre can get quite loud and busy, especially during the day and on weekend nights. Upmarket hotels tend to have more peaceful locations, usually outside town along the shores of Lake Titicaca, which can make for a very relaxing stay.

CENTRAL PUNO

Inka's Rest Pasaje San Carlos 158 ☎051 368 720, ⌨inkasresthostel.com. This intimate hostel has myriad rooms tucked away on various floors; the simple dorms all have shared bath, while there are comfortable mini-apartments with living area for larger groups. There's a billiards table, and kitchen for guests' use. Dorms S/26, doubles S/60

Kuntur Inn Jr Ayacucho 708 ☎051 351 209, ⌨kunturinn.com. This friendly, spick-and-span place offers nicely decorated rooms with faux-parquet floors. Colourful carpets add a little character, while splashes of red paint brighten up the rooms. All rooms are en suite with flat-screen TV, and some have lake views. S/172

Lucky House Jr Titicaca 144 ☎051 353 552, ⌨luckyyourhouse.com. This is a very decent guesthouse with a cosy living area adorned with a few trinkets and an old wooden bar where guests are encouraged to mingle. The simple rooms are clean and welcoming, and you can use the kitchen if you want – all you need to do is ask. S/120

Posada Kusillos Jr Federico More 162 ☎051 364 579. This small, homely place has ten simple but pleasant en-suite rooms and two little patios. Wicker baskets and the owner's collection of masks from around the world adorn the communal areas. S/120

Qelqatani Jr Tarapacá 355 ☎051 366 172, ⌨qelqatani .com. Just a short walk from the main square, this place has hallways furnished with couches, paintings and potted plants. Rooms are welcoming and comfortable, although rather overpriced for what you get. The wi-fi reaches most of the rooms. S/257

Quechua's Backpackers Jr Independencia 301 ☎051 352 194, ⌨quechuasbackpackers.com. This clean and friendly hostel has just one cosy six-bed dorm with wooden lockers; the large window overlooking town means it has plenty of light, and there's a small balcony with lake views. There's free all-day tea, book exchange, laundry service (S/7 per kg) and a fully equipped, open-plan kitchen for guest use. Dorms S/35, doubles S/87

Royal Inn Hotel Jr Ayacucho 438 ☎051 364 574, ⌨royalinnhoteles.com. Central Puno's most upmarket option features polished wooden floors, solid beds with headboards and lamps made of goat leather. The hallways are decorated with large paintings and there's a computer for guests' use on each floor. Service is friendly and professional. S/330

Suites Antonio Jr Arequipa 840 ☎051 351 767, ⌨sanantoniosuitespuno.com. Paintings of life on Lake Titicaca brighten up the public areas of this hotel, while a handful of crafts and odds and ends, including shoe-shaped vases, decorate the stairway. There's a communal area with fireplace, a kitchen for guests' use and free infusions on each floor. S/130

Tierra Viva Jr Grau 270 ☎051 368 005, ⌨tierravivahoteles.com. This is one of the best hotels in central Puno, offering welcoming rooms with king-size beds draped with alpaca blankets. Walls are decorated with *kipus*, a set of hanging Inca cords that were used in a similar way to an abacus. The corridors are embellished with draped fabrics from the island of Taquile, and the slightly more spacious superior rooms (S/453) have tea- and coffee-making facilities, fridge and flat-screen TV. S/393

AROUND PUNO

★**Casa Andina Private Collection** Av Sesquicentenario 1970 ☎051 363 992, ⊛casa-andina .com. On the shores of Lake Titicaca, this peaceful hotel offers accommodation in comfortably furnished rooms with modern amenities. The hotel restaurant serves excellent meals, too, and there's a lovely outdoor area that is particularly appealing on a crisp sunny day. S/550

Hotel Libertador Isla Esteves s/n ☎051 367 780, ⊛libertador.com.pe. Located on a private island linked to the mainland by bridge, the real draw at this hotel is the excellent view of Lake Titicaca from the restaurant's floor-to-ceiling glass panels. Overall, the hotel decor is rather outmoded, although the smallish rooms are comfortable nonetheless. S/715

Sonesta Posadas del Inca Av Sesquicentenario 610,

Sector Huaje ☎051 364 111, ⊛sonestaperu.com. Located about 2km northeast of town, the carpeted rooms here have comfortable solid mattresses, and most have lake views. The pleasant garden area with views over the lake is a nice spot to take in the crisp morning air, although breakfast is rather bland. S/695

Titilaka Distrito Platería, Chucuito Peninsula ☎01 700 5106, ⊛titilaka.com. This luxurious three-storey lodge on a remote peninsula on Lake Titicaca offers lake-view rooms facing the islands of Taquile and Amantani and the Bolivian Cordillera Real to the east. The interiors are stylishly furnished with local artwork and modern amenities, and all rooms have stunning lake views. S/1450

★**Yavari B&B** ☎051 369 329, ⊛yavari.org. The stunning British-built *Yavari* gunship (see p.190) offers accommodation in four cabins that accommodate seven guests. The interior of the boat has been immaculately restored to its original splendour – it's not every day you get to stay in a B&B on the world's highest navigable lake. Recommended. US$45 per person per night

EATING

There are plenty of restaurants in Puno, although only a handful of places are particularly worth recommending. The food here is generally nothing to write home about, but the local delicacies of trout and kingfish (*pejerey*) are worth trying and are available in most restaurants.

Balcones de Puno Jr Libertad 354 ☎051 365 300, ⊛balconesdepuno.com. This restaurant hosts daily folkloric dance shows (7.30–9pm) featuring incredible costumes that you probably wouldn't see otherwise. The food is excellent too, and the menu includes a great trout and kingfish ceviche (S/30) and alpaca medallions accompanied by *quinoa* cooked with milk and cheese risotto-style with stir-fried vegetables and gooseberry sauce (S/40). Don't forget to try the delicious *quinoa* ice cream (S/15) and the coca mousse (S/11). Daily 10am–10pm.

La Casa del Corregidor Jr Deustua 576 ☎051 351 921, ⊛cafebar.casadelcorregidor.pe. Located within a beautifully restored building, this café-bar is a pleasant spot for an afternoon *chicha* (S/4) or a freshly squeezed juice (S/7); the café area features lanterns and board games, and there are shaded tables on the patio. There's a quirky bar area that's a good spot for a beer (S/10), with upturned funnels as lampshades, cushioned seating and walls plastered with vinyl discs. Sadly, though, the food is average. Mon–Sat 9am–9pm.

La Casona Jr Lima 423, 2nd floor ☎051 351 108, ⊛lacasona-restaurant.com. This large family-run restaurant in the heart of town has been going strong for over two decades; the interior walls are adorned with a collection of old irons, sewing machines and typewriters, and the menu includes local dishes including trout in crispy *kiwicha* (Andean cereal) coated with passionfruit sauce, mash with fennel and vegetables (S/32). Daily noon–9pm.

Cevichería Mareas Jr Cajamarca 448 ☎051 777 000. Seafood and fresh fish travel to this bustling cevichería daily from Ilo on the coast. Some ceviche dishes are also made with lake fish, and, as would be expected, the menu includes a range of tasty ceviches (S/11), as well as other fish-based dishes including rice with seafood (S/16). Daily 9am–4pm.

La Choza de Oscar Jr Libertad 340 ☎051 351 199, ⊛lachozadeoscar.com. Sister establishment to *Balcones*, this place also has lively *peña* shows; tucked away at the back of the restaurant is a bustling cheap and cheerful *pollería*, serving tasty chicken (S/15 for a quarter) spit-roasted in front of your eyes. Daily 7.30am–9pm.

Loving Hut Jr Choquehuanca 188 ☎051 353 523, ⊛lovinghut.com/pe. This simple vegan restaurant gets particularly busy at lunchtime, and offers tasty vegan cuisine at very reasonable prices. The lunch menu will set you back S/15, or you can choose individual dishes for about S/7. Mon–Sat 8am–6.30pm.

Mojsa Jr Lima 635, 2nd floor ☎051 363 182, ⊛mojsarestaurant.com. It translates as "delicious" in Aymara, and they wouldn't be lying. On the main square, this cosy restaurant with wooden interiors offers tasty *palta mojsa* (avocado and marinated chicken in tomato served with creole sauce; S/16) and *truchicausa* (mashed potatoes with yellow spicy pepper served with grilled trout, avocado and creole sauce; S/28). Daily 10am–10pm.

Ricos Pan Jr Moquegua 334. This popular bakery offers a selection of delectable cakes and pies, including lemon,

3

apple or spinach (S/6) to be taken away or consumed at the little tables. There are *empañadas* (S/2.50), too, as well as

plenty of hot drinks and infusions (S/2.50). Mon–Sat 6am–9.30pm, Sun 3–9.30pm.

DRINKING AND NIGHTLIFE

Nightlife centres around Jirón Lima, a pedestrian precinct where the locals, young and old alike, hang out, parading up and down past the hawkers selling woollen sweaters, craft goods, cigarettes and sweets.

Ekekos Jr Lima 355, 2nd floor ☎051 365 986. *Ekekos* offers snacks, drinks, cable TV, books and games; it also shows films and favours a soundtrack of rock, salsa, reggae, trance and techno music. Daily 5pm–4am.

Kamizaraky Jr Grau 158. A dark, cavernous bar with live music on weekend nights from 9pm. The main musical flavour is rock, although bands also play reggae, country, jazz and blues. Cocktails from S/13. Daily 5pm–midnight.

Positive Jr Lima 378 ☎051 950 329. This place has plenty of character – the walls are plastered with travellers' notes and coins, and it hums with custom in the evenings. It's a great spot for a beer (S/15), although the food is pretty average. Daily 7am–2am.

Teatro Municipal Block 1 of Arequipa. Puno's Teatro Municipal hosts folklore music, dance and other cultural events. For details of what's on, check at the tourist information office (see p.191).

SHOPPING

Artesanía There are plenty of craft shops along Jr Lima; another good spot to buy artesanía is at the stalls just by the port.
Instrumentos Musicales Cárdenas Fernández Jr

Arbulú 311B, Parque Pino ☎051 368 452. This little shop on Parque Pino sells traditional Andean musical instruments. Daily 9am–2pm & 4–9pm.

DIRECTORY

Consulate Bolivia, Jr Arequipa 136 ☎051 351 251 (Mon–Fri 8.30am–2pm).
Health Medicentro Tourist's Health, Jr Moquegua 191 (☎051 365 909, ⊕th.pe), or the Hospital Regional, Av El Sol 1022 (☎051 369 696).
Immigration Jr Ayacucho 270 ☎051 357 103 (Mon–Fri 8am–1pm and 3–4pm).
Internet Google X, Jr Arequipa 666 and Jr Puno (daily 7am–10pm; S/1 per hr).

Money and exchange Banco Continental, Jr Lima and Libertad; Banco de Credito, Jr Lima and Av Grau; Interbank, Jr Lima 444.
Police The 24hr Tourist Police are at Jr Deustua 588 (☎051 352 303).
Post office Jr Moquegua 269 (Mon–Fri 8am–7pm, Sat 8am–noon).
Taxis Millennium ☎051 353 134; Taxi Tour Puno ☎051 369 000.

Sillustani

Scattered all around Lake Titicaca you'll find *chullpas*, gargantuan white-stone towers up to 10m in height in which the ancient Colla people, who dominated the region before the Incas, buried their dead. Some of the most spectacular are at **SILLUSTANI**, set on a little peninsula in Lake Umayo overlooking Titicaca, 30km northwest of Puno. This ancient temple/cemetery consists of a ring of stones more than five hundred years old – some of which have been tumbled by earthquakes or, more recently, by tomb robbers intent on stealing the rich goods (ceramics, jewellery and a few weapons) buried with important mummies. Two styles predominate at this site: the honeycomb *chullpas* and those whose superb stonework was influenced by the advance of the Inca Empire. The former are set aside from the rest and characterized by large stone slabs around a central core; some of them are carved, but most are simply plastered with white mud and small stones. The later, Inca-type stonework is more complicated and in some cases you can see the elaborate corner-jointing typical of Cusco masonry. If you want to **camp** overnight at Sillustani (though remember how cold it can be), the site guard will show you where to pitch your tent. It's a magnificent place to wake up, with the morning sun rising over the snowcapped Cordillera Real on the Bolivian side of Titicaca.

CLOCKWISE FROM TOP LEFT LOCALS ON AMANTANI (P.198); EL MISTI, NEAR AREQUIPA (P.175); MONASTERIO DE SANTA CATALINA, AREQUIPA (P.160) >

By colectivo The easiest way to get here is on a guided tour from Puno (see p.190); alternatively, you can take a colectivo towards Juliaca from Puno's Jr Lampa and Pasaje Maldonado (every 20min) and ask the driver to let you off at Desvío Sillustani (15min). At this junction, cross the road and catch a colectivo to Atuncolla (10min), from where you'll have to change again for another colectivo to Sillustani (10min). Alternatively, you can hire a colectivo from Desvío Sillustani directly to Sillustani (approx S/20).

Uros islands

The man-made floating **UROS ISLANDS** have been inhabited since their construction centuries ago by Uros Indians retreating from more powerful neighbours like the Incas. They are now home to a dwindling and much-abused Indian population. Although there are about 48 of these islands, most guided tours limit themselves to the largest, **Huacavacani**, where several families live alongside a floating Seventh-Day Adventist missionary school.

The islands are made from layer upon layer of **totora reeds**, the dominant plant in the shallows of Titicaca and a source of food (the inner juicy bits near the roots), as well as the basic material for roofing, walling and fishing rafts. During the rainy season months of November to February it's not unusual for some of the islands to move about the surface of the lake.

By boat You can visit independently with the skipper of one of the many launches that leave from the port in Puno about every thirty minutes (S/5 one way).

Tours The easiest way to get to the islands is on a short two- to three-hour trip (from S/25–30) with one of the tour agencies in Puno (see p.190).

Taquile

One of Titicaca's non-floating islands, **TAQUILE** is a peaceful place that sees fewer tourists than the Uros. Located 25–30km across the water from Puno it lies just beyond the outer edge of the Gulf of Chucuito. Taquile is arguably the most attractive of the islands hereabouts, measuring about 1km by 7km, and looking from some angles like a huge ribbed whale, large and bulbous to the east, tapering to its western tail end. The horizontal striations are produced by significant amounts of ancient terracing along the steep-sided shores. Such terraces are at an even greater premium here in the middle of the lake where soil erosion would otherwise slowly kill the island's largely self-sufficient agricultural economy, of which potatoes, corn, broad

---

THE UROS

There are only six hundred **Uros** people living on the islands these days and a lot of the population is mixed-race, with Quechua and Aymara blood. When the Incas controlled the region, they considered the Uros so poor – almost subhuman – that the only tribute required of them was a section of hollow cane filled with lice.

Life on the islands has certainly never been easy: the inhabitants have to go some distance to find **fresh water**, and the bottoms of the reed islands rot so rapidly that fresh matting has to be constantly added above. Islands last around twelve to fifteen years and it takes two months of communal work to start a new one.

More than half the islanders have converted to **Catholicism** but the largest community is dominated by its Adventist school. Forty years ago the Uros were a proud **fishing people**, in many ways the guardians of Titicaca, but the 1980s, particularly, saw a rapid devastation of their traditional values. However, things have improved over recent years and you do get a glimpse of a very unusual way of life. Note that lots of the people you may meet actually live on the mainland, only travelling out to sell their wares to tourists.

beans and hardy *quinoa* are the main crops. Without good soil Taquile could become like the main floating islands, depending almost exclusively on tourism for its income. Today, the island is still very traditional. There is no grid-connected electricity on the island, though there is a solar-powered community loudspeaker and a growing number of individual houses with solar lighting; it's therefore a good idea to take a torch, matches and candles.

The island has two main ports: **Puerto Chilcano Doc** (on the west or Puno side of the island) and **El Otro Puerto** (on the north side, used mostly by tour agency boats because it has an easier and equally panoramic access climb). Arriving via Puerto Chilcano Doc, the main heart of the island is reached via 525 gruelling steps up a steep hill from the small stone harbour; this can easily take an hour of slow walking. When you've recovered your breath, you will eventually appreciate the spectacular view of the southeast of the island where you can see the hilltop ruins of **Uray K'ari**, built of stone in the Tiahuanaco era around 800 AD; looking to the west you may glimpse the larger, slightly higher ruins of **Hanan K'ari**. On arrival, before climbing the stairs, you'll be met by a committee of locals who delegate various native families to look after particular travellers – be aware that your family may live in basic conditions and speak no Spanish, let alone English (Quechua being the first language).

Brief history

The island has been inhabited for over ten thousand years, with agriculture being introduced around 4000 BC. Some three thousand years ago it was inhabited by the Pukara culture and the first stone terraces were built here. It was dominated by the Aymara-speaking Tiahuanaco culture until the thirteenth century, when the Incas conquered it and introduced the Quechua language. In 1580, the island was bought by Pedro Gonzalez de Taquile and so came under Spanish influence.

During the 1930s the island was used as a safe place of exile/prison for troublesome characters such as former president Sánchez Cerro, and it wasn't until 1937 that the residents – the local descendants of the original inhabitants – regained legal ownership by buying it back.

ARRIVAL AND TOURS · TAQUILE

By boat There are daily boats from the port in Puno (departing at 7am, returning at 2pm; 3hr; S/25 return). Alternatively, you can go on an organized trip with one of the tour companies listed (see p.190). The sun's rays reflected off the lake are strong, so it's a good idea to protect your head and shoulders during this voyage.

Tour guides There are some indigenous Taquileño tourist guides, many of whom now speak English, so it's not essential to book a visit to Taquile via a travel agent in Puno. The quality can be just as good or even better by arranging a visit to Taquile directly with the islanders: this way you can help keep the economic benefit of tourism on the island itself. Once you arrive, ask around at the port or head to the main square and ask there.

ACCOMMODATION

Homestays Many visitors choose to stay a night or two in bed and breakfast accommodation (from around S/45, plus S/20 for each meal) in islanders' homes. The only way to guarantee a place to stay is to book in advance through one of Puno's tour agencies (see p.190); if you arrive on spec, you can ask the relevant island authorities or talk to the boat's captain and you may be lucky, but don't bank on it. Sleeping bags and toilet paper are recommended, and fresh fruit and vegetables are appreciated by the host islanders.

EATING AND SHOPPING

Restaurants Away from the plaza there are more than twenty restaurants, or eating houses, dotted around the island, most serving the classic local dish of *sopa de quinoa* or *pejerey* fish with French fries.

Shops There are a few small stores that sell artesanía, mostly weavings, and a couple of places to eat around the small plaza.

WEAVING AND KNITTING ON TAQUILE

Although they grow abundant maize, potatoes, wheat and barley, most of Taquile's population of 1200 people are also weavers and knitters of fine **alpaca wool**, renowned for their excellent cloth. You can still watch the locals drop-spin, a common form of hand-spinning that produces incredibly fine thread for their special cloth. The men sport black woollen trousers fastened with elaborate waistbands woven in pinks, reds and greens, while the women wear beautiful black headscarves, sweaters, dark shawls and up to eight skirts at the same time, trimmed usually with shocking-pink or bright-red tassels and fringes. You can tell if a man is married or single by the colour of his **woollen hat**, or *chullo*, the former's being all red and the latter's also having white; single men usually weave their own *chullos*. The community authorities or officials wear black sombreros on top of their red *chullos* and carry a staff of office.

Amantani

Like nearby Taquile, **AMANTANI**, a basket-weavers' island and the largest on the lake, has managed to retain some degree of cultural isolation and autonomous control over the tourist trade. Amantani is the less visited of these two islands and consequently has fewer facilities and costs slightly more to reach by boat. Of course, tourism has had its effect on the local population, so it's not uncommon to be offered drinks, then charged later, or for the children to sing you songs without being asked, expecting to be paid. The ancient **agricultural terraces** are excellently maintained, and traditional stone masonry is still practised, as are the old Inca systems of agriculture, labour and ritual trade. The islanders eat mainly vegetables, with meat and fruit being rare commodities, and the women dress in colourful clothes, very distinctively woven.

The island is dominated by two small hills: one is the **Temple of Pachamama** (Mother Earth) and the other the **Temple of Pachatata** (Father Earth). Around February 20, the islanders celebrate their main festival with half the 5000-strong population going to one hill, the other half gathering at the other. Following ancient ceremonies, the two halves then gather together to celebrate their origins with traditional and colourful music and dance.

ARRIVAL AND DEPARTURE
AMANTANI

By boat Boats for Amantani usually leave Puno daily at 9am, returning between 4 and 4.30pm; as usual, check with the captain for the time they plan to depart from the islands. You can go on an organized trip with one of the tour companies listed (see p.190), but the agencies are at least twice as expensive. It's a good idea to protect your head and shoulders from the sun on the journey over.

ACCOMMODATION AND EATING

Homestays Currently the only accommodation is in islanders' houses though there are plans to build a hostel. These can be booked in advance (S/84/US$30 per person, including boat and accommodation) via most Puno-based tour companies (see p.190).

Food shops There are no restaurants, but you can buy basic supplies at the artesanía trading post in the heart of the island.

Juliaca

There's no particular reason to stop in **JULIACA**, in many ways an uninspiring and geographically very flat settlement, but at the same time it's hard to avoid. This is the first town out of Puno towards Cusco, less than an hour away across a grassy pampa. The wild, flat and relatively barren terrain here makes it easy to imagine a straggling column of Spanish cavalry and foot soldiers followed by a thousand Inca warriors – Diego de Almagro's fated expedition to Chile in the 1530s. Today, much as it always was, the plain is scattered with tiny isolated communities, many of them with conical kilns, self-sufficient even down to kitchenware.

Inland from the lakeside, this is not an inviting town, looking like a large but down-at-heel, desert-bound work camp. There are some good **artesanía** stalls and shops on the Plaza Bolognesi, and excellent woollen goods can be purchased extremely cheaply, especially at the **Monday market**. The daily market around the train station is worth a browse and sells just about everything – from stuffed iguanas to second-hand bikes.

ARRIVAL AND DEPARTURE   JULIACA

By plane If you fly to Titicaca, you'll arrive at Aeropuerto Manco Capac, about 2km north of town. Flights depart most days for Lima, Arequipa and Cusco with LAN (ⓦlan.com) and Avianca (ⓦavianca.com). A taxi to the airport is about S/15.

By train If you're going by rail to Cusco from Puno, you have to pass through Juliaca en route; no one really gets off here though.

By bus The Terminal Terrestre is at Jr San Martín and Av Miraflores. Cruz del Sur (ⓣ051 502 536) has services to

Arequipa and Lima (1 daily; 18hr), while a number of companies serve Cusco, including Cristobal del Sur (ⓣ051 323 702; 7hr). Wayra (ⓣ958 314 516) has services to Puerto Maldonado (2 daily; 12hr).

By colectivo Colectivos leave from Puno's Jr Lampa and Pasaje Maldonado (every 20min; 45min), dropping passengers off at Plaza Bolognesi.and Real Plaza.

By taxi A taxi from Puno will set you back around S/80 (45min).

ACCOMMODATION

Royal Inn Hotel Jr San Román 158 ⓣ054 321 561, ⓦroyalinnhoteles.com. A surprisingly classy hotel with heating, carpets, private bathrooms and reasonably good

service. This is the best place to sleep if you get stranded here and need to sample one of Juliaca's several bland establishments. S/330

South to Bolivia

The most popular routes to Bolivia involve overland road travel, crossing the frontier either at **Yunguyo** or at **Desaguadero**. En route to either you'll pass by some of Titicaca's more interesting colonial settlements, each with its own individual style of architecture. The lakeside stretch between Puno and the Bolivian frontier at Desaguadero is known – also for linguistic reasons – as the **Corredor Aymara**. This sector is full of fascinating but unfortunately slowly decaying colonial relics, particularly the fine churches of Chucuito, Acora, Ilave, Juli, Pomata and Zepita. The more commonly used of the two frontier crossings is Yunguyo.

Chucuito

CHUCUITO, 20km south of Puno, is dwarfed by its intensive hillside terracing and the huge igneous boulders poised behind the brick and adobe houses. It was once a colonial town and the main plaza retains the **pillory** (*picota*) where the severed heads of executed criminals were displayed. Close to this there's a **sundial**, erected in 1831 to help the local Aymara people regulate to an 8am to 5pm work day. The base is made from stones taken from the Inca Templo de Fertilidad. Also on the plaza is the **Iglesia Santo Domingo**, constructed in 1780 and displaying a very poor image of a puma.

Templo de Fertilidad

Located behind the *Hotel Taypikala*, the **Templo de Fertilidad** remains Chucuito's greatest treasure. Inside the temple's main stone walls are around a hundred stone phalluses, row upon row jammed within the temple space, ranged like seats in a theatre. Some of the larger ones may have had particular ritual significance, and locals say that women who have difficulty getting pregnant still come here to pray for help on the giant phalluses.

ARRIVAL AND DEPARTURE   CHUCUITO

By bus/colectivo Colectivos from Puno (every 15min; 25min) drop passengers off at Chucuito's Plaza de Armas. Buses between Puno and the frontier (at Yunguyo and

Desaguadero) drop off and pick up on the main street, one block from the Templo de Fertilidad.

THE GATEWAY OF AMARU MURU

Coming from Puno, beyond the bridge over the Río Ilave, the road cuts 60km across the plain towards Juli, passing by some unusual rock formations scattered across the altiplano of the Titicaca basin, many of which have ritual significance for the local Aymara. The most important of these is the **Gateway of Aramu Muru**, a doorway-like alcove carved into the rock and said by indigenous mystics to serve as a dimensional link to the ancestors, a belief shared by new agers, who view it as the Andean "star gate", a kind of link to non-Earthly beings and other worlds; it is very hard to find, without a local guide or tour leader.

Ilave

About two-thirds of the way between Puno and Juli you pass through **ILAVE**, where a major side-road heads off directly down to the coast for Tacna (320km) and Moquegua (231km). Ilave is quite an important market town and has a large **Sunday market** selling colourful clothing and coca leaves, and also hosts a few shamanic fortune-tellers. The large Plaza de Armas hosts a statue to Coronel Francisco Bolognesi, hero of the Arica battles between Peru and Chile, while half a block to the south, the ancient and crumbling **Iglesia de San Miguel** has an impressive cupola and belfry.

ARRIVAL AND DEPARTURE   ILAVE

By bus Colectivos from Puno's Terminal Zonal drop passengers off at Ilave's Terminal Terrestre (every 30min; most departures 7–9am & 5–7pm; 1hr 30min). From here it's possible to catch services to Tacna and Moquegua on the coast.

Juli

A few kilometres on from the Aramu Muru rock (see box above) is the relatively large town of **JULI**, now bypassed by a new road, but nestling attractively between gigantic round-topped and terraced hills. Juli is also known as Pequeña Roma (Little Rome) because of the seven prominent mountains immediately surrounding it, each one of them of spiritual significance to the indigenous inhabitants in terms of magic, healing and fertility. Perhaps because of this, the **Jesuits** chose Juli as the site for a major missionary training centre, which prepared missionaries for trips to the remoter regions of Bolivia and Paraguay. The concept they developed, a form of community evangelization, was at least partly inspired by the Inca organizational system and was extremely influential throughout the seventeenth and eighteenth centuries. The Jesuits' political and religious power is reflected in the almost surreal extravagance of the church architecture.

Iglesia de San Pedro

Plaza de Armas • Daily 8am–5pm • Free

Fronting the town's large, open plaza is the stone-built parish church of **San Pedro**, marked by its intricately carved Plateresque side-altars. Constructed in 1560, it has an impressive cupola, and the cool, serene interior, awash with gold leaf, is home to many superb examples of Cusqueña-school artwork. Behind the altar there's a wealth of silver and gold, and the patterned woodwork drips with seashells, fruits and angels. In front of this church you'll often see local shamanic fortune-tellers.

Iglesia San Juan

Plazuela de San Juan • Tues–Sun 8am–5pm • S/8

Juli's numerous other churches display superb examples of Indian influence, particularly the huge brick and adobe **Iglesia San Juan**, with its *mestizo* stonework on some of the doors and windows. Cold and musty but with a rather surreal interior, due in part to the play of light through its few high windows, this church was founded in 1775 but is now an excellent **museum of religious art and architecture**, which handsomely rewards the inquisitive visitor.

ARRIVAL AND DEPARTURE
JULI

By bus Buses from Puno's Terminal Zonal (every 30min; 2hr) drop off at the Plaza de Armas.

Pomata

Twenty kilometres on from Juli lies the historic town of **POMATA**, with its pink granite church of **Santiago Apóstol**, built in 1763. Outside the church, in a prominent location overlooking the lake, is a circular stone construction known as **La Glorieta**; crumbling today, it's still the site where local authorities meet for ceremonial purposes. Pomata's name is derived from the Aymara word for "puma", and you'll see the puma symbol all over the fountain in the Plaza de Armas and outside the church. If you happen to be around the area in October, try to get to Pomata for the **Fiesta de la Virgen de Rosaria** on the first Sunday of the month, a splendid celebration with processions, music and folk dancing, as well as the usual drinking and feasting.

ARRIVAL AND DEPARTURE
POMATA

By colectivo From Puno's Terminal Zonal, catch a colectivo to Yunguyo (services leave every 20min or so), and hop off in Pomata (a journey of 1hr 30min).

3

CROSSING THE BOLIVIAN BORDER
SOUTH TO BOLIVIA

VIA YUNGUYO–COPACABANA

From Puno catch a colectivo from the Terminal Zonal (every 20min; 2hr 45min). The actual border is about 2km away; take a mototaxi (10min; S/2). Note the Peruvian border is open 8am–6pm Peruvian time, while the Bolivian border is open 7am–7pm Bolivian time (+1 from Peru), so make sure you time your arrival well. From Kasani on the Bolivian side there are regular colectivos to Copacabana (20min).

Changing money There are a handful of casas de cambio in town, but most are at the border itself.

VIA DESAGUADERO–LA PAZ

From Puno catch a colectivo to Desaguadero from the Terminal Sonal (every 20min; 3hr). Note that here too the Peruvian border is open 8am–6pm Peruvian time, while the Bolivian border is open 7am–7pm Bolivian time (+1 from Peru), so make sure you time your arrival well. Once in Bolivia, you can pick up a bus on to La Paz (3–4hr).

Changing money There are a few casas de cambio in town, more at the border.

ACCOMMODATION

YUNGUYO

San Andrés Jr Grau 516 ☎ 051 556 009. A basic *hostal* offering very simple rooms with communal bathrooms, aimed at the odd traveller who is unexpectedly stuck at the border. **S/40**

DESAGUADERO

El Sol Av Cultura 117 ☎ 01 551 045. A simple, friendly *hostal* offering double or twin rooms with private bath. Staff can advise on border crossings if required. **S/40**

Cusco and around

FIESTA DE LA VIRGEN DEL CARMEN, PAUCARTAMBO

Cusco and around

Known to the Incas as the "navel of the world", colourful Cusco was built by the Spanish on the remains of Inca temples and palaces, and is as rich in human activity today as it must have been at the height of the empire. One of South America's biggest tourist destinations, the city boasts a thriving Andean culture, and Inca architecture and colonial treasures galore, not to mention exclusive access to the mighty Machu Picchu, an unmissable highlight of any trip to Peru. In high season – June to September – the entire Sacred Valley swarms with visitors. It might be difficult to avoid the crowds, but Cusco's magnificent history and ancient feel may well tempt you to consider extending your stay.

Enclosed between high hills, Cusco's heart is the **Plaza de Armas**. Directly above it, the imposing ceremonial centre and fortress of **Sacsayhuaman** dominates the hillscape. Once the Incas' capital, Cusco is now home to a rich mix of traditional culture, lively nightlife and an endless variety of museums, walks and tours.

The wider region of Cusco is mainly mountainous, with several peaks over 6000m, all of which the Incas considered sacred. The entire region is **high altitude** and even the city of Cusco sits at 3399m, an altitude which needs to be treated with respect, particularly if arriving by air from sea level (see box, p.210). Within easy access of the city, there are dozens of enticing destinations. The **Sacred Valley** of the Río Urubamba is the obvious first choice, with the citadel of **Machu Picchu** as the ultimate goal, but there are hundreds of other magnificent Inca ruins – **Pisac** and **Ollantaytambo** in particular – set against glorious Andean panoramas.

The Cusco mountain region boasts some of the country's finest **trekking**. The **Inca Trail** to Machu Picchu is by far the best known and most popular, but there are excellent **alternative trails** all starting less than a day's overland travel from Cusco. The stunning Inca remains of **Choquequirao**, in the Río Apurímac area, is arguably the best alternative archeological destination, with tours leaving from Cusco more or less daily. **Salcantay** to the north, and **Ausangate**, visible on the city's southern horizon, are also appealing options.

East of Cusco, the Andean mountains slope steeply down into the lowland **Amazon rainforest**, where protected areas are helping to maintain some of the world's most biodiverse wilderness areas. In particular, the Reserva Nacional Tambopata–Candamo

MACHU PICCHU

Highlights

❶ San Blas Take in the scene of Cusco's vibrant artists' quarter from a bench beside the church in Plazoleta San Blas. **See p.217**

❷ Whitewater rafting A fast rafting trip down one of Cusco's whitewater rivers through awesome Andean scenery is an unmissable experience. **See p.223**

❸ Pisac Standing at this Inca citadel offers one of Peru's most amazing panoramas, along the Sacred Valley and down onto the beautiful little market town of the same name. **See p.237**

❹ Trek to Machu Picchu The Inca Trail is just one of many breathtaking paths in the Andes

around Cusco; plenty of spectacular alternative treks have opened in recent years. **See p.250 & p.264**

❺ Machu Picchu Words never adequately describe this awe-inspiring Inca citadel; magically set against forested mountain peaks and distant glacial summits, it's dwarfed only by the sky. **See p.255**

❻ Paucartambo festival During the Fiesta de la Virgen del Carmen this normally quiet town changes into a colourful, haunting display of music and surreal outfits. **See p.270**

HIGHLIGHTS ARE MARKED ON THE MAP ON P.206

(see p.440), or the slightly nearer Manu Biosphere Reserve (see p.442), are among the best and most accessible ecotourism destinations. South of Cusco are the pre-Inca sites at **Tipón** and **Pikillacta**, nearly as spectacular as those in the Sacred Valley but far less visited.

The **best time to visit** Cusco and the surrounding area is during the dry season (May–Sept), when it's warm with clear skies during the day but relatively cold at night. During the wet season (Oct–April) it doesn't rain every day, but when it does, downpours are heavy.

Cusco

Nestling majestically in the belly of a highland valley and fed by two rivers, **CUSCO**'s unique layout was designed by the Incas in the form of a puma. Many of the city's finest Inca architectural treasures were so masterfully constructed out of local stone that they are still in great shape today, and the city is ripe for exploring: one minute you're walking down a shadowy, stone-walled alley, the next you burst onto a plaza full of brightly dressed dancers from the countryside, joining in what, at times, seems like the endless carnival and religious **festival celebrations** for which Cusco is famous (see box, p.218).

Nearly every site you'll want to visit is within walking distance of the main **Plaza de Armas**, and you can easily cover the main features of each quarter of the city in half a

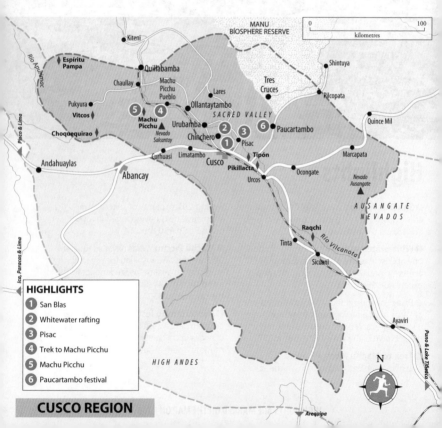

HIGHLIGHTS
1. San Blas
2. Whitewater rafting
3. Pisac
4. Trek to Machu Picchu
5. Machu Picchu
6. Paucartambo festival

CUSCO REGION

day. You should be able to see most of Cusco town in two or three active days, perhaps allowing a little extra time for hanging out in the bars and shops en route.

Brief history

The Cusco Valley and the Incas are synonymous in many people's minds, but the area was populated well before the Incas arrived on the scene and built their empire on the toil and ingenuity of previous peoples.

Founding Cusco

The **Killki**, who dominated the region from around 700–800 AD, while primarily agrarian, also built temple structures from the hard local diorite and andesite stone. Some of these structures still survive, while others were incorporated into later Inca constructions – the sun temple of Q'orikancha, for example, was built on the foundations of a Killki sun temple.

According to Inca legend, Cusco was founded by **Manco Capac** and his sister Mama Occlo around 1200 AD. Over the next two hundred years the valley was home to the Inca tribe, one of many localized groups then dominating the Peruvian sierra.

Building Cusco

It wasn't until **Pachacuti** assumed leadership of the Incas in 1438 that Cusco became the centre of an expanding empire and, with the Inca army, took religious and political control of the surrounding valleys and regions. As Pachacuti pushed the frontier of Inca territory outwards, he also masterminded the design of imperial Cusco, canalizing the Saphi and the Tullumayo, two rivers that ran down the valley, and building the centre of the city between them. Cusco's city plan was conceived in the form of a puma, a sacred animal: **Sacsayhuaman**, an important ritual centre and citadel, is the jagged, tooth-packed head; **Pumachupan**, the sacred cat's tail, lies at the junction of the city's two rivers; between these two sites lies **Q'orikancha**, the **Temple of the Sun**, reproductive centre of the Inca universe, the loins of this sacred beast; the heart of the puma was **Huacapata**, a ceremonial square approximate in both size and position to the present-day **Plaza de Armas**. Four main roads radiated from the square, one to each corner of the empire.

The overall achievement was remarkable, a planned city without rival, at the centre of a huge empire; and in building their capital the Incas endowed Cusco with some of its finest structures. Stone palaces and houses lined streets which ran straight and narrow, with water channels to drain off the heavy rains. It was so solidly built that much of ancient Cusco is still visible today, particularly in the stone walls of what were once palaces and temples.

The Spanish Conquest

In 1532, when the Spanish arrived in Peru, Cusco was a thriving city, and capital of one of the world's biggest empires. The new arrivals were astonished: the city's beauty surpassed anything they had seen before in the New World; the stonework was better than any in Spain; and precious metals, used in a sacred context across the city, were in abundance throughout Q'orikancha. They lost no time in plundering its fantastic wealth. **Atahualpa**, the emperor at the time, was captured by Spanish conquistadores in Cajamarca while en route to Cusco, returning from bloody battles in the northern extremity of the empire. Hearing from the Emperor Atahualpa himself of Cusco's great wealth as the centre of Inca religious and political power, **Francisco Pizarro** reached the capital on November 15, 1533.

The Spanish city was officially founded on March 23, 1534. Cusco was divided up among 88 of Pizarro's men who chose to remain there as settlers. **Manco Inca**, a blood relative of Atahualpa – who was murdered by Pizarro (see p.486) – was set up as a puppet ruler, governing from a new palace on the hill just below Sacsayhuaman. After

4

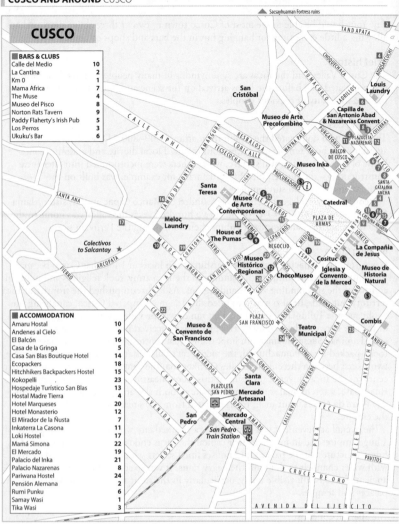

▲ Sacsayhuaman Fortress ruins

CUSCO

■ BARS & CLUBS

Calle del Medio	10
La Cantina	2
Km 0	1
Mama Africa	7
The Muse	4
Museo del Pisco	8
Norton Rats Tavern	9
Paddy Flaherty's Irish Pub	5
Los Perros	3
Ukuku's Bar	6

■ ACCOMMODATION

Amaru Hostal	10
Andenes al Cielo	9
El Balcón	16
Casa de la Gringa	5
Casa San Blas Boutique Hotel	14
Ecopackers	18
Hitchhikers Backpackers Hostel	15
Kokopelli	23
Hospedaje Turístico San Blas	13
Hostal Madre Tierra	4
Hotel Marqueses	20
Hotel Monasterio	12
El Mirador de la Ñusta	7
Inkaterra La Casona	11
Loki Hostel	17
Mamá Simona	22
El Mercado	19
Palacio del Inka	21
Palacio Nazarenas	8
Pariwana Hostel	24
Pensión Alemana	2
Rumi Punku	6
Samay Wasi	1
Tika Wasi	3

Pizarro's departure, and following twelve months of power struggles, his sons Juan and Gonzalo came out on top and were then free to abuse Manco and his subjects, which eventually provoked the Incas to open resistance. In April 1536 Manco fled to Yucay, in the Sacred Valley, to gather forces for the **Great Rebellion**.

Within days, the two hundred Spanish defenders, with only eighty horses, were surrounded in Cusco by over 100,000 Inca warriors. On May 6, Manco's men laid siege to the city. After a week, a few hundred mounted Spanish soldiers launched a desperate counterattack on the Inca base in Sacsayhuaman and, incredibly, defeated the stronghold, putting some 1500 warriors to the sword as they took it.

Spanish-controlled Cusco never again came under such serious threat from its indigenous population, but its battles were far from over. By the end of the rains the following year, a rival conquistador, Almagro, had seized Cusco for himself until Francisco Pizarro defeated the rebel Spanish troops a few months later, and

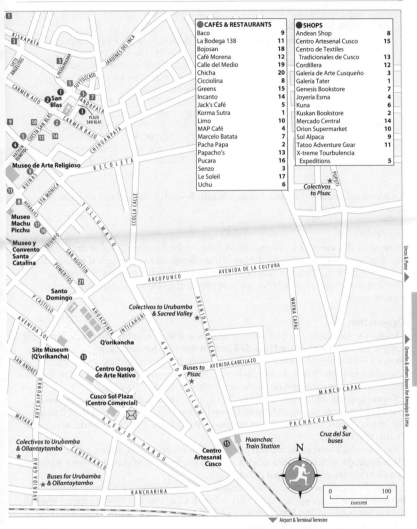

CAFÉS & RESTAURANTS	
Baco	9
La Bodega 138	11
Bojosan	18
Café Morena	12
Calle del Medio	19
Chicha	20
Cicciolina	8
Greens	15
Incanto	14
Jack's Café	5
Korma Sutra	1
Limo	10
MAP Café	4
Marcelo Batata	7
Pacha Papa	2
Papacho's	13
Pucara	16
Senzo	3
Le Soleil	17
Uchu	6

SHOPS	
Andean Shop	8
Centro Artesanal Cusco	15
Centro de Textiles Tradicionales de Cusco	13
Cordillera	12
Galería de Arte Cusqueño	3
Galería Tater	1
Genesis Bookstore	7
Joyería Esma	4
Kuna	6
Kuskan Bookstore	2
Mercado Central	14
Orion Supermarket	10
Sol Alpaca	9
Tatoo Adventure Gear	11
X-treme Tourbulencia Expeditions	5

had Almagro garrotted in the main plaza. Around the same time, a diehard group of rebel Incas established itself in Vilcabamba where they held out until 1572, when the Spanish colonial viceroy, Toledo, captured the leader **Tupac Amaru** and had him beheaded in the Plaza de Armas.

Post-Conquest Cusco

From then on the city was left in relative peace, ravaged only by the great **earthquake** of 1650. After this dramatic tremor, remarkably illustrated on a huge canvas in La Catedral de Cusco, **Bishop Mollinedo** was largely responsible for the reconstruction of the city, and his influence is also closely associated with Cusco's most creative years of art. The **Cusqueña school** (see box, p.213), which emerged from his patronage, flourished for the next two hundred years, and much of its finer work, produced by native Quechua and *mestizo* artists such as Diego Quispe Tito Inca, Juan Espinosa de

ALTITUDE SICKNESS

Soroche, or **altitude sickness** (see p.45), is a reality for most people arriving in Cusco by plane from sea level and needs to be treated with respect. It's vital to take it easy, not eating or drinking much on arrival, even sleeping a whole day just to assist acclimatization (**coca tea** is a good local remedy). After three days at this height most people have adjusted sufficiently to tackle moderate hikes at similar or lesser altitudes. Anyone considering hiking the major mountains around Cusco will need time to adjust again to their higher base camps.

If you do encounter altitude-related health problems, many hotels and restaurants have **oxygen cylinders** to help; alternatively, for serious cases, try the Clinica Peruano Suiza (English spoken) at Calle Meson de la Estrella 168 (open 24hr; ☎084 237 009, ⓦclinicaperuano suiza.com), which also has a dedicated medical network whose details can be accessed at ⓦo2medicalnetwork.com, and the Clinica Cima at Av Pardo 978 (☎084 255 550).

los Monteros, Fabian Ruiz and Antonio Sinchi Roca, is exhibited in museums and churches around the city.

The modern age

In spite of this cultural heritage, Cusco only received international attention after the discovery of **Machu Picchu** during Hiram Bingham's archeological expedition in 1911 (see p.255). With the advent of air travel and global tourism, Cusco was slowly transformed from a quiet colonial city in the remote Andes into a major tourist centre.

Orientation

Despite the seemingly complex street structure, it doesn't take long to get to grips with Cusco. The area **south of the Plaza de Armas to Q'orikancha** starts along the broad **Avenida Sol** running downhill and southeast from the corner of the plaza by the university and Iglesia de la Compañía towards the Inca sun temple at Q'orikancha, Huanchac train station and on to the airport in the south.

Running uphill and southwest from the top of Avenida Sol, the area encompassing **Plaza San Francisco** and the Mercado Central follows Calle Mantas past the Plaza and the Iglesia de Santa Clara, and then continues towards the Mercado Central and San Pedro train station.

Just one block west of the central plaza, you'll find the smaller, leafier, neighbouring **Plaza Regocijo**, which has Inca origins and is home to some of the city's finest mansions as well as the modest municipal palace.

From the northeast corner of Plaza de Armas, Calle Triunfo leads steeply uphill through a classic Inca stone-walled alley before leading through cobbled streets towards the artesan barrio of **San Blas**. One route here from the Plaza de Armas takes you via the tiny but elegant **Plaza Nazarenas**.

Heading northwest along **Calle Plateros**, uphill from Plaza de Armas, you'll pass through some really charming streets that lead toward the fortress of Sacsayhuaman above the city.

Plaza de Armas

Cusco's modern and ancient centre, the **Plaza de Armas** – whose location corresponds roughly to that of the ceremonial *Huacapata*, the Incas' ancient central plaza – is the natural place to get your bearings. With the unmistakeable ruins of **Sacsayhuaman** towering above, you can always find your way back to the plaza simply by locating the fortress or, at night, the illuminated white figure of Christ that stands beside it on the horizon. The plaza is always busy, its northern and western sides filled with shops and restaurants.

The plaza's exposed northeastern edge is dominated by the squat **Catedral** while the smaller **Templo de la Compañía de Jesús**, with its impressive pair of belfries, sits at the southeastern end.

Portal de Panes
Plaza de Armas

Circling the plaza, the **Portal de Panes** is a covered cloister pavement, like those frequently found around Spanish colonial squares, where the buildings tend to have an upper-storey overhang, supported by stone pillars or arches, creating rain-free and sun-shaded walking space virtually all the way around. Usually the *portales* host processions of boys trying their best to sell postcards, and waiters and waitresses attempting to drag passing tourists into their particular dive.

The Portal de Panes used to be part of the palace of Pachacuti, the ancient walls of which can still be seen from inside the *Roma Restaurant* close to the corner of the plaza and Calle Plateros.

Catedral
Plaza de Armas • Daily 10am–6pm • S/25; S/12.50 with ISIC card

Cusco's **Catedral** sits solidly on the foundations of the Inca Viracocha palace, its massive lines looking fortress-like in comparison with the delicate form of the nearby Compañía. Construction began in 1560; the cathedral was built in the shape of a Latin cross with a three-aisled nave supported by only fourteen pillars. The entrance is through the **Triunfo Chapel**, the first Spanish church to be built in Cusco. Check out its finely carved granite altar and the huge canvas depicting the terrible 1650 earthquake, before moving into the main cathedral to see the intricately carved pulpit, beautiful cedarwood seats and Neoclassical high altar, made entirely of finely beaten embossed silver, as well as some of the finest paintings of the **Cusqueña school**.

In the **Sacristy**, on the right of the nave, there's a large, dark painting of the Crucifixion attributed to Van Dyck. Ten smaller chapels surround the nave, including the **Capilla de la Concepción Inmaculada** (Chapel of the Immaculate Conception) and the **Capilla del Señor de los Temblores** (Chapel of the Lord of Earthquakes), the latter housing a 26-kilogram crucifix made of solid gold and encrusted with precious stones. To the left of the cathedral is the adjoining eighteenth-century **Iglesia de Jesús María**, a relatively small extension to the main church; here you'll find a sombre collection of murals and a lavish main altar.

Templo de la Compañía de Jesús
Plaza de Armas • Mon–Fri 9am–5.15pm, Sat & Sun 9am–11pm & 1–5.15pm • S/15; S/10 with ISIC card

Looking downhill from the centre of the plaza, the **Templo de la Compañía de Jesus** dominates the Cusco skyline. First built over the foundations of Amara Cancha – originally Huayna Capac's Palace of the Serpents – in the late 1570s, it was resurrected over fifteen years after the earthquake of 1650, which largely destroyed the original version, itself constructed in a Latin cross shape with two belfries. The **interior** is cool

---

ICONS AND FOLKLORE

The cathedral's appeal lies as much in its **folklore and legends** as in its tangible sights. Local myth claims that an Indian chief is still imprisoned in the right-hand tower, awaiting the day when he can restore the glory of the Inca Empire. The building also houses the huge, miraculous gold and bronze **bell of María Angola**, named after a freed African slave girl and reputed to be one of the largest church bells in the world. And on the cathedral's massive main doors, native craftsmen have left their own pagan adornment – a carved puma's head – representing one of the most important religious motifs and gods found throughout ancient Peru.

and dark, with a grand gold-leaf altarpiece; a fine wooden pulpit displaying a relief of Christ, high vaulting and numerous paintings of the Cusqueña school; and a transept ending in a stylish Baroque cupola. The gilded altarpieces are made of fine cedarwood and the church contains interesting oil paintings of the Peruvian Princess Isabel Ñusta. Its most impressive features, though, are the two majestic **towers** of the main facade, a superb example of Spanish-colonial Baroque design, which has often been described in more glowing terms than the neighbouring Catedral's. On the left-hand side of the church, the **Capilla de la Virgen de Lourdes**, restored in 1894, is used mostly as an exhibition centre for local crafts, as well as for dances and readings.

Museo de Historia Natural

Paraninfo Universitario, Plaza de Armas • Mon–Fri 9am–2.30pm • S/3

Alongside La Compañía, an early Jesuit university building houses the **Museo de Historia Natural**. The entrance is off an inner courtyard, up a small flight of stairs to the left. The exhibits cover Peru's coast, the Andes and the Amazon jungle, with a particularly good selection of stuffed mammals, reptiles and birds. With over 150 animals, the collection is relatively extensive, although travellers who are in Cusco for just a few days will probably want to prioritize other sights.

Museo Inka

Cuesta del Almirante 103, C Ataúd and C Córdoba del Tucumán • Mon–Fri 8am–7pm, Sat 9am–4pm • S/10 • ☎ 084 237 380

North of the cathedral you'll find one of the city's most beautiful colonial mansions, **El Palacio del Almirante** (the Admiral's Palace). This palace now houses the **Museo Inka**, which boasts 10,000 catalogued specimens and features excellent exhibits of mummies, trepanned skulls, Inca textiles, a set of forty green-turquoise figurines from the Huari settlement of Pikillacta and a range of Inca wooden *quero* vases (slightly tapering drinking vessels). There are also displays of ceramics, early silver metalwork and gold figurines, but it's the spacious, organized layout and the imaginative, well-interpreted presentation that make this one of the best museums in Cusco for understanding the development of civilization in the Andes. Frequent temporary exhibitions are held here, too, including live alpaca spinning and weaving demonstrations by local women.

Constructed on Inca foundations – this time the Waypar stronghold, where the Spanish were besieged by Manco's forces in 1536 – the **building** itself is noteworthy for its simple but well-executed Plateresque facade, surmounted by two imposing Spanish coats of arms and a mullioned external balcony.

Convento de Santa Catalina de Sena

Leading southeast from the Plaza de Armas, Callejón Loreto separates La Compañía church from the tall, stone walls of the ancient Temple of the Sun Virgins, or **Acllahuasi,** where the Sun Virgins used to make *chicha* beer for the Lord Inca. Today, the Acllahuasi building is occupied by the **Convento de Santa Catalina de Sena**, built in 1610, with its small but grand side-entrance half a short block down Calle Santa Catalina Angosta; just under thirty sisters still live and worship here in isolation.

Museo y Convento de Santa Catalina

C Santa Catalina Angosta 401 • Mon–Sat 8.30am–5.30pm, Sun 2–5pm • S/8

Inside the convent, the **Museo y Convento de Santa Catalina** features a splendid collection of paintings from the **Cusqueña school** (see box opposite), as well as an impressive Renaissance altarpiece and several gigantic seventeenth-century tapestries depicting the union of Indian and Spanish cultures. The blending of cultures is a theme that runs throughout much of the museum's fascinating artwork and is particularly

THE CUSQUEÑA SCHOOL

Colonial Cusco evolved into an exceptional centre for architecture and art. The era's paintings in particular are curious for the way they adorn human and angelic figures in elaborate lacy garments and blend traditional and ancient with colonial and Spanish elements. They are frequently brooding and quite bloody, and by the mid-seventeenth century had evolved into a recognizable school of painting.

The **Cusqueña art movement** dedicated itself to beautifying church and convent walls with fantastic and highly moralistic painting, mainly using oils. The Cusqueña school is best known for portraits or religious scenes with dark backgrounds, serious (even tortured-looking) subjects and a profusion of gold-leaf decoration. Influences came from European émigrés – mainly Spanish and Italian – notably Juan de Illescas, Bernardo Bitti and Mateo Perez de Alessio. At the close of the seventeenth century, the school came under the direction of **Bishop Manuel Mollinedo**. Bringing a number of original paintings (including some by El Greco) with him from his parish in Spain, the bishop was responsible for commissioning **Basilio Santa Cruz**'s fine 1698 reproduction of the *Virgen de la Almudena*, which still hangs behind the choir in Cusco's Catedral. He also commissioned the extraordinarily carved cedarwood pulpit in the church at San Blas.

The top Cusqueña artists were **Bernardo Bitti** (1548–1610), an Italian who is often considered the "father of Cusqueña art" and who introduced the Mannerist style to Peru, and **Diego Quispe Tito Inca** (1611–81), a *mestizo* painter who was influenced by the Spanish Flamenco school and whose paintings were vital tools of communication for priests attempting to convert Indians to Catholicism. Bitti's work is on display in the Museo Historico Regional, while some of Quispe's works can be seen in rooms off the second courtyard in the Religious Art Museum at the Archbishop's Palace in Cusco. The equally renowned **Mauricio García** (painting until the mid-eighteenth century) helped spur the form into a fuller *mestizo* synthesis, mixing Spanish and Indian artistic forms. Many of the eighteenth- and nineteenth-century Cusqueña-*mestizo* works display bold compositions and colours.

By the eighteenth century the style had been disseminated as far afield as Quito in Ecuador, Santiago in Chile and even into Argentina, making it a truly South American art form and one of the most distinctive indigenous arts in the Americas.

evident in the Cusqueña paintings. Another common feature of much of the Cusqueña art here is the disproportionate, downward-looking, blood-covered head, body and limbs of the seventeenth-century depictions of Christ, which represent the suffering and low social position of the Andean Indians and originate from early colonial days when Indians were not permitted to look Spaniards in the eyes.

Another highlight of the museum, on the first floor at the top of the stairs, is a large fold-up box containing miniature three-dimensional religious and mythological images depicting everything from the Garden of Eden to an image of God with a red flowing cape and dark beard, and a white dove and angels playing drums, Andean flutes and pianos.

Museo Machu Picchu

Santa Catalina Ancha 320 • Mon–Sat 9am–5pm • S/20 • ☎ 084 255 535

A number of artefacts that Hiram Bingham unearthed during the 1911 expedition to Machu Picchu are now on display at the fascinating **Museo Machu Picchu**. There are a number of informative videos too – it's worth heading here before travelling to the ruins to get a clearer idea of what lies behind the Inca marvel that is Machu Picchu. The exhibition includes over 350 pieces that were returned to the city from the University of Yale in 2010, along with local Inca artefacts that were unearthed during the restoration of the eighteenth-century Casa Concha, in which the museum is housed today.

The Q'orikancha complex

C Av Sol and C Santo Domingo • Mon–Sat 8.30am–5.30pm, Sun 2–5pm • S/10; S/5 with ISIC card • ☏ 084 249 176

The main Inca temple for worship of major deities and a supreme example of Inca stonework underlying colonial buildings can be found just a short walk from the Plaza de Armas, through the Inca walls of Callejón Loreto, then along the busy Pampa del Castillo. You can't miss the **Q'orikancha complex**, with the Convento de Santo Domingo rising imposingly from its impressive walls, which the conquistadores made lower to make way for their uninspiring seventeenth-century Baroque church – a poor contrast to the still-imposing Inca masonry evident in the foundations and chambers of the Temple of the Sun.

Brief history

Prior to the Incas, the Wari culture had already dedicated the site with its own sun temple, known as Inticancha (*inti* meaning "sun" and *cancha* meaning "enclosure"). Before the conquistadores set their gold-hungry eyes on it, Q'orikancha must have been even more breathtaking, consisting as it did of four small sanctuaries and a larger temple set around a central courtyard. This whole complex was encircled on the inside walls by a cornice of gold, hence the temple's name (Q'orikancha means "golden enclosure").

Q'orikancha's position in the Cusco Valley was carefully planned. Dozens of *ceques* (power lines, in many ways similar to ley lines, though in Cusco they appear to have been related to imperial genealogy) radiate from the temple towards more than 350 sacred *huacas*, special stones, springs, tombs and ancient quarries. In addition, during every summer solstice, the sun's rays shine directly into a niche – the **tabernacle** – in which only the Inca emperor (often referred to as *the* Inca) was permitted to sit. Mummies of dead Inca rulers were seated in niches at eye level along the walls of the actual temple, the principal idols from every conquered province were held "hostage" here, and every emperor married his wives in the temple before assuming the throne. The niches no longer exist, though there are some in the walls of the nearby Temple of the Moon, where mummies of the emperor's concubines were kept in a foetal position.

Punchau golden sun disc

Still visible today, there's a large, slightly trapezoidal niche on the inside of the curved section of the retaining wall, close to the chamber identified as the Temple of the Sun, where there once stood a huge, gold disc in the shape of the sun, **Punchau**, which was worshipped by the Incas. Punchau had two companions in the temple: a golden image of creator god **Viracocha**, on the right; and another, representing **Illapa**, god of thunder, to the left. Below the temple was an artificial garden in which everything was made of gold or silver and encrusted with precious jewels, from depictions of llamas and shepherds to the tiniest details of clumps of earth and weeds, including snails and butterflies. Not surprisingly, none of this survived the arrival of the Spanish.

Q'orikancha site museum

Av Sol • Daily 9am–6pm • Entry by Cusco Tourist Ticket (see box, p.221) • It's a 2min walk downhill from the complex reception to the underground museum entrance on block 3 of Av Sol

Though one of Cusco's smaller and less interesting museums, the **Q'orikancha site museum**, or Museo Arqueológico de Q'orikancha, does contain a number of interesting pieces. The first section is pre-Inca, mainly stone and ceramic exhibits; the second is Inca, with wooden, ceramic and some metallurgic crafts; in the third, archeological excavations are illustrated and interpreted; and the fourth houses a mummy and some bi-chrome ceramics of the Killki era (around 800 AD), which reflect the art of the pre-Inca Wari culture.

From the museum you can access the **garden**, which, though little more than a green, open, grassy space just outside the main walls of Q'orikancha, has a particularly beautiful pre-Inca spring and bath that dates to the Wari period, providing evidence of the importance of Q'orikancha before the Incas arrived on the Andean scene.

Iglesia y Convento de la Merced

Plazoleta Espinar, C Mantas • Mon–Sat 8am–12.30pm & 2–5.30pm • S/6 • ☎ 084 231 821

Ten minutes' walk southwest of the Plaza de Armas is the **Iglesia y Convento de la Merced**, which sits peacefully amid the bustle of one of Cusco's more interesting quarters. First raised with Pizarro's financial assistance on top of the Inca site Limipata in 1536, it was rebuilt some 25 years after the 1650 earthquake in a rich combination of Baroque and Renaissance styles by such native artesans as Alonso Casay and Francisco Monya.

The facade is exceptionally ornate and the roof is endowed with an unusual Baroque spire, while **inside** there's a beautiful star-studded ceiling and a huge silver cross, which is adored and kissed by a shuffling crowd. The monastery's highlight, however, is a breathtaking 1720s **monstrance** standing a metre high and crafted by Spanish jeweller Juan de Olmos, who used over 600 pearls, more than 1500 diamonds and upwards of 22kg of solid gold. The monastery also possesses a fine collection of **Cusqueña paintings**, particularly in the cloisters and vestry, and an exceptionally gorgeous white-stone cloister.

Museo y Convento de San Francisco

Plaza San Francisco • Mon–Sat 9am–1pm & 3–6pm • S/6 • ☎ 054 221 361

Southwest of the city centre is the **Plaza San Francisco,** frequently filled with food stalls that couldn't be squeezed into the central market or along Calle Santa Clara. The square's southwestern side is dominated by the simply adorned **Museo y Convento de San Francisco**, built between 1645 and 1652. Inside, two large cloisters boast some of the better colonial paintings by local masters such as Diego Quispe Tito, Marcos Zapata and Juan Espinosa de los Monteros, the latter being celebrated for his massive works on canvas, one or two of which are on display here.

Templo de Santa Clara

C Santa Clara

The small but beautiful **Templo de Santa Clara** was originally built around a single nave in 1558 by *mestizo* and indigenous craftsmen under the guidance of the architect Brother Manuel Pablo. Partly restored in 2005, it contains a gold-laminated altar, small mirrors covering most of the interior, and a few canvases, although it remains closed to visitors. The **outside walls**, however, show more interesting details: finely cut Inca blocks support the upper, cruder stonework, and four andesite columns, much cracked over the centuries, complete the doorway. The belfry is so time-worn that weeds and wildflowers have taken permanent root.

Templo de San Pedro

C Santa Clara and C Chaparro • Mon–Sat 7.30am–5.30pm • Free

In the busy market area next to San Pedro train station stands the sixteenth-century colonial **Templo de San Pedro**, whose steps are normally crowded with Quechua market traders. The interior is decorated with paintings, sculptures, gold-leaf and wooden carvings and an elaborate, carved pulpit. Relatively austere, with only a single nave, the church's main claim to fame is that somewhere among the stones of its twin towers are ancient blocks dragged here from the small Inca fort of Picchu.

Mercado Central

C Santa Clara and C Chaparro • Daily 6am–6pm

The covered Mercado Central bustles with custom at most times of the day, especially in the mornings. Stalls sell every imaginable practical item, from plentiful and exotic foodstuffs to herbalist kiosks that stock everything from lucky charms to jungle medicines. The food stalls at the bottom end of the indoor market offer some of the best and cheapest **street meals** in Peru, while the juice stalls at the top end serve up a delicious range of tropical smoothies.

Plaza Regocijo

A block southwest of the Plaza de Armas, **Plaza Regocijo**, today a pleasant garden square sheltering a statue of Colonel Francisco Bolognesi, a famous Peruvian war martyr, was originally the Inca *cusipata*, an area cleared for dancing and festivities beside the Incas' ancient central plaza. Regocijo is dominated on its northwestern side by an attractively arched municipality building housing the **Museo de Arte Contemporáneo**, with a traditional Inca rainbow flag flying from its roof. Opposite this is the venerable old *Hotel Cusco*, under refurbishment but formerly the grand, state-run *Hotel de Turistas*, while on the southwest corner of the plaza lies an impressive mansion where more Inca stones mingle with colonial construction, home to the Museo Histórico Regional y Casa Garcilaso.

Museo Histórico Regional y Casa Garcilaso

Plaza Regocijo and C Heladeros • Daily 8am–5pm • Entry by Cusco Tourist Ticket (see box, p.221) • ☎ 084 223 245

Once the residence of **Garcilaso de la Vega**, a prolific half-Inca (his mother may have been an Inca princess), half-Spanish poet and author, the mansion now known as the **Museo Histórico Regional y Casa Garcilaso** is home to significant regional archeological finds and much of Cusco's historic art.

Fascinating **pre-Inca ceramics** from all over Peru are displayed here, as well as a **Nazca mummy** in a foetal position with typically long (1.5m) hair, embalming herbs and unctures, black ceramics with incised designs from the early Cusco culture (1000–200 BC) and a number of **Inca artefacts** such as *bolas*, maces, architects' plumb-lines and square water-dishes used for finding horizontal levels on buildings. The museum also displays gold bracelets discovered at Machu Picchu in 1995, some gold and silver llama statuettes found in 1996 in the Plaza de Armas when reconstructing the central fountain and golden pumas and figurines from Sacsayhuaman. From the **colonial era** there are some weavings, wooden *quero* drinking vessels and dancing masks.

The main exhibition rooms upstairs house mainly period furniture and a multitude of **Cusqueña paintings**, which span the range from the rather dull (religious adorations) to the utterly spectacular. As you progress through the works you'll notice the rapid intrusion of cannons, gunpowder and proliferation of violence appearing throughout the eighteenth century, something which was reflected in Cusco art as a microcosm of what happened across the colonial world – emanating from Europe as part of the general march of technological "progress".

Museo de Arte Contemporáneo

Plaza Regocijo • Mon–Sat 9am–6pm • Entry by Cusco Tourist Ticket (see box, p.221)

The **Museo de Arte Contemporáneo**, in the municipality building on Plaza Regocijo, is a welcome and relatively new feature in Cusco, and an outlet for the many talented local artists. **Sala 1** displays images of Cusco, mainly paintings but occasional photos of subjects like Inca dancers as well as abstract features and some sculpture. **Sala 2** is dedicated to non-Cusco-inspired contemporary art, some of it very abstract but with exhibits changing quite regularly; the *sala* (room) leads off into a large courtyard with a typically attractive colonial fountain; here you'll find glass cases with dolls in traditional costumes, some regional variations of dance masks (from Paucartambo dance groups, for example) and models of buildings in different Cusco styles. The upstairs **Sala 3** houses more images of Cusco, both ancient and modern.

ChocoMuseo

Garcilaso 210, 2nd floor • Daily 10am–7pm • Free; workshops S/75 for 2hr • ☎ 084 244 765, ⊕ chocomuseo.com

A few steps from Plaza Regocijo, the **ChocoMuseo** has a range of interpretative displays on the history of cacao, starting with the Maya's love of this plant in Central America. The museum also organizes **workshops** on chocolate making and tours to cacao plantations in the Cusco region, and provides the opportunity to see artisanal chocolate production first-hand in the on-site **factory**, from cacao bean to chocolate bar.

Iglesia de Santa Teresa

C Siete Cuartones • Daily 6am–6pm • Free

The **Iglesia de Santa Teresa** is an attractive but neglected church with stone walls, the upper half of which have paintings featuring St Teresa. Inside, the small brick ceiling has a beautifully crafted dome and there's a gold-leaf altar inset with paintings. The small **chapel** next door is worth a look for its intricately painted walls (featuring yet more images of St Teresa), usually beautifully candlelit.

Museo de Arte Precolombino (MAP)

Plaza las Nazarenas • Daily 8am–10pm • S/20; S/10 with ISIC card • ☎ 084 233 210

The small, quiet **Plaza Nazarenas** is home to the unmistakeable **Casa Cabrera**, an eighteenth-century mansion built on top of a ninth-century temple pyramid, which has been transformed into the **Museo de Arte Precolombino** at the top end of this small square. The museum boasts many masterpieces dating from 1250 BC to 1532 AD, including gold and other precious metals and jewellery, displayed in chronological order. Some of the new exhibits, the Larco Collection, have come from the Museo Larco in Lima (see p.76). There's an interesting exhibit exploring the history of urban architecture in this Inca imperial capital city. Frequent temporary exhibitions are also held here.

Capilla de San Antonio Abad and the former Nazarenas Convent

Plaza Nazarenas

On the northeastern side of Plaza Nazarenas, the ancient, subtly ornate **Capilla de San Antonio Abad** was connected to a religious school before becoming part of the university in the seventeenth century. The chapel now forms part of the *Hotel Monasterio* (see p.224), and is technically only open to hotel guests, although you may be able to take a peek inside if you ask nicely at the hotel reception. Just a few steps north is the upmarket *Belmond Palacio Nazarenas*, where nuns lived until 1977, when they moved to smaller quarters. Separating the two hotels is the Inca passage of Siete Culebras (Seven Snakes) that leads onto Choquechaca.

Barrio San Blas

Originally known as T'oqokachi ("salty hole"), the **San Blas** barrio was the first parish to be established by the Spanish in Cusco and one of twelve administrative sectors in the Inca capital. After the Conquest it became the residence for many defeated Inca leaders. It rapidly grew into one of the more attractive districts in the city, reflecting strong *mestizo* and colonial influences in its architecture and high-quality **artesanía** – even today it's known as the *barrio de los artesanos* (artesans' quarter). Hit hard by the

1950 earthquake, it has been substantially restored, and in 1993 it was given a major face-lift that returned it to its former glory. The process of rebuilding continues, with many old houses being converted to hostels, shops and restaurants.

Templo de San Blas

Cuesta de San Blas • Mon–Sat 8am–6pm, Sun 10am–6pm • S/10; S/5 with ISIC card

The highlight of the **Templo de San Blas** is an incredibly intricate pulpit, carved from a block of cedarwood in a complicated Churrigueresque style; its detail includes a

---

FIESTAS IN THE CUSCO REGION

As the imperial capital during Inca times, Cusco was the most important place of pilgrimage in South America, a status it retains today. During Easter, June and Christmas, the city centre becomes the focus for relentless **fiestas and carnivals** celebrated with extravagant processions blending pagan pre-Columbian and Catholic colonial cultures.

Around Jan 20 Adoración de los Reyes (Adoration of the Magi). Ornate and elaborate processions leave from Templo de San Blas and parade through Cusco.

Last week of Jan Pera Chapch'y (Festival of the Pear). A harvest festival in San Sebastián, 4km southeast of Cusco, with lively street stalls and processions.

First week of March Festival de Durasno (Festival of the Peach). Food stalls and folk dancing in Yanahuara and Urubamba.

Holy Week Semana Santa. On Easter Monday there's a particularly splendid procession through Cusco, with a rich and evocative mix of Indian and Catholic iconography. The following Thursday a second procession celebrates the city's patron saint, El Señor de los Temblores (Lord of Earthquakes), and on Good Friday, street stalls sell many different traditional dishes.

May 2–3 Cruz Velacuy, or Fiesta de las Cruces (Festival of the Cross). All church and sanctuary crosses in Cusco and the provinces are veiled for a day, followed by traditional festivities with dancing and feasting in most communities. Particularly splendid in Ollantaytambo.

Weekend before Corpus Christi Qoyllur Rit'i (Snow Star, or Ice Festival). Held on the full-moon weekend prior to Corpus Christi (see below) in an isolated valley above the road from Cusco to the Amazon town of Puerto Maldonado. Live music continues for days, several processions, and bands and dancers from various communities make an annual pilgrimage to recharge spiritually. As it involves camping at around 4600m at the foot of a glacier, it's only for the adventurous; some tour operators organize trips, but it's primarily a Quechua festival, with villagers arriving in their thousands in the weeks running up to it.

Corpus Christi (nine weeks after Easter). Imposed by the Spanish to replace the Inca tradition of parading ancestral mummies. Saints' effigies are carried through the streets of Cusco, even as the local *mayordomos*

(ritual community leaders) throw parties and feasts combining elements of religiosity with outright hedonism. The effigies are then left inside the cathedral for eight days, after which they are taken back to their respective churches, accompanied by musicians, dancers and exploding firecrackers.

Second week of June Cusqueña International Beer and Music Festival. Lively, with big Latin pop and jazz names, at its best from Thursday to Sunday.

June 16–22 Traditional folk festivals in Raqchi and Sicuani.

June 20–30 Fiesta de Huancaro. An agricultural show packed with locals and good fun, based in the Huancaro sector of Cusco (S/5 taxi ride from Plaza de Armas, or go down Av Sol and turn right at the roundabout before the airport).

Last week of June Cusco Carnival. Daily processions and folk dancers, plus lively music on the streets throughout the day and night, peaking with Inti Raymi (see below).

June 24 Inti Raymi. Popular, commercial fiesta re-enacting the Inca Festival of the Sun in the grounds of Sacsayhuaman.

July 15–18 Virgen del Carmen. Dance and music festival celebrated all over the highlands, but at its best in Paucartambo.

July 28 Peruvian Independence Day. Festivities nationwide, not least in Cusco.

Sept 14–18 Señor de Huanca. Music, dancing, pilgrimages and processions take place all over the region but are especially lively in Calca, with a fair in the Sacred Valley.

First week of Dec Yawar Fiesta. A *corrida de toros* (bull fight) at the end of the week in Paruro, Cotabambas and Chumbivilcas during which a condor, representing indigenous culture, is tied to the back of a bull, symbolizing Spanish colonial influence. The gory spectacle is no short of blood – bulls are often slaughtered and condors injured and killed, threatening a species that is already in decline.

cherub, a sun disc, faces and bunches of grapes, believed to have been carved by native craftsman Tomas Tuyro Tupa in the seventeenth century.

Calle Suytuccato

Outside the Templo de San Blas, along **Calle Suytuccato** (the continuation of Cuesta San Blas), there are a few art workshops and galleries, the most notable of which is **Galería Olave**, at no. 651 (Mon–Sat 10.30am–7pm). The **Museo de Cerámica** (daily 10am–6pm), Carmen Alto 133, is worth checking out for its pottery.

Plazoleta San Blas

At the San Blas barrio's centre, on the southeast side of the Iglesia San Blas, lies the **Plazoleta San Blas**, with 49 gargoyles set on a fountain that's laid out in the form of a *chakana*, or Inca cross, with four corners and a hole at its centre. On the *plazoleta*, the **Museo Taller Hilario Mendivil** (Mon–Sat 10am–6pm) contains a number of Cusqueña paintings, as well as some interesting murals and religious icons.

Hathun Rumiyoq

Go down the Cuesta de San Blas and continue over the intersection with Choquechaca, then head straight on until you come to the narrow alley

One of the main streets in ancient Cusco, **Hathun Rumiyoq** provides classic examples of superb Inca **stonework**: the large cut boulders on the museum side, about halfway along, boast one that has twelve angles in its jointing with the stones around it. Not just earthquake-resistant, it is both a much-photographed ruin and a work of art in its own right.

4

Museo de Arte Religioso del Arzobispado

C Triunfo and Palacio • Mon–Sat 8am–6pm, Sun 10am–6pm • S/10; S/5 with ISIC card • ☎ 084 231 615

At the end of Hathun Rumiyoq, and just one block from the Plaza de Armas, along Calle Triunfo, you'll find the broad doors of the **Museo de Arte Religioso del Arzobispado**, housed in a superb Arabesque-style mansion built on the impressive foundations of Hathun Rumiyoq palace. Once home to Brother Vicente de Valarde and the marquises of Rocafuert, and later the archbishop's residence, the museum now contains a significant collection of **paintings**, mostly from the Cusqueña School. There are stunning mosaics in some of the period rooms, and other significant features include the elaborate gateway and the gold-leaf craftsmanship on the chapel's altar.

ARRIVAL AND DEPARTURE   CUSCO

Arriving in Cusco is always an exhilarating experience. If coming straight from sea level, there's the physical effect of the **altitude** (see box, p.210), but, more than that, there's a sense of historic imperial glory reflected in people and architecture alike from the moment you step into the city. By far the majority of visitors arrive by plane from Lima or by bus from Lima, Arequipa or Puno. The **airport and main bus station** (Terminal Terrestre) are both located in the southeast of the city, downhill from the Plaza de Armas and Cusco's bustling heart. Buses, colectivos and taxis are readily available to connect with hotels.

BY PLANE

Aeropuerto Internacional Velasco Astete ☎ 084 222 611. The airport is about 5km southeast of the city centre. A taxi to the centre should be about S/30. Regular colectivos also leave from outside the airport car park (45min; S/0.70), travelling along Av Sol to Ayacucho, two blocks from the Plaza de Armas. Note that the airport is full of tour touts, who should be avoided.

Airlines LAN (ⓦ lan.com), Avianca (ⓦ avianca.com), Peruvian Airlines (ⓦ peruvian.pe), Star Peru (ⓦ starperu .com), Andes Air (ⓦ andesair.com) and Amazonas (ⓦ amazonas.com) serve the airport.

Destinations Arequipa (3 daily; 1hr 30min); Juliaca (1 daily; 50min); La Paz (daily except Sat; 1hr 30min); Lima (several daily; 1hr); Puerto Maldonado (3 daily; 40min).

BY TRAIN

Huanchac station If you're coming in by train from Puno, you'll arrive at the Huanchac train station in the southeast of the city; you can hail a taxi on the street outside (around S/5 to the centre), or turn left out of the station and walk about a hundred metres to Av Sol, from where it's a 15–20min walk to the Plaza de Armas in the heart of the city centre.

Trains to Machu Picchu All Machu Picchu trains (see box, p.254) start and finish outside Cusco city, either from Poroy station (15min by taxi from Cusco) or Ollantaytambo (2–3hr by car or colectivo from Cusco). There are two competing rail companies that offer the Machu Picchu service: PeruRail and Inca Rail. The former has trains from both Poroy and Ollantaytambo, while Inca Rail only serves Ollantaytambo station in the Sacred Valley (see p.248).

Train tickets PeruRail has a ticket office on the Plaza de Armas at Portal de Carnes 214 (daily 7am–10pm) and also at Wanchaq train station on Av Pachacutec (Mon–Fri 7am–5pm, Sat & Sun 7am–noon; call centre ☎084 581 414, ⓦ perurail.com), selling Puno and Machu Picchu tickets. To travel to either Puno or Machu Picchu with PeruRail (see box, p.256) it's best to buy well in advance. Inca Rail has an office on the Plaza de Armas at Portal de Panes 105 (Mon–Fri 9am–9pm, Sat 9am–7pm, Sun 9am–2pm; ☎084 233 030 or ☎084 581 860 ⓦ incarail .com), although note its services only depart from Ollantaytambo.

Destinations: Machu Picchu Pueblo (6–12 daily; 3–5hr) via Ollantaytambo; Puno (1 daily: April–Oct Mon, Wed, Fri & Sat; Nov–March Mon, Wed & Sat at 8am; 10hr).

BY BUS

Inter-regional and international buses With the exception of Cruz del Sur (see opposite), all inter-regional and international buses arrive at and depart from the Terminal Terrestre at Av Vallegos Santoni, block 2 (☎084 224 471), southeast of the centre, close to the Pachacutec monument and roundabout (*óvalo*) and roughly halfway between the Plaza de Armas and the airport. Taxis from here to the city centre cost S/5, or you can walk from the centre in about half an hour. Alternatively, catch a colectivo marked "Correcaminos" which drops passengers off at C Almadro between Sol and Bernardo. If you're travelling to the bus station from the centre, colectivos leave from C Ayacucho between San Andrés and Av Sol. Cruz del Sur

buses operate both from the Terminal Terrestre and from their own independent depot at Av Industrial 121 in Cusco's Bancopata suburb.

Sacred Valley buses and colectivos Regular buses and colectivos travel to Pisac (every 15min; 45min–1hr) and Calca (every 15min; 1hr 30min) from Puputi s/n, while colectivos to Urubamba (every 20min; 1hr 40min) leave from Pavitos passing through Chinchero (45min). Note that departure points for colectivos change regularly – check with the tourist office for the latest departure locations.

Destinations Abancay (several daily; 5hr); Andahuaylas (4 daily; 9hr); Arequipa (several daily; 10hr); Ayacucho (3 daily; 18hr); Copacabana, Bolivia (6 daily; 10hr); Desaguadero (Thursdays at 7.30pm; 9hr); Ica (2 daily; 16hr); Ilo (2 daily; 15hr); Juliaca (2 daily; 5hr); La Paz, Bolivia (7 daily; 12hr); Lima (several daily; 21hr); Nazca (3 daily; 13hr); Puerto Maldonado (several daily; 10hr); Puno (several daily; 6hr); Río Branco, Brazil (Mon & Thurs at noon, Fri at 3pm; 20hr); São Paolo (Fri at 3pm; 3 days); Tacna (2 daily; 15hr).

BUS OPERATORS

Civa Terminal Terrestre ☎084 249 961. Services to Arequipa, Lima and Puerto Maldonado.

Cruz del Sur Av Industrial 121, Bancopata & Terminal Terrestre ☎084 248 255, ⓦ cruzdelsur.com.pe. Arequipa, Lima and Puno.

Expreso Los Chankas Terminal Terrestre ☎084 262 909. Services to Abancay, Andahuaylas, Ayacucho and Puerto Maldonado.

Expreso Turismo San Martín ☎984 612 520. Services to Arequipa, Desaguadero, Puno and Tacna.

Oltursa Terminal Terrestre ☎084 608 313, ⓦ oltursa .pe. Services to Abancay, Arequipa, Ica, Lima and Nazca.

Ormeño Terminal Terrestre ☎084 241 426, ⓦ grupo -ormeno.com.pe. Buses to Lima, Río Branco (Brazil) and São Paulo (Brazil).

San Cristóbal Terminal Terrestre ☎084 229 763. Services to Arequipa, Ilo and Juliaca.

Tepsa Terminal Terrestre ☎084 224 534 ⓦ tepsa.com .pe. Services to Arequipa, Ica, Lima, Nazca and Puerto Maldonado.

Transzela Terminal Terrestre ☎084 238 223, ⓦ transzela.com.pe. Services to Arequipa, Copacabana (Bolivia), La Paz (Bolivia), Puerto Maldonado and Puno.

GETTING AROUND

On foot Cusco's centre is small enough to walk around. Although it is well spread out down the valley and it might take more than an hour to get from one end to the other, most of the interesting sights are within a 10- to 15-min walk of the Plaza de Armas.

By taxi Taxis can be waved down on any street, particularly on the Plaza de Armas, Avenida Sol and around the market

end of Plaza San Francisco, although it's always best to call a reliable company in advance as scams are common; rides within Cusco centre cost around S/3–4, slightly more for outlying suburbs and around S/70–80 to Sacsayhuaman, Quenko and Tambo Machay for a 4hr round trip. To book a taxi try Aló Cusco (☎084 222 222), Taxi Turismo (☎084 245 000) or Oqarina (☎084 255 000).

CUSCO TOURIST TICKET

The **Cusco Tourist Ticket**, or **Boleto Turístico General – Cusco** (S/130 for ten days, students S/70), is a vital purchase for most visitors. In some ways it's a bit of a rip-off, but it's the only way to get into many of the city's and region's main attractions, covering some sixteen destinations including the **archeological sites** of the Sacred Valley (Pisac and Ollantaytambo) as well as Sacsayhuaman, Qenko, Tambo Machay, Puca Pucara, Chinchero, Moray, Pikillacta and Tipón. The ticket also affords free entry to **museums** including the Museo de Arte Popular, Museo de Sitio Q'orikancha, the Museo de Arte Contemporáneo and the Museo Histórico Regional. It does not, however, give entry to the cathedral, or Q'orikancha main temple site. It comes with useful **maps** and other information, including opening times. A number of cheaper boletos parciales (partial tourist tickets) cost S/70 and take in fewer sights (although note their validity is only one or two days). Tickets can be bought from COSITUC at Avenida Sol 103 (☎084 227037; daily 8am–6pm).

By bus and colectivo The city bus system is incredibly difficult to fathom, though it's cheap, fast and has several networks extending across the entire city. Largely unregulated, the buses are mainly minibuses chalking up their destinations on the front windscreens. Most useful are the buses and colectivos that run up and down Av Sol every couple of minutes during daylight hours, stopping at street corners if they have any seats left; they can be hailed on virtually any corner along the route.

By bike Eric Adventures (see p.222) rents out bikes for US$45/day; Berenice Tours, Garcilaso 278 (☎084 240 364) rents out bikes for US$15–25/day, while Party Bike Travel, Carmen Alto 246, San Blas (☎084 272 862) charges US$15–36/day.

By car and motorbike Some of the more remote and scenic valleys can be reached by car or motorbike with a map rather than a guide. The following organize car and motorbike rental: Manu, Av Sol 520 (☎084 233 382, ⓦ manurentacar.com); Peru Moto Tours, Saphi 578 (☎084 232 742, ⓦ perumototours.com); Cusco Moto Tour Peru, Saphi 592 (☎084 227 025).

INFORMATION

iPerú is at Portal de Harinas 177 on the Plaza de Armas (Mon–Fri 9am–7pm, Sat & Sun 9am–1pm; ☎084 252 974 ⓔ iperucusco@promperu.gob.pe); they also have a couple of kiosks in the main hall of the airport as well as at arrivals (Daily 6am–5pm; ☎084 237 364 ⓔ iperucuscoapto @promperu.gob.pe). The Cuscoperu **website** is another good source of information: ⓦ cuscoperu.com.

South American Explorers' Club Atoqsaycuchi 670, San Blas (☎084 245 484, ⓦ saexplorers.org). Offers good information sheets, trip reports and files on virtually everything about Cusco and Peru, including transport, trekking, hotels, internet cafés and tour companies. Membership fees would be covered by the discount SE Club (South American Explorers' Club) members get with some companies on just one tour to the Manu Biosphere Reserve.

TOUR OPERATORS AND TRAVEL AGENTS

Tours in and around Cusco range from a half-day city tour to a full-on adventure down to the Amazon. **Prices** range from US$30 to over US$200 a day, and service and facilities vary considerably, so check exactly what's provided, whether **insurance** is included and whether the guide speaks English. The majority of operators and agents are strung along three sides of the Plaza de Armas, along Portal de Panes, Portal de Confiturias and Portal Comercio, up Procuradores and along calles Plateros and Suecia. Although prices vary, many are selling places on the same tours and treks, so always hunt around. Avoid the **tour touts** at the airport or in the plaza at Cusco, and check out the operators in advance at the South American Explorers' Club (see above); members of the club also receive a discount with some outfits. For popular treks you need to **book well in advance** (at least six months ahead – nine months is preferable – for the **Inca Trail**). The companies listed below have been around for some time; there are also a few Lima-based operators in this area (see p.81).

Andean Treks ☎+1 800 683 8148 or ☎084 600 500, ⓦ andeantreks.com. US-based agency founded in 1980 whose partner company based in Cusco operates under the name of Inca Tours and Travel Adventures. They have top-quality options for the Inca Trail (5 days/4 nights from US$875) and operate alternative treks including Choquequirao, Ausangate, Salcantay and an off-the-beaten track Moonstone to Machu Picchu trek, taking in the Inca ruins at Quillarumiyoc (literally "moonstone").

Andina Travel Plazoleta Santa Catalina 219 ☎084 251 892, ⓦ andinatravel.com. Reputable Andina is constantly working at opening and developing new alternatives to remote areas, including Quillatambo. Part of the profits goes towards community projects including building new schools, reforestation projects with native queñua (polylepis) and reintroduction of native Andean camelids, namely alpacas and llamas. A reliable backpacker choice.

Apumayo Expediciones Jr Ricardo Palma 11, Urb Santa Monica, Wanchaq ☎084 246 018, ⓦapumayo .com. Expert operators offering trekking in the Sacred Valley region, mountain biking around Cusco and the Sacred Valley, historical and archeological tours, tours for disabled people (with wheelchair support for visiting major sites), horseriding and rafting on the ríos Urubamba and Apurimac. They can customize their trips to suit your agenda, though note that they usually only work with pre-booked groups.

Aspiring Adventures Apartado 611 ☎084 224 514, ⓦaspiringadventures.com. Offers half- and one-day gastronomic and "Alternative Cusco" tours to discover more about the city's hidden attractions, unique 3–4 day trips to mysterious religious festivities such as Paucartambo and Qoyllur Riti where entranced costume dancing goes on for days, and one- and two-week mountain biking, cultural, family and generalist tours.

Colibri Tour Choquechaca 229, 2nd floor ☎084 255 579, ⓦcolibritour.com. Specialists on the Inca Trail, and will arrange transport and collection from hotel. Also offers treks to Salcantay, Ausangate, Choquequirao and Vilcabamba.

Eric Adventures Urb Santa María A1-6, San Sebastián ☎084 272 862, ⓦericadventures.com. A good selection of tours, from the Inca Trail to trekking, kayaking, paragliding and mountain biking. They also rent out bikes, camping equipment and 4WDs, and have a good reputation for rafting. A day on the Urubamba river can cost as little as US$55.

Expediciones Vilca C Plateros 359 ☎084 244 751, ⓦmanuvilcaperu.com. A well-established trekking company with a variety of treks, albeit specializing in expeditions to the Manu Biosphere Reserve (see p.442). They can rent you any camping gear you need.

Explorandes Paseo Zarzuela Q-2 Huancaro ☎084 238 380, ⓦexplorandes.com. Operating since 1975, award-winning Explorandes is very professional and offers a range of tours and treks across Peru's most fascinating landscapes. In the Cusco area, these are the Inca Trail (5 days from US$787), Salcantay (5 days) and Choquequirao (5 days). They also offer mountain climbing, mountain biking, stand-up paddle, kayaking and rafting expeditions (see box, p.82).

Manu Expeditions Jr Los Geranios 2G, Urbanización Mariscal Gamarra ☎084 224 135, ⓦmanuexpeditions .com and ⓦbirding-in-peru.com. This company specializes in both trips to Manu in the rainforest (see p.442) and birding expeditions, as well as horseriding and

mountain adventure tours, including trips to Espíritu Pampa, the Inca site of Choquequirao through the Vilcabamba mountains, to Machu Picchu from Ollantaytambo via Anacachcocha and the Huaynay peaks, as well as more traditional treks like the Inca Trail.

Manu Nature Tours Av Pardo 1046 ☎084 252 721, ⓦmanuperu.com. An award-winning, nature-based adventure travel company, running tours to the jungle, particularly Manu (see p.442), plus mountain biking, birdwatching and rafting. It also operates a garden café next to its offices.

MAYUC Portal Confituras 211 ☎084 232 666 (or toll free from US and Canada ☎1 888 493 2109), ⓦmayuc .com. Highly reliable outfit with the experience to organize any tour or trek of your choice, from the Inca Trail to visiting the Tambopata–Candamo area in the jungle of Madre de Dios. Whitewater rafting is their speciality, with standard scheduled 3-day/2-night excursions from about US$480.

Milla Turismo Av Pardo 800 ☎084 231 710, ⓦmillaturismo.com. Will organize travel arrangements, tours, volunteer work and cultural tourist-related activities.

Mountain Lodges of Peru Av Emilio Cavenencia 225, Office 3220, San Isidro, Lima 27 ☎001 421 6952, ⓦmountainlodgesofperu.com. MLP organizes trekking and equestrian trips in comfort and style. It offers the only lodge-to-lodge trek to Machu Picchu, staying in luxurious lodges along the way, collaborating closely with local communities (one of which shares lodge ownership). Their latest adventure programme, the Lares trek, offers accommodation in stylish lodges while providing immersion in cultural, natural and archeological attractions, from snow peaks and glacial lakes to visiting traditional weavers in colourful dress.

Peru Planet C Garcilaso 210, Office 201 ☎084 251145, ⓦperu-planet.net. A well-respected Belgian-Peruvian travel agency offering the usual city tours as well as a wide range of trek options around the Sacred Valley, Salcantay, Lares, Choquequirao, Machu Picchu, Inca Trail, horseriding and rafting.

SAS Travel C Garcilaso 270, just below Plaza San Francisco ☎084 249 194, ⓦsastravelperu.com. One of the most reliable and professional tour and trek operators in Cusco, SAS specializes in the Inca Trail (4 days from US$640), but also visit Salcantay, Choquequirao, Ausangate and Vilcabamba, as well as the main jungle destinations. All good value.

Terra Explorer Urbanización Santa Ursula D4, Distrito de Wanchaq ☎084 237 352, ⓦterra explorerperu.com. Adventure travel agency specializing in high-end trips, including trekking in the Andes, rafting expeditions, lake kayaking and mountain biking. They also organize family trips.

United Mice Av Pachacuteq 424 ☎084 221 139, ⓦunitedmice.com. Specializing in guided tours of the

ACTIVITIES AROUND CUSCO

The Cusco region and nearby cloud forest and lowland Amazon provide a fantastic range of **activities**, from river-based ecotourism and whitewater kayaking to mountain biking, hiking and horseriding, not to mention white-knuckle experiences of the spiritual variety.

HIKING AND HORSERIDING

The mountains to the south and the north of Cusco are full of amazing **trekking trails**, some of them little touched, most of them still rarely walked (see p.264). Less adventurous **walks** or **horse rides** are possible to Qenko, Tambo Machay, Pukapukara and Chacan, in the hills above Cusco and in the nearby Sacred Valley. Many **jungle trip operators** are based in Cusco (see opposite).

WHITEWATER RAFTING

Cusco is also a great **whitewater rafting** centre, with easy access to classes 2 to 5 (rivers are generally rated from class 1 – very easy – to class 5 – very difficult/borderline dangerous) around Ollantaytambo on the Río Urubamba and classes 1 to 3 between Huambutio and Pisac, on the Río Vilcanota. From Calca to Urubamba the river runs classes 2 to 3, but this rises to 5 in the rainy season. Calca to Pisac (Huaran) and Ollantaytambo to Chilca are among the most popular routes, while the most dangerous are further afield on the Río Apurimac. The easiest stretch is from Echarate to San Baray, which passes by Quillabamba. Costs range from around US$40 to about US$200 a day, with price usually reflecting quality, but it's always recommended to use a reputable and well-established rafting company such as Terra Explorer (see opposite). Remember that most **travel insurance policies** exclude this kind of adventure activity, and always ensure that you are fully equipped with a safety kayak, helmets and lifejackets.

BUNGEE JUMPING

Bungee jumping is big in Cusco. The tallest bungee jump facility in the Americas (122m) is offered by Action Valley Cusco, Santa Teresa 325 (☎084 240 835, ⓦactionvalley.com), just 11km outside the city centre.

CANOPY ZIPLINE

Ziplining has become a popular activity in recent years in Peru. Located 15km from Machu Picchu, Cola de Mono (☎084 786 973, ⓦcanopyperu.com), just 2km from the town of Santa Teresa, was Peru's first zipline and is today one of South America's highest. With over 2500m of cables in seven sections and with speeds reaching 60km/hour, this is the place to give it a go.

HEALING PLANT RETREATS

Although less prevalent than around Iquitos (see box, p.475), it is possible to take part in ayahuasca and San Pedro retreats in the Sacred Valley. One benefit of this is that mosquitoes and other bugs are less prevalent in the Andes than in the Amazon. Neither ayahuasca nor San Pedro is for the faint-hearted; the effects (not always pleasant) of both plants can last for many hours. Choose your retreat carefully – each shaman is different and the retreats vary in length and intensity. The website ⓦayaadvisor.org is a good source of reviews.

Inca Trail, this company is reasonably priced (some discounts for students), with good guides, many of whom speak English. Food is of a high standard and their camping equipment is fine. They also offer 4-day treks to Ausangate, as well as treks approaching Machu Picchu via Salcantay.
X-treme Tourbulencia Plateros 364 ☎084 224 362, ⓦx-tremetourbulencia.com. Offers a variety of tours and adventure expeditions with the aim of promoting sustainable tourism and protecting the local environment: Inca Trail, Salcantay, Lares, Choquequirao and Ausangate, as well as the Inka Jungle Trail and trips throughout the Sacred Valley.

ACCOMMODATION

Cusco offers a plethora of accommodation options for all budgets, from backpackers' pads to luxurious five-star hotels with all the services you would expect in an upmarket Western hotel. You can find slightly pricier and more high-end places in the area east of the Plaza around San Blas and Choquechaca in the artists' quarter.

HOTELS & GUESTHOUSES

Amaru Hostal Cuesta de San Blas 541 ☎084 225 933, ⓦamaruhostal.com. Located in a colonial building with a couple of patios with benches and pretty flowers, this guesthouse has a calm atmosphere in the heart of San Blas. Rooms are clean and great value, with intricately decorated wooden beds and brightly coloured abstract paintings. **S/174**

★**Andenes al Cielo** Choquechaca 176 ☎084 222 237, ⓦandenesalcielo.com. A wonderful option located in the heart of Cusco offering spacious, tastefully decorated rooms with hardwood floors or carpets that give onto a pleasant courtyard. The two deluxe rooms (S/334) feature wooden beams and fireplaces, as well as balconies with street views. **S/247**

★**El Balcón** Tambo de Montero 222 ☎084 236 738, ⓦbalconcusco.com. This lovely guesthouse with a leafy garden area with wooden benches offers rustic rooms adorned with woven fabrics and local materials. There's a long balcony that runs the length of the building from where they are lovely views over the city rooftops. Staff are exceptionally friendly. **S/200**

Casa de la Gringa Pasñapakana 148, San Blas ☎084 241 168, ⓦcasadelagringa.com. A bright blue door opens up onto a pleasant breakfast area, while a purple-coloured corridor with wind chimes singing in the breeze leads to smallish rooms with hand painted murals. There's an annexe with a suite, and staff are friendly and helpful. Doubles **S/90**, suite **S/205**

Casa San Blas Boutique Hotel Tocuyeros 566, San Blas ☎084 254 852, ⓦcasasanblas.com. Located in the picturesque district of San Blas, this lovely boutique hotel offers twelve rooms with sturdy wooden beds and walls adorned with textiles that give onto the leafy interior courtyard. The suites have lovely city views. Doubles **S/388**, suites **S/565**

Hospedaje Turístico San Blas Cuesta San Blas, San Blas 526 ☎084 225 781, ⓦsanblascusco.com. Located in San Blas, this friendly place features a glass-covered courtyard with sofas and armchairs that is a good place to meet fellow travellers. Rooms are a bit poky but overall it's a decent lower-to-mid-range option. **S/130**

★**Hotel Marqueses** C Garcilaso 256 ☎084 264 249, ⓦhotelmarqueses.com. This charming three-star hotel is located in a beautiful colonial house dating back to the end of the sixteenth century (much of the original architecture has been preserved, along with some impressive frescoes). The en-suite rooms are warm and welcoming, with dark wooden furniture and local materials, and staff are exceptionally friendly and helpful. **S/336**

★**Inkaterra La Casona Cusco** Plazoleta Nazarenas 167 ☎084 234 010, ⓦinkaterra.com. Located in a beautifully restored sixteenth-century colonial manor house, this upmarket hotel consists of eleven sumptuous suites that give onto a pretty courtyard. The decor incorporates sumptuous colonial furnishings in an intimate environment – the hotel keeps its doors closed at all times of the day as it functions as a private manor house. Each room contains a stone fireplace, heated flooring and a large marble bathroom, while wholesome dishes (mains from S/50) made with locally sourced ingredients are served in the pleasant dining area. **S/1200**

Hostal Madre Tierra Atoqsaycuchi 647A, San Blas ☎084 248 452, ⓦhostalmadretierra.com. Located high up in the district of San Blas, with its cobbled streets and picturesque walkways, this snug little place features only seven rooms with wooden furnishings and en-suite facilities. Guests mingle over breakfast, which is served at the communal table in the open-plan kitchen area. **S/183**

★**El Mercado** 7 Cuartones 306 ☎084 582 640, ⓦelmercadotunqui.com. Located on the site of a former food market, this stylish hotel brims with character. The restaurant is decorated with weighing scales and a juice bar reminiscent of a market stall, while in the evenings a voguish bonfire is lit in the internal patio. Rooms are tastefully furnished with quirky paintings and modern amenities including individual wi-fi modems. **S/730**

El Mirador de la Ñusta Tandapata 682 ☎084 248 039, ⓔelmiradordelanusta.cusco@hotmail.com. This intimate little guesthouse, painted in mellow hues of blue, yellow and pink is superbly located overlooking the Plazoleta San Blas. The agreeable rooms are warm and welcoming, featuring wooden beds with woolly blankets and wicker lamps. **S/70**

Hotel Monasterio C Palacio 136, Plazoleta Nazarenas ☎084 604 000, ⓦbelmond.com. With rooms and suites set around four stunning sixteenth-century monastery cloisters, this smart hotel, whose interiors are decorated with antiques and religious paintings, houses a gilded chapel. Rooms are equipped with state-of-the-art amenities, including oxygen enrichment to fight high altitude and marble bathrooms. **S/1270**

Palacio del Inka Plazoleta Santo Domingo 259 ☎084 604 000, ⓦlibertador.com.pe. Located just across the road from the Q'orikancha, this sumptuous hotel is set in a thoroughly renovated mansion with a spacious lobby with knobbly, genuine Inca stonework. Rooms are grand and stylish, the buffet breakfast is excellent and there's an indoor pool, too. **S/1200**

★**Palacio Nazarenas** Plaza Nazarenas 144 ☎084 582 222, ⓦbelmond.com. Part of the Belmond chain of hotels, this intimate stylish hotel is located in a former palace and convent with 55 plush suites set around seven cloistered courtyards landscaped with Andean flowers and herbs. Each room is enriched with oxygen, ensuring guests easily adapt to Cusco's altitude. There's an inviting outdoor

heated pool (this is the only hotel in Cusco to boast this facility) set around a pretty courtyard, which also houses the *Senzo* restaurant (see p.228). S/1960

Pensión Alemana Tandapata 260 ☎ 084 226 861, ⓦ pension-alemana-cuzco.com. This German-run guesthouse offers well-appointed rooms, some of which are set around a small garden area that brims with colourful flowers. The location is particularly peaceful, high up in San Blas – there are nice views over town from some of the rooms, too. S/210

★ **Rumi Punku** Choquechaca 339 ☎ 084 221 102, ⓦ rumipunku.com. A welcoming establishment built on an old Inca temple site in one of Cusco's most attractive streets offering rooms set around a series of pretty courtyards with hanging potted plants. Rooms are stylish for the price, with hardwood floors and private bathrooms, and there's a lounge area with TV and fireplace, as well as a Finnish sauna, hot tub and gym. S/290

Tika Wasi Tandapata 491 ☎ 084 231 609, ⓦ tikawasi .com. It's Quechua for "the house of flowers" – it does indeed have a pretty garden area which is a perfect spot to sit back and relax with a book in hand. The individually themed rooms are rather fun, such as the eucalyptus room in autumnal hues decorated with real eucalyptus trunks and tasteful murals, although others may be a bit too much for some, such as the religious-themed room with a painting of Christ and a blue ceiling above representing the sky. S/67

HOSTELS

Ecopackers Santa Teresa 375 ☎ 084 231 800, ⓦ ecopackersperu.com. A central and modern hostel with female-only and mixed dorms sleeping 4 to 18, with light wooden beds and lockers set around an attractive courtyard. There are sunbeds, table tennis and billiards, and rates include breakfast. Dorms S/33, doubles S/120

Hitchhikers Backpackers Hostel Saphi 440 ☎ 084 260 079, ⓦ hhikersperu.com. This small intimate hostel with a series of itsy-bitsy courtyards and walls decorated with pretty photos of Inca crafts. All rooms are en suite, including dorms, and woolly blankets are provided to keep warm. Dorms S/28, doubles S/84

Kokopelli San Andrés 260 ☎ 084 224 473, ⓦ hostelkokopelli.com. This popular hostel has four- to twelve-bed dorms, with pricier rooms set further away from the happening bar, where customers tend to linger until the early hours. Facilities include a billiards table, table football, a mini cinema with comfortable lounge chairs and plenty of daily events from rock'n'roll nights to Peruvian nights where you can learn how to make potent piscos to the sound of criolla music. Dorms S/25, doubles S/140

Loki Hostel Santa Ana 601 ☎ 084 243 705, ⓦ lokihostel .com. A friendly, lively hostel with dorms and doubles set around the courtyard of a beautifully restored colonial building. Facilities include a TV room, table tennis and a small gym. The comfortable dorms have under-bed lockers, and there are plenty of activities including bingo, karaoke, quiz nights and beer pong. Dorms S/21, doubles S/90

Mamá Simona Ceniza 364 ☎ 084 260 408, ⓦ mamasimona.com. The doors of this peaceful hostel open up onto a lobby area with an internal patio featuring armchairs, fun murals and colourful beanbags and masks. Doubles and dorms have lovely parquet floors and light wooden beds, and are kept spick and span. There's a bright red kitchen for guests' use, too. Dorms S/30, doubles S/80

Pariwana Hostel Av Meson de la Estrella 136 ☎ 084 233 751, ⓦ pariwana-hostel.com. The dorms and private rooms at this pleasant hostel are set around a pretty patio embellished with flowers and colourful beanbags. The atmosphere is welcoming and laidback, and there are plenty of activities and events to meet other travellers including yoga, beer pong and Sunday barbecue (S/15) as well as a happening bar and restaurant. Dorms S/27, doubles S/130

Samay Wasi Atoqsaycuchi 416 ☎ 084 253 108, ⓦ samaywasiperu.com. This pleasant hostel high up in San Blas offers four- and six-bed dorms with en-suite bathrooms. The real winners here, however, are the private rooms – welcoming and cosy with exposed stone walls and wonderful views over the city from the top floor balcony. There's a kitchen for guests' use, free airport and bus pick-up for guests who stay two or more nights, and rates include breakfast. Dorms S/33, doubles S/82

EATING

Local cuisine Cusco prides itself on its traditional dishes, which have evolved this century into a *novo andino* cuisine, fusing the best ingredients of the Andes with exquisite Mediterranean and even Argentinian influences. Generally speaking, trout is plentiful, reasonably priced and often excellent, and roast guinea pig (*cuy*) can usually be ordered, along with international dishes such as pizza.

Self-catering The central market by San Pedro train station (Mon–Sat 6am–6pm, Sun 7am–4pm) sells a wonderful variety of meats, tropical and imported fruits, local vegetables, Andean cheeses and other basics. The market also has a wide range of daytime hot-food stalls where you can get superb, freshly squeezed juices.

Where to eat Eating out in Cusco is enjoyable, and restaurants range from cheap-and-cheerful pizza joints to exceptionally fine gourmet establishments. Many of the best restaurants and bars are within a block or two of the Plaza de Armas and uphill towards San Blas; the more central places serve anything from a toasted cheese sandwich to authentic Andean or criolla dishes. *Quintas* – basic local eating houses – serve mostly traditional Peruvian food, full of spice and character. It's difficult, if not impossible, to categorize some of the establishments in Cusco as distinctly cafés, restaurants or bars since many fulfil all three functions, occasionally simultaneously, sometimes varying between different hours of the day.

CAFÉS AND RESTAURANTS

Baco Ruinas 465 ☎084 242 808, ⓦcicciolinacuzco .com. This stylish and atmospheric bistro-cum-restaurant is decorated with quirky paintings by a Dutch artist who calls Cusco his home. The menu includes great alpaca burgers (S/32) as well as pizzas with imaginative toppings such as lamb with rocket (S/36), along with home-made desserts (from S/18); there's an extensive wine list, too. Daily 3–11pm.

La Bodega 138 Herrajes 138 ☎084 260 272. Set on two floors, this popular spot with little wooden tables serves great salads (S/23), as well as wood-fire pizzas (S/32) and calzones (S/29), along with delectable desserts (try the Nutella cheesecake; S/15). There are over thirty types of beer on offer, including an excellent range of craft beers from the Sacred Valley. Daily noon–10.30pm.

Bojosan C San Agustín 275 ☎084 246 502. With an open kitchen that aims to recreate Japanese ambience and cuisine, this little udon bar is the perfect spot for a warming bowl of noodles on a cold Cusco evening. There are seven types of udon (S/20) to choose from, namely beef, duck, curry, chicken, seaweed and pork, accompanied by Japanese green tea, beer or sake. Thurs–Tues 12.30–3.30pm & 6.30–10.30pm.

Café Morena C Plateros 348B ☎084 437 832. This café, lit by dozens of dangling light bulbs, specializes in tasty sandwiches with a great choice of fillings including pork, chicken and a veggie option served on focaccia bread. Other light dishes include soups (S/19), salads (S/20) and *empañadas* (S/10). Mon–Sat 9.30am–10pm.

Calle del Medio C del Medio 113 ☎084 248 340, ⓦcalledelmediorestaurante.com. This excellent restaurant-bar right on the plaza serves contemporary Peruvian cuisine in a particularly tasteful setting with quirky wallpaper, recycled furniture and a balcony overlooking the plaza. Ingredients are fresh from the Sacred Valley and the menu includes alpaca, llama, trout, *cuy* and *quinoa*; try the slow-roasted pork belly marinated in fig and chilli (S/49). Daily 11am–3am.

Chicha Plaza Regocijo 261, 2nd floor ☎084 240 520, ⓦchicha.com.pe. Renowned chef Gastón Acurio is behind one of the city's best restaurants – expect excellent ceviche (S/43), causa (S/34) and grilled octopus (S/39) dishes as well as meat favourites including *lomo saltado* (S/56) and pork *adobo* (S/46). The atmosphere is overall pretty relaxed. Daily noon–11pm.

★**Cicciolina** C Triunfo 393 ☎084 239 510, ⓦcicciolinacuzco.com. This award-winning restaurant serves excellent Mediterranean and Peruvian dishes with a twist, including tagliolini tinted with squid ink and sautéed with prawns and coconut milk (S/39). The bustling tapas bar, with chilli and garlic strands dangling from the ceiling, offers sandwiches, salads and wine by the glass, while the adjacent fine dining room is a touch smarter with white linen tablecloths. The ground-floor bakery serves home-made breads (S/8) and superb breakfasts (S/16). Daily 8–11am, noon–3pm & 6–10pm.

Greens Santa Catalina Angosta 135 ☎084 243 379, ⓦcuscorestaurants.com. A bustling stylish restaurant with recycled Coke bottles as lamps serving innovative *novo andino* and Mediterranean dishes, using as many organic and green ingredients as possible. There are plenty of veggie options too, such as a vegetable wrap with grilled veg, lettuce and hummus (S/25), as well as seasonal vegetable curry (S/38). Daily 8am–11pm.

Incanto Santa Catalina Angosta 135 ☎084 254 753. This stylish restaurant with laidback tunes and a large wood-fire oven in the centre of the dining area serves Italian and Peruvian cuisine with a twist. The menu includes imaginative pizzas such as alpaca pepperoni (S/36) and ossobuco served with cream pappardelle (S/55), along with a number of delectable desserts including profiteroles (S/19). Daily 11am–11pm.

★**Jack's Café** Corner of Choquechaca and Cuesta San Blas ☎084 254 606. This excellent gringo café serves consistently good dishes in a welcoming cosy interior. The all-day breakfasts are particularly good, as are the hearty soups (S/16) and tasty sandwiches (S/15). The Mediterranean salad with grilled veg, avocado and greens (S/19) is particularly good. The café is a pleasant spot to just sit back and read a book with a tea in hand. Get ready to queue. Daily 7.30am–11.30pm.

Korma Sutra Tandapata 909 ☎084 233 023. It's not every day you see crispy tandoori guinea pig (S/24) on the menu. Cusco's main curry house serves plenty of Indian favourites including samosas (S/12), chicken tikka masala (S/27) and lamb rogan josh (S/30). Mon–Sat 1–10pm.

★**Limo** Portal de Carnes 236, 2nd floor ☎084 240 668, ⓦcuscorestaurants.com. Located just beside the cathedral, this stylish place is one of Cusco's best restaurants with lovely views over the plaza from the dining area. The speciality here is fish, and the menu includes sushi (S/20), ceviche (S/38) and other creatively presented dishes including superb tuna tartare (S/38). The drinks menu features pisco-based cocktails (S/20) only. Daily 11am–11pm.

MAP Café Plazoleta Las Nazarenas 231 ☎084 242 476, ⓦcuscorestaurants.com. Located in the pretty courtyard of the Museo de Arte Precolombino, this smart restaurant with soft lighting and mellow background music serves

4

creatively presented Peruvian dishes; the signature mushroom *capchi* soup is made with Andean mushrooms, fava beans, potatoes and cheese, topped with soft pastry and crispy black *quinoa* (S/34). Daily 11.30am–3pm & 7–10pm.

Marcelo Batata Palacio 121, 2nd floor ☎ 084 222 424. This popular restaurant with black and red undertones has a wonderful rooftop terrace with panoramic views over Cusco – a great spot for a post-prandial beer (S/8) or a pisco sour (S/18). The international menu includes grilled lamb ribs served with mash (S/44) and spicy pork *adobo* (S/43). Daily 12.30–11pm.

Pacha Papa Plazoleta San Blas 120 ☎ 084 241 318, ⓦ cuscorestaurants.com. On the picturesque Plazoleta San Blas, this popular restaurant is set around an attractive inner courtyard shaded by cherry trees, and serves Peruvian favourites including alpaca and *cuy*, as well as grilled lamb. Often has wonderful Andean live harp music. Mains from S/40. Daily 11.30am–10pm.

Papacho's Portal de Belén 115 ☎ 084 245 359, ⓦ papachos.com. This quirky burger bar overlooking the square is decorated with funky retro furnishings, including old school posters and discs, as well as dangling lamps and colourful paintings. The tasty burgers come with sixteen different fillings including pork and chicken accompanied by tangerine ketchup with lemon grass and chilli pepper, plus four tasty veggie burgers (S/30), nicely rounded off with an ice-cream sundae (S/23). Mon–Fri noon–midnight, Sat & Sun 11am–midnight.

Pucara Plateros 309 ☎ 084 222 027. This cosy restaurant with wooden interiors and dim lighting is a great spot to try reasonably priced local dishes in a pleasant setting. The *quinoa* soup is particularly good (S/15), and the menu includes Peruvian favourites such as *causa rellena* (stuffed potato with tuna salad; S/18), along with a range of tasty desserts (S/9). Daily noon–10pm.

Senzo Palacio Nazarenas, Palacio 144 ☎ 084 582 222, ⓦ belmond.com. Located within the stylish Belmond *Palacio Nazarenas* hotel, *Senzo* serves traditional Peruvian dishes in an upmarket setting overlooking the hotel's outdoor pool area. The menu includes *chupe de paiche*, a traditional jungle fish soup (S/58), *choclo con queso* (fried cheese with sautéed corn; S/41) and a creatively presented strawberry and eucalyptus sorbet with popped *quinoa* (S/39) that is simply exquisite. Daily 5am–10pm.

Lo Soleil C San Agustín 275 ☎ 084 240 543, ⓦ restaurantelesoleilcusco.com. Traditional gourmet French cuisine – a small part of the ingredients here is flown in from France, including snails, although the majority of produce is rigorously selected daily from the local market. The five-course tasting menu (S/135) features foie gras and neck of duck confit, while the menu includes French specialities such as *canard à l'orange* (roast duck served with an orange sauce; S/69). The wine list features labels exclusively from France. Thurs–Tues 12.30–3pm & 7–10.30pm.

Uchu Palacio 135 ☎ 084 246 598. This steakhouse tucked away on a little courtyard that gives onto C Palacio offers great sizzling steaks served hot on stone slabs (S/47) in a smart if a bit kitsch interior with chandeliers and upholstered green and brown sofas. Daily 12.30–10pm.

DRINKING, NIGHTLIFE AND ENTERTAINMENT

Apart from Lima, no Peruvian town has as varied a nightlife as Cusco. The Plaza de Armas is a hive of activity until the early hours, even during the week. Most venues in the city are simply **bars** with a dancefloor and sometimes a stage, but their styles vary enormously, from Andean folk spots with panpipe music to reggae or jazz joints, as well as more conventional **clubs**. Most places are within staggering distance of each other, and sampling them is an important part of any stay in Cusco. Most really get going between 10 and 11pm, then keep on going until 2 or 3am.

★**Calle del Medio** C del Medio 113 ☎ 084 248 340, ⓦ calledelmediorestaurante.com. The welcoming bar and lounge of this appealing restaurant is decked out in recycled furniture with a touch of retro, and features over thirty colourful pisco jars lining the bar. Barmen exclusively rustle up pisco-based drinks (S/22). There's a small balcony area overlooking the plaza, which is the perfect spot for a sundowner. Daily 11am–3am.

La Cantina Saphi 554 ☎ 084 242 075. This Italian-run wine bar is a good spot to sit back and enjoy a glass of Italian red (S/15) on a cold Cusco evening. There are great cheese and salami platters (S/60), too. Daily 6–11pm.

Km 0 Tandapata 100, San Blas ☎ 084 238 239. This cosy itsy-bitsy bar and restaurant is decked out in warm red undertones; the walls are packed with paintings and customers sip on cocktails at high wooden tables enjoying the live music shows (daily 10.30pm–midnight), which include an eclectic mix of latino, blues, jazz, reggae and rock'n'roll. The menu includes Peruvian dishes and Thai curry (S/24). Daily 6pm–2am.

Mama Africa Portal de Panes 109, 3rd floor, Plaza de Armas. Right on the main square, this is a popular club that goes on until the early hours of the morning. The main musical flavour is pop, and there are salsa classes 9–11pm. The second floor bar/club, *Mushrooms*, plays house and electro, although it's a bit seedy. Fri & Sat cover charge S/10–20. Daily 9pm–5am.

The Muse C Triunfo 338, 2nd floor ☎ 084 242 030, ⓦ themusecuscoweebly.com. This grungy café lounge and bar regularly hosts Peruvian and international bands who play all manner of music including latino, salsa, meringue and afro-Cuban – to name a few. There's a restaurant area serving local and international dishes (S/15), as well as a karaoke room. Daily 10am–4am.

Museo del Pisco Santa Catalina Ancha 398 ☏ 084 262 709, ⓦ museodelpisco.org. Not exactly a museum, but nearly – with three types of pisco from over forty bodegas, this is Cusco's pisco bar par excellence, offering pisco tastings and live music – criolla, jazz, rock and blues – daily (9.30–11pm). There is tapas (S/16) to accompany the drinks, as well as more substantial mains, too (S/24). Daily noon–12.30pm, Thurs, Fri & Sat until 1am.

Norton Rats Tavern Santa Catalina Angosta 116, 2nd floor ☏ 084 246 204. This pub is a popular spot for a late afternoon lager (S/25) on the little balcony overlooking the main square. Its mostly male clientele come here to show their skills at the pub's three dartboards, play billiards or watch sports on satellite TV. The menu includes burgers (S/12), chilli con carne (S/14) and burritos (S/14), and there are over thirty types of beer (S/25) and ciders (S/40), too. Daily 7.30am–2am.

★ **Paddy Flaherty's Irish Pub** C Triunfo 124 ☏ 084 225 361, ⓦ paddysirishbarcusco.com. At 11,156ft, this pub proudly boasts it's the highest Irish-owned pub on the planet. Its cosy wood-panelled interior is jam-packed with pictures and Irish artefacts. The atmosphere is pleasant and generally very busy, especially at weekends, when Guinness (S/18) flows abundantly. The menu includes shepherd's pie (S/17.50) and cheeseburgers (S/17). Daily 10am–2am.

Los Perros Tecsecocha 436 ☏ 084 241 447. This trendy hangout in red and black undertones is a great spot to grab a beer (S/9) or a pisco (S/15). The walls are decorated with bright colourful paintings, while large decorative glass jars are dotted around the premises. You can nibble on some tasty oriental snacks here too, including chilli rolls (S/19) and spicy wonton (S/19). Daily 11am–midnight.

Ukuku's Bar Plateros 316 ☏ 084 254 911, ⓦ ukukusbar .com. A highly popular venue with one of the best atmospheres in Cusco, teeming with energetic revellers most nights by around 11pm, when the music gets going. There's a small dancefloor, a seating area and a long bar, with music ranging from live Andean folk with panpipes, drums and *charangos* (small Andean stringed instruments) to DJs or taped rock. Daily 8pm–6am.

OTHER ENTERTAINMENT VENUES

Alliance Française Av de la Cultura 804 ☏ 084 243 887, ⓦ alianzafrancesacusco.org.pe. Runs a full programme of events including music, films, exhibitions, theatre and music.

Dance Performances Centro Qosqo de Arte Nativo, Av Sol 604 ☏ 084 227 901. During major fiestas you'll encounter colourfully costumed folk-dancing groups in the streets; at other times, the Centro Qosqo is the only place that offers regular folkloric dance shows. Entrance with Cusco Tourist Ticket or S/25 per show. Daily 6.30–8pm.

Teatro Municipal Mesón de la Estrella 149 ☏ 084 231 847. The municipal theatre of Cusco occasionally holds folkloric shows and events. Check with the tourist office for an updated schedule.

SHOPPING

Areas Most of the touristy artesanía and jewellery shops are concentrated in streets like Plateros around the Plaza de Armas and up Triunfo, though calles Herraje (first right as you head towards San Blas) and San Agustín have slightly cheaper but decent shops with leather and alpaca work. It's worth heading off the beaten track, particularly around San Blas or the upper end of Tullumayo, to find outlets hidden in the backstreets.

Markets The main street-market day for artesanía is Sat (10am–6pm). The central market, selling fresh produce, is

CRAFT-SHOPPING IN CUSCO

Crafts and artesanía are Cusco's stock in trade, with the best value and range of **alpaca clothing** in Peru, apart perhaps from Puno. It's an ideal place to pick up **weavings** or **antique cloths**, traditional **musical instruments** like panpipes and colourful bags and **leather crafts**. There are artesanía (craft shops) all over the centre, but the best prices and fullest range are found at the **Centro Artesanal Cusco** (daily 8am–8pm) at the corner of Huanchac and Tullumayo, close to the huge sun-disc fountain on Avenida Sol. This large building brings together arguably the largest and best-value collection of artesanía under one roof in Peru; it's a nice, clean and relatively hassle-free shopping environment very close to the train ticket office at Huanchac station.

Another good part of town for quality artesanía is the barrio of **San Blas**. This is the traditional artisan area of Cusco, home to a number of jewellers and art and antique shops. The Cuesta San Blas itself contains some of the finest artesanía, selling new and old oil paintings, while Hathun Rumiyoq has more good shops at its bottom end. There are some funky shops around the San Blas *plazoleta* too. The main street-market day for artesanía is Saturday (10am–6pm).

4

at San Pedro (see below). Out of town there are good markets for artesanía at Pisac and Chinchero; both have craft stands daily, although the main market days are Sun and Thurs, respectively (see p.237 and p.245), when campesinos from the surrounding villages descend into the Sacred Valley to sell fresh fruit and veg produce.

Prices and haggling In the markets and at street stalls you can often get up to twenty per cent off, and even in the smarter shops it's quite acceptable to bargain a little. If you're worried about carrying an expensive purchase around town, it's fine to ask the shopkeeper to bring the goods to your hotel so that the transaction can take place in relative safety.

ALPACA

Andean Shop Santa Teresa 321 ☎084 244 873, ✉1Andeanshop@gmail.com. This pleasant shop sells top-quality baby alpaca scarves and other clothing accessories. Daily 9am–9pm.

Kuna Portal de Panes 127 ☎084 243 191, ⓦkuna.com. One of the best places to buy alpaca products, this shop with branches throughout Peru specializes in upscale alpaca fashions, with high-quality scarves, jumpers, hats and coats. The priciest item on sale is a *vicuña* scarf, made of one of the world's finest wools, costing about US$1000. Daily 9am–10pm.

Sol Alpaca Santa Teresa 317 ⓦsolalpaca.com. With a number of branches across town and throughout the Sacred Valley, this upmarket shop is a safe bet if you're after genuine alpaca wool – prices are high, but so is the quality.

BOOKS

Genesis Bookstore Santa Catalina Ancha 307 ☎084 257 971. Sells books in English, particularly guides, history books and material on birds or wildlife; it's also a post office agent and has stationery. Daily 9am–9pm.

Kuskan Bookstore Plaza San Blas 630A ☎084 253 320. This store has some fascinating books in English, particularly focusing on travel, culture and biodiversity. Daily 8am–8pm.

CAMPING EQUIPMENT

Rental or purchase of camping equipment is easy in Cusco, but you may be asked to leave your passport as a deposit on more expensive items; always get a proper receipt. For basics such as pots, pans, plates and so on, try the stalls in Monjaspata, less than half a block from the bottom end of San Pedro market, while others such as buckets, bowls and sheets are sold in various shops along C Concebidayoq,

close to the San Pedro market area.

Cordillera Garcilaso 210 ☎084 244 133, ⓦcordillerastores.com. A decent store with a range of good-quality camping equipment and accessories. Mon–Fri 9am–9pm.

Tatoo Adventure Gear Portal Espinar 144 ☎084 236 703, ⓦpe.tatoo.ws. A well-stocked camping shop selling trekking and mountain-climbing shoes, as well as backpacks and camping equipment. Daily 9.30am–9pm.

X-treme Tourbulencia Expeditions Plateros 364 ☎084 222 405, ⓦx-tremetourbulencia.com. A decent range of used mountain camping equipment. Daily 10am–8pm.

CRAFTS, ANTIQUES AND JEWELLERY

Centro Artesanal Cusco Last block of Av Sol and Tullumayo. A plethora of stalls selling a range of crafts as well as blankets and other accessories. Daily 8am–8pm.

Centro de Textiles Tradicionales de Cusco Av Sol 603 ☎084 228 117, ⓦtextilescusco.org. A not-for-profit organization that aims to keep weaving traditions alive by promoting fine textiles by local communities and artisans. The majority of the sale price goes directly to the communities. Prices are a bit higher than in shops but are also of superior quality and the profits go to the women who work on each piece. Mon–Fri 7.30am–8.30pm, Sat & Sun 8.30am–7.30pm.

Galería de Arte Cusqueño Plazoleta San Blas 114 ☎084 237857. This shop in San Blas displays a range of antiques, from furniture to textiles. Mon–Sat 10am–1pm & 4–8pm.

Galería Tater Suytuccato 705B ☎084 506 228. Artist Tater Camilo Vera Vizcarra displays his work at his gallery in San Blas – ceramics are available for purchase. He also has a ceramic workshop at Tungasuca Z4 in Urbanización Tupac Amaru. Mon–Sat 10am–2pm & 4–8pm.

Joyería Esma Hatun Rumiyoc 120 ☎084 260 824. A fun little shop selling hand-designed Peruvian jewellery. Mon–Sat 9.30am–8pm.

FOOD

Mercado Central Plazoleta San Pedro. The best place for generally excellent and very cheap food – including all the main typical Peruvian dishes like *cau cau* (tripe), rice with meat and veg, and *papas a la huancaina* (see p.33). Mon–Sat 6am–6pm, Sun 7am–4pm.

Orion Supermarket Meloc 417. A centrally located supermarket offering a range of goods, from foodstuffs to toiletries. It also has a branch at Belén 494. Daily 7.30am–10pm.

DIRECTORY

Consulates Bolivia, Av Oswaldo Baca 101 (☎084 231 845); Brazil, Jr Las Gardenias D13, 3rd floor (☎084 221 390); Netherlands, Lechugal 405, 4th floor (☎084 236 540);

UK, Jr Los Geranios 2G, Mariscal Gamarra (☎084 224 135); US, Av Pardo 845 (☎084 231 474).

Health The Hospital Regional is on Av de la Cultura

(☎084 231455, 084 223030 or 084 223691). Among the city's best private clinics are CIMA, Av Pardo 978 (☎084 255 550, ⓦcima-clinic.com); Clínica San José, Av Los Incas 1408B (☎084 253 295, ⓦsanjose.com.pe) and the Clínica Peruano Suiza, Av Peru K3, Urb Quispicanchis (☎084 242 114 ⓦcps.com.pe).

Immigration Migraciones, Av Sol s/n (Mon–Fri 8am–4.30pm; ☎084 222 741).

Internet Virtually all restaurants, cafés and hotels have wi-fi. Most hotels have computers for guests' use, too.

Language schools Amigos Spanish School, Zaguan del Cielo B-23 (☎084 225 053, ⓦspanishcusco.com), is a not-for-profit institution which funds education and food for local young people through its teaching of Spanish; family stays can also be organized if required. Staff speak English, Dutch, German, French and Japanese. The South American Spanish School, based at Carmen Alto 112, San Blas (☎084 223 012, ⓦsasschool.org), provides excellent teaching along with hostel or family-home-based accommodation where required. Amauta Spanish at Suecia 480 (☎084 262 345, ⓦamautaspanish.com) also offers group and individual Spanish lessons.

Laundry Lavandería Louis at Choquechaca 264 (Mon–Sat 8am–8pm; S/3 per kg); Lavandería Meloc at Meloc 488 (☎084 251 733).

Money and exchange For ATMs, try the 24hr Scotiabank ATM at the top of Av Sol (no. 104); the BCP tourist centre on Plaza de Armas has several machines at the corner of Portal de Harinas with Procuradores; Global Net ATMs at Portal de Panes 115 and Portal Comercio 117, both at Plaza de Armas. For banks, try Interbanc, Av Sol 380 – good for travellers' cheques, exchange and has an ATM; Banco de Credito, Av Sol 189 (has ATMs); Banco Continental, Av Sol 366, changes cash and most travellers' cheques. For faster service on cash and travellers' cheque exchange, try hotels or casas de cambio. There are several casas de cambio along Portal Comercio at the Plaza de Armas. Street *cambistas* can be found on blocks 2 and 3 of Av Sol, around the main banks, but take great care here.

Police The 24hr tourist police are at Plaza Túpac Amaru s/n (☎084 235 123).

Post office The main office is at Av Sol 800 (Mon–Sat 7.30am–8pm; Sun 9am–2pm).

Inca sites near Cusco

4

The megalithic fortress of **Sacsayhuaman**, which looks down onto the red-tiled roofs of Cusco from high above the city, is the closest and most impressive of several historic sites scattered around the Cusco hills. However, there are four other major Inca sites in the area. Not much more than a stone's throw beyond Sacsayhuaman lie the great *huaca* of **Qenko** and the less-visited Salapunco, thought by some to be a moon temple. A few kilometres further on, at what almost certainly formed the outer limits of the Inca's home estate, you come to the small, fortified hunting lodge of **Pukapukara** and the stunning imperial baths of **Tambo Machay**.

Sacsayhuaman

Daily 7am–6pm • Entry by Cusco Tourist Ticket (see box, p.221)

The walled complex of **SACSAYHUAMAN** forms the head of Cusco's puma (the Inca city was designed in the shape of a puma), whose fierce-looking teeth point away from the city. The name Sacsayhuaman is of disputed origin, with different groups holding that it means either "satiated falcon", "speckled head" or "city of stone".

Once the site of a bloody battle between Inca leaders and the Spanish conquistadores, today the most dramatic event to take place at Sacsayhuaman is the colourful – if overly commercial – **Inti Raymi festival** in June (see box, p.218). However, throughout the year, you may stumble across various **sun ceremonies** being performed here by local mystics.

SACSAYHUAMAN IN NUMBERS

The chronicler Cieza de León, writing in the 1550s, estimated that some twenty thousand men had been involved in Sacsayhuaman's construction: **four thousand** cutting blocks from quarries; **six thousand** dragging them on rollers to the site; and another **ten thousand** working on finishing and fitting the blocks into position. According to legend, some **three thousand** lives were lost while dragging just one huge stone.

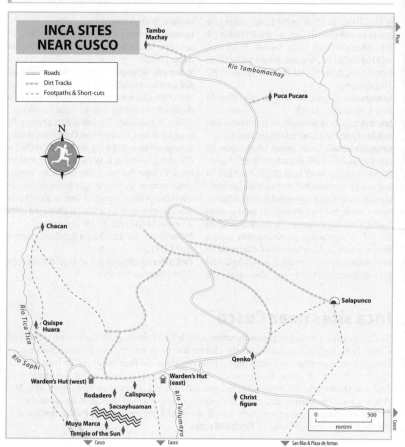

INCA SITES NEAR CUSCO

Roads
Dirt Tracks
Footpaths & Short-cuts

Tambo Machay
Río Tambomachay
Puca Pucara
Chacan
Salapunco
Quispe Huara
Río Tica Tica
Río Saphi
Qenko
Warden's Hut (west)
Warden's Hut (east)
Rodadero
Calispucyo
Christ figure
Sacsayhuaman
Río Tullumayo
Muyu Marca
Temple of the Sun
0   500
metres
Cusco
Cusco
San Blas & Plaza de Armas

Brief history

It was the **Emperor Pachacuti** who began work on Sacsayhuaman in the 1440s, although it took nearly a century of creative work to finish it. Various types of rock were used, including enormous diorite blocks from nearby for the outer walls, Yucay limestone from more than 15km away for the foundations, and dark andesite, some of it from over 30km away at Rumicolca, for the inner buildings and towers. First, boulders were split by boring holes with stone or cane rods and wet sand; next, wooden wedges were inserted into these holes and saturated to crack the rocks into more manageable sizes; finally the blocks were shifted into place with levers. With only natural fibre ropes, stone hammers and bronze chisels, it would have been an enormous undertaking.

During the fateful **battle of 1536**, Juan Pizarro, Francisco's son, was killed as he charged the main gate in a surprise assault, and a leading Inca nobleman, armed with a Spanish sword and shield, caused havoc by repulsing every enemy who tried to scale Muyu Marca, the last tower left in Inca hands. Having sworn to fight to the death, he leapt from the top when defeat seemed inevitable, rather than accept humiliation and dishonour. After the battle the esplanade was covered in native corpses: food for vultures and inspiration for the Cusco coat of arms, which, since 1540, has been bordered by eight **condors** "in memory of the fact that when the castle was taken these birds descended to eat the natives who had died in it". The conquistadores wasted little time in dismantling most of the inner structures of the fortress, using the stones to build Spanish Cusco.

The walls

Protected by such a steep approach from the town, the fortress only needed **defensive walls** on one side. Nevertheless, this "wall" is one of South America's archeological treasures, actually formed by three massive, parallel stone ramparts zigzagging together for some 600 metres across the plateau just over the other side of the mountaintop from Cusco city and the valley below. These zigzag walls, incorporating the most monumental and megalithic stones used in ancient Peru, form the boundary of what was originally designed as a "spiritual distillation" of the ancient city below, with many sectors named after areas of imperial Cusco.

Little of the inner structures remain, yet these enormous ramparts stand twenty metres high, quite undamaged by past battles, earthquakes and the passage of time. The strength of the mortarless stonework – one block weighs more than three hundred tonnes – is matched by the brilliance of its design: the **zigzags**, casting shadows in the afternoon sun, not only look like jagged cats' teeth, but also seem to have been cleverly designed to expose the flanks of any attacking force. Recently, however, many sacred and ritual objects excavated here have caused archeologists to consider Sacsayhuaman as more of a **ceremonial centre** than a fortress, the distinctive, jagged form of these outer walls possibly symbolizing the important deity of lightning.

The towers and temple

Originally, the inner "fort" was covered in buildings, a maze of tiny streets dominated by three major towers. The tower of **Muyu Marca**, whose foundations can still be seen clearly, was round, over 30m tall and with three concentric circles of wall, the outer one roughly 24m in diameter. An imperial residence, it apparently had lavish inner chambers and a constant supply of fresh water, carried up through subterranean channels. The other two towers – **Salla Marca** and **Paunca Marca** – had rectangular bases about 20m long and were essentially warriors' barracks, and all three were painted in vivid colours, had thatched roofs and were interconnected by underground passages: in its entirety, the inner fortress could have housed as many as ten thousand people under siege. At the rear of this sector, looking directly down into Cusco and the valley, was a **temple dedicated to the sun**, reckoned by some to be the most important shrine in the entire Inca Empire and the most sacred sector of Sacsayhuaman. Excavation of these sites continues, but it's still very difficult to make out anything but the circular tower base.

The Rodadero, Qocha Chincanas and Calispucyo

In front of the main defensive walls, a flat expanse of grassy ground – the esplanade – divides the fortress from a large outcrop of volcanic diorite. Intricately carved in places, and scarred with deep glacial striations, this rock, called the **Rodadero** ("sliding place"), was the site of an Inca throne. Originally there was a stone parapet surrounding this important *huaca*, and it's thought that the emperor would have sat here to oversee ceremonial gatherings at fiesta times, when there would have been processions, wrestling matches and running competitions. On the far side of this huge outcrop are larger recreational sliding areas, smoothed by the many centuries of Inca – and now tourists' – backsides.

From here you can see another large circular space called **Qocha Chincanas**, possibly an Inca graveyard, and on its far side the sacred spring of **Calispucyo**, where ceremonies to initiate boys into manhood were held. Excavations here have uncovered crystals and shells (some of the latter all the way from Ecuador), a sign usually associated with water veneration.

Qenko

Daily 7am–5.30pm • Entry by Cusco Tourist Ticket (see box, p.221)

The large limestone outcrop of **QENKO** was another important Inca *huaca*. This great stone, carved with a complex pattern of steps, seats, geometric reliefs and puma designs, illustrates the critical role of the rock cult in the realm of Inca cosmological beliefs (the surrounding foothills are dotted with carved rocks and elaborate stone terraces). The name of this *huaca* derives from the Quechua word *quenqo*, meaning "labyrinth" or "zigzag", and refers to the patterns laboriously carved into the upper, western edge of the stone. At an annual festival priests would pour sacrificial llama blood into a bowl at the serpent-like top of the main zigzag channel; if it flowed out through the left-hand bifurcation, this was a bad omen for the fertility of the year to come. If, on the other hand, it continued the full length of the channel and poured onto the rocks below, this was a good omen.

The stone may also be associated with solstice and equinox ceremonies, fertility rites and even marriage rituals (there's a twin seat close to the top of Qenko which looks very much like a lovers' kissing bench). Right on top of the stone, two prominent round nodules are carved onto a plinth. These appear to be mini versions of **intihuatanas** ("hitching posts" of the sun), found at many Inca sacred sites – local guides claim that on the **summer solstice**, at around 8am, the nodules' shadow looks like a puma's face and a condor with wings outstretched at the same time. Along with the serpent-like divinatory channels, this would complete the three main layers of the Inca cosmos: sky (condor), earth (puma) and the underworld (snake).

The tunnels and caves

Beneath Qenko are several **tunnels and caves**, replete with impressive carved niches and steps, which may have been places for spiritual contemplation and communication with the forces of life and earth. It's been suggested that some of the niches may have been where the **mummies** of lesser nobles were kept.

The amphitheatre

At the top end of the *huaca*, behind the channelled section, the Incas constructed an impressive, if relatively small, semicircular **amphitheatre** with nineteen vaulted niches (probably seats for priests or nobles) facing in towards the impressive limestone. At the heart of the amphitheatre rises a natural **standing stone**, which from some angles looks like a frog (representative of the life-giving and cleansing power of rain) and from others like a puma, both creatures of great importance to pre-Conquest Peru.

Salapunco and around

Daily 24hr • Free

Yet another sacred *huaca*, though off the beaten track, the large rock outcrop of **SALAPUNCO** – also known as the Temple of the Moon and locally called Laqo – contains a number of small caves where the rock has been painstakingly carved. You can see worn relief work with puma and snake motifs on the external rock faces, while the caves hold altar-like platforms and niches that were probably used to house mummies. The largest of the caves is thought to have been a venue for ceremonies celebrating the full moon, as it sometimes is today, when an eerie silver light filters into the usually dark interior. Close to Salapunco there's another site, **K'usilluchayoq**, which has some more rock carvings.

Chacan and Quispe Huara

Daily 24hr • Free

An important but little-visited Inca site, **CHACAN** lies about 5km from Sacsayhuaman on the opposite side of the fortress from Qenko and the road to Tambo Machay.

Chacan itself was a revered spring, and you can see a fair amount of terracing, some carved rocks and a few buildings in the immediate vicinity; like Tambo Machay, it demonstrates the importance of water as an ever-changing, life-giving force in Inca religion. A pleasant but more difficult walk (10min) leads down the Tica Tica stream to **Quispe Huara** ("crystal loincloth"), where a two- to three-metre-high pyramid shape has been cut into the rock. Close by are some Inca stone walls, probably once part of a ritual bathing location. It's easy to get lost visiting these two sights – you're better off going with a guide (see p.221).

Pukapukara

Daily 7am–6pm • Entry by Cusco Tourist Ticket (see box, p.221)

A relatively small ruin, **PUKAPUKARA**, meaning "Red Fort", is around 11km from the city, impressively situated overlooking the Cusco Valley, right beside the main Cusco–Pisac road. A good example of how the Incas combined recreation and spirituality along with social control and military defence, Pukapukara is well worth the trip.

Although in many ways reminiscent of a small European castle, with a commanding **esplanade** topping its semicircle of protective wall, Pukapukara is more likely to have been a hunting lodge for the emperor than simply a defensive position. Thought to have been built by the Emperor Pachacutec, it commands views towards glaciers to the south of the Cusco Valley. Easily defended on three sides, it could have contained only a relatively small garrison and may have been a guard post between Cusco and the Sacred Valley, which lies to the northeast; it could also have had a sacred function, as it has excellent **views** towards the *apu* of Ausangate and is ideally placed to keep tabs on the flow of people and produce from the Sacred Valley to Cusco.

Tambo Machay

Daily 7am–6pm • Entry by Cusco Tourist Ticket (see box, p.221)

One of the more impressive Inca baths, at 3765m **TAMBO MACHAY**, or Temple of the Waters, is thought to have been a place for ritual as well as possibly also for physical cleansing and purification. Situated at a spring near the Incas' hunting lodge, its main construction lies in a sheltered gully where some superb Inca masonry again emphasizes their fascination with water.

The ruins basically consist of three tiered **platforms**. The top one holds four trapezoidal niches that were likely used to place statues of gods; on the next level, underground water emerges directly from a hole at the base of the stonework, and from here cascades down to the bottom platform. On this platform the spring water splits into two channels, both pouring the last metre down to ground level. This may have been a site for **ritual bathing**; the quality of the stonework suggests that its use was possibly restricted to the higher nobility, who perhaps used the baths only on ceremonial occasions.

About 1km further up the gully, you'll come to a small **grotto** where there's a pool large enough for bathing, even in the dry season. While it shows no sign of Inca stonework, the hills to either side of the stream are dotted with stone terraces and caves, one or two of which still have remnants of walls at their entrance. In Inca, *machay* means "cave", suggesting that these were an important local feature, perhaps as sources of water for Tambo Machay and Pukapukara.

ARRIVAL AND DEPARTURE   **INCA SITES NEAR CUSCO**

ON FOOT

These sites are an energetic day's walk from Cusco, but   you'll probably want to devote a whole day to Sacsayhuaman and leave the others until you're more

4

adjusted to the rarefied air. You could also take a taxi from the centre of Cusco up to Tambo Machay (S/25–30; 15min), and make your way down on foot from there.

Sacsayhuaman Although it looks relatively close to central Cusco, it's quite a steep 40min, 2km climb up to the ruins of Sacsayhuaman from the Plaza de Armas. The simplest route is up C Suecia, then right along the narrow cobbled street of Wayna Pata to Pumacurco, which heads steeply up to a small café-bar with a balcony that commands superb views over the city. It's only another 10min from the café, following the signposted steps all the way up to the ruins. By now you're beyond Cusco's built-up areas and walking in countryside, and there's a well-worn path and a crude stairway that takes you right up to the heart of the fortress.

Qenko An easy 20min walk from Sacsayhuaman. Head towards the Cusco–Pisac road along a track from the warden's hut on the northeastern edge of Sacsayhuaman, and Qenko is just over the other side of the main road; the route is straightforward but poorly signposted.

Salapunco Walk for 20min uphill and through the trees above Qenko, to the right of the small hill, along the path (keeping the houses to your right), then come out onto the fields and turn right. It's also possible to walk down to the Plaza de Armas from nearby K'usilluchayoq via interconnecting trails that initially go through some new barrios above the main Cusco–Pisac road, then down to San Blas.

Chacan Chacan can be safely, though not easily, reached in the dry season (May–Sept) by following the main road from the Rodadero at Sacsayhuaman for about 50m; turn left on the dirt track, walk for about 30min or so until you see a small artificial lagoon on your left. Continue walking up the road for another 5–10 min; you will see a path on your left. Follow this path for about 15min until you reach Chacan.

Quispe Huara A difficult walk leads from Chacan down the Tica Tica stream (keep to the right-hand side of the stream and stay well above it) to Quispe Huara. You really need a local map to find your way with any certainty.

Pukapukara Between one and two hours' cross-country walk, uphill from Sacsayhuaman and Qenko (longer if you keep to the sinuous main road).

Tambo Machay Walk for less than 15min along a signposted track that leads off the main road just north of Pukapukara.

BY BUS

If you'd rather start from the top and work your way downhill, it's possible to take one of the regular buses from Cusco to Pisac and Urubamba. Empresa Clorinda buses leave from C Puputi 208, one block below Recoleta and two blocks up from Av de la Cultura at the junction with Ejercicios, just beyond the Estadio Universitario. Other regular buses depart from Tullumayo 207. Ask to be dropped off at the highest of the sites, Tambo Machay, from where it's a relatively easy 2hr walk back into the centre of Cusco, or at Qenko, which is closer to Sacsayhuaman and the city.

BY TRANVÍA

A wooden bus which resembles a tram car – Tranvía de Cusco (Mon–Sat 8.30am, 10am, 11.30am, 2pm, 3.30pm, 5pm & 6.30pm; 1hr 15min; S/25, students with ISIC card S/15; ☎ 084 223 840) – takes a scenic route from Plaza Regocijo up through the historic centre to Sacsayhuaman and back most days (a good option to avoid the tiring experience of walking up there before you've really acclimatized to the altitude), visiting nearly forty other places in Cusco en route.

BY HORSEBACK TOUR

You could also take a horseback tour (around S/40–50 for a couple of hours), incorporating most of these sites. Tours usually start and finish at Sacsayhuaman or Qenko (S/7–8 taxi ride from the centre of Cusco).

The Sacred Valley

The **SACRED VALLEY**, or Vilcamayo to the Incas, about 30km northwest of Cusco, traces its winding, astonishingly beautiful course from here down towards Urubamba, Ollantaytambo and eventually **Machu Picchu** (see p.255), the most famous ruin in South America and a place that – no matter how jaded you are or how commercial it seems – is never anything short of awe-inspiring. The steep-sided river valley opens out into a narrow but very fertile alluvial plain, which was well exploited agriculturally by the Incas. Even within 30km or so of the valley, there are several microclimates allowing specializations in different fruits, maizes and local plants. The **river** itself starts in the high Andes south of Cusco and is called the Vilcanota river until it reaches the Sacred Valley; from here on downriver it's known as the Río Urubamba, a magnificent and energetic torrent which flows on right down into the jungle to merge with other major headwaters of the Amazon.

GETTING TO AND AROUND THE SACRED VALLEY

The Sacred Valley and Machu Picchu need to be approached differently, though it is quite possible, even logical, to start in one and then move on to the other. There are three main **transport hubs** in the Sacred Valley – Pisac, Urubamba and Ollantaytambo – all best reached by colectivo minibuses or taxis from Cusco. Travelling up and down the valley between them is simple enough; pick up a colectivo, taxi or local bus to follow the one main road that hugs the valley floor, keeping fairly close to the Río Urubamba. **Machu Picchu** (see p.255) is further down the valley and is almost exclusively accessible on foot – typically the Inca Trail hike – or by rail.

Standing guard over the two extremes of the Sacred Valley, the ancient **Inca citadels** of Pisac and Ollantaytambo perch high above the stunning Río Vilcanota–Urubamba and are among the most evocative ruins in Peru. **Pisac** itself is a small, pretty town with one of Peru's best artesanía markets, just 30km northeast of Cusco, close to the end of the Río Vilcanota's wild run from Urcos. Further downstream are the ancient villages of **Calca**, **Yucay** and **Urubamba**, the last of which has the most visitors' facilities and a developing reputation as a spiritual and meditation centre, yet somehow still retains its traditional Andean charm.

At the far northern end of the Sacred Valley, even the magnificent ancient town of **Ollantaytambo** is overwhelmed by the astounding temple-fortress clinging to the sheer cliffs beside it. The town is a very pleasant place to spend some time, with a decent choice of restaurants, and it is a convenient location in the heart of great trekking country. It makes an ideal base from which to take a tent and trek above one of the Urubamba's minor tributaries, or else tackle one of the **Salcantay** trails.

Beyond Ollantaytambo the route becomes too tortuous for any road to follow. Here, the valley closes in around the rail tracks, and the Río Urubamba begins to race and twist below **Machu Picchu** itself (see p.255).

Awana Kancha

Km 23 Carretera Cusco–Pisac • Daily 9am–5.30pm • ☎ 084 632 990 • ⊕ awanakancha.com

About 23km from Cusco and 7km before you reach Pisac, where the road starts steeply down into the Sacred Valley, **Awana Kancha** offers a rare opportunity to see alpacas and llamas up close, as well as traditional weaving in practice. Quality alpaca wool products are for sale too.

Pisac

A vital Inca road once snaked its way up the canyon that enters the Sacred Valley at **PISAC**, and the ruined **citadel**, which sits at the entrance to the gorge, controlled a strategic route connecting the Inca Empire with Paucartambo, on the borders of the eastern jungle. Less than an hour from Cusco by bus, the town is now most commonly visited – apart from a look at the citadel – for its morning **market**, which takes place three times a week.

In addition, the main local **fiesta** – Virgen del Carmen (from around July 15–18) – is a good alternative to the simultaneous but more remote Paucartambo festival of the same name (see box, p.270), with processions, music, dance groups, the usual firecracker celebrations and food stalls around the plaza.

Plaza Constitución

Apart from the road and river bridge, the hub of Pisac activity is around **Plaza Constitución**, where you'll find most of the restaurants and the few hotels that exist, as well as the popular **market** and the town's quaint **church**.

Iglesia San Pedro Apóstol

Plaza Constitución

Commerce bustles around the **Iglesia San Pedro Apóstol**, an unusually narrow concrete church located in Pisac's central market plaza, which is dominated by an ancient and massive *pisonay* tree. The church is named for St Peter, the patron saint of Pisac.

Pisac market

Plaza Constitución • Craft market daily 8am–5pm

The thriving **market** is held in and around the town's main square, where you can buy hand-painted ceramic beads and pick up the occasional bargain. There are a number of excellent artesanía stands open daily, selling all manner of goods from baby alpaca blankets to jumpers. The best day to visit the market is on a Sunday, when locals descend onto the town to sell their fresh produce.

Pisac's citadel

Daily 7am–6pm • Entry by Cusco Tourist Ticket (see box, p.221)

Set high above a valley floor patchworked by patterned fields and rimmed by centuries of terracing amid giant landslides, the **citadel** displays magnificent stonework – water ducts and steps have been cut out of solid rock – and **panoramas**. The citadel takes around an hour and a half to **climb up to** – only attempt it if you're fit and already well adjusted to the altitude. Alternatively, take a **tour** – try one of the agents in Cusco (see p.221) – or pick up a taxi or colectivo from the river bridge.

From the saddle on the hill, you can see over the Sacred Valley to the north: wide and flat at the base, but towering towards the heavens into green and rocky pinnacles. To the south, the valley closes in, but the mountains continue, massive and steep-sided, casting shadows on one another. Below the saddle, a semicircle of buildings is gracefully positioned on a large natural balcony under row upon row of fine stone terraces thought to represent a partridge's wing (*pisac* meaning "partridge").

Templo del Sol

In the upper sector of the ruins, the citadel's **Templo del Sol** (Temple of the Sun) is the equal of anything at Machu Picchu, and more than repays the exertions of the steep climb (20–30min from the car park). Reached by many of the dozens of paths that crisscross their way up through the citadel, it's poised in a flattish saddle on a great spur protruding north–south into the Sacred Valley. The temple was built around an outcrop of volcanic rock, its peak carved into a **"hitching post"** for the sun. The hitching post alone is intriguing: the angles of its base suggest that it may have been used for keeping track of important stars, or for calculating the changing seasons with the accuracy so critical to the smooth running of the Inca Empire. Above the temple lie

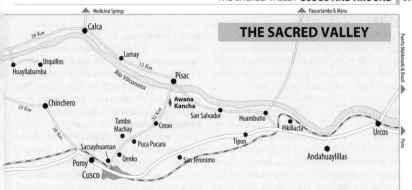

still more ruins, largely unexcavated, and among the higher crevices and rocky overhangs several ancient burial sites are hidden.

ARRIVAL AND GETTING AROUND   PISAC

By bus Buses are much slower than colectivos, and take about 1hr 30 min from Cusco (every 30min).

By colectivo Colectivo minibuses leave from Puputi in Cusco (every 15min; 45min), dropping passengers off on Av Amazonas to the west of town. If you're going to the citadel, take a taxi or colectivo from Av Amazonas up to the site car park, just below the main ruins. Leaving Pisac for Cusco or going on down the valley to Calca and Urubamba, if you haven't got a taxi or tour bus organized, wait on Av Amazonas and pick up a colectivo, bus or taxi as they pass.

On foot If you want to walk up to the citadel from the village (2hr or more), start on the path that leads off, uphill from Plaza Constitución, along the left flank of Iglesia San Pedro Apóstol.

By taxi Taxis cost S/60–70 one-way from Cusco (45min).

By tour Many people arrive in Pisac with an organized tour from Cusco (see p.221).

ACCOMMODATION

The only time when accommodation in Pisac may be hard to find is in **September**, when the village fills up with pilgrims heading to the nearby sanctuary of Huanca, home of a small shrine which is held very sacred by local inhabitants. In and around Pisac there's a surprising selection of places to stay.

Hospedaje Chaska Wasi Av Amazonas s/n ☎ 985 903 868, ⊛ pisachotel.com. This pleasant *hospedaje* is Pisac's best budget option, with warm and welcoming rooms set around a large courtyard. There's a kitchen for guests' use, an outdoor lounge hut with cushioned seating and a meditation room decked out in mellow colours. Dorms S/30, doubles S/110

Hotel Royal Inka 2km northeast of Pisac ☎ 084 203 064, ⊛ royalinkahotel.pe. A series of pretty flowered walkways here lead to comfortable rooms with brightly painted doors. Facilities include two large jacuzzis, table tennis, table football, a 98-person cinema and an Olympic-size pool that is also open to non-guests (Mon–Fri 8am–4pm, Sat & Sun 9am–5pm). It's possible to camp here, too. Doubles S/277; camping S/25 per person.

★ **Melissa Wasi** Sector Matará ☎ 084 797 589, ⊛ melissa-wasi.com. This is a lovely place to stay with a large garden and pretty rooms with clay tiles decorated with local materials. There are also duplex bungalows sleeping four. The restaurant is built around natural rock,

and the owners' son, a shaman, hosts Ayahuasca ceremonies, too. There's a barbeque area, as well as yoga classes and a massage centre. Bungalows S/375, doubles S/275

Paz y Luz 1km southeast of Pisac ☎ 084 203 204, ⊛ pazyluzperu.com. This hotel and healing centre offers healing workshops as well as reiki, shiatsu, yoga and astrology sessions. It's a quiet and relaxing place to hang out, with its own salad and herb garden and use of kitchen for guests. The spick-and-span rooms are nicely decorated, with wooden beams, warm colours and en-suite bathrooms. S/190

Pisac Inn Plaza Constitución 333 ☎ 084 203 062, ⊛ pisacinn.com. This is an excellent option right in the heart of town, offering eleven lovely rooms featuring wooden furniture and natural materials, including rustic lamps made with goat leather. The small lounge and TV area has sofas and a bamboo roof, and the hotel's restaurant, *Cuchara de Palo*, is one of the best in town. S/182

EATING AND DRINKING

Café Mullu Plaza de Armas 352 ☎084 203 073, ⊚mullu .pe. This laidback art café right on the main square has wonderful views over the market from its little balcony. The cuisine is international with an emphasis on eastern dishes prepared using local products, including Thai curry (S/27), wok of alpaca (S/39) and pad Thai (S/32). Daily 9am–9pm.

Cuchara de Palo Plaza Constitución 333 ☎084 203 062, ⊚pisacinn.com/restaurant. This cosy, welcoming restaurant with a warming fireplace serves wonderfully presented Andean dishes both in the dining area and on the small patio full of potted plants and flowers. The menu includes *quinoa* soup (S/22) and *lomo saltado* (beef loin strips sautéed with onion, tomato, yellow chilli), served with fries and rice; S/50). Pizzas (S/18) are cooked every Sun in the clay oven. Daily 7am–9pm.

Doña Clorinda La Rinconada ☎084 203 051, ⊚restaurant_dona_clorinda_eirl@yahoo.es. This pleasant restaurant about 1km from town has seating in an open-fronted area with tables spilling out onto the garden. The cuisine here is Andean, with a number of *quinoa*-based dishes, beef and trout, as well as some vegetarian options. Mains from S/22. Daily 9am–5pm.

Horno Pumachayoc Av Federico Zamalloa s/n ☎984 012 575. This bakery and restaurant serves tasty hand-made *empañadas* (S/4) made with natural local ingredients. The dough is made from seven types of flour, including *quinoa* and coca, and there are five different fillings to choose from, including cheese and tomato and tropical fruits. The *chicha morada* is particularly good at S/4 a glass. Daily 6am–6pm.

Intihuatana Lounge C Pardo 601 ☎993 075 352. This laidback vegetarian café and restaurant features colourful dining areas that give onto an interior garden dotted with beanbags. The menu includes healthy juices (S/6), as well as plenty of veggie dishes such as tacos with guacamole, black beans, cheese and tortilla (S/14). They also rent tastefully furnished rooms that are kept in spick-and-span condition (S/190). Sun–Fri 9.30am–7.30pm.

Ulrike's C Pardo 613 ☎084 203 195. This German-run place with colourful partitioned dining areas set over two floors offers international dishes including a number of veggie options. Thin-crust pizzas are baked in the wood-burning oven on Tues, Thurs, Sat and Sun, and the menu includes curries (S/15), salads (S/15) and Peruvian *causas* (S/12). There's a good-value set-lunch menu for S/22, and all-day breakfast, too. Daily 8am–9pm.

Lamay and Calca

Take any colectivo, minibus or bus heading down the valley from the town side of the Pisac river bridge (Calca 30min)

Known for its medicinal springs, the first significant village between Pisac and Urubamba is **Lamay**, just 12km away. High above this village, on the other side of the Río Vilcanota and just out of sight, are the beautiful Inca terraces of Huchiq'osqo. A little further down the road you come to the larger village of **Calca**, where there is nothing much of interest to tourists. Moving down the valley from here the climate improves and you see pears, peaches and cherries growing in abundance. In July and August vast piles of maize sit beside the road waiting to be used as cattle feed.

Machacancha

The popular **thermal baths** of **Machacanca** are within an hour and a half's walk of Calca, signposted from the town. Situated under the hanging glaciers of Mount Sahuasiray, this place was favoured by the Incas for the fertility of its soil, and you can still see plenty of maize cultivation here.

■ ACCOMMODATION		● CAFÉS & RESTAURANTS	
Hospedaje Chaska Wasi	2	Café Mullu	4
Melissa Wasi	3	Cuchara de Palo	5
Paz y Luz	4	Doña Clorinda	1
Pisac Inn	5	Horno Pumachayoc	6
Hotel Royal Inka	1	Intihuatana Lounge	2
		Ulrike's	3

INCA FIESTAS

Around the end of September and start of October every year local **fiestas** and celebrations take place around Lamay and Calca, which date back at least to early Inca times. The main local ritual theme for the festival is **water**, and there are strong links to a mythic experience high in the hills and tied to the moving shadows of **Mount Pitusiray**: every year around the beginning of October, the mountain casts shadows over neighbouring peaks and cliffs. Over several days the shadow of Pitusiray, considered to be a solar clock, moves in a dynamic and very clear representation of a prostrate Inca being leapt upon and transformed by a black puma or jaguar; it has to be seen to be believed. With this visual effect on the landscape in mind, a festival is now held on the first Sunday in October and based at the **Inca ruins of Urco**, also dedicated to water, which are located a 2km walk above the village of Calca. For information on the festival ask at the Cusco tourist information offices (see p.221).

Yucay

The small town of **Yucay,** 3.5km east of Urubamba, had its moment in Peruvian history when, under the Incas, Huayna Capac, father of Huascar and Atahualpa, had his palace here. You can admire the ruined but finely dressed stone walls of another **Inca palace** (probably the country home of Sayri Tupac, though also associated with an Inca princess) on the Plaza Manco II.

Urubamba

About 80km from Cusco via Pisac or around 60km via Chinchero, **URUBAMBA** is only a short way down the main road from Yucay's Plaza Manco II, and it is here that the Río Vilcanota becomes the Río Urubamba (though many people still refer to this stretch as the Vilcanota). While it has little in the way of obvious historic interest, the town has good **facilities** and is situated in the shadow of the beautiful Chicon and Pumahuanca glaciers. At weekends there's a large **market** on Jirón Palacio, while Cerámicas Seminario (Av Berriozábal 405, ☎084 201 002, ⓦceramicaseminario.com; daily 8am–7pm) gives visitors an insight into ancient pottery techniques and has a range of products for sale.

Plaza de Armas

The laidback and attractive **Plaza de Armas** has palm trees and pines surrounded by interesting topiary. At the heart of the plaza is a small fountain topped by a maize plant sculpture, but everything defers to the red sandstone **Iglesia San Pedro**, with its stacked columns below two small belfries. The church's cool interior has a vast, three-tier gold-leaf altar, and at midday light streams through the glass-topped cupola.

ARRIVAL
URUBAMBA

By bus The Terminal Terrestre is to the west of the town centre. Buses connect Pisac with Urubamba (every 20min; 1hr 30min); Ollantaytambo (20min; 30min); for Calca (40min) and Chincero (1hr), catch a Cusco-bound bus.

By train PeruRail trains depart to Machu Picchu Pueblo from the *Tambo del Inka* hotel in Urubamba several times a week, taking roughly 2hr 30min each way. Check ⓦperurail.com for the latest schedules.

By colectivo Colectivos to Urubamba leave from C Pavitos in Cusco (every 20min; 2hr) from about 5–6am.

By taxi Taxis from Cusco to Urubamba charge around S/90.

ACCOMMODATION

URUBAMBA

Hotel Tambo del Inka Av Ferrocarril ☎084 201 071 or ☎084 201 126, ⓦlibertador.com.pe. A large resort hotel with over a hundred rooms, mainly well-appointed bungalows, and a conference centre with internet access, a pool and tennis courts. **S/900**

Hospedaje Los Jardines Av Convención 459 ☎084 201 331, ⓦhttp://losjardines.weebly.com. A very pleasant budget choice a few blocks east of the main square with rooms giving onto a verdant garden area dotted with chairs and parasols. Rooms are simply furnished but welcoming, and all feature private facilities and hot-water showers. **S/90**

Hostal Los Perales Pasaje Arenales 102 **☎**084 201 151, **w**ecolodgeurubamba.com. This pleasant guesthouse features six neat rooms set around a large overgrown garden. There's table tennis and a billiards table, too. The congenial owner speaks some English. **S/70**

OUTSIDE URUBAMBA

★**Belmond Hotel Rio Sagrado** Km 75.8, Carretera Urubamba-Ollantaytambo **☎**084 201 631, **w**belmond .com. Located on the banks of the Urubamba River, this top-end hotel with lush tranquil gardens home to grazing alpacas is built using natural materials. Constructed from natural stone and wood, the elegant sun-lit rooms all offer stunning views of the river and the surrounding mountains. There's an inviting outdoor heated pool, along with a spa with jacuzzi where it's easy to wallow away for longer than planned, taking in the marvellous garden views. **S/1065**

La Capilla Lodge Rumichaca Km 72 **☎**084 633 164, **w**capillalodge.com. A secluded Peruvian-English owned place where rooms, set around an attractive leafy garden, feature dream catchers, private bathrooms and wooden or carpeted floors. The hotel's *Alma* pub has a very British touch to it, with draped flags and walls adorned with dozens of paintings, and there are board games and a book exchange, too. The hotel also has secure parking facilities. **S/155**

★**K'uychi Rumi** Km 71.5 Sector Rumichaca **☎**084 201 169, **w**urubamba.com. This lovely guesthouse has seven welcoming *casitas* dotted around a garden area with pebbled walkways. The cosy chalets sleeping four feature kitchenette and living area, and three friendly dogs guard the premises day and night. **S/495**

Qawana Lodge Km 57.2 Carretera Pisac–Urubamba **☎**084 632 086 or **☎**974 791 456, **w**qawana.com. This tranquil, welcoming lodge has a wonderful riverside location. The hotel restaurant, serving a range of Peruvian dishes, overlooks the gushing Urubamba River, while rooms have farmland or garden views and mostly feature stone and wooden interiors. **S/300**

Sol & Luna Fundo Huincho Lote A5, **☎**084 201 620, **w**hotelsolyluna.com. An upmarket hotel offering three categories of rooms dotted around a lush garden area bursting with colourful flowers; the stylishly decorated deluxe rooms feature wonderful artworks and fireplaces, while the premium rooms have unique wooden tables originally used as saints' altars during religious celebrations. The hotel's *Wayra* restaurant has a well-stocked wine cellar, where wine-tasting sessions are regularly held. **S/850**

Villa Urubamba Camino Real s/n, Rumichaca Baja **☎**084 205 133, **w**villaurubamba.com. The well-appointed pads here are set around a large garden area, with a couple of rooms featuring exposed rock that adds a pleasant touch. There are four domes where yoga and

ACCOMMODATION		CAFÉS & RESTAURANTS	
Belmond Hotel Rio Sagrado	6	El Huacatay	7
Hotel Tambo del Inka	8	Kaia	6
Hospedaje Los Jardines	9	Kampu	1
Hostal Los Perales	7	Paca Paca	3
K'uychi Rumi	1	Q'anela	5
La Capilla Lodge	2	Red Valentina	2
Qawana Lodge	10	Tres Keros	4
Sol & Luna	3		
Villa Urubamba	5		
Willka Tika	5		

meditation sessions, healing ceremonies, seminars and workshops take place. **S/285**

Willka Tika Paradero Rumichaka ☎+1 707 202 5340 (international), ⓦwillkatika.com. This peaceful zen of a place with a stunning garden offers a range of outdoor activities and encourages spiritual practices. It's the ideal place to switch off from the outside world while living in well-appointed surrounds, where you can take part in ceremonies led by Andean healers while nurturing the body and soul with freshly picked organic fruit and veg from the garden. There are two yoga studios, and the hotel offers all-inclusive ten-day yoga packages, too. **S/987**

EATING AND DRINKING

★**El Huacatay** Jr Arica 620 ☎084 201 790, ⓦelhuacatay.com. An excellent choice, with tables set around a leafy garden area that is the perfect spot to while away a few hours over a refreshing juice. The innovative cuisine uses local produce, incorporating Mediterranean, Asian and Peruvian influences, with ricotta croquettes (S/24) and green lima bean salad with duck prosciutto (S/24) featured on the menu. Mon–Sat 12.30–9.30pm.

Kaia Av Berriozabal 111 ☎084 201 387. A child-friendly restaurant specializing in organic and veggie dishes, along with invigorating juices and smoothies. The atmosphere is welcoming and laidback, with leafy lounge areas and colourful decor. The menu includes zucchini carpaccio (S/12), quinotto (*quinoa* risotto with vegetables; S/22) and quesadillas (S/12). There's also a daily set menu (S/18–24). Tues–Sun noon–9pm

Kampu Jr Sagrario 342 ☎974 955 977. This laidback curry place a stone's throw away from the main square has chairs splattered with paint and seating at wooden tables in a series of little dining areas. The menu, scribbled on the board in colourful chalk, includes a range of curries including beef (S/40), chicken (S/35) and vegetarian (S/30). Fri–Wed 1–9pm.

Paca Paca Av Mariscal Castilla 640 ☎084 201 181. A great choice, with clay oven pizzas (S/24) and a particularly tasty *lomo a las cuatro pimientas* (loin of beef with four pepper sauce) accompanied by *quinoa* risotto; (S/40) served in a pleasant setting with wooden tables and an eclectic choice of knick-knacks decorating the walls. Tues–Sun 1–9pm.

Q'anela Jr Grau 654 ☎084 201 373. A welcoming place with a little internal garden area in which the management hope they will soon be able to seat guests too, although the crisp mountain area means you may want to bring a warm jumper. The cuisine is creole, and includes staples such as *ají de gallina* (S/33). Daily noon–10pm.

Red Valentina Jr Grau 323 ☎980 964 175. The small entrance of this atmospheric bar opens up onto a larger room with bamboo ceiling, stone floors and wooden chairs that brims with character. Things liven up on Wed & Fri eve when local live bands take centre stage. A beer is about S/10. Daily 9am–3pm & 6–9.30pm.

★**Tres Keros** Av Torrechayoc ☎084 201 701. This superb restaurant is one of the very best in the Sacred Valley and is not to be missed. The warm atmospheric interior features candle-lit tables and a fireplace, while beautiful ceramic plates adorn the walls. The food is all home-made, using natural produce from the Sacred Valley or high-quality imported ingredients – the *lomo saltado* (S/42) is simply exceptional, as is the trout with butter sauce (S/38), and there are plenty of veggie dishes too from home-made pastas with pesto to curries. The pisco sours are also worth a try. Wed–Mon 12.30–3.30pm & 6.30–9.30pm.

Around Urubamba

Because of its convenient location and plentiful facilities, Urubamba makes an ideal base from which to explore the mountains and lower hills around the Sacred Valley, which are filled with sites of jaw-dropping splendour. The eastern side of the valley is formed by the **Cordillera Urubamba**, a range of snowcapped peaks dominated by the summits of Chicon and Veronica. Many of the ravines can be hiked, alone or with local guides (found only through the main hotels and hospedajes) and on the trek up from the town you can take in stupendous views of Chicon.

Moray

Daily 7am–6pm • Entry by Cusco Tourist Ticket (see box, p.221) • Best visited as part of a private tour of the Sacred Valley

A stunning Inca site, part agricultural centre and part ceremonial, **Moray** lies about 6km west of Maras village on the Chinchero side of the river, within a two- to three-hour walk from Urubamba. The ruins are deep, bowl-like depressions in the earth, the largest comprising seven concentric circular stone terraces, facing inward and diminishing in radius like a multi-layered roulette wheel.

Salinas de Maras

4km walk northeast from Moray • Best visited as part of a private tour of the Sacred Valley

The **Salinas de Maras** (Maras salt pans), still in use after more than four hundred years, are situated 4km on from the village of Maras, and a similar distance from Moray. Cross the river by the footbridge in the village, turn right, then after a little over 100m downstream along the riverbank, turn left past the cemetery and up the canyon along the salty creek. After this you cross the stream and follow the path cut into the cliffside to reach the salt pans, which are soon visible if still a considerable uphill hike away. The trail offers spectacular views of the valley and mountains, while the Inca salt pans themselves are set gracefully against an imposing mountain backdrop. A **scenic trail** (about an hour's walk) leads down through the salt pans and on to the Urubamba River below, where there's a footbridge across to the village of Tarabamba, which is on the road for Urubamba (6km) or Ollantaytambo; colectivos pass every twenty minutes or so in both directions.

Chinchero

CHINCHERO ("Village of the Rainbow"), an old colonial settlement with a great market, lies 3762m above sea level, 28km (40min) northwest of Cusco and off the main road, overlooking the Sacred Valley, with the Vilcabamba range and the snowcapped peak of Salcantay dominating the horizon to the west. The bus ride here takes you up to the Pampa de Anta, once a huge lake but now relatively dry pasture, surrounded by snowcapped *nevadas*. The town itself is a small, rustic place, where the local women, who crowd the main plaza during the market, still wear traditional dress. Largely built of stone and adobe, the town blends perfectly with the magnificent display of Inca architecture, ruins and megalithic carved rocks, relics of the Inca veneration of nature deities. The best time to visit is on September 8 for the lively traditional **fiesta**. Failing that, the Sunday-morning **market** in the lower part of town, reached along Calle Manco II, is smaller and less touristy than Pisac's but has attractive local craftwork for sale.

Plaza Principal

Uphill from the market, along the cobbled steps and streets, you'll find a vast **plaza**, which may have been the original Inca marketplace. It's bounded on one side by an impressive wall reminiscent of Sacsayhuaman's ramparts, though not as massive – it too was constructed on three levels, and ten classical Inca trapezoidal niches can be seen along its surface. On the western perimeter of the plaza, the raised Inca stonework is dominated by a carved **stone throne**, near which are puma and monkey formations.

Iglesia de Chinchero

Tues, Thurs & Sun 8am–5pm • Free (donations welcome)

Dating from the early seventeenth century, the colonial adobe **Iglesia de Chinchero** was built on top of an Inca temple or palace, perhaps belonging to the Inca emperor **Tupac Yupanqui**, who particularly favoured Chinchero as an out-of-town resort – most of the area's aqueducts and terraces, many of which are still in use today, were built at his command. The church itself boasts frescoes and **paintings**, which, though decaying, are still very beautiful and evocative of the town's colonial past. Many pertain to the **Cusqueña school** and celebrated local artist Mateo Cuihuanito, the most interesting depicting the forces led by local chief Pumacahua against the rebel Tupac Amaru II in the late eighteenth century.

ARRIVAL AND DEPARTURE   **CHINCHERO**

By colectivo Colectivos to Urubamba leave from Cusco's C Pavitos, passing through Chincero (every 20min; 45min).

By taxi Taxis from Cusco to Chinchero charge around S/50.

ACCOMMODATION AND EATING

★**La Casa de Barro** C Miraflores 147 ☎ 084 306 031, ⓦ lacasadebarro.com. This homely lodge is an excellent place to base yourself as you explore the Sacred Valley. Rooms, with floral wall designs, mellow lighting and woolly blankets, are warm and welcoming, while the restaurant, open to non-guests, serves excellent creole and international dishes in a cosy setting with fireplace. S/255

Ollantaytambo and around

The picturesque little town of **OLLANTAYTAMBO** with its cobblestone streets and ancient irrigation canals serves as an excellent base for trekking and biking. Coming down the valley from Urubamba the river runs smoothly between a series of impressive Inca terraces that gradually diminish in size. Just before the town, the rail line reappears and the road climbs a small hill to an ancient **plaza**.

As one of the region's tourist hotspots, and a popular overnight stop en route to Machu Picchu (see p.255), Ollantaytambo can get very busy in high season, making it hard to escape the scores of other travellers. At heart, though, it's a small but still very traditional settlement, worth enjoying over a few days, particularly during its highly colourful **fiestas** (see box below), when local folk-dancing takes place in the main plaza. Many women still wear traditional clothing, and it's common to see them gather in the plaza with their intricately woven *manta* shawls, black-and-red skirts with colourful zigzag patterns and inverted red and black hats.

Beyond Ollantaytambo, the Sacred Valley becomes a subtropical, raging river course, surrounded by towering mountains and dominated by the snowcapped peak of Salcantay; the town is also a popular base for **rafting** trips (see box, p.249).

Brief history

The valley here was occupied by a number of pre-Inca cultures, notably the Chanapata (800–300 BC), the Qotacalla (500–900 AD) and the Killki (900–1420 AD), after which the Incas dominated only until the 1530s, when the Spanish arrived.

The legend of Ollantay

Legend has it that **Ollantay** was a rebel Inca general who took arms against Pachacutec over the affections of the Lord Inca's daughter, the Nusta Cusi Collyu. However, historical evidence shows that a fourteen-kilometre canal, that still feeds the town today, was built to bring water here from the Laguna de Yanacocha, which was probably Pachacutec's private estate. The later Inca Huayna Capac is thought to have been responsible for the trapezoidal Plaza Maynyaraqui and the largely unfinished but impressive and megalithic temples.

A strategic location

Ollantaytambo was built as an Inca **administrative centre** rather than a town and is laid out in the form of a maize corn cob: it's one of the few surviving examples of an **Inca grid system**, with a plan that can be seen from vantage points high above it, especially

---

OLLANTAYTAMBO'S FIESTAS

Ollantaytambo's vibrant **fiestas** are a sight to behold, particularly the Festival of the Cross, Corpus Christi and Ollantaytambo Raymi (generally on the Sunday after Cusco's Inti Raymi), and at Christmas, when locals wear flowers and decorative grasses in their hats. On the **Fiesta de Reyes**, around January 6, there's a solemn procession around town of the three *Niños Reyes* (Child Kings), sacred effigies, one of which is brought down from the sacred site of Marcaquocha, about 10km away in the Patacancha Valley, the day before.

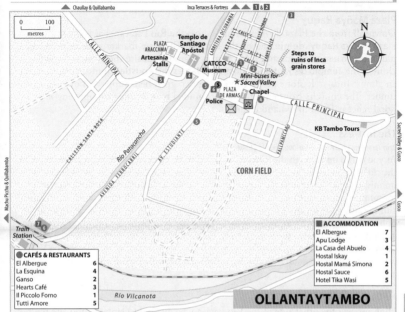

Chaullay & Quillabamba — Inca Terraces & Fortress — 1 & 2

Templo de Santiago Apóstol

PLAZA ARACCAMA

Artesanía Stalls

CATCCO Museum

Steps to ruins of Inca grain stores

Mini-buses for Sacred Valley

PLAZA DE ARMAS

Police

Chapel

CALLE PRINCIPAL

KB Tambo Tours

CORN FIELD

Train Station

Machu Picchu & Quillabamba

Río Patacancha

AVENIDA FERROCARRIL

CALLE PRINCIPAL

CALLEJON SANTA ROSA

AV. ESTUDIANTE

CALLE JANACANCHO

Sacred Valley & Cusco

Cusco

Río Vilcanota

OLLANTAYTAMBO

4

■ ACCOMMODATION

El Albergue	7
Apu Lodge	3
La Casa del Abuelo	4
Hostal Iskay	1
Hostal Mamá Simona	2
Hostal Sauce	6
Hotel Tika Wasi	5

● CAFÉS & RESTAURANTS

El Albergue	6
La Esquina	4
Ganso	2
Hearts Café	3
Il Piccolo Forno	1
Tutti Amore	5

from the hill opposite the fortress. An incredibly fertile sector of the Urubamba Valley, at 2800m above sea level and with comfortable temperatures of 11–23°C (52–73°F), good alluvial soils and water resources, this area was also the gateway to the **Antisuyo** (the Amazon corner of the Inca Empire) and a centre for tribute-gathering from the surrounding valleys.

As strategic protection for the entrance to the lower Urubamba Valley and an alternative gateway into the Amazon via the Pantiacolla Pass, this was the only Inca stronghold to have successfully resisted persistent Spanish attacks.

Rebel Inca Manco

After the unsuccessful siege of Cusco in 1536–37 (see p.207), the rebel Inca **Manco** and his die-hard force withdrew here, with **Hernando Pizarro** (Francisco's brother), some seventy horsemen, thirty foot-soldiers and a large contingent of native forces in hot pursuit. As they approached, they found that not only had the Incas diverted the Río Patacancha, making the valley below the fortress impassable, but they had also joined forces with neighbouring jungle tribes to form a massive army. After several desperate attempts to storm the stronghold, Pizarro and his men uncharacteristically slunk away under cover of darkness, leaving much of their equipment behind. However, the Spanish came back with reinforcements, and in 1537 Manco retreated further down the valley to Vitcos and Vilcabamba. In 1540, Ollantaytambo was entrusted to **Hernando Pizarro**, brother of the conquistador leader.

Plaza de Armas

The **Plaza de Armas** is the centre of civic life. Backstreets radiating from here are littered with stone water channels, which still come in very handy during the rainy season, carrying the gushing streams tidily away from the town and down to the Urubamba River.

Plaza Mañya Raquy

Downhill from the Plaza de Armas, just across the Río Patacancha, is the old Inca **Plaza Mañya Raquy**, dominated by the fortress. There are market stalls in the plaza plus a few artesanía shops and cafés nearby, mainly opposite the attractive small church, the **Templo de Santiago Apóstol (St James the Apostle)**. Built in 1620, it has an almost Inca-style stone belfry containing two great bells supported on an ancient timber. The church's front entrance is surrounded by a simple yet appealing *mestizo* floral relief painted in red and cream.

The fortress

Daily 7am–6pm • Entry with Cusco Tourist Ticket (see box, p.221)

As you climb up through the **fortress**, the solid stone terraces and the natural contours of the cliff remain frighteningly impressive. Above them, huge red granite blocks mark the unfinished sun temple near the top, where, according to legend, the internal organs of mummified Incas were buried. A dangerous path leads from this upper level around the cliff towards a large sector of agricultural terracing which follows the Río Patacancha uphill. From up above you can see down to the large Inca plaza and the impressive stone aqueducts which carried the water supply. Between here and the river you see the **Andenes de Mollequasa terraces** which, when viewed from the other side of the Urubamba Valley (a twenty-minute walk up the track from the train station), look like a pyramid.

Around Ollantaytambo

High up over the other side of the Río Patacancha, behind Ollantaytambo, are rows of **ruined buildings** originally thought to have been prisons but now considered likely to have been granaries. In front of these, it's quite easy to make out a gigantic, rather grumpy-looking **profile of a face** carved out of the rock, possibly an Inca sculpture of Wiraccochan, the mythical messenger from **Viracocha**, the major creator-god of Peru (see p.501). According to sixteenth- and seventeeth-century histories, such an image was indeed once carved, representing him as a man of great authority; this particular image's frown certainly implies presence, and this part of the mountain was also known as Wiraccochan Orcco ("peak of Viracocha's messenger"). From here, looking back towards the main Ollantaytambo fortress, it's possible to see the mountain, rocks and terracing forming the **image of a mother llama** with a young llama, apparently representing the myth of Catachillay, which relates to the water cycle and the Milky Way. *The Sacred Valley of the Incas – Myths and Symbols* (available in most Cusco bookshops), written by archeologists Fernando and Edgar Salazar, is a useful companion for interpreting the sites in this part of the valley.

ARRIVAL AND DEPARTURE

OLLANTAYTAMBO AND AROUND

BY TRAIN

The trains connecting Cusco with Ollantaytambo and Machu Picchu start at Poroy, 20–30min by taxi from Cusco. Ollantaytambo's train station is a few hundred metres down Av Estación (also known as Av Ferrocarril), about a 10min walk west of the main plaza.

Companies PeruRail and Inca Rail both offer the Ollantaytambo–Machu Picchu Pueblo route (roughly 2hr 20min), with slight variations in prices and timings, depending on the company, service level, season and day of the week. Each offers online booking, though they also have ticket offices in central Cusco (see Cusco train tickets p.220).

Tickets To be on the safe side, it's important to buy tickets well in advance (weeks ahead during high season) online

– from a tour agency (see p.221) or direct from one of the railway companies above – since carriages are often fully booked in high season. PeruRail also offers the exclusive Hiram Bingham train service (from US$475); check current timings and costs online. Return or one-way tickets are available, giving visitors the opportunity to stay overnight or longer in Machu Picchu.

BY BUS

Afternoon buses to Cusco (2hr) leave regularly from the small yard just outside the train station, often coinciding with the train timetable. In the mornings the buses depart mainly from Ollantaytambo's main plaza.

BY COLECTIVO
Colectivos from Cusco's C Pavitos travel to Ollantaytambo. Heading back to Cusco, head to the main plaza where you will find car and minibus colectivos (1hr 40min–2hr).

BY TAXI
Taxis from Cusco to Ollantaytambo charge about S/90. You can pick up a taxi in Ollantaytambo outside the train station.

INFORMATION AND TOURS

Tourist information At the time of writing there was no tourist information office in Ollantaytambo. Your best bet is to ask at your hotel or at KB Tambo Tours.
Tour operator KB Tambo Tours, Principal s/n

(☎084 204 133, ⓦkbperu.com) is by far the most experienced operator in the area, specializing in rafting. They organize trekking and mountain biking tours too; all activities start from around US$45/day

ACCOMMODATION

★ **El Albergue** Ollantaytambo train station ☎084 204 014, ⓦelalbergue.com. Located in Ollantaytambo station, this wonderful gem of a place offers rustic yet stylishly furnished rooms that give onto a leafy garden of passionflower, fuchsia and peach trees daily visited by hummingbirds. Paintings by North American owner Wendy

Weeks brighten up the premises, and the organic farm with chickens, sheep, pigs, alpaca and a vegetable garden supplies the hotel restaurant with fresh produce. **S/288**
★ **Apu Lodge** Lares s/n ☎084 797 162, ⓦapulodge .com. Tucked away off a quiet pedestrian street, this tranquil lodge is set in a lovely verdant area surrounded by

ACTIVITIES AROUND OLLANTAYTAMBO

Ollantaytambo is surrounded by stunning countryside and skyscraping mountain peaks, and offers a wealth of interesting **day-trip** options.

WALKING
It's easy enough just to choose a path leading up into the hills to the east and see where you get to, remembering, of course, that you will need a tent or have to get back to town by nightfall. Any route will provide a good **hike**, bringing you into close contact with local people in their gardens. There are also a number of organized **tours**, available from Ollantaytambo (see above) as well as from agents in Cusco.

TREKKING
The area around Ollantaytambo is an excellent spot to begin **trekking** into the hills. Here you can do hikes of half a day to a week or more; all have Inca ruins along the way. For a half or full day, try hiking from town up the Río Patacancha to the little-visited Inca ruins of **Pumamarca**, on the left of the river where the Río Yuramayu merges with the Patacancha under the shadows of the Nevada Helancoma. From here the main track carries on along the right bank of the Río Patacancha through various small peasant hamlets – Pallata, Colqueracay, Marcacocha, Huilloc and Patacancha – before crossing the pass, with the Nevada Colque Cruz on the right-hand side. It then follows the ríos Huacahuasi and Tropoche down to the valley and community of **Lares**, just before which are some Inca baths. Beyond the village are several more ruins en route to Ampares, from where you can either walk back to Urubamba, travel by road back to Cusco, or head down towards Quillabamba. It's at least a two-day walk one way from Ollantaytambo to Ampares, and you'll need camping equipment and food, as there are no facilities at all on the route. Other good day hikes are to Intihuatana (see below). Multi-day hikes can also be launched from nearby Chilca (Km 77).

HORSERIDING
The Inca **quarries of Cachiqata** can be reached in four hours on horseback with a Cusco or Ollantaytambo tour company (see p.221 & above). It's also possible to camp here and visit the site of an **Inca gateway** or **Intihuatana**. There are also the nearer ruins of **Pinkuylluna**, less than an hour away by horse, or the **Pumamarca** Inca ruins about half a day away.

RIVER RAFTING
Ollantaytambo is a centre for **river rafting**, organized largely by KB Tours (see above). Alternatively, arrange a rafting trip with one of the Cusco-based tour companies (see p.221). The river around Ollantaytambo is class 2–3 in the dry season and 3–4 during the rainy period (Nov–March).

mountains, with great views of Ollantaytambo's iconic face carved out of rock. Andean-themed paintings by a local artist are displayed throughout, and rooms feature wooden floorboards, a dresser and en-suite bathrooms. Most look over the town's rooftops to the city ruins, and locally made yogurt and granola are served for breakfast. The hotel regularly hosts writers and yoga groups, too. **S/190**

La Casa del Abuelo Convención 143 ☎ 084 436 747, ✉ lacasadelabuelo78@gmail.com. Right in the centre of town, this place offers tiled smallish rooms with puffy duvets and rain showers. Some have tiny little balconies, barely big enough to stand on. Room 301 is one of the most appealing, with a slanted roof that gives it a cosy feel. **S/165**

Hostal Iskay Patacalle s/n ☎ 084 204 004, ⓦ iskaygroup.com. A lovely little place offering seven rustic rooms on an old Inca site, all with private bathroom and some with bare stone walls. Single rooms are on the smallish side – it's wise to take a look at a couple before settling in. **S/120**

Hostal Mamá Simona Av Ocobamba s/n ☎ 084 436 383, ⓦ mamasimona.com. A short walk north of town, this peaceful hostel offers comfortable four and six-bed

dorms with sturdy beds and colourful blankets. The soothing sound of water is heard in most rooms, some of which have balconies. There's a fully equipped kitchen, a garden with hammocks and a barbecue set for guests, along with all-day coca tea and lockers for those wanting to leave their belongings as they head to Machu Picchu. Dorms **S/36**, doubles **S/90**

Hostal Sauce C Ventiderio 248 ☎ 084 204 044, ⓦ hostalsauce.com.pe. Colourful woolly hats decorate the walls of the living area of this small guesthouse, adding a pinch of fun. The six rooms have orange-coloured walls and wooden flooring, and three face the town's ruins. All are simply furnished with bare walls although the wooden beams add a cosy touch. There are home-made jams and yogurt for breakfast, and the hotel also offers laundry service (S/5/kg). Slightly overpriced for what you get. **S/340**

Hotel Tika Wasi Convención s/n ☎ 084 204 166, ⓦ tikawasihotel.com. This pleasant hotel offers two beautiful Inca rooms with original walls and niches adorned with statuettes. These cost S/60 more than the standard rooms, which are welcoming too, although how often do you get to sleep in a historical Inca room? **S/175**

EATING AND DRINKING

★ **El Albergue** Ollantaytambo train station ☎ 084 204 014 ⓦ elalbergue.com. This pleasant restaurant is without a doubt Ollantaytambo's best – ingredients are sourced directly from the farm at the back, including *quinoa*, corn and potatoes, and the interior is warm and pleasant. The menu includes delicious *causitas* (S/23) with three toppings, namely guacamole, grilled trout and *ají de gallina*. There are plenty of vegetarian options too, and guests can also reserve a *pachamanca* meal in advance. This is also a great spot to grab some freshly made sandwiches for the train journey to Machu Picchu Pueblo. Daily 5.30am–3.30pm & 6–9pm.

La Esquina Plaza de Armas. Baked goods fresh from the oven every day, including *empañadas* (S/6), breads and brownies (S/7), while the coffee is sourced from a local artisanal producer. Salads (S/13), soups (S/10) and sandwiches (S/12), as well as all-day breakfasts (S/9), are on offer. Daily 7.30am–9pm.

Ganso Waqta s/n ☎ 084 795 432. A quirky, atmospheric bar set on two floors with swing seats, dream catchers and a fireman's pole which first-floor customers are encouraged

to use when heading down to the ground floor. The drinks menu inevitably includes pisco sours (S/17), and there are pizzas (S/10) too for those feeling peckish. Occasional Andean live music. Daily 7pm–3am.

Hearts Café Av Ventiderio s/n. This wonderful little café serves chunky soups (S/10), huge salads (S/16), and a range of international dishes (mains from S/16), including plenty of veggie options. The bread is freshly baked and the cookies and pies (S/8) are all home-made. Profits go to the local community. Free wi-fi. Daily 7am–8.45pm.

Il Piccolo Forno C del Medio 120 ☎ 996 400 150. This Italian-Peruvian owned place is a great spot for a pizza (S/15), lasagne (S/23) or one of the many delectable desserts that can be consumed at little wooden tables. The shelves are lined with jars of pasta sauces and packets of local coffee – available for purchase – and there are plenty of gluten free options, too. Tues–Sun 1–9pm.

Tutti Amore Av Estación s/n. This little ice-cream joint produces over eighty flavours a year, solely using local produce including all manner of seasonal fruits. S/5 per scoop or two for S/8. Daily 8am–5pm.

The Inca Trail

Even though it's just one among a multitude of paths across the Andes, the fabulous treasure of Machu Picchu (see p.255) at the end of its 43km path makes the **INCA TRAIL** the world's most famous trek. Most people visit the site on a day-tour by train from Cusco, Ollantaytambo or Urubamba (see box, p.254), but if you're reasonably fit

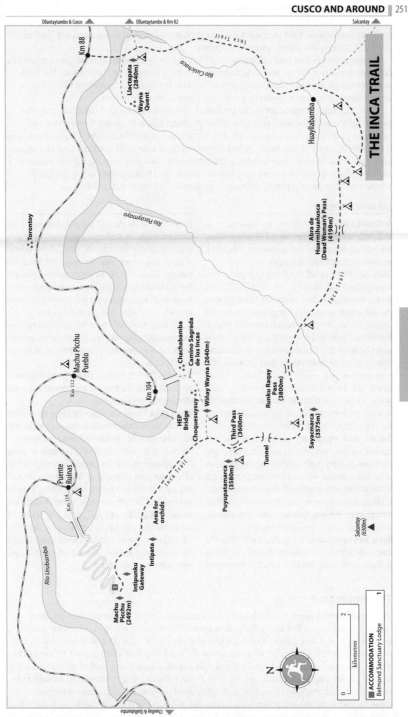

THE INCA TRAIL

Ollantaytambo & Cusco   Ollantaytambo & Km 82   Salcantay

Km 88

Llactapata
(2840m)

Wayna Quent

Río Cusichaca

Huayllabamba

Inca Trail

Torontoy

Río Pacaymayo

Abra de
Huarmihuañusca
(Dead Woman's Pass)
(4198m)

Inca Trail

4

Machu Picchu
Pueblo

Km 112

Chachabamba

Camino Sagrada
de los Incas (2640m)

Km 104

Wiñay Wayna

Runku Raqay
Pass
(3800m)

HEP
Bridge

Choquesuysuy

Third Pass
(3600m)

Sayacmarca
(3575m)

Puente
Ruinas

Tunnel

Km 114

Puyupatamarca
(3580m)

Inca Trail

Río Urubamba

Area for
orchids

Salcantay
(6300m)

Intipata

Intipunku
Gateway

Machu
Picchu
(2492m)

N

0   1   2
kilometres

■ ACCOMMODATION
Belmond Sanctuary Lodge   1

Chaullay & Quillabamba

and can dedicate at least four days to the experience, arriving along the Inca Trail offers the most atmospheric and rewarding option.

The downside of the trail's popularity is that you have to **book** at least nine months in advance and can only go with a **tour group** run by a licensed tour operator. The trail involves tough altitude trekking at times, but this is rewarded by spectacular scenery, deep valleys, glaciated mountain peaks and remote Inca structures.

Doing the trail in **four days** is the preferred option for most, and the most common tour length offered by tour agencies. More pleasant still is to spend five or six days, taking in everything as you go along. If you can only spare three days, you'll be pushing it the whole way – it can be done but it's gruelling. If this is all the time you can spare, give yourself a head start by catching the afternoon train and heading up the Cusichaca Valley as far as possible the evening before. There are 16 **campsites** along the trail; where you stay the night will ultimately be decided by your trail guide.

INFORMATION

Acclimatization It's important to make time to acclimatize to the altitude (see box, p.210) before tackling the Inca Trail or any other high Andean trek, especially if you've flown straight up from sea level.

Costs For a basic Inca Trail tour a reasonable price is from around US$450 (low season) to as much as US$650 (high season) for a standard three- or four-day trek. If you want the best, expect to pay more. Competition between the agencies has seen the price drop at times, which tends to manifest as a lower level of service and, potentially, lower wages for the porters. With the present levels of demand, however, prices are tending to rise. Most companies offer good value in their guiding service, food, equipment quality and the all-inclusiveness of their price. Some agency prices include things like transport or entry to the Inca Trail and Machu Picchu in their price, and others add this as an extra, so check details before booking.

Porters and equipment Trekking companies will organize porters and maybe mules to help carry equipment. So many people walk this route every year that toilets have now been built, and hikers are strongly urged to take all their rubbish away with them – there's no room left for burying any more tin cans. Porters can be organized through most trekking companies and they normally charge about US$70 for the four-day trek.

Rules and restrictions The sanctuary authorities (the Unidad de Gestión del Santuario Histórico de Machu Picchu) have imposed a limit of a maximum of five hundred people a day on the Inca Trail (including trekkers, porters, cooks and guides). In addition, it is mandatory for trekkers to go with a tour or licensed guide (see p.221): the old days of going it alone are gone. Be aware that within the Santuario Histórico de Machu Picchu, which incorporates the entire trail, you must only camp at a designated site.

Tours Most people select a tour to suit them from among the multitude of agencies registered for the Inca Trail (see p.221); the company will take care of everything including your registration, but demand is so great that it is essential to book at least nine months in advance and make your booking deposit.

Websites Check ⓦ machupicchu.gob.pe for background on Machu Picchu, the Inca Trail and alternative sites like Choquequirao (see box, p.265).

When to go Choose your season for hiking the Inca Trail carefully. May is the best month to venture on a hike here, with clear views, fine weather and verdant surroundings. Between June and September it's usually a pretty cosmopolitan stretch of mountainside, with travellers from all over the globe converging on Machu Picchu the hard way, but from mid-June to early August the trail is simply very busy (and the campsites noisy), especially on the last stretch. From October until April, in the rainy season, it's less crowded but also, naturally, quite a bit wetter. Locals will tell you that the best time to hike the trail is during a full moon, and it certainly adds a more romantic, even mystical feeling to your journey.

The main trail

The usual **starting point** for the Inca Trail is a small station at the hamlet and bridge at Q'orihuayrachina, at **Km 88** on the railline from Ollantaytambo and Poroy. Some tours arrive here by car and start at Km 82, where the road stops. The train stop is hailed by the guards and a small footbridge sees you across the tumbling Río Urubamba. Once over the bridge, the main path leads to the left through a small eucalyptus wood, then around the base of the Inca ruins of Llactapata – worth a visit for archeology enthusiasts, though most people save their energy for the trail and other archeological remains ahead – before crossing and then following the Río Cusichaca upstream along its left bank.

It's a good two hours' steep climb to **Huayllabamba**, the only inhabited village on the route and the best place to hire horses or mules for the most difficult climb on the whole trail, the nearby **Dead Woman's Pass**. This section of the valley is rich in Inca terracing, from which rises an occasional ancient stone building. To reach Huayllabamba you have to cross a well-marked bridge onto the right bank of the Cusichaca.

Many groups spend their first night at Huayllabamba campsite, but if you want to gain distance and time for the second day, there are three commonly used **campsites**: one at Llulluchayoc, also known as **Three White Stones**, where the trail crosses the Río Huayruro, just half a kilometre above its confluence with the Llullucha stream; another slightly higher site, just below Llulluchpampa, where there are toilets and space for several tents; or, slightly higher again, actually on the pampa where there's plenty more camping space – a good spot for seeing rabbit-like *viscachas* playing among the rocks. All of these campsites are on the trail towards the first and highest pass, but only the top one is within sight of it.

The first pass

It takes five hours or so to get from Huayllabamba to the Abra de Huarmihuañusca, **the first pass** (4200m) and the highest point on the trail. This is the hardest part of the walk – leave it (or at least some of it) for the second day, especially if you're feeling the effects of the altitude. The views from the pass itself are stupendous, but if you're tempted to hang around savouring them, it's a good idea to sit well out of the cutting wind (many a trekker has caught a bad chill here). From here the trail drops steeply down, keeping to the left of the stream into the Pacamayo Valley where, by the river, there's an attractive spot to **camp**, and where you can see playful **spectacled bears** if you're very lucky, or take a break before continuing.

The second pass

A winding, tiring track up from the Pacamayo Valley takes you to the **second pass** – Abra de Runkuracay – just above the interesting circular ruins of the same name. About an hour beyond the second pass, a flight of stone steps leads up to the Inca ruins of **Sayacmarca**. This is an impressive spot to **camp**, near the remains of a stone aqueduct that supplied water to the ancient settlement (the best spots are by the stream just below the ruins).

The third pass

From Sayacmarca, make your way gently down into increasingly dense cloud forest where delicate orchids and other exotic flora begin to appear among the trees. By the time you get to the **third pass** – which, compared with the previous two, has very little incline – you're following a fine, smoothly worn flagstone path where at one point an astonishing tunnel, carved through solid rock by the Incas, lets you avoid an otherwise impossible climb.

The trail winds down to the impressive ruin of **Puyupatamarca** – "Town Above the Clouds" – where there are five small stone baths and, in the wet season, constant fresh

---

INCA TRAIL WILDLIFE

Acting as a bio-corridor between the Cusco Andes, the Sacred Valley and the lowland Amazon forest, the **Santuario Histórico de Machu Picchu** possesses over 370 bird species, 47 mammal species and over seven hundred butterfly species. Some of the more notable residents include the **cock-of-the-rock** (*Rupicola peruviana*, known as *tunkis* in the Quechua-speaking Andes), **spectacled bear** (*Tremarctos ornatus*) and condor (*Vultur gryphus*). In addition, there are around three hundred different species of orchid hidden up in the trees of the cloud forest.

THE TRAIN JOURNEY TO MACHU PICCHU

The competitive services offered by the three Cusco-based train operators – **PeruRail**, **Inca Rail** and **Machu Picchu Train** (see p.220) – between Cusco and Machu Picchu provide one of the finest mountain train journeys in the world, with all the thrills and vistas associated with riding tracks through fantastic scenery, along with very good service and comfortable, well-kept carriages.

The longest of the train options (the others leave from Ollantaytambo and Urubamba), only offered by PeruRail, rumbles out of **Poroy station**, 15–20 minutes by taxi from Cusco centre. The wagons zigzag their way through the backstreets, where little houses cling to the steep valley slopes. It takes a while to rise out of the teacup-like valley, but once it reaches the high plateau above, the train rolls through fields and past highland villages before eventually dropping rapidly down into the **Urubamba Valley** via several major track switchbacks, which means you get to see some of the same scenery twice.

The train reaches the Sacred Valley floor just before getting into **Ollantaytambo**, where from the windows you can already see scores of impressively terraced fields and, in the distance, more Inca temple and storehouse constructions. Ollantaytambo's pretty train station is right next to the river, and here you can expect to be greeted by a handful of Quechua women selling woollen crafts. The train continues down the valley, stopping briefly at Km 88, where the **Inca Trail** starts (see p.250), then follows the Urubamba River as the valley gets tighter (which is why there's no road) and the mountain becomes more and more forested, as well as steeper and seemingly taller. The end of the line is the station at **Machu Picchu Pueblo** (also known as **Aguas Calientes**), a busy little town crowded into the valley just a short bus ride from the ruins themselves (see p.260). From Cusco (Poroy Station) the journey takes four hours; it's two hours from Ollantaytambo and three hours from Urubamba. Whichever route you're taking, buy **tickets** well in advance online (see p.220).

running water. There are places to **camp** actually on the pass (above the ruins), commanding stunning views across the Urubamba Valley and, in the other direction, towards the snowcaps of Salcantay (Wild Mountain): this is probably one of the most magical camps on the trail, given good weather, and it's not unusual to see deer feeding here.

Wiñay Wayna

It's a very rough, two- or three-hour descent along a non-Inca track to the next ruin, a citadel almost as impressive as Machu Picchu, **Wiñay Wayna** – "Forever Young" – another place with fresh water, as well as the official *Trekkers Hostal*.

Consisting of only two major groups of architectural structures – a lower and an upper sector – Wiñay Wayna's most visible features are **stone baths** with apparently as many as nineteen springs feeding them, all set amid several layers of fine Inca terracing. Nearby there's also a small waterfall created by streams coming down from the heights of Puyupatamarca. Much like today, it is believed that Wiñay Wayna was used by Incas as a washing, cleansing and resting point before arriving at the grand Machu Picchu citadel.

This is usually the spot for the **last night of camping**, and, especially in high season, the crowds mean that it's a good idea to pitch your tent soon after lunch, but don't be surprised if someone pitches theirs right across your doorway. To reach Machu Picchu for sunrise the next day you'll have to get up very early with a torch to avoid the rush.

Intipunku to Machu Picchu

A well-marked track from Wiñay Wayna takes a right fork for about two more hours through sumptuous vegetated slopes to the stone archway entrance called

Intipunku (Gateway of the Sun), from where you get your first sight of Machu Picchu – a stupendous moment, however exhausted you might be. Aim to get to Machu Picchu well before 9.30am, when the first hordes arrive off the train from Cusco, if possible.

Machu Picchu

Daily 6am–5pm • S/126, student S/63; combined entry with Wayna Picchu S/150, student with ISIC card S/75 • ⓦ machupicchu.gob.pe

MACHU PICCHU is one of the greatest of all South American tourist attractions: beautiful stone architecture enhanced by the Incas' exploitation of local 250-million-year-old rocks of grey-white granite with a high content of quartz, silica and feldspar, set against a vast, scenic backdrop of dark-green forested mountains that spike up from the deep valleys of the Urubamba and its tributaries. The distant glacial summits are dwarfed only by the huge sky. The site's mysterious origins are central to its enduring appeal, but even without knowing too much about its history or archeology, or the specifics of each feature, it's quite possible to enjoy a visit to Machu Picchu: for many, it's enough just to absorb the mystical atmosphere.

Brief history

The name Machu Picchu apparently means simply Old or Ancient Mountain. With many legends and theories surrounding the position of the site, most archeologists agree that its **sacred geography and astronomy** were auspicious factors in helping the Inca Pachacuti decide to build this citadel here at 2492m. It's thought that agricultural influences as well as geo-sacred indicators prevailed, and that the site secured a decent supply of sacred coca and maize for the Inca nobles and priests in Cusco.

The discovery of Machu Picchu

Never discovered by the Spanish conquerors, for many centuries the site of Machu Picchu lay forgotten, except by local Indians and settlers, until it was found on July 24, 1911 by the US explorer **Hiram Bingham**. It was a fantastic find, not least because the site was still relatively intact, without the usual ravages of either Spanish conquistadores or tomb robbers. Accompanied only by two locals, Bingham left his base camp around 10am and crossed a bridge so dodgy that he crawled over it on his hands and knees before climbing a precipitous slope until they reached the ridge at around midday. After resting at a small hut, he received hospitality from a local peasant who described an extensive system of terraces where they had found good fertile soil for their crops. Bingham was led to the site by an 11-year-old local boy, Pablito Alvarez, but it didn't take him long to see that he had come across some important ancient Inca terraces – over a hundred of which had recently been cleared of forest for subsistence crops. After a little more exploration Bingham found the fine white stonework and began to realize that this might be the place he was looking for.

MACHU PICCHU TICKETS

In spite of the huge numbers of visitors – 2500 a day in high season – Machu Picchu is large enough to absorb its visitors without it being a scrum. Due to its popularity and attempts to limit visitor numbers because of the potential environmental impact, however, **booking ahead** is a good idea. The website ⓦ machupicchu.gob.pe allows you to check availability. You cannot, however, book tickets online; you need to either do so through a travel agency or in person in Cusco or at the INC in Machu Picchu Pueblo (cash only; see p.262) or in Cusco opposite the stadium at Condominio Huáscar 238 (cash and cards accepted; ☎084 236 061; Mon–Sat 7am–7.30pm).

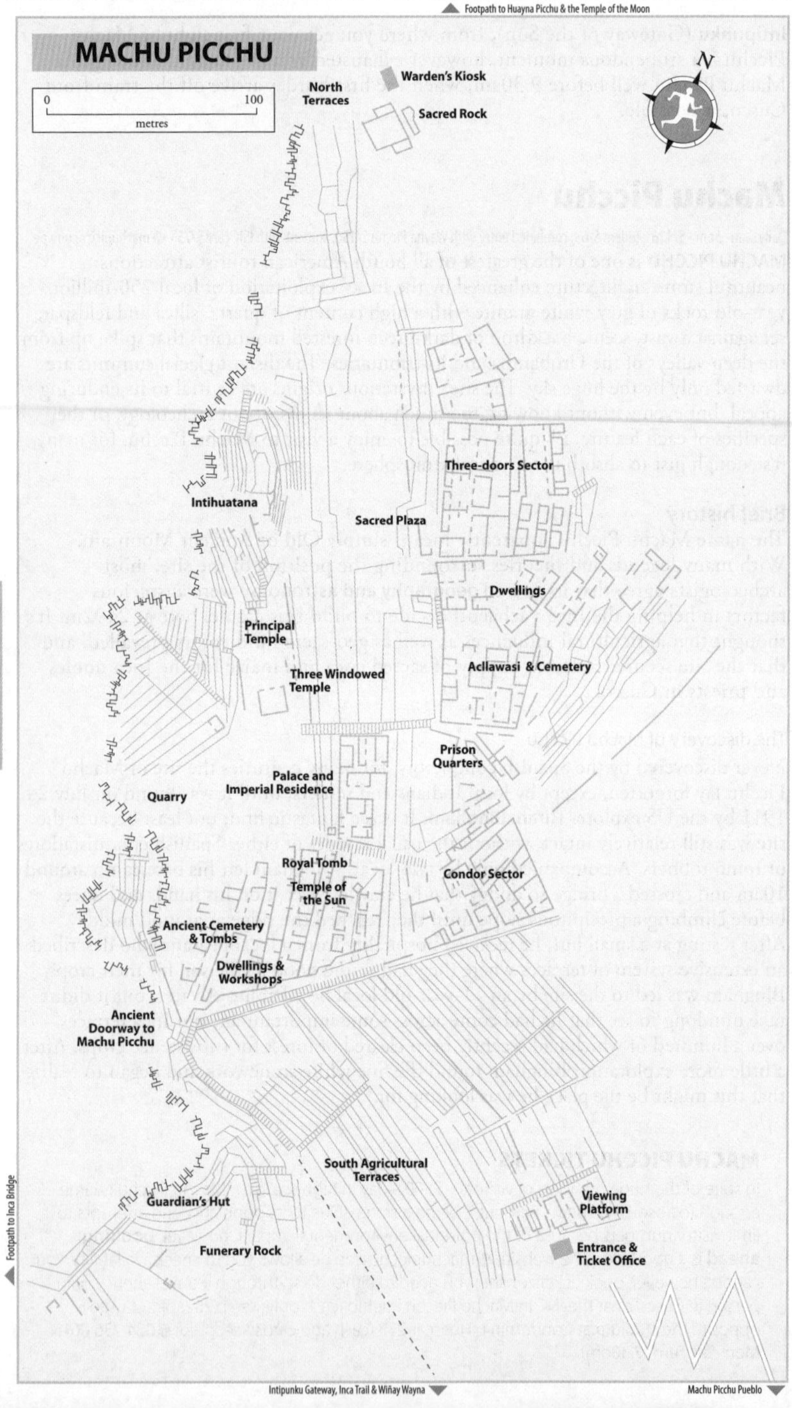

Footpath to Huayna Picchu & the Temple of the Moon
MACHU PICCHU
0
100
metres
N
Warden's Kiosk
North Terraces
Sacred Rock
Three-doors Sector
Intihuatana
Sacred Plaza
Dwellings
Principal Temple
Acllawasi & Cemetery
Three Windowed Temple
Prison Quarters
Palace and Imperial Residence
Quarry
Royal Tomb
Condor Sector
Temple of the Sun
Ancient Cemetery & Tombs
Dwellings & Workshops
Ancient Doorway to Machu Picchu
South Agricultural Terraces
Viewing Platform
Guardian's Hut
Funerary Rock
Entrance & Ticket Office
Footpath to Inca Bridge
Intipunku Gateway, Inca Trail & Wiñay Wayna
Machu Picchu Pueblo

Origins of Machu Picchu

Bingham first theorized that Machu Picchu was the lost city of **Vilcabamba**, the site of the Incas' last refuge from the Spanish conquistadores. Not until another American expedition surveyed the ruins around Machu Picchu in the 1940s did serious doubts begin to arise over this assertion, and more recently the site of the Incas' final stronghold has been shown to be Espíritu Pampa in the Amazon jungle (see p.271).

Meanwhile, it was speculated that Machu Picchu was perhaps the best preserved of a series of **agricultural centres** that served Cusco in its prime. The city was conceived and built in the mid-fifteenth century by **Emperor Pachacuti**, the first to expand the empire beyond the Sacred Valley towards the forested gold-lands. With crop fertility, mountains and nature so sacred to the Incas, an agricultural centre as important as Machu Picchu would easily have merited the site's fine stonework and temple precincts. It was clearly also a **ritual centre**, given the layout and quantity of temples; but for the Incas it was usual not to separate things we consider economic tasks from more conventional religious activities. So, Machu Picchu represents to many archeologists the most classical and best-preserved remains in existence of a citadel used by the Incas as both a religious temple site and an agricultural (perhaps experimental) centre.

The ruins

Though more than 1000m lower than Cusco, Machu Picchu seems much higher, constructed as it is on dizzying slopes overlooking a U-curve in the Río Urubamba. More than a hundred flights of steep stone steps interconnect its palaces, temples, storehouses and terraces, and the outstanding views command not only the valley below in both directions but also extend to the snowy peaks around Salcantay. Wherever you stand in the ruins, you can see spectacular **terraces** (some of which are once again being cultivated) slicing across ridiculously steep cliffs, transforming mountains into suspended gardens.

Though it would take a lot to detract from Machu Picchu's incredible beauty and unsurpassed location, it is a zealously supervised place, with the site guards frequently blowing whistles at visitors who have deviated from the main pathways. The best way to enjoy the ruins – while avoiding the ire of the guards – is to hire a **guide** (see p.252) at the entrance to the site, or buy the **map** from the ticket office and stick to its routes.

The Temple of the Sun

The **Temple of the Sun**, also known as the Torreon, is a wonderful, semicircular, walled, tower-like temple displaying some of Machu Picchu's finest granite stonework. Constructed to incorporate polyhedrons and trapezoidal window niches, the temple's carved steps and smoothly joined stone blocks fit neatly into the existing relief of a natural boulder that served as some kind of altar and also marks the entrance to a small cave. A window off this temple provides views of both the June solstice sunrise and the constellation of the Pleiades, which rises from here over the nearby peak of Huayna

---

THREATS TO MACHU PICCHU

This most dramatic and enchanting of Inca citadels, suspended on an extravagantly terraced saddle between two prominent peaks, is believed to be in danger of **collapse**. The original Inca inhabitants temporarily stabilized the mountainside, transforming some of the geological faults into **drainage channels**. They also joined many of the construction stones together, using elaborate multi-angled techniques, making them more resistant to both tremors and landslides. Nevertheless, these spots remain weak, and significant damage can be seen on nearby buildings. The National Institute of Culture, which administers Machu Picchu, acknowledges the problems, but correcting them is an ongoing process.

Picchu. The Pleiades are still a very important Andean astronomical symbol relating to crop fertility: locals use the constellation as a kind of annual signpost in the agricultural calendar, giving information about when to plant crops and when the rains will come.

The Royal Tomb

Below the Temple of the Sun is a cave known as the **Royal Tomb**, despite the fact that no graves or human remains have ever been found there. In fact, it probably represented access to the spiritual heart of the mountains, like the cave at the Temple of the Moon (see opposite).

The funerary rock

Retracing your steps 20m or so back from the Temple of the Sun and following a flight of stone stairs directly uphill, then left along the track towards Intipunku (see opposite), brings you to a path on the right, which climbs up to the thatched **guardian's hut**. This hut is associated with a modestly carved rock known as the **funerary rock** and a nearby graveyard where Hiram Bingham (see p.255) found evidence of many burials, some of which were obviously royal.

The Sacred Plaza

Arguably the most enthralling sector of the ruins, the **Three-Windowed Temple** (Templo de Tres Ventanas), part of the complex based around the **Sacred Plaza** (Plaza Sagrada), is located back down in the centre of the site, the next major Inca construction after the Temple of the Sun. Dominating the southeastern edge of the plaza, the attractive Three-Windowed Temple has unusually large windows looking east towards the mountains beyond the Urubamba River valley. From here it's a short stroll to the **Principal Temple** (Templo Principal), so called because of the fine stonework of its three high main walls, the most easterly of which looks onto the Sacred Plaza. Unusually (as most ancient temples in the Americas face east), the main opening of this temple faces south, and white sand, often thought to represent the ocean, has been found on the temple floor, suggesting that it may have been allied symbolically to the Río Urubamba: water and the sea.

The Intihuatana

A minute or so uphill from the Principal Temple along an elaborately carved stone stairway brings you to one of the jewels of the site, the **Intihuatana**, also known as the **"hitching post of the sun"**. This fascinating carved rock, built on a rise above the Sacred Plaza, is similar to those created by the Incas in all their important ritual centres, but is one of the very few not to have been discovered and destroyed by the conquistadores. This unique and very beautiful survivor, set in a tower-like position, overlooks the Sacred Plaza, the Río Urubamba and the sacred peak of Huayna Picchu.

The Intihuatana's base is said to have been carved in the shape of a map of the Inca Empire, though few archeologists agree with this. Its main purpose was as an **astro-agricultural clock** for viewing the complex interrelationships between the movements of the planets and constellations. It is also thought by some to be a symbolic representation of the spirit of the mountain on which Machu Picchu was built – by all accounts a very powerful spot both in terms of sacred geography and its astrological function. The Intihuatana appears to be aligned with four important **mountains**: the snowcapped mountain range of La Verónica lies directly to the east, with the sun rising behind its main summit during the equinoxes; directly south, though not actually visible from here, sits the father of all mountains in this part of Peru, Salcantay, a few days' walk away; to the west, the sun sets behind the important peak of Pumasillo during the December solstice; and due north stands the majestic peak of Huayna Picchu. The rock evidently kept track of the annual cycles, with its basic orientation northwest to southeast, plus four vertices pointing to the four directions.

> **SUNRISE OVER MACHU PICCHU**
>
> It's easy enough to get into the site before **sunrise**, since the sun rarely rises over the mountains to shed its rays over Machu Picchu before 7am. Make your way to the "hitching post" of the sun before dawn for an unforgettable sunrise that will quickly make you forget the hike through the pre-dawn gloom – bring a torch if you plan to try it.

The Sacred Rock

Following the steps down from the Intihuatana and passing through the Sacred Plaza towards the northern terraces brings you in a few minutes to the **Sacred Rock** (Piedra Sagrado), below the access point to Huayna Picchu. A three-metre-high and seven-metre-wide lozenge of rock sticking out of the earth like a sculptured wall, little is known for sure about the Sacred Rock, but it is thought to have had a ritual function; its outline is strikingly similar to the Incas' sacred mountain of Putukusi, which towers behind it in the east.

Huayna Picchu

The prominent peak of **Huayna Picchu** juts out over the Urubamba Valley at the northern end of the Machu Picchu site, and is easily scaled by any reasonably energetic person. The record for this vigorous and rewarding climb is 22 minutes, but most people take at least an hour. Access to this sacred mountain is restricted to four hundred people a day (the first two hundred are expected to get back down by 10am so that the second two hundred can then go up); register for the climb with the guardian in the hut just behind the Sacred Rock. From the summit, there's an awe-inspiring **panorama**, and it's a great place from which to get an overview of the ruins suspended between the mountains among stupendous forested Andean scenery.

The Temple of the Moon

Accessed in the same way as Huayna Picchu, but about one-third of the way up, another little track leads to the left and down to the stunning **Temple of the Moon** (Templo de la Luna), hidden in a grotto hanging magically above the Río Urubamba, some 400m beneath the pinnacle of Huayna Picchu. Not many visitors make it this far and it's probably wise to have a **guide** (and if you've already walked up Huayna Picchu, you might want to save this for another day: it's at least another 45 minutes each way and not that easy going at times). The guardian by the Sacred Rock will often take people for a small fee (around US$1/person, provided there are two or more). Once you reach the temple, you'll be rewarded by some of the best stonework in the entire complex, the level of craftsmanship hinting at the site's importance to the Inca.

The temple's name comes from the fact that it is often lit up by the moonlight, but some archeologists believe the structure was probably dedicated to the spirit of the mountain. The main sector of the temple is in the mouth of a natural **cave**, where there are five niches set into an elaborate white-granite stone wall. There's usually evidence – small piles of maize, coca leaves and tobacco – that people are still making offerings at these niches. In the centre of the cave there's a rock carved like a throne, beside which are five cut steps leading into the darker recesses, where you can see more carved rocks and stone walls, nowadays inaccessible. Immediately to the front of the cave is a small **plaza** with another cut-stone throne and an altar. Outside, steps either side of the massive boulder lead above the cave, from where you can see a broad, stone-walled **room** running along one side of the cave boulder. There are more buildings and beautiful little stone sanctuaries just down a flight of steps from this part of the complex.

Intipunku

If you don't have the time or energy to climb Huayna Picchu or visit the Temple of the Moon, head back to the guardian's hut on the other side of the site and take the path

4

below it, which climbs gently for thirty minutes or so, up to **Intipunku**, the main entrance to Machu Picchu from the Inca Trail. This offers an incredible view over the entire site, with the unmistakeable shape of Huayna Picchu in the background.

Machu Picchu Pueblo

Many people base themselves at the settlement of **MACHU PICCHU PUEBLO** (previously known as **Aguas Calientes**), connected to Machu Picchu by bus, in order to visit the ruins at a more leisurely pace or in more depth. Its warm, humid climate and surrounding landscape of towering mountains covered in cloud forest make it a welcome change from Cusco. The town's explosive growth has pretty well reached the limits of the valley here; there's very little flat land that hasn't been built on or covered in concrete. Not surprisingly, this boom town has a lively, bustling feel and enough restaurants and bars to satisfy a small army.

The thermal baths

Av Pachacutec • Daily 5am–8pm • S/10

The main attraction in these parts – apart from Machu Picchu itself – is the natural **thermal bath**, which is particularly enjoyable after a few days on the Inca Trail or a hot afternoon up at Machu Picchu, although it can get very crowded. You can find several communal baths of varying temperatures right at the end of the main drag of Avenida Pachacutec, around 750m uphill from the town's small plaza.

Trail to Putukusi

Closed on rainy days

A **trail** up the sacred mountain of **Putukusi** starts just outside town, a couple of hundred yards down on the left if you follow the rail track towards the ruins. The walk offers stupendous views of the town and across to Machu Picchu; allow an hour and a half each way. Note it is not for the faint-hearted as the trail is very steep in parts (some sections have been replaced by ladders) and very narrow.

ARRIVAL AND GETTING AROUND   MACHU PICCHU

BY TRAIN

If travelling all the way to Machu Pichu from Poroy near Cusco, Ollantaytambo or Urubamba by train you'll get off at Machu Picchu Pueblo station, located in the nearest town to the ruins, which has experienced explosive growth over the last decade or so. You walk through a craft market area from the station and over a footbridge; below the bridge you'll see the buses that head up to the ruins. You can also buy bus tickets here.

Destinations Ollantaytambo (6–12 daily; 2hr–2hr 30min); Poroy (3–6 daily; 3–4hr); Urubamba (occasionally scheduled; 2–3hr).

BY BUS

From Machu Picchu Pueblo Head through the market stalls and cross the Río Aguas Calientes by a footbridge. Tickets can be bought just below this from a small window, where there's usually a queue to help identify it, and from where buses usually depart. The first buses leave at 5.20am and continue every 10min or so according to demand until about 4pm, returning continuously until the last bus at

5.30pm (S/30 one way, S/60 return).

From Cusco The Turismo Ampay bus from Cusco (Urb Pucutupampa B-11, Santiago; ☎ 084 245 7344; S/15) to Santa María (5 daily; 6–9hr) goes via Ollantaytambo before crossing the mountains east of the Urubamba Valley. From the high pass at Abra Malaga, the bus drops down to Santa María. From here there are colectivos (1hr; S/20) to the larger settlement of Santa Teresa, from where it is possible to walk to Machu Picchu (see below).

ON FOOT

From Machu Picchu Pueblo It's possible to walk from Machu Picchu Pueblo to the ruins, but it'll take one and a half to three hours, depending on how fit you are and whether you take the very steep direct path or follow the more roundabout paved road.

From Santa Teresa If you've taken the bus from Cusco to Santa Teresa (see opposite), you can do the rest of the journey to Machu Picchu on foot. From Santa Teresa you follow the Río Urubamba upstream for 8km (1hr 30min–2hr) to a hydroelectric power station. Colectivos catering to

workers commuting to the hydroelectric plant run daily along this route (20min; S/3), though the road is frequently washed away in the height of the rainy season (Dec–March/ April). Continue upriver from here to an INC hut where you need to register, then follow the path along the rail line a further 10–11km (2–3hr) to Machu Picchu Pueblo.

INFORMATION AND TOURS

Tourist information iPeru is at Av Pachacutec s/n (☎084 211 104; ✉iperumachupicchu@promperu.gov.pe; Mon–Sat 9am–1pm & 2–6pm, Sun 9am–1pm).

Machu Picchu Tickets The INC (Instituto Nacional de Cultura) office just off the main square at Av Pachacutec 123 (☎084 211 196; daily 5.20am–8.40pm) sells tickets for Machu Picchu entry (cash only; S/126, student S/63;

combined entry with Wayna Picchu S/150, student S/75). If you stay overnight in Machu Picchu Pueblo before visiting the site, buy your ticket as soon as you arrive in town as this will save you time in the morning.

Tour operators Numerous companies offer tours covering Machu Picchu and the Inca Trail (see p.221). Most of the hotels also organize tours of the site or have links with operators.

ACCOMMODATION

MACHU PICCHU PUEBLO

Although there is an overwhelming choice of places to stay in Machu Picchu Pueblo, there can be a lot of competition for lodgings during the high season (June–Sept), when large groups of travellers often turn up and take over entire hotels. Coming to town on an early train will give you some increased choice in where to stay, but for the better places

try and book at least a week or two, if not months, in advance.

HOTELS & GUESTHOUSES

Adela's Hostal Av Prolongación Imperio de los Incas s/n ☎084 211291, ✉adelas_hostal@hotmail.com. This small budget option right by the train station features

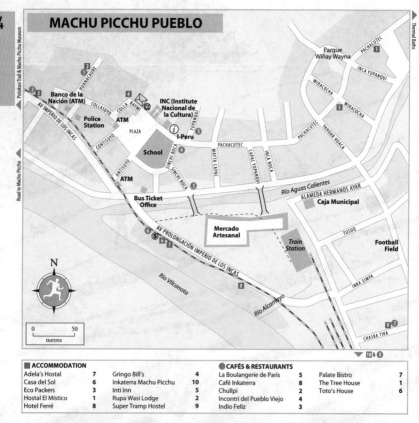

■ ACCOMMODATION				● CAFÉS & RESTAURANTS			
Adela's Hostal	7	Gringo Bill's	4	La Boulangerie de Paris	5	Palate Bistro	7
Casa del Sol	6	Inkaterra Machu Picchu	10	Café Inkaterra	8	The Tree House	1
Eco Packers	3	Inti Inn	5	Chullpi	2	Toto's House	6
Hostal El Místico	1	Rupa Wasi Lodge	2	Incontri del Pueblo Viejo	4		
Hotel Ferré	8	Super Tramp Hostel	9	Indio Feliz	3		

yellow and claret-coloured rooms with matching bedspreads. There are only eight rooms, which lends the place an intimate feel, and there are great views to be had over the river (make sure you ask for a river-view room). **S/130**

Casa del Sol Av Imperio de los Incas 608 ☎084 211 118, ⓦcasadelsolhotels.com. Set on seven floors, this modern hotel features welcoming rooms with wooden floors, cosy armchairs and hand-woven framed fabrics from Ayacucho. Bathrooms are equipped with rain showers and stone sinks, and the double-glazing ensures peace and quiet from the honking train and bustle of the city streets. The spa features a steam room and jacuzzi. **S/1220**

Gringo Bill's Colla Raymi 104 ☎084 211 046, ⓦgringobills.com. This intimate establishment is one of the most interesting choices in town, with bar, restaurant and rooms, with paintings of orchids in each, forming an appealing complex built into the lower hillside with pebbly walkways and wooden balustrades. There is a small open-air jacuzzi and a leafy terrace with barbecue facilities. They also offer laundry service at S/10 per kg. **S/280**

Hotel Ferré Av Imperio de los Incas 634 ☎084 211 337, ⓦhotelferremachupicchu.com. A newly built hotel that is very comfortable indeed and prices – for Machu Picchu – are very reasonable; rooms are spick and span and all feature fridge, TV and safe. Some have views on the interior corridor, which means they can be a bit dark; river-view rooms are without a doubt worth the extra S/60 – room 306 is particularly appealing. **S/390**

Hostal El Místico Av Pachacutec 814 ☎084 211 051, ⓦelmisticomachupicchu.com. This pleasant guesthouse features ten rooms spread across three floors with a little lounge area on each; the walls are decorated with psychedelic paintings, and the friendly owner, who runs a jewellery shop right next door, organizes complimentary mystical tours around town. **S/90**

Inkaterra Machu Picchu Km 110 by the rail line on the western edge of the settlement ☎084 211 122, Lima ☎01 610 0400, ⓦinkaterra.com. This smart eco-friendly hotel features well-appointed rooms set in five hectares of tropical gardens and cloud forest with jacuzzi and a small pool, and a cosy lobby area scattered with books and fireplaces. The grounds are dotted with bird feeders, attracting beautiful humming birds that flutter around in the early mornings. The hotel's orchid garden has a whopping 372 species of orchids, and also houses a bear rescue project. The excellent restaurant serves tea from the hotel's very own tea plantation. **S/960**

Inti Inn Av Pachacutec s/n ☎084 211 137, ⓦgrupointi .com. On the town's main drag, this is a pleasant option that has recently been renovated. The corridors are atmospherically lit with low lighting, and the interiors feature stone floors and wooden beams. Rooms are comfortable although they can get a little noisy. **S/464**

★**Rupa Wasi Lodge** Jr Huanacaure 105 ☎084 211 101, ⓦrupawasi.net. The eco-friendly owners of this lovely lodge have done a great job at integrating the accommodation with the surrounding environment. Wooden rooms with en-suite bathrooms are set on a slope in a lush tropical garden, and some feature small balconies with pretty views. The attached restaurant, *The Tree House*, serves superb Peruvian dishes with a twist, and they offer two-hour cooking classes too (US$70/person). **S/240**

HOSTELS

Eco Packers Av Imperio de los Incas 136 ☎084 211 121, ⓦecopackersperu.com. A popular place with dorms and doubles giving onto narrow corridors that wind their way up to the rooftop terrace with billiards table and cable TV. Dorms have wooden beds tightly packed together, while the more comfortable doubles feature en-suite bathrooms – if you're after some quiet ask for a room facing the back of the building. Dorms **S/43**, doubles **S/150**

Super Tramp Hostel Chaska Tika, at Plaza de la Cultura ☎084 435 830, ⓦsupertramphostel.com. This popular hostel with brightly painted murals offers a range of dorm rooms sleeping eight to twelve. Doubles, all with shared bath, are small but comfortable. There's a great little rooftop terrace with recycled furniture, a communal kitchen, a lounge area with cable TV, book exchange, wi-fi and an attached burger restaurant, too. Dorms **S/30**, doubles **S/85**

AROUND MACHU PICCHU PUEBLO

Belmond Sanctuary Lodge Right by the ruins of Machu Picchu ☎084 211 038, ⓦbelmond.com. This exclusive lodge is the only accommodation adjacent to the ruins, allowing easy access to the citadel at sunrise and at sunset. Set amid lush gardens, most rooms have mountain views and some feature private terraces. There's a jacuzzi nestled among greenery from where there are views of the citadel, while the massage meditation temple looks over the cloud forest. Plenty of activities on offer including birdwatching and orchid walks. Rates are full board. **S/3385**

EATING AND DRINKING

There are scores of restaurants in Machu Picchu Pueblo; don't be surprised to be harassed by waiters trying to entice you in as you walk down the street. Most establishments offer pretty average fare; the restaurants outlined below are particularly worth seeking out.

★ **La Boulangerie de Paris** Jr Sinchi Rica ☎ 084 797 798, ⊛ laboulangeriedeparis.net. This French-run bakery is the best spot in town to grab a freshly baked croissant (S/2.50) or a pain au chocolat (S/3.50). As well as all manner of sweet delights there are plenty of savoury snacks too, including quiche (S/10.50) – it's a great place to stock up on some goodies for the train journey back to Cusco. Daily 5am–9pm.

★ **Café Inkaterra** Km 110 by the rail line on the southeastern edge of the settlement ☎ 084 211 122, ⊛ inkaterra.com. Tucked away behind the train station, this atmospheric café and restaurant overlooking the murmuring Río Vilcanota serves excellent international and Peruvian dishes in a welcoming thatched-roof building. Mains from S/25. Daily 11am–9pm.

Chullpi Av Imperio de los Incas 140 ☎ 084 211 350, ⊛ chullpirestaurant.com. Serving Peruvian and *novoandina* (see p.226) dishes, this smartish establishment serves creatively presented dishes. There are plenty of meat and fish options including alpaca medallions grilled in port sauce and fresh trout fillet served with mash. The S/65 menu consisting of three courses will ensure you leave with a full belly. Daily 11am–10pm.

Incontri del Pueblo Viejo Av Pachacutec s/n ☎ 084 211 072. This Italian- and Peruvian-owned place serves traditional Italian dishes such as home-made tagliatelle (S/33) and gnocchi al ragù (S/30). The handmade pastas are kneaded right in front of customers' eyes, and the pizza dough is left to leaven for 24 hours, resulting in delicious thin-crust pizzas (S/25) that are cooked in a wood-fire oven. There are great organic beers from Peru and beyond, too. Daily noon–1pm.

★ **Indio Feliz** Lloque Yupanqui 103 ☎ 084 211 090, ⊛ indiofeliz.com. This French-owned restaurant bursts with character; the walls are plastered with business cards and the premises jam-packed with curios. Customers enjoy the excellent French–Peruvian cuisine in a series of rooms with pretty hand-painted furniture, and there's an excellent three-course set menu at S/64.50. Daily noon–10pm.

Palate Bistro Chaska Tika, at Plaza de la Cultura ☎ 084 435 830. This cosy burger joint adjacent to *Super Tramp Hostel* serves excellent burgers with fries (S/20); there are veggie burgers too, as well as pizzas (S/20). They also prepare Machu Picchu lunch boxes for S/30. Tues–Sun noon–10pm.

Toto's House Av Imperio de los Incas ☎ 084 211 020. A vast but warm and welcoming restaurant with great views of the river and a crackling open fire to grill meats; they offer an expensive but quite good buffet lunch every day (noon–4pm; S/60). Daily noon–10pm.

★ **The Tree House** Jr Huanacaure 105 ☎ 084 435 849, ⊛ thetreehouse-peru.com. The menu at one of the town's best restaurants is scribbled on blackboards while large jars of fermented piscos line the bar shelf. The cuisine is *novoandina* with a touch of international, with dishes such as *quinoa* tabule and falafel (S/32) and tournedos de alpaca (grilled alpaca wrapped in bacon) in Andean chimichurri dressing (S/52). There's also a raw food menu with sushi (S/35) and fruit rolls (S/35). This is also a great place to order a box lunch for Machu Picchu outings, delivered for free at any hotel in town (S/37). Daily 4.30–10pm.

DIRECTORY

Internet Try Cyber World on the plaza (daily 8am–10pm; S/3 per hr).

Laundry Most hostels and hotels will offer this, but there are some laundries dotted around. Note that prices here are much higher than in Cusco.

Left luggage Next to the entrance to the ruins (no backpacks or camping equipment are allowed inside; price per item S/5).

Money and exchange BCP on Av Los Incas 600, next to *Toto's*, Banco de la Nación at Av Los Incas 540 by the police station and Caja Municipal by the Mercado Artesanal all have ATMs, but sometimes run out of money, especially at weekends. There's also an ATM in the Panamericana pharmacy on the main plaza (daily 8am–9pm).

Police Av Imperio de los Incas, just down from the old train station (☎ 211 178).

Post office On the western end of the plaza, with erratic opening hours – it seems to be closed more often than open.

Alternative treks to the Inca Trail

There are a number of **alternative trekking routes** that have been developed by Cusco-based adventure tour operators (see p.221) in response to the desperate over-demand for the Inca Trail. The most popular of these is **Choquequirao**, and like the Inca Trail, this trek ends at a fabulous ancient citadel. Treks around the sacred glaciated mountain of **Salcantay** are also well developed and, to some extent, overlap with and link to the Inca Trail itself. Much less walked, but equally breathtaking, is **Ausangate**, another sacred snow-covered peak (with a convenient looping trail) that on a clear day can be seen from Cusco dominating the southern horizon. Another popular trek is the route from Ollantaytambo to **Lares** (see box, p.249). As for **cost**, these treks are similar in price to the Inca Trail, starting from a minimum of about US$80–100 a day.

Choquequirao

An increasingly popular alternative to the Inca Trail, the hike to **Choquequirao** can be made with a trekking tour of **three to four days**; these leave Cusco on demand and pretty much daily during tourist season. Not quite as spectacular as Machu Picchu, this is still an impressive Inca citadel whose name in Quechua means "Cradle of Gold". Sitting among fine terraces under a glaciated peak of the Salcantay range, less than half the original remains have been uncovered from centuries of vegetation, making a visit here similar to what Hiram Bingham may have experienced at Machu Picchu when he discovered the site back in 1911 (see p.255).

Brief history

Located 1750m above the Apurímac River and 3104m above sea level in the district of Vilcabamba, Choquequirao is thought to have been a **rural retreat** for the Inca emperor as well as a **ceremonial centre**. It was built in the late fifteenth century and almost certainly had an important political, military and economic role, controlling people and produce between the rainforest communities of the Ashaninka (see p.511), who still live further down the Apurimac River, and the Andean towns and villages of the Incas. It's easy to imagine coca, macaw feathers, manioc, salt and other Ashaninka products making their way to Cusco via Choquequirao.

Hiram Bingham came to Choquequirao in 1910 on his search for lost Inca cities. Regardless of the exquisite stonework of the ceremonial complex and the megalithic agricultural terracing, Bingham – as have many archeologists since – failed to see just how important a citadel Choquequirao actually was. Evidence from digs here suggest that a large population continuously inhabited Choquequirao and nearby settlements, even after the Spanish Conquest.

The trek to Choquequirao

The most **direct route** up is along the Abancay road from Cusco – about four hours – to Cachora in Apurímac, over 100km from Cusco and some 93km north of Abancay; from here it's a further 30km (15–20 hours) of heavy but stunningly beautiful trekking to the remains of the Choquequirao citadel. A longer and even more **scenic route** involves taking a twelve-day hike from Huancacalle and Pukyura and then over the Pumasillo range, through Yanama, Minas Victoria, Choquequirao and across the Apurímac ending in Cachora.

Taking the direct route, the first two hours are spent hiking to Capuliyo, where, at 2915m, there are fantastic panoramas over the Apurímac Valley. The trail descends almost 1500m from here to Playa Rosalina on the banks of the Río Apurímac, where it's possible to camp the first night. The second day has the most gruelling uphill

---

CAMINO SAGRADO DE LOS INCAS

The **Camino Sagrado de los Incas**, a truncated Inca Trail, starts at Km 104 of the Panamerican Highway, 8km from Machu Picchu. The footbridge here (roughly US$50 entry, US$25 for students, free for children under 12; includes entry to Machu Picchu) leads to a steep climb (4–6hr) past Chachabamba to reach Wiñay Wayna (see p.254), where most people camp. From here the route joins the remainder of the Inca Trail, which can be reached easily in another two to four hours.

walking – about five hours as far as Raqaypata and a further two or three to Choquequirao itself.

The site
Daily 7am–4pm • S/39

Consisting of nine main sectors, the **site** was a political and religious centre, well served by a complex system of aqueducts, canals and springs. Most of the buildings are set around the main ceremonial courtyard or plaza and are surrounded by well-preserved and stylish Inca agricultural terracing.

The return journey
You can go in and come out the same way in three to four days, or as an alternative, leave Choquequirao via a different, more or less circular, route following the path straight down from the ruins to the river bridge at San Ignacio. The small town of **Huanipaca**, with colectivos for Abancay, is a further two to three hours' steep uphill walk from here. Alternatively, Choquequirao can be approached this way (it's a faster route than via Cachora) and, in a reverse circular route, you can then exit via Cachora.

Salcantay

Irregular colectivos to Salcantay leave from Cusco's C Arcopata (2.5–3hr) with mostly morning departures; you can take a ride in a truck from Mollepata as far as Soraypampa, cutting out the first 8hr of the usual trek, for around S/20, but trucks arrive irregularly

The **SALCANTAY** mountain (6271m) is one of the Cusco region's main *apus*, or gods. Its splendid snowcapped peak dominates the landscape to the northwest of Cusco and it makes for relatively peaceful trekking territory. The main route joins the Machu Picchu train line and the Urubamba Valley with the lesser-visited village of Mollepata in the Río Apurímac watershed. The trek usually takes from **five to seven days** and offers greater contact with local people, a wider range of ecological niches to pass through and higher paths than the Inca Trail: a good option for more adventurous trekkers who have already acclimatized.

The trail
Most people start on the Urubamba side of Machu Picchu at Km 82, where the Inca Trail also starts (see p.250). From here you can follow the **Inca Trail path** up the Cusichaca Valley, continuing straight uphill from the hamlet of Huayllabamba, ignoring the main Inca Trail that turns west and right here, up towards Dead Woman's Pass – Abra de Huarmihuañusca. Throughout the trail, the landscape and scenery are very similar to the Inca Trail, though this route brings you much closer to the edge of the glaciers. The trail is steep and hard, up to the high pass at 5000m, which takes you around the southern edge of **Salcantay glacier**, before descending directly south to the village of **Mollepata**.

The trek is increasingly approached **in reverse**, with guides and mules hired at Mollepata where there is less competition for them than there is on the Huayllabamba side; this route means you finish up in the Urubamba Valley, between Machu Picchu and Ollantaytambo. There are no official **camping** sites en route, but plenty of good tent sites and several traditional stopping-off spots.

Lares

There are several options for trekking in the **Lares Valley**, lasting two to five days, and all offer splendid views of snow-capped peaks and green valleys. The hikes allow you to properly experience village life in the Andes. You'll pass through communities where you can stay with local families and purchase traditional crafts. The hot springs in Lares make for a relaxing end to any trek in the area. Some tour

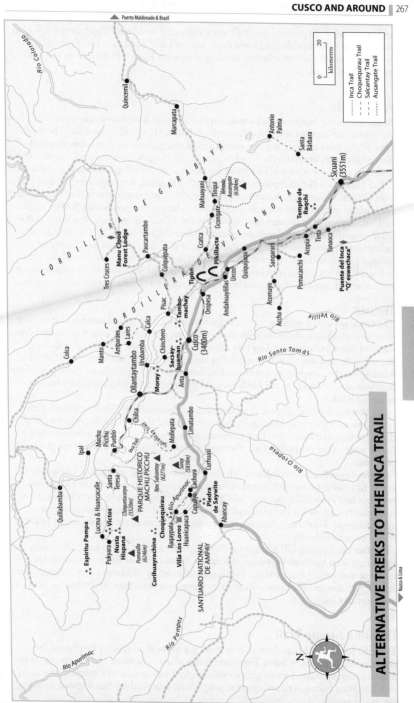

ALTERNATIVE TREKS TO THE INCA TRAIL

operators sell a three-day Lares trek with a day-trip to Machu Picchu on the fourth day, but do not be misled; in most cases you will still need to travel for two to five hours by bus and/or train before arriving at Machu Picchu Pueblo from the end point of your trail.

Ausangate

The start point of the trail, Tinqui, is reached by a 3–4hr bus drive from Cusco via Urcos, although departures are irregular

An important mountain god for the Incas, **AUSANGATE** is still revered daily by locals. One of the most challenging and exciting treks in southern Peru, this **five-day trail** is also relatively quiet: you'll see very few people, apart from the occasional animal herder, once you leave the start and end point for this trail at the village of **Tinqui** at 3800m.

The **Ausangate Circuit** explores the Cordillera Vilcanota, weaving around many peaks over 6000m. Ausangate, the highest peak at 6384m, remains at the hub of the standard trail. Many of the camps are over 4600m and there are two passes over 5000m to be tackled. A good **map** is essential – the best is the *PERU Topographic Survey 1:100,000–28-T*, available from the South American Explorers' Club (see p.221) – and a local **guide** strongly recommended. The management at Tinqui's *Hostal Ausangate* can arrange guides, mules and a muleteer (*arriero*). Some **supplies** are now available at the trailhead, but it's still safer to bring everything you need with you; there's more choice in Cusco, but some food and cooking utensils could be purchased en route in Urcos.

The trail

The **first day**'s uphill walking from Tinqui brings you to a natural campsite on a valley floor almost 4500m above sea level close to the hot springs near Upis with tremendous views of Nevado Ausangate. **Day two** requires about six hours of walking, following the valley up and over into the next valley through the high pass of Arapa (4800m) heading for the camping area at the red-coloured lake of Laguna Jatun Pucacocha; from here you can see and hear the Nevado Ausangate's western ice-falls against a backdrop of alpaca herds.

Day three tackles the highest of all the passes – Palomani (5170m) – early on. From here there are views over Laguna Ausangatecocha, and the walking continues up and down, passing the Ausangate base camp en route. From Palomani it is three or four hours' walk to the next campsite, offering some of the best views towards the glaciated peak itself.

Day four continues downhill towards the Pitumarca Valley, which you follow left uphill to a campsite beyond Jampa, a remote settlement way beyond the electricity grid, but just this side of the magical Campa Pass (5050m), where centuries' worth of stone piles or cairns left by locals and travellers adorn the landscape honouring the mountain god. From here there are spectacular views towards the snowcapped peaks of Puka Punta and Tres Picos.

Day five takes you uphill again through the pass and down beside Lake Minaparayoc. From here it's a three- or four-hour descent to the campsite at Pacchanta where there are some welcoming hot springs, traditionally enjoyed by trekkers as they near the end of this trail. Beyond Pacchanta, it's another three-hour walk back to Tinqui for road transport to Cusco.

The Inka Jungle Trail

The Inka Jungle Trail lasts three to four days, going south to Machu Picchu via the peaceful jungle towns of Santa Teresa and Santa María. The name is a misnomer, as the trail runs through cloud forest rather than jungle. Tours consist of a mixture of walking and mountain biking, and are ideal for people who want activity but without spending too much money.

A great way to save some extra soles is to do the trail independently. From Cusco you take a bus towards Quillabamba and get off at Santa María (5–6hr; S/20; S/35 by minivan); the town is pretty unattractive and there's no real reason to stay overnight here. Instead, you can easily hop onto a taxi heading to Santa Teresa (1hr; S/20), where there is plenty of cheap accommodation and some wonderful natural hot springs (S/10) outside town. Combis (30min; S/3) from Santa Teresa run daily to take workers to the hydroelectric plant and meet the trains to Machu Picchu Pueblo (ask around for the latest schedule).

If you're with a tour, on the first day you'll go by private bus to Abra Málaga, the high point between Ollantaytambo and Santa María, before going on an exhilarating four-hour downhill ride to Santa María and then proceeding to Santa Teresa the next day.

Towards the jungle

The two major places to visit **northeast of Cusco** are **Paucartambo**, 112km from Cusco, and **Tres Cruces**, another 50km beyond Paucartambo. The road between the two follows the **Kosnipata Valley** ("Valley of Smoke"), then continues through cloudy tropical mountain scenery to the mission of Shintuya on the edge of the **Manu Biosphere Reserve** (see p.442). Legend has it that the Kosnipata enchants anyone who drinks from its waters at Paucartambo, drawing them to return again and again.

The area along the Río Urubamba from Machu Picchu onwards, to the **north**, is a quiet, relatively accessible corner of the Peruvian wilderness. As you descend from Ollantaytambo, the vegetation along the valley turns gradually into **jungle**, thickening and getting greener by the kilometre, as the air gets steadily warmer and more humid. Most people heading down here get as far as the town of **Quillabamba**, but the road continues deeper into the rainforest where it meets the navigable jungle river at **Ivochote** (see p.447). Many come to this region to explore its mountains, cloud forest and rainforest areas, either to check out known Inca ruins or to search out some new ones. It's relatively easy to visit the hilltop ruins of the palace at **Vitcos**, a site of Inca blood sacrifices, and possible – though an expedition of six days or more – to explore the more remote ruins at **Espíritu Pampa**, now thought to be the site of the legendary lost city of Vilcabamba.

Paucartambo

Eternally spring-like because of the combination of altitude and proximity to tropical forest, the pretty village of **PAUCARTAMBO** ("Village of the Flowers") is located some 130km from Cusco in a wild and remote Andean region, and guards a major entrance to the **jungle zone of Manu**. A silver-mining colony, run by slave labour during the

---

NEW DISCOVERIES

Major Inca sites are still being discovered in this jungle region. In April 2002 British explorer **Hugh Thomson** – author of *The White Rock* (see p.514) – and American archeologist **Gary Ziegler**, following rumours of a **lost city**, led an expedition, which discovered an Inca city in the virtually inaccessible valley bottom at the confluence of the ríos Yanama and Blanco in the Vilcabamba region. Apparently seen briefly by **Hiram Bingham** nearly a hundred years ago, its coordinates were never recorded and this settlement of forty main buildings set around a central plaza hadn't been spotted since. Although very difficult to access – due to river erosion – there appears to have been an Inca road running through the valley, probably connecting this site to the great Inca citadel of **Choquequirao** (see p.265). This settlement is believed to have been Manco Inca's hideout during his rebellion against the conquistadores, which lasted until his execution in Cusco in 1572 (see p.207).

seventeenth and eighteenth centuries, it's now a popular destination that is at its best in the dry season between May and September, particularly in mid-July when the annual **Fiesta de la Virgen del Carmen** takes place (see box below); visitors arrive in their thousands and the village is transformed from a peaceful habitation into a huge mass of frenzied, costumed dancers. Even if you don't make it to Paucartambo for the festival, you can still see the ruined *chullpa* burial towers at **Machu Cruz**, an hour's walk from Paucartambo; ask in the village for directions. Travellers rarely make it here outside festival time, unless en route to the rainforest by road.

Plaza Principal

The beautiful main **plaza**, with its white buildings and traditional blue balconies, holds concrete **monuments** depicting the characters who perform at the fiesta – demon-masked dancers, malaria victims, lawyers, tourists and just about anything that grabs the imagination of the local communities. Also on the plaza is the rather austere **church**, restored in 1998 and splendid in its own way, simple yet full of large Cusqueña paintings. It's also the residence of the sacred **image of the Virgen del Carmen**, unusual in its Indian (rather than European) appearance. When the pope visited Peru in the mid-1980s, it was loaded onto a truck and driven to within 30km of Cusco, then paraded on foot to the city centre so that the pope could bless the image. When the Fiesta de la Virgen del Carmen is on, hotels in town are always fully booked and their prices hiked, but it's possible to rent out spaces in local residents' homes or find a site to **camp**. It is always best to take a tent, in case all rooms are full. You can seek the help of an agency in Cusco to book a hotel for you although note that you'll need to do so well in advance (at least 2–3 months).

4

ARRIVAL AND INFORMATION   PAUCARTAMBO

By bus Transportes Gallitos de las Rocas buses leave from Av Diagonal Angamos 1952 in Cusco; (☎ 084 226 895) daily to Paucartambo (3–4hr) and three times a week to Pilcopata (see p.444), the first major settlement (6–8hr on from Paucartambo) as you go down into the jungle. Buses

generally stop off in Paucartambo's marketplace.
Tourist information During festival times, a tourist information point can usually be found near the stone bridge which leads over the river into the main part of town, en route to the plaza.

FIESTA DE LA VIRGEN DEL CARMEN

Paucartambo spends the first six months of every year gearing up for the **Fiesta de la Virgen del Carmen**. It's an essentially female festival: tradition has it that a wealthy young woman, who had been on her way to Paucartambo to trade a silver dish, found a beautiful (if body-less) head that spoke to her once she'd placed it on the dish. Arriving in the town, people gathered around her and witnessed rays of light shining from the head, and henceforth it was honoured with prayer, incense and a wooden body for it to sit on.

The energetic, hypnotic **festival** lasts three or four days – usually July 16–19, but check with the tourist office in Cusco (see p.221) – and features throngs of locals in distinctive **traditional costumes**, with **market stalls** and a small **fair** springing up near the church. Clamouring down the streets are throngs of intricately costumed and masked **dancers and musicians**, the best known of whom are the black-masked **Capaq Negro**, recalling the African slaves who once worked the nearby silver mines. Note the grotesque blue-eyed masks and outlandish costumes acting out a parody of the white man's powers – **malaria**, a post-Conquest problem, tends to be a central theme – in which an old man suffers terrible agonies until a Western medic appears on the scene, with the inevitable hypodermic in his hand. If he manages to save the old man (a rare occurrence) it's usually due to a dramatic muddling of prescriptions by his dancing assistants – and thus does Andean fate triumph over science.

On Saturday afternoon there's a **procession of the Virgen del Carmen** itself, with a brass band playing mournful melodies as petals and emotion are showered on the icon of the Virgin – which symbolizes worship of Pachamama as much as devotion to Christianity. The whole event culminates on Sunday afternoon with the **dances of the guerreros** (warriors), during which good triumphs over evil for another year.

Tres Cruces

The natural special effects during sunrise at **TRES CRUCES** are in their own way as magnificent a spectacle as the Fiesta de la Virgen del Carmen (see box opposite). At 3739m above sea level, on the last mountain ridge before the eastern edge of the Amazon forest, the **view** is a marvel at any time: by day a vast panorama over the start of a massive cloud forest with all its weird and wonderful vegetation; by night an enormous star-studded jewel. Seen from the highest edge of the **Manu Biosphere Reserve**, the **sunrise** is spectacular, particularly around the southern hemisphere's winter solstice in June: multicoloured, with multiple suns, it's an incredible light show that lasts for hours. The only **accommodation** in Tres Cruces is an empty house that's used as a visitors' shelter, which fills up very fast at Paucartambo and solstice festival times, when **camping** is the only real option, so take a warm sleeping bag, a tent and enough food.

ARRIVAL AND DEPARTURE · TRES CRUCES

By bus Transport to Tres Cruces can be a problem, except during the Paucartambo fiesta in July; there are weekly departures from Cusco to Paucartambo (4–5hr). Check the latest schedule with the tourist office), from where there are colectivos to Tres Cruces (1hr 30min–2hr).

By tour Cusco tour operators (see p.221) can organize a trip.

Vitcos and Espíritu Pampa

Lying at the edge of the jungle, the archeological site of Vitcos is where ruler-in-exile Manco Inca settled after fleeing Cusco and Ollantaytambo; he was subsequently murdered here in 1544 by Spanish conquistadores. Nearby is Espíritu Pampa (formerly Vilcabamba), the last refuge of the Inca Empire that fell to the Spanish in 1572. The easiest way to see the **Vitcos and Espíritu Pampa ruins** is on a guided tour with an adventure tour company (see p.221). If you'd rather travel more independently, it is possible to travel to Vilcabamba, the jump-off point to the ruins, by bus, although expedition-type preparation is required: you should hire a local **guide** (best done through Cusco tour agents) and possibly even mules. There are no services or facilities as such at either location, and neither is staffed by permanent on-site guardians.

Vitcos

Daily 24hr · Free

In 1911, after discovering Machu Picchu, **Hiram Bingham** set out down the Urubamba Valley to Chaullay, then up the Vilcabamba Valley to Pukyura, where he expected to find more Inca ruins. What he found – **VITCOS** (known locally as Rosapata) – was a relatively small but clearly palatial ruin, based around a trapezoidal plaza spread across a flat-topped spur. Down below the ruins, Bingham was shown by local guides a spring flowing from beneath a vast, **white granite boulder** intricately carved in typical Inca style and surrounded by the remains of an impressive Inca temple. This fifteen-metre-long and eight-metre-high sacred white rock – called Chuquipalta by the Incas – was a great oracle where **blood sacrifices** and other religious rituals took place. According to early historical chronicles, these rituals had so infuriated two Spanish priests who witnessed them that they exorcized the rock and set its temple sanctuary on fire.

Espíritu Pampa

Daily 24hr · Free

The lost city of **ESPÍRITU PAMPA** was the last refuge of the Incas, and was brought to attention in Hiram Bingham's book *The Lost City of the Incas*. After briefly exploring some of the outer ruins at Espíritu Pampa, Bingham decided they must have been built by Manco Inca's followers and deduced that they were post-Conquest Inca constructions since many of the roofs were Spanish-tiled. Believing that he had already found the lost city of **Vilcabamba** he was searching for at Machu Picchu, Bingham paid little attention to these newer discoveries.

Consequently, as the site was accessible only by mule, Espíritu Pampa remained covered in thick jungle vegetation until 1964, when serious exploration was undertaken by US archeological explorer **Gene Savoy**. He found a massive ruined complex with over sixty main buildings and some three hundred houses, along with temples, plazas, wells and a main street. Clearly this was the largest Inca refuge in the Vilcabamba area, and Savoy rapidly became convinced of its identity as the true site of the last Inca stronghold. More conclusive evidence has since been provided by the English geographer and historian John Hemming who, using the chronicles, was able to match descriptions of Vilcabamba, its climate and altitude, precisely with those of Espíritu Pampa.

ARRIVAL AND DEPARTURE   VITCOS AND ESPÍRITU PAMPA

By tour Tours are best arranged through one of the companies in Cusco (see p.221).
By colectivo Catch a colectivo from Cusco to Quillabamba

(5–6hr). From here hop on another colectivo to Espíritu Pampa (2–3hr). From Espíritu Pampa it's just 5km to Vitcos.

South from Cusco

The first 150km of the road (and rail) south from Cusco towards Lake Titicaca (see p.186) passes through the beautiful valleys of Huatanay and Vilcanota, from where the legendary founders of the Inca Empire are said to have emerged. A region outstanding for its natural beauty and rich in magnificent archeological sites, it's easily accessible from Cusco and offers endless possibilities for exploration or random wandering. The whole area is ideal for **camping and trekking**, and in any case, only the rustic towns of **Urcos** and **Sicuani** are large enough to provide reasonable accommodation (see p.276 and p.277).

About 20km east of Vilcanota are the superb Inca remains of **Tipón** lie high above the road, little visited but extensive and evocative. Closer to the road, the Huari city of **Pikillacta** is easier to find and worthy of an hour or two. Beyond Urcos but before Sicuani, a rather dull transport hub of a town, the great **Temple of Raqchi** still stands unusually high as a monument to Inca architectural abilities.

ARRIVAL AND GETTING AROUND   SOUTH FROM CUSCO

BY BUS
As the trains are slow, infrequent and don't stop at all towns, most people travel on one of the frequent, and cheaper, buses or minibuses. Many of the bus options are inter-regional carriers (see box, p.220).
Inka Express The best option is offered by Inka Express,

Urb El Ovalo, Av La Paz C-23 (☎084 247 887, ⓦinkaexpress.com), which has quality buses linking Cusco with Puno, but also offers opportunities to stop off at some of the tourist sites below, including Tipón and Raqchi (see p.274 and p.276), en route, with a bilingual tour guide.

San Sebastián

Heading south from Cusco by road, after about 5km you pass through the little pueblo of **San Sebastián**. Originally a small, separate village, it has now become a suburb of the city. It has an impressive **church**, ornamented with Baroque stonework, six Neoclassical columns and two squat belfries. It was apparently built on the site of a chapel erected by the Pizarros in memory of their victory over Almagro. These days San Sebastián is celebrated with processions and prayers throughout the month of Jaunuary, often providing a colourful spectacle.

OPPOSITE COLOURFUL COSTUMES AT THE FIESTA DE LA VIRGEN DEL CARMEN, PAUCARTAMBO (P.270) >

SCENIC ROUTES TO PUNO AND LIMA

Even if you aren't planning to spend time around Lake Titicaca, the rail journey south to **Puno** (see p.188) is worth taking. The journey starts in the Cusco region and takes around twelve hours, covering a soul-stirring route that climbs slowly through stunning green river valleys to a desolate landscape to the pass, beyond the town of Sicuani. From here it rolls down onto the altiplano, a flat high plain studded wih adobe houses and large herds of llama and alpaca, before reaching Lake Titicaca and its port city of Puno.

If **Lima** is your destination, consider the twenty-hour direct highland route northwest from Cusco through Abancay and then down to the coast at Nazca. Known as the Nazca-Cusco Corridor, it offers access to a range of potential stopovers on the way: the archeological sites of Choquequirao and Sahuite; the city of Abancay and protected mountain forest area of Ampay; the thermal baths at Chaullanca and the alpaca and vicuña centre at Puquio; and, of course, the mysterious archeological sites around Nazca itself.

Oropesa

The next place of any interest beyond San Sebastián is picturesque **Oropesa**, some 25km on, traditionally a town of bakers, whose adobe **church**, boasting a uniquely attractive three-tiered belfry with cacti growing out of it, is notable for its intricately carved pulpit and the beautiful, Cusqueña-esque interior murals which look to have been painted between 1580 and 1630. On the left side of the church there's a pretty little chapel, the Capilla de Jesús. In early Inca days Oropesa was home to a well-known rebel clan, the Pinaguas, who had to be subdued by Pachacutec before he could safely build his country residence at Tipón (see below).

Tipón ruins

Daily 7am–6pm • Entry by Cusco Tourist Ticket (see box, p.221) • Colectivos leave from Cusco's Pampa de Castilla (1hr 30min), dropping you off at the main square; from here you'll have to walk up to the ruins (40min)

Both in setting and architectural design, the **TIPÓN RUINS** are one of the most impressive Inca sites. With no village or habitation in sight, and fresh running water, it's also a breathtaking place to **camp**.

The lower ruins

Well hidden in a natural shelf high above the Huatanay Valley, the **lower sector** of the ruins is a stunning sight: a series of neat agricultural terraces, watered by stone-lined channels, all astonishingly preserved and many still in use. The impressive stone terracing reeks of the Incas' domination over an obviously massive and subservient labour pool; yet at the same time it's clearly little more than an elaborate attempt to increase crop yield. At the back of the lower ruins, water flows from a stone-faced "mouth" around a **spring** – probably an aqueduct subterraneously diverted from above. The entire complex is designed around this spring, reached by a path from the last terrace.

The reservoir and temple block

Another sector of the ruins contains a **reservoir** and **temple block** centred on a large volcanic rock – presumably some kind of *huaca*. Although the stonework in the temple seems cruder than that of the agricultural terracing, its location is still beneficial. By contrast, the construction of the reservoir is sophisticated, as it was originally built to hold nine hundred cubic metres of water which gradually dispersed along stone channels to the Inca "farm" directly below.

The upper ruins

Coming off the back of the reservoir, a large, tapering stone **aqueduct** crosses a small gully before continuing uphill – about thirty minutes' walk – to a vast zone of

unexcavated terraces and dwellings. Beyond these, over the lip of the hill, you come to another level of the upper valley literally covered in Inca terracing, dwellings and large stone storehouses. Equivalent in size to the lower ruins, these are still used by locals who have built their own houses among the ruins. So impressive is the terracing at Tipón that some archeologists believe it was an Inca **experimental agricultural centre**, much like Moray (see p.244), as well as a citadel.

ARRIVAL AND DEPARTURE

THE TIPÓN TEMPLES

By bus Hop off about 5min beyond Oropesa (you can also flag buses down in Oropesa, but many will be full), then walk east towards the entrance to the site, signposted from the main road, but higher up the hillside with a reception hut.

Pikillacta

Daily 7am–6pm • Entry by Cusco Tourist Ticket (see box, p.221) • Beside the main road (ask the bus driver to drop you off)

About 7km south of Oropesa, the pre-Inca ruins of **PIKILLACTA**, alongside those of Rumicolca, can be seen alongside the road. After passing the Paucartambo turn-off, near the ruins of an ancient storehouse and the small red-roofed pueblo of **Huacarpay**, the road climbs to a ledge overlooking a wide alluvial plain and **Lucre Lake** (now a weekend resort for Cusco's workers). At this point the road traces the margin of a stone wall defending the pre-Inca settlement of Pikillacta.

Spread over an area of at least fifty hectares, Pikillacta, or "The Place of the Flea", was built by people of the Huari culture around 800 AD, before the rise of the Incas. Its unique, geometrically designed **terraces** surround a group of bulky two-storey constructions: apparently these were entered by ladders reaching up to doorways set well off the ground in the first storey – very unusual in ancient Peru. Many of the walls are built of small cut stones joined with mud mortar, and among the most interesting finds here were several round turquoise **statuettes**. These days the city is in ruins but it seems evident still that much of the site was taken up by barrack-like quarters. When the Incas arrived early in the fifteenth century they modified the site to suit their own purposes, possibly even building the aqueduct that once connected Pikillacta with the ruined gateway of Rumicolca, which straddles a narrow pass by the road, fifteen minutes' walk further south.

Rumicolca

Daily 24hr • Free • Right beside the main road (ask the bus driver to drop you off)

The massive defensive passage of **RUMICOLCA** was initially constructed by the Huari people and served as a southern entrance to – and frontier of – their empire. Later it became an **Inca checkpoint**, regulating the flow of people and goods into the Cusco Valley: no one was permitted to enter or leave the valley via Rumicolca between sunset and sunrise. The Incas improved on the rather crude Huari stonework of the original **gateway**, using regular blocks of polished andesite from a local quarry. The gateway still stands, rearing up to twelve solid metres above the ground, and is one of the most impressive of all Inca constructions.

Andahuaylillas

Catch a bus from opposite Cusco's General Hospital to Urcos or from opposite the Estadio General to Sicuani and ask the driver where to get off (every 30min; 1hr) • Andahuaylillas church 7.30am–5.30pm • S/15; student with ISIC card S/10; ticket grants access to Huaro church

In the tranquil and well-preserved village of **ANDAHUAYLILLAS**, an adobe-towered church sits above an attractive **plaza**, fronted by colonial houses. Built in the early seventeenth century on the site of an Inca temple, the **Iglesia de San Pedro** has an exterior balcony from which the priests would deliver sermons. While it's fairly small, with only one nave, it is nevertheless a magnificent example of provincial colonial art. Huge **Cusqueña canvases** decorate the upper walls, while below are some unusual murals, slightly faded over the centuries; the ceiling, painted with Spanish flower designs, contrasts strikingly with the great Baroque altar.

Huaro

Catch a bus from opposite Cusco's General Hospital to Urcos or from opposite the Estadio General to Sicuani and ask the driver where to get off (every 30min; 1hr) • Huaro church 8am–noon & 1–5.30pm • S/15; student with ISIC card S/10; ticket grants access to Andahuaylillas church

To the south, the road leaves the Río Huatanay and enters the Vilcanota Valley. **HUARO**, crouched at the foot of a steep bend in the road 3km from Andahuaylillas, has a much smaller **church** whose interior is completely covered with colourful **murals** of religious iconography, angels and saints; the massive gold-leaf altarpiece dominates the entire place as you enter.

Urcos

Climbing over the hill from Huaro (see above) to Urcos, you can see **boulders** which have been gathered together in mounds, to clear the ground for the simple ox-pulled ploughs which are still used here. The road descends to cruise past **Lake Urcos** before reaching the town that shares the lake's name. According to legend, the Inca Huascar threw his heavy gold chain into these waters after learning that strange bearded aliens – Pizarro and his crew – had arrived in Peru. Between lake and town, a simple **chapel** now stands poised at the top of a small hillock: if you find it open, go inside to see several excellent Cusqueña paintings.

The town of **URCOS**, resting on the valley floor and surrounded by weirdly sculpted hills, is centred on the **Plaza de Armas**, where a number of huge old trees give shade to Indians selling bread, soup, oranges and vegetables. On one side of the plaza, which is particularly busy during the town's excellent, traditional **Sunday market**, there's a large, crumbling old church; on the other, low adobe buildings.

Templo de Raqchi

Daily 7am–5pm • S/15 • Sicuani-bound buses pass here (every 20min; 3hr)

Between Urcos and Sicuani the road passes through **San Pedro de Cacha**, the nearest village (4km) to the imposing ruins of the **TEMPLO DE RAQCHI**, built in honour of Viracocha, the Inca creator-god (see box below). The temple was supposedly built to appease the god after he had caused the nearby volcano of Quimsa Chata to spew out fiery boulders in a fit of anger, and even now massive **volcanic boulders** and ancient lava flows scar the landscape as a constant reminder.

VIRACOCHA'S HUACA

One of the unusually shaped hills surrounding Urcos is named after the creator-god **Viracocha**, as he is said to have stood on its summit and ordered beings to emerge from the hill, thus creating the town's first inhabitants. In tribute, an ornate **huaca**, with a gold bench, was constructed to house a statue to the god, and it was here that the eighth Inca emperor received a divinatory vision in which Viracocha appeared to him to announce that "great good fortune awaited him and his descendants". In this way the emperor obtained his imperial name, **Viracocha Inca**, and also supposedly his first inspiration to conquer non-Inca territory, though it was his son, Pachacuti, who carried the empire to its greatest heights.

 With its adobe walls still standing over 12m high on top of polished stone foundations, and the **site** scattered with numerous other buildings and plazas, such as barracks, cylindrical warehouses, a palace, baths and aqueducts, Raqchi was clearly an important **religious centre**. Today the only ritual left is the annual **Raqchi Festival** (second week of June), a dramatic, untouristy fiesta comprising three to four days of folkloric music and dance – performed by groups congregating here from as far away as Bolivia to compete on the central stage. The performances are well stage, but the site, in a boggy field, can be mayhem, with hundreds of food stalls, a funfair, Quechua women selling *chicha* maize beer – and their drunken customers staggering through the tightly knit crowds.

Sicuani

Several buses daily between Sicuani and Cusco (3hr) as well as Puno (4–5hr); train is the slowest and most expensive option and, although it stops briefly at Sicuani, few if any tourists get off here, since they are obliged to buy a ticket all the way to Puno (see p.188).

 About 20km from Raqchi, **SICUANI** is capital of the province of Canchis and quite a thriving agricultural and market town, not entirely typical of the settlements in the Vilcanota Valley. Its busy **Sunday market** is renowned for cheap and excellent woollen goods, which you may also be offered on the train if you pass through Sicuani between Puno and Cusco. Although not a particularly exciting place in itself – with too many tin roofs and an austere atmosphere – the people are friendly and it makes an excellent **base for trekking** into snowcapped mountain terrain, being close to the vast Nevada Vilcanota mountain range which separates the Titicaca Basin from the Cusco Valley.

 The train journey south continues towards Puno and Lake Titicaca (see p.186), with the Vilcanota Valley beginning to close in around the line as the tracks climb **La Raya Pass** (4300m), before dropping down into the desolate *pampa* that covers much of inland southern Peru.

4

The Central Sierra

PLAZA DE ARMAS, HUANCAVELICA

5

The Central Sierra

Peppered with traditional towns and cities sitting in remote valleys, the green and mountainous Central Sierra region boasts some of Peru's finest archeological sites and colonial buildings. Although significantly fewer travellers make it here compared with hotspots like Cusco and Machu Picchu, anyone with the time to spare will find this region a worthwhile destination in its own right, rather than just somewhere to stop en route to the central selva (see p.448). As well as fantastic mountain scenery, this amalgam of regions in the central Peruvian Andes offer endless walking country, a caving opportunity and a gateway into the country's Amazon rainforest.

Almost all travellers from Lima enter the Central Sierra by road, along the much-improved **Carretera Central**. The road passes close to the enigmatic rock formations centring on **Marcahuasi** and the village of **San Pedro de Casta** before climbing over the high pass at Ticlio. The old train – the "Tren de la Sierra" – now only rarely takes passengers up to the city of Huancayo.

The most attractive hub in the Sierra Central is the laidback town of **Tarma**, which has a relatively pleasant climate influenced by the cloud forest to the east, and is a major nodal point for pioneers from the jungle, traders and, to a lesser extent, tourists. To the north, pleasant **Huánuco** serves as a good base for exploring some of Peru's most interesting archeological remains, and **Tingo María** is the gateway to the jungle port of Pucallpa. To the southwest of Tarma lies the largest city in the northern half of the Central Sierra, **Huancayo**, high up in the Andes. South of Huancayo are the two most traditional of all the Central Sierra's towns: **Ayacucho** – one of the cultural jewels of the Andes, replete with colonial churches and some of Peru's finest artesan crafts – and **Huancavelica**. Immediately north of Huancayo lies the astonishing **Jauja Valley**, which has beautiful scenery, striped by fabulous coloured furls of mountain.

GETTING AROUND   THE CENTRAL SIERRA

Most people will travel this region by bus. Bar unpredictable events like landslides in the rainy season (Dec–March) or miners' union strikes, a car or bus will get over the Andes faster than the train (see p.282). All buses from Lima have to travel by the often-congested Carretera Central, up past some large mines and over the high pass at Ticlio before descending to La Oroya. The train follows the same route. Once up in the Sierra Central, apart from the Lima–Huancayo railway, the only option for travel is by road. The area is well served by regular bus companies and most of the larger towns have colectivos or minibuses connecting them, with a more informal service and without fixed departure times.

BY BUS
Cruz del Sur and Ormeño run regular buses between Lima and Huancayo. Other bus companies connect between main centres within the Central Sierra. Turismo Central joins Huánayo with Huánuco; Palomino links Lima with Andahuaylas, Abancay and Ayacucho, although if you're travelling to Cusco from Ayacucho it's quicker to catch a combi via Andahuaylas and Abancay.

BY COLECTIVO
There are colectivo services between most neighbouring major towns and cities in the Central Sierra, but they are harder to find and without regular departure times. In Huancayo they tend to leave from C Real, a little beyond the centre of town; in Lima they start and end at Yerbadero.

Highlights

❶ Lima–Huancayo train journey The last
remaining working rail line in the region, this
breathtaking high-altitude train journey is one
of the finest in the world. **See p.283**

❷ Marcahuasi Reports of UFO sightings on this
high plateau covered in unusual rock formations
make for out-of-this-world weekend camping.
See p.283

❸ Tarma An attractive little colonial town,
known as La Perla de los Andes, is famous for its
fantastic Easter Sunday procession and
associated flower "paintings" that carpet the
roads. **See p.284**

❹ San Pedro de Cajas This scenic and remote
village is home to many craftspeople who
produce some of Peru's superb modern
weavings. **See p.284**

❺ Reserva Paisajística Nor Yauyos Cochas
Spectacular cascades, natural dams and blue
lagoons in this stunning reserve bursting with
flora and fauna. **See p.290**

❻ Ayacucho One of the most traditional and
architecturally fascinating cities in the Peruvian
Andes – renowned for around forty impressive
churches as well as boisterous religious fiestas.
See p.294

HIGHLIGHTS ARE MARKED ON THE MAP ON P.282

5

BY TRAIN

The world-famous Lima-to-Huancayo railway line ("El Tren de la Sierra") currently runs trains from Lima to Huancayo about twice a month (usually Fri or Sat) between April and September a breathtaking 11hr journey.

Information Precise itineraries, up-to-date prices and tickets can be obtained from FCCA (Ferrocarril Central

Andino) by phone or online (☎01 226 6363 ext 222, ⊛ferrocarrilcentral.com.pe) or in person at the Lima office (Av José Galvez Barrenechea 566, 5th floor, San Isidro).

Altitude sickness You're more likely to suffer from *soroche* – altitude sickness (see p.45) – if you enter the Central Sierra by train, due to the relatively slow climb through the high Ticlio Pass (over 4800m). To avoid breathlessness and

CENTRAL SIERRA REGION

HIGHLIGHTS

1. Lima–Huancayo train journey
2. Marcahuasi
3. Tarma
4. San Pedro de Cajas
5. Reserva Paisajística Nor Yauyos Cochas
6. Ayacucho

0   100
kilometres

5

THE ANDES RAIL LINE

The original opening of the Lima-to-Huancayo **rail line** into the Andes in the late nineteenth century had a huge impact on the region and was a major feat of engineering. For President Balta of Peru and many of his contemporaries in 1868, the iron fingers of a rail line, "if attached to the hand of Lima would instantly squeeze out all the wealth of the Andes, and the whistle of the locomotives would awaken the Indian race from its centuries-old lethargy". Consequently, when the American rail entrepreneur **Henry Meiggs** (aptly called the "Yankee Pizarro") arrived on the scene, it was decided that coastal guano deposits would be sold off to finance a new line, one that faced technical problems (ie, the peaks and troughs of the Andes) never previously encountered by engineers. The man really responsible for the success of this massive project was the Polish engineer, Ernest Malinowski. Utilizing timber from Oregon and the labour of thousands of Chinese workers (the basis of Peru's present Chinese communities), Malinowski's skill and determination finished Meiggs's rail line, over a thirty-year period. An extraordinary accomplishment, it nevertheless produced a mountain of debt that bound Peru more closely to the New York and London banking worlds than to its own hinterland and peasant population.

headaches, or the even worse effects of *soroche*, it's advisable to take the first few days over 3000m pretty easy before doing any hiking or other strenuous activities.

Tickets There are two classes of ticket: Touristic (S/350 return; S/235 one way) and Classic (S/195 return; S/120 one way).

The route to Tarma

Vehicles take four to six hours to cross the high pass at Ticlio, after which they drop in less than an hour to the unsightly and mining-contaminated town and pit stop of **La Oroya**. Just beyond here the road splits three ways: north to **Cerro de Pasco** and **Huánuco**; south to **Huancayo**, **Huancavelica** and, for the travel-hardened, **Ayacucho**; or, eastwards towards **Tarma**, which is just another hour or two further.

Marcahuasi and around

S/10 entrance fee

MARCAHUASI (4100m) is a high plateau that makes a fantastic weekend camping jaunt and is one of the more adventurous but popular excursions from Lima. Its main attractions are incredible, mysterious **rock formations**, which, particularly by moonlight, take on weird shapes – llamas, human faces, turtles, a hippopotamus and even a human figure known as Peca Gasha, a monument to humanity. Located 90km east of Lima (40km beyond Chosica), the easiest way to visit this amazing site in the hard-to-access Santa Eulalia Valley is on a day-trip from the capital (see p.81). The second week of October sees the start of the annual Festival del Agua, eight days of celebrations with music, dance and festivities.

San Pedro de Casta

Only a few kilometres from Marcahuasi (2hr 30min–3hr trek), **San Pedro de Casta** makes a good overnight stop – unless you choose to camp at Marcahuasi (take a good sleeping bag – it can get very chilly). It's a small and simple Andean village, quaint but without much choice in its limited range of facilities. There is a basic, municipally run hotel in town, and a handful of people rent out rooms in their homes. Your best bet is to ask around when you arrive.

ARRIVAL AND INFORMATION   **MARCAHUASI AND AROUND**

By bus There are no direct buses from Lima to Marcahuasi/ San Pedro. Instead, take a colectivo to Chosica (50min)

from between the 3rd and 4th blocks of Av Pasco colón, east of Bolognesi in Lima or hop on the Coasters minibus

5

marked Chosica (1hr 30min). From C Libertad, a block north of Chosica's Parque Echinique, a local bus departs at 9am for San Pedro (3hr).

Tourist information There's an Oficina de Información on the main plaza in San Pedro de Casta which tends to have erratic opening hours; it is normally open early in the morning and around lunchtime. This is where you will have to pay your S/10 fee for Marcahuasi. If you're looking for a guide, head to *La Cabañita* restaurant on the main square and ask for Jorge.

Tour operator The friendly TEBAC (Trekking and Backpacking Club), Jr Huascar 1152, Jesús María, Lima (☏ 01 423 2515 or ☏ 943 866 794, ⊕ angelfire.com/mi2/tebac) runs one- to three-day trips to Marcahuasi and throughout Peru; it's a great source of information on the country, too.

La Oroya

Not a particularly inviting place, **LA OROYA** is a small, desolate mining town that gets fiercely cold at night. Located in a dreary spot above the treeline, some four hours or so by steep uphill road from Lima, La Oroya is some 50km beyond the highest point, the pass or *abra* of Ticlio (4758m). The only possible reason to stop here is to have lunch in one of the many roadside cafés.

Tarma and around

Known locally as "La Perla de los Andes", **TARMA** is by far the nicest mountain town in this part of Peru, with warm temperatures and an abundance of wild and farmed flowers, sitting on the edge of the Andes almost within spitting distance of the Amazon forest. The town makes a good living from its traditional textile and leather industries, and from growing flowers for export as well as for its own use. Although connected with the **Juan Santos Atahualpas rebellion** in the 1740s and 1750s, today Tarma is a quiet place, disturbed only by the flow of trucks climbing up from the Amazon Basin loaded with timber, coffee, chocolate or oranges. The town is particularly famous for an Easter Sunday procession, starting from the main plaza; the streets are covered by carpets of dazzling flowers depicting various local, religious or mythic themes.

The scenery **around Tarma** constitutes one of Peru's most beautiful Andean regions, with green rather than snow-capped mountains stretching down from high, craggy limestone outcrops into steep canyons forged by Amazon tributaries powering their way down to the Atlantic. It's nevertheless always a good idea to check with your embassy in Lima for up-to-the-minute intelligence on this area, since the occasional terrorist column has been known to be active in its remoter sectors.

Palcamayo to San Pedro de Cajas

Colectivos run here from Av Francisco de Paula Otero and Jr Pablo Bermudez in Tarma (every 30min; 45min)

The rural village of **Palcamayo** makes an interesting day-trip from Tarma, though it's better appreciated if you camp overnight. From here it's an hour's climb to **La Gruta de Huagapo**, the country's deepest explored **caves**; if dry they are generally accessible for about 180m without specialized equipment, or up to 1.8km with a guide and full speleological kit. If you've got your own transport, continue 20km along the same road (the only road in the valley) west to the beautiful village of **San Pedro de Cajas**, where craftspeople produce superb-quality weavings. As an example of how landscapes can influence local art forms, the village lies in a valley neatly divided into patchwork field-systems – an exact model of the local textile style.

Acobamba

Church daily 8am–6pm · Free · Colectivo from the Mercado Modelo in Tarma (every 15min; 15min); tell the driver you're heading to the church and he will tell you where to get off, as it's 1km after the town centre

Within day-tripping distance from Tarma (12km) is the small settlement of **Acobamba**, home of the **Sanctuary of the Lord of Muruhuay**, a small church built in 1972 around a rock painting where a vision of Christ on the cross led to this site becoming a major

5

centre of pilgrimage. The chapel has an altar with weavings representing the Resurrection and the Last Supper. Some of the restaurants by the church serve excellent *cuy* and *pachamanca.*

ARRIVAL AND INFORMATION

BY BUS
The Terminal Terrestre (☎ 064 322 170) is on Av Vienrich. Destinations Huancayo (hourly; 3hr); La Merced (hourly; 2hr); Lima (several daily with morning and evening departures; 7hr); Satipo (several daily; 4hr).

BY COLECTIVO
Colectivos serving San Pedro de Cajas stop off at Av Francisco de Paula Otero and Jr Moquegua (every 30min 8am–4pm; 1hr 30min). To get to Huánuco catch a colectivo to Cerro de Pasco (every 30min 5am–3pm; 3hr) from Tarma's Av Castilla close to the Terminal Terrestre; from

TARMA AND AROUND

Cerro de Pasco you'll have to hop on another colectivo to Huánuco (every 30min; 2hr30min).

INFORMATION
Tourist information Municipal office on the plaza at Jr Dos de Mayo 755 (Mon–Fri 8am–1pm & 3–6pm; ☎ 064 321 010).

Tours Max Aventura at Jr Dos de Mayo 682 (☎ 064 323 908, ⍵ maxaventuraperu.com) organizes a range of full-day tours; the most popular is to the Valle de las Flores (S/45), which takes in a number of sights including San Pedro de Cajas (opposite).

ACCOMMODATION

TARMA
Hostal Corazón Av Castilla 194B ☎ 064 322 528. Just a few steps from the bus station, the colour-coded rooms at this place are good value; all come with hot running water and private bathrooms. $\overline{S/50}$

Hostal El Vuelo del Condor Jr Dos de Mayo 471 ☎ 064 322 399, ⍵ hotelelvuelodelcondor.com/el-hostal.php. This comfortable guesthouse a few steps from the Plaza de Armas makes for an excellent budget choice. The en-suite rooms are warm and welcoming, as are the staff, and there's wi-fi throughout. $\overline{S/60}$

Hotel Los Portales Av Ramón Castilla 512 ☎ 064 321411, ⍵ losportaleshoteles.com.pe. A short walk from the main square, Tarma's most comfortable hotel offers 46 comfortable rooms and suites in an attractive yellow building with garden and an attached *pollería*. The in-house restaurant is highly rated too, and there's wi-fi throughout, as well as a business centre and parking facilities. $\overline{S/350}$

Hotel Victoire's Jr Amazonas 548 ☎ 064 323 648. The brand-new rooms here feature parquet floors and green bedspreads, and come with clean en-suite bathrooms. Don't be afraid to ask for a discount, as staff will invariably oblige. The cabinet at reception displays ancient vases and

stonework from the area. $\overline{S/80}$

AROUND TARMA
Casa Hacienda La Florida Km 39, Carretera Central ☎ 01 344 1358 or ☎ 064 341 041, ⍵ haciendalaflorida .com. Some 6km from Tarma on the Acobamba road towards Chanchamayo, this family-run, eco-friendly hacienda occupying forty hectares is a working farm; guests can help milk the cows in the early morning, and the farm's own yogurt is served for breakfast. It's also a cultural centre, with art exhibitions and occasional historical and literary readings. Rooms are welcoming and comfortable, decked out with rustic furniture and local artefacts. Home-cooked meals, using fresh produce from the veg garden, must be ordered one day in advance. Doubles $\overline{S/233}$, camping $\overline{S/15}$ per person

Hacienda Santa María Sacsamarca, 1.2km from Tarma ☎ 01 445 1214 or ☎ 064 321 232, ⍵ haciendasantamaria.com. This beautiful hacienda features comfortable rooms set around a courtyard; the barn has been converted into a welcoming living area decorated with Peruvian rugs, while the Salón de los Recuerdos, or Room of Memories, houses antique furniture and curios, including paintings and old irons. $\overline{S/240}$

EATING

Check out the Mercado Modelo (daily 6am–8pm), which has cheap stalls serving local dishes for about S/10. There are many *chifa* restaurants or *pollerías* located within a couple of blocks' radius of the Plaza de Armas.

★**Daylo** Av Castilla 118 ☎ 064 323 048. This place proved so popular it had to relocate to larger premises; the extensive menu includes excellent freshwater trout ceviche (S/25) served with yucca, grilled or crispy trout (S/15) and salmon trout in garlic cream (S/15). Daily 7am–midnight.

Señorial Jr Huánuco 138 ☎ 064 323 130. One of the city's most reliable restaurants, *Señorial* offers good-standard Peruvian cuisine in the centre of town; the interior is oddly reminiscent of a US tavern with neon lights and retro furnishings. Mains S/15. Daily 8am–4pm & 6–11.30pm.

5

South of Tarma

The bustling city of **Huancayo** is the natural hub of the mountainous and remote region **south of Tarma**. Nearby **Jauja Valley** is significantly more beautiful, less polluted and friendlier. Further afield, **Ayacucho** is a must for anyone interested in colonial architecture, particularly fine churches; while **Huancavelica** offers a slightly darker history lesson – the area has suffered from extreme exploitation both in colonial times, with the mines, as well as in the 1980s and 1990s when terrorism was at a peak. The area is still occasionally visited by remnants of the Shining Path terrorist group (see box, p.493), but there have been no related problems for tourists in recent years. The trip out here by train (some 130km south of Huancayo), one of the world's highest railway journeys, passes through some stark yet stunning landscapes.

Huancayo

A large commercial city with over 350,000 inhabitants, **HUANCAYO** (3241m) is the capital of the Junín *departamento*. An important market centre thriving on agricultural produce and dealing in vast quantities of wheat, the city makes a good base for exploring the Mantaro Valley and experiencing the region's distinct culture. While the area is rich in pre-Columbian remains, and the cereal and textile potential of the region has long been exploited, the city itself is mostly relatively modern, with very little of architectural or historical interest. It is

HUANCAYO

0 — 200 metres

■ **ACCOMMODATION**
La Casa de la Abuela — 3
Hostal El Marquéz — 4
Hotel Presidente — 5
Posada Junco y Capuli — 2
Tuki Llajta Hotel — 1

● **CAFÉS & RESTAURANTS**
La Cabaña — 3
Coqui Café — 4
Detrás de la Catedral — 5
Huancahuasi — 1
Leopardo — 6
La Tullpa — 2

Capilla La Merced
LC Busre (airline office)
Catedral de Huancayo
PLAZA CONSTITUCIÓN
Peru Bus
BCP Bank
Colectivos to Tarma
Municipal Building & Artesan Market
PLAZA HUAMANMARCA
Iglesia María Inmaculada
Ancient Huanca Culture Wall
Train Station (Lima)

Terminal Los Andes
& Museo del Colegio Salesiano
Feria Dominical (Market)
Hospital
Parque de la Identidad de Huancayo, Cerro de la Libertad & Torre Torre
Train Station (Huancavelica), Wari Willka Sanctuary & Museum

still a lively enough place with a busy market and even some nightlife at weekends. It's also worth trying to time your trip to coincide with the splendid **Fiesta de las Cruces** each May, when Huancayo erupts in a succession of boisterous processions, parties and festivities.

Brief history

The region around Huancayo was dominated by the Huanca people from around 1200 AD, and the Huari culture before that, though it wasn't until Pachacuti's forces arrived in the fifteenth century that the Inca Empire took control. Occupied by the Spanish from 1537, Huancayo was formally founded in 1572 by Jeronimo de Silva, next to the older and these days relatively small town of Jauja (see p.291). In 1824, the **Battle of Junín** was fought close to Huancayo, when patriotic revolutionaries overcame royalist and Spanish forces. Apart from the comings and goings of the Catholic Church, Huancayo remained little more than a staging point until the rail line arrived in 1909, transforming it slowly but surely during the twentieth century into a city whose economy was based on the export of agrarian foodstuffs and craft goods.

More so than any other Peruvian city – except perhaps Ayacucho – Huancayo was paralysed in the years of **terror during the 1980s and 1990s**. As home to a major army base, it became the heart of operations in what was then a military emergency zone. In 1999, an extensive army operation captured the then leader of **Sendero Luminoso**, Oscar Ramírez Durand, who had taken over from Abimael Guzmán in 1992.

Plaza de la Constitución

Plaza de la Constitución – named in honour of the 1812 Liberal Constitution of Cádiz – is where you'll find monuments in honour of Mariscal Ramón Castilla (who abolished slavery in Huancayo in 1854), surrounded by ornamental plants of local origin, like *quishuar* and *retama*. Surrounded by the Neoclassical **Catedral de la Ciudad de Huancayo** (daily 7.30–9.30am & 5–7.30pm; free) and some of the town's major public buildings and offices, it was once home to the Feria Dominical market (see below), which was shifted in the mid-1990s to alleviate traffic problems.

Calle Real

Calle Real is the main drag running on the western edge of Plaza de la Constitución; it's here you'll find the **Capilla La Merced** (daily 9am–noon & 3–6.30pm; free), a colonial church, once the site for the preparation and signing of the 1839 Peruvian Constitution, and now designated a historic monument.

Plaza Huamanmarca

Plaza Huamanmarca sits at the heart of the city and is the oldest plaza, founded with the town back in 1572. On April 22, 1882, three local heroes – Enrique Rosado Zárate, Vicente Samaniego Vivas and Tomás Gutarra – were shot here by the Chilean army. Today the square is surrounded by public buildings, the Municipality, the central post office and the old *Hotel de Turismo*.

Museo del Colegio Salesiano

Prolongación Arequipa 10 • Mon–Fri 9am–1pm & 3–6pm, Sat 9am–noon • S/5 • ☎ 064 247 763

The **Museo del Colegio Salesiano**, in the residential northern district of El Tambo, is an excellent natural history museum with almost a thousand exhibits of local flora and fauna as well as archeological objects, hundreds of fossils, paintings, sculptures and a selection of interesting rocks and minerals.

Feria Dominical market

Blocks 2–12, Av Huancavelica • Sun 10am–5pm

Established in 1572 to assist the commerce of the local population, the market still sells fruit and vegetables, as well as a good selection of woollen and alpaca clothes and

5

blankets, superb weavings and some silver jewellery. Like most Peruvian city markets, it is the hub of activity early in the morning, and the wealth of tropical and Andean produce makes it exotic and satisfying to see and sense.

Parque de la Identidad de Huancayo

Taxi S/10 each way – more with a wait

Just 5km northeast from the city centre, in the Urbanización San Antonio, the **Parque de la Identidad de Huancayo** covers nearly 6000 hectares, much of it green space open for public enjoyment. The main entrance is in the form of a giant gourd, one of the typical regional artesanía products, and inside there's a *mirador* (viewing platform), some shady pergolas, cacti and the Laguna de Amalu. The entire park was created in honour of the local *wanka* style of music and the musicians themselves.

ARRIVAL AND DEPARTURE   HUANCAYO

BY BUS

Bus companies Most buses from Lima, including Oltursa (☎064 601 504, ⓦoltursa.pe), use the Terminal Terrestre, Av Evitamiento Norte s/n, El Tambo. Cruz del Sur has its own terminal at Av Ferrocarril 151 (☎064 223 367, ⓦcruzdelsur .com.pe). Expreso Molina serves Ayacucho from its office at Jr Angaraes 334 (☎064 224 501); Turismo Central is located at Jr Ayacucho 274 (☎064 223 128) and serves Huanuco, Tingo María, Pucallpa and Satipo.

Destinations Ayacucho (1 daily; 8hr); Huancavelica (several daily; 2–3hr); Huánuco (1 daily; 7hr); Lima via Jauja (several daily; 6–7hr); Pucallpa (1 daily; 15hr); Satipo (several daily; 5–6hr); Tingo María (1 daily; 8–10hr).

BY COLECTIVO

Most colectivos leave from the Terminal Los Andes on Av Ferrocarril just north of the centre.

Destinations Chanchamayo (every 30min; 3hr); Cochas Chico and Cochas Grandes (every 15min; 40min); Jauja

(every 30min; 40min); La Oroya (every 15min; 1hr 30min); Tarma (every 15min; 1hr 30min–2hr).

BY TRAIN

Train tickets are best bought online (ⓦferrocarrilcentral .com.pe).

Trains to and from Lima Serve the train station on Av Ferrocarril 461, within walking distance of the city centre.

Destinations Lima (once monthly April–Sept; 11hr).

BY PLANE

Flights from Lima to Huancayo (2 daily; 1hr) land at Franciso Carle airport in Jauja, 45km northwest of the city, served by LC Perù, Av Ayacucho 322, Huancayo (☎064 214 514, ⓦlcperu.pe), and Andes Air (ⓦandesair.com). Colectivos to Huancayo (30min; S/60) and Jauja (5min; S/5) meet incoming flights.

GETTING AROUND, INFORMATION AND TOURS

By taxi or bike The easiest and safest way of getting around is by taxi – or on foot in the very centre – though you can also cycle. Incas del Perú (see opposite), charges US$8/half day or US$12/full day.

Tourist information Dircetur, Jr Pachitea 201, at the Lima train station (Mon–Fri 8am–1pm & 2.30–5.30pm;

☎064 222 575).

Tour operators and guides Incas del Perú, Av Giraldez 675 (☎064 223 303, ⓦincasdelperu.com), and Dargui Tours, Jr Ancash 367, Plaza Constitución (☎064 233 705, ⓦdarguitours.com), offer trips throughout the region. Both agencies also organize car rental.

ACCOMMODATION

HUANCAYO

The best Huancayo offers in accommodation is its choice between rambling old or modern traditional city-centre hotels and a more familial setting in smaller outlying hostels. It doesn't offer anything spectacular in terms of rooms with views; for that you need to get out of town.

La Casa la Abuela Prolongación Cusco 794 and José Gálvez 420 ☎064 234 383, ⓦincasdelperu.org. This backpacker favourite offers accommodation in a large dorm room with woven Peruvian blankets and en-suite bathroom, as well as simple doubles with private bath.

There's a living room and small kitchen for guests' use, as well as a larger communal area with TV and a billiards table. There's a pleasant garden, too, with hammocks. Dorms <u>S/30</u>, doubles <u>S/70</u>

Hostal El Marquéz Jr Puno 294 ☎064 219 026, ⓦelmarquezhuancayo.com. Definitely a hotel and not a hostel, this is a modernized central choice offering large, comfy beds with crisp linen, nicely decorated rooms, laundry service and parking facilities. Staff are friendly, and the location – just behind the plaza – can't be beat. <u>S/210</u>

Hotel Presidente C Real 1138 ☎064 231 275,

ⓦhotelpresidente.com.pe. Attracting business types, central Huancayo's most upmarket option offers clean, carpeted rooms with dark wooden furniture. Service is friendly, and there are parking facilities. **S/265**

★**Posada Junco y Capuli Julio** C Tello 414, El Tambo ☎064 244 368. Tucked away on a little side-street to the north of town, this is a lovely budget *posada* with neat and tidy rooms with wooden floorboards, flat-screen TV and private bath. The welcoming entrance area is decorated with small statues and a couple of chessboards. **S/60**

OUTSIDE HUANCAYO

Tuki Llajta Hotel Av Centenario s/n, San Gerónimo de Tunan ☎064 797 107, ⓦtukillajta.com. Perched on a hillside to the north of Huancayo overlooking the town, this welcoming hotel offers accommodation in spacious rooms, all of which are equipped with fireplace – a welcome addition on cooler nights. Food is served in the bright dining area with large windows that look out over the city. It's a great spot to get away from the chaos of Huancayo. The helpful staff organize tours, too. **S/250**

EATING

La Cabaña Av Giraldez 675 ☎064 223 303. This cosy restaurant with wooden benches is packed with curios and odds and ends including rows of lanterns, old radios, jukeboxes and wine demijohns. The menu features Peruvian and international dishes, including sandwiches (S/12), burgers (S/10) and grilled meats (S/25). There is seating in the little garden-cum-patio area at the back, too. Daily 9am–midnight.

Coqui Café Jr Puno 296 and Centro Comercial Real Plaza. This popular café-bakery serves all manner of cakes (S/6), sandwiches (S/14) and coffees (S/3.50) in a welcoming setting just a few steps behind the cathedral. There's another branch at the Lima–Huancayo rail station in the Centro Comercial Real Plaza. Mon–Sat 7am–10.30pm, Sun 7am–1pm & 6–10.30pm.

Detrás de la Catedral Jr Ancash 335 ☎064 212 969. Nestled away on a small side-street just behind the cathedral, this is a great central restaurant offering Peruvian staples (S/16) and pasta dishes (S/20) in a welcoming setting. Mon–Sat noon–10pm, Sun noon–4pm.

Huancahuasi Av Mariscal Castilla 2222, El Tambo ☎064 244 826. This atmospheric restaurant buzzes with custom, particularly at the weekend when there's live music and traditional dance shows (1–3pm). Waiters are dressed in colourful gilets and food is served in an attractive indoor room with wooden beams or at outdoor tables with pretty Peruvian tablecloths. Mains S/25. Daily 9am–7pm.

Leopardo Jirones Huánuco and Libertad ☎064 235 488, ⓦleopardorestaurante.com. This well-established restaurant with a peach-coloured interior has been serving traditional Peruvian dishes for more than thirty years. There's a wide selection of ceviche dishes (S/27), as well as plenty of meat mains (S/21). Daily 6.30am–6.30pm.

La Tullpa Jr Atahualpa 145, El Tambo ☎064 253 649, ⓦlatullpa.com. A popular local restaurant with seating both indoors and out in the interior patio, offering all manner of trout dishes, from tasty ceviche (S/31) to fillet (S/22), along with chicken (S/22) and *cuy* dishes (S/33). Daily 11am–4.30pm.

DIRECTORY

Health Hospital Regional, Av Daniel Carrión 1552 ☎064 222 157.

Language schools Incas del Perú, Av Giraldez 675 (☎064 223 303, ⓦincasdelperu.org).

Money and exchange Banco de Credito, C Real 1039, is best. To change dollars, try your hotel or the street *cambistas* along C Real.

Police Tourist Police, Av Ferrocarril 580 ☎064 219 851.

Post office Centro Cívico Foco 2, Plaza Huamanmarca (Mon–Sat 8am–8pm).

Around Huancayo

There is plenty to see in the area around Huancayo, including the ancient **Wari Willka Sanctuary** just south of the city, and the stunning eighteenth-century **Convento de Santa Rosa de Ocopa**. It's well worth heading to **Cochas Chico and Cochas Grandes** for a morning or afternoon to see skilled craftsmen making beautiful, intricately carved gourds that make for great souvenirs. The surrounding countryside also offers excellent hiking opportunities in the Cordillera Huaytapallana and the Reserva Paisajística Nor Yauyos Cochas.

Wari Willka Sanctuary and Museum

Tues–Sun 9am–1pm & 2.30–5.30pm • S/3 • Taxi from Huancayo S/10

Some 6km south of Huancayo, near the present-day pueblo of **Huari**, stands the **Wari Willka sanctuary** constructed by the Waris between 700 and 1200 AD, and

5

subsequently occupied by the Wanka people (1200–1460) and then probably by the Incas. The grounds are thought to have been used as a religious sanctuary where sacrifices – including of children and dogs – took place. The interesting little **museum** in the town square houses a collection of ceramic fragments and a mummy of a young woman (circa 600–700) in her 20s, whose injuries indicate she was probably sacrificed.

Convento de Santa Rosa de Ocopa

Visitable on guided tour only Mon & Wed–Sun 9am, 10am, 11am, 3pm, 4pm & 5pm (1hr) • S/5 • Colectivos to Santa Rosa from C Calixto in Huancayo (1hr), 22km north of Huancayo

Founded in 1725 and located some 25km northwest of Huancayo, the **Convento de Santa Rosa de Ocopa** took some twenty years to build. The church was the centre of the Franciscan mission into the Amazon, until their work was halted by the Wars of Independence (see p.488), after which the mission villages in the jungle disintegrated and most of the indigenous people returned to the forest. Guided tours take in the convent's two pretty cloisters and the plethora of rooms that give onto them, including a chapel, a canteen with brightly coloured wall paintings, a small printing press, a library with 30,000 titles and a couple of rooms displaying stuffed birds, anacondas, crocodiles and other exotic species from the jungle.

A trip to the *convento* can be conveniently combined with a visit to the nearby village of **San Jerónimo**, about 12km west, well known for its workshops of fine silver jewellery (daily 8.30am–9pm).

Cochas Chico and Cochas Grandes

Colectivo from Huancayo's Terminal Los Andes on Av Ferrocarril (every 15min; 40min)

A good day-trip from Huancayo is to the local villages of **Cochas Chico and Cochas Grandes**, whose speciality is crafted, carved gourds. Strangely, Cochas Grandes is the smaller of the two villages, and you have to ask around if you want to buy gourds here. You can buy straight from cooperatives or from individual artisans; expect to pay anything from S/4 up to S/2500 for the finer gourds, and if you are ordering some to be made, you'll have to pay half the money in advance. The etchings and craftsmanship on the more detailed gourds is incredible in its microscopic depth, creativity and artistic skill. On some, whole rural scenes, like the harvest, marriage and shamanic healing are represented in tiny storyboard format. The less expensive, simpler gourds have fairly common geometric designs, or bird, animal and flower forms etched boldly across their curvaceous surfaces.

Cordillera Huaytapallana

Private tour from Huancayo (see p.288)

About 29km northeast of Huancayo lies the Cordillera Huaytapallana mountain range where snow blankets the ground at about 5150m by the peaks of Lazuhuntay (5557m) and Yanahucsha (5530m). Here the landscape is peppered with beautiful emerald lagoons, deep gorges and scenic rivers, including the River Shullcas that flows towards Huancayo. It's a 5.5km walk over 4500m through beautiful landscape that is among the most elevated in the Central Andes, home to vicuñas, dozens of species of bird and lush vegetation.

Reserva Paisajística Nor Yauyos Cochas

Private tour from Huancayo (see p.288)

Occupying an area of 2213 square kilometres, the **Reserva Paisajística Nor Yauyos Cochas** is located in the Junín region between 2500 and 5700m above sea level. The main attractions here are the spectacular cascades, natural dams and blue lagoons that the River Cañete forms at its source. There are excellent bird-watching opportunities as well as beautiful views of Uscho Canyon. The landscape reserve also harbours a plethora of Andean flora and fauna, including *vicuñas*, Andean foxes and herons. The reserve can be visited as part of a full-day tour from Huancayo; it's also possible to camp here.

Jauja

5

Forty kilometres northwest of Huancayo is **JAUJA**, a little colonial town that was the capital of Peru before the founding of Lima. Surrounded by some gorgeous countryside, Jauja is a likeable place, whose past is reflected in its unspoilt architecture, with many of the colonial-style buildings painted light blue. A much smaller and more languid town than Huancayo, its streets are narrow and picturesque, and the people friendly. Today, Jauja is more renowned for its traditional and well-stocked Sunday and Wednesday markets.

Capilla de Cristo Pobre

Between calles San Martín and Colina • Open during Mass times

The **Capilla de Cristo Pobre** shares some similarities with Notre Dame de Paris and, perhaps a tenuous claim to fame: Gothic in style, it was also the first concrete religious construction in the Central Sierra.

Laguna de Paca

10–15min by colectivo (S/1.50) from Jauja • Boats S/10 per hr

If you fancy exploring the landscape around Jauja, it's possible to rent boats on the nearby **Laguna de Paca** and row out to the Isla de Amor; according to local legend, this lake is the home of a mermaid who lures men to their deaths. The lake is surrounded by *totora* reeds and brimming with birdlife. The shoreline is lined with cafés serving decent trout meals, and, at weekends, *pachamanca* (meat and vegetables placed in a hole in the earth on preheated hot rocks and covered with soil for slow cooking) is served.

Tunanmarca

30min by taxi from Jauja (S/25 return)

Some 17km northwest of Jauja, just outside the town of Concho, are the archeological remains of **Tunanmarca**. The ancient settlement was home to an estimated population of 8000–13000 between 1200 and 1400 AD and boasts circular constructions as well as aqueducts and other pre-Inca water works. Located on a mountain pass surrounded by waterfalls at 3900m, Tunanmarca is one of three pre-Inca defensive constructions. It is thought to have been the main base for the Xauxa culture, centred high up in the Valley of Yanamarca, to the north of the fertile Mantaro Valley.

ARRIVAL, GETTING AROUND AND INFORMATION   JAUJA

By bus Buses serve the Terminal Terrestre on Av Ricardo Palma. Lima-bound buses from Huancayo pick up passengers in Jauja, with most departures in the early mornings and evenings.
Destinations Cerro de Pasco (hourly; 4hr); Huancayo (several daily; 45min); Lima (several daily; 6hr).

By colectivo Colectivos use the Terminal Terrestre on Av Ricardo Palma, with frequent services to Huancayo (every 15min; 45min).
Tourist information At the Municipality, Jr Ayacucho 856 on the main plaza (Mon–Fri 8am–1pm & 3–5pm; ☎ 064 362 075 ext 213).

ACCOMMODATION AND EATING

El Mantaro Jr Tarapacá ☎ 064 362 671. This atmospheric restaurant with black-and-white prints of old Jauja offers a good-value set-lunch menu for S/10; food is served in two rooms, and there's frequent live music. Daily 11am–5pm.
Villarreal Hotel Jr Villarreal 593 ☎ 064 361 550,

✉ hotelvillarrealeirl@hotmail.com. A few blocks east of the city centre, this is a reliable option with spick-and-span tiled rooms kitted out in dark furnishings; all have flat-screen TVs, en-suite facilities and wi-fi, and staff are friendly and welcoming. <u>S/75</u>

Huancavelica

Remote **HUANCAVELICA**, at 3676m, is almost purely indigenous in its ethnic make-up, which is surprising considering its long colonial history and a fairly impressive array of Spanish-style architecture. There's little of specific interest in the town itself, except the

5

Sunday market, which sells local food, jungle fruits and carved gourds. A couple of pleasant walks from town will bring you to the natural hot springs on the hill north of the river, or the weaving cooperative, 4km away at Totoral. Local mines (see below) are an attraction, too.

Brief history

Originally occupied by hunter-gatherers from about 5000 years ago, the area then turned to sedentary cultivation as the local population was, initially, taken over by the Huari people around 1100 AD, a highly organized culture that reached here from the Ayacucho Valley. The Huanca people arrived on the scene in the fifteenth century, providing fierce resistance when they were attacked and finally conquered by the Inca. The weight of its colonial past, however, lies more heavily on the region's shoulders.

After mercury deposits were discovered here in 1563, the town began producing **ore** for the silver mines of Peru, replacing expensive imports previously used in the mining process. In just over a hundred years, so many indigenous labourers had died of mercury poisoning that the pits could hardly keep going: after the generations of locals bound to work by the *mitayo* system of virtual slavery had been literally used up and thrown away, the salaries required to attract new workers made many of the mines unprofitable.

Today the mines are working again and the ore is taken by truck to Pisco on the coast. The Mina de la Muerte, as the **Santa Barbara mines** tend to be called around Huancavelica, are also an attraction in their own right, located several kilometres southeast of town (about 1hr 30min by foot); the shield of the Spanish Crown sits unashamedly engraved in stone over the main entrance to this ghostly settlement. There's plenty to explore, but as with all mines, some sections are dangerous and not visitor-friendly, and it's best to ask local advice before setting off.

Plaza de Armas

Huancavelica's main sights are around the **Plaza de Armas**, where you'll find the two-storey Cabildo buildings, the **Capilla de la Virgen de los Dolores** and, at the heart of the square, a stone *pileta* in octagonal form incorporating two waterspouts, each portraying an Indian face, water gushing from their respective mouths.

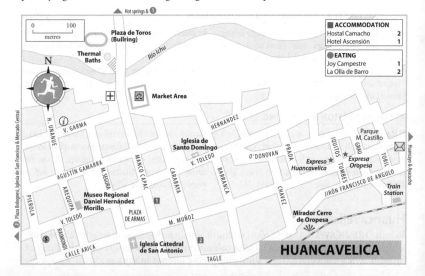

ANDES TRAVEL WARNING

It's best to travel through the Andes by day, although if you're confined to night-time travel choose your transport wisely: it's possible to hitch rides on trucks or take cheap local buses, but these are more at risk of being stopped and robbed during night journeys. The Huancayo-Huancavelica-Ayacucho stretch of road is particularly subject to robberies as buses wind their way through isolated mountain plains, making them an easy target for muggers.

Iglesia Catedral de San Antonio

Plaza de Armas • Mon–Sat 7am–5.15pm, or for Mass on Sun at 5.30am, 8am, 9.30am & 5.15pm

The seventeenth-century **Iglesia Catedral de San Antonio** features a fine altar and pulpit and some excellent paintings. Construction started in 1673, and it took a hundred years to complete. These days it's home to the sacred image of the city's patron – Nuestra Señora de las Mercedes. The elaborate gold-leaf altar was carved from wood, and the silver sheets on display beside it are from the Cusqueña and Huamanguina schools (see box, p.213). There is a distinct Baroque style in the volcanic stone craftsmanship, and religious paintings decorate the interior representing Heaven, Purgatory, Hell, the Last Supper and the Crucifixion.

Iglesia de San Francisco

Plaza Bolognesi • Open daily for Mass only 5–6.15pm

The **Iglesia de San Francisco**, which along with Santo Domingo (see below) is connected to the cathedral via an underground passage, was built on the Plaza Bolognesi in 1774 by the Franciscan Order. Posessing a single nave and some fancy Baroque and Churrigueresque *retablos* of wood and gold leaf, it has just about survived some major earthquakes. During the nineteenth-century war with Chile, this church was commandeered by the Peruvian army, who sold its fine collection of musical instruments to finance the war effort. Today, the steps of San Francisco are the site, on December 24 and 25, of the awe-inspiring, traditional scissor-dancing performances (*danza tijera*), generally done by men wielding two long machete-like swords.

Iglesia de Santo Domingo

C Toledo • Open daily for Mass only 5–6.15pm

Santo Domingo is a church and convent complex, connected to the cathedral via an underground passage and founded in 1601, just thirty years after the city was established. The entrance is made from red stone brought from the Pucarumi quarry. Inside there are fine paintings, brought from Rome, of the Virgen del Rosario and the patron St Dominic, as well as a fine Baroque altar with some gold-leaf adornment; in the sacristy you can find a painting dating from 1666 representing *El Señor de la Sentencia y Resurrección*.

Museo Regional Daniel Hernández Morillo

Plazuela San Juan de Dios • Tues–Sun 8am–1pm & 2.30–8pm • S/3 • ☎ 067 453 420

The small **Museo Regional Daniel Hernández Morillo** sits in the Instituto Nacional de Cultura building one block from the Plaza de Armas, and contains archeological exhibits, fossils from the Tertiary period, petrified marine species and displays on pre-Inca Andean cultures. As well as the archeology and anthropology section, this museum also boasts a room of popular art, showing paintings and objects depicting local culture.

ARRIVAL AND INFORMATION   HUANCAVELICA

By bus Megabus at Av Muñoz 662 (☎ 067 451 411) connects Lima with Huancavelica, while Oropesa, at Av Muñoz 610 (☎ 067 369 082), has buses from Ica, Lima and Huancayo; Molina at Av Muñoz 1004 (☎ 067 452 613) has services from Lima and Ayacucho. Note that buses are frequently held up and robbed on the Huancavelica–Ayacucho road, especially at nighttime.

Destinations Ayacucho (daily at midnight; 7–9hr); Huancayo (1 daily; 5hr); Ica (2 daily; 8hr); Lima (4 daily with evening departures; 12hr).

5

Tourist information Dircetur, Jr Victoria Gamarra 444 (Mon–Fri 8am–1pm & 2.30–5.30pm; ☎ 067 452 938).
Tours Turismo Andino organizes tours in and around

Huancavelica; it has an office in Huancayo at C Real 261 (☎ 064 224 419, ⓦ turismo-andino.com).

ACCOMMODATION

Hotel Ascensión Jr Manco Cápac 481 ☎ 067 453 103, ✉ hotelascension@hotmail.com. Right on the Plaza de Armas, this is one of the city's best options, offering sturdy beds with locally woven blankets and chocolate-coloured furnishings. All rooms are en suite. **S/70**

Hotel Presidente Plaza de Armas ☎ 067 452 760, ⓦ huancavelicaes.hotelpresidente.com.pe. This is a clean and well-established place with large, modern-styled rooms all with wi-fi, cable TV and private bathroom. Room service and minibar are available. **S/245**

EATING

Joy Campestre Av Los Incas 870 ☎ 067 454 101. Probably the best restaurant in town, this is a pleasant spot with seating in a welcoming garden with views. Joy's bestseller is *pachamanca* (S/20), a hearty stew of meat and vegetables baked in hot stones under the ground, although there are plenty of other options, such as soup (S/10) and

chicken dishes (S/12). Daily 8am–6pm.
La Olla de Barro Jr Agustín Gamarra 305 ☎ 958 943 558. This first-floor restaurant serves traditional dishes in a simple interior brightened up with woven tablecloths of Peruvian design. The menu includes *cuy* (S/20), beef steak (S/12) and chicken (S/13). Daily 11am–3pm.

Ayacucho

Roughly halfway between Cusco and Lima, **AYACUCHO** ("Purple Soul", in the Quechua language) sits in the Andes around 2800m high in one of Peru's most archeologically important valleys, with evidence such as ancient stone tools found in nearby caves at Pikimachay, which suggest that the region has been occupied for over 20,000 years. Its **climate**, despite the altitude, is pleasant all year round – dry and temperate with blue skies nearly every day – and temperatures average 16°C (60°F). The surrounding hills are covered with cacti, broom bushes and agave plants, adding a distinctive atmosphere to the city.

Despite the political problems of the last few years, most people on the streets of Ayacucho, although quiet and reserved (seemingly saving their energy for the city's boisterous **fiestas**), are helpful, friendly and kind. You'll find few people speak any English; Quechua is the city's first language, though most of the town's inhabitants can also speak some Spanish.

Brief history

Ayacucho was the centre of the Huari culture, which emerged in the region around 700 AD and spread its powerful and evocative religious symbolism throughout most of Peru over the next three or four hundred years. After the demise of the Huari, the ancient city later became a major Inca administrative centre. The Spanish originally selected a different nearby site for the city at Huamanguilla; but this was abandoned in 1540 in favour of the present location. Ayacucho's strategic location, vitally important to both the Incas and the Spanish colonials, meant that the city grew very wealthy as miners and administrators decided to put down roots here, eventually sponsoring the exquisite and unique wealth of the city's **churches**, which demonstrate the clearly high level of masonry and woodworking skills of the local craftspeople.

The bloody **Battle of Ayacucho**, which took place near here on the Pampa de Quinoa in 1824, finally released Peru from the shackles of Spain. The armies met early in December, when Viceroy José de la Serna attacked Sucre's Republican force in three columns. The pro-Spanish soldiers were, however, unable to hold off the Republican forces who captured the viceroy with relative ease. Ayacucho was the last part of Peru to be liberated from colonial power.

Though quiet these days, Ayacucho was also a radical university town with a left-wing tradition going back at least fifty years, known around the world for the civil war

▲ Bus Terminal

AYACUCHO

0   200
          metres

Museo de la
Memoria

Museo de
Arqueología

University

INDEPENDENCIA

JIRÓN QUINUA

MANCO CAPAC

Cruz del Sur
Buses ★

JIRÓN LIBERTAD

Pisco ◀

Combis to
Andahuaylas
and Agency

JIRÓN ASAMBLEA

PASS. CÁCERES

CRD ALEGRIA

Huari & buses ▶

JIRÓN MARISCAL CACERES

JIRÓN SOL

1

✉

JIRÓN GARCILAZO DE LA VEGA

Iglesia de
Santo Domingo

❶ 2

JIRÓN M P BELLIDO

Galeria de
Arte Popular

1

❷

JIRÓN CALLAO

$

JIRÓN CUSCO

JIRÓN ECO PIZARRO

Airport, Abancay & Cusco ▶

❸

PLAZA
DE
ARMAS

❹ 3

JIRÓN LIMA

ⓘ

Catedral

JIRÓN AREQUIPA

Jesuit Templo de la Compañia

$

Tourist
Police

Centro Cultural San Cristóbal ❺

$ @

Conquistadores

JIRÓN 9 DE DICIEMBRE

JIRÓN SAN MARTIN

Museo de Arte
Popular Joaquín
Lopez Antay

4

JIRÓN TRES MÁSCARAS

Plaza More ❻

CALLE EL NAZARENO

5

JIRÓN GRAU

Arco de
Triunfo

JIRÓN C F VIVANCO

JR. LOND RES

★ *Combis to*
Airport

Market
Area

Iglesia
San Francisco
de Asis

RAYMONDI

JIRÓN 28 DE JULIO

S J DE DIOS

CORCOBADO

JIRÓN 2 DE MAYO

CHORRO

ITANA

Templo de
San Cristóbal

Barrio
Santa Ana

● CAFÉS & RESTAURANTS

La Casona	2
Mamma Mia	6
La Miel	3
El Nino	1
Niñachay	5
Via Via Café	4

■ ACCOMMODATION

Hotel Rivera	2
Hotel Sevilla	1
Misky Samay	5
Tres Máscaras	4
Via Via Hotel	3

■ BAR

| Taberna Magía Negra | 1 |

5

between terrorists and the Peruvian armed forces during the 1980s (see p.493). Most civilians in the region remember this era as one where they were trapped between two evils – the terrorists on the one hand and the retaliatory military on the other. Because of this, several villages were annihilated by one side or the other. A large proportion of villagers from remote settlements in the region consequently decided to leave the area, a move which they hoped would offer them relative safety. Despite efforts by Fujimori's government to rehabilitate these communities and entice people back from Lima to their rural homes in the 1990s, many of them remain in the capital today.

Catedral

Mon–Sat 10am–noon & 4–6pm, Sun open for Mass only • Free

Splendid churches and mansions pack together in dense blocks around the central **Plaza de Armas** (also known as the **Plaza Mayor**) at whose centre rests a monument to Mariscal José Sucre. From here you can see the fine stonework of the **Catedral**, just off the Plaza Mayor, which is of more interest. Built of red or pink stone in its central section and grey stone for its towers between 1612 and 1671, it has a fine, three-aisled nave culminating in a stunning Baroque gold-leaf altarpiece.

Templo de San Cristóbal

Jr 28 de Julio 651 • Opens sporadically for Mass • Free

The 1540 **Templo de San Cristóbal** was the first church built in Ayacucho. It has a nave whose roof is covered with stone and adobe; within the church are the remains of men killed during the 1542 Battle of Chupas, one of the bloodiest battles ever fought against the Spanish conquistadores. There's only one small tower, topped by a gold-painted domed belfry. At the time of writing, the church was being restored.

Iglesia de Santo Domingo

Jr 9 de Diciembre • Mon–Fri 9am–noon & 4–7pm, Sat 9am–noon, Sun open for Mass only at 7am & 6.30pm • Free

The **Iglesia de Santo Domingo** was founded in 1548 and possesses one of the most beautiful exteriors in the city, with three arches of brick and lime, said to be where heretics were hanged and tortured during the Spanish Inquisition. Inside, the church houses a Baroque and Churrigueresque gold-leaf altar and two images – *El Señor del Santo Sepulcro* and the *Virgen Dolorosa* – only brought out for the Easter processions.

Templo Jesuita de la Compañía

Jr 28 de Julio • Mon–Sat 10am–12.30pm & 6–7pm, Sun 7–8am & 9am–12.30pm • Free

The **Templo Jesuita de la Compañía**, built in 1605, is renowned for its distinctive Churrigueresque-style main altar, but even the front exterior facade is one of the city's most complex and colourful, with a red-painted stone entrance held tight between two stout stone towers.

Museo de Arte Popular Joaquín Lopez Antay

Portal Independencia 72 • Mon–Fri 7.30am–1pm & 2–4.30pm • Free

The **Museo de Arte Popular Joaquín Lopez Antay** features an impressive range of artworks from the Ayacucho region, including woodcarvings, ceramics and religious dioramas, as well as papier-mâché and photographs of twentieth-century Ayacucho. A number of the paintings on display were created by acclaimed Peruvian artist Joaquín López Antay (1897–1981), who was born in Ayacucho and awarded the National Prize of Culture in 1974, shortly before his death.

Museo de Arqueología

Av Independencia 502 • Tues–Sun 9am–1pm & 3–5pm • S/3 • ☏ 066 312 056

The **Museo de Arqueología**, or Museo Hipolito Unanue, is located in the university's botanical gardens. It's a small museum stuffed full of local archeological finds, mainly

5

ceramics, dating from several millennia ago, plus exhibits from the Chavín, Huarpa, Nazca and Inca eras.

Museo de la Memoria

Prolongaciom Libertad 1229 • Mon–Fri 9am–1pm & 3–6pm • S/2 • ☎ 066 317 170

The harrowing **Museo de la Memoria** focuses on the socio-political violence inflicted by the Shining Path revolutionary movement in the 1980s and 90s (see box, p.493). The little museum is home to a number of displays including photographs of the dead and missing, as well as artworks on the conflict and a replica of a torture cell. A wall chart details the history of ANFASEP, the non-profit organization that runs the museum. Mothers and wives of the deceased and missing meet here regularly to share their experiences and lend support to one another. You can purchase the women's handmade clothes and crafts in the little shop upstairs.

ARRIVAL AND GETTING AROUND	AYACUCHO

BY PLANE

Most overseas visitors arrive in Ayacucho by plane from Lima. The airport (☎ 066 312 418) is 4km from town. Regular combis (every 15min; 10min) connect it to Puente Nuevo on Jr Vivanco; a taxi is about S/6. LAN, LC Perú and Star Perú serve the city. Currently the only destination is Lima (5 daily; 35min) although Star Perú is due to launch a direct service to Cusco at the end of 2015.

BY BUS

Most buses use the Terminal Municipal Los Libertadores de America at Av Pérez de Cuellar s/n (☎ 066 312 666), with the exception of the well-established Cruz del Sur which serves

Lima (3 daily) from its own terminal at Jr Mariscal Cáceres 1204 (☎ 066 312 813). Palomino (☎ 066 313 899) travels to Lima and Ica; Antezana Hermanos (☎ 066 311 348) also serves Ica; Turismo Central (☎ 066 317 873) serves Huancayo; Expreso Los Chankas (☎ 066 401 943) serves Cusco. Expreso Molina (☎ 066 319 989) serves Huancavelica, although this company has a poor safety record and the route itself is often the target of night-time robberies. To get into town from the bus terminal catch a taxi (10min; S/10).

Destinations Abancay (2 daily; 7–8hr); Andahuaylas (2 daily; 5–6hr); Cusco (3 daily; 12–16hr); Huancavelica (1 daily; 8hr); Huancayo (3 daily; 10hr); Huanta (3 daily; 1hr); Ica (3 daily; 6hr); Lima (several daily; 8–9hr).

ARTS AND CRAFTS

Many visitors come for Ayacucho's thriving **craft industry**, mainly woven rugs and *retablos* (finely worked little wooden boxes containing intricate three-dimensional religious scenes made mainly from papier-mâché). If you've got the time to spare, however, it's more interesting and less expensive to visit some of the actual **craft workshops** and buy from the artisans themselves. Most of these workshops are found in the barrio of **Santa Ana**, just uphill from the Plaza de Armas: locals are always happy to guide visitors in the right direction. Some of the best-quality *retablos* are not all that expensive, but if you want one of their more complicated modern pieces it could cost as much as US$300, and take up to three months to complete.

RUGS

Edwin Sulca – arguably the best-known weaver here – lives opposite the church on the Plaza Santa Ana; his work sells from around US$100 (almost double in Lima's shops), and many of his designs graphically depict the recent political horrors around Ayacucho.

Gerado Fernandez Palomino is another excellent weaver who has a store in his house and workshop located on Jr Paris 600, also in Santa Ana.

ALABASTER CARVINGS

Alabaster carvings – known in Peru as **Huamanga stone carvings** – are another speciality of Ayacucho. Try Señor Pizarro, Jr San Cristóbal 215, who has a reputation as one of the best carvers in town. The craft cooperative Ahuacllacta, Huanca Solar 130, is also worth checking out.

ARTESANÍA MARKETS

Head to the following: Plazoleta María Pardo de Bellido; the first block of Jirón Paris; second block of Pasaje Bolognesi; and the first two of Jirón Asamblea.

5

BY COMBI

Combis to Andahuaylas and Abancay leave from Pasaje Cáceres just off Jr Mariscal Cáceres, with departures between 6–7am, 1–2pm and 6–7pm.

Destinations Abancay (10hr); Andahuaylas (6hr).

INFORMATION AND TOURS

Tourist information The helpful iPeru office is located in the Municipalidad building, Portal Municipal 45, Plaza de Armas (Mon–Sat 9am–6pm, Sun 9am–1pm; ☎ 066 318 305, ✉ iperuayacucho@promperu.gob.pe); there's also a tourist information kiosk at the airport, although it opens only for morning flights (roughly 6.30–7.30am).

Tour operators One of the easiest ways to visit the sites around Ayacucho is to take a guided tour. A number of companies offer half-day tours to Pikimachay and Huari

(see p.299) for about S/40, Quinua for about S/35 and Vilcasayhuamán and Intihuatana for about S/65. Operators include: A&R Tours, Jr 9 de Diciembre 130 (☎ 066 311 300, ✇ viajesartours.com); Net Travel, Jr 9 de Diciembre 123 (☎ 066 326 316, ✇ netravel.com.pe); Urpillay Tours, Jr 28 de Julio 262 (☎ 066 315 074, ✇ ayacuchoviajes.com); Wari Tours, Jr Lima 138B (☎ 066 311 415, ✇ waritoursayacucho .blogspot.com); and Wily Tours, Jr 9 de Diciembre 209, Parque Luís Carranza (☎ 066 314 075, ✇ wilytours.com).

ACCOMMODATION

Finding a room in Ayacucho is easy enough outside the Easter period when, because of the colourful religious festivals (see box below), the town is bursting at the seams with visitors from Lima and elsewhere.

Hotel Rivera Jr Callao 316 ☎ 066 316 255, ✇ hotelriveraperu.com. Three blocks west of the main square, this hotel has bare-brick stone walls, a polished wooden staircase and 38 comfortable rooms with flat-screen TV and carpets. Rates include American breakfast. S/140

Hotel Sevilla Jr Libertad 635 ☎ 066 314 388, ✇ hotelsevillaperu.com. The real attraction here is the beautiful courtyard dotted with dozens of pretty potted plants and beautiful wooden chests. Rooms are comfortable and mostly decorated with local or chintzy paintings; rates include breakfast. S/90

Misky Samay Jr Carlos F. Vivanco 145 ☎ 066 313 335, ✇ miskysamay.com. Located just across from the Mercado Central and tucked away in a little courtyard lined with shops, this place offers simple but welcoming rooms with private bath that are very good value. S/60

Tres Máscaras Jr Tres Máscaras 194 ☎ 066 312 921, ✉ hoteltresmascaras@yahoo.com. This lovely guesthouse has plenty of character – rooms give onto a lush garden area with prickly pears, apple and orange trees, cacti and bougainvillea, to name a few, while ceramics and the odd curio are displayed in the corridor. Two parrots and three chirpy dogs further add to the atmosphere. Breakfast is an extra S/6. S/71

Via Via Hotel Portal Constitución 4 ☎ 066 312 834, ✇ viaviacafe.com. The rooms at this popular place, all named after continents and regions of Ayacucho, give onto a bustling courtyard where meals from the *Via Via Café* are served; some feature open-plan bathrooms, while the larger family rooms are set on two floors. There's a book exchange, all-day water and tea, and local crafts and souvenirs on sale in support of NGOs and a local women's association. S/150

EATING AND DRINKING

Food and nightlife are both surprisingly good in Ayacucho, with the city's distinctive cuisine including *puca picante*, made from pork and potatoes seasoned with yellow chilli peppers and ground toasted peanuts, and the local *chorizo*, which is prepared with minced pork soaked with yellow chilli and vinegar, then fried in butter and served with diced fried potatoes. The courtyard complex of cafés and shops – Complejo Turístico San Cristóbal – at Jr 28 de Julio 178, offers a popular place for eating out.

FESTIVALS AND MUSIC IN AYACUCHO

If you can be in Ayacucho for **Semana Santa**, the Holy Week beginning the Friday before Easter, you'll see fabulous daily processions, pageants and nightly candlelit processions centred on the Catedral. But beware of the beautiful procession of the **Virgen Dolores** (Our Lady of Sorrows), which takes place the Friday before Palm Sunday: pebbles are fired at the crowd (particularly at children and foreigners) by expert slingers so that onlookers take on the pain of La Madre de Dios, and so supposedly reduce her suffering. Around May 23, there is the elaborate religious procession of the **Fiesta de las Cruces**, when festivities often involve the local "scissors" folkdance performed by two men, each wielding a rather dangerous pair of cutlasses.

La Casona Jr Bellido 463 ☎ 066 312 733. This place gets particularly busy at lunchtime for its good-value set lunch of local dishes for S/12; à la carte mains start at about the same price, although note that service can be slow. Daily 11am–10pm.

Mamma Mia Plaza More, Jr 28 de Julio 262 ☎ 066 311 067. On the pretty Plaza More, home to a number of restaurants, this is one of the city's few options for pizzas and pasta dishes. The setting is pleasant, and there are plenty of cocktails to choose from too. Daily 4pm–midnight.

La Miel Portal Constitución 11–12 ☎ 066 317 183. Right on the main square, this is a popular spot that buzzes at all times of day for its tasty cakes (S/6), freshly squeezed juices (S/5) and good coffees. Daily 10am–10pm.

El Nino Jr 9 de Diciembre 205 ☎ 066 314 537. One of Ayacucho's most appealing restaurants offers seating on a pleasant patio with views of the pretty Iglesia de Santo Domingo – a great spot for a pisco sour (S/12) as the sun sets. The ground-floor seating area is decorated with local masks and wooden benches, and the menu is heavy on meat dishes, although at about S/40 a pop it doesn't come cheap. Daily 11am–2pm & 5–11pm.

Niñachay Centro Turístico Cultural San Cristóbal de Huamaga, Jr 28 de Julio 178 ☎ 066 403 171. Located within the San Cristóbal cultural centre that also houses a number of other restaurants, this is a safe option with tables spilling onto the courtyard offering a range of tasty local dishes. Mains S/16. Daily 8am–10pm.

Taberna Magía Negra Jr 9 de Diciembre 293. This popular pizza and bar venue gets busy over the weekends, when locals and tourists alike come to drink beer and listen to good live music. Mon–Sat 4pm–midnight.

Via Via Café Portal Constitución 4 ☎ 066 312 834, ⊛ viaviacafe.com. With wonderful views of the main plaza, this is one of the city's best restaurants, offering local and international dishes including excellent Belgian stew (S/21) and a particularly good *quinoto*, or *quinoa* risotto (S/15), as well as a selection of alpaca dishes (S/12). There are great fruit and vegetable juices (S/7) too, and inventive home-made ice-cream flavours including pisco sour (S/2 per scoop). There's regular live acoustic music, too (Thurs–Sat 7–11pm). Daily 7am–midnight.

DIRECTORY

Health Hospital Central, Av Independencia 355 (☎ 066 312 180).

Internet Conquistadores, Dos de Mayo 172 (daily 8am–9pm; S/1 per hr; ☎ 066 527 683).

Money and exchange There's an ATM at the Banco de Credito on the Plaza Mayor and at Caja Municipal also on the square. Several shops on the Plaza de Armas will change dollars and euros.

Post office Jr Asamblea 293, two blocks from the plaza (Mon–Fri 8am–7pm, Sat 8am–6pm).

Tourist police Jr Arequipa and Dos de Mayo (daily 8am–10pm; ☎ 066 315 845).

Around Ayacucho

Although the city itself is certainly the main pull, there are some quite fascinating places **near Ayacucho** that are possible to visit. Having said that, it's always a good idea to check with the tourist office (see opposite) beforehand on whether or not it's safe to travel in the rural environs of Ayacucho. At the time of writing, the region had been politically stable for over twelve years, but the situation is open to change and some villages are more sensitive than others.

GETTING AROUND   **AROUND AYACUCHO**

By organized tour The best way to travel in the area around Ayacucho is with one of the local tour companies and a guide (see opposite).

By car If you have your own transport or rent a vehicle, you'll need good maps.

Pikimachay and Huari

Huari museum Daily 9am–5pm • S/3

The cave of **Pikimachay**, 24km northwest of Ayacucho, on the road to Huanta, where archeologists have found human (dated to 15,000 BC) and gigantic animal remains, is best visited on a guided tour with one of the tour companies (see opposite). This is also true of the ancient city of **Huari** (sometimes written "Wari"), about 20km north of Ayacucho on the road to Huancayo. Historians claim that this site, which covers about 2000 hectares, used to house some 50,000 people just over a thousand years ago. You can still make out the ancient streets, plazas, some reservoirs, canals and large structures. The small site **museum** displays skulls and stone weapons found here in the 1960s.

Quinua

Located about 37km northeast of Ayacucho, the charming and sleepy village of **QUINUA** is a bus ride (1hr) away, through acres of tuna cactus, which is abundantly farmed here for both its delicious fruit (prickly pear) and the red dye (cochineal) extracted from the *cochamilla* larvae that thrive at the base of the cactus leaves. The site of the historic nineteenth-century **Battle of Ayacucho**, just outside town on the pampa, is marked by a striking obelisk, unmistakeable at 44m tall. There are still some **artisans** working in Quinua: at San Pedro Ceramics (at the foot of the hill leading to the obelisk) it's often possible to look round the workshops, or try Mamerto Sánchez's workshop on Jirón Sucre.

Vilcasayhuamán and Intihuatana
Daily 9am–5pm • Vilcasayhuamaán S/3; Intihuatana S/2

About 120km from Quinua, some four hours by road, is **Vilcasayhuamán**, a pre-Conquest construction with a Temple of the Sun, Temple of the Moon and a ceremonial pyramid. Vilcasayhuamán was an Inca administrative centre once home to 40,000 people. The central plaza was the focus for ceremonies and two very important buildings stood round it: the Sun Temple (Templo del Sol) and the Ushnu, a truncated pyramid. On the upper platform of this pyramid there's a large stone with unique carvings, thought once to have been covered with gold leaf. Originally, the city was constructed in the form of a falcon with the Ushnu located at the head. Another 25km on from Vilcasayhuamán, at a site called **Intihuatana**, there's another archeological complex, with a palace, artificial lake and a stone bath. This site reveals very fine Inca stonework in terracing and palatial doorways.

East to Cusco

It takes 20 to 28 hours to travel from Ayacucho to Cusco via **Andahuaylas** and **Abancay**, a distance of almost 600km. From Abancay, the rest of the journey to Cusco is a little less than 200km, usually taking five or six hours and passing through archeologically interesting terrain en route: shortly before crossing into the *departamento* of Cusco the road goes through the village of **Carahuasi** where the community of Concacha (3500m) is home to the archeological complex of Sahuite, comprising three massive, beautifully worked granite boulders, the best of which graphically depicts an Inca village (though the boulders have been partially defaced in recent years). Nearby, at Conoc, there are hot medicinal springs.

Andahuaylas and around

It's a 250km (6hr) haul from Ayacucho across mountain passes and through several valleys to **ANDAHUAYLAS**, a small town that serves as the airport for the larger Abancay. There's little to see or do here, despite the backdrop of splendid highland scenery. The main church, **Catedral de San Pedro**, reflects a plain colonial style and the nearby plaza possesses a *pileta* cut from a solid piece of stone. Another fine example of *sillar* stone construction, the **Puente Colonial El Chumbao** road bridge gives access to the Nazca road and the airport.

Sondor
45min by bus from Andahuaylas

Some 21km from Andahuaylas, the archeological remains of **Sondor** lie in the mountains about 2km beyond Laguna Pacucha at 3200m. This region – the province of Cotabambas, and specifically the village of Coyllurqui – is also home to the Yawar Fiesta, a dramatic festival that takes place every July, usually near the end of the month. The mythic re-enactment and community event involves capturing a live condor and tying it to the back of a bull, the latter representing the conquistadores and the condor being indigenous to Peru. Legend says that the condor kills the bull, but in real life the bull ends up killing the condor. The fiesta is very much frowned upon given the mistreatment of animals, and it looks like the tradition will die out.

ARRIVAL AND INFORMATION

By bus The Terminal Terrestre is at Av Malecón Mil Amores 235 and Av José Gátvez. Expreso Los Chankas (☎83 722 441) serves Cusco and Ayacucho.

Destinations Ayacucho (several daily; 7hr); Cusco (several daily; 5hr); Lima (several daily; 15–17hr).

By combi The quickest way to get to Ayacucho is by combi; to get to Cusco catch a combi to Abancay, and then a bus or

ANDAHUAYLAS AND AROUND

another combi from there.

Destinations Abancay (every 45min; 4hr); Ayacucho (every 45min; 6hr).

Tourist information Dircetur is located at Jr Guillermo Cáceres Tresierra 284 (Mon–Fri 7.30am–1pm & 2–4.15pm; ☎83 421 627).

ACCOMMODATION

La Mansión Casa Hotel Av Peru 667 ☎83 205 613, ⓦlamansioncasahotel.com. A decent choice in Andahuaylas, offering clean and comfortable rooms,

parking facilities, good service and a pleasant garden area. **S/110**

Abancay and around

About 150km east of Andahuaylas is **ABANCAY**, a large, bustling town at 2378m above sea level. Despite few sights or tourist facilities (with Cusco so close, the town hosts relatively few tourists), it's nevertheless worth a stop as it's within striking range of a number of stunning sites, not least Choquequirao.

Choquequirao

The superb Inca ruins of **Choquequirao** overlook the Apurimac Canyon and provide a fantastic trek with archeological interest, one which competes well as an alternative to the Inca Trail (see p.250). Choquequirao is best approached with a planned expedition, hiring local guides and mules, or through one of the Cusco tour operators (see p.221).

Santuario Nacional de Ampay

Accessed from a track about 5 or 6km north from Abancay • S/10 • Take a taxi or bus from Abancay (30–45min; taxi S/10)

The **Santuario Nacional de Ampay** is a protected area boasting forests, orchids and bromeliads, as well as foxes, deer, spectacled bears, *viscachas*, falcons and owls. The forest here is almost 4000 hectares of protected land mostly covered in endangered *intimpa* trees. It also contains waterfalls, glaciers and swampy areas. The Nevado Ampay, the glacial peak that dominates the landscape here, stands at 5235m tall. There's a small **visitor's centre** at the entrance, where you will have to pay the S/10 entrance fee.

ARRIVAL AND INFORMATION

By bus The Terminal Terrestre is on Av Tupac Amaru. Cruz del Sur (☎83 324 877) serves Lima, Nazca and Ica.

Destinations Cusco (several daily; 5hr); Lima (several daily; 15–17hr); Nazca (several daily; 8–10hr); Puquio (several daily; 9–10hr).

By combi The quickest way to get to Ayacucho is by combi via Andahuaylas; these leave from the Terminal Terrestre,

ABANCAY AND AROUND

while services to Cusco leave from Avenida Nuñez.

Destinations Andahuaylas (every 45min from about 5–6am until 3pm; 4hr); Cusco (hourly; 4hr 30min).

Tourist information There's a tourist information point at the Terminal Terrestre (Mon–Sat 7.30am–1pm & 2.30–7pm; ☎83 504 890); Dircetur is located at Av Arenas 121 (Mon–Fri 7.15am–1pm & 2.30–4.30pm; ☎83 321 664).

ACCOMMODATION

Abmale Hostal Jr Libertad 101 ☎83 323 979, ⓔabmale-hs@hotmail.com. This green block has some of the best rooms in town – welcoming, clean and good value with en-suite bathrooms, and right on the main square. **S/90**

El Peregrino Apart Hotel Jr Andrés Avelino Cáceres

390 ☎83 502 610. This modern hotel just a short walk from the main square offers comfortable tiled apartments with fully equipped kitchenette and living area. The premises are kept clean, there's wi-fi throughout, and staff are friendly. **S/130**

5

West of Abancay

Cusco is four or five hours east of Abancay; travelling west it's a relatively short hop to Puquio and from there down to Nazca on the coast, or even direct to Lima. The small town of **Chalhaunca** sits beside a popular thermal bath at a crossroads below Abancay, just before the serious mountain climbs start on the route to **Puquio**.

Chalhuanca

Catch a combi from Av Brasil in Abancay (every 30min; 2hr)

CHALHUANCA is a small town in a deep valley a couple of hours downhill from Abancay en route towards Puquio and Nazca. Its claim as a stopping point rests mainly in the clean, and reputedly healing, hot thermal springs that can be visited just 2km from the town itself (taxi from the main plaza S/5–8).

Puquio

Take a Nazca- or Lima-bound bus from Abancay and hop off here (6hr)

PUQUIO lies 180km west, over the Andes, from Chalhaunca. It is a base for exploring alpaca and *vicuña* land – particularly Pampas Galeras (see box, p.38). With the many surrounding mines, the area is rich in treasures but, more importantly, great varieties of fruits and vegetables in different valleys of the region. There are also small volcanoes and even condor-viewing points within a day or so of the town.

North of Tarma

North of Tarma there are two main routes: closest is the steep road which heads northeast down from the Andes into the Central Selva of Chanchamayo and beyond to a large region with its own possible but adventurous overland routes. The other goes back up to the crossroads just before La Oroya and then heads north to Cerro de Pasco and Huánuco, interesting for its nearby archeological remains, such as Tantamayo, and itself another important gateway to the jungle region (see p.306).

Reserva Nacional de Junín

The **Reserva Nacional de Junín** is located some 85km northwest of Tarma on the La Oroya-to-Cerro de Pasco road; this is an excellent trip if you can afford the time and car rental or tour (see p.285). Located at around 4100m above sea level on the Pampa de Junín, it's packed with aquatic birds around the lakes as well as being home to plenty of *viscachas* in its 5300 hectares. It's possible to **wild camp** here (always asking local permission first), but there are no facilities at all.

Huánuco and around

The charming modern city of **HUÁNUCO**, more than 100km east of the deserted Inca town of the same name, and around 400km from Lima, sits nestled in a beautiful Andean valley some 1900m above sea level. It's a relatively peaceful place, located on the left bank of the sparkling Río Huallaga, and depending for its livelihood on forestry, tea and coca, along with a little low-key tourism. Founded by the Spaniard Gómez de Alvarado in August 1539, the city contains no real sights, save the usual handful of fine old churches and a small natural history museum. There are plenty of fascinating excursions in the area – notably, the 4000-year-old **Temple of Kotosh**.

Iglesia de San Francisco
Plaza de Armas • Daily 6–10am & 5–8pm • Free

The sixteenth-century **Iglesia de San Francisco** houses the tomb of the town's founder and shows a strong indigenous influence, its altars featuring richly carved native fruits – avocados, papayas and pomegranates. It also displays a small collection of sixteenth-century paintings. Externally, it is not as impressive and doesn't look as old as it is, with a plain facade, painted mustard right up to its two towers.

Iglesia de la Merced
C Hermilio Valdizan • Daily 6–10am & 5–8pm • Free

The **Iglesia de la Merced** lies some three blocks south and west from the Plaza de Armas. It was built in 1566, in the Romantic style, and it's worth a look around if only for its spectacular Neoclassical gold-leaf altarpiece; there are also two notable Cusqueña-style (see box, p.213) religious paintings on display. From the outside, the church is small and simple, painted cream.

Iglesia de San Cristóbal
C Damaso Beraun • Daily hours of Mass only • Free

The **Iglesia de San Cristóbal**, three blocks west of Plaza de Armas, has some fine gold-leaf altarpieces, and is said to be built on the site where the chief of the Chupacos tribe once lived and where Portuguese priest Pablo Coimbra celebrated the first Mass in the region. The first-ever Mass to be said in Huánuco was on this site on August 15, 1539, just seven years after the conquest of Peru. Some of the interior woodwork depicts faces and hands.

Museo de Ciencias
Jr General Prado 495 • Mon–Sat 8am–noon & 3–7pm • S/5

The natural history museum, **Museo de Ciencias**, houses regional archeological finds, mainly pottery, as well as a small display of Andean flora and fauna including some dried and some stuffed animals from the region. Established with the help of expert taxidermists back in 1947, there are brilliant examples of stuffed condors, eagles, sloths and armadillos, and also butterfly collections. The museum was closed at the time of research due to renovations and financial constraints; it is not known whether it will reopen or not.

The Temple of Kotosh
Daily 9am–5.15pm • S/5 • Taxi from Huánuco S/10

Just 6km from Huánuco along the La Unión road, the fascinating, though poorly maintained, **TEMPLE OF KOTOSH** lies in ruins on the banks of the Río Tingo. At over 4000 years old, this site predates the Chavín era by more than a thousand years. A more or less permanent settlement existed here throughout the Chavín era (though without the monumental masonry and sculpture of that period) and Inca occupation, right up to the Conquest. The most remarkable feature of the Kotosh complex is the **crossed-hands symbol** carved prominently onto a stone – the gracefully executed insignia of a very early culture about which archeologists know next to nothing – which now lies in the **Museo Nacional de Arqueología, Antropología e Historia del Peru** in Lima (see p.76). The site today consists of three sacred stone-built enclosures in generally poor condition; but with a little imagination and/or a good local guide, it is both atmospheric and fascinating to explore one of the most ancient temple sites in Peru.

ARRIVAL AND DEPARTURE   **HUÁNUCO AND AROUND**

By plane Aeropuerto Alférez FAP David Figueroa Fernandini (☎ 062 513 066) is 6km out of town, and served by LC Busre, Jr Dos de Mayo 1321 (☎ 062 518 113). There are weekly (1hr) flights from Lima.

5

FIESTAS IN HUÁNUCO

If you can, you should aim to be in Huánuco around August 15, when **carnival week** begins and the city's normal tranquillity explodes into a wild fiesta binge. **Peruvian Independence Day** (July 28) is also a good time to be here, when traditional dances like the *chunco* take place throughout the streets. On January 1, 6 and 18, you can witness the **Dance of the Blacks** (El Baile de los Negritos) in which various local dance groups, dressed in colourful costumes with black masks (representing the slaves brought to work in the area's mines) run and dance throughout the main streets of the city; food stalls stay open and drinking continues all day and most of the night.

By bus There is no central bus station in Huánuco; each operator uses its own terminal. GM Internacional is at Av 28 de Julio 535 (☎062 519 770) and serves Lima and Tingo María; Turismo Central is at Jr Tarapacá 598 (☎062 511 806) and serves Pucallpa, Huancayo and Tingo María; Turismo Unión is at Jr Tarapacá 449 (☎062 514 540) and serves La Unión and Tantamayo.

Destinations Huancayo (1 daily; 8–10hr); La Unión (1 daily; 5–6hr); Lima (several daily; 8–10hr); Pulcallpa (1 daily; 11hr); Tantamayo (1 daily; 7–10hr); Tingo María (1 daily; 2–3hr).

By colectivo Colectivos are the best way to get from Huánuco to Tingo María; they leave and drop off from the first block of C Prado. There are more bus options to Pucallpa from Tingo María, so it may be worth hopping onto a colectivo to Tingo and finding a bus there.

INFORMATION AND TOURS

Tourist information There's a Dircetur office at Jr Bolívar 381 (Mon–Fri 8am–1pm & 3–6pm; ☎062 512 980, ⓦdirceturhuanuco.gob.pe)

Tour operators Adventure and Expeditions, Jr Los Nogales Mz. N Lote 33, Los Portales, Amarilis, Huánuco (☎062 512 826, ⓦadventureandexpeditionsperu.com).

ACCOMMODATION

HUANUCO

Gran Hotel Huánuco Jr Damaso Beraun ☎062 514 222, ⓦgrandhotelhuanuco.com. Right on the plaza is this comfortable hotel in a pretty colonial building shaded by old trees; rooms are quite spacious and kept clean, with wi-fi throughout. Facilities include a swimming pool and a great restaurant serving local cuisine. S/230

Grima Hotel Jr Dámaso Beraún 880 ☎062 513 649, ⓦgrimahotel.pe. This modern hotel in the centre of town is an excellent choice, featuring spotless rooms with modern amenities; all have flat-screen TV and private facilities, and buffet breakfast is served on the first-floor mezzanine. S/120

Hotel Trapiche Jr General Prado 636 ☎062 517 091 ⓔhoteltrapichehuanuco@hotmail.com. A reliable central option offering accommodation over two floors. The

clean, comfortable and spacious rooms are decked out in modern furnishings with splashes of bright colour; there's wi-fi throughout and laundry service, too. S/140

AROUND HUANUCO

Casa Hacienda Shismay Shismay, 19km east of Huánuco ☎062 631 174 or ☎962 367 734, ⓦshismay .com. Built in 1859 by German immigrants, this wonderful hacienda was expropriated by the government in 1970 and lovingly restored; today, profits are shared between the building's maintenance and other community projects, students acts as guides to the surrounding sites, and local women prepare meals for guests. Accommodation is in attractively furnished rooms, and there's also a mini museum recreating the hacienda's pre-1970 days. S/180

EATING

Marhana Jr Dos de Mayo 1064 ☎999 664 420. A stone's throw from the plaza, this restaurant and bar offers well-presented Peruvian and international cuisine in a pleasant enough setting. Mains S/25. Daily 7am–midnight.

Tradiciones Huanuqueñas Jr Huallayco 2444

☎062 515 953. This large restaurant on the road towards the airport serves hearty portions of local food, namely the *cuy* (S/20); there are a number of other dishes to choose from too, including chicken (S/15), duck (S/20) and freshwater trout (S/15). Daily 10.30am–5.30pm.

La Unión

A small market town high up on a cold and bleak pampa, **LA UNIÓN** is a base for visiting the Inca ruins of Huánuco Viejo; they are a tough – and not recommended due to precipitous mountain roads – three- to four-hour hike away. La Unión has a few cafés and a couple of hostels.

Huánuco Viejo

Take a taxi from Plaza de Armas, La Unión (S/15–20) • Daily 8am–6pm • S/4

Huánuco Viejo sits high up on the edge of a desolate pampa and is one of the most complete existing examples of an Inca provincial capital and administrative centre. The site gives a powerful impression of a once-thriving city – even though it's been a ghost town for four hundred years. The grey stone houses and **platform temples** are set out in a roughly circular pattern radiating from a gigantic *unsu* (Inca throne) in the middle of a plaza. To the north are the **military barracks** and beyond that the remains of suburban dwellings. Directly east of the plaza is the palace and temple known as Incahuasi, and next to this is the Acllahuasi, a separate enclosure devoted to the Chosen Women, or Virgins of the Sun. Behind this, and running straight through the Incahuasi, is a man-made water channel diverted from the small Río Huachac. On the opposite side of the plaza you can make out the extensive administrative quarters.

Poised on the southern hillside above the main complex are more than five hundred **storehouses** where all sorts of produce and treasure were kept as tribute for the emperor and sacrifices to the sun. Well away from the damp of the valley floor, and separated from each other by a few metres to minimize the risk of fire, they also command impressive views across the plain.

Brief history

Virtually untouched by the Spanish conquistadores, the city became a centre of native dissent. Illa Tupac, a relative of the rebel Inca Manco and one of the unsung heroes of the indigenous resistance, maintained clandestine Inca rule around Huánuco Viejo until at least 1545. The Spanish built their own colonial administrative centre – modern Huánuco – at a much lower altitude, more suitable for their unacclimatized lungs and with slightly easier access to Cusco and Lima. Huánuco grew thoroughly rich, but was nevertheless regarded by the colonial Peruvians as one of those remote outposts (like Chile) where criminals, or anyone unpopular with officialdom, would be sent into lengthy exile.

ARRIVAL AND DEPARTURE LA UNIÓN

By bus Buses from Huánuco (sporadic departures, about 3–4 daily; 5–6hr) link with La Unión daily; all arrive at the same terminal on Jr Comercio.

By colectivo Colectivos arrive at the same terminal on Jr Comercio.

ACCOMMODATION

Hospedaje Shamuy Punay Jr Comercio 1318. One of La Unión's safest bets for a night or two, this place offers simple rooms. The *El Hornito* restaurant, just next door at no. 1317, is a reliable spot for a bite to eat. **S/50**

Tantamayo

About 150km north of Huánuco, poised in the mountainous region above the higher reaches of the Río Marañón, lies the small village of **TANTAMAYO**, with its extensive ruins nearby.

The precise age of the remote **ruins of Tantamayo** is unknown. Its buildings appear to fit into the Tiahuanaco-Huari phase, which would make them some 1200 years old, but physically they form no part of this widespread cultural movement, and the site is considered to have developed separately, probably originating from tribes migrating to the Andes from the jungle and adapting to a new environment over a long period of time. It is also thought that the ruins might reveal archeological links to Chavín de Huantar (see p.335) and Kotosh.

The architectural development of some four centuries can be clearly seen – growing from the simplest of structures to complex edifices. The thirty separate, massive constructions make an impressive scene, offset by the cloud forest and jungle

5

flourishing along the banks of the Marañón just a little further to the north. Tall buildings dot the entire area – some clearly **watchtowers** looking over the Marañón, one of Peru's most important rivers and a major headwater of the Amazon, others with less obvious functions, built for religious reasons as temple-palaces, perhaps, or as storehouses and fortresses. One of the major constructions, just across the Tantamayo stream on a hill facing the village, was named **Pirira** by the Incas who conquered the area in the fifteenth century. At its heart there are concentric circles of carved stone, while the walls and surrounding houses are all grouped in a circular formation – clearly this was once an important centre for religious ritual. The **main building** rises some 10m on three levels, its bluff facade broken only by large window niches and by centuries of weathering.

ARRIVAL AND DEPARTURE   TANTAMAYO

By bus Tantamayo is served by a handful of minivans and combis from Huánuco; these leave from the corner of jirones San Martín and Tarapacá, with most departures around 6am (and then irregularly every 2hr or so; 4–5hr).

Several combi-colectivos and buses also run daily from La Unión to Tantamayo (6–7hr); these pick up and drop off from the main terminal on Jr Comercio.

Into the jungle

The Amazon is the obvious place to move on to from Huánuco and the surrounding area, unless you're heading back to Lima and the coast. The spiralling descent north is stunning, with views across the jungle, as thrilling as if from a small plane. By the time the bus reaches the town of **Tingo María**, a possible stopover en route to Pucallpa (see p.458), the Río Huallaga has become a broad tropical river, navigable downstream in shallow canoes or by balsa raft. And the tropical atmosphere, in the shadow of the forested ridges and limestone crags of the **Bella Durmiente** mountain, is delightful. From Tingo María you can continue the 260km directly northeast on the dirt road through virgin forest, going through the **Pass of Padre Abad**, with its glorious waterfalls, along the way to Pucallpa, jumping-off point for expeditions deep into the seemingly limitless wilderness of tropical jungle (see Chapter Eight).

Tingo María

Once known as the "Garden City", because of the ease with which gardens, tropical fruit, vegetables and wild flora grow in such abundance, the ramshackle settlement of **TINGO MARÍA**, 130km north of Huánuco, lies at the foot of the Bella Durmiente (Sleeping Beauty) mountain. According to legend, this is the place where the lovesick Princess Nunash awaits the waking kiss of Kunyaq, the sorcerer. These days the town welcomes more travellers than ever due to the decreased activity in the region's cocaine trade. However, that said, even the road on to Pucallpa from Tingo still sees the occasional armed robbery of buses travelling by night.

Despite Tingo María's striking setting, it is a tatty, ugly town, on which the ravages of Western civilization have left their mark. Dominated by sawmills and plywood factories financed by multinational corporations, with its forest of TV aerials sticking out from the rooftops, the town displays symbols of relative affluence, but the tin roofs and crumbling walls across the township betray the poverty of the majority of its inhabitants. There's little for visitors to see, other than the **Cueva de las Lechuzas** (Owls' Cave; daily 8am–6pm, last entry at 5pm; S/10), the vast, picturesque home to a flock of rare nocturnal parrots (you'll need a torch), 14km out of town. To get here, catch a mototaxi from the city's Parque Ramón Castilla (S/2.50). Tingo María's major **fiesta** period is the last week of July – a lively and fun time to be in town, but on no account leave your baggage unattended.

ARRIVAL AND DEPARTURE

By bus Each bus company has its own terminal. The following all serve Lima: GM Internacional at Av Raymondi 740 (☎ 062 561 895, ⓦ gminternacional.com.pe); Bahía Bus Continental at Jr General Prado 1085 (☎ 062 562 780); León de Huánuco, Pimentel 164 (☎ 062 562 030); Transmar, Av Enrique Pimentel 147 (☎ 062 564 733, ⓦ transmar.com.pe). Turismo Central (Av Raymondi Cuadra 9 ☎ 062 562 668, ⓦ turismocentral.com.pe) serves Huancayo. Be aware that local buses travelling at night are sometimes robbed at

gunpoint, which is at the very least an unpleasant experience. Destinations Huancayo (1–2 daily; 8–10hr); Lima (several daily; 10–12hr).

By colectivo Colectivos leave and arrive at all times of day and night connecting Tingo María with both Pucallpa and Huánuco from Av Raymondi, about five blocks from the Plaza de Armas.

Destinations Huánuco (every 15min; 2hr); Pucallpa (every 15min; 5hr); Tarapoto (every 15min; 6–7hr).

INFORMATION AND TOURS

Tourist information Dircetur, Av Sven Ericson 158 (Mon–Fri 8am–1pm & 2.30–5.30pm; ☎ 062 562 310, ⓔ perucata@hotmail.com).

Tours Mecsa Osha Tours, Alameda
430, ⓦ toursmecsaosha.com; Nuna
☎ 062 785 278, ⓦ tingomarianuna

ACCOMMODATION

Green Paradise Hotel Av Raymondi 687 ☎ 062 406 818, ⓦ greenparadisehotel.com. This friendly central hotel in a modern block offers smallish but clean and welcoming rooms with private bath. Breakfast is served on an open-fronted terrace, which provides a welcome little breeze in Tingo María's heat. **S/60**

Madera Verde Hotel Av Universitaria s/n, 2km south of Tingo María ☎ 062 562774 or ☎ 0662 561800, ⓦ maderaverdehotel.com. Two kilometres south of Tingo María, this rustic wooden lodge offers accommodation in rooms, two-room bungalows (sleeping four; S/320) or three-room cabañas (sleeping five; S/380); rooms are decorated with local materials and brightened up with

colourful Peruvian paintings. W
hectares is a rehabilitation centre,
and monkeys. **S/150**

Villa Jennifer Km 3.4 Monte
☎ 062 794 714 or ☎ 962 603 50
Covering an area of ten hectares,
offers comfortable, tasteful room
orange trees; there's an alligator
turtles, and facilities include mi
pitch, volleyball court and two s
which is nestled among trees by
good spot for a refreshing dip. **S/1**

MONOPOLY

A60R501592748C

FREE Shutterfly 4.5 x 5 Magnet Reward!
Turn the photos you love into photo books,
cards and gifts at shutterfly.com/monopoly

Enter promo code at shutterfly.com/monopoly. Offer ends June 30, 2017.

AL2D-7SPE-31J3-HXDF8E

Offer expires June 30, 2017 (11:59 P.M. PT). Offer is good for one free 4.5x5 magnet through shutterfly.com or our mobile-friendly site. This offer code can only be entered once. Taxes, shipping and handling will apply. Not valid on other magnet sizes, stationary or glass magnets, prepaid items, other products, prior purchases and orders made on Shutterfly apps. Cannot be redeemed for cash or combined with select offers or credits. Not valid for resale. We reserve the right to modify or replace any part of these terms and conditions without notice. Shutterfly is not responsible for lost or stolen promotion coupons.

A48C

A60R501592748C

SHOP, PLAY, WIN!

Huaraz, the cordilleras and the Ancash coast

MOUNTAINS OF THE CORDILLERA BLANCA

Huaraz, the cordilleras and the Ancash coast

It is the majestic snow-capped peaks of the Cordillera Blanca that draw most visitors to this region – many of them to follow the area's awesome trekking trails and some to experience mountaineering in the high Andes (or "Andinismo"). The mountains are accessed via an immense desert coastline, where pyramids and ancient fortresses are scattered withineasy reach of several small resorts linked by vast, empty beaches. Between the coast and the Cordillera Blanca, sits the barren, dry and dark Cordillera Negra. Sliced north to south by these parallel ranges, the centre of Ancash is focused on the Huaraz Valley, known locally as the Callejón de Huaylas. The city of Huaraz offers most of the facilities required for exploring the valley and surrounding mountains, though there are more rural alternatives.

The *departamento* of Ancash was a rural backwater when it was created in 1839. These days, the main industries are fishing (mainly restricted to Chimbote, Peru's largest fishing port), tourism (everywhere but Chimbote), mining (gold, silver, copper and zinc) and agriculture (primarily the cultivation of wheat, potatoes, maize corn and pulses, but also over forty percent of Peru's commercial marigold flowers). The region has a population of just over one million, with 250,000 of these people living in or around **Chimbote**.

For Peruvian and overseas visitors alike, Ancash offers more in terms of **trekking** and **climbing**, beautiful snowcapped scenery, "alpine" flora and fauna and glaciated valleys than anywhere else in the country. It is also extremely rich in history and **pre-Columbian remains** as well as possessing a truly traditional living culture.Given the severe earthquake damage this area has suffered throughout the twentieth century, it may lack some of the colonial charm seen in Cusco, Arequipa, Cajamarca and Ayacucho, yet more than makes up for it with the majesty and scale of its scenery. At around 3000m above sea level, it is important to acclimatize to the **altitude** before undertaking any major hikes.

Nestling in the valleys, the *departamento*'s capital, **Huaraz** – a six- or seven-hour drive north from Lima – makes an ideal base for exploring the region. It's the place to stock up, hire guides and mules or relax after a breathtaking expedition. Besides being close to scores of exhilarating mountain trails, the city is also near the ancient Andean treasure, **Chavín de Huantar**, an impressive stone temple complex that was at the centre of a culturally significant puma-worshipping religious movement just over 2500 years ago.

MOUNTAIN BIKING NEAR HUARAZ

Highlights

❶ Monterrey and Chancos Relaxing in either of these two natural thermal baths is both a healthy and a hedonistic experience to remember. **See p.320**

❷ Cordillera Blanca Hiking or climbing in this mountainous region is as scenic an adventure as you could hope to find anywhere outside the Himalayas. **See p.321**

❸ Las Lagunas de Llanganuco These calm, turquoise-coloured glacial lakes sit 3850m above sea level, dramatically surrounded by Peru's highest peaks. **See p.328**

❹ Huascarán Dividing the Amazon Basin from the Pacific watershed, this mountain is the highest peak in Peru. **See p.328**

❺ Caraz A quaint, attractive town known for its honey and milk products, quietly settled below the enormous Huandoy Glacier and close to the little-visited ruins of Tumshucaico. **See p.331**

❻ Chavín de Huantar One of the most important ancient temple sites in the Andes – associated with a cult dedicated primarily to a terrifying feline god. **See p.335**

❼ The Sechín ruins A unique temple site whose outer wall is clad with some of the most gruesome ancient artwork to be found anywhere in South America. **See p.342**

HIGHLIGHTS ARE MARKED ON THE MAP ON P.312

Huaraz

Situated in the perfectly steep-sided Callejón de Huaylas valley, **HUARAZ** – 400km from Lima – is the focal point of inland Ancash. Only a day's bus ride from either Lima or Trujillo, it's one of the best places in Peru to base yourself if you have any interest in **outdoor adventure** or just sightseeing. As a market town and magnet for hikers, bikers, canoeists and climbers, the city centre has a naturally lively atmosphere, making it the ideal springboard for exploring the surrounding mountainous region; besides the stunning mountain scenery, the area boasts spectacular ruins, natural thermal baths and beautiful glacial lakes. The valley is dominated by the **Cordillera Blanca**, the world's highest tropical mountain range, and **Huascarán**, Peru's highest peak. The region is best experienced between May and September when the skies are nearly always blue and it rains very little. Between October and April, however, it's often cloudy and most afternoons you can expect some rain.

Brief history

Occupied since at least 12,000 years ago, the area around Huaraz was responsible for significant cultural development during the Chavín era (particularly 1500–500 BC), although the Incas didn't arrive here until the middle of the fifteenth century AD. Following the **Spanish conquest** of Peru, and up until less than a century ago, Huaraz remained a fairly isolated community, barricaded to the east by the dazzling snowcapped peaks of the Cordillera Blanca and separated from the coast by the dry, dark Cordillera Negra. Between these two mountain chains the powerful Río Santa valley, known as the Callejón de Huaylas, is a region with strong traditions of local independence.

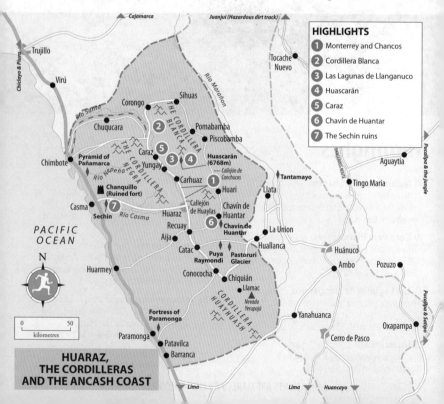

HIGHLIGHTS

1. Monterrey and Chancos
2. Cordillera Blanca
3. Las Lagunas de Llanganuco
4. Huascarán
5. Caraz
6. Chavín de Huantar
7. The Sechin ruins

HUARAZ, THE CORDILLERAS AND THE ANCASH COAST

For several months in 1885, the people of the Callejón waged a **guerrilla war** against the Lima authorities, during which the whole valley fell into rebel hands. The revolt was sparked by a native leader, the charismatic **Pedro Pablo Atusparia**, and thirteen other village mayors, who protested against excessive taxation and labour abuses. After they were sent to prison and humiliated by having their braided hair (a traditional sign of status) cut off, the local peasants overran Huaraz, freeing their chieftains, expelling all officials and looting the mansions of wealthy landlords and merchants (many of them expatriate Englishmen who had been here since the Wars of Independence). The rebellion was eventually quashed by an army battalion from the coast, which recaptured the city while the Indians were celebrating their annual fiesta. Even today, Atusparia's memory survives close to local hearts, and inhabitants of the area's remote villages remain unimpressed by the central government's attempts to control the region.

Downtown Huaraz

Although well over 3000m above sea level, Huaraz has a somewhat cosmopolitan, and very busy, city centre. It has developed rapidly in terms of tourism and commerce since the completion of the highway through the river basin from Paramonga, and the opening of mainly US- and Canadian-owned zinc, silver and gold mines in both the Cordillera Negra and the Callejón de Conchucos. Even so, most tourism activity is geared towards goings-on out of town, like trips to Chavín de Huantar or mountaineering expeditions to the glaciated peaks and trekking country that surrounds Huaraz.

Avenida Luzuriaga is the town centre's north–south axis, where most of the restaurants, nightlife and tour agencies are based. The Parque Ginebra is set just behind Luzuriaga and the **Plaza de Armas**; the plaza is pleasant but something of an afterthought in terms of city planning and not yet fully integrated into the network of roads.

Virtually the entire city was levelled by the **earthquake** of 1970, and the old houses have been replaced with single-storey modern structures topped with gleaming tin roofs. Surrounded by eucalyptus groves and fields, it's still not quite the vision it once was, but it's a decent enough place in which to recuperate from the rigours of hard travel. There are many easy **walks** just outside of town, and if you fancy an afternoon's stroll you can simply go out to the eastern edge and follow one of the paths or streams uphill.

Museo Arqueológico de Ancash

Av Luzuriaga 762 • Mon–Sat 9am–5pm, Sun 9am–2pm • S/5 • ☎ 043 421 551

Huaraz's major cultural attraction is the **Museo Arqueológico de Ancash**, facing the modern Plaza de Armas. Fronting attractive, landscaped gardens that are full of stones removed from Recuay tombs and temples, this small but interesting museum contains a superb collection of Chavín, Chimu, Wari, Mochica and Recuay **ceramics**, as well as some expertly trepanned skulls. It also displays an abundance of the finely chiselled stone monoliths typical of this mountain region, most of them products of the Recuay and Chavín cultures. There's also a model of the Guitarrero Cave, a local site showing evidence of human occupation around 10,000 BC. One of its most curious exhibits is a *goniometro*, an early version of the surveyor's theodolite, probably over a thousand years old and used for finding alignments and exact ninety-degree angles in building construction.

La Catedral

Plaza de Armas • Daily 7am–7pm • Free

On the other side of the Plaza de Armas from the museum stands the **Catedral**. Completely rebuilt after being destroyed in the 1970 earthquake, it has nothing special to see inside, but its vast blue-tiled roof makes a good landmark and, if you look closely, appears to mirror one of the glaciated mountain peaks, the Nevado Huanstán (6395m), behind it.

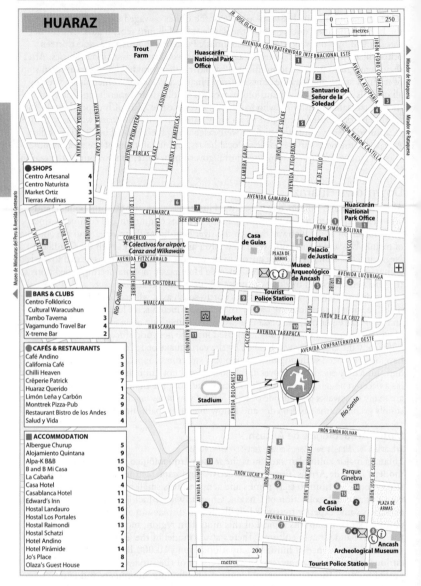

HUARAZ

SHOPS

Centro Artesanal	4
Centro Naturista	1
Market Ortiz	3
Tierras Andinas	2

BARS & CLUBS

Centro Folklorico Cultural Waracushun	1
Tambo Taverna	3
Vagamundo Travel Bar	4
X-treme Bar	2

CAFÉS & RESTAURANTS

Café Andino	5
California Café	3
Chilli Heaven	6
Crêperie Patrick	7
Huaraz Querido	1
Limón Leña y Carbón	2
Monttrek Pizza-Pub	9
Restaurant Bistro de los Andes	8
Salud y Vida	4

ACCOMMODATION

Albergue Churup	5
Alojamiento Quintana	9
Alpa-K B&B	15
B and B Mi Casa	10
La Cabaña	1
Casa Hotel	4
Casablanca Hotel	11
Edward's Inn	12
Hostal Landauro	16
Hostal Los Portales	6
Hostal Raimondi	13
Hostal Schatzi	7
Hotel Andino	3
Hotel Pirámide	14
Jo's Place	8
Olaza's Guest House	2

Museo de Miniaturas del Peru

Block 7 of Av Centenario, in grounds of Gran Hotel Huascarán • Mon–Fri 8am–1pm & 3–6pm • S/3

The second of the town's museums to merit a visit is the **Museo de Miniaturas del Peru**, in the gardens of the *Gran Hotel Huascarán*, close to the town exit en route down the valley along Avenida Fitzcarrald. The museum contains an interesting collection of pre-Hispanic art from the Huaraz region and a range of local folk art and crafts, including fine red Callejón de Huaylas ceramics. It also displays a small model of Yungay (see p.326) prior to the entire town being buried under a mudslide as a result of the 1970 earthquake.

Santuario del Señor de la Soledad

Plazuela del Señor de la Soledad • Daily 8am–1pm & 3–6pm • Free • ☎ 043 728 878

Uphill in the eastern part of town, at the Parque de la Soledad, is the **Santuario del Señor de la Soledad,** a gleaming church that was rebuilt after two earthquakes, in 1725 and 1970. The modern building houses biblical murals and the powerful sixteenth-century religious image of *El Señor de la Soledad.*

Trout Farm

Av Confraternidad Internacional Oeste • Daily 8am–5pm • 25¢, includes guided tour • A 15min walk up Av Raimondi then across the Río Quillcay bridge and down Av Confraternidad Internacional Oeste

It is worth the stroll to the regional **Trout Farm** (or Estación Pesquería), run by the Ministerio de Pesquería. It breeds thousands of rainbow trout every year and you can observe the process from beginning to end (more interesting than you might think); much of the excellent trout available in the restaurants of Huaraz comes from here.

Mirador de Rataquenua

Follow Av Villón out beyond the cemetery and up through the woods to the cross. Taxis (S/10–20 one way) will also take you there and back, which is safer than walking if you're on your own

There are one or two vantage points on the hills around the city of Huaraz, but the best and most accessible is the **Mirador de Rataquenua**, about a two-hour walk each way. It is not advisable to walk alone since there have been muggings reported on this route. Notwithstanding, it commands a splendid location, high above the town to the southeast, and looks out over the Callejón de Huaylas.

ARRIVAL AND DEPARTURE   HUARAZ

BY PLANE

There are daily flights from Lima to Huaraz with LC Perú (Av Pablo Carriquiry 857, San Isidro, Lima; ☎01 204 1313, ⓦ lcperu.pe). The flight lands at a small airstrip close to the village of Anta, some 23km north of Huaraz; from here it's 30min into the city by colectivo (S/2.50) or bus, both of which leave from the main road outside the airstrip, or 25min by taxi (S/35). Colectivos to the airport leave Huaraz from the corner of Jr 13 Diciembre and Av Fitzcarrald before the river.

BY BUS

Most people arrive by bus from Lima or Trujillo. The most comfortable bus service offered by Cruz del Sur; Movil Tours and Expreso Ancash also offer day and night buses and a range of services. All long-range buses come in at and leave from (or close to) their company's offices (see opposite). Local buses connect Huaraz with other towns along the valley – Carhuaz, Yungay and Caraz. These can be caught from just over the main river bridge from the town centre, on either side of the main road (Av Fitzcarrald), beside the Río Quillcay. Buses to Chiquián are run by Chiquián Tours from block 1 of C Huascarán, near the market, and leave every hour or so.

Destinations Carhuaz (hourly; 45min); Casma (daily 4–5hr; S/15–20); Catac (hourly; 1hr 20min); Chimbote (daily 5–7hr; S/20–35); Chavín (daily; 2–3hr); Chiquián (daily; 3–4hr); Huánuco (daily; 12–14hr); Huari (daily; 4hr); La Unión (daily; 8hr); Lima (6 daily; 8hr; S/40–80);

Piscobamba (daily; 8–10hr); Pomabamba (daily; 8–10hr); Pomacha (daily; 3hr 40min); Sihuas (daily; 10hr); Trujillo (daily 8–10hr; S/35–70).

BUS OPERATORS

Chavín Express Jr Mariscal Cáceres 328 (☎ 043 424 652). Services to Sihuas, Chavín and Huari.

Civa Jr Julian de Morales 650 (☎043 429 253). Services to Lima.

Colectivos Comité 14 Av Fitzcarrald 216 (☎043 421 202). Services to Lima and Trujillo.

Cruz del Sur Jr Lucar y Torré 585 (☎043 428 726). The best services for Lima and Trujillo.

Empresa Condor de Chavín Jr Tarapaca 312 (☎043 422039). Services to Chavín and Lima.

Empresa Huandoy Av Fitzcarrald 261 (☎043 727 507). Services to Chimbote and Caraz.

Empresa Moreno Av Raimondi 858 (☎043 721 590). Services to Casma.

Empresa Rapido Cáceres 380 (☎043 422 887). Services to Chiquián, Huallanca and La Unión.

Empresa Rosario Jr Caraz 605. Services to Pomabamba, La Unión and Huánuco.

Empresa Sandoval Tarapaca 582 (☎043 426 930). Services to Catac, Chavín, Pomacha and Huari.

Expresso Ancash/Ormeño Av Raimondi 853 (☎043 421 102). Services to Lima and Caraz.

6

Movil Tours Av Raimondi 730 (☎043 422 555). Services to Lima, Chimbote and Trujillo.

Rodríguez Services to Chimbote and Caraz.

Turismo Chimbote Services to Trujillo, Caraz and Chimbote.

Turismo Huaraz Jr Caraz 605. Services to Caraz, Piscobamba, Pomabamba and Chimbote.

BY COLECTIVO

Colectivos Comité 14 run daily services here from Jr Leticia in Lima Centro and also to and from Trujillo. Colectivos also connect all the main towns and villages to the north – Carhuaz (50min), Yungay (1hr 10min) and Caraz (1hr 30min) – at very reasonable rates, departing when full (about every 20min; up to S/10); these can be caught from just over the main river bridge from the town centre, on either side of the main road (Av Fitzcarrald), beside the Río Quillcay. Just before the same bridge, colectivos heading south to Catac (80min; S/4) and Olleros (20–30min; S/8) can be caught daily every 30min from the end of Jr Cáceres, just below the market area.

GETTING AROUND

On foot Much of Huaraz town can be easily negotiated on foot once you've acclimatized to the altitude (3091m); however, some of the more remote sectors should not be walked alone at night since incidents of mugging and rape have, albeit rarely, been reported here.

By colectivo For short journeys within the city, the best option is one of the regular colectivos, which run on fixed routes along avenidas Luzuriaga and Centenario (S/1).

By taxi Using taxis in and around the city costs around S/3–5. A long-distance taxi ride, say from Huaraz to Caraz, would cost at least S/50–70 during daylight, and taxis are also available by the day from around S/100 upwards.

INFORMATION AND TOURS

INFORMATION

National Institute of Culture Av Luzuriaga 766 (☎043 421 829). The office responsible for ancient monuments provides information about remote ruins.

Tourist information Plaza de Armas (Mon–Sat 8am–6.30pm, Sun 8am–2pm; ☎043 428 812, ⓦregionancash.gob.pe). The staff are usually helpful and stock photocopies of trekking maps. The Tourist Police (☎043 421 341) also have maps and information at the back of the same building by the plaza.

TOUR OPERATORS

There are many tour operators in Huaraz who can assist with tours and treks around the city; Pony's Expeditions in Caraz (see p.333) is one of the best such operators.

Caillou Aventure Parque Ginebra ☎043 421 214. Rock climbing, trekking, Andinismo (high Andes trekking and climbing) and mountain biking.

Casa das Guías Parque Ginebra 28-G ☎043 421 811, ⓦcasadeguias.com.pe. Located on a quiet little plaza in the streets behind Av Luzuriaga, this is a centre for local guides and mountaineers, with an attached café.

Monttrek Av Luzuriaga 646 (upstairs) ☎043 421 124, ⓦmonttrek.com.pe. Offers professional climbing, guides, treks, horseriding, river-rafting and snowboarding in the region. It also has a climbing wall, stocks new and used camping and climbing equipment, and the office is a great place to meet other trekkers.

Mountain Bike Adventures Jr Lucre y Torre 530 ☎043 424 259, ⓦchakinaniperu.com. Organizes bike tours with mountain bikes to rent as well as a variety of alternative routes for cyclists with particular interests, including cross-country, single track and up- or downhill options. English-speaking guides are available and there's the bonus of a book exchange in the office.

Pablo Tours Av Luzuriaga 501 ☎043 421 145, ⓦpablotours.com. One of the best agencies for standard tours, Pablo Tours is particularly good for organized treks and canoeing, but also offers local cultural and city tours. Note that they get booked up very quickly.

Peruvian Andes Adventures Jr José Olaya 532 ☎043 421 864, ⓦperuvianandes.com. This outfit offers a combination of trekking, climbing and day-trips to sites around the region, plus flights and bus tickets.

ACCOMMODATION

Even in the high season, around August, it's rarely difficult to find accommodation at a reasonable price, though rates do rise during the **Semana Turística** (or Semana del Andinismo) in June and between November and January when many Peruvians tend to visit. There are really three main areas providing accommodation in the urban area: west of the main streets avenidas Fitzcarrald and Luzuriaga; east of these streets; and another sector, away from the centre, up the Jirón José de Sucre hill to the east. From the Plaza de Armas along Av Luzuriaga there are countless hostels and many smaller places renting out rooms; outside high season it is definitely worth bargaining. There are some peaceful places to choose from out of town, too, some with a garden or **thermal springs**, particularly those around Monterrey.

WEST OF FITZCARRALD AND LUZURIAGA

Alojamiento Quintana Mariscal Cáceres 411 ☎043 426 060, ⓦhostal-quintana.com. An increasingly popular backpacker joint, less than three blocks from the

TOURS AND ADVENTURE ACTIVITIES AROUND HUARAZ

The most popular **tours** around Huaraz are to the Llanganuco Lakes (8hr; $10–15 per person), Chavín de Huantar (9–11hr; US$10–15 per person, including lunch in Chavín) and to the **thermal baths** at Chancos (4hr; from US$8) and Caraz (6hr; from US$10). You can also take a rather commercialized tour to the Pastoruri Glacier, 70km from Huaraz at 5240m (6–8hr return; from US$10 per person). Sadly, the glacier's ice is actually retreating these days, so although worth a visit, it's not as spectacular as it used to be. A new route around Pastoruri known as the **Ruta del Cambio Climatico** (Climate Change Route) was partially reopened in 2011; you can get to the edge of the glacier now, but you can't touch it. There are mules available (S/5) to help visitors along the route. It's worth remembering that Pastoruri is very high and can be bitterly cold, so make sure you're well acclimatized to the altitude, and take warm clothing with you.

The Pastoruri tour usually includes a visit to see **Puya raimondii** plants (see box, p.330) as well.

ADVENTURE ACTIVITIES

In a region as exciting as this in terms of **outdoor adventure**, most people come for something active, namely trekking (see box, p.327), climbing, mountain biking, canoeing or even parapenting. Adventure activities should really be done in association with reputable **local tour agencies** and/or local guides. Always check on **inclusive costs** (and whether these include entry fees, food, porters etc) and if the guide leading your tour speaks English or another language you understand. Some companies may charge more if they consider their service superior. There's greater price variation in the more adventurous tours, treks, biking, mountaineering, canoeing and river-rafting trips, though tariffs generally start at around US$40–60 per half-day.

Canoeing For canoeing, the most popular section of the Río Santa, which runs along the valley separating the two massive cordilleras, lies between the villages of Jangas and Caraz, navigable between May and October most years with rapids class 2 and 3.

Llama-packing If a three-day trek with llamas carrying your camping equipment appeals to you, then check out Peru Llama Trek at Pasaje Huaullac, Nueva Florida (☎43 425 661, ⓦperullamatrek.com), a llama-packing initiative designed to promote eco-tourism in the region; you can also ask for details in the Casa de Guías, Parque Ginebra 28-G (☎43 421 811).

Mountain biking The Callejón de Huaylas offers one of Peru's most scenic bike rides, with most routes here going over 3500m; Llanganuco (3800m) from Yungay is popular, as is Carhuaz to the Abra de Punta Olímpica (4800m). The sun is very hot here, so always use good sunglasses and sunblock.

Parapenting If you fancy parapenting, the Huaraz region is an ideal place (mostly around Caraz and Yungay, particularly around the Pan de Azúcar); the best local contact is Alberto Sotelo, contactable through Monttrek (see opposite).

Plaza de Armas. It is clean, comfortable and well managed, and most rooms have a private bathroom. S/80

B and B Mi Casa Av Tarapaca (also known as 27 de Noviembre) 773 ☎043 423 375, ⓦmicasahuaraz.jimdo .com. Just three blocks west of the Plaza de Armas, this place is distinguished by very friendly owners who provide excellent service and have expert cartographical information as well as general tourist info. There's also free wi-fi in rooms and a dining room serving breakfasts (included in price), as well as 24hr hot water and private bathrooms. S/80

Casablanca Hotel Av Tarapaca 138 ☎043 422 602, ⓦhuaraz.com/casablanca. A comfortable and upmarket hotel with fine wood-beamed ceilings. Used by a lot of tour groups, it actually seems rather out of place on this downmarket street. All rooms have a private bathroom and there's a good restaurant with included breakfast. S/350

Edward's Inn Av Bolognesi 121 ☎043 422 692, ⓦedwardsinn.com. One of the most popular trekkers' hostels, located just below the market area and offering all sorts of services, including up-to-the-minute tourist information, in a very convivial atmosphere. Rooms come with private bathroom and wi-fi, and hot water is almost always available. The owner, who speaks English, French and Italian, is a highly experienced trekker, climber and mountain rescuer. S/70

EAST OF FITZCARRALD AND LUZURIAGA

Alpa-K B&B C José de Sucre 320 ☎043 421 629, ⓦalpa-k.org. Alpa-K caters to the mountaineering crowd with ample treks, but you can stay just to feel far from the crowds. The modern rooms are spacious and have small balconies. The clean designer bathrooms have marble showers and are shared with only one other room. There is a communal kitchen and rooftop, while the intercom entry on Parque Ginebra keep things secure. **S/70**

Hostal Landauro Jr José de Sucre 109 ☎043 421 212, ✉willemmi@yahoo.es. A popular place right on the Plaza de Armas, with small but well-decorated rooms (with or without bathroom) set along narrow balconies boasting views over the town towards the Cordillera Blanca. **S/60**

Hostal Los Portales Av Raimondi 903 ☎043 428 184. A spacious, if dimly lit, three-star hotel, well situated for most bus terminals. Rooms are clean with private bathrooms and large, well-sprung beds and there's also a large, safe luggage store for trekkers, as well as a restaurant. **S/130**

Hostal Raimondi Av Raimondi 820 ☎043 721 082. This hostel is large, clean and full of character, with a spacious, old-fashioned lobby. Rooms themselves are well-appointed if a little dark, with private bathrooms. **S/75**

Hostal Schatzi Jr Simón Bolívar 419 ☎043 423 074, ✇hostalschatzi.com. A lovely, very friendly little place set around a lush garden patio with small but tidy and nicely furnished rooms; those on the second floor are located on a wraparound wooden balcony with parquetry floors and some views across the garden, town and valley. **S/70**

Hotel Pirámide Parque Ginebra 22 ☎043 428 853, ✉hotelpiramide_peru@yahoo.es. The rooms here, equipped with standard private bathrooms and wi-fi, are a bit boxy but it's a good choice if you want a leafy plaza and good eating options on your doorstep. Little English spoken. **S/50**

Jo's Place Jr Daniel Villaizan 276 ☎043 425 505, ✇josplacehuaraz.com. Located 10min from the town centre – over the river bridge, on the fourth street on the right – *Jo's Place* is very relaxed, with comfortable rooms and a secure atmosphere making for great value, as well as popularity with backpackers. The staff can help organize tours and there is a large garden, a terrace and views across to the Cordillera Blanca. English newspapers and breakfasts are available. Dorms **S/25**, doubles **S/50**

EAST OF AVENIDA GAMARRA

Albergue Churup Jr Amadeo Figueroa 1257, La Soledad ☎043 424 200, ✇churup.com. Just a 5min walk from Plaza de Armas, this great-value establishment has a family atmosphere, a garden, lovely wood-burning stove, laundry, kitchen and left-luggage facilities as well as panoramic views. It also has lots of info on local trekking. **S/55**

★**Hotel Andino** Jr Pedro Cochachín 357 ☎043 421 662, ✇hotelandino.com. An uphill hike away from the centre of town, albeit with the reward of beautiful views over the Cordillera Blanca and plush quarters in the best hotel in town. There are a variety of rooms to choose from, with or without terraces and fireplaces, and there's also a gourmet restaurant serving delicious food with a Swiss influence. **S/338**

★**La Cabaña** Jr José de Sucre 1224 ☎043 423 428, ✉edgon175@hotmail.com. A popular and very friendly *pensión* with safe, comfortable accommodation, a dining room and hot water all day. Rooms have private bathrooms and TV, while guests also have access to kitchen and laundry facilities, plus a dining room. **S/40**

Casa Hotel C Alejandro Manguina 1467, in front of Hotel Andino ☎043 429 709. A five-storey building with panoramic views of Huaraz from the roof patio. A pleasant communal area on the ground floor offers a TV, small library and a billiard table. Rooms come with breakfast and have private bathrooms with 24hr hot water, and there's a laundry available. **S/140**

Olaza's Guest House Jr Julio Arguedas 1242, La Soledad ☎043 422 529, ✇olazas.com. Nice, large rooms here – very clean and with private bathrooms and wi-fi as well as access to the kitchen and laundry. This place is also a good source of local information, enjoys a roaring fire in the communal living space and has a roof terrace that is great for enjoying the spectacular views and mixing with fellow travellers over tea or breakfast. **S/100**

EATING

★**Café Andino** Lucar y Torre 530 ☎043 421 203. A popular upstairs café with library and games, serving breakfasts, good coffee, juices and Mexican food. A good place to meet other travellers, trekkers and climbers, or just find a quiet corner in the sprawling space. Daily 9am–10pm.

California Café C 28 de Julio 562 ☎043 428 354. A good place for wi-fi and mingling with other travellers; the coffee is excellent, there's trekking information on offer and a relaxed atmosphere. Try the all-day American breakfast or waffles, especially if you've worked up an appetite after a few days' hiking. Daily 7.30am–7pm.

Chilli Heaven Parque Ginebra 28. The generous servings of spicy curries (Thai and Indian) and Mexican dishes (all around S/30) at this homely, English/Peruvian-owned restaurant will breathe life back into any weary hiker. The authentic tastes make it a popular spot with travellers on the quiet plaza. Daily 1–10pm.

Crêperie Patrick Av Luzuriaga 422. A centrally located establishment close to the corner with Av Raimondi, *Crêperie Patrick* serves guinea pig, rabbit *al vino* and fondues in addition to excellent crêpes, salads and sandwiches. Daily 10.30am–9.30pm.

Huaraz Querido Jr Simón Bolívar 981. Easily the best spot in town for fresh fish and seafood. The ceviche is generally delicious, but there's a wide range of other sea, lake and farmed fish options (starting at around S/15 a main dish). Daily 9am–10pm.

Limón Leña y Carbón Av Luzuriaga 1002. Out on a limb at the southern end of the main drag, this is another really good seafood restaurant that serves fresh fish delivered from Chimbote; the menu also includes local trout, meat dishes and pizzas in the evening. Daily 11am–9pm.

★**Monttrek Pizza-Pub** Av Luzuriaga 646 ☎043 421 124. A spacious place, very popular with trekkers and one of the town's top tour and climbing operators (see p.316). It also boasts a useful noticeboard for contacting like-minded backpackers, as well as maps and aerial photos of the region. The food is delicious and the music good, and there's even a climbing wall. Daily 8am–10pm.

Restaurant Bistro de los Andes Jr Julian de Morales 823 ☎ 043 426 249. A great place for breakfast, with seats outside, good yogurt, coffee and pancakes; also popular during the evening. Features a book exchange too. Mon–Sat 7.30am–9pm approx, Sun noon–9pm approx.

Salud y Vida Jr Leonisa Lescano 632, near Caceres. A dark, simple, good-value place that's filled with locals and worth a visit whether you're vegetarian or not. The standard meat-free stir-fries, salads, soups and soya meat dishes (mains around S/10–15) also feature in the set-menu meals, a steal at S/7, especially for dinner. Mon–Sat 11am–9pm.

DRINKING AND NIGHTLIFE

There's a lively nightlife scene in Huaraz, with several **peñas** hosting traditional Andean music, as well as a few **clubs** where locals and tourists can relax, keep warm and unwind during the evenings or at weekends. Nightlife joints start to open from 7pm and can go on until 3am.

Centro Folklórico Cultural Waracushun Jr Bolívar 1101, Belén, Huaraz. The folklore centre in Huaraz helps make local and regional music and dance culture more accessible. It generally has live music and dance shows at weekends, and most days serves reasonable meals and snacks. Daily 11am–11pm.

Tambo Taverna Jr José de la Mar 776. A restaurant-*peña* serving good drinks, with a great party spirit, a mix of popular sounds and occasional live music – a mix of Latin, rock and pop. Daily 6pm–midnight.

★**Vagamundo Travel Bar** Jr Julian de Morales 753. Arguably the most trendy and popular bar in Huaraz these days, *Vagamundo* serves great sandwiches as well as a wide range of cocktails. Daily 7pm–late.

X-treme Bar Avenidas Uribe and Luzuriaga. A popular cocktail lounge and dancefloor spinning everything from rock and pop to jazz, blues and Latin – one of Huaraz's best bars. Daily 8pm–2am.

SHOPPING

Huaraz is a noted **crafts centre**, producing, in particular, very reasonably priced, handmade leather goods (custom made if you've got a few days to wait around). Other bargains include woollen hats, scarves and jumpers, embroidered blankets and interesting replicas of the Chavín stone carvings. Most of these items can be bought from the stalls in the small **artesanía market** in covered walkways set back off Avenida Luzuriaga (daily 2pm–dusk) or, for more choice, in the **Mercado Modelo** two blocks down Avenida Raimondi from Avenida Luzuriaga. Huaraz is also renowned for its **food**, in particular its excellent local cheese, honey and *manjar blanco* (a traditional sweet made out of condensed milk). These can all be bought in the **food market**, in the backstreets around Avenida José de San Martín (daily 6am–6pm).

Centro Artesanal Next to the post office on the plaza. Sells textiles, ceramics, jewellery, stone- and leather-work – most of it made locally in the valley. Mon–Sat 10am–6pm.

FIESTAS IN AND AROUND HUARAZ

Throughout the year various **fiestas** take place in the city and its surrounding villages and hamlets. They are always bright, energetic occasions, with *chicha* and *aguardiente* flowing freely, as well as roast pig, bullfights and vigorous communal dancing, with the townsfolk dressed in outrageous masks and costumes. The main festival in the city of Huaraz is usually in the first week of February and celebrates **Carnival**. In June (dates vary, so check with the tourist office for exact dates), Huaraz hosts the **Semana del Andinismo** (Andean Mountaineering and Skiing Week), which includes trekking, climbing and national and international ski competitions, on the Pastoruri Glacier.

Caraz has its own Semana Turística, usually in the third week of June. Note that during this month accommodation and restaurant prices in Huaraz and Caraz increase considerably. Other festivals include the **Aniversario de Huaraz**, in July (usually on the 25th), when there are a multitude of civic and cultural events in the city, plus the annual folklore celebrations in the first week of August for Coyllur-Huaraz. The fiesta for the **Virgen de la Asunción** in Huata and Chancas takes place during mid-August. Late September sees the festival of the **Virgen de las Mercedes**, celebrated in Carhuaz, as well as other rural get-togethers you'll often come across en route to sites and ruins in the Callejón de Huaylas.

Centro Naturista Av Fitzcarrald 356. Good for natural medicines, yogurt, herbs and eco-friendly soaps and cosmetics; some of these products are locally manufactured using plant combinations based on traditional remedies. Mon–Fri 9am–7pm.

Market Ortiz Av Luzuriaga 401. One of the best supermarkets in town with everything from wine to trail mix on sale. Daily 8am–9pm.

Tierras Andinas Parque Ginebra. Has some fine handicrafts and local artwork. Mon–Sat 10am–5pm.

DIRECTORY

Health For emergencies, go to the hospital on Av Luzuriaga, block 8 (☎ 043 421861 or ☎ 043 421290) or San Pedro Clinic, Huaylas 172 (☎ 043 428 811). For non-urgent medical treatment try Dr Simon Komori, Jr 28 de Julio 602 (24hr), or try the surgery at Av Luzuriaga 618 (Mon–Fri 9am–5pm). For dental treatment there's the Centro Odontologico Olident, Av Luzuriaga 410–204 (☎ 043 424 918).

High Altitude Rescue Call ☎ 043 493 327; Yungay branch ☎ 043 493 333.

Internet Wi-Fi California Café, Jr 28 de Julio 562, offers local, national and international phone calling at very reasonable prices. There are several other internet cafés along Av Luzuriaga and also at Parque Ginebra.

Laundry Lavandería BB, Jr la Mar 674, is the best; otherwise, try Lavandería Huaraz, Av Fitzcarrald, close to the bridge, or Lavandería El Amigo, on the corner of jirones Simón Bolívar and José de Sucre.

Money and exchange Banco Wiese, Jr José de Sucre 766; Interbanc, on Plaza de Armas; Banco de Credito, Av Luzuriaga 691; Banco de la Nación, Av Luzuriaga. All banks open Mon–Fri 9am–6pm. *Cambistas* gather where Jr Julian de Morales and Av Luzuriaga meet, or try the casa de cambio at Luzuriaga 614 for good rates on dollars.

Police The Tourist Police are on the Plaza de Armas at Jr Larrea y Loredo 716 (☎ 043 421 341 ext 315); National Police are at Jr José de Sucre, block 2 (☎ 043 421 330).

Post office Plaza de Armas, Av Luzuriaga 702 (Mon–Sat 8am–8pm).

Telephones Locutorio Emtelser, Jr José de Sucre 797 (daily 7am–11pm).

Around Huaraz

There are a number of worthwhile sights within easy reach of Huaraz. Only 7km north are the natural thermal baths of **Monterrey**; higher into the hills, you can explore the inner labyrinths of the dramatic **Wilkawain temple**. On the other side of the valley, **Punta Callan** offers magnificent views over the Cordillera Blanca, while to the south of the city you can see the intriguing, cactus-like **Puya raimondii**.

Monterrey

There's no town in **Monterrey** as such, just a street of a few properties, some of which have been converted or purpose-built as hostels or restaurants. At the top end of this street are the **thermal baths**, the reason there's any settlement here at all.

Monterrey thermal baths

Central Monterrey • Daily 7am–6pm • From around S/5

The vast **Monterrey thermal baths** include two natural swimming pools and a number of individual and family bathing rooms. Luxuriating in these slightly sulphurous hot springs can be the ideal way to recover from an arduous mountain-trekking expedition, but make sure you are fully acclimatized, otherwise the effect on your blood pressure can worsen any altitude sickness. If you're staying at the wonderful old *Real Hotel Baños Termales Monterrey* (see opposite), the baths are free. There's also an impressive waterfall just ten minutes' walk behind the hotel and baths.

ARRIVAL AND DEPARTURE — MONTERREY

By colectivo Monterrey is 15min by colectivo (S/1.5) from the centre of Huaraz; services depart frequently (every 10min or so) from the corner of avenidas Fitzcarrald and Raimondi.

ACCOMMODATION AND EATING

★Hostal El Patio de Monterrey Av Monterrey ⓣ 043 424 965, ⓦ elpatio.com.pe; reservations ⓣ 01 448 0254. Just a couple of hundred metres from Monterrey's thermal baths and only a few kilometres from Huaraz, this luxurious neo-colonial complex of clean, attractive rooms with iron bedsteads and more expensive bungalows, is based around an attractive patio and lovely gardens. Bungalows S/360, doubles S/220

Hotel Monterrey Av Monterrey ⓣ 043 427 690. Staff serve very reasonable dishes in some style in this elegant, old-fashioned restaurant. Daily 7.30am–9pm.

El Monte Rey Opposite Artesanía Johao (the ceramic workshop on the main access lane to the baths). Arguably the best restaurant in town, this welcoming place serves great local food at excellent prices. Daily 9am–7pm.

Real Hotel Baños Termales Monterrey Av Monterrey ⓣ 043 427 690. An old hotel full of character and style and actually attached to the thermal baths (residents have free access). The fine rooms have hot showers and there's a splendid restaurant overlooking the heated pool. They also have bungalows, which cost a bit more. S/160

Wilkawain temple

Situated some 8km from Huaraz, **Wilkawain temple** is an unusual two-storey construction, with a few small houses around it, set against the edge of a great bluff. With a torch you can check out some of its inner chambers, where you'll see ramps, ventilation shafts and the stone nails that hold it all together. Most of the rooms, however, are still inaccessible, filled with the rubble and debris of at least a thousand years. The temple base is only about 11m by 16m, sloping up to large, slanted roof slabs, long since covered with earth and rocks to form an irregular domed top. The construction is a small replica of the Castillo at Chavín de Huantar (see p.335), with four superimposed platforms and stairways, and a projecting course of stones near the apex, with a recessed one below it. There was once a row of cat heads carved beneath this, which is a typical design of the Huari-Tiahuanaco culture that spread up here from the coast sometime between 600 and 1000 AD.

ARRIVAL AND DEPARTURE — WILKAWAIN TEMPLE

By colectivo Colectivos for Wilkawain leave Huaraz from the corner of calles Comercio and 13 de Diciembre.

By taxi If there are four or five of you, a round-trip by taxi will cost about S/20–40 (depending on waiting time).

On foot Follow Av Centenario downhill from Av Fitzcarrald, then turn right up a track (just about suitable for cars) a few hundred metres beyond the *Real Hotel Huascarán*. From here, it's about an hour's winding stroll to the signposted ruins.

Punta Callan

Some 24km west of Huaraz, **Punta Callan** is the classic local viewpoint. No other spot can quite match its astonishing views across the Cordillera Blanca, ideally saved for a really clear afternoon, when you can best see Huascarán's towering ice cap. The grazing land that surrounds the area is as pleasant as you could find for a picnic.

ARRIVAL AND DEPARTURE — PUNTA CALLAN

By bus Punta Callan can be reached in about 2hr on the Casma bus (S/8) from Av Raimondi 336. Ask the driver to drop you off at Callan, shortly before the village of Pira along the road to Casma; from here it's a 20min walk up the path to the promontory. It's a relatively easy walk of a few hours back down the main road to Huaraz. Passing trucks or buses will usually pick up anyone who waves them down en route. Go early in the day, if you want to be sure you can get a bus back.

Cordillera Blanca

The **Cordillera Blanca** extends its icy chain of summits for 140 to 160km north of Huaraz. The highest range in the tropical world, the Cordillera consists of around 35 peaks poking their snowy heads over the 6000m mark, and until early this century,

6

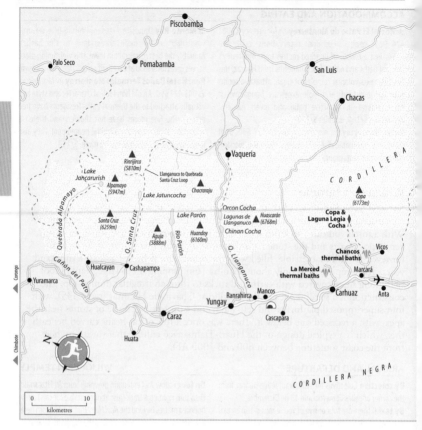

when the glaciers began to recede, this white crest could be seen from the Pacific. The **Callejón de Huaylas** is the valley that sits between the Cordillera Blanca and the Cordillera Negra mountain ranges. Under the western shadow of the Cordillera Blanca lie the northern valley Callejón towns, including **Carhauz**, **Yungay** and **Caraz**. Small and rustic, these towns generally boast attractive accommodation and busy little markets, and provide access to ten snow-free passes in the Cordillera Blanca; combining any two of these passes makes for a superb week's trekking. Yungay and Caraz in particular are both popular bases for trekkers.

Of the many mountain lakes in the Cordillera Blanca, **Lake Parón**, above Caraz, is renowned as the most beautiful. Above Yungay, and against the sensational backdrop of Peru's highest peak, **Huascarán** (6768m), are the equally magnificent **Lagunas de Llanganuco**, whose waters change colour according to the time of year and the sun's daily movements, and are among the most accessible of the Cordillera Blanca's three hundred or so glacial lakes.

The number of possible **hikes** into the Cordillera depends mostly on your own initiative and resourcefulness. There are several common routes, some of which are outlined below; anything more adventurous requires a local guide or a tour with one of the local operators. **Maps** of the area, published by the Instituto Geográfico Militar, are good enough to allow you to plot your own routes. The most popular hike is the **Llanganuco-to-Quebrada Santa Cruz Loop** (see p.330), which begins at Yungay and ends at Caraz.

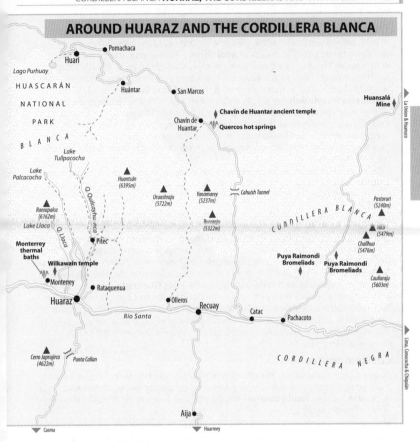

AROUND HUARAZ AND THE CORDILLERA BLANCA

Chancos thermal baths

Chancos, Marcará • Daily 8am–6pm • S/2–5 • Take a bus or colectivo from the first block of Av Fitzcarrald or the market in Huaraz, along the valley towards Yungay or Caraz; get off at the village of Marcará and follow the rough road uphill for about 4km, passing several small peasant settlements en route, until you reach the baths

Known traditionally as the Fuente de Juventud (Fountain of Youth), the **Chancos thermal baths**, 30km north of Huaraz, consist of a series of natural saunas inside caves, with great pools gushing hot water in a beautiful stream. It is claimed that the thermal waters are excellent for respiratory problems, but you don't have to be ill to enjoy them, and they make an ideal end to a day's strenuous trekking.

Laguna Legia Cocha

From Chancos a small track leads off to the hamlet of Ullmey, following the contours of the Legiamayo stream to the upper limit of cultivation and beyond into the barren zone directly below the glaciers. Keeping about 500m to the right of the stream, it takes ninety minutes to two hours to reach **Laguna Legia Cocha**. Hung between two vast glaciers at 4706m above sea level and fed by their icy melted water, the lake is an exhilarating spot, with the added bonus of amazing views across the Santa Valley to Carhuaz in the north, Huaraz in the south and Chancos directly below. If you leave Huaraz early in the morning, you can enjoy a fine day-trip, stopping at Chancos for a picnic lunch, after walking an hour from Marcará, then returning again the same way.

6

TREKKING AND CLIMBING ROUTES IN THE CORDILLERAS

In 1932, when a German expedition became the first group to successfully scale Huascarán (see p.328), the concept of **Andinismo** – Andean mountaineering – was born. You don't have to be a mountaineer to enjoy the high Andes of Ancash, however, and there is plenty of scope for trekking and climbing in the two major mountain chains accessible from Huaraz as well; the closest is the **Cordillera Blanca** (see p.321). The **Cordillerra Huayhuash** (see p.339), about 50km south of that range, is still relatively off the beaten tourist trail and *andinistas* claim it to be one of the most spectacular trekking routes in the world. In order to hike in the Parque Nacional Huascarán, you need to get **permission** first from the park office (Parque Nacional Huascarán, Jr Federico Sal y Rosas 555) and the Casa de Guías in Huaraz (see box, p.317); both can also provide maps and information.

If you intend to hike at all, it's essential to spend at least a couple of days acclimatizing to the **altitude** beforehand; for high mountain climbing, this should be extended to at least five days. Although Huaraz itself is 3060m above sea level, most of the Cordilleras' more impressive peaks are over 6000m.

TREKKING ROUTES

One of the most popular trekking routes, the **Llanganuco-to-Santa Cruz Loop** (see p.330), is a well-trodden trail offering spectacular scenery, some fine places to camp and a relatively easy walk that can be done in under a week, even by inexperienced hikers. The **Hualcayan-to-Pomabamba hike** (see p.331) offers a much longer alternative and is equally rewarding. There are shorter walks, such as the trails around the **Pitec Quebrada**, within easy distance of Huaraz, and a number of other loops like the **Llanganuco-to-Chancos** trek. Experienced hikers could also tackle the circular **Cordillera Huayhuash** route. Detailed information on all these walks is available from the South American Explorers' Club in Lima (see p.81) or, in Huaraz itself, from the Casa de Guías (see p.327), the tourist office (see p.316) or tour companies (see p.316).

CLIMBING ROUTES

To give a flavour of what you may expect from mountain climbing in the Cordillera Blanca, the expeditions below are some of the most popular among serious mountaineers. Remember to take a **local guide** (see box, p.327) if you do any of these; they're listed in increasing order of difficulty.

Pisco One of the easier climbs, up to 5752m, this is a good way to cut your teeth in the Cordillera Blanca. Little more than a hard trek, really, with access via the Llanganuco Valley (3800m), with a duration of only three days. Rated easy to moderate.

Urus A two-day climb reaching heights of around 5500m; access is via Collon to Quebrada de Ishinca and it takes only two days. Rated easy to moderate for the peaks Ishinca and Urus; or moderate to difficult if you tackle Tocllaraju (6034m).

Alpamayo A serious and quite technical mountain rising to 5947m, and requiring good acclimatization on an easier climb first. Access is from Cashapampa (accessible by bus from Caraz), and it usually takes around eight or nine days. Rated as difficult.

Huascarán The south summit at 6768m is the classic route and really requires thorough acclimatization. Access is via Mancos (from where it's an hour by bus to the village of Musho), and it normally demands a good week to tackle effectively. Rated, not surprisingly, as difficult.

ACCOMMODATION AND EATING

CHANCOS THERMAL BATHS

Camping There's no accommodation in Chancos, but the valley bus service is good enough to get you back to Huaraz within an hour or so, or you could camp (ask permission to camp on one of the grassy patches up- or downhill from the baths).

Restaurants There are a couple of basic restaurants on hand that are famous for their strong *chicha*, and are particularly popular with locals on Sunday afternoons.

Carhuaz and around

One of the major towns along the Callejón de Huaylas, **CARHUAZ**, some 30km from both Huaraz and Yungay, has an attractive, central Plaza de Armas, adorned with palm trees, roses and labyrinths of low-cut hedges and dominated by the solid, concrete Iglesia de San Pedro on its south side.

The market
On Sundays the streets to the north and west of the plaza are home to a thriving traditional **market**, where Andean and tropical foodstuffs, herbs and craft (in particular, gourd bowls) can be bought very cheaply. The colourfully dressed women here often sell live guinea pigs from small nets at their feet, and wear a variety of wide-brimmed hats – ones with blue bands indicate that they are married, ones with red bands show that they are single. Many also wear glass beads, on their hats or around their necks, as a sign of wealth.

Cave of Hombre Guitarrero
In the 1980s, a cave was discovered a few kilometres north of Carhuaz, on the other side of the Río Santa in the Cordillera Negra. Containing the bones of mastodons and llamas and suggesting human occupation dating from as far back as 12,000 BC, it is situated close to a natural rock formation that looks vaguely like a guitar, and the site is now known as the **cave of Hombre Guitarrero** (Guitar Man).

Mancos
Some 9km further north of Carhuaz, over a river, the road comes to the village of **MANCOS**. The village has an unusually attractive plaza, with palm trees and a quaint, modern church with twin belfries sitting under the watchful eye of the glistening glacier of Huascarán. The village's main **fiesta** (Aug 12–16) is in honour of its patron, San Royal de Mancos, and the plaza becomes the focus of highly colourful religious processions, dancing and, later, bullfighting.

ARRIVAL AND DEPARTURE
CARHUAZ AND AROUND

CARHUAZ
By colectivo Combi colectivos to Huaraz (S/3, 40min), Chancos (S/2) and Caraz (S/2.50) arrive at, and depart from, a stop one block west beyond the market side of the plaza.

By bus Buses to Lima, Huaraz and Caraz leave from a terminal on block 2 of Av La Merced, which is a continuation of the road from the market side of the plaza to the main highway.

CAVE OF HOMBRE GUITARRERA
On foot This archeological site can be accessed in just over an hour's walk, beyond the sports stadium in Carhuaz and up the stream past the unusual church.

MANCOS
By bus/colectivo Located on the main valley road between Carhuaz and Yungay, you'll need to ask your bus or colectivo driver to drop you in the village.

ACCOMMODATION AND EATING

CARHUAZ
El Abuelo Jr 9 de Diciembre 257, by the plaza ☎043 394 456, ⓦ elabuelohostal.com. This is a modern, two-storey building with a dining room, comfortable beds and good hot-water supplies. Rooms are stylish without going over the top, and service is attentive as well as friendly. **S/190**

Casa de Pocha Located at the foot of Hualcan mountain, about 1.5km above Carhuaz ☎943 613 058, ✉ lacasadepocha@yahoo.com. A lovely eco-ranch offering accommodation in a traditional adobe lodge with eight spacious rooms under red-tiled roofs. There's a sauna, 12m swimming pool, solar cookers and horseriding, and the hot springs of La Merced are nearby. The owner speaks Spanish, English, French and Italian. **S/120**

La Eskina Cafe On the plaza ☎956 928 330. The friendly owner lived in the US, speaks English and can recommend local specialities, such as steamed chicken with milk, rice and potatoes (S/8). You can also get salads, desserts, coffee and juices. Daily 9am–7pm.

Hostal La Merced Jr Ucayali 724 ☎043 394 241. This centrally located place has commodious rooms with or without private bathrooms. Rooms are plain and service is good, with a locked room to leave bags in while trekking. **S/40**

MANCOS
Casa Alojamiento On the plaza. Offers clean, comfortable rooms and shared bathrooms. Though there are several restaurants around, none is especially good. **S/35**

Yungay

Fifty-eight kilometres up the Callejón de Huaylas from Huaraz, and just past Mancos, **YUNGAY** was an attractive, traditional small town until it was obliterated in seconds on May 31, 1970, during a massive earthquake. This was not the first catastrophe to assault the so-called "Pearl of the Huaylas Corridor"; in 1872 it was almost completely wiped out by an avalanche, and on a fiesta day in 1962 another avalanche buried some five thousand people in the neighbouring village of Ranrahirca. The 1970 quake arrived in the midst of a festival and also caused a landslide, and although casualties proved impossible to calculate with any real accuracy, it's thought that over 70,000 people died. Almost the entire population of Yungay, around 26,000, disappeared almost instantaneously, though a few of the town's children survived because they were at a circus located just above the town, which fortunately escaped the landslide. Almost eighty percent of the buildings in neighbouring Huaraz and much of Carhuaz were also razed to the ground by the earthquake.

The new town, an uninviting conglomeration of modern buildings – including some ninety prefabricated cabins sent as relief aid from the former Soviet Union – has been built around a concrete Plaza de Armas a few kilometres from the original site. Yungay still cowers beneath the peak of Huascarán, but it is hoped that its new location is more sheltered from further dangers than its predecessor. The best reason for staying here is to make the trip up to **Las Lagunas de Llanganuco** and **Parque Nacional Huascarán**.

Old town of Yungay

Visible from the main road, before arriving at the new town of Yungay • Daily 8am–6pm • S/2

On the way into town from Carhuaz, a car park and memorial monument mark the entrance to the site of the buried **old town of Yungay**, which has developed into one of the region's major tourist attractions. The site, entered through a large, blue concrete archway, is covered with a grey flow of mud and moraine, now dry and solid, with a few stunted palm trees to mark where the old Plaza de Armas once stood. Thousands of rose bushes have been planted over the site – a gift of the Japanese government. Local guidebooks show before-and-after photos of the scene, but it doesn't take a lot of imagination to reconstruct the horror. You can still see a few things like an upside-down, partially destroyed school bus, stuck in the mud. The graveyard of Campo Santo, above the site, which predates the 1970 quake, gives the best vantage point over the devastation. A tall statue of Christ holds out its arms from the graveyard towards the deadly peak of Huascarán itself, as if pleading for no further horrors.

ARRIVAL AND DEPARTURE   YUNGAY

By bus/colectivo Buses and colectivos all stop and pick up passengers on Jr 28 de Julio en route between Huaraz and Caraz. From Carhuaz (S/2.50). Colectivos for Las Lagunas de Llanganuco (55min; S/5) leave from the same spot, or the Plaza de Armas, usually between 7 and 8.30am.

ACCOMMODATION AND EATING

Café Pilar On the plaza. This large space is good for breakfast and snacks like sandwiches, tamales (maize cakes) and cakes. Daily 8am–6pm.

Hostal Gledel Av Arias Graziani ☎ 043 393 048. A very friendly budget hostel at the northern end of town. Upstairs rooms are best, and though all rooms share toilet facilities, the hostel is spotlessly clean and a good place to meet trekkers and climbers. S̲/̲3̲0̲

Hostal Yungay Jr Santo Domingo 1, on the Plaza de Armas ☎ 043 393 053. Well located and with private bathrooms, hot water, colour TV and laundry service, they have decent-quality rooms and a terrace with clotheslines for hanging your wet garments. It also gives out free maps and information on the area. S̲/̲3̲5̲

Restaurant Alpamayo Av Arias Graziani, in the Caraz end of town. This place has excellent fish meals including fried trout from local fish farms, but also serves other standard mains. Daily 10am–5pm.

ORGANIZING A TREK IN THE CORDILLERAS

People die and get lost on these mountains regularly, so ideally you'll be trekking with a **local guide**, perhaps with a tour group, who will ensure you have the right equipment for the terrain and local climatic conditions. If this is not the case, then you need to take responsibility for having good boots, appropriate clothing (including waterproofs), a warm sleeping bag, good mountain tent and other equipment (eg crampons and ice axe).

Wherever you end up, be sure to pay heed to the rules of **responsible trekking**: carry away your **waste**, particularly above the snow line. Note too that you should always use a **camping stove** – campfires are strictly prohibited in Parque Nacional Huascarán, and wood is scarce anyway. Just as important, though, is to realize that the **solar irradiation** in this part of the Andes is stronger than that found in the North American Rockies, European Alps or even the Himalayas. This creates unique glacier conditions, making the ice here less stable and necessitating an **experienced local guide** for the safety of any serious climbing or ice-walking expedition. It's also vital to **be fit**, particularly if you are going it alone.

COSTS

There are three levels of **guide** available: certified mountain guides, who cost upwards of US$80/day; mountain guides undergoing the one-year trial period after training, from US$50/day; and trekking guides, who cost from US$35/day. Note that these costs don't include your transport or accommodation. **Porters** cost between US$20 and US$35/day, depending on whether they are leaders or assistants, and are not supposed to climb over 6000m. **Mule drivers** (*arrieros*) charge from US$18/US$25 a day, plus around US$10/day per animal. Expedition **cooks** usually charge the same as *arrieros*.

INFORMATION

Both the Casa de Guías (see below) and the Parque Nacional Huascarán office (see p.331) can give you advice on the best and safest areas for trekking, since this region is not without its **political danger zones**; you also need to obtain permission from them before trekking in the national park. Tour operators offering guided treks can be found in the Huaraz section (see p.316).

Ideally you should have detailed maps – available from the Casa de Guías (see below) – and one or other of the following excellent guidebooks: *Trails of the Cordillera Blanca and Huayhuash*, *Classic Climbs of the Cordillera Blanca* or *The High Andes: A Guide for Climbers* (see p.515).

AOTUM (Asociación Peruana de Operadores de Turismo de Montaña) Based in the *Hotel Andino* (see p.318), in Huaraz. Offers very useful assistance to climbers. Other Peruvian mountaineering associations are all based in Lima (see box, p.82).

Casa de Guías (Mountain Guides) Parque Ginebra 28-G, Huaraz ☎ 43 421 811. The best-organized association of mountain guides in Peru offering plenty of local expertise and the Andean Mountain Rescue Corps on hand.

Mountain Institute Ricardo Palma 100, Pedregal district of Huaraz, south of Av Villón ☎ 43 423 446. A mainly conservation-based organization whose focus is the Peruvian Andes and the Cordillera Blanca in particular.

Trekking and Backpacking Club Jr Los Libertadores 134, Independencia, Huaraz ☎ 943 866 794. Provides information for independent travellers interested in the region's archeology, trekking, backpacking and climbing.

TREKKING GUIDES

Alberto Cafferata Trekking guide contactable through Pony's Expeditions in Caraz (see p.333).

Oscar Ciccomi Based in Lima and contactable through Viajes Vivencial, Los Cerezos 480, Chaclacayo, Lima (☎ 01 497 2394).

Eduardo Figueroa Contactable via *Edward's Inn*, Huaraz (see p.317).

David Gonzáles Castromonte, Pasaje Coral Vega 354, Huarupampa, Huaraz (☎ 43 422 213).

HIGH MOUNTAIN GUIDES

High Mountain Guides (members of UIAGM – Unión Internacional de Asociaciones de Guías de Montaña), contactable through the Casa de Guías (see above), include:

Selio Billón One of the founders of La Asociación de Guías and the Casa de Guías, with 25 years' experience.

Michel Burger Owner of the *Bistro de los Andes*

restaurant in Huaraz; offers trekking and fishing.

Arista Monasterio Provides customized guiding services.

Parque Nacional Huascarán

Daily 6am–6pm • US$1.50 for day-visitors, US$20 for trekkers or mountaineers • Permission must be obtained from the park office (see p.331) and Casa de Guías in Huaraz before trekking or climbing here

Parque Nacional Huascarán is home to the Lagunas de Llanganuco, two stunning, deep-blue lakes, as well as perhaps Peru's most awe-inspiring peak, glaciated Huascarán. On the way up to the level of the lakes you get a dramatic view across the valley and can clearly make out the path of devastation from the 1970 earthquake. The last part of the drive – starkly beautiful but no fun for vertigo sufferers – slices through rocky crevices, and snakes around breathtaking precipices surrounded by small, wind-bent *quenual* trees and orchid bromeliads known locally as *weclla*. Well before reaching the lakes, at Km 19 you pass through the entrance to the national park itself, located over 600m below the level of the lakes; from here it's another thirty minutes or so by bus or truck to the lakes.

Las Lagunas de Llanganuco

At 3850m above sea level, the **Lagunas de Llanganuco** are only 26km northeast of Yungay (83km from Huaraz), but take a good ninety minutes to reach by bus or truck, on a road that crawls up beside a canyon that is the result of thousands of years of Huascarán's meltwater.

The first lake you come to after the park entrance is **Chinan Cocha**, named after a legendary princess. You can rent **rowing boats** by the car park here to venture onto the blue waters (80¢ for 15min), and, if you're hungry, take a picnic from the **food stalls** at the lakeside nearby. The road continues around Chinan Cocha's left bank and for a couple of kilometres on to the second lake, **Orcon Cocha**, named after a prince who fell in love with Chinan. The road ends here and a **loop trail** begins (see p.330). A third, much smaller, lake was created between the two big ones, as a result of an avalanche caused by the 1970 earthquake, which also killed a group of hikers who were camped between the two lakes.

Huascarán

Immediately to the south of the lakes is the unmistakable sight of **Huascarán**, whose imposing ice-cap tempts many people to make the difficult climb of 3km to the top. Surrounding Huascarán are scores of lesser, glaciated mountains that stretch for almost 200km and divide the Amazon Basin from the Pacific watershed.

LODGES IN THE CORDILLERA BLANCA

The two **lodges** listed below both offer an exciting opportunity to stay in relative comfort right on the edge of the Cordillera Blanca's wilderness. *Lazy Dog Inn* is closer to Huaraz and is right on the edge of Parque Nacional Huascarán. *LLanganuco Mountain Lodge* is also on the edge of the national park, but is much closer to the Lagunas de Llanganuco and Huascarán.

Lazy Dog Inn ☎ 943 789 330, ⊚ thelazydoginn .com. Some 10km east of Huaraz, it offers transport from the city, or you can take a taxi here (S/20–30); there's a sign at Km 12, a few kilometres beyond Wilkawain temple. The cabins are comfortable but you can also stay inside the main adobe-built lodge. The service is excellent and the setting fantastic – it borders the Huascarán National Park (30min from Huaraz). There are cheaper rooms with shared bathrooms. S/310

★**Llanganuco Mountain Lodge** Keushu Lake, Huandoy ⊛ llanganucomountainlodge.com. A fantastic lodge catering to everyone who wants to stay in comfort by the lake, *Llanganuco Mountain Lodge* is located just underneath the Huascarán and Huandoy glaciers (contact in advance for transport or take a taxi). Accommodation is available in suites, rooms and dorms, and the lodge also offers great food, value and service (the restaurant is excellent) plus a library, games, DVDs and outward-bound activities including adventure trails organized on demand. Dorms S/35, camping S/15 per person, doubles S/315

The Llanganuco-to-Santa Cruz Loop

The **Llanganuco-to-Santa Cruz Loop** starts at the clearly marked track leading off from the end of the road along the left bank of Orcon Cocha (see p.328). The entire trek shouldn't take more than about five days for a healthy (and acclimatized) backpacker, but it's a perfect hike to take at your own pace. It's essential to carry all your food, camping equipment and, ideally, a medical kit and emergency survival bag. Along the route there are hundreds of potential campsites. The best time to attempt this trek is in the dry season, between April and October, unless you enjoy getting stuck in mud and being soaked to the skin.

From **Orcon Cocha** the main path climbs the Portachuelo de Llanganuco pass (4767m), before dropping to the enchanting beauty of the Quebrada Morococha (a *quebrada* is a river gully) through the tiny settlement of **Vaqueria**. From here you can go on to Colcabamba and Pomabamba (but only by diverting from the main loop trail), which are settlements located in the Callejón de Conchucos – though not in the rainy season, when you may well find yourself stranded. Most people prefer to continue on the loop back to the Callejón de Huaylas via Santa Cruz.

Continuing from Vaqueria the main loop trail subsequently heads north from Vaqueria up the Quebrada Huaripampa, where you'll probably camp the first night. From here it goes around the icecap of **Chacraraju** (6000m) and along a stupendous rocky canyon with a marshy bottom, snowy mountain peaks to the west and Cerro Mellairca to the east.

On the third or fourth day, following the stream uphill, with the lakes of Morococha and Huiscash on your left, you pass down into the **Pacific watershed** along the **Quebrada Santa Cruz**, eventually emerging, after perhaps another night's rest, beside the calm waters of Lake Grande (Lake Jatuncocha). Tracing the left bank and continuing down this perfect glacial valley for about another eight hours, you'll come to the village of **Cashapampa**, which has very basic accommodation, but don't bank on this since it can't be booked

---

THE PUYA RAIMONDII

The gigantic and relatively rare **Puya raimondii** plant, reaching up to 12m in height and with a lifespan of around forty years, is found in Parque Nacional Huascarán. Most people assume the *Puya raimondii* is a type of cactus, but it is, in fact, the world's largest **bromeliad**, or member of the pineapple family. Known as *cuncush* or *cunco* to locals (and *Pourretia gigantea* to botanists), it only grows between altitudes of 3700m and 4200m, and is unique to this region. May is the best month to see them, when they are in full bloom and average 8000 flowers and six million seeds per plant. Dotted about the **Quebrada Pachacoto** slopes (some 50km southeast of Huaraz) like candles on an altar, the plants look rather like upside-down trees, with the bushy part as a base and a phallic flowering stem pointing to the sky. Outside of late April, May and early June, the plants can prove disappointing, often looking like burned-out stumps after dropping their flowers and seeds, but the surrounding scenery remains sensational, boasting grasses, rocks, lakes, llamas and the odd hummingbird.

TOURS

By far the easiest way to see the *Puya raimondii* is on an **organized tour** with one of the companies listed (see p.316). Alternatively, you could take a combi colectivo to Catac, leaving daily every thirty minutes from the end of Jirón Cáceres in Huaraz (roughly S/3.50). From Catac, 45km south of Huaraz, there are a few buses and trucks each day down the **La Unión** road, which passes right by the plants. Alternatively, it's possible to get off the combi colectivo 5km beyond Catac at Pachacoto (where there are a couple of cafés often used as pit stops by truck drivers) and hitch from here along the dirt track that leads off the main road across barren grasslands. This track is well travelled by trucks on their way to the mining settlement of Huansala, and after about 15–20km – roughly an hour's drive – into this isolated region, you'll be surrounded by the giant bromeliads. From here, you can either continue on to La Unión (see p.304), via the Pastoruri Glacier, or return to Huaraz by hitching back to the main road.

before walking there. From here it's just a short step (about 2km) to the inviting and very hot (but temperature-controllable) thermal baths of **Huancarhuaz** (daily 8am–5pm; S/3), and there's a road or a more direct three-hour path across the low hills south to Caraz.

The Hualcayan-to-Pomabamba hike

The **Hualcayan-to-Pomabamba hike** is one of the longest in the Cordillera Blanca and requires good acclimatization as well as fitness. It takes about a week to cover the route's total distance of around 78km – altitudes vary between 3100 and 4850m. Starting at Cashapampa, near Hualcayan (with an archeological complex at 3140m), the route takes seven to ten days, taking in great views of the Cordillera Negra on the first day's uphill, zigzag, hiking, passing turquoise lakes and with views over the Santa Cruz glacier (6259m). The trail terminates at the village of Pomabamba, where there are thermal baths, a basic hotel and a road.

6

ARRIVAL AND INFORMATION	PARQUE NACIONAL HUASCARÁN
Parque Nacional Huascarán office Jr Federico Sal y Rosas 555, by corner with Belén, Huaraz ☎ 043 722 086. If you're going to trek in Parque Nacional Huascarán, you'll need to register here and at the Casa de Guías in Huaraz (see box, p.327) beforehand.	**By bus** You can get to Hualcayan (3100m) and Cashapampa from Caraz by bus (1hr 45min), leaving from the corner of Grau with Santa Cruz, two or three times every morning. Pomabamba is connected by Los Andes bus with Yungay (daily; 4–6hr; S/18); there are sometimes colectivos, too.

ACCOMMODATION	
THE HUALCAYAN-TO-POMABAMBA HIKE **Camping** Campsites (free) along the way include:	Jamacuna (4050m), Osoruri (4550m), Jancanrurish (4200m), Huillca (4000m) and Yanacollpa (3850m).

Caraz and around

The attractive town of **CARAZ**, less than 20km down the Santa Valley from Yungay, sits at an altitude of 2285m, well below the enormous Huandoy Glacier. Mainly visited for the access it gives to a fantastic hiking hinterland, it is also well known throughout Peru for its honey and milk products. Palm trees and flowers adorn a colonial-looking **Plaza de Armas**, which has survived well from the ravages of several major earthquakes. The plaza makes the town worth visiting in its own right, especially to escape busy Huaraz. A small daily **market** (6.30am–5pm), three blocks north of the plaza, is usually vibrant with activity, good for fresh food, colourful fabrics, traditional gourd bowls, religious candles and hats. A twenty-minute walk up the hill on the north side of town, dodging house dogs, rewards you with good views over Caraz.

Tumshucaico

A couple of kilometres northeast of Caraz along 28 de Julio, close to the Laguna Parón turn-off, lie the weathered ruins of **Tumshucaico**, probably the largest ruins in the Callejón de Hualyas. A possible ceremonial centre, dating from the formative period of 1800 BC, replete with galleries and worked stone walls, it may well also have had a defensive function given its dominating position overlooking the valley. These days its edges have been eaten away by the peri-urban growth of Caraz and the extension of local cultivated land.

Huata

Nine kilometres across the Río Santa from Caraz, set on the lower slopes of the Cordillera Negra, the small settlement of **HUATA** is a typical rural village with regular truck connections from the market area in Caraz. It serves as a good starting point for a number of easy walks, such as the 8km stroll up to the unassuming lakes of Yanacocha and Huaytacocha or, perhaps more interestingly, north about 5km along a path up Cerro Muchanacoc to the small Inca ruins of Cantu.

CARAZ

CAFÉS & RESTAURANTS
Café Oasis	1
Café de Rat	2
Café El Turista	3
Restaurant SuruBar	4

ACCOMMODATION
Hostal Chamanna	1
Hostal Chavín	4
Hostal Perla de los Andes	3
Hostal San Marco	4
Los Pinos Lodge	2

Laguna Parón

Some 30km, more or less, east of Caraz, the deep-blue **Laguna Parón** (4185m) is sunk resplendently into a gigantic glacial cirque, hemmed in on three sides by some of the Cordillera Blanca's highest icecaps. A short walk east gives views of the pyramid peak of **Artesonraju**, the supposed inspiration for the Paramount Picture's logo swirling with stars.

ARRIVAL AND DEPARTURE   CARAZ AND AROUND

By bus Most of the bus offices are along jirones Daniel Villar and Cordova, within a block or two of the Plaza de Armas: Chinchasuyo serves Trujillo; Empresa Turismo goes to Lima and Chimbote; Ancash to Lima; Movil Tours to Huraz and Lima; Region Norte runs buses to Yungay, Huaraz and Recuay; and Transporte Moreno to Chimbote.

By colectivo Colectivos for Huaraz leave from just behind the market roughly every 30min (1hr 30min; S/10). Services from Yungay arrive every 15–30min (20min; S/2).

TUMSHUCAICO

By taxi Tumshucaico is just a 15min drive from Caraz

plaza. If you aren't with a tour bus and don't have your own transport the best option is a taxi (S/5–8 one way, more for waiting).

HUATA

By taxi Huata is a 20min drive from Caraz (S/8–10 one way).

LAGUNA PARÓN

By bus/colectivo Buses and colectivos (6am; S/5 one way) travel from Caraz market up to Pueblo Parón, from where it's a hike of 9km (3hr) up to the lake. The last transport back from Pueblo Parón to Caraz is usually at noon–1pm. This means it's not possible to make the return trip without a form of your own transport and tours are the better option.

By taxi Taxis to the lake (about S/20–30 per person) can be found most days at the Plaza de Armas in Caraz.

INFORMATION AND TOURS

INFORMATION

Tourist information The office in the Plaza de Armas (Mon–Sat 7.45am–1pm & 2.30–5.30pm; ☎ 043 391 029) stocks maps and brochures covering local attractions and some of the hikes (including the relatively demanding 6–8hr Patapata walk).

TOUR OPERATORS

For trekking guides, local information or help organizing and fitting out an expedition, there are two excellent options with a wealth of expert local knowledge.

Pony's Expeditions Jr Sucre 1266, Plaza de Armas ☎ 043 391 642, ⊛ ponyexpeditions.com. A very professional organization that both fits out and guides climbing, trekking and mountain-biking expeditions in the area. An excellent source of local trekking and climbing information, it also runs treks in other regions, such as the Cordillera Huayhuash, the Inca Trail and Ausangate.

Apu Aventura Parque San Martín 103 ☎ 043 391 130, ⊛ apuaventura.pe. Another excellent local option, Apu Aventura organizes guides, porters, cooks and equipment for expeditions in the Cordillera Blanca and elsewhere in Peru.

ACCOMMODATION

★ **Hostal Chamanna** A little out of town down Av 28 de Julio, at Av Nueva Victoria 185 ☎ 943 595 343, ⊛ chamanna.com. A rather different place, set in a lovely labyrinth of gardens, streams and patios. Not all rooms have a private bathroom but they are very stylish, adorned by ethnic murals; great meals available by prior arrangement. S/150

Hostal Chavín Jr San Martín 1135 ☎ 043 391 171. Close to the plaza, clean, well organized and with wi-fi, this hostel is good value, and some rooms have a private bathroom. Breakfasts and travel assistance also available. S/50

Hostal Perla de los Andes Jr Daniel Villar 179, Plaza de Armas ☎ 043 392 007, ✉ hostalperladelosandes @hotmail.com. The balcony rooms at *Perla* have fantastic views onto the Plaza de Armas, but unfortunately suffer from street noise, even late at night. Bring earplugs or choose one of the equally comfortable inside rooms. All have hot water, private bathroom, wi-fi and TV. There's also a very nice breakfast restaurant. S/55

Hostal San Marco Jr San Martín 1133, Plaza de Armas ☎ 942 879 247. A great place to rest, close to the action. Quiet, light-filled back rooms look onto a courtyard, and boast soft beds, and bathrooms with good hot water. S/45

Los Pinos Lodge Parque Jr San Martín 103 ☎ 043 391 130. One of the least expensive options in town, *Los Pinos Lodge* is a youth hostel that also offers camping spaces and internet facilities. There are shared rooms and also private ones. Camping S/7 per person, dorms S/20, doubles S/55

EATING

Café Oasis Jr Antonio Raimondi 425 ☎ 043 391 785. Just a small stone's throw from the plaza, this café is good for snacks and also has four rooms that it rents out (price on enquiry). Daily 8am–9pm.

Café de Rat Jr Sucre 1266. Just down at the bottom southwestern edge of the Plaza de Armas, this café serves decent pasta, pizza, pancakes and vegetarian food, as well as having a dartboard, maps, guidebooks, music and internet access. Daily 8am–8pm.

Café El Turista Jr San Martín 1117. A great place for early morning hot snacks, full breakfasts and coffee. The staff are friendly and the service is good. Daily 7.30am–noon & 6–9pm.

Restaurant SuruBar Jr Daniel Villar 224. Just off the Plaza de Armas, this family-run restaurant serves reasonably priced lunches and evening meals from a menu of Peruvian and international food. Daily 11am–9pm.

Cañon del Pato

The first canyon village is Huallanca, reached by daily buses (see p.315) from Huaraz; from here, it's 8km on to Yuramarca where the road divides: one route branches off west along a rough road to Chimbote (another 140km) on the coast, or you can continue along the valley to Corongo and the Callejón de Conchucos

One of Peru's most exciting roads runs north from Caraz to Huallanca, squeezing through the spectacular **Cañon del Pato** (Duck's Canyon). An enormous rocky gorge cut from solid rock, its impressive path curves around the Cordillera Negra for most of the 50km between Caraz and Huallanca. Sheer cliff-faces rise thousands of metres on either side while the road passes through some 39 tunnels – an average of one

6

every kilometre. Situated within the canyon is one of Peru's most important hydroelectric power plants; the heart of these works, invisible from the road, is buried 600m deep in the cliff wall. Unfortunately, the road is often closed for a number of reasons – causes include terrorists, bandits, landslides in the rainy season or just the sheer poor quality of the road surface. Much of the first section has been improved in recent years, but from Huallanca to Chimbote it's more like a dry riverbed than a dirt track. Check with the tourist office in Huaraz and local bus companies (see p.315) about the physical and political condition of the road before attempting this journey.

Callejón de Conchucos

To the east of the Cordillera Blanca, roughly parallel to the Callejón de Huaylas, runs another long natural corridor, the **Callejón de Conchucos**. Virtually inaccessible in the wet season, and off the beaten track even for the most hardened of backpackers, the valley represents quite a challenge, and while it features the town of **Pomabamba** in the north and the spectacular ruins at **Chavín de Huantar** just beyond its southern limit, there's little of interest between the two. The villages of **Piscobamba** (Valley or Plain of the Birds) and **Huari** are likely to appeal only as food stops on the long haul (141km) through barren mountains between Pomabamba and Chavín.

Brief history

The Callejón de Conchucos was out of bounds to travellers between 1988 and 1993, when it was under almost complete Sendero Luminoso **terrorist control**; many of the locals were forced to flee the valley after actual or threatened violence from the terrorists. The region's more distant history was equally turbulent and cut off from the rest of Peru, particularly from the seat of colonial and Republican power on the coast. Until the Conquest, this region was home to one of the fiercest ancient tribes – the **Conchucos** – who surged down the Santa Valley and besieged the Spanish city of Trujillo in 1536. By the end of the sixteenth century, however, even the fearless Conchuco warriors had been reduced to virtual slavery by the colonial *encomendero* system.

Pomabamba

The small town of **POMABAMBA**, 3000m up in dauntingly hilly countryside, is surrounded by little-known archeological remains that display common roots with Chavín de Huantar; try Pony's Expeditions in Caraz (see p.333) for further information on these, as well as maps, equipment and advice on trekking in this region. Today the town makes an excellent trekking base; from here you can connect with the **Llanganuco-to-Santa Cruz Loop** (see p.330) by following tracks southwest to either Colcabamba or Punta Unión. Alternatively, for a hard day's hike above Pomabamba, you can walk up to the stone remains of **Yaino**, an immense fortress of megalithic rock. On a clear day you can just about make out this site from the Plaza de Armas in Pomabamba; it appears as a tiny rocky outcrop high on the distant horizon. The climb takes longer than you may imagine, but locals will point out short cuts along the way.

ARRIVAL AND DEPARTURE   **POMABAMBA**

By bus Direct Empresa Los Andes buses to Pomabamba leave from the Plaza de Armas in Yungay at 8.30–9am, while Turismo Huaraz in Huaraz (see p.316) go to Piscobamba and Pomabamba. Alternatively, you can get here from Huaraz via Chavín, on a bus from Lima that comes north up the Callejón de Conchucos more or less every other day.

ACCOMMODATION

Hostal Estrada Vidal C Huaraz 209 ☎ 043 804 615. Located just one block from the small main plaza, this place is basic, but pleasant and clean. **S/25**

Hostal Pomabamba Huamachuco 338 ☎ 043 751 276. Just off the Plaza de Armas, *Hostal Pomabamba* offers simple accommodation, with clean double and single rooms. **S/50**

Chavín de Huantar

Chavín • Tues–Sun 9am–4pm • S/10 • ☎ 043 754 042

A three- to four-hour journey from Huaraz, and only 30km southeast of Huari (see p.339), the magnificent temple complex of **CHAVÍN DE HUANTAR** is the most important Peruvian site associated with the Chavín cult (see box, p.338). Although partially destroyed by earthquakes, floods and erosion from the Río Mosna, enough of the ruins survive to make them a fascinating sight and one of the most important ones in Peru's pre-history. Though the on-site **Sala de Exposición** features ceramics, textiles and stone pieces relating to the cultural influences of the Chavín, Huaras, Recuay and Huari, it is the **Chavín** culture that evolved and elaborated its own brand of religious cultism on and around this magnificent site during the first millennium BC. This religious cult also influenced subsequent cultural development throughout Peru, right up until the Spanish Conquest some 2500 years later (see p.486).

The pretty **village** of Chavín de Huantar, with its whitewashed walls and traditional tiled roofs, is just a couple of hundred metres from the ruins and has a reasonable supply of basic amenities.

Brief history

The original temple was built here around 900 BC, though it was not until around 400 BC that the complex was substantially enlarged and its cultural style fixed. Some archeologists claim that the specific layout of the temple, a U-shaped ceremonial courtyard facing east and based around a raised stone platform, was directly influenced by what was, in 1200 BC, the largest architectural monument in the New World, at Sechin Alto (see p.342). By 300 BC, Sechin Alto had been abandoned and Chavín was at the height of its power and one of the world's largest religious centres, with about three thousand resident priests and temple attendants. The U-shaped temples were probably dedicated to powerful mountain spirits or deities, who controlled meteorological phenomena, in particular rainfall, vital to the survival and wealth of the people.

The temple area

The complex's main temple building consists of a central rectangular block with two wings projecting out to the east. The large, southern wing, known as the **Castillo**, is the

OLLEROS TO CHAVÍN DE HUANTAR TREK

6

GETTING TO CHAVÍN DE HUANTAR

If you have the time, the journey to **Chavín de Huantar** is almost as rewarding as exploring the archeological site itself; the road has to climb out of the Huaraz Valley and cross over the mountains before dropping quite steeply to the modern-day village and remains of Chavín. There is also the option of reaching the ruins on foot from Olleros.

THE ROAD FROM HUARAZ

The vast majority of people approach the temple complex from **Huaraz**; buses (see p.315) turn off the main Huaraz-to-Lima road at the town of Catac. From here they take a poorly maintained road that crosses over the small Río Yana Yacu (Black Water River) and then starts climbing to the beautiful lake of **Querococha** (*quero* is Quechua for "teeth", and relates to the teeth-like rock formation visible nearby), which looks towards two prominent mountain peaks – Yanamarey and Pucaraju ("Red Glacier" in Quechua). From here the road, little more than a track now, climbs further before passing through the **Tunél de Cahuish**, which cuts through the solid rock of a mountain to emerge in the Callejón de Conchucos, to some spectacular but quite terrifying views. A couple of the more dangerous and precipitous curves in the road are known as the Curva del Diablo and Salvate Si Puedes ("Save yourself if you can"), from which you can deduce that this journey isn't for the squeamish or for vertigo sufferers.

OLLEROS-TO-CHAVÍN DE HUANTAR TREK

If you are feeling adventurous there is a two- to four-day trail over the hills from **Olleros** to Chavín. It follows the Río Negro up to Punta Yanashallash (4700m), cuts down into the Marañón watershed along the Quebrada Shongopampa, and where this meets the Jato stream coming from the north, the route follows the combined waters (from here known as the Río Huachesca) straight down, southwest to the Chavín ruins another 1500m below. It's quite a **hike**, so take maps and ideally a guide and pack-llamas (see box, p.327). A good account of this walk is given in Hilary Bradt's *Backpacking and Trekking in Peru and Bolivia* (see p.515).

most conspicuous feature of the site: massive, almost pyramid-shaped, the platform was built of dressed stone with gargoyles attached, though few remain now.

Some way in front of the Castillo, down three main flights of steps, the **Plaza Hundida**, or "sunken plaza", covers about 250 square metres with a rectangular, stepped platform to either side. Here, the thousands of pilgrims thought to have worshipped at Chavín would gather during the appropriate fiestas. And it was here that the famous Tello Obelisk, now in the Museo de Arqueología, Antropología e Historia in Lima (see p.76), was found, next to an altar in the shape of a jaguar and bedecked with seven cavities forming a pattern similar to that of the Orion constellation.

Standing in the Plaza Hundida, facing towards the Castillo, you'll see on your right the **original temple**, now just a palatial ruin dwarfed by the neighbouring Castillo. It was first examined by Julio Tello in 1919 when it was still buried under cultivated fields; during 1945 a vast flood reburied most of it and the place was damaged again by the 1970 earthquake and the rains of 1983. Among the fascinating recent finds from the area are bone snuff tubes, beads, pendants, needles, ceremonial shells (imported from Ecuador) and some quartz crystals associated with ritual sites. One quartz crystal covered in red pigment was found in a grave, placed after death in the mouth of the deceased.

The subterranean chambers

Behind the original temple, two entrances lead to a series of underground passages and **subterranean chambers**. The passage on the right leads down to an underground chamber, containing the awe-inspiring Lanzon, a prism-shaped 4.5m block of carved white granite that tapers down from a broad feline head to a point stuck in the ground. The entrance on the left takes you into the labyrinthine inner chambers, which run underneath the Castillo on several levels connected by ramps and steps. In the seven major subterranean rooms, you'll need a torch to get a decent look at the carvings and the granite sculptures (even when the electric lighting is switched on), while all around you can hear the sound of water dripping.

Another large stone slab that was originally discovered at Chavín in 1873 – the Estela Raymondi – is now in the Museo Nacional de Arqueología, Antropología e Historia in Lima; this was the first and most spectacular of all the impressive carved stones to be found. The most vivid of the carvings remaining at the site are the **gargoyles** (known as Cabeza Clavos) along the outer stone walls of the Castillo sector, guardians of the temple, which again display feline and bird-like characteristics.

ARRIVAL AND INFORMATION

CHAVÍN DE HUANTAR

By bus Empresa Condor de Chavín, Empresa Huascarán, Chavín Express and Empresa Sandoval buses leave Huaraz daily around 10am (3–4hr; S/10–15 one way) for Chavín, while all the tour companies (see p.316) in Huaraz offer a slightly faster, though more expensive, service (3hr; S/35–50 /return). Getting back to Huaraz or Catac, there are buses daily from Chavín, more or less on the hour from 3 to 6pm.

Tourist information There's a small tourist information office on the corner of the Plaza de Armas, next to the market, though it doesn't have regular hours. Detailed advice and information on the site and hiking in the area are best obtained from the relevant organizations in Huaraz (see p.316) or, in Lima, from the South American Explorers' Club (see p.81).

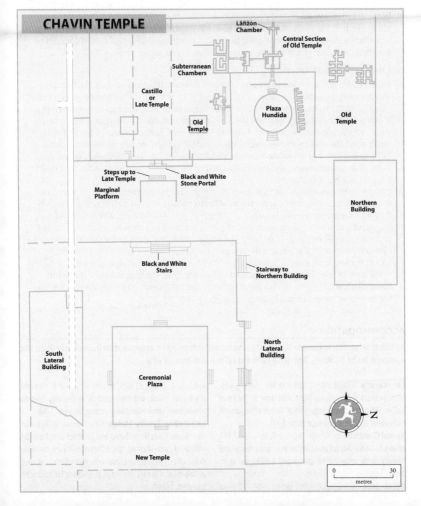

6

THE CHAVÍN CULT

The **Chavín cult**, whose iconography spread across much of Peru, was not a coherent pan-Peruvian religion, but more of a widespread – and unevenly interpreted – cult of the feline god. Chavín had a strong impact on the Paracas culture and later on the Nazca and Mochica civilizations. Theories as to the origin of its inspiration range from extraterrestrial intervention to the more likely infiltration of ideas and individuals or entire tribes from Central America. There is a resemblance between the ceramics found at Chavín and those of a similar date from Tlatilco in **Mexico**, yet there are no comparable Mexican stone constructions as ancient as these Peruvian wonders. More probable, and the theory expounded by medical doctor and Peruvian archeologist Julio Tello (1880–1947), is that the cult initially came up into the Andes (then down to the coast) from the Amazon Basin via the Marañón Valley. The inspiration for the beliefs themselves, which appear to be in the power of totemic or animistic gods and demons, may well have come from visionary experiences sparked by the ingestion of **hallucinogens**: one of the stone reliefs at Chavín portrays a feline deity or fanged warrior holding a section of the psychotropic mescalin cactus San Pedro, still used by *curanderos* today for the invocation of the spirit world. This feline deity was almost certainly associated with the shamanic practice of visionary transformation from human into animal form for magical and healing purposes, usually achieved by the use of hallucinogenic brews; the most powerful animal form that could be assumed, of course, was the big cat, whether a puma or a jaguar.

CHAVÍN ICONOGRAPHY

Most theories about the **iconography** of Chavín de Huantar's stone slabs, all of which are very intricate, distinctive in style and highly abstract, agree that the Chavíns worshipped three major gods: the moon (represented by a fish), the sun (depicted as an eagle or a hawk) and an overlord, or creator divinity, normally shown as a fanged cat, possibly a jaguar. It seems very likely that each god was linked with a distinct level of the Chavín cosmos: the fish with the underworld, the eagle with the celestial forces and the cat with earthly power. This is only a calculated guess, and ethnographic evidence from the Amazon Basin suggests that each of these main gods may have also been associated with a different subgroup within the Chavín tribe or priesthood as a whole.

Chavín itself may or may not have been the centre of the movement, but it was obviously at the very least an outstanding **ceremonial focus** for what was an early agricultural society, thriving on relatively recently domesticated foods as well as cotton, and well-positioned topographically to control the exchange of plants, materials and ideas between communities in the Amazon, Andes and Pacific coast. The name "Chavín" comes from the Quechua *chaupin*, meaning navel or focal point, and the complex might have been a sacred shrine to which natives flocked in pilgrimage during festivals, much as they do today, visiting important *huacas* in the sierra at specific times in the annual agricultural cycle. The appearance of the **Orion constellation** on Chavín carvings fits this theory, since it appears on the skyline just prior to the traditional harvest period in the Peruvian mountains.

ACCOMMODATION

It's sometimes possible to **camp** by the Baños Quercos thermal springs (ask for an update at the Huaraz Tourist Office, tour agencies or in Chavín village), 2km up the valley and a 20min stroll from the village.

La Casona Wiracocha 130 ☎043 454 116, ⓦlacasonachavin.com.pe. Right next door to the town hall on the plaza, this relatively small hostel offers private bathrooms and has a well-kept patio. S/60
Hostal Chavín Jr San Martín (previously Inca Roca) 141 ☎043 454 055. Not all that comfortable, but popular and friendly, with some shared spaces and a courtyard at its heart. S/60
Hotel Inca Wiracocha 170 ☎043 454 021 or

☎01 574 2735, ⓦhotelincachavin.com. A pleasant place with small well-kept gardens and a very friendly atmosphere; some rooms have private showers. S/60
Konchukos Tambo Lodge San Marcos ☎043 454 631. Some 10km from Chavín and a further 2km from the village of San Marcos, this Conchucos-based trekking lodge offers archeological and educational tours as well as day-hikes. Contact the lodge in advance for help with transfers. S/240

EATING

La Portada C 17 de Enero Sur 311. Based in an ageing mansion, *La Portada* offers good, simple, local food including soups, meat and rice. The service is very welcoming and there are some tables in the courtyard. Mon–Sat 10.30am–5.30pm.

Restaurant Chavín Turístico C 17 de Enero Sur 439. As the name suggests, this place has a menu geared towards visitors to town. There is a small central patio garden, service is swift and the ambience pleasant. Daily 7.30am–8pm.

Restaurant La Ramada C 17 de Enero Sur 577. Centrally located and popular with locals and tourists alike, with fresh trout served most days. Daily 8am–8pm.

North from Chavín

There are buses every hour from Chavín to San Marcos (20min; S/5) and Huari (1hr; S/8), or you can walk to San Marcos in well under 2hr; to continue on to Pomabamba from Huari, there are buses every other day, usually leaving at 9pm (7hr; S/18)

Some 8km north of Chavín is the lovely village of **San Marcos**, a good base for mountain hiking. From San Marcos you can climb up another 300m in altitude to the smaller community of **Carhuayoc**, a 100-year-old village whose population specializes in the production of fine textiles – mainly blankets and rugs (it's a 9hr return journey). About 35km from San Marcos, the town of **Huari** is a good base for a short trek to the scenic Lago Purhuay; it's only 8km from the town and a climb of some 400m, but it usually takes between five and six hours to get there and back.

Cordillera Huayhuash

To the south of Huaraz, the **Cordillera Huayhuash** offers much less frequented but just as stunning trekking trails as those in the Cordillera Blanca. Most treks start in the small town of **Chiquián**, 2400m above sea level. The most popular trek hereabouts is the **Chiquián Loop** (see box, p.340), which leaves Chiquián heading for Llamac and the entire Cordillera loop. There is also an alternative trek from Chiquián that is much easier (see below).

The mountains here, although slightly lower than the Cordillera Blanca and covering a much smaller area, nevertheless rise breathtakingly to 6634m at the **Nevada Yerupajá**, some 50km southeast of Chiquián as the crow flies. Yerupajá actually forms the watershed between the Cordillera Huayhuash to the north and the lower-altitude Cordillera Raura to the south. Large and stunning lakes, flocks of alpaca, herds of cattle and some sheep can be seen along the way. High levels of fitness and some experience are required for hiking or climbing in this region and it's always best to tackle it as part of a team, or at least to have a **local guide** along. The guide will help to avoid the rather irritating dogs that look after the animals in these remote hills and his presence will also provide protection against the possible, but unlikely, threat of robbery.

Chiquián

A very small and traditional Andean town, **CHIQUIÁN** is quiet (except during the town's festivals), reserved and very pretty. One popular Huayhuash trek from Chiquián follows a route from **Llamac** to Pampa de Llamac (via a very difficult pass), then on to the lake of **Jahuacocha**, where trout fishing is possible. Taking about five days, the scenery on the trek can only be described as breathtaking; the hiking itself is quite hard. The only downside is that you have to walk Chiquián–Llamac twice, and between Rondoy and Llamac a mining company has destroyed much of the beautiful countryside, apparently also polluting the river as well as building a rather ugly road. More information can be obtained from the Casa de Guías in Huaraz (see box, p.327). Most people who come this far, though, prefer to do the **Chiquián Loop** (see box, p.340), which entails a tough couple of weeks, though the really fit might manage it in ten days at a push.

ARRIVAL AND DEPARTURE
CHIQUIÁN

By bus Chiquián is easily reached by bus with Empresa   Rapido, at Mariscal Cáceres 312 in Huaraz (6 daily; 3hr).

ACCOMMODATION AND EATING

After the town of Chiquián, it's virtually impossible to buy food, so it's a good idea to get most of this in **Huaraz** or in **Lima**, before arriving, supplementing when you arrive here with extras such as bread, dry biscuits, dairy products (including good local cheeses), rice and pasta.

6

THE CHIQUIÁN LOOP

One of the least-visited and most difficult trails, the **Chiquián Loop** lies at altitudes between 2750m and 5000m. It covers a distance of 164–186km and takes some fourteen days to hike (give or take a few, depending on your fitness, walking ability and desire). Rated as Class 4 (difficult), the route, as the name suggests, starts and finishes in Chiquián. Note that maps are essential and local guides with mules advisable. It is also possible to do the trek in sixteen days if you'd like to take things a little easier.

Day 1: Chiquián to Llamac This is an easy first-day walk. The wide and clearly marked path takes hikers to the far end of the valley. After crossing three times from one valley to the other, a short way up will lead walkers to Llamac, a typical highland village.

Day 2: Llamac to Matacancha A two-hour descent leads to another little Andean village called Pocpa, from where walkers must take the left bank of the river and start climbing to the campsite. The first mountain that appears is the Ninashanca at 5607m (18,391ft). The camping spot is at the far end of this dry and treeless valley.

Day 3: Matacancha to Janca The first ascent to the Cacananpunta Pass (La Abra Cacananpunta) at 4880m (16,006ft) is difficult and best reached before noon; descent to the camp does not require a major effort.

Day 4: Janca to Carhuacocha This day involves significant trekking up and back down, offering views of almost the entire scenery of the Cordillera Huayhuash. Arriving at the lakeside camp beside Carhuacocha, the Cordillera is clearly visible.

Day 5: Carhuacocha to Carnicero and Rinconada Leaving the lake at Carhuacocha in the morning, the next pass opens out to the Valle Carnicero. A not very steep, and beautiful, climb takes the hiker to the low Rinconada pass that forms visually spectacular rocky scenery.

Day 6: Carnicero to Huayhuash and Altuspata The descent continues to the next valley via the pass of Punta Carnicero (4600m), passing several small lakes and rivers along the way to the village of Huayhuash (4350m) and continuing to Altuspata, which has good camping.

Day 7: Altuspata to Lago Viconga Leaving the Altuspata campsite first thing, the ascent continues towards one of the highest passes on the route, which leads the way to the Lago Viconga. Walking around the lake through the narrow valley one reaches the next camping spot.

Day 8: Lago Viconga to Valle Huanacpatay A very long way and one of the toughest hikes on the route, this is where one crosses the Abra de Cuyoc pass at 5100m (16,728ft) next to the mountain of Nevado Cuyoc and close to Puscanturpa at 5442m (17,854ft). Descending from the pass, a small, steep and difficult corridor leads to the Valle Huanacpatay.

Days 9 and 10: Abra del Diablo Mudo Two days must be set aside for climbing two of the peaks around the Abra del Diablo Mudo pass to reach Huanacpatay (4500m).

Day 11: Huanacpatay to Huatiac Another long trekking day, but downhill overall, takes you from the high Valle Huanacpatay to a lower one at Huatiac (3800m). After a deep descent into the endless valley of the Huallapa River one starts seeing trees and plants, with the trail passing close by Huallapa village.

Day 12: Huatiac to Jahuacocha Leaving the pleasant Huatiac campsite, the trail continues upwards again to the Abra del Diablo Mudo pass at 5000m (16,400ft), an area bereft of plant life. Everything is downhill from the pass until the lake at Jahuacocha and past it, to camp.

Day 13: Lago Jahuacocha to Llamac After almost two weeks the path crosses again into Llamac village. There are two paths from Jahuacocha which lead back to Llamac's campsite: one is direct and very steep and is done in a shorter time, while the second one is longer but with no major or sudden descents.

Day 14: Llamac to Chiquián and Huaraz A repeated stretch, which also formed the first day's hike: a tough but marvellous trek through the Cordillera Huayhuash.

CHIQUIÁN FIESTAS

In late August and early September there are some colourful fiestas in the town, for the **Virgen de Santa Rosa**, during the last day of which there is always a **bullfight**, with the local football stadium being transformed into an arena. The aim of the game is, as with most rural Peruvian bullfights, just to play with the bull (without hurting him) and this is done not only by the *toreador*, but by anyone who feels the urge to get involved (local youth, drunk men); they can challenge the bull with their poncho, which guarantees a lot of excitement and fun, with the public scattering when the irritated bull comes too close.

6

Hotel Los Nogales Jr Comercio 1301 ☎ 043 447 121, ✉ hotel_nogales_chiquian@yahoo.com.pe. Friendly and safe, this is a good alternative to *San Miguel* (see opposite), with a choice of rooms with TV, and with or without private bathroom. **S/35**

El Refugio de Bolognesi Tarapaca 471. This is the best

of a limited set of small restaurants, offering perhaps the nicest set-lunch menus. Daily 7am–7pm.

San Miguel Jr Comercio 233 ☎ 043 747 001. Arranged around a patio, this rustic place has reasonably clean and comfortable beds and a nice little garden. **S/40**

The Ancash coast

The **Ancash coast** is a largely barren desert strip that quickly rises into Andean foothills when you head east and away from the ocean. Most people going this way will be travelling between Lima and either Huaraz (6–7hr) or Trujillo (8hr). Huaraz is reached by a turn-off from the Panamerican Highway following a well-maintained road that climbs furiously to the breathless heights of the Callejón de Huaylas. There is a small beach resort near **Barranca**, and **Casma** and **Chimbote** have some intriguing archeological sites nearby, and offer alternative routes up to Huaraz.

Barranca and around

The only likely reason to stop off at **BARRANCA** is as part of a visit to the nearby **Fortress of Paramonga**, the best preserved of all Peru's coastal outposts, built originally to guard the southern limit of the powerful Chimu Empire. To explore the ruins, it's best to base yourself in the town, where there are a few simple hotels and two or three places to eat.

Five kilometres north of Barranca is the smaller town of **PATAVILCA**, where Bolívar planned his campaign to liberate Peru. The main paved road to Huaraz and the Cordillera Blanca leaves the Panamerican Highway here and heads up into the Andes.

Fortress of Paramonga

7km north of Barranca • Daily: Fortress 8am–5.30pm; museum 8am–5pm • S/8 • To get from Barranca to Paramonga, take the efficient local bus service, which leaves from the garage at the northern end of town, every hour or so (10–15min; S/2)

The **Fortress of Paramonga** sits less than 1km from the ocean and looks in many ways like a feudal castle. Constructed entirely from adobe, its walls within walls run around the contours of a natural hillock and are similar in style and situation to the Sun Temple of Pachacamac (see p.97). As you climb up from the road, you'll see the main entrance to the fortress on the right by the site's small **museum** and ticket office.

Heading into the labyrinthine **ruins**, you'll find the rooms and sections get smaller and narrower the closer you get to the top – and the original **palace-temple**. From here there are commanding views over the desert coast and across vast sugar-cane fields, formerly belonging to the US-owned Grace Corporation, once owners of nearly a third of Peru's sugar production. In contrast to the verdant verdure of these fields, irrigated by the Río Fortaleza, the fortress stands out in the landscape like a huge, dusty yellow pyramid.

6

There are differences of opinion as to whether the fort had a military function or was purely a ritual centre, but as most pre-Conquest cultures built their places of worship around the natural personality of the landscape (rocks, water, geomorphic features and so on), it seems likely that the Chimu built it on an older *huaca* (ancient sacred site), both as a fortified ritual shrine and to mark the southern boundary of their empire. In the late fifteenth century, it was conquered by the **Incas**, who built a road down from the Callejón de Huaylas. Arriving in 1533 en route from Cajamarca to Pachacamac, Hernando Pizarro, the first Spaniard to see Paramonga, described it as "a strong fort with seven encircling walls painted with many forms both inside and outside, with portals well built like those of Spain and two tigers painted at the principal doorways". There are still red- and yellow-based geometric murals visible on some of the walls in the upper sector, as well as some chessboard-style patterns.

ARRIVAL AND ACCOMMODATION   BARRANCA AND AROUND

By bus/colectivo Nearly all buses and colectivos on their way between Lima and Trujillo or Huaraz stop at Barranca. There are several buses daily to Casma (2hr), Chimbote (3hr), Huaraz (4–5hr) and Lima (3hr) from here.

Hotel Jefferson Jr Lima 946 ☎01 235 2184. An inexpensive establishment with quite comfortable rooms. **S/65**

Casma and around

The town of **CASMA**, 170km north of Barranca, marks the mouth of the well-irrigated Sechin River Valley. Surrounded by corn and cotton fields, this small settlement is peculiar in that most of its buildings are just one storey high and all are modern. Formerly the port for the Callejón de Huaylas, the town was razed by the 1970 earthquake, whose epicentre was just offshore. There's not a lot of interest here and little reason to break your journey, other than to try the local speciality of duck ceviche (flakes of duck meat soaked deliciously in lime and orange juice) or to explore the nearby ruins, such as the temple complex of Sechin, the ancient fort of Chanquillo and the Pañamarca pyramid, 20km north.

The Sechin ruins

5km southeast from Casma • Daily: Ruins 8am–5pm; Museo de Sitio Max Uhle 8am–5.30pm • S/5

A partially reconstructed temple complex, the main section of the **Sechin ruins** is unusually stuck at the bottom of a hill, and consists of an outer wall clad with around ninety monolithic slabs engraved with sometimes monstrous representations of particularly nasty and bellicose warriors, along with their mutilated sacrificial victims or prisoners of war. Some of these stones, dating from between 1800 and 800 BC, stand 4m high. Hidden behind the standing stones is an interesting inner sanctuary – a rectangular building consisting of a series of superimposed platforms with a central stairway on either side. The site also contains the small **Museo de Sitio Max Uhle**, which displays photographs of the complex plus some of the artefacts uncovered here, as well as information and exhibits on Moche, Huari, Chimu, Casma and Inca cultures.

Some of the ceremonial centres at Sechin were built before 1400 BC, including the massive, U-shaped **Sechin Alto complex** (21km away near Buena Vista Alta; not accessible via public transport), at the time the largest construction in the entire Americas. Ancient coastal constructions usually favoured adobe as a building material, making this site rare in its extensive use of granite stone. Around 300m long by 250m wide, the massive stone-faced platform pre-dates the similar ceremonial centre at Chavín de Huantar (see p.335), possibly by as much as four hundred years. This means that Chavín could not have been the original source of the temple architectural style, and that much of the iconography and legends associated with what is known as the Chavín cultural phase of Peruvian prehistory actually began 3500 years ago down here on the desert coast.

Pampa de Llamas

Several lesser-known archeological sites dot the Sechin Valley, whose maze of ancient sandy roadways constituted an important pre-Inca junction. The remains of a huge complex of dwellings can be found on the **Pampa de Llamas**, though all you will see nowadays are the walls of adobe huts, deserted more than a thousand years ago. At **Mojeque**, you can see a terraced pyramid with stone stairs and feline and snake designs.

Fort of Chanquillo

6

Some 12km southeast of Casma lies the ruined, possibly pre-Mochica fort of **Chanquillo**, around which you can wander freely. It's an amazing ruin set in a commanding position on a barren hill, with four walls in concentric rings and watchtowers in the middle, keeping an eye over the desert below. Less than one kilometre below the fort stand thirteen towers in a long line.

Pañamarca pyramid

At Km 395 of the Panamericana Norte, a turn-off on the right leads 11km to the ruined adobe pyramid of **Pañamarca**, an impressive monument to the Mochica culture, dating from around 500 AD. Three large painted panels can be seen here, and on a nearby wall a long procession of warriors has been painted – but all this artwork has been badly damaged by rain.

ARRIVAL AND DEPARTURE
CASMA AND AROUND

CASMA

By bus Turismo Chimbote buses, at block 1, Av Luís Ormeño, run at least every hour to Lima (6hr) and Chimbote (40min); for Huaraz, Huandoy buses, Av Luís Ormeño 158 (☎043 712 336), take the fastest normal route, finishing at Caraz; while Empresa Moreno buses serve Huaraz three times a week via the scenic but dusty track over the Cordillera Negra via the Callan Pass (6–8hr).

THE SECHIN RUINS

On foot Walk south along the Panamerican La for 3km, then up the signposted side road to Huaraz for about the same distance; the walk should take just over an hour.

By taxi If you're not up to the walk here, your best option is to take a mototaxi from Casma, (S/5 one way). Alternatively, there are taxis from the Plaza de Armas, for around $10–15 return, including a wait of an hour or so.

By colectivo There are no buses, but some local colectivos come here in the mornings from the market area of Casma.

PAMPA DE LLAMAS AND MOJEQUE

By taxi Both Mojeque and Pampa de Llamas are best visited from Casma by taxi; expect to pay around S/30 (return).

CHANQUILLO

By truck Trucks leave for Chanquillo every morning at around 9am from the Petro Perú filling station in Casma – ask the driver to drop you off at "El Castillo", from where it's a 30min walk uphill to the fort.

FORT OF CHANQUILLO

By taxi From Casma your taxi should take the turning east from the Panamericana Norte at Km 361; the driver will have to wait since it is unlikely there will be others at the site (S/15 one way, plus S/5–10 for the wait).

PAÑAMARCA PYRAMID

By taxi This is not an easy site to visit; it is best to get a taxi from the Plaza de Armas in Casma for around S/15–20.

ACCOMMODATION

CASMA

Hospedaje Las Dunas Ormeno 505 ☎043 711 057. On the route to the Sechin ruins this place is well run with a good restaurant, and is only 10min from town by car or taxi. **S/70**

Hostal Las Aldas Panamericana Norte Km 347 ☎01 442 8523, ✇lasaldas.com. Some 30km from Casma, this fun hostel is located near a pleasant beach at Playa Las Aldas (turn off the Panamericana Norte at Km 345); some of the bungalows face the ocean and are right on the beach. **S/60**

Hostal Gregori C Luís Ormeño 530 ☎043 711 073. Very clean and quiet hostel with comfortable rooms in a modern building with an airy and pleasant lobby; service is good too. **S/55**

Hotel El Farol Tupac Amaru 450 ☎043 711 064, ✉hostalfarol@yahoo.com. Just two blocks from the Plaza de Armas, the only hotel in Casma is friendly and clean, with TVs and private bathrooms, a summer pool and a decent restaurant which sometimes serves *ceviche de pato*. **S/65**

6

Chimbote

Elderly locals say that **CHIMBOTE** – another 25km beyond the turn-off to the Pañamarca pyramid – was once a beautiful coastal bay, with a rustic fishing port and fine extensive beach. You can still get a sense of this on the southern Panamericana approach, but the smell and industrial sprawl created by the unplanned fishing boom over thirty years ago undeniably dominates the senses. Chimbote has more than thirty **fish-packing factories**, which explains the rather unbearable stench of stale fish. Despite the crisis in the fishing industry since the early 1970s – overfishing and El Niño have led to bans and strict catch limits for the fishermen – Chimbote accounts for more than 75 percent of Peru's fishing-related activity. Most travellers stay in Chimbote one night at most; the town is smelly and offers little of interest to visitors, apart perhaps from some attractive **marble sculptures** which adorn the central Boulevard Isla Blanca.

Chimbote's development constitutes the country's most spectacular **urban growth** outside Lima. Initially stimulated by the Chimbote–Huallanca rail line (built in 1922), a nearby hydroelectric plant and government planning for an anticipated rise in the anchovy- and tuna-fishing industry, the population grew rapidly from 5000 in 1940 to 60,000 in 1961 (swollen by squatter settlers from the mountains). Yet even Chimbote was virtually razed to the ground during the 1970 earthquake (see p.326).

ARRIVAL AND INFORMATION   CHIMBOTE

By plane The airport, where you can get daily flights to (or from) Lima and Trujillo, can be found at Km 421 (☎043 311 844 or ☎043 311 062).

By bus Most important is knowing how to get out of town. Most buses call at and leave from the Terminal Terrestre El Chimbador, a few kilometres south of the city centre on Av de los Pescadores on the Carretera Panamericana. All the coastal buses travelling north to Trujillo (3hr north) and south to Lima along the Panamerican Hwy stop here; it can be very busy. Turismo Huaraz run direct Chimbote–Huaraz buses, daily (one daytime, one at night) from Av Pardo 1713 (☎043 321 235). Movil Tours, Turismo Chimbote, Expresso Huandoy and Trans Moreno all run daily buses to Huaraz via Pativilca and Casma, as well as (mostly nightly) services to Caraz via Huallanca and the Cañon del Pato, a very rough road) from Jr Pardo, between jirones José Galvez and Manuel Ruiz.

By colectivo Colectivos to Trujillo (2–3hr away) leave regularly from C Enrique Palacios, near the Plaza de Armas, while colectivos to Lima hang around on Manuel Ruiz, one block towards the sea off Av Prado.

Tourist information Bolognesi 421 (Mon–Sat 9am–5.30pm). Can advise on transport to nearby sites and sometimes stocks town and regional maps. Limited information can also be found at ⓦ chimboteonline.com.

ACCOMMODATION

Gran Chimú Av José Galvez 109 ☎043 321 741. Dominating the Plaza 28 de Julio, this large hotel is reasonably priced, offering comfortable rooms and mod cons, and its restaurant, though not cheap, serves some of the best food found along this part of the coast; try the ceviche or the criolla dishes such as *aji de gallina*. **S̲/̲1̲8̲0̲**

Hostal El Ruedo Lote 15, Urbino Los Pinos ☎043 335 560. Located a little way from the noisy town centre, this basic establishment is usually relatively free of fishy smells. **S̲/̲6̲5̲**

Hotel La Casona Av San Pedro 246 ☎043 322 655. Located in the suburb of Miramar Bajo, this stylish and very comfortable hotel offers all modern conveniences. **S̲/̲1̲2̲0̲**

The Santa and Viru valleys

The valleys formed by the rivers **Santa** and **Viru** provide relief against the sun-blasted desert on the road north between Chimbote and Trujillo. Despite the bleak terrain and climate the roadside towards Trujillo is fast filling up with new settlements – a kind of ribbon development between two busy markets and population centres. The desert itself, beyond the road, is rarely visited, yet littered with **archeological remains**.

Great Wall of Peru

Twenty kilometres north of Chimbote, the Panamericana crosses a rocky outcrop into the Santa Valley, where an enormous defensive wall known as the **Great Wall of**

Peru – a stone and adobe structure more than 50km long and thought to be over a thousand years old – rises from the sands of the desert. The enormous structure was first noticed in 1931 by the Shippee-Johnson Aerial Photographic Expedition, and there are many theories about its construction and purpose. Archeologist Julio Tello thought it was pre-Chimu, since it seems unlikely that the Chimu would have built such a lengthy defensive wall so far inside the limits of their empire. It may also, as the historian Garcilaso de la Vega believed, have been built by the Spaniards as a defence against the threat of Inca invasion from the coast or from the Callejón de Huaylas. The wall stretches from Tambo Real near the Río Santa estuary in the west up to Chuqucara in the east, where there are scattered remains of pyramids, fortresses, temples and stone houses.

Further up the valley – albeit far off the beaten track, with no tourism infrastructure whatsoever – lies a double-walled **construction** with outer turrets, discovered by Gene Savoy's aerial expedition in the late 1950s. Savoy reported finding 42 stone-built strongholds in the higher Santa Valley in only two days' flying, evidence that supports historians' claims that this was the most populated valley on the coast prior to the Spanish Conquest. Hard to believe today, it seems more probable if you bear in mind that this desert region, still alive with wildlife such as desert foxes and condors, is fed by the largest and most reliable of the coastal rivers.

Viru

The Viru Valley's main town is the eponymous **VIRU**, a small place at Km 515 of the Panamericana Norte, with a bridge over the riverbed, which in the dry season looks as though it has never seen rain. The name Viru is believed by many to be the original source of the modern name Peru. According to the chroniclers, the Spanish conquistadores met a raft of fishermen out on the sea here, before landing in Peru. When the Spanish tried to find out from the fishermen where they came from, apparently they said "Viru, Viru".

An impressive cultural centre around 300 AD, when it was occupied by the Gallinazo or Viru people, today the town offers very little to the tourist. The most interesting ruin in the area is the **Grupo Gallinazo** near Tomabal, 24km east of Viru up a side road just north of the town's bridge. Here in the valley you can see the dwellings, murals and pyramids of a significant religious and administrative centre, its internal layout derived from kinship networks (with different clans responsible for different sectors of the settlement). The site covers an area of four square kilometres and archeologists estimate that over ten thousand people sometimes lived here at the same time. You can also make out the adobe walls and ceremonial platform of a Gallinazo temple, on one of the hilltops at Tomabal.

ARRIVAL AND DEPARTURE   THE SANTA AND VIRU VALLEYS

GREAT WALL OF PERU

By bus To see the wall, take any Trujillo bus north from Chimbote (see opposite) along the Panamericana Norte, and get off when you see a bridge over the Río Santa. From here, head upstream for three or four hours and you'll arrive at the best surviving section of the wall, just to the

west of the Hacienda Tanguche farm, where the piled stone is cemented with mud to more than 4m high in places.

VIRU

By bus The road between Chimbote and Trujillo runs straight through Viru, so just take any bus and get off there.

Trujillo and the north

CHAN CHAN

Trujillo and the north

Northern Peru is packed with unique treasures – cultural, archeological and natural. Blessed with fewer tourists and better coastal weather than either Lima or the south (particularly in the high season – December to February), the area encompasses city oases along the coast, secluded villages in the Andes – where you may well be the first foreigner to pass through for years – and is brimming over with imposing and important pre-Inca sites, some of them only discovered in the last decade or two. For many, the biggest attraction will be the beautiful and trendy beaches or the perfectly formed surf rolling in just offshore. For others, it's the scenery, archeology and the opportunity to get off the beaten tourist trail.

7

Trujillo is located on the seaward edge of the vast desert plain at the mouth of the Moche Valley. Its attraction lies mainly in its nearby ruins – notably **Chan Chan** and the huge, sacred pyramids of the **Huaca del Sol** and **Huaca de la Luna** – but also partly in the city's colonial centre, and some excellent, laidback outlying beach communities. **Huanchaco**, only 12km from Trujillo, is a good case in point, a fishing village turned surf town fronting on long sandy beaches and with massive ancient ruins just down the road.

There are established bus **touring routes** through the Andean region above Trujillo, all of which present the option of winding through the beautifully situated mountain town of **Cajamarca**. It was here that Pizarro first encountered and captured the Inca Emperor Atahualpa, beginning the Spanish conquest of Peru. Cajamarca is also a springboard for visiting the smaller town of **Chachapoyas** and the ruined citadel complex of **Kuélap**, arguably the single most overwhelming pre-Columbian site in Peru. Beyond, there are possible routes down to Amazon headwaters and the jungle towns of **Tarapoto** and even **Iquitos** – long and arduous journeys.

The coastal strip north of Trujillo, up to **Tumbes** by the Ecuadorian border, is for the most part a seemingly endless **desert** plain, interrupted by isolated villages and new squatter settlements, but only two substantial towns, **Chiclayo** and **Piura**. Newly discovered archeological sites around Chiclayo possess some of the coast's most important temple ruins, pyramids and nobles' tombs, the latter containing a wealth of precious-metal ceremonial items, and there are some excellent regional museums such as the Museo de las Tumbas, not far from Chiclayo. Northern Peru has Peru's best beaches, with party town **Máncora** throbbing at the heart of them and luxurious **Las Pocitas** lazing just next door. To the south are surf getaways **Chichama** and **Lobitos** and

SURFING AT MÁNCORA BEACH

Highlights

❶ **Chan Chan** Located by the ocean near the city of Trujillo, this massive adobe city was built by the Chimu culture in the thirteenth century. **See p.365**

❷ **Kuélap** Way off the beaten track, this majestic mountaintop citadel rivals Machu Picchu for its setting and archeological interest. **See p.386**

❸ **Museo de las Tumbas** An excellent museum whose exhibits include precious objects of gold and silver, as well as a replica of the royal tomb of the Lord of Sipán. **See p.400**

❹ **Batán Grande** On the eastern edge of the Americas' largest dry forest, and right next to the beautiful Río de la Leche, ancient pyramids stand as an impressive monument to the ceremonial heart of Sicán culture. **See p.402**

❺ **Valley of the Pyramids** Standing in the hot dry desert of northern Peru is this magnificent collection of adobe pyramids from the Sicán culture, dating around 1100 AD. **See p.403**

❻ **Máncora and Pocitas** Peru's trendiest beach and surf resort, Máncora has warm water, strong sunshine and hot nightlife, while Pocitas is tranquil and palm-lined. **See p.414 & p.416**

HIGHLIGHTS ARE MARKED ON THE MAP ON PP.350–351

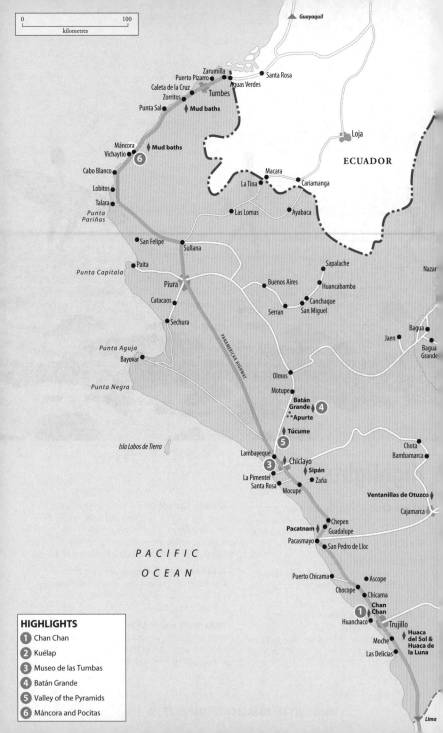

HIGHLIGHTS

1. Chan Chan
2. Kuélap
3. Museo de las Tumbas
4. Batán Grande
5. Valley of the Pyramids
6. Máncora and Pocitas

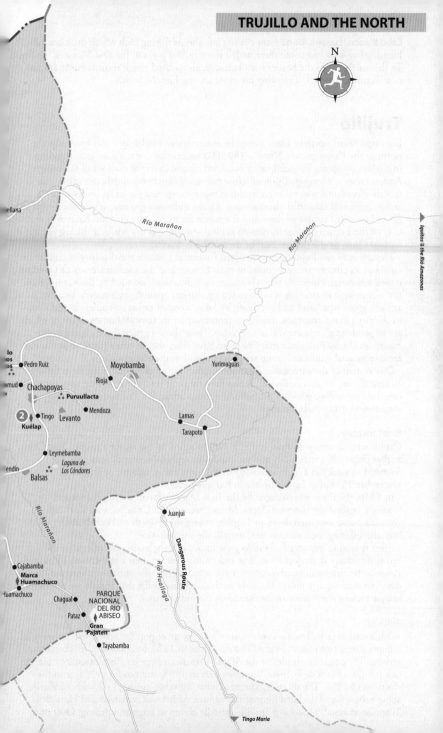

N

ellana

Río Marañon

Río Marañon

Iquitos & the Río Amazonas

lo
os
os

● Pedro Ruiz

mud

Chachapoyas

Moyobamba

Rioja

Yurimaguas

Puruullacta

2 ● Tingo
Kuélap

Mendoza

Levanto

Lamas

Tarapoto

● Leymebamba

endín

Balsas

*Laguna de
Los Cóndores*

Río Marañon

● Juanjui

Dangerous Route

Río Huallaga

● Cajabamba

**Marca
Huamachuco**

Huamachuco

Chagual ●

PARQUE
NACIONAL
DEL RIO
ABISEO

Pataz ●

**Gran
Pajaten**

● Tayabamba

▼ *Tingo Maria*

Cabo Blanco, famous for its giant curling left and its fishing club which once hosted Hemingway who had come there with a team to film parts of the *Old Man and the Sea*. To the north, up to the border with Ecuador, are isolated beach retreats **Punta Sal** and near Tumbes, **Zorritos**, a growing favourite among Limeño youth.

Trujillo

Just eight hours north of Lima along the Panamerican Highway – also known in the north as the Panamericana Norte – **TRUJILLO** looks every bit the oasis it is, standing in a relatively green, irrigated valley bounded by arid desert at the foot of the brown Andes. Despite a long tradition of leftist politics, today Peru's northern capital only sees the occasional street protest, and it is more recognized for its lavish colonial architecture and colourful old mansions. Lively and cosmopolitan, it's small enough to get to know in a couple of days, and is renown for its friendly citizens. Known as the City of the Eternal Spring, its **climate** is ideal – warm and dry without the fog you get around Lima, or the intense heat of the northern deserts.

The city may not have the international flavour of Lima or the diversity of culture or race, but its citizens are very proud of their history, and the local university **La Libertad** is well respected, especially when it comes to archeology. Founded by Bolívar in 1824, the picturesque institution is surrounded by elegant, Spanish-style streets, lined with ancient green ficus trees and overhung by long, wooden-railed balconies. In addition to the city's many **churches**, Trujillo is renowned for its **colonial houses**, most of which are in good repair and are still in use today. These should generally be visited in the mornings (Mon–Fri), since many of them have other uses at other times of day; some are commercial banks and some are simply closed in the afternoons.

One or two of the surrounding communities, which make their living from fishing or agriculture, are also celebrated across Peru for their traditional healing arts, usually based on *curanderos* who use the hallucinogenic cactus, San Pedro, for diagnosing and sometimes curing their patients.

Brief history

On his second voyage to Peru in 1528, **Pizarro** sailed by the site of ancient Chan Chan, at that point still a major city and an important regional centre of Inca rule. He returned to establish a Spanish colony in the same valley, naming it Trujillo in December 1534 after his birthplace in Extremadura.

In 1536, the town was besieged by the Inca Manco's forces during the second rebellion against the conquistadores. Many thousands of Conchuco warriors, allied with the Incas, swarmed down to Trujillo, killing the Spanish and collaborators on the way and offering their victims to Catequil, the tribal deity.

After surviving this attack, Trujillo grew to become the main port of call for the Spanish treasure fleets, sailors wining and dining here on their way between Lima and Panama. By the seventeenth century it was a walled city of some three thousand houses covering three square miles. The only sections of those walls that remain are the **Herrera rampart** and a small piece of the facade on Avenida España.

APRA

With a restless past, Trujillo continued to be a centre of popular rebellion, declaring its independence from Spain in the Plaza de Armas in 1820, long before the Liberators arrived. The enigmatic leader of the **APRA** – American Popular Revolutionary Alliance (see p.492) – Haya de la Torre, was born here in 1895, and ran for president in the elections of 1931. The dictator, Sánchez Cerro, however, counted the votes (unfairly, some believe), and declared himself the winner. APRA was outlawed and Haya de la Torre imprisoned, provoking Trujillo's middle classes to stage an uprising. Over one

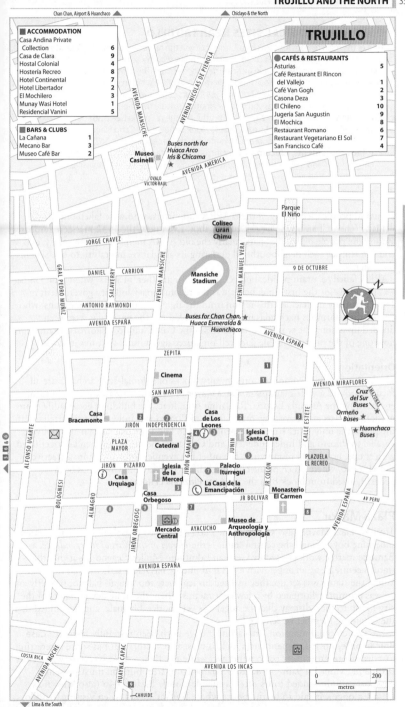

Chan Chan, Airport & Huanchaco ▲   ▲ Chiclayo & the North

TRUJILLO

■ ACCOMMODATION
Casa Andina Private Collection	6
Casa de Clara	9
Hostal Colonial	4
Hostería Recreo	8
Hotel Continental	7
Hotel Libertador	2
El Mochilero	3
Munay Wasi Hotel	1
Residencial Vanini	5

■ BARS & CLUBS
La Cañana	1
Mecano Bar	3
Museo Café Bar	2

● CAFÉS & RESTAURANTS
Asturias	5
Café Restaurant El Rincon del Vallejo	1
Café Van Gogh	2
Casona Deza	3
El Chileno	10
Jugeria San Augustin	9
El Mochica	8
Restaurant Romano	6
Restaurant Vegetariano El Sol	7
San Francisco Café	4

Museo Casinelli

Buses north for Huaca Arco Iris & Chicama ★

OVALO VICTOR RAUL

Parque El Niño

7

Coliseo Gran Chimu

JORGE CHAVEZ

DANIEL   CARRION

9 DE OCTUBRE

GRAL. PEDRO MUÑIZ

SALAVERRY

Mansiche Stadium

ANTONIO RAYMONDI

AVENIDA ESPAÑA

Buses for Chan Chan, Huaca Esmeralda & Huanchaco ★

AVENIDA ESPAÑA

ZEPITA

AVENIDA MIRAFLORES

Cinema

Cruz del Sur Buses ★

SAN MARTIN

Ormeño Buses ★

Casa Bracamonte

Casa de Los Leones

Huanchaco Buses ★

JIRÓN INDEPENDENCIA

Iglesia Santa Clara

ALFONSO UGARTE

PLAZA MAYOR

Catedral

JUNIN

PLAZUELA EL RECREO

BOLOGNESI

JIRÓN PIZARRO

Casa Urquiaga

Iglesia de la Merced

Palacio Iturregui

ALMAGRO

Casa Orbegoso

La Casa de la Emancipación

Monasterio El Carmen

JR BOLIVAR

JIRÓN ORBEGOSO

Mercado Central

AYACUCHO

Museo de Arqueología y Anthropologia

AV PERU

AVENIDA ESPAÑA

COSTA RICA MOCHE

AVENIDA MOCHE

HUAYNA CAPAC

AVENIDA LOS INCAS

CAHUIDE

0   200
metres

▼ Lima & the South

TOP ARCHEOLOGICAL SITES NEAR TRUJILLO

One of the main reasons for coming to Trujillo is to visit the numerous **archeological sites** dotted around the nearby Moche and Chicama valleys. In many ways these sites are more impressive than the ruins around Cusco – and most are more ancient too. The pyramids, courtyards and high walls of the various sites are all constructed from adobe bricks which have suffered from the occasional rains over the last eight hundred years or so, consequently requiring a little imagination to mentally reconstruct them as you wander around. Here are the three to aim for:

Chan Chan A gigantic adobe city on the northern edge of Trujillo (see p.365).

Huaca del Sol/Huaca de la Luna Standing alone beneath the Cerro Blanco hill south of Trujillo these are the largest mud-brick pyramids in the Americas (see p.362).

Pre-Inca settlements, Chicama Valley Incredible remnants of vast pre-Inca irrigation canals, temples and early settlement sites existing in stark contrast to the massive, green sugar-cane plantations of the haciendas (see p.369).

7

thousand people died, many of them APRA supporters, who were taken out to the fields of Chan Chan by the truckload and shot. Even now, the 1932 massacre resonates among the people of Trujillo, particularly the old APRA members and the army, and you can still see each neighbourhood declaring its allegiance, in graffiti, to one side or the other.

APRA failed to attain political power in Peru for another 54 years, when Alan García was president for the first time; but it was the revolutionary military government in 1969 that truly unshackled this region from the tight grip of a few **sugar barons**, who owned the enormous haciendas in the Chicama Valley. The haciendas were then divided up among the worker co-operatives – the Casa Grande, a showcase example, is now one of the most profitable and well-organized agricultural ventures in Peru.

Orientation

The heart of Trujillo comprises some twenty blocks of colonial-style architecture all focused around a wide main plaza, **Plaza Mayor** or Plaza de Armas, which is in turn encircled by the Avenida España. Radiating from here, the buildings get steadily more modern and less attractive. The main streets of Pizarro and Independencia originate at the plaza; the only other streets you really need to know are San Martín and Bolívar, parallel to Pizarro and Independencia, and Gamarra, the main commercial street lined with shops, hotels and restaurants. The other big avenue, older and more attractive, is **Jirón Pizarro**, where much of the city's nightlife is centred and which has been pedestrianized from block 8 to the pleasant **Plazuela El Recreo**.

Plaza Mayor

Trujillo's **Plaza Mayor** (also known as the Plaza de Armas) is packed with sharp-witted shoeshine boys around the central statue – the *Heroes of the Wars of Independence*, a Baroque marble work created by German Edmundo Muller. Legend has it that the statue's centrepiece, an angel with a torch of liberty, has had a rather tough time of it. When the statue was set up, they realized his legs were too long to balance properly and he was promptly shortened by a few centimetres. Then, the more devout ladies of the city found to their dismay that the angel was very noticeably male, and demanded that the offending member be removed.

The two colonial mansions that front it have both been tastefully restored: **Casa Bracamonte**, on Jr Independencia 441, is closed to visitors but has some interesting cast-ironwork around its patio windows, while the Banco de la Nación-owned **Casa Urquiaga** (Mon–Fri 9am–3pm, Sat 9.30am–1pm; free, but you must present a passport; 30min guided tours often available), on Jr Pizarro 446 (also known as Casa Calonge), is said to be the house where Bolívar stayed when visiting Trujillo;

it's also home to some first-class Rococo-style furniture and a fine collection of ancient ceramics.

La Catedral

Plaza Mayor • Daily 7–11.45am & 4–7pm **Museum** Mon–Fri 9am–1pm & 4–7pm, Sat 9am–1pm • S/4

Plaza Mayor is home to **La Catedral**, built in the mid-seventeenth century, then rebuilt the following century after earthquake damage. Known locally as the Basílica Menor, it's plain by Peruvian standards but houses some colourful Baroque sculptures and a handful of paintings by the Quiteña school (a deeply religious style of painting that originated in eighteenth-century Quito). The paintings that cover the roof of the Cathedral are particularly impressive. To the right of the main entrance of the cathedral, the **Museo de Catedral** exhibits a range of mainly eighteenth- and nineteenth-century religious paintings and sculptures. The tour (only in Spanish) included in the museum's entry fee can explain a little of the history of the rather drab collection in the small room, but also includes a visit down into the crypt below which hosts seventeenth- and eighteenth-century paintings, murals depicting funeral rites and a rather morbid selection of paintings of decapitated martyrs.

Casa Orbegoso

Jr Orbegoso 553 • Closed to public, only opening for art shows

Between Plaza Major and the Central Market stands the most impressive of Trujillo's colonial houses – the **Casa Orbegoso**, the home of **Luís José Orbegoso**, former president of Peru. Born into one of Trujillo's wealthiest founding families, Orbegoso fought for independence and became president of the republic in 1833 with the support of the liberal faction. However, he proved to be the most ineffective of all Peruvian leaders, resented by his aristocratic bearing by the *mestizo* generals, and from 1833 to 1839, although still officially president, he lost control of the country – first in civil war, then to the Bolivian army, and finally to a combined rebel and Chilean force. Unfortunately, today, unless your visit happens to coincide with an art show, you will only be able to appreciate its impeccable yellow-painted exterior with elaborate window frames and an intricately carved wooden box balcony.

Mercado Central and Mercado Mayorista

Cnr of Ayacucho and Gamarra • Mon–Sat 7am–5pm

Trujillo's main market, the **Mercado Central** (known locally as the Mercado de los Brujos: the Witches' Market) is only two blocks east of the Plaza Mayor. As well as selling most essentials, such as juices, food and clothing, it has an interesting line in **herbal stalls** and healing or magical items, not to mention unionized shoe-cleaners. There's a second, much busier market, the **Mercado Mayorista**, further out, on Avenida Costa Rica in the southeast corner of town.

Museo de Arqueología y Antropología

Jr Junín 682 • Mon–Fri 9am–5pm, Sat & public holidays 9am–2pm • S/5; no fixed tours, but call beforehand and they may be able to organize one • ☏ 044 474 850

The university's excellent **Museo de Arqueología y Antropología** specializes in ceramics, early metallurgy, textiles and feather work. It is located in Casa Risco, a colonial mansion donated by the Peruvian government to the university of Trujillo in 1995. The main hall provides a chronological review of the archeological finds of the north coast, while four further rooms host temporary exhibitions of current work and new discoveries. Well worth visiting for some solid background information before going on any further tours in the area.

La Casa de la Emancipación

Jr Pizarro 610 • Mon–Sat 9am–1pm & 4–8pm • Free

East of the main plaza stands an impressive mansion, **La Casa de la Emancipación**. Remodelled in the mid-nineteenth century by the priest Pedro Madalengoitia (the reason it's also sometimes known as the Casa Madalengoitia), it is now head office of the Banco Continental. The main courtyard and entrance demonstrate a symmetrical and austere design, while the wide gallery has some impressive marble flooring. At the entrance are a couple of late eighteenth-century murals depicting peasant life, and paintings or historical photographs are usually exhibited in at least one of its rooms.

Palacio Iturregui

Jr Pizarro 688 • Daily 8.30am–10am • S/5

Two blocks east of the Plaza Mayor is the **Palacio Iturregui**, a striking mid-nineteenth-century mansion. Built by the army general Don Juan Manuel de Iturregui y Aguilarte, the house is used today by the city's exclusive Central Club. The room to the right of the entry usually hosts a small but excellent collection of local modern paintings. The highlight of the building is its pseudo-classical courtyard, encircled by superb galleries, with tall columns and an open roof, which provides a wonderful view of the blue desert sky. The club maintains very limited entry hours, but you can pop in any time during the day to appreciate the courtyard and the two rooms just off the courtyard.

Plazuela El Recreo

Eastern end of Jr Pizarro

Five blocks from the Plaza Mayor, there's a small, attractive square known as the **Plazuela El Recreo** where, under the shade of some vast 130-year-old ficus trees, a number of **bars** and food stalls act like a magnet for young couples in the evenings. This little plaza was, and still is, an *estanque de agua* – a water distribution point – built during colonial days, but tapping into even more ancient irrigation works.

FIESTAS IN TRUJILLO

Trujillo's main **fiestas** turn the town into even more of a relaxed playground than it is normally, with the **marinera** dance featuring prominently in most celebrations. This regional dance originated in Trujillo and is accompanied by a combination of Andalucian, African and aboriginal music played on the *cajón* (rhythm box) and guitar. Energetic and very sexual – this traditional dance represents the seduction of an elegant, upper-class woman by a male servant – the *marinera* involves dancers holding handkerchiefs above their heads and skilfully prancing around each other. You'll see it performed in *peñas* all over the country but rarely with the same spirit and conviction as here in Trujillo. The last week in January, sometimes running into February (check with the tourist information office in Trujillo, for any particular year), is the main **Festival de la Marinera**. During this time there's a National Marinera Competition – el Concurso Nacional de Marinera – taking place in the city over several weeks, with dance academies from all over Peru.

The main **religious fiestas** are in October and December, with October 17 seeing the procession of El Señor de los Milagros, and the first two weeks of December being devoted to the patron saint of Huanchaco – another good excuse for wild parties in this beach resort. February, as everywhere, is **Carnival** time, with even more *marinera* evenings taking place throughout Trujillo. The end of June sees a week-long celebration of the patron saint of the fishermen, San Pedro, which takes place along the coast and is particularly festive in Huanchaco.

Monasterio El Carmen

C Colón and C Bolívar • Closed to the public

Less than two blocks southeast of where the pedestrian walkway Jirón Pizarro ends stands the most stunning of the city's religious buildings, the **Monasterio El Carmen**, considered by many to be the most superb religious building in the north of Peru. Built in 1759 but damaged by an earthquake in the same year, its two brick towers were then rebuilt using bamboo for safety in case they toppled again. The church was also built above ground level to save it from El Niño's periodic flooding.

Casa de los Leones

Jr Independencia 628 • Daily noon–midnight • It is now a restaurant, *Casona Deza* (see p.359) and to be able to explore you will need to order food or drinks

Just one block from the plaza stands the **Casa de los Leones**, a colonial mansion also known as the Casona Ganoza Chopitea, which is larger and more labyrinthine than it looks from the outside. There are two open-air courtyards to explore and the walls are decorated with some excellent modern art.

Museo Casinelli

Nicolás de Pierola 601 • Daily 9.30am–1pm & 3–7pm • S/7

The most curious museum in Trujillo is set in the middle of the road, in the basement of the Mobil petrol station on the Ovalo Victor Raul, just north of the large Mansiche Stadium. **Museo Casinelli** is simply stuffed with pottery and artefacts spanning thousands of years, collected from local *huaqueros*. The Salinar, Viru, Mochica, Chimu, Nazca, Huari, Recuay and Inca cultures are all represented, with highlights including **Mochica pots** with graphic images of daily life, people, animals and anthropomorphic deities, and an exquisite range of **Chimu silver artefacts**, including a tiny set of panpipes.

Mural Mosaico

Av Juan Pablo II and Jesús de Nazareth • free

Along two exterior walls of the university of Trujillo, artists Rafael Hastings and Carlos de Mar have created the world's largest mosaic mural, completed with the help of thousands of students over the span of more than twenty years. It is an impressive sight, with over 3000square metres covered in 1cm by 1cm tiles making up a series of images – the early works were mostly pre-Hispanic themed, while the later images range from volcanoes and hurricanes to a levitating sleeper.

ARRIVAL AND DEPARTURE   TRUJILLO

BY PLANE

Aeropuerto Carlos Martínez de Pinillos (☎ 044 464 224; daily 7am–9pm) is about 10km from Trujillo, near Huanchaco. The only airline that serves the airport is LAN (Diego de Almagro 490; ☎ 044 221 469; Mon–Fri 9am–7pm & Sat 9am–1pm). Taxis into the city will cost around S/15–20, or you can get a bus, which leaves every 20min (approx 6am–7pm) daily from the roundabout just outside the airport gates (S/1.50).
Destinations Lima (daily; 1hr 40min).

BY BUS

Buses arrive from the south at the new Terrapuerto on the Panamericana Norte Km 558. From there a taxi into town costs S/8. Heading north, most bus companies have terminals close to the centre of town near the Mansiche Stadium, on avenidas Daniel Carrion or España to the southwest, or east of it along avenidas America Norte or Ejercito. You need to check with the bus company when buying tickets whether it's best to pick up the bus at the depot or at the terminal south of town.

Bus companies Cruz del Sur, Amazonas 437 (☎ 044 261 801) serves Lima, Máncora, Piura and Guayaquil; Excluciva, Av Ejercito 285 (☎ 044 251 402) is the best luxury service to Lima; Oltursa, Av Ejercito 342 (☎ 044 263 055) serves the whole coast up to Tumbes (excluding Piura). Others include Emtrafesa, Jr Pizarro 476 (☎ 044 607 270 or ☎ 044 235 182), a good and reliable service to Chiclayo (every 30min)

as well as Lima, Chimbote, Pacasmayo, Guadalupe, Cajamarca, Piura, Máncora and Tumbes; Linea, Av America Sur 2857 (☎ 044 297 000) for Cajamarca, Chiclayo, Huaraz, Piura and Chimbote; Transportes Fuentes, Av Ricardo Palma 767 (☎ 044 204 581) for Huamachuco; Movil Tours, Av America Sur 3959 (☎ 044 286 538) is the safest and most comfortable for Nuevo Cajamarca, Moyobamba, Tarapoto and Chachapoyas, and even runs to Cusco.
Destinations Cajamarca (several daily; 6–8hr); Chachapoyas (daily; 14hr); Chiclayo (12 daily; 3hr); Guayaquil (midnight on

Sun, Mon, Wed and Fri; 18hr); Lima (12 daily; 9hr); Piura, via Chiclayo (8 daily; 6hr); Máncora (several daily; 6hr); Tarapoto (daily; 18hr); Tumbes (daily; 10hr).

BY COLECTIVO
Colectivos connecting with towns to the north mostly leave from and end up on Avenida España. If you're arriving by day it's fine to walk to the city centre, though at night it's best to take a taxi (S/5–6).

INFORMATION AND TOURS

Tourist information iPeru office at Jr Diego de Almagro 420 (Mon–Sat 8am–7pm, Sun 8am–2pm; ☎ 044 294 561, ✉ iperutrujillo@promperu.gob.pe) on the Plaza Mayor. The Tourist Police is at POLTUR, Jr Independencia 630 (Mon–Fri 8am–7pm; ☎ 044 291 705). The official Camara Regional de Turismo (☎ 044 203 718; Mon–Fri 9am–1pm & 4–8pm, Sat 9am–1pm) is next door to the Tourist Police at Independencia 628.
Tour operators and guides Most companies offer 3hr tours to Chan Chan and Huanchaco for around S/25 per person (including the site museum, Huaca Arco Iris and

Huaca Esmeralda), and to huacas del Sol and Luna from S/25. There is usually a discount for a combined, full-day tour. For Chicama sites, expect to pay S/50 plus. Recommended operators include: America Tours, Jr Pizarro 476 (☎ 044 235 182); Clara Brava's Tours at *Casa de Clara* (see opposite); Guía Tours, Independencia 580 (☎ 044 234 856); Turismo Carolina, Jr Pizarro 536 (☎ 044 226 599, ⓦ turismocarolina.com); and Peru Routes, Av San Martín 455, Office 5 (☎ 044 250 000, ⓦ peruroutes.com). A tour with an English-speaking guide costs extra and needs to be arranged in advance.

GETTING AROUND

By taxi Taxis cost less than S/6 for rides within Trujillo and can be hailed anywhere, but for safety and fair, set prices, stick with the official 'radio' taxis (that have a telephone number on the roof). Try Sonrisa (☎ 044 233 000) or Taxi

Seguro (☎ 044 253 473).
By car Car rental is available at Turismo Carolina, Jr Pizarro 536 (☎ 044 226 599, ⓦ turismocarolina.com).

ACCOMMODATION

The best place to stay in Trujillo is around Plaza Mayor in the centre of the city. However, many people prefer to stay out of the city centre at the nearby beach resort of Huanchaco (see p.363).

CENTRAL TRUJILLO
★ **Hostal Colonial** Jr Independencia 618 ☎ 044 258 261, ⓦ hostalcolonial.com.pe. An attractive, colonial-style place with colourfully painted walls, white-trimmed balconies and striped pillars, all around a pleasant green central courtyard. Some English-speaking staff members. Rooms are fine but for guaranteed peace and quiet get a room at the back. S/110
Hostería Recreo C Estete 647 ☎ 044 220 055, ⓦ hotelrecreo.com.pe. Away from the centre but still only four blocks from the Plaza Mayor, this is a very comfortable hotel with friendly service and its own restaurant. Offers free airport pickup. S/120
Hotel Continental Jr Gamarra 663 ☎ 044 241 607. Plain, blocky grey building, but centrally located and popular with Peruvian business types. Rooms are clean with private bath, TV and reliable hot water. Breakfast is included. S/110
★ **Hotel Libertador** Jr Independencia 485 ☎ 044 232 741, ⓦ libertador.com.pe. Right on the plaza, this place is particularly grand, and completely revived thanks to a 2014

refurbishment, with excellent service and a superb restaurant renowned for its criolla dishes. The large, comfortable rooms have all modern conveniences and great beds. S/300
El Mochilero Jr Independencia 887 ☎ 044 297 842. Rooms are very basic, lack natural light and are a little scruffy, but the staff are friendly and there's a pleasant open-air courtyard and snack bar at the entrance for lounging in. You also have a better chance of meeting fellow travellers here, as opposed to the hotels. Breakfast extra. Dorms S/20, doubles S/40
Munay Wasi Hotel Jr Colon 50 ☎ 044 231 462, ⓦ munaywasihostel.com. Near the edge of the historic centre, the location isn't ideal, but friendly owners, a comfortable price as well as good wi-fi and a basic breakfast make this a welcome choice for the budget-conscious avoiding the backpacker vibe. Impeccably clean. Dorms S/30, doubles S/80
Residencial Vanini Av Larco 237 ☎ 044 200 878, ✉ enriqueva@hotmail.com. A little outside the downtown area, but a very good-value, family-run hostel. There's a choice of private bath, while the cheapest rooms

are actually small rooms on the roof terrace. $\overline{S/100}$

FURTHER AFIELD

Casa Andina Private Collection Av El Golf 591, Urb Las Flores del Golf III ☎ 044 480 760, ⓦ casa-andina .com. Trujillo's newest luxury hotel, aimed at business travellers. Plush carpeted halls, large-scale photos of Chan Chan on the walls and a spacious lobby filled with top-class staff. The most comfortable and modern rooms in town, with quality furnishings and rain showers. Outstanding breakfast buffet. $\overline{S/330}$

★**Casa de Clara** Cahuide 495, Santa María, Trujillo ☎ 044 299 997 or T 044 243 347, ⓦ hostal-casadeclara.com. Located near Huayna Capac 542, this is very nice bargain accommodation, with private bath, breakfast and internet available. Owner Clara, an archeologist, is very well informed about local places of interest, and will help organize reliable and affordable tours. $\overline{S/70}$

EATING AND DRINKING

Some of the liveliest restaurants and bars are along jirones Independencia, Pizarro, Bolívar and Ayacucho, to the east of Plaza Mayor. A speciality of the city is tasty, reasonably priced seafood, particularly ceviche, which is probably best appreciated on the beach at nearby Huanchaco (see p.363). Goat and beans is a local speciality, too; if you get the chance try *cabrito con frijoles*, a truly traditional dish of goat marinated in *chicha* beer and vinegar and served with beans cooked with onions and garlic. There's a good supermarket for general provisions at Pizarro 700.

7

Asturias Jr Pizarro 739. Delicious fruit juices plus alcoholic drinks, lunchtime meals (S/10) and snacks at this busy coffee bar. Mon–Sat 7am–7pm.

Café Restaurant El Rincon del Vallejo Jr Orbegoso 311 ☎ 044 292 972. A local institution set in a beautiful old building, both with the classic corner local and the original home of Trujillo's most famous poet, Cesar Vallejo, just next door. Great for traditional local meals or a classic Trujillo breakfast (S/12). Quick, quality service. Mon–Sat 7am–3pm and 5–11pm, Sun 7am–3pm.

Café Van Gogh Jr Independencia 533 ☎ 976 478 939. The best coffee in town and plenty of sweet treats to fill up on after a day exploring the centre. Friendly and quick service. Mon–Sat 8.30am–9.30pm, Sun 8.30am–midday.

Casona Deza Jr Independencia 630 ☎ 044 474 756. A first-rate Italian restaurant set in a historic building dating back to 1635. Two gorgeous open-air patios to dine in and the walls decorated with impressive artwork. Best for a coffee and sandwich during the day to appreciate the building, but also a good choice in the evening for quality pizza (S/25). Daily noon–midnight.

El Chileno Ayacucho 581. Outside the market, another classic, and by the same owners as *San Agustín* (see below). Similarly, nothing fancy, just great home-style ice cream, wonderfully rich and tasty. Daily 8am–9pm.

Jugería San Agustín Jr Bolívar 522 ☎ 044 259 591. Trujillo's most famous juice bar, a few blocks from the plaza, it's best known for its *sandwich de pavo* (turkey sandwich; S/8). Don't miss it. Daily 8am–1pm and 4.15–8.30pm.

El Mochica Bolívar 462. A smart restaurant extremely popular with local tourists serving exquisite criolla dishes and local cuisine – if you're in luck they'll have *cabrito con frijoles* (S/34); sometimes local bands play here live. Daily 11am–9pm.

Restaurant Romano Criollo C Esatos Unidos 162 ☎ 044 244 207. Much better than the *Romano* on Jr Pizarro, this place cooks up abundant, tasty Peruvian dishes, look out for the *causa* – mashed yellow potatoes with a seafood and avo filling – or creole classics like the *tacu tacu* – a fried rice and bean cake usually topped with an egg or a beef cutlet (S/32). Mon–Fri 12–4pm, Sat and Sun 12–5pm.

Restaurant Vegetariano El Sol Jr Pizarro 660. Typical local diner, serving up reasonably priced vegetarian and vegan food, mostly based on rice, alfalfa, soya, maize and fresh vegetables. It's particularly popular with locals at lunchtime when it offers a cheap lunch special for just S/5. Mon–Sat 8.30am–4.30pm, Sun 8.30am–4pm.

San Francisco Café Jr Gamarra 433 ☎ 044 252 195. Offers a lunch menu with interesting variety and though more expensive than the average, the food is more refined and delicious. For just S/11 you get a salad or potato in a creamy yellow chili *huancaína* sauce as a starter, mains that range from standard chicken and rice to more original meatballs in a creamy chilli sauce, something sweet to finish up and a drink. Good, friendly service in a long, airy, hall with heavy wooden rafters and wagon-wheel chandeliers that must have once hung in the entrance to a magnificent colonial home. Mon–Sat 11am–8pm.

NIGHTLIFE AND ENTERTAINMENT

Trujillo has a fairly active nightlife, with several *peñas* and nightclubs celebrating local culture, dance and music, as well as Latin rhythms and the latest global popular sounds. The city is also well known worldwide for its January *marinera* dance fiesta (see box, p.356) and occasional international dance jamborees.

★**La Cañana** San Martín 791 ☎ 044 232 503. A highly popular restaurant-*peña* (as well as a discotheque) that does excellent meals; it has a great atmosphere and good, danceable folklore shows accompanied by an orchestra that generally start after 10pm and carry on into the early hours. The best shows and liveliest crowds are on Fri and Sat. Mon–Sat 8pm–2am.

Mecano Bar Jr Gamarra 574 ☎ 044 201 652. A great bar with mainly Latin, rock, pop, merengue, bachata and salsa music that keeps the crowd dancing all night. Best on Thursday nights when it's a little quieter.

Thurs–Sat from 9pm.

Museo Café Bar Jr Independencia 701 ☎ 044 346 741. An old-style, wood-heavy bohemian bar created by local artist Ricardo Rojas Maza; go for a beer, a sandwich and long conversations. On Thursdays a live jazz band sets up in the corner. Mon–Thurs 9am–11pm, Fri & Sat 9am–1am.

DIRECTORY

Consulates UK (honorary consul), at Jr Alfonso Ugarte 310 (☎ 044 245 935).

Health Hospital Belén de Trujillo, Bolívar 350 ☎ 044 245 748 (24hr); Hospital Regional Docente de Trujillo, Av Manseriche 795 ☎ 044 231 581 (24hr).

Immigration Av Larco 1220, Urb Los Pinos, for visa renewals.

Internet There are several internet cafés along Jr Pizarro between the Plaza Mayor and Gamarra.

Language school Trujillo Language School ☎ 044 280 015, ⊕ peru-language-school.com. Based in a quiet neighbourhood quite far from the centre, this offers Spanish courses to all levels.

Laundry Lavandarias Unidas, at Jr Pizarro 683, and Lavandería El Carmen, Jr Pizarro 759.

Money and exchange Banco de Credito, Jr Gamarra 562; BCP, Jr Gamarra 562; Scotiabank, Jr Pizarro 314; Banco de la Nación, Jr Almagro 297. The Casa de Cambios Martelli, Jr Bolívar 665, gives the best rate in town for dollars cash, or try the *cambistas* (though be very careful, especially after dark) on the corner of Jr Pizarro and Gamarra, or on the Plaza Mayor. A safer bet are the numerous casas de cambio on block 6 of Pizarro.

Post office Serpost (Mon–Sat 8am–7pm), Jr Independencia 286, a block and a half southwest of the plaza.

Around Trujillo

The beaches close to Trujillo have seen a lot of fast and unattractive development recently and though there remain some nice empty stretches, they are somewhat spoilt by the strong smell from the nearby marshes. It's best just to head straight out to **Huanchaco** for beach time. For those in search of sand and seafood south of the city, the villages of **Moche** and **Las Delicias** are within easy reach.

Moche and Las Delicias

From Trujillo (S/1; 25min), catch the direct van (hourly) marked "Delicias" from the corner of avenidas Moche and Los Incas. The best choice is a taxi (S/25–30).

After crossing the Río Moche's estuary, 2km south of Trujillo, you'll come across the settlements of **MOCHE** and **LAS DELICIAS**, both within an easy bus ride of the Huaca del Sol and Huaca de la Luna (see p.362). Moche is a small village some 4km south of the city, slightly inland from the ocean, blessed with several **restaurants** serving freshly prepared seafood. Close by, Las Delicias, 5km south of Trujillo, has a long, empty **beach** and a handful of reasonable restaurants. Las Delicias's main claim to fame is that the *curandero* El Tuno once lived at Lambayeque 18, right on the beach.

Huacas del Moche

Colectivos (S/1.50) leave from the south side of Ovalo Grau (every 10–15min) at the southern entrance of the Panamericana Norte into Trujillo city. Some go all the way to the Huaca de la Luna, but many prefer to drop you off on the road, within sight, but still a 10–15min walk away

Five kilometres south of Trujillo, in a barren desert landscape beside the Río Moche, two temples really bring ancient Peru to life. Collectively known as the **Huacas del Moche**, these sites make a fine day's outing and shouldn't be missed even if you only have a passing interest in archeology or the ancient civilizations of Peru. The stunning **Huaca del Sol** (Temple of the Sun) is the largest adobe structure in the Americas, and easily the

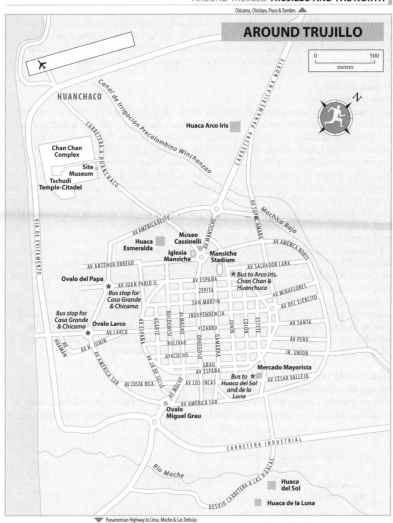

most impressive of the many pyramids on the Peruvian coast. Its twin, the **Huaca de la Luna** (Temple of the Moon), is smaller, but more complex and brilliantly frescoed.

Brief history

After more than eighteen years of excavation, the Huaca de la Luna is now believed to have been developed in two main phases: platform I and three plazas (know collectively as the old temple) around 600 AD; platform III by around 900 AD.

The complex is believed to have been the capital, or most important ceremonial and urban centre, for the Moche culture, at its peak between 400 and 600 AD. Although very much associated with the Moche culture and nation (100–600 AD), however, there is evidence of earlier occupation at these sites, dating back two thousand years to the Salinar and Gallinazo cultures, indicated by constructions underlying the *huacas*. The area continued to be held in high regard after the collapse of the Moche culture, with signs of

Wari, Chimu and Inca offerings here demonstrating a continued importance. The latest theory suggests that these *huacas* were mainly ceremonial centres, separated physically by a large graveyard and an associated urban settlement. Finds in this intermediate zone have so far revealed some fine structures, plus pottery workshops and storehouses.

Huaca del Sol

Closed at the time of writing

The **Huaca del Sol** is presently off limits to visitors as archeologists are still investigating the area, but it's an amazing sight from the grounds below or even in the distance from the Huaca de la Luna, which is very much open to the public. Built by the Mochica around 500 AD, and extremely weathered, its pyramid edges still slope at a sharp 77 degrees to the horizon. Although still an enormous structure, what you see today is about thirty percent of the original construction. On top of the base platform is the demolished stump of a four-sided, stepped pyramid, surmounted about 50m above the desert by a ceremonial platform. From the top of this platform you can clearly see how the Río Moche was diverted by the Spanish in 1602, in order to erode the *huaca* and find treasure. They were quite successful at washing away a large section of the site, but found precious little except adobe bricks.

Estimates of the pyramid's brickwork vary, but it is reckoned to contain somewhere between 50 million and 140 million adobe blocks, each of which was marked in any one of a hundred different ways – probably with the maker's distinguishing signs. It must have required a massively well-organized labour supply to put together – Calancha, a Spanish historian, wrote that 200,000 workers were required. How the Mochica priests and architects decided on the shape of the *huaca* is unknown, but if you look from the main road at its form against the silhouette of Cerro Blanco, there is a remarkable similarity between the two, and if you look at the *huaca* sideways from the vantage point of the Huaca de la Luna, it has the same general outline as the hills behind.

Huaca de la Luna

Daily 9am–4pm • S/10; a 45min guided tour is available, tip expected

Clinging to the bottom of Cerro Blanco, just 500m from Huaca del Sol (see above), is **Huaca de la Luna**, a ritual and ceremonial centre that was built around the same time as

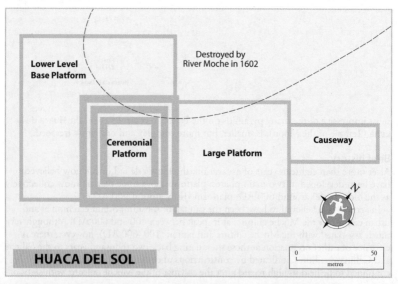

Lower Level
Base Platform

Destroyed by
River Moche in 1602

Ceremonial
Platform

Large Platform

Causeway

HUACA DEL SOL

0   50
metres

its neighbour. What you see today is only part of an older complex of interior rooms built over six centuries that included a maze of interconnected patios, some covered and lavishly adorned with painted friezes. The **friezes** are still the most striking feature of the site, rhomboid in shape and dominated by an anthropomorphic face surrounded by symbols representing nature spirits, such as the ray fish (symbol of water), pelicans (symbol of air) and serpent (symbol of earth). Its feline fangs and boggle-eyes are stylizations dating back to the early Chavín cult and it's similar to an image known to the Moche as **Ai-Apaec**, master of life and death. The god that kept the human world in order, he has been frequently linked with human sacrifice, and in 1995 archeologists found 42 skeletons of sacrificial victims here. Sediment found in their graves indicates that these sacrifices took place during an El Niño weather phenomenon, something that would have threatened the economic and political stability of the nation. Ceramics dug up from the vast graveyard that extends between the two *huacas* and around the base of Cerro Blanco suggest that this might have also been a site for a cult of the dead. Cerro Blanco itself may have been considered a link to deity.

Behind the *huaca* are some frescoed rooms, discovered in the early 1990s, displaying multicoloured murals (mostly reds and blues). The most famous of these paintings has been called *The Rebellion of the Artefacts* because, as is fairly common on Mochica ceramics, all sorts of objects are depicted attacking human beings, getting their revenge, or rebelling. Over 6000 square metres of polychrome reliefs have been uncovered.

Museo Huacas de Moche
Close to the Huaca de la Luna • Daily 9am–4pm • S/3 • ☎ 044 221 269 or ☎ 971 492 924 • ⓦ huacasdemoche.pe

The new **Museo Huacas de Moche**, built in a pyramid style to look like Moche architecture, displays some fine ceramics – check out the warrior duck and the blind shaman – as well as a feline cat-cloak of gold and feathers. The museum combines exhibition rooms with an investigations centre, communal space and a theatre.

Huanchaco

Although no longer exactly a tropical paradise, **HUANCHACO**, 12km west of Trujillo, is still quite a pleasant beach town, with a thriving surfer and backpacker scene. Until the 1970s, Huanchaco was a tiny fishing village, quiet and little known to tourists. Today it consists of half-finished adobe houses, concrete hotels and streets slowly spreading back towards Trujillo, and makes an excellent base for visiting many of the sites around the region, in particular the nearby ruins of **Chan Chan**.

A good time to visit Huanchaco is at the end of June for the **fiesta** of the patron saint of fishermen, San Pedro, when a large *totora* raft comes ashore accompanied by a smaller flotilla of *caballitos* (see p.364). But the best weather here, and the most crowded and expensive time to visit, is arguably between December and March. The town is always lively, with people on the beach, some surfers, fishermen and travellers hanging around the restaurants.

Iglesia Soroco
A 15min walk uphill from the seafront • Mon–Sat 8am–6pm

The town's only historical sight is the old, square **Iglesia Soroco**, perched high on the coastal cliffs. The second church in Peru to be built by the Spanish, it was built in 1540 on top of a pre-Inca temple dedicated to the idol of the Golden Fish, and was rebuilt after its destruction during the earthquakes of 1619–70.

The waterfront
Jetty S/0.5; boat trips S/10

Huanchaco's picture-perfect heart is a long pier, where fishermen and tourists jostle for the best positions, while the entrance is crowded with hawkers of trinkets and ice creams. Just next door, stacked along the beach are rows of *caballitos del mar* – the ancient seagoing rafts designed by the Mochica – still used by locals today. They are constructed out of four cigar-shaped bundles of *totora* reeds, tied together into an arc tapering at each end. The fishermen kneel or sit at the stern and paddle, using the surf for occasional bursts of motion. The local boat-builders here are the last who know the craft of making *caballitos* to the original design of the Mochica, and the best can assemble a seaworthy craft in 30 minutes. Some of the fishermen offer ten- to fifteen-minute trips on the back of their *caballitos*.

ARRIVAL AND DEPARTURE   HUANCHACO

Be aware that due to the quite rapid growth of the town, street and block numbers are in a state of transition, so it's quite easy to get confused by Huanchaco addresses.

By bus Southwest of the Plaza de Armas in Trujillo, where Independencia meets España, you can get a combi with an A on the windshield that takes you directly to Huanchaco. To catch the colourful red and yellow bus, cross Av España and head two blocks further, at Juan Pablo II and Jesús Nazareth (S/1.5; 45min). Returning, catch either bus or combi at the waterfront near the pier; look out for the bus marked 'H corazón', this takes the shortest route back to where you boarded.

By taxi From Trujillo, taxis are around S/15–20.

ACCOMMODATION

The town is well served by the kind of accommodation range you'd normally expect at a popular beach resort. Many families also put people up in private rooms; these can be identified by the signs reading "Alquila Cuarto" on houses, particularly in the summer (Dec–Feb).

Casa Colonial Av La Rivera 514 ☎ 044 461 015. Higher-end rooms with great balconies and sea views. Quality art from the owner's Lima gallery adorns the walls. Some good bargains to be had out of season; ask about the smaller sea-view room on the ground floor. Good breakfast and food at the restaurant downstairs. **S/220**

★ **Casa Fresh** Av La Rivera 322 ☎ 945 917 150, ⓦ casafresh.pe. Located near the beginning of Rivera where the street noise is lower and the views and sound of the surf are better. Simple, comfortable rooms with hot water and wi-fi; breakfast is included. Board rental and Spanish available. A great deck for relaxing with a drink. Dorms **S/20**, doubles **S/60**

La Gringa de Huanchaco Av La Rivera 850 ☎ 044 462 325. A busy backpackers' with a nice bar and social area, right across from the pier. The dorms and kitchen are quite dark, and could do with more care, but the sea-view rooms are good. The main attraction here is the rooftop camping with amazing views. Camping **S/15**, dorms **S/15**, doubles **S/40**

Hospedaje Familiar La Casa Suiza Los Pinos 308 ☎ 044 639 713, ⓦ lacasasuiza.com. One of the best, friendliest budget places in Huanchaco, with a range of different rooms (some with bath), a rooftop terrace and a book exchange. There are laundry and internet facilities, boards for rent, and the breakfast is delicious. The staff speak English. **S/85**

Hostal Los Esteros Larco 870 ☎ 044 461 300. An ageing but still good option, where the tidy rooms all come with private bath and hot water. Worth spending the extra for the rooms with views of the sea and pier. The restaurant downstairs serves one of the best ceviches in town for just S/15. **S/100**

Hostal Solange Los Ficus 258 ☎ 044 638 918. This is a small, very basic, but easy-going and friendly family-run hostel situated just two blocks from the beach, where you can do your own cooking if you wish, though there is a small café that serves Mexican food. Breakfast for an extra S/10. **S/30**

Hotel Bracamonte Los Olivos 160 ☎ 044 461 162, ⓦ hotelbracamonte.com.pe. A peaceful complex of different-sized chalets with solar-heated showers. Very welcoming for children, it has a pool, a games room, internet access, laundry facilities, a good restaurant and terraces with views over the ocean. A bit isolated and pricey; only for those who really want to avoid the noise of town. **S/202**

★ **Oceanus** Los Cerezos 105 ☎ 044 461 653, ⓦ hospedajeoceano1.com. Family run, comfortable and popular *Oceanus* is a long block away from the beachfront, which can be a blessing on busier days. The *cremoladas* (a rough sorbet) downstairs are amazing; try the *lúcuma* or the coco. **S/30**

★ **Surf Hostel Meri** Av La Rivera 720 ☎ 044 538 675, ⓦ surfhostelmeri.com. The top choice for backpackers and surfers, a cool young atmosphere, good music and a deck with views over the beach. Rooms are clean and pleasant and the price is more than right. Even if you don't stay here, it is worth coming for the cheap and delicious breakfasts, everything from home-made granola, to bacon and eggs and – of course – banana pancakes. Dorms **S/30**, doubles **S/60**

EATING AND DRINKING

There are restaurants all along the front in Huanchaco, and not surprisingly, seafood is the local speciality, including excellent crab, and you can often see women and children up to their waists in the sea collecting shellfish. The seafront towards the pier from *Big Ben* (see below) is lined with restaurants, and the quality is much the same; just choose the one with the music and atmosphere you like the best. Nightlife is focused along the main avenue, La Rivera, south of the pier.

Chocolate Av Rivera 752 ☎ 044 462 420. A small but very friendly café, they serve great snacks and breakfasts and good coffee, and the staff are a mine of local information; sometimes some B&B rooms available. Daily 7.30am–6pm.

Huanchaco Beach Restaurant Malecón Larco 602 ☎ 044 461 484. Very tasty fish dishes (ceviche S/35), and excellent views across the ocean and up to the clifftop Iglesia Soroco. Daily 11am–7pm.

Restaurant Big Ben Av Lorco 836. Serves probably the best and certainly the most expensive seafood dishes (averaging around S/60) in Huanchaco, including excellent crab and sea urchin if you're lucky. Daily 11am–5pm.

Restaurant El Caribe Atahualpa 100. Just around the corner from the seafront avenue to the north of the pier, this restaurant has great ceviche (S/22) and is very popular with locals. Mon–Sat 10am–6pm.

Restaurant Mar Azul Malecón Larco 600 ☎ 044 462 446. Among the best-positioned seafront restaurants, with a balcony overlooking the *caballitos del mar* and the beach; you're paying a little extra for the location, but the food is good, especially the selection of seafood dishes – everything from fresh and spicy ceviches to grilled fish a lo macho (with a spicy mixed seafood sauce) and grilled octopus (S/30–40). Daily 11am–6.30pm.

Trattoria Italiana Violeta Los Ficus 537 ☎ 948 701 047. Nothing fancy, this tiny place with a few plastic tables serves up great fresh pasta and pizzas (S/18–25) from the hands of an Italian cook. Daily 6–11pm.

INFORMATION AND TOURS

Tourist information An all-in-one stop for info, maps, tours, money exchange and bus tickets, Huanchaco Tours at Av La Rivera (Mon–Sat 8am–7pm, Sun 8am–2pm; ☎ 044 462405, 🌐 huanchacotours.com).

The Chan Chan complex

Daily 9am–4pm • Taxis from Trujillo cost S/20, or a half-day for around S/75. The orange and yellow Huanchaco-bound microbus (S/1.5) from Av España and Independencia or Pizarro in Trujillo goes past the main Chan Chan sites. Tell the driver where you want to get off.

The ruined city of **CHAN CHAN** stretches across a large sector of the Moche Valley, beginning almost as soon as you leave Trujillo northwards on the Huanchaco road, and ending just a couple of kilometres from Huanchaco. A huge complex even today, its main focus and museum site is the **Tschudi** sector (see p.367), which needs only a little imagination to raise its weathered mud walls to their original grandeur. Not far from Tschudi, **Huaca La Esmeralda** displays different features, being a ceremonial or ritual pyramid rather than a citadel. The third sector, the **Huaca Arco Iris** (or **El Dragón**), on the other side of this enormous ruined city, was similar in function to Esmeralda but has a unique design that has been restored with relish, if not historical perfection.

Brief history

Chan Chan was the capital city of the **Chimu Empire**, an urban civilization that appeared on the Peruvian coast around 1100 AD. Chimu cities and towns throughout the region stretched from Tumbes in the north to as far south as Paramonga. Their cities were always elaborately planned, with large, flat-topped buildings for the nobility and intricately decorated adobe pyramids serving as temples. Recognized as fine goldsmiths by the Incas, the Chimu panelled their temples with gold and cultivated palace gardens where even the plants and animals were made from precious metals. The city walls were brightly painted, and the style of architecture and relief decoration is sometimes ascribed to the fact that the Mochica (who pre-dated the Chimu in this valley by several centuries) migrated from Central America into this area, bringing with them knowledge and ideas from a more advanced civilization, like the Maya.

7

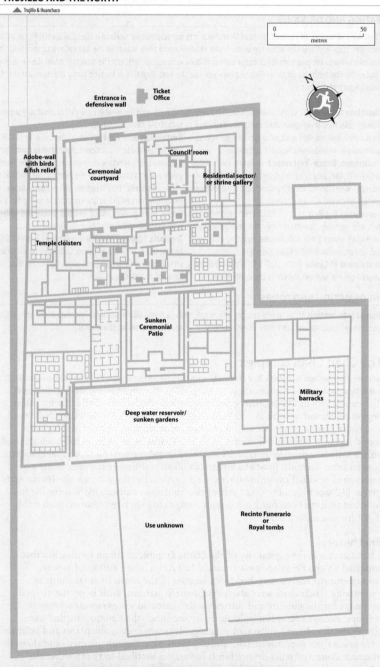

0 ——————————— 50
metres

N

Ticket
Office

Entrance in
defensive wall

Adobe-wall
with birds
& fish relief

'Council' room

Ceremonial
courtyard

Residential sector/
or shrine gallery

Temple cloisters

Sunken
Ceremonial
Patio

Military
barracks

Deep water reservoir/
sunken gardens

Recinto Funerario
or
Royal tombs

Use unknown

CHAN CHAN TSCHUDI TEMPLE-CITADEL

Birth of a city

According to one legend, the city was founded by **Taycanamu**, who arrived by boat with his royal fleet; after establishing an empire, he left his son, Si-Um, in command and then disappeared over the western horizon. Another legend has it that Chan Chan's construction was inspired by an original creator-deity of the same name, a dragon who made the sun and the moon and whose earthly manifestation is a rainbow. Whatever the impulse behind Chan Chan, it remains one of the world's marvels and, in its heyday, was one of the largest pre-Columbian cities in the Americas.

The Chimu inherited ideas and techniques from a host of previous cultures along the coast, including the Mochica, and, most importantly, adapted the techniques from many generations of trial and error in irrigating the Moche Valley. In the desert, access to a regular water supply was critical in the development of an urban civilization like that of Chan Chan, whose very existence depended on extracting water not only from the Río Moche but also, via a complicated system of canals and aqueducts, from the neighbouring Chicama Valley.

By 1450, when the Chimu Empire stretched from the Río Zarumilla in the north to the Río Chancay in the south and covered around 40,000 square kilometres, Chan Chan was the centre of a chain of provincial capitals. These were gradually incorporated into the Inca Empire between 1460 and 1480.

7

Death of a city

The events leading to the city's demise are better documented than those of its birth: in the 1470s **Tupac Yupanqui** led the Inca armies down from the mountains in the east and cut off the aqueducts supplying Chan Chan with its vital water supply. After lengthy discussions, the Chimu council managed to persuade its leader against going out to fight the Incas, knowing full well that resistance would be met with brutality, and surrender with peaceful takeover. The Chimu were quickly deprived of their chieftains, many of them taken to Cusco (along with the highly skilled metallurgists) to be indoctrinated into Inca ways. Sixty years later when the first Spaniards rode through Chan Chan they found only a ghost town full of dust and legend.

Museo di Sitio

A few hundred metres before the entrance to the Tschudi temple-citadel

The **Museo de Sitio** is a good place to start your visit to Chan Chan. It offers an interesting eight-minute multimedia show in Spanish, and uses scale replica models, ceramics and other archeological finds to reconstruct life in the hot but irrigated desert before modern Trujillo was built.

Tschudi (Nik Am) temple-citadel

Get off the Huanchaco bus at the concrete Tschudi/Chan Chan signpost about 2km beyond the outer suburbs. From here, follow the track to the left of the road for 10–15min until you see the ticket office (on the left), next to the high defensive walls around the inner temple-citadel

The best place to get an idea of what Chan Chan must have been like is the **Tschudi temple-citadel**, even though it's now stuck out in the desert among high ruined walls, dusty streets, gateways, decrepit dwellings and open graves.

Following the marked route around the citadel through a maze of corridors, chambers, and amazingly large plazas, you will begin to form your own picture of this highly organized ancient civilization. For example, in the courtyard just past the entrance gateway, some 25 seats are set into niches at regular intervals along the walls. By sitting in one niche and whispering to someone in another, you can witness an unusual acoustic effect: how this simply designed **council room** amplifies all sounds, making the niches seem like they're connected by adobe intercoms.

Fishing-net motifs are repeated throughout the citadel's design, particularly in the **sunken ceremonial patio** (an antechamber before the entrance to the *audiencias*, or little temples area), and show how important the sea was to the Chimu people, both mythologically and as a major resource. Dedicated to divinities and designed to hold offerings and tributes, the **audiencias** lead to the **main ceremonial courtyard** and also to the corridor of fish and bird designs.

The westernmost open point of the site is the burial area, known as the **Recinto Funerario**, and was the most sacred part of Tschudi, where the tomb of El Señor Chimo and his wives was located. Beyond the citadel extend large areas of untended ruins that are dangerous for foreigners – some, certainly, have been robbed after wandering off alone.

Huaca La Esmeralda

Get off the Huacachina bus at the colonial church of San Salvador de Mansiche, at blocks 14 and 15 of Av Mansiche, then follow the path along the right-hand side of the church for three blocks (through the modern barrio of Mansiche), until you reach the *huaca*.

One of the most beautiful, and possibly the most venerated of Chimu temples, **Huaca La Esmeralda** (The Emerald Temple) lies in ruins a couple of kilometres before Tschudi, just off the main Trujillo-to-Huanchaco road. Unlike Tschudi, the *huaca*, or sacred temple, is on the very edge of town, stuck between the outer suburbs and the first cornfields. It was built in the twelfth or early thirteenth century – at about the same time as the Tschudi temple-citadel – and is one of the most important of the *huacas* scattered around Trujillo. Uncovered only in 1923, its adobe walls and decorations were severely damaged in the freak rains of 1925 and 1983. Now you can only just make out what must have been an impressive multicoloured **facade**. All the relief work on the adobe walls is original, and shows marine-related motifs including friezes of fishing nets containing fish, waves, a flying pelican, a sea otter and frequent repetitive patterns of geometrical arabesques.

The *huaca* has an unusually complex structure, with two main platforms, a number of surrounding walls and several sloping pathways giving access to each section. From the top platform, which was obviously a place of worship and possibly the cover to a royal tomb, you can see west across the valley to the graveyards of Chan Chan, out to sea, over the cultivated fields around the site and into the primitive brick factory next door. Only some shells and *chaquiras* (stone and coral necklaces) were found when the *huaca* was officially dug out some years ago, long after centuries of *huaqueros* (treasure hunters) had exhausted its more valuable goods. These grave robbers nearly always precede the archeologists. In fact, archeologists are often drawn to the sites they eventually excavate by the trail of treasures that flow from the grave robbers through dealers' hands into the market in Lima and beyond.

Huaca Arco Iris (or Huaca del Dragon)

Due to safety considerations (the outskirts of Trujillo have seen an increase in gang-related crime and muggings recently) it is best to take a taxi (S/10–15).

The **Huaca Arco Iris** (Rainbow Temple) is the most fully restored ruin of the Chan Chan complex and one of the oldest sectors at 1100 years old, located just to the left of the Panamericana, about 4km north of Trujillo in the middle of the urban district of La Esperanza. The *huaca* consists of two tiers: the **first tier** is made up of fourteen rectangular chambers, possibly used for storing corn and precious metals for ritual purposes, while a path slopes up to the **second tier**, a flat-topped platform used as a ceremonial area where sacrifices were held and the gods apparently spoke. From here, there is a wide view over the valley, towards the ocean, Trujillo and the city of Chan Chan.

Several interpretations have been made of the **central motif**, which is repeated throughout the *huaca* – some consider it a dragon, some a centipede and some a rainbow. Most of the main **temple inner walls** have been restored, and they are covered with the re-created central motif. The outer walls are decorated in the same way, with identical friezes cut into the adobe, in a design that looks like a multi-legged serpent arching over two lizard-type beings.

DIRECTORY   **THE CHAN CHAN COMPLEX**

Facilities There's a small interpretive centre at the Tschudi complex entrance, as well as toilets, a cafetería and souvenirs, plus a life-size model of a Chimu warrior in full regalia.

Guided tours Easily arranged (around S/10 for the museum); guides for the Tschudi complex (S/30 for a group of one to three people) usually hang around at the Tschudi entrance, and, if you want, will also take you round the *huacas*.

Tickets Entrance to the three archeological sites of the wider Chan Chan complex and the Museo de Sitio is included on the same ticket (S/10), called the Talon Visitante, which is valid for only two days (but you can try asking for an extension if you need more time). Although you can visit each sector separately, there are only two ticket offices, one at the entrance of Museo de Sitio, the other at the entrance to Tschudi temple-citadel.

Chicama Valley

The Chicama Valley, north of the Río Moche and about 35km from Trujillo, is full of **huacas** and ancient sites, the most famous being the **Huaca El Brujo**. The valley is also home to the remains of fortresses and an irrigation system possibly dating back nearly 6000 years when the Río Chicama was once connected to the fields of Chan Chan by a vast system of canals and aqueducts over 90km long. Today, however, the region looks like a single enormous sugar-cane field, although in fact it's divided among a number of large sugar-producing co-operatives, originally family-owned **haciendas** that were redistributed during the military government's agrarian reforms in 1969. Even more laidback, the isolated seaside village of **Puerto Chicama**, 65km north of Trujillo, offers excellent surfing opportunities.

Huaca El Brujo complex

50km north of Trujillo • Mon–Sat 9am–4pm; museum Mon–Sat 9am–5pm, entry included in site ticket • S/10 • From Trujillo, take a bus to Chocope from the Santa Cruz (ex-Chicago) bus terminal on Av America Sur. Once there, to get to the El Brujo complex, take a colectivo to Magdalena de Cao (every 30min; S/1.5), about 5km from the site and the nearest place that local colectivos pass through. From Magdalena, a mototaxi will take you and wait for the return for S/15.

The **Huaca El Brujo**, whose name means "Temple of the Wizard", is a Mochica-built complex of associated adobe temple ruins incorporating the Huaca Cao Viejo to the south, plus the huacas Cortada and Prieto, slightly to the north. Most of the recent discoveries have been made in Huaca Cao Viejo, most notably a female mummy who was clearly a powerful shamanic leader, her face, hands and legs being tattooed with spiders and snakes. This is now on display in a small onsite **museum** (Museo Cao).

To get to the *huaca*, you have to pass through the nearby village of **Magdalena de Cao** – the ideal place to sample *chicha del año*, an extra-strong form of **maize beer** brewed in the valley.

The huacas

Three main ceremonial *huacas* make up the Huaca El Brujo site: Cortada, Cao Viejo and Prieta. Some of the walls on these *huacas* are adorned with figures in high relief and painted murals, discovered here as recently as 1990. On the top, third layer of the

---

SUGAR AND THE TRUJILLO REGION

Sugar cane was first brought to Peru from India by the Spanish in the seventeenth century and quickly took root as the region's main crop. Until early in the twentieth century, the haciendas were connected with Trujillo by a British-operated rail line, whose lumbering old wagons used to rumble down to Trujillo full of molasses and return loaded with crude oil; they were, incidentally, never washed between loads. Although the region still produces nearly half of Peru's sugar, it has diversified as well. These days, Chicama is also well known for the fine Cascas semi-seco **wine** it produces. The haciendas are also renowned for the breeding of *caballos de paso* – **horses** reared to compete in dressage and trotting contests – a long-established sport that's still popular with Peruvian high society.

Huaca Cortada, there's a painted character with startled eyes, a sacrificial knife in one hand and a decapitated head in the other (decapitation apparently being common practice among the Mochica). The **Huaca Cao Viejo** is a larger pyramid, topped by a ceremonial platform some 30m high, and clearly of great significance to the Mochica ceremonial world and religious hierarchy.

Quite literally a heap of rubbish, **La Huaca Prieta** sits at the edge of the ocean, ten minutes' walk west of the main Huaca El Brujo site. It may be a dump, but it is one that has been accumulating rubbish for some 6500 years, and is crowded with evidence and clues about the evolution of culture and human activity on this coast. This small, dark hill is about 12m high and owes its discolouration to thousands of years of decomposing organic remains. On the top, there are signs of subterranean dwellings, long since excavated by archeologists Larco Hoyle and Junius Bird.

Puerto Chicama

PUERTO CHICAMA (also known as **Puerto Malabrigo**), 13km northwest of Paijan and 74km north of Trujillo, is a small fishing village that once served as a port for the sugar haciendas (see box, p.369), but is now much better known as a **surfers'** centre, offering some of the best surfing waves on Peru's Pacific coast. The place has a real lack of facilities, though, and few boards to hire locally – which won't affect serious surfers, who generally bring their own. The surf here is said to have "the longest left-hand breaking surf in the world", often reaching heights of over 2m and running for over 2km at times. Novice surfers may want to check out the gentler waters of Máncora (see p.414).

GETTING AROUND   THE CHICAMA VALLEY

While there are buses and colectivos serving the Chicama Valley, it is a good day-trip from Trujillo and many people prefer to go on a guided tour to visit the Huacas (see p.362) or to hire a taxi with driver and guide for the day (S/90).

By bus From Trujillo, catch a van from Terminal Santa Cruz (ex-Chicago) on Av America del Sur to Puerto Malabrigo (S/5.50; 2hr).

By taxi You can usually find taxis in Chicama or Chocope who'll take you to the sites for around S/20 an hour. It might cost more per hour from Trujillo.

ACCOMMODATION

Chicama Surf Hotel and Spa Chicama ☎ 044 576 206, ⓦ chicamasurf.com. A beach resort with twenty rooms, a spa and pool. Relatively upmarket for Chicama, it has wi-fi and a decent restaurant. They offer surf lessons at S/75 for two hours including gear and trips to nearby waves when it's quiet in Chicama itself (half-day S/420 for 4–5 people). **S/390**

Hostal Los Delfines Chicama ☎ 044 343 044. Good sea views and friendly service; relatively comfortable for a beach hostel, with jacuzzis in some rooms and a swimming pool. **S/180**

Hostal El Hombre Chicama ☎ 044 576 077. Managed by local surfer "El Hombre", this was the first surfers' lodgings in Chicama; it is still basic but quite comfortable and the service good. Great sea views from some rooms. Singles with private bath. **S/40**

Cajamarca

A grand Andean town, **CAJAMARCA** is second only to Cusco in the grace of its architecture and the soft drama of its mountain scenery. The city's stone-based architecture reflects the cold nights up here – charming as it all is, with elaborate stone filigree mansions, churches and old Baroque facades. Almost Mediterranean in appearance, Cajamarca, at 2720m above sea level, squats below high mountains in a neat valley.

Proud and historic Cajamarca has intrinsic interest as the place where Pizarro captured and ransomed the Inca Emperor, Atahualpa, for gold, before killing him anyway. Gold has been an issue here since Pizarro arrived. Today the operations of

CLOCKWISE FROM TOP LEFT HUANCHACO WATERFRONT (P.363); DANCING AT A LOCAL FESTIVAL (P.356); TRADITIONAL ARCHITECTURE IN TRUJILLO (P.352) >

7

CAJAMARCA

SHOPPING

Mercado Artesanal	1
Quinde Ex	2

0 — 100 metres

ACCOMMODATION

Albergue Baños del Inca	8
Hospedaje Los Jazmines	7
Hostal El Cabildo	12
Hostal El Portada del Sol	4/14
Hostal El Portal de Marqués	9
Hostal Jusovi	5
Hostal Los Balcones de la Recoleta	13
Hostal Plaza	6
Hotel Casablanca	11
Hotel Costa del Sol	10
Hotel Laguna Seca	2
Los Pinos Inn	3
Posada del Puruay	1

NIGHTLIFE

Peña Tisné	2
Peña Usha Usha	1

CAFÉS & RESTAURANTS

Cascanuez	1
Chifa Hong Kong	2
Don Paco	6
Heladería Holanda	4
El Marengo/	
Marenguito Pizzeria	11/10
Om Gri	5
Pez Loco	8
Q'llpu Café Lounge	12
Restaurant El Zarco	3
Salas	7
Sanguchon.com	9

University Museum

Central Market

Palacio de Los Condes de Uceda

Catedral

PLAZA DE ARMAS

Scotiabank

Iglesia & Convent San Francisco & La Dolorosa

El Museo del Art Religioso

Cuarto del Rescate

Complejo de Belén

Museo Archeológico I Ethnográfico

Cerro Santa Apolonia

Combis to Baños del Inca

ATAHUALPA'S LAST DAYS

Atahualpa, the last Inca lord, was in Cajamarca in late 1532, relaxing at the hot springs, when news came of **Pizarro** dragging his 62 horsemen and 106 foot soldiers high up into the mountains. Atahualpa's spies and runners kept him well informed of their movements, and he could quite easily have destroyed the small band of weary aliens in one of the rocky passes to the west of Cajamarca. Instead he waited patiently until Friday, November 15, when a dishevelled group entered the silent streets of the deserted Inca city.

For the first time, Pizarro saw Atahualpa's camp, with its sea of cotton tents, and an army of men and long spears. Estimates varied, but there were between 30,000 and 80,000 Inca warriors, outnumbering the Spanish by at least two hundred to one.

Pizarro was planning his coup along the same lines that had been so successful for Cortés in Mexico: he would capture Atahualpa and use him to control the realm. The plaza in Cajamarca was perfect, as it was surrounded by long, low buildings on three sides, so Pizarro stationed his men there. Leaving most of his troops outside on the plain, Atahualpa entered the plaza with some five thousand men, unarmed except for small battle-axes, slings and pebble pouches. He was carried into the city by eighty noblemen in an ornate carriage – its wooden poles covered in silver, the floor and walls with gold and brilliantly coloured parrot feathers. The emperor himself was poised on a small stool, richly dressed with a crown placed upon his head and a thick string of magnificent emeralds around his aristocratic neck. Understandably bewildered to see no bearded men and not one horse in sight he shouted, "Where are they?"

A moment later, the Dominican friar, **Vicente de Valverde**, came out into the plaza; with a great lack of reverence to a man he considered a heathen in league with the Devil, he invited Atahualpa to dine with Pizarro. The Lord Inca declined the offer, saying that he wouldn't move until the Spanish returned all the objects they had already stolen from his people. The friar handed Atahualpa his Bible and began preaching unintelligibly to the Inca. After examining this strange object Atahualpa threw it angrily to the floor. As Vicente de Valverde moved away, screaming – "Come out, Christians! Come at these enemy dogs who reject the things of God. – two cannons signalled the start of what quickly became a **massacre**. The Spanish horsemen hacked their way through flesh to overturn the litter and capture the emperor. Knocking down a two-metre-thick wall, many of the Inca troops fled onto the surrounding plain with the cavalry at their heels. Spanish foot soldiers set about killing those left in the square with speed and ferocity. Not one Inca raised a weapon against the Spanish. Atahualpa, apparently an experienced warrior-leader, had badly underestimated his opponents' crazy ambitions and technological superiority – steel swords, muskets, cannons and horsepower.

Taken prisoner by the conquistadores after the deaths of 7000 or so of his followers and aware of the Spanish lust for gold, Atahualpa offered to buy his freedom by filling a large chamber with the precious metal, and it took a year for this ransom to be gathered, with priceless objects melted down and turned into bullion. Atahualpa had good reason to fear his captors' treachery, and sent messages to his followers in Quito to come and free him. These messages were intercepted by the Spanish who sentenced him to death by being burnt at the stake. In the end, the sentence was changed to garrotting as Atahualpa accepted a last-minute baptism. The help that he sought never came and the Spanish justified murdering the Inca ruler by claiming that Atahualpa won his title by treachery against his own brother and that they, in fact, were freeing the Incas from Atahualpa's 'tyranny'. These events were dramatized in the 1964 British play, *The Royal Hunt of the Sun* and also in the 1969 film version of the play.

massive **gold mines** in the region are generating protest; there are grave concerns in the area that the gold industry is polluting the land and groundwater.

Brief history

As far back as 1000 BC the fertile Cajamarca Basin was occupied by well-organized indigenous cultures, the earliest sign of the Chavín culture's influence on the northern mountains. The existing sites, scattered all about this region, are evidence of advanced civilizations capable of producing elaborate stone constructions without hard metal tools, and reveal permanent settlement from the **Chavín** era right through until the arrival of the conquering **Inca** army in the 1460s.

The Incas

For seventy years after the Incas' arrival in the 1460s, Cajamarca developed into an important provincial garrison town, evidently much favoured by Inca emperors as a stopover on their way along the Royal Highway between Cusco and Quito. With its hot springs, it proved a convenient spot for rest and recuperation after the frequent Inca battles with "barbarians" in the eastern forests. The city was endowed with sun temples and sumptuous palaces, so their ruler's presence must have been felt even when the supreme Inca was over 1000km away to the south in the capital of his empire.

Plaza de Armas

The city is laid out in a grid system centred around the **Plaza de Armas**, which was built on the site of the original triangular courtyard where Pizarro captured the Inca leader Atahualpa in 1532.

La Catedral de Cajamarca

Plaza de Armas • Daily 8–11am & 6–9pm • Free

On the northwest side of the plaza is the late seventeenth-century **Catedral de Cajamarca**, its walls incorporating various pieces of Inca masonry, and its interior distinguished only by a splendid Churrigueresque altar created by Spanish craftsmen. Its Plateresque Baroque facade is the most elaborate of all of Cajamarca's churches.

Iglesia San Francisco and Museo de Arte Religioso

Plaza de Armas • Mon–Fri 9am–noon & 4–6pm • Church free, museum S/5

Opposite the cathedral on Plaza de Armas is the elaborate Plateresque Baroque **Iglesia San Francisco**, in whose sanctuary the bones of Atahualpa are thought to lie, though they were originally buried in the church's cemetery. Attached to the church, the **Convento de San Francisco** houses a **museum** devoted to religious art. A guide will happily take you into the crypt to view the bones of the church's benefactors, the catacombs where the Franciscan monks are seeing out eternity (some entombed as recently as 2001) and several rooms around the attractive cloisters where you can view examples of the Cusco, Cajamarca and Quito schools of art from the sixteenth to eighteenth centuries. See if you can spot the *Cristo de la Columna*, with a four-legged Christ, and Satan's head in the painting depicting San Jerónimo.

La Dolorosa

Plaza de Armas • Mon–Fri 10am–5pm • Free

One of Cajamarca's unique features was that, until relatively recently, none of the churches had towers, in order to avoid the colonial tax rigidly imposed on "completed" religious buildings. The eighteenth-century chapel of **La Dolorosa**, next to Iglesia San Francisco, followed this pattern; it does, however, display some of Cajamarca's finest examples of stone filigree, both outside and in.

TICKETS IN CAJAMARCA

A single **ticket** (S/5) allows entrance to three of Cajamarca's main attractions, **El Cuarto del Rescate**, the **Iglesia Belén** and the **Museo Arqueológico i Etnográfico**, the latter two of which form part of the **Compejo de Belén**. The ticket can be bought at either the El Cuarto del Rescate or the complex.

El Cuarto del Rescate (Atahualpa's Ransom Room)

Amalia Puga 722 • Tue–Sat 9am–1pm & 3–8pm, Sun 9am–noon • S/5 joint ticket (see box opposite)

The most famous sight in town, the **El Cuarto del Rescate** is the only Inca construction still standing in Cajamarca. Lying just off the Plaza de Armas, across the road from the Iglesia San Francisco, the Ransom Room is a small rectangular room with Inca stonework in the backyard of a colonial building. It has long been claimed that this is the room which Atahualpa, as Pizarro's prisoner, promised to fill with gold in return for his freedom, but historians are still in disagreement about whether this was just Atahualpa's prison cell. There is, however, a line drawn on the wall at the height to which it was supposed to be filled with treasure, and you can also see the stone on which Atahualpa is thought to have been executed. The room's trapezoidal niches and doorways are classic Inca constructions. A painting at the entrance to the site depicts Atahualpa being burnt at the stake – the fate, to which he was originally sentenced (see box, p.372).

Compejo de Belén

C Belén • Mon–Fri 8.30am–noon & 4–6pm, Sat & Sun 8.30am–noon • S/5 joint ticket (see box opposite)

The **Compejo de Belén** (Belén Complex) comprises the former Hospital de Hombres, which has an exceptionally attractive stone-faced patio with fountains, a small medical museum, the tourist office and the **Iglesia Belén**, whose lavish interior boasts a tall cupola replete with oversized angels and a particularly graphic depiction of a bloodied, crucified Jesus.

The former hospital is of particular interest: inside there are 21 small, cell-like niches, presumably used by patients, and too small for people over 1.5m in height. A separate room inside the building is dedicated to bold, colourful Andean scenes painted by Cajamarcan artist Andrés Zevallos.

Museo Arqueológico i Etnográfico

C Belén and C Santisteban • Tue & Wed 9am–1pm & 3–8pm, Thurs–Sat 9am–8pm, Sun 9am–1pm • S/5 joint ticket (see box opposite)

Located in what used to be the Hospital de Mujeres, over the road from the Complejo de Belén, the **Museo Arqueológico I Etnográfico** displays ceramics and weavings from different pre-Inca civilizations, from the Nazca in the south to the Chachapoyas in the north (and see if you can spot the Cajamarca ossuary containing the mummy of a child). The cloister showcases the anthropomorphic and zoomorphic pottery of the Mochica and Lambayeque peoples, while the room dedicated to ethnography exhibits regional crafts such as basket weaving, mask-making for Carnaval and textiles. Look out for the elaborate stone carvings that flank the archway at the entrance to the museum, which depict two mythical women, each with four breasts – allegedly a symbol of fertility.

Cerro Santa Apolonia

Parque Ecología • Daily 7am–7pm • S/1

A two-block stroll up Jr 2 de Mayo from the Plaza de Armas takes you to a path that snakes its way up the **Cerro Santa Apolonia**, a hill that overlooks the city and offers great views across the valley. At the top of the hill are the terraced gardens known as the **Parque Ecología**, whose entrance is beside the Iglesia Santisima Virgen de Fatima, an appealing blue-and-white chapel at the top of the steps. At the highest point in the park you'll find what is thought to have been a sacrificial stone dating from around 1000 BC, popularly known as the Inca's Throne.

ARRIVAL AND DEPARTURE	CAJAMARCA
BY PLANE The airport is 4km out of town, on Av Arequipa. It is served	from Lima by LAN, Jr Comercio 832 (⊕lan.com; Mon–Fri 9am–7pm, Sat 9am–1pm), and LC Perú, Jr Comercio 1024

(ⓦlcperu.pe; Mon–Sat 8am–6pm). The quickest and cheapest way to and from the airport is by mototaxi (S/5). Destinations Lima (5 daily; 1hr 20min).

BY BUS/COLECTIVO

Most bus terminals are located at or around the third block of Av Atahualpa, a major arterial route running almost directly east out of the city.

Bus companies Cruz del Sur, Av Atahualpa 844 (ⓣ076 362 024, ⓦcruzdelsur.com.pe) runs to Lima via Trujillo at 7pm; Civa, Ayacucho 753 (ⓣ067 361 460, ⓦciva.com.pe), Tepsa, Sucre 422 (ⓣ067 363 306, ⓦwww.tepsa.com.pe) and Línea, Atahualpa 306 (ⓣ076 366 100, ⓦtransporteslinea.com.pe) all run overnight cama-buses to Lima, with Línea being the most comfortable and departing at 6pm and 6.30pm; Línea also runs services to Chiclayo and Trujillo; Transportes Chiclayo, Atahualpa 283 (ⓣ067 364 628, ⓦwww.transporteschiclayo.com) runs a night service to Chicalyo with good onward connections to Tumbes via Máncora; Virgen del Carmen, Atahualpa 333A (ⓣ067 413 243, ⓦturismovirgendelcarmen.com.pe) runs direct services to Cajamarca via Celendín and Leymebamba; Transportes Horna, Atahualpa 312 (ⓣ067 363 218) and Transportes Rojas, Atahualpa 309 (ⓣ067 340 548) serve Cajabamba, with Horna continuing directly to Huamachuco once daily.

Destinations Celendín (numerous daily; 2hr 30min); Chachapoyas (2 daily, 10–11hr); Chiclayo (8 daily; 6hr); Huamachuco (1 daily; 6hr); Leymebamba (2 daily at 4am and 3pm; 8hr 30min); Lima (at least 10 daily; 16hr); Piura (at least 5 daily; 9hr); Trujillo (at least 10 daily; 6hr).

INFORMATION AND TOURS

Tourist information The very helpful tourist office, inside the Compejo de Belén (Mon–Sat 7.30am–1pm & 3–5pm; ⓣ076 362 903), has some basic maps of the region. Staff are happy to explain how to reach outlying attractions independently. Some English spoken.

Tour operators All the companies offer pretty much the same array of tours, and most of them will pool clients. Bike Cajamarca (ⓣ076 369 361, ⓦbikecajamarca.blogspot.com) offers mountain-bike trips in the surrounding mountains; Catequil Tours (ⓣ076 363 958, ⓦcatequiltours.com) organizes everything from guided city tours to community tourism in the nearby countryside; Cumbe Mayo Tours (Jr Amalia Puga 635 ⓣ076 362 938) offers the normal range of excursions.

ACCOMMODATION

Most of Cajamarca's accommodation is in the centre of the city, around the Plaza de Armas, although there are also some interesting options slightly out of town.

IN CAJAMARCA

Hospedaje Los Jazmines Amazonas 775 ⓣ076 361812, ⓦhospedajelosjazmines.com.pe. A comfortable hostel in a converted colonial house surrounds a leafy courtyard with an antique doll collection. The excellent *Espresso Bar* on the premises serves some of the best coffee in town. Rooms are simple en suites. This place is associated with a charity that supports less-able children. **S/80**

Hostal Los Balcones de la Recoleta Amalia Puga 1050 ⓣ076 363 302. A beautifully restored, late nineteenth-century building wrapped around a courtyard full of flowers. All rooms have private bath and some have period furniture. Good service too. **S/110**

Hostal El Cabildo Jr Junín 1062 ⓣ076 762 442. Set around an attractive courtyard filled with greenery and statuary, this rambling old mansion offers a clutch of well-maintained yet somewhat musty rooms with modern showers and polished wooden floors. **S/130**

Hostal Jusovi Jr Amazonas 637 ⓣ076 362 920. Looks like a concrete monstrosity from the outside, but inside the singles, doubles and triples are pleasant and spotless and come with cable TV and wi-fi. **S/70**

Hostal Plaza Amalia Puga 669 ⓣ076 362 058. At this House of Chintz, rooms are basic but generous and come with plastic flowers and teddy bears. Some of the rooms look out over the plaza from the little balconies with geranium pots (note, hot water only in mornings and evenings in the shared bathrooms). **S/45**

Hostal El Portada del Sol Pisagua 731 ⓣ076 363 395, ⓦhostalportadadelsol.com. A charming colonial house with well-kept wooden floors, ceiling beams and an attractive covered patio where visitors can enjoy breakfast. All rooms have private bath, and there's also good internet access. They have an associated rural hacienda lodging of same name (see opposite). **S/135**

★ **Hostal El Portal de Marqués** C Comercio 644 ⓣ076 368 464, ⓦportaldelmarques.com. A formidable stone gateway leads you into the immaculate courtyard of this restored colonial house, surrounded by two floors of modern, carpeted rooms decked out in warm colours and with welcome touches of contemporary art. **S/241**

Hotel Casablanca Jr Dos de Mayo 446 ⓣ076 331 295. A fine old mansion right on the plaza, with dated and somewhat dark yet spacious rooms and a casino downstairs. The rooms surrounding the courtyard get more light. The showers are hot and powerful and the service is friendly. **S/140**

Hotel Costa del Sol Jr Cruz del Piedra 707 ⓣ076 362 472, ⓦcostadelsolperu.com. Cajamarca's plushest in-town option has a you-couldn't-be-more-central location, and inside it's an international-standard four-star hotel, complete with some English-speaking service, snug, carpeted en suites with cable TV, small pool, spa offering massages and facials and a good restaurant serving a mix of regional and European dishes. Overpriced for what it is but it's hard to fault the amenities or the location. S/566

Los Pinos Inn Jr La Mar 521 ☎076 365 992, ⓦ lospinosinn.com. Tucked away down a quiet street, this mansion combines Old World elegance in the form of gilded mirrors, antique furniture and a rather splendid staircase with Old World kitsch (the suits of armour in the lounge) and modern amenities (cable TV, wi-fi). Choose from the cheaper old wing or the more elaborate new wing. Doubles S/120, suites S/270

OUT OF TOWN

★Albergue Baños del Inca Located behind the thermal bath complex ☎076 348 385, ⓦctbinca.com .pe. A number of rooms (doubles and family rooms), as well as two-person bungalows, all very comfortable and with their own built-in thermal bathrooms, TV, minibar, bedroom and living room. Many of the chalets afford stunning views of, and direct access to, the complex of atmospheric steaming baths. Doubles S/60, bungalows S/150

Hostal El Portada del Sol At Km 6 on road from Cajamarca to Cumbe Mayo ☎076 363 395, ⓦ hostalportadadelsol.com. Based in a plot of partly wooded land, by the village of Cajamarquino, this charming *albergue* has been lovingly built with mainly local materials in traditional hacienda style with patio and wooden balconies. All rooms have private bath, and there's good wi-fi access. S/135

Hotel Laguna Seca Manco Capac 10988 ☎076 584 300, ⓦlagunaseca.com.pe. Very close to the Banos del Inca, this is a good place to rest up; the water in the rooms is heated by the thermal springs, the hotel has its own outdoor thermal pool, spa, and natural-steam Turkish baths. Service is very good. S/445

Posada del Puruay 5km north of the city ☎076 367 028, ⓦposadapuruay.com.pe. A country mansion converted into a luxury hotel museum. All rooms have colonial furniture and iron bedsteads, and are decorated in warm ochres and yellows. Besides its sculpted grounds and lovely interior, this gorgeous mansion is notable for its ecological approach (they have their own organic garden) and range of activities for guests, from horseriding to mountain biking. S/360

EATING AND DRINKING

Cajamarca is famous for its dairy products – including the widest variety of cheese in Peru. It's often served as *choclo con queso*, where you literally get a slab of cheese with a big cob of corn – a delicious snack. Other dishes include *caldo verde* (green broth) – something of an acquired taste – made from potato, egg, herbs and quesillo cheese, and *picante de papas con cuy* (potatoes with peanut and chilli sauce with fried guinea pig).

Cascanuez Amalia Puga 554 ☎076 946 089. Some of the best coffee and cake in town, in a refined café. Also good for lunchtime sandwiches, *humitas* and three types of breakfast (S/14–16). Daily 7.30am–7pm.

Chifa Hong Kong Jr Batán 133 ☎076 340 932. Its decor may be 'generic Chinese' but the menu consists mostly of genuine Cantonese dishes (the chef hails from Canton) as well as the obligatory *chifa* (Peruvian-Chinese) creations. The sizzling dishes stand out and if you've been living on a diet of *yuca* and potatoes, you may be thrilled to see glass noodles, fresh broccoli and a dozen flavours of bubble tea. Mains from S/12. Daily noon–11pm.

★Don Paco Puga 726 ☎076 362 655. The menu at this popular hangout, festooned with oodles of fake greenery, is among the most imaginative in town. You can choose from the likes of Philly cheese steak and 1/4 *cuy* with spicy potatoes, or you can opt for the signature *novocaxamarquino* (New Cajamarcan) dishes such as seared duck breast with elderberry sauce and fish fillet with Andean mash and oyster-and-passion fruit sauce. Mains from S/13–30. Daily 9am–10pm.

Heladería Holanda Amalia Puga 657, on the plaza. There's a real artisan at work here preparing some excellent ice cream using local milk and fresh tropical fruit. It's hard to go wrong with *maracuyá* (passion fruit) or *lúcuma*

(eggfruit). Cones from S/3. Daily 10am–8pm.

El Marengo/Marenguito Pizzeria Jr Junín 1201 ☎076 368 045, & Junín 1184 ☎076 344 251. This tiny pizzeria, warmed by a giant wood-burning oven, is so popular it has two locales around the corner from each other; both get packed with locals after the best pizza in town (from S/16), washed down with sangria. Daily 5–11pm.

Om Gri Jr Amazonas 858. Modesty is not one of chef/owner Tito's attributes since he claims to cook 'the best pasta in the world'. We're not sure about 'the world', but it certainly is some of the best pasta in town, served while he chats to you. Mains from S/15. Daily noon–11pm.

Pez Loco Jr San Martín 333 ☎076 361 806. This smart little restaurant is a lunchtime favourite with the Cajamarca business set, serving ample portions of a dozen or so different ceviches, as well as huge portions of rice dishes (try the *arroz con conchas negras*) and *chicharrón de pescado* (fried, battered fish bits). In the evenings, the menu turns meaty with mixed grill offerings and *anticuchos* (skewers). Mains from S/15. Mon–Sat noon–4pm & 7–11pm.

Q'illpu Café Lounge Jr Santisteban 105 ☎076 313 327. With its crimson-coloured easy chairs, winning location, an extensive selection of coffees, frappés, hot chocolates and a smattering of international nibbles (lasagne, ciabatta chicken sandwiches, waffles, cupcakes), this is a good, linger-worthy spot (also partly because continents may drift before you get your coffee). Coffees S/10. Mon–Sat 9am–8pm.

Restaurant El Zarco Jr del Batán 170. One of the few local cafés to stand out in Cajamarca, *El Zarco* is always packed with locals. It plays a wide range of mostly Latin music and offers an enormous variety of tasty, large dishes, including excellent trout, served in a refined, 1920s atmosphere. Mains from S/ 20. Daily 7.30am–11pm.

Salas Cruz de Piedra 639 ☎ 076 362 867. *Salas* has been around since 1947 and is still run by the same family. It's a local institution and their repertoire of regional dishes is hard to fault. There's *cuy* with potato and rice stew (S/28), dish-of-the-day specials are a steal at S/7, and there are sandwiches and light bites as well as more substantial meals. Daily 7am–10.30pm.

Sanguchon.com Jr Junín 1137 ☎ 076 343 066, ⓦ sanguchon.com.pe. This lively hole-in-the-wall-cum-bar specializes in humungous sandwiches, true to its name. And what sandwiches they are! Choose from overflowing burgers, grilled chicken sandwiches (the Californichicken stands out) or really push the boat out with Vito Corleone – an epic creation comprising steak, double cheese, eggs and more. Sandwiches S/9–15. Mon–Sat 7–11.30pm.

NIGHTLIFE AND ENTERTAINMENT

Peña Tisné Jr San Martín 265. This is neither a real *peña* nor a real bar, but a one-of-a-kind Peruvian experience that should not be missed. Knock on the unmarked door and Don Victor will lead you through his house to his bohemian back garden, full of cosy tables and memorabilia soaked in Cajamarcan history. Everyone is welcome here, from tourists to poets to the mayor. Try the home-made *macerado* – a delicious liquor made from fermenting tomatillo (an exotic fruit) and sugar (pitcher S/16). Daily 9am–midnight.

★ **Peña Usha Usha** Amalia Puga 320. This is the best venue in town for live Peruvian, especially criolla music, as well as Cuban troubadour-style performances. A small space particularly busy at weekends but also entertaining during the week when owner Jaime Valera inspires locals and tourists alike with his incredibly talented and versatile guitar playing and singing. Often lit only by candles, this bar has a cosy and inviting atmosphere. Wed–Sat 8pm–2am.

SHOPPING

Mercado Artesanal Jr 2 de Mayo 255. This collection of stalls is a good bet for quality ponchos, sweaters and other woollen goodies; the rest is mass-produced tat. Daily 10am–7pm.

Quinde Ex Jr Dos de Mayo 264. A decent artesanía shop with a good selection of textiles, bags and shawls.

DIRECTORY

Banks and exchange BCP, Jr Apurímac 717; Interbank, Jr 2 de Mayo 546 (good for changing money); Banco de La Nación, Jr Pisagua 552; Banco Continental, Jr Tarapaca 747.
Hospital Clínica Limatambo, Jr Puno 263, ☎ 076 362 241.

Private, high-standard 24hr care.
Post office SERPOST, at Jr Apurímac 626.
Tourist police Jr El Comercio 1013 (☎ 076 507 826).

Around Cajamarca

Within a short distance of Cajamarca are several attractions that can easily be visited on a day-trip from the city. The most popular trip from Cajamarca is to the steaming-hot thermal baths of **Baños del Inca**, just 6km from the city centre. A four-kilometre walk from Cajamarca lies the small village of **Aylambo**, known for its ceramics workshops, where you can try your hand at making your own pots. Further out are the impressive aqueduct at **Cumbe Mayo**, the ancient temple at **Kuntur Huasi** and the 'windows' into the world of the dead: the two ancient necropolises of **Ventanillas de Otuzco** and **Ventanillas de Combayo**.

Baños del Inca and around

6km east of Cajamarca • 15min bus ride from block 10 of Amazonas; local buses and colectivos leave when full, usually every 10min or so (S/1.50) • **Baths** Daily 6am–8pm • S/6–25 • ⓦ ctbinca.com.pe

Many of the ruins around Cajamarca are related to water, in a way that seems to both honour it in a religious sense and use it in a practical way. A prime example of this is the **BAÑOS DEL INCA**, where the Inca ruler allegedly recuperated from war wounds. The baths, which actually date from pre-Inca times, have long been popular with locals and wallowing in the thermal waters is a glorious way to spend a few hours (mornings are best to avoid the crowds). There's a restored Inca bath within the complex, but the stonework, though very good, is not original. It was from here that the Inca army marched to their doom against Pizarro and co. You can choose between using the public pool (S/6), cleanest on Mondays and Fridays; and private little pools (S/6–25). Sauna (S/10) and massages (S/20) are also on offer and there's a decent guesthouse attached (see p.377).

Ventanillas de Otuzco and Ventanillas de Combayo

Daily 9am–5pm • S/5 • Direct colectivos leave from the Plaza de la Recoleta for the Ventanillas (S/2) when full

The **Ventanillas de Otuzco**, 8km from Cajamarca, are a huge pre-Inca necropolis where the dead chieftains of the Cajamarca culture were buried in niches (windows), sometimes metres deep, cut by hand into the volcanic rock. They can be reached either directly by colectivo or via an enjoyable two-hour (one way) walk along the road leading north from outside the Baños del Inca (ask for directions). Twelve kilometres further east from the Ventanillas de Otuzco are the **Ventanillas de Combayo**, an even bigger necropolis; colectivos pass nearby but you have to ask the driver to drop you off in the right place and then walk up; otherwise it's a four-hour walk from Otuzco.

Aylambo

Frequent buses from Av Independencia in Cajamarca (15min; S/2)

A four-kilometre walk along Avenida R. Castilla to the south of Cajamarca brings you to the small village of **AYLAMBO**, known for its ceramics workshops. You can buy a

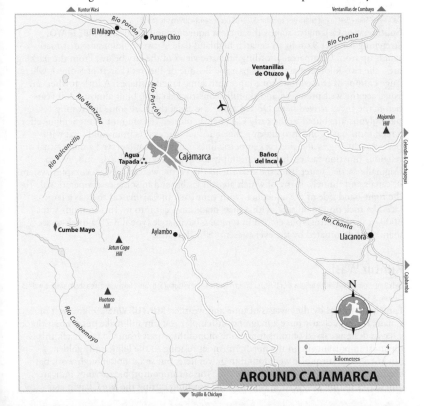

AROUND CAJAMARCA

FIESTAS IN CAJAMARCA

Cajamarca likes to party. Its wildest festival is **Carnaval**, which is celebrated at the beginning of Lent and tends to coincide with the Carnaval in Río. It's a week-long party of parades, cultural events, music, dancing and water fights. Anybody is fair game, so if you're in town at the height of celebrations, expect to be soaked with water guns, water balloons, buckets of paint and more. Book accommodation in advance. Another good time to visit Cajamarca is during May or June for the **Festival of Corpus Christi**. Until the early twentieth century this was the country's premier festival, before it was superseded by the traditional Inca sun festival, Inti Raymi, held at Sacsayhuaman in Cusco. Corpus Christi nevertheless actually coincided with the sun festival and is traditionally led by the elders of the Canachin family, who, in the Cajamarca area, were directly descended from local pre-Inca chieftains. The procession here still attracts locals from all around, but increasing commercialism is eating away at its traditional roots. Nevertheless it's fun, and visited by relatively few non-Peruvian tourists, with plenty of parties, bullfights, *caballos de paso* meetings and an interesting trade fair.

7

wide range of locally made earthenware products or even have a go at making your own pottery. Special workshops are also laid on for children; ask at one of the tour agents in Cajamarca for details (see p.376). There are plenty of **buses** here from Cajamarca if you want to save your legs for the many trails that wind around the village through attractive, forested land.

Cumbe Mayo

Daily 9am–5pm • Best to visit with a tour operator (S/20–25 per person, including site entry)

Southwest of Cajamarca stands the ancient aqueduct and canal of **CUMBE MAYO**, stretching for over 9km in an isolated highland dale. A twenty-kilometre dirt road winds up from Cajamarca, affording fantastic views of the city below. From the parking area, the two-kilometre trail loops past the Bosque de Piedras (Forest of Stones), where huge clumps of eroded limestone taper into some fanciful shapes. A little further on, you'll see the well-preserved and skilfully constructed **canal**, built almost 1200 years before the Incas arrived here. Dotted along the canal there are some interesting **petroglyphs** attributed to the early Cajamarca culture. The amount of meticulous effort which must have gone into crafting the aqueduct, cut as it is from solid rock with perfect right angles and precise geometric lines, suggests that it served a more ritual or religious function rather than being simply for irrigation purposes. Cumbe Mayo originally carried water from the Atlantic to the Pacific watershed via a complex system of canals and tunnels, many of which are still visible and in some cases operational. To the right-hand side of the aqueduct (with your back to Cajamarca) there is a large face-like rock on the hillside, with a man-made **cave** cut into it. This contains some 3000-year-old petroglyphs etched in typical Chavín style (you'll need a torch to see them) and dominated by the ever-present feline features.

Kuntur Wasi

Daily 9am–5pm • S/5 • Visit via full-day tour (S/90) or take a colectivo to the village of San Pablo, from where it's a short downhill walk to the ruins

Largely destroyed by the ravages of time and weather, **KUNTUR WASI**, 93km west of Cajamarca, was clearly once a magnificent temple. You can still make out a variation on Chavín designs carved onto its four stone monoliths. Apart from Chavín itself, this is the most important site in the northern Andes relating to the feline cult; golden ornaments and turquoise were found in graves here, but so far not enough work has been done to give a precise date to the site. The anthropomorphic carvings indicate differences in time, suggesting Kuntur Wasi was built during the late Chavín era, around 400 BC. Whatever its age, the pyramid is an imposing ruin amid exhilarating countryside. There's a small site museum displaying mostly replicas of pieces uncovered here by archeologists plus maps of the site and photographs of the Japanese dig. Public transport is infrequent, so tours are the easiest option.

South from Cajamarca

It's a long but rewarding journey south from Cajamarca to the small town of **Huamachuco**, jumping-off point for visiting the archeological site of **Marcahuamachuco** as well as the remarkable, rarely visited and very remote ruins of **Gran Pajatén**. The small colonial town of Cajabamba is the only other place of significance en route, but its main function is as a place to change buses.

Huamachuco

Infamous in Peru as the site of the Peruvian army's last-ditch stand against the Chilean conquerors back in 1879, **HUAMACHUCO**, at 3180m, is a fairly typical Andean market town, surrounded by partly forested hills and a patchwork of fields on steep slopes. The site of the battle is now largely covered by the small airport, while the large Plaza de Armas in the centre of town possesses an interesting colonial archway in one corner, which the Liberator Símon Bolívar once rode through. Now, however, it's flanked by the modern cathedral.

Markahuamachuco

10km northwest from Huamachuco • daily 6am–6pm • S/5 • A taxi will take you 5–6km (S/15–20), then walk the rest of the rough road; or 3hr walk one way • Ask at your guesthouse for 4WD transport (around S/60 for up to 4 people, waiting time extra)

The dramatic circular fort of **Markahuamachuco**, located on top of one of several mountains dominating the town, is considered to be of great archeological significance as the most important site relating to the Markahuamachuco culture, thought to have developed independently of its neighbours. Some 3km long, the **ruins** date back to around 300 BC, when they probably began life as an important ceremonial centre, with additions dating from between 600 and 800 AD. The fort was adopted possibly as an administrative outpost during the Huari-Tiahuanaco era (600–1100 AD), although it evidently maintained its independence from the powerful Chachapoyas nation, who lived in the high forested regions to the north and east of here (see p.383). An impressive, commanding and easily defended position, Markahuamachuco is also protected by a massive eight-metre-high wall surrounding its more vulnerable approaches. The *convento* complex, which consists of five circular buildings of varying sizes towards the northern end of the hill, is a later construction and was possibly home to a pre-Inca elite ruler and his selected concubines; the largest building has been partially reconstructed.

ARRIVAL AND DEPARTURE   HUAMACHUCO

By bus Transportes Horna, Carrion 1101 (☎ 067 440 061) runs one daily bus to Cajamarca and also runs services to Trujillo; alternatively, to reach Cajamarca, take any bus to Cajabamba and change there.

Destinations Cajabamba (numerous daily; 1hr); Cajamarca (1 daily; 6hr); Trujillo (numerous daily; 6hr).

FIESTAS IN HUAMACHUCO

On the first weekend in August the **Fiesta de Waman Raymi** is held at nearby Wiracochapampa, bringing many people from the town and countryside to the Inti Raymi-style celebrations. Other festivals in the region include the **Fiesta de Huamachuco** (celebrating the founding of the city) on August 13–20, a week of festivities including a superb firework display on August 14 and aggressive male *turcos* dancers during the procession.

7

ACCOMMODATION AND EATING

Café Doña Emilia Plaza de Armas. Snug, friendly café serving decent coffee and a great selection of desserts; their chocolate cake really stands out. Cake from S/3. Daily 8am–8pm.

Hostal Grand Colonial Jr Castilla 525 ☎076 522 202. Just off the Plaza de Armas, this colonial house may not be grand, but its ten rooms are arranged around a pleasant courtyard with fountain and has good enough rooms with or without bath. Good restaurant on-site. Double ‾S/60‾

Hostal Huamachuco Castilla 354 ☎076 440 559, ⓦ hostalhuamachucocentenario.com. Close to the Plaza de Armas, this appealing guesthouse attracts younger travellers with its clutch of swing-a-cat singles, doubles and triples, set around a quiet courtyard. ‾S/50‾

Gran Pajatén

Discovered in the 1960s, the remote archeological site of Gran Pajatén is difficult to reach and rewards those who are successful. Added to the World Monuments list in 2014, and inhabited as early as 200 BC, this important Chachapoyas site consists of sixteen typical circular structures, as well as terraced structures with elaborate decoration, both built mainly of a slate-type stone. One of the round structures is thought to have been a temple, another living quarters. Many of the walls features elaborate slate mosaics (similar to those found around Kuélap; see p.386), with geometric and anthropomorphic figures that have been created by the way in which these frequently thin stones are placed in the walls. Some of the buildings had once been elaborately painted in red, yellow, white and black and Mausoleum no. 5 still retains six curious *pinchidos* (*caoba*-wood sculptures) dangling from the rafters, depicting nude men with elaborate headgear, arms folded over their stomachs and exposed genitalia. Their purpose is unknown and you can see a lifesize example at the Museo de Leymebamba (see p.388).

ARRIVAL AND DEPARTURE

GRAN PAJATÉN

By bus and mule A fairly rough road connects Huamachuco with the village of Patáz, reachable by several combis weekly. In Patáz you can hire mules and guides for the trek to Gran Pajatén, which is a three-day walk one way, making this a true expedition (roughly S/100 per day).

Chachapoyas and around

The thriving market town of **CHACHAPOYAS**, at 2334m high up in the Andes, is first and foremost a springboard for a wealth of nearby pre-Columbian remains. West of Chachapoyas lie the **Pueblo de los Muertos** and **Karajía**, two impressive cliff-face burial centres for the elite of the Chachapoyas. However, the most famous and most worthwhile of all the Chachapoyan archeological remains is **Kuélap**, a fabulous, huge

---

THE TWO ROADS TO CHACHAPOYAS

There are two routes up to Chachapoyas from the south; the far longer and less exciting route is the road leaving the coast from Chiclayo and Piura via Olmos, Jaen and Bagua; this route has fewer and lower passes but is not terribly scenic, and is more prone to landslides during the rainy season.

A fascinating **alternative route to Chachapoyas** is the direct scenic route – a precarious one-lane highway (with spots to pull over) from Cajamarca that passes through Celendín and Leymebamba, winding its way up and down several massive valleys and passes. This road is completely paved but there's a reason why the driver's assistant hands out travel sickness bags at the start of the journey: the curves can be nausea-inducing – many locals tend to be sick – and it's best if you have a head for heights, given the sheer drop to one side, which is stunning or terrifying, depending on your outlook. Just to up the risks stake, this scenic route is also run overnight (wear warm clothes and bring a blanket). Passing via the market town of Celendin, the road descends into the Marañón Valley and the smaller town of Balsas. Climbing again, the bus comes through Leymebamba and reaches heights of almost 4000m before descending to the town of Chachapoyas.

citadel complex. South of here lie **Balsas** and **Leymebamba**. To some extent, the ancient culture lives on in some of the remote, traditional communities like **La Jalca**, 76km south of Chachapoyas. Less than 30km north of Chachapoyas gush the fabulous **Cataratas de Gocta**, the tallest falls in Peru.

The town is centred around the tranquil **Plaza de Armas**, surrounded by the cathedral and the municipal buildings and with a colonial bronze fountain as its centrepiece: a monument to Toribio Rodríguez de Mendoza. Born here in 1750, he is considered the main source of Peru's own ideological inspiration behind independence from its colonial master, Spain. The town's main church of interest, the **Iglesia de Santa Ana**, Jr Santa Ana 1056, was built in 1569 by the Spanish to ensure the commitment of Chachapoyas' indigenous population's to Christianity.

Brief history

In Aymara, Chachapoyas means "the cloud people", perhaps a description of the fair-skinned tribes who used to dominate this region, living in one of at least seven major cities (like Kuélap, Magdalena and Purunllacta), each one located high up above the Utcubamba Valley or a tributary of this, on prominent, dramatic peaks and ridges. Many of the local inhabitants still have a light-coloured complexion and remarkably pale faces. The Chachapoyas people, despite building great fortifications, were eventually subdued by the empire-building Incas. **Chachapoyas** was once a colonial possession rich with gold and silver mines as well as extremely fertile alluvial soil, before falling into decline during the Republican era.

ARRIVAL AND GETTING AROUND CHACHAPOYAS

By bus The best of the bus companies, the comfortable Movil Tours buses at Libertad 464 (☎041 478 545, ⓦmoviltours.com.pe) serve Lima (11am), Chiclayo (8pm) and Trujillo (7.30pm), while Civa at Salamanca 956 (☎041 478 048) also runs to Lima (1pm) and Chiclayo (6.30pm). Buses go via Pedro Ruíz rather than the shorter route via Cajamarca. To get to Tarapoto, take a direct colectivo or switch to a bus in Pedro Ruíz.

Destinations Chiclayo (4 daily; 9hr); Lima (2 daily; 22hr); Trujillo (2–3 daily; 12hr).

By colectivo Minibuses and shared cars to regional destinations depart from the Terminal Terrestre, around 10 blocks from the Plaza de Armas. Vírgen del Carmen (☎041 413 243) serves Cajamarca; Turismo Selva (☎961 659 443) serves Tarapoto; Trotamundo (☎956 918 759), Raymi Express (☎981 882 572) and Cristo Luz del Mundo (☎041 095 342) run to Leymebamba;

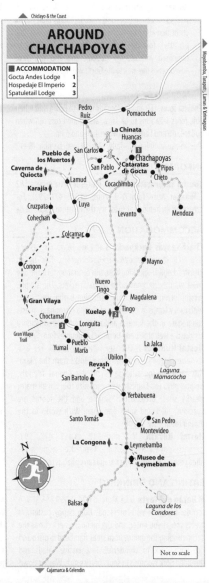

Chiclayo & the Coast

AROUND CHACHAPOYAS

■ ACCOMMODATION
Gocta Andes Lodge	1
Hospedaje El Imperio	2
Spatuletail Lodge	3

Pomacochas
Pedro Ruíz
La Chinata
Huancas
Pueblo de los Muertos — San Carlos
Chachapoyas
Caverna de Quiocta — San Pablo — Cataratas de Gocta — Pipos
Lamud — Cocachimba — Cheto
Karajía
Cruzpata — Luya
Cohechan — Levanto — Mendoza
Colcamar
Congon — Mayno
Nuevo Tingo
Gran Vilaya — Magdalena
Choctamal — Kuelap — Tingo
Gran Vilaya Trail — Longuita
Yumal — Pueblo María — La Jalca
Ubilon — Laguna Mamacocha
Revash
San Bartolo
Yerbabuena
Santo Tomás — San Pedro Montevideo
La Congona — Leymebamba
Museo de Leymebamba
Balsas — Laguna de los Condores

Not to scale

Cajamarca & Celendin

Moyobamba, Tarapoti, Lamas & Yurimaguas

7

7

TOURS FROM CHACHAPOYAS

There are numerous tour operators dotted around the Plaza de Armas, all of which offer standard day-trips at standard prices to Kuélap (S/35), Karajía combined with either Pueblo de Los Muertos or the Quiocta Cave (S/70), Gocta waterfall (S/40), Revash combined with the Museo de Leymebamba (S/90); some offer more specialized trips. The above prices cover transport and guide; entrance fees and lunch are extra. Not all companies and guides are certified, however, and not all guides speak English. Below are two certified tour agencies with good reputations who employ bilingual tour guides.

Amazon Expeditions Jr Ortiz Arrieta 508 ☎041 798 718, ⊛amazonexpedition.com.pe. Highly professional outfit that also runs four-day treks to Gran Vilaya (S/800 per day), four-day treks to Laguna de los Cóndores combined with Kuélap (S/900), and also the more adventurous day-trek to the Gocta waterfall (see p.386).

Turismo Explorer Grau 509 ☎041 478 162, ⊛turismoexplorerperu.com. Experienced, competent operator that also runs popular day-trips to Kuélap, Karajía, Gocta and Revash, as well as multi-day explorations of Gran Vilaya.

Chinata Tours, TED and Diplomáticos run to Pedro Ruíz when full, Tours Tella runs to La Jalca, and shared curs run when full to Luya and Lamud between 4am and 6pm.
Destinations Jalca (2 daily; 2hr); Leymebamba (8–12 daily; 2hr); Lamud (several daily; 2hr); Pedro Ruíz (numerous daily; 1hr); Tarapoto (5 daily; 8hr).
By taxi Taxis around town charge a flat rate of S/3.

INFORMATION

Tourist information iPeru's office, Jr Ortiz Arrieta 582 (Mon–Sat 8am–1pm & 3–7pm; ☎041 477 292). For advice on archeological sites, try the Instituto Nacional de Cultura, Jr Junín 817 (Mon–Fri 9am–6pm).
Website The useful website ⊛camayocperu.com is run by the Camayoc Foundation.

ACCOMMODATION

Chachapoyas Backpackers Jr 2 de Mayo 639 ☎041 478 879 ⊛chachapoyasbackpackers.com. Run by an effusive, English-speaking host, this central hostel is the one most warmly recommended by backpackers. The simple, swamp-green rooms (some with own bathrooms) come with funky lamps in the shape of Karajía sarcophagi, guests congregate in the kitchen and small lounge, and laundry service is a welcome perk. Dorm **S/18**, doubles from **S/40**
Hostal Ñuñurco Jr Ortíz Arrieta 186 ☎041 477 845 ⊛nunurcotravellers.com. Three blocks from the plaza, this rambling guesthouse is run by several friendly, helpful guys (no English) who organize tours to all major nearby sites. Breakfast is simple and the rooms are spacious, tiled and spick and span. Wi-fi works in the dining room only. **S/100**
Hostal Revash Jr Grau 517 ☎041 477 391, ⊛chachapoyaskuelap.com.pe. Centred on a greenery-filled courtyard featuring a Karajía sarcophagus replica, this

guesthouse couldn't be more central. It's renowned for the having the best hot showers in town, and the spacious rooms (the cheapest singles are S/40) come with properly comfortable beds. There's a buffet spread for breakfast and a rather persistent in-house tour agency. **S/120**
Posada del Arriero Jr Grau 636 ☎041 478 945, Wposadadelarriero.net. Set back from the street and centred around a well-tended leafy courtyard, this quiet three-storey guesthouse features compact en suites in warm yellows with cable TV. **S/140**
La Xalca Hotel Jr Grau 940 ☎041 479 106 ⊛laxalcahotel.com. Adding a touch of Old World charm to Chachapoyas' range of lodgings, this handsome mansion sports antique furnishings, chandeliers in the lounge, an immaculate inner courtyard and seriously spacious rooms – some carpeted, some tiled – with strangely low beds and cable TV. Service is professional, and the breakfast buffet features regional specialities such as *humitas*. **S/170**

EATING AND DRINKING

El Batán del Tayta Jr La Merced 604 ☎959 865 539. A corridor inscribed with messages from happy customers greets you as you enter, and the menu is as eclectic as the decor, running the gamut from steak flambéed in pisco and rice with duck to wonderful, imaginative salads and shredded pork wontons in sour cherry sauce. Wash it down

with pineapple sangria or one of their signature sours. Mains from S/15. Daily noon–11pm.
★**Café Fusiones** Chincha Alta 445 ⊛cafefusiones .com. This bohemian hangout specializes in largely organic 'slow food'. Come here for spicy lentil burgers, fresh guacamole and hummus, ample fresh juices, chunky

sandwiches, ample breakfasts and great teas and coffees. Wi-fi and book exchange make it even more linger-worthy. Mains from S/10. Mon–Sat 7am–noon & 3–9pm.

El Tejado Santo Domingo 424 ☏ 041 477 592. Really good traditional Peruvian and local cuisine served in a warm and friendly ambience around a patio. The speciality here is several takes on *tacu tacu*, a rice and beans dish.

Mains from S/12. Mon–Sat noon–4pm & 7–9pm.

La Tushpa Jr Ortiz Arrieta 753 ☏ 041 777 198. A magnet for the carnivorously inclined, this restaurant specializes in meat dishes such as *cuy* (S/40), *chicharones* (deep-fried pork), steak and *anticuchos de corazón* (oxheart kebabs). It's not gourmet (the meat can be tough) but it'll do in a pinch. Mains S/7–20. Mon–Sat 1–10pm.

DIRECTORY

Internet Plenty of internet cafés on and around the Plaza de Armas.

Money and exchange BCP is on Triunfo, seven blocks from the Plaza de Armas and next to the hospital. Banco de la Nación is at Ayacucho and 2 de Mayo. Both have global ATMs.

Post office Grau 561 (Mon–Sat 8am–7pm).

Karajía

S/5 • It's easiest to go via organized tour (see box opposite) from Chachapoyas. Alternatively, catch a shared car to Luya and then (an infrequent) one to Cruzpata

A characteristic of the Chachapoyas region are the ancient **sarcophagi**, elaborately painted clay coffins moulded around a cone made of wooden poles, dating back to the fifteenth century and often stuck inaccessibly into horizontal crevices high up along cliff faces to prevent desecration by grave robbers. There are over 250 sarcophagi sites in the region, of which the only accessible one is the **Karajía** site, 46km southwest of Chachapoyas.

From the plaza in the village of Cruz Pata, it's a one-kilometre descent via dirt road and steep steps to the narrow walkway hugging the cliff. Thirty metres above you, you can see a row of six sarcophagi (there were eight but two were destroyed) with heads reminiscent of Easter Island's moai. Up to 2m in height, they house the mummies of the most important individuals, such as chieftains, warriors and shamans, as well as their most prized belongings. The two skulls above them and one to the right are thought to be trophy skulls. Walk to the far end of the walkway; from there you'll be able to see another five sarcophagi to the left of the main group – these are far less elaborate and have been thoroughly desecrated. To the left of those there's a solitary sarcophagus, hidden in the shrubbery.

Caverna de Quiocta

10km north of Lamud • S/5 • Best reached by combined Karajía tour (see box, p.384)

The **Caverna de Quiocta**, reachable via a muddy, rutted road up from Lamud, is known both for its otherworldly rock formations and mortal remains. The cave is 23m high at its highest point and 55m deep, and consists of five chambers. In the first chamber are skulls and bones, neatly piled on ledges – the remains of a few Chachapoyas people. Overhead, the cave ceiling sparkles with a myriad tiny constellations, actually specs of metal ore. Proceeding deeper into the cave is really muddy going (which is why tour companies stop in Luya to pick up rubber boots); you cross streams, and the deeper you go, the more outlandish the rock formations become, hence the fanciful names of "Beer Mug", "Castles", "Chamber of the Pharaoh" and more. The final chamber features the largest stalagmite formation of them all, looking rather like a Gothic meringue.

Pueblo de los Muertos

S/5 • Take a shared car to Lamud, from where it's a 45min walk down and 1hr 30min walk back up • Tours combine visits to Pueblo de los Muertos with Karajía during the dry season

The **PUEBLO DE LOS MUERTOS** (City of the Dead), located some 30km to the north of Chachapoyas and about 3km from Lamud, is where you'll find overgrown roundhouse foundations plus **sarcophagi**, some up to 2m high and carved with human faces. Six were originally found here and three have been put back in their previous sites to stare blankly across the valley from a natural fault in the rock face. Each one has been carefully moulded into an elongated egg-like shape from a mixture of mud and vegetable fibres, then painted purple and white with geometric zigzags and other superimposed designs.

Cataratas de Gocta

S/10 • Take a colectivo to Pedro Ruíz and double back by mototaxi to Cocachimba or San Pablo, or take a tour from Chachapoyas (S/70)

The **Cataratas de Gocta** (771m) claim to be the fifth tallest falls in the world. Only revealed to the outside world in 2002, local legend says that it is protected by an immense siren-like serpent. Getting to a good viewpoint – from where you can make out the main two tiers of the falls (231m above and another 540m below) – requires some hiking. The walk starts in the hamlet of Cocachimba; from here it's a six-kilometre hike to the base of the falls, but if you want to explore higher or return via San Pablo hamlet on the other side of the valley, you will need at least four to six hours. The hike goes through attractive cloud-forest terrain where *gallitos de la roca* (Peru's emblematic bird) and many other feathered species flit about.

Kuélap

Daily 8am–5pm • S/15 • The easiest way to visit is by day-tour from Chachapoyas (see box, p.384)

The main attraction for most travellers in the Chachapoyas region is the partially restored ruin of **KUÉLAP**, one of the most overwhelming pre-Inca sites in Peru, originally inhabited by the Chachapoyas people – a seemingly impregnable stone citadel sitting atop a limestone mountain, with exceptional views of the valleys below. Just 40km south of Chachapoyas, the ruins were discovered in 1843, above the tiny village of **Tingo** in the remote and verdant Utcubamba Valley by Judge Juan Crisóstomo Nieto.

Built sometime between 500 AD and 1493, Kuélap was the strongest, most easily defended of all Peruvian fortress cities, something that can be seen in the narrowing defensive form of the main entry passageways, though walls may have shifted over the centuries due to damage done by the elements.

The site

It has been calculated that some 700,000 tonnes of stone were used to build this fortress and to this day, it is not known where the Chachapoyas people obtained this stone. An estimated four thousand people would have lived here at its height, working mainly as farmers, builders and artisans and living in little, round stone houses.

Kuélap is 700m long and the site's enormous **walls** thrust 20m high, and are constructed from gigantic limestone slabs arranged in geometric patterns, with some sections faced with rectangular granite blocks over forty layers high. The average wall thickness is around 80cm and the largest stone 2m thick.

Inside the ruins lie the remains of some four hundred round stone **houses** which originally sported conical grass roofs (see the reconstructed dwelling), some, thought to be the houses of the nobility, decorated with a distinctive diamond and zigzag pattern. The smaller stone circles served a funerary function. Elsewhere, you may spot small carved animal heads, condor designs, deer-eye symbols and intricate serpent figures. These are similar in style to the better-known Kogi villages of today's northern Colombia; and, indeed, there are thought to be linguistic connections between the Kogi and the Chachapoyas peoples, and possible links to a Caribbean or even Maya influence. A typical circular house features a stone grinder, a cellar-like hole – some were used as food storage and some for funerary purposes, and a squat, narrow stone tunnel used as a guinea-pig hutch.

The upper part of the citadel was restricted to the most privileged ranks in Chachapoyas society and features a seven-metre-high watchtower at the north end of the fortress inside which human remains have been found, as well as several rectangular buildings, thought to have been used for ceremonial purposes. At the citadel's south end, there is a unique structure with fine, curved outer walls, which is believed to have been a temple, or at least to have had a ceremonial function. Inside the temple and accessible from the roof is an inverted, truncated cone containing a large, bottle-shaped cavity (known as El Tintero or inkwell), possibly a place of sacrifice, since archeologists have found human bones there and llama remains nearby. Just up from the temple are several more circular houses, believed to have been the dwellings of the priests.

ARRIVAL AND DEPARTURE   KUÉLAP

By colectivo Colectivos run from the Terminal Terrestre in Chachapoyas (usually leaving between 6 and 11am) pass through Nuevo Tingo and continue their winding, precipitous way on a circular anticlockwise route via the village of Choctamal to Pueblo María. Colectivos run frequently from Tingo Viejo to Chachapoyas.

On foot It's possible to hike up to Kuélap from Tingo Viejo; the 9.8km trail is well signposted but a steep, shadeless slog (around 4hr up and about 2hr back down). Leave early to avoid the mid-morning sun, and remember to carry all the water you'll need with you. Alternatively, you can hike up to Kuélap from Pueblo María; it's a 2hr hike up a gently inclining dirt road that passes through Cuchapampa, Quisango and Malcapampa hamlets.

By organized tour By far the easiest option, though it does mean that you'll be exploring the ruins during the heat of the day with all the other tour groups.

ACCOMMODATION AND EATING

KUÉLAP

Hospedaje El Imperio No phone. Basic, friendly little place beneath the Kuélap ruins. Bring own sleeping bag if possible. Meals (S/5–10) available on request. It's also free to camp next to the nearby INC hostel. **S/15** per person

AROUND KUÉLAP

Gocta Andes Lodge Cocachimba ☎ 041 630 552 ⓦ goctalodge.com. The location of this lodge is second to none, with superb views of the Gocta waterfall and spacious, bright rooms with colourful textiles lining the two sides of the little infinity pool. **S/250**

Hospedajes Pueblo María. No phone. Several families in the community offer bed and breakfast to visitors. They are usually very good, with plenty of blankets and quite comfortable beds in traditional wooden buildings; meals available for around S/7. **S/20** per person

Spatuletail Lodge Kuélap road Km 20, Choctamal

☎995 237 268 or ☎1 866 396 9582 (US), ⓦ marvelousspatuletail.com. A great lodge with seven individually decorated rooms, an orchidarium, telescope observatory and grounds overflowing with bougainvillea with a hot tub for guest use. Private tours to Kuélap offered. **S/150**

Gran Vilaya

Colectivos drop you off at the village of Choctamal or Cruz Pata • From here it is expedition-style trekking, with or without horses or mules and with a local guide • 4-day guided treks from Chachapoyas cost S/800

The collection of archeological remains known as **GRAN VILAYA** – a superb complex of almost entirely unexcavated ruins scattered over a wide area – are found in the lush mountain valleys west of Chachapoyas. About thirty of these sites are of note, and companies in Chachapoyas run four-day treks into the valley, starting from Cruz Pata and paying a visit to Karajía before crossing a 3000m pass into the splendid Valle Belén. The trek includes staying overnight in very simple accommodation in the villages of Congon and Choctamal en route, visits to important ruins, such as Pirquilla and horse trekking (or hiking, if you prefer) between Congon and the ruins of Lanche, followed by a trek to Choctamal and a visit to Kuélap. This gives you a good taste of Gran Vilaya, but if you're keen on seeing more of the valley's ruins or spending more time in Gran Vilaya, then consider looking for a guide and mules in either Cruz Pata or Choctamal and taking camping gear and food with you.

La Jalca

There are only a couple of direct combis from Chachapoyas (leaving around 3pm, returning at 5am and 7am), which requires overnighting at one of the very basic guesthouses, but you can also take any Leymebamba-bound combi, get off at the turn-off, and walk up to La Jalca (around 3hr).

Two hours south by road from Chachapoyas, the traditional village of **La Jalca** is within walking distance of a number of ruins. The folklore capital of the region, La Jalca also lays claim to some amazing fourteenth-century stone walls and a seventeenth-century stone-built **church**, with characteristic Chachapoyan zigzags. The houses in the village, built in typical Chachapoyas fashion along the ridge, are lovely, conical thatched-roofed constructions with walls of *tapial*-type mudwork.

Leymebamba and around

The cute cobblestoned village of **LEYMEBAMBA**, some 80km south of Chachapoyas along the scenic road to Cajamarca, is a good place to break the journey. The land around Leymebamba is rich in archeological sites, the most important being La Congona and Revash. Leymebamba can also be used as a jumping-off point for visiting the spectacular Laguna de los Cóndores, though both are regularly included in organized tours from Chachapoyas (see box, p.384).

Museo de Leymebamba

Daily 10am–4.30pm • S/15 • 5km south of Leymebabma; take a mototaxi from the Chachapoyas plaza (S/5)

This superb **museum** is the home to the 219 Chachapoyas mummies, around 800 years old, from the mausoleum found near the **Laguna de los Condores** in 1996 (see opposite). They are remarkably well preserved (some still have eyes) and while many are still wrapped in their original shrouds embroidered with human faces, others – including two babies – are uncovered and seem to be peeking through their fingers at you from behind glass. Other exhibits focus on Chachapoyas and Inca pottery, ritual and household objects and centuries-old weavings. A fascinating display depicts the pick of the region's archeological sites – Karajía, La Petaca, Gran Pajatén – in miniature, and you may also spot two trepanned skulls, a mummified dog and Inca bone flutes. Labels are in English, German and Spanish, and the museum is housed in a beautiful building created using traditional materials and construction techniques including stonework, timber and *tapial*.

La Congona

5hr return hike from Leymebamba

Up from Leymebamba along a trail that begins at the bottom end of Calle 16 de Julio, **La Congona** is an overgrown site featuring the circular houses of the Chachapoyas as well as a lookout tower which can be climbed for superb views of the valley. Inside the houses there are niches, believed to have been used for storing sacred objects, and many houses feature the distinctive diamond patterns favoured by the Chachapoyas culture. The two-hour trail is reasonably easy to follow but it's not a bad idea to ask around Leymebamba for a guide (around S/100) for the half-day.

Revash

Accessed either via 5km uphill hike from the turnoff to the Santo Tomás village or via a level 3km walk from San Bartolo village

Consisting of several red-and-white mudbrick *chullpas* (funerary buildings) that look remarkably like cheerful cottages, **Revash** is a thirteenth-century burial site, built by the Revash culture (contemporaneous with the Chachapoyas people), where skeletal remains were found by archeologists (even if the tombs themselves had been looted) and where rock paintings decorate the cliff behind the tombs. Due to lack of public transport to the villages, it's easiest to take a tour that drops you off either at the Santo Tomás or the San Bartolo trailhead.

Laguna de los Cóndores

Accessed via a 3-day, 2-night trek/horseride from Leymebamba (S/450–500) or as a 4-day, 3-night trek from Chachapoyas that takes in Kuélap as well (S/900)

This gorgeous highland lake, fringed with cloud forest, was the location of a remarkable archeological find in 1996, when some local *campesinos* stumbled upon six Chachapoyas tombs perched on a ledge above the water. These tombs turned out to contain a treasure trove of mummies and funerary objects, which you can view at the Museo de Leymebamba (see opposite). The lake is a tough but beautiful ten- to twelve-hour uphill trek from Leymebamba; guided three-day treks involve a day's stay at the lake and exploration of the area. Enquire about guides and horses at the museum, *La Casona de Leymebamba or Kentitambo* (see below), or else join a guided trek from Chachapoyas (see box, p.384).

ARRIVAL AND DEPARTURE LEYMEBAMBA

By bus Four companies run colectivos from Chachapoyas to Leymebamba's Plaza de Armas; of these, Vírgen del Carmen (☎ 076 413 243) and Amazonas Express continue to Cajamarca but only Vírgen is recommended. Vírgen operates small buses rather than minivans and switches to a proper bus in Celendín. Raymi Express (☎ 981 882 572) has the most Chachapoyas–Leymebamba departures.
Destinations Cajamarca (daily at 8am and 10pm; 8–10hr); Chachapoyas (8–12 daily; 2hr).

ACCOMMODATION AND EATING

La Casona de Leymebamba Jr Amazonas 223 ☎ 041 830 106, ☻ casonadeleymebamba.com. Run by the indefatigable Nelly, this beautiful house dates back to 1906, with heavy wooden beams, a tranquil inner courtyard overflowing with flowers and a hanging orchid garden – the owner's passion. Most beds come with antique, intricately carved wooden headboards and the breakfast spread features home-made dairy products. Other meals can be arranged on request and the owner can put you in touch with the pick of local guides if you wish to visit Revash, the Laguna de los Cóndores or other local attractions. S̲/̲1̲8̲0̲
KentiKafé opposite the Museo de Leymebamba. By far the best place for coffee or a light meal, this café sits uphill from the Museo de Leymebamba, and besides enjoying the excellent coffee, chunky sandwiches and home-made cakes, you can also observe seventeen different species of

humming bird at feeders strategically placed amid the greenery. Mains from S/15. Daily 8.30am–5.30pm.

Kentitambo next to KentiKafé ☎ 971 118 259, ⓦ kentitambo.com. Surrounded by lush gardens, this boutique guesthouse consists of just two bungalows, both with king-sized beds, rain showers, and hammocks out front. The host is a multilingual historian who can tell you all about the Laguna de los Cóndores mummies. S/300

Sabores de Misqui Jr Amazonas 380 ☎ 953 552 111. Half a block from the Plaza de Armas, this is the best place to eat in Leymebamba proper. The proprietress whips up such classics as *lomo saltado*, grilled trout and even a lentil omelette, preceded by a generous bowl of soup. Three-course meal S/10. Mon–Sat noon–10pm.

SHOPPING

A.M.A.L. Jr San Agustín 429. Right on the plaza, this is the main outlet for the local women's co-operative that specializes in high-quality weavings, scarves and bags. A small selection of their work is also available at the Museo de Leymebamba. Daily 9am–6pm.

Tarapoto

TARAPOTO, known as the "City of Palms", is a sweltering, busy jungle town that makes a good base from which to explore the surrounding villages and waterfalls, prepare for a spell in the jungle or do some whitewater rafting on the Río Mayo. It also has excellent road connections with the jungle port of Yurimaguas, the starting point for one of Peru's best Amazon river trips to Iquitos (see p.461) via the remote rainforest haven of **Reserva Nacional de Pacaya-Samiria** (see p.471).

Lamas

Take a colectivo from Tarapoto's Jr Urgarge, block 10 (S/6; 30min) or go with a tour (see box, p.384) for S/35

Surrounded by large pineapple plantations, **LAMAS**, a small village 20km up into the forested hills from Tarapoto is very popular with tour groups. Tours typically stop at the Plaza de Armas where a statue of Inca leader Pachacutec is depicted shaking hands with a conquistador – takes great liberties with history. After a brief stop at the small history museum, visitors are whisked off to the *mirador* overlooking the town before descending to an incongruous-looking brick castle built here by an Italian expatriate. A final stop involves mingling with the inhabitants of Barrio Wayco, reputedly the direct descendants of the Chanka tribe, who escaped from the Andes to this region in the fifteenth century, fleeing the conquering Inca army. They typically put on a short music show, with the dressed-up children showing off traditional dance steps and encouraging audience participation; there are also some traditional (and not so traditional) handicrafts for sale. The best month to visit is August when the village **Fiesta de Santa Rosa de Lima** is in full swing.

Cataratas de Ahushiyacu and Cataratas de Huacamaillo

Easiest accessed by tour from Tarapoto (S/30–40)

The forty-metre **Cataratas de Ahuashiyacu** are a popular and scenic local swimming spot; they are situated along the road east towards Yurimaguas, and you can get any Yurimaguas-bound bus or colectivo to drop you off. The **Cataratas de Huacamaillo** are trickier to get to, with a two-hour trek that involves river crossings; this one is easiest done by tour (S/65).

THE ROAD SOUTH FROM TARAPOTO: TRAVEL UPDATE

While several years ago the route **south from Tarapoto** via Juanjui (150km) and Tingo María (a further 350km) had a reputation for being the most dangerous road in Peru due to robberies by narcotraffickers, at the time of research the mostly paved road was deemed safe to travel on, even at night, since narcotrafficking action has moved to a different region of Peru. However, get the most up-to-date information on the ground before taking a bus south.

DOWNRIVER TO IQUITOS

From Yurimaguas, you can travel all the way to **Iquitos** by river, your best and most comfortable bet being Transportes Eduardo (☎ 065 351 270; S/60 per hammock on 2nd deck, S/120 per hammock on top deck, S/250 for a cabin; a two- to three-day trip). Check boat departures directly at the La Boca port, find the captain and arrange details directly with him; don't pay anyone apart from the captain. The price includes basic food (it's a good idea to bring your own, as well as own hammock, bottled water, high-factor sun screen and sun hat; if you want to try fishing along the way, lines and hooks are sold in the town's *ferreterías*.

The scenery en route is electric: the river gets steadily wider and slower, especially once it joins Río Marañón, and the vegetation on the riverbanks more and more dense. En route you can break your journey at the small settlement of Lagunas (12hr), the starting point for trips into the huge Reserva Nacional de Pacaya-Samiria and a place where you can find basic accommodation and knowledgeable guides to take you into the reserve for around S/150 per day for boat, guide and basic accommodation in the jungle. You can catch a smaller, faster boat to Lagunas (around S/120; 4hr) from the port of Garcilazo in Yurimaguas, just southeast of the Plaza de Armas.

7

ARRIVAL AND DEPARTURE

TARAPOTO

By plane Tarapoto airport is 5km from the centre of town. A mototaxi into town costs S/4–5. Lan (ⓦlan.com) has twice-daily flights to Lima while Star Peru (ⓦstarperu .com) flies daily to Iquitos as well as twice daily to Lima.
Destinations Iquitos (daily; 1hr); Lima (4 daily; 1hr).
By bus Most bus companies operate from block 8 of Av Salaverry (S/2 by mototaxi from the centre), with departures for Lima, Chiclayo, Pucallpa and Trujillo between 7am and 6pm. To get to Chachapoyas, change at Pedro Ruíz or take a combi (see opposite). Movil Tours, Av Salaverry 880 (☎042 529 193, ⓦmoviltours.com) is the

most comfortable option; Civa, Av Salaverry 840 (☎042 522 269) is another good bet, while TSP, Aviación 100 (☎979 639 716) serves Pucallpa.
Destinations Chiclayo (numerous daily; 14hr); Lima (numerous daily; 25–30hr); Pucallpa (daily at 8am; 15hr); Trujillo (numerous daily; 15–18hr).
By colectivo Turismo Selva, Jr Alfonso Ugarte 1128 (☎042 530 100) has combis running to Yurimaguas and directly to Chachapoyas.
Destinations Chachapoyas (3 daily at 7am, 10am and noon; 8hr); Yurimaguas (7 daily, 2hr).

ACCOMMODATION

Casa de Palos Jr Prado 155 ☎ 949 317 681. With a Pan-like statue waiting by the entrance to the lush inner courtyard that overflows with greenery, this characterful guesthouse is all rustic chic, with individual touches in its nine rooms and an appealing breakfast terrace. **S/110**
★ **El Mirador** Jr San Pablo de la Cruz 517 ☎042 522 177. With its hammock-hung terrace overlooking the sea of green in the valley below, this guesthouse is made all the sweeter by the motherly matriarch. Individually decorated rooms are spotless and spacious

(particularly the a/c doubles), the extensive breakfast features eggs, fruit salad and fresh fruit juice, and your hosts can help you organize tours and transport. **S/100**
La Posada Inn Jr San Martín 146 ☎042 522 234. Half a block from the main plaza, the rooms at this friendly budget hotel are arranged around an inner courtyard, which blocks the noise from the street outside. Choose from basic fan-cooled en suites on the ground floor or the a/c, air-freshener-scented rooms upstairs. Wi-fi comes and goes like the three resident felines. **S/120**

EATING AND DRINKING

The Jr San Pablo de la Cruz Solidus Jr Lamas intersection is lined with bars pumping loud music and serving jungle-themed cocktails.

Brava Grilled Jr San Martín 615 ☎042 524 231. Sometimes all you really want is a plate of spicy chicken wings and a Coliseum-sized Oreo milkshake. This crimson night-owl magnet does that and more; the *tacacho* express – chicken skewers with fried plantains is popular with locals while the English menu, Cobb salad, Caesar salad and ample home-made burgers overflowing with toppings are a hit with homesick travellers. Mains from S/10. Daily 6–11pm.

Estarbarts Cajue Jr San Pablo de la Cruz 243 ☎042 341 052. With a leafy courtyard out front, this sedate café mocks Starbucks, but more importantly it serves an impressive range of coffees (ristretto, cortado, Americano, espresso are all present and correct), iced coffees, milkshakes and fruit juices. Sustenance is limited to a range of sandwiches, crepes and ample breakfasts. Coffee from S/5. Daily 8.30am–noon & 5.30pm–midnight.

★**Limón y Aji** Jr A A Morey 158 ☎042 529 762. This smart new cevicheria is a welcome addition to Tarapoto's dining scene. Choose from a dozen different ceviches (the classic with black clams and *leche de pantera* is wonderful), rice dishes (green rice with squid stands out), *tacu tacu* dishes and more. The service is friendly and attentive. Mains from S/20. Tues–Sun 12.30–5pm.

La Patarashka Jr San Pablo de la Cruz 362 ⓦlapatarashka.com. Atmospherically lit, breezy restaurant shrouded in greenery, specializing in jungle dishes such as *patarashka* (fish steamed in a leaf with tomatoes, garlic, onions and sweet peppers) and smoked wild pork with *patacones* (balls of mashed, fried green plantains). Mains from S/20. Daily noon–3pm & 7–11pm.

DIRECTORY

Internet The best internet café is probably Mundonet, one block from the Plaza Mayor at Jr San Martín 205.

Money and exchange There are several banks within half a block from the Plaza de Armas, including Scotiabank and BCP on the first block of Hurtado, both with ATMs.

Post office Jr San Martín 482 (Mon–Sat 8am–7pm).

Yurimaguas

7

From Tarapoto it's another 140km north along a paved road to the frontier town of **YURIMAGUAS**. This bustling market town has little to recommend it, other than its **three ports**, giving access to the Río Huallaga. The most important is the downriver port of **La Boca**, from where the Iquitos-bound cargo boats leave. The port is located thirteen blocks north of the town centre, or a S/2 ride in a mototaxi.

ARRIVAL AND INFORMATION   YURIMAGUAS

By bus/colectivo Buses, colectivos and combis (S/35) depart from the southern outskirts of town in Yurimaguas, along the Tarapoto road. Several combi companies, including the reliable Turismo Selva (Pje Los Claveles 104, ☎065 758 710), run between Tarapoto and Yurimaguas several times daily (2hr).

ACCOMMODATION AND EATING

Hotel Omaguas Jr Tacna 128 ☎956 889 972. This central budget hotel is four blocks from the waterfront and while its rooms belong to the instantly unmemorable, basic, tiled category, they are clean, air-conditioned and come with wi-fi and cable TV. S/75

★**Hotel Río Huallaga** C Arica 111 ☎065 353 951, ⓦriohuallagahotel.com. Catering to all traveller needs, Yurimaguas' smartest option has plenty of perks – from a swimming pool to laundry service, a small cinema and in-house tour agency. A/c rooms are bright, airy and decked out in creams and lime green and the restaurant serves an ambitious mix of international, regional and classic Peruvian dishes. S/220

L'Nute & Listo Tnte César López 103 ☎065 353 399. The pick of the town's eateries, this is a popular local spot for regional dishes that come with buffers of *yuca* and rice, as well as more imaginative offerings such as the *tortilla de camarones* (shrimp omelette). Their fresh fruit juices are superb. Mains from S/15. Daily noon–10pm.

The northern desert

The **northern desert** remains one of the least-visited areas of Peru, mainly because of its distance from Lima and Cusco, the traditional hubs of Peru's tourist trail, but it is still an invaluable destination for its distinctive landscape, wildlife, archeology and history.

Northern Peru has some excellent **museums**, besides the stunning, if harsh, coastal beauty of its desert environment, which itself contains the largest dry forest in the Americas, almost entirely consisting of *algarrobo* (carob) trees. The main cities of **Chiclayo** and **Piura** (the first Spanish settlement in Peru) are lively commercial centres, serving not only the desert coast but large areas of the Andes as well. If, like a lot of travellers, you decide to bus straight through from Trujillo to the Ecuadorian border beyond **Tumbes** (or vice versa) in a single journey, you'll be missing out on some unique attractions.

The coastal resorts, such as the very trendy and lively **Máncora** and quieter, posher **Punta Sal** are among the best reasons for stopping. Other options include **Cabo Blanco**

and, further south **La Pimentel**, Chiclayo's closest beach, or small-town Zorritos to the north. Whatever the beach experience you're looking for, be it an all-night party, a yoga retreat, a surf vacation or just complete peace and quiet, you can find it somewhere along the Panamericana where the country's warmest and richest seas lap up against the tropical dry forest. The real treasures of the region, however, are the archeological remains, particularly the **Valley of the Pyramids** at **Túcume** and the older pyramid complex of **Batán Grande**, two immense pre-Inca ceremonial centres within easy reach of Chiclayo. Equally alluring is the **Temple of Sipán**, where some of Peru's finest gold and silver artefacts were found within the last fifteen years.

Pacasmayo and around

Some 10km north of the town of San Pedro de Lloc, which is famous for its stuffed lizards and great ham, the Panamericana passes by the growing port town of **Pacasmayo**; many buses pull in here to pick up passengers and it is a possible stop-off en route between Trujillo and Chiclayo. If you have your own car, it's a good place to stop for some great seafood and a cold drink and take twenty minutes to explore the seafront promenade. The town isn't particularly attractive, but beach and promenade are pleasant and the old jetty is considered the largest and most attractive surviving pier on the Peruvian coast. The local surf conditions are good and nearby Poemape has a famous wave that old surfers tell long stories about. There are a few hotels here, if you do decide to spend some time to enjoy the surf and the generally chilled atmosphere.

Pakatnamu

Free • Take a colectivo or bus from Pacasmayo, then 6km walk from the main highway to the site or take a taxi (S/20–30 with short wait)

A few kilometres north of Pacasmayo, just before the village of Guadalupe, a track leads off left to the well-preserved ruins of **Pakatnamu** (City of Sanctuaries), overlooking the mouth of the Río Jequetepeque. Being off the main road and far from any major towns, the ruins of this abandoned city have survived relatively untouched by treasure hunters or curious browsers. The remains include pyramids, palaces, storehouses and dwellings. The place was first occupied during the Gallinazo period (around 350 AD), then was subsequently conquered by the Mochica and Chimu cultures. It gets very hot around midday, and there's little shade and **no food** or drink available at the site, so bring your own.

ARRIVAL AND DEPARTURE
PACASMAYO AND AROUND

By bus From Trujillo take the regular Emtrafesa, Av Tupac Amaru 185 (☎ 044 607 270), service to Chiclayo (every 30min, S/8), which will drop you off at Leoncito Prado and 28 de Julio. From there a taxi to the beachfront will cost around S/5.
Bus companies Most buses stop at the main bus terminal two block north of 28 de Julio.
Destinations All destinations are served by Emtrafesa, which runs all day. Cajamarca (5hr); Chiclayo (1–2hr); Trujillo (2hr).

ACCOMMODATION AND EATING

Tabaris Adolfo King, cnr of Ayacucho. A typical little family-owned seafood restaurant, known throughout the region for making a killer ceviche and for grilled grouper freshly caught nearby (S/30–40). Daily 9am–9.30pm.
Hotel Pakatnamu Malecón Grau 103 ☎ 044 522 368. This hotel has an attractive wooden veranda and sea views; rooms are comfortable but simple, with plenty of carpet cover plus cable TV and private hot showers. S̲/̲1̲3̲0̲
Hotel El Mirador Aurelio Herrera 10 ☎ 044 521 883, ⓦ perupacasmayo.com. One of the most popular options among the passing surfer crowd, this large yellow building with wooden balconies has great sea views from the terrace upstairs. The rooms are quite bare, with white brick walls and basic furnishings, but are clean and comfortable. S̲/̲1̲2̲0̲

Chiclayo

The commercial centre of northern Peru, **CHICLAYO** is better famed for its banks than its heritage. Nevertheless, it has its own attractions, even if most of the city is an urban

ATTRACTIONS AROUND CHICLAYO

Most places of interest in the region can be reached independently by taking a **colectivo** from the market area of Chiclayo, but it's a very time-consuming process; you'll find it much easier to see all the archeological sites if you've got your own transport. You'll get the most out of these by going with a knowledgeable local **guide** on an organized tour from Chiclayo. **Taxi** drivers can also be hired by the day or half-day (usually around S/60 for half-day and S/150 full day, but it depends on negotiation and, in particular, how much actual driving time).

sprawl modernizing and growing rapidly. The city has an incredibly busy feel to it, with people and traffic moving fast and noisily everywhere during daylight hours. Tourists tend to attract attention in the main streets, not least because they aren't seen very often.

Parque Principal and around

The city's heart is the **Parque Principal**, where there is a futuristic fountain that's elegantly lit at night. You'll also find the Neoclassical **Catedral** here, built in 1869 and with its main doorway supported by Doric columns, and the **Palacio Municipal**,

7

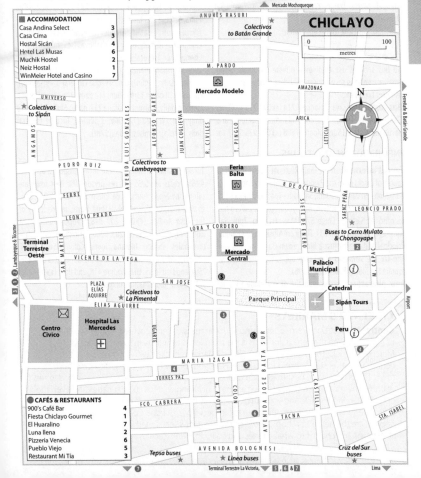

CHICLAYO

ACCOMMODATION	
Casa Andina Select	3
Casa Cima	5
Hostal Sicán	4
Hotel Las Musas	6
Muchik Hostel	2
Neiz Hostal	1
WinMeier Hotel and Casino	7

CAFÉS & RESTAURANTS	
900's Café Bar	4
Fiesta Chiclayo Gourmet	1
El Huaralino	7
Luna llena	2
Pizzeria Venecia	6
Pueblo Viejo	5
Restaurant Mi Tía	3

a Republican edifice built in 1919. Along Calle San José you'll find the **Convento Franciscano Santa María**, built in the early seventeenth century but destroyed, apart from the second cloister, by El Niño rains in 1961.

La Verónica and the Plazuela Elías Aguirre

Six blocks directly west of the Parque Principal, there's the small, attractive chapel of **La Verónica** (daily 7–10am and 6–8pm; free), Calle Torres Paz. Built at the end of the nineteenth century, its most notable feature is the altarpiece of silver- and gold-leaf. In the **Plazuela Elías Aguirre**, just around the corner, there's a statue in honour of the *comandante* of this name, who was a local hero serving the Republicans in the Battle of Angamos during the War of the Pacific.

ARRIVAL AND DEPARTURE   CHICLAYO

BY PLANE

José Abelardo Quiñones González Airport is 2km east of town on Av Bolognesi (☎074 233 192; 24hr), and easily reached by taxi for S/15–20. Flights are with LAN Perú, C Manuel María Izaga 770 (Mon–Fri 9am–7pm, Sat 9am–1pm; ☎074 274 875).

Destinations Lima (daily; 1hr 30min).

BY BUS

All bus services use their own private terminals, while smaller minivans serve closer local destinations and leave from set terminals.

Bus companies Civa, Bolognesi 714 (☎074 223 434), for Chachapoyas, Lima, Tarapoto, Máncora, Tumbes and Gayuaquil; Cruz del Sur, Bolognesi 888 (☎074 225 508), for

Lima; Movil Tours, Bolognesi 195 (☎074 271 940), for Chachapoyas, Bagua, Moyobamba and Tarapoto; Oltursa, Av Vincente de la Vega 101 (☎074 236 244), has an excellent service to Los Organos, Máncora and Tumbes; Transportes Chiclayo, Av Lora y Lora s/n (☎074 223 632) is the best for Puira, Sullana and Talara (hourly departures).

Destinations Batán Grande (several daily; 40min), Cajamarca (10 daily; 6hr); Chachapoyas (several daily; 9hr); Chongoyape (several daily; 1hr); Ferreñafe (several daily; 20min); Huancabamba (2 weekly; 15hr); La Pimentel (several daily; 15min); Lambayeque (several daily; 20min); Lima (8–10 daily; 13hr); Piura (12 daily; 3hr 30min); Sipán (several daily; 25min); Sullana (12 daily; 5hr); Talara (12 daily; 6hr); Trujillo (12 daily; 3 30min); Túcume (several daily; 45min); Tumbes (8 daily; 7hr).

INFORMATION AND TOURS

Tourist information The main Regional Tourist Office is a couple of blocks from the Parque Principal on Av Sáenz Peña 838 (Mon–Fri 9am–5.30pm, Sat 9am–1pm; ☎074 233 132 or ☎074 238 112, ⓦregionlambayeque.gob.pe). iPeru has an office at Siete de Enero 579 (Mon–Fri 9am–7pm, Sat 9am–2pm; ☎074 205 703). There are kiosks in the Parque Principal and nearby just a block down Balta Sur. You can also try the *WinMeier Hotel* (see opposite). Alternatively, contact the Tourist Police (see p.398).

Tour operators Tours around the area include trips to

Túcume, Batán Grande and the local museums, and last 4–8hr; costs are S/35–75 per person. The best tours are offered by Sipán Tours, 7 de Enero 772 (☎074 229 053, ⓦsipantours.com), and InkaNatura Travel, in the lobby of the *Casa Andina* (☎074 209 948, ⊜opcix@inkanatura .com), or in Lima (☎01 203 5000, ⓦinkanatura). Other companies include Indiana Tours, Colón 556 (☎074 222991), who also have a kiosk at the airport (☎074 238 750), and Lizu Tours, Elías Aguirre 418, 2nd floor (☎074 228 871, ⊜lizu_tours@latinmail.com).

CHICLAYO'S MARKETS

Central Market Daily 7am–6pm. Along with the massive semi-covered market lanes – part of which is called the Feria Balta – this is the main focus of activity in town. Known as the Mercado Modelo, the main part of the Central Market is packed with food vendors at the centre, and other stalls around the outside. Here you can find some of the best ceviche in town. This is one of the best markets in the north – and a revelation if you've just arrived in the country. There's a whole section of live animals, including wild fox cubs, canaries and even the occasional condor chick, and you can't miss the ray fish, known as *la guitarra*, hanging up to dry in the sun before being made into a local speciality, *pescado seco*. But the most compelling displays are the herbalists' shops, or *mercado de brujos* (witches' market), selling everything from herbs and charms to whale bones and hallucinogenic cacti.

GETTING AROUND

By bus Buses connecting Chiclayo with La Pimentel and Lambayeque use the Terminal Terrestre Oeste, on the first block of Calle San José, while most other close local destinations are reached by minibuses leaving from Terminal Epsel, Nicolas de Pierola and Avenida Sáenz Peña.

By car Lima Aero Rent a Car Perú, Av Bolognesi 1462 (☎ 074 271 547).

By taxi There are plenty of taxis in the streets, but as always, it is better to call one. Try Chiclayo Taxi (☎ 074 265 410), Taxi Sipán Tours (☎ 074 781 100) or Taxi Seguro (☎ 074 232 244).

ACCOMMODATION

Finding a place to stay is relatively simple in Chiclayo, although most are geared towards the business traveller, meaning that quality budget accommodation isn't really an option. If you want peace and quiet, or to camp, you may prefer one of the out-of-town options like the beautiful *Hospedaje Rural Los Horcones* (see p.406). La Pimental and the calm of the seaside are also just 15min away. In the city itself, most of the reasonably priced hotels are clustered around the Plaza de Armas.

★**Casa Andina Select** (formerly Gran Hotel Chiclayo) Av Federico Villareal 115 ☎ 074 234 911, ⓦ casa-andina .com. The best, most luxurious hotel in town, even if it is a little way from the centre. Recently renovated and incorporated into the usually excellent Casa Andina chain. You get spacious, very comfortable rooms with polished wooden floors, excellent showers, a fine restaurant, decent swimming pool, wi-fi in rooms, a business centre and even a little casino-bar. S/240

★**Casa Cima** C Los Mangos 161, apt 501, Urb Santa Victoria ☎ 074 602 244, ⓔ infocima.ingles.cix@gmail .com. Located in a slightly quieter, safe neighbourhood, some ten blocks from the plaza, rooms are up in the owner's penthouse, with a terrace offering great views over the city. There are just three rooms (one en-suite), all impeccable and simply comfortable. Helpful hosts Liam and Teófila go above and beyond the call of duty. S/96

Hostal Sicán Av María Izaga 356 ☎ 074 208 741. Nicely decorated, central and friendly, it has TVs in rooms, fans (or S/10 more for a/c) and communal internet access. The quietest beds are at the top, and the price includes breakfast. S/65

Hotel Las Musas Los Faiques 101, Urb Santa Victoria ☎ 074 231 548. Upmarket lodgings that are a little less expensive than you'd expect, with excellent service, big rooms and beds with a/c and quick wi-fi in rooms, a cool lobby and casino. S/200

Muchik Hostel Jr Vicente de la Vega 1127 ☎ 074 272 119, ⓦ muchik-hostel.minihostels.com. The most common choice for backpackers in town. Everything is kept clean, the staff are friendly, and it's located in a safe area. Dorms S/25, doubles S/60

Neiz Hostal Pedro Ruiz 756 ☎ 074 229 441. Solid value, the rooms are clean and big enough, have fans, flat-screen TVs and hot water. There's a lot of clashing gold and pale green colours and if you're lucky, swan-shaped towels, but the staff are welcoming and helpful. S/90

WinMeier Hotel and Casino (formerly Garza) Bolognesi 756 ☎ 074 228 172, ⓦ winmeier.pe. Very central and pretty comfortable, with a pool and sauna, two restaurants serving well-prepared and -presented local creole dishes and fresh seafood, and staff who provide useful tourist information. Their main draw is their casino which gets quite a lot of traffic. They also rent out cars and jeeps. S/295

EATING AND DRINKING

The best thing to do in Chiclayo is eat: some of the most flavourful Peruvian dishes come from this region and reach back deep into their Moche heritage. The Moche were among the first cultures to domesticate the local Muscovy duck, and the *seco de pato* stew is a local favourite. Being close to the ocean, seafood is also on every menu, and one local speciality is rehydrated dried fish (*pescado seco*), often prepared from flat ray fish, with potatoes.

900's Café Bar Av Izaga 900 ☎ 074 209 268. Quality and stylish Peruvian food, and some fine cocktails, but really, its all about the coffee and desserts (S/8.50) – the best in town. Mon–Sat 8am–3.30pm & 5.30–11pm.

★**Fiesta Chiclayo Gourmet** Av Salaverry 1820 ☎ 074 201 970. This is where celebrity chef Hector Solís started his empire, and it remains the best place to eat refined, creative versions of the best local dishes (S/100–120 for a starter, mains and dessert). He breeds his own ducks and goats at his nearby farm and serves up stunning food in an fine-dining atmosphere. Don't miss the *ceviche caliente* (S/60), a grouper ceviche flash-grilled in its own juices in an open banana leaf. Tues–Sun 11am–3pm & 6–11pm.

El Huaralino La Libertad 155, Urb Santa Victoria ☎ 074 270 330. Offers *tortilla de raya* and *pato a la Nortena* (duck with rice and vegetables Northern Peru style). Prices start at S/30–40. Come early for a tasty set breakfast. Mon–Sat 8.30am–9.30pm.

Luna llena Block 10, Av Miguel Grau ☎ 074 233 988. Peruvian-Chinese food resturant, (*chifas*) are a standard throughout Peru, but rarely outside Lima do they rise to anything above mediocre – *Luna Llena* does, and then some. Great Chinese food and local variants, quick, professional service; you'll want to go back. Rice dishes (*arroz chaufa*) around S/12 and fried noodles around S/20. Daily noon–3pm and 6.30–11pm.

7

Pizzeria Venecia Av José Balta 365 ☎ 074 233384. Just a few blocks down from the Parque Principal, this is the best of Chiclayo's numerous pizza parlours; cosy in the evenings with small tables and a large pizza oven, but fills up quickly. Efficient service and a choice of wines and other drinks. Daily 6.30–11.45pm.

Pueblo Viejo María Izaga 900 ☎ 074 229 863. With top criolla cooking, this place is excellent, though it's better still when there's live music on Fridays. It has a wide-ranging menu which varies over time (dishes from S/40). Best to book in advance. Tues–Sat 7–11pm.

★ **Restaurant Mi Tía** C Elías Aguirre 662 ☎ 074 205 712. You'll find this place easily in the evenings by the queue snaking along outside, but skip that, they're here for the fast food window; you want to head inside, grab a table and get choosing from their extensive menu. The space is quite small, and can get a little cramped as it is hugely popular, but friendly service and the best traditional Chiclayo food in town makes sharing elbow space well worth it. Try the *arroz con pato* (S/32), roast local duck with savoury, cilantro perfumed rice, or any of the goat stews (*seco de cabrito*; S/32–40) which get their famous flavour from an overnight marinade in chicha. Mon–Sat 8am–11pm.

DIRECTORY

Health The hospital is at C Hipolito Unanue 180 ☎ 074 237 776 (24hr).

Internet Click-Click, close to the plaza at San José 604, upstairs; and at San José 104.

Money and exchange The main banks are concentrated around the Parque Principal. *Cambistas* are on the corners of the Parque Principal, particularly Av José Balta, or there's the casa de cambio Hugo Barandiaran at Av Balta 641A (Mon–Fri 9.30am–5pm) next to the Banco Continental.

Post office Elías Aguirre 140, seven blocks west of the plaza (Mon–Sat 8am–8pm, Sun 8am–2pm).

Tourist Police Sáenz Peña 830 ☎ 074 227 615 (Mon–Sat 8am–6pm); also on call 24hr.

La Pimentel and around

An attractive beach resort just 11km southwest of Chiclayo, **La Pimentel** is a pleasant settlement with an attractive colonial-style centre around the **Plaza Diego Ferre**. More importantly, though, it offers a decent **beach** for swimming and **surfing** (competitions take place in Dec and Jan). The town is known for its small-scale fishing industry, some of it using the traditional *caballitos del mar* (made from *totora* reeds). For a small fee (S/1) you can access the long pier, nearly 100 years old, that divides the seafront *malecón* in two, where you can watch the fishermen.

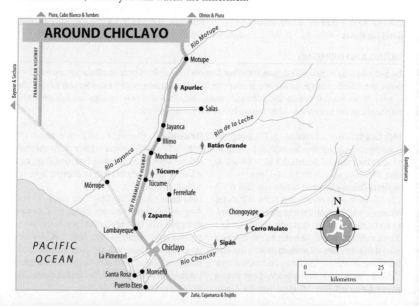

AROUND CHICLAYO

More picturesque is the small fishing village of **La Caleta Santa Rosa**, about 5km south of La Pimentel. Here the beach is crowded with colourful boats and fishermen mending nets; the best and freshest **ceviche** in the Chiclayo area is served in the restaurants on the seafront here.

The area known as **El Faro** (the Lighthouse), slightly to the south of La Caleta Santa Rosa, is the best location for surfing. Continuing from here along the road inland for about 5km, you come to the small town of **Monsefú**, known as the "city of flowers" because of the local cottage industry that supplies blooms to the area. It's also known for its fine straw hats, straw-rolled cigarettes and the quality of its cotton, all of which you can buy at the daily **market**.

About 4km south from Monsefú you come to the colonial village of **Etén** and its nearby ruined church, the Capilla del Milagro, built following a local's vision of the Christ Child in 1649. Southwest, towards the sea, lie the wide avenues of largely derelict **Puerto Etén**, just another 4km away, where there are abandoned nineteenth-century train carriages.

ARRIVAL AND DEPARTURE   LA PIMENTEL AND AROUND

By bus Buses depart regularly from block one of Calle San José in Chiclayo(S/1.5; 20min).

By colectivo Regular colectivos leave from Calle Elias Aguirre and Avenida Luis Gonzales in Chiclavo (S/2; 15min)

ACCOMMODATION AND EATING

★ **Casona del Muelle** C Nueva Estación 116 ☎ 074 458 168, ⓦ casonadelmuelle.com. The best option in Pimentel, a beautiful old house from the 1920s with wooden floors and plenty of decoration that takes you right back to that era, or at least, thereabouts. It's not luxury accommodation, but it's comfortable, the service is great, and you're within spitting distance of the pier. **S/100**

Hostal Garuda Jr Quiñones 109 ☎ 074 619 850. Clean and comfortable, if simple rooms, most around a small interior garden. A good breakfast of fresh bread, jams, juice and eggs included; a block away from the seafront and beach. **S/110**

La Tienda del Pato Malecón Seoane, next to the Capitanía de Puerto. The local's 'local' (and it has been for nearly thirty years), right on the *malecón*, the seafood and duck dishes are great (S/20–40). Daily noon–5pm and 7.30pm–12.30am.

Lambayeque

The old colonial town of **LAMBAYEQUE**, 12km from Chiclayo city, must have been a grand place before it fell into decay last century; fortunately, it seems on the road to recovery, helped by its popular museums and vibrant Sunday **markets**. Buildings worth seeing here include the early eighteenth-century **Iglesia de San Pedro**, parallel to the main square between 2 de Mayo and 8 de Octubre, which is still holding up and is the most impressive edifice in the town, with two attractive front towers and fourteen balconies.

Lambayeque's casonas

The dusty streets of Lambayeque are better known for their handful of colonial *casonas*, such as **La Casa Cúneo** (8 de Octubre 328), and a few doors down **La Casa Descalzi**, which has a fine *algarrobo* doorway in typical Lambayeque Baroque style. **La Casa de la Logia Masónica** (Masonic Lodge), at the corner of calles 2 de Mayo and San Martín, is also worth checking out for its superb balcony, which has lasted for about four hundred years and, at 67m, is thought to be the longest in Peru.

Museo Arqueológico Nacional Brüning

Block 7, Av Huamachuco • Daily 9am–5pm • S/8 • ☎ 074 282 110

Lambayeque's highlights are its two museums. The oldest, though quite new itself, is the modern **Museo Arqueológico Nacional Brüning**. Named after its founder Hans Heinrich Brüning, an expert in the Mochica language and culture, the museum has superb collections of early ceramics, many of which have only recently resurfaced and been put on display.

7

Museo de las Tumbas Reales de Sipán

Av Juan Pablo Vizcardo y Guzmán 895 • Tues–Sun 9am–5pm • S/10 • ☎ 074 283 978, ⓦ museotumbasrealessipan.pe

The **Museo de las Tumbas Reales de Sipán**, or Museum of the Royal Tombs of Sipán, is an imposing concrete construction in the form of a semi-sunken or truncated pyramid, reflecting the form and style of the treasures it holds inside. This mix of modernity and indigenous pre-Columbian influence is a fantastic starting-point for exploring the archeology of the valley. You'll need a good hour or two to see and experience all the exhibits, which include a large collection of gold, silver and copper objects from the tomb of **El Señor de Sipán** (see below), including his main emblem, a staff known as **El Cetro Cuchillo**, found stuck to the bones of his right hand in his tomb. The tomb itself is also reproduced as one of the museum's centrepieces down on the bottom of the three floors. The top floor mainly exhibits ceramics, while the second floor is dedicated to El Señor de Sipán's ornaments and treasures. Background music accompanies you around the museum circuit using instruments and sounds associated with pre-Hispanic cultures of the region. A musical finale can usually be caught on the ground floor.

The Lambayeque Valley has long been renowned for turning up pre-Columbian metallurgy – particularly gold pieces from the neighbouring hill graveyard of **Zacamé** – and local treasure-hunters have sometimes gone so far as to use bulldozers to dig them out; but it's the addition of the Sipán treasures that's given the biggest boost to Lambayeque's reputation, and the museum is now one of the finest in South America.

ARRIVAL AND DEPARTURE
LAMBAYEQUE

By colectivo From Chiclayo, take the short combi ride north from Calle San José, opposite the Plazuela Elías Aguirre, six blocks west of Parque Principal (S/2.50).

EATING

Lambayeque is famous for its sweet pastry cakes – filled with *manjar blanca* (a very popular condensed-milk product) and touted under the unlikely name of *King-Kongs*. In any of the town's streets, you'll be bombarded by street vendors pushing out piles of the cake, shouting "King-Kong! King-Kong!"

El Cantaro C Dos de Mayo 180 ☎ 074 282 196. An excellent lunchtime restaurant whether you go for the set menus or à la carte; known by most taxi drivers, this is one of the most traditional restaurants in the region, serving ceviche, duck (S/22), goat (S/22) and other local specialities. Daily 11am–5pm.

The Temple of Sipán (La Huaca Rajada)

Tues–Sun 9am–5pm • S/8 • Combi colectivos to Sipán (25min; S/2.50) leave Chiclayo from the Epsel terminal

The **TEMPLE OF SIPÁN**, 33km southeast of Chiclayo, discovered in 1987 by archeologist Walter Alva has proved to be one of the richest **tombs** in the entire Americas. Every important individual buried here, mostly Mochica nobles from around 200–600 AD, was interred lying flat with his or her own precious-metal grave objects, such as gold and silver goblets, headdresses, breastplates and jewellery including turquoise and lapis lazuli, themselves now on show in the **Museo de las Tumbas Reales de Sipán** (see above). The most important grave uncovered was that of a noble known today as **El Señor de Sipán**, the Lord of Sipán. He was buried along with a great many fine gold and silver decorative objects adorned with semi-precious stones and shells from the Ecuadorian coast.

There are two large adobe **pyramids**, including the Huaca Rajada, in front of which there was once a royal tomb; the place certainly gives you a feel for the people who lived here almost two millennia ago, and it's one of the few sites in Peru whose treasures were not entirely plundered by either the conquistadores or more recent grave robbers. There's also a **site museum**, displaying photos and illustrations of the excavation work plus replicas of some of the discoveries.

Pampagrande and around

Not open to the public • Buses to Chongoyape leave Chiclayo from the Epsel terminal (S/5; 1hr 20min)

Pampagrande was one of the largest and most active Mochica administrative and ceremonial centres in the region and was populated by thousands. Located in the desert some 20km (more or less) west of the Temple of Sipán (see opposite), it can be reached along dusty tracks, but it is currently closed to all but the archelogists working there. Also worth a visit is the site of **Cerro Mulato**, near the hill town of **Chongoyape**, 80km out of Chiclayo along the attractive Chancay Valley. From Chongoyape, another dirt road traces an alternative route through the desert to Cerro Mulato. Here you can see some impressive Chavín **petroglyphs**, and in the surrounding region, a number of Chavín graves dating from the fifth century BC.

Reserva Nacional Chaparrí

Entry S/10 per person, guide for a 3hr tour S/50 for 1–10 people; the lodge costs S/700 for one night, S/1200 for two nights for two people, includes a local Spanish-speaking guide and all meals • Buses to Chongoyape leave Chiclayo from the Epsel terminal (S/5; 1hr 20min), tell the driver you are going to Chaparrí and he will let you off at Aroturch, the reserve's main administrative office. Alternatively, and more comfortably, the reserve can organize transport for S/480 for the round trip to Chiclayo.

Chaparrí was Peru's first privately owned reserve in 1999, and is an inspiring example of a community-run project making great strides in protecting communal land and changing local attitudes on the value of conservation. Set in over 34,000 hectares of land owned by the local community, Chaparrí is a birdwatchers' paradise, with over 250

7

THE SICÁN CULTURE

The **Sicán culture**, thought to descend from the Mochica (see p.482), is associated with the Naymlap dynasty, based on a wide-reaching political confederacy emanating from the Lambayeque Valley between around 800 and 1300 AD. These people produced alloys of gold, silver and arsenic-copper on a scale unprecedented in pre-Hispanic America. The name Sicán actually means "House of the Moon" in the Mochica language. Legend has it that a leader called **Naymlap** arrived by sea with a fleet of balsa boats, his own royal retinue and a green female stone idol. Naymlap set about building temples and palaces near the sea in the Lambayeque Valley. The region was then successfully governed by Naymlap's twelve grandsons, until one of them was tempted by a witch to move the green stone idol. Legend has it that this provoked a month of heavy rains and flash floods, rather like the effects of El Niño today, bringing great disease and death in its wake. Indeed, glacial ice cores analysed in the Andes above here have indicated the likelihood of a powerful El Niño current around 1100 AD.

The Sicán civilization, like the Mochica, depended on a high level of **irrigation technology**. The civilization also had its own copper money and sophisticated ceramics, many of which featured an image of the flying **Lord of Sicán**. The main thrust of the Lord of Sicán designs is a well-dressed man, possibly Naymlap himself, with small wings, a nose like a bird's beak and, sometimes, talons rather than feet. The Sicán culture showed a marked change in its burial practices from that of the Mochica, almost certainly signifying a change in the prevalent belief in an afterlife. While the Mochica people were buried in a lying position – like the Mochica warrior in his splendid tomb at Sipán (see opposite) – the new Sicán style was to inter its dead in a sitting position. Excavations of Sicán sites in the last decade have also revealed such rare artefacts as 22 "tumis" (semicircular bladed ceremonial knives with an anthropomorphic figure stabbing where a handle should be).

The Sicán monetary system, the flying Lord of Sicán image and much of the culture's religious and political infrastructures were all abandoned after the dramatic environmental disasters caused by El Niño around 1100 AD. **Batán Grande**, the culture's largest and most impressive city, was partly washed away, and a fabulous new centre, a massive city of over twenty adobe pyramids at **Túcume** (see p.403), was constructed in the Leche Valley. This relatively short-lived culture was taken over by Chimu warriors from the south around 1370 AD, who absorbed the Lambayeque Valley, some of the Piura Valley area and about two-thirds of the Peruvian desert coast into their empire.

endemic species to be found within its boundaries and seventy endemic species. Among the various terrestrial inhabitants, the stars are the spectacled bears, reintroduced to the region here in the reserve, and although most of the population is scattered a day's hike or more away, it is possible you'll be able to see some in the recuperation area where rescued bears are prepared for reintroduction into the wild. For the really persistent and lucky, there are a few puma and ocelot around, although they are mostly only seen by the local camera traps. Accommodation is available in luxurious rustic cabins with adobe walls and bamboo ceilings, and a stay of a few nights is simply the best way to enjoy the peace and beauty of Peru's least-known ecosystem.

Ferreñafe and around

Combis to Ferreñafe leave Chiclayo from the Epsel terminal and colectivo cars leave from C Leoncio Prado 1159 and Av Sáenz Peña (20min; S/2.50). From town, a mototaxi gets you to the museum (10min; S/1.50).

Founded in 1550 by Captain Alfonso de Osorio, **FERREÑAFE**, 18km northeast of Chiclayo, was once known as the "land of two faiths" because of the local tradition of believing first in the power of spirits and second in the Catholic Church. Curiously, Ferreñafe is also home to more Miss Peru winners than any other town in the country.

Museo Nacional de Sicán

Tues–Sun 9am–5pm · S/8 · ☎ 074 286 469

Ferreñafe is best known for its excellent **Museo Nacional de Sicán**, which has an audiovisual introduction and a large collection of exhibits, mostly models depicting daily life and burials of the Sicán people (see box, p.401), a great way to get a visual concept before or after visiting the local archeological sites themselves. One central room is full of genuine treasures, including the famous ceremonial headdresses and masks.

Santuario Historico Bosque de Pomac

Daily 8am–6pm · S/10, a guide from the interpretative centre, through the forest and to the *huacas*, S/30 · Interpretative centre ☎ 074 286 182

The site at **BATÁN GRANDE** inside the forest sanctuary, 57km northeast of Chiclayo, incorporates over twenty pre-Inca temple pyramids within one corner of what extends to the largest dry forest in the Americas, the **Bosque de Pomac**. There's an **interpretative centre** at the main entrance, which has a small archeological museum with a scale model of the site.

Part of the beauty of this site comes from its sitting at the heart of an ancient forest, dominated by *algarrobo* trees, spreading out over some 13,400 hectares, a veritable oasis in the middle of the desert landscape. Over ninety percent of Peru's ancient gold artefacts are estimated to have come from here – you'll notice there are thousands of holes, dug over the centuries by treasure hunters. Batán Grande is also known to have developed its own copper-smelting works, which produced large quantities of flat copper plates – *naipes* – that were between 5 and 10cm long. These were believed to have been used and exported to Ecuador as a kind of monetary system.

Brief history

The **Sicán culture** arose to fill the void left by the demise of the Mochica culture around 700 AD (see box, p.401), and were the driving force in the region from 800 to 1100 AD, based here at Batán Grande. Known to archeologists as the Initial Lambayeque Period, this era was clearly a flourishing one judging by the beauty and extent of the pyramids here. Nevertheless, Batán Grande was abandoned in the twelfth century and the Sicán moved across the valley to Túcume (see p.403), probably following a deluge of rains (El Niño) causing devastation, epidemics and a lack of faith in the power of the ruling elite. This fits neatly with the legend of the Sicán leader Naymlap's descendants, who evidently brought this on themselves by sacrilegious behaviour. There is also some evidence that the pyramids were deliberately burnt, supporting the latter theory.

The site

The main part of the **site** that you visit today was mostly built between 750 and 1250 AD, and comprises the Huaca el Oro, Huaca Rodillona, Huaca Corte and the Huaca Las Ventanas, where the famous **Tumi de Oro** was uncovered in 1936. The tomb of **El Señor de Sicán** (not to be confused with the tomb of El Señor de Sipán; see p.400), on the north side of the Huaca l Oro, contained a noble with two women, two children and five golden crowns; these are exhibited in the excellent **museum** (see opposite) in Ferreñafe. From the top of these pyramids you can just about make out the form of the ancient ceremonial plaza on the ground below.

Bosque de Pomac

The **Pomac Forest** is the largest dry forest in western South America. A kilometre or so in from the interpretative centre you'll find the oldest *algarrobo* tree in the forest, the **árbol milenario**; over 500 years old, its spreading, gnarled mass is still the site for pagan rituals, judging from the offerings hanging from its twisted boughs, but it's also the focus of the **Fiesta de las Cruces** on May 3. The reserve is home to over forty species of bird such as mockingbirds, cardinals, burrowing owls and humming birds, and most visitors at least see some iguanas and lizards scuttling into the undergrowth. Rarer, but still present, are wild foxes, deer and anteaters. There's also a **mirador** (viewing platform) in the heart of the forest, from where it's possible to make out many of the larger *huacas*. Although there is hostel accommodation at the interpretative centre, it's rarely available or open: you'll have to turn up and chance it. There is a camping area outside, however. The café here, selling basic snacks, is not always functioning, so bring a picnic.

7

ARRIVAL AND TOURS	SANTUARIO HISTORICO BOSQUE DE POMAC

By car Take the new northern road from Ferreñafe to reach Batán Grande; it's a 15–20min drive. There are two routes into the forest; one passes the interpretative centre, while another goes via Huaca el Oro, and comes from the nearby village of Illimo, the next settlement north of Túcume. You'll need a decent car, preferably but not essentially 4WD, and a local driver or good map. If you take this route you'll be rewarded by close contact with small, scattered desert communities, mainly goat herders and peasant farmers, many of whose houses are still built out of adobe and lath. **By colectivo** Combis to Batán Grande pueblo (10km beyond the site) leave from the Epsel terminal in Chiclayo (40min; S/4) – go as early as possible and ask to be dropped at the interpretative centre.
Tours To visit the site in just one day, it's best to take a guided tour from Chiclayo or Ferreñafe.

Túcume

Daily 9am–5pm, though in reality the site is not fenced off and so accessible 24hr • Cost varies depending on the route chosen: Route A museum and *mirador* S/8; Route B museum and Huaca las Balsas S/8; Route C covering all three for S/10

The site of **TÚCUME**, also known as the **Valley of the Pyramids**, contains 26 adobe pyramids, many clustered around the hill of **El Purgatorio** (197m), also known as Cerro La Raya (after a ray fish that lives within it, according to legend), and is located some 33km north from Chiclayo. Although the ticket office closes at 4.30pm and the museum shortly after this, the site is accessible after these hours (being part of the local landscape and dissected by small paths connecting villages and homesteads), with the main sectors clearly marked by good interpretative signs.

Túcume's modern settlement, based alongside the old Panamerican Highway, lies just a couple of kilometres west of the Valley of the Pyramids, and doesn't have much to offer visitors except a handful of accommodation and eating options (see p.406).

Brief history

Covering more than two hundred hectares, Túcume was occupied initially by the **Sicán culture**, which began building here around 1100 AD after abandoning Batán Grande (see p.402). During this time, known as the Second Lambayeque Period, the focus of

7

construction moved to Túcume where an elite controlled a complex administrative system and cleared large areas of *algarrobo* forest (as is still the case today in the immediate vicinity of the Valley of the Pyramids and Cerro El Purgatorio at Túcume). Reed seafaring vessels were also essential for the development of this new, powerful elite. The Sicán people were clearly expert **seamen** and traded along the coast as far as Ecuador, Colombia and quite probably Central America; to the east, they traded with the sierra and the jungle regions beyond. They were also expert **metallurgists** working with gold, silver, copper and precious stones, and their elaborate funerary masks are astonishingly vivid and beautiful.

At Túcume's peak, in the thirteenth and early fourteenth centuries, it was probably a focus of annual pilgrimage for a large section of the coastal population, whose Sicán

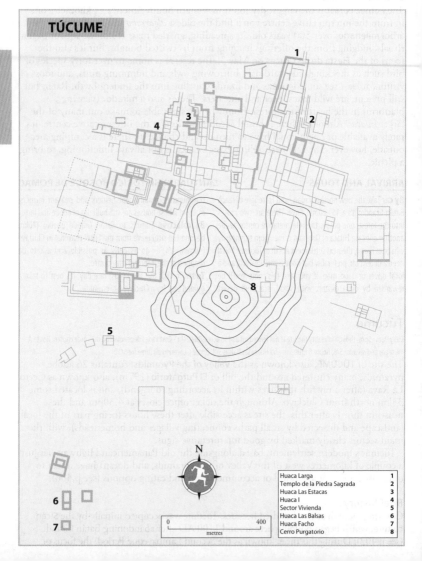

TÚCUME

Huaca Larga	1
Templo de la Piedra Sagrada	2
Huaca Las Estacas	3
Huaca I	4
Sector Vivienda	5
Huaca Las Balsas	6
Huaca Facho	7
Cerro Purgatorio	8

0 — 400
metres

leaders were high priests with great agro-astrological understanding, adept administrators, a warrior elite, and expert artisans.

It wasn't long, however, before things changed, and around 1375 AD the **Chimu** invaded from the south. Within another hundred years the **Inca** had arrived, though they took some twenty years to conquer the Chimu, during which time it appears that Túcume played an important role in the ensuing military, magical and diplomatic intrigues. Afterwards, the Inca transported many Chimu warriors to remote outposts in the Andes, in order to maximize the Incas' political control and minimize the chances of rebellion. By the time the **Spanish** arrived, just over half a century later, Túcume's time had already passed. When the Spanish chronicler, Pedro Cieza de León, stopped here in 1547, it was already in ruins and abandoned.

The site

From Túcume's plaza, follow the right-hand road to the site; it's a dusty 2km walk. Alternatively, take a mototaxi or combi colectivo for S/2. At the end of the fields, the road divides: right leads to the museum and ticket office

Today, Túcume remains an extensive site with the labyrinthine ruins of walls and courtyards still quite visible, if slightly rain-washed by the impact of heavy El Niño weather cycles, and you can easily spend two or three hours exploring. The site has two clearly defined sectors: North is characterized by the large monumental structures; South has predominantly simpler structures and common graveyards. The adobe bricks utilized were loaf-shaped, each with their maker's mark, indicating control and accounting for labour and tribute to the elite. Some of the pyramids – most notably Huaca Las Balsas – have up to seven phases of construction, showing that building went on more or less continuously.

El Purgatorio hill

There's a **viewing point**, reached by a twisting path that leads up **El Purgatorio hill**, from where you can get a good view of the whole city. This hill, circular and cone-shaped, at the very centre of the occupied area, was and still is considered by locals to be a sacred mountain. Access to it was restricted originally, though there is evidence of later Inca constructions, for example an altar site. It is still visited these days by the local *curanderos*, healing wizards who utilize shamanic techniques and the psychoactive San Pedro cactus in their weekly rituals, which researchers believe are similar to those of their ancestors and which could be one possible explanation for the name El Purgatorio (the place of the purge).

Museo di Sitio

Daily 9am–5pm • ☎ 074 830 250, ⊕ museodesitiotucume.com

The **Museo de Sitio**, at the entrance to the site, has exhibits relating to the work of **Thor Heyerdahl**, who found in Túcume the inspiration for his *Kon Tiki* expedition in 1946 when he sailed a raft built in the style of ancient Peruvian boats from Callao, near Lima, right across the Pacific Ocean to Polynesia, as he tried to prove a link between civilizations on either side of the Pacific. The museum also covers the work of archeologist Wendell Bennett, who in the late 1930s was the first person to excavate scientifically at the site. More esoterically, Túcume has a local reputation for **magical power**, and a section of the museum has been devoted to a display of local *curanderismo*. There's also an attractive picnic area, and a ceramic workshop where they use 2500-year-old techniques. The museum was constructed to reflect the style – known as *la ramada* – of colonial chapels in this region, built by local indigenous craftsmen centuries ago and using much the same materials.

ARRIVAL AND INFORMATION   TÚCUME

By colectivo From Lambayeque, take a combi from the market on the Panamericana Norte (15min; S/2.50). From Chiclayo, take one of the colectivos marked "Túcume" (45min; S/2.50), which leave every 30min or so from a yard on Las Amapolas, just off block 13 of Av Leguía and near the Óvalo de Pescador.

Tourist information Well-signposted tourist information centre (daily 8am–5pm) on the main road, Av Federico Villareal, just before the turn-off to the plaza.

ACCOMMODATION AND EATING

Hospedaje Las Balsas Augusto B Leguía 149 ☎074 422 056. Cheap decor and furnishings match the low price, but the rooms are clean and have fans, wi-fi and private bathrooms. Just two blocks from the plaza, a perfect choice for overnighting near the ruins. S̲/50̲

Hospedaje Rural Los Horcones North of Túcume archeological site ☎951 831 705, ⓦloshorconesde tucume.com. Luxurious rooms plus camping sites, shower blocks and local home-cooked food available here;

buildings are constructed with traditional materials in a style reflecting that of the pyramid site next door. A very good breakfast is included. Doubles S̲/360̲, camping S̲/30̲

Restaurant Campestre On the road to the Museo di Sitio ☎949 811 602. This rural restaurant is all that's great about eating in Peru. Plastic chairs under a woven bamboo roof, a friendly, lively atmosphere and big plates of unbeatably tasty food. Try going in a group, so you can try lots of different dishes, or just get the spit-roasted pig. Mon–Sat 9am–5.30pm.

DIRECTORY

Money and exchange The only places to change money in town are the Banco de la Nación, half a block south of the plaza, and the Ferretería Don José, just before the police station and petrol garage at the northern end of town.

Shamanic healing This is a strong local tradition and one renowned healer, Don Victor Bravo, who helped to design

the shamanic section of the museum's exhibits (see p.405), lives very close to the ruins of Túcume; anyone seriously interested in participating in one of his *mesa* ceremonies (see box below) could try asking for an introduction through the *Hospedaje Rural Los Horcones* (see above).

Túcume Viejo

Turn left along the sand track at the fork in the road just before you get to Túcume's site museum (30min walk)

Although there are no tourist facilities as such, the Túcume ruins in the village of **Túcume Viejo**, less than 2km from Lambayeque, make for an interesting walk. Check out the crumbling colonial adobe walls and a once-painted adobe brick gateway as well as the church, all of which have an elegant and rather grandiose feel, suggesting perhaps that the early colonists were trying to compete for attention with the Valley of the Pyramids.

Piura

The city of **PIURA** feels very distinct from the rest of the country, cut off to the south by the formidable Sechura Desert, and to the east by the Huancabamba mountains. **Francisco Pizarro** spent ten days in Piura in 1532 en route to his fateful meeting with the Inca overlord, Atahualpa, at Cajamarca (see box, p.373). By 1534 the city, then known as **San Miguel de Piura**, had well over two hundred Spanish inhabitants,

---

HEALING SESSIONS IN SALAS

Salas is known locally as the capital of folklore medicine on the coast of Peru. Here the ancient traditions of **curanderismo** are so strong that it's the major source of income for the village. Most nights of the week, but especially Tuesdays and Fridays, there'll be healing sessions going on in at least one of the houses in the village, generally starting around 10pm and ending at roughly 4am. The sessions, or *mesas*, are based on the ingestion of the hallucinogenic **San Pedro cactus** and other natural plants or herbs, and they do cost money (anything up to US$200 a night, though the amount is usually fixed and can be divided between as many as five to ten participants). Combining healing with divination, the *curanderos* utilize techniques and traditions handed down from generation to generation from the ancient Sicán culture.

Salas is 20min by car from Túcume; take a back road for 17km off the old Panamerican Highway at Km 47 (27km north of Túcume). To contact a *curandero* about participating in a session, the best bet is to ask a local tour operator, or a trustworthy taxi driver from Túcume, to take you to the village one afternoon to see what can be arranged.

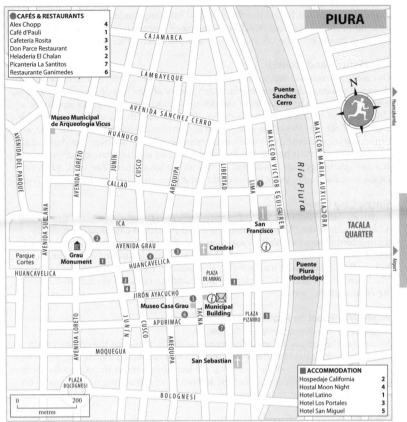

CAFÉS & RESTAURANTS	
Alex Chopp	4
Café d'Pauli	1
Cafetería Rosita	3
Don Parce Restaurant	5
Heladería El Chalan	2
Picantería La Santitos	7
Restaurante Ganímedes	6

ACCOMMODATION	
Hospedaje California	2
Hostal Moon Night	4
Hotel Latino	1
Hotel Los Portales	3
Hotel San Miguel	5

including the first Spanish women to arrive in Peru. As early as the 1560s, there was a flourishing trade in the excellent indigenous **Tanguis cotton**, and Piura today still produces a third of the nation's cotton.

The city has a strong oasis atmosphere, entirely dependent on the vagaries of the **Río Piura** – known colloquially since Pizarro's time as the Río Loco, or Crazy River. At only 29m above sea level, modern **Piura** is divided by a sometimes dry riverbed. Most of the action and all the main sights are on the west bank. With temperatures of up to 38°C (100°F) from January to March, the region is known for its particularly wide-brimmed, finely woven straw sombreros, worn by everyone from the mayor to local goat-herders. You'll have plenty of opportunities to see these in **Semana de Piura** (first two weeks of Oct), when the town is in high spirits. Sweaty and easy-going, Piura is fine as a stopover, but most travellers arrive with the beach in their sights, and would be forgiven for moving rapidly along.

Plaza de Armas

The spacious and attractive **Plaza de Armas** is shaded by tall tamarind trees planted well over a hundred years ago. On the plaza you'll find a "Statue of Liberty", also known as *La Pola* (The Pole), and the **Catedral de Piura** (Mon–Fri 7am–8pm, Sat & Sun 8am–noon; free), where the town's poorest folk tend to beg. Though not especially beautiful, the cathedral boasts impressive bronze nails decorating its main doors, and inside, the spectacularly tasteless gilt altars and intricate wooden pulpit are worth a look. Surrounding the plaza, you'll see some pastel-coloured, low, colonial buildings that clash madly with the tall, modern glass-and-concrete office buildings nearby.

Plaza Pizarro and around

One block towards the river from the Plaza de Armas, along Jirón Ayacucho, a delightful elongated square, called **Plaza Pizarro**, is also known as the Plaza de Tres Culturas. Every evening the Piurans promenade up and down here, chatting beneath tall shady trees. One block east of here is the Río Piura, usually little more than a trickle of water with a few piles of rubbish plus white egrets, gulls and terns searching for food. The riverbed is large, however, indicating that when Piura's rare rains arrive, the river rises dramatically; people who build their homes too close to the dry bed regularly have them washed away. Puente Piura bridge connects central Piura with the less aesthetic east-bank quarter of **Tacala**, renowned principally for the quality and strength of its fermented *chicha* beer.

Museo Casa Grau

Tacna 662 • Mon–Fri 8am–1pm & 3–6pm, Sat & Sun 8am–noon • S/2 • ☎ 073 326 541

A block south of the Plaza de Armas, you'll find the **Museo Casa Grau**, nineteenth-century birthplace of **Admiral Miguel Grau**, one of the heroes of the War of the Pacific (1879–80), in which Chile took control of Peru's valuable nitrate fields in the south and cut Bolivia's access to the Pacific. The museum, a reconstruction of the house which was destroyed in a 1912 earthquake, includes a model of the British-built ship, the *Huascar*, Peru's only successful blockade runner, as well as various military artefacts.

Museo Municipal de Arqueologia Vicús

Av Sullana and Jr Huánuco • Mon–Sat 9am–5pm, Sun 9am–1pm • S/4

An array of the region's archeological treasures, and in particular the ceramics from Cerro Vicus, is displayed at the **Museo Municipal de Arqueologia Vicús**, one block west of Avenida Loreto. One of the rooms has artefacts uncovered at the necropolis Vicús at Chulucanas, another is dedicated to the archeology of metallurgy, and another to 64 ancient gold objects, including jewellery, cups and pincers.

The market

One block north of Av Sánchez Cerro • Best Mon–Sat 6.30–11am

The town's daily **market**, in the north of the city, is worth a visit for its straw hats (see p.407), well made in Santo Domingo, and ceramics from the villages of Chulucanas and Simbila, plus a variety of leather crafts.

ARRIVAL AND DEPARTURE   **PIURA**

BY PLANE

Piura airport (☎ 073 344 503) is 2km east of the city. The LAN Perú office is in the Plaza Vea at the Real Plaza shopping centre on Av Sánchez Cerro (☎ 977 295 338) and Peruvian Airlines at C Libertad 777 (☎ 073 322 385). A taxi into the centre costs S/10–15.

Destinations Lima (2 daily; 2hr); Trujillo (1 daily; 1hr).

BY BUS

El Dorado buses from Trujillo and Tumbes, Dorado Express buses from Tumbes, Sullana and Aguas Verdes and Transporte Chiclayo buses all arrive around blocks 11 and 12 of Av Sánchez Cerro. All other buses arrive at their companies' offices (see below).

Bus companies CIAL, Bolognesi 817 (☎ 073 304 250),

for Huaraz, Lima and Tumbes; CIFA, Av Loreto 1485 (☎ 972 894 616) for Machala and Guayaquil; Cruz del Sur, Circunvalación 160, with an office at the corner of Bolognesi with Lima (bus passes both on way through town), just a few blocks south of the Plaza de Armas in the centre (☎ 073 337 094), for Lima and the coast; Empresa de Transporte LOJA, Av Loreto 1241 (☎ 073 333 260); Emtrafesa, Los Naranjos 255, Urb Club Grau (☎ 073 337 093), for Chiclayo, Trujillo and Tumbes; EPPO, Av Panamericana 243 (☎ 073 304 543 or ☎ 969 633 355), the usual choice for Talara, Los Organos and Máncora, but often without a/c; Linea, Av Sánchez Cerro 1215 (☎ 073 327 821), for Chiclayo, Trujillo and Tumbes; Tepsa, Av Loreto 1195 (☎ 073 306 345), for Trujillo and Tumbes; Transportes Chiclayo, Av Sánchez Cerro 1121 (☎ 073 308 455) the most reliable and frequent to Chiclayo; Turismo Díaz, Av

Loreto 1485 (☎ 073 302 834) for Cajamarca and Tarapoto. **Destinations** Cajamarca (daily; 9hr); Chiclayo (every 30min; 3hr); Guayaquil (4 daily; 10hr); Huancabamba (2–3 daily; 12hr); La Tina and Loja (4 daily; 10–12hr); Lima (8 daily; 13–15hrs); Loja, Ecuador (2 daily; 8–9hr;) Talara and Máncora (every 30min; 1hr 30min–3hr); Tarapoto (daily;

18hr); Trujillo (3 daily; 6–7hr); Tumbes (8 daily; 4–6hr).

BY COLECTIVO

Colectivos, mainly for Tumbes and Talara, arrive and depart from the middle of the road at block 11 of Av Sánchez Cerro, a 10min stroll from the centre of town.

GETTING AROUND AND INFORMATION

By mototaxi The quickest way of getting around the city is by the ubiquitous mototaxi, which you can hail just about anywhere for S/2.

By taxi In-town taxi rides are set at around S/4; or call Taxi Seguro ☎ 073 676 800.

Tourist information The best choice is iPeru at Jr

Ayacucho and C Libertad just off the corner of the plaza (Mon–Sat 9am–6pm, Sun 9am–1pm; ☎ 073 320 249). Local tour operators (see below) can also be of some use.

Tour operators Piura Tours, C Arequipa 978 (☎ 073 326 778); Domiruth Travel Service, C Ayacucho 560 (☎ 073 321 926).

ACCOMMODATION

A wide range of hotels and hostels are spread throughout the town, with most of the cheaper ones on or around Av Loreto or within a few blocks of Av Grau and the Plaza de Armas.

Hospedaje California Junín 837 ☎ 073 301 673. A family-run establishment, brightly painted and decorated with plastic flowers, giving it a somewhat kitschy feel. It's good value and popular with backpackers; private baths with cold water, ceiling fans and wi-fi. **S/60**

Hostal Moon Night Junín 899 ☎ 073 336 174. Hotels with this kind of name in Peru are generally aiming for the lovers' market, but it's still comfortable and pretty central, offering more than average mod cons and clean, spacious rooms with private bath and TV. **S/60**

★ **Hotel Latino** Huancavelica 720 ☎ 073 335 114, ✉ hoslatino@hotmail.com. A large, fairly modern establishment, *Latino* is centrally located close to good breakfast and dinner options and a supermarket a few

blocks away. All the usual facilities, including fan, TV and wi-fi. The staff at reception are particularly helpful and accommodating. **S/90**

Hotel Los Portales C Libertad 875 ☎ 073 321 161, ⓦ hotelportalespiura.com. A luxury hotel set in a lovely old building; the best rooms are around an internal courtyard, but all are first rate, if overpriced. The restaurant with tall glass doors overlooks the pool and makes for a great place to breakfast. **S/470**

Hotel San Miguel Lima 1007, and Apurímac ☎ 073 305 122. A decently priced, unstylish but comfortable hotel including some rooms with a view of the plaza. There's also a cafetería and all rooms have private baths with good hot water, wi-fi, a/c and TVs. **S/110**

EATING AND DRINKING

Most of Piura's restaurants and cafés are near the Plaza de Armas, with many of the cafés specializing in delicious ice cream. Piura's speciality is a very sweet toffee-like delicacy, called *natilla*, bought from street stalls around the city. There's a supermarket, good for general provisions, by the Grau monument. In the evenings, you'll find most Piurans strolling around the main streets, mingling in the plazas and drinking in the cheap bars along the roads around Junín.

Alex Chopp Huancavelica 538 ☎ 073 332 538. A popular venue with a friendly atmosphere, serving good draught beers and fine seafood all day. Ceviche S/32–42. Daily 10am–10pm.

Café d'Pauli Lima 541 ☎ 073 322 210. A small but smart café serving pricey but delicious ice creams, cakes, teas and coffee; don't miss their lemon pie (S/7) and their cheesecake (S/8). Daily 9am–8pm.

Cafetería Rosita Av Grau 223. Dishes up heavenly sandwiches and green tamales, and has a few veggie options as well as great breakfasts. Daily 7.30am–9pm.

Don Parce Restaurant C Tacna 646 ☎ 073 300 842. A graceful old building just off the plaza, with three small but sunlit rooms that buzz over lunch thanks to a great menu of local classics (average S/30); particularly well known for their

roast pork sandwiches (S/12) and the *ronda criolla* a mix of four different traditional northern dishes (S/48). Daily 7.30am–11pm.

Heladería El Chalan Av Grau 452. Excellent service in a bright and busy atmosphere; a great choice for breakfast (S/9–14), or try their sandwiches, juices and ice creams. They also have a newer place behind the cathedral. Daily 8am–11pm.

Picantería La Santitos C La Libertad 1001 ☎ 073 309 475. This place serves a good choice of traditional creole dishes such *as majado de yuca* (mashed *yuca* with pieces of pork), *seco de chavelo* (mashed plantain with pieces of beef), both a bargain at S/18, and of course, a great ceviche, in a renovated colonial house. Daily 10am–6.30pm.

Restaurante Ganímedes C Apurímac 468. The best

7

restaurant in town for vegetarian meals; try the stuffed avocados or the Locro de Zapallo (a pumpkin stew flavoured with Peruvian yello chili). Lunch menu S/8. Friendly service, but cash only. Mon–Sat 10.30am–5pm.

DIRECTORY

Internet There's a large, busy internet café at Sánchez Cerro 265 (daily 9am–11pm).

Money and exchange The Banco Continental is on the Plaza de Armas, at the corner of Ayacucho and Tacna. *Cambistas* are at block 7 of Av Arequipa, near the corner of Av Grau; but a safer best are the casas de cambio between blocks 4 and 7 of Av Arequia.

Police Av Sánchez Cerro block 12 (☎ 072 307 641).

Post office Plaza de Armas, on the corner of C Libertad and Ayacucho (Mon–Sat 8am–4pm).

Catacaos

Just 12km south of Piura is the friendly, dusty little town of **CATACAOS**, worth a visit principally for its excellent, vast **market** (best at weekends 10am–4pm). Just off the main plaza, the market sells everything from food to crafts, even filigree gold- and silver-work, with the colourful hammocks hanging about the square being a particularly good buy. The town is renowned locally for its **picanterías** (traditional restaurants), which serve all sorts of local delicacies, such as *tamalitos verdes* (little green-corn pancakes), fish-balls, *chifles* (plantain chips), goat (*seco de cabrito*) and the local *chicha* beer. While you're here you could also try a Peruvian favourite, particularly common here, *algarrobina*, a sweet syrup usually used as a honey substitute its often mixed into fruit smoothies. Made from the seed pods of the tree that dominates the northern desert, the *algarrobo*, a type of carob, it is reputed to have various health benefits and is available from bars and street stalls.

ARRIVAL AND DEPARTURE   CATACAOS

By colectivo Regular combi colectivos for Catacaos leave Piura when full, usually every 20min or so (S/1.50; 20min), from block 12 of Av Sánchez Cerro, or from Av Loreto 1292 and Tumbes.

EATING

La Chayo San Francisco 493 (near the church). Most locals agree that this is one of the best places to get your teeth into Piura cuisine, which tends to be seafood-heavy, but they also do a fair bit of turkey and, like most of the

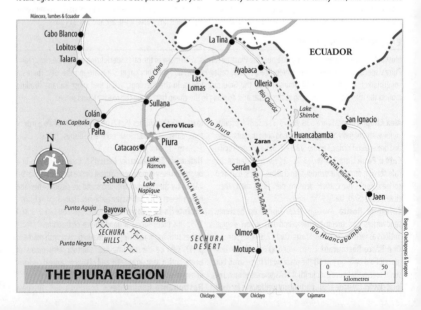

THE PIURA REGION

HOW PIZARRO FOUND ATAHUALPA

It was at Serran, then a small Inca administrative centre in the hills above Piura, that Francisco **Pizarro** waited in 1532 for the return of a small troop of soldiers he had sent up the Inca Royal Highway on a discovery mission. It took the soldiers, led by **Hernando de Soto**, just two days and a night to reach the town of Cajas, now lost in the region around Huancabamba and Lake Shimbe.

At Cajas, the Spaniards gained their first insight into the grandeur and power of the Inca Empire, although, under orders from Atahualpa, the town's two thousand-warrior Inca garrison had slunk away into the mountains. The Spanish were not slow to discover the most impressive Inca buildings – a sacred convent of over five hundred virgins who had been chosen at an early age to dedicate their lives to the Inca religion. The soldiers raped at will, provoking the Inca diplomat who was accompanying De Soto to threaten the troops with death for such sacrilege, telling them they were only 300km from Atahualpa's camp at Cajamarca. This information about Atahualpa's whereabouts was exactly what De Soto had been seeking. After a brief visit to the adjacent, even more impressive, Inca town of Huancabamba – where a tollgate collected duties along the Royal Highway – he returned with the Inca diplomat to rejoin Pizarro. Realizing that he had provided the Spanish with vital information, the Inca diplomat agreed to take them to Atahualpa's camp – a disastrous decision resulting in the massacre at Cajamarca (see box, p.373).

northern region, use a lot of goat and duck, often accompanied by plantain in various forms and frequently cooked with *cilantro*. *La Chayo* still cooks over wood fires, adding an extra smoky flavour. Don't miss the *chicha* – this fermented maize beer is an acquired taste, but can be quite good if well made and fresh. Daily 10am–6pm.

Sullana

Leaving Piura, the Panamericana Norte heads directly north, passing through the large town of **SULLANA** after 40km. This major transport junction has little of interest to travellers, except to connect with the inland route up into the mountains to La Tina and Ecuador. If you do stop, take a quick look at the **Plaza de Armas**, which boasts fine views over the Río Chira, and is the location for the old church of La Santísima Trinidad.

ARRIVAL AND DEPARTURE

By bus EPPO, C Nicolás de Piérola 257 (☎073 502 522; ⓦwww.eppo.com.pe) runs buses every 30 min to Máncora (via Talara, 3hrs) and Piura (40min).
By colectivo There are regular combis from Av Lama to Piura, while the faster colectivos cost slightly more. Combis for the inland border crossing with Ecuador (see p.423) at La Tina leave in the morning from Av Buenos Aires and Calle 4 (several daily; 2hr).

Talara and Lobitos

TALARA, 70km further north, has been ruined by recent growth – the trees and cliffs are dotted with plastic bags, fertilizer plants cut the skyline and the smell near the port is overpowering. Until 1940, it was no more than a small fishing hamlet, though its deep-water harbour and tar pits had been used since Pizarro's time for caulking wooden ships. Pizarro had chosen the site for the first Spanish settlement in Peru, but it proved too unhealthy and he was forced to look elsewhere, eventually hitting on Piura (see p.406). Talara's **oil reserves**, which you'll see being worked on- and off-shore along the coast, were directly responsible for Peru's last military coup in 1968. President Belaunde, in his first term of office, had given subsoil concessions to the multinational company IPC, declaring that "if this is foreign imperialism what we need is more, not less of it." A curious logic, it led to the accusation that he had signed an agreement "unacceptable to true Peruvians". Within two months of the affair, and as a direct consequence, he was deposed and exiled. The new revolutionary government nationalized IPC and declared the Act of Talara null and void.

The only real reason to get off in Talara is to head on to the isolated surf enclave of **LOBITOS** twenty minutes further up the coast. A collection of hotels and a few basic places to eat line the shore. The beach receives some day-visitors from Talara, but is mostly filled with surfers lazing about, eyes fixed on the waves. Non-surfers, bring a good book and enjoy the peace and quiet. The fishermen at the pier sometimes take people out for S/25.

ARRIVAL AND DEPARTURE   TALARA AND LOBITOS

Take the EPPO bus to Talara from Piura (2hr) or Sullana (1hr 20min). From the Talara terminal, buses leave all day back to Piura (S/9) and up the coast to El Alto (for Cabo Blanco), Los Organos and Máncora (1hr 30min; S/7.50). Colectivos to Lobitos are across the fruit market, while combis leave from near the flower market (S/4). Mototaxis waiting outside the EPPO station will enthusiastically offer to take you for S/25.

ACCOMMODATION AND EATING

Eating options are basic, but the fish is generally fresh. Try a local place near the pier or stick to the hotels.

★**La Casona** Up on the hill overlooking the beach ☎973 416 737, ⓦcasonadelobitos.com. The patio of this sprawling, slightly run-down, but charming old wooden house has the best views over the beach and the waves. There is a very laidback and friendly collective vibe, drawing surfers and travellers from all over. Dorms S/25, doubles S/60

Hotel Relajate Nuevo Lobitos beach ☎946 318 240. With Its feet in the sand, this is the best-set-up budget place on the beach. They have a small shop and money exchange, a decent restaurant and board rental. Dorms S/30, doubles S/80

Lobitos Lodge Nuevo Lobitos beach ☎991 702 989, ⓦlobitoslodge.com.pe. Spacious and stylish rooms in a compound right on the beach, this is affordable luxury away from it all. S/180

Cabo Blanco

Thirty kilometres or so north of Talara, there's a turning off the highway to the old fishing hotspot of **CABO BLANCO**. Thomas Stokes, a British resident and fanatical fisherman, discovered the place in 1935, and it was a very popular resort in the postwar years. **Hemingway** stayed for a month in 1951 while filming parts of *Old Man and the Sea*, while two years later the largest fish ever caught with a rod was landed here – a 710-kilo black marlin. While the fishing has declined continuously since those glory days, and the famous Cabo Blanco fishing club that housed the celebrities has long since closed down, it is still worth casting a line out there. Most tourism in Cabo Blanco these days, however, is from surfers looking to ride its famous left tube.

From here to Tumbes the Panamericana cuts across a further stretch of desert, for the most part keeping tightly to the Pacific coastline. It's a straight road, except for the occasional detour around bridges destroyed by the 1998 El Niño. To the right of the road looms a long hill, the **Cerros de Amotape**, named after a local chief whom Pizarro had killed in 1532 as an example to potential rebels.

ARRIVAL AND DEPARTURE   CABO BLANCO

Located just over halfway between Talara and Máncora at Km 1137 of the Panamericana Norte, take the EPPO bus from Piura to El Alto (3hr). From here, 50m ahead, white minivans run into Cabo Blanco every 20min, 7am–7pm; S/2.

ACCOMMODATION AND EATING

Hotel El Merlin Km 1136.5, Cabo Blanco ☎073 256 188, ⓦelmerlin.webs.com. A really nice place right on the beach, with stone floors, bamboo and *estera* (reeds) for the nine rooms overlooking the ocean. There's wi-fi and cable TV, kayaks available for use and excellent boat-based fishing trips arranged. S/140

Restaurante Cabo Blanco Km 1136.5, Cabo Blanco. Just 50m from *Hotel El Merlin*, this place has the best reputation locally for seafood; try the superb ceviches. Daily, lunch only.

Máncora

🌐 vivamancora.com

Once just an attractive roadside fishing port, **MÁNCORA** is now the most fashionable beach in Peru, attracting an international surf crowd. It's a highly welcome and very enjoyable stopover when travelling along the north coast, well served by public transport, and spread out along the Panamericana, parallel to a beautiful sandy beach.

As the highway passes through town, it is first Avenida Piura, lined with stylish restaurants, funky cafés, a few of the cheaper backpackers' and an obligatory hippie market selling some decent crafts and jewellery. Further north it becomes Avenida Grau, where most buses have their depots and where you'll find cheaper local restaurants and, one block away, the market.

Heading down to the central beach, the bars here are the heart of Máncora's non-stop party, particularly ferocious during the summer months. The main beach has grown considerably thinner over the years as hotels encroach ever closer, and tends to be quite packed, while the waves are full of competing surfers. Those who look for a peaceful patch of sand and prefer the sound of the sea as their soundtrack (instead of thumping *cumbia*) will have to shell out for the pricey but luxurious hotels on Máncora's southern beaches, the palm-lined Las Pocitas or Vichayito, or head north to Punta Sal, Cancas or Zorritos.

ARRIVAL AND DEPARTURE   MÁNCORA

BY BUS

Comng from the south – Lima, Chiclayo or Piura – there are several buses daily. Excluciva has the best service (2nd level, almost 180° reclining seats and personal TV), as well as Cruz del Sur and Oltursa. From Tumbes, buses and colectivos to Máncora leave frequently from Avenida Tumbes Norte, but the return is better in one of the minibuses.

Bus companies The bus companies are all in the main street, Avenida Piura, where you can buy tickets for their selection of daily and nightly services up or down the coast, connecting Tumbes with Lima and the major cities in between. Transportes EPPO Piura 679 (☎ 073 258 140) has buses every 30 minutes to Piura, stopping at Los Organos, El Alto, Talara and Sullana. Cruz del Sur, Av Grau 208 (☎ 073 258 232), and Civa, Av Piura 472 (☎ 073 258 524), go to Trujillo, Lima and Guayaquil. Cifa, Grau 212 (☎ 941 816 863) goes direct to Guayaquil; Oltursa, Av Piura 509

(☎ 073 258 212) connects with Piura, Chiclayo, Trujillo and Lima. Tepsa, Av Grau 113 (☎ 073 258 672), runs to Lima.

Destinations Chiclayo (several daily; 5–7hr); Guayaquil (several daily; 8hr); Lima (several daily; 18hr); Los Organos (several daily; 30min); Piura (several daily; 3–4hr); Talara (several daily; 1hr); Trujillo (4 weekly; 9–10hr); Tumbes (several daily; 1hr 30min–2hr).

BY COLECTIVO

From Tumbes, colectivo vans leave from around block 3 of Avenida Tumbes Norte (2hr; S/12–20). From Máncora, these same vans run to Piura (3hr; S/30) and even to the airport for an extra S/15. The most reliable company is SerTour at Piura 270. For those looking to save a few Soles, cars and beat-up minibuses run between Máncora and Tumbes all day, stopping anywhere in between.

ACCOMMODATION

The cheapest hotels in Máncora are along Avenida Piura, with a couple of big party hostels near the entrance just after the bridge (with the exception of the infamous Point Hostel, out north of town on Playa El Amor). Heading to the beach, to the north are first a few run-down old motels that fill up with party-intent locals over the holidays, while a block or two further on the places become more refined, with some decent, cheaper options set back from the sea. Past the pier, to the south, hotels become more exclusive and ever pricier as the beach becomes emptier at Las Pocitas and on to palm-lined Vichayito.

Del Wawa ☎ 073 258 427, 🌐 delwawa.com. Right in the middle of the main beach, this is the place to be seen lounging on your deckchair sipping a cocktail from your private beach bar, while the crowds jostle for space on the busy beach just metres away. Rooms are cool and stylish and most have great beach views. **S/180**

Hotel Sunset Av Antigua Panamericana Norte 196 ☎ 073 258111, 🌐 sunsetmancora.com. This is a stylish boutique hotel on a secluded beach, with a good clifftop restaurant and bar terrace with a small pool and very fine service. With great views all round, this is the perfect place for a relaxed beach getaway. **S/210**

★ **Kichic** Las Pocitas ☎ 073 411 518, 🌐 kichic.com. Every detail of this tiny boutique hotel is refined; gorgeous and exuding calm, it is set in lush green grounds and has a pool overlooking the beach. The focus here is on rejuvenating the spirit, offering massages, yoga and a healthy menu from the superb vegetarian restaurant. **S/600**

7

★**Laguna Surf Camp** C Acceso Veraniego s/n ☎994 015 628, @pilarinmancora@yahoo.es. One of the best for location and price in Máncora; just half a block from the beach, you can hear the sea, but generally not the noise from the parties just up the road. The bamboo and palm-thatched bungalows are set in a calm, hammock-filled area around a small but adequate pool. Dutch cook "Pepe" offers amazing breakfasts and lunches with generous, tasty portions. Dorms <u>S/30</u>, doubles <u>S/90</u>

Misfit Hostel Playa El Amor ☎073 496 938, ⓦmisfithostel.com. The four wooden A-frame huts with decidedly trippy interior murals have quickly become the most sought-after budget accommodation in Máncora. A fair bit north of town, and set right on the beach, the vibe is intimate but always festive. Book well in advance. Dorms <u>S/32</u>, doubles <u>S/102</u>

Punta Ballenas Inn Punta Ballenas ☎073 630 844, @puntaballenasmancora@gmail.com. One of the first hotels in town, its location south of town and just metres from the waves is still unbeatable. The installations are showing their age a little, but in a pleasant, beach-cottage kind of way. Make sure you get a room at the front. Check for good out-of-season discounts. <u>S/140</u>

EATING AND DRINKING

Comercial Marlon II, next to the ATM and Municipal building, has a superb range of groceries, including wholemeal bread, local honey and wines, although prices are high. For fruit, skip the vendors on Avenida Piura and walk further down to the local market. For eating out, there's a surplus of restaurants in the centre of town, mainly along the Panamericana. There is a hectic nightlife scene based in the bars, beachside hotels, backpacker hostels and on the beach itself, especially during Peruvian holiday times; it's easy to find – just follow the sounds after dark.

El Atelier Vino Bar Av Piura 360 ☎984 088 339. Another bastion of calm cool on the avenue, *El Atelier* could be in any major city, with its decor heavy on recycled wooden crates. It's not just a pretty face: the food is great,

ACTIVITIES IN MÁNCORA

Máncora enjoys warm waters and its position is blessed as the place where northern tropical currents meet with the much, much cooler southern one: at Lobitos, the next beach down the coast from Cabo Blanco (30km south of Máncora), the sea is cold. This geographical position gives Máncora near-perfect surf conditions at times, with barrel waves achieving up to 4m in height. Although fairly safe, there are offshore currents which surfing novices are advised to watch out for (ask one of the surf teachers before venturing out). **Kite-surfing** has also boomed here, and Máncora is now recognized as an international destination for the sport. To hire gear, find surf tours or get surf lessons check ⓦvivamancora.com, or try:

Del Wawa (see opposite) Offers surf lessons from around S/50 an hour (board rentals S/15–20hr).
Laguna Surf Camp ☎994 015 628, @pilarinmancora@yahoo.es. Offers rentals, trips and lessons. Pilar is a well-loved local who is particularly good with kids, but can help all ages and levels.
Octopus Surf Tours ☎994 005 518, ⓦoctopussurftours.com. Operated by experienced Peruvian surfer Marco Antonio Ravizza, aka "Octopus"; they tend to offer surfing packages including food and accommodation.
Wild K ☎999 109 002, ⓦwild-kitesurf-peru.com. One-stop shop for all kitesurfing needs, including rentals, training for all levels and multi-day safaris. They also offer stand-up paddle lessons and board rental.

When the sea is flat and the wind dies, you still have plenty of options. Head out to nearby El Ñuro to swim with turtles. Around the pier at this little fishing village south of Los Organosa surprising number of green turtles gather most days to feed on the fishermen's scraps. For a small fee (S/5), you can walk down the pier to check them out or even jump into the water and swim with them. Be sure to give them some space, they are wild animals and you may get a well-deserved nip. Go on your own: take the EPPO bus to Los Organos and from there, a mototaxi to El Ñuro. Otherwise most local tour agencies along Avenida Piura will take you out there, or go all in for a half-day snorkelling trip with Spondylous Dive School (☎999 891 268, ⓦbuceaenperu.com; S/100).

Bike tours or rental is at Amancay, Av Piura 220 (☎947 946 470, ⓦamancaybikes.com). Eco Fundo La Caprichosa (Av Grau s/n ☎073 258 574, ⓦecofundolacaprichosa.com) is a lodge set a little way north of Máncora that specializes in adventure activities – they offer ziplining, a monstrous climbing wall, quad bikes and a large property left to the local wildlife and allowing pursuits like hikes and birdwatching.

with roots in French and Peruvian cuisines. Even if you're not hungry, go for the cheese, wine or cocktails; live music some nights. Tues–Sun 6pm–1am.

The Bird House Beachfront just south of the Hostal Sol y Mar. This extremely popular spot is divided into shops, bars and cafés, mostly franchised out, which offer a wide range of international dishes (the breakfasts at *Green Eggs and Ham* are among the best in town, if pricey at S/15), as well as local cuisine (try the fish and seafood at *Willka* up on the first floor); there's also a surf shop, cocktail bar, great smoothies at *Papa Mo's Milk Bar* and a pleasant beachside, shaded lounge area. Daily 8am–10pm.

Don Santiago Pizzería C Acceso Veraniego, next to Sunray Hotel. Not much more than a large wooden shack with a few tables, but the large, wood-fired clay oven at the back is the only furniture really necessary here. The Argentine baker-cum-owner makes killer breads (if you can get your hands on one) and the best pizzas in town, at unfathomably cheap prices (S/16–22). And you can bring your own beer. Tues–Sat 8pm–late.

Nylamp Av Piura 476. A holdout from the Máncora of 20 years ago, this simple menu restaurant does just what it promises on the whiteboard outside, a S/10, two-course lunch, abundant and tasty. Daily lunch time.

La Sirena de Juan Av Piura 316 ☎ 073 258 173. A standout on the crowded Av Piura, *La Sirena de Juan* serves impressive food in a stylish two-storey location. Best loved for their tuna steaks, cooked to near-raw perfection. Dishes average S/30–50. Tues–Sun 7pm–11pm.

7

DIRECTORY

Internet USHPA Internet, Av Piura 372 (daily 9am–10pm).
Money and exchange Banco de la Nación, block 5 of Av Piura (Mon–Fri 8am–6pm); there are at least five ATMs scattered about Máncora. The best exchange rate in town is at Punto Pollo Piura 609 (daily, 9.30am–3pm & 5–11.30pm); and they even make a pretty good *pollo a la brasa* (the classic Peruvian fast-food chicken cooked on a rotisserie over coals and rubbed with a light spice).
Telephones The Locutorio Público telephone office (daily 8am–10pm) and shop is on block 5 of Av Piura opposite the small church.
Tourist Police Av Piura 330 ☎ 073 496 926.

Las Pocitas and Vichayito

Take the rough (old Panamerican) highway on the right just as you leave Máncora; mototaxis will charge S/3–S/8, depending on how far you want to go; alternatively, you could walk from Máncora along the coast, but make sure you take water with you

Máncora's two satellite beaches, **LAS POCITAS** and **VICHAYITO**, are probably what you were hoping for when you planned your trip here. Las Pocitas basically begins once you pass the pier, and the isolation grows as you head south. They make for a relaxing alternative, with good swimming, some surf and lovely coastal scenery, but staying here is pricey. Some of the hotels have excellent restaurants where you can stop for lunch. The restaurant at *Arennas* (🌐 arennasmancora.com) is a real treat offering creative, gourmet food, superbly presented and prepared. The stylishly designed restaurant is set on a wooden deck next to a large pool with palms and the empty beach in the foreground.

Poza de Barro (mud baths)

Open access daily 24hr; basic toilets and a changing hut • S/3 • Take a taxi from Máncora or ride a horse (the latter through a local tour company; see box, p.415). The entry road to the mud baths is off the Panamericana, just north of Máncora next to the "Comunidad Máncora Campesino" sign by the bridge

If the beach isn't relaxing enough, you can always head to the local **mud baths**. Set 11km from the main road and surrounded by hills and *algarrobo* trees, the warm natural bath appeared in the shaft following oil extraction in the 1980s. It's now visited for its cleansing subterranean waters (no sign of oil today).

Punta Sal

Located some 2km along a track from Km 1187 of the Panamericana, **PUNTA SAL**, considered by many to be the best **beach** in Peru, has extensive sands and attractive rocky outcrops, swarming with crabs at low tide. It's a safe place to swim and a heavenly spot for diving in warm, clear waters. In the low season you'll probably have the beautiful beach pretty much to yourself; in high season it's a good idea to book your accommodation in advance.

The waters off Punta Sal are known for their high concentration of striped and black marlin. **Fishing trips** can be arranged (a yacht for four people costs between US$400 and US$1000 from North Shore Peru Expeditions (☎961 770 728, ⓦnorthshore.pe), with prices based on what you're hoping to catch and how far out to sea you wish to go. Between July and October, Punta Sal also makes an excellent base for **whale watching**, as humpbacks come up from the Antarctic to calve. Trips can be arranged with North Shore Expeditions in Punta Sal or Pacifico Adventures in Los Organos (☎073 257 686, ⓦpacificoadventures.com; S/120 per person).

ACCOMMODATION AND EATING   PUNTA SAL

There are a couple of small bodegas in Punta Sal, so drinks and general groceries can be bought without leaving the beach area.

Hospedaje Hua Punta Sal ☎072 540 043, ⓦhua-puntasal.com. Located towards the middle of the beach, *Hua* is a good mid-range choice, with a main wooden building; some rooms have ocean views. Service is very good, plus there's a restaurant which serves seafood (S/20–30) and great fresh juices during the day and at night whips out pasta and tasty pizzas (S/25–30). Camping is only for pre-arranged tour groups. **S/170**

Punta Sal Club Hotel Panamericana Norte Km 1192 ☎072 596 700, ⓦpuntasal.com.pe. At the northern end of the point, this rather exclusive place offers comfortable cabin-style accommodation right on the beach, a pool, a fantastic bar and restaurant facilities; it also offers fishing, horseriding and snorkelling. **S/330**

Las Terrazas Punta Sal ☎072 507 701, ⓦlasterrazasdepuntasal.com.pe. Down near the far end of the beach, this is the best budget choice. They are located in the second row so you miss the cooling ocean breeze but the view is still pleasant with a patch of sea and sunset visible through a huge of honganville or nothing fancy and a little run down, but friendly, and the English owner is a deft hand in the kitchen, making good pizzas (S/22); ask about a daily lunch dish (S/12). **S/170**

★Yemaya Panamericana Norte Km 1198 ☎981 848 008, ⓦyemayaperu.com. A luxurious small boutique hotel past the fishing village of Cancas a few kilometres north of Punta Sal. Just eight bungalows on a spacious plot guarantee absolute peace and individual attention; all meals included at their excellent restaurant by the pool, overlooking the beach. **S/561**

ARRIVAL AND DEPARTURE

BUS
From Tumbes, go with the comfortable, air-conditioned minivans that run along the coast; try Sertur, Av Tumbes Norte 302 (☎072 521 455; 1hr; S/25).

COLECTIVO
Colectivo cars leave from in front of the Cruz del Sur station in Máncora (30min; S/5) and leave you on the highway outside the city. For an extra charge, the driver will drop you off right by the beach. If not, a mototaxi costs S/5.

Tumbes
About 30km from the Ecuadorian border and 287km north of Piura, **TUMBES**, separated from the rest of Peru by the sluggish brown River Tumbes which you cross as you enter, is usually considered a mere pit stop for overland travellers, offering decent restaurants and better money-changing options than at the Ecuadorian frontier. However, the city has a significant history and, is somewhat friendlier than most border settlements. On top of that, it's close to two very distinct and unique forests and protected areas: the **Santuario Nacional los Manglares de Tumbes** and the **Zona Reservada de Tumbes**. The settlement of **Zorritos** is strung out along the seafront and Panamericana some 28km south of Tumbes; as well as a long, empty and quite beautiful beach, this town is the point of access to some ancient, still-working natural mud baths.

The area can get very hot and humid between December and March, while the rest of the year it offers a pleasant heat, compared with much of Peru's southern coast. The sea is warm and mosquitoes can be bothersome between September and January. Locals tend to be laidback and spontaneous, a trait reflected in the local traditions such as **las cumananas**, an expression in popular verse, often by song with a guitar. The verse is expected to be sparky, romantic, comical and even sad, but most importantly, spur of the moment and rap-like.

7

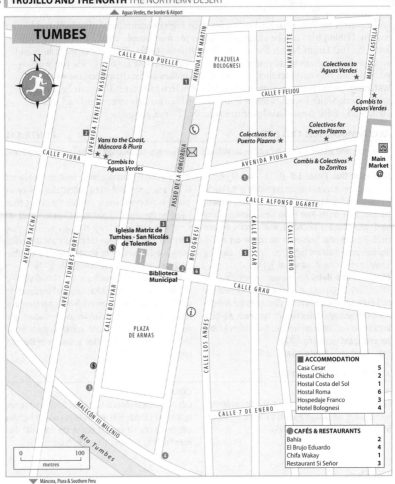

Aguas Verdes, the border & Airport

TUMBES

N

CALLE ABAD PUELLE

AVENIDA SAN MARTIN

PLAZUELA
BOLOGNESI

NAVARETTE

MARISCAL CASTILLA

CALLE F FEIJOU

*Colectivos to
Aguas Verdes* ★

★ *Combis to
Aguas Verdes*

AVENIDA TENIENTE VASQUEZ

1

2

★ ★ *Vans to the Coast,
Máncora & Piura*

CALLE PIURA

*Combis to
Aguas Verdes*

PASEO DE LA CONCORDIA

*Colectivos for
Puerto Pizarro* ★

*Colectivos for
Puerto Pizarro* ★

AVENIDA PIURA

Combis & Colectivos ★
to Zorritos

Main
Market
@

AVENIDA TACNA

AVENIDA TUMBES NORTE

CALLE ALFONSO UGARTE

3

**Iglesia Matriz de
Tumbes - San Nicolás
de Tolentino** $

4

BOLOGNESI

5

CALLE HUASCAR

CALLE BODERO

2

6

**Biblioteca
Municipal**

CALLE GRAU

CALLE BOLIVAR

ⓘ

PLAZA
DE ARMAS

CALLE LOS ANDES

$

3

MALECÓN III MILENIO

CALLE 7 DE ENERO

Río Tumbes

4

0   100
metres

■ **ACCOMMODATION**
Casa Cesar   5
Hostal Chicho   2
Hostal Costa del Sol   1
Hostal Roma   6
Hospedaje Franco   3
Hotel Bolognesi   4

● **CAFÉS & RESTAURANTS**
Bahía   2
El Brujo Eduardo   4
Chifa Wakay   1
Restaurant Si Señor   3

Máncora, Piura & Southern Peru

Brief history

Pizarro didn't actually set foot in Tumbes when it was first discovered by the Spanish in 1527. He preferred to cast his eyes along the Inca city's adobe walls, its carefully irrigated fields and its shining temple, from the comfort and safety of his ship. However, with the help of translators he set about learning as much as he could about Peru and the Incas during this initial contact.

The Spaniards who did go ashore made reports of such grandeur that Pizarro at first refused to believe them, sending instead the more reliable Greek Conquistador, **Pedro de Candia**. Dubious descriptions of the temple, lined with gold and silver sheets, were confirmed by Candia, who also gave the people of Tumbes their first taste of European technological might – firing his musket to smash a wooden board to pieces. Pizarro had all the evidence he needed; he returned to Spain to obtain royal consent and support for his projected conquest.

The Tumbes people hadn't always been controlled by the Incas. The area was originally inhabited by the **Tallanes**, related to coastal tribes from Ecuador who are still known for their unusual lip and nose ornaments. In 1450 they were conquered for the first time – by the **Chimu**. Thirteen years later came the **Incas**, organized by Tupac Inca, who bulldozed the locals into religious, economic and even architectural conformity in order to create their most northerly coastal terminus. A fortress, temple and sun convent were built, and the town was colonized with loyal subjects from other regions – a typical Inca ploy, which they called the *mitimaes* system. The valley had an efficient irrigation programme, allowing the inhabitants to grow, among other things, bananas, corn and squash.

Pizarro longed to add his name to the list of Tumbes' conquerors, yet after landing on the coast of Ecuador in 1532 with a royal warrant to conquer and convert, and despite the previous friendly contact, some of the Spanish were killed by natives as they tried to land. Moreover, when they reached the city it was completely deserted with many buildings destroyed, and, more painfully for Pizarro, no sign of gold. It seems likely that Tumbes' destruction prior to Pizarro's arrival was the result of inter-tribal warfare directly related to the **Inca Civil War**. This, a war of succession between Atahualpa and his half-brother, the legitimate heir, Huascar, was to make Pizarro's role as conqueror a great deal easier, and he took the town of Tumbes without a struggle.

7

Plaza de Armas

Tumbes is jumbled and chaotic, but at least around the broad **Plaza de Armas**, bounded by large trees, there is some peace and people gather to sit and chat and suck on *marcianos*, deliciously refreshing iced sticks made from local fruit – try the *lúcuma* (an ovaloid, green-skinned fruit with bright orange flesh that has a rich, sweet flavour somewhere between sweet potato, caramel and maple syrup). Young kids skate on the far side of the plaza, while at the opposite end you might find an old trumpet player filling the space with his music as he busks for a few soles. Beyond lies the rather plain **Iglesia Matriz de Tumbes–San Nicolás de Tolentino**, built in the seventeenth century but restored in 1995, making it now one of the most modernized churches in northern Peru. It has an understated Baroque facade and both cupolas are covered in mosaics.

Located in the amphitheatre or stage at the southern end on the main plaza, the **municipal mural** entitled *Encuentro de Dos Mundos* (Encounter of Two Worlds) depicts a bold and vivid jungle, conquistador- and Inca-inspired scene symbolizing the first contact between Spain and ancient Peru and in particular the Battle of the Mangroves. Leading off eastwards from the northern edge of the plaza is Calle Grau, an attractive old-fashioned hotchpotch of a street, lined with wooden colonial buildings.

Malecón

The slightly grubby raised **Malecón** promenade runs along the high riverbanks of the Río Tumbes, a block beyond the southern end of the Plaza de Armas. At the western end of the Malecón, you can see a massive Modernist **sculpture**, *Tumbes Paraiso del Amor y el Eterno Verano* (Tumbes Paradise of Love and Eternal Summer), depicting a pair of lovers kissing.

BORDER RELATIONS WITH ECUADOR

Tumbes was the first town to be "conquered" by the Spanish and has maintained its importance ever since – originally as the gateway to the Inca Empire and more recently through its strategic position on the contentious **frontier with Ecuador**. Despite three regional wars (in 1859, 1941–42 and 1997–98), the exact line of the border remains a source of controversy. Maps of the frontier vary depending on which country you buy them in, with the two countries claiming a disparity of up to 150km in some places along the border. The traditional enmity between Peru and Ecuador and the continuing dispute over the border mean that Tumbes has a strong Peruvian army presence and a consequent strict **ban on photography** anywhere near military or frontier installations.

7

ARRIVAL AND GETTING AROUND

BY PLANE
Aeropuerto Pedro Canga Rodríguez, Av Panamericana Norte 1276 (☎072 525 102), is just north of the city. LAN Perú, Jr Bolognesi 250 (☎072 524 481), has flights to and from Lima. A taxi into town (15min) should cost around S/20. Taxis to Punta Sal cost around S/90 and take about an hour.
Destinations Lima (4 flights weekly; 2hr 30min); Trujillo (daily; 1hr).

BY BUS
Most buses coming to Tumbes arrive at offices along Av Tumbes Norte (also known as Av Teniente Vásquez), or along Piura.
Bus companies CIAL, Av Tumbes Norte 958 (☎072 526 350), for Lima; Civa, Av Tumbes Norte 518 (☎072 525 120), and Cruz del Sur, Av Tumbes Norte 319 (☎072 526 200), among the best for Lima and Guayaquil; El Dorado, Av Tacna 351 (☎072 523 480), for Piura, Chiclayo and Trujillo, with some coastal stops on the way; Oltursa, Av Tumbes Norte 936 (☎072 523 046), for luxurious travel to Lima and all

TUMBES AND AROUND

major northern destinations; Ormeño, Av Tumbes Norte 1187 (☎072 522 894), similar to Oltursa, but also Guayaquil.
Destinations Aguas Verdes (hourly; 30min); Chiclayo (8 daily; 8hr); Guayaquil (4 daily; 6hr); Lima (8 daily; 20hr); Máncora (several daily; 1–2hr); Piura (6 daily; 4hr); Puerto Pizarro (hourly; 15min); Trujillo (4 daily; 12hr).

BY VAN
Sertur vans (more comfortable than combis and colectivos) pull in at Av Tumbes Norte 302 (☎072 521 455) and leave when full to Máncora, Sullana and Piura.

BY CAR
San José Rent a Car, Av Tumbes Norte 486 (☎072 522 321, ⓦrentacarsanjose.pe).

BY TAXI AND MOTOTAXI
SeguriTaxi (☎072 630 298) is one of the companies recommended by iPeru. You can also hail one of the many mototaxis, which will take you anywhere in the city for around S/2.

INFORMATION AND TOURS

Tourist information iPeru have an office on the 3rd floor in the Malecón III Milenio (☎072 506 721; ⓔiperutumbes @promperu.gob.pe).
Tour operators Tumbes Tours, Av Tumbes 334 (☎072 524 837, ⓦtumbestours.com), runs a number of tours including a four-day/three-night trip exploring the Puerto

Pizarro mangrove swamp (see opposite), as well as local beaches from S/55 per person per day, depending on size of group. Preference Tours, Grau 427 (☎072 525 518), is good for general tourist information and tickets, and organizes most standard local tour packages.

ACCOMMODATION

Central Tumbes has plenty of places to stay. The best spots are within a few blocks from the Plaza de Armas; best not go much further abroad as the the buildings are quite run down and the traffic is chaotic and noisy. The most attractive beach near Tumbes, Zorritos has become popular with young Limeño sun-seekers and is lively over the summer months.

CENTRAL TUMBES
Casa César C Huascar 313 ☎072 522 883, ⓦcasacesartumbes.com. Still looking new and modern from a recent renovation, rooms are spacious with big, comfortable beds and a/c. Good service, decent breakfast and they have a secure parking lot across the road. **S/160**
Hospedaje Franco Paseo la Concordia 105 ☎072 525 295. On the pedestrian avenue off the Plaza de Armas, it is considerably quieter here. Nothing standout, just spacious rooms with very welcome ceiling fans; cold water only. **S/80**
Hostal Chicho Av Tumbes Norte 327 ☎074 522 282. On the noisy and dirty main road close to the bus stations; basic rooms, but fine if you're on a tight budget. **S/45**
Hostal Costa del Sol Av San Martín 275 ☎072 523 991, ⓦcostadelsolperu.com. Located on the Plazuela Bolognesi, the *Costa del Sol* is about as luxurious as it gets here, offering very comfortable rooms with a/c, private baths and cable TV, as well as a nice garden patio and pool. **S/200**
Hostal Roma Bolognesi 425 ☎072 524 137. Right on

the Plaza de Armas, this is solid budget choice, even if the staff are quite surly. The rooms have decent showers and are quite spacious; no a/c but there are fans. **S/70**
Hotel Bolognesi Bolognesi 221 ☎072 633 837. Friendly service and spotless rooms with a/c or fan. Hot water, good wi-fi and just 100m from the corner of the plaza. **S/80**

ZORRITOS
Los Balcones de Zorritos Panamericana Norte 1230, Bocapan ☎072 500 761, ⓦbalconesdezorritos.com. Located south of Zorritos, this place is right on the beach with a welcoming pool, wooden deck and lounging area facing the sea just 20m away. Great service. **S/190**
★**La Casa del Grillo Tres Puntas** Av Los Pinos 563, Zorritos ☎072 544 222, ⓦcasagrillo.net. A few kilometres before Zorritos town, *Tres Puntas* is a laidback eco-lodge set on a beautiful beach with spacious wood and bamboo cabins that blend in with the large open space surrounding the hostel. Shaded campsites with hammocks are just 20m from

the waves. Some good vegetarian food at their restaurant and free yoga in the afternoons. Camping **S/15**, Bungalow **S/100 Casa Kresala** Zorritos, Barrio El Pacífico ☎ 072 500 801, ⓦ casakresala.com. In central Zorritos, and just off the beach, this is a colourful and simple surfer hostel. Green, shady common areas with hammocks and good wi-fi. **S/70**

EATING AND DRINKING

Tumbes has some excellent restaurants and is the best place in Peru to try *conchas negras* – the black clams found only in these coastal waters, where they grow on the roots of mangroves.

Bahía C Grau 309 ☎ 072 504 216. A popular eating and drinking spot with a cool, shaded patio overlooking Plaza de Armas; serves quality local dishes, fresh seafood and colourful cocktails with a happy hour. Usually has a very good lunchtime set menu (S/12). Occasional live music events at weekends. Mon–Sat 8am–midnight.

★ **El Brujo Eduardo** Jr malecón Benavides 850 ☎ 072 522 829. Probably the best reason to stop in Tumbes – superb seafood with some interesting creations you won't easily find outside of Lima with prices ranging from S/30–50 for mains. Impeccable service, although it does get very busy. Oddly located in the far corner of the plaza where Bolognesi meets the malecón, but with a nice view over the river. Mon–Sat 9am–midnight.

Chifa Wakay C Huascar 417 ☎ 072 522 829. Dishes up well-priced, tasty Chinese food in a well-cared-for ambience; serving the usual Chino-Peruvian delights such as *cien flores* and *wantan kamlu*. Daily 6–11pm.

Restaurant Si Señor C Bolívar 115 ☎ 976 678 640. Serves mostly beer and seafood, right on the Plaza de Armas and is open late into the night. The food is tasty, but for freshness, stick to eating at lunch time. Daily 7am–2am.

DIRECTORY

Consulate Jr Bolívar 129, 3rd floor, Plaza de Armas ☎ 072 523 022 (Mon–Fri 9am–4pm).
Internet Internet Bolognesi, Jr Bolognesi 225, 9am–11pm.
Money and exchange There are a number of banks, ATMs and even a Moneygram service lining the plaza on Jr Bolívar.

Cambistas are at the corner of Bolívar with Piura and an official casa de cambio is Cambios Internacionales, Jr Bolívar 259 (Mon–Fri 8.30am–6.30pm, Sat 8.30am–1pm).
Police Av Mayor Novoa and C Zarumilla ☎ 072 522 525.
Post office Av San Martín 208 (Mon–Sat 8am–8pm).

Puerto Pizarro

PUERTO PIZARRO, 13km northeast of Tumbes, is worth a visit if you have time to kill, though it has no specific link with the conquistador it's named after, and the waterfront today is full of rubbish. The boat trips offered to the Isla de Amor (see below) can be pleasant; just choose your guide carefully and go at high tide. The late afternoon is the best time to see the birds as they return home to roost. If, however, you only have time for one mangrove outing, the Santuario Nacional los Manglares de Tumbes (see box, p.422) is generally more attractive.

An ancient fishing port, Puerto Pizarro was a commercial harbour until swamps grew out to sea over the last few centuries, making it inaccessible for large boats and permanently disconnecting Tumbes from the Pacific.

ARRIVAL AND DEPARTURE

PUERTO PIZARRO

Colectivos leave regularly for Puerto Pizarro (S/2.50; 15min) from C Huascar, just across Av Piura in Tumbes. Taxis cost around S/10–15 from Tumbes.

ACCOMMODATION AND EATING

Hospedaje Bayside Malecón, overlooking Puerto Pizarro ☎ 072 543 045. This hotel is right on the waterfront; it has a pool, private bathrooms, palm trees and a restaurant-café. They can advise on fishing and boat excursions. **S/170**

Isla de Amor

Boats run to Isla de Amor from Puerto Pizarro; buy tickets (S/70 per boat minimum, more for a more spacious and comfortable boat) from the information and ticket booth on the seafront

From Puerto Pizarro you can take slow but pleasant **boat trips** out to the **ISLA DE AMOR**, where there's a bathing beach and a café. The boat operators tell you the history of the area and the mangroves themselves, as well as point out wildlife like the magnificent frigate bird (also called scissor-tail) and the occasional white iguana languishing among the mangroves. The tour will also take you through **mangrove creeks** where you'll see the *rhizopora* tree's dense root system. The centre for the protection of Peru's only indigenous, and **endangered**, **crocodile** (*Crocodylus acutus americano)* is neglected and a bit depressing. There are very few of these crocodiles left in the wild (where they can live for a hundred years), having been hunted in the past for their skin, and the centre has bred around 225 in captivity. It's possible to see the crocodiles at most life stages, with the largest growing to around 3m.

TUMBES PROTECTED AREAS

The Tumbes region is well endowed with natural resources, not least the three major **protected areas** of the Santuario Nacional los Manglares de Tumbes, the Parque Nacional Cerros Amotape and the Zona Reservada de Tumbes. These, plus the El Angulo Hunting Reserve, encompass many habitats only found in this small corner of the country. If you're short of time, it is just about possible to travel between these in just a day going with a local tour company. As of writing, there is no entry fee for the reserves, but you will have to register at a small SERNANP post, the local government conservation agency. For more info contact the iPeru office in Tumbes (see p.420) or the main SERNANP office in Tumbes (☎072 526 489).

THE SANTUARIO NACIONAL LOS MANGLARES DE TUMBES

The **Santuario Nacional los Manglares de Tumbes** comprises most of the remaining **mangrove swamps** left in Peru, which are under serious threat from fishing and farming (shrimp farming in particular). The best way to visit the sanctuary is via Puerto 25, fifteen minutes from Aguas Verdes. There are five species of mangrove here, of which the red mangrove is the most common and this is where the *conchas negras* thrive, although the 1998 El Niño weather introduced large amounts of fresh water into the shell beds here, causing significant damage. The mangroves also contain over two hundred bird species, including eight endemic species, notably the rather splendid mangrove eagle.

Combis run from Tumbes on block four of Avenida Mariscal Castillo, just past the market, across from the church, or in Bolívar to Aguas Verdes (S/2.50; 30min). From here, head to the iPeru post (☎072 632 537), where they can call a reliable mototaxi which will take you to Puerto 25 for S/10, and later return you to Aguas Verde (S/10). At the SERNANP office you need to pay a S/10 entry fee and choose your boat operator. A two- to three-hour trip through the mangroves will cost S/60 and a longer trip all the way out to Punta Capones, where there is more birdlife (4–5hr), will cost S/120 (price per boat, for up to four people). A short stroll over a raised walkway is available at no cost if you just want a glimpse of the mangroves.

ZONA RESERVADA DE TUMBES

This reserve extends right up to the Ecuadorian border and covers over 75,000 hectares of mainly tropical forest. The best route is inland, due south from Tumbes via Pampas de Hospital and El Caucho to El Narranjo and Figueroa on the border, but transport is infrequent, making visits only really possible with a tour. Potential sightings include monkeys, many bird species, small cats and snakes, though the **Río Tumbes crocodile** is a highly endangered species, found only at two sites along this river. There is some small hope for this unique creature in the form of a local breeding programme, but the whole area is under threat from gold mining, mainly from across the border in Ecuador at the headwaters of the river. Pollution from Tumbes, too, is generating further disturbance.

PARQUE NACIONAL CERROS DE AMOTAPE

Home to the best-preserved region of dry forest anywhere along the Pacific coast of South America, the **Parque Nacional Cerros de Amotape** contains six other distinct habitats that cover over 90,000 hectares. Access is via Rica Playa at the SERNANP post, 1hr 20 min south of Tumbes (36km), but public transport is rare and slow. Essentially, unless you have your own car, you need to go with a tour. Animals here include black parrots, desert foxes, deer, white-backed squirrels, *tigrillos* (ocelots), pumas and white-winged turkeys. Remember to take all your drinking and other **water** needs with you when entering this zone.

Baños de Barro Medicinal Hervideros (Medicinal Mud Baths)

Not currently recommended for visits as they are undergoing repairs and upgrades (estimated to be done mid-2015) and the road is particularly bad • Turn off the Panamericana Norte at Bocapan, Km 1214; signpost reads "Parque Nacional Cerros de Amotape"; the baths are about 4km down this road. Walking, taxi or mototaxi from Zorritos are the only alternatives apart from going with a tour group from Tumbes or Máncora.

Located 40km south of Tumbes, these little-visited **mud baths** are reputedly very good for your skin. Surrounded by hills and *algarrobo* trees, this is a really peaceful and relaxing spot. The *pozos de barro* (mud baths) were discovered by the archeologist Raymondi in 1882, though were almost certainly used for centuries before that. There are several mud baths, with a lower pool for washing down. Temperatures and health effects vary pool by pool; some of this is noted on small wooden signs showing an analysis of the mud.

The Peru–Ecuador border

Crossing the **Peru–Ecuador border** is relatively simple in either direction. You have the choice of crossing at the busy frontier settlement of **Aguas Verdes**, easily done with little effort thanks to long-distance international buses plying the route, or at the crossing between **La Tina** and **Macará**, which is a very pleasant alternative, its main advantage being the scenery en route to Loja.

CROSSING THE BORDER

AT AGUAS VERDES

By bus The best and safest way to enter Ecuador is to take an international bus from Tumbes (or Máncora) to Guayaquil of Machala which waits for you as you do the exit and entry process at the CEBAF (Centro Binacional de Atención Fronteriza) border control. The entry and exit is in the same building and is open 24hr. To go on to other destinations, take a bus to Machala, and from there, you have connections to all destinations.

By colectivo Combis (S/2.50) and colectivo cars (S/4) for the border leave Tumbes from block four of Av Mariscal Castillo, just past the market and leave you in Aguas Verdes. Once here, it is a short stroll across the Puente Internacional (international bridge) and on the other side you take one of the yellow taxis to the CEBAF control point (10min; US$3–5). Get your stamps and head to Huaquillas (the Ecuadorian equivalent of Aguas Verdes) and choose a bus for any Ecuadorian destination. Note that the risk of mugging or fraud makes travelling by taxi to the control point an undesirable option; it is much easier and more pleasant to just take a direct international bus from Tumbes or Máncora.

By taxi A taxi from Tumbes to the border bridge (taxis are not allowed over the two bridges into Huaquillas, Ecuador) costs S/30.

Entry/exit stamps The CEBAF border control (☎ 072 597 900) for both exit and entry stamps is on the Ecuadorian side of the bridge and is open daily, 24hr.

Customs The main Peruvian customs point is actually a concrete complex in the middle of the desert between the villages of Cancas and Máncora, more than 50km south of the border. When it is operating, buses are pulled over and passengers have to get out, often having to show documents to the customs police, while the bus and selected items of luggage are searched for contraband

goods. This rarely takes more than 20 minutes.

Money and exchange Since Ecuador dollarized its currency, exchange has become much easier. Change your remaining nuevos soles to dollars in Tumbes before leaving as the moneychangers by the bridge are a hassle and you open yourself up to fraudulent notes and pickpockets. Similarly, when leaving Ecuador, change at your first major Peruvian destination, or at least at an official exchange in Aguas Verdes.

VIA LA TINA AND MACARÁ

By colectivo The crossing is most conveniently approached by combi from Sullana, leaving from the Terminal Terrestre in Av Buenos Aires, not far from the main market, departing regularly between 6am and 6pm (128km; almost 2hr; S/15). A short mototaxi ride (S/1; 5min) connects small La Tina with the international bridge and immigration facilities.

Macará The Ecuadorian town of Macará is located some 4km from the border; mototaxis (10min; 70¢) take people into town. Buses on to Loja (5hr) depart from Macará. Alternatively, there are also buses direct to Loja from Piura with Transportes Loja (Av Loreto 1241 ☎ 073 333 260; 2 daily; 8–9hr; S/30). The journey between the border and Macará is extremely hot – it's only a few kilometres, but if the sun's out, take water to drink. There are a couple of hostels in Macará.

Entry/exit stamps The Peruvian and Ecuadorian immigration offices are open 24hr; the frontier is based on a river bridge with the Peruvian immigration on the Peruvian end of the bridge. Hand in your tourist card and get an exit stamp in your passport here, then walk over the bridge to the Ecuadorian immigration facility. Coming into Peru you may have to have your completed tourist card stamped by the national police.

Money and exchange You can change money in Macará, and in La Tina at the bank (Mon–Fri 9am–4pm).

The jungle

AERIAL VIEW OF IQUITOS

The jungle

The Amazon, the rainforest, the selva, the jungle, the green hell (*el infierno verde*): all attempt to name this huge, vibrant swathe of Peru. Whether you explore it up close, from the ground or a boat, or fly over it in a plane, the Peruvian jungle seems endless. Well over half of the country is covered by dense tropical rainforest, and this jungle region, sharing the western edge of the Amazon with Colombia, Ecuador and Brazil, forms part of what is probably the most biodiverse region on Earth. Jaguars, anteaters and tapirs still roam the forests, huge anacondas lurk in the swamps, toothy caimans sunbathe along riverbanks, and trees rise like giants from the forest floor. Many indigenous communities still live scattered throughout the Peruvian section of the Amazon, surviving primarily by hunting and fishing.

The jungle of southeastern Peru is plentifully supplied with lodges, guides, boats and flights. Cusco is arguably the best departure point for trips into the **southern selva**, with air and road access to the frontier town of **Puerto Maldonado** – a great base for visiting the nearby forests of **Madre de Dios**, which boast the **Reserva Nacional Tambopata–Candamo** and the **Parque Nacional Bahuaja-Sonene**, an enormous tract of virgin rainforest close to the Bolivian border. Many naturalists believe that this region is the most biodiverse on Earth, and thus the best place to head for wildlife. Reachable overland from Cusco, the **Manu Biosphere Reserve and National Park** runs from cloud forest on the slopes of the Andes down to relative lowland forest. For a quicker and cheaper taste of the jungle, you can travel by bus from Cusco via Ollantaytambo to **Quillabamba**, on the **Río Urubamba**, which flows north along the foot of the Andes, through the dangerous but unforgettable whitewater rapids of the **Pongo de Mainique**.

North of here lies **Pucallpa**, a rapidly growing, industrialized jungle town in the **central selva**, best reached by scheduled flights or the fully paved road from Lima. Another sector of this stunning central jungle region – **Chanchamayo** – is only eight hours by road from Lima, and is blessed with crystalline rivers, Peru's best coffee, numerous protected areas for birdwatching and good road links. Winding fast but precariously down from the Andean heights of Tarma, the Carretera Central is paved all the way to **Satipo**, a jungle frontier town, relatively close to the **Río Tambo**, the jumping-off point for off-the-beaten-track adventures. En route, the road passes through the cloud forest via **La Merced**, from where there are connections to quasi-European **Oxapampa,** the fascinating Tyrolean settlement of **Pozuzo** and **Villa Rica**, Peru's Coffee Central.

RÍO TAMBOPATA

Highlights

❶ Río Tambopata You'll be hard-pushed to find anywhere as rich in flora and fauna as the rainforest around some of the lodges on this stunning Amazonian river. **See p.440**

❷ Manu Biosphere Reserve An excellent place to experience a truly pristine rainforest and spot plenty of jungle wildlife – from giant otters in secluded lakes to caimans sunning themselves on the riverbanks. **See p.442**

❸ The central selva Taste Peru's best coffee in Villa Rica or La Merced or discover the country's Tyrolean roots in Pozuzo on a trip around the central selva. **See p.448**

❹ Pampa Hermosa Lodge Just eight hours' drive from Lima, this sumptuous cloud-forest lodge, one of the jewels of Peru, offers access to a cock-of-the-rock refuge, where Peru's national birds dance every evening. **See p.450**

❺ Iquitos A fun, vivacious city, ridiculously hot during the day, with an equally sizzling bar and club scene when the sun goes down, and animal rescue centres on the outskirts. **See p.461**

❻ Dolphin-watching Quite common in the rivers around Iquitos, pink river dolphins and blue dolphins are a fantastic sight as they leap around your boat. **See p.470**

❼ Ayahuasca healing Hearing a shaman's ancient chants waft under the moonlit jungle canopy while drinking the brew from a jungle vine is a powerful hallucinatory experience. **See p.475**

HIGHLIGHTS ARE MARKED ON THE MAP ON P.428

The main access point to the **northern selva** is **Iquitos**, at the heart of the largest chunk of lowland jungle – the largest city in the world that can only be reached by riverboat or plane. The northern selva can also be reached from the northern Peruvian coast via an adventurous route that takes the Río Huallaga from Yurimaguas (see p.392), a three- to four-day boat journey that can be broken by a visit to the immense **Reserva Nacional Pacaya Samiria** at the heart of the upper Amazon, a spectacular, little-visited wildlife haven, or via a river journey of similar length from Pucallpa along Río Ucayali. The northern selva is also the most organized and established of the Peruvian Amazon's tourist destinations, with many reputable companies offering a range of jungle visits, from luxury lodges and cruises (see p.473) to no-frills survival expeditions.

THE JUNGLE REGION

HIGHLIGHTS

1. Río Tambopata
2. Manu Biosphere Reserve
3. The central selva
4. Pampa Hermosa Lodge
5. Iquitos
6. Dolphin-watching
7. Ayahuasca healing

BEST OF THE JUNGLE

Given the breadth of options, it's not easy to decide which bit of the jungle to head for. Your three main criteria will probably be budget, ease of access (see p.430) and the nature of jungle experience you're after, whether it's a few days in a luxury lodge, exploring the rivers by boat or a back-to-nature week of wildlife-spotting. Below are the best places for…

Cash-strapped travellers Satipo or Puerto Maldonado; both can be reached with ease by bus. p.452 & p.432.

Trips of three days or less Puerto Maldonado, Iquitos or Satipo/Oxapampa. p.432, p.460 & p.452.

Off-the-beaten-track adventure Pucallpa, Iquitos and Puerto Maldonado are the best starting points; book through an established tour company. p.458, p.460 & p.432.

Wonderful wildlife The Manu Biosphere Reserve, Reserva Nacional Tambopata–Candamo or Reserva Nacional Pacaya Samiria. p.442, p.440 & p.471.

Blow-the-budget luxury Iquitos and Puerto Maldonado/Tambopata are great for top-flight jungle tours. p.460 & p.432.

Brief history

Many archaeologists believe that the initial spark for the evolution of Peru's high cultures came from the jungle. Evidence from **Chavín**, **Chachapoyas** and **Tantamayo** cultures seems to back up such a theory – ancient Andean people certainly had continuous contact with the jungle areas – and the **Incas** were unable to dominate the tribes, their main contact being peaceful trade in treasured items such as feathers, gold, medicinal plants and the sacred coca leaf. At the time of the **Spanish Conquest**, long-term settlements existed along all the major jungle rivers, with people living in large groups to farm the rich alluvial soils.

Early colonization

For centuries, the Peruvian jungle resisted major colonization. **Alonso de Alvarado** successfully led the first Spanish expedition, cutting a trail through from Chachapoyas to Moyobamba in 1537, but most incursions ended in utter disaster, defeated by disease, the ferocity of the indigenous peoples, the danger of the rivers, the climate and wild animals. Ultimately, apart from white-man's epidemics (which spread much faster than the men themselves), the early conquistadores had relatively little impact on the populations of the Peruvian Amazon. Only **Orellana**, one of the first Spaniards to lead exploratory expeditions into the Peruvian Amazon, managed to glimpse the reality of the rainforest, though even he seemed to misunderstand it when he was attacked by a tribe of blonde women, one of whom managed to hit him in the eye with a blow-gun dart. These "women" are now thought to be the men of the Yagua tribe (from near Iquitos), who wear straw-coloured, grass-like skirts and headdresses.

The impact of the Church

By the early eighteenth century the **Catholic Church** had made deep but vulnerable inroads into the rainforest regions. Resistance to this culminated in 1742 with an **indigenous uprising** in the central selva led by an enigmatic character from the Andes calling himself **Juan Santos Atahualpa**. Missions were destroyed, missionaries and colonists killed, and Spanish military expeditions defeated. The result was that the central rainforest remained under the control of the indigenous population for nearly a century more.

The rubber boom

As "white man's" technology advanced, so too did the possibilities of conquering Amazonia. The 1830s saw the beginning of a century of massive and painful exploitation of the forest and its population by **rubber barons**. Many of these wealthy men were European, eager to gain control of the raw material desperately needed following the discovery of the vulcanization process. Moreover, during this era the jungle regions of Peru were better connected to Brazil, Bolivia, the Atlantic and

---

AMAZON ECOLOGY: THE BASICS

At about six times the size of England, or approximately the size of California, the tangled, sweltering **Amazon Basin** rarely fails to capture the imagination of anyone who ventures beneath its dense canopy. In the **lowland areas**, away from the seasonally flooded riverbanks, the landscape is dominated by red, loamy soil, which can reach depths of 50m. Reaching upwards from this, the **primary forest** – mostly comprising a huge array of tropical palms, with scatterings of larger, emergent tree species – regularly achieves evergreen canopy heights of 50m. At ground level the vegetation is relatively open (mostly saplings, herbs and woody shrubs), since the trees tend to branch high up, restricting the amount of light available. At marginally **higher altitudes**, a large belt of **cloud forest** (*ceja de selva*) sweeps the eastern edges of the Andes, the most biodiverse of the rainforest zones.

---

ultimately Europe, than they were to Lima or the Pacific coast. The peak of the boom, from the 1880s to just before World War I, had a prolonged effect. Treating the local indigenous communities as little more than slaves, men like the notorious **Fitzcarrald** (see box, p.435) made overnight fortunes.

Modern colonization

Nineteenth-century colonialism also saw the progression of the **extractive frontier** along the navigable rivers, which involved short-term economic exploitation based on the extraction of other natural materials, such as timber and animal skins; coupled to this was the advance of the **agricultural frontier** down from the Andes. Both kinds of expansion assumed that Amazonia was a limitless source of natural resources and an empty wilderness – misapprehensions that still exist today.

Coca barons

When the Peruvian economy began to suffer in the mid-1980s, foreign credit ended, and those with substantial private capital fled, mainly to the US. The government, then led by the young Alan García, was forced to abandon the jungle region, and both its colonist and indigenous inhabitants were left to survive by themselves. This effectively opened the doors for the **coca barons**, who had already established themselves during the 1970s in the Huallaga Valley, and who moved into the gap left by government aid in the other valleys of the *ceja de selva* (edge of the jungle) – notably the Pichis-Palcazu and the Apurimac-Ene. Over the subsequent decade, illicit coca production was responsible for some ten percent of the deforestation that occurred in the Peruvian Amazon during the entire twentieth century; furthermore, trade in this lucrative crop led to significant corruption and supported the rise of **terrorism**.

The twenty-first century

Clearing the forest for agriculture continues, and in Madre de Dios **gold mining** ravages the jungle. By the turn of the century, a massive desert had appeared around Huaypetue, previously a small-time frontier mining town. The neighbouring communities of Amarakaeri (who have been panning for gold in a small-scale, sustainable fashion for more than thirty years) are in danger of losing their land and natural resources. Attempts by NGOs and pro-indigenous lawyers to maintain the boundaries of reserves and communities are constantly thwarted by colonists, who are supported by local government.

GETTING TO THE JUNGLE

By plane Flying to the main jungle towns – Iquitos (1hr 40min), Puerto Maldonado (1hr 40min), Tarapoto (1hr) and Pucallpa (1hr) – from Lima (Puerto Maldonado is also reachable from Cusco; 1hr) is relatively inexpensive (from around US$100 one way) and can save a long bus journey (Iquitos is only reachable by plane or boat).

By bus or colectivo The central selva (La Merced, Oxapampa, Satipo) is easily reachable by paved road from Lima (8–10hr), while Tarapoto and Yurimaguas are also reachable by paved road form Lima (the long way),

Pucallpa and Cajamarca via Pedro Ruíz. Parts of the southern selva (Manu Biosphere Reserve, Quillabamba) are reachable from Cusco by bus (the former also by boat), while Puerto Maldonado is only 10hr by bus along a good paved road from Cusco and 12hr from Juliaca (near Puno).

By boat You can reach Iquitos easily by boat from the frontier with Brazil and Colombia (see p.477) or else by slow boat from Pucallpa (see p.459) and Yurimaguas (see p.392).

GETTING AROUND THE JUNGLE

BY BOAT

The three most common forms of river transport are canoes (*canoas*), speedboats (*deslizadoras*) and larger riverboats (*lanchas*). Whichever method you choose, it's a good idea to make sure you can get along with the boatman (*piloto*) or captain, and that he really does know the rivers.

By canoe Canoes can be anything from a small dugout with a paddle, useful for moving along small creeks and rivers, to a large 18m canoe with panelled sides and a *peque-peque* (on-board engine) or a more powerful outboard motor. Travelling in a smaller canoe requires either reliable local guides or a good tour company with professional guides.

By speedboat Speedboats are considerably faster and more manoeuvrable than canoes, but also more expensive.

By riverboat Riverboats come in a range of sizes and vary considerably in their river-worthiness: always have a good look at the boat before buying a ticket or embarking on a journey. The best are the Iquitos-based tour boats, with cabins for up to thirty passengers, dining rooms, bars, sun lounges and even jacuzzis on board. Next best are the larger vessels such as Henry boats, with up to three decks, with hammock spaces and a few cabins (for which you pay two to three times as much); cabins are rarely more than airless boxes, so you'll want to sleep in a hammock anyway, but may wish to rent a cabin just for the purpose of storing your luggage. Always try to get a spot as close as possible to the front of the boat, away from the noise of the motor. On the larger riverboats (especially between Pucallpa and Iquitos, or Tabatinga and Iquitos) you can save money on hotels by hanging around in your hammock, as most captains allow passengers to sling one up and sleep on board for a day or two before departure.

ON FOOT

Walking is slow and difficult in the forest, and should only be attempted with an experienced tour guide or local person willing to guide you. People rarely get from A to B on foot, since river travel is the fastest and safest route in much of the rainforest.

Getting lost Losing your bearings on walking trails in the forest is a genuine danger, even for locals. By straying less than a hundred metres from your lodge, camp, the river or your guide, you can find yourself completely surrounded by a seemingly impenetrable tangle of undergrowth. If there are any, one trail looks very much like the next to the unaccustomed eye. If you're with a group who will look for you when they realize you are lost, a sensible strategy is to shout, blow a whistle (always carry one!) or bang the base of big buttress-root trees as indigenous people do when they get lost on hunting forages. If no one is likely to come looking for you, find moving water and follow it downstream to the main river, where there's more probability of finding a settlement or passing boat. If you get caught out overnight, the best places to sleep are: beside a fire on the riverbank; in a nest you could make for yourself in between the buttress roots of a large tree; higher up in a tree that isn't crawling with biting ants; in a hammock.

8

JUNGLE ESSENTIALS

- Anti-diarrhoea medicine (such as Lomotil or Imodium)
- Certificate of inoculation against yellow fever (essential if you're planning on crossing into Brazil overland)
- Malaria pills (start course in advance as directed by your doctor)
- Insect repellent containing DEET
- Suitable clothing (socks, trousers and long sleeves in the evenings)
- Sunhat
- Toilet paper
- Torch and spare batteries
- Waterproof poncho
- Whistle
- Multipurpose knife (with can and bottle opener)
- Plastic bags for packing and lining your bags (a watertight box is best for camera equipment and other delicate valuables)
- Waterproof matches and a back-up gas lighter
- Gifts for people you might encounter (batteries, knives, fish-hooks and line, and so on)
- Insect-bite ointment (antihistamines, tiger balm or *mentol china*)
- Running shoes; trekking sandals (rubber boots for jungle outings are provided by jungle lodges)

INDIGENOUS PEOPLES OF THE JUNGLE

Outside the few main towns of the Peruvian jungle, there are few sizeable settlements, and the population remains dominated by about fifty **indigenous groups**. For most, the jungle offers a **semi-nomadic** existence, and in terms of material possessions, they have, need and want very little. Communities are scattered, with groups of between ten and two hundred people, and their sites shift every few years. For **subsistence** they depend on small, cultivated plots, fish from the rivers and game from the forest, including wild pigs, deer, monkeys and a great range of edible birds. The main species of edible jungle fish are *sabalo* or doncella (oversized catfish), *carachama* (an armoured walking catfish), the feisty piranha and the giant *zungaro* and *paiche* – the latter, at up to 200kg, being the world's largest scaled freshwater fish. In fact, food is so abundant that jungle-dwellers generally spend no more than three to four days a week engaged in subsistence activities, which, as some anthropologists like to point out, makes them "relatively affluent".

After centuries of **external influence** (missionaries, gold-seekers, rubber barons, cash-crop colonists, cocaine smugglers, soldiers, oil companies, illegal loggers, documentary makers, anthropologists and now tourists), most indigenous peoples speak Spanish and live fairly conventional, westernized lives. While many have been sucked into the money-based labour market, however, others, increasingly under threat, have struggled for cultural integrity and **territorial rights**; some – voluntarily isolated or uncontacted – have retreated as far as they are able beyond the world's enclosing frontier. Today they are struggling as their traditional and last remaining hunting grounds are infiltrated by oil companies and loggers.

8 Madre de Dios

A large, forested region, with a manic climate (usually searingly hot and humid, but with sudden cold spells – *friajes* – between June and August, due to icy winds coming down from the Andean glaciers), the **southern selva** has only been systematically explored since the 1950s.

Named after the broad river that flows through the heart of the southern jungle, the still relatively wild *departamento* of **MADRE DE DIOS** is centred on the fast-growing river town of **Puerto Maldonado**, near the Bolivian border and just 180m above sea level. Most visitors come for the nearby **wildlife**, either in the strictly protected **Manu Biosphere Reserve** – still essentially an expedition zone – and the cheaper and easy-to-access **Reserva Nacional Tambopata–Candamo**. Both offer some of the most luxuriant jungle and richest flora and fauna in the world. Another massive protected area, the **Parque Nacional Bahuaja-Sonene**, is adjacent to Tambopata.

Easily accessible from several jungle lodges (or by chartering a boat), **Lago Sandoval** and the huge expanse of **Lago Valencia** are both great wildlife spots east along the Río Madre de Dios and close to the Bolivian border. At the least, you're likely to spot a few caimans and the strange hoatzin bird, and if you're very lucky, larger mammals such as capybara, tapir or, less likely, jaguar – and at Valencia, you can fish for piranha. A little further southeast lies the **Pampas del Heath**, the only tropical grassland within Peru. The Río Madre de Dios itself is fed by two main tributaries, the **Río Manu** and the **Río Alto Madre de Dios**, which roll off the Paucartambo Ridge just north of Cusco. West of this ridge, the **Río Urubamba** watershed starts and its river flows on past Machu Picchu and down to the jungle area around the town of **Quillabamba**, before entering lowland Amazon beyond the rapids of **Pongo de Mainique**.

Puerto Maldonado

A frontier colonist town with strong links to the Cusco region, **PUERTO MALDONADO** has a fervour for bubbly jungle *chicha* music. With an economy originally based on unsustainable lumber and gold extraction, the early twentieth-century rubber boom and highly sustainable Brazil-nut gathering from the rivers and forests of Madre de

Dios, Puerto Maldonado has grown enormously from a small, laidback outpost of civilization to a busy market town.

Today, swollen by the arrival of businesses thanks to the Interoceanic Highway linking Peru to Brazil, it's the thriving capital of a region that feels very much on the threshold of major upheavals.

The town itself is centred around a pleasant Plaza de Armas but has few specific attractions, and most visitors come here primarily to head into the jungle and stay in a **lodge** (see p.436).

The port
Follow Jirón Billinghurst one block towards the river from the main plaza, and head down the steep steps to the main **port** area, situated on the **Río Madre de Dios**, and offering an otherwise rare glimpse of the river. There used to be a lot of boat traffic, ferrying people across the river, now replaced by the **suspension bridge** (Puente Intercontinental), built recently as part of the Interoceanic Highway.

Obelisco
Jirones Fitzcarrald and Madre de Dios • Daily 9am–5pm • S/2

This distinctly phallic concrete-and-glass **Obelisco** rises 30m above the city in the middle of two busy streets. It's well worth ascending the tower for a 360-degree view of the colourful houses, the jungle, the river and the corrugated iron roofs of Puerto Maldonado.

Mercado Central
Block 4 of Jr Ica • Daily 6.30am–4pm

The **Mercado Central**, just eight short blocks from the Plaza de Armas, is large, busy and brimming over with jungle produce, including Brazil nuts; it also has a couple of rainforest medicine practitioners. A few stalls offer fresh fruit juice.

8

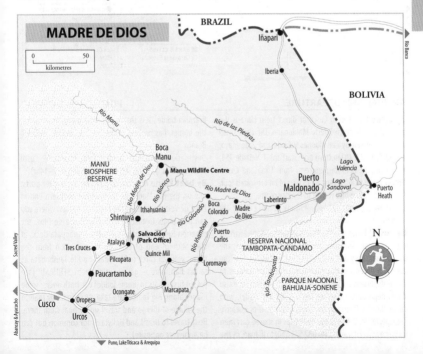

8

PUERTO MALDONADO

Río Madre de Dios

Port area
(Madre de Dios)

Police

Viewing Platform

PLAZA GRAU

Capitania
del Puerto

Municipal Building

Interbank

Teatro
Municipal

Cinema

PLAZA
DE ARMAS

Scotiabank

BCP

LAMBAYEQUE

CUSCO

2 DE MAYO

PIURA

G PRADA

ERNESTO RIVERO

J TRONCOSO

MOQUEGUA

TACNA

ICA

AV FITZCARRALD

Money
Change

Mercado
Central

LEÓN DE VELARDE

PUNO

PUNO

AREQUIPA

26 DE DICIEMBRE

LORETO

CARRION

BILLINGHURST

PUENTE INTERCONTINENTAL

Airport, Laberinto & Cusco buses

Immigration Office

Obelisco & Transportes M. D'Acre

N

0   200
metres

Port Area (Tambopata) & 7

ACCOMMODATION
Anaconda Jungle Lodge	3
Cabaña Quinta	4
Hostal Paititi	6
Hotel Centenario	2
Kapievi Eco Village	7
Tambopata Hostel	5
Wasai	1

CAFÉS & RESTAURANTS
Burgos's House	3
La Casa Nostra	7
Cevichería El Califa	1
Chifa Wa Seng	6
Los Gustitos del Cura	2
Pizzeria Chez Maggy	4
Pollos a la Brasa la Estrella	5

BARS & CLUBS
La Casa de la Cerveza	2
Witite	1

ARRIVAL AND DEPARTURE

PUERTO MALDONADO

By plane Flying from Cusco or direct from Lima is the quickest way to reach Puerto Maldonado. The city's small airport is served by Lan (jirones Velarde and 2 de Mayo; ☎ 082 573 677, ⊚ lan.com) and StarPerú (C Velarde 151; ☎ 082 573 564, ⊚ starperu.com) from Lima and Cusco. Unless you're being picked up as part of an organized tour, mototaxis (S/8) whisk you off to the city centre.

Destinations Cusco (2 daily; 45min); Lima (2 daily; 1hr 40min).

By bus All buses serving Peruvian destinations arrive at the Terminal Terrestre, several blocks north of the Interoceanic Hwy and a S/2 ride on a motorbike from the centre. A dozen bus companies run overnight services to Cusco, departing at around 8.30pm and 9pm; there are also direct departures to Juliaca (6pm & 6.30pm daily), with connections to Puno and Arequipa. At the time of research, Transportes M. D'Acre made daily trips in shared cars from its office at Av Fitzcarrald (☎ 082 571 560) to Iñapari, by the

Brazilian border, less than a 3hr drive away; Assis, across the border, has onward connections to Brasília and Río Branco.

Destinations Brazilian border (see opposite); Cusco (numerous daily; 10hr); Juliaca (several daily; 12–14hr).

By boat Puerto Maldonado has two main river ports: one on the Río Madre de Dios, at the northern end of León de Velarde, just off the Plaza de Armas, where you can hire boats to take you up Río Madre de Dios; the other on Río Tambopata. From the Tambopata dock, at the southern end of León de Velarde, 2km from the plaza, you can catch public boats up Río Tambopata as far as Baltimore – get a permit from SERNAMP (see p.436) first. Boats to jungle lodges use both docks; some lodges along Río Tambopata take passengers by road to the village of Ifierno and travel up by boat from there. Boat travel to Brazil and Bolivia is not common but can be done (see opposite).

CROSSING INTO BRAZIL AND BOLIVIA

INTO BRAZIL

If heading to Brazil overland, all visitors must present yellow fever certificates.

From Puerto Maldonado to the border Catch a shared car (see opposite) to the border town of Iñapari, around 2hr 30min from Puerto Maldonado, and get an exit stamp from the Peruvian border post (Mon–Fri 8.30am–noon & 2.30–7pm, Sat & Sun 9am–noon & 2.30–6pm). Book transport to the border at least a day in advance. To enter Brazil Americans need a Brazilian visa, which must be obtained in advance in Lima (see p.96) or in the United States. It's only 2km from Iñapari to the Brazilian Federal Police and customs (colectivos available from the main plaza in Iñapari). Change Peruvian money before leaving Peru. Assis, across the border from Iñapari, has better lodgings than Iñapari (though still basic).

From the border to Brazil Get stamped into Brazil in Assis. From Assis there's public transport plying the 112km to Brasília, a much larger town that also connects via a walkable bridge with the Bolivian free-trade-zone town of Cobija. From Brasiléia, colectivos and buses for Río Branco leave regularly from near the Ponte Augusto do Araujó.

Destinations Iñapari and the border (several shared cars daily from 4am; 2hr 30min).

INTO BOLIVIA

By boat It's possible to travel into Bolivia on one of the cargo boats that leave more or less every week from Puerto Maldonado (there are occasional cargo and passenger boats that go all the way to Riberalta, though not during the "dry" months of July–Sept) or else you can hire a boat to take you to Puerto Pardo (around US$100), the last frontier Peruvian settlement. First, get your Peruvian exit stamp from the Puerto Maldonado police and Migraciones offices (see p.438). From Puerto Pardo it's a short hop by boat to the Bolivian frontier post of Puerto Heath (get your Bolivian entry stamp here) from where you continue by river to Riberalta (a week or so), or take public transport north to Cobija via Chivé. From Riberalta there are land and air connections to the rest of Bolivia, as well as river or road access into Brazil via the Río Madeira or Guajará-Mirim. Alternatively, you can cross into Brasiléia in Brazil (see opposite), catch a ferry to Cobija in Bolivia, and then combine overland and boat travel to Riberalta. Americans need a visa to enter Bolivia, which can be obtained at land border crossings for US$135 in cash.

GETTING AROUND AND INFORMATION

By mototaxi/motorbike The quickest way of getting around Puerto Maldonado is by mototaxi (S/2–3 in town, S/7 to the airport, but check before getting in) or passenger-carrying motorbikes (S/1.50–2 in town).

Tourist information The airport has a tourist information kiosk (rarely staffed). For permits to travel by river into the jungle call at the Captanía del Puerto on León de Velarde, between avenidas González Prada and Dos de

8

THE SAGA OF FITZCARRALD

While the infamous rubber baron, **Fitzcarrald** (often mistakenly called Fitzcarraldo), is associated with the founding of Puerto Maldonado, he actually died some twelve years before the event; his story is, however, relevant to the development of this region. While working rubber on the Río Urubamba, Fitzcarrald caught the gold bug after hearing rumours from local Ashaninka and Machiguenga Indians of an **Inca fort** protecting vast treasures, possibly around the Río Purus. Setting out along the Mishagua, a tributary of the Río Urubamba, he managed to reach its source, and from there walked over the ridge to a new watershed which he took to be the Purus, though it was in fact the Río Cashpajali, a tributary of the Río Manu. Leaving men to clear a path, he returned to Iquitos, and in 1884 came back to the region on a boat called *La Contamana*. He took the boat apart, and, with the aid of over a thousand Asháninka and other indigenous people carried it across to the "Purus". But, as he cruised down, attacked by tribes at several points, Fitzcarrald slowly began to realize that the river was not the Purus – a fact confirmed when he eventually bumped into a Bolivian rubber collector.

Though he'd ended up on the wrong river, Fitzcarrald had discovered a link connecting the two great Amazonian watersheds. In Europe, the discovery was heralded as a great step forward in the exploration of South America, but for Peru it meant more **rubber**, a quicker route for its export and the beginning of the end for Madre de Dios's indigenous tribes. Puerto Maldonado was founded in 1902, and as exploitation of the region's rubber peaked, so too was there an increase in population of workers and merchants, with Madre de Dios ultimately becoming a *departamento* of Peru in 1912. German director **Werner Herzog** thought this historical episode a fitting subject for celluloid, and in 1982 directed the epic *Fitzcarraldo*.

MADRE DE DIOS'S GOLD

Every rainy season the swollen rivers of Madre de Dios deposit a heavy layer of **gold dust** along their banks, and those who have been quick enough to stake claims on the best stretches have made substantial fortunes. In such areas there are thousands of **unregulated miners**, using large front-loader earth-moving machines, destroying a large section of the forest, and doing so very quickly.

Gold lust is not a new phenomenon here – the gold-rich rivers have brought Andean Indians and occasional European explorers to the region for centuries. The Inca Emperor Tupac Yupanqui is known to have discovered the Río Madre de Dios, naming it the Amarymayo ("serpent river"), and may well have sourced some of the Empire's gold from around here.

Mayo (Mon–Sat 8am–6pm).

National park information The local SERNANP office (dealing with national protected areas) is at Av 28 de Julio 875 (☎ 082 573 278, ⓦ sernapt.gob.pe/sernamp. Entry to the national parks of this region is either organized by your tour company or paid for at the relevant river entry points, but this office has info on the protected areas.

ACCOMMODATION

★**Anaconda Jungle Lodge** Airport road ☎ 082 792 726, ⓦ anacondajunglelodge.com. Within a 10min walk of the airport (and about 6km from Puerto Maldonado's centre), *Anaconda Jungle Lodge* accommodates its visitors in attractive traditional palm-roofed bungalows set on stilts above the ground within pleasant jungle gardens, complete with several species of resident monkey. There's a swimming pool and a restaurant that serves authentic Thai cuisine. S̲/160

Cabaña Quinta Jr Cusco 535 ☎ 082 571 045, ⓦ hotelcabanaquinta.com. Close to the centre, this orange, two-storey creation is one of the more popular hotels in town. Rooms are comfortable, some have fans – the more expensive ones a/c – and all are complemented by a small attractive garden. There's also an excellent bar-restaurant, wi-fi, a small pool and sauna. S̲/180

Hostal Paititi Jr Velarde 290 and Jr Prada ☎ 082 574 667. Colourful central guesthouse on a busy street, with spacious rooms and large windows, guest internet and even a small gym. The on-site café is decent and a basic breakfast is included. You can opt for cheaper fan-cooled rooms. S̲/140

Hotel Centenario Av Dos de Mayo 744 ☎ 082 574 731, ⓦ hotelcentenario.com.pe. Modern, business-style hotel several blocks out of the centre, complete with rooftop pool surrounded by greenery and spick-and-span rooms with shiny floors, cable TV and swan-shaped towels. Some English spoken. S̲/170

Kapieivi Eco Village Carretera Tambopata Km1.5 ☎ 082 795 650, ⓦ ecoaldeakapieivi.blogspot.com. Part-yoga and part-ayahuasca retreat, this chilled-out place sits in its own patch of jungle off the dirt road leading to Infierno (10min by mototaxi). Expect rustic cabins with mosquito nets, solar-heated showers, wind chimes dangling from trees and home-cooked meals on request. S̲/100 per person

★**Tambopata Hostel** Av 26 de Diciembre 234 ☎ 082 574 201, ⓦ tambopatahostel.com. A great-value pad for budget travellers in a very central cedarwood-built house with dorms, private rooms (some with own bathrooms) with mozzie nets and hammocks in the garden. There's free wi-fi, a communal kitchen and an outside terrace. Breakfasts are included in the price, you can bone up on your Peruvian slang by reading the wall, and tours to Lago Sandoval and Colorado clay lick are organized. Dorms S̲/30, doubles S̲/80

Wasai Parque Grau on Jr Billinghurst ☎ 082 572 290, ⓦ wasai.com. The best of the higher-end options, offering fine views over the Río Madre de Dios, and an apple-shaped swimming pool with a waterfall and bar set among trees. All rooms are cabin-style with TV and shower, and staff here also organize local tours and run the *Wasai Lodge* (see p.442). S̲/210

EATING AND DRINKING

Manioc and fish are staple foods in the town's **restaurants**. A variety of river fish is always available, even in ceviche form, though there is some concern in the region about river pollution from the unofficial gold mining. Venison (try *estofado de venado*) and wild boar fresh from the forest are often on the menu too.

★**Burgos's House** Av 26 de Diciembre, cuadra 1. In a new location and surrounded by lush greenery, this is the nicest place to eat in town, with an extensive menu of dishes heavily influenced by jungle ingredients (*juanes* with wild pig and criollo salad, grilled fish with star fruit sauce) and an evening buffet (pick a main and then help yourself to fried *yuca* and sweet potato, salads and more). The exotic cocktails (maracuya sour, for example) pack a punch. Daily noon–3pm & 6–10pm.

La Casa Nostra Jr Velarde 515 ☎ 082 573 833. A popular little café with evocative photos of turn-of-the-century Puerto Maldonado, a range of tasty cakes, tropical fruit juices (including mango, passionfruit, pineapple and local favourite *carambola* for around S/3 a glass), as well as tamales and *papas rellenas* (stuffed potatoes). It also serves pretty good coffee and Peruvian breakfasts with a side of ill grace. Daily 7am–1pm & 4–11pm.

Cevichería El Califa Jr Piura 266 ☎ 082 571 119. A popular local lunchtime spot, *El Califa* is a garden-based restaurant, slightly hidden away, serving a variety of national and international dishes (from around S/25), including riverfish ceviche, palm heart, pig's-head soup and a range of *refresco* drinks made from tropical fruits. Mon–Sat 11am–5pm.

Chifa Wa Seng Av Dos de Mayo 253. This popular *chifa* successfully combines traditional Chinese meals with an abundance of jungle foodstuffs. Good selection of noodle and rice dishes. Mains from S/15. Daily 11.30am–9pm.

Los Gustitos del Cura C Loreto 258. Right on the Plaza de Armas, this place is particularly good for ice cream, but it also serves tamales and other inexpensive light bites. Ice cream S/2 per scoop. Daily 8am–8pm.

Pizzería Chez Maggy Jr Carrión 271. This is arguably Puerto Maldonado's best pizzeria, with ample portions of wood-fired pizza, calzones and an array of pastas. Only open in the evening, as the oven makes the place, erm, an oven during daytime. Pizzas from S/20. Daily 6–10pm.

Pollos a la Brasa la Estrella Jr Velarde 474. Perpetually popular grilled chicken joint, and it's fine as long as you don't order anything more ambitious than chicken and chips. Quarter chicken S/7. Daily noon–9.30pm.

DRINKING AND NIGHTLIFE

There's a surprisingly busy **nightlife** in this laidback town, especially at weekends, with venues blaring rock, reggae, chicha, cumbia or Latin pop. Things tend to really kick off around midnight on Friday and Saturday nights. Many bars are either on or around the plaza.

La Casa de la Cerveza Jirones Velarde and Carrión. Popular two-storey watering hole right on the plaza, with a good range of beers and some stronger options if you feel like courting oblivion. Daily 6pm–late.

Witite Jr Velarde 151. This old stalwart, with Shipibo designs adorning the walls and a surprisingly advanced sound system playing the whole range of Latino music, is still one of the best places in town to hit the dancefloor. Entry is usually free. Fri & Sat 7pm–5/6am.

8

MADRE DE DIOS'S INDIGENOUS GROUPS

Off the main Madre de Dios waterways, within the system of smaller tributaries and streams, live a variety of different **indigenous groups**. All are depleted in numbers due to contact with Western diseases and influences, such as pollution of their rivers, environmental destruction by large-scale gold-mining and new waves of exploration for oil. While some have been completely wiped out over the last twenty years, several have maintained their isolation. These groups have recently come to worldwide attention as the international press have highlighted the plight of "the uncontacted".

If you go anywhere in the jungle, especially on an organized tour, you're likely to stop off at a **tribal village** for at least half an hour or so, and the more you know about the people, the more you'll get out of the visit. Downstream from Puerto Maldonado, the most populous indigenous group are the **Ese Eja** (often wrongly, and derogatorily, called "Huarayos" by *colonos*). Originally semi-nomadic hunters and gatherers, the Ese Eja were well-known warriors who fought the Incas and, later on, the Spanish expedition of Alvarez Maldonado – eventually establishing fairly friendly and respectful relationships with both. Under Fitzcarrald's reign, they suffered greatly through the **engaño system**, which tricked them into slave labour through credit offers on knives, machetes, pots and pans, which then took years, or in some cases a lifetime, to work off. Quite often, indigenous people were kidnapped, forced to sign sham contracts and live out short, brutal lives as slaves, only to be replaced by others like themselves when they died from overwork and maltreatment.

Upstream from Puerto Maldonado live several indigenous groups, known collectively (again, wrongly and derogatorily) as the "Mashcos" but actually comprising at least five separate linguistic groups – the **Huachipaeri**, **Amarakaeri**, **Sapitoyeri**, **Arasayri** and **Toyeri**. All typically use long bows – over 1.5m – and lengthy arrows, and most settlements will also have a shotgun or two these days, since less time can be dedicated to hunting when they are panning for gold or working timber for *colonos*. Traditionally, they wore long bark-cloth robes and had long hair, and the men often stuck eight feathers into the skin around their lips, making them look distinctively fierce and cat-like. Many Huachipaeri and Amarakaeri groups are now actively engaging with the outside world on their own terms, and some of their young men and women have gone through university education and subsequently returned to their native villages.

DIRECTORY

Immigration Oficina de Migraciones is at Av 28 de Julio 467 (Mon–Fri 8am–1pm; ☎ 082 571 069).

Money and exchange There are three banks on the plaza: Scotiabank, Interbank and BCP, all with ATMs. There are casas de cambio at jirones Prada and Puno gives standard rates for US$.

Post office Jr Velarde 675, opposite the corner of Jr Troncoso (Mon–Sat 8am–8pm, Sun 8am–3pm).

Around Puerto Maldonado

Madre de Dios boasts spectacular virgin **lowland rainforest** and exceptional **wildlife**. A range of lodges, some excellent local guides and ecologists, plus indigenous cultures are all within a few hours of Puerto Maldonado. Serious **jungle trips** can be made here with relative ease, and this part of the Amazon offers easy and uniquely rewarding access to relatively undisturbed rainforest. Most travellers come to Puerto Maldonado in order to stay in a jungle lodge, either on the Río Madre de Dios or the Río Tambopata. The former offers greater ease of access from Puerto Maldonado, and good wildlife-viewing opportunities nearby on Lago Sandoval, Lago Valencia and Río Heath, while the latter is spectacular for its remoteness away from human habitation and there's an even better chance of seeing the jungle fauna, particularly inside the Tambopata Reserve proper.

Lago Sandoval

1hr downriver from Puerto Maldonado (1hr 30min on the return), plus 40min–1hr walk

A short way downriver from Puerto Maldonado is **Lago Sandoval**, a large lake where the Ministry of Agriculture have introduced the large *paiche* fish. You can walk here from the drop-off point on the Río Madre de Dios; during the rainy season, the 3km track turns into a mudbath and rubber boots are essential. By the lake, a caretaker watches over several large rowing boats that can hold up to a dozen people. The wildlife is at its best early in the morning, so it helps to stay either next to Lago Sandoval or at one of the nearby lodges (see p.440) that run tours here. There's a fair amount of birdlife to be seen, including hoatzins and the occasional toucan, as well as a family of **giant otters**.

You can come here as part of a tour run by a lodge or else you can charter a boat for around S/120 in Puerto Maldonado for several people and have it pick you up later.

Lago Valencia and around

60km from Puerto Maldonado along Río Madre de Dios; 6–8hr by canoe with a *peque-peque*, or around 2hr in a *lancha* with an outboard

Travelling by boat from Puerto Maldonado to the huge lake of **Lago Valencia**, you can stop off to watch some gold-panners on the Río Madre de Dios and visit a small settlement of **Ese Eja**; about thirty minutes beyond, you turn off the main river into a narrow channel that connects with the lake.

Towards sunset it's quite common to see caimans basking on the muddy banks, an occasional **puma** if you're lucky, or the largest rodent in the world, a **capybara**. Up in

---

WILDLIFE ON THE LAKES

Both Lago Valencia and Lago Sandoval are superbly endowed with **birdlife**. In addition to the hoatzin (see opposite) you might spot kingfishers, cormorants, herons, egrets, pink flamingoes, skimmers, macaws, toucans, parrots and gavilans.

Behind the wall of trees along the banks hide **deer**, **wild pigs** and **tapir**, all of them spotted occasionally. If you're lucky enough to catch a glimpse of a tapir you'll be seeing one of South America's strangest creatures – almost the size of a cow, with an elongated rubbery nose and spiky mane. In fact, the tapir is known in the jungle as a *sachavaca* ("forest cow" – *sacha* is Quechua for "forest" and *vaca* is Spanish for "cow").

There are caimans and larger fish in the lake, but the easiest fish to catch are **piranhas** – all you need is some line, a hook and a chunk of unsalted meat; throw this into the lake and you've got yourself a piranha.

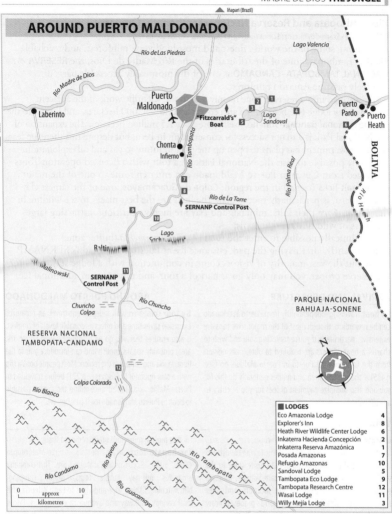

▲ Iñapari (Brazil)

AROUND PUERTO MALDONADO

Río de Las Piedras

Lago Valencia

Río Madre de Dios

Cusco

Laberinto

Puerto
Maldonado

"Fitzcarrald's
Boat"

Lago
Sandoval

Puerto
Pardo

Puerto
Heath

BOLIVIA

Río Heath

Río Palma Real

Chonta

Infierno

Río Tambopata

7

8

Río de La Torre
SERNANP Control Post

9

10

Lago
Sachavacayoc

Baltimore

Río Malinowski

**SERNANP
Control Post**

11

Chuncho
Colpa

Río Chuncho

PARQUE NACIONAL
BAHUAJA-SONENE

8

RESERVA NACIONAL
TAMBOPATA-CANDAMO

12

Colpa Colorado

Río Blanco

Río Tavara

Río Candamo

Río Guacamayo

Río Tambopata

N

| 0 | approx | 10 |

kilometres

■ LODGES	
Eco Amazonia Lodge	4
Explorer's Inn	8
Heath River Wildlife Center Lodge	6
Inkaterra Hacienda Concepción	2
Inkaterra Reserva Amazónica	1
Posada Amazonas	7
Refugio Amazonas	10
Sandoval Lodge	5
Tambopata Eco Lodge	9
Tambopata Research Centre	12
Wasai Lodge	11
Willy Mejía Lodge	3

the trees around the channel lie hundreds of **hoatzin** birds, or *gallos* as they are called locally – large, ungainly creatures with orange and brown plumage, long wings and distinctive spiky crests. Some lodges (see p.440) organize full-day tours to the lake that combine bird watching with some excellent fishing.

Río Heath and Parque Nacional Bahuaja-Sonene
Less than 2hr from Lago Valencia in a motorized *lancha*

Further up from Lago Valencia and skirting the Peru–Bolivia border is the **Río Heath**, a national rainforest sanctuary that passes through the remote **Parque Nacional Bahuaja-Sonene**, a superb place for wildlife watching and well worth the effort of getting there. The only place to stay in the park is the *Heath River Wildlife Center Lodge*, run by InkaNatura (see p.446). Pay your entrance fee at the SERNANP office in Puerto Maldonado (see p.436).

Río Tambopata and Reserva Nacional Tambopata–Candamo

S/100 entry fee • Reached by motorized canoe from Puerto Maldonado • ⓦ tambopata.com

Containing some of the world's finest and most biodiverse rainforest, and reachable via Río Tambopata, one of the tributaries of the Río Madre de Dios, the **RESERVA NACIONAL TAMBOPATA–CANDAMO** is one of the most easily accessible parts of relatively pristine Amazon rainforest.

Transformed into a reserved zone mainly due to the scientific work of the adjacent *Explorer's Inn* lodge (see below), the area covers around 250,000 hectares, and is next to the **Parque Nacional Bahuaja-Sonene**, itself more than 1.5 million hectares. The expansion of the National Park is a major success for conservation in Peru, but despite this there are fears that the government has plans to open up the park in future to gas and oil exploitation.

It's only possible to visit the National Park on a **tour** with a licensed operator. Tours organized from Cusco or Puerto Maldonado can enter en route to one of the major macaw **salt-licks** (*colpas*) in the region; **Colpa de Guacamayos**, one of the largest clay licks in Peru, is particularly spectacular. The licks are the best places to see wildlife in the jungle, since their salts, minerals and clay are highly nutritious, attracting large numbers of wild birds and animals.

It's technically possible to enter the *zona de amortiguamento* (buffer zone) independently, after paying the park entrance fee at Puerto Maldonado's SERNAMP office, but the vast majority of visitors come in conjunction with a lodge stay. To enter the reserve proper, you may only go as part of a tour, and must pay an additional fee.

ARRIVAL AND DEPARTURE

By boat Travelling independently from Puerto Maldonado can be rewarding, though most of the major river trips are expensive, particularly if you're travelling solo and wish to charter a boat. Visitors are required to obtain permission from the Capitanía del Puerto in Puerto Maldonado (see p.435) – though boatmen and guides generally do this for you and also organize payment of fees for you at entry to any protected areas.

AROUND PUERTO MALDONADO

By tour Compared with independent travel, an organized excursion saves time and offers reasonable levels of comfort. It also ensures that you go with someone who knows the area, probably speaks English and can introduce you to the flora, fauna and culture of the region. Most people book a trip with a tour operator in Cusco (see p.221) before travelling to Puerto Maldonado, or in advance online, though it is possible to book in Puerto Maldonado itself (see below).

TOURS

Inotawa Expeditions Av Aeropuerto, Puerto Maldonado ☎ 082 572 511, ⓦ inotawaexpeditions.com. Located on the Río Tambopata quite close to the start of the Parque Nacional Bahuaja-Sonene, Inotawa operates a nice lodge in a good location, and offer expeditions to Colpa Colorado, the world's biggest macaw salt-lick a further 8hr into the forest from the lodge. Prices start at US$280 per person for two nights, US$380 for five nights; minimum group required is six.

Tambopata Tours Jr Velarde 173, Puerto Maldonado ☎ 082 502 475, ⓦ tambopatatours.com. This company organizes full-day jungle tours, jungle camping, birdwatching, fishing trips and visits to Lago Valencia, the local canopy walkway and ayahuasca ceremonies. Prices depend on service level and lodge accommodation, but expect to pay US$100–250 a day per person.

ACCOMMODATION

RÍO MADRE DE DIOS

Eco Amazonia Lodge C Garcilazo 210, Oficina 206, Cusco ☎ 084 236 159 ⓦ ecoamazonia.com.pe. Less than 2hr downriver of Puerto Maldonado, this large establishment offers fifty comfortable bungalows. The area abounds in stunning oxbow lakes, and while it can't claim the variety of flora and fauna of the Reserva Nacional Tambopata–Candamo, it is recommended for birdwatching. Packages usually include visits to Lago Apu Victor, Monkey Island, caiman-spotting and more. Two nights from US$295 per person

Explorer's Inn ☎ 082 573 029, ⓦ explorersinn.com. Located within the Reserva Nacional Tambopata–Candamo, some 58km (about 3hr) in a motorized *canoa* upriver from Puerto Maldonado, this intimate, well-organized lodge, which has been around since 1975, is surrounded by a 38km network of jungle trails and sits in an area of staggering biodiversity, with 620 species of bird spotted in the surrounding jungle, and a nearby macaw clay-lick. Spanish- or English-speaking guides are available, the food is good, and accommodation is generally in twin rooms with private bath. Enquire about rates for

8

special-interest visitors (eg ornithologists). Two nights from US$299 per person

★ **Inkaterra Hacienda Concepción** C Andalucía 174, Miraflores, Lima ☎01 610 0400, ⦿inkaterra.com. Around 45min downstream of Puerto Maldonado along the Río Madre de Dios, this is an intimate, luxurious lodge comprising fan-cooled, individual bungalows and cheaper rooms at the lodge itself. Nature outings include trips to Lago Sandoval, canopy walkway, caiman-spotting on the river, night walks in the jungle and more. Service is fantastic and the food is very good. Two nights from US$370 per person

Inkaterra Reserva Amazónica C Andalucía 174, Miraflores, Lima ☎01 610 0400, ⦿inkaterra.com. One of the Peruvian jungle's most luxurious and stylish lodges (Mick Jagger stayed here in 2011), located an hour or so downstream from Puerto Maldonado on the Río Madre de Dios, the original Inkaterra lodge consists of luxurious fan-cooled bungalows (and larger suites), a palatial main lodge building with restaurant, bar and lounge areas, and a massage/spa centre. The food is some of the best in the Amazon and there's an excellent range of half- and full-day excursions on offer, including guided walking trails and night walks, plus visits to Lago Sandoval, as well as evening caiman-spotting cruises on the river and full-day outings to Lago Valencia (at extra cost). The lodge is surrounded by its own protected rainforest area and boasts a canopy walkway. Two nights from US$541 per person

Willy Mejía Cepa Lodge Jr Velarde 487, Puerto Maldonado ☎082 684 700. Operated by Ceiba Tours, this rustic-style hostel houses up to twenty guests in bungalow-style accommodation with shared facilities on the side of Lago Sandoval; perfect for canoe exploration of the lake. It's rarely full, so it's fine to just turn up here by canoe from Puerto Maldonado without prior arrangement (get the boatman to drop you off on the trail from the Tambopata riverbank). Per person, per night including food from US$25

RÍO TAMBOPATA

Posada Amazonas Contact through Rainforest Expeditions, Av Aeropuerto, La Joya Km 6, Puerto Maldonado US freephone ☎0877 231 9251, ⦿perunature.com. The nearest of Rainforest Expedition's lodges to Puerto Maldonado, 45min by boat, is fully owned

and managed by the Ese Eja indigenous community of Infierno. Comfortable rooms come with hammocks and mosquito nets, there's a canopy tower, a series of forest trails and access to a nearby ethno-botanical garden. Massage and other treatments are available, and it's also possible to organize trips combining this lodge with the more remote *Refugio Amazonas* (see below) and the most distant of all the region's lodges – the *Tambopata Research Centre* (see below). Two nights from US$432 per person

Refugio Amazonas Contact through Rainforest Expeditions, Av Aeropuerto, La Joya Km6, Puerto Maldonado US freephone ☎0877 231 9251, ⦿peru nature.com. Run by Rainforest Expeditions and 4hr away from Puerto Maldonado, this is the most luxurious of the company's three lodges, a splendid mix of traditional hut design and extravagant architectural beauty, with 32 spacious rooms with large comfortable beds under mosquito nets opening out onto the forest, plus a great dining room and busy bar. A range of activities is on offer, including bird-watching at a clay-lick, kayaking on the Tambopata River (no experience required), canopy climbing and mountain biking trails. The lodge is close to two lakes where otters are sometimes spotted, and also has an engaging educational trail for kids. Three nights from US$616 per person

Tambopata Eco Lodge C Nueva Baja 432, Cusco ☎084 245 695, ⦿tambopatalodge.com. Just over the river from the Reserva Nacional Tambopata–Candamo, nearly 4hr from Puerto Maldonado and 12km upstream from the *Explorer's Inn*, this lodge has comfortable, individual cabin-style accommodation. Activities include wildlife-spotting on forest walks, kayaking and birdwatching on Lago Condenado, going up the tree platforms and caiman-spotting in the evenings. Two nights from US$437 per person

★ **Tambopata Research Centre** Contact through Rainforest Expeditions, Av Aeropuerto, La Joya Km 6, Puerto Maldonado US freephone ☎0877 231 9251, ⦿perunature.com. The remotest of the Rainforest Expeditions lodges, this comfortable eighteen-room lodge sits in the heart of the Tambopata Nature Reserve, in an area of great bird and mammal diversity. It's located 500m from the world's biggest macaw *colpa*, the Colpa Colorado, and there's an excellent chance of spotting five species of monkey, peccaries, capybara, agouti and even the occasional jaguar. A minimum of

8

CHOOSING A LODGE

The quality of the **jungle experience** varies from river to river and from lodge to lodge. Most companies offer full board and include transfers, though it is a good idea to verify the level of service online and talk to other travellers. You should also check what's included, and what **extra costs** you'll be liable for once you're there; alcoholic beverage prices can be high. Remember, too, that conditions can be rustic and relatively open to the elements: **sleeping arrangements** range from bunk rooms to luxurious doubles with mosquito nets, solar-powered showers, fans and hammocks. **Food** is generally good, though you may want to take additional snacks. Electricity is generator-powered and tends only to be on at certain times of day.

six days is recommended, since it takes a full day by canoe both up and down river. Three nights from US$788 per person

Wasai Lodge Contact through the *Wasai* hotel in Puerto Maldonado (see p.436). Four hours or 120km upriver from Puerto Maldonado, this luxurious lodge consists of 21 airy cabins, a pleasant jungle bar and dining area, a hammock-festooned lounge with wi-fi, 20km of walking trails around the lodge and a canopy tower for all-encompassing jungle views. There are kayaks for rent and an Amazon adventure circuit (ziplines, etc), and tours are available on request (at extra cost) to the Chuncho *colpa*, Lago Sandoval and the nearby indigenous community of Baltimore. Two days one night from US$265 per person

LAGO SANDOVAL

Sandoval Lodge InkaNatura, C Manuel Bañon 461, San Isidro, Lima ☎ 01 203 5000, ⓦ inkanatura.com. On the shores of Lago Sandoval, and accessed by canoe after the 3km walk (see p.438), this lodge has a privileged location on a small hill surrounded by primary forest and

gives you exclusive access to the lake in the very early morning and late afternoon, best hours for wildlife viewing and photography. The lodge has one large, airy communal building as a bar and dining room, plus electricity and hot water. Most groups spend time on the lake or explore the small, well-trodden surrounding trail system with multilingual guides. Two nights from US$325 per person

RÍO HEATH

Heath River Wildlife Center Lodge InkaNatura, C Manuel Bañon 461, San Isidro, Lima ☎ 01 203 5000, ⓦ inkanatura.com. The only eco-lodge on the Río Heath, consisting of ten simple but comfortable rooms, is run by the Ese'eja indigenous community, and there's some great birdwatching to be had from the floating hide nearby, with hundreds of parrots and dozens of macaws flocking to one of the best clay-licks in the world. Other attractions include wildlife spotting from the trails around the lodge; stays here are usually part of multi-day jungle ventures with InkaNatura. Two nights from US$355 per person

8 Manu Biosphere Reserve

Eco-tours in the **MANU BIOSPHERE RESERVE** don't come cheap, but represent good value when you consider its remoteness and the abundance of **wildlife** that thrives in its almost two million hectares of virgin cloud- and rainforest, a uniquely varied environment that ranges from crystalline cloud-forest streams and waterfalls down to slow-moving, chocolate-brown rivers in the dense lowland jungle. Created in 1973 as a national park, it was made a UNESCO World Heritage Site in 1987.

The only permanent residents within this vast area are the teeming forest wildlife; a few virtually uncontacted indigenous groups who have split off from their major tribal units (Yaminahuas, Amahuacas and Matsiguenka); the park guards; and the scientists at a biological research station just inside the park on the beautiful Lago Cocha Cashu.

The reserve is divided into three zones. By far the largest, comprising eighty percent of the park, is **Zone A** (zona natural), the core zone, the **Parque Nacional Manu**, which is strictly preserved in its natural state. A few biologists are allowed in for research purposes and several Matsiguenka groups live inside Zone A, some of whom have virtually no contact with outsiders. **Zone B** (zona reservada) is a Buffer Zone, ten percent of the park, set aside mainly for controlled research and tourism, with several lodges located within that zone. The final ten percent, **Zone C** (zona cultural) is the Transitional Zone, an area of human settlement for controlled traditional use, with

---

JUNGLE PERMITS FOR INDEPENDENT TRAVEL

To enter some of the more remote and sensitive **protected areas**, such as the **Reserva Nacional Pacaya Samiria**, or the **Manu** and **Parque Nacional Bahuaja-Sonene**, official permission is essential, and a small daily **fee** (usually around S/35) payable either in advance or at entry points located on the main rivers. As a tourist, this will usually be handled for you by your **tour company**. Independent travel within these areas is discouraged, but if you want to enter for research purposes you will need to do this directly. For all Peruvian jungle protected areas it's best to contact the SERNAMP office of whichever locality you plan to travel in. It's also possible to contact SERNANP in Lima (C 17, 355 Urb El Palomar, San Isidro (☎ 01 717 7500, ⓦ sernanp.gob.pe) but you have to do it well in advance, whereas local offices can dispense permits considerably faster.

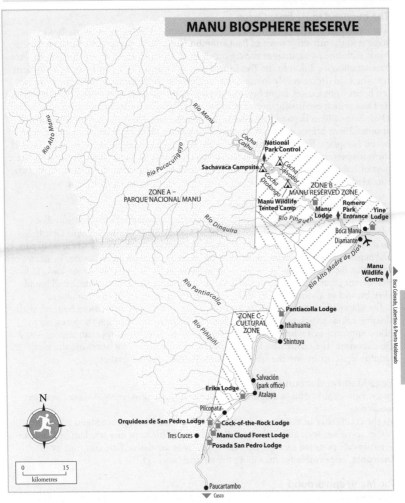

MANU BIOSPHERE RESERVE

Río Manu

Río Alto Manu

Río Pucacungoyo

Cocha Cashu

National Park Control

Sachavaca Campsite

Cocha Salvador

Cocha Otorongo

ZONE A – PARQUE NACIONAL MANU

ZONE B – MANU RESERVED ZONE

Manu Wildlife Tented Camp

Manu Lodge

Romero Park Entrance

Yine Lodge

Río Dinquira

Río Pinquen

Boca Manu

Diamante

Río Alto Madre de Dios

Manu Wildlife Centre

Boca Colorado, Laberinto & Puerto Maldonado

Río Pantiacolla

ZONE C – CULTURAL ZONE

Pantiacolla Lodge

Ithahuania

Río Pinipini

Shintuya

Salvación (park office)

Erika Lodge

Atalaya

Pilcopata

Orquideas de San Pedro Lodge

Cock-of-the-Rock Lodge

Tres Cruces

Manu Cloud Forest Lodge

Posada San Pedro Lodge

N

Paucartambo

Cusco

0   15
kilometres

8

Boca Manu village marking the boundary between Zones A and B. Tourists are allowed into zones B and C only as part of organized visits with guides, following the basic rules of non-interference with human, animal or vegetable life.

The interior of the protected area is only accessible by **boat**, so any expedition to Manu is very much in the hands of the gods, due to the temperamental jungle environment; the **rainy season** is from December to March, and visits are best organized between May and August when it's much drier, although at that time the temperatures often exceed 30°C (86°F).

Pretty much the only way to visit Manu National Park is by joining an **organized tour** through one of the main Cusco agents (see p.221). Most tours currently enter the area by fast boats (4–6hr) from Puerto Maldonado, since the **airstrip** at Boca Manu is presently not being used for tours (the available charter planes are currently monopolized by oil companies). In theory, flights will resume if prices go down, but for the time being, a number of tours choose instead to fly with scheduled flights to **Puerto Maldonado**, then travel by boat upriver to Manu or else enter and leave by boat.

The overland route from Cusco

The road route to Manu from Cusco is highly scenic. The first four- to six-hour stage is to the attractive town of **Paucartambo** (see p.269), over stupendous narrow roads with fine panoramas of the region's largest glaciated mountain of Ausungate. From Paucartambo it's 25km to the **Tres Cruces** turn-off (see p.271), at the reserve's southern tip. The road drops steeply to the quiet jungle town of **Pilcopata**, a journey of around ten hours from Cusco. From here the terrain is fairly level as it skirts the Río Alto Madre de Dios, which eventually merges with the Río Manu to form the great Río Madre de Dios. Some 20km beyond Pilcopata is the smaller riverside settlement of **Atalaya** and another 20km brings you to the pueblo of **Salvación**, 28km before Shintuya, where the Manu Biosphere Reserve has an **office** and where your guide will usually be expected to show his permits. From Shintuya, the route continues another 15km or so to the river port of Itahuania where the road finishes. From here, it's another 55–60km by boat via Río Madre de Dios to Boca Manu and the entry to the national park itself.

Manu Wildlife Centre and around

Some 10km outside the park and further downstream (around 30min–1hr) from Boca Manu along the Río Alto Madre de Dios is the **Manu Wildlife Centre**, a comfortable lodge used by various tour companies (see p.445). It's close to a superb **salt-lick** where small **parrots** and larger, colourful **macaws** can be seen, and claims to be strategically located in an area of forest that has the highest diversity of microhabitats in the Manu: *tierra-firme* (lowland forest that doesn't get flooded), transitional flood plain, *varzea* and bamboo forest are all found close by, and an astounding 530 bird species have been recorded in one year alone.

The **Blanquillo** macaw-and-parrot salt-lick is only thirty minutes away by river, with floating blinds to access the wildlife. About an hour's walk through the forest there's also a large salt-lick where you can see tapirs – even rarer creatures than jaguars – and Brocket deer. The centre also features mobile canopy towers for watching the local wildlife right up among the treetops, where jungle creatures gather.

Boca Manu and around

4hr down the Río Alto Madre de Dios (from Shintuya) or 6–8hr up the Río Madre de Dios (from Puerto Maldonado) in a *lancha* with outboard motor

At the confluence of the ríos Alto Madre de Dios and Manu, **Boca Manu** is a mere 300m above sea level and little more than a small settlement of a few families (and an internet café powered by a generator!). Close by is the native Yiné community of **Diamante**, responsible for managing the airstrip (see p.443).

Río Manu and around

Heading deep into Zone B of the park, **Río Manu** is perhaps your best bet for spotting such wildlife as jaguar (if you're lucky, you may see one sunning itself on the banks of the river), howler, dusky titi, spider, emperor tamarin, squirrel, capuchin and other monkeys, and giant otters that dwell in Cocha Otorongo and Cocha Salvador – two oxbow lakes typically visited during an extended trip into Manu.

The journey to Puerto Maldonado

Tour companies that use this route will have their own fast boats (6–8hr). The only settlements en route are **Boca Colorado** at the confluence of the ríos Colorado and Alto Madre de Dios, a small gold-miners' service town, followed by Madre de Dios, and then Inambari and Laberinto, near Puerto Maldonado.

ARRIVAL AND INFORMATION   **MANU BIOSPHERE RESERVE**

Manu is among the most easily reached parts of relatively pristine Amazon rainforest offering high levels of biodiversity. From Cusco, Manu is either a day's journey by bus then a day more by canoe, or a thirty-minute flight and up to six hours in a speedboat.

By boat It is possible to travel independently on the rivers by picking up a boat at Shintuya or one of the other riverside towns. This won't allow you to enter the Manu National Park area, but you can hop aboard a cargo-bearing canoe from Atalaya, Shintuya and Diamante downriver from Manu to Puerto Maldonado for around S/10 per hr.

Tourist information The Manu National Park Office is at Av Cinco Loc Chacacomos, F2-4, Larapa Grande, San Jerónimo, Cusco (☎084 274 509, ⓦvistimanu.com). Entrance to the reserve is by organized tour, and it's virtually impossible to get permission to go it alone. The entrance fee of US$60 is either included in the price of tours or paid to the tour company. If you're a naturalist, a photographer or can demonstrate a serious interest, then it is sometimes possible to gain a special permit for restricted areas; contact SERNANP in Lima (see box, p.442).

TOURS

There are quite a few **organized tours** competing for travellers who want to visit Manu; however, only a few are authorized to operate within Manu National Park, while others claim to take tourists to Manu but in fact only run tours to the Manu Wildlife Centre, which isn't actually within the park. The options listed below have a good reputation both for the way they treat their tourists and the delicate ecology of the rainforest itself. Numbers are limited annually to around 3000 visitors, so it's a good idea to book well in advance. Prices include transport, lodging, guides and food, unless stated otherwise.

MANU WILDLIFE AND FLORA

For **flora and fauna**, the Manu is pretty much unbeatable in South America, home to over 5000 flowering plants, 1200 species of butterfly, 1000 types of bird and 200 kinds of mammal. Rich in macaw salt-licks and otter lagoons, it's also home to prowling jaguars, thirteen species of monkey and seven species of macaw, and contains several species in danger of extinction, such as the giant otter and the black caiman. The highlight of most organized visits to Manu is the trail network and lakes of **Cocha Salvador** (the largest of Manu's oxbows, at 3.5km long) and **Cocha Otorongo**, both bountiful jungle areas rich in animal, water and birdlife.

OTORONGO OTTERS

The **Cocha Otorongo** lake is known for the **giant otters** that live there, one of the world's most endangered species. The otters are also bio-indicators of the environment, since they only live where there is clean, healthy water and a wide choice of fish. Only the oldest female of the group is mated with, so reproduction is very slow – the "queen" otters only have two or three cubs a year, usually around October, which can be expected to live for around thirty years. The top-ranking male otters are responsible for defending the group and do very little fishing, taking the catch from younger males instead.

Although they appear friendly as they play in their large family groups, the otters can be very aggressive, able to keep jaguars at bay and kill caimans that approach their lakeside nesting holes. Canoeing is not permitted, but there is a **floating platform** which can be manoeuvred to observe the otters fishing and playing from a safe distance (though your guide has to book a time for this): 30–50m is good enough to watch and take photos, though as this is Manu's most popular tourist area, you're likely to meet other groups and there can be severe competition for access to the platform.

OTHER WILDLIFE

Other wildlife to look out for includes the plentiful **caimans**, including the 2–3m white alligators and the rarer 3–5m black ones, and you can usually spot several species of **monkey** (including dusky titis, woolly monkeys, red howlers, brown capuchins and the larger spider monkeys known locally as *maquisapas*). Sometimes big mammals such as **capybaras** or **white-lipped peccaries** (*sajinos*) also lurk in the undergrowth.

GIANT TREES

The flora of Manu is as outstanding as its fauna. Huge **cedar trees** can be seen along the trails, covered in hand-like vines climbing up their vast trunks (most of the cedars were removed between 1930 and 1963, before it became a protected area). The giant **catahua trees**, many over 150 years old, are traditionally the preferred choice for making dugout canoes – and some are large enough to make three or four; their bulbous white trunks seem to reach endlessly up to the rainforest canopy.

8

InkaNatura Travel C Manuel Bañon 461, San Isidro, Lima ☎ 01 203 5000, ⓦ inkanatura.com. This outfit offers customized travel, from four to five days, operating from the Manu Wildlife Centre, where one of the nearby highlights is the world's largest tapir salt-lick. It also accommodates people at the *Cock of the Rock Lodge*, 6hr by road from Cusco, in one of the best cloud-forest locations for birdwatching, and its *Manu Wildlife Tented Camp* is located several hours down Río Manu in Zone B, near an oxbow lake with thirteen monkey species living nearby and a good chance of spotting a jaguar. Some trips start from Cusco while others start from Puerto Maldonado. Six nights deep in Manu National Park $2597 per person.

Manu Adventures C Plateros 356, Cusco ☎ 084 261 640, ⓦ manuadventures.com. Jungle-trip specialist and one of the first operators to run trips into Manu, with its own vehicles, boats and multilingual guides and three lodges throughout the park that allow visitors to experience different ecological habitats – from the *Orquideas de San Pedro Lodge* in the cloud forest and *Erika Lodge* in Zone C to the *Sajino Campsite* in Zone B, on the banks of Cocha Salvador – ideal for wildlife spotting. It runs three- to eight-day trips into Manu. Four days, three nights $405 per person.

Manu Expeditions Jr Los Geranios 2G, Urb. Mariscal Gamarra Primero Etapa, Cusco ☎ 084 225 990, ⓦ manuexpeditions.com. One of the best and the most responsible companies, run by British ornithologist Barry Walker and his wife. They offer five-, six- and nine-day lodge-based and tented camp expeditions into Zone B and to the Manu Wildlife Centre, as well as specialist birding tours, with top-quality service and bilingual naturalist guides. The superb nine-day trip includes stays at the *Cocha Salvador Tented Camp*, visits to clay-licks for macaw and tapir spotting and other wildlife spotting on oxbow lakes. Five days, four nights US$1835 per person.

Manu Nature Tours Av Pardo 1046, Cusco ☎ 084 252 721, ⓦ manuperu.com. A pioneer in Manu since 1985, this responsible operator owns the *Manu Cloud Forest Lodge* as well as the *Manu Lodge* on Río Manu, within Zone B. Tours range from three to eight days, the latter including birdwatching along the 20km of trails around Manu Lodge spotting giant otters on the oxbow lakes in Zone B. It can also incorporate whitewater rafting and mountain biking into its tours for an extra fee. Seven-night tours from US$934 per person.

Pantiacolla Tours C Garcilaso 265, 2nd floor, Office 12, Cusco ☎ 084 238 323, ⓦ pantiacolla.com. An established company with an excellent reputation, knowledgeable guides and three lodges in the Manu Biosphere Reserve: *Posada San Pedro Lodge*, *Pantiacolla Lodge*, *Yine Lodge* (near the Boca Manu landing strip, used as a base for exploring Zone B) and also the basic *Sachavaca Campsite* in the Reserved Zone, even deeper in Zone B, six hours up Río Manu. It specializes in seven- and nine-day tours of Zone B, complete with birdwatching at clay-licks and animal watching on the oxbow lakes, as well as a five-day tour of Zone C and three days in the cloud forest. Five days, four nights US$760 per person.

Río Urubamba and around

Traditionally the home of the Matsiguenka and the Piro, the **Río Urubamba** rolls down from the Incas' Sacred Valley to the humid lower Andean slopes around the town of **Quillabamba**. The river remains unnavigable for another 80km or so, with regular buses following a dirt road that continues deeper down into the jungle via the settlement of **Kiteni**, where the Río Urubamba becomes navigable again, to the even smaller frontier settlement of **Ivochote**. From here on, the river becomes the main means of transport, through the Amazon Basin right to the Atlantic, interrupted only by the impressive **Pongo de Mainique** whitewater rapids, just a few hours downstream from Ivochote. These rapids are generally too dangerous to pass between November and March.

Most of the Urubamba has been colonized as far as the *pongo*, and much of it beyond has suffered more or less permanent exploitation of one sort or another – rubber, cattle, oil or gas – for over a hundred years. Travel-wise, it still remains a relatively quiet and untouristed region.

Quillabamba

A rapidly expanding market town, growing fat on profits from coffee, tropical fruits, chocolate and, to an increasing extent, narcotrafficking, **QUILLABAMBA** is the only Peruvian jungle town that's easily accessible by road from Cusco: the main attraction here is a trip to the Pongo de Mainique rapids. Coming from Cusco, the road, though completely paved, ribbons its narrow, precipitous way over the magical Abra Malaga – the main pass, before descending into the distinctly warmer, junglier Urubamba Valley. The town itself, though a good place to stock up on necessities at the market before

8

heading further into the jungle, is unremarkable, though it does have a leafy and pleasant **Plaza de Armas**, with its shady fountain statue of the town's little-known benefactor, Don Martín Pio Concha.

A few kilometres out of town, the beautiful waterfalls of **Pacchac** and **Siete Tinajas** (in order of proximity to Quillabamba) are accessed just off the main road; take a combi or colectivo towards Echarati and ask to be dropped off.

ARRIVAL AND DEPARTURE   QUILLABAMBA

By bus Buses from the terminal on C Lorena in Cusco terminate at Quillabamba's Terminal Terrestre at jirones 25 de Julio and Lima, passing by the plaza in Ollantaytambo en route.

By colectivo Minibuses and shared cars from Cusco leave from within a couple of blocks of the C Lorena terminal, along C Inca. In Quillabamba they depart from the block of Jr 25 de Julio closest to the Plaza de Banderas, four blocks along Jr Torre from Plaza Grau in Quillabamba from 4am onwards when full. Shared cars to Kiteni (with onward connections to Pongo de Mainique) leave from the first block of C Palma, by the market, at the ungodly hours of 2am or 10pm.

Destinations Cusco (several daily; 4–5hr); Kiteni (several daily; 5hr); Ollantaytambo (several daily; 2hr 30min).

ACCOMMODATION AND EATING

Chifa Mio Jr San Martín 333. The pick of the town's *chifas* has a very decent selection of rice and noodle dishes (prawn with vegetable hits the spot) with a free wonton soup thrown in and a breezy courtyard location. Mains from S/11. Daily noon–9pm.

Heladería Misky Next to the market. One of the town's best ice-cream joints, with two dozen delectable flavours, coffee and cake. Daily 8.30am–9pm.

Hostal Alto Jr Urubamba 2 de Mayo 333 ☏ 084 281 131. One of two decent choices in town, with fan-cooled or a/c rooms encircling a small inner courtyard and helpful staff. S/75

Hostal Don Carlos Jr Libertad 556 ☏ 084 281 150, ⓦ hostaldoncarlosquillabamba.com. Just up from the Plaza de Armas, this is a cosy, friendly and popular place. Rooms are smart and face a leafy courtyard. S/100

8

Ivochote and around

The road continues down into the jungle from Quillabamba via Kiteni (6–7hr) to the village of **Ivochote**, the staging point for the Pongo de Mainique; look for a boatman in the Ivochote port area. Boats to the *pongo* tend to set off early in the morning, as travelling there and back takes up much of the day. At the time of writing, the road to Kiteni and beyond wasn't considered hugely safe due to increased narcotrafficking activity, so check what the situation is on the ground before setting off.

Travelling down the river from Ivochote, just before you reach the *pongo* there's a community at **San Idriato**. The people here, known as the Israelites, founded their village around a biblical sect; the men leave their hair long and, like Rastafarians, they twist it up under expandable peaked caps. Across the Urubamba from San Idriato the small community of **Shinguriato**, upstream from the Río Yuyato mouth, is the official entrance to the *pongo* itself.

Pongo de Mainique

The awe-inspiring **Pongo de Mainique rapids** – a very challenging 2km of a (barely) navigable river in the entire Amazonian river system – are hazardous at any time of year, and difficult to pass during the rainy season (Nov–March).

As you approach, you'll see a forested mountain range directly in front of you; the river speeds up, and as you get closer, it's possible to make out the great cut made through the range over the millennia by the powerful Urubamba. Then, before you realize, the boat is whisked into a long **canyon** with soaring rocky cliffs on either side: gigantic volcanic boulders look like wet monsters of molten steel; imaginary stone faces can be seen shimmering under cascades; and the danger of the *pongo* slips by almost unnoticed, as the walls of the canyon will absorb all your attention. The main hazard is a drop of about 2m, which is seen and then crossed in a split second. Now and then boats are overturned at this dangerous drop – although even then locals somehow manage to come upstream in small, non-motorized dugouts.

ARRIVAL AND DEPARTURE

IVOCHOTE AND PONGO DE MAINIQUE

By organized tour If you want to take an organized tour or whitewater-rafting trip down through the *pongo*, it's best to do this in Cusco with one of the rafting companies (see box, p.223).

By bus or colectivo To get to Ivochote from Quillabamba, buses and colectivos leave from Quillabamba's northern bus depot (daily 8–10am).

By boat Boats regularly take goods and people from the

river port at Ivochote to the gas operations and lower Urubamba communities through the *pongo* most days between May and October, and it's often possible to pay a small fee for a ride on one, though you then need to find a way to get back; it's far easier to pay a boatman to take you there and back (from S/80 per person, depending on the number of people you're with and your bargaining powers).

The central selva

The obvious appeal of the central selva is its ease of overland access and proximity to Lima. Directly east of the capital, the region is endowed with an array of rainforest eco-niches. The large and modern jungle city of **Pucallpa** lies in lowland rainforest, while the nearby oxbow lake **Lago Yarinacocha** provides a fine spot to watch schools of dolphins or travel deeper into the jungle in search of other wildlife. Pucallpa is also a main point of departure for trips downriver to the larger destination of **Iquitos** (see p.461), a 1000km, three-day journey.

Closer to Lima yet less explored by tourists, the **Chanchamayo** region – famous for its fantastic coffee – offers stunning forested mountain scenery, fast-running rivers and trees dripping with epiphytes. A steep road descends from Tarma down to the jungle gateway towns of **San Ramón** and **La Merced**, separated by a ten-minute drive. From here you can travel north, visiting the unique Austro-German settlements of **Pozuzo** and **Oxapampa**, both rich agricultural centres located within a mosaic of little-visited protected areas, including the stunningly beautiful **Parque Nacional Yanachaga-Chemillén**. Apart from Pozuzo, rough roads connect these towns to Pucallpa via Villa Rica, Puerto Bermudez and Puerto Inca.

East from San Ramón and La Merced, an easier paved road heads towards the lower forest region, focused on the frontier town of **Satipo**, where the Asháninka often come to town to sell produce and buy supplies. Near Satipo are scores of indigenous communities, mainly Asháninka, and some of South America's finest **waterfalls**; Puerto Prado and Atalaya are also the gateway for adventurous river travel.

The Chanchamayo Valley

The **CHANCHAMAYO VALLEY**, only 300km from Lima and 750m above sea level, marks the real beginning of the central selva directly east of the capital. Some Franciscan monks settled here in 1635 but kept coming into conflict with the region's indigenous communities. These days access to the main towns of San Ramón and La Merced is straightforward.

San Ramón

The settler town **SAN RAMÓN** is more tranquil and less "happening" than its larger twin La Merced (see p.451), just ten minutes further by bus down the Chanchamayo Valley – the latter is the communications hub with road connections deeper into the jungle and a better choice of lodgings and dining venues.

Founded originally as a fort in 1849, to assist the colonization of the region in the face of fierce indigenous resistance, San Ramón is centred around the leafy **Plaza Mayor** that features a Chinese-pagoda-esque construction. There are several waterfalls within easy reach of town, the best being **El Tirol**.

Catarata El Tirol

Take a mototaxi from San Ramón (around S/5) for 2.8km, then walk the remaining 2.2km

About 5km from San Ramón, the **Catarata El Tirol** waterfalls enjoy a 35m drop into an attractive plunge pool. The falls are accessed by a pleasant 45-minute country walk from the riverside village of Playa Hermosa, along a dirt track surrounded by orchids and lianas.

ARRIVAL AND DEPARTURE   SAN RAMÓN

By bus Direct buses running from Lima (see p.79) and Huancayo in the Sierra stop in San Ramón en route to and from La Merced (see opposite for details).
Destinations Huancayo (several daily; 4hr 30min); La Merced (many daily; 15–20min); Lima (several daily; 7hr 30min–8hr 30min).

By colectivo Shared cars (S/3) link the twin towns of San Ramón and La Merced throughout the day. Mototaxis cost S/7.

ACCOMMODATION AND EATING

Chanchamayo-Italia Ristorante Jr Tarma 592 ☎ 964 417 217. The legacy of Italian colonists, this Italian restaurant is excellent for mainly home-made pastas and pizzas as well as good coffee and wine. Mains from S/20. Daily noon–3pm & 7–10pm.

Chifa Felipe Siu C Progreso 440 ☎ 064 331 078. Based in an attractive, airy space on two storeys and overlooking a small jungle garden, the San Ramón branch of this La Merced institution serves up equally good Chinese food

– considered the best *chifa* in the region by locals. There are set meals at lunchtimes (around S/12). Mains from S/20. Daily 11.30am–9.30pm.

Hotel Conquistador C Progreso 298 ☎ 064 331 157. This brick-and-concrete creation is still the best hotel in town (not that there's much competition). Expect simple, clean, fan-cooled en suites with reliable hot water and a basic breakfast. **S/70**

Pampa Hermosa and around

About 20km (2–3hr) along a fairly rough road from San Ramón there's the **Santuario Nacional de Pampa Hermosa**, an area of verdant virgin cloud forest. Covering some 11,000 hectares, this national forest sanctuary is blessed with a fabulous jungle-style **lodge** (see below). Several impressive waterfalls bisect the reserve's unusually rich vegetation, including orchids, royal palms, lianas and giant ferns, and the reserve also boasts what is considered to be the **oldest cedar tree** in South America, fondly known as *el abuelo* (the grandfather); a breathtaking sight, it's so wide at its base that it takes sixteen people to circle its circumference hand in hand.

Various **treks** using local hill paths can also be planned to start or finish at *Pampa Hermosa Lodge*, which is only a few hours' walk from the end of forest cover and the start of mountain scenery; the Andean community of Ninabamba is less than six hours' trek. Slightly nearer, a trek to the tiny settlement of Alto Perú offers possible glimpses of spectacled bears and access to pre-Columbian remains dating back over 5000 years.

ARRIVAL AND DEPARTURE   PAMPA HERMOSA AND AROUND

By 4WD Accessible by 4WD vehicles – the lodge (see below) can arrange transport – it takes around 2hr to reach Pampa Hermosa from San Ramón, crossing the Puente Victoria bridge and following first the Oxabamba River, then climbing up beside the bubbling Ulcumayo gorge.

By colectivo Combis only go to Pampa Hermosa (also known as Nueva Italia) on Thursday and Saturday mornings, departing from next to the crossroads with the military plane monument at around 5am (4–5hr).

ACCOMMODATION

Pampa Hermosa Lodge 1hr 30min by track from San Ramón ☎ 01 273 7878, ⊛ pampahermosalodge.com. On the edge of the Santuario Nacional de Pampa Hermosa are these beautiful wooden bungalows all in natural materials with palm-frond roofs set around a sumptuous pagoda-like restaurant, with great food. Within a 20min

walk of the lodge Peru's national bird – the vermillion cock-of-the-rock – can be seen every afternoon. Abseiling down waterfalls and floating in huge tyres down the river is also possible. Guiding service and all meals are included in the price. Advance bookings only. Per person **S/320**

La Merced and around

The market town of **LA MERCED**, some 10km further down the Chanchamayo Valley, is larger and busier than San Ramón, with more than sixteen thousand inhabitants, a thriving Saturday **market** a couple of blocks behind the main street, and several restaurants and bars crowded around the Plaza de Armas. On the opposite side of the town from Río Chanchamayo, a winding cobbled road runs up to the **Miradór La Cruz**, topped with an enormous cross and giving you a bird's-eye view of La Merced's tin roofs and the forested mountains beyond (S/5 return by mototaxi).

Zhaveta Yard

10min from La Merced by mototaxi (S/5) • Daily 8am–5.30pm • Entry by tour only; S/5

About 9km out of town on the Satipo/Oxapampa road, this well-organized butterfly farm also features some rescued jungle wildlife – a spider monkey, a woolly monkey, macaws, birds of prey, a peccary and river otter. All were illegally owned, confiscated by the police and given to Zhaveta Yard for rehabilitation; those animals that can be rehabilitated are later released into the wild. En route, 2km out of La Merced, you pass **Puente Quimiri,** a rickety 1905 pedestrian suspension bridge across the muddy swirls of Río Chanchamayo; on the other side there's a nice walk that takes you to two lots of three waterfalls, depending on which fork in the trail you take; it's an hour and a half's climb either way.

ARRIVAL AND GETTING AROUND
LA MERCED AND AROUND

By bus La Merced is easily accessible by bus from Lima via Tarma. Expresos Molina Unión and Transporte La Merced both have separate terminals along the main road leading from La Merced to San Ramón and offer *bus-cama* and semi-*cama* services departing around 8–9am and 9–11pm; Molina is the most comfortable. All other buses, colectivos and combis leave from the Terminal Terrestre (Terminal Royal Bus).
Destinations Huancayo (several daily; 5hr); Lima (at least 12 daily; 7–8hr); Oxapampa (2–3 daily; 2hr); Pucallpa (1 weekly via Puerto Inca; 20–30hr); San Ramón (many daily; 15–20min); Satipo (several daily; 2–3hr); Tarma (at least 24 daily; 1–2hr).

By colectivo Colectivo cars link the twin towns of San Ramón and La Merced 24hr daily, leaving from within one block of each town's main plaza, and colectivo cars and slower combis also reach most regional destinations. Colectivos leave from inside the Terminal Terrestre for Oxapampa, San Ramón, Villa Rica, Puerto Bermudez and Satipo via Pichanaki (doublecheck that the colectivo is going all the way to Satipo or you'll have to change in Pichnaki).
Destinations Oxapampa (numerous daily; 1hr 30min); Puerto Bermudez (2 daily at 2am; 5hr); Satipo (numerous daily; 2hr); Villa Rica (numerous daily; 1hr).

ACCOMMODATION

Fundo San José Av Circunvalación s/n ☎ 064 531 816, ⓦ fundosanjose.com.pe. Located high up on the hillside to the left as you come into La Merced from San Ramón, this plush hotel offers quality bungalow accommodation with lovely views across the valley and a great swimming pool. **S/390**
Heliconia Hotel Jr Junín 992 ☎ 064 531 394, ⓦ heliconiahotel.com. The flashest of in-town options and overlooking Parque Incarnación, *Heliconia* offers vast, beige rooms with large doubles, fridges, a/c, TVs and equally spacious bathrooms. Receptionists are friendly and

breakfast is included. **S/150**
Hospedaje Santa Rosa Jr 2 de Mayo 447 ☎ 064 531 012. The pick of the local cheapies, *Santa Rosa* has S/20 rooms if you don't mind sharing a shower, and marginally more expensive en suites, all with cable TV and wi-fi. Miracle of miracles, all rooms have windows. **S/30**
Hotel El Paraíso Jr Junín 550 ☎ 064 532 245. As close as you get to heaven in La Merced, with spotless tiled en suites overlooking the church on the main plaza, a/c, fans, flat-screen TVs and a warm welcome. **S/50**

EATING, DRINKING AND NIGHTLIFE

Cafeteria y Chocolatería Chanchamayo Highland Coffee Jirones Ancash and Tarma. If you don't make it to its coffee factory-cum-produce store, you can still pick up some excellent Peruvian coffee, fruit preserves and chocolates at this café, and sample a cup of the delicious brew (S/2.50) or a fresh juice (S/1.50–2.50), with tamales and burgers as snacks. Daily 7.30am–10pm.

Chifa Felipe Siu Jr Junín 121. Locals proclaim this to be the best *chifa* in town, and if you taste its glass noodles with shrimp and broccoli, it's difficult to argue with that. The wonton soup and main combos (S/12.50–19.50) are excellent value and the *chicha morada* is unadulterated black corn goodness. Mains around S/20. Daily noon–11pm.
Kametsa Av Puente Herreria 1 ☎ 064 532 015. As you

8

CHANCHAMAYO VALLEY COFFEE

An additional reason to come to La Merced is to sample its celebrated local brew. The Chanchamayo Valley famously produces some of Peru's best gourmet coffee – smooth, medium-bodied, slightly nutty in flavour – including the world's most expensive bean, **Café Misha**, which sells for $1400 per kilo. This exclusive bean passes through the digestive system of the coati, a member of the racoon family, which gives the coffee an intense aroma and takes away the bitterness. In La Merced proper, you can organize a tour of the Chanchamayo Highland Coffee factory (Urb. San Carlos, just off the main road towards Oxapampa and Satipo, up a short dirt track; ☎064 531 198, ⌨highlandproducts.com.pe) if you phone in advance. Otherwise, its vast retail outlet sells a bewildering array of coffees (including Café Misha), as well as local jams and liqueurs (coffee-flavoured included), honeys, raw cocoa paste and some of the smoothest, most intense coffee ice cream in Peru.

cross the bridge heading from La Merced towards San Ramón, you'll spot this thatched-roofed club on the other side of the river. On weekends the place heaves with local youths to the sounds of trance, reggaeton, pop, rap and rock; best after midnight. Fri–Sun 8pm–3am.

Los Koquis Jr Tarma 376. Set back from the Plaza de Armas, this greenery-festooned, family-run spot serves enormous portions of classic dishes such as *picante de cuy* and *asado de res*; vegetarians might be tempted by the *tallarines verdes* (spaghetti in Peruvian-style pesto). Mains S/13–21. Daily 11am–11pm.

Shambari Campa Jr Tarma 383. On the Plaza de Armas, this popular restaurant is decorated with early twentieth-century photos of La Merced and has an extensive menu of both traditional dishes (*cecina* – pork – with *juanes* and fried plantains) and jungle flavours, such as river-fish ceviche, *chancho* (wild pig) and *zamaño* (a medium-sized forest rodent). Mains S/19–29. Daily 7am–11pm.

Satipo

A real jungle frontier town, **SATIPO** is the jumping-off point for really off-the-beaten-track river travel into the jungle, but not a town to linger in (or wander around after dark – narcotrafficking activity along the nearby Río Ene occasionally brings some insalubrious characters here). The settlement was first developed to service colonists and settlers in the 1940s, and continues in similar vein today, providing an economic and social centre for a widely scattered population of over forty thousand colonists and Asháninka people, with supplies of tools and food, medical facilities and banks.

In the 1940s, the first dirt road extended here from Huancayo, but it wasn't until the 1970s that a road was opened from Lima via La Merced. With the surfacing of the Carretera Marginal road all the way from Lima over a decade ago, many more recent settlers have moved into the region, but the rate of development is putting significant pressure on the last surviving groups of traditional forest dwellers, mainly the **Asháninka**, who have mostly taken up plots of land and either compete with the relatively newcomer farmers or live in one of the ever-shrinking zones with very little contact with the rest of Peru. You can often see the Asháninka, in town to buy supplies and trade, sometimes still dressed in their reddish-brown or cream *cushma* robes.

ARRIVAL AND DEPARTURE   SATIPO

By bus and colectivo Satipo is accessible direct by bus from Lima; Expresos Molina Unión and Transmar are the best of the half-dozen companies that offer overnight *bus-camas*; buses to Lima tend to depart at 8.30pm, 9pm and 9.30pm. Turismo Central are the only buses to make the arduous journey to Pucallpa via the Carretera Marginal. Buses arrive in Satipo at the Terminal Terrestre, on Jr Leguia, seven blocks from the plaza, as do the vast majority of colectivos, shared cars and pickups. Pickup trucks leave early in the morning for Atalaya.
Destinations Atalaya (1–2 daily; 9hr); Huancayo (at least

10 daily; 6–8hr); La Merced (at least 20 daily; 2–3hr); Lima (10–12 daily; 10–12hr); Pucallpa (1 daily at 6pm; 19hr).
By shared car Shared cars to La Merced and Pichanaki depart when full from the corner of jirones Irazola and Bolognesi, a block downhill from the plaza. Shared cars to Puerto Ocopa, Puerto Prado, Atalaya and Puerto Bermudez depart from Jr Bolognesi.
Destinations Atalaya (several daily; 7–9hr); La Merced (several daily; 2hr); Pichanaki (several daily; 1hr); Puerto Bermudez (several daily; 8hr); Puerto Ocopa (several daily; 2hr).

ACCOMMODATION

Hostal Palmero Jr Manuel Prado 228 ☎064 545 020. The rooms are basic but clean and come with balconies and hot showers, but the real treasures are the owners who are happy to share their knowledge of the area and to arrange tours of the local petroglyphs and waterfalls. The location is central as can be, within half a block of the main plaza. Cheaper rooms with shared facilities are available. S̄/50

Hotel Brassia Jr Los Incas 535 ☎064 545 787, ⓦbrassiahotel.com. Clean and secure, this two-star hotel comes with cream-coloured a/c rooms, cable TV, hot water and good wi-fi. Service is very pleasant and they'll even wash your dirty togs for you. S̄/60

★**Hotel San Luis** Jr Grau 173 ☎064 545 319, ⓦsanluishotelsatipo.com. The nicest of Satipo's digs, this family-run hotel has quiet a/c rooms with crimson accents, on-site café, wi-fi, secure parking and even money-changing facilities. S̄/90

EATING AND DRINKING

El Bosque Jr Prado 554. Found inside a large courtyard full of greenery and away from the bustle of the street, this restaurant specializes in grilled meat dishes (the ribs aren't bad at all), as well as jungle dishes such as *doncella* ceviche and *tacacho* (a pork dish) with fried cassava, washed down with overly sweet regional fruit juices. Mains from S/20. Daily noon–10pm.

Chifa Sui Kao Jr Irazola 80. Right on the plaza and accessed through a red, horseshoe-shaped gateway, Satipo's most popular *chifa* does decent takes on a cornucopia of rice and noodle dishes. Mains from S/17. Daily noon–10pm.

Frutoz Jr Bolognesi 163 ☎064 781 197. You know it's a cool place because it spells its name with a "z". But seriously, this is a colourful and pleasant café with a large array of tropical juices on offer, as well as coffee, burgers and chicken and *chicharrón* sandwiches. Juices from S/3. Daily noon–3pm.

Rosemay Restaurant Jirones Las Incas and San Martín. Locally appreciated for its ample bowls of *caldo de gallina* (chicken soup), this informal joint does S/5 breakfasts and lunches – solid portions of fried fish, chicken and *chanco* (wild pig). Daily 8am–4pm.

Around Satipo

Satipo sits in the middle of a beautiful valley, the best way to get a feel for which is by following a **footpath** from the other side of the suspension bridge, two blocks from the plaza, which leads over the river from behind the market area, to some of the plantations beyond town. Other attractions beyond Satipo tend to be for the very adventurous, with plenty of time to spare.

The scenic route to Huancayo

Instead of retracing your steps from Satipo via La Merced and San Ramón, you can follow a breathtaking direct road to **Huancayo**; the rough road passes Toldopampa at 4200m, and the village of Comas before joining the main paved road between Tarma and Huancayo. This route is served by very scarce public transport.

Puerto Ocopa, Puerto Prado and around

Satipo is the southernmost large town on the jungle-bound Carretera Marginal, and a dirt road continues to **Puerto Ocopa** (a small river port originally founded by Franciscan missionaries in 1918) and further on to **Puerto Prado** which, for the last few years, has been the main port and a strategic location for travelling deeper into the forest along Río Tambo (while Río Ene is currently best avoided due to narco-activity). If you wish to travel to the Asháninka settlement of Betanya, known for its natural swimming pools, roughly halfway between Puerto Prado and Atalaya, you need to obtain permission from the Albergue de Asháninka in Satipo or risk a glacial welcome.

Atalaya

Tiny **Atalaya**, reachable either by boat down the **Río Tambo** or the loggers' road from Satipo (these days passable by pickup truck year-round), is way off the tourist trail: facilities are few and you need to bring all supplies with you. From Atalaya there are occasional boats down Río Ucayali to Pucallpa (p.458) that take two to three days to travel the 450km; facilities are very basic and it's best to ask in Satipo about the current political situation.

By bus and colectivo From Satipo, at least six bus companies make several daily journeys to Huancayo from the Terminal Terrestre (at least 10 daily; 6–8hr). Colectivos run to Puerto Prado via Puerto Ocopa (several daily; 2hr 15min), while pickup trucks depart daily for Atalaya early in the morning (1–2 daily; 9hr).

By boat From Puerto Prado motorized canoes leave for the Tambo and Ene rivers. Boats head to Atalaya (around 8hr) and Pucallpa (2–3 days).

Oxapampa

Some 78km by road (2hr) north of La Merced lies the small settlement of **OXAPAMPA**, a pleasant and well-organized frontier town, situated on the banks of the Río Chontabamba, some 1800m above sea level; wealthy residents from Lima buy land on the outskirts and build holiday ranches here. The area was settled by two hundred immigrants from Prussia in the mid-nineteenth century and evidence of these German roots is present both in the language still spoken by some of the descendants, and in the blue eyes and light hair of many inhabitants.

Oxapampa is situated around a beautiful, leafy square, complete with towering araucaría trees, and the frequently cool climate, combined with the vista of mist creeping along the surrounding mountains, gives the town a bit of an Alpine feel. This is dairy country, and a good place to feast on local cheeses, yogurts and honey.

Oxapampa's main local **fiesta** takes place at the end of August; on the thirtieth, the town celebrates its founding, while on the following day the traditional **Torneo de Cintas** takes place, when local young men compete on horseback to collect ribbons from a post.

8

By bus Oxapampa is reached via Expreso Molina Unión, Lobato and Transportes Merced buses from Lima via La Merced, among others. Transportes Edatur (☎ 964 863 041) runs to Huancayo. All buses pull in at the Terminal Terrestre in Jr Loechle, one block off the main road, Av San Martín, and a few blocks from the Plaza de Armas. There are convenient overnight departures for Lima at around 8pm.

Destinations Huancayo (2–6 daily; 6–7hr); La Merced (several daily; 3hr); Lima (several daily; 9–12hr).

By colectivo Colectivos and shared cars to La Merced, Villa Rica and Puerto Bermúdez leave throughout the day when full from the Terminal Terrestre. For Pozuzo, colectivos Yanachaga (☎ 963 646 551) leave from Av San Martín 501, while Transportes Santa Rosa (☎ 994 645 523) departs from Av San Martín 463.

Destinations La Merced (numerous daily; 2hr–2hr 30min); Pozuzo (7 daily; 3–4hr); Villa Rica (several daily; 1hr 20min).

By mototaxi Getting from the Terminal Terrestre to the centre costs a flat fare of S/.1.

INFORMATION AND TOURS

Tourist information For tourist information on Oxapampa and around, try the websites ⓦ oxapampa.pe and ⓦ oxapampaonline.com. Peru's protected-area agency SERNANP has a park office in Oxapampa, on the third block of Jr Pozuzo (☎ 063 462 544, ⓦ sernanp.gob.pe).

Tour operators There are four tour companies all running similar tours around the region – to Villa Rica, Pozuzo and the waterfalls around La Merced and Chontabamba. A decent bet is Polka Tours, on the first block of Av Mariscal Castilla on the Plaza de Armas (☎ 976 006 078); it also has a few mountain bikes for rent and sells the coffee for which the region is so famous.

ACCOMMODATION

Albergue Turístico Böttger Av Mariscal Castilla, block 6 ☎ 063 462 377. Five blocks' walk from the plaza, this *albergue* is based in a luxurious modern mansion built and panelled largely from cedar and *diablo fuerte* wood; it serves ample breakfasts, there's a good restaurant on-site, rooms are spacious and super-clean, and there's a splendid suite above the bar. S̲/̲1̲4̲0̲

★**Carolina Egg Gasthaus** Av San Martín 1085 ☎ 063 462 331, ⓦ carolinaegg.com. A lovely complex of en-suite rooms and bungalows, hidden amidst lush vegetation in a gated property across the main road from the Terminal Terrestre. This is an exceptionally friendly and well-run place (managed by a family descended from the original nineteenth-century colonists); there's a good restaurant during high season and the breakfasts are amazing. Doubles S̲/̲2̲3̲0̲, four-person bungalow S̲/̲5̲2̲0̲

Edelweiss Miraflores Km 53, Lote 58, just as you come into the entrance to town from the La Merced direction ☎ 063 462 567, ⓦ posadaedelweiss.com. A 100-year-old cedarwood house with forty beds based in chalets around a garden, with hammocks and a barbecue. There's also a guest lounge with TV, and a restaurant serving German and Italian dishes. S/120

Hospedaje Don Calucho Av San Martín 411 ☎ 063 462 109. Conveniently located near the plaza, just off the main road, this simple, secure guesthouse is run by a larger-than-life character who happens to be the president of the local cockfighting association. Best for

sound sleepers, as his prize cocks are resident in the appealing little garden and make themselves known at around dawn. S/60

Hospedaje Ruffner Jr Bolívar s/n, cuadra 5 ☎ 063 221 002. Handsome, red-brick guesthouse just three blocks from the plaza. Simple rooms come with balconies (facing the street or out back), exposed brick walls and hot showers. Per person S/30

EATING AND DRINKING

Your cheapest dining bet is to head one block south of the plaza along Jirón Bolognesi to the Mercado Municipal, where you can pick up S/5 lunches and fresh fruit and veg.

La Casa de Baco In the Miraflores suburb on the way into town at Km 2.5. Easily reached by mototaxi, this great garden restaurant is locally famous for its grilled meat dishes. The *parilla* mix, which includes chicken, smoked pork and *chorizo*, can generously feed two. Mains from S/20. Thurs–Sun 11.30am–9.30pm.

Ceja de Selva Jirones Castilla and Grau. It's difficult to pigeonhole this establishment, part-café serving an extensive selection of rooibos, oolong and herbal teas, decent coffee, and delicious cheese and smoked meat *empañadas*, and part-deli selling a huge array of local cheeses, yogurts and honey. Its beers span Europe and South America, too. Daily 9am–9pm.

La Nonna Jr Grau s/n, cuadra 1. Just off the Plaza de Armas, this is Oxapampa's (very good) answer to a trattoria.

Think imaginative pizzas with some locally exotic ingredients (mozzarella, smoked pork), spinach and ricotta lasagne, oxtail ravioli and more. A boon for vegetarians and full of surprises: the wine list even features some nice reds from Chile's Casillero del Diablo. Daily noon–3pm & 5–9pm.

★**El Rinconcito Oxapampino** Av San Martín s/n, cuadra 5 ☎ 063 462 155. This new kid on the block is homely, spotless and has daily specials scrawled cheerfully on the blackboard in coloured chalk. A fantastic place to taste criollo dishes such as *chicharrón de dorado* (fried chunks of dorado fish) and *cecina con patacones* (pork with green plantain fritters); the smoked ribs with star-fruit sauce are a delight, as are the fresh fruit juices. Mains S/19–28. Tues–Sun 8am–9pm.

Villa Rica and around

The town of **VILLA RICA**, some 36km southeast from Oxapampa, in the *ceja de selva* (edge of the jungle) next to an immense, shallow reed lake that's ideal for recreational boating, offers overland access to the Pichis and Palcazu valleys, the region's principal producers of coffee. The oversized coffeepot that graces the Plaza de Armas is testimony to the bean's importance in the local economy, and the coffee grown around Villa Rica is considered to be Peru's best.

There's a small place that roasts and grinds its own beans on Jirón San Carlos and Avenida Padre Salas, a couple of blocks from the Plaza de Armas, while the tourist office on the square has details of local *fincas* (coffee farms), a short mototaxi drive out of town, where you can sample local coffee and even stay the night (see below).

In terms of other attractions, only 12km from town you'll find the **Catarata El Encanto** (the "Spell" or "Enchantment" Waterfall), which has three sets of falls; rainbows frequently appear here, and there are deep, dangerous plunge pools.

ARRIVAL AND INFORMATION

By combi and colectivo Villa Rica is well connected to Oxapampa (1hr 20min) and La Merced (1hr) by frequent combis and colectivos.

VILLA RICA AND AROUND

Tourist information The tourist office on the Plaza de Armas (daily 8am–1pm & 2.30–5pm) has information on the local *fincas*.

ACCOMMODATION

Finca Santa Rosa ☎ 999 788 930, ⊕ finca santarosaperu.com. An excellent place to stay, where you can take guided tours of the coffee farm, go birdwatching

or hiking in the forest on the property and stay in simple but comfortable double and triple rooms. Breakfast is included in the price. S/100

Parque Nacional Yanachaga-Chemillén

Around 8km from Pozuzo proper, accessed via the Huampal sector in the Cañon de Huancabamba (as well as other routes) • Entrance fee S/20, payable at the SENAMP office • Get any Pozuzo–Oxapampa colectivo to drop you off by the entrance

Some 30km north of Oxapampa is the southern boundary of the **Parque Nacional Yanachaga-Chemillén**, a 122,000-hectare reserve dominated by dark mountains and vivid landscapes, where grasslands and cloud forest merge and separate. Established as a protected area in 1986, there are some hiking trails here and it may be possible to camp. Best visited in the dry season (May–Sept), there are vast quantities of bromeliads, orchids and cedars, as well as dwarf brocket deer, giant rats and even the odd spectacled bear, some jaguar and around 427 bird species, including a significant variety of hummingbirds. It's also home to a number of Yanesha communities.

Pozuzo

Some 80km further north from Oxapampa, and down into the rainforest at 823m above sea level, **POZUZO** is a slice of Tyrol-meets-the tropics. Reached via a rough road that crosses over several rivers and streams (which sometimes flow directly across the road) as it loops down through the greenery, the vista of wooden chalets with sloping Tyrolean roofs has endured ever since the first **Austrian and German colonists** arrived here in the mid-nineteenth century (see box opposite).

Pozuzo is a popular destination for Peruvian, Austrian and German tourists, particularly during the lively festival in the last week of July commemorating the founding of the town. It's a gorgeous little settlement, very unlike other Peruvian towns in size: it's compact, no more than two blocks wide; its streets are noticeably spotless and orderly; its chalet-style houses sport colourful gardens and flowers in window boxes; there's a noticeable absence of mototaxis; and it's surrounded by greenery-clad mountains wreathed in low-hanging mist.

When the road from Oxapampa crosses the river, it first reaches tiny **PRUSIA**, a German settlement linked to Pozuzo proper by the best 3km of paved road in rural Peru. Pozuzo itself is centred around the leafy **Plaza de Armas**, complete with a water, wheel and ship commemorating the colonists' voyage. Other places to explore include the fine **Iglesia San José**, built in stone and wood during 1875; the **Museo Schafferer** (daily 9am–11am & 3–5pm; S/3), which focuses on the colonists' history and displays photos and curios of the indigenous peoples; the very Germanic **Casa Budweiser** with its stylish chimney; and the neat, colourful little **cemetery**. Among the most noteworthy of the **colonists' houses**, perhaps the Casa Típica Palmatambo and the Casa Típica Egg Vogt are among the most interesting. As for scenic walks, take the turn-off towards the river next to the playschool and cross the **Puente Emperador Guillermo I**; a couple of trails start from the other side of the river, including a fifteen-minute walk up to a chapel that affords fantastic views over the whole of Pozuzo.

ARRIVAL AND INFORMATION   POZUZO AND PRUSIA

By colectivo Two colectivo companies run between Oxapampa and Pozuzo daily. Transportes Yanachaga (Av Los Colonos 560 ☎ 965 287 686) leaves Oxapampa at 7am, 9.30am and 1pm, returning from Pozuzo at 4am, 10am and 3pm. Transportes Santa Rosa (Av Los Colonos 351, ☎ 968 908 759) leaves Pozuzo at 6am, 10am, 1pm and 3pm. The journey takes 3–4hr but delays due to landslides are common during the rainy months (Dec–March).

Tourist information For local information, check out ⓦ pozuzo.pe, or contact Prusia Tours in Lima (☎ 01 445 6670, ⓦ prusiatours.com).

ACCOMMODATION

Pozuzo and Prusia have fifteen places to stay in total, which is remarkable for such tiny settlments; book well ahead for July's festivities.

Albergue Frau Maria Egg Av Los Colonos ☎ 063 287 559, ⓦ pozuzo.com. Accommodation here is in attractive wooden chalets, with lush gardens surrounding a little pool. The food served is exceptionally good, and Frau Maria

POZUZO'S TYROLEAN ROOTS

Back in the 1850s, Baron Schutz von Holzhausren of Germany and the then President of Peru, General Ramón Castilla, developed a grand plan to establish settlements deep in the jungle. The original **deal between Germany and Peru** required Peru to build roads, schools and churches; while the Austro-Germans needed to be of Catholic religion, have some kind of office and impeccable reputation.

The first group, comprising two hundred **Tyrolean** and one hundred Prussian immigrants, left Europe in 1857 on the British ship *Norton*, arriving in Lima on July 28. During the overland journey, cutting their way through jungle, almost half the colonists died of disease, accident or exhaustion. The town of **Pozuzo** was founded in 1859 when the area was ripe with virgin forest and crystalline rivers owned by the Yanesha people. Nine years later, a second group of immigrants arrived to reinforce the original population, which had been left, more or less abandoned, by the Peruvian authorities. The colonists began to expand their population and territory; first, **Oxapampa** was founded in 1891 by the Bottger family, then others went on to found **Villa Rica** in 1928.

Today the economy of Pozuzo is based on beef cattle and agriculture; but **lederhosen** are worn for fiestas and **Tyrolean dances** are still performed, particularly during the annual festival on July 25 – creating a peculiar combination of European rusticism (the local dance and music is still strongly influenced by the German colonial heritage) and native Peruvian culture. Moreover, many of the older generation of this unusual town's present inhabitants speak a nineteenth-century form of German, eat the best sausages in Peru and dance the polka.

can organize hikes to her ancestral home of Casa Palmatambo, cock-of-the-rock spotting by the Pozas de Guacamayo (see below) and more. **S/80**

★**Hospedaje Haus Köhel** C José Egg s/n ☎ 063 287 604. Appealing, flower-festooned chalet run by a welcoming family that is the pillar of the local community. The wood-panelled rooms are simple but come with reliable hot water, and a large breakfast with fresh fruit juice is included. **S/60**

El Mango C Pacificación 185 ☎ 063 287 528. This pleasant, wood-built place offers excellent rooms, a restaurant serving criollo dishes and Germanic-style specialities and the lady of the house is renowned for her great smoked sausages and smoked pork. **S/60**

Tierra Verde Lodge C José Egg s/n ☎ 01 726 1316, ⓦ hotelpozuzo.com. In an idyllic riverside location, this cluster of cheery cottages around a pool is Pozuzo's most upscale lodging option, several kilometres from Pozuzo proper and a stroll across the bridge to Prusia. Tour options include jungle-trekking, whitewater rafting and swimming in waterfalls and the proximity to Pozuzo's only disco, *Crazy Eddy's*, means that this is a nightlife option whether you like it or not. Two-person cottages **S/120**

EATING AND DRINKING

Cervecería C José Egg s/n. Remarkably, Pozuzo has its own microbrewery that specializes in exactly one kind of blond beer – the Dörchen. It's a very informal outdoor spot; pick a pew by the vats and ask for a mug of the stuff (S/5). No set hours.

Restorante Típico Prusia Av Cristóbal Johann 110 ☎ 064 631 251. Ignore the clichéd name of the first restaurant you reach from the turn-off into Prusia, and sit down to a meal that includes Pozuzo's famous sausages and smoked pork with fried plantains, *yuca* and delicious home-made cheese, all washed down with quitoquito juice. The proprietress is a descendant of Tyrolean colonists and speaks German. Mains around S/15. Daily noon–10pm.

Restorante Santa Rosita Av Los Colonos s/n ☎ 940 062 803. The pick of Pozuzo's criollo restaurants, this friendly spot is a good bet for local specialities such as *pachamanca de chancho* (a pork dish). The cheap daily menu includes soup and main (S/6–12) but if you really feel like pushing the boat out, go for the *mixto Pozucino* – a heaped plate of juicy sausages, smoked chicken and pork with fried plantains and *yuca* (S/20). Daily 7am–10pm.

Around Pozuzo

Reachable from Prusia, the main attraction is the **Catarata Delfín**, which has an 80m drop and is an hour's walk from the Delfín hydroelectric plant by the Cañon de Huancabamba, itself an hour or so's walk from the village; you can swim in the pool beneath the falls. At **Pozas de Guacamayo**, a fifteen-minute walk from Prusia, there's a natural habitat for the cock-of-the-rock bird which can be seen most afternoons.

En route to Pozuzo from La Merced, the road passes through the small town of **Huancabamba**, starting point for a four- or five-day trek up into the high Andes on an old Inca road crossing the Cordillera Huaguruncho via the Abra Anilcocha pass (4500m) towards Lago Chinchaycocha and Cerro de Pasco.

Pucallpa

A sprawling, hot and dusty city with over 400,000 inhabitants, **PUCALLPA** is a decent base for travellers who wish to visit **Lago Yarinacocha** (see p.460), a ten-minute mototaxi drive away. If you stay a little while, it's difficult not to appreciate the entrepreneurial optimism of this burgeoning jungle frontier city and its unvarnished waterfront activity. The Plaza de Armas features a construction of concrete and glass that is the town's modern **cathedral**; opinions divide as to whether it's cutting edge or hideous.

Pucallpa's annual festival for visitors – the **Semana Turística de la Region Ucayali** – is usually held in the last week of September, offering mostly artesanía and forest-produce markets, as well as folklore, music and dance.

Brief history

Long an impenetrable refuge for the **Cashibo**, Pucallpa was developed as a camp for rubber gatherers at the beginning of the twentieth century. In 1930 the town was connected to Lima by road (850km of it), and since then its expansion has been intense and unstoppable. Sawmills surround the city and spread up the main highway towards Tingo María and the mountains, and there's an impressive floating harbour at the nearby port of **La Hoyada**, where larger commercial vessels dock. In the twenty-first century, the city has been one of the main routes for lumber travelling from the Peruvian Amazon to Lima and the Pacific coast for export markets. Cattle-ranching is also big around here, putting increasing pressure on the rainforest's ecosystems and biodiversity.

Shops and markets

If you have an hour or so to while away in the town itself, both the downtown **food market** on Jirón Independencia and the older central **market** on Dos de Mayo are worth checking out; the latter in particular comprises varied stalls full of jungle produce. The port next to the central **Parque San Martín** bustles with activity by day, with great bunches of plantains being unloaded from cargo ships, delicious smells wafting from the food stalls, a mini fairground in the park and people playing roulette and cards. For **craft shopping**, artesanía can be found at the **Feria Municipal Artesanal** in the pedestrian passageway between Independencia and Libertad, closest to Udayali. Shipibo women hang out on the plaza in front of *Hotel El Castillo*, selling colourful weavings and other trinkets.

Museo Agustín Rivas

Jr Tarapacá 861 • Mon–Sat 10am–noon & 3–5pm • Free

There are works by the Pucallpa-born wood sculptor **Agustín Rivas** at his house – fantastic, twisted creations featuring humans and jungle creatures, inspired by Rivas' work with ayahuasca (he is also a shaman). The museum keeps erratic hours, though.

ARRIVAL AND DEPARTURE	PUCALLPA

By air The easiest way to get into town from Pucallpa airport, 5km west of town, is by mototaxi (15min; S/5–6) or taxi (10min; S/20). LAN Perú, at the corner of Jr Tarapacá 805 (☎061 579 840, ⓦlan.com), operates flights between Pucallpa and Lima, while Peruvian Airlines (Jr Tarapacá 805 ☎061 579 840) serves both Iquitos and Lima daily. Star Perú, Jr 7 de Junio 865 (☎061 590 589, ⓦstarperu.com), flies here from Tarapoto, Lima and Iquitos once a week.

Destinations Iquitos (1 daily; 1hr); Lima (2 daily; 1hr); Tarapoto (1 daily; 1hr 20min).

By bus There are direct services between Pucallpa and Lima via the sealed road that passes through Huánuco and Tingo María; however, while conditions were said to be okay at the time of research, in recent years there have been a number of holdups along the Pucallpa–Tingo María section of the road, so it's best to travel it during daylight hours. For years the mostly sealed road that branches off north to Tarapoto from just north of Tingo María also had a reputation for armed holdups, but at the time of research was deemed safe, particularly during the day. Several bus companies offer services to Lima and Tarapoto; Transmar (Raimondi 793; ☎ 061 579 778) is supposedly the most comfortable.

Destinations Lima via Tinga María (at least 12 daily; 17–20hr); Tarapoto (Mon, Wed & Fri at 7pm; 19hr).

By boat The operational port depends mostly on the height of the river and during the high-water season (Jan–April) many boats dock in front of the central Parque San Martín. Henry boats (☎ 980 253 420) to Iquitos dock at Puerto Henry, around ten blocks north of the city centre (S/2 by mototaxi). Henry boats depart downriver to Iquitos three times weekly (Mon, Wed & Fri); the journey takes three days, and it costs S/100 to sling your hammock (buy one at the Pucallpa market) or S/400 for a cabin for up to four people. Buy your ticket in the unmarked office by the port. Food is included in the price, but since it's of rather poor quality, you're better off bringing your own. As for smaller boats, their precise destinations can be identified directly in the port by notices on (or in front of) each boat; it's a matter of finding the right boat, then talking to the captain about prices and schedule.

GETTING AROUND AND INFORMATION

By mototaxi Ubiquitous mototaxis charge S/1–2 for short hops in town and S/5 to get out to Lago Yarinacocha.

Tourist information ⌕ pucallpa.com is a moderately useful website.

Tour operators Laser Viajes, Jr Raimondi 399 and Jr Tarapacá (☎ 061 571 120, ⌕ laserviajes.pe), offers some multi-day tours around Pucallpa and sells travel tickets.

Services Interbank (jirones Ucayali and Raimondi), Banco Continental (across the street) and BCP (jirones Tarapacá and Raimondi) have ATMs and exchange US dollars. The post office is at Av San Martín 418.

ACCOMMODATION

★ **Del Castillo Plaza Hotel** Jr Independencia 550 ☎ 061 573 141, ⌕ delcastilloplazahotel.com. Overlooking the plaza and the controversial modern cathedral, this is one of Pucallpa's best hotels, with vast, spotless a/c rooms, bright splashes of colour and swan-shaped towels. If you fancy a romantic night in with your sweetie, they'll strew flower petals on the bed. S̲/̲1̲8̲0̲

Grand Hotel Mercedes Jr Raimondi 610 ☎ 061 575 120, ⌕ granhotelmercedes.com. One of Pucallpa's best upmarket options, Mercedes has a great swimming pool, lovely jungle gardens, a reasonable restaurant and bar. The rooms are comfortable and clean, and come with cable TV and fridges. Prices halve in the off-season. S̲/̲3̲1̲0̲

Hospedaje Barbtur Jr Raimondi 670 ☎ 061 572 532. Central cheapie run by a friendly family. Your room may or may not have a window, but it will have cable TV, cold showers and wi-fi. S/30 doubles with shared bath also available. S̲/̲4̲0̲

Hospedaje Komby Jr Ucayali 360 ☎ 061 571 562, ⌕ kombypucallpa.com. In spite of being on a busy street a couple of blocks from the plaza, many rooms are quiet as they face an inner courtyard, and the amenities – wi-fi, cable TV, fridges – make up for the lack of a scenic view. Cheaper, fan-only rooms are available and airport drop-off is included in the price. S̲/̲1̲0̲0̲

Hospedaje El Virrey Av San Martín 552 ☎ 061 575 611, ⌕ elvirreypucallpa.com. Located between the plaza and the waterfront Parque San Martín, this guesthouse has simple, comfortable rooms, a swimming pool and a decent restaurant serving local specialities. S̲/̲1̲5̲0̲

8

EATING

Like all jungle cities, Pucallpa has developed a cuisine of its own; one of the unique dishes you can find in some of these restaurants is *inchicapi* – a chicken soup made with peanuts, manioc and coriander leaves. Try the local speciality *patarashca* (fresh fish cooked in *bijao* leaves).

Los Antojitos de Odisa Jr Tarapacá 863 ☎ 061 572 194. Friendly, colourful little café where you can grab a plate of roast chicken/cecina/fried fish with *patacones* (fried green plantain) and a drink for S/12. They offer delivery, too. Daily noon–3pm & 7–10pm.

Bekanwe Jr Inmaculada 671 ☎ 061 577 424. With its ayahuasca-themed decor, this smart café serves anything from spicy chicken wings to grilled *paiche*, complete with an excellent selection of home-made sauces. The ample helpings of *chicharrón de pescado* with *patacones* are a good bet. Daily 8.30am–3.30pm & 6.30–10pm.

Chez Maggy Jr Inmaculada 643 ☎ 061 754 958. The first thing that catches your eye is the massive stone oven at the front of the restaurant where the chefs toil to produce a wide selection of very good pizza and calzones the size of your head. The tropical sangria is an excellent accompaniment. Medium pizza from S/20. Daily 7–11pm.

Chifa Dragón del Oro Jr Inmaculada 668 ☎ 061 574 841. The pick of the city's Chinese-Peruvian establishments, with attentive staff, an extensive menu of noodle, rice, meat and seafood dishes and proper, stock-based wonton soup. Portions are ample. Mains from S/25. Daily 12.30–11.30pm.

Pez Dorado Jr Bolívar, between jirones Huascár and Tarapacá. This tiny blue cevichería with three tables is a one-man show; come here earlier rather than later for *arroz* *con mariscos, chicharrón de pescado* and ceviche, as he occasionally runs out in the evenings. The two-course menu is a steal at S/12. Tues–Sun noon–3pm & 7–9pm.

Parque Natural y Museo Regional de Pucallpa

Barboncocha • Daily 8am–5pm • S/5 • S/4–5 by mototaxi

Some 6km out of town, along the highway towards Lima, there's a small lakeside settlement and zoological park at Barboncocha, reachable by a very muddy road. Known as the **Parque Natural y Museo Regional de Pucallpa**, it consists of almost two hundred hectares of lakeside reserve, with a small museum featuring Shipibo pottery, a children's playground and a rather depressing collection of caged wildlife, so this isn't for everyone. It was under renovation at the time of research.

Yarinacocha

Some 9km from Pucallpa, the appealing **YARINACOCHA** oxbow lake is Pucallpa's biggest attraction. **Dolphins** are a common enough sight if you take a boat out onto the lake, and there are numerous small **Shipibo communities** scattered around its perimeter, some, such as San Francisco, easily reachable by road. A narrow river channel connects the lake to rivers further on.

Puerto Callao

The lakeside village, **Puerto Callao**, is more like a suburb of Pucallpa – an urban sprawl with the greenery on the Plaza de Armas pruned into shapes of wild beasts.

There's a ramshackle charm to the waterfront where you can watch villagers loading up boats with produce. There also a little market and a cluster of boats down the south end of the lake, with local guides waiting to whisk visitors off on short jaunts or even multi-day adventures. If you follow the dirt road past the boats, it eventually ends in a leafy cul-de-sac after passing several large restaurants over the water and jungle bars blaring music. It's worth a visit as a day-trip, but unless you're going on a multi-day boating adventure into the jungle, the *chicha*-blaring bars are unlikely to keep you occupied for long.

Moroti-Shobo Crafts Co-operative

Plaza Yarina, two blocks from Malecón Callao • Daily 8am–9pm

The settlement boasts one of the best jungle Indian craft workshops in the Amazon, the **Moroti-Shobo Crafts Co-operative** – a project operated by the local Shipibo and Conibo Indians. Located on the side of the main plaza, the stalls mostly sell psychedelic Shipibo weavings, though you can also find a few examples of beautifully moulded ceramics.

ARRIVAL AND DEPARTURE	**YARINACOCHA**

By mototaxi Though it is served by buses and colectivos, by far the quickest and easiest way to reach Yarinacocha is to take a mototaxi from Pucallpa (15min; S/4–5).

BOAT TRIPS FROM PUERTO CALLAO

The guides lurking near their boats will approach you as you reach the lake with proposals of boat trips. The standard hour-long jaunt (S/30 for up to five people) includes dolphin-spotting plus a chance to see sloths on a small island near the southern lake shore. More adventurous options include two- and three-day ventures down rivers beyond the lake, with overnight stays in Shipibo villages, piranha-fishing on the Canal Negro, animal-watching along Río Ucayali and jungle trekking/camping. Congenial Mario (☏ 961 571 880) – owner of the *Los 3 Hermanos* boat – and his son run such trips (very little English spoken); it's a bare-bones adventure (S/200 for three days, two nights) and a number of other operators offer something similar.

ACCOMMODATION AND EATING

Most accommodation in Puerto Callao is ramshackle at best, so it's worth staying in a lodge further out. Waterside restaurants have pretty much identical menus, but visitors seem to favour the *Anaconda*.

Ecolodge Amazónico Jene Shobo Yarinacocha, lakeside ☎972 900 739, ⌨jeneshobo.com.pe. This comfortable lodge has a restaurant, library and stylish en-suite rooms, organizes bonfires and drum-dancing, and will pick up from Pucallpa airport; it also has boat transport for the lake and runs short local tours. **S̲/̲3̲5̲0̲**

La Maloka Malecón Yarinacocha ☎061 569 900. At the end of the leafy cul-de-sac, this is the only appealing place to stay in Puerto Callao. The simple, wi-fi-enabled rooms sit on stilts above the water, there's a pleasant restaurant and they've even done away with their g̲h̲a̲s̲t̲l̲y̲ little zoo (with the exception of a tortoise or two). **S̲/̲1̲8̲0̲**

The northern selva

At the "island" city of Iquitos, by far the largest and most exciting of Peru's jungle towns, there are few sights as magnificent as the **Río Amazonas**. Its tributaries start well up in the Andes, and when they join together several hours upstream from the town, the river is already several kilometres wide. The town's location, only 104m above sea level yet thousands of miles from the ocean and surrounded in all directions by brilliant green forest and hemmed in by the maze of rivers, streams and lagoons, makes for a stunning entry to the **NORTHERN SELVA**.

Much of **Iquitos's** appeal derives from its being the starting point for excursions into the **rainforest** (see p.473), but the town is an interesting place in its own right, if only for the lively local people and magnificent architecture. It's a buzzing, cosmopolitan tourist town, connected to the rest of the world by river and air only: the kind of place that lives up to all your expectations of a jungle town, from its elegant reminders of the rubber-boom years to the atmospheric shantytown suburb of **Puerto Belén**, one of Werner Herzog's main locations for his 1982 film *Fitzcarraldo*, where you can buy almost anything, from fuel to ayahuasca medicines.

Even without venturing into the jungle you can acquaint yourself with the jungle wildlife at legitimate **animal rescue centres** around Iquitos, but beware of the fakes (see box, p.470).

The town has a friendly café and club scene, interesting museums and beautiful, late nineteenth- and early twentieth-century buildings, and the surrounding region has some great island and lagoon **beaches**, a range of easy excursions into the rainforest and the possibility of continuing down the Amazon into **Colombia or Brazil**. The area has also become something of a **spiritual focus**, particularly for gringos seeking a visionary experience with one of the many local shamans who use the sacred and powerful hallucinogenic ayahuasca vine in their psycho-healing sessions (see box, p.475).

Unlike most of the Peruvian selva, the **climate** here is little affected by the Andean topography, so there is no rainy season as such; instead, the year is divided into "high water" (Dec–May) and "low water" (June–Nov) seasons. The upshot is that the weather is always hot and humid, with temperatures averaging 23–30°C (74–86°F) and with an annual rainfall of about 2600mm. Most visitors come between May and August, but the high-water months are perhaps the best time for seeing **wildlife**, because the animals are crowded into smaller areas of dry land, though the low-water months are best for fishing.

Iquitos

Self-confident and likeable, **IQUITOS** is a modern, spread-out city of almost half a million people, built on a wide, flat river plain. Only the heart of the city, around the main plaza, contains older, architecturally interesting buildings, but the river port and market area of **Belén** boasts rustic wooden huts on stilts – a classic image of Iquitos.

If it weren't for the few stalls and shops selling jungle craft goods it would be hard to know that this place was once dominated by hunter-gatherer **tribes** like the Iquito, Yaguar, Bora and Witito who initially defended their territory against the early Spanish missionaries and explorers.

Brief history

Though founded in 1757 under the name of San Pablo de los Napeanos, the present centre of Iquitos was established in 1864. By the end of the nineteenth century Iquitos was, along with Manaus in Brazil, one of *the* great rubber towns, built on the misery and countless deaths of indigenous people who were used by the rubber barons as de facto slaves. From that era of grandeur a number of structures survive, but during the last century the town veered between prosperity (as far back as 1938, when the area was explored for oil) and the depths of economic depression. However, its strategic position on the Amazon, which makes it accessible to large ocean-going ships from the distant Atlantic, has ensured its continued importance. From the 1940s to the 1960s, Iquitos was buoyed by the export of timber, tobacco and Brazil nuts, and dabbling in the trade of wild animals, tropical fish and birds, as well as an insecticide called *barbasco*, long used by natives as a fish poison, while from the 1960s, an oil boom helped Iquitos to regain some degree of prosperity, helped along by tourism, particularly in recent years.

Plaza de Armas

Iquitos has several squares, but the heart of the city is the central **Plaza de Armas**, still weirdly dominated by the towering presence of a bright blue, abandoned and dilapidated high-rise **hotel**, built during the boom of the early 1980s, before the economy slumped and terrorism temporarily slowed tourism in the region. The plaza comes alive at night with hundreds of little lights.

On the southwest side of the plaza, the **Iglesia Matriz** (daily 7am–5pm), the main Catholic church, houses paintings by the Loretano (Loreto is the *departamento* Iquitos is located in) artists Américo Pinasco and César Calvo de Araujo, depicting biblical scenes.

IQUITOS FIESTAS

Iquitos throws some good annual festivals. The carnival known as **Omagua** (local dialect for "lowland swamp") has grown vigorously over recent years and now involves not only townspeople, but hundreds of indigenous people as well, with plenty of chanting and dancing. The main thrust of activities is on the Friday, Saturday and Sunday before Ash Wednesday, and on Monday the town celebrates with the traditional Umisha dance around a sacred tree selected for the purpose. It's similar to maypole dancing in Britain, though in Iquitos the dancers strike the tree with machetes; when it eventually falls, children dive in to grab their share of the many gifts suspended from it.

Perhaps the best time to visit Iquitos, however, is at the end of June (supposedly June 23–24, but actually spread over three or four days), when the main **Fiesta de San Juan** takes place. The focus is on the small artesanía market of San Juan (the patron saint of Iquitos), some 4km from the city and quite close to the airport. It's the traditional time for partying and for eating *juanes*, delicious little balls of rice and chicken wrapped in jungle leaves; the best place for these is in San Juan itself. June is also the month for **Iquitos Week**: seven days of celebrations around the Fiesta de San Juan, though tending to spread right across the month.

In October the local tourist board organizes an **international rafting competition**, which draws enthusiasts from every continent for a five-hour, 19km river race between Nauta and Iquitos in hand-built craft. At the end of the month there's the **Espiritos de La Selva** (Spirits of the Jungle) festival, which coincides with Hallowe'en and All Souls, and involves street processions with costumes depicting mythological figures, plus the usual communal drinking and eating.

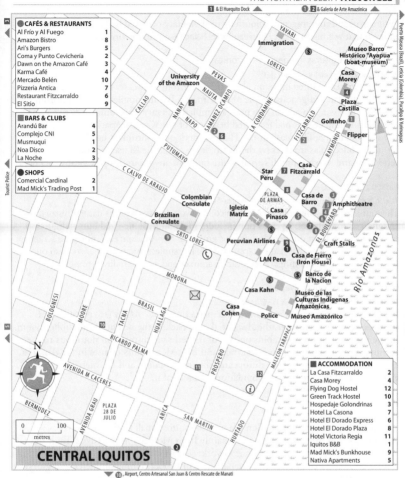

CAFÉS & RESTAURANTS
Al Frío y Al Fuego	1
Amazon Bistro	8
Ari's Burgers	5
Coma y Punto Cevichería	2
Dawn on the Amazon Café	3
Karma Café	4
Mercado Belén	10
Pizzeria Antica	7
Restaurant Fitzcarraldo	6
El Sitio	9

BARS & CLUBS
Arandú Bar	4
Complejo CNI	5
Musmuqui	1
Noa Disco	2
La Noche	3

SHOPS
Comercial Cardinal	2
Mad Mick's Trading Post	1

ACCOMMODATION
La Casa Fitzcarraldo	2
Casa Morey	4
Flying Dog Hostel	12
Green Track Hostel	10
Hospedaje Golondrinas	3
Hotel La Casona	7
Hotel El Dorado Express	6
Hotel El Dorado Plaza	8
Hotel Victoria Regia	11
Iquitos B&B	1
Mad Mick's Bunkhouse	9
Nativa Apartments	5

CENTRAL IQUITOS

8

Airport, Centro Artesanal San Juan & Centro Rescate de Manatí

Casa de Fierro

On the southeast corner of the plaza, you'll find the eyecatching **Casa de Fierro** (Iron House), hard to miss with its silvery sides glinting in the afternoon sunshine. Designed by Gustave Eiffel for the 1889 Paris exhibition, it was later shipped in pieces to Iquitos and reconstructed here in the 1890s by one of the local rubber barons. It now houses a pharmacy.

The riverfront

One block southeast of Plaza de Armas are the two best sections of the **old riverfront**, El Boulevard and Malecón Tarapacá, both of which have been recently restored to some of their former glory. **El Boulevard** is the busier of the two areas, especially at night, full of bars and restaurants and with a small **amphitheatre** with live entertainment most nights, from capoeira demonstrations to breakdancing. In the evenings this pedestrian stretch fills with a whirlwind of strolling locals, people playing roulette, tourists having their photos taken with gussied-up llamas and hippie travellers sprawled on benches with their battered rucksacks.

The **Malecón Tarapacá** boasts some fine old mansions, one of which, at no. 262, with lovely nineteenth-century *azulejo* work, is now one of the town's better bakeries. On the corner with

Putumayo stands the gorgeous, colourfully tiled, military-occupied building (no photos allowed) that was once the Art Nouveau **Hotel Palace** – one of the city's historical icons.

Museo de las Culturas Indígenas Amazónicas
Malecón Tarapacá 332 • Daily 8am–7.30pm • S/15

The excellent two-storey museum along the waterfront showcases the culture and rituals of forty different indigenous people of the Amazon Basin, complete with captions in English. Here you can admire the pre-Columbian funerary urns found at Peru's Valencia site, the splendid ceremonial feathered headgear of the Wayana-Apari and the Kaiapo and the totem-pole-like mask of the Tikuna, check out a shrunken head of the kind formerly collected as trophies by the Jivaro, learn about the Matses poison frog ceremony, and much more. It's an absolute must for anyone anthropologically inclined.

Museo Amazónico
Malecón Tarapacá 382 • Mon–Sat 9am–12.30pm & 2.30–5pm • S/3

The municipal museum, **Museo Amazónico**, is devoted to the region's natural history and indigenous cultures. Its collection includes some unusual life-sized human figures in traditional dress from different indigenous groups of the Amazon; each fibreglass sculpture was made from a cast that had encapsulated the live subject for an hour or so. Also on display are some oil paintings, a few stuffed animals and a small military museum.

Museo Barco Histórico "Ayapua"
Plaza Ramón Castilla • Daily 9am–5pm • S/15 • ⓦ fundoamazonia.org

Docked by the waterfront across the little plaza from *Casa Morey* (see p.466) is this triple-decked 1906 **steamer**, the *Ayapua*, dating back to the height of the rubber boom. Inside the air-conditioned cabins on two of its decks are displays on notorious rubber barons such as Carlos Fermín Fitzcarrald and Luis Morey, missionaries in the Amazon, exploration of the Amazon by Europeans, the rubber boom and the merciless exploitation of the indigenous populations because of it.

Casa Cohen
Jirones Próspero and Morona

The quaint, one-storey **Casa Cohen** is a nod to Iquitos' small Sephardic Jewish community that came to the Amazon mainly from Morocco in the 1870s. Built in 1905 and beautifully adorned with ironwork, colourful *azulejos* (tiles) and *pilastras* (mural-covered pillars), it reflects the past days of rubber-boom commerce and glory; these days it's a less-than-glamorous supermarket.

Casa Kahn
Block 1 of Jr Sargento Lores

The **Casa Kahn** is a particularly fine example of the Portuguese tile decoration that adorns many of the late eighteenth- and early nineteenth-century buildings, some of which are brilliantly extravagant in their Moorish inspiration.

Casa Fitzcarrald
Jr Napo 200–212

Once home to the legendary rubber baron of the same name, sadly the **Casa Fitzcarrald** is not open to the public. It was built of adobe and *quincha* (cane or bamboo plastered with mud) and has a central patio with arches, plus ceilings of roughly sawn wood.

Belén
The most memorable part of town – best visited around 7am when it's most active – **Belén** looms out of central Iquitos at a point where the Amazon, until recently, joined the Río Itaya inlet. Consisting almost entirely of **wooden huts** raised on stilts and, until

a few years ago, also floating on rafts, the district has earned fame among travellers as the "Venice of the Peruvian Jungle". Actually, besides being built over the water, it has very little in common with European glamour; it has changed little over its hundred or so years, remaining a poor shanty settlement trading in basics like bananas, manioc, fish, turtles and crocodile meat. While filming *Fitzcarraldo* here, Werner Herzog merely had to make sure that no motorized canoes appeared on screen: virtually everything else, including the style of the *barriada* dwellings, looks exactly the way it did during the nineteenth century.

Mercado Belén

4–5min in a mototaxi (S/2) from Plaza de Armas

A somewhat insalubrious grid of pungent, narrow streets lined with produce, the **market** adjacent to the floating shantytown makes for a fascinating wander and a cheap and exotic place to eat (see p.468). Not all of it is pleasant: you may see some dismembered river turtles headed for the soup pot, and one section of the market features cages full of jungle animals, some of which end up in "animal rescue centres" (see box, p.470) while others are destined to be illegal pets. Unfortunately, buying them and trying to donate them to legitimate rescue centres or setting them free only helps to fuel the illegal animal trade.

Ask for directions to **Pasaje Paquito**, the busy herbalist alley in the heart of the market, synthesizing the rich flavour of the place. Here you'll find scores of competing stalls selling an enormous variety of natural jungle medicines, as well as some of the town's cheapest artesanía.

Galería de Arte Amazónica

C Trujillo 438 • Call for an appointment on ☎ 065 253120 • Free

In the Punchana sector of Iquitos, the **Galería de Arte Amazónica** exhibits the work of the Peruvian painter **Francisco Grippa**, as well as that of other national and local artists. Grippa, who lives and works mainly in Pevas (see p.474), arrived in the Amazon in the late 1970s after being educated in Europe and the US, and his work, described variously as figurative and expressionist, displays an obsession with light and colour, focusing on subjects such as Shipibo Indians, jungle birds and rainforest landscapes.

ARRIVAL AND DEPARTURE   IQUITOS

BY BOAT

Iquitos is Peru's largest and busiest river port city and there are three main passenger ports. Cargo boats upstream to Yurimaguas, Pucallpa via Lagunas and cargo boats upstream to Tabatinga, Brazil and Leticia, Colombia, via Pevas depart from the main Puerto Masusa (Av La Marina), some eleven blocks northeast of the Plaza de Armas. Occasionally there are also cargo boats all the way to Manaus, Brazil. Henry boats (☎ 965 678 622) to Pucallpa have their own port on Av La Marina, not far from the city centre. Finally, speedboats to Leticia and Tabatinga (the tri-border, p.476) leave from the Puerto Embarcadero. There are tips on travelling by boat in the main jungle listings (see p.431).

Boat companies The two speedboat companies serving Santa Rosa at the tri-border (see p.476) have their offices on Av Raymondi: Flipper, at no. 350 (☎ 065 766 303), and Golfinho, at no. 378 (☎ 065 225 118); their speedboats depart on consecutive days (except Mon) at 5am (S/200).

Destinations Leticia/Tabatinga by speedboat (Tues–Sun; 8–9hr); Leticia/Tabatinga by cargo boat (2–3 weekly; 2 days); Pevas (2–3 weekly; 12hr); Pucallpa (at least 3 weekly; 4–7 days); Yurimaguas (weekly; 3–6 days).

BY PLANE

Flights land at Iquitos airport (Aeropuerto Internacional Francisco Secada Vignetta), 6km southwest of town. Flights are met by taxis (S/15–20) and mototaxis (S/10). Iquitos is served by flights from Lima with LAN Perú, Jr Prospero 232 (☎ 065 232 421), flights from Lima and Pucallpa with Star Perú, Jr Napo 256 (☎ 065 236 208) and Peruvian Airlines, Jr Prospero 215 (☎ 065 480 111); Star Perú also flies to Tarapoto; and flights from Panama City with Copa Airlines (🌐 copaair.com). There are rumours of a new small-plane airline starting flights from Iquitos to Manaus and Iquitos to Cusco, but this is yet to happen.

Destinations Lima (several daily; 1hr 49min); Panama City (2 weekly on Wed & Sat; 4hr 30min); Pucallpa (2 daily; 1–2hr); Tarapoto (daily; 1hr).

8

GETTING AROUND

By mototaxi For getting around town, the ubiquitous mototaxis charge S/10 from the airport and S/2 for short hops within town.

By canoe If you want to get onto the river itself, you can hire a canoe from the port at Bellavista (see p.470).

INFORMATION AND TOURS

Tourist information There's a helpful tourist information kiosk at the airport (daily 8am–9pm; ☎ 065 260251), and the main iPeru tourist office is at C Napo 161 (Mon–Sat 9am–6pm, Sun 9am–1pm; ☎ 065 236 144). *Dawn on the Amazon Café* (see p.468) acts as an unofficial clearing house of information; owner Bill is happy to recommend ecologically friendly attractions and to steer people away from less-than-reputable ayahuasca retreats.

National park information The SERNAMP office for the Reserva Nacional Pacaya-Samiria office is at Jr Chávez 930–942 (☎ 065 223 555). It's good for maps, information on the reserve and permission to enter it (S/30 per day).

Tours A number of tour companies arrange tours of Iquitos and its environs, and there are also independent guides offering their services (see box, p.473).

Useful resources There's a free monthly English-language newspaper for Iquitos (🌐 iquitostimes.com), run by UK expat Mike Collis and to be found at many hotels, guesthouses and cafés. There's also the monthly *The Amazon River* (🌐 theamazonrivermonthly.com), another free English-language newspaper that's an entertaining collection of articles on all things Amazonian (some to be taken with a pinch of salt) and a decent breakdown of restaurant listings.

ACCOMMODATION

HOTELS AND GUESTHOUSES

★ **La Casa Fitzcarraldo** Av La Marina 2153 ☎ 065 601 138, 🌐 lacasafitzcarraldo.com. Hidden within a lush garden that blocks off much of the city's bustle, this characterful, luxurious B&B runs with the theme from Hertzog's film (in fact, the cast and crew were resident here when *Fitzcarraldo* was being filmed). There are only three individually decorated rooms and a bungalow (Mick Jagger had the Blue Room, Klaus Kinski the Green Room and Hertzog took the spacious bungalow), a very clean swimming pool, plus great food, drinks, lovely orchid-rich gardens and a three-level treehouse with panoramic views. Various European languages spoken. S/300

★ **Casa Morey** C Loreto 200 ☎ 065 231 913, 🌐 casamorey.com. This gorgeous rubber-boom mansion from 1913 – all Georgian chic mixed with Amazonian motifs – has been converted to a boutique hotel with fourteen spacious, light-filled rooms with some period furniture and thoroughly modern bathrooms. The secluded pool with its faux-Grecian columns and fountain is perfect for a quiet swim and visitors and guests alike are welcome to peek into the handsome library. US$95

Hospedaje Golondrinas Jr Putumayo 1024 ☎ 065 236 428, 🌐 hospedajegolondrinas.com. Friendly guesthouse that's nine to ten blocks from the plaza, with a greenery-filled courtyard, large swimming pool, guest kitchen and compact, basic private singles, doubles and triples. Could be cleaner, but really good value for the money and the owners run a rustic jungle lodge. S/40

Hotel La Casona Jr Fitzcarrald 147 ☎ 065 223 283, 🌐 hotellacasonaiquitos.com.pe. A stone's throw from the plaza, this is a large, rambling budget hotel with an inner courtyard (a good place to hang out with fellow travellers), psychedelic Shipibo weavings and Bora masks on walls, simple en-suite rooms (some with a/c) and helpful staff. There's a smaller, cheaper branch of *La Casona* across the street. S/105

Hotel El Dorado Express Jr Napo 362 ☎ 065 232 574, 🌐 eldoradohoteles.com. The smaller, cheaper offshoot of the celebrated *El Dorado* (see below) has a quiet range of rooms set back from the road, a swimming pool surrounded by greenery, a café serving light bites and vegetarian dishes, and guest computers in the a/c lobby. The rooms are stylish and carpeted, with modern bathrooms and a/c. Doubles US$104, suites US$238

Hotel El Dorado Plaza Jr Napo 258, Plaza de Armas ☎ 065 222 555, 🌐 eldoradohoteles.com. As well as being the first five-star in Iquitos, this is the most central splurgeworthy option. Rooms are large and spacious with excellent showers, a/c, cable TV and large beds, and the superbly cool lobby has a glass lift rising to all six floors. The service is as professional as you'd expect, and *El Dorado* boasts a nice pool, a *maloca*-style bar and a quality restaurant, as well as some fantastic rainforest-inspired paintings by local artist Francisco Grippa (see p.474). Doubles US$255, suites US$480

Hotel Victoria Regia Jr Palma 252 ☎ 065 231 983, 🌐 victoriaregiahotel.com. One of Iquitos's more luxurious options, this smart hotel is decked out in purples and shades of mustard and the rooms are stylish, with excellent beds and baths in the bathrooms (the suite comes with a jacuzzi). There's also a small pool and two very good restaurants on site. S/250

Iquitos B&B Jr Prado 231 🌐 iquitosbnb.com. Run by a friendly Dutch jungle guide and ayhuasca enthusiast, this is one of the best backpacker digs in town. Rooms are modest

en suites, quiet and clean, and your host is a treasure trove of local information. S/35

Nativa Apartments Jr Nanay 144 ☎ 065 600 270, ⓦnativaapartments.com. Run by a friendly and helpful family, this secure guesthouse is just a few blocks from the plaza and comes with clean, colourful, wi-fi equipped studio apartments with kitchenettes, which can be rented for a single night or for weeks at a time. Tea and coffee available for guests. S/150

HOSTELS

Flying Dog Hostel Jr Tarapacá 592 ☎ 065 223 755, ⓦflyingdogperu.com. Bona fide offshoot of the Lima/Cusco/Arequipa hostel chain, complete with colourful rooms (some with bathroom), spacious guest lounge with graffitied testimonies from happy travellers, guest kitchen

and plenty of *buena onda* (good vibes). Dorms S̲/25, doubles S̲/90

★**Green Track Hostel** Jr Palma 516 ☎ 065 600 805, ⓦgreentrack-jungle.com. Popular backpacker haunt a short distance from the plaza with all facilities that backpackers have come to expect: a/c guest lounge, wi-fi, security lockers, guest kitchen, secure rooms and dorms, as well as an appealing courtyard filled with greenery. As a bonus, *Green Track* has its own jungle lodge (see p.476) in the Tapiche Reserve and the owner is renowned for his efforts to protect the local wildlife. Dorms S̲/25, doubles S̲/105

Mad Mick's Bunkhouse Jr Putumayo 163 ☎ 965 754 976. With a super-central location just off the Plaza de Armas, the bunkhouse consists of a single fan-cooled bunkroom with eight beds, shared bathroom and guest computer. Cheap as chips and reputable besides. Dorms S̲/15

EATING AND DRINKING

Food in Iquitos is exceptionally good for a jungle town, specializing in **fish dishes** but catering pretty well to any taste. Unfortunately, many of the **local delicacies** are now in danger of disappearing entirely from the rivers around Iquitos – notably, river turtle and alligator, though the tasty *paiche* fish – the largest scaled fish in the world – is now more readily available due to breeding programmes. Note that *Dawn on the Amazon Café*, *Karma Café* and *Amazon Bistro* are particularly good places to avoid the Inca's Revenge, as they use filtered water for everything, including ice cubes and washing produce.

★**Al Frío y Al Fuego** Av la Marina 138 ☎ 965 607 474, ⓦalfrioyalfuego.com. This is an excellent restaurant that floats on the Río Itaya and focuses on imaginative jungle cuisine. Choose from the likes of doncella-filled ravioli, the classic *patarasca* dish and *cecina con tacacho* (smoked pork with fried green plantains), washed down with generously poured fresh tropical juices. Take a mototaxi to the Av La Marina address and catch a boat from the dock downstairs to the restaurant; there's a swimming pool at the restaurant, so you may wish to linger. Mains from S/20. Mon 6–9pm, Tues–Sat noon–3pm & 6–9pm, Sun noon–3pm.

Amazon Bistro Malecón Tarapacá 268 ☎ 065 600 785. Housed in the gorgeous Casa del Fierro, this restaurant combines Old World charm with high ceilings, an imposing bar and an eclectic menu of international dishes. *Patarashka* (fish steamed with manioc in a palm leaf) sits comfortably alongside Argentinian steak, Caesar salad and doncella fish in lemon sauce; the dessert list features profiteroles and tipples include Belgian beer. Very popular with travellers and the local expat community. Daily 8am–midnight.

Ari's Burgers Jr Prospero 127. Actually serving more than burgers (which are very average), including dishes with a variety of river fish, plus the best French fries in town. It's hugely popular with the locals and also sells some of the best ice cream in town (S/2 a scoop). Daily 8am–midnight.

Coma y Punto Cevichería Jr Napo 488 ☎ 065 225 268. A popular lunchtime spot that serves some of the Iquitos' best ceviche made from different types of river fish. Other dishes include generous portions of *arroz con mariscos* (seafood rice) and *chicharrón de pescado* (chunks of fried,

battered fish). Mains from S/15. Daily noon–5pm.

★**Dawn on the Amazon Café** Malecón Maldonado 185 ☎ 065 600 057. This wonderfully relaxed spot on the waterfront is hugely popular, not just for its varied menu, which makes great use of fresh local produce and runs the gamut from American-style breakfasts and ample salads to spicy Mexican fajitas, falafel burgers and grilled fish, but also for the genuine warmth of owner Bill, who's a fantastic source of local information. In the evenings, the tables out front are a good place for a beer and act as an expat magnet. Ayahuasca diets are catered for. Mon–Sat 7.30am–11pm.

★**Karma Café** Jr Napo 138 ☎ 065 223 663. All psychedelic wall hangings, beanbags and bright colours, the only thing that would complete this "Eastern" ambience would be the delicate strains of the sitar. There's plenty to please vegetarians (falafel burgers, veggie curry) and meat eaters alike, plus welcome spice in the form of Thai dishes, voluminous fruit juices and salads, and in the evening the place gets so packed with offbeat travellers that you'll be lucky to find a spare beanbag to sprawl on. Mains from S/15. Daily 12.30pm–midnight.

Mercado Belén Jirones Prospero and 9 de Diciembre. The chaotic Mercado Belén is a great spot for cheap eats, particularly generous helpings of fresh fruit juices (try the *jugo especial* – jungle juice), and real jungle staples of juicy Amazon grubs on a stick, *sikisapa* – fried leafcutter ants, rice-studded *morcilla* (black pudding) and more. Daily 7am–5pm.

Pizzeria Antica Jr Napo, between the plaza and the Malecón ☎ 065 241 988. A large space with ceiling fans and driftwood decor, this Italian joint has an extensive menu of wood-fired pizzas, pastas and immense calzones, including good vegetarian options and some dishes incorporating jungle ingredients. The immense oven makes it a bit too hot for lunchtimes, but the nice bar on the second level is perfect for hiding out in the evenings. Mains from S/19. Daily 11am–1am.

Restaurant Fitzcarraldo Jr Napo 100 ⊕065 236 536. Inside a historic rubber-boom building right on the Malecón, this fan-cooled, smart restaurant serves some excellent jungle dishes, such as grilled fish with *patacones* (skip the tasteless *tiradito*, though), and the not-so-jungly crepes Suzette for dessert. Mains from S/20. Daily noon–midnight.

El Sitio Jr Lores, block 4. A very creative snack bar/restaurant, run by the family of the recently deceased Argentinian owner – inexpensive and with delicious *anticuchos*, tamales, *juanes* and fruit juices; best to get there before 9pm, or you'll miss out on the tastiest treats. Mains from S/10. Daily 10am–11pm.

NIGHTLIFE

While mainly an extension of eating out and meeting friends in the main streets, the **nightlife** in Iquitos is vibrant, and there are a number of discos, clubs and bars worth knowing about. They're quite easy to locate, especially after 11pm when things generally get going in the downtown areas, particularly around the Plaza de Armas and nearby Malecón Tarapacá.

BARS AND CLUBS

Arandú Bar Malecón Maldonado 113. Psychedelic wall paintings, an extensive cocktail list and a great people-watching location on the *malecón* make this a very popular watering hole. Daily 5pm–late.

Complejo CNI Jr Mariscal Cáceres, block 13. More of a covered outdoor arena, this gives a flavour of what the Iquitos youth get up to at weekends, with more than a thousand people dancing all night to mostly live salsa, *chicha* and *cumbia* bands, but with significant Brazilian influence creeping in. Take a mototaxi (S/4). Thurs–Sat 9pm–3am.

Musmuqui Jr Raimondi 382. This lively two-storey bar is very popular with locals and famous for its cocktails that feature all sorts of jungle plants and are served in odd-shaped glasses. Some have alleged aphrodisiac properties, so it might be worth bringing your squeeze here. Daily 8pm–late.

Noa Disco Jr Fitzcarrald 298. Easily identified after 11.30pm by the huge number of flashy motorbikes lined up outside, this is Iquitos's liveliest club, attracting young and old, gringo and *Iquiteño* alike. It has three bars and plays lots of Latino music, including the latest *technocumbia*. S/20 entrance. Mon–Sat 10pm–late.

La Noche Malecón Maldonado 177. Overlooking the waterfront, this bar/restaurant is perfect for people-watching. The food is only so-so, but it's hard to beat the view from the upstairs balcony and the strong cocktails. Daily 7.30am–late.

8

SHOPPING

Centro Artesanal San Juan Some 2km east of the airport along the main road. A popular souvenir market consisting of a couple dozen stalls. You can pick up some Shipibo embroidery here; the only other items here that are not mass-produced tat are the vases carved out of beautiful tropical hardwoods, some of them true works of art. Daily roughly 9/10am–6pm.

Comercial Cardinal Jr Prospero 300. Sells fishing tackle, compasses and knives. Daily 9am–6pm.

Craft stalls Malecón Maldonado s/n. The craft stalls on the waterfront sell a really good selection of psychedelic Shipibo embroidery, the designs allegedly inspired by ayahuasca visions. No set hours but typically mid-morning until around 9–10pm; shorter hours on Sun.

Mad Mick's Trading Post Jr Putumayo 184B. This small shop has been established to provide the basic essentials for a jungle trip, including rubber boots, rainproof ponchos, sunhats, fishing tackle, etc. Will buy items back if they are in good shape. Daily 8am–8pm.

DIRECTORY

Consulates Brazil, Jr Lores 363 (⊕065 235 151); Colombia, C Calvo de Araujo 431 (⊕065 231 461).

Health Clinica Ana Stahl, Av La Marina 285 (⊕065 252 535) is a good 24hr private clinic. TrámazonDoctor, Jr Bolívar 222 (⊕959 464 131, ⓦtramazondoctor.com), is a 24hr emergency callout service, with doctors able to come to your lodgings if necessary. There are two pharmacies right on the Plaza de Armas.

Immigration Oficinia de Migraciónes is at Jr Mariscal Cáceres, cuadra 18 (⊕065 235 371). Come here to extend or renew your Peruvian tourist card or visa.

Internet Cyber, Jr Putumayo at Condamine, is a large and popular internet facility open into the wee hours.

Laundry Lavandería Imperial, Jr Nauta, cuadra 1 (Mon–Sat 8am–8pm).

Money and exchange Banco de Credito, Jr Putumayo 201; Banco de la Nación, Jr Condamine, cuadra 4; Banco Continental, Jr Próspero, cuadra 4, and Interbank, Jr Próspero, cuadra 1, all have global ATMs. Banks also change US dollars at competitive rates. Casas de cambio along Jr Próspero between C Lores and Jr Brasil also give competitive rates but there's more of a chance of being slipped counterfeit money.

Police Tourist Police, C Lores 834 (⊕065 242 081); central police station, C Morona 126 (⊕065 231 123).

Post office SERPOST, C Arica 402 (Mon–Fri 8am–6pm, Sat 8am–4.30pm).

Around Iquitos

The massive river system around Iquitos offers some of the best access to **Indian villages**, **lodges** and **primary rainforest** in the entire Amazon. For those with ample time and money, the Reserva Nacional Pacaya-Samiria is one of the more distant but rewarding places for eco-safari tours; but there are also towns up and down the river, most notably Pevas, which is en route towards Brazil.

If you want to go it alone, colectivo boats run up and down the **Amazon River** more or less daily, and although you won't get deep into the forest without a **guide**, you can visit some of the larger river settlements on your own.

Many visitors to Iquitos come to stay at one of the **jungle lodges**, which sit either on the Río Amazon or its tributaries and are a great way of getting to know the jungle with the help of experienced guides and spotting local wildlife.

Bellavista and around

15min by mototaxi (S/5) from Plaza de Armas

Some 4km northeast of the centre of Iquitos, the suburb of **Bellavista**, on the Río Nanay, is the main access point for smaller boats to all the rivers. There's a small **market** selling jungle products, including endangered species – grilled baby caimans, river turtle eggs, plus jungle delicacies such as fat Amazonian grubs on a skewer. There are some bars and shops clustered around the Bellavista port, where you can **hire canoes** for short trips at around S/25 an hour.

From Bellavista you can set out by canoe ferry for **Playa Nanay**, the best beach around Iquitos, popular with locals but not too clean, or else to the village of Padre Cocha, from which you can walk to the Pipintuwasi Butterfly Farm (see below).

You can also hire a canoe to take you to the confluence of the mud-brown Río Amazon and the clear blue Río Nanay, just a few minutes away from Bellavista; the abundant fish where the two rivers meet attract pink river dolphins and it's easy to spot them.

Pilpintuwasi Butterfly Farm & Amazon Animal Orphanage

Near the village of Padre Cocha • Tues–Sun 9am–4pm • S/20, S/10 for students with ISIC card • ☎ 965 932 999, ⓦ amazonanimalorphanage.org • 20min by boat from Bellavista

The fascinating **Pilpintuwasi Butterfly Farm** is a hugely worthwhile non-profit organization: both a breeding centre for numerous species of Amazonian butterflies and a genuine jungle animal rescue centre. Access is by guided tour only (9.30am, 11am, 12.30pm, 1.30pm and 2.45pm); volunteers lead you through the butterfly enclosure where you're likely to spot

---

ANIMAL RESCUE CENTRES

One of Iquitos' main draws is seeing wild animals in their natural habitat, most easily done from reputable jungle lodges. If you don't have the time to get out into the wild, it is still possible to get a taste for the Amazon wildlife by visiting the three reputable, genuine animal rescue centres around Iquitos: the **Pilpintawasi Butterfly Farm** (see above), the **Centro Rescate de Manatí** (see opposite) and the **Isla de los Monos** (see opposite). However, numerous tour companies offer less salubrious animal encounters in the form of visits to self-proclaimed "animal rescue centres" where you're offered the opportunity to wrap an anaconda or python around yourself or hold a sloth or monkey for that exotic holiday snap. These are nothing more than decrepit zoos, with animals purchased from poachers. The welfare of the unhappy creatures is not high on the list of the owners' concerns as dead animals are easily replaced. The guide who takes you around may tell you that the animals are there for rehabilitation and release into the wild, but that is not true. When the Serpentario, one of such "rescue centres", had its animals confiscated by the authorities, the cages were replenished with other "rescued" creatures within three days. These places are best avoided, since visiting them perpetuates the illegal animal trade in endangered species and dooms the monkeys, sloths, macaws and snakes to a short life in a cage; as for snakes, being handled by visitors covered in sun cream and insect repellent is bad for their skin.

AROUND IQUITOS

LODGES

Amazon Refuge	10
Botanical Lodge	4
Cumaceba Lodge	7
Explorama ACTS Field Station	1
Explorama Ceiba Tops	3
Explorama Lodge	2
ExplorNapo Lodge	1
Heliconia Amazon River Lodge	5
Muyuna Lodge	9
Otorongo Lodge	8
San Pedro Lodge	6
Tapiche Lodge	11

the camouflaged owl butterfly and the large, iridescent-winged blue morpho. You are then shown the rescued anteater, sloths, coatí, Pedro Bello (the jaguar raised from an orphaned cub) and several species of monkey, all taken in as orphans and victims of poaching. Do not approach the red aukari monkeys or the howler monkey as they can bite.

You can visit either as part of a tour or take a boat to Padre Cocha, walk through the village, turn left towards the water tower and follow the road all the way to Pilpintuwasi (10min in total).

Centro de Rescate de Manatí

Around 2km past the airport • Mon noon–3pm, Tues–Sun 9am–3pm • S/20 entry • S/10 by mototaxi

Its efforts supported by a Californian aquarium, this hard-working animal rescue centre specializes principally in the rehabilitation of orphaned baby manatees, whom they take in after their mothers are killed by poachers. The baby manatees are nursed back to health and kept until they are around 2 years old; when they are ready to fend for themselves, they are released into the wild. Entry is by Spanish-speaking tour; there are some labelled medicinal plants, a fun learning area for children and a few other rescued animals, comprising a tailless macaw and some monkeys. You can also purchase a pot full of aquatic plants that the manatees particularly like, and feed them by hand.

La Isla de los Monos (Monkey Island)

2hr upriver from Iquitos; office at Sargento Lores 752, Iquitos • Free; donations are hugely appreciated • ☎ 065 235 529, ⓦ monkeyislandperu .com • Take a speedboat from the Puerto de Productores to Varadero and call ☎ 965 779 610 when setting off so that they can pick you up at Varadero and take you across the river to the island, or else take a tour with Dawn on the Amazon (see p.473) or another tour company

This wonderful, family-run initiative consists of an island a couple of hours upriver from Iquitos, where they have planted all the fruit trees that eight species of monkey feed from. The organization takes in animals rescued from poachers, nurses them back to health and releases them into the wild if feasible. Otherwise, the monkeys (howlers, tamarins, spider monkeys, woolly monkeys and more) are free to roam the island and many of them interact with humans, coming down from the trees to take fruit from you. It's a fantastic day out; Monkey Island does not charge entry but they greatly appreciate donations and take in volunteers.

Beware of fake Monkey Island: some boat operators in Iquitos balk at the long journey (2hr–2hr 30min there, 1hr 30min back) and instead take you to a disreputable place close to Iquitos that's full of monkeys purchased from poachers.

Reserva Nacional Pacaya-Samiria

S/30 per day from SERNANP or the park office in Iquitos (see p.466) or Santa Rosa if travelling from Lagunas • ⓦ pacaya-samiria.com

The huge **RESERVA NACIONAL PACAYA-SAMIRIA** comprises around two million hectares of virgin rainforest (about 1.5 percent of the total landmass of Peru) leading up to the confluence between the ríos Marañón and Huallaga, two of the largest Amazon headwaters and possessing between them the largest protected area of seasonally flooded jungle in the Peruvian Amazon. The reserve is crisscrossed by half a dozen rivers and countless creeks and is dotted with numerous oxbow lakes; it's famous for its abundance of wildlife, particularly pink and grey dolphins, river turtles, manatees, caimans, numerous species of monkey and an astounding 450-plus species of bird. Away from human settlement, there's a good chance of spotting jaguars and other big mammals.

To do the reserve justice you ideally need a week, or at least several days; half-day visits from Iquitos don't even scratch the surface and you're just as likely to spot river dolphins during any short river jaunt.

The reserve is a swampland during the **rainy season** (Dec–May), when the streams and rivers rise; it becomes easier to spot reptiles and there's more bird activity on account of cloudy weather. Mammals are easier to spot during the drier months when they come to the river and creeks to drink; the drier months are also the best time to go fishing. The hottest months are February to June.

This region is home to the **Cocoma**, whose main settlement is **Tipishca**, where the native community is now directly involved in eco-tourism. They can be hired as guides and will provide rustic accommodation, but can only be contacted by asking on arrival. Visitors should be aware that around 50,000 people, mostly **indigenous communities**, still live in the reserve's forest; they are the local residents, and their territory and customs should be respected.

INDIGENOUS COMMUNITIES AROUND IQUITOS

With all organized visits offered by numerous tour agencies to indigenous **villages** in this area, you can expect the inhabitants to put on a quick show, with a few traditional dances and some singing, before they try to sell you their handicrafts (sometimes over-enthusiastically). Prices range from S/5 to S/35 for necklaces, feathered items (mostly illegal to take out of the country), bark-cloth drawings, string bags (often excellent value) and blowguns; most people buy something, since there's no charge for the visit.

While the experience may leave you feeling somewhat ambivalent – the men, and particularly the women, only discard Western clothes for the performances – it's a preferable situation to the times when visits were imposed on communities by unscrupulous tour companies, and it has become a way of preserving the language and traditional costume. Visitors are now these indigenous groups' major source of income, and the Bora and Yaguar have both found a niche within the local tourist industry.

EXPLORING THE JUNGLE AROUND IQUITOS

ORGANIZED TOURS

Short tours in the area (which can be arranged with most accommodation options) include boat trips from Bellavista up the Río Momón to visit a community of **Yaguar or Bora Indians** at San Andrés; boat trips to Isla de Los Monos (see p.471) and to Pilpintuwasi Butterfly Farm (see p.470) with dolphin-spotting thrown in. Unfortunately, many operators also offer trips to disreputable "animal rescue centres" such as Serpentario (see box, p.470). All places visited on short boat trips are places you can also get to under your own steam, but for **longer tours** beyond the limited network of roads around Iquitos, you'll have to take an organized trip with a lodge operator, go on a river cruise or hire a freelance guide, and tours are indispensable when it comes to taking part in specialized activities, such as fishing for peacock bass – the holy grail of the Amazon's fish – or visiting the Pacaya-Samiria reserve, since only a few ecologically responsible outfits have permission to operate there.

Always deal with an established company or agent – check out which outfits are registered at the tourist office in Iquitos (see p.466) – and insist on a written contract and receipt. If your jungle trip doesn't match what the agency led you to believe when selling you the tickets, it would help future visitors if you report this to the local tourist office and/or the 24hr hotline of the **Tourist Protection Service** in Iquitos (☎065 233 409). A few of the reputable tour operators with **riverboats** and services in the Iquitos area are listed below.

Amazon Voyagers ☎0866 725 3255 in the US, ⓦamazoncruise.net. Choose from such luxurious riverboats as the *M/V Aqua* and the *M/V Zafiro*, with their spacious suites, gourmet cuisine and naturalist bilingual guides. Depending on the time of year and water levels, these cruises may pass through the Pacaya-Samiria reserve and along the Amazonas, Yarapa and Ucayali rivers. Four-day cruise from US$2239.

Dawn on the Amazon Jr Malecón Maldonado 185 ☎065 223 730, ⓦdawnontheamazon.com. Passionate about the local ecology, Bill Grimes and his team are happy to organize custom-made tours depending on your interests, be it fishing for peacock bass, day-trips in the surrounding area, multi-day cruises into the Pacaya-Samiria reserve on the comfortable *Selva Viva* boat with cabins or swinging a hammock on the smaller *Dawn on the Amazon*. Ideal for independent travellers, families and small groups. From US$120 per person, per day.

Green Tracks ☎970 884 6107 in the US, ⓦgreentracks.com. Mid-range operator offering multi-day cruises on the Amazon (4–8 days) and into the Reserva Nacional Pacaya-Samiria on its half-dozen, multi-deck, luxury riverboats. You don't spend all your time on board; guided hikes in the jungle and small-boat wildlife watching excursions are part of the package. Four-day cruise from US$3299.

INDEPENDENT BOAT TRAVEL

If you're thinking of hiring a boat and heading down Río Amazonas or Río Napo, stopping at various small communities en route, it's doable but costly; you'll pay at least US$80–90 per person for day. There's an almost infinite amount of jungle to be rewardingly explored in any direction from Iquitos, and one of the less-visited but nevertheless interesting areas lies **east between Iquitos and the Brazilian border**; having your own boat allows far greater potential for exploration, since the public boats plying this stretch of the Amazon River rarely stop and certainly don't allow any time for passengers to explore. If you do want to stop off and spend some time here, **Pevas** (see p.474) is a possible base for making river trips more or less independently, at least without going through an Iquitos tour company, though it's always a good idea to make use of local guides.

FINDING A RELIABLE GUIDE

In Iquitos you will be approached by a plethora of self-styled guides and touts trying to persuade you to take their tours. Many of them can be unpleasantly persistent, bordering on aggressive, and many work for sub-par establishments for commissions. It's best to ask for recommendations at reputable hotels and traveller hubs such as the *Dawn on the Amazon Café* (see p.468) and talk to other travellers. Check that a guide has a licence (they are all supposed to have one) and ask around about a particular guide's reputation as they don't tend to carry references. Many of the top guides are snapped up by the best jungle lodges. One reputable independent guide who comes warmly recommended by travellers is Gerson Pizango (☎965 012 225, ⓦamazonjungleguide.com), known for his independent style; he runs a small family business and does tailor-made trips that can include visits to indigenous communities, including his own. You're looking to pay at least US$55 per day for a reputable guide.

ARRIVAL AND INFORMATION	RESERVA PACAYA SAMIRIA

By organized tour Jungle lodges located upriver from the city (see below) and various riverboat tour companies in Iquitos (see p.473) offer visits to the reserve.

By bus and boat Take a bus from Iquitos as far as Nauta (2–3hr), which is located on the Río Marañón a little upstream from the confluence with the Río Ucayali, before it turns into the Amazon. From Nauta, it's two to three days by boat along the Río Marañón to Lagunas (S/50–150 hammock/shared cabin), a riverine settlement that is more easily accessed by

regular boat between Yurimaguas (see p.392; 12hr) and Iquitos. Boats travelling between Nauta and Lagunas run along the western edge of the reserve for most of the route. From Lagunas, expect to pay around S/150–170 per day for guide, boat and simple lodgings (food is extra). You should come well prepared with mosquito nets, hammocks, insect repellent and all the necessary food and medicines.

Information The reserve office in Iquitos (see p.466) provides maps and information on the region.

Pevas

The only way here is by riverboat (larger boats 15hr, speedboats 3hr 30min), or with an organized tour from Iquitos (see p.473)

Downstream from Iquitos, some 150km to the east, lies attractive, palm-thatched **PEVAS**, the oldest town in the Peruvian Amazon and still a frontier settlement populated largely by indigenous folk. The economy here is based primarily on fishing (visit the **market** where produce is brought in by boat every day), and dugout **canoes** are the main form of transport, some still propelled by characteristically ovoid-bladed and beautifully carved paddles rather than motors. Renowned artist **Francisco Grippa**, whose work is exhibited at the Amazon Art Gallery in Iquitos (see p.465) and at the *Hotel El Dorado Plaza* (see p.466), lives and has a gallery in Pevas; he's a larger than life character, hugely charming, and if he takes a liking to you he may let you stay in the spare rooms at his home. Otherwise, pretty much your only bet is the basic *Casa Loma* (see opposite).

The surrounding flood forest is home to hundreds of **caimans** and significant **birdlife**, including several types of parrots, eagles and kingfishers. The area is also good for **butterfly watching**, and November, in particular, is a great time to study orchids and bromeliads in bloom.

ACCOMMODATION	AROUND IQUITOS

Guided tours require some kind of camp setup or tourist **lodge** facilities. There are two main types of jungle experience available from Iquitos – what Peruvian tour operators describe as "**conventional**" (focusing on lodge stays) and what they describe as "**adventure trips**" (going deeper into the jungle). Bear in mind that during the low-water season some jungle lodges close as they are located on the smaller river tributaries and become inaccessible by boat. Prices are given according to the minimum stay required, which varies from lodge to lodge, depending on its distance from Iquitos.

Amazon Refuge toll-free in the US ☎0800 771 3100, ⓦ amazonrefuge.com. A great lodge owned in collaboration with the San Juan de Yanayacu community, the *Amazon Refuge* is 1hr 30min by boat from Iquitos up the relatively remote Río Yanayacu. Surrounded by a 800-hectare nature reserve, the lodge's buildings are constructed using naturally felled trees

and thatched-palm roofs. Accommodation is in private bungalows, each with modern bathroom facilities. The English-speaking naturalist guides are top-rate and, not least because of the lodge's proximity to the park, wildlife and cultural treks into the Reserva Nacional Pacaya-Samiria are a speciality. Four-night wildlife eco-tour based here from US$588 per person

---

THE WITOTO AND THE BORA

The **Witoto and the Bora**, largely concentrated around Pevas, arrived here in the 1930s after being relocated from the Colombian Amazon. They are now in virtually everyday contact with the riverine society of Pevas, producing quality goods for sale to passers-by and yet retaining much of their traditional culture of songs, dances and legends, plus significant ethno-pharmacological practice in rainforest medicine. The nearby Bora village of **Puca Urquillo** is a good example, a large settlement based around a Baptist church and school, whose founders moved here from the Colombian side of the Río Putumayo during the hardships of the rubber era rather than be enslaved. A number of local indigenous groups can be visited close to Pevas, including the Bora, the Witoto and the less-known Ocainas. **Costs** are from around US$80 per person per day, with extra for speedboat transport from Iquitos.

SHAMANS AND AYAHUASCA SESSIONS

Ayahuasca is a jungle vine (*Banisteriopsis caapi*) that grows in the Western Amazon region and has been used for thousands of years as a "teacher plant", gaining a worldwide reputation for divination, inspiration and healing of physical, emotional and spiritual ailments. The vine is generally mixed with other jungle plants to enhance its powers and transform it into a bitter-tasting hallucinogenic brew, usually taken in a public session with a shaman.

Each indigenous community in the area around Iquitos has a shaman and Ayahuasca **retreats** have long been a booming business here, initially attracting backpackers and hippies when they first appeared on the radar of Western travellers but now popular with well-heeled tourists prepared to spend hundreds of dollars on a spiritual detox. There are dozens of retreats around Iquitos, some of them very upmarket, with plush accommodation and a cleansing superfood diet, others more basic. Few accept visitors who are unable to commit to less than three or four days.

While the vast majority of participants report positive – even life-changing – experiences it's important to be aware that, if ayahuasca is mixed with a particular plant, or if you have an allergic reaction, it can lead to dangerously high blood pressure and even, in rare cases, death. It is at the very least a purging experience (most participants vomit profusely) and since the plant is a powerful **hallucinogen**, stronger than LSD, you may undergo hours of intense and sometimes uncomfortable visions. It's therefore important not only to feel comfortable with the scene and setting, but also with the person leading a session, particularly given the lack of recognized qualifications for practitioners.

Though it's difficult to give specific recommendations, the **Temple of the Way of Light** (W templeofthewayoflight.org), out beyond Iquitos airport, has a good reputation for combining ayahuasca ceremonies with charitable and environmental work; the majority of the shamans are Shipibo women, which is a bonus for female visitors. There are also some well-known local ayahuasca guides, including **Francisco Montes** and the internationally renowned **Agustín Rivas**, a famous sculptor who has dedicated more than thirty years to working with ayahuasca. In addition, many if not most of the **jungle lodges and camps** around Iquitos regularly organize ayahuasca sessions, but talk to fellow travellers about their experience before committing yourself to anything. W **ayaadvisor.org** is a forum dedicated to ayahuasca retreats and a good starting point.

8

Casa Loma Pevas (no phone). Pretty much your only bet in Pevas is this basic guesthouse, found on the outskirts of town on a small hill; the owner can take your piranha fishing. Ask locals for directions. **S/20** per person

Cumaceba Lodges Putumayo 184, Iquitos ☎ 065 232 229, W cumaceba.com. A highly recommended budget option, with the fifteen-room *Cumaceba Lodge*, 35km downstream from Iquitos, consisting of private rustic bungalows and communal area with hammocks. Its *Botanical Lodge*, further downstream 90km from town, has a particular emphasis on rainforest plants, complete with large swimming pool and its own botanical garden. Both run visits to local Yaguar villages and organize jungle walks; bird- and dolphin-watching also form part of their programmes. Optional extras include multi-day trips to the Reserva Nacional Pacaya-Samiria and ayahuasca sessions. Three days, two nights **US$370**

Explorama ACTS Field Station (Amazon Conservatory for Tropical Studies) Explorama, Av La Marina 340, Iquitos ☎ 065 252 530, W explorama.com. An hour's walk from the company's *ExplorNapo Lodge* (see p.476), this establishment owns some 750 hectares of primary forest and was designed for research, though it's available for short visits and is quite comfortable, with twenty rooms and shared dining and bathroom facilities. There's a medicinal plant trail

with an information booklet, but the really special feature is the well-maintained canopy walkway, whose topmost platform is 35m high. Unless you're a research scientist, you're likely to stay at this lodge as part of a multi-day Explorama package that includes other lodges. **US$140** per person

Explorama Ceiba Tops Explorama, Av La Marina 340, Iquitos ☎ 065 252 530, W explorama.com. Explorama has more than forty years' experience and of its four lodges, this is the most luxurious, located some 40km from Iquitos. Facilities include a fantastic jungle swimming pool with water slide, and proper bar and dining areas, surrounded by primary forest. Accommodation is in smart bungalows with a/c; wi-fi is available. This lodge is very popular with families and can be visited in conjunction with other Explorama lodges. Two days, one night **US$360** per person

Explorama Lodge Explorama, Av La Marina 340, Iquitos ☎ 065 252 530, W explorama.com. In a 195-hectare reserve 90km from Iquitos, this was Explorama's first lodge. Well equipped, it retains its rustic charm and acts as a base camp for long-range programmes. Bora talking drums announce mealtimes in the dining room, and guides often play Peruvian music in the bar during the evenings. The 55 bedrooms (no locks) are simple but attractive, with individual mosquito nets and cold-water showers. Staff can arrange for you to swim with dolphins in the Amazon, plus there are night walks and visits to the nearby Yaguar Indians. Can be visited in conjunction with other Explorama lodges. Three days, two nights US$475 per person

ExplorNapo Lodge Explorama, Av La Marina 340, Iquitos ☎ 065 252 530, ⓦexplorama.com. Over 145km from Iquitos, on the Río Sucusari (Orejon for "way in and out"). This lodge controls 3000 hectares of surrounding forest, the ExplorNapo Reserve, and its palm-roofed buildings, hammock areas and dining room/bar are linked by thatch-covered walkway. From here there's easy access (less than a 1hr walk) to the canopy walkway at the *Explorama ACTS Field Station* (see p.475); and a 2hr walk into the forest there is a jungle camp – *ExplorTambos* – where visitors can have a night out in the middle of the forest. Can be visited in conjunction with other Explorama lodges; price depends on size of group, length of trip and number of lodges visited. Five days, four nights US$1125 per person

Heliconia Amazon River Lodge ☎ 01 421 9195, ⓦheliconialodge.com.pe. A small, intimate lodge, 80km downriver from Iquitos, with accommodation in twin rooms with private bathrooms and a swimming pool. Its multi-day programmes include jungle hikes, night boat rides, piranha fishing and visits to nearby indigenous communities. Three days, two nights US$385 per person

Muyuna Lodge Putumayo 163, Iquitos ☎ 065 242 858, ⓦmuyuna.com. Some 120km upriver from Iquitos, up a tributary called Yanayacu, this lodge is fairly close to the Reserva Nacional Pacaya-Samiria. Accommodation is in attractive cabins, with private mosquito-proofed rooms, en-suite bathrooms and tiled showers. It offers jungle walking, dolphin-spotting river safaris, and other traditional excursions including piranha fishing, searching out giant lily plants and alligator-spotting. Most guides come from local indigenous communities, and the lodge works hard to distinguish itself from competitors, as a protector of wild animals' right to remain free rather than be kept in captivity.

Three days, two nights from US$890 per person

★ **Otorongo Lodge** Depto 203, Putumayo 163, Iquitos ☎ 065 224 192, ⓦotorongoexpeditions.com. Some 100km upriver from Iquitos, down a tributary, this intimate lodge consists of just twelve rooms, insect-proofed with fine mesh and with individual mosquito nets. The food is fantastic, each guest is given a bilingual guide to help decide on activities, which range from swimming with river dolphins, canoeing in a flooded forest, fishing for peacock bass and piranha and learning about jungle medicinal plants. The owner, falconer Anthony, runs jungle survival courses and extreme fishing trips, and can imitate a huge number of bird calls; he's also extremely passionate about conservation. Five days, four nights US$790 per person

San Pedro Lodge 1hr north of Iquitos by car and boat ☎ 955 628 164, ⓦsanpedrolodge.com. A recommended budget option, *San Pedro Lodge* is located a short way downstream from Iquitos, and its accommodation consists of rustic thatched bungalows with cold-water showers and rooms for just twelve guests. You can visit the nearby indigenous village of Padre Cocha on foot, and optional trips include boat rides on the Momón River and visits to the manatee rescue centre (see p.471). Two-person bungalow S/150

★ **Tapiche Lodge** Ricardo Palma 516 ☎ 065 600 805, ⓦtapichejungle.com. Located up the Ucayali and Tapiche tributaries, 404km upriver from Iquitos inside the Tapiche Reserve – a new protected area created in 2010 – this fantastic lodge is located further in the jungle than any other and while the accommodation is not ultra-luxurious (oversized Brazilian hammocks or private, mesh-protected cabins), it's second to none when it comes to proximity to rare and endangered wildlife. Human impact is kept to a minimum, guests have access to the whole of 1540-acre property, and the owners, Deborah and Katoo, are really passionate about conservation. Trekking and canoeing are on offer and the emphasis is on animal- and bird-spotting. Five days, four nights US$600 per person

The three-way frontier

Exiting or entering Peru by river via Brazil or Colombia has become increasingly popular in recent years, and inevitably means crossing the **three-way frontier**, nearly 300km from Iquitos. Some boats from Iquitos go all the way to **Leticia (Colombia)** or **Tabatinga (Brazil)**, but many stop at one of the two small Peruvian frontier settlements of **Santa Rosa** or **Isla Islandia**. Some big *lancha* boats pull in at Isla Islandia, opposite Benjamin Constant (on the Brazilian side of the frontier) while the *rapido* speedboats from Iquitos finish their journeys at Santa Rosa.

Leticia, Colombia

Having grown rich on tourism and contraband (mostly cocaine), **LETICIA** is the much more exciting place to stay, given the choice between it and Tabatinga. It's a lively jungle town with *cumbia* and salsa music blasting out all over the place, a good selection of guesthouses and restaurants, scope for trekking in pristine jungle, visiting indigenous communities and an animal sanctuary.

THREE-WAY FRONTIER

Tabatinga, Brazil

More spread out than Leticia, and a stroll of several blocks away (the two towns blend into one another), **TABATINGA** is an unpretty urban sprawl, and travellers prefer to hop over the border to Leticia for the duration of their stay. There are no border formalities between Leticia and Tabatinga; in fact, you don't even require a Colombian or Brazilian visa if you're not planning on travelling further than Leticia/Tabatinga and intend on turning around and taking a boat back to Iquitos.

CROSSING THE BORDER INTO COLOMBIA AND BRAZIL

BY BOAT

The cheapest route downriver from Iquitos is by standard cargo boat (2–3 days) to Isla Islandia, swinging your hammock on one of the decks (S/40–50 per day). The much faster, and marginally more expensive alternative is to take a *lancha rapida*, a big speedboat to Santa Rosa; two companies (see p.465) depart on alternate days (S/200; 10hr downstream; 12hr coming back upriver). Motorized canoes connect Santa Rosa with Tabatinga and Leticia (15–20min) and also Isla Islandia to Leticia or Tabatinga (40min–1hr).

From Tabatinga Boats sail downriver to Manaus; it's a four- to seven-day journey that costs US$100–350 depending on the size and condition of the boat, and whether or not you require a cabin; check departure schedule at the port. If you're coming from Iquitos on a boat that's continuing all the way to Manaus, boats typically stop for the night at Benjamin Constant. Let the captain know whether or not you need to go into Tabatinga to get stamped into Brazil.

From Leticia You can take one of the infrequent boats to Puerto Asis (10–12 days) from where there are buses to Mocoa and Pasto, with onward connections to Popayán, Cali and Bogotá.

BY AIR

Tabatinga to Manaus There are daily flights (1hr 40min) between Tabatinga and Manaus with Azul Linhas Aereas Brasileiras (ⓦ voeazul.com.br).

Leticia (Colombia) to Bogotá There are one or two daily flights (2hr) between Leticia and Bogotá with LAN (ⓦ lan.com) and Avianca (ⓦ avianca.com).

CUSTOMS

Get an exit stamp from Peru at Santa Rosa if you haven't already done so at the Iquitos office (see p.469), or get an entry stamp and tourist card if arriving. Brazilian entry and exit formalities are processed at the Policia Federal office, Av da Amizade (ⓣ 097 3412 2180; daily 7am–noon & 2–6pm); if you're entering Brazil you'll usually be asked to show an exit ticket or prove that you have sufficient funds to pay for your stay. Americans need a visa to enter Brazil, which must be obtained in Lima or the US in advance; it may be possible to obtain Brazilian visas from the consul in Iquitos (see p.469) but this was not the case at the time of research.

To officially enter Colombia, take a short mototaxi ride to Leticia's airport and get a Colombian tourist card from the immigration office there (daily 8am–6pm).

PIPE PLAYER, SACRED VALLEY

Contexts

History

The first Peruvians were descendants of the nomadic tribes who crossed into the Americas during the last Ice Age (40,000–15,000 BC), when a combination of ice packs and low sea levels exposed a neck of solid "land" that spanned what's now the Bering Strait. Following herds of game animals from Siberia into what must have been a relative paradise of fertile coast, wild forest, mountain and savanna, successive generations continued south through Central America. Some made their way down along the Andes, into the Amazon, and out onto the more fertile areas of the Peruvian and Ecuadorian coast, while others found their niches en route.

In a number of tribes there seem to be cultural memories of these long migrations, encapsulated in their traditional mythologies. There is archeological evidence of human occupation in Peru dating back to around 20,000–15,000 BC, concentrated in the **Ayacucho Valley** where these early Peruvians lived in caves or out in the open. Around 12,000 BC, slightly to the north in the **Chillon Valley** (just above modern Lima), comes the first evidence of significant craft skills – stone blades and knives for hunting. At this time there were probably similar groups of hunter tribes in the mountains and jungle too, but the climatic conditions of these zones make it unlikely that any significant remains will ever be found.

The difficulties of traversing the rugged terrain between the highlands and coast evidently proved little problem for the early Peruvians. From 8000 to 2000 BC, **migratory bands** of hunters and gatherers alternated between camps in the lowlands during the harsh mountain winters, and highland summer "resorts", their actual movements well synchronized with those of wild animal herds. One important mountain encampment from this **Incipient Era** has been discovered at **Lauricocha**, near Huánuco, at an altitude of over 4000m. Here the art of working stone – eventually producing very fine blades and arrow points – seems to have been sophisticated, while at the same time a growing cultural imagination found expression in cave paintings depicting animals, hunting scenes and even dances. Down on the coast at this time other groups were living on the greener *lomas* belts of the desert in places like **Chilca** to the south, and in the mangrove swamps around **Tumbes** to the north.

The emergence of cultism

An awareness of the potential uses of plants began to emerge around **5000 BC** with the **cultivation** of seeds and tubers (the potato being one of the most important "discoveries" later taken to Europe), to be followed over the next two millennia by the introduction, presumably from the Amazon, of gourds, Lima beans, then squashes, peanuts and eventually cotton. Towards the end of this period a climatic

20,000–15,000 BC	12,000 BC	8000 BC
The country's earliest archeological evidence of human occupation dates to this period.	Significant craft skills develop in the Chillon Valley, not far from modern Lima.	A transhumant population alternates between lowland camps during harsh mountain winters and highland summer "resorts".

shift turned the coast into a much more arid belt and forced those living there to try their hand at **agriculture** in the fertile riverbeds, a process to some extent paralleled in the mountains.

With a stable agricultural base, permanent settlements sprang up all along the coast, notably at **Chicama**, **Asia** and **Paracas**, and in the sierra at **Kotosh**. The population began to mushroom, and with it came a new consciousness, perhaps influenced by cultural developments within the Amazon Basin to the east: **cultism** – the burial of the dead in mummy form, the capturing of trophy heads and the building of grand religious structures – made its first appearance. At the same time there were also overwhelming technological advances in the spheres of weaving, tool-making and ornamental design.

The pyramids of Caral

Possibly the most important discovery since Machu Picchu, the **pyramids of Caral** were rediscovered in 1911 – this site represents human achievements that occurred four

---

THE CHAVÍN CULT

From around 1200 BC to 200 AD – the **Formative Era** – agriculture and village life were established in Peru. Ceramics were invented, and the regions slowly began to integrate, mainly due to the widespread reach of a religious movement – the **Chavín Cult**. Remarkable in that it seems to have spread without the use of military force, the cult was based on the worship of nature spirits, and an all-powerful **feline creator-god**. This feline image rapidly exerted its influence over the northern half of Peru and initiated a period of inter-relations between people in fertile basins in the Andes and some of the coastal valleys. How and where the cult originated is uncertain, though it seems probable that it began in the eastern jungles, possibly spreading to the Andes (and eventually the coast) along the upper Río Marañón. There may well have been a significant movement of people and trade goods between these areas and the rainforest regions, too, as evidenced by the many **jungle-bird feathers** incorporated into capes and headdresses found on the coast. More recent theories, however, suggest that the flow may have been in the opposite direction, starting on the coast. The stone and adobe temples, for instance, in the Sechin area, pre-date the Chavín era, yet seem to be culturally linked.

The Chavín Cult was responsible for excellent progress in **stone carving** and **metallurgy** (copper, gold and silver) and, significantly, a ubiquity of temples and pyramids emerged as religious and cultural centres. The most important known centre was the temple complex at **Chavín de Huantar** (see p.335) in Ancash, though a similar one was built at **Kotosh** (see p.303) near Huánuco; the cult's influence seems to have spread over the northern highlands and coast from Chiclayo down as far as the Paracas Peninsula (where it had a particularly strong impact). There were immense local variations in the expressions of the Chavín Cult: elaborate metallurgy in the far north; adobe buildings on stone platforms in the river valleys; excellent ceramics from Chicama; and the extravagant stone engravings from Chavín itself.

Towards the end of the Chavín phase, an experimental period saw new cultural centres attempting to establish themselves as independent powers with their own distinct cultures. This gave birth to Gallinazo settlements in the Viru Valley; the Paracas culture on the south coast (with its beautiful and highly advanced textile technology based around a cult of the dead); and the early years of Tiahuanaco development in the Lake Titicaca region. These three cultural upsurges laid the necessary foundations for the flourishing civilizations of the subsequent Classical Era.

5000 BC	**2600 BC**	**1800 BC to 200 AD**
Plants like cotton are domesticated and stable settlements are characteristic.	Radiocarbon dating proves that the ancient pyramids of Caral were fully functioning for around five hundred years from this date.	The Chavín Cult is responsible for progress in stone carving and metallurgy. Temples and pyramids emerge as religious and cultural centres at Chavín de Huantar, Kotosh and Sechin.

thousand years earlier than the Incas appeared. These stone-built ceremonial structures were flourishing a hundred years before the Great Pyramid at Giza was built in Egypt.

Located in the Supe Valley 120km north of Lima, 22km inland from the ocean, the site has been proved to have been radiocarbon dating fully functioning for approximately five hundred years, from around 2600 BC, complete with six stone platform mounds, with **ceremonial plazas** below and irrigation channels serving the surrounding fields. First discovered in 1905, Caral was then largely ignored by archeologists because, though large, no gold or even ceramics had ever been unearthed there. It was, in fact, a pre-ceramic site whose importance resided in another technology, that of the early **domestication of plants**, including cotton, squashes, beans and guava. Some of the best artefacts discovered here, in a ceremonial fire pit by the circular amphitheatre, include 32 flutes made from pelican and animal bones, and engraved with the figures of birds and monkeys, demonstrating a connection with the Amazon region even this long ago.

At its heyday it's thought that at least **three thousand people** were living in Caral. If the other seventeen so far unexcavated sites in the area had held similar-sized populations, then the total population living, working and worshipping in the Supe Valley around 4600 years ago might have been as high as 20,000 or even more. The complex appears to have been abandoned quite rapidly after about five hundred years of booming occupation; theories as to why include the possibility of drought, which would have forced the inhabitants to move to another valley in search of available water and even more fertile soils.

The Classical Era

A diverse period – and one marked by intense development in almost every field – the **Classical Era** (200–1100 AD) saw the emergence of numerous distinct cultures, both on the coast and in the sierra. The best-documented of these cultures, though not necessarily the most powerful, were the **Mochica and Nazca cultures** (see box, p.482) – both probably descendants of the coastal Paracas culture – and the **Tiahuanaco**, all forebears of the better-known Inca. In recent years, though, archeological discoveries in the Lambayeque Valley on the north coast have revealed important ceremonial centres – particularly the massive sacred complex of truncated pyramids at **Batán Grande** originating from the **Sicán culture** (see box, p.401).

In the north, the Valley of the Pyramids, or **Túcume** (see p.406), was a major ceremonial centre, covering more than two hundred hectares. Initially begun by the Sicán culture, who started building here around 1100 after abandoning their earlier centre at Batán Grande, it reached its peak in the thirteenth and early fourteenth centuries, during the power vacuum in the Mochica Valley, between the decline of the Mochica and the rise of the Chimu. Archeologists believe that this must have been a time of abundance and population growth in this desert region, with optimum weather conditions for agriculture, the improvement of irrigation techniques and plentiful seafood.

Intertribal warfare

An increasing prevalence of **intertribal warfare** characterized the era's later period, culminating in the erection of defensive forts and a multiplication of ceremonial sites,

200–1100	300	1200
Classical cultures emerge throughout the land. The Nazca Lines and Cahuachi complex are developed on the coast.	Technological advances in the Viru Valley and Paracas mean every known form of non-machine weaving is used in textiles.	The Inca Empire is founded by the mysterious Manco Capac. An age of great city building begins.

including over sixty large pyramids in the Lima area. The **Huaca Pucllana** (see p.69) is one of these pyramids, a vast pre-Inca adobe mound that can be visited in the suburb of Miraflores, in Lima. It has a hollow core running through its cross-section and is

CLASSICAL CULTURES

THE MOHICA CULTURE

The **Mochica culture** has left the fullest evidence of its social and domestic life, all aspects of which, including its work and religion, are vividly represented in highly realistic pottery. The peak of their influence came around 500 to 600 AD, when they had cultural and military control of the coast from Piura in the north to the Nepena Valley in the south. The first real urban culture in Peru, its members maintained a firm hierarchy, an elite group combining both secular and sacred power. Ordinary people cultivated land around clusters of dwelling sites, dominated by sacred pyramids – man-made *huacas* dedicated to the gods. The key to the elite's position was probably their organization of large **irrigation projects**, essential to the survival of relatively large population centres in the arid desert of the north coast. In the Mochica region, nature and the world of the ancestors seem the dominant cultural elements; occasional human sacrifices were offered and trophy heads were captured in battle.

THE NAZCA CULTURE

More or less contemporaneous with the Mochica, the **Nazca culture** bloomed for several hundred years on the south coast. The Nazca are thought to be responsible for the astonishing lines and drawings etched into the Pampa de San José, though little is known for certain about their society or general way of life. The Nazca did, however, build an impressive temple complex in the desert at **Cahuachi**, and their burial sites have turned up thousands of beautiful ceramics whose abstract designs can be compared only to the quality and content of earlier Paracas textiles.

THE SICÁN CULTURE

Contemporaneous with the Mochica, to the south, there is also strong evidence that the **Sicán culture** revered the same demonic spirit or god, named **Ai-Apaec** in the Mochica language (the "Winged Decapitator"), who kept the world of human life and death in order. Ai-Apaec is also associated with the veritable treasure-trove found in the royal tombs at Sipán, just south of Lambayeque, and those of the **Vicús** culture, to the north, near Piura.

THE TIAHUANUCO CULTURE

Contemporaneous with the other classical cultures, but also pre-dating them, the **Tiahuanaco culture** was named after its sacred centre on the shore of Lake Titicaca. The Tiahuanaco culture, and in particular its central site of pilgrimage, was evidently active between 300 BC and 300 AD and then lasted for another 600 years. The last 500 years coincided with the classical Mochica period – with which, initially at least, it peacefully coexisted. Tiahuanaco textiles and pottery spread along the desert, modifying both Mochica and Nazca styles and bending them into more sophisticated shapes and abstract patterns. The main emphasis in Tiahuanaco pottery and stonework was on symbolic elements featuring condors, pumas and snakes – more than likely the culture's main **gods**, representing their respective spheres of the sky, earth and underworld. In this there seem obvious echoes of the deified natural phenomena of the earlier Chavín cult.

1438–1532	1513	1527
Expansion of the Inca Empire from Cusco, north into Ecuador and south into Chile. Inca Highway constructed from Colombia to Chile, parts of which are still in existence.	The Spaniard Francisco Pizarro stumbles upon and names the Pacific Ocean while on an exploratory expedition in Panama.	Huayna Capac dies of smallpox; civil war breaks out.

thought to have been constructed in the shape of an enormous frog, a symbol of the rain god, who spoke to priests through a tube connected to the cavern.

Although initially peaceable, the **Tiahuanaco** culture is associated in its decadent phase (900–1000 AD) with militarism. This seems most likely due to conflict with neighbouring powerful tribes, like the **Huari** who were based further north. The ruins at Huari cover some eight square kilometres and include high-walled enclosures of field stones laid and plastered with mud and decorated by just a few stone statues, suggesting that the Huari were warlike, or at least needed to defend their town.

The Chimu era

Eventually Huari-Tiahuanaco influence on the coast was uprooted and overturned by the emergence of three youthful mini-empires – the **Chimu**, the **Cuismancu** and the **Chincha**. In the mountains its influence mysteriously disappeared to pave the way for the separate growth of relatively large tribal units such as the **Colla** (around Lake Titicaca), the **Inca** (around Cusco) and the **Chanca** (near Ayacucho).

Partly for defensive reasons, this period of isolated development sparked off a city-building urge which became almost compulsive by the Imperial Period in the thirteenth century. The most spectacular urban complex was **Chan Chan** (see p.365), near modern Trujillo, built by the Chimu on the side of the river opposite earlier Mochica temples. Indicating a much greater sophistication in social control, the internal structure of the culture's clan-based society was reflected in the complex's intricate layout. By now, with a working knowledge of bronze manufacture, the Chimu spread their domain from Chan Chan to Tumbes in the north and Paramonga in the south – dominating nearly half the Peruvian coastline. To the south they were bounded by the **Cuismancu**, less powerful, though capable of building similar citadels (such as Cajamarquilla near Lima) and of comparable attainment in craft industries. Further down the coastline, the **Chincha** – known also as the **Ica culture** – also produced fine monuments and administrative centres in the Chincha and Pisco valleys. The lower rainfall on the southern coast, however, didn't permit the Chincha state – or (to an extent) the Cuismancu – to create urban complexes anything near the size of Chan Chan.

The Incas

With the **Inca Empire** (1200–1532 AD) came the culmination of Peru's city-building phase and the beginnings of a kind of Peruvian unity, as the Incas, although originally a tribe of no more than around 40,000, gradually took over each of the separate coastal empires. One of the last to go – almost bloodlessly, and just sixty years before the Spanish conquest – was the Chimu empire, which for much of this **Imperial Period** was a powerful rival.

Based in the valleys around Cusco, the Incas were, for the first two centuries of their existence, much like any other of the larger mountain tribes. Fiercely protective of their independence, they maintained a somewhat feudal society, tightly controlled by rigid religious tenets, though often disrupted by inter tribal conflict. The founder of the dynasty – around 1200 AD – was **Manco Capac**, who passed into Inca mythology as a cultural hero. Historically, however, little is known about Inca developments or

1532	1533	1535
Spanish conquistadores, led by Pizarro, set foot on Peruvian soil for the first time and make their way overland to the Inca town of Cajamarca.	Pizarro brings Atahualpa to trial; the Spanish baptize and then kill him.	Foundation of Lima – its colonial architecture draws heavily on Spanish influences, though native craftsmen also leave their mark.

achievements until the accession in 1438 of Pachacuti, and the onset of their great era of expansion.

Inca expansion

Pachacuti, most innovative of all the Inca emperors, was the first to expand the Incas' traditional tribal territory. The beginnings of this expansion were in fact not of his making but the response to a threatened invasion by the powerful, neighbouring Chanca during the reign of his father, **Viracocha**. Viracocha, feeling the odds to be overwhelming, left Cusco under Pachacuti's control, withdrawing to the refuge of Calca along the Río Urubamba. Pachacuti, however, won a legendary victory – Inca chronicles record that the very stones of the battlefield rose up in his defence – and, having vanquished the most powerful force in the region, he shortly took the Inca crown for himself.

Within three decades Pachacuti had consolidated his power over the entire sierra region from Cajamarca to Titicaca, defeating in the process all main imperial rivals except for the Chimu. At the same time the empire's capital at **Cusco** was spectacularly developed, with the evacuation and destruction of all villages within a ten-kilometre radius, a massive programme of agricultural terracing (watched over by a skyline of agro-calendrical towers) and the construction of unrivalled palaces and temples.

Inca territory expanded north into Ecuador, almost reaching Quito, under the next emperor – **Tupac Yupanqui** – who also took his troops down the coast, overwhelming the Chimu and capturing the holy shrine of Pachacamac. Not surprisingly the coastal cultures influenced the Incas perhaps as much as the Incas influenced them, particularly in the sphere of craft industries. Even compared to Pachacuti, Tupac Yupanqui was nevertheless an outstandingly imaginative and able ruler. During the 22 years of his reign (1471–93) he pushed Inca control southwards as far as the Río Maule in Chile; instigated the first proper census of the empire and set up the decimal-based administrative system; introduced the division of labour and land between the state, the gods and the local *ayllus*; invented the concept of "chosen women", or *mamaconas* (see p.498); inaugurated a new class of respected individuals (the *yanaconas*). An empire had been unified not just physically but also administratively and ideologically.

Huayna Capac and civil war

At the end of the fifteenth century the Inca Empire was thriving, as vital as any civilization before or since. Its politico-religious authority was finely tuned, extracting what it needed from its millions of subjects and giving what was necessary to maintain the status quo – be it brute force, protection or food. The only obvious problem inherent in the Inca system of unification and domination was one of over-extension. When **Huayna Capac** continued Tupac Yupanqui's expansion to the north he created a new Inca city at **Quito**, one which he personally preferred to Cusco and which laid the seed for a division of loyalties within Inca society. At this point in history, the Inca Empire was probably the largest in the world, even though it had neither horses nor wheel technology. The empire was over 5500km long, stretching from southern Colombia right down to northern Chile, with Inca highways covering distances of around 30,000km in all.

1541	1569	1572
Pizarro is assassinated by displeased conquistadores; for the next seven years the country is rent by civil war.	Francisco Toledo arrives in Peru as viceroy with a view to reforming the colonial system.	After fierce fighting and a near escape, Tupac Amaru is captured, brought to trial in Cusco and subsequently beheaded – an act by Toledo that was disavowed by the Spanish Crown.

THE INCA EMPERORS

Manco Capac (c.1200 AD) Legendary founder of the Incas and cultural hero; we have little actual information on him or his life.

Sinchi Roca (1230–60) His name means Magnificent Warrior; nevertheless, he was unable to expand the Inca territorial base.

Lloque Yupanqui (1260–90) This Inca failed to expand the Inca Empire and also worsened relations with some of the neighbouring tribes.

Mayta Capac (1290–1320) He inherited imperial throne at a tender age, and an uncle took command until he reached maturity.

Capac Yupanqui (1320–50) Considered a Machiavellian Inca, since, as the son of Mayta Capac's sister, he was not in direct line to inherit the throne, but nevertheless took it by force.

Inca Roca (1350–80) The first to actually bear the title "Inca". Some of his palace still exists beside the modern Plaza de Armas in Cusco.

Yahuar Huaca (1380–1400) His claim to fame was crying tears of blood after being captured by a neighbouring tribe when he was 8 years old; he managed to escape but did little building in Cusco and was ultimately assassinated.

Viracocha Inca (1400–38) He took the sacred name of the creator-god Viracocha after having a dream. He had to escape from his position when it was taken over briefly by the rival Chanca tribe from the Abancay region, and died in isolation.

Pachacuti (1438–71) Also called Pachacutec, he was the Inca who really created the empire; he expanded its territorial base from the Cusco Valley, began its true megalithic architectural heritage, and developed the social order required to take over and run other parts of Peru and beyond.

Tupac Yupanqui (1471–93) Pachacuti's son, he was responsible for extending the empire north into Ecuador and took over the Chimu dynasty on Peru's north coast.

Huayna Capac (1493–1525) Much of his reign focused on maintaining the northern end of the empire; in fact, he was in Quito when he first heard of strange sightings of white men in boats off the Peruvian shores. He died of smallpox before naming a successor.

Huascar (1525–32) Huascar was appointed Inca Emperor, but there were many other pretenders, including Atahualpa, who defeated him in battle just before Pizarro landed (see p.486).

Atahualpa (1532–33) The shortest reign of any Inca was terminated by the conquistadores in Cajamarca (see box, p.373).

Almost as a natural progression from over-extending the empire in this way, divisions in Inca society came to a head even before Huayna Capac's death. Ruling the empire from Quito, along with his favourite son **Atahualpa**, Huayna Capac installed another son, **Huascar**, at Cusco. In the last year of his life he tried to formalize the division – ensuring an inheritance at Quito for Atahualpa – but this was fiercely resisted by Huascar, legitimate heir to the title of Lord Inca and the empire, and by many of the influential Cusco priests and nobles. In 1527, when Huayna Capac died of "the white man's disease", smallpox, which had swept down overland from Mexico in the previous seven years, killing over thirty percent of the indigenous population, civil war broke out. Atahualpa, backed by his father's army, was by far the stronger and immediately won a major victory at the Río Bamba – a battle that, it was said, left the plain littered with human bones for over a hundred years. A still bloodier battle, however, took place along the Río Apurímac at Cotabamba in 1532. This was the decisive victory for Atahualpa, and with his army he retired to relax at the hot baths near Cajamarca. Here, informed of a strange-looking, alien band, successors of the

1742	**1780**	**1819**
Juan Santos Atahualpa, a *mestizo* from Cusco who had travelled the world as a young man, rouses groups of forest Indians to rebellion.	Another *mestizo*, José Gabriel Condorcanqui, leads a rebellion around Cusco. Within a year he is executed.	The first rebel invaders land at Paracas. Ica, Huánuco and the north of Peru soon opt for independence.

bearded adventurers whose presence had been noted during the reign of Huayna Capac, he waited with his followers.

Francisco Pizarro arrives

Francisco Pizarro, along with two dozen soldiers, stumbled upon and named the Pacific Ocean in 1513 while on an exploratory expedition in Panama. From that moment his determination, fired by native tales of a fabulously rich land to the south, was set. Within eleven years he had found himself financial sponsors and set sail down the Pacific coast with the priest Hernando de Luque and Diego Almagro.

With remarkable determination, having survived several disastrous attempts, the three explorers eventually landed at **Tumbes** in 1532. A few months later a small, Pizarro-led band of Spaniards (less than two hundred men), arrived at the Inca city of **Cajamarca** to meet the leader of what they were rapidly realizing was a mighty empire. En route to Cajamarca, Pizarro had learned of the Inca civil wars and of Atahualpa's recent victory over his brother Huascar. This rift within the empire provided the key to success that Pizarro was looking for.

Pizarro seizes control

The day after their arrival, in what at first appeared to be a lunatic endeavour, Pizarro and his men massacred thousands of **Inca warriors** and captured Atahualpa. Although ridiculously outnumbered, the Spanish had the advantages of surprise, steel, cannons, and, above all, mounted cavalry. The decisive battle was over in a matter of hours: with Atahualpa prisoner, Pizarro was effectively in control of the Inca Empire. Atahualpa was promised his freedom if he could fill the famous Ransom Room at Cajamarca with **gold**. Caravans overladen with the precious metal arrived from all over the land and within six months the room was filled: a treasure worth over 1.5 million pesos, which was already enough to make each of the conquerors extremely wealthy. Pizarro, however, chose to keep the Inca leader as a hostage in case of Indian revolt, amid growing suspicions that Atahualpa was inciting his generals to attack the Spanish. Atahualpa almost certainly did send messages to his chiefs in Cusco, including orders to execute his brother Huascar who was already in captivity there. Under pressure from his worried captains, Pizarro brought Atahualpa to trial in July 1533, a mockery of justice in which he was given a free choice: to be burned alive as a pagan or strangled as a Christian. They baptized him and then killed him.

With nothing left to keep him in Cajamarca, Pizarro made his way through the Andes to Cusco where he crowned a puppet emperor, **Manco Inca**, of royal Indian blood. After all the practice the Spanish had in imposing their culture on the Aztecs in Mexico, it took them only a few years to replace the Inca Empire with a working colonial mechanism. Now that the Inca civil wars were over, the natives seemed happy to retire quietly into the hills and get back to the land. However, more than wars, **disease** was responsible for the almost total lack of initial reaction to the new conquerors. The native population of Peru had dropped from some 32 million in 1520 to only five million by 1548 – a decline due mainly to new European ailments such as smallpox, measles, bubonic plague, whooping cough and influenza.

1821	1824	1826
The great liberators – San Martín from the south and Bolívar from the north – enter the capital without a struggle. San Martín proclaims Peruvian independence on July 28.	Spanish resistance to independence is extinguished at the battles of Junín and Ayacucho.	Bolívar remains dictator of the Andean Confederation until 1826.

Colonial Peru

Peru's vast wealth, of resources as well as treasure, was recognized early on by the Spanish. Between the sixteenth and seventeenth centuries Spain established only two Viceroyalties in the Americas: first in Mexico, then shortly afterwards in Peru. Queen Isabella indirectly laid the original foundations for the political administration of Peru in 1503 when she authorized the initiation of an **encomienda system**, which meant that successful Spanish conquerors could extract tribute for the Crown and personal service in return for converting the natives to Christianity. They were not, however, given the titles to the land itself. As governor of Peru, Pizarro used the *encomienda* system to grant large groups of Indians to his favourite soldier-companions.

Colonial society

In 1541 Pizarro was assassinated by a disgruntled faction among the conquistadores who looked to **Diego Almagro** as their leader, and for the next seven years the nascent colonial society was struck by civil war. In response, the first **viceroy** – Blasco Nuñez de Vela – was sent from Spain in 1544. His risk was to seek a new legal commissioner and to secure the colony's loyalty to Spain; his fate was to be killed by Gonzalo Pizarro, brother of Francisco. But royalist forces, now under Pedro de la Gasca, eventually prevailed – Gonzalo was captured and executed, and Crown control firmly re-established. During the sixteenth and seventeenth centuries, **Peruvian society** was being transformed by the growth of new generations: creoles, descendants of Spaniards born in Peru, and *mestizos*, of mixed Spanish and native blood, created a new class

---

CATHOLIC CULTISM

Despite the evangelistic zeal of the Spanish, religion changed little for the majority of the native population. Although Inca ceremonies, pilgrimages and public rituals were outlawed, their mystical and magical base endured. Each region quickly reverted to the **pre-Inca cults** deep-rooted in their culture and cosmology. Over the centuries the people learnt to absorb symbolic elements of the **Catholic faith** into their beliefs and rituals – allowing them, once again, to worship relatively freely. Magic, herbalism and divination have always managed to continue strongly at the village level, and have successfully pervaded modern Peruvian thought, language and practice (the Peruvian World Cup football squad in 1982 enlisted – in vain – the magical aid of a *curandero*). At the elite level, the Spanish continued their fervent attempts to convert the entire population to their own ritualistic religion. They were, however, more successful with the rapidly growing *mestizo* population, who shared the same cultural aspirations.

Miraculous occurrences became a conspicuous feature in the popular Peruvian Catholic Church, the greatest example being **Our Lord of Miracles (El Señor des los Milagros)**, a cult that originated among the black population of colonial Lima. In the devastating earthquake of 1665, an anonymous mural of the Crucifixion on the wall of a chapel in the poorest quarter was supposedly the only structure left standing. The belief that this was a direct sign from God took hold among the local populace, and Our Lord of Miracles remains the most revered image in Peru. Thousands of devotees process through the streets of Lima and other Peruvian towns every October, and even today many women dress in purple throughout the month to honour Our Lord of Miracles.

1827	1845	1856
Within a year of Bolívar's withdrawal Peruvians vote for the liberal General La Mar as president.	Ramón Castilla is the first president to bring any real strength to his office. The country begins to develop on the rising wave of a booming export in guano fertilizer, made of bird droppings.	A new moderate constitution is approved. Castilla begins his second term of office.

structure. In the coastal valleys where populations had been ravaged by European diseases, slaves were imported from Africa. There were over 1500 black slaves in Lima alone by 1554. At the same time, as a result of the civil wars and periodic Indian revolts, over a third of the original conquerors had lost their lives by 1550.

In return for the salvation of their souls, the native population were expected to surrender their bodies to the Spanish. Some forms of service (*mita*) were simply continuations of Inca tradition – from keeping the streets clean to working in textile mills. But the most feared was a new introduction, the *mita de minas* – **forced work in the mines**. With the discovery of the "mountain of silver" at Potosí (now in Bolivia) in 1545, and of mercury deposits at Huancavelica in 1563, it reached new heights. Forced off their smallholdings, few Indians who left to work in the mines ever returned. Indeed, the mercury mines at Huancavelica were so dangerous that the quality of their toxic ore could be measured by the number of weekly deaths. Those who were taken to Potosí had to be chained together to stop them from escaping: if they were injured, their bodies were cut from the shackles by sword to save precious time. Around three million Indians worked in Potosí and Huancavelica alone; some had to walk over 1000km from Cusco to Potosí for the privilege of working themselves to death.

Francisco Toledo becomes viceroy

In 1569, **Francisco Toledo** arrived in Peru to become viceroy. His aim was to reform the colonial system so as to increase royal revenue while at the same time improving the lot of the native population. Before he could get on with that, however, he had to quash a rapidly developing threat to the colony – the appearance of a **neo-Inca state** (see box opposite). Toledo's next task was to firmly establish the viceregal position – something that outlasted him by some two centuries. He toured highland Peru seeking ways to improve Crown control, starting with an attempt to curb the excesses of the *encomenderos* and their tax-collecting *curacas* (hereditary local chieftains) by implementing a programme of **reducciones** – the physical resettlement of Indians in new towns and villages. Hundreds of thousands of peasants – perhaps millions – were forced to move from remote hamlets into large conglomerations, or *reducciones*, in convenient locations. Priests, or *corregidores*, were placed in charge of them, undercutting the power of the *encomenderos*. Toledo also established a new elected position – the local mayor (or *varayoc*) – in an attempt to displace the *curacas*. The *varayoc*, however, was not necessarily a good colonial tool in that, even more than the *curacas*, his interests were rooted firmly in the *ayllu* (extended family or clan, usually village-based) and in his own neighbours, rather than in the wealth of some distant kingdom.

Peruvian independence

The end of the eighteenth century saw profound changes throughout the world. The North American colonies had gained their independence from Britain; France had been rocked by a people's revolution; and liberal ideas were spreading everywhere. Inflammatory newspapers and periodicals began to appear on the streets of Lima, and discontent was expressed at all levels of society. A strong sense of **Peruvian nationalism** emerged in the pages of *Mercurio Peruano* (first printed in the 1790s), a concept that

1860	1870s	1872	1879
Sugar and cotton are exported from coastal plantations and guano exports are also substantial.	Construction of the high-altitude rail lines and other engineering projects. First exploitation of Amazonian rubber.	Peru's first civilian president – Manuel Pardo – assumes power.	Peru cannot pay off its growing foreign debt.

REBEL INCAS

After an unsuccessful uprising in 1536, **Manco Inca**, Pizarro's puppet emperor, had disappeared with a few thousand loyal subjects into the remote mountainous regions of Vilcabamba, northwest of Cusco. With the full regalia of high priests, virgins of the sun and the golden idol of Punchau (the sun god), he maintained a **rebel Inca state** and built himself impressive new palaces and fortresses between Vitcos and Espíritu Pampa – well beyond the reach of colonial power. Although not a substantial threat to the colony, Manco's forces repeatedly raided nearby settlements and robbed travellers on the roads between Cusco and Lima.

Manco himself died at the hands of a **Spanish outlaw**, a guest at Vilcabamba who hoped to win himself a pardon from the Crown. But the neo-Inca state continued under the leadership of Manco's son, **Sairi Tupac**, who assumed the imperial fringe at the age of 10. Tempted out of Vilcabamba in 1557, Sairi Tupac was offered a palace and a wealthy life by the Spanish in return for giving up his refuge and subversive aims. He died a young man, only three years after turning to Christianity and laying aside his father's cause. Meanwhile **Titu Cusi**, one of Manco's illegitimate sons, declared himself emperor and took control in Vilcabamba.

Eventually, Titu Cusi began to open his doors. First he allowed two Spanish friars to enter his camp, and then, in 1571, negotiations were opened for a return to Cusco when an emissary arrived from Viceroy Toledo. The talks broke down before the year was out and Toledo decided to send an army into Vilcabamba to rout the Incas. They arrived to find that Titu Cusi was already dead and his brother, **Tupac Amaru**, was the new emperor. After fierce fighting and a near escape, Tupac Amaru was captured and brought to trial in Cusco. Accused of plotting to overthrow the Spanish and of inciting his followers to raid towns, Tupac Amaru was **beheaded** as soon as possible – an act by Toledo that was disavowed by the Spanish Crown and which caused much distress in Peru.

was vital to the coming changes. Even the architecture of Lima had changed in the mid-eighteenth century, as if to welcome the new era. Wide avenues suddenly appeared, public parks were opened, and palatial salons became the focus for the discourse of gentlemen. The philosophy of the Enlightenment was slowly but surely pervading attitudes even in remote Peru.

When, in 1808, Napoleon took control of Spain, the authorities and elites in all the Spanish colonies found themselves in a new and unprecedented position. Was their loyalty to Spain or to its rightful king? And just who was the rightful king now? The American War of Independence, the French Revolution and Napoleon's invasion of Spain all pointed towards the opportunity of throwing off the shackles of colonialism, and by the time Ferdinand returned to the Spanish throne in 1814, royalist troops were struggling to maintain order throughout South America. Venezuela and Argentina had already declared their independence, and in 1817 San Martín liberated Chile by force. It was only a matter of time before one of the great liberators – **San Martín** in the south or **Bolívar** in the north – reached Peru.

San Martín was the first to do so. Having already liberated Argentina and Chile, he contracted an English naval officer, Lord Cochrane, to attack Lima. By September 1819 the first rebel invaders had landed at Paracas. Ica, Huánuco and then the north of Peru soon opted for independence, and the royalists, cut off in Lima, retreated into the mountains. Entering the capital without a struggle, San Martín proclaimed Peruvian **independence** on July 28, 1821.

1879–83	**1883**
Chile declares war on Bolivia and Peru as a result of arguments about nitrates mined in Bolivia. By 1880 Bolivia had been defeated, and by 1881 the Chilean army occupied Lima, finally defeating Peru in the Battle of Huamachuco in 1884.	The Treaty of Ancón brings the War of the Pacific to a close. As a result, Bolivia loses access to the sea and Peru's southern border is significantly shortened.

INDIGENOUS REBELLION IN THE EIGHTEENTH CENTURY

When the Habsburg monarchy gave way to the Bourbon kings in Spain at the beginning of the eighteenth century, shivers of protest seemed to reverberate deep in the Peruvian hinterland. There were a number of serious **native rebellions** against colonial rule during the next hundred years. One of the most important, though least known, was that led by **Juan Santos Atahualpa**, a *mestizo* from Cusco. Juan Santos had travelled to Spain, Africa and, some say, to England as a young man in the service of a wealthy Jesuit priest. Returning to Peru in 1740 he was imbued with revolutionary fervour and moved into the high jungle region between Tarma and the Río Ucayali where he roused the forest Indians to rebellion. Throwing out the whites, he established a millenarian cult and, with an Indian army recruited from several tribes, successfully repelled all attacks by the authorities. Although never extending his powers beyond Tarma, he lived a free man until his death in 1756.

In 1780, another *mestizo*, José Gabriel Condorcanqui, led a rebellion, calling himself **Tupac Amaru II**. Whipping up the already inflamed peasant opinion around Cusco into a revolutionary frenzy, he imprisoned a local *corregidor* before going on to massacre a troop of nearly six hundred royalist soldiers. Within a year Tupac Amaru II had been captured and executed but his rebellion had demonstrated both a definite weakness in colonial control and a high degree of popular unrest. Over the next decade several administrative reforms were to alter the situation, at least superficially: the *repartimiento* and the *corregimiento* systems were abolished. In 1784, Charles III appointed a French nobleman – Teodoro de Croix – as the new viceroy to Peru and divided the country into seven *intendencias* containing 52 provinces. This created tighter direct royal control, but also unwittingly provided the pattern for the Republican state of federated *departamentos*.

The Republic

Once Peruvian independence had been declared, San Martín immediately assumed political control of the fledgling nation. With the title "Protector of Peru" he set about devising a workable **constitution** for the new nation – at one point even considering importing European royalty to establish a new monarchy. A libertarian as well as a liberator, San Martín declared freedom for slaves' children, abolished Indian service (*mita*) and even outlawed the term "Indian". But in practice, with royalist troops still controlling large sectors of the sierra, his approach did more to frighten the establishment than it did to help the slaves and peasants whose problems remain, even now, deeply rooted in their social and territorial inheritance.

The development of a relatively stable **political system** took virtually the rest of the nineteenth century, although Spanish resistance to independence was finally extinguished at the battles of Junín and Ayacucho in 1824. By this time, San Martín had given up the power game, handing political control over to **Simón Bolívar**, a man of enormous force with definite tendencies towards megalomania. Between them, Bolívar and his right-hand man, Sucre, divided Peru in half, with Sucre first president of the upper sector, renamed Bolivia. Bolívar himself remained dictator of a vast Andean Confederation – encompassing Colombia, Venezuela, Ecuador, Peru and Bolivia – until 1826. Within a year of his withdrawal, however, the Peruvians had torn up his controversial constitution and voted for the liberal **General La Mar** as president.

1908	1890–1930	1932
The powerful oligarch Augusto Leguía rises to power and is elected president.	Much modernization in Lima (including the building of the Presidential Palace), and grandiose public buildings are developed elsewhere.	The Trujillo middle class lead a violent uprising against the sugar barons and working conditions on the plantations.

Political power games

On La Mar's heels raced a generation of *caudillos*, military men, often *mestizos* of middle-class origins who had achieved recognition (on either side) in the battles for independence. Peru was plunged deep into a period of domestic and foreign plotting and counterplotting, while the economy and some of the nation's finest natural resources withered away.

Ramón Castilla was the first president to bring any real strength to his office. After he assumed power in 1845 the country began to develop more positively on the rising wave of a booming export in guano fertilizer (made of bird droppings). In 1856, a new moderate constitution was approved and Castilla began his second term of office in an atmosphere of growth and hope – there were rail lines to be built and the Amazon waterways to be opened up. Sugar and cotton became important exports from coastal plantations and guano deposits alone yielded a revenue of US$15 million in 1860. Castilla abolished Indian tribute and managed to emancipate slaves without social-economic disruption by buying them from their "owners"; guano income proved useful for this compensation.

His successors fared less happily. President Balta (1868–72) oversaw the connection then of most of Peru's rail lines, but overspent so freely on these and a variety of other public and engineering works that it left the country on the brink of economic collapse. In the 1872 elections an attempted military coup was spontaneously crushed by a civilian mob, and Peru's first civilian president – the laissez-faire capitalist **Manuel Pardo** – assumed power.

The Peruvian Corporation

Modern Peru is generally considered to have been born in 1895 with the forced resignation of **General Cáceres**, who was twice President of Peru (1886–90 and 1894–95). However, the seeds of industrial development had been laid under his rule, albeit by foreigners. In 1890 an international plan was formulated to bail Peru out of its bankruptcy. The **Peruvian Corporation** was formed in London and assumed the US$50 million national debt in return for "control of the national economy". Foreign

---

THE WAR OF THE PACIFIC

By the late nineteenth century Peru's **foreign debt**, particularly to England, had grown enormously. Even though interest could be paid in guano, there simply wasn't enough. To make matters considerably worse, Peru went to war with Chile in 1879. Lasting over four years, this "**War of the Pacific**" was basically a battle for the rich nitrate deposits located in Bolivian territory. Peru had pressured its ally Bolivia into imposing an export tax on nitrates mined by the Chilean-British Corporation. Chile's answer was to occupy the area and declare war on Peru and Bolivia. Victorious on land and at sea, Chilean forces had occupied Lima by the beginning of 1881 and the Peruvian president had fled to Europe. By 1883 Peru "lay helpless under the boots of its conquerors", and only a diplomatic rescue seemed possible.

The **Treaty of Ancón**, possibly Peru's greatest national humiliation, brought the war to a close in October 1883. Peru was forced to accept the cloistering of an independent Bolivia high up in the Andes, with no land link to the Pacific, and the even harder loss of the nitrate fields to Chile.

1940s	1948	1963
Inflation is out of control; during the 1940s the cost of living in Peru rises by 262 percent.	General Odría leads a coup d'état from Arequipa and forms a military junta.	Revolutionary Hugo Blanco creates nearly 150 syndicates around Cusco, whose peasant members work their own individual plots.

companies took over the rail lines, navigation on Lake Titicaca, vast quantities of guano and were given free use of seven Peruvian ports for 66 years as well as the opportunity to start exploiting the rubber resources of the Amazon Basin. Under Nicolás de Piérola (president 1879–81 and 1895–99), some sort of stability had begun to return by the end of the nineteenth century.

The twentieth century

In the early years of the twentieth century, Peru was run by an **oligarchical clan** of big businessmen and great landowners. Fortunes were made in a wide range of enterprises, exploiting above all, sugar along the coast, minerals from the mountains and rubber from the jungle. Meanwhile, the lot of the ordinary individual worsened dramatically. The lives of the mountain peasants became more difficult – the jungle Indians lived like slaves on the rubber plantations and the owners of sugar plantations were abusing their wealth and power on the coast. In 1932, the Trujillo middle class led a **violent uprising** against the sugar barons and the primitive working conditions on the plantations. It was suppressed by the army, and nearly five thousand lives are thought to have been lost in the uprising.

The rise of the **APRA** – the American Popular Revolutionary Alliance – which had instigated the Trujillo uprising, and the growing popularity of its leader, **Haya de la Torre**, kept the nation occupied during World War II: the unholy alliance between the monied establishment and APRA has been known as the "marriage of convenience" ever since. More radical feeling was aroused in the provinces by **Hugo Blanco**, when his followers created nearly 150 syndicates, whose peasant members began to work their own individual plots and refused to work for the hacienda owners. The second phase of Blanco's "reform" was to take physical control of the **haciendas**, mostly in areas so isolated that the authorities were powerless to intervene. Blanco was finally arrested in 1963 but the effects of his peasant revolt outlived him: in the future, Peruvian governments were to take agrarian reform far more seriously.

In Lima, the **elections** of 1962 had resulted in an interesting deadlock, with Haya de la Torre getting 33 percent of the votes, Belaunde 32 percent and Odría 28.5 percent. Almost inevitably, the army took control. Belaunde stood again in the 1963 elections and was in power until 1969.

Land reform and the military regime

By the mid-1960s, many intellectuals and government officials saw the agrarian situation as an urgent economic problem as well as a matter of social justice. Even the army believed that **land reform** was a prerequisite for the development of a larger market, without which any genuine industrial development would prove impossible. President Belaunde didn't agree. On October 3, 1968, tanks smashed through the gates into the courtyard of the Presidential Palace. General Velasco and the army seized power, deporting Belaunde and ensuring that Haya de la Torre could not even participate in the forthcoming elections.

The new government, revolutionary for a **military regime**, gave the land back to the workers in 1969. The great plantations were turned virtually overnight into **cooperatives**, in an attempt to create a genuinely self-determining peasant class.

1968	1969	1978
On October 3, tanks smash into the Presidential Palace; General Velasco and the army seize power.	The new government gives land back to the workers. Great plantations are turned into cooperatives virtually overnight.	Peru knock Scotland out of the Argentine football World Cup by beating the boys in blue 3–1.

At the same time guerrilla leaders were brought to trial, political activity was banned in the universities, indigenous banks were controlled, foreign banks nationalized and diplomatic relations established with East European countries. By the end of military rule, in 1980, the land-reform programme had done much to abolish the large capitalist landholding system.

The 1970s and 1980s

After twelve years of military government the 1980 elections resulted in a centre-right alliance between Acción Popular and the Popular Christian Party. **Belaunde** resumed the presidency, having become an established celebrity during his years of exile and having built up, too, an impressive array of international contacts. The policy of his government was to increase the pace of development still further, and in particular to

---

SENDERO LUMINOSO

Sendero Luminoso (the Shining Path), founded in 1980, persistently discounted the possibility of change through the ballot box. In 1976 it adopted armed struggle as the only means to achieve its anti-feudal, anti-imperial revolution in Peru. Following the line of the Chinese Gang of Four, Sendero was led by **Abimael Guzmán** (alias Comrade Gonzalo), whose ideas it claimed to be in the direct lineage of Marx, Lenin and Chairman Mao. Originally a brilliant philosophy lecturer from Ayacucho (specializing in the Kantian theory of space), before his capture by the authorities in the early 1990s Gonzalo lived mainly underground, rarely seen even by Senderistas themselves.

Rejecting Belaunde's style of technological development as imperialist and the United Left as "parliamentary cretins", the group carried out attacks on business interests, local officials, police posts and anything regarded as outside interference with the self-determination of the peasantry. On the whole, members were recruited from the poorest areas of the country and from the **Quechua-speaking population**, coming together only for their paramilitary operations and melting back afterwards into the obscurity of their communities.

Although strategic points in **Lima** were frequently attacked – police stations, petrochemical plants and power lines – Sendero's main centre of activity was in the sierra around **Ayacucho** and **Huanta**, subsequently spreading into the remote regions around the central selva and a little further south in **Vilcabamba** – site of the last Inca resistance, a traditional hideout for rebels, and the centre of Hugo Blanco's activities in the 1960s.

Sendero was very active during the late 1980s and early 1990s, when it had some 10,000–15,000 **secret members**. Guzmán's success lay partly in his use of **Inca millennial mythology** and partly in the power vacuum left after the implementation of the agrarian reform and the resulting unrest and instability. The group's power and popular appeal advanced throughout the 1980s, spreading its wings over most of central Peru, much of the jungle, and to a certain extent into many of the northern and southern provincial towns.

Much of Sendero's funding came from the **cocaine trade**. Vast quantities of coca leaves are grown and partially processed all along the margins of the Peruvian jungle. Much of this is flown clandestinely into Colombia where the processing is completed and the finished product exported to North America and Europe. The thousands of peasants who came down from the Andes to make a new life in the tropical forest throughout the 1980s found that **coca** was by far the most lucrative cash crop. The cocaine barons paid peasants more than they could earn elsewhere and at the same time bought protection from Sendero (some say at a rate of up to US$10,000 per clandestine plane-load).

1980

After twelve years of military government, elections result in a centre-right alliance between Acción Popular and the Popular Christian Party. Abimael Guzmán launches the revolutionary wing of Peru's communist party – the Shining Path.

1982

Peru play in the World Cup finals in Spain, but despite having a normally exciting side, they play as if they have lead boots.

emulate Brazilian success in opening up the Amazon – building new roads and exploiting the untold wealth in terms of oil, minerals, timber and agriculture. But **inflation** continued as an apparently insuperable problem, and Belaunde fared little better in coming to terms with either the parliamentary Marxists of the United Left or the escalating guerrilla movement led by Sendero Luminoso (see box, p.493).

The 1980s saw the growth of two major threats to the political and moral backbone of the nation – one through **terrorism**, the other through the growth of the **cocaine industry**.

Belaunde lost the 1985 elections, with APRA (see p.492) taking power for the first time and the United Left also getting a large percentage of the votes. Led by a young, highly popular new president, **Alan García**, the APRA government took office riding a massive wave of hope. Sendero Luminoso, however, continued to step up its tactics of anti-democratic terrorism, and the isolation of Lima and the coast from much of the sierra and jungle regions became a very real threat. By 1985, new urban-based terrorist groups like the **Movimiento Revolucionario Tupac Amaru** (**MRTA**) began to make their presence felt in the shantytowns around Lima. The MRTA had less success than the Senderistas, losing several of their leaders to Lima's prison cells. Their military confidence and capacity were also devastated when a contingent of some 62 MRTA militants was caught in an army ambush in April 1988; only eight survived from among two truckloads. To make things worse, a right-wing death squad – the **Rodrigo Franco Commando** (**RFC**) – appeared on the scene in 1988, evidently made up of disaffected police officers, army personnel and even one or two Apristas (APRA members). Meanwhile, the once young and popular President García got himself into a financial mess and went into exile, having been accused by the Peruvian judiciary of high-level corruption and possibly even "misplacing" millions of dollars belonging to the people of Peru.

The 1990s

The year 1990 proved to be a turning point for Peru with the surprise electoral victory by an entirely new party – Cambio 90 (Change 90), formed only months before the election – led by a young college professor of Japanese descent, **Alberto Fujimori**. Fujimori implemented an economic shock strategy and the price of many basics such as flour and fuel trebled overnight. Fujimori did, however, manage to turn the nation around and gain an international confidence in Peru, reflected in the country's stock exchange – one of the fastest-growing and most active in the Americas.

THE JAPANESE EMBASSY HOSTAGE CRISIS

The mid-1990s was also the time when the **MRTA** terrorists battled with Fujimori and his government. On December 17, 1996, the MRTA really hit the headlines when they infiltrated the **Japanese ambassador's residence**, which they held under siege for 126 days, with over three hundred hostages. Some of these were released after negotiation, but Fujimori refused to give in to MRTA demands for the freedom of hundreds of their jailed comrades. Peruvian forces stormed the building in March 1997 as the terrorists were playing football inside the residence, massacring them all, with only one hostage perishing in the attack. Fujimori's reputation as a hard man and a successful leader shot to new heights.

1990	**1990s**	**1992**
Fujimori gains a surprise victory over Mario Vargas LLosa in the presidential elections.	Fujimori improves roads and takes a firm line with the terrorist groups Sendero Luminoso and MRTA.	After twelve very bloody years Sendero's leader Abimael Guzmán is captured in a Lima hideout, watching TV in his pyjamas.

However, the real turning point of the decade was the capture of Sendero's leader **Abimael Guzmán** in September 1992. He was captured at his Lima hideout (a dance school) by General Vidal's secret anti-terrorist police, DINCOTE; even Fujimori didn't know about the raid until it had been successfully completed. With Guzmán in jail, and presented very publicly on TV as a defeated man, the political tide shifted. The international press no longer described Peru as a country where terrorists looked poised to take over, and Fujimori went from strength to strength, while Sendero's activities were reduced to little more than the occasional car bomb in Lima as they were hounded by the military in their remote hideouts along the eastern edges of the Peruvian Andes. All this was a massive boost to Fujimori's popularity in the elections of 1995 he gained over sixty percent of the vote. Perhaps it was also a recognition that his strong policies had paid off as far as the economy was concerned – inflation dipped from a record rate of 2777 percent in 1989 to 10 percent in 1996.

Fujimori continued to grow in popularity, despite Peru going to **war with Ecuador** briefly in January 1995, May 1997 and, more seriously, in 1998. The Ecuadorian army, which was accused of starting the fighting, imposed significant losses on the Peruvian forces. This dispute was inflamed by the presence of huge oilfields in the region, currently on what the Peruvians claim is their side of the border, a claim the Ecuadorians bitterly dispute: Ecuadorian maps continue to show the border much further south than Peruvian maps. The two countries signed a formal peace treaty in 1998, although the dispute remains fresh in most people's minds.

The twenty-first century

The run-up to the **elections** of April 9, 2000, was marked by Fujimori's controversial decision to stand for a **third term** of office, despite constitutional term limits. He reasoned that the constitution was introduced during his second term, thus he was entitled to stand for one more. Even with his firm control of the media (especially TV), he encountered strong opposition in the person of **Alejandro Toledo**, a *serrano* (of mountain Indian blood) Perú Posible candidate representing the interests of Andean cities and communities. Toledo had worked his way up from humble beginnings to become a UN and World Bank economist before standing for president; such was the worry over his popularity that a smear campaign surfaced a few weeks before the voting, accusing him of shunning an illegitimate daughter and organizing a disastrous financial pyramid scheme in the early 1990s.

Fujimori polled 49.87 percent of the vote, missing outright victory by just 14,000 votes; Toledo followed behind with just over 40 percent. There were unproven allegations of **fraud** and **vote rigging**, and Toledo eventually withdrew from the contest. However, Fujimori was forced to resign in November 2000 following revelations that his head of intelligence, **Vladimiro Montesinos**, had been videotaped bribing politicians before the last election and had also secreted hundreds of millions of dollars (believed to be drug money) in Swiss and other bank accounts around the world. It quickly became clear that Montesinos had exerted almost complete **control** of the president, the army, the intelligence service and the cocaine mafia during the preceding few years. Soon afterwards, Fujimori fled to Japan.

2000	2000–2003
The run-up to the April elections is marked by Fujimori's controversial decision to stand for a third term of office, despite constitutional term limits. By November, Fujimori is forced to resign following revelations of bribery and drug-money laundering.	Fujimori flees to Japan. The economy is unstable and there are protests over the country's coca eradication programme.

PERU'S WHITE GOLD

Coca, the plant from which cocaine is derived, has come a long way since the Incas distributed this "divine plant" across fourteenth-century Andean Peru. Presented as a gift from the gods, coca was also used to exploit slave labour under Spanish rule: without it the Indians would never have worked in the gruelling conditions of colonial mines such as Potosí.

The isolation of the active ingredient in coca, cocaine, in 1859, began an era of intense **medical experimentation**. Its numbing effects have been appreciated by dental patients around the world, and even Pope Leo XIII enjoyed a bottle of the coca wine produced by an Italian physician, who amassed a great fortune from its sale in the nineteenth century. On a more popular level, coca was one of the essential ingredients in Coca-Cola until 1906.

Today, **cocaine** is one of the most fashionable – and expensive – illegal drugs. From its humble origins cocaine has become very big business. Unofficially, it may well be the biggest export for countries like Peru and Bolivia, where coca grows best in the Andes and along the edge of the jungle. While most mountain peasants always cultivated a little for personal use, many have now become dependent on it for obvious economic reasons: coca is still the most profitable cash crop and is readily bought by middlemen operating for extremely wealthy cocaine barons. A constant flow of semi-refined coca paste leaves Peru aboard Amazon riverboats or ocean yachts bound for places like Panama and Mexico or in unmarked light aircraft heading for laboratories in Colombia. For some rural farmers, it is the most profitable subsistence crop; for others cocaine is a scourge, bringing violence, the mobsters and deforestation in its wake.

New elections were held in April 2001, which **Toledo** won easily, inheriting a cynical populace and a troubled domestic situation, with slow economic growth and deteriorating social conditions. Despite lack of popular support and with little or no backing from Peru's powerful elite business classes, Toledo clung onto his office until 2006, when in a general election he was replaced, amazingly, by an older and much plumper **Alan García** – the very same man and ex-president who left Peru and his first term of office in disgrace back in 1988. Meanwhile, Fujimori returned to South America via Chile in late 2005, and was arrested on arrival. Charged with human rights abuses and corruption (including payments to members of Congress and illegal wiretapping), he was extradited to Peru in 2007; he was convicted and locked up despite being ill. Similarly, legal action was taken against his once right-hand man, Montesinos, who also remains locked up.

In 2011 Ollanta Humala was elected president with 51.5 percent of the votes on the second round against Keiko Fujimori (the ex-president's daughter). Upon his election, Peru's stock exchange fell amongst fears of the new president's socialist and nationalist tendencies. Groundless fears it turns out, as Humala, ever the political chameleon, maintained his predecessors' economic policies and generally toed the line put forward by Miguel Castilla, the minister of economy and the most powerful figure in Humala's government. There hasn't, however, been much progress on the less positive facts: Peru has become the main producer and trafficker of illegal cocaine (see box above); the massive inequality in incomes continues to grow; and Peru's mineral, timber and petroleum assets are being sold off cheaply. In fact, Humala's approval ratings fell consistently during the first half of his mandate, reaching its lowest point in December 2013, with 70 percent of the voters actively disapproving

2006	2006–2011	2009
Political elections are held – ex-president Alan García wins, taking office for the second time.	President García is seen by many as putting Peru's natural resources out to auction and denies the existence of "uncontacted" Indians.	Fujimori sentenced to 25 years in prison on charges of human rights abuses and widespread corruption.

his leadership. A police corruption scandal in late 2013 contributed to this drop in popularity, and has raised awareness on how little the government has done to fight crime and improve security.

In early 2014, the International Court of Justice´s ruling on the border conflict with Chile, by which Peru gained sovereignty rights over a maritime area that accounted for 70 percent of Peru's request, gave a boost to the government´s popularity.

In the past years, Peru has been slowly increasing its participation as host of international meetings. After successfully hosting the United Nations Climate Change Conference, COP20, in December 2014, it has been chosen to host the tenth Presidential Summit of the Pacific Alliance, the Annual Meeting of the Board of Governors of the World Bank Group (WGB) in 2015, and the United Nations Conference on Trade and Development in 2016. Further down the line, Lima has also been chosen to be the host of the 2019 Pan-American Games.

GREENPEACE BLURRING THE LINES

Coinciding with the COP20 summit on December 2014, and in the hope of increasing pressure during the Climate Change negotiations being held in Lima, Greenpeace activists entered a strictly prohibited area of the Nazca Lines World Heritage Site and placed a giant message next to the figure of the Hummingbird. Meant to be read from the sky, it stated, "Time for change, the future is renewable." The publicity stunt, which might have damaged the ancient and very fragile lines carved more than 1500 years ago, sparked international criticism and was strongly rejected by the Peruvian Government who considered it a "slap in the face at everything Peruvians consider sacred". Despite Greenpeace´s fulsome apology for the offence caused, the stunt resulted in calls for legal action, and the Ministry of Culture has since released new footage showing the damage caused at the site.

2011	2012	2014
Ollanta Humala wins the presidential elections.	Solid economic growth from the exploitation of Peru's resources is creating conflict with local communities. Five people are killed when police open fire on a crowd of protesters in Cajamarca.	Peru hosts the rather ineffectual COP20 in Lima; its conservation credibility continues to look shaky.

Inca culture

In less than a century, the Incas developed and knitted together a vast empire peopled by something like twenty million Indians, that was to endure from 1200 to 1532. They established an imperial religion in relative harmony with those of their subject tribes; erected monolithic fortresses, salubrious palaces and temples; and, astonishingly, evolved a viable economy – strong enough to maintain a top-heavy elite in almost godlike grandeur. To understand these achievements and get some idea of what they must have meant in Peru five or six hundred years ago, you really have to see for yourself their surviving heritage: the stones of Inca ruins and roads; the cultural objects in the museums of Lima and Cusco; and their living descendants who still work the soil and speak Quechua – the language used by the Incas to unify their empire.

Inca society

The Inca Empire rapidly developed a **hierarchical structure**. At the highest level it was governed by the **Sapa Inca**, son of the sun and direct descendant of the god Viracocha. Under him were the priest-nobles – the royal *ayllu* or kin-group who filled most of the important administrative and religious posts – and, working for them, regional *ayllu* chiefs (*curacas* or *orejones*), responsible for controlling tribute from the peasant base. The Inca nobles were fond of relaxing in thermal baths, of hunting holidays and of conspicuous eating and drinking whenever the religious calendar permitted. *Ayllu* chiefs were often unrelated to the royal Inca lineage, but their position was normally hereditary. As lesser nobles (*curacas*) they were allowed to wear earplugs and special ornate headbands; their task was to both protect and exploit the commoners, and they themselves were free of labour service. One-third of the land belonged to the emperor and the state; another to the high priests, gods and the sun; the last third was for the *ayllu* themselves.

In their conquests the Incas absorbed **craftsmen** from every corner of the empire: goldsmiths, potters, carpenters, sculptors, masons and *quipumayocs* (accountants) were frequently removed from their homes to work directly for the emperor in Cusco. These skilled men lost no time in developing into a new and entirely separate class of citizen. The work of even the lowest servant in the palace was highly regulated by a rigid division of labour.

Special regulations affected both **senior citizens** and **people with disabilities**. Around the age of fifty, a man was likely to pass into the category of "old". He was no longer capable of undertaking a normal workload, he wasn't expected to pay taxes, and he could always depend on support from the official storehouses. Nevertheless, the community still made small demands by using him to collect firewood and other such tasks, in much the same way the kids were expected to help out around the house and in the fields. In fact, children and old people often worked together, the young learning directly from the old. Disabled people were obliged to work within their potential – the blind, for instance, might de-husk maize or clean cotton. Inca law also bound people with disabilities to marry those with similar disadvantages.

Inca women

Throughout the empire young girls, usually about 9 or 10 years old, were constantly selected for their beauty and serene intelligence. Those deemed perfect enough were taken to an *acllahuasi* – a special sanctuary for the "**chosen women**" – where they were trained in specific tasks, including the spinning and weaving of fine cloth, and the higher culinary arts. Most chosen women were destined ultimately to become *mamaconas* (Virgins of the Sun) or the concubines of either nobles or the Sapa Inca himself. Occasionally some of them were sacrificed by strangulation in order to appease the gods.

For most **Inca women** their allotted role was simply that of peasant/domestic work and rearing children. Women weren't counted in the census; for the Incas, a household was represented by the man and only he was obliged to fulfil tribute duties on behalf of the *ayllu*.

The Inca diet

The Inca diet was essentially **vegetarian**, based on the staple potato but encompassing a range of other foods like *quinoa*, beans, squash, sweet potatoes, avocados, tomatoes and manioc. In the highlands, emphasis was on root crops like potatoes, which have been known to survive in temperatures as low as 15°C (59°F) at over 5000m. On the valley floors and lower slopes of the Andes, maize cultivation predominated.

The importance of maize both as a food crop and for making *chicha* increased dramatically under the Incas; previously it had been grown for ceremony and ritual exchange, as a status rather than a staple crop. The use of **coca** was restricted to the priests and Inca elite. Coca is a mild narcotic stimulant which effectively dulls the body against cold, hunger and tiredness when the leaves are chewed in the mouth with a catalyst such as lime or calcium. The Incas believed its leaves possessed magical properties; they could be cast to divine future events, offered as a gift to the wind, the earth or the mountain *apu*, and they could be used in witchcraft.

As well as coca, their "divine plant", the Incas had their own special hallucinogen: **vilca** (meaning "sacred" in Quechua). The *vilca* tree (probably *Anadenanthera colubrina*) grows in the cloud-forest zones on the eastern slopes of the Peruvian Andes. The Incas used a snuff made from the seeds, which was generally blown up the nostrils of the participant by a helper. Evidently the Inca priests used *vilca* to bring on visions and make contact with the gods and spirit world.

Economy, agriculture and building

The main **resources** available to the Inca Empire were agricultural land and labour, mines (mainly gold, silver or copper) and fresh water, abundant everywhere except along the desert coast. With careful manipulation of these resources, the Incas managed to keep things moving the way they wanted. Tribute in the form of **service** (*mita*) played a crucial role in maintaining the empire and pressurizing its subjects into ambitious building and irrigation projects. Some were so grand that they would have been impossible without the demanding whip of a totalitarian state.

Although a certain degree of local barter was allowed, the state regulated the distribution of every important product. The astonishing Inca **highways** were one key to this economic success. Some of the tracks were nearly 8m wide and at the time of the Spanish Conquest the main Royal Highway ran some 5000km, from the Río Ancasmayo in Colombia down the backbone of the Andes to the coast, at a point south of the present-day Santiago in Chile. The Incas never used the wheel, but gigantic **llama caravans** were a common sight tramping along the roads, each animal carrying up to 50kg of cargo.

Every corner of the Inca domain was easily accessible via branch roads, all designed or taken over and unified with one intention – to dominate and administer an enormous empire. **Runners** were posted at *chasqui* stations, and *tambo* rest-houses punctuated the road at intervals of between 2km and 15km. Fresh fish was relayed on foot from the coast and messages were sent with runners from Quito to Cusco (2000km) in less than six days. The more difficult mountain canyons were crossed on bridges suspended from cables braided out of jungle lianas (creeping vines) and high passes were – and still are – frequently reached by incredible stairways cut into solid rock cliffs.

Agricultural terracing

The primary sector in the economy was inevitably **agriculture** and in this the Incas made two major advances: large terracing projects created the opportunity for agricultural specialists to experiment with new crops and methods of cultivation, and the transport system allowed a revolution in distribution. Massive agricultural **terracing projects** were going on continuously in Inca-dominated mountain regions. The best examples of these are in the Cusco area at Tipón, Moray, Ollantaytambo, Pisac and Cusichaca. Beyond the aesthetic beauty of Inca stone terraces, they have distinct practical advantages. Terraced hillsides minimize erosion from landslides, and using well-engineered stone channels gives complete control over irrigation.

Inca masonry

Today, however, it is Inca construction that forms their lasting heritage: vast **building projects** masterminded by high-ranking nobles and architects, and supervised by expert masons with an almost limitless pool of peasant labour. Without paper, the architects resorted to imposing their imagination onto clay or stone, making miniature models of the more important constructions – good examples of these can be seen in Cusco museums. More importantly, **Inca masonry** survives throughout Peru, most spectacularly at the fortress of Sacsayhuaman above Cusco, and on the coast in the Achirana aqueduct, which even today still brings water down to the Ica Valley from high up in the Andes.

Arts and crafts

Surprisingly, Inca masonry was rarely carved or adorned in any way. Smaller stone items, however, were frequently ornate and beautiful. High technical standards were achieved, too, in **pottery**. Around Cusco especially, the art of creating and glazing ceramics was highly developed. They were not so advanced artistically, however; Inca designs generally lack imagination and variety, tending to have been mass-produced from models evolved by previous cultures. The most common pottery object was the *aryballus*, a large jar with a conical base and a wide neck, thought to have been used chiefly for storing *chicha*. Its decoration was usually geometric, often associated with the backbone of a fish: the central spine of the pattern was adorned with rows of spikes radiating from either side. Fine plates were made with anthropomorphic handles, and large numbers of cylindrically tapering goblets – *keros* – were manufactured, though these were often of cedar wood rather than pottery.

Refinements in **metallurgy**, like the ceramics industry, were mostly developed by craftsmen absorbed from different corners of the empire. The Chimu were particularly respected by the Incas for their superb metalwork. Within the empire, bronze and copper were used for axe-blades and *tumi* knives; gold and silver were restricted to ritual use and for nobles.

Religion

The Inca **religion** was easily capable of incorporating the religious features of most subjugated regions. The Incas merely superimposed their variety of mystical, yet inherently practical, elements onto those they came across. At the very top of the **religio-social hierarchy** was the Villac Uma, the high priest of Cusco, usually a brother of the Sapa Inca himself. Under him were perhaps hundreds of high priests, all nobles of royal blood who were responsible for ceremonies, temples, shrines, divination, curing and sacrifice within the realm, and below them were the ordinary priests and chosen women. At the base of the hierarchy, and probably the most numerous of all religious personalities, were the **curanderos**, local healers practising herbal medicine and magic, and making sacrifices to small regional *huacas* (sacred sites or temples).

Most **religious festivals** were calendar-based and marked by processions, sacrifices and dances. The Incas were aware of lunar time and the solar year, although they generally used the blooming of a special cactus and the stars to gauge the correct time to begin planting. Sacrifices to the gods normally consisted of llamas, *cuys* or *chicha* – only occasionally were chosen women and other adults killed. Once every year, however, young children were apparently sacrificed in the most important sacred centres.

Divination was a vital role played by priests and *curanderos* at all levels of the religious hierarchy. Soothsayers were expected to talk with the spirits and often used a hallucinogenic snuff from the *vilca* tree to achieve a trance-like state. Everything from a crackling fire to the glance of a lizard was seen as a potential omen, and treated as such by making a little offering of coca leaves, coca spittle or *chicha*. There were specific problems which divination was considered particularly accurate in solving: retrieving lost things; predicting the outcome of certain events (including military expeditions); and the diagnosis of illness.

Gods and symbols

The main religious novelty introduced with Inca domination was their demand to be recognized as direct descendants of the creator-god **Viracocha**. A claim to divine ancestry was, to the Incas, a valid excuse for military and cultural expansion. They felt no need to destroy the *huacas* and oracles of subjugated peoples; on the contrary, certain sacred sites were recognized as intrinsically holy, as powerful places for communication with the spirit world. When ancient shrines like Pachacamac, near Lima, were absorbed into the empire they were simply turned over to worship on imperial terms.

The **sun** is the most obvious symbol of Inca belief, a chief deity and the visible head of the state religion. The sun's role was overt, as life-giver to an agriculturally based empire, and its cycle was intricately related to agrarian practice and annual ritual patterns. To think of the Inca religion as essentially sun worship, though, would be far too simplistic. There were distinct **layers** in Inca cosmology: the level of creation, the astral level and the earthly dimension. The first, highest, level corresponds to Viracocha as the creator-god who brought life to the world and society to mankind. Below this, on the astral level, are the celestial gods: the sun itself, the moon and certain stars (particularly the Pleiades, patrons of fertility). The earthly dimension, although that of man, was no less magical, endowed with important *huacas* and shrines which might take the form of unusual rocks or peaks, caves, tombs, mummies and natural springs.

Peruvian music

Latin America's oldest musical traditions are those of the Amerindians of the Andes. Their music is best known outside these countries through the characteristic panpipes of poncho-clad folklore groups. However, there's a multitude of rhythms and popular music alive in Peru that deserve a lot more recognition, including *huayno*, *chicha*, *cumbia*, Afro-Peruvian and even reggaeton.

For most people outside Latin America the sound of the Andes is that of bamboo panpipes and *quena* flutes. What is most remarkable is that these instruments have been used to create music in various parts of this large area of mountains – which stretch 7200km from Venezuela down to southernmost Chile – since before the time of the Incas. Pre-Conquest Andean instruments – conch-shell trumpets, shakers which used nuts for rattles, ocarinas, wind instruments and drums – are ever-present in museum collections.

Andean music can be divided roughly into three types: first, that which is of **indigenous origin**, found mostly among rural Amerindian peoples still living very much by the seasons; secondly, music of **European origin**; and thirdly, **mestizo music**, which continues to fuse the indigenous with the European in a whole host of ways. In general, Quechua people have more vocal music than the Aymara.

Traditional music

Panpipes, known by the Aymara as *siku*, by the Quechua as *antara* and by the Spanish as *zampoña*, are ancient instruments, and archeologists have unearthed them tuned to a variety of scales. Simple **notched-end flutes**, or *quenas*, are another independent innovation of the Andean highlands found in both rural and urban areas. The most important pre-Hispanic instrument, they were traditionally made of fragile bamboo (though often these days from plumbers' PVC water pipes) and played in the dry season, with *tarkas* (vertical flutes – like a shrill recorder) taking over in the wet. *Quenas* are played solo or in ritual groups and remain tremendously popular today, with many virtuoso techniques.

MUSIC AT FESTIVALS

Peru's many **festivals** are a rewarding source of traditional music. One of the best takes place in January on the **Isla Amantani** in Lake Titicaca, its exact date, as is often the case in the Andean highlands, determined by astronomical events. The festival occurs during a period often called the "time of protection", when the rainy season has finally begun. It is related to the cleansing of the pasturage and water sources; stone fences are repaired, walking paths repaved, and the stone effigies and crosses that guard the planting fields replaced or repaired. A single-file "parade" of individuals covers the entire island, stopping to appease the deities and provide necessary maintenance at each site. At the front are local nonprofessional musicians, all male, playing drums and flutes of various types.

Some festivals are celebrated on a larger scale. On the day of the June solstice (midwinter in the Andes) the Inca would ceremonially tie the sun to a stone and coax it to return south, bringing warmer weather and the new planting season. **Inti Raymi**, the Festival of the Sun, is still observed in every nook and cranny in the Andean republics, from the capital city to the most isolated hamlet. The celebration, following a solemn ritual that may include a llama sacrifice, is more of a carnival than anything else. Parades of musicians, both professional bands and thrown-together collages of amateurs, fill the streets. You will be expected to drink and dance until you drop, or hide in your room. This kind of party can run for several days, so be prepared.

Large **marching bands** of drums and panpipes, playing in the cooperative "back and forth" leader/follower style that captivated the Spanish in the 1500s, can still be seen and heard today. The drums are deep-sounding, double-headed instruments known as *bombos* or *wankaras*. These bands exist for parades at life-cycle fiestas, weddings and dances in the regions surrounding the Peruvian–Bolivian frontier and around Lake Titicaca. Apart from their use at fiestas, panpipes are played mainly in the dry season, from April to October.

Folk music festivals to attract and entertain the tourist trade are a quite different experience to music in the village context. While positively disseminating the music, they have introduced the notion of judging and the concept of "best" musicianship – ideas totally at odds with rural community values of diversity in musical repertoire, style and dress.

Charangos and mermaids
The **charango** is another major Andean instrument whose bright, zingy sounds are familiar worldwide. This small guitar – with five pairs of strings – was created in imitation of early guitars and lutes brought by the Spanish colonizers, which Amerindian musicians were taught to play in the churches. Its small size is due to its traditional manufacture from armadillo shells, while its sound quality comes from the indigenous aesthetic that has favoured high pitches from the pre-Columbian period through to the present.

In rural areas in southern Peru, particularly in the Titicaca region and province of Canas, the *charango* is the main instrument – used by young **single men** to woo and court the female of choice. Some villagers construct the sound box in the shape of a **mermaid**, including her head and fish tail, to invest their *charango* with supernatural power. When young men go courting at the weekly markets in larger villages they will not only dress in their finest clothes, but dress up their *charangos* in elaborate coloured ribbons.

Song and brass
Most **singing** in the Andes is done by women, and the preferred style is very high-pitched – almost falsetto to Western ears. There are songs for potato-growing, reaping barley, threshing wheat, marking cattle, sheep and goats, for building houses, for traditional dances and funerals and for many other ceremonies.

Huaynos and orquestas típicas
Visit the Peruvian central sierra and you find a music as lively and energetic as the busy market towns it comes from, and largely unknown outside the country. These songs and dances are **huaynos**, one of the few musical forms that reach back to pre-Conquest times, although the **orquestas típicas** that play them, from sierra towns like Huancayo, Ayacucho and Pucará, include saxophones, clarinets and trumpets alongside traditional instruments like violins, *charangos* and the large Amerindian harp. The buoyant, swinging rhythms of *huayno* songs are deceptive, for the lyrics fuse joy and sorrow; sung in a mixture of Spanish and Quechua, they tell of unhappy love and betrayal, celebrate passion and often deliver homespun philosophy.

Afro-Peruvian music
Afro-Peruvian music has its roots in the communities of black slaves brought to work in the mines along the Peruvian coast. As such, it's a fair way from the Andes, culturally and geographically. However, as it developed, particularly in the twentieth century, it drew on Andean and Spanish, as well as African traditions, while its modern exponents also have affinities with Andean *nueva canción*. The music was little known even in Peru until the 1950s, when it was popularized by the seminal performer Nicomedes Santa Cruz, whose body of work was taken a step further in the 1970s by the group Perú Negro. Internationally, it has had a recent airing through David Byrne's Luaka Bop label, issuing the compilation, *Perú Negro*, and solo albums by the now world-renowned **Susana Baca**.

Nicomedes Santa Cruz is the towering figure in the development of Afro-Peruvian music. A poet, musician and journalist, he was the first true musicologist to assert an Afro-Peruvian cultural identity through black music and dance, producing books and recordings of contemporary black music and culture in Peru. In 1964 he recorded a four-album set *Cumanana*, now regarded as the bible of Afro-Peruvian music. Santa Cruz himself followed in the footsteps of **Porfirio Vásquez**, who came to Lima in 1920 and was an early pioneer of the movement to regain the lost cultural identity of Afro-Peruvians. A composer of *décimas*, singer, guitarist, *cajonero* (box player) and *zapateador* (dancer), he founded the Academia Folklórica in Lima in 1949. Through Santa Cruz's work and that of the group **Perú Negro** and the singer and composer **Chabuca Granda**, Latin America came to know Afro-Peruvian dances, the names of which were given to their songs, such as *Toro Mata*, *Samba-malató*, *El Alcatraz* and *Festejo*.

Chicha and Cumbia

Chicha, the fermented maize beer, has given its name to a hugely popular brew of Andean tropical music, one which has recently spread to wider Anglophone world music circles. The music's origins lie in the rapidly urbanizing Amazon of the late 1960s, in places like Iquitos and Pucallpa, where bands such as **Los Mirlos** and **Juaneco y Su Combo** fused *cumbia* (local versions of the original Colombian dance), traditional highland *huayno* and Western rock and psychedelia. In the 1970s, mass migration carried *chicha* to Lima, and by the mid-1980s, it had become the most widespread urban music in Peru. Most bands have lead and rhythm guitars, electric bass, electric organ, a *timbales* and conga player, one or more vocalists (who may play percussion) and, if they can, a synthesizer. While most lyrics are about love in all its aspects, nearly all songs actually reveal an aspect of the harshness of the Amerindian experience – displacement, hardship, loneliness and exploitation.

Chicha, and, more recently, the Peruvian version of *cumbia* (which is clearly more *cumbia* than *chicha*), has taken root and also achieved international acclaim. In Peru itself, this belated international recognition has witnessed a resurgence in interest in seminal artists like Juaneco y Su Combo, currently feted by the Lima cognoscenti and the subject of their own recent Barbès retrospective, *Juaneco y Su Combo: Masters of Chicha Volume 1*. The label even has its own in-house band, Chicha Libre, whose excellent debut, *¡Sonido Amazonico!*, was released in early 2008. In the last few years, Peruvian *cumbia* artists, like Barreto and also the Hermanos Yaipen, have become very popular. In 2012, during the Selvámonos Festival, a new group of *cumbia* musicians was formed: Cumbia All Stars. Its members are veterans of Peruvian *cumbia* from the 1970s, and their psychedelic brand of *cumbia* hit a chord not only locally but also internationally.

Reggaeton

More rap than reggae, **reggaeton** is popular with the urban youth of Peru today. With Jamaican reggae roots, this sexually explicit and fairly macho genre began life in Panama and Puerto Rico in the late 1980s. Spreading slowly in underground fashion it gradually became popular all over Latin America until breaking through into radio and TV music channels in the twenty-first century. It hit the clubs of Lima between 2007 and 2011, scandalizing the Catholic establishment there with its sexually explicit *el perreo* dancing. If you sample the nightlife in Lima's clubs, you're bound to find this music style thriving in the early hours.

Original material written by Jan Fairley, with thanks to Thomas Turino and Raúl Romero, Gilka Wara Céspedes, Martín Morales and Margaret Bullen. Adapted from the *Rough Guide to World Music*, Vol 2. with additional contributions by Brendon Griffin. Re-edited by Claire Jenkins, 2012.

Natural Peru

Peru's varied ecological niches span an incredible range of climate and terrain; the Amazon region covers 60 percent of Peru's land surface, yet has only 12 percent of its population; the highlands cover 28 percent of the land but are home to only 36 percent of the country's people; the desert coast, where 52 percent of Peruvians live, comprises a mere 12 percent of its land area. Between these three major zones, the ecological reality is continuous intergradation, encompassing literally dozens of unique habitats. Mankind has occupied Peru for perhaps twenty thousand years, but there has been less disturbance there, until relatively recently, than in most other parts of our planet, which makes it a top-class ecotourist and wildlife photo-safari destination.

The coast

Peru's **coast** is characterized by abundant sea life and by the contrasting scarcity of terrestrial plants and animals. The **Humboldt current** runs virtually the length of Peru, bringing cold water up from the depths of the Pacific Ocean and causing any moisture to condense out over the sea, depriving the mainland coastal strip and lower western mountain slopes of rainfall. Along with this cold water, large quantities of nutrients are carried up to the surface, helping to sustain a rich planktonic community able to support vast numbers of fish, preyed upon in their turn by a variety of coastal birds: gulls, terns, pelicans, boobies, cormorants and wading birds are always present along the beaches. One beautiful specimen, the **Inca tern**, although usually well camouflaged as it sits high up on inaccessible sea cliffs, is nevertheless very common in the Lima area. The **Humboldt penguin**, with grey rather than black features, is a rarer sight – shyer than its more southerly cousins, it is normally found in isolated rocky coves or on offshore islands. Competing with the birds for fish are schools of dolphins, sea lion colonies and the occasional coastal otter. Dolphins and sea lions are often spotted off even the most crowded of beaches or scavenging around the fishermen's jetty at Chorrillos, near Lima.

One of the most fascinating features of Peruvian birdlife is the number of vast, **high-density colonies**: although the number of species is quite small, their total population is enormous. Many thousands of birds can be seen nesting on islands like the Ballestas, off the Paracas Peninsula, or simply covering the ocean with a flapping, diving carpet of energetic feathers. This huge bird population, and the **Guanay cormorant** in particular, is responsible for depositing mountains of guano (bird droppings), which form a traditional and potent source of natural fertilizer.

The coastal desert

In contrast to these rich waters the **coastal desert** lies stark and barren. Here you find only a few trees and shrubs; you'll need endless patience to find wild animals other than birds. The most common animals are feral **goats**, once domesticated but now living wild, and **burros** (donkeys) introduced by the Spanish. A more exciting sight is the attractively coloured **coral snake** – shy but deadly and covered with black and orange hoops. Most animals are more active after sunset; when out in the desert you can hear the eerily plaintive call of the **huerequeque** (Peruvian thick-knee bird), and

> ## EL NIÑO
>
> In order to understand the Peruvian coastal desert you have to bear in mind the phenomenon of **El Niño**, a periodic climatic shift caused by the displacement of the cold Humboldt current by warmer equatorial waters; it last occurred in 1998 and the predicted return in 2014 never materialized, although most agree that an event is imminent. El Niño causes the plankton and fish communities either to disperse to other locations or to collapse entirely. At such a period the shore rapidly becomes littered with carrion, since many of the sea mammals and birds are unable to survive in the limited environment. Scavenging condors and vultures, on the other hand, thrive, as does the desert, where rain falls in deluges along the coast, with a consequent bloom of vegetation and rapid growth in animal populations. When the Humboldt current returns, the desert dries up and its animal populations decline to normal sizes (another temporary feast for the scavengers). While it used to be at least ten years before this cycle was repeated, global warming over the last two decades has witnessed the pattern becoming much more erratic. Generally considered a freak phenomenon, El Niño is probably better understood as an integral part of coastal ecology; without it the desert would be a far more barren and static environment, virtually incapable of supporting life.

the barking of the little **desert fox** – alarmingly similar to the sound of car tyres screeching to a halt. By day you might see several species of small birds, a favourite being the vermilion-headed **Peruvian flycatcher**. Near water – rivers, estuaries and lagoons – desert wildlife is at its most populous. In addition to residents such as **flamingoes**, **herons** and **egrets**, many migrant birds pause in these havens between October and March on their journeys south and then back north.

The mountains

In the **Peruvian Andes** there is an incredible variety of habitats. That this is a mountain area of true extremes becomes immediately obvious if you fly across, or along, the Andes towards Lima, the land below shifting from high *puna* to cloud forest to riparian valleys and eucalyptus tracts (trees introduced from Australia in the 1880s). The complexity of the whole makes it incredibly difficult to formulate any overall description that isn't essentially misleading: climate and vegetation vary according to altitude, latitude and local characteristics.

The Andes divides vertically into three main regions, identified by the Incas from top to bottom as the Puna, the Qeswa and the Yunka. The **Puna**, roughly 3800–4300m above sea level, has an average temperature of 3–6°C (37–43°F), and annual rainfall of 500–1000mm. Typical animals here include the main Peruvian cameloids – llamas, alpacas, *guanacos* and *vicuñas* – while crops that grow well here include the potato and *quinoa* grain. At 2500–3500m, the **Qeswa** has average temperatures of around 13°C (55°F), and a similar level of rainfall at 500–1200mm. The traditional forest here, including Andean pine, is not abundant and has been largely displaced by the imported Australian eucalyptus tree; the main cultivated crops include maize, potatoes and the nutritious *kiwicha* grain. The *ceja de selva* (cloud forest to high forest on the eastern side of the Andes) forms the lower-lying **Yunka**, at 1200–2500m, and has at least twice as much rain as the other two regions and abundant wildlife, including Peru's national bird, the red-crested *gallito de las rocas* (cock-of-the-rock). Plant life, too, is prolific, not least the region's orchids. On the western side of the Andes there is much less rainfall and it's not technically known as the Yunka, but it does share some characteristics: both sides have wild river canes (*caña brava*), and both are suitable for cultivating banana, pineapple, *yuca* and coca.

Mountain flora and fauna

Much of the Andes has been settled for over two thousand years – and hunter tribes go back another eight thousand years before this – so larger predators are rare, though still present in small numbers in the more remote regions. Among the most exciting you might actually see are the **mountain cats**, especially the **puma**, which lives at most altitudes and in a surprising number of habitats. Other more remote predators include the shaggy-looking **maned wolf** and the likeable **spectacled bear**, which inhabits the moister forested areas of the Andes and actually prefers eating vegetation to people.

The most visible animals in the mountains, besides sheep and cattle, are the cameloids – the wild **vicuña** and **guanaco**, and the domesticated **llama** and **alpaca**. Although these species are clearly related, zoologists disagree on whether or not the alpaca and llama are domesticated forms of their wild relatives. Domesticated they are, however, and have been so for thousands of years; studies reveal that cameloids appeared in North America some forty to fifty million years ago, crossing the Bering Straits long before any humans did. From these early forms the present species have evolved in Peru, Bolivia, Chile, Argentina and Ecuador, and there are now over three million llamas – 33 percent in Peru and a further 63 percent over the border in Bolivia. The alpaca population is just under four million, with 87 percent in Peru and only 11 percent in Bolivia. Of the two wild cameloids, the *vicuña* is the smaller and rarer, living only at the highest altitudes (up to 4500m) and with a population of just over 100,000. There are 4000 *guanaco* in Peru, compared to over 500,000 in Argentina alone.

Andean deer are quite common in the higher valleys and with luck you may even come across the rare **mountain tapir**. Smaller animals tend to be confined to particular habitats – rabbit-like **viscachas**, for example, to rocky outcrops; **squirrels** to wooded valleys; and **chinchillas** (Peruvian chipmunks) to higher altitudes.

Most birds also tend to restrict themselves to specific habitats. The **Andean goose** and **duck** are quite common in marshy areas, along with many species of wader and migratory waterfowl. A particular favourite is the elegant, very pink, **Andean flamingo**, which can usually be spotted from the road between Arequipa and Puno where they turn Lake Salinas into one great red mass. In addition, many species of passerine can be found alongside small streams. Perhaps the most striking of them is the **dipper**, which hunts underwater for larval insects along the stream bed, popping up to a rock every so often for air and a rest. At lower elevations, especially in and around cultivated areas, the **ovenbird** (or horneo) constructs its nest from mud and grasses in the shape of an old-fashioned oven; while in open spaces many birds of prey can be spotted, the comical **caracara**, **buzzard-eagle** and the magical **red-backed hawk** among them. **Andean condors** are actually quite difficult to see up close as, although not especially rare, they tend to soar at tremendous heights for most of the day, landing only on high, inaccessible cliffs, or at carcasses after making sure that no one is around to disturb them. A glimpse of this magnificent bird soaring overhead will come only through frequent searching with binoculars, perhaps in relatively unpopulated areas or at one of the better-known sites such as the Cruz del Condor viewing platform in the Colca Canyon (see p.181).

Tropical rainforest

Descending the eastern edge of the Andes, you pass through the distinct habitats of the Puna, Qeswa and Yunka before reaching the lowland jungle or **rainforest**. In spite of its rich and luxuriant appearance, the rainforest is in fact extremely fragile. Almost all the nutrients are recycled by rapid decomposition (with the aid of the damp climate and a prodigious supply of insect labour) back into the vegetation, thereby creating a nutrient-poor soil that is highly susceptible to large-scale disturbance. When the forest is cleared, for example – usually in an attempt to colonize the area and turn it into viable farmland – there is not only heavy soil erosion to contend with but also a limited amount of nutrients in the earth (only enough for five years of good harvests and twenty years' poorer farming at the most). Natives of the rainforest have evolved cultural mechanisms by which, on the whole, these problems are avoided: they tend to live in small, dispersed groups, move their gardens every few years and obey sophisticated social controls to limit the chances of overhunting any one zone or any particular species.

Around eighty percent of the Amazon rainforest was still intact at the start of the twenty-first century, but for every **hardwood** logged in this forest, an average of 120 other trees are destroyed and left unused or simply burnt. Over an acre per second of this magnificent forest is burnt or bulldozed, equating to an area the size of Great Britain **every year**, even though this makes little economic sense in the long term. According to the late rainforest specialist Dr Alwyn Gentry, just 2.5 acres of primary rainforest could yield up to US$9000 a year from sustainable harvesting of wild fruits, saps, resins and timber – yet the average income for the same area from ranching or plantations in the Amazon is a meagre US$30 a year.

Amazon flora and fauna

The most distinctive attribute of the Amazon Basin is its overwhelming abundance of plant and animal species. Over six thousand species of plants have been reported in one small 250-acre tract of forest, and there are at least a thousand species of birds and dozens of types of monkeys and bats spread about the Peruvian Amazon. There are several reasons for this marvellous **natural diversity** of flora and fauna; most obviously, it is warm, there is abundant sunlight and large quantities of mineral nutrients are washed down from the Andes – ideal conditions for forest growth. Secondly, the rainforest has enormous structural diversity, with layers of vegetation from the forest floor to the canopy 30m above, providing a vast number of niches to fill. Thirdly, since there is such a variety of habitat as you descend the Andes, the changes in altitude mean a great diversity of localized ecosystems. With the rainforest being stable over longer periods of time than temperate areas (there was no Ice Age here, nor any prolonged periods of drought), the fauna has had the freedom to evolve, and to adapt to often very specialized local conditions.

But if the Amazon Basin is where most of the plant and animal species are in Peru, it is not easy to see them. Movement through the vegetation is limited to narrow trails and along the rivers in a boat. The riverbanks and flood plains are richly diverse areas: here you are likely to see **caimans, macaws, toucans, oropendulas, terns, horned screamers** and the primitive **hoatzins** – birds whose young are born with claws at the wrist to enable them to climb up from the water into the branches of overhanging trees. You should catch sight, too, of one of a variety of **hawks** and at least two or three species of **monkeys** (perhaps the **spider monkey**, the **howler** or the **capuchin**). With a lot of luck and more determined observation you may spot a rare **giant river otter, river dolphin,** or **capybara,** or maybe even one of the **jungle cats.**

In the jungle proper you're more likely to find mammals such as the **peccary** (wild pig), **tapir, tamandua tree sloth** and the second largest cat in the world, the incredibly powerful **spotted jaguar.** Characteristic of the deeper forest zones, too, are many species of bird, including **hummingbirds** (more common in the forested Andean foothills), **manakins** and **trogons,** though the effects of widespread hunting make it difficult to see these around any of the larger settlements. Logging is proving to be another major problem for the forest fauna – since valuable trees are dispersed among vast areas of other species in the rainforest, a very large area must be disturbed to yield a relatively small amount of timber. Deeper into the forest, however, and the further you are from human habitation, a glimpse of any of these animals is quite possible. Most of the bird activity occurs in the canopy, 30 to 40m above the ground, but platforms such as the **canopy walkway** at the Amazon Explorama ACTS Field Station (see p.475) and another, newer one at Inkaterra's Reserva Amazonica (see p.441), on the Río Madre de Dios, make things a little easier.

CONSERVATION AND ENVIRONMENTAL POLITICS IN PERU

Climate change is already having serious impacts on Peru's priceless environment and the country has been ranked in a recent UNDP report as third globally in terms of risk to climate-change-related impact.

DIMINISHING GLACIERS

The glaciers are retreating fast. South America possesses more than 99 percent of the world's tropical glaciers, with over seventy percent of these located in Peru, where they act as a reservoir of meltwater which provides two very vital resources: on the one hand it gives the water for drinking, agriculture and hydroelectricity for urban areas, industry and agriculture in the Andes and along the desert coast, even during the dry season; on other hand, and in the opposite direction, the glaciers feed the main headwaters of the Amazon Basin. With the glaciers diminishing, problems are beginning already in both directions – water shortages on the coast and very low dry-season river levels in the Amazon. The Peruvian glaciers, essential stores of the planet's most basic resource, have been described by Lonnie Thompson (an Ohio State University glaciologist) as the "water towers of the world". Nevertheless, Peru's most important glacier – Pastoruri (see box, p.217), near the city of Huaraz – and previously the country's main ski resort, has finally split itself into two halves, retreating at an incredible 20m every year, it has lost more than half of its surface area since 1995 and will almost certainly vanish completely before 2020. CONAM, Peru's National Environment Agency, estimates that by 2025, Peru will be the first country in South America to experience "permanent water stress", principally, of course, along the urbanized coastal belt.

GROUND AND WATER POLLUTION

Ground and water **pollution**, among the worst in the world, has become a concern around some of Peru's Andean mining towns. La Oroya, just four hours by road from Lima, has been a major mining centre since 1922 when the US Cerro de Paso Corporation established its first smelter here. The three plants operating around La Oroya were once claimed by the Ministry of Energy and Mines to be producing around 1.5 tonnes of lead and over 800 tonnes of sulphur dioxide every day. These levels of pollution are significantly greater than is permitted under Peruvian law, and blood samples from newborn babies in the town of La Oroya found over 8.8 micrograms of lead per 100 millilitres, very close to the maximum a baby can cope with without damaging its cognitive abilities. Other mines, mainly in the Mantaro river basin, close to La Oroya, pour contaminated waters downstream, affecting the health of indigenous and settler populations on the Amazon headwaters.

Deforestation

According to the UN Food and Agriculture Organization (FAO), 53.1 percent of Peru is forested. Of this, 88.5 percent is classified as **primary forest**, the most biodiverse and carbon-dense form. **Deforestation** is responsible for nineteen percent of present global carbon dioxide emissions; alongside this there's the obvious travesty of concomitant destruction of forest habitats and biodiversity – Peru has some 2937 known species of amphibians, birds, mammals and reptiles – and of the home of many indigenous peoples. Despite Peru's vested interest in mitigating climate change, logging of the Amazon region continues apace, up to eighty percent of it possibly illegal but whitewashed with official documents by the time the timber reaches Lima and the port of Callao for export. In total, between 1990 and 2010, Peru lost 3.1 percent of its forest cover. Combating these excesses may well be the biggest challenge for the present government.

In June 2014, the government announced a package of economic proposals aimed at reactivating the economy following a drop in the country´s growth rate. The government vowed the proposals would not change environmental standards, but this has been highly disputed by environmental NGOs. The government has also received criticism over its approach to illegal mining and logging. A 2012 World Bank report estimated that as much as eighty percent of Peru's logging exports are harvested illegally. The issue gained momentum in September 2014 after the killing

---

MEGADAMS

The Brazilian electricity company Electrobras has an agreement with Peru to build at least six **megadams** to generate electricity in the Peruvian Amazon over the coming years. The plan is that eighty percent of the electricity produced, initially at least, be exported to Brazil to power **aluminium plants** in the western Brazilian Amazon. The dams are so big, however, that their social and environmental impact would be devastating, and the project is seen as another of ex-President García's big thumbs-down to the environment and indigenous Peruvian communities. Currently there are some seventy dams planned for the Amazon basin over the next forty years. More information on the most controversial of these megadam proposals can be found on these websites:

Ⓦ internationalrivers.org   Ⓦ latinamericacurrentevents.com
Ⓦ rainforestfoundationuk.org   Ⓦ indigenouspeoplesissues.com

---

of Edwin Chota, environmental advocate and indigenous leader, along with three other colleagues, while trying to protect a remote region of the Amazon jungle from illegal logging.

In September, some good news seemed to arise, in the form of an agreement between Peru, Norway and Germany in which Humala pledged to make his country carbon-neutral by 2021, and pledged to grant land title of five million acres to indigenous tribes in the Amazon. In return, Norway and Germany have pledged hundreds of millions of dollars for verified results in the next six years. Considering, however, the government's big-business-friendly approach, that Humala will be out of office in 2016, and the frequent lack of continuity between governments, NGOs have remained sceptical.

Illegal gold mining

Peru's worst example of **illegal gold mining** is found in the southeastern jungles of Madre de Dios, home to the Amarakaeri people, where monster-sized machinery is transforming one of the Amazon's most biodiverse regions into a huge muddy scar. A number of gold miners have already moved into the unique Tambopata Reserved Zone, a protected jungle area where giant otters, howler monkeys, king vultures, anacondas and jaguars are regularly spotted. All plant life around each mine is turned into gravel, known in Peru as *cancha*, for just a few ounces of gold a day. Front-loading machines move up to about thirty metres depth of soil, which is then washed on a wooden sluice where high-pressure hoses separate the silt and gold from mud and gravel. **Mercury**, added at this stage to facilitate gold extraction, is later burnt off, causing river and air pollution. The mines are totally unregulated, and the richer, more established mining families tend to run the show, having the money to import large machines upriver from Brazil or by air from Chile.

The **indigenous tribes** are losing control of their territory to an ever-increasing stream of these miners and settlers coming down from the high Andes. As the mercury pollution and suspended mud from the mines upstream kill the life-giving rivers, they have to go deeper and deeper into the forest for fish, traditionally their main source of protein. Beatings and death threats from the miners and police are not uncommon.

There is a hope that improved **gold-mining technology** can stem the tide of destruction in these areas; mercury levels in Amazon rivers and their associated food chains are rising at an alarming rate. However, with raw mercury available for only US$13 a kilo there is little obvious economic incentive to find ways of using less-hazardous materials. Pressure by international **environmental groups**, and the publicity they generate, make some difference, but greater political willpower and more holistic, inclusive solutions than the current hard-line approach are needed to truly resolve the issue.

INDIGENOUS RIGHTS AND THE DESTRUCTION OF THE RAINFOREST

The indigenous people of the Peruvian jungles are being pushed off their land by an endless combination of slash-and-burn colonization, megadam builders, big oil companies, gold miners, timber extractors, coca farmers organized by drug-trafficking barons and, at times, "revolutionary" political groups. All along the main rivers and jungle roads, settlers are flooding into the area. In their wake, forcing land-title agreements to which they have no right, are the main timber companies and multinational oil corporations. In large tracts of the jungle the fragile selva ecology has already been destroyed; in others the tribes have been more subtly disrupted as they become dependent on outside consumer goods and trade, or by the imposition of evangelical proselytizing groups, and the Indian way of life is being destroyed.

In response to the dire situation of indigenous communities, self-determination groups sprang up throughout the 1970s and 1980s, such as AIDESEP (Inter-ethnic Association for the Development of the Peruvian Amazon) and CONAP (Coalition of Indigenous Nationalities of the Peruvian Amazon).

In May 2008, Alan García's government very publicly created Peru's first **Ministry of the Environment** during the Lima-based European Union–Latin America and the Caribbean Summit whose main focus was climate change. This was third a direct attempt for Peru to access new and future global funds for conservation, rather than a serious effort to protect the country's rainforests and mega-biodiversity. Within weeks of the new ministry's creation, the government also announced plans to open up community-owned lands for commercial investment by making fundamental changes to the law of **land ownership** in the Andes and Amazon regions – a move which was integral to the new free-trade agreement between Peru and the US. The concept is straightforward: without long-term ownership of large areas of land, big corporations are simply unlikely to invest in massive agribusiness schemes such as soya production and the cultivation of crops for biofuels.

Voluntarily isolated peoples

Many of Peru's indigenous peoples, like the Ashaninka and Aguaruna-Huambisa, stand firm against exploitation and invasion from outside influences. The Peruvian Amazon is home to approximately fifteen uncontacted tribes with up to 15,000 people. But more and more previously uncontacted or voluntarily isolated Indians are having their land invaded by loggers, drug trafficking or oil companies and the threat of encountering diseases to which they have no resistance is growing.

The region of Madre de Dios in particular, has seen a sharp increase in the number of "encounters" with isolated tribes in the past few years. The Mashco-Piro tribe has visited neighbouring villages at least four times during 2014, the last one of which saw an unprecedented number of uncontacted people, estimated at two hundred, attack the village of Monte Salgado whose population had to be evacuated.

Books

There are few books published exclusively about Peru and very few works by Peruvian writers ever make it into English. Many of the classic works on Peruvian and Inca history are now out of print (o/p), though frequently one comes across them in libraries around the world or in bookshops in Lima and Cusco. Travel books, coffee-table editions and country guides are also generally available in Lima bookshops. Others can be obtained through the South American Explorers' Club (see p.49), who also have specialist and out-of-print articles, books, maps and documents. Titles marked ★ are especially recommended.

INCA AND ANCIENT HISTORY

Anthony Aveni *Nasca: Eighth Wonder of the World*. Contains much on the history of the Nazca people and explores the complex relationships between water, worship, social order and the environment. Written by a leading scholar who has spent twenty years excavating here.

Kathleen Berrin *The Spirit of Ancient Peru: Treasures from the Museo Arqueológico Rafael Larco Herrera* (o/p). Essentially a detailed exhibition catalogue with essays by reputable Andeanists and plenty of quality illustrations and photographs representing one of Peru's finest collections of mainly pre-Inca artefacts.

Hiram Bingham *Lost City of the Incas*. The classic introduction to Machu Picchu: the exploration accounts are interesting but many of the theories should be taken with a pinch of salt. Widely available in Peru.

Peter T. Bradley *The Lure of Peru: Maritime Intrusion into the South Sea 1598–1701* (o/p). A historical account of how the worldwide fame of the country's Inca treasures attracted Dutch, French and English would-be settlers, explorers, merchants and even pirates to the seas and shores of Peru. Includes descriptions of naval blockades of Lima and various waves of buccaneers and their adventures in search of Peru.

Richard Burger *Chavín and the Origins of Andean Civilisation*. A collection of erudite essays – essential reading for anyone seriously interested in Peruvian prehistory.

★Geoffrey Hext Sutherland Bushnell *Peru* (o/p). A classic, concise introduction to the main social and technological developments in Peru from 2500 BC to 1500 AD; well illustrated, if dated in some aspects.

Pedro de Cieza de Leon *The Discovery and Conquest of Peru (Latin America in Transition)*. A new paperback version of the classic post-Conquest chronicler account.

Evan Hadingham *Lines to the Mountain Gods: Nasca and the Mysteries of Peru*. One of the more down-to-earth books on the Nazca Lines, including maps and illustrations.

★John Hemming *The Conquest of the Incas*. The authoritative narrative tale of the Spanish Conquest, very readably brought to life from a mass of original sources.

Thor Heyerdahl, Daniel Sandweiss and **Alfredo Navárez** *Pyramids of Túcume*. A recently published description of the archeological site at Túcume plus the life and society of the civilization that created this important ceremonial and political centre around 1000 years ago. Widely available in Peruvian bookshops.

Richard Keatinge (ed) *Peruvian Prehistory*. One of the most up-to-date and reputable books on the ancient civilizations of Peru – a collection of serious academic essays on various cultures and cultural concepts through the millennia prior to the Inca era.

Ann Kendall *Everyday Life of the Incas* (o/p). Accessible, very general description of Peru under Inca domination.

Alfred L. Kroeber and **Donald Collier** *The Archeology and Pottery of Nazca, Peru: Alfred Kroeber's 1926 Expedition*. A historical perspective on the archeology of Peru.

Kim MacQuarrie *The Last Days of the Incas*. Available in both hardback and paperback, this is a thoroughly researched and highly dramatic account of Francisco Pizarro's conquest, depicting the Inca rebellion and subsequent guerrilla war. The book also covers the modern search for lost Inca cities.

J. Alden Mason *Ancient Civilisations of Peru*. Reprinted in 1991, an excellent summary of the country's history from the Stone Age through to the Inca Empire.

Michael E. Moseley *The Incas and Their Ancestors*. A fine overview of Peru before the Spanish Conquest, which makes full use of good maps, diagrams, sketches, motifs and photos.

Keith Muscutt *Warriors of the Clouds: A Lost Civilization in the Upper Amazon of Peru*. Some superb photos of the ruins and environment left behind by the amazing Chachapoyas culture of northern Peru.

William Hickling Prescott *History of the Conquest of Peru*. Hemming's main predecessor – a nineteenth-century classic that remains a good read, if you can find a copy.

Johan Reinhard *Nasca Lines: A New Perspective on Their Origin and Meaning*. Original theories about the Lines and ancient mountain gods. The same author also wrote *The Sacred Centre: Machu Picchu*, a fascinating book, drawing on anthropology, archeology, geography and astronomy to reach highly probable conclusions about the sacred geology and topography of the Cusco region, and how this appears to have been related to Inca architecture, in particular Machu Picchu.

Gene Savoy *Antisuyo: The Search for the Lost Cities of the Amazon* (o/p). Exciting account of Savoy's important explorations, plus loads of historical detail.

★**Garcilasco de la Vega** *The Royal Commentaries of the Incas* (2 vols; o/p). Many good libraries have a copy of this, the most readable and fascinating of contemporary historical sources. Written shortly after the Conquest, by a "Spaniard" of essentially Inca blood, this work is the best eyewitness account of life and beliefs among the Incas.

Oscar Medina Zevallos *The Enigma of Machu Picchu*. Written by a Peruvian explorer and historical writer, this book tries to answer some of the difficult questions posed by Machu Picchu.

MODERN HISTORY AND SOCIETY

Americas Watch *Peru under Fire; Human Rights since the Return to Democracy*. A good summary of Peruvian politics in the 1980s.

Susan E. Benner and **Kathy S. Leonard** *Fire from the Andes: Short Fiction by Women from Bolivia, Ecuador, and Peru*. A fascinating read featuring unique and passionate writing.

Sally Bowen and **Jane Holligan** *The Imperfect Spy: the many lives of Vladimiro Montesinos*. Tracing the emergence of Montesinos, who virtually ran Peru throughout the 1990s as head of SIN (Servicio de Inteligencia Nacional), this well-researched book covers his upbringing and career in a highly engaging and accessible style. It provides a fascinating insight into corruption and power in the CIA and the mafia, as manifested in Peru.

Eduardo Calderón *Eduardo El Curandero: The Words of a Peruvian Healer*. Peru's most famous shaman – El Tuno – outlines his teachings and beliefs in his own words.

Catherine M Conaghan *Fujimori's Peru: Deception in the Public Sphere*. A very readable account of the lesser-known, manipulative side of Fujimori's time in power, his brutalizing of Peru's democratic institutions and eventual downfall.

Carlos Cumes and **Romulo Lizarraga Valencia** *Pachamama's Children: Mother Earth and Her Children of the Andes in Peru*. A New Age look at the culture, roots and shamanistic aspects of modern Peru.

Holligan de Díaz-Limaco *Peru in Focus*. A good (if short) general reader on Peru's history, politics, culture and environment.

James Higgins *Lima: a cultural and literary history*. A scholarly book showing great affection for Lima, carefully weaving together both its culture and social history. It guides the reader through Lima's historical sites with particular emphasis on the colonial era, and culminating with a section on modern-day culture.

★**F. Bruce Lamb** and **Manuel Córdova-Rios** *The Wizard of the Upper Amazon*. Masterful reconstruction of the true story of Manuel Córdova-Rios – "Ino Moxo" – a famous herbal healer and *ayahuascero* from Iquitos who was kidnapped as a young boy and brought up by Indians in the early twentieth century. Offers significant insight into indigenous psychedelic healing traditions.

E. Luís Martín *The Kingdom of the Sun: A Short History of Peru* (o/p). The best general history of Peru, concentrating on the post-Conquest period until the 1980s.

Nicole Maxwell *Witch-Doctor's Apprentice* (o/p). A very personal and detailed account of the author's research into the healing plants used by Amazonian Peruvian tribes; a highly informative book on plant lore.

Sewell H. Menzel *Fire in the Andes: U.S. Foreign Policy and Cocaine Politics in Bolivia and Peru*. A good summary of US anti-cocaine activities in these two countries, written by a credible academic.

David Scott Palmer (ed) *Shining Path of Peru*. A modern history compilation of meticulously detailed essays and articles by Latin American academics and journalists on the early and middle phases of Sendero Luminoso's civil war in Peru.

Michael Reid *Peru: Paths to Poverty* (o/p). A succinct analysis tracing Peru's economic and security crisis of the early 1980s back to the military government of General Velasco.

Orin Starn, Carlos Degregori and **Robin Kirk** (eds) *The Peru Reader: History, Culture, Politics*. One of the best overviews yet of Peruvian history and politics, with writing by characters as diverse as Mario Vargas Llosa and Abimael Guzmán (imprisoned ex-leader of Sendero Luminoso).

Kimberly Theidon *Intimate Enemies, Violence and Reconciliation in Peru*. An excellent account of divisions left in the Andean communities following the Shining Path insurgency.

FLORA AND FAUNA

Allen Altman and **B. Swift** *Checklist of the Birds of Peru*. A useful summary with photos of different habitats.

J.L. Castner, S.L. Timme and **J.A. Duke** *A Field Guide to Medicinal and Useful Plants of the Upper Amazon*. Of interest to enthusiasts and scientists alike, this book contains handy colour illustrations.

L.H. Emmons *Neotropical Rainforest Mammals: A Field Guide*. An excellent paperback with over 250 pages of authoritative text and illustrations.

M. Koepke *The Birds of the Department of Lima*. A small but classic guide, for many years the only one available that covered many of Peru's species, and still good for its excellent illustrations.

★**Thomas Schulenberg, Douglas Stotz, Daniel Lane, John O'Neill et al.** *Birds of Peru* (Princeton Field Guide). The most comprehensive and up-to-date guide to the over 1800 species of birds found in Peru, with excellent colour illustrations to aid identification.

★**Richard E. Schultes** and **Robert F. Raffauf** *The Healing Forest*. An excellent and erudite large-format paperback on many of the Amazon's most interesting plants. It's well illustrated with exquisite photographs and is a relatively easy read.

Richard E. Schultes and **Robert F. Raffauf** *Vine of the Soul*. One of the best large-format books about the indigenous use of the hallucinogenic plant ayahuasca.

Thomas Valqui *Where to Watch Birds in Peru*. Divided into seven sections or regions of Peru, it covers 151 of the most important birding sites, featuring maps and details on how to reach the locations as well as where to stay nearby. Naturally, it also gives plenty of information on what birds to look for and thorough descriptions of birds and their habitats. Incorporates an up-to-date Peru bird checklist.

Barry Walker and **Jon Fjeldsa** *Birds of Machu Picchu*. A splendid full-colour booklet focusing on the birdlife found in Peru's best-known national sanctuary and the area within which the Inca Trail is located.

Walter Wust *Manu: el último refugio*. This is an excellent coffee-table book on the wildlife and flora of Manu National Park by one of Peru's foremost wildlife photographers. Available in most good bookshops in Lima and Cusco.

TRAVEL

Timothy E. Albright and **Jeff Tenlow** *Dancing Bears and the Pilgrims Progress in the Andes: Transformation on the Road to Qolloriti*. A slightly dry report on the Snow Star annual festival of Qoyllur Rit'i, which is attended by tens of thousands of Andean peasants at the start of every dry season.

Christopher Isherwood *The Condor and the Cows* (o/p). A diary of Isherwood's South American trip after World War II, most of which took place in Peru. Like Paul Theroux, Isherwood eventually arrives in Buenos Aires, to meet Jorge Luis Borges.

John Lane *A Very Peruvian Practice*. This comical and well-written autobiographical travel book about Lane's work as adviser to a new ladies' health clinic in Lima paints a colourful picture of life in Peru – from bullfights to funerals, and the rainforest to Andean mountaintops.

Patrick Leigh Fermor *Three Letters from the Andes*. Three long letters written from Peru in 1971, describing the experiences of a rather upper-crust mountaineering expedition.

Dervla Murphy *Eight Feet in the Andes*. An enjoyable account of a rather adventurous journey Dervla Murphy made across the Andes with her young daughter and a mule. It can't compare with her India books, though.

Matthew Parris *Inca Kola, A Traveller's Tale of Peru*. Very

amusing description of travelling in Peru, with a perspicacious look at Peruvian culture, past and present.

Tom Pow *In the Palace of Serpents: An Experience of Peru*. A well-written insight into travelling in Peru, spoilt only by the fact that Tom Pow was ripped off in Cusco and lost his original notes. Consequently he didn't have as wonderful a time as he might have and seems to miss the beauty of the Peruvian landscapes and the wealth of history and culture.

Paul Theroux *The Old Patagonian Express*. Theroux didn't much like Peru, nor Peruvians, but for all the self-obsessed pique and disgust for most of humanity, at his best – being sick in trains – he is highly entertaining.

★**Hugh Thomson** *The White Rock*. One of the best travelogues on Peru for some time, focusing mainly on the archeological explorations and theories of an English Peruvianist.

George Woodcock *Incas and Other Men* (o/p). An enjoyable, light-hearted tour, mixing modern and ancient history, and travel anecdotes. Still a good introduction to Peru over fifty years later.

★**Ronald Wright** *Cut Stones and Crossroads: A Journey in the Two Worlds of Peru*. An enlightened travel book and probably the best general travelogue writing on Peru over the last few decades, largely due to the author's depth of knowledge of his subject.

PERUVIAN WRITERS

Martín Adán *The Cardboard House*. A poetic novel based in Lima and written by one of South America's best living poets.

Ciro Alegria *Broad and Alien is the World*. Another good book to travel with, this is a distinguished 1970s novel offering persuasive insight into life in the Peruvian highlands.

José María Arguedas *Deep Rivers* and *Yawar Fiesta*. Arguedas is an *indigenista* – writing for and about the native peoples. *Yawar Fiesta* focuses on one of the most impressive Andean peasant ceremonial cycles, involving the annual rite of pitching a live condor against a bull (the condor representing the indigenous Indians and the bull the Spanish conquistadores).

Cesar Vallejo *Collected Poems of Cesar Vallejo.* Peru's one internationally renowned poet – and deservedly so. Romantic but highly innovative in style, his writing translates beautifully.

Mario Vargas Llosa *Death in the Andes, A Fish in the Water, Aunt Julia and the Scriptwriter, The Time of the Hero, Captain Pantoja and the Special Service, The Green House, The Real Life of Alejandro Mayta, The War of the End of the World, Who Killed Palomino Molero?* The best-known and the most brilliant of contemporary Peruvian writers, Vargas Llosa is essentially a novelist but has also written on Peruvian society, run his own current-affairs TV programme in Lima and even made a (rather average) feature film. *Death in the Andes* deals with Sendero Luminoso and Peruvian politics in

a style that goes quite a long way towards illuminating popular Peruvian thinking in the late 1980s and early 1990s. His ebullient memoir, *A Fish in the Water*, describes, among other things, Vargas Llosa's experience in unsuccessfully running for the Peruvian presidency. *Aunt Julia*, the best known of his novels to be translated into English, is a fabulous book, a grand and comic novel spiralling out from the stories and exploits of a Bolivian scriptwriter who arrives in Lima to work on Peruvian radio soap operas. In part, too, it is autobiographical, full of insights and goings-on in Miraflores society. Essential reading – and perfect for long Peruvian journeys. His latest novel – *The Way to Paradise (El Paraiso en la Otra Esquina)* – is a fictional re-creation of the life and times of Flora Tristan and Paul Gauguin.

NOVELS SET IN PERU

Jordan Jacobs *Samantha Sutton and the Labyrinth of Lies.* A great read for young travellers to Peru, this novel is part Nancy Drew, part Indiana Jones, following a teenage girl in a detailed and well-researched adventure with her uncle in the ruins of Chavín de Huantar.

★ **Peter Mathiessen** *At Play in the Fields of the Lord.* A celebrated American novel, which catches the energy and magic of the Peruvian selva.

James Redfield *The Celestine Prophecy.* A best-selling

novel that uses Peru as a backdrop. Despite not having much to say about Peru, it was a popular topic of conversation among travellers in the 1990s; some were actually inspired to visit Peru from having read this intriguing book, which expresses with some clarity many New Age concepts and beliefs. Unfortunately the book's descriptions of the Peruvian people, landscapes, forests and culture bear so little relationship to reality that it feels as though the author has never been anywhere near the country.

SPECIALIST GUIDES

Flor Arcaya de Deliot *The Food and Cooking of Peru: traditions, ingredients, tastes & techniques.* A colourful book full of well-illustrated recipes, with alternative ingredients suggested for foods not readily available outside Peru.

John Biggar *The High Andes: A Guide for Climbers.* The first comprehensive climbing guide to the main peaks of the Andes, with a main focus on Peru but also covering Bolivia, Ecuador, Chile, Argentina, Colombia and Venezuela.

Ben Box *Cusco and the Inca Trail.* A good general guide to Peru's most popular destination.

Hilary and **George Bradt** *Backpacking and Trekking in Peru and Bolivia.* Detailed and excellent coverage of some of Peru's most rewarding hikes – worth taking if you're remotely interested in the idea, and good anyway for background on wildlife and flora.

Charles Brod *Apus and Incas: A Cultural Walking and Trekking Guide to Cusco.* An interesting selection of walks in the Cusco area.

Richard Danbury *The Inca Trail: Cusco and Machu Picchu.* Highly informative and smoothly written guide to this trekking destination, with fine contextual pieces. Also includes practical information for Lima.

★ **Peter Frost** *Exploring Cusco.* A very practical and stimulating site-by-site guide to the whole Cusco area

(where it is widely available in bookstores). Unreservedly recommended if you're spending more than a few days in the region, and also for armchair archeologists back home.

Peter Frost and **Jim Bartle** *Machu Picchu Historic Sanctuary.* A well-written and beautifully photographed coffee-table book on South America's most alluring archeological site.

Bradley C. Johnson *Classic Climbs of the Cordillera Blanca.* Available in paperback only, this is a must for anyone seriously wanting to climb in Peru's most popular mountaineering destination.

Latin Works *Machu Picchu Guide.* A small booklet with accurate detail on the various compounds within the archeological site.

Copeland Marks *Exotic Kitchens of Peru.* Takes a close look at Peruvian food, cooking and culture, and describes the variety of the country's kitchens.

David Mazel *Pure and Perpetual Snow: Two Climbs in the Andes.* Climbing reports on Ausangate and Alpamayo peaks. Available locally or from the South American Explorers' Club (see p.49).

Lynn Meisch *A Traveller's Guide to El Dorado and the Incan Empire.* Huge paperback full of fascinating detail – well worth reading before visiting Peru.

Language

Although Peru is officially a Spanish-speaking nation, a large proportion of its population, possibly more than half, regard Spanish as their second language. When the conquistadores arrived, Quechua, the official language of the Inca Empire, was widely spoken everywhere but the jungle. Originally known as Runasimi (from *runa*, "person", and *simis*, "mouth"), it was given the name Quechua – which means "high Andean valleys" – by the Spanish.

Quechua was not, however, the only pre-Columbian tongue. There were, and still are, well over **thirty languages** within the jungle area and, up until the late nineteenth century, **Mochica** had been widely spoken on the north coast for at least 1500 years.

With such a rich linguistic history it is not surprising to find non-European words intruding constantly into any Peruvian conversation. **Cancha**, for instance, the Inca word for "courtyard", is still commonly used to refer to most sporting areas – *la cancha de basketball*, for example. Other linguistic survivors have even reached the English language: **llama**, **condor**, **puma** and **pampa** among them. Perhaps more interesting is the great wealth of traditional **creole slang** – utilized with equal vigour at all levels of society. This complex speech, much like Cockney rhyming slang, is difficult to catch without almost complete fluency in Spanish, though one phrase you may find useful for directing a taxi driver is *de fresa alfonso* – literally translatable as "of strawberry, Alfonso" but actually meaning "straight on" (*de frente al fondo*).

Once you get into it, **Spanish** is the easiest language there is – and in Peru people are eager to understand even the most faltering attempt. You'll be further helped by the fact that South Americans speak relatively slowly (at least compared with Spanish people in Spain) and that there's no need to get your tongue round the lisping pronunciation.

Pronunciation

The rules of **pronunciation** are pretty straightforward and, once you get to know them, strictly observed. Unless there's an accent, words ending in d, l, r and z are **stressed** on the last syllable, all others on the second last. All **vowels** are pure and short.

A somewhere between the "A" sound of back and that of father

E as in get

I as in police

O as in hot

U as in rule

C is soft before E and I, hard otherwise: **cerca** is pronounced "serka"

G works the same way, a guttural "H" sound (like the ch in loch) before E or I, a hard G elsewhere – **gigante** becomes "higante"

H is always silent

J is the same sound as a guttural G: **jamón** is pronounced "hamon"

LL sounds like an English Y: **tortilla** is pronounced "torteeya"

N is as in English unless it has a tilde (accent) over it, when it becomes NY: **mañana** sounds like "manyana"

QU is pronounced like an English K

R is rolled, RR doubly so

V sounds more like B, **vino** becoming "beano"

X is slightly softer than in English – sometimes almost SH – except between vowels in place names where it has an "H" sound – for example México (Meh-Hee-Ko) or Oaxaca

Z is the same as a soft C, so **cerveza** becomes "servesa"

Below is a list of a few essential words and phrases, though if you're travelling for any length of time a **dictionary** or phrase book is obviously a worthwhile investment – try the *Dictionary of Latin American Spanish* (University of Chicago Press). Bear in mind that in

Spanish CH, LL and Ñ count as separate letters and are listed after the Cs, Ls and Ns respectively.

WORDS AND PHRASES

BASICS

Yes	Sí
No	No
Please	Por favor
Thank you	Gracias
Where...?	¿Dónde...?
When...?	¿Cuándo...?
What...?	¿Qué...?
How much...?	¿Cuánto...?
Do you have the time?	¿Tiene la hora?
Here	Aquí
There	Allí
This	Este
That	Eso
Now	Ahora
Later	Más tarde
Open	Abierto/a
Closed	Cerrado/a
With	Con
Without	Sin
Good	Buen(o)/a
Bad	Mal(o)/a
Big	Gran(de)
Small	Pequeño/a
More	Más
Less	Menos
Today	Hoy
Tomorrow	Mañana
Yesterday	Ayer

GREETINGS AND RESPONSES

Hello	Hola
Goodbye	Adiós
Good morning	Buenos días
Good afternoon/night	Buenas tardes/noches
See you later	Hasta luego
Sorry	Lo siento/discúlpeme
Excuse me	Con permiso/perdón
How are you?	¿Como está (usted)?
I (don't) understand	(No) Entiendo
Not at all	De nada
Do you speak English?	¿Habla (usted) inglés?
I don't speak Spanish	No hablo español
My name is ...	Me llamo ...
What's your name?	¿Como se llama usted?
I am English	Soy inglés(a)
...American	...americano/a
...Australian	...australiano/a
...Canadian	...canadiense
...Irish	...irlandés(a)
...New Zealander	...neozelandés(a)
...Scottish	...escocés(a)
...Welsh	...galés(a)

TRANSPORT AND DIRECTIONS

Do you know...?	¿Sabe...?
I don't know	No sé
How do I get to...?	Por dónde se va a...?
Left, right, straight on	Izquierda, derecha, derecho
Where is...?	¿Dónde está...?
...the bus station	...la estación de autobuses
...the train station	...la estación de ferrocarriles
...the nearest bank	...el banco más cercano
...the post office	...el correo
...the toilet	...el baño/sanitario
Where does the bus to... leave from?	¿De dónde sale el camión para...?
Is this the train for Lima?	¿Es éste el tren para Lima?
I'd like a (return) ticket to...	Querría un boleto (de) ida y vuelta) para...
What time does it leave (arrive in...)?	¿A qué hora sale (llega en...)?

ACCOMMODATION, RESTAURANTS AND SHOPPING

I want	Quiero
I'd like	Querría
There is (is there)?	(¿)Hay(?)
Give me...	Deme...
(one like that)	(uno así)
Do you have...?	Tiene...?
...a room	...un cuarto
...with two beds/ double bed...	...con dos camas/ cama matrimonial
It's for one person (two people)	es para una persona (dos personas)
...for one night (one week)	...para una noche (una semana)
It's fine, how much is it?	¿Está bien, cuánto es?
It's too expensive	Es demasiado caro
Don't you have anything cheaper?	¿No tiene algo más barato?
Can one... ?	¿Se puede...?
...camp (near here?)	¿...acampar aquí (cerca)?
Is there a hotel nearby?	¿Hay un hotel aquí cerca?
What is there to eat?	¿Qué hay para comer?
What's that?	¿Qué es eso?

What's this called in Spanish?	¿Como se llama este en Castillano?

USEFUL ACCOMMODATION TERMS

Desk fan or ceiling fan	Ventilador
Air-conditioned	Aire-acondicionado
Baño colectivo/compartido	Shared bath

Hot water	Agua caliente
Cold water	Agua fría
Double bed	Cama matrimonial
Single bed	Sencillo
Single room	Cuarto simple
Taxes	Impuestos
Check-out time	Hora de salida

FOOD AND DRINK

BASICS

Arroz	Rice
Avena	Oats (porridge)
Galletas	Biscuits
Harina	Flour
Huevos	Eggs
fritos	fried
duros	hard-boiled
pasados	lightly boiled
revueltos	scrambled
Mermelada	Jam
Miel	Honey
Mostaza	Mustard
Pan (integral)	Bread (brown)
Picante de…	spicy dish of…
Queso	Cheese

SOUP (SOPAS) AND STARTERS

Caldo	Broth
Caldo de gallina	Chicken broth
Causa	Mashed potatoes and shrimp
Conchas a la parmesana	Scallops with Parmesan
Huevos a la rusa	Egg salad
Inchicapi	Appetizing jungle soup made from chicken, peanuts, manioc (yuca) and fresh coriander herb
Palta	Avocado
Palta rellena	Stuffed avocado
Papa rellena	Stuffed fried potato
Sopa a la criolla	Noodles, vegetables and meat

SEAFOOD (MARISCOS) AND FISH (PESCADO)

Calamares	Squid
Camarones	Shrimp
Cangrejo	Crab
Ceviche	Marinated seafood
Chaufa de mariscos cojinova	Chinese rice with seafood
Corvina	Sea bass
Erizo	Sea urchin
Jalea	Large dish of fish with onion
Langosta	Lobster
Langostino a lo macho	Crayfish in spicy shellfish sauce
Lenguado	Sole
Paiche	Large jungle river fish
Tiradito	Ceviche without onion or sweet potato
Tollo	Small shark
Zungarro	Large jungle river fish

MEAT (CARNES)

Adobo	Meat/fish in mild chilli sauce
Ají de gallina	Chicken in chilli sauce
Anticuchos	Skewered heart (usually lamb)
Bifstek (bistek)	Steak
Cabrito	Goat
Carapulcra	Pork, chicken and potato casserole
Carne a lo pobre	Steak, fries, egg and banana
Carne de res	Beef
Chicharrones	Deep-fried pork skins
Conejo	Rabbit
Cordero	Lamb
Cuy	Guinea pig (a traditional dish)
Estofado	Stewed meat (usually served with rice)
Higado	Liver
Jamón	Ham
Lechón	Pork
Lomo asado	Roast beef
Lomo saltado	Sautéed beef
Mollejitos	Gizzard
Pachamanca	Meat and vegetables, cooked over hot, buried stones
Parillada	Grilled meat
Pato	Duck
Pavo	Turkey
Pollo (a la brasa)	Chicken (spit-roasted)
Tocino	Bacon
Venado	Venison

VEGETABLES (LEGUMBRES) AND SIDE DISHES

Ají	Chilli
Camote	Sweet potato
Cebolla	Onion
Choclo	Corn on the cob
Fideos	Noodles
Frijoles	Beans
Hongos	Mushrooms
Lechuga	Lettuce
Papa rellena	Fried potato balls, stuffed with olives, egg and mincemeat
Tallarines	Spaghetti noodles
Tomates	Tomatoes
Yuca a la Huancaina	Manioc (like a yam) in spicy cheese sauce

FRUIT

Chirimoya	Custard apple (green and fleshy outside, tastes like strawberries and cream)
Lucuma	Small nutty fruit (used in ice creams and cakes)
Maracuya	Passion fruit
Palta	Avocado
Piña	Pineapple
Tuna	Pear-like cactus fruit (refreshing but full of hard little seeds)

SWEETS (DULCES)

Barquillo	Ice cream cone
Flan	Crème caramel
Helado	Ice cream
Keke	Cake
Manjar blanco	Sweetened condensed milk
Mazamorra morada	Fruit/maize jelly
Panqueques	Pancakes
Picarones	Doughnuts with syrup

SNACKS (BOCADILLOS)

Castañas	Brazil nuts
Chifle	Fried banana slices
Empañada	Meat or cheese pie
Hamburguesa	Hamburger
Salchipapas	Potatoes, sliced frankfurter sausage and condiments
Sandwich de butifara	Ham and onion sandwich
Sandwich de lechón	Pork salad sandwich
Tamale	Maize-flour roll stuffed with olives, egg, meat and vegetables
Tortilla	Omelette-cum-pancake
Tostadas	Toast

FRUIT JUICES (JUGOS)

Especial	Fruit, milk, sometimes beer
Fresa	Strawberry
Higo	Fig
Manzana	Apple
Melon	Melon
Naranja	Orange
Papaya	Papaya
Piña	Pineapple
Platano	Banana
Surtido	Mixed
Toronja	Grapefruit
Zanahoria	Carrot

BEVERAGES (BEBIDAS)

Agua	Water
Água mineral	Mineral water
Algarrobina	*Algarrobo*-fruit drink
Café	Coffee
Cerveza	Beer
Chicha de jora	Fermented maize beer
Chicha morada	Maize soft drink
Chilcano de pisco	Pisco with lemonade
Chopp	Draught beer
Cuba libre	Rum and Coke
Gaseosa	Soft carbonated drink
Leche	Milk
Limonada	Real lemonade
Masato	Fermented manioc beer
Pisco	White-grape brandy
Ponche	Punch
Ron	Rum
Té	Tea
....con leche	....with milk
....de anis	....aniseed tea
....de limón	....lemon tea
....hierba luisa	....lemon-grass tea
....manzanilla	....camomile tea

NUMBERS AND DAYS

1	un/uno, una		4	cuatro
2	dos		5	cinco
3	tres		6	seis

7	siete	90	noventa
8	ocho	100	cien(to)
9	nueve	101	ciento uno
10	diez	200	doscientos
11	once	201	doscientos uno
12	doce	500	quinientos
13	trece	1000	mil
14	catorce	2000	dos mil
15	quince	first	primero/a
16	dieciséis	second	segundo/a
20	veinte	third	tercero/a
21	veintiuno	Monday	lunes
30	treinta	Tuesday	martes
40	cuarenta	Wednesday	miércoles
50	cincuenta	Thursday	jueves
60	sesenta	Friday	viernes
70	setenta	Saturday	sábado
80	ochenta	Sunday	domingo

GLOSSARY OF PERUVIAN TERMS

Aguajina Refreshing palm-fruit drink

Apu Mountain god

Ayllu Kinship group, or clan

Barrio Suburb, or sometimes shantytown

Burro Donkey

Cacique Headman

Callejón Corridor, or narrow street

Campesino Peasant, country-dweller, someone who works in the fields

Ceja de la selva Edge of the jungle

Chacra Cultivated garden or plot

Chamba Slang for work

Chaquiras Pre-Columbian stone or coral beads

Chicha Maize beer, or a form of Peruvian music

Chifa Peruvian-Chinese restaurant

Colectivo Collective taxi

Cordillera Mountain range

Curaca Chief

Curandero Healer

Empresa Company

Extranjero Foreigner

Farmacia Chemist

Flaco/a Skinny (common nickname)

Gordo/a Fat (common nickname)

Gringo A European or North American

Hacienda Estate

Huaca Sacred spot or object

Huaco Pre-Columbian artefact

Huaquero Someone who digs or looks for *huacos*

Jirón Road

Lomas Place where vegetation grows with moisture from the air rather than from rainfall or irrigation

Mamacona Inca Sun Virgin

Masato Manioc beer

El monte The forest

Pachamama Mother earth

Paiche The world's largest freshwater fish, often found on jungle menus

Pakucho Jungle variant of "gringo"

Peña Nightclub with live music

Plata Silver; slang for "cash"

Poblado Settlement

Pongo Whitewater rapids

Pueblos jóvenes Shantytowns

Puna Barren Andean heights

Quebrada Stream

Remolino Whirlpool

Selva Jungle

Selvático Jungle-dweller

Serrano Mountain-dweller

Shushupero "Drunk" or inebriated individual, from the deadly *shushupe* snake

Sierra Mountains

Siete raices Strong medicinal drink

Soroche Altitude sickness

Tambo Inca Highway rest-house

Tienda Shop

Tipishca Oxbow lake

Tramites Red tape, bureaucracy

Varzea Forest which gets regularly flooded

Small print and index

A ROUGH GUIDE TO ROUGH GUIDES

Published in 1982, the first Rough Guide – to Greece – was a student scheme that became a publishing phenomenon. Mark Ellingham, a recent graduate in English from Bristol University, had been travelling in Greece the previous summer and couldn't find the right guidebook. With a small group of friends he wrote his own guide, combining a highly contemporary, journalistic style with a thoroughly practical approach to travellers' needs.

The immediate success of the book spawned a series that rapidly covered dozens of destinations. And, in addition to impecunious backpackers, Rough Guides soon acquired a much broader readership that relished the guides' wit and inquisitiveness as much as their enthusiastic, critical approach and value-for-money ethos.

These days, Rough Guides include recommendations from budget to luxury and cover more than 120 destinations around the globe, as well as producing an ever-growing range of ebooks.

Visit **roughguides.com** to find all our latest books, read articles, get inspired and share travel tips with the Rough Guides community.

Rough Guide credits

Editors: Greg Dickinson, Ann-Marie Shaw
Layout: Jessica Subramanian
Cartography: Rajesh Chhibber
Picture editors: Yoshimi Kanazawa, Michelle Bhatia
Proofreader: Jennifer Speake
Managing editor: Andy Turner
Assistant editor: Sharon Sonam

Production: Jimmy Lao
Cover design: Nicole Newman, Jessica Subramanian
Editorial assistant: Freya Godfrey
Senior pre-press designer: Dan May
Programme manager: Gareth Lowe
Publisher: Keith Drew
Publishing director: Georgina Dee

Publishing information

This ninth edition published October 2015 by
Rough Guides Ltd,
80 Strand, London WC2R 0RL
11, Community Centre, Panchsheel Park,
New Delhi 110017, India
Distributed by Penguin Random House
Penguin Books Ltd,
80 Strand, London WC2R 0RL
Penguin Group (USA)
345 Hudson Street, NY 10014, USA
Penguin Group (Australia)
250 Camberwell Road, Camberwell,
Victoria 3124, Australia
Penguin Group (NZ)
67 Apollo Drive, Mairangi Bay, Auckland 1310,
New Zealand
Penguin Group (South Africa)
Block D, Rosebank Office Park, 181 Jan Smuts Avenue,
Parktown North, Gauteng, South Africa 2193
Rough Guides is represented in Canada by Tourmaline
Editions Inc. 662 King Street West, Suite 304, Toronto,
Ontario M5V 1M7
Printed in Singapore

© Rough Guides 2015
Maps © Rough Guides
No part of this book may be reproduced in any form
without permission from the publisher except for the
quotation of brief passages in reviews.
536pp includes index
A catalogue record for this book is available from the
British Library
ISBN: 978-0-24118-168-3
The publishers and authors have done their best to
ensure the accuracy and currency of all the information
in **The Rough Guide to Peru**, however, they can accept
no responsibility for any loss, injury, or inconvenience
sustained by any traveller as a result of information or
advice contained in the guide.
1 3 5 7 9 8 6 4 2

MIX
Paper from
responsible sources
FSC
www.fsc.org   FSC™ C018179

Help us update

We've gone to a lot of effort to ensure that the ninth edition of **The Rough Guide to Peru** is accurate and up-to-date. However, things change – places get "discovered", opening hours are notoriously fickle, restaurants and rooms raise prices or lower standards. If you feel we've got it wrong or left something out, we'd like to know, and if you can remember the address, the price, the hours, the phone number, so much the better.

Please send your comments with the subject line "**Rough Guide Peru Update**" to @ mail@uk.roughguides .com. We'll credit all contributions and send a copy of the next edition (or any other Rough Guide if you prefer) for the very best emails.

Find more travel information, connect with fellow travellers and plan your trip on Ⓦ roughguides.com.

ABOUT THE AUTHORS

Kiki Deere holds an MA in Latin American literature and has been travelling to South America on a regular basis since 2006. She has visited remote corners of Peru, from the little explored Cotahuasi Canyon, one of the deepest in the world, to isolated llama-herding communities in the Andes. Kiki is co-author of the *Rough Guide to Brazil* and tweets about her travels at @kikideere.

Anna Kaminski has been travelling in Peru since the early 2000s. Equally comfortable trekking around highland villages or on a riverboat on the Amazon, she is an ardent fan of new Peruvian cuisine and has been to every Gastón Acurio and Virgilio Martínez restaurant. Past Rough Guides assignments have found her on the Inca Trail, above the Nazca Lines and visiting indigenous communities in the jungle.

Phillip Tang began visiting Latin America in 2002 and is also an author on the *Rough Guide to South America On a Budget* as well as other guidebooks on the region and various guidebooks to Asia, including the *Rough Guide to Thailand*. More at ⓦphilliptang.co.uk. He calls both Mexico City and Sydney home.

Greg de Villiers has spent the past five years living in and travelling around the Southern Cone – Peru, Chile, Bolivia, Uruguay, Brazil, and Argentina. He hails from South Africa but currently works between Lima and Buenos Aires as a freelance food photographer and writer. He is also co-author of a guide to the wines and wineries of Uruguay.

This guide is dedicated to Dilwyn Jenkins, original author of the *Rough Guide to Peru*, who died on 12 November 2014 aged 57. A champion of Peru's indigenous peoples, particularly of the Ashaninka tribe of the western Amazon, Dilwyn had a lifelong connection with the country and will be deeply missed. For information on Dilwyn's work to protect Peru's rainforests visit ⓦcoolearth.org.

Acknowledgements

Kiki Deere wishes to thank Ric and Bernard at Peru for Less; Richard for his company and all the long days' driving up in the Andes; Mountain Lodges of Peru for hosting me on such a wonderful trek to Machu Picchu; Whilder Alarico for being such an excellent guide and for his jovial company on our trek; Boneth for her patience and company as she guided me around the Sacred Valley's beautiful Inca sights; Edwin from Pablo Tours in Arequipa for helping out with my itinerary and for his excellent organizational skills; his brother Yamil for the great pizzas, and Pablo for the fun company on the trek down to (and back up – just about!) Sangalle Oasis; Gustavo for kindly taking me around the Colca Canyon; Mayra for her company in Cotahuasi; all the friendly helpful staff at the iPeru offices throughout the country; the Rough Guides team in London for commissioning me to travel to such a beautiful part of the world; and last but not least Budgie for his support over the years and for putting up with a fiancée who nipped off to Peru for over a month just two days after he proposed.

Anna Kaminski I'd like to thank everyone who helped me en route, including Rupert for his invaluable help and advice on the Central Selva; Bill in Iquitos for all his local knowledge, support and great breakfasts; Inkaterra and Muyuna Lodge for their gracious hospitality; the courageous driver who ferried me to Pozuzo and back in one piece in the rainy landslide season; Marianne for the Manu info; the knowledgeable Amazon Expeditions in Chachapoyas for first-class tours of the area; my delightful hostess at El Mirador in Tarapoto and to Mike, Monica, Duncan and Saudy for being my home away from home in Lima.

Phillip Tang Muchísimas gracias a Ernesto A. Alanis Cataño por tu ayuda, tu compañía y los buenos momentos de sanguches, muñecas antiguas, sonrisas de tic tac, precipicios, ceniceros raros y aventuras chidas. Big thanks to Ann-Marie Shaw for her hard work, patience and guidance in editing, and Mani Ramaswamy for having me on board.

Readers' updates

Thanks to all the readers who have taken the time to write in with comments and suggestions (and apologies if we've inadvertently omitted or misspelt anyone's name):

Tais Briceño; Carl Callaway; Peter Castro; Sue Conner; Maggie Dawson; Dan & Lois Easley; Denise Fussen; Sukhreet Ghuman; Kelly Grainger; Rand Hoffman; Ruth Horwitz; Kevin Hurley; Laura Joseph; Matthys Katrien; Michael Keating; Anita Kelles-Viitanen; Eyal Keshet; Kirsty Kothakota; Camden Luxford; Scott Mafater; Tom Nurick; Louis Otis; Amélie Ranger; Paul Rogers; Anna Sampy; Bill Scolding; Katy Shorthouse; Nicolas Vandenbroucque; Roy van der Meijs; Kelly Wiebe; Roland Zimmermann.

Photo credits

All photos © Rough Guides except the following:
(Key: t-top; c-centre; b-bottom; l-left; r-right)

1 AWL Images/Nigel Pavitt
2 AWL Images/Alex Robinson
4 Getty Images/Altrendo
5 Axiom Photographic Agency/Paul Miles
9 Dorling Kindersley/Demetrio Carrasco (b)
11 Getty Images/David Tipling (t)
12 Corbis/Mike Theiss/National Geographic Society
13 Corbis/Konrad Wothe (t); Gregory de Villiers (c)
14 Alamy Images/Travel (b)
15 Robert Harding Picture Library/Glow Images (t); Alamy Images/neiljohn (bl)
16 Alamy Images/John Warburton-Lee Photography (tl); SuperStock/Jason Langley (br)
17 AWL Images/Nigel Pavitt (t)
18 Getty Images/Aurora Creative (t)
19 Robert Harding Picture Library/Richard Maschmeyer (t); AWL Images/Paul Harris (b)
20 SuperStock/Eye Ubiquitous (t)
21 Getty Images/Bjorn Holland (tr)
22 SuperStock/Johannes Pfatschbacher
24 4Corners/Orient/SIME
52–53 Getty Images/Juergen Ritterbach
73 Photoshot/Cuboimages (t); AWL Images/John Coletti (b)
93 AWL Images/Danita Delimont (tr); Getty Images/Aurora Creative/Axel Fassio (b)
121 Getty Images/Jacek Kadaj
137 Dorling Kindersley/Linda Whitwam (t); NHPA/Photoshot/Kevin Schafer (b)
139 Dorling Kindersley/Linda Whitwam
152–153 Alamy Images/David A. Barnes

155 Alamy Images/Hemis
167 Corbis/Nigel Pavitt (t)
183 Corbis/Ed Kashi
225 Corbis/Hugh Sitton (b)
243 SuperStock/Stefano Torrione (b)
278–279 Dorling Kindersley/Demetrio Carrasco
308–309 AWL Images/Aurora Photos
311 Corbis/Marcos Ferro
329 Dorling Kindersley/Michel Burger (t, b)
346–347 4Corners/Stefano Torrione/SIME
349 AWL Images/Andrew Watson
371 Corbis/JAI/Andrew Watson (tl); Corbis/National Geographic Society/Abraham Nowitz (tr); Alamy Images/ J.Enrique Molina (b)
393 Corbis/Stephan Knödler (t)
413 Alamy Images/National Geographic Image Collection (tr); AWL Images/Andrew Watson (b)
424–425 Getty Images/Paul Harris
427 NHPA/Photoshot/Andre Baertschi
449 SuperStock/MIVA Stock (t); Getty Images/Frans Lemmens (bl); FLPA/David Tipling (br)
467 AWL Images/Paul Harris (tl); SuperStock/Wolfgang Kaehler (tr); AWL Images/Aurora Photos (b)

Front cover and Spine Woman in Chinchero © Getty Images/Frans Lemmens
Back cover Amazon River, Iquitos © AWL Images/Paul Harris (t); Andean cock-of-the-rock © FLPA/John Holmes (bl); Chan Chan detail © Robert Harding Picture Library/ Robert Frerck (br)

Index

Maps are marked in grey

Map symbols

The symbols below are used on maps throughout the book

———	International boundary	ⓘ	Information office	‧‧‧‧‧	Funicular line
– – –	Chapter division boundary	★	Bus/taxi	▲	Mountain peak
▬▬▬	Motorway	@	Internet access	⋀⋀	Spring
———	Major road	ⓒ	Telephone office	⌒	Cave
———	Minor road	⋏	Campsite	⁞	Ruins
▬▬▬	Pedestrian road	🏝	Beach		Cliff
▬●▬	4 Wheel drive	⛳	Golf course	⋀	Arch
———	Railway	⭣	Viewpoint		Market
⌣	Bridge	⌂	Lodge	$	Bank
— —	Ferry route	♦	Museum		Building
– – – –	Footpath	▪	Tower		Church
———	Ruins	🏛	Monument	⬭	Stadium
✈	Airport	> <	Pass		Park
✉	Post office	⌃⌃	Mountain range		Saltpan
✚	Hospital				Glacier

Listings key

- ■ Accommodation
- ● Café/restaurant
- ■ Bar/club & live music venue/ gay club/club & peña
- ● Shop

Transportation Across all of Peru
1st Class Service, 24/7

Services include:

Airport pickup and dropoff
Hourly rates
City Tours
Full Day Tours
Country-wide travel

www.arviritours.com
arviritours@gmail.com

0051-1-4223804
(51) 996568744

PABLO TOUR

PERU

The specialist in Peru
Explore Peru avoiding the tourist crowd.

Respecting nature and creating jobs
for local people.

Tailor-made arragements:
tours - treks and climbing

Telephone: (51) (54) 203737 Cellphone: (51) 941414048
E-mail: pablotour@hotmail.com
Address: Jerusalen 400-AB-1 Arequipa - Peru

www.pablotour.com

Peru for Less

BUILDING MAGICAL MEMORIES

Over 15 YEARS OF EXPERIENCE **in Peru travel with expert travel advisors**

Over 2,000 outstanding testimonials
Fully customizable vacations
24-hour customer support

USA toll free
+1-877-269-0309

www.peruforless.com
travel@latinamericaforless.com

UK
+44-203-002-0571

WORLDWIDE
+1-817-230-4971